BLACK THEATRE USA

THE FREE PRESS

New York London Toronto Sydney Tokyo Singapore

BLACK THEATRE USA

PLAYS BY AFRICAN AMERICANS

The Recent Period
1935–Today

Revised and Expanded Edition

Edited by

JAMES V. HATCH
TED SHINE

THE FREE PRESS
A Division of Simon & Schuster Inc.
1230 Avenue of the Americas
New York, NY 10020

Designed by Carla Bolte

Manufactured in the United States of America

10 9 8 7 6 5 4 3 2

Library of Congress Cataloging-in-Publication Data

Black theatre USA : plays by African Americans from 1847 to today /
[edited by] James V. Hatch, Ted Shine. —Rev. and expanded ed.
p. cm.
Rev. ed. of: Black theater, U.S.A.
Paperback ed. issued in 2 vols. Vol. 1: The early period,
1847–1938; v. 2: The recent period, 1937–today.
Includes bibliographical references and index.
ISBN 0–684–82306–3 (cloth).—ISBN 0–684–82308–X (pbk. : v. 1).—
ISBN 0–684–82307–1 (pbk. : v. 2)
1. American drama—Afro-American authors. 2. Afro-Americans—
Drama. I. Hatch, James Vernon. II. Shine, Ted.
III. Title: Black theater, U.S.A.
PS628.N4B56 1996
812.008' 03520396073—dc20 95–40329
CIP

ISBN 0–684–82307–1

The editors of this anthology have consistently capitalized "Black" when it represents "Negro" or "African American" in documents, plays, and headnotes.

This book is dedicated to James "Beanie" Butcher, Owen Vincent Dodson, Winona Lee Fletcher, Errol Gaston Hill, Thomas D. Pawley III, and Anne Cooke Reid. Their scholarship, integrity, and devotion to preparing students to excel in the theatre arts made them giants in the American theatre.

CONTENTS

MODERN WOMEN WRITING ON WOMEN

BLACK THEATRE FOR BLACK PEOPLE

NEW PLAYS, NEW IDEAS, NEW FORMS

FOREWORD

When the 1st edition of this work came out I was elated because, the historical continuum of Black Art is very much underdocumented. For instance, of all the great Afro American writers there is none save Du Bois (and in a somewhat restricted-by-cost, little-known edition) whose works have been reissued in the uniform "classic" editions.

The fact that there was a work, of some admirable scholarship, that sought to at least sum up and present some of the notable works of Black dramatists. (Ah, now if we could only get around to putting together a national Afro American Repertory Theater, so that these works could be seen, could tour, could go into the schools . . . but then that is work we are working on, I hope?)

I used the 1st edition in many of my classes through the years and still instantly recommend it for Black lit and drama courses. This new edition, in two volumes, in paper, promises, on the surface, to be more accessible, so that is cause for more elation. The editors have shown themselves to be genuinely "on the case," again re-presenting a historic selection of what they feel to be some of the outstanding dramatic works produced by Afro American authors.

But as much as I celebrate the event and the work and the authors. (Ted Shine, in fact, is an "old" schoolmate of mine, years past from "The Capstone" [of Negro Education] they used to call it, Howard University. We witnessed Baldwin's *Amen Corner* make its first appearance down there, and I guess were both touched by it forever.) Still I would like to make some critical remarks, call them scholarly responses to the whole, not out of any petty pedanticism, but only out of a genuine desire to enhance the presentation.

Drama is the most interactive (media word) form of Art, simply because it presents persons, human beings in something presuming ongoing life. All literature is an ideological reflection of real life (to paraphrase Mao). Black literature, here Black Drama, gives an ideological portrait of Black life; Afro American drama, of the lives and history, the material social life and psychological development of the Afro American people.

So that if we understand that Black Americans have gone through three distinctive political upsurges in our history here in the United States: The nineteenth-century Anti Slavery movement, which culminated in the Civil War and Reconstruction. The early 20th century, which focused as The Harlem Renaissance, where a distinct Afro American modernism rooted in the "Black Consciousness" that Du Bois had spawned and Garvey had popularized and Langston had made great poetry. And then the Black Arts Movement that accompanied and reflected Malcolm X, The Black Panthers, Dr.

King's marches, a literature and art that reflected the real turbulence and political upsurge of the Civil Rights and Black Liberation Movements.

An anthology truly reflecting this historical span and motion should carry the works that try to dig into the essence of those times, dig deeper than the superficial newspaper lies (usually of the rulers) to say whatever was not and whatever is whatever, but we still rule.

These volumes do this, to a great extent. I simply want to mention what is not and why they should be. Though, some of the suggestions I made were taken up, but others I felt should be mentioned.

Zora[1] was missing at first. I wanted *Mule Bone,* which many of the buppie/academic negroes do not like because it talks of uneducated peasants. But what about being an uneducated peasant masquerading as a Professor at Slave Money University teaching that Afro American literature is a marginal form, a kind of Henry James/Derrida scrub team? Forget that.

I thought that "Yes We Can" as the title of the early twentieth century plays was corny. Though my dialogist said well that's what they (those dramatists) thought. Well. . . . but I wd say they had no doubt what they could do, they thought the restrainers needed assurance, if the title has any relevance.

In the section titled "Legend and History," I could not understand how Charlie Fuller's *A Soldier's Play* (which I confess I dislike and have written an essay on to explain) could be placed, anachronistically, into a group of plays from the 20s and 30s. If they wanted Fuller, *The Brownsville Raid* is a better play in my view, certainly it is not the "Hail, The Negro Middleclass," drumbeater that *SP* is.

Along with that, I wondered where was Ted Ward's *Our Lan'* (although they do have the great *Big White Fog*). Ted Ward is one of the great, dig it, great writers of any nationality and any time. The reason his plays don't get done . . . well, it's like Robeson said, "Two things these people don't like about me, my views and my nationality." Ward was a Red, like they say, Black & Red. Ain't Black bad enough?

Also, William Branch's important play, *In Splendid Error* is gone from this edition. This play about Fred Douglass and John Brown is pantheonic in impact and certainly its "Legend and History" qualities should go unchallenged, even as text.

Under "Social Justice," I wondered why there were not more of the Federal Theater Project plays. *Fog* was one, but Roosevelt sent Harry Hopkins to squash it in Chicago it was so Black and Red.

But this is the root of one aspect of Black national oppression. That we do not have our own venues and networks and theaters and tours. Our art is formidable, but still kept to the margin because we have not achieved self reliance for the Black Arts, as predicate for the Self Determination of Afro America itself. Self Determination must be first, because even to struggle for complete democracy as Americans, the oppressed must, themselves, put together the united fronts and organizations of struggle. That is the 1st degree of self determination. Malcolm called for Self Determination, Self Respect, and Self Defense. The Self Respect can only come with creation of self reliant institutions that will carry Revolutionary Art and make Cultural Revolution. This is the only real education an oppressed people can have. The formal public education of the

1. The plays of Zora Neale Hurston, Charles Fuller, and Theodore Ward appear in *Black Theatre USA: The Early Period, 1847–1938.*

U.S. is at best flawed with the lies and distortions of bourgeois class ideology and racism. So that a few years after the last political upsurge the people make, through the schools or lack of schools, films, television, sick negroes, and regular U.S. nazis, they can preach the end of the Civil Rights movement and the natural hegemony of the petty bourgeois. Just as Du Bois said they did after the Civil War: For 60 years pushed the humiliation and plantation stereotype slave portrait of the Afro American people (from Sambo to *Birth of a Nation*) to justify the destruction of the reconstruction.

Self Defense is not just military. It begins with organizations and institutions for true self consciousness (again, Du Bois) to break down the "double consciousness," i.e., seeing yrself through the eyes of people that hate you. The great Afro American dramatists do just that. They cut through the sickening double consciousness (as Langston said in "The Negro Artist & The Racial Mountain") and talk to us about our actual origins and history, draw out our actual intelligence, touch our real feelings. This is why Confucius said, "If the people hear the wrong music the Empire will fall." That's why there's so little real jazz on the stations. Why they cover and hide and melt it down into fusion. The same with all the deep democratic voices of the Black artists. And drama, the most ambitious, because it uses real folks. When revolutionary drama appears it usually means the other (real) thing is about or already on.

Under "Comedy as Protest" I wanted Ben Caldwell's *The First Militant Preacher,* which was one of the most performed plays of the 60's Black Arts Movement. I know personally, I directed it, and did performances up and down the West Coast and the East. There can be no registration of this, because we were in cultural centers, schools, playgrounds, people's houses, right where we belonged. And that is what must rehappen. The arts, the drama, must not wait around for the murderers to discover them so they can make its creators honorary murderers, or real ones. We must do it ourselves.

Dig, for instance, the quality of the "black films & drama" on the slavemasters' circuits these days. From *House Party 100* to *Living Color,* it's mostly minstrelsy. Compare them to *CornBread Earl & Me* or *The Education of Sonny Carson* or *Buck & The Preacher.* Or *A Raisin in the Sun, Blues for Mister Charlie, Dutchman* to what passes as Black drama on the stages of dying-killerville.

The editors happily also included Caldwell's little masterpiece. (It needs to be played in every church in the country.) In that same category, I wondered where was Loften Mitchell.

Under "Modern Black Women," Toni Morrison is one of the most important playwrights around, though I know her plays have not been seen. Like Billie sd, you aint got "your own," you in the wind. But Toni's Emmett Till play cries to be included, not to mention, performed. We saw a performance up off somewhere in the SUNY complex. You know the deal, give you a perf, but none really.

Under very big mistakes, I'd say the decision not to include *Blues for Mister Charlie* is the heavy. This is a great play, one that marks, very clearly and indelibly, a transition in the mindset of the Afro American people. The play is ideological struggle between Dr. King and Malcolm, in Jimmy's dissociative and sexually oriented perception. A struggle over the youth of the movement. Which way, non violence or self defense? After this play Jimmy was demoted to the margins of US literature by the living dead.

Under "Black Theatre For Black People," where is Marvin X, Ron Milner, Sonia Sanchez, Rob Penny, Oyamo, Larry Neal, some of the people who actually picked up the Black Arts Movement and carried Black Theatre across the country?

We could go on with our carping. Where is Wesley, where are the Harrises, Cleage, J. Franklin. And certainly, of the new folks, Lawrence Holder, that hard working young man shoulda made the set. But my informant sd, they had a space problem. (Like I told you, Billie sd, you aint got yr own. . . . &c)

But put all these things I sd in yr notes, and be thankful for the considerable gifts these two energetic archivists have provided. I was deeply thankful to see Du Bois's *Ethiopia.* It would be a great project for the churches and Board of Educations to collaborate on. But like the lady sd. . . .

What is important though, is that collections such as these should be made mandatory in all Black Studies programs and in schools across the country, especially those where Black folks are. This is the deep education we need and must have, to stimulate a true self consciousness and begin again to push our Sisyphus-like burden up the mountain, again. But unlike Sisyphus, one day soon the rock wont be coming back down.

—AMIRI BARAKA

ACKNOWLEDGMENTS

The editors are grateful to Vanessa Jackson and Judy Blum for secretarial assistance; to Celia Knight, Ellen Simon, and Lori Williams for copy editing; to Whitney LeBlanc, Thomas Pawley, Robert West, Tisch Jones, Freda Scott Giles, Leo Hamalian, and John Graziano for editorial and critical analysis; to Beth Anderson, our chief editor, for steering us safely through this book's voyage; and finally to Dr. Oscar Brockett, who was our mentor in history and research at the University of Iowa.

SOCIAL PROTEST

Langston Hughes • Richard Wright • Paul Green

Three years before America entered World War II, playwright Owen Dodson mocked the celebration of the Emancipation Proclamation's seventy-fifth anniversary with these lines:

This is a rusty time to sing in:
A rusty broken hingeless time:
The temperamental doors of liberty undone,
Undone and lying before the lintels
Of the doorway in this winter like dead gangsters.

From this present will the future be sent
Like a trained pigeon flying from tomorrow
To now and this sorrow:
A terrible message waving from his neck[1]

Clearly, African Americans had not yet received the fruits of emancipation. In the rural Southland, the penury of sharecropping had circumvented the Fourteenth Amendment. In the Northland, penury of unemployment imprisoned families in the prison of city tenements. Black playwrights implored and warned audiences that change must come, and come soon, or a great tribute would be exacted from a nation in default. Some looked to the labor unions for salvation.

In 1937, Conrad Seiler wrote *Sweetland,* the story of Chet Jackson, who, decorated for bravery in the war, comes home to the Neill plantation where he sees the sharecropper peonage. When his wartime buddy Sam is lynched as an agitator, Chet realizes that his place is in the rank and file of the sharecropper's union. *Sweetland,* produced at the Lafayette Theatre in Harlem, ran for six months.

1. Owen Dodson, "Seventy-Five Years Is a Long Stretch of Land," *Trend* (Chicago: University of Chicago Press, 1939).

In August of 1938, Hughes wrote *The Organizer, A Blues Opera in One Act,* an anthem dedicated to organizing the Black cotton pickers of the South. James P. Johnson composed the music. The opera, like Clifford Odets's *Waiting for Lefty,* begins with workers waiting for the man who will lead them out of a deadening spiritual slavery. The International Ladies' Garment Workers Union staged the premiere in 1940 at Carnegie Hall.

In the North, three great Chicago plays by African Americans portrayed the urban blight of segregated housing: *Big White Fog* (1938), *Native Son* (1941), and *A Raisin in the Sun* (1959). In each, the anger of families trapped in tenements spills out and into the larger society. "From this present will the future be sent." In 1941 the Japanese bombed Pearl Harbor, and America was pushed into both war and new racial policies.

"Racial tolerance," the government stressed, was necessary for America's war effort. Many African Americans agreed: America would not win a war abroad if there were race riots in our own cities. Blacks, however, co-opted Winston Churchill's "V" for victory sign, extending it to a double "V/V," meaning that there must be victory in the war overseas *and also* victory in the racial "war" at home where Blacks had been expected to tolerate a segregated armed services, nonemployment in war industries, and continued discrimination in housing and education. A. Philip Randolph, president of the Brotherhood of Sleeping Car Porters, scheduled a march on Washington for June 30, 1941; 50,000 people were to protest directly to Congress and the president. On June 25, President Roosevelt, unable to call off the march, signed Executive Order 8802, setting up the Fair Employment Practices Commission, aimed at ending discrimination in government employment and in industries with government contracts. But in 1943, the failure to remedy Black grievances erupted with rebellions in Harlem and Detroit.

Poet Witter Bynner's verse caught the mood:

On a train in Texas German prisoners eat
With white American soldiers, seat by seat,
While Black American soldiers sit apart—
The White men eating meat, the Black men Heart.

Meanwhile, socially relevant theatre of the 1930s, like Lucky Strike green, had gone off to war. Many entertainers joined the USO (United Service Organizations, 1941–1945) and toured military installations at home and overseas. Black artists presented programs to segregated American servicemen but rarely did whites perform for Blacks. Actor/director Dick Campbell organized over sixty-five all-Black USO camp shows. The Stage Door Canteen in New York City was one of the few cabarets where Black and white servicemen could enjoy entertainment together. In 1942, a Black seaman at Great Lakes Training Station, Owen Dodson, wrote and directed eleven spectacles (among them *Freedom the Banner* and *The Ballad of Dorie Miller*) designed to raise the morale of the Negro sailors. James W. Butcher at Fort Huachuca in Arizona served as a theatre consultant with the Special Services Division of the U.S. Army.

On Broadway, Jane White in *Strange Fruit* (1945), Canada Lee in *On Whitman Avenue* (1946), and Ethel Waters in *The Member of the Wedding* (1950) received critical praise, as did Gordon Heath as the returning war veteran acting under Elia Kazan's direction in *Deep Are the Roots* (1945). Canada Lee, cast in *The Duchess of Malfi* (1946), played in whiteface, the same year that Ossie Davis made his Broadway debut in *Jeb* (1946). Paul Robeson in 1943 set a record for all *Othello* productions, with 296 performances. Yet, a few years later, the same Paul Robeson and his concert audience were assaulted with rocks and bottles by a racist crowd in Peekskill, New York, while state police stood by and watched.

In Broadway musicals like *Carmen Jones* (1943) and *Cabin in the Sky* (1940), white playwrights continued to exploit exotic Negro characters. Others substituted suffering Negroes for exotic Negroes in condescending plays like *Lost in the Stars* (1949), *The Respectful Prostitute* (1946), and *South Pacific* (1943). A few dramatists assayed changes of attitude; *Finian's Rainbow* (1947) used satire to tickle the problem.

Significant Black employment on Broadway happened only in shows with all-Black casts: *Carmen Jones* (1943), *St. Louis Woman* (1946), and *Anna Lucasta* (1944), which ran nearly 1,000 performances.

African Americans sought ways to promote their own theatres by organizing the American Negro Theatre (see introduction to *On Strivers Row*) and The Negro Playwrights Company (see introduction to *Big White Fog*). Only two plays by Black playwrights were produced on Broadway in the 1940s: Theodore Ward's *Our Lan'* (1947) and Richard Wright's *Native Son* (1941).

By the end of the decade, the slogan "racial tolerance" had been discarded. With President Truman's order to end segregation in the armed services, "integration" became the buzz word, but America still had promises to keep.

MULATTO
1935

Langston Hughes (1898–1967)

In 1863, in an attempt to defeat Abraham Lincoln and the Republican Party's bid for reelection, David Croly and George Wakeman, two journalists from the *New York World*, manufactured the word "miscegenation" for a pamphlet they claimed had been written by abolitionist Democrats. The journalists' thesis was that the newly freed slaves would want to mate with "your white daughter," creating an America fouled by a race of mixed blood, that is, "Negro blood." In the years following the Civil War, states passed laws defining who was a Negro. Louisiana declared anyone with 1⁄16 Negro blood to be a Negro and forbade interracial marriage.[1]

In two short stories—"Red-headed Baby" and "Father and Son"—Langston Hughes addressed the difficulties of being racially mixed in America. Himself a descendant of mixed-race ancestry, he chose to be identified with African Americans regardless of their color. Professor Leslie Sanders has observed that the specific idea for a play on that subject probably came to Hughes while he was staying with the director Jasper Deeter at the Hedgerow Theatre in Rose Valley, Pennsylvania. There he watched the rehearsals of Paul Green's *In Abraham's Bosom*, a Pulitzer Prize–winning three-act play (1927), that presented a self-righteous man who resembled Hughes's own father in that he disliked poor Black people and found white people intolerable. Apparently angered by Green's play, Langston Hughes created a young protagonist of mixed-blood who identified as Black, while insisting that he was entitled to all the rights that whites enjoyed, even if he had to die for them.[2]

Mulatto is unique among Hughes's nearly one hundred theatre pieces. It is an early play (perhaps his second), using conventional European structure, a form Hughes soon abandoned for more narrative forms. And it is a tragedy, while nearly all of Hughes's other plays were comedies or musicals.

1. See Dion Boucicault's play *The Octoroon* (1859) for a dramatic playing out of this thesis.

2. Leslie Catherine Sanders *The Development of Black Theater in America: From Shadows to Selves* (Baton Rouge: Louisiana State University Press, 1988).

Hughes never had an opportunity to rewrite before the play opened on Broadway October 24, 1935. Optioned and rewritten by a white producer, Martin Jones, the play was put into rehearsal without Hughes's participation. The corrupted version, which now included a gratuitous rape, changed the play from tragedy to melodrama. Despite negative and mixed reviews, *Mulatto* enjoyed 373 performances on Broadway, giving it the longest run of any play by a Black until Lorraine Hansberry's *A Raisin in the Sun* in 1959. *Mulatto* then toured the United States for eight months and later was produced in Italy by Italian actors, where it ran for two years. The play's New York success can be attributed to Hughes's bold choice of subject, plus the play's cast, which featured two of Black theatre's most talented actors, Mercedes Gilbert and Rose McClendon. The composer Jan Meyerowitz so admired the drama, he adapted it into a successful opera, *The Barrier*.

3. Jay Plum, "Accounting for the Audience in Historical Reconstruction: Martin Jones's Production of Langston Hughes's *Mulatto*," *Theatre Survey* 36, No. 1 (May 1995). In this article Plum persuasively demonstrates that audience members, according to their racial biases, received different messages.

Unlike many of Hughes's political plays (see *Don't You Want To Be Free?*), *Mulatto* is representational; it has a plot that develops toward a core confrontation. Through empathy and story, the audience is led to the thesis: racism, not miscegenation, is the problem.[3]

"Cross," Langston Hughes's poem about mixed race, written during the early period in which he wrote *Mulatto*, presents the play's dilemma.

My old man's a white old man
And my old mother's black.
If ever I cursed my white old man
I take my curses back.

If ever I cursed my black old mother
And wished she were in hell,
I'm sorry for that evil wish
And now I wish her well.

My old man died in a fine big house,
My ma died in a shack.
I wonder where I'm gonna die,
Being neither white nor black?[4]

4. Langston Hughes, *The Weary Blues* (New York: Alfred A. Knopf, 1931).

Mulatto
A Tragedy of the Deep South

Langston Hughes

Characters

COLONEL THOMAS NORWOOD, *plantation owner, a still vigorous man of about sixty, nervous, refined, quick-tempered, and commanding; a widower who is the father of four living mulatto children by his Negro housekeeper*

CORA LEWIS, *a brown woman in her forties who has kept the house and been the mistress of Colonel Norwood for some thirty years*

WILLIAM LEWIS, *the oldest son of Cora Lewis and the Colonel; a fat, easy-going, soft-looking mulatto of twenty-eight; married*

SALLIE LEWIS, *the seventeen-year-old daughter, very light with sandy hair and freckles, who could pass for white*

ROBERT LEWIS, *eighteen, the youngest boy; strong and well-built; a light mulatto with ivory-yellow skin and proud thin features like his father's; as tall as the Colonel, with the same gray-blue eyes, but with curly black hair instead of brown; of a fiery, impetuous temper—immature and willful—resenting his blood and the circumstances of his birth*

FRED HIGGINS, *a close friend of Colonel Norwood; a county politician; fat and elderly, conventionally Southern*

SAM, *an old Negro retainer, a personal servant of the Colonel*

BILLY, *the small son of William Lewis; a chubby brown kid about five*

TALBOT, *the overseer*

MOSE, *an elderly Negro, chauffeur for Mr. Higgins*

A STOREKEEPER

AN UNDERTAKER

UNDERTAKER'S HELPER, *voice offstage only*

THE MOB

Act One

TIME *An afternoon in early fall.*

THE SETTING *The living room of the Big House on a plantation in Georgia. Rear center of the room, a vestibule with double doors leading to the porch; at each side of the doors, a large window with lace curtains and green shades; at left a broad flight of stairs leading to the second floor; near the stairs, downstage, a doorway leading to the dining room and kitchen; opposite, at right of stage, a door to the library. The room is furnished in the long out-dated horsehair and walnut style of the nineties; a crystal chandelier, a large old-fashioned rug, a marble-topped table, upholstered chairs. At the right there is a small cabinet. It is a very clean, but somewhat shabby and rather depressing room, dominated by a large oil painting of* NORWOOD'S *wife of his youth on the center wall. The windows are raised. The afternoon sunlight streams in.*

ACTION *As the curtain rises, the stage is empty. The door at the right opens and* COLONEL NORWOOD *enters, crossing the stage toward the stairs, his watch in his hand. Looking up, he shouts:*

NORWOOD Cora! Oh, Cora!

CORA *(heard above)* Yes, sir, Colonel Tom.

NORWOOD I want to know if that child of yours means to leave here this afternoon?

CORA *(at head of steps now)* Yes, sir, she's goin' directly. I's gettin' her ready now, packin' up an' all. 'Course, she wants to tell you good-bye 'fore she leaves.

NORWOOD Well, send her down here. Who's going to drive her to the railroad? The train leaves at three—and it's after two now. You ought to know you can't drive ten miles in no time.

CORA *(above)* Her brother's gonna drive her. Bert. He ought to be back here most any time now with the Ford.

NORWOOD *(stopping on his way back to the library)* Ought to be *back* here? Where's he gone?

CORA *(coming downstairs nervously)* Why, he driv in town 'fore noon, Colonel Tom. Said he were lookin' for some tubes or somethin' 'nother by de mornin' mail for de radio he's been riggin' up out in de shed.

NORWOOD Who gave him permission to be driving off in the middle of the morning? I bought that Ford to be used when I gave orders for it to be used, not . . .

CORA Yes, sir, Colonel Tom, but . . .

NORWOOD But what? *(pausing. Then deliberately)* Cora, if you want that hardheaded yellow son of yours to get along around here, he'd better listen to me. He's no more than any other Black buck on this plantation—due to work like the rest of 'em. I don't take such a performance from nobody under me—driving off in the middle of the day to town, after I've told him to bend his back in that cotton. How's Talbot going to keep the rest of those darkies working right if that boy's allowed to set that kind of an example? Just because Bert's your son, and I've been damn fool enough to send him off to school for five or six years, he thinks he has a right to privileges, acting as if he owned this place since he's been back here this summer.

CORA But, Colonel Tom . . .

NORWOOD Yes, I know what you're going to say. I don't give a damn about him! There's no nigger child of mine, yours, ours—no darkie—going to disobey me. I put him in that field to work, and he'll stay on this plantation till I get ready to let him go. I'll tell Talbot to use the whip on him, too, if he needs it. If it hadn't been that he's yours, he'd-a had a taste of it the other day. Talbot's a damn good overseer, and no saucy, lazy Nigras stay on this plantation and get away with it. *(to* CORA*)* Go on back upstairs and see about getting Sallie out of here. Another word from you and I won't send your *(sarcastically)* pretty little half-white daughter anywhere, either. Schools for darkies! Huh! If you take that boy of yours for an example, they do 'em more harm than good. He's learned nothing in college but impudence, and he'll stay here on this place and work for me awhile before he gets back to any more schools. *(he starts across the room)*

CORA Yes, sir, Colonel Tom. *(hesitating)* But he's just young, sir. And he was mighty broke up when you said last week he couldn't go back to de campus. *(*COLONEL NORWOOD *turns and looks at* CORA *commandingly. Understanding, she murmurs)* Yes, sir. *(She starts upstairs, but turns back)* Can't I run and fix you a cool drink, Colonel Tom?

NORWOOD No, damn you! Sam'll do it.

CORA *(sweetly)* Go set down in de cool, then, Colonel. 'Taint good for you to be going' on this way in de heat. I'll talk to Robert maself soon's he comes in. He don't mean nothing—just smart and young and kinder careless, Colonel Tom, like ma mother said you used to be when you was eighteen.

NORWOOD Get on upstairs, Cora. Do I have to speak again? Get on! *(he pulls the cord of the servants' bell)*

CORA *(on the steps)* Does you still be in the mind to tell Sallie goodbye?

NORWOOD Send her down here as I told you. *(impatiently)* Where's Sam? Send him here first. *(fuming)* Looks like he takes his time to answer that bell. You colored folks are running the house to suit yourself nowadays.

CORA *(coming downstairs again and going toward door under the steps)* I'll get Sam for you.

*(*CORA *exits left.* NORWOOD *paces nervously across the floor. Goes to the window and looks out down the road. Takes a cigar from his pocket, sits in a chair with it unlighted, scowling. Rises, goes toward servants' bell and rings it again violently as* SAM *enters, out of breath)*

NORWOOD What the hell kind of a tortoise race is this? I suppose you were out in the sun somewhere sleeping?

SAM No, sah, Colonel Norwood. Just tryin' to get Miss Sallie's valises down to de yard so's we can put 'em in de Ford, sah.

NORWOOD *(out of patience)* Huh! Darkies waiting on darkies! I can't get service in my own house. Very well. *(loudly)* Bring me some whiskey and soda, and ice in a glass. Is that damn Frigidaire working right? Or is Livonia still too thickheaded to know how to run it? Any ice cubes in the thing?

SAM Yes, sah, Colonel, yes sah. *(backing to-*

ward door left) 'Scuse me, please sah, but *(as* NORWOOD *turns toward library)* Cora say for me to ask you is it all right to bring that big old trunk what you give Sallie down by de front steps. We ain't been able to tote it down them narrer little back steps, sah. Cora, say, can we bring it down de front way through here?

NORWOOD No other way? (SAM *shakes his head)* Then pack it on through to the back, quick. Don't let me catch you carrying any of Sallie's baggage out of that front door here. You-all'll be wanting to go in and out the front way next. *(turning away, complaining to himself)* Darkies have been getting mighty fresh in this part of the country since the war. The damn Germans should've . . . *(to* SAM*)* Don't take that trunk out that front door.

SAM *(evilly, in a cunning voice)* I's seen Robert usin' de front door—when you ain't here, and he comes up from de cabin to see his mammy.

(SALLIE, *the daughter, appears at the top of the stairs, but hesitates about coming down)*

NORWOOD Oh, you have, have you? Let me catch him and I'll break his young neck for him. *(yelling at* SAM*)* Didn't I tell you some whiskey and soda an hour ago?

(SAM *exits left.* SALLIE *comes shyly down the stairs and approaches her father. She is dressed in a little country-style coat-suit ready for traveling. Her features are Negroid, although her skin is very fair.* COLONEL NORWOOD *gazes down at her without saying a word as she comes meekly toward him, half frightened)*

SALLIE I just wanted to tell you goodbye, Colonel Norwood, and thank you for letting me go back to school another year, and for letting me work here in the house all summer where mama is. (NORWOOD *says nothing. The girl continues in a strained voice as if making a speech)* You mighty nice to us colored folks certainly, and mama says you the best white man in Georgia. *(still* NORWOOD *says nothing. The girl continues)* You been mighty nice to your—I mean to us colored children, letting my sister and me go off to school. The principal says I'm doing pretty well and next year I can go to Normal and learn to be a teacher. *(raising her eyes)* You reckon I can, Colonel Tom?

NORWOOD Stand up straight and let me see how you look. *(backing away)* Hum-m-m! Getting kinder grown, ain't you? Do they teach you in that school to have good manners, and not be afraid to work, *and to respect white folks?*

SALLIE Yes, sir, I been taking up cooking and sewing, too.

NORWOOD Well, that's good. As I recall it, that school turned your sister out a right smart cook. Cora tells me she's got a good job in some big hotel in Chicago. I'm thinking about you going on up North there with her in a year or two. You're getting too old to be around here, and too womanish. *(he puts his hands on her arms as if feeling her flesh)*

SALLIE *(drawing back slightly)* But I want to live here with mama. I want to teach school in that there empty school house by the Cross Roads what hasn't had a teacher for five years.

(SAM *has been standing with the door cracked, overhearing the conversation. He enters with the drink and places it on the table, right.* NORWOOD *sits down, leaving the girl standing, as* SAM *pours out a drink)*

NORWOOD Don't get that into your head, now. There's been no teacher there for years—and there won't be any teacher there, either. Cotton teaches these pickaninnies enough around here. Some of 'em's too smart as it is. The only reason I did have a teacher there once was to get you young ones o' Cora's educated. I gave you all a chance and I hope you appreciate it. *(he takes a long drink)* Don't know why I did it. No other white man in these parts ever did it, as I know of. *(to* SAM*)* Get out of here! (SAM *exits left)* Guess I couldn't stand to see Cora's kids working around here dumb as the rest of these no good darkies—need a dozen of 'em to chop one row of cotton, or to keep a house clean. Or maybe I didn't want to see Talbot eyeing you gals. *(taking another drink)* Anyhow, I'm glad you and Bertha turned out right well. Yes, hum-m-m! *(straightening up)* You know I tried to do something for those brothers of yours, too, but William's stupid as an ox—good for work, though—and that Robert's just an impudent, hardheaded, yellow young fool. I'm gonna break his damn neck for him if he don't watch out. Or else put Talbot on him.

SALLIE *(suddenly frightened)* Please sir, don't put the overseer on Bert, Colonel Tom. He was the smartest boy at school, Bert was. On the football team, too. Please, sir, Colonel Tom. Let brother work here in the house, or somewhere else where Talbot can't mistreat him. He ain't used . . .

NORWOOD *(rising)* Telling me what to do, heh? *(staring at her sternly)* I'll use the back of my hand across your face if you don't hush. *(he takes another drink. The noise of a Ford is heard outside)* That's Bert now, I reckon. He's to take you to the railroad line, and while you're riding with him, you better put some sense into his head. And tell him I want to see him as soon as he gets back here. *(*CORA *enters left with a bundle and an umbrella.* SAM *and* WILLIAM *come downstairs with a big square trunk, and exit hurriedly, left)*

SALLIE Yes, sir, I'll tell him.

CORA Colonel Tom, Sallie ain't got much time now. *(to the girl)* Come on, chile. Bert's here. Yo' big brother and Sam and Livonia and everybody's all waiting at de back door to say goodbye. And your baggage is being packed in. *(noise of another car is heard outside)* Who else is that there coming up de drive? *(*CORA *looks out the window)* Mr. Higgins' car, Colonel Tom. Reckon he's coming to see you . . . Hurry up out o' this front room, Sallie. Here, take these things of your'n *(hands her the bundle and parasol)* while I opens de door for Mr. Higgins. *(in a whisper)* Hurry up, chile! Get out! *(*NORWOOD *turns toward the front door as* CORA *goes to open it)*

SALLIE *(shyly to her father)* Goodbye, Colonel Tom.

NORWOOD *(his eyes on the front door, scarcely noticing the departing* SALLIE, *he motions)* Yes, yes, goodbye! Get on now! *(*CORA *opens the front door as her daughter exits left)* Well, well! Howdy do, Fred. Come in, come in! *(*CORA *holds the outer door of the vestibule wide as* FRED HIGGINS *enters with rheumatic dignity, supported on the arm of his chauffeur,* MOSE, *a very black Negro in a slouchy uniform.* CORA *closes the door and exits left hurriedly, following* SALLIE*)*

NORWOOD *(smiling)* How's the rheumatiz today? Women or licker or heat must've made it worse—from the looks of your speed!

HIGGINS *(testily, sitting down puffing and blowing in a big chair)* I'm in no mood for fooling, Tom, not now. *(to* MOSE*)* All right. *(the* CHAUFFEUR *exits front.* HIGGINS *continues angrily)* Norwood, that damned yellow nigger buck of yours that drives that new Ford tried his best just now to push my car off the road, then got in front of me and blew dust in my face for the last mile coming down to your gate, trying to beat me in here—which he did. Such a deliberate piece of impudence I don't know if I've ever seen out of a nigger before in all the sixty years I've lived in this county. *(the noise of the Ford is heard going out the drive, and the cries of the* NEGROES *shouting farewells to* SALLIE. HIGGINS *listens indignantly)* What kind of crazy coons have you got on your place, anyhow? Sounds like a Black Baptist picnic to me. *(pointing to the window with his cane)* Tom, listen to that.

NORWOOD *(flushing)* I apologize to you, Fred, for each and every one of my darkies. *(*SAM *enters with more ice and another glass)* Permit me to offer you a drink. I realize I've got to tighten down here.

HIGGINS Mose tells me that was Cora's boy in that Ford—and that young Black fool is what I was coming here to talk to you about today. That boy! He's not gonna be around here long—not the way he's acting. The white folks in town'll see to that. Knowing he's one of your yard niggers, Norwood, I thought I ought to come and tell you. The white folks at the Junction aren't intending to put up with him much longer. And I don't know what good the jail would do him once he got in there.

NORWOOD *(tensely)* What do you mean, Fred—jail? Don't I always take care of the folks on my plantation without any help from the Junction's police force? Talbot can do more with an unruly Black buck than your marshal.

HIGGINS Warn't lookin' at it that way, Tom. I was thinking how weak the doors to that jail is. They've broke 'em down and lynched four niggers to my memory since it's been built. After what happened this morning, you better keep that yellow young fool out o' town from now on. It might not be safe for him around there—today, nor no other time.

NORWOOD What the hell? *(perturbed)* He went in just now to take his sister to the depot. Damn it, I hope no ruffians'll break up my new Ford. What was it, Fred, about this morning?

HIGGINS You haven't heard? Why, it's all over town already. He sassed out Miss Gray in the post office over a box of radio tubes that come by mail.

NORWOOD He did, heh?

HIGGINS Seems like the stuff was sent C.O.D. and got here all smashed up, so he wouldn't take it. Paid his money first before he saw the box was broke. Then wanted the money order back. Seems like the post office can't give money orders back—rule against it. Your nigger started to argue, and the girl at the window—Miss Gray—got scared and yelled for some of the mail clerks. They threw Bert out of the office, that's all. But that's enough. Lucky nothing more didn't happen. *(indignantly)* That Bert needs a damn good beating—talking back to a white woman—and I'd like to give it to him myself, the way he kicked the dust up in my eyes all the way down the road coming out here. He was mad, I reckon. That's one yellow buck don't know his place, Tom, and it's your fault he don't—sending 'em off to be educated.

NORWOOD Well, by God, I'll show him. I wish I'd have known it before he left here just now.

HIGGINS Well, he's sure got mighty aggravating ways for a buck his color to have. Drives down the main street and don't stop for nobody, white or Black. Comes in my store and if he ain't waited on as quick as the white folks are, he walks out and tells the clerk his money's as good as a white man's any day. Said last week standing out on my store front that he wasn't *all* nigger nohow; said his name was Norwood—not Lewis, like the rest of his family—and part of your plantation here would be his when you passed out—and all that kind of stuff, boasting to the walleyed coons listening to him.

NORWOOD *(astounded)* Well, I'll be damned!

HIGGINS Now, Tom, you know that don't go 'round these parts 'o Georgia, nor nowhere else in the South. A darkie's got to keep in his place down here. Ruinous to other niggers hearing that talk, too. All this postwar propaganda on the radio about freedom and democracy—why the niggers think it's meant for them! And that Eleanor Roosevelt, she ought to been muzzled. She's driving our niggers crazy—your boy included! Crazy! Talking about civil rights. Ain't been no race trouble in our country for three years—since the Deekin's lynching—but I'm telling you, Norwood, you better see that that buck of yours goes away from here. I'm speaking on the quiet, but I can see ahead. And what happened this morning about them radio tubes wasn't none too good.

NORWOOD *(beside himself with rage)* A Black ape! I . . . I . . .

HIGGINS You been too decent to your darkies, Norwood. That's what's the matter with you. And then the whole county suffers from a lot of impudent bucks who take lessons from your crowd. Folks been kicking about that, too. Guess you know it. Maybe that's the reason you didn't get that nomination for committeeman a few years back.

NORWOOD Maybe 'tis, Higgins. *(rising and pacing the room)* God damn niggers! *(furiously)* Everything turns on niggers, niggers, niggers! No wonder Yankees call this the Black Belt! *(he pours a large drink of whiskey)*

HIGGINS *(soothingly)* Well, let's change the subject. Hand me my glass, there, too.

NORWOOD Pardon me, Fred. *(he puts ice in his friend's glass and passes him the bottle)*

HIGGINS Tom, you get excited too easy for warm weather . . . Don't ever show Black folks they got you going, though. I think sometimes that's where you make your mistake. Keep calm, keep calm—and then you command. Best plantation manager I ever had never raised his voice to a nigger—and they were scared to death of him.

NORWOOD Have a smoke. *(pushes cigars toward* HIGGINS*)*

HIGGINS You ought've married again, Tom—brought a white woman out here on this damn place o' yours. A woman could help you run things. Women have soft ways, but they can keep things humming. Nothing but Blacks in the house—a man gets soft like niggers are inside. *(puffing at cigar)* And living with a colored woman! Of course, I know we all have 'em—I didn't know you could make use of a white girl till I was past twenty. Thought too much o' white women for that—but I've given many a yellow gal a baby in my time. *(long puff at cigar)* But for a man's own house you need a wife, not a Black woman.

NORWOOD Reckon you're right, Fred, but it's too late to marry again now. *(shrugging his shoulders)* Let's get off of darkies and women for awhile. How's crops? *(sitting down)* How's politics going?

HIGGINS Well, I guess you know the Republicans is trying to stir up trouble for us in Washington. I wish the South had more men like Bilbo and Rankin there. But, say, by the way, Lawyer Hotchkiss wants to see us both about that budget money next week. He's got some real Canadian stuff at his office, in his filing case, too—brought back from his vacation last summer. Taste better'n this old mountain juice we get around here. Not meaning to insult your drinks, Tom, but just remarking. I serve the same as you myself, label and all.

NORWOOD *(laughing)* I'll have you know, sir, that this is prewar licker, sir!

HIGGINS Hum-m-m! Well, it's got me feelin' better'n I did when I come in here—whatever it is. *(puffs at his cigar)* Say, how's your cotton this year?

NORWOOD Doin' right well, specially down in the south field. Why not drive out that road when you leave and take a look at it? I'll ride down with you. I want to see Talbot, anyhow.

HIGGINS Well, let's be starting. I got to be back at the Junction by four o'clock. Promised to let that boy of mine have the car to drive over to Thomasville for a dance tonight.

NORWOOD One more shot before we go. *(he pours out drinks)* The young ones must have their fling, I reckon. When you and I grew up down here it used to be a carriage and the best pair of black horses when you took the ladies out—now it's an automobile. That's a good lookin' new car of yours, too.

HIGGINS Right nice.

NORWOOD Been thinking about getting a new one myself, but money's been kinder tight this year, and conditions are none too good yet, either. Reckon that's why everybody's so restless. *(he walks toward stairs calling)* Cora! Oh, Cora! . . . If I didn't have a few thousand put away, I'd feel the pinch myself. *(as* CORA *appears on the stairs)* Bring me my glasses up there by the side of my bed . . . Better whistle for Mose, hadn't I, Higgins? He's probably 'round back with some of his women. *(winking)* You know I got some nice Black women in this yard.

HIGGINS Oh, no, not Mose. I got my servants trained to stay in their places—right where I want 'em—while they're working for me. Just open the door and tell him to come in here and help me out. *(*NORWOOD *goes to the door and calls the* CHAUFFEUR. MOSE *enters and assists his master out to the car.* CORA *appears with the glasses, goes to the vestibule and gets the* COLONEL*'s hat and cane which she hands him)*

NORWOOD *(to* CORA*)* I want to see that boy o' yours soon as I get back. That won't be long, either. And tell him to put up that Ford of mine and don't touch it again.

CORA Yes, sir, I'll have him waiting here. *(in a whisper)* It's hot weather, Colonel Tom. Too much of this licker makes your heart upset. It ain't good for you, you know. *(*NORWOOD *pays her no attention as he exits toward the car. The noise of the departing motor is heard.* CORA *begins to tidy up the room. She takes a glass from a side table. She picks up a doily that was beneath the glass and looks at it long and lovingly. Suddenly she goes to the door left and calls toward the kitchen)* William, you William! Come'ere, I want to show you something. Make haste, son. *(as* CORA *goes back toward the table, her eldest son,* WILLIAM *enters carrying a five-year-old boy)* Look here at this purty doily yo' sister made this summer while she been here. She done learned all about sewing and making purty things at school. Ain't it nice, son?

WILLIAM Sho' is. Sallie takes after you, I reckon. She's a smart little crittur, ma. *(sighs)* De Lawd knows, I was dumb at school. *(to his child)* Get down, Billy, you's too heavy. *(he puts the boy on the floor)* This here sewin's really fine.

BILLY *(running toward the big upholstered chair and jumping up and down on the spring seat)* Gityap! I's a mule driver. Haw! Gee!

CORA You Billy, get out of that chair 'fore I skins you alive. Get on into de kitchen, sah.

BILLY I'm playin' horsie, grandma. *(jumps up in the chair)* Horsie! Horsie!

CORA Get! That's de Colonel's favorite chair. If he knows any little darkie's been jumpin' on it, he raise sand. Get on, now.

BILLY Ole Colonel's ma grandpa, ain't he? Ain' he ma white grandpa?

WILLIAM *(snatching the child out of the chair)* Boy, I'm gonna fan your hide if you don't hush!

CORA Sh-ss-s! You, Billy, hush yo' mouth! Chile, where you hear that? *(to her son)* Some o' you all been talking too much in front o' this chile. *(to the boy)* Honey, go on in de kitchen till yo' daddy come. Get a cookie from 'Vonia and set down on de back porch. *(little* BILLY *exits left)*

WILLIAM Ma, you know it 'twarn't me told him. Bert's the one been goin' all over de plantation since he come back from Atlanta remindin' folks right out we's Colonel Norwood's chilluns.

CORA *(catching her breath)* Huh!

WILLIAM He comes down to my shack tellin' Billy and Marybell they got a white man for grandpa. He's gonna get my chilluns in trouble sho'—like he got himself in trouble when Colonel Tom whipped him.

CORA Ten or 'leven years ago, warn't it?

WILLIAM And Bert's *sho'* in trouble now. Can't go back to that college like he could-a if he'd-a had any sense. You can't fool with white folks—and de Colonel ain't never really liked Bert since that there first time he beat him, either.

CORA No, he ain't. Leastwise, he ain't understood him. *(musing sadly in a low voice)* Time Bert was 'bout seven, warn't it? Just a little bigger'n yo' Billy.

WILLIAM Yes.

CORA Went runnin' up to Colonel Tom out in de horse stables when de Colonel was showin' off his horses—I 'members so well—to fine white company from town. Lawd, that boy's always been foolish! He went runnin' up and grabbed a-holt de Colonel and yelled right in front o' de white folks' faces, "O, papa, Cora say de dinner's ready, papa!" Ain't never called him papa before, and I don't know where he got it from. And Colonel Tom knocked him right backwards under de horse's feet.

WILLIAM And when de company were gone, he beat that boy unmerciful.

CORA I thought sho' he were gonna kill ma chile that day. And he were mad at me, too, for months. Said I was teaching you chilluns who they pappy were. Up till then Bert had been his favorite little colored child 'round here.

WILLIAM Sho' had.

CORA But he never liked him no more. That's why he sent him off to school so soon to stay, winter and summer, all these years. I had to beg and plead to have him home this summer—but I's sorry now I ever got that boy back here again.

WILLIAM He's sho' growed more like de Colonel all de time, ain't he? Bert thinks he's a real white man hisself now. Look at de first thing he did when he come home, he ain't seen de Colonel in six years—and Bert sticks out his hand fo' to shake hands with him!

CORA Lawd! That chile!

WILLIAM Just like white folks! And de Colonel turns his back and walks off. Can't blame him. He ain't used to such doings from colored folks. God knows what's got into Bert since he come back. He's acting like a fool—just like he was a boss man 'round here. Won't even say "Yes, sir" and "No, sir" no more to de white folks. Talbot asked him warn't he gonna work in de field this mornin'. Bert say "No!" and turn and walk away. White man so mad, I could see him nearly foam at de mouth. If he warn't yo' chile, ma, he'd been knocked in de head fo' now.

CORA You's right.

WILLIAM And you can't talk to him. I tried to tell him something the other day, but he just laughed at me, and said we's all just scared niggers on this plantation. Says he ain't no nigger, nohow. He's a Norwood. He's half white, and he's gonna act like it. *(in amazement at his brother's daring)* And this is Georgia, too!

CORA I's scared to death for de boy, William. I don't know what to do. De Colonel says he won't send him off to school no mo'. Says he's mo' sassy and impudent now than any nigger he ever seed. Bert never has been like you was, and de girls, quiet and sensible like you knowed you had to be. *(she sits down)* De Colonel say he's gonna make Bert stay here now and work on this plantation like de rest of his niggers. He's gonna show him what color he is. Like that time when he beat him for callin' him "papa." He says he's gwine to teach him his place and make de boy know where he belongs. Seems like me or you can't show him. Colonel Tom has to take him in hand, or these white folks'll kill him around here and then—oh, My God!

WILLIAM A nigger's just got to know his place in de South, that's all, ain't he, ma?

CORA Yes, son. That's all, I reckon.

WILLIAM And ma brother's one damn fool nigger. Don't seems like he knows nothin'. He's gonna ruin us all 'round here. Makin' it bad for everybody.

CORA Oh, Lawd, have mercy! *(beginning to*

cry) I don't know what to do. De way he's acting up can't go on. Way he's acting to de Colonel can't last. Somethin's gonna happen to ma chile. I had a bad dream last night, too, and I looked out and seed de moon all red with blood. I seed a path o' living blood across this house, I tell you, in my sleep. Oh, Lawd, have mercy! *(sobbing)* Oh, Lawd, help me in ma troubles. *(the noise of the returning Ford is heard outside.* CORA *looks up, rises, and goes to the window)* There's de chile now, William. Run out to de back door and tell him I wants to see him. Bring him in here where Sam and Livonia and de rest of 'em won't hear ever'thing we's sayin'. I got to talk to ma boy. He's ma baby boy, and he don't know de way.

(Exit WILLIAM *through the door left.* CORA *is wiping her eyes and pulling herself together when the front door is flung open with a bang and* ROBERT *enters)*

ROBERT *(running to his mother and hugging her teasingly)* Hello, ma! Your daughter got off, and I've come back to keep you company in the parlor! Bring out the cookies and lemonade. *Mister* Norwood's here!

CORA *(beginning to sob anew)* Take yo' hands off me, boy! Why don't you mind? Why don't you mind me?

ROBERT *(suddenly serious, backing away)* Why, mamma, what's the matter? Did I scare you? Your eyes are all wet! Has somebody been telling you 'bout this morning?

CORA *(not heeding his words)* Why don't you mind me, son? Ain't I told you and told you not to come in that front door, never? *(suddenly angry)* Will somebody have to beat it into you? What's got wrong with you when you was away at that school? What am I gonna do?

ROBERT *(carelessly)* Oh, I knew that the Colonel wasn't here. I passed him and old man Higgins on the road down by the south patch. He wouldn't even look at me when I waved at him. *(half playfully)* Anyhow, isn't this my old man's house? Ain't I his son and heir? *(grandly, strutting around)* Am I not Mr. Norwood, Junior?

CORA *(utterly serious)* I believes you goin' crazy, Bert. I believes you wants to get us all killed or run away or something awful like that. I believes . . . (WILLIAM *enters left)*

WILLIAM Where's Bert? He ain't come round back—*(seeing his brother in the room)* How'd you get in here?

ROBERT *(grinning)* Houses have front doors.

WILLIAM Oh, usin' de front door like de white folks, heh? You gwine do that once too much.

ROBERT Yes, like de white folks. What's a front door for, you rabbit-hearted coon?

WILLIAM Rabbit-hearted coon's better'n a dead coon any day.

ROBERT I wouldn't say so. Besides you and me's only half coons, anyhow, big boy. And I'm gonna act like my white half, not my Black half. Get me, kid?

WILLIAM Well, you ain't gonna act like it long here in de middle o' Georgy. And you ain't gonna act like it when de Colonel's around, either.

ROBERT Oh, no? My stay down here'll be short and sweet, boy, short and sweet. The old man won't send me away to college no more—so you think I'm gonna stick around and work in the fields? Like fun? I might stay here awhile and teach some o' you darkies to think like men, maybe—till it gets too much for the old Colonel—but no more bowing down to white folks for me—not Robert Norwood.

CORA Hush, son!

ROBERT Certainly not right on my own old man's plantation—Georgia or no Georgia.

WILLIAM *(scornfully)* I hears you.

ROBERT *You* can do it if you want to, but I'm ashamed of you. I've been away from here for six years. *(boasting)* I've learned something, seen people in Atlanta, and Richmond, and Washington where the football team went—real colored people who don't have to take off their hats to white folks or let 'em go to bed with their sisters—like that young Higgins boy, asking me what night Sallie was comin' to town. A damn cracker! *(to* CORA*)* 'Scuse me, ma. *(continuing)* Back here in these woods maybe Sam and Livonia and you and mama and everybody's got their places fixed for 'em, but not me. *(seriously)* Nobody's gonna fix a place for me. I'm old man Norwood's son. Nobody fixed a place for him. *(playfully again)* Look at me. I'm a 'fay boy. *(pretends to shake his hair back)* See these gray eyes? I got the right to everything everybody else has. *(punch-*

ing his brother in the belly) Don't talk to me, old slavery-time Uncle Tom.

WILLIAM *(resentfully)* I ain't playin', boy. *(pushes younger brother back with some force)* I ain't playin' a-tall.

CORA All right, chilluns, stop. Stop! And William, you take Billy and go on home. 'Vonia's got to get supper and she don't like no young-uns under feet in de kitchen. I wants to talk to Bert in here now 'fore Colonel Tom gets back. *(exit* WILLIAM *left.* CORA *continues to* BERT*)* Sit down, child, right here a minute, and listen.

ROBERT *(sitting down)* All right, ma.

CORA Hard as I's worked and begged and humbled maself to get de Colonel to keep you chilluns in school, you comes home wid yo' head full o' stubbornness and yo' mouth full o' sass for me an' de white folks an' everybody. You know can't no colored boy here talk like you's been doin' to no white folks, let alone to de Colonel and that old devil of a Talbot. They ain't gonna stand fo' yo' sass. Not only you, but I 'spects we's all gwine to pay fo' it, every colored soul on this place. I was scared to death today fo' yo' sister, Sallie, scared de Colonel warn't gwine to let her go back to school, neither, 'count o' yo' doins, but he did, thank Gawd—and then you come near makin' her miss de train. Did she have time to get her ticket and all?

ROBERT Sure! Had to drive like sin to get there with her, though. I didn't mean to be late getting back here for her, ma, but I had a little run-in about them radio tubes in town.

CORA *(worried)* What's that?

ROBERT The tubes was smashed when I got 'em, and I had already made out my money order, so the woman in the post office wouldn't give the three dollars back to me. All I did was explain to her that we could send the tubes back—but she got hot because there were two or three white folks waiting behind me to get stamps, I guess. So she yells at me to move on and not give her any of my "educated nigger talk." So I said "I'm going to finish showing you these tubes before I move on"—and then she screamed and called the mail clerk working in the back, and told him to throw me out. *(boasting)* He didn't do it by himself, though. Had to call all the white loafers out in the square to get me through that door.

CORA *(fearfully)* Lawd have mercy!

ROBERT Guess if I hadn't-a had the Ford then, they'd've beat me half-to-death, but when I saw how many crackers there was, I jumped in the car and beat it on away.

CORA Thank God for that!

ROBERT Not even a football man *(half boasting)* like me could tackle the whole junction. 'Bout a dozen colored guys standing around, too, and not one of 'em would help me—the dumb jiggaboos! They been telling me ever since I been here *(imitating darky talk)* "You can't argue wid whut folks, man. You better stay out o' this Junction. You must ain't got no sense, nigger! You's a fool" . . . Maybe I am a fool, ma—but I didn't want to come back here nohow.

CORA I's sorry I sent for you.

ROBERT Besides you, there ain't nobody in this country but a lot of evil white folks and cowardly niggers. *(earnestly)* I'm no nigger, anyhow, am I, ma? I'm half white. The Colonel's my father—the richest man in the county—and I'm not going to take a lot of stuff from nobody if I do have to stay here, not from the old man either. He thinks I ought to be out there in the sun working, with Talbot standing over me like I belonged in the chain gang. Well, he's got another thought coming! *(stubbornly)* I'm a Norwood—not a field-hand nigger.

CORA You means you ain't workin' no mo'?

ROBERT *(flaring)* No, I'm not going to work in the fields. What did he send me away to school for—just to come back here and be his servant, or pick his hills of cotton?

CORA He sent you away to de school because *I* asked him and begged him, and got down on my knees to him, that's why. *(quietly)* And now I just wants to make you see some sense, if you can. I knows, honey, you reads in de books and de papers, and you knows a lot more'n I do. But, chile, you's in Georgy—and I don't see how it is you don't know where you's at. This ain't up North—and even up yonder where we hears it's so fine, yo' sister has to pass for white to get along good.

ROBERT *(bitterly)* I know it.

CORA She ain't workin' in no hotel kitchen like de Colonel thinks. She's in a office typewriting. And Sallie's studyin' de typewriter, too, at de school, but yo' pappy don't know it. I knows we ain't s'posed to study nothin' but cookin' and hard workin' here in Georgy.

That's all I ever done, or knowed about. I been workin' on this very place all ma life—even 'fore I come to live in this big house. When de Colonel's wife died, I come here, and borned you chilluns. And de Colonel's been real good to me in his way. Let you all sleep in this house with me when you was little, and sent you all off to school when you growed up. Ain't no white man in this county done that with his cullud chilluns before, far as I can know. But you—Robert, be awful, awful careful! When de Colonel comes back, in a few minutes, he wants to talk to you. Talk right to him, boy. Talk like you was colored, 'cause you ain't white.

ROBERT *(angrily)* And I'm not Black either. Look at me, mama. *(rising and throwing up his arms)* Don't I look like my father? Ain't I as light as he is? Ain't my eyes gray like his eyes are? *(the noise of a car is heard outside)* Ain't this our house?

CORA That's him now. *(agitated)* Hurry, chile, and let's we get out of this room. Come on through yonder to the kitchen. *(she starts toward the door left)* And I'll tell him you're here.

ROBERT I don't want to run into the kitchen. Isn't this our house? *(as CORA crosses hurriedly left, ROBERT goes toward the front door)* The Ford is parked out in front, anyway.

CORA *(at the door left to the rear of the house)* Robert! Robert! *(as ROBERT nears the front door, COLONEL NORWOOD enters, almost runs into the boy, stops at the threshold and stares unbelievingly at his son. CORA backs up against the door left)*

NORWOOD Get out of here! *(He points toward the door to rear of the house where CORA is standing)*

ROBERT *(half smiling)* Didn't you want to talk to me?

NORWOOD Get out of here!

ROBERT Not that way. *(the COLONEL raises his cane to strike the boy. CORA screams. ROBERT draws himself up his full height, taller than the old man and looking very much like him, pale and proud. The man and the boy face each other. NORWOOD does not strike)*

NORWOOD *(in a hoarse whisper)* Get out of here. *(his hand is trembling as he points)*

CORA Robert! Come on, son, come on! Oh, my God, come on. *(opening the door left)*

ROBERT Not that way, ma. *(ROBERT walks proudly out the front door. NORWOOD, in an impotent rage, crosses the room to a small cabinet right, opens it nervously with a key from his pocket, takes out a pistol, and starts toward the front door. CORA overtakes him, seizes his arm, stops him)*

CORA He's our son, Tom. *(she sinks slowly to her knees, holding his body)* Remember, he's our son.

(Curtain.)

Act Two

Scene One

TIME *After supper. Sunset.*

SETTING *The same.*

ACTION *As the curtain rises, the stage is empty. Through the windows the late afternoon sun makes two bright paths toward the footlights. SAM, carrying a tray bearing a whiskey bottle and a bowl of ice, enters left and crosses toward the library. He stoops at the door right, listens a moment, knocks, then opens the door and goes in. In a moment SAM returns. As he leaves the library, he is heard replying to a request of NORWOOD's.*

SAM Yes, sah, Colonel! Sho' will, sah! Right away, sah! Yes, sah, I'll tell him. *(he closes the door and crosses the stage muttering to himself)* Six o'clock. Most nigh that now. Better tell Cora to get that boy right in here. Can't nobody else do nothin' with that fool Bert but Cora. *(he exits left. Can be heard calling)* Cora! You, Cora . . .

(Again the stage is empty. Offstage, outside, the bark of a dog is heard, the sound of Negroes singing down the road, the cry of a child. The breeze moves the shadows of leaves and tree limbs across the sunlit paths from the windows. The door left opens and CORA enters, followed by ROBERT)

CORA *(softly to ROBERT behind her in the dining room)* It's all right, son. He ain't come out yet, but it's nearly six, and that's when he said he wanted you, but I was afraid maybe you was gonna be late. I sent for you to come up here to de house and eat supper with me in de kitchen. Where'd you eat yo' vittuals at, chile?

ROBERT Down at Willie's house, ma. After

the old man tried to hit me you still want me to hang around and eat up here?

CORA I wanted you to be here on time, honey, that's all. *(she is very nervous)* I kinder likes to have you eat with me sometimes, too, but you ain't et up here more'n once this summer. But this evenin' I just wanted you to be here when de Colonel sent word for you, 'cause we's done had enough trouble today.

ROBERT He's not here on time, himself, is he?

CORA He's in de library. Sam couldn't get him to eat no supper tonight, and I ain't seen him a-tall.

ROBERT Maybe he wants to see me in the library, then.

CORA You know he don't 'low no colored folks in there 'mongst his books and things 'cept Sam. Some o' his white friends goes in there, but none o' us.

ROBERT Maybe he wants to see *me* in there, though.

CORA Can't you never talk sense, Robert? This ain't no time for foolin' and jokin'. Nearly thirty years in this house and I ain't never been in there myself, not once, 'mongst the Colonel's papers. *(the clock strikes six)* Stand over yonder and wait till he comes out. I's gwine on upstairs now, so's he can talk to you. And don't aggravate him no mo' fo' God's sake. Agree to whatever he say. I's scared fo' you, chile, de way you been actin', and de fool tricks you done today, and de trouble about de post office besides. Don't aggravate him. Fo' yo' sake, honey, 'cause I loves you—and fo' all de po' colored folks on this place what has such a hard time when his humors get on him—agree to whatever he say, will you, Bert?

ROBERT All right, ma. *(voice rising)* But he better not start to hit me again.

CORA Shs-ss-s! He'll hear you! He's right in there.

ROBERT *(sullenly)* This was the day I ought to have started back to school—like my sister. I stayed my summer out here, didn't I? Why didn't he keep his promise to me? You said if I came home I could go back to college again.

CORA Shs-ss-s! He'll be here now. Don't say nothin', chile. I's done all I could.

ROBERT All right, ma.

CORA *(approaching the stairs)* I'll be in ma room, honey, where I can hear you when you goes out. I'll come down to de back door and see you 'fore you goes back to de shack. Don't aggravate him, chile.

(She ascends the stairs. The boy sits down sullenly, left, and stares at the door opposite from which his father must enter. The clock strikes the quarter after six. The shadows of the window curtains have lengthened on the carpet. The sunshine has deepened to a pale orange, and the light paths grow less distinct across the floor. The boy sits up straight in his chair. He looks at the library door. It opens. NORWOOD *enters. He is bent and pale. He looks across the room and sees the boy. Suddenly he straightens up. The old commanding look comes into his face. He strides directly across the room toward his son. The boy, half afraid, half defiant, yet sure of himself, rises. Now that* ROBERT *is standing, the white man turns, goes back to a chair near the table, right, and seats himself. He takes out a cigar, cuts off the end and lights it, and in a voice of mixed condescension and contempt, he speaks to his son.* ROBERT *remains standing near the chair)*

NORWOOD I don't want to have to beat you another time as I did when you were a child. The next time I might not be able to control myself. I might kill you if I touched you again. I been runnin' this plantation for thirty-five years, and I never had to beat a Nigra as old as you are. I never had to beat one of Cora's children either—but you. The rest of 'em had sense 'nough to keep out of my sight, and to speak to me like they should . . . I don't have any trouble with my colored folks. Never have trouble. They do what I say, or what Mr. Talbot says, and that's all there is to it. I give 'em a chance. If they turn in crops they get paid. If they're workin' for wages, they get paid. If they want to spend their money on licker, or buy an old car, or fix up their cabins, they can. Do what they choose long as they know their places and it don't hinder their work. And to Cora's young ones I give all the chances any colored folks ever had in these parts. More'n many a white child's had. I sent you all off to school. Let Bertha go on up North when she got grown and educated. Intend to let Sallie do the same. Gave your brother William that house he's living in when he got married, pay him for his work, help him out if he needs it. None of my darkies suffer. Sent you to college. Would have kept on, would have sent you back today, but I don't intend to pay for no darky, or white boy either if I had one, that acts the way you've been acting. And certainly for no Black fool. Now I want to know what's wrong with you? I don't usually talk about what I'm going to do with anybody on this place. It's my habit to tell people *what to do,* not discuss it with 'em. But I want to know what's the matter with you—whether you're crazy or not. In that case, you'll have to be locked up. And if you aren't, you'll have to change your ways a damn sight or it won't be safe for you here, and you know it—venting your impudence on white women, parking the car in front of my door, driving like mad through the Junction, and going, everywhere, just as you please. Now, I'm going to let you talk to me, but I want you to talk right.

ROBERT *(still standing)* What do you mean, "talk right?"

NORWOOD I mean talk like a nigger should to a white man.

ROBERT Oh! But I'm not a nigger, Colonel Tom. I'm your son.

NORWOOD *(testily)* You're Cora's boy.

ROBERT Women don't have children by themselves.

NORWOOD Nigger women don't know the fathers. You're a bastard.

*(*ROBERT *clenches his fist.* NORWOOD *turns toward the drawer where the pistol is, takes it out, and lays it on the table. The wind blows the lace curtains at the windows and sweeps the shadows of falling leaves across the paths of sunlight on the floor)*

ROBERT I've heard that before. I've heard it from Negroes, and I've heard it from white folks. Now I hear it from you. *(slowly)* You're talking about my mother.

NORWOOD I'm talking about Cora, yes. Her children are bastards.

ROBERT *(quickly)* And you're their father. *(angrily)* How come I look like you, if you're not my father?

NORWOOD Don't shout at me, boy. I can hear you. *(half smiling)* How come your skin is yellow and your elbows rusty? How come they threw you out of the post office today for talking to a white woman? How come you're the crazy young buck you are?

ROBERT They had no right to throw me out. I asked for my money back when I saw the broken tubes. Just as you had no right to raise that cane today when I was standing at the door of this house where *you* live, while *I* have to sleep in a shack down the road with the field hands. *(slowly)* But my mother sleeps with you.

NORWOOD You don't like it?

ROBERT No, I don't like it.

NORWOOD What can you do about it?

ROBERT *(after a pause)* I'd like to kill all the white men in the world.

NORWOOD *(starting)* Niggers like you are hung to trees.

ROBERT I'm not a nigger.

NORWOOD You don't like your own race? *(*ROBERT *is silent)* Yet you don't like white folks either?

ROBERT *(defiantly)* You think I ought to?

NORWOOD You evidently don't like me.

ROBERT *(boyishly)* I used to like you, when I first knew you were my father, when I was a little kid, before that time you beat me under the feet of your horses. *(slowly)* I liked you until then.

NORWOOD *(a little pleased)* So you did, heh? *(fingering his pistol)* A pickaninny calling me "papa." I should've broken your young neck for that first time. I should've broken your head for you today, too—since I didn't then.

ROBERT *(laughing scornfully)* You should've broken my head!

NORWOOD Should've gotten rid of you before this. But you was Cora's child. I tried to help you. *(aggrieved)* I treated you decent, schooled you. Paid for it. But tonight you'll get the hell off this place and stay off. Get the hell out of this county. *(suddenly furious)* Get out of this state. Don't let me lay eyes on you again. Get out of here now. Talbot and the storekeeper are coming up here this evening to talk cotton with me. I'll tell Talbot to *see* that you go. That's all. *(*NORWOOD *motions toward the door, left)* Tell Sam to come in here when you go out. Tell him to make a light here.

ROBERT *(impudently)* *Ring* for Sam—I'm not going through the kitchen. *(he starts toward the front door)* I'm not your servant. You're not going to tell me what to do. You're not going to have Talbot run me off the place like a field hand you don't want to use any more.

NORWOOD *(springing between his son and the front door, pistol in hand)* You Black bastard! *(*ROBERT *goes toward him calmly, grasps his father's arm and twists it until the gun falls to the floor. The older man bends backward in *startled fury and pain)* Don't you dare put your . . .

ROBERT *(laughing)* Why don't you shoot, papa? *(louder)* Why don't you shoot?

NORWOOD *(gasping as he struggles, fighting back)* . . . Black . . . hands . . . on . . . you . . .

ROBERT *(hysterically, as he takes his father by the throat)* Why don't you shoot, papa? *(*NORWOOD*'s hands claw the air helplessly.* ROBERT *chokes the struggling white man until his body grows limp)* Why don't you shoot? *(laughing)* Why don't you shoot? Huh? Why?

*(*CORA *appears at the top of the stairs, hearing the commotion. She screams)*

CORA Oh, my God! *(she rushes down.* ROBERT *drops the body of his father at her feet in a path of flame from the setting sun.* CORA *starts and stares in horror)*

ROBERT *(wildly)* Why didn't he shoot, mama? He didn't want *me* to live. Why didn't he shoot? *(laughing)* He was the boss. Telling me what to do. Why didn't he shoot, then? He was the white man.

CORA *(falling on the body)* Colonel Tom! Colonel Tom! Tom! Tom! *(gazes across the corpse at her son)* He's yo' father, Bert.

ROBERT He's dead. The white man's dead. My father's dead. *(laughing)* I'm living.

CORA Tom! Tom! Tom!

ROBERT Niggers are living. He's dead. *(picks up the pistol)* This is what he wanted to kill me with, but he's dead. I can use it now. Use it on all the white men in the world, because they'll be coming looking for me now. *(stuffs the pistol into his shirt)* They'll want me now.

CORA *(rising and running toward her boy)* Quick, chile, out that way *(pointing toward the front door)* so they won't see you in de kitchen. Make for de swamp, honey. Cross de fields fo' de swamp. Go de crick way. In runnin' water, dogs can't smell no tracks. Hurry, chile!

ROBERT Yes, mama. I can go out the front way now, easy. But if I see they gonna get me before I can reach the swamp, I'm coming back here, mama, and *(proudly)* let them take me out of my father's house—if they can. *(pats the gun under his shirt)* They're not going to string me up to some roadside tree for the crackers to laugh at.

CORA *(moaning aloud)* Oh, O-o-o! Hurry! Hurry, chile!

ROBERT I'm going, ma. *(he opens the door. The sunset streams in like a river of blood)*

CORA Run, chile!

ROBERT Not out of my father's house. *(he exits slowly, tall and straight against the sun)*

CORA Fo' God's sake, hurry chile! *(glancing down the road)* Lawd have mercy! There's Talbot and de storekeeper in de drive. They sees my boy! *(moaning)* They sees ma boy. *(relieved)* But thank God, they's passin' him! *(*CORA *backs up against the wall in the vestibule. She stands as if petrified as* TALBOT *and the* STOREKEEPER *enter)*

TALBOT Hello, Cora. What's the matter with you? Where's that damn fool boy o' your'n goin', coming out the front door like he owned the house? What's the matter with you, woman? Can't you talk? Can't you talk? Where's Norwood? Let's have some light in this dark place. *(he reaches behind the door and turns on the lights.* CORA *remains backed up against the wall, looking out into the twilight, watching* ROBERT *as he goes across the field)* Good God, Jim! Look at this! *(The two white men stop in horror before the sight of* NORWOOD*'s body on the floor)*

STOREKEEPER He's blue in the face. *(bends over the body)* That nigger we saw walking out the door! *(rising excitedly)* That nigger bastard of Cora's . . . *(stooping over the body again)* Why the Colonel's dead!

TALBOT That nigger! *(rushes toward the door)* He's running toward the swamp now . . . We'll get him . . . Telephone town—there, in the library. Telephone the sheriff. Get men, white men, after that nigger.

*(*STOREKEEPER *rushes into the library. He can be heard talking excitedly on the phone.)*

STOREKEEPER Sheriff! Sheriff! Is this the sheriff? I'm calling from Norwood's plantation. That nigger, Bert, has just killed Norwood—and run, headed for the swamp. Notify the gas station at the crossroads! Tell the boys at the sawmill to head him off at the creek. Warn everybody to be on the lookout. Call your deputies! Yes! Yes! Spread a dragnet. Get out the dogs. Meanwhile we'll start after him. *(he slams the phone down and comes back into the room)* Cora, where's Norwood's car? In the barn? *(*CORA *does not answer)*

TALBOT Talk, you Black bitch!

(She remains silent. TALBOT *runs, yelling and talking, out into the yard, followed by the* STOREKEEPER. *Sounds of excited shouting outside, and the roar of a motor rushing down the drive. In the sky the twilight deepens into early night.* CORA *stands looking into the darkness)*

CORA My boy can't get to de swamp now. They's telephoned the white folks down that way. So he'll come back home now. Maybe he'll turn into de crick and follow de branch home directly. *(protectively)* But they shan't get him. I'll make a place for to hide him. I'll make a place upstairs down under de floor, under ma bed. In a minute ma boy'll be runnin' from de white folks with their hounds and their ropes and their guns and everything they uses to kill po' colored folks with. *(distressed)* Ma boy'll be out there runnin'. *(turning to the body on the floor)* Colonel Tom, you hear me? Our boy, out there runnin'. *(fiercely) You* said he was ma boy—*ma* bastard boy. I heard you . . . but he's yours too . . . but yonder in de dark runnin'—runnin' from yo' people, from white people. *(pleadingly)* Why don't you get up and stop 'em? He's *your* boy. His eyes is gray—like your eyes. He's tall like you's tall. He's proud like you's proud. And he's runnin'—runnin' from po' white trash what ain't worth de little finger o' nobody what's got your blood in 'em, Tom. *(demandingly)* Why don't you get up from there and stop 'em, Colonel Tom? What's that you say? He ain't your chile? He's ma bastard chile? My yellow bastard chile? *(proudly)* Yes, he's mine. But don't call him that. Don't you touch him. Don't you put your white hands on him. You's beat him enough, and cussed him enough. Don't you touch him now. He *is* ma boy, and no white folks gonna touch him now. That's finished. I'm gonna make a place for him upstairs under ma bed. *(backs away from the body toward the stairs)* He's ma chile. Don't you come in ma bedroom while he's up there. Don't you come to my bed no mo'. I calls you to help me now, and you just lays there. I calls you for to wake up, and you just lays there. Whenever you called me, in de night, I woke up. When you called for me to love, I always reached out ma arms fo' you. I borned you five chilluns and now one of 'em is out yonder in de dark runnin' from yo' people. Our youngest boy out yonder in de dark runnin'. *(accusingly)* He's runnin' from you, too. You said he warn't your'n—he's just Cora's po' little yellow bastard. But he *is* your'n, Colonel Tom. *(sadly)* And he's runnin' from you. You are out yonder in de dark *(points toward the door)* runnin' our chile, with de hounds and de gun in yo' hand, and Talbot's followin' 'hind you with a rope to hang Robert with. *(confidently)* I been sleepin' with you too long, Colonel Tom, not to know that this ain't you layin' down there with yo' eyes shut on de floor. You can't fool me—you ain't never been so still like this before—you's out yonder runnin' ma boy. *(scornfully)* Colonel Thomas Norwood, runnin' ma boy through de fields in de dark, runnin' ma poor little helpless Bert through de fields in de dark to lynch him . . . Damn you, Colonel Norwood! *(backing slowly up the stairs, staring at the rigid body below her)* Damn you, Thomas Norwood! God damn you!

(Curtain)

Scene Two

TIME *One hour later. Night.*

SETTING *The same.*

ACTION *As the curtain rises, the* UNDERTAKER *is talking to* SAM *at the outer door. All through this act the approaching cries of the manhunt are heard.*

UNDERTAKER Reckon there won't be no orders to bring his corpse back out here, Sam. None of us ain't seen Talbot or Mr. Higgins, but I'm sure they'll be having the funeral in town. The coroner told us to bring the body into the Junction. Ain't nothin' but niggers left out here now.

SAM *(very frightened)* Yes, sah! Yes, sah! You's right, sah! Nothin' but us niggers, sah!

UNDERTAKER The Colonel didn't have no relatives far as you know, did he, Sam?

SAM No, sah. Ain't had none. No, sah! You's right, sah!

UNDERTAKER Well, you got everything o' his locked up around here, ain't you? Too bad there ain't no white folks about to look after the Colonel's stuff, but every white man that's able to walk's out with the posse. They'll have that young nigger swingin' before ten.

SAM *(trembling)* Yes, sah, yes, sah! I 'spects so. Yes, sah!

UNDERTAKER Say, where's that woman the Colonel's been living with—where's that Black housekeeper, Cora, that murderin' bastard's mother?

SAM She here, sah! She's up in her room.

UNDERTAKER *(curiously)* I'd like to see how she looks. Get her down here. Say, how about a little drink before we start that ride back to town, for me and my partner out there with the body?

SAM Cora got de keys to all de licker, sah!

UNDERTAKER Well, get her down here then, double quick! *(*SAM *goes up the stairs. The* UNDERTAKER *leans in the front doorway talking to his partner outside in the wagon)* Bad business, a white man having saucy nigger children on his hands, and his Black woman living in his own house.

VOICE OUTSIDE Damn right, Charlie.

UNDERTAKER Norwood didn't have a gang o' yellow gals, though, like Higgins and some o' these other big bugs. Just this one bitch far's I know, livin' with him damn near like a wife. Didn't even have much company out here. And they tell me ain't been a white woman stayed here overnight since his wife died when I was a baby. *(*SAM*'s shuffle is heard on the stairs)* Here comes a drink, I reckon, boy. You needn't get down off the ambulance. I'll have Sam bring it out there to you. *(*SAM *descends followed by* CORA *who comes down the stairs. She says nothing. The* UNDERTAKER *looks up grinning at* CORA*)* Well, so you're the Cora that's got these educated nigger children? Hum-m! Well, I guess you'll see one of 'em swinging full of bullet holes when you wake up in the morning. They'll probably hang him to that tree down here by the Colonel's gate—'cause they tell me he strutted right out the front gate past that tree after the murder. Or maybe they'll burn him. How'd you like to see him swinging there roasted in the morning when you wake up, girlie?

CORA *(calmly)* Is that all you wanted to say to me?

UNDERTAKER Don't get smart! Maybe you think there's nobody to boss you now. We gonna have a little drink before we go. Get out a bottle of rye.

CORA I takes ma orders from Colonel Norwood, sir.

UNDERTAKER Well, you'll take no more orders from him. He's dead out there in my wagon—so get along and get the bottle.

CORA He's out yonder with de mob, not in your wagon.

UNDERTAKER I tell you he's in my wagon!

CORA He's out there with de mob.

UNDERTAKER God damn! *(to his partner outside)* I believe this Black woman's gone crazy in here. *(to* CORA*)* Get the keys out for that licker, and be quick about it! *(*CORA *does not move.* SAM *looks from one to the other, frightened)*

VOICE OUTSIDE Aw, to hell with the licker, Charlie. Come on, let's start back to town. We want to get in some of that excitement, too. They should've found that nigger by now—and I want to see 'em drag him out here.

UNDERTAKER All right, Jim. *(to* CORA *and* SAM*)* Don't you all go to bed until you see that bonfire. You niggers are getting besides yourselves around Polk County. We'll burn a few more of you if you don't be careful. *(he exits, and the noise of the dead-wagon going down the road is heard)*

SAM Oh, Lawd, hab mercy on me! I prays, Lawd hab mercy! O, ma Lawd, ma Lawd, ma Lawd! Cora, is you a fool? *Is* you a fool? Why didn't you give de mens de licker, riled as these white folks is? In ma old age is I gonna be burnt by de crackers? Lawd, is I sinned? Lawd, what has I done? *(suddenly stops moaning and becomes schemingly calm)* I don't have to stay here tonight, does I? I done locked up de Colonel's library, and he can't be wantin' nothin'. No, ma Lawd, he won't want nothin' now. He's with Jesus—or with de devil, one. *(to* CORA*)* I's gwine on away from here. Sam's gwine in town to his chilluns' house, and I ain't gwine by no road either. I gwine through de holler where I don't have to pass no white folks.

CORA Yes, Samuel, you go on. De Colonel can get his own drinks when he comes back tonight.

SAM *(bucking his eyes in astonishment at* CORA*)* Lawd God Jesus!

(He bolts out of the room as fast as his old legs will carry him. CORA *comes downstairs, looks for a long moment out into the darkness, then closes the front door and draws the blinds. She looks down at the spot where the* COLONEL*'s body lay)*

CORA All de colored folks are runnin' from you tonight. Po' Colonel Tom, you too old now to be out with de mob. You got no business goin', but you had to go, I reckon. I 'members that time they hung Luke Jordon, you sent yo' dogs out to hunt him. The next day you killed all de dogs. You were kinder softhearted. Said you didn't like that kind of sport. Told me in bed one night you could hear them dogs howlin' in yo' sleep. But de time they burnt de courthouse when that po' little cullud boy was locked up in it cause they said he hugged a white girl, you was with 'em again. Said you had to go help 'em. Now you's out chasin' ma boy. *(as she stands at the window, she sees a passing figure)* There goes yo' other woman, Colonel Tom, Livonia is runnin' from you too, now. She would've wanted you last night. Been wantin' you again ever since she got old and fat and you stopped layin' with her and put her in the kitchen to cook. Don't think I don't know, Colonel Tom. Don't think I don't remember them nights when you used to sleep in that cabin down by de spring. I knew 'Vonia was there with you. I ain't no fool, Colonel Tom. But she ain't bore you no chilluns. I'm de one that bore 'em. *(musing)* White mens and colored womens, and little bastard chilluns—that's de old way of de South—but it's ending now. Three of your yellow brothers yo' father had by Aunt Sallie Deal—what had to come and do your laundry to make her livin'—you got colored relatives scattered all over this county. Them de ways o' de South—mixtries, mixtries. *(WILLIAM enters left, silently, as his mother talks. She is sitting in a chair now. Without looking up)* Is that you, William?

WILLIAM Yes, ma, it's me.

CORA Is you runnin' from him, too?

WILLIAM *(hesitatingly)* Well, ma, you see . . . don't you think kinder . . . well, I reckon I ought to take Libby and ma babies on down to de church house with Reverend Martin and them, or else get 'long to town if I can hitch up them mules. They's scared to be out here, my wife and her ma. All de folks done gone from de houses down yonder by de branch, and you can hear de hounds a bayin' off yonder by de swamp, and cars is tearin' up that road, and de white folks is yellin' and hollerin' and carryin' on somethin' terrible over toward de brook. I done told Robert 'bout his foolishness. They's gonna hang him sure. Don't you think you better be comin' with us, ma. That is, do you want to? 'Course we can go by ourselves, and maybe you wants to stay here and take care o' de big house. I don't want to leave you, ma, but I . . . I . . .

CORA Yo' brother'll be back, son, then I won't be by myself.

WILLIAM *(bewildered by his mother's sureness)* I thought Bert went . . . I thought he run . . . I thought . . .

CORA No, honey. He went, but they ain't gonna get him out there. I sees him comin' back here now, to be with me. I's gwine to guard him 'till he can get away.

WILLIAM Then de white folks'll come here, too.

CORA Yes, de Colonel'll come back here sure. *(the deep baying of the hounds is heard at a distance through the night)* Colonel Tom will come after his son.

WILLIAM My God, ma! Come with us to town.

CORA Go on, William, go on! Don't wait for them to get back. You never was much like neither one o' them—neither de Colonel or Bert—you's mo' like de field hands. Too much o' ma blood in you, I guess. You never liked Bert much, neither, and you always was afraid of de Colonel. Go on, son, and hide yo' wife and her ma and your chilluns. Ain't nothin' gonna hurt you. You never did go against nobody. Neither did I, till tonight. Tried to live right and not hurt a soul, white or colored. *(addressing space)* I tried to live right, Lord. *(angrily)* Tried to live right, Lord. *(throws out her arms resentfully as if to say, "and this is what you give me.")* What's de matter, Lawd, you ain't with me?

(The hounds are heard howling again)

WILLIAM I'm gone, ma. *(He exits fearfully as his mother talks)*

CORA *(bending over the spot on the floor where the COLONEL has lain. She calls)* Colonel Tom! Colonel Tom! Colonel Tom! Look! Bertha and Sallie and William and Bert, all your chilluns, runnin' from you, and you layin' on de floor there, dead! *(pointing)* Out yonder with the mob, dead. And when you come home, upstairs in my bed on top of my body, dead. *(goes to the window, returns, sits down, and begins to speak as if remembering a far-off dream)* Colonel Thomas Norwood! I'm just poor Cora Lewis,

Colonel Norwood. Little black Cora Lewis, Colonel Norwood. I'm just fifteen years old. Thirty years ago, you put your hands on me to feel my breasts, and you say, "You a pretty little piece of flesh, ain't you? Black and sweet, ain't you?" And I lift up ma face, and you pull me to you, and we laid down under the trees that night, and I wonder if your wife'll know when you go back up the road into the big house. And I wonder if my mama'll know it, when I go back to our cabin. Mama said she nursed you when you was a baby, just like she nursed me. And I loved you in the dark, down there under that tree by de gate, afraid of you and proud of you, feelin' your gray eyes lookin' at me in de dark. Then I cried and cried and told ma mother about it, but she didn't take it hard like I thought she'd take it. She said fine white mens like de young Colonel always took good care o' their colored womens. She said it was better than marryin' some Black field hand and workin' all your life in de cotton and cane. Better even than havin' a job like ma had, takin' care o' de white chilluns. Takin' care o' you, Colonel Tom. *(as* CORA *speaks, the sound of the approaching mob gradually grow louder and louder. Auto horns, the howling of dogs, the far-off shouts of men, full of malignant force and power, increase in volume)* And I was happy because I liked you, 'cause you was tall and proud, 'cause you said I was sweet to you and called me purty. And when yo' wife died—de Mrs. Norwood *(scornfully)* that never bore you any chilluns, the pale beautiful Mrs. Norwood that was like a slender pine tree in de winter frost . . . I knowed you wanted me. I was full with child by you then—William, it was—our first boy. And ma mammy said, go up there and keep de house for Colonel Tom, sweep de floors and make de beds, and by and by, you won't have to sweep de floors and make no beds. And what ma mammy said was right. It all come true. Sam and Rusus and 'Vonia and Lucy did de waitin' on you and me, and de washin' and de cleanin' and de cookin'. And all I did was a little sewin' now and then, and a little preservin' in de summer and a little makin' of pies and sweet cakes and things you like to eat on Christmas. And de years went by. And I was always ready for you when you come to me in de night. And we had them chilluns, your chilluns and mine, Tom Norwood, all of 'em! William, born dark like me, dumb like me, and then Baby John what died; then Bertha, white and smart like you; and then Bert with your eyes and your ways and your temper, and mighty nigh your color; then Sallie, nearly white, too, and smart, and purty. But Bert was yo' chile! He was always yo' child . . . Good-looking, and kind, and headstrong, and strange, and stubborn, and proud like you, and de one I could love most 'cause he needed de most lovin'. And he wanted to call you "papa"; and I tried to teach him no, but he did it anyhow and *(sternly)* you beat him, Colonel Thomas Norwood. And he growed up with de beatin' in his heart, and your eyes in his head, and your ways, and your pride. And this summer he looked like you that time I first knowed you down by de road under them trees, young and fiery and proud. There was no touchin' Bert, just like there was no touchin' you. I could only love him, like I loved you. I could only love him. But I couldn't talk to him, because he hated you. He had your ways—and you beat him! After you beat that chile, then you died, Colonel Norwood. You died here in this house, and you been living dead a long time. You lived dead. *(her voice rises above the nearing sounds of the mob)* And when I said this evenin', "Get up! Why don't you help me?" You'd done been dead a long time—a long time before you laid down on this floor, here, with the breath choked out o' you—and Bert standin' over you living, living, living. That's why you hated him. And you want to kill him. Always, you wanted to kill him. Out there with de hounds and de torches and de cars and de guns, you want to kill ma boy. But you won't kill him! He's comin' home first. He's comin' home to me. He's comin' home! *(outside the noise is tremendous now, the lights of autos flash on the window curtains, there are shouts and cries.* CORA *sits, tense, in the middle of the room)* He's comin' home!

A MAN'S VOICE *(outside)* He's somewhere on this lot.

ANOTHER VOICE Don't shoot, men. We want to get him alive.

VOICE Close in on him. He must be in them bushes by the house.

FIRST VOICE Porch! Porch! Porch! There he is yonder—running to the door!

(Suddenly shots are heard. The door bursts open and ROBERT *enters, firing back into the darkness. The shots are returned by the mob, breaking the windows. Flares, lights, voices, curses, screams)*

VOICES Nigger! Nigger! Nigger! Get the nigger!

*(*CORA *rushes toward the door and bolts it after her son's entrance)*

CORA *(leaning against the door)* I was waiting for you, honey. Yo' hiding place is all ready, upstairs, under ma bed, under de floor. I sawed a place there fo' you. They can't find you there. Hurry—before yo' father comes.

ROBERT *(panting)* No time to hide, ma. They're at the door now. They'll be coming up the back way, too. *(sounds of knocking and the breaking of glass)* They'll be coming in the windows. They'll be coming in everywhere. And only one bullet is left, ma. It's for me.

CORA Yes, it's fo' you, chile. Save it. Go upstairs in mama's room. Lay on ma bed and rest.

ROBERT *(going slowly toward the stairs with the pistol in his hand)* Goodnight, ma. I'm awful tired of running, ma. They been chasing me for hours.

CORA Goodnight, son.

*(*CORA *follows him to the foot of the steps. The door begins to give at the forcing of the mob. As* ROBERT *disappears above, it bursts open. A great crowd of white men pour into the room with guns, ropes, clubs, flashlights, and knives.* CORA *turns on the stairs, facing them quietly.* TALBOT, *the leader of the mob, stops)*

TALBOT Be careful, men. He's armed. *(to* CORA*)* Where is that yellow bastard of yours—upstairs?

CORA Yes, he's going to sleep. Be quiet, you all. Wait. *(she bars the way with outspread arms)*

TALBOT *(harshly)* Wait, hell! Come on, boys, let's go! *(a single shot is heard upstairs)* What's that?

CORA *(calmly)* My boy . . . is gone . . . to sleep!

*(*TALBOT *and some of the men rush up the stairway,* CORA *makes a final gesture of love toward the room above. Yelling and shouting, through all the doors and windows, a great crowd pours into the room. The roar of the mob fills the house, the whole night, the whole world. Suddenly* TALBOT *returns at the top of the steps and a hush falls over the crowd)*

TALBOT Too late, men. We're just a little too late.

(A sigh of disappointment rises from the mob. TALBOT *comes down the stairs, walks up to* CORA *and slaps her once across the face. She does not move. It is as though no human hand can touch her again. Curtain)*

NATIVE SON
1941

Paul Green (1894–1981)
Richard Wright (1909–1960)

Herman Mankiewicz and John Houseman had just completed the manuscript for *Citizen Kane* when they decided that they would like to adapt Richard Wright's popular new novel, *Native Son,* for the stage. Houseman contacted Wright for permission to write the script, only to discover that this right had already been granted to Paul Green. Houseman was disappointed but recognized that Green was a reasonable choice considering his honest and sensitive treatment of Black characters, and his having won the Pulitzer Prize for his folk play about Black family life, *In Abraham's Bosom.* Still he wondered if Green, who had a "Southern, rural attitude" toward America's race problem, was the right person to bring such a revolutionary and violent work to life. But agreements had been made, so Houseman's focus now would be obtaining the rights to produce the play.

Wright was invited to Green's home in Chapel Hill, North Carolina, to serve in an advisory capacity while Green worked on the manuscript. They became collaborators. Wright had agreed to certain stipulations that Green made before agreeing to do the script: (1) that he be allowed to make Bigger Thomas, at least in part, responsible for his action, and (2) that he could add humor to the communist scenes.

Houseman went to Chapel Hill to secure producing rights to *Native Son.* He met with Wright and Green and, to his dismay, discovered that Green's notion of what *Native Son* should be was absolutely contrary to Wright's intent. Wright's premise in the novel had been that Negroes like Bigger Thomas could only escape the highly organized repressive structure in which they lived through an act of violence. Green would not, morally or artistically, accept this.

Wright, of course, disagreed with Green, but said nothing. When Houseman asked him why he had not spoken up, Wright's reply was that under no circumstances would he risk a public disagreement with a man like Paul Green. There were too many people on both sides anxious to enjoy a dogfight between a successful Black intellectual and a white Southern writer of progressive reputation—an avowed "friend" of the Negro people.[1]

The first draft of the script, filled with additions and modifications, was not to Houseman's liking, nor were the changes and deletions made in the next draft. What disturbed Houseman most was the change in the moral attitude from that in the novel, and the way Green changed the ending. Wright ended his novel with Bigger Thomas accepting what life had made of him, but in Green's version Bigger is given "'lyric' delusions of grandeur in which he saw himself as 'a Black God, single and alone.'"[2] This folksy treatment of the characters and watermelon image was considered racist and offensive. Even so, Green absolutely refused to change the ending, leaving Houseman at his wits' end. He implored Wright to confront Green, but true to his word, Wright remained neutral, steering clear of the infighting between playwright and producer. He vowed to withdraw the play from production rather than fight with Green.

Houseman's enthusiasm for the play returned once Orson Welles, the director, began preparations for the production. With Green not present during rehearsals, Houseman and Wright rewrote parts of the script keeping it faithful to the novel and Wright's revolutionary concept.

Green was in the audience for the final rehearsal of the play and was enraged by what he saw. At the production meeting the following morning, he insisted that they return to his original script and that his ending be restored. His demands were rejected and the play opened on March 24, 1941, as rehearsed. This Mercury Theatre production starred Canada Lee and ran for ninety-seven performances. After touring major cities across the country, it returned to New York, opening again on October 23, 1942, for eighty-four performances.

Canada Lee, cast as Bigger Thomas, received unanimous praise from the critics. Nearly everything else in the play was controversial. Was the script merely a vehicle for communist propaganda? Had Orson Welles gimmicked the production and sensationalized the story? Was the audience let off the hook or accused of complicity in the murder of Bigger Thomas?

In 1969, Paul Green revised *Native Son,* changing the context to a 1960s Black power struggle. The version published here is the original.

1. John Houseman, *Run-Through* (New York: Simon & Schuster, 1972), pp. 464–465.

2. Ibid., p. 466.

Native Son

Cast of Characters

BIGGER THOMAS, *Negro youth about twenty or twenty-one years old*
HANNAH THOMAS, *his mother, fifty-five*
VERA THOMAS, *his sister, sixteen*
BUDDY THOMAS, *his brother, twelve*
CLARA MEARS, *his sweetheart, twenty*
JACK HENSON, "G. H." RANKIN, GUS MITCHELL } *cronies of* BIGGER *and about his age*
ERNIE JONES, *a cafe and night club owner*
HENRY G. DALTON, *a capitalist, about fifty-five*
ELLEN DALTON, *his wife, about fifty*
MARY DALTON, *their daughter, twenty-two or three*
PEGGY MACAULIFFE, *the* DALTON *cook and maid, forty*
JAN ERLONE, *a labor leader, twenty-eight*
JEFF BRITTEN, *a private detective and local politician, forty-five*
DAVID A. BUCKLEY, *state's attorney, forty*
EDWARD MAX, *an elderly lawyer*
MISS EMMET, *a social worker*
A NEWSPAPERMAN
OTHER NEWSPAPERMEN, NEIGHBORS, GUARDS, A JUDGE, AND OTHERS

TIME *The present*

PLACE *The Black Belt of Chicago*

Scene One

(The THOMAS *bedroom, an early mid-winter morning. In the darkness of the theater, a strident alarm clock begins ringing. It continues a while and then dies out as the curtain rises upon a small poverty-stricken apartment house in the crowded Black Belt of Chicago's South Side. A door at the right leads into the hallway, and at the right center is a pallet of quilts upon which two of the* THOMAS *family,* BIGGER *and* BUDDY*, sleep. Farther back and at the right is a rusty iron bed upon which* VERA *and* HANNAH *sleep, and at the center rear is a small dresser with a dull and splotched mirror. At the left rear, screened from view by a cheap chintz curtain is a corner nook with a gas stove, a sink, and shelves for groceries. A drop-leaf table, covered with an oil-cloth, is against the wall at the left front. There are a couple of chairs, a box and a chest about the room. The plastered walls are cracked and show the lathing here and there. A few crayon likenesses of dead relatives are on the wall—*BIGGER*'s father, his grandfather and grandmother. And in clear dominance above the one bed at the right rear is a large colored lithograph of Jesus Christ hanging on the Cross, with the motto—"I am the Resurrection and the Life." A flower pot on the sill of the window at the left center with a single red geranium is the room's one pretense to beauty. As the curtain rises, the family is busy getting dressed and preparing breakfast. The muffled form of* BIGGER THOMAS *lies bundled under a quilt on the pallet. Far away in the distance, the chimes of a great clock are heard ringing)*

HANNAH *(the middle-aged careworn mother who is busy at the stove, and still wearing her flannel nightgown)* You children hurry up. That old clock done struck the half-past. Hear me, Vera?

VERA Yes, Ma. *(*VERA *is a slender brown-skinned girl of sixteen, dressed in a pink cotton nightgown)*

HANNAH And you too, Buddy. I got a big washing on my hands today. *(*BUDDY*, a dark sober little fellow of twelve, is standing by the stove buttoning his shirt with one hand and warming the other at the gas flame. He is shivering from the morning chill)*

BUDDY Yessum.

HANNAH And, Vera, you got to git to that sewing class. *(*BUDDY *sneezes)* Yes, look at that boy, caught cold again sleeping on that old floor. Told you better sleep with me and Vera at the bed foot. *(*HANNAH *is now fastening her skirt which she has pulled on over her nightgown)* Turn your head, son, so we can get our clothes on. *(silently* BUDDY *turns and looks toward the pallet where* BIGGER *lies, buttoning his shirt the while. The sleeping* BIGGER *turns over, muttering under his quilt and stuffs a pillow against his head)*

VERA Ma wants you to get up too, Bigger. Somebody'll stumble on you lying there. *(she pulls her dress over her head and slips her cotton nightgown off underneath it.* HANNAH *looks toward the pallet and sighs)*

HANNAH Get the milk from the hall, Buddy.

BUDDY Yessum. *(he quickly pulls on his little old coat, his lips blubbering from the cold.* HANNAH *pushes the table out from the wall and begins setting a few dishes on it.* BUDDY *goes out as* HANNAH *calls after him)*

HANNAH Take the empty bottle. Every time I got to tell you. *(he turns, picks up a bottle by the door and disappears)* And, Vera, spread up the bed. *(she begins singing her shrill morning song as she works)*

> Jordan River, chilly and col'
> Chill the body but not the soul—
> Every time I feel the spirit
> Moving in my heart I will pray.

BIGGER *(muttering from his pallet)* How the hell can a man sleep with all this racket?

VERA *(a little testily)* Who'd want to sleep when the rest of us have to work so hard?

BIGGER *(growling)* Yeah, start right in soon's I git my eyes open! *(he covers his head with the quilt again)*

HANNAH Let him alone, Vera.

VERA It's the truth, Ma. He ought to be up looking for a job.

HANNAH Well, he's got his application in down at the relief station.

VERA But he ought to get out—hunt for work—Maybe ask that truck man to take him back, and we'd have something for Christmas!

BIGGER *(sitting suddenly up)* And him sassing at me? *(*BIGGER *is a dark muscular young fellow of some twenty or twenty-one with deep-set eyes and sensitive heavy face. He is dressed in rumpled trousers, shirt and socks)*

VERA Thought it was you sassing at him?

BIGGER You go to—*(muttering darkly)* The white boys got all the good runs—They don't want no niggers driving trucks down to Florida—

HANNAH Maybe you'd better get up, son.

BIGGER Might as well—all the tongues clanging like fire bells. *(*HANNAH *goes out.* BIGGER *rises and stands over his shoes, kicks one into place with his foot, and then rams his left foot down halfway into it. He stomps against the side of the wall to get the shoe on. A pot clatters to the floor behind the curtain, bang-a-lang-lang)* These old shoes wet from that snow four days ago. I was looking for a job then.

VERA *(who is now putting things on the table)* Well, knocking the house down won't dry 'em. *(*BIGGER *stomps his right foot against the wall to get his other shoe on.* BUDDY *enters at the right with a bottle of milk)*

BUDDY *(coming up to the table and helping* VERA*)* Goody, peaches to go with them cornflakes.

VERA And we better go slow on 'em, too. That relief box got to last till Saturday. *(*BUDDY *ducks into the alcove and out again with a couple of glasses and pours the milk.* BIGGER *stands smoking and staring before him.* HANNAH *returns, still singing her song.)*

HANNAH

> By thy bleeding breast and side,
> By the awful death he died—
> Every time I feel the spirit
> Moving in my heart I will pray.

(She hands her towel to VERA, *who takes it and goes out at the right.* BUDDY *strains at the can of peaches with a large pocket knife.* HANNAH *starts working busily at the breakfast)* Gimme that knife—And get away from this table until you done washed yourself—Go on. Vera's got the towel. *(*BUDDY *shies away and goes out.* HANNAH *appraises the knife an instant in her hand)* Why any human being wants to carry around a knife as big as this, I don't see. Why you give it to him, Bigger?

BIGGER *(mumbling)* He wanted to tote it a little bit. *(*HANNAH *opens the can.* BIGGER *now sits bent over in a chair smoking and idly turning the pages of a movie magazine spread on the floor before him. She looks over at him)*

HANNAH Bigger, try for one time to roll that pallet up. No telling when Miss Emmet might come by.

BIGGER *(still lazily reading)* That old case worker ain't studying 'bout us.

HANNAH She got us on relief—and kept us from starving. *(*VERA *comes in again.* BIGGER *rises and rushes out at the right, bumping into somebody in the hall. A flooding high-pitched woman's voice fills the air with a whorl of words)*

VOICE Heigh—you! Yeh, look at you, just look at you—a-tromping and a scrouging. I'm ahead of you and you knows it! Git back in there and wait your turn, boy. *(*BIGGER *turns back and stands sheepishly in the door)*

VERA *(with a biting little laugh)* Reckon Sister Temple told him his manners.

BIGGER *(wrathfully)* All right now, and what's so funny about that old woman with the toilet trots? *(*BUDDY *enters)*

BUDDY Here's yo' towel, Bigger. *(*BIGGER *grabs the towel, balls it up and hurls it across the room, then goes over to the chest, sits down and resumes his magazine.* VERA *and* BUDDY *help their mother at the table, passing in and out of the alcove with a few dishes and food)*

VERA *(coming from the stove)* And that's another thing he ain't got—no respect.

HANNAH Sister Temple lives with her Lord.

BIGGER And her Epsom Salts! Eats it like oatmeal. Jack says so.

VERA Yeh, and that Jack's breaking his grandma's heart like you're breaking Ma's.

BIGGER I wish you'd stop being a little snot, dirting up where you don't belong.

HANNAH *(opening a box of cornflakes)* That's no way to speak to your own sister, son, and she getting to be a young lady now. *(*BIGGER *flaps his magazine over irritatedly)*

VERA If you was the kind of man Ma always hoped you'd be, you'd not have to wait for your turn to go to the bathroom. You'd be up early and get there first. But no—you'd rather hang around Ernie's place with Jack and that low-life gang and let us live on relief.

HANNAH Hush, Vera.

BIGGER Yeh, hush—always hush. *(muttering)* Relief didn't say more'n forty people got to use the same toilet every morning—lining up like women to see Clark Gable. *(with sudden viciousness as he flings his arm around)* It's the way the white folks built these old buildings!

VERA Now don't start cussing the white folks again . . .

HANNAH They what keep us alive right this minute. *(he gets up and strides into the hall.* HANNAH *wags her head dolefully)* Now here we go again. Said to myself last night, we was gonna quit fussing at him. Don't do no good.

VERA How can we help it and seem like some strange devil growing in him all the time. *(her voice filled with angry earnestness)* He gets more like a stranger to us every day. He ain't never got a smile for anybody. And there's that Clara woman he runs with. Here I try to make myself respectable and be somebody, and he—

HANNAH Oh, Lord, I don't know. *(calling contritely)* Come on back, son. Le's try to eat in peace, Vera.

BUDDY *(piping up)* Bigger says we ain't got nothing to smile about, says that's what wrong with the niggers—always smiling, and nothing to smile about. *(he leans over, smells the peaches, and wrinkles his nose in delight)*

HANNAH Shut yo' mouth, boy.

BUDDY That's what he say—

HANNAH Yeh, he say a lot he hadn't ought to. If the white folks ever hear him—

VERA And some these days they're gonna hear him—

HANNAH Bigger needs God in him, that's what. I've prayed, and Sister Temple's prayed, and Reverend Hammond's put up special prayers for him. Yeh, God's what he needs, po' boy.

BIGGER *(who has reappeared in the door)* God! *(flinging out a gesture, his voice rising mockingly)* Yeh, you got him hanging on the wall there—the white folk's God!

VERA Yeh, every morning he gets up like something mad at the world.

HANNAH *(with a touch of piteousness as she looks fervently at the picture on the wall, her lips moving audibly, quoting)* "I am the Resurrection and the Life." Your pa knowed that, son, your pa lived by it.

BIGGER And he died by it. *(half chanting, mockingly)* "They hung his head on the thorny cross, the red blood trickled down."

HANNAH Bigger, stop that!

VERA *(quickly)* come on, le's eat breakfast.

HANNAH This ain't the way to start the day off.

BIGGER Way you start every day—when I'm around.

BUDDY *(uncertainly)* Yeh, let's eat! *(they sit to the table.* HANNAH *lifts the family Bible from the top of the chest and opens it. Suddenly there comes a thin, dry rattling sound in the wall at the rear. They all sit listening an instant.* BUDDY *calls out)* Listen!

BIGGER Yeah, that's old man Dalton, all right. *(hacking a hunk of bread off from the loaf and buttering it)* If that old rat stick his head out this time, I'm gonna scrush it for him.

HANNAH *(reading)* "I have trodden the winepress alone; and of people there was none with me; for I will tread them in mine anger, and trample them in my fury; and their blood shall be sprinkled upon my garments, and I will stain—" *(the noise in the wall is heard again)* "—all my raiment. For the day of vengeance is in my heart, and the year of my redeemer is come—And I will tread down the people in mine anger, and make them drunk in my fury, and I will bring down their strength to the earth." Blessed be the name of the Lord. *(the noise in the wall is heard still again)*

BUDDY *(whispering)* That's him, aw right.

HANNAH *(closing the Bible)* Bow your heads. *(*BUDDY *and* VERA *bow their heads.* BIGGER *sits munching his bread and staring moodily before him.* HANNAH*'s words rise in deep humility)* Lord our Father in Heaven, we thank Thee for the food You have prepared for the nourishment of our humble bodies. We thank Thee for the many blessings of thy loving grace and mercy. Guide our poor feet in the path of righteousness for your sake. Bless this home, this food, these children You gave me. Help me to raise them up for a pride and witness to their Lawd. And thine be the power and the glory forever and ever—Amen. *(they all begin eating as* HANNAH *lifts her gaze again to Jesus on the wall. Suddenly* BIGGER *springs out of his chair with a shout)*

BIGGER There he go! *(he lunges across the room, flings himself over the bed and begins jabbing in the corner with his foot. Then, springing back, he seizes an old baseball bat from the floor.* BUDDY *grabs the bread knife and hops up)*

BUDDY *(as* VERA *and* HANNAH *jump to their feet)* Where is he? Where is he?

BIGGER He's our meat this time. We got his hole stopped up.

HANNAH *(shakily)* There he goes.

VERA *(with a squeal)* Where, Ma, where?

BIGGER *(creeping toward the trunk)* The sonofabitch, I see his shiny eye. *(there is a knock on the door, but no one heeds it.* BIGGER *lunges behind the trunk and strikes a shattering blow against the floor. There is a scramble as* BUDDY *rushes across the room and peers under the bed.* BIGGER *creeps forward, his whole body tensely alive)*

BUDDY *(pointing)* Yonder—yonder—

BIGGER *(bending down)* Jesus, look at them teeth! *(he grabs the end of the bed with one hand and swings it around the room)* He's behind that box now. *(his voice is charged with a harsh intensity. Again there is a knock at the door)*

VERA *(half-weeping)* Let him go, Bigger. Let him go.

HANNAH *(piteously)* Unstop the hole, let him out.

BIGGER Gimme that skillet, quick! *(*BUDDY *rushes over to the alcove and hands him the skillet.* BIGGER *takes aim, and hurls it into the corner)*

BUDDY *(excitedly)* You hit him, you hit him! *(the door opens silently and a smallish young white woman, carrying a black portfolio in her hands stands in the doorway. She looks inquiringly and then half-frightenedly at the scene before her. Now* BIGGER *creeps toward the kitchen nook.* HANNAH *and* VERA *have their arms about each other, watching him breathlessly.* BIGGER *stands waiting, poised, his hand raised)*

BIGGER *(his feet weaving to the right and left)* Yeah, there you sit on your hind legs and gnashing them tushes at me—I'm gonna beat your brains out—Wheeooh! *(with a yell he jumps forward and strikes with flailing, lightning blows along the curtain edge on the floor)*

HANNAH Bigger, Bigger!

BIGGER *(lifting the rat up and holding it by the tail, a murmuring chant running from his lips)* I got you, old man Dalton, got you that time! I put out your light, mashed you into a mushy, bloody pudding. You dead now—dead, dead, dead, dead—

VERA Stop him, Ma! *(the woman in the door now stands shaken and weakly leaning against the lintel)* Look, Ma!

HANNAH *(moaning)* Mercy sake, Bigger. Here's Miss Emmet.

BIGGER Try to run now—try to bite me—just try it, you black, fat, slimy, ratty, greasy— *(his words gradually die out as he looks up and sees* MISS EMMET. *She comes on into the room)*

HANNAH Miss Emmet!—Bigger, take that thing out of here right now!

MISS EMMET I came a little early—before you got to work. *(she is a kindly young woman, serious-faced and tired)*

BUDDY We just killed a rat. Yessum. *(with a touch of boyish pride)* Bigger done it. Ain't he a big one?

BIGGER *(softly)* That scutter could cut your throat—the biggest one we ever killed. *(holding him up)* See him, Miss Emmet?

MISS EMMET Yes, I see it. *(drawing back)* Better throw it away.

BIGGER *(feeling him)* See how fat he is—feeding on garbage. They get more to eat than we do. Yeh, old Dalton, you're going to the incinerator and there ain't no coming back. *(he shakes the rat at* VERA *and she squeals)*

MISS EMMET *(quietly)* Why do you call it Dalton, Bigger?

BIGGER Just call 'em that.

BUDDY Yessum. Last week us killed another rat in here—we calls 'em "Old Man Dalton"—the big man what owns all the houses round here—

HANNAH I said to him, "Anyhow, Bigger, you might leastwise say 'Mr. Dalton.'" *(a small meek smile passes around* MISS EMMET*'s lips)* Sit down, Ma'am.

MISS EMMET Yes, considering Mr. Dalton's kindness to the people of your race. *(she sits down and opens her portfolio)*

BIGGER *(softly)* Kind—*(flaring up)* I wish old Dalton'd show up around here sometime—I'd fix 'im up—Like I did that rat—

VERA Hush, Bigger!

HANNAH *(soothingly)* He don't mean nothing by it, Miss Emmet—

BUDDY Gimme heah, Bigger.

BIGGER *(now beginning to grow silent again, the excitement dying in him)* Okay. *(he hands the rat to* BUDDY *who takes it proudly and goes out.* BIGGER *sits down on the chest, finishing a hunk of buttered bread)*

HANNAH *(watching* MISS EMMET *eagerly, holding her cup of coffee in her hand)* I pray the Lord you got some good news for us, ma'am.

MISS EMMET I hope so.

HANNAH Bless you, ma'am. I knowed you'd help us.

MISS EMMET Just a final question or two. Bigger, about your application. As head of the house—*(she takes out a double-leaved form sheet and untops her fountain pen.* VERA *leaves the table and goes over to the mirror)*

BIGGER *(with a little laugh)* We ain't got nothin' but this one room, and there ain't no head to it.

MISS EMMET But as soon as we place you in a job, Bigger, you'll feel differently.

BIGGER *(fumbling with the movie magazine)* What kind of job I going to get?

MISS EMMET Mr. Dalton is interested in placing his jobless tenants.

BIGGER *(with the faintest touch of a snicker)* Yessum.

HANNAH *(happily)* Hear that, Bigger? *(she sets her coffee cup down and wipes her hands on her apron.* BUDDY *reappears and goes back to his bowl of cornflakes)*

MISS EMMET *(as she looks at her wrist watch)* There's an opening with Mr. Dalton's family itself—the job of chauffeur. You might get that place. According to the record here, you're a first-rate driver.

BUDDY He sure can drive. *(snapping his fingers)* She's gone from here. Hot dog!

MISS EMMET But we must supply Mr. Dalton with all the facts. Here under previous history you failed to mention that matter of reform school, Bigger.

BIGGER Yeh, yeh—I knowed they was gonna find that out. Jesus! You white folks know everythin'.

MISS EMMET When did it happen? We must have the facts.

VERA Go ahead, Bigger. Tell the lady.

BIGGER You tell her, Ma. I done forgot them things.

HANNAH It was a year ago last June, ma'am. That old no 'count Gus Mitchell fellow told on him. *(eagerly)* But please, Miss Emmet—

MISS EMMET *(writing)* Three months term, ending June 15th, 1939. Metropolitan Home for the Detention of Juvenile Delinquents—Theft—Taking of three automobile tires from a colored garage—Is that right?

BIGGER *(with a faint touch of mockery)* Yessum, that must be about right.

MISS EMMET And you haven't had any other trouble since, Bigger?

BIGGER No'm—

MISS EMMET *(holds out her fountain pen)* Now please sign here.

BIGGER *(with apparent reluctance as he takes the pen)* I done signed that paper once.

MISS EMMET Yes, but this is added material and we must follow the Washington rules.

BIGGER Sure if the big man in Washington say so. He the boss. *(with a flourish in the air, he writes his name)*

MISS EMMET *(taking the blank, breathing on it, and then giving it a little drying wave in the air)* I'll send Mr. Dalton a confidential report recommending you, Bigger. In fact, I'll take it down to his office this morning.

HANNAH *(joy breaking over her face)* God bless you, ma'am. I been praying to hear something, and now to know that Bigger gonna have a good job—*(touching her hands together evangelically)* Bless the Lord, bless the Lord. Bigger will make a new start—From now on he will, ma'am. Won't you, son?

BUDDY *(with fervent admiration)* You gonna drive Mr. Dalton's big car, Bigger. *(suddenly putting his hands up on the steering wheel of an imaginary car and driving it around the room)* Swoos-s-hh, look out, everybody—old twelve-cylinders coming round the curve. *(he bumps into* MISS EMMET *who stands up with a little gentle laugh)*

HANNAH Look out, boy, you 'bout to run over the lady!

BIGGER *(flinging up his hand and grinning as he adopts the attitude of a traffic cop, at the same time blowing a sharp whistle through his teeth)* Hey, what you mean running through that red light? Pull up heah and lemme see your license, boy. *(he scuffs* BUDDY*'s hair a bit in spontaneous friendliness; then his face grows heavy again)* But, pshaw, I ain't gonna get that job.

MISS EMMET Now good-by, Mrs. Thomas. Good-by, Bigger. You'll hear as soon as I contact Mr. Dalton. Keep your head up—*(she smiles wanly at them and goes out)*

HANNAH *(following her to the door)* Bless you, ma'am, bless you—whole soul and body—*(she closes the door and turns happily about the room)* And my prayers are answered. I knowed they'd be. *(she begins piling the household wash rapidly into a sheet)*

VERA *(coming by* BIGGER *and stopping with deep earnestness)* Maybe this is the real break. We are all so glad, Bigger. And we can quit living in one room like pigs.

BIGGER Aw, cut it out.

VERA Good-by, Ma. *(she goes by her mother, gives her a little pecking kiss, and then turning gives* BIGGER*'s arm an affectionate squeeze)* And you'll help me pay for my domestic science, won't you?

HANNAH Sure he will.

VERA Yes. Come on, Buddy, time you was out selling your papers.

HANNAH *(jubilantly)* Ain't it the truth? And let's all hustle. *(*BIGGER *is now sitting at the table idly marking across the movie magazine with a pencil)*

BUDDY *(putting on his overcoat and cap)* 'Bye, Ma. *(standing in front of* BIGGER*)* You lemme ride in that old Dusenberg sometime?

BIGGER *(spreading out an imaginary document in front of him and beginning to write gravely)* Have to examine the archives of the Commitment Home first. How the hell I know what you been doing on the sly?

BUDDY *(his face crinkling into a smile)* Bigger you sure a case. Look, Ma, Bigger's smiling.

BIGGER Hell, I ain't smiling none. *(*BUDDY *scampers out after* VERA*)*

HANNAH *(laying a coin on the table by him)* Here, son, take this fifty cents. Run down there to the corner and get me two bars of that hard soap, a bottle of bluing, and a box of starch, and a can of Red Devil lye, and make a bee-line back to the basement. Sister Temple and me will be needing it for the work. *(*BIGGER *continues to scrawl with his pencil)* Hear me?

BIGGER Yeh.

HANNAH *(turning to him, her voice affectionate and serious)* Bigger, that good white lady is right. From now on, you're the real head of the house. She gonna get you that job. I ain't gonna be with you always, trying to make a home for you children. And Vera and Buddy has got to have protection. Hear me, son? *(she lifts the bundled sheet of clothes over her shoulder)*

BIGGER Uhm—

HANNAH I'll be too old to work soon. *(laying a hand gently on his shoulder)* And some day yet you'll believe like me—my boy—*(she bends over, touches him lightly on the hair with her lips and goes silently and suddenly out. For an instant he sits stock still. His hand goes up into the air, as if to feel the top of his head, and then comes down on the table in a clenched fist. He looks upward at the picture of Christ on the wall. He begins to study it closely, and gradually a wry twisting smile slides around his lips.*

BIGGER *(reading)* "I am the Resurrection and the Life"—Uhm—*(he gets sharply up and puts on his old leather coat and cap. The chimes begin to ring again. He stands listening)* They ringing your bells, Lawd—*(as if irritated by some inner thought, he slaps the coin down on the table)* Heads I do, tails I don't. *(disgustedly)* Heads. *(he gives a little laugh, shakes his shoulders and spits angrily at the stove. A signal whistle comes up from outside the window at the left. It is repeated. He stands in indecision a moment and then goes over and looks out. Finally he raises his hand in a sort of fascist salute and waves it across the pane)* Okay, be right with you, Jack! *(he turns back toward the bed, pulls forth a wooden packing box and unlocks it. He takes out a pistol, and looks at it and then back at the picture)* Here's what you didn't have—but I got it! *(hurriedly he crams it into his blouse.* HANNAH *comes in still carrying the sheet of clothes slung over her shoulder)*

HANNAH *(to herself)* Seem like my mind failing away. Forgot my washboard again. *(queryingly)* What you up to, boy? *(without answering* BIGGER *kicks the box back under the bed and goes quickly out. Something in his actions disturbs* HANNAH. *She gazes worriedly after him and then hurries to the door and calls)* Bigger! *(more loudly)* Bigger! *(but there is no answer. Slowly and heavily she turns into the room again. Dropping the bundle of clothes, she hurries into the hall, calling)* Come back here, boy!

(The chimes continue to ring. Fadeout)

Scene Two

(A street, that afternoon. The chimes die away as the scene opens again on a street and sidewalk in front of Ernie's Kitchen Shack, somewhere on Indiana Avenue near 47th Street. At the right front the gullet of a narrow alleyway leads back into the shadows. And at the mouth of the alleyway sits a garbage can, looking like a squat molar in its maw, across which is a string label saying "Keep Our City Clean." The entrance to Ernie's place of business is through a door in the center with windows on either side. Adjoining the "shack" is an empty building with a boarded-up window on which are posters announcing the candidacy of two men for the office of state's attorney for Cook County. One of the men depicted is middle-aged, of imposing bearing, and declared to be "The Party's Choice." The other is somewhat elderly, less commanding, and announced to be "The People's Choice." Their names written in large letters respectively are David A. Buckley and Edward Max. At the left front is a hydrant and near it a steel lamp-post topped above with the usual globular glass. The sounds of a busy thoroughfare are heard off at the left—a streetcar clanging, automobile horns, now and then a tremulous roar of a heavy truck, and once or twice the siren of a squad or ambulance car—a great wash of droning sound.

When the curtain rises, BIGGER *and sportly* JACK HENSON, *one of his buddies, are seen leaning against the wall near the left rear. Their caps are pulled down and coat collars turned up to warm them in the splotch of winter sun that shines upon them and the wall. Now and then they look up and down the street with watchful, roving eyes)*

BIGGER *(spitting and looking at his watch)* Time G.H. was here.

JACK They'll be here. Everything's jake. *(softly)* Passed old Blum's while ago—setting back in there like a crab.

BIGGER *(looking carefully about him)* Yeh, I seen him. Back to the door—bent over by the cash register working in his books. How much you think we get?

JACK Hundred fifty bucks anyhow. It's a cinch.

BIGGER Cinch—and a white man. Don't seem right.

JACK Getting up into big time, boy. *(he laughs)*

BIGGER Uhm—twenty minutes till. Gimme another cigarette, Jack.

JACK *(peering at him)* Twenty minutes till—*(narrowly)*—and ain't no gun in it. *(he pulls out a package of cigarettes)* This is our second pack already.

BIGGER *(taking a cigarette)* Who said a gun?

JACK Nobody. Somebody get killed—then the hot seat. *(whistling)* Jesus! *(*BIGGER *stares at him)*

BIGGER That Gus Mitchell—old tongue wags at both ends. He keep mo' out of trouble just wagging one end. *(he lights up his cigarette and holds the match for* JACK*)*

JACK Gus got mighty sharp eyes, though. *(after a few draws)* Gosh, you shake like an old woman. And what your hands doing sweating so?

BIGGER *(throwing down the match)* Hell. Light it yourself. *(*JACK *lights up.* CLARA MEARS, *an attractive, kindly young Negro girl, comes in at the right, carrying a package under one arm. She smiles brightly at* BIGGER *and stops)*

CLARA Hy, Bigger.

JACK Hy, Clara.

BIGGER *(nonchalantly)* Hy, Clara.

CLARA Thought I'd find you here.

BIGGER Smart girl—

CLARA Missed you last night, honey.

BIGGER I was busy. *(she puts out a hand and touches him affectionately on the arm)*

CLARA Gonna see you tonight?

BIGGER Maybe.

JACK *(laughs)* Maybe.

CLARA *(with a slap in the air at* JACK*)* The

Burtons got a house full of company for Christmas—but I'll get off. Maybe we'll go to a picture? *(looking at her wrist watch and then up at the sun)* Gee, I got to hurry. *(giving* BIGGER*'s arm a farewell squeeze)* It's a date.

BIGGER *(still nonchalantly)* Okay. *(she gazes deep into his face and then hurries out at the left)*

JACK Shucks, that gal loves the very ground you walk on.

BIGGER It don't matter.

JACK Uh?

BIGGER Love 'em and leave 'em.

JACK Not Clara.

BIGGER Huh?

JACK Nothing. *(They puff in silence a moment and then stare off before them.* BIGGER *runs his fingers around inside his collar and twists his head)* Kinder warm today—for December.

BIGGER Almost like summer . . . *(sharply)* Summer or winter—all the same. *(he pulls out his dollar watch again)*

JACK Yeh, all the same. Quit looking at that old watch—time never pass. *(he chuckles)*

BIGGER Now what? *(he spits)*

JACK Gus say he don't want you in on the job neither—too nervous, he say.

BIGGER Lousy runt!

JACK Say you too hair-trigger. Now keep your shirt on and quit that spitting. There he come. *(*JACK *straightens up and stares off as* GUS *comes briskly into the scene from the left. He is a small-sized Negro about Bigger's age and wears his cap turned round like a baseball catcher. As he enters he cups his right hand to his mouth as though holding an imaginary telephone transmitter and his left hand to his ear with a receiver. He grins as he bows)*

GUS Hello-hello.

JACK *(responding quickly and pantomiming)* Hello—Yes—uhm—old Gus boy—

GUS Who's speaking?

JACK Why—er—this is the president of the United States of America.

GUS Oh, yes suh, Mr. President. What's on your mind?

JACK I'm calling a cabinet meeting this afternoon at three o'clock—as secretary of state you must be there!

BIGGER *(satirically)* Hah-hah.

GUS Well, now, Mr. President, I'm pretty busy. Bombs falling all over Europe. I'm thinking of sending that old Hitler another note.

JACK And them Japs—they . . .

BIGGER *(pantomiming like the others)* Hello, Mr. President. I just cut in from the sidelines and heard what you said. Better wait about that war business. The niggers is raising sand all over the country! You better put them down first.

JACK Oh, if it's about the niggers, Mr. Willkie, we'll wait on the war!

BIGGER *(satirically)* Yes, suh. At a time like this, we Republicans and Democrats got to pull together!

GUS Reckon we can do without you, Mr. Willkie. *(they bow about in sudden and rich physical laughter, slapping their thighs, their knees easy and bent)*

JACK Lawd, Lawd, Lawd—

BIGGER I bet that's just how they talk.

JACK Sho, it is—*(*ERNIE *comes to the rear door, and stands looking out. He is a stoutish phlegmatic Negro of fifty or more)*

ERNIE 'Bout time to open up here, and how you speck me to have any customers and you all wallowing all over the pavement?

BIGGER Aw, go suck something.

ERNIE *(angrily)* I don't want none of your back-talk, Bigger Thomas.

BIGGER Three o'clock our zero hour—ten minutes and we go.

ERNIE Ten minutes then, 'fore I call a cop. *(he turns back into the shadow)* You're up to devilment, I know you. *(he disappears)*

BIGGER *(muttering)* Sonofabitch. *(turning toward* GUS *and staring at him with hard bright eyes)* So you don't want Mr. Willkie in on the deal—huh—meaning me?

GUS Aw, I was just joking, Bigger.

BIGGER You wanter live and keep doing well— . . . drop the joking. *(he pauses a moment)* But, hell, I ain't against no war. I'd just soon fight as to stand here waiting all day.

JACK Fight who?

BIGGER Hell, anybody. I'd just soon take a gun and pop off a few of these white folks—old Blum too. Eight minutes to three . . . Goddammit! I feel old Blum gnawing round my liver here.

JACK *(softly)* Yeh, and in your lungs and throat too—like fire. We gonna spit him out in a few minutes now.

BIGGER Sometime you can hardly breathe. you know what—sometime—*(with sudden anger)* Where's G.H.? Goddammit. I'm ready for old Blum!

JACK Christ, don't talk so loud. Ernie'll hear you. We got five minutes yet. *(they are silent for a moment.* BIGGER *tilts back his face and the sun shines full upon it.* JACK *stares up at the sky and sneezes twice)*

GUS That's sign o' bad luck!

BIGGER *(yelling)* Go to hell! Superstition—you niggers—signs, wonders—Look up there—the white man's sign.

JACK What?

BIGGER *(dramatically)* That airplane—writing on the sky—like a little finger—*(they all three look up)* So high up, looks like a little bird. *(waving his hands)* Sailing and looping and zooming—And that white smoke coming out of his tail—*(he walks restlessly about)*

JACK *(reading—afar off)* "Use Speed Gasoline"—

BIGGER *(exultantly)* Speed! That's what them white boys got!

GUS *(whispering)* Daredevils—

BIGGER Go on, boys, fly them planes, fly 'em to the end of the world, fly 'em smack into the sun! I'm with you. Goddam! *(he stares up, the sunlight on his face)*

GUS *(unable to let well enough alone, doffing his cap in a mock bow to* BIGGER*)* Yessuh! If you wasn't *Black* and if you had some *money* and if they'd let you go to that *aviation* school, you might could be with 'em.

BIGGER *(fiercely)* Yeh, keep on, keep on now!

JACK *(flexing his hands as though holding onto controls, he makes the sound of an airplane motor)* Thrr—hu-hu-hu-hu—

GUS Wish I could fly now!

*(*BIGGER *joins* JACK *in the roar of the plane, primping his lips.* GUS *also joins in, and for a moment the sound of the motor goes on uninterruptedly.* G.H.*, a darkish heavy-set young Negro comes in at the left. He lifts one hand in a mocking "Heil Hitler" salute, holding his nose with the other.* BIGGER *sees him and barks out an order)*

BIGGER You pilot!

G.H. *(falling in with the game)* Yessuh!

BIGGER Give her the stick and pull right over! *(he bends over, squinting, as if peering down through glasses from a great height)* Machine gunner, give that crowd down there on Michigan Boulevard some hot lead.

JACK Yessuh! *(making the rat-tat-tat of a machine gun)* Rat-tat-tat-tat-tat-tat, rat-tat-tat-tat-tat—

BIGGER Looks at the white folks fall—*(he speaks in a half singsong as he turns with growing excitement about him—exultantly)* Now we gonna dive-bomb that Tribune Tower. *(he leads off with the zooming roar of an airplane throttle opened at full speed. The others join in.* BIGGER *cries out wildly)* Turn 'em loose! *(he makes a kicking motion downward with his foot, and then in a high whine depicts the passage of the bombs earthward. They all make the "boom" of the explosion together)*

GUS *(bent over, staring down)* Lawd, look at the smoke.

BIGGER A direct hit, sergeant. *(loudly)* Look at the fires—things flying through air—houses—people—streetcars—hunks of sidewalk and pavements. Goddam! Whoom—Tracer bullets. *(yelling)* Look out! There come the fighter planes! *(frantically pulling his pistol)* Cold steel! Watch the turn—Put it through the navel. *(the three boys look at him and then spring back in fear, their playful spirit suddenly gone)*

G.H. That crazy fool!

GUS *(pointing)* Look he's got a gun. I knowed it. *(*BIGGER *continues to aim about him. The others mumble in half fear)*

BIGGER *(hunching out his shoulder and running at* JACK *who dodges him)* Crash him! Crash him!

GUS *(throwing out his hands in fear)* Put up that gun, fool!

BIGGER *(whirling and leveling the gun at* GUS*)* Ride into 'em or I'll shoot your lights out. *(he gives a high wild laugh)*

G.H. Bigger, for Christ's sake! Somebody'll see you!

GUS I told you he's crazy! Now just look at him!—

BIGGER *(advancing upon* GUS *with gun leveled)* You sonofabitch, don't you call me crazy—

GUS *(backing away toward the other two boys, who stare at him silently)* He's yellow. He's scared to rob a white man, that how come he brung that gun. *(he moves behind* JACK*)* I told you to leave him out of it. *(*BIGGER *puts up his gun and suddenly darts out his hand, seizes* GUS *by the collar, and bangs his head against the wall)*

BIGGER *(his face working in violent rage, as he pulls his knife again)* I don't need no gun. Yellow, huh? *(pushing the knife against* GUS*'s stomach)* Take it back.

JACK That ain't no way to play, Bigger.

BIGGER Who the hell said I was playing?

GUS Please, Bigger. I was just joking.

BIGGER *(his lips snarled back over his teeth)* Want me to cut your belly button out?

G.H. Aw, leave him alone, Bigger.

BIGGER Put your hands up. Way up! *(*GUS *swallows and stretches his hands high along the wall. He stares out with wide frightened eyes, and sweat begins to trickle down his temples. His lips hang open and loose)* Shut them liver lips.

GUS *(in a tense whisper)* Bigger!

BIGGER *(pressing the point of the knife deeper against his belly)* Take it back. Say "I'm a lying sonofabitch."

GUS *(with a moan)* Quit!

BIGGER Say it, say it.

G.H. *(staring horrified at him)* For Christ's sake, Bigger!

BIGGER Take it back. Say it. *(*GUS *begins to slump down along the wall.* BIGGER *jabs him slightly. He straightens up quickly with a howl)* Say, "I'm a lying sonofabitch."

GUS I'm—I'm a lying sonofabitch. *(his arm falls down and his head slumps forward.* BIGGER *releases him)*

BIGGER Next time you whimper on me I'm gonna kill you. Now scat. *(hissing)* You ain't gonna be in on this. I'll take your share of the haul. *(he starts at* GUS *again, who gazes wildly around him a moment and then flies out of the scene at the right. For a while they are all silent. The noise of the city rolls in across the scene)* Goddammit, somebody, say something!

JACK *(watching him)* Don't cuss at us.

BIGGER I am cussing at you. Come on, will you?

G.H. *(angrily)* Aw, lay off! *(somewhere from a tower a clock booms three times. They listen, stock still)*

BIGGER All right, zero hour.

G.H. I ain't going nowhere—now.

BIGGER Hundred fifty bucks waiting in that cash drawer. *(they eye him in cold silence)* Goddammit, you scared?

JACK Yeh, we was gonna walk in quiet—"Hand over your money," we say, and then back out. Now, you bring along a gun and a knife—maybe kill somebody and put us in the 'lectric chair *(laughing harshly)* who's scared? *(he pulls a sort of wooden peg from his pocket and throws it into the alley)*

BIGGER Just one more word out of you. *(laughing hysterically)* So you all turn against me—huh? I knowed you bastards was scared! I'll do it by myself—Just watch. And when I do, don't nobody even speak to me, don't ask me for time to die, you hear? *(*ERNIE *comes to the door)*

ERNIE Bigger, get away from here.

BIGGER *(whirling on him and jerking out his knife)* Make me!

ERNIE I'll fix you this time—*(he turns around and reaches up as if to lift a hidden weapon down from above the door. But* BIGGER *springs forward, grabs him and jerks him out to the sidewalk. With a swipe of his knife, he cuts off a piece of* ERNIE*'s coat and holds it up, yelling)*

BIGGER This is a sample of the cloth. Wanta see a sample of the meat?

ERNIE *(gasping)* I'll get my gun—I'll shoot you—

G.H. Let's go, Come on. *(*BUDDY *comes running to the scene carrying a bundle of papers under his arm and an envelope in his hand. He stops for an instant and looks at the scene, and then hurries forward)*

BUDDY Bigger—that lady come by the house—sent a message for you. *(*BIGGER *stares at* ERNIE *and chuckles, at the same time reaches out and takes the letter from* BUDDY. BUDDY *looks off, then springs away out at the left, calling)* Paper, mister, paper!

BIGGER You all keep quiet while I read my mail. *(he backs off a few steps and opens the letter with a rip of his knife)* Good Gordon gin! *(the others watch him)* Old Man Dalton wants to see me at my convenience—immediately if not sooner. *(shouting out at them)* Damn all of you now—you can all go to hell. I'm gonna be driving for a millionaire, and don't you speak to me no more, none of you. Hear me? *(he laughs and spits)* I spit in your slimy faces—a bunch of yellow cowards.

JACK *(placatingly, as he edges forward)* Is it a job for real, Bigger?

BIGGER And when I go riding by, tip your hats—you'd better—yeh, you had—*(*ERNIE *has been edging back into the door)* Yeh, get your gun, Ernie. I ain't afraid of it—I'm finished with all you cheesy little punks—I'm on my way now—*(he makes an upward gesture, then feeling in his coat pocket, pulls out a coin and scornfully throws it at them)* Here, take this fifty cents and buy you some hash. *(he turns and goes quickly out at the left)*

ERNIE On his way now—*(mopping his forehead)* Somebody gonna kill that fool yet.

JACK Or he's gonna kill somebody. Takes more'n a job to cure what ails him!

G.H. *(picking up the piece of money from the pavement)* Come on, let's get something to drink, Jack.

JACK And a nickel for some canned music.

G.H. Old boogie-woogie take the pressure off.

ERNIE *(still staring in the direction* BIGGER *has gone)* Yeh, come on in. What'll you have? *(the boys start into the cafe. The automatic phonograph immediately begins playing a drum-beaten blues song, and continues. Fadeout)*

Scene Three

(The following morning. As the blues music dies away, the curtain rises on the sun-filled spotless DALTON *breakfast room. To the left is a door which opens into the dining room, and to the right another door leading into the kitchen and back hall. In the center room is a wide triple window, giving a view beyond of the* DALTON *private grounds. The table in the center room is decorated with a vase of hot-house poinsettia, and by the window is a canary's cage.*

When the curtain rises, MR. *and* MRS. DALTON *are seated at the table and* PEGGY *is making toast on an electric toaster at the right. A portable tea wagon, with plates and hot dishes, is just behind her.* PEGGY *is the Irish cook and maid. She is about forty years old and wears a blue dress with white apron, collar and cap—the typical maid's uniform.* MR. DALTON *is holding an application form in one hand and a coffee cup in the other. He is about fifty-five or sixty and wears a pair of pince-nez be-ribboned glasses on the bridge of his nose.* MRS. DALTON *is middle-aged, thin, almost ascetic, and dressed in flowing white, with a knitted shawl draped loosely about her shoulders. She holds a white pet cat in the crook of her arm, and one pallid hand fumbles at the food in front of her. Her eyes are staring and blinkless.* BIGGER, *dressed as usual in his old black leather jacket, is standing before them with his cap in his hand)*

DALTON *(reading in a hurried slurring tone)* Twenty years of age—grammar school education—poor student but learns quickly when he applies himself—*(he glances at* BIGGER*)* Counted as head of the house—color complex—father killed in a race riot in Jackson, Mississippi, August 15th, 1930. *(he looks up again, clearing his throat)* Quite a lot of background factors, Ellen.

MRS. DALTON *(quietly)* Yes.

BIGGER *(mumbling uncertainly)* Yessuh, they told me to bring it.

*(*PEGGY *sets a glass of milk by* MRS. DALTON *and re-fills* MR. DALTON'*s coffee cup)*

DALTON *(as* DALTON *goes on,* BIGGER *now and then lifts his slumbrous eyes and gives* MRS. DALTON'*s sightless face a somewhat awed and inquiring look)* Knows how to obey orders but is of unstable equilibrium as to disposition. *(chuckling)* Never mind all those words, Bigger—part of the new social philosophy. Uh, what kind of car did you drive last?

BIGGER A truck, sir.

DALTON Got your license?

BIGGER *(showing it)* Yessuh, I can drive most any kind. I can handle a Dusenberg right off.

DALTON I have a Buick.

BIGGER Yessuh.

DALTON Now, Bigger, about this reform school business. Just forget it. I was a boy myself once, and God knows I got into plenty of jams.

MRS. DALTON *(softly)* But he's colored, Henry.

DALTON I know, I know, Ellen. *(looking at his watch and rising)* I've got to be getting on down to the office. They're threatening to rent strike over on Prairie Avenue . . . Old man Max's labor speeches . . . Peggy, suppose you show Bigger around. Let him try his hand at the furnace. *(to* MRS. DALTON*)* He suits me all right, Ellen. Bigger, I always leave the final decision in these matters to Mrs. Dalton.

BIGGER Yessuh. *(a buzzer on the back wall sounds a sudden thur-rrh.* PEGGY *turns quickly)*

DALTON No you don't. Mary will have her breakfast here.

PEGGY Yes, sir.

DALTON No more of this breakfast in bed business.

MRS. DALTON *(always in her gentle unhurried manner)* She was out late last night—at the university—

DALTON She can get up just the same—*(he comes over and kisses* MRS. DALTON *on the forehead)* What about those flowers you wanted me to take down to be entered?

MRS. DALTON I'll show you. *(she rises and goes out with him.* BIGGER *watches them go, and*

PEGGY *starts clearing the table. The buzzer begins ringing again, and* BIGGER *glances at it)*

PEGGY *(shaking her head)* I know—in my soft heart I want to answer it. But Mr. Dalton's right—We've got to—Want one of my hot rolls?

BIGGER No'm—no'm—I ain't hungry.

PEGGY *(deftly buttering a roll and sticking it out to him)* Take it. *(he takes it with a slow hand and bites into it)* Good?

BIGGER Yessum—Sure mighty good. *(the sound of an automatic furnace turning itself on in a great windy draught comes up from below.* BIGGER *stands listening to it)*

PEGGY That's the furnace. It works by machinery. One of your jobs will be looking after it . . . keeping it stoked with the ashes cleaned out.

BIGGER Yessum. I learn machinery easy.

PEGGY I hope you're going to like it here.

BIGGER Yessum.

PEGGY *(still working at her duties)* Before I forget it, Miss Mary's going to Detroit tomorrow. You'll have to come early in the morning and drive her to the La Salle Street Station.

BIGGER Yessum.

PEGGY That'll be one of your jobs—looking after Miss Mary.

BIGGER Yessum.

PEGGY She's not a bit like her folks. Drives her father crazy! Runs around with a wild bunch of radicals. But she's good-hearted—she'll learn better. She'll marry and settle down one of these days.

BIGGER Yessum.

PEGGY Now Mrs. Dalton—you'll like her. She's wonderful.

BIGGER She—she can't see, can she?

PEGGY *(pouring herself a cup of coffee and drinking from it)* She's blind. Went blind years ago when her second child was born. It died, and she's been blind ever since. Never talks much, but she loves people and tries to help them. Loves that cat and her piano and her flowers. *(she sets her cup down and wipes her hands on her apron.* MRS. DALTON *comes feeling her way in from the left dressed as before and still carrying the white cat.* BIGGER *rises abruptly, clattering the dishes on the table)*

MRS. DALTON Have you told the young man his duties, Peggy?

PEGGY Part of 'em, ma'am. I haven't spoke about the flowers yet.

MRS. DALTON Yes, Bigger. You are to water the flowers every morning.

BIGGER Yessum.

PEGGY I'll start the cleaning, Ma'am.

(MRS. DALTON *makes her way along the table and sits down.* PEGGY *goes out at the right.* MRS. DALTON *takes one of the blossoms from the vase on the table and strokes it against her cheek)*

MRS. DALTON *(detached)* Flowers are wonderful creatures, Bigger. Each with a personality of its own. You'll learn to love them while you are here.

BIGGER *(in almost mumbling incoherence)* Yessum. *(he looks about him and nervously lifts a glass of water from the little table. He drinks and watches* MRS. DALTON *over the rim)*

MRS. DALTON Bigger, we've decided to engage you. This is your new start.

BIGGER Yessum. . . .

MRS. DALTON Now you are one of us—a member of the family—We'll do all in our power to help you find your way in this new life.

BIGGER *(spasmodically)* Yessum. Thank you, ma'am.

MRS. DALTON *(her face tilted up, as if drinking in the sunlight that pours through the window. Reminiscently)* Bigger, I used to teach school, and I once had a colored boy in one of my classes who was so distrustful that he carried a knife and a gun.

BIGGER Huh? *(the glass of water drops from his hand and crashes to the floor)* Oh—*(he bends down in a scramble to pick up the glass, but his eyes remain on her face. His hands feel blindly among the splinters, gathering them. He stands up again, his knees bent a little)* I'm sorry, ma'am. I broke one of your glasses.

MRS. DALTON *(quietly)* That's all right—accidents will happen. *(rising)* That is all, Bigger. You have the job. Your pay will be twenty dollars a week, which will go to your mother. There will be five dollars more for yourself. You will have every second Sunday off. Is that clear?

BIGGER *(still in a whisper)* Yessum.

MRS. DALTON *(turning)* And if you're ever bothered about anything, come to me and we'll talk it over. We have a lot of books in the library. You can read any you like.

BIGGER No'm. Yessum.

MRS. DALTON You don't have to read them. Peggy'll show you the rest of the routine. *(she turns and moves slowly out at the left.* BIGGER *stares after her as the door closes. Then he begins to look about him; goes over to a table, picks up a silver knife and weighs it in his hand)*

BIGGER Uhm—*(he puts down the knife, glancing apprehensively at the door. Then he goes over to the sideboard and quickly opens two of the drawers and peers into them. He hears someone coming and quickly closes the drawers.* MARY DALTON *enters from the left, dressed in a flowing red robe, opened at the bosom. It blows and trails behind her. Her hair is bunchy and tousled, and she is puffing a cigarette.* MARY *is a slender, pale-faced girl of some twenty-two or three, with wide, restless dark eyes. Her lips are rouged heavily, and her fingernails done to a deep vermilion. Her whole appearance denotes a sense of boredom and weary child-like disillusionment. She comes on over to the table, then stops and glances at* BIGGER. *He takes a back step)* Yessum.

MARY *(quenching her cigarette in a coffee cup)* I'm not going to hurt you—(BIGGER *stands with downcast eyes, saying nothing.* MARY *pours herself a cup of coffee, pulls a little tin box from her pocket and puts a couple of aspirin tablets into her mouth. She gazes over at* BIGGER *as she gulps from her cup)* What's your name?

BIGGER Bigger—Bigger Thomas, ma'am.

MARY Funny name—Where'd you get it?

BIGGER *(without looking up)* They just give it to me, ma'am.

MARY *(sitting down and picking idly at a roll)* Our new chauffeur?

BIGGER Yessum.

MARY Do you belong to a union?

BIGGER No'm—No'm, I ain't never fooled with them folks, ma'am.

MARY Better join a union or Father'll exploit your shirt off. My name's Mary Dalton. And I've got the most God-awful hangover in the world. Did you ever get drunk, Bigger?

BIGGER *(uncertainly)* No'm.

MARY Has Mother hired you?

BIGGER Yessum.

MARY Well, don't take the job. *(now* BIGGER *looks at her)* I mean it. You'd better keep away from us—from Mother. She'll try to give you a serious, ambitious soul—make you want to be something in the world. And you've got no chance to be anything. None of you colored people have—Where do you live?

BIGGER Over on Indiana Avenue.

MARY You know, some time I'd like to meet some colored people—You know, Bigger, sometimes I drive down South Park way, and I look at all those brick buildings crowded with Black people, and I wonder what's going on inside of them. Just think, I live ten blocks from you, and I know nothing about you. I've been all over the world, and I don't know how people live ten blocks from me.

BIGGER *(swallowing)* Yessum.

MARY *(mockingly)* "Yessum, yessum"—Don't you work in this house. Do you hear me? They made a law-abiding punk out of Green. I'll have you meet Jan Erlone and Max and some of our friends. We're having a celebration down at Ernie's tonight. D'you know where it is?

BIGGER Yessum.

MARY You'll drive me down there—

BIGGER Got to—got to stick to my job.

MARY That's your job—to take me where I want to go. (BIGGER *blinks helplessly at her)* Have you got a girl, Bigger? (BIGGER *stares at her)* Bigger, how do you colored people feel about the way you have to live? Do you ever get real mad? Why don't you talk? Oh, maybe I'm not saying the right things, but what are the right things to say? I don't know. Bigger—say something. . . . How is it that two human beings can stand a foot from each other and not speak the same language? Bigger, what are you thinking about? What are you feeling? (BIGGER *doesn't answer)* D'you think I'm crazy?

BIGGER No . . . No, ma'am!

MARY And you won't be like Green, will you, with your hat in your hand? Who knows, you might be a leader among your own people. And I'd have a part in it. Mother's little spoiled darling'd have a part in it . . . Tonight, Bigger, you're going to meet Max, a man who can tell you things . . .

BIGGER Yessum.

MARY And I appoint you a committee of one to look after me—get me home. If I should happen to drink too much—Hell, I always drink too much.

BIGGER Got to stick to my job.

MARY Your job is to do what I tell you!

(PEGGY *comes in at the left)*

PEGGY *(sighing)* Is your head better?

MARY No.

PEGGY I'll get you an aspirin.

MARY I've had one . . .

PEGGY I wanted to bring your breakfast up, darlin', but your father—

MARY Go away and leave me alone!

PEGGY *(after a moment, quietly)* Come with me, Bigger, and I'll show you about the furnace.

BIGGER Yessum. *(in the distance, in a room upstairs, a piano begins to play a sentimental piece.* MARY *shudders)*

PEGGY And the flowers.

BIGGER Yessum. *(he follows her abjectly out. The piano continues to play.* MARY *lights a cigarette and stands smoking, gazing before her)*

MARY *(quietly)* Yassum . . . yassum . . .

(The piano continues to play. Fadeout)

Scene Four

(The bedroom of MARY DALTON, *before dawn, a day later. When the curtain rises, the piano stops playing. At the left front is a door opening into the hall, and to the left, and set at an angle from the audience, is* MARY'S *bed draped in ghostly white and raised like a dais or bier. At the center rear is a filmy curtained window, and to the right of that a huge oblong mirror, so tilted that its depths are discernible, but only a vague blur of images is reflected in it. In front of the mirror is a delicately-patterned chaise longue and stool. An entrance to the dressing-room is at the right front. The walls of the bedroom are cold and dead, and the whole scene is bathed in the snowy city's pallid light which glimmers through the window)*

BIGGER'S VOICE *(in hushed anxiety)* Please, Miss Dalton. Please, stand up and walk. Is this your room? *(her voice, stiff-lipped and almost mechanical, is heard in the hall at the left, drunkenly)*

MARY'S VOICE A great celebration, Bigger. God, I'm drunk!

BIGGER'S VOICE *(tense and in a hushed pleading)* Sh-sh—*(*MARY *appears in the door, her hat awry, her hair hanging down, her eyes set in a frozen stare and her face mask-like and dead. She grasps the lintel with her right hand. She has some pamphlets in her hand)*

MARY And you're drunk, too, Bigger. *(jerking with her left hand)* It's a victory, Bigger. Hooray for the rent strike. Hooray for our side!

BIGGER For Christ sake! *(still unseen, his voice a sort of moan)* This ain't my job, Miss Dalton.

MARY It is your job—to see me home—safe home. *(she pulls* BIGGER *on into the room. His head is lowered, his face somewhat averted from her. On his left arm he carries* MARY'S *red handbag, hung by its handle. He is dressed in his chauffeur's uniform, his cap off)* The people are strong, Bigger—you and me—thousands like us—Poor Father—Gimme a drink. Why don't you give me a drink? *(she reaches for the handbag)*

BIGGER No'm.

MARY *(rocking her head from right to left, mockingly)* Yessum—yessum—My father—a landlord that walks like a man—And we had a big celebration, didn't we? Here, Bigger, I want you to read these—The road to freedom—

BIGGER *(moaning again)* Lemme go, Miss Dalton. *(suddenly his head snaps about him as if he hears an enemy in the dark)* I got to go—ain't my job—got to get out of here.

MARY *(stuffing pamphlets into* BIGGER'S *pocket)* Here, take those! Put them in your pocket! *(*BIGGER *pulls away)* What are you scared of? You don't frighten me, Bigger. I frighten you, now—See, it's all turned around. Crazy world, isn't it?

BIGGER This your room, Miss Dalton? They kill me—kill me—they find me in here—

MARY *(insistently)* Know what I am?

BIGGER *(peeping furtively out from beneath his brows)* I dunno—No'm—I dunno.

MARY I'm what the Russians call "the penitent rich"—I feed the poor—*(her hands go out as if scattering largesse to a begging world, and she strews the pamphlets about the room)* And I'm drunk—and I'm dead—drunk and dead—inside I am—*(giggling, as though at herself)* I'm just a girl falling to pieces—*(shaking her head)* I want to talk—Trouble with the world, Bigger—Nobody to talk to—Mother and Father—they—talk up to God in the sky—I talk down—way, way down to you at the bottom—*(with wild, emotional impulsiveness)* Oh, I wish I was Black—Honest, I do—Black like you—down there with you—to start all over again—a new life—*(she puts out her hand toward him. He shivers and stands helplessly paralyzed. She touches his hair)* Your hair is hard. Like little black wires—I know—It has to be hard—tough—to stand it—*(she touches his cheek)*

BIGGER *(in a whispering scream)* Naw—Naw. *(the air of his lungs hisses through his lips and dies, as it were, in an echoing supplication. His face glistens more brightly with the sweat that drenches it. He spits emptily)*

MARY *(looking at her hand)* See, not shoe polish—it don't come off. *(now touching her own cheek and gazing at her crooked, spread-out fingers and wagging her head hopelessly)* There's a difference, and there's not a difference—*(his eyes are lifted, gazing blindly at her)* Bigger, what are you thinking—what are you feeling? *(she begins to weep noiselessly)*

BIGGER *(moaning, twisting his shoulders as if in the grip of some overpowering, aching pain. Gasping)* Lemme go.

MARY Yes, that's what I want—to break through and find you—

BIGGER *(as he speaks,* MARY *falls, and he lifts her suddenly into his arms)* Ain't my job—ain't my job—

MARY Your arms—hard—hurt—make me feel safe—and hurt—I want to suffer—begin all over again—home—take me home *(singing)* "Swing low, sweet chariot, coming for to carry me home—" That's Mother's favorite song . . . *(with a cry)* Mother! *(her eyes blare wide with fear)* Let me go! Let me—*(but still his arms, as if against his will, hold to her.* MARY *is now staring at him coldly)* Who are you? *(lifting a weak hand, she strikes him blindly in the face)* Stop—*(shrieking)* Stop it! *(wiggling like a rubber thing, queerly alive, the breath goes out of her. Her head falls back and she lies still and limp in his arms. For a moment* BIGGER *does not move. Fascinatedly, he gazes at her face, his lips open and breathless)*

BIGGER *(he jerks his face away from hers, and lowers her feet to the floor; but the upper part of her body hangs over his arm. He looks frantically about him, then eases and half-drags her to the bed. A sob rises into his throat)* Miss Mary—Mary—Mary—Miss Dalton—*(with his head still bowed, his hands go up and onto her reclining figure. Whispering, as his head flies up)* Gotta get away—get away quick. *(now, as if from some interminable distance deep in the house, comes the sound of* MRS. DALTON*'s gentle voice)*

MRS. DALTON'S VOICE Mary!—Is that you, Mary?

*(*BIGGER *springs up terrified. The door at the left swings open and the blur of* MRS. DALTON*'s tall form stands there in its white dressing gown. And now, as if the calling voice had penetrated into* MARY*'s deep unconsciousness, the bed heaves and a murmur rises from it.* BIGGER*'s whole body grows taut, caught in a flooding horror of fear. He stares at* MRS. DALTON *with wide eyes, and as she moves farther into the room he backs noiselessly around the bed from her, the palms of his hands outstretched as if in piteous supplication before her unseeing vision, and his lips making a gasping, soundless cry. For an instant the scene is silent.* MRS. DALTON *clasps her long fingers in front of her and stands listening at the bed)*

MRS. DALTON *(in her normal voice)* Mary? Where are you? *(*BIGGER *remains across the bed from* MRS. DALTON, *his face tilted and his eyes glued in awe upon the white figure. One of his hands is half-raised, the fingers weakly open as if an object he had been holding had just dropped from them.* MRS. DALTON *calls again)* Mary, are you asleep? *(there is no answer from the bed. The white figure turns slowly and seems to look about the room.* BIGGER *shrinks back into the shadows as if unable to face the blinding condemnation of that sightless face.* MRS. DALTON *feels toward the bed, and then, as if touching* MARY *through the air itself, suddenly draws back)* You've been drinking. You reek of liquor. *(*BIGGER *carries his right hand to his mouth as if about to scream.The white figure now sits brokenly down on the edge of the bed. Her hand goes out and rests lovingly on* MARY*'s brow)* My poor child—why do I fail you? Sleep—sleep then. *(rising, she fumbles for the coverlet, spreads it over* MARY*'s feet and turns back toward the door. A low sigh of relief passes through* BIGGER*'s lips.* MRS. DALTON *wheels about)* What is it? *(the sleeping figure lifts a hand and mumbles as if waking up. Quick as a flash and with an instinctive action,* BIGGER *picks up a pillow and pushes it down against* MARY*'s face. Her hands flash in the gloom, clawing helplessly at his arms. But he holds the pillow against her, heedless of her struggle, his face turned watchfully toward* MRS. DALTON. *She takes a step back toward the bed, then stops—in alarm)* Mary—are you ill? *(*MARY*'s form on the bed moves, and there is a sound of a heavy breath. A quick, muscular taughtness in* BIGGER*'s entire body indicates the enormous strength with which he is holding the pillow. The white hands continue to clutch futilely at his wrists.* MRS. DALTON*'s voice calls out sharply)* What is it, Mary? *(pause)* Mary! *(listening. A long pause. The white hands have fallen limp by the pillow now)* Good night, Mary. I'll call you early for your train.

(She moves silently from the room. There is a loud sound as the door closes behind her. For a moment there is no sound or movement; then with a deep, short gasp of relieved tension, BIGGER *falls to the floor, catching the weight of his body upon his hands and knees. His chest heaves in and out as though he had just completed a hard foot-race. Gradually, his breathing subsides, and he stands slowly up, looking at the door. His body is relaxed now, the burden of fear gone from him. Then he looks toward the bed, his whole attitude changing, his body becoming taut again. He takes a step forward, then stops uncertainly. He stares at the white form, his face now devoid of that former hard concentration. With a quick movement, he springs to the bed, bends, and stares down at* MARY'S *face. Slowly his hand goes up into the air, the fingers sensitively poised, until again he assumes the same position in which he was standing and looking when the white blur of* MRS. DALTON *first roused him. He stares anxiously at* MARY'S *face, as though a dreadful knowledge were on the threshold of his consciousness. His right hand moves timidly toward* MARY *and touches her, then is jerked quickly away. He touches her head, gently rolls it from side to side, then puts his hands behind him as if they had suffered some strange and sudden hurt)*

BIGGER *(in a whisper)* Naw—naw—*(for a moment he stands looking at the still form, as though it had in some manner deeply offended him. Once more he places his hand upon* MARY'S *head. This time it remains there and his body does not move. He mumbles frenziedly)* Naw—naw—naw—*(he is silent for an instant, then whispers)* I didn't do it—*(he takes a quick step back)* I didn't, I tell you, I didn't. Wake up, wake up, Miss Dalton. *(his voice takes on a note of pleading)* Miss Dalton, Miss Mary—*(for a second he stands, then straightens up suddenly. He turns, walks swiftly to the door, opens it, and looks out into the darkness. All is quiet. He walks back to the center of the room and stands looking at the bed. He mumbles piteously)* Naw—naw—naw—I didn't do it—I didn't go to do it—*(in a clear, sober, deep voice, as if all his faculties were suddenly alive)* They'll say I done it—I'm Black and they'll say I done it—*(again he bends over the bed)* I didn't go to do it. You know I didn't. I'm just working here. I didn't want to come here to work. You know I didn't. I was scared—I didn't want to come to your room—you made me come—*(his voice dies out of him in a sob, and he is silent. Far away a clock booms the hour. Slowly his body straightens with intent and purpose. Looking back over his shoulder, at the door, he slides his hands under* MARY'S *body and lifts her in his arms. He turns undecidedly about and sees himself in a mirror on the dressing-table)* Don't you look at me—don't say I done it—I didn't, I tell you—*(for a moment the image in the mirror holds him fascinated. He clasps* MARY *tightly to him as if to protect her and himself. Then suddenly, vehemently, to the image in the mirror, as the hum of the furnace switching itself on is heard below)* Naw—ain't nothin' happened—*(he listens to the furnace draft. He jerks his head up as if struck by a smashing thought. He goes through the door with the body of* MARY *in his arms, and the sound of the furnace draft continues. Fadeout)*

Scene Five

(The sound of the furnace draft dissolves gradually into the metallic tingling of a telephone. The curtain rises on the DALTON *study. Afternoon of the same day. At the right of the room are bookshelves, and at the left a fireplace in which some logs are burning. There is a large flat-topped desk in the rear center and across the back a glass partition looking into the fairy-land of flowers and plants of the conservatory. The conservatory is bathed in golden artificial sunlight. On a table near the partition, in which there is a glass door on the right, is a large bouquet of flowers spilling luxuriously over)*

DALTON *is standing by the desk using the telephone.* MRS. DALTON *is sitting in a chair, bolt upright, listening)*

DALTON No, she's not here. *(he pauses, then hangs up the receiver and turns to* MRS. DALTON*)* Well, that's final. She didn't go to Detroit, Ellen.

MRS. DALTON *(with a tremor in her voice)* Mary had been drinking again last night, Henry. When I came into her room—

DALTON Yes, yes—maybe that Erlone fellow knows something. She was out with him last night.

MRS. DALTON He was down at the station waiting to see her off. He called up—

DALTON Well, Britten ought to be back any

minute. (PEGGY *comes in with a tray at the right front. Her face shows signs of recent weeping)*

PEGGY Here's your tea, Mrs. Dalton—

MRS. DALTON *(with a gesture)* No thank you, Peggy.

PEGGY But you must eat and drink, Mrs. Dalton.

MRS. DALTON No, thank you.

PEGGY Mr. Jan Erlone just phoned again—said he was coming right over. He seems worried too. *(she turns and hurriedly goes out, meeting* BRITTEN *in the doorway. She stops.* BRITTEN *comes on in. He is a little man of forty or forty-five, with a thin florid face, and given to a flashy watch chain and ring. He goes over to the fireplace and shakes a bit of snow from his hat and coat)*

BRITTEN Snow's pouring down, all right—regular blizzard for old Santa Claus. Well, Mr. Dalton, looks like Buckley better get busy. That labor crowd's talking up this fellow Edward Max.

DALTON I know, I know—What did you find out at the station, Britten?

BRITTEN Nothing. Absolutely nothing. *(a sob breaks from* PEGGY. *She goes out)* Mmm—I don't understand that car sitting out there, the window open—must have been there for hours—snow four inches deep on the top—I measured it. Your chauffeur says he brought Miss Dalton home about two-thirty.

MRS. DALTON About two-thirty this morning. I heard the clock strike. Later I went to her room.

BRITTEN Ahm—By the way, that colored boy—is he all right?

DALTON He seems all right.

BRITTEN Yeh, he does—dumb-like—Seems to know his place.

DALTON We have his complete record. I talked to him. I'm sure he's all right.

*(*PEGGY *comes in and listens. While they are talking,* BIGGER *slowly enters the conservatory at the rear. He has a watering can in his hand and goes about quietly and methodically watering the flowers. But even in his nonchalant and detached manner, we sense that he is straining every sense and nerve to hear the words of the group in the study)*

BRITTEN *(to* PEGGY*)* And what do you think of this colored boy?

PEGGY He's just like all colored boys to me.

BRITTEN Is he polite? Does he pull off his cap when he comes into the house?

PEGGY Yes, sir.

BRITTEN Does he seem to be acting at any time? I mean, does he appear like he's more ignorant than he really is?

PEGGY I don't know, Mr. Britten.

BRITTEN I'd like to talk to that boy again.

PEGGY *(gesturing toward the rear glass door of the conservatory)* He's out there.

BRITTEN *(in a loud voice)* Come in here, boy! *(*BIGGER *turns, opens the glass door and comes slowly through, still carrying the watering can in his hand.* BRITTEN *turns to him and shouts)* I want to ask you some more questions!

BIGGER *(blinking and staring back)* Yessuh.

BRITTEN What time do you say you took Miss Dalton from here last night?

BIGGER About eight-thirty, suh.

BRITTEN You drove her to her night class at the University? *(*BIGGER *hangs his head and makes no answer)* Open your mouth and talk, boy. *(he puts out a placating hand to the* DALTONS. *They wait)*

BIGGER Well, Mister, you see—I'm just working here.

BRITTEN You told me that before. You drove her to school, didn't you? *(*BIGGER *still makes no answer)* I asked you a question, boy!

BIGGER *(his face strangely alert and yet impassive)* No, suh. I didn't drive her to school.

BRITTEN Where did you drive her?

BIGGER Well, suh, she told me after I got as far as the Park to turn around and take her to the loop.

DALTON *(his lips parted in surprise)* She didn't go to school?

BIGGER No, suh.

BRITTEN Huh?

DALTON Why didn't you tell me this before, Bigger?

BIGGER *(quietly)* She told me not to.

BRITTEN Where did you take her, then?

BIGGER To the Loop, suh.

BRITTEN Whereabouts in the Loop?

BIGGER To Lake Street.

BRITTEN Do you remember the number?

BIGGER Sixteen, I think, suh.

BRITTEN *(rubbing his chin)* That's a good boy—Uhm—Sixteen Lake Street, then?

BIGGER Yessuh.

BRITTEN *(kindly)* Say, boy, your water is pouring out on the floor.

BIGGER Thank you, suh. Yessuh! *(he jerks the watering can up and hugs it in front of him)*

BRITTEN How long was she in this place—Number Sixteen?

BIGGER 'Bout half an hour, I reckon, suh.

BRITTEN Then what happened?

BIGGER *(quietly)* Then they came out.

BRITTEN They?

BIGGER Her and this—this Mr. Jan.

BRITTEN Jan Erlone.

DALTON Jan Erlone—that's a friend of hers—

BRITTEN *(he looks triumphantly around him)* And then you drove 'em to—?

BIGGER He wanted to drive and she told me to let him.

BRITTEN And where did they go?

BIGGER To the speaking—to hear that man—Mr. Max—

BRITTEN Ah-hah—Erlone's one of his crowd—Hear that, Mr. Dalton?—And then where did you go?

BIGGER Mr. Jan drove to Ernie's Kitchen Shack.

BRITTEN And how long did you stay there?

BIGGER Well, we must have stayed—

BRITTEN We? Didn't you wait outside in the car?

BIGGER Naw, suh. You see, Mister, I did what they told me. I was only working for 'em.

BRITTEN And then what did you do?

BIGGER They made me eat with 'em. I didn't want to, Mister, I swear I didn't want to. They kept worrying me until I went in and had a drink with 'em.

BRITTEN *(with a placating gesture toward* MRS. DALTON) A drink, eh? So they were drinking—

BIGGER Farewell party and Christmas and all—

BRITTEN And then you brought them home here?

BIGGER Yessuh.

MRS. DALTON *(in sad, but firm graciousness)* How intoxicated was Miss Dalton, Bigger?

BIGGER *(not looking at her)* She—she couldn't hardly stand up—up—ma'am.

BRITTEN And he—this Erlone—he helped her to her room? Huh? *(*PEGGY *bows her head in her apron)*

DALTON That's all right, Bigger. Go ahead and tell us.

BIGGER Yessuh.

BRITTEN She had passed out, huh?

BIGGER Well, yes, suh. I 'spect you'd call it that.

BRITTEN *(conclusively)* And they told you to leave the car outside, huh?

BIGGER Yes, suh, he told me to leave the car. And I could go on home, get my things, and come back this morning.

BRITTEN How was this Erlone acting? Drunk, eh?

BIGGER Yes, suh, I guess he was drunk. *(suddenly* BRITTEN *takes from his pocket a small batch of pamphlets and holds them under* BIGGER*'s nose)*

BRITTEN Where did you get these?

BIGGER I ain't never seen them things before.

BRITTEN Oh, yeah? I got 'em out of your overcoat pocket—in the basement. Is that your coat?

BIGGER Yessuh.

BRITTEN Is that the coat you were wearing last night?

BIGGER Yessuh.

BRITTEN Then where did you get them?

BIGGER Miss Dalton, she gave 'em to me, but I didn't read 'em—

BRITTEN What unit are you in?

BIGGER *(backing away)* Suh?

BRITTEN *(savagely)* Come on, Comrade. Tell me what unit are you in? *(*BIGGER *stares at him in speechless amazement)* Who's your organizer?

BIGGER I don't know what you mean, suh!

DALTON Britten, he doesn't know anything about that.

BRITTEN Didn't you know this Erlone before you came to work here?

BIGGER Naw, suh, naw, suh—You got me wrong, sir. I ain't never fooled around with them folks. The ones at the meeting last night was the first ones I ever met, so help me God.

(Now BRITTEN *comes pushing nearer to* BIGGER *till he has forced him back against the wall at the right. He looks him squarely in the eye, then grabs him by the collar and rams his head against the wall)*

BRITTEN Come on, gimme the facts. Tell me about Miss Dalton and that Erlone. What did he do to her?

BIGGER Naw, suh, I ain't—I don't know—Naw, suh.

DALTON *(sternly)* That's enough, Britten.

BRITTEN Okay. I guess he's all right. *(smiling kindly at* BIGGER*)* Just playing a little, son. *(*BIGGER *gulps and stares at him)* If you say he's okey, then he's okey with me, Mr. Dalton. *(to* BIGGER*)* You say Erlone told you to leave the car in the drive and then he helped Miss Dalton up to the steps.

BIGGER Yes, suh.

BRITTEN And did he go away?

BIGGER He helped her up the steps, suh, and—uh, she was just about passed out.

BRITTEN And he went with her into the house?

BIGGER Yes, suh—*(he suddenly stops and stares toward the door at the right front.* JAN ERLONE *enters. His manner is nervous and agitated, and his face is pale)*

JAN What are you telling these people, Bigger Thomas?

BRITTEN Oh, so you walked right in?

JAN *(ignoring him)* What's all this about? Have you heard anything from Mary—Miss Dalton?

BRITTEN *(savagely)* You're just in time to tell us. *(*JAN *stares at* BIGGER, *who straightens up and gazes fearlessly before him.* JAN *looks around)*

JAN What's happened? Tell me.

BRITTEN Take it easy. You got plenty of time. I know your kind—you like to rush in and have things your way. *(he turns to* BIGGER*)* Bigger, is this the man that came home with Miss Dalton last night? *(*JAN*'s lips part. He stares at* BRITTEN, *then at* BIGGER*)*

BIGGER *(without flinching)* Yes, suh. *(*JAN *stares at* BIGGER *with wide incredulous eyes)*

JAN You didn't bring me here, Bigger. Why do you tell them that? *(crossing to* MRS. DALTON*)* Mrs. Dalton, I'm worried too. That's why I'm here. What is this? *(to* BRITTEN*)* What are you making this boy lie for?

BRITTEN Where is Miss Dalton, Erlone?

JAN She was supposed to go to Detroit this morning, to see her grandmother.

BRITTEN We know that. But she didn't go. Did you see Miss Dalton last night?

JAN *(hesitating)* No.

BRITTEN But you were with her and with this Negro boy—at Ernie's Kitchen Shack.

JAN All right then, I saw her. So what?

BRITTEN *(sarcastically)* So you saw her. Where is she now?

JAN If she's not in Detroit, I don't know where she is.

BRITTEN You and Miss Dalton were drunk last night.

JAN Oh, come on! We weren't drunk. We just had a little to drink.

BRITTEN You brought her home about two in the morning.

JAN *(after a pause)* No. *(*BIGGER *is seen to take a quick step backward and his hand takes hold of the knob on the glass door)*

DALTON Mr. Erlone, we know my daughter was drunk last night when you brought her here. She was too drunk to leave here by herself. We know that. Now do you know where she is?

JAN *(stammering)* I—I didn't come here last night.

BRITTEN But you were with her and she was drunk. Do you mean you left her in that condition?

JAN *(hesitating and swallowing)* Well, I came as far as the door with her. I had to go to a meeting. I took the trolley. Had to hurry. *(*JAN *turns to* BIGGER*)* Bigger, what are you telling these people? *(*BIGGER *makes no answer)*

MRS. DALTON *(in an agitated voice)* I'll see you in my room, Henry—please. *(*PEGGY *comes over to her, helps her up and assists her from the room. Just before she leaves,* MRS. DALTON *turns and gazes toward* JAN *with her sightless eyes. Then lowering her head, she goes away with* PEGGY*)*

JAN *(beseechingly around him)* Bigger, didn't you get Miss Dalton home safely? What's happened to her? *(*BIGGER *gazes stonily at him and does not answer.* JAN *seems to read a strange and ultimate antagonism in* BIGGER*'s face, for he gradually lowers his head and stares at the floor)*

BRITTEN *(chuckling)* So Bigger brought her home and you didn't?

JAN Yes.

BRITTEN You're a liar, Erlone. First you say you didn't see her, then you did. Then you didn't bring her home, then you did. Then again you didn't—Come on, what's your game?

JAN *(in a low desolate voice as he stares about him)* I was trying to protect her.

BRITTEN You're trying to protect yourself, and making a damn poor job of it.

JAN I didn't come here, I tell you.

BRITTEN You got Miss Dalton drunk, Erlone—you brought her here early this morning. You told the boy to leave the car out in the driveway. You went inside and went upstairs with her, and now she's disappeared. Where is she? *(*JAN *looks at him with staring, bewildered eyes)*

JAN Listen, I told you all I know.

DALTON *(stepping forward)* Erlone, you and I don't agree on certain things. Let's forget that. I want to know where my daughter is.

JAN I tell you I don't know, Mr. Dalton. *(*DALTON *throws up his hands in futile, desperate anger)*

DALTON We'll see you upstairs later, Britten. *(he goes out)*

BRITTEN *(blocking the way to the door and glaring at* JAN *as he yells)* Get over there! *(*JAN *backs away from his menacing look)* Now listen to me, you goddam red—

JAN I tell you I don't know where she is!

BRITTEN All right. You don't know now—eh? But you will know, and you'll know damn soon. We've a way of handling your kind—*(he turns to go as* PEGGY *appears in the door)*

PEGGY Mr. Dalton said please come up. And you better look after the furnace, Bigger. It needs tending—

BRITTEN Okay. That's all I got to say now, Erlone. *(he follows* PEGGY *out. For a moment,* JAN *stares at the floor.* BIGGER *watches him with steady, smoldering eyes. In the street outside, a chorus begins singing a Christmas carol. Slowly* BIGGER*'s hand goes up and slides into his coat and rests there. Presently* JAN *looks up)*

JAN Bigger.

BIGGER *(in a low humming voice)* Go on away from here, Mr. Jan. Go on way.

JAN What's all this about, Bigger? Why did you tell those lies?

BIGGER You heard me.

JAN I haven't done anything to you, have I? Where's Mary?

BIGGER *(mumbling)* I don't want to talk to you.

JAN *(desperately)* But what have I done to you?

BIGGER I don't want to talk to you. *(with a sharp cry)* Get out!

JAN Listen, Bigger. If these people are bothering you, just tell me. Don't be scared. We are used to this sort of persecution. Mr. Max will help you in your rights. He knows their crooked law. Listen, now. Tell me about it. Come on, we'll go out and get a cup of coffee and talk it over. *(*JAN *comes toward him.* BIGGER *suddenly whips out his gun, and* JAN *stops with white face)* For God's sake, man, what are you doing?

BIGGER I don't need you—that Mr. Max neither—*(hoarsely)* Get out!

JAN I haven't bothered you. Don't—

BIGGER *(his voice tense and hysterical)* Leave me alone.

JAN *(backing away from him)* For Christ's sake, man!

BIGGER *(his voice rising almost to a scream)* Get away from here! Now! Now!

*(*JAN *backs farther away, then turns and goes rapidly out at the right front, looking back over his shoulder with hurt and helpless eyes. For a moment* BIGGER *stands still, then slowly his hand replaces the pistol in his coat. In the basement below the windy draft of the furnace begins blowing.* BIGGER *jerks his head up with a shudder, listening. Gradually a low moaning sound rises from his lips. For a moment he remains so, then wheeling quickly, he goes into the conservatory and passes out of sight through the flowers at the right rear, leaving the watering can sitting on the floor. The music of the carol singers comes in more strongly from the street and continues. Fadeout)*

Scene Six

(The music of the carol singers melts into the evangelical fervor of a Negro song service in a church across the street. The curtain rises upon CLARA MEARS*' one-room kitchenette apartment. A bed is at the left rear, a window by it, and a dresser at the right front next to the door. In the right rear are a sink and little table. It is night, a few hours later.* CLARA *is standing in front of her mirror arranging her hair. She is partly dressed.* BIGGER *is sitting on the edge of the bed dressed in trousers and undershirt. His shoulders are hunched over. The Negro song service continues intermittently throughout the scene)*

CLARA *(glancing over at* BIGGER*'s coat hanging on the chair at the left)* Look, puddles of water dripped all over the floor from your coat. *(she moves the chair and coat over near the radiator, then goes back to the mirror)*

BIGGER *(muttering musingly)* Yeh, like a little brown doll talking about a wet coat and puddles on the floor—rain and snow, they don't matter. *(he flings out a clenched fist and bangs the railing of the bed.* CLARA *turns toward him questioningly)*

CLARA Bigger, what's wrong with you?

BIGGER *(musingly)* She asks me what's wrong—yeh, what's wrong?

CLARA You don't seem like yourself—You *ain't* yourself—

BIGGER All right, I ain't. I'm different, then.

CLARA *(tripping swiftly over and dropping on her knees by him)* Bigger, honey, don't be like that. Don't stay away from me. You stay away from me for two days—then when you show up—

BIGGER Aw, can it.

CLARA All the time I loved you in my arms there, seemed like you full of something different.

BIGGER You done had all you want from me now, and I better go.

CLARA *(impulsively grabbing his hand and kissing it)* Please, Bigger, I don't mean to make you mad. I want to make you happy—that's all I want. You know that. I know your folks tries to turn you against me—say I ain't no good.

BIGGER *(growling, he turns and seizes her roughly by the shoulders, his voice a mixture of anguish and cruelty and bitter love)* Goddam it, you know why I come here—'Cause I can't help it. I wish I could help it—Now I wish I could—*(springing up)*

CLARA Bigger, what's the matter? Don't you love me no more?

BIGGER Sometimes I do love you—Then I feel you holding me down—pulling at me—

CLARA *(half weeping)* I don't—I don't—

BIGGER And it's your little soft baby-talk again—fumbling around my heart—and then we get some liquor—and end up by kissing and going to bed. You all around me—Like a swamp sucking me under—Can't see—Can't think—Goddam, I hate it! I hate it! Wish it was different. Now I do.

CLARA *(echoing)* Now! How come you keep saying "now" all the time? *(*BIGGER *stares unseeingly.* CLARA'*s inquiring, begging eyes are fastened on his face. He breaks into hoarse, raucous laughter and pounds his knees with his fists.* CLARA *(whispering)* How come you laughing like that? *(she shudders)*

BIGGER Yeh, I'm laughing—laughing at everybody—everybody in the whole damn world. Laughing at you.

CLARA *(piteously)* Please, Bigger. *(frantically)* Bigger, you talk wild, drunk-like—

BIGGER *(gesturing)* That little old bottle of whisky? Hunh, didn't even feel it.

CLARA Why don't you try to sleep some? I'll fix you supper. You tired. Your po' face all tight, and yo' eyes full of blood. *(she rises and stands by his side)*

BIGGER *(his arm clutching around her as though suddenly doubting everything)* You love me, Clara?

CLARA You know that. *(she bends and kisses him on the forehead)* And it ain't things you give me and all that money don't matter. *(indicating the dresser)* It don't matter at all. *(her arm is tight along his side. Suddenly she draws it away with an exclamation)* Something hard in your pocket, Bigger. You got a gun—*(gasping)* Is that why you got all that money? Rob somebody?

BIGGER I ain't, I tell you. *(snickering)* Maybe they give me something in advance on my job.

CLARA Who? *(looking at him sharply)* Old white gal I seen you eating with, down at Ernie's last night?

BIGGER Maybe.

CLARA *((in fierce jealousy)* She's crazy. Her face say she's crazy.

BIGGER *(sharply)* Aw, don't worry 'bout her.

CLARA *(anxiously)* Leave her alone, honey. She'll get you in trouble.

BIGGER Nunh-unh.

CLARA Say, Bigger, where is this you working—the Dalton place?

BIGGER *(sharply)* How come you want to know that?

CLARA I just like to know, honey! How come you don't want to talk none!

BIGGER Over there on Drexel . . .

CLARA That's where them rich folks live . . . That's where they had that kidnapping last year.

BIGGER Huh?

CLARA Kidnap that girl—and tried to get money from her folks?

BIGGER *(staring off)* Tried to get money. Yeh, yeh, I remember. *(springing up)* Money! Goddamit. Everybody talking about it—papers with headlines, telephones ringing. Yeh, let 'em ring—ringing all over America, asking, asking about Bigger. The bells ringing; they'll sound the sirens and the ambulances beat their gongs.

CLARA Bigger! Bigger! *(in sharp and unbelieving reproof)* There's something wrong, make you talk like that.

BIGGER *(turning to her and speaking almost kindly, as he touches her face affectionately)* Yeh, Clara, plenty wrong. I tell you now, and you stay with me?

CLARA What is it, Bigger?

BIGGER *(shouting)* You stay with me, I say?

CLARA Yes, anything, Bigger. I stay with you.

BIGGER Sit down. *(she sinks obediently to the bed)* Listen, now. I'm a fool to tell you, but I got to tell you. *(queerly)* Got to tell somebody. I don't know what's gonna happen, Clara. *(suddenly matter-of-factly)* Maybe I got to get out of town soon.

CLARA What you done?

BIGGER Right now, it come to me, you help me, you and me together—nobody won't know—we be safe then, money make us safe.

CLARA *(her eyes wide and still)* What you talking about?

BIGGER *(turning and beginning to pace the floor)* Listen. This gal where I work—this Dalton gal she crazy. Crazier'n hell, see? Father's a rich man—millionaire—*(pauses)* Millionaire—*(shouting his words out again)* And she's done run off—Always hanging around with them reds—maybe done run off with one of 'em.

CLARA I told you.

BIGGER Nobody don't know where she's gone. So last night I—maybe she give me money to hush my mouth. See? They throw money around everywhere. They don't care none. Just pay in advance maybe.

CLARA I don't care none, Bigger. It ain't the money.

BIGGER *(shouting)* Shut your damn mouth. *(pulling the back of his hand nervously across his lips)* They don't know where she is—so, they sit worrying. All day they been worrying. The old man pacing the floor like me now. *(a harsh laugh breaking from him)* But I'm walking different. See? Different. And that blind woman—holding them white flower hands together and crying out, "Where's my daughter?" And that detective tromping about, mashing things down. "Where is she?" they saying. They don't know. I know.

CLARA *(crying out)* Bigger, what you talking about? What you done?

BIGGER I tell you. They think she's kidnapped. Yeh, them reds got her. I heard 'em say so. Gonna ask for money, see? Plenty.

CLARA *(pleadingly)* Maybe she'll show up, Bigger. She'll come back.

BIGGER *(waving his hand excitedly)* Don't worry about that. Yeh, money. They got plenty of dough. They won't miss it. And we get some of it. How come? Then you and me—we's free. Goddamit, free! You hear me? Free like them. *(suddenly sitting down and turning excitedly and close to her)* One of them old empty buildings over there—Yeh, 36 Place and Michigan—door open all the time. I'll write 'em a letter, and we'll wait for 'em there.

CLARA *(weeping)* But you can't do that, Bigger. They'll catch you. They'll never stop looking. The white folks never stop looking—

BIGGER Yeh, but looking for the wrong folks.

CLARA But you know where the girl is. She'll show up.

BIGGER She won't.

CLARA How you know?

BIGGER She just won't.

CLARA Bigger, you ain't done nothing to that girl, has you?

BIGGER *(throwing back his hand)* Say that again and I'll slap you through the floor. Yeh, I'll get the pencil and paper—*(springing up and moving toward the dresser)* Write them a letter—print it. Think they sharp, huh? We see. We see. *(he rummages in the dresser.* CLARA *gazes helplessly at him, words beginning to break through her dying sobs)*

CLARA Bigger, what you doing? What you doing to me?

BIGGER *(unheedingly)* Here she is. *(he gets the paper and pencil. Looking about him for a place to write, he drops down on the floor and spreads the sheet out, biting the pencil ruminatively the while)*

CLARA All you ever caused me was trouble—just plain black trouble. I been a fool—just a blind, dumb, Black, drunk fool; and I'll go on being a fool 'cause I love you—love you clean down to hell—ain't never had nobody but you—nobody in my arms but you, close against me but you—*(she moves unsteadily over and stands behind him. Falling down on her knees, she lays her face against the back of his neck, her arms around him)*

BIGGER Shut up, now. I got to write. No. I'll print it—with my left hand. Yeh, I'll sign the note "Red." They're all scared of Reds. You see it in the newspapers—*(exultantly)* Won't ever think we done it. Think we too scared. *(excitedly)* We ain't scared, is we, Clara? Ain't scared to do anything. *(writing)* "Dear Sir." Ha! Ha! Naw, just "Sir." *(cocking his head)* Look at that word. A few more of them and the whole world turn upside-down, and we done it. Big headlines in the papers, police running around like chickens with their heads cut off—and all the time we stay back watching, waiting to pick up the dough where they put it. *(his voice rising to a croon which mockingly apes the rhythm of the distant singing)* Twenty years, up and down the dark alleys, like a rat. Nobody hear us—*(CLARA slides further down on the floor beside him, her face buried protectively and protectedly against him)*—nobody hear you, nobody pay any attention to you, and the white folks walking high and mighty don't even know we're alive. Now they cut the pigeon wing the way we say—

CLARA *(moaning)* Bigger, Bigger! *(she falls sobbing on the floor)*

BIGGER *(his head raised, staring off, his face alight with his vision)* Like bars falling away—like doors swinging open, and walls falling down. And all the big cars and all the big buildings, and the finery and the marching up and down, and the big churches and the bells ringing and the millionaires walking in and out bowing low before their God—Hunh-huh. It ain't God now, it's Bigger. Bigger, that's my name! *(CLARA's sobs break hopelessly through the room. BIGGER bends his head and begins to write)* "Sir:—We got your daughter—say nothing—the ransom is—"

(The song service comes more loudly into the room. Fadeout)

Scene Seven

(The song service dies away, and the curtain comes up on the basement of the Dalton home, the next night. The walls of the scene are painted a solid, glistening gray; the ceiling is high, and crossed by the tubes of many white asbestos-covered pipes. To the left rear is a squat iron furnace, with dull baleful eye of the fire showing through its isinglass door and reflecting on the wall. Behind it is the jutting angle of the coal bin. At the center rear are steps leading up to the kitchen pantry. At the center right is a door leading to the outside. To the left, near the stairs, are trunks, boxes, and piles of old newspapers, and on the opposite side of the stairs, clothes are hanging to dry.

When the curtain rises, BIGGER is seen standing by the furnace, motionless and looking intently before him. He starts in terror as the door at the upper center rear opens and BRITTEN stands looking down into the reddish gloom)

BRITTEN That you, Bigger?

BIGGER Oh—*(he whirls and backs quickly to the wall, his hands groping for the ax that hangs within reach. He comes to himself quickly)* Yessuh. Yessuh.

BRITTEN *(descending the stairs)* Fixing the furnace?

BIGGER *(still gripping the ax in his right hand)* Yessuh.

BRITTEN *(with a little laugh)* What? With the ax?

BIGGER *(in confusion)* No suh—no, suh—Huh—I—*(he breaks off, hangs the ax back on the wall and picks up the shovel)*

BRITTEN You sure jumped like the devil was after you. *(coming over to the furnace)* Yeh, I reckon you are a little on edge. Dogonne it, I'm nervous as a cat myself with all this "Who shot John" around here. *(BIGGER still stands with the shovel in his hand, watching his movements. BRITTEN opens the furnace and stoops to gaze inside. BIGGER quickly gets behind him with the shovel and slowly raises it. BRITTEN clangs the door shut and straightens up)* No wonder the house is freezing upstairs—a ton of ashes banked up in there.

BIGGER *(lowering the shovel and backing away, his eyes fastened intently upon BRITTEN's face)* Yessuh, I'm gonna fix it right away.

BRITTEN *(as a pounding begins on the door at the right)* What's that? Just listen to 'em. Goddam newspapermen. *(the pounding continues)* Say, Bigger, did you lock that gate to the driveway? *(before BIGGER can answer, the door at the right opens and several newspapermen crowd their way in, some of them with cameras. BRITTEN tries to stop them)* You can't come in. Get out and stay out.

VOICE We're in, Mr. Britten.

(One of them is a lean, lynx-eyed, horse-trader type of man with an old dark felt hat set back on

his head. BIGGER *backs slowly away to the wall at the left and stands alert in the shadow. As the scene progresses, the* NEWSPAPERMAN *begins to watch* BIGGER*)*

BRITTEN Now, listen here, boys. This is Mr. Dalton's home. And Mr. Dalton's got no statement to make.

VOICES What's the dope? Come on. What's going on?

BRITTEN Nothing! *(the* FIRST NEWSPAPERMAN *pushes forward, a cigarette in his mouth and snow on his old hat and coat. He wanders aimlessly around the scene)*

VOICE How about that red you picked up?

SECOND VOICE Jan Erlone?

THIRD VOICE Was she sleeping with him?

VOICE He says he didn't even come here that night. Says he's got witnesses. Says you had him arrested because he's a Communist.

BRITTEN *(shouting)* I don't know a thing—not a goddam thing.

(The reporters have their pads and pencils out. They crowd around BRITTEN*, shooting questions at him)*

VOICES When was she seen last?
Can we get a picture of her room?
Is the girl really missing?
Or is that a publicity stunt, Britten?

(a flash bulb goes off in BRITTEN*'s face. He blinks and backs away)*

BRITTEN Hey, steady, boys.

VOICE What's the matter?

BRITTEN I only work here. For Christ's sake, give me a break. *(another flash bulb explodes in his face)*

VOICE Then talk.

ANOTHER VOICE Maybe this boy'll talk.

BRITTEN He don't know a damn thing.

VOICE Say, Mike, what do you think?

BIGGER *(in a hard, cold voice)* My name ain't Mike.

VOICE That's the Thomas boy. Bigger Thomas.

VOICE I'd like to ask you a few questions, Mr. Thomas. *(*BIGGER *makes no reply)*

BRITTEN He's dumb. He don't know nothing. *(a bulb goes off in* BIGGER*'s face.* BIGGER *dodges, throwing his hands before his eyes)*

BRITTEN *(helplessly)* Cut it out, will you? Listen, boys—they're worried about the girl—Mrs. Dalton's ill. The whole house is upset—*(a newspaperman walks over to* BIGGER *and slips something into his hand)*

VOICE Come on, boy. Give us a break.

BRITTEN *(hurrying forward)* No, none of that. *(he snatches the money from* BIGGER*'s fingers and returns it to the newspaperman)* Take your damn money back. *(*BIGGER *inches away from them, his head lowered. All fall abruptly silent as the door at the upper center opens and* MR. DALTON*—old, weary, and shaken—stands framed in the light, the red shadows flickering across his wan features. He holds a white piece of paper tremblingly in his hand. The photographers begin hastily loading their cameras)*

DALTON Gentlemen—*(they all watch him, waiting, as he descends the steps.* BRITTEN *moves to his side with the protection of the law. Several flash bulbs now blind the scene as* DALTON *lifts his hand, emphasizing his words)* Please, gentlemen—just a moment. *(pause)* I am ready to make a statement now. *(his voice fails, then goes on)* I want you to listen carefully—*(pause)* The way you gentlemen handle this will mean life or death to someone—someone very dear to me. *(the bulbs flash again, making* DALTON *blink and lose the train of his thought. Pencils are already flying over their pads.* MRS. DALTON*, dressed in white, holding the white cat in her arms, appears in the doorway and descends the stairs and stops. One photographer is on his knees, pointing his camera upwards.* PEGGY*'s face also comes timidly into the doorway, looking down.* BIGGER *remains silent by the wall, his right hand going now and then to his lips in a nervous gesture)* Gentlemen, I have just phoned the police and requested that Mr. Erlone be released immediately. I want it known and understood publicly that I have no charges to prefer against him. It is of the utmost importance that this be understood. I hope your papers will carry the story. Further, I want to announce publicly that I apologize for his arrest and inconvenience. Gentlemen, our daughter, Mary Dalton—*(his voice fails)*—has been kidnapped. *(there is a commotion in the basement.* BRITTEN *confirms the news with a sage nod of his head as if he knew all the time)*

VOICE How do you know, Mr. Dalton?

VOICE When did it happen?

DALTON *(recovering himself)* We think it happened early Sunday morning.

VOICE How much are they asking?

DALTON Ten thousand dollars.

VOICE Have you any idea who they are?

DALTON We know nothing.

VOICE Have you received any word from her, Mr. Dalton?

DALTON No, not directly, but we *have* heard from the kidnapers.

VOICE Is that the letter there?

DALTON Yes, this is it.

VOICE Did it come through the mail? How did you get it?

DALTON Someone left it under the door.

VOICE When?

DALTON An hour ago.

VOICE Can we see it?

DALTON The instructions for the delivery of the money are here, and I have been cautioned not to make them public. But you can say in your papers that these instructions will be followed, and I shall pay the ransom.

VOICE How is the note signed? *(there is silence)*

DALTON It's signed "Red."

VOICES Red! Do you know who it is? What does that mean?

DALTON No.

VOICE Do you think some Communist did it, Mr. Dalton?

DALTON I don't know. I am not positively blaming anybody. If my daughter is returned, I'll ask no questions of anyone. Now that's all, gentlemen—all—*(with a final wave of his hand, he turns and follows* MRS. DALTON *up the steps. There is a babble of noise among the newspapermen)*

VOICES *(swirling around the confused* BRITTEN*)* Get a shot of her room. Climb a tree if you have to. And play up the blind mother and the cat. *(the newspapermen begin rushing out of the basement at the right.* BRITTEN *stands guarding the entrance up the stairs at the rear)* Hell, this is bigger than the Loeb-Leopold case. Do you believe it? What do you think?

BRITTEN *(half-forcing, half-following them out)* Come on, fellows, have a heart. Give the old man a break.

(And now the newspapermen have all scrambled out except the FIRST NEWSPAPERMAN, *who stands gazing with apparent idleness at* BIGGER*'s form in the shadow. He turns and strolls over toward the door at the right, whistling aimlessly, through his teeth.* BRITTEN *mops his forehead and goes hurriedly up the stairs and out at the rear.* BIGGER *comes tremblingly forward and stands in front of the furnace, gazing at the red, gleaming light. And now we see that the* FIRST NEWSPAPERMAN *has stopped in the shadow at the right and is looking back at* BIGGER. PEGGY *comes swiftly down the steps)*

PEGGY Bigger!

BIGGER Huh? *(whirling again)*

PEGGY For goodness sake, get the fire going.

PEGGY Yessum.

PEGGY Now! Mrs. Dalton's had to wear her shawl all day to keep warm. *(she picks up the shovel and hands it to him)* Go ahead. It won't bite you—*(at the tone of her voice the* FIRST NEWSPAPERMAN *looks around)* I'll have your supper ready soon.

BIGGER *(taking the shovel mechanically)* Yessum.

(She goes hurriedly up the stairs. BIGGER *stands holding the shovel in his hand. He bends down, reaches out to open the door, then takes his hand away and backs off. The lean figure of the* FIRST NEWSPAPERMAN *comes strolling back out of the shadows at the right)*

FIRST NEWSPAPERMAN What's the trouble, boy? *(*BIGGER *springs around, the shovel flying instinctively up in the air as if about to strike something)*

BIGGER *(dropping the shovel swiftly down, its edge hitting the top of his foot)* Nothing, suh—Nothing, suh. *(his foot, as though a separate and painful part of him, lifts itself up from the floor and wiggles in its shoe, then grows still again)*

FIRST NEWSPAPERMAN Awful nervous, huh?

BIGGER Naw, suh. Naw, suh, I ain't nervous.

FIRST NEWSPAPERMAN Have a cigarette.

BIGGER Nawsuh, nawsuh.

FIRST NEWSPAPERMAN *(pulling one out and lighting it, then holding the package out to* BIGGER*)* Don't smoke?

BIGGER Yessuh. *(he takes one of the cigarettes, his hand trembling in spite of itself)*

FIRST NEWSPAPERMAN Here, let me light it for you. *(he strikes a match, and holds it for* BIGGER, *staring keenly at his face)* Sort of warm, ain't you?

BIGGER Naw, suh.

FIRST NEWSPAPERMAN You're sweating a lot.

And I'm freezing. You're supposed to tend the furnace, ain't you?

BIGGER Yessuh.

FIRST NEWSPAPERMAN *(staring at him)* Then why don't you do it?

BIGGER *(without moving)* Yessuh.

FIRST NEWSPAPERMAN Sit down, son. I want to talk with you a little. *(he pulls a couple of chairs out from the rear, sits in one, and motions* BIGGER *to the other.* BIGGER *sinks quietly down, breathing heavily. He sucks the smoke of the cigarette deep into his lungs, and as if through that action gaining control of himself, he lifts his face and looks directly at his questioner)*

BIGGER *(in a clear hard voice)* How come you want to talk to me?

FIRST NEWSPAPERMAN Just a few questions. You know anything connected with this story is news. Say, what do you think of private property?

BIGGER Suh? Naw, suh, I don't own no property.

FIRST NEWSPAPERMAN *(soothingly)* Sure, sure. *(puffing on his cigarette, his eyes crinkling into a gentle smile)* Tell me, what do *you* think of Miss Dalton? I've heard she was sort of wild.

BIGGER *(quickly)* Nawsuh, nawsuh. She was a mighty fine lady.

FIRST NEWSPAPERMAN *(coolly, blowing a ring of smoke)* Why do you say she *was*?

BIGGER I—uh—I mean she was fine to me.

FIRST NEWSPAPERMAN Yes, the Daltons are mighty fine folks. *(as though veering off from the subject)* What did old Max talk about at that meeting last night?

BIGGER Suh?

FIRST NEWSPAPERMAN Some of his radical ideas? What did he say to you—well, about the rich and the poor?

BIGGER Well, suh, he told me that some day there'd be no more rich folks and no more poor folks, if folks could get together . . .

FIRST NEWSPAPERMAN Here's hoping, son—especially about the poor.

BIGGER And he said that a Black man could have a chance to get a good job like anybody else—and stand up high and equal.

FIRST NEWSPAPERMAN And there wouldn't be any more lynchings?

BIGGER Yessuh, no more lynchings.

FIRST NEWSPAPERMAN And what did the girl, Miss Dalton, say?

BIGGER She said so too.

FIRST NEWSPAPERMAN And what did he say to you about white women?

BIGGER Nothing, suh, nothing.

FIRST NEWSPAPERMAN *(sighing)* Too bad! You know, Bigger, such things as this ought to be a warning to this country. Here was a happy family, living in peace, loving their neighbor, with one daughter—a beautiful daughter—You agree with that, don't you, Bigger?

BIGGER Yessuh.

FIRST NEWSPAPERMAN Yes, it's a warning to us. You might say she was a martyr, died to help us to see the error of our ways. We've got to learn to treat people better in this country—raise up the oppressed, give them a chance. From what I've heard, Mary Dalton thought like that, too. (BIGGER *now and then gives him a queer, questioning, baffled look)* What do you think has happened to her?

BIGGER I don't know, suh.

FIRST NEWSPAPERMAN Look, that cigarette's burning your fingers. (BIGGER *drops it like a hot coal. The* FIRST NEWSPAPERMAN *offers him another.* BIGGER *shakes his head)* They must have killed her, don't you think?

BIGGER *(spasmodically)* They must've done it, sir.

FIRST NEWSPAPERMAN Who?

BIGGER Them reds, sir.

FIRST NEWSPAPERMAN And then write a note signing their name to it. You don't think you'd do that, do you, Bigger? *(his voice is low and cool and insinuating)*

BIGGER Nawsuh, nawsuh.

FIRST NEWSPAPERMAN *(hunching his chair confidentially up toward* BIGGER*)* Just suppose you had killed her, Bigger—

BIGGER *(wildly)* Nawsuh, I didn't do it. I didn't do it!

FIRST NEWSPAPERMAN Aw, take it easy. Just suppose I had killed her. Now that we both agree she's dead. Well, what would I do? *(he rises slowly out of his chair, pushes his hands into his pockets, and begins walking slowly back and forth in a weaving semicircle around* BIGGER, *his hat tilted back on his head)* Let me see. Yes, I need money. I'd write a ransom note, collect that before they found out she'd been murdered. Wouldn't you do it that way, Bigger?

BIGGER Nawsuh.

FIRST NEWSPAPERMAN What would you do?

BIGGER I didn't do it.

FIRST NEWSPAPERMAN I'm just imagining. Where were we? Oh, she's murdered. So now, we've got to dispose of the body—no traces—nobody ever to know. Well, what about a trunk—ship it off somewhere? Nunh-unh, that wouldn't do. What about weights—sink her to the bottom of the lake? Nunh-unh, they always rise to the surface. Bury her? No, that's too difficult. Somebody see you. What is it that wipes away all traces, Bigger?

BIGGER Dunno, sir.

FIRST NEWSPAPERMAN I'll tell you—fire. *(whirling and snapping his fingers)* Yeh, that's what I'd do—I'd burn the body up. Wouldn't you, Bigger? *(with sudden loudness)* Go ahead and shake the ashes down, like the woman said. *(*BIGGER*'s head sinks lower still, his shoulders shaking. With a click the thermostat turns the furnace fan on. There is a deep, blowing draft of sound.* BIGGER *springs out of his chair. The* FIRST NEWSPAPERMAN *looks at him wonderingly)* Come on, now. Shake 'em down. *(flipping a coin in his hand)* Bet you two bits you won't. *(*BIGGER *bends puppet-like down and reaches for the shovel. The* FIRST NEWSPAPERMAN *steps briskly over and lifts down the ax, and weighs it idly in his hand.* BIGGER *turns slowly around. The* FIRST NEWSPAPERMAN *smiles at him)* This is a good ax, Bigger. Old Kelly. I used to chop with one like this when I was a kid, back on the farm. And I was good at trapping in the winter—used to catch a lot. *(and now in desperation,* BIGGER *turns fiercely back to the furnace, flings open the door and plunges the shovel into the blinding bank of glowing, red-hot ashes. A puff of dust sails out and settles about the room. Then flinging the shovel down, he hysterically seizes the upright grate handle and shakes it with a great clatter)* Hell of a lot of ashes in there, boy.

BIGGER *(breathing deeply)* It's all fixed now. Draws fine—everything be warmed up now. *(yelling at the ceiling above him)* Miss Peggy, the furnace okay now! Listen at her sing! *(making a puffing noise with his lips)* She's putting on the steam now! Going to town. Goddam, Goddam. *(he begins whistling cheerily)*

FIRST NEWSPAPERMAN *(hanging the ax behind him and strolling over again)* Sing on, boy, sounds mighty good.

BIGGER *(joy breaking in his voice)* Yessuh, and I can do the boogie-woogie if I'm pushed. Listen to that old coal roll on down! The old valve creeping up—soon be popping off. Hear them drivers roll. *(*BRITTEN *comes hurriedly down the steps at the rear)*

BRITTEN What's going on here? Hell of a time to be singing. *(the* FIRST NEWSPAPERMAN *is now standing by the pile of ashes idly stirring them with the toe of his shoe)*

FIRST NEWSPAPERMAN He's a croon-baby. Come on, baby, sing us some more.

BIGGER Got to clean up now. *(he grabs a broom from behind the furnace and goes to work. The* NEWSPAPERMAN *bends down and picks something out of the ashes)*

BRITTEN So you're still here, huh?

FIRST NEWSPAPERMAN Yeh, just poking around—looking for my story.

BRITTEN *(sarcastically)* Ain't found it, I reckon.

FIRST NEWSPAPERMAN Maybe—according to deduction—

BRITTEN Hell of a note. We just called up the jail and that Erlone fellow won't leave. He's raising hell—

FIRST NEWSPAPERMAN Says this Bigger boy's been lying, don't he? *(he stares at a tiny object he holds between his fingers.* BIGGER *stops stock-still, staring at the* NEWSPAPERMAN, *caught again suddenly in the grip of his fear)*

BRITTEN How'd you know? That's just what he said.

FIRST NEWSPAPERMAN *(holding his hand out toward* BRITTEN*)* Here's an earring, Britten. It might interest you. *(*BIGGER*'s mouth flies open and a horrified gasp breaks from him.* BRITTEN *takes the earring and looks at it inquiringly)*

BRITTEN Where'd you get it?

FIRST NEWSPAPERMAN Just picked it up. Tell him where I got it, Bigger.

BIGGER *(screaming)* Let me out of here! Let me out! *(he staggers as if about to fall, then stumbles drunkenly across the room and flies through the door yelling as he goes)* I didn't do it! I didn't do it!

BRITTEN *(pushing back his hat)* Holy smoke! What's the matter with him—having a fit or something?

FIRST NEWSPAPERMAN You'd better catch him. He killed Mary Dalton and burned her in that furnace.

(BRITTEN *stares at him, dumbfounded, then pulling a whistle from his pocket begins blowing it wildly as he rushes toward the door at the right. In the distance other whistles begin to sound continuously. Fadeout)*

Scene Eight

(The sounds of commotion and pursuit die away, as the curtain rises. It is the next night—an empty room on the top floor of an abandoned house. The rear wall of the room has collapsed and gives a view of a ruined balcony at the back, with frozen roof-tops, chimneys, and a stretch of night sky beyond. Remaining in the extreme left of this rear wall is a jagged section, on which is hanging a once ornate and gilded picture frame, now cankered and dark from the beatings of the weather. The frame contains a semblance of a family portrait. Part of the wall at the right rear leans forward, and in, to form a sort of shelter. In the shadow at the right front is the distorted shape of a doorframe. The color of the scene runs from thick black shadow at the right to a diffused yellowish glare in the center and back. The wind moans intermittently. From the deep canyon below, comes the muffled drone of the great city, punctuated by the auto horn, a snatch of radio music, and vague wandering noises—all hushed and muted down by the thick snow enveloping the world. The room is lit up at intervals by the changing colors of what is evidently a large electric sign on a neighboring roof. Less noticeable at first, is the faint light from a revolving beacon far away.

When the curtain rises, BIGGER *is seen standing half-crouched in the shadow of the wall at the right rear. An old piece of rotted blanket is pulled protectingly around his shoulders, and his feet are tied up in pieces of wrapped tow-sacking. He is peering out toward the rear and listening, as if some sound had just disturbed him and he is trying to discover what it is. The glint of his pistol barrel shows from beneath the blanket where he holds it in his hand. Presently he turns and begins to pace up and down, beating himself with his arms to keep from freezing. A mumble of words rises from his lips)*

BIGGER Pshaw, nothing but that old piece of tin banging. They ain't found me yet! From the first jump I out-figure 'em. *(stopping)* Uhm—everything sleepy and 'way off—*(with sudden loudness)* I ain't scared, naw. They all scared, feeling me in the night, feel me walking behind 'em. . . . And everywhere, the bulls is searching them old nigger houses—Indiana, Calumet, Prairie, Wabash! Ha! But I ain't 'mong the niggers. *(calling softly)* Clara! *(he listens at the door at the right)* Why don't she come on here? *(he sinks down on an old box and pulls his blanket shiveringly about him. The flopping tin bangs off at the left. He springs instinctively and nervously up, then sits down again)* Ain't nothing—that old tin banging again, hanging loose and ready to fall. Fall on down, old tin, but I ain't gonna fall. They ain't gonna get me *(gazing back over his shoulder at the night sky. Chuckling with low and bitter irony)* They smart, them white folks! Yeh, they get the niggers. But maybe not too smart—*(he spits in the air. He beats his arms about him and stares out into the night)* That's right! Flash away, old sign! "Sun-kissed oranges." Ha! I'll be in them orange-groves soon . . . with the sun on my back! *(he raises his head more and sees far away, above him, the revolving beam of the beacon in the sky)* Uhmm—an' look at that old Lindbergh beacon, shining there 'way out through the darkness—*(musingly)* Old Lindbergh he knowed the way. Boiling icy water below him, the thunder and the lightning, the freezing and the hail around him. Keep on driving—riding through. *(imitating the sound of an airplane propeller with his numbed lips)* V-r-r-rh-h-h-h! V-r-r-r-ruh-uh-uh! Yes, he made it, got there. And all the people running and shouting, and the headlights switching and sweeping the sky! Old Lindbergh—he made it—got home, safe home. He not scared! *(snapping his head up, his hollow eyes burning through the shadows before him)* Aw, I ain't scared neither! *(he laughs)* An' when I light, ain't goin' to be no lot of people running to me with flowers! Hell, no! When I come, they run! Run like Hell! *(laughs. And now from the depths of the great city below comes the sound of a siren. He springs around, the piece of rotted blanket falling from his shoulders. He grips his gun tightly in his hand and crouching down, moves swiftly to the window at the left. Inching his head up against the sill, he peers over. The sound dies away. He turns from the window)* Sure, nothing but a' ambulance! Another fool white man done broke his neck somewhere. *(he moves back toward the box, flapping his arms like a bird to restore the circulation of his blood. A soft sound of fumbling footsteps is heard at the right. Holding his pistol, he backs away, keeping his eyes fastened on the door. The footsteps come nearer, then stop. He calls out softly)* That you, Clara?

CLARA'S VOICE *(outside)* Open the door. *(he springs over, unbars the door, and lets* CLARA *in. Ramming the bar of plank back in place, he grabs a package from her)*

BIGGER Okay?

CLARA *(in a low dull voice)* Eat something, Bigger. *(with shaking, eager hands, he opens the bag of food and begins devouring the sandwiches she has brought)*

BIGGER Thought you was never coming back. And me sitting here freezing to death. Things going 'round in my head! How everything look?

CLARA Go ahead and eat—

BIGGER *(his mouth full of food)* Anybody notice you?

CLARA Went to a new delicatessen—Thirty-ninth and Indiana.

BIGGER And you come back under the El like I told you?

CLARA I come back that way.

BIGGER Get the papers?

CLARA Here's some liquor—you 'bout froze. *(she pulls a bottle from her pocket. He grabs it, unstops it and drinks half of it swiftly down, then lays the bottle on the floor. She stands with her hands shoved by each other into her coat sleeves, looking at him)*

BIGGER Where the papers? I ask you.

CLARA Didn't get 'em, Bigger.

BIGGER Damn it, told you to—See what they say?

CLARA They got your picture.

BIGGER On the front page?

CLARA On the front page.

BIGGER Reckon they have. And big headlines—huh?

CLARA Big headlines, black—*(her mouth twists with pain)*

BIGGER Humm. Where they think I hid?

CLARA Section down by Ernie's all surrounded.

BIGGER Hah-knowed it. Dumb nuts. If them cops' brains was dynamite, wouldn't have enough to make 'em sneeze! *(angrily)* Why'n hell didn't you bring me that paper? *(she stares at him with dull, dead eyes, saying nothing)* What's the matter? What time is it?

CLARA Forgot to wind my watch.

BIGGER What the big clock down there say?

CLARA Ten till one, it say.

BIGGER Ten more minutes and I'm gone from here. Ten more minutes and that big old sign out there goes off, and I make it 'cross that old stairway over there in the dark to the next building and down that long alley.

CLARA *(piteously)* Then what, Bigger?

BIGGER I find somebody with a car—*(with the gun, he indicates a jab in the side)* He drive me till I say stop. Then I catch a train to the west—Still got that money?

CLARA I got it.

BIGGER How much?

CLARA 'Bout ninety dollars.

BIGGER Gimme. *(she pulls it out of her pocket and hands it to him)*

CLARA Bigger, you can't make it that way—You can't.

BIGGER Goddamit, what do you think? Set here and freeze stiff as a poolstick and wait for 'em to come and pick me up? I got everything figured to the minute. *(now from the city below comes the sound of the siren again. It continues longer than before. He jerks his head around)* Don't like the sound of that. Jesus, won't that sign hurry and go off?

CLARA Bigger, you can't do it.

BIGGER *(with a shout)* Cut that out!

CLARA They offer ten thousand dollars reward—paper say.

BIGGER *(after an instant of silence)* Uhm—They want me bad. Well, they ain't gonna get me. *(thoughtfully)* Ten thousand—same we put in that kidnap note—

CLARA It say you killed her, Bigger.

BIGGER All right, then, I killed her. I didn't mean to. *(angrily)* But hell, we got no time to talk about that. Got to keep my mind clear, my feet free. *(he bends down and begins unwrapping the sacking from around his feet)*

CLARA You told me you wasn't never gonna kill nobody, Bigger. *(she chokes down the sob that keeps rising up in her throat)*

BIGGER I tell you, I wasn't trying to kill her. It was an accident—

CLARA Accident—

BIGGER She was drunk—passed out cold—She was so drunk she didn't even know where she was—And her ma might hear her bumbling about.

CLARA And what she do?

BIGGER Nothing—I just put her on the bed and her blind ma come in—*(shuddering)* Blind. She came in and I got scared. *(his voice quickening)* Yeh, her ma come into the room—had her hands stretched out like. So I just pushed the pillow hard over the gal's mouth to keep her from talking. *(there is a pause. His voice drops to a low note of helpless confession)* Then when she left I looked at that gal and she was dead—that's all—it happened just like that—*(he looks at* CLARA *as though imploring her belief)* She was dead!

CLARA You—you smothered her.

BIGGER Yeh, I reckon I did—I reckon I did—but I didn't mean to—I swear to God I didn't. *(in a hopeless tone)* But what difference do it make? Nobody'll believe me. I'm Black and they'll say—*(flinging a rag savagely away)*

CLARA The paper say—

BIGGER Yeah, I know what they say. They say rape. But I didn't . . . I never touch that girl. *(pause)* And then when I see she dead, I, oh . . . Clara, I didn't know what to do—I took her to the basement and put her in the furnace—burnt her up. *(*CLARA *stares at him, her fist stuffed against her mouth as if to keep herself from screaming)* Jesus, I couldn't help it! *(he stands up suddenly)* It don't seem like I really done it now—really it don't seem like I done it. *(he looks off, his face hard and tense)* Maybe I didn't do it. Maybe I just think I did. Maybe somebody else did all that—*(his body relaxes and his shoulders slump)* But I did, Yeh . . . *(he goes on unwinding the rags. She gazes at him, her eyes filled with their nameless look of horror and despair)*

CLARA *(as if with stiffened tongue)* You—you said you was never going to kill—you said—

BIGGER What the hell difference do it make now? I got to scram! *(he looks anxiously off at rear)* Damn snow quit falling hours ago—Roads be cleared up now. Jesus, that blizzard—like it stopped all the traffic to keep me shut up here. *(he picks up the bottle and takes another drink)*

CLARA *(monotonously)* You can't get away. You got to walk down—meet 'em—tell 'em how it happened—

BIGGER *(with a wild laugh)* And they believe me, huh? Goddamit, I stick my head out that door, my life ain't worth a snowflake in hell. They shoot me down like a dog. Jesus, that tin keeps banging. *(and now a strange light flares into the scene an instant and then is gone.* BIGGER *leaps to his feet with a cry)* What the hell was that! *(across the dark blue sky at the rear, a tall, slender cone of penciled light begins weaving back and forth. It continues its slow and monotonous sweep a moment like a gigantic metronome finger silently ticking out the minutes of* BIGGER*'s life, and then is gone. He turns and stares at it)* Look at that light moving. *(he tilts the bottle again, finishes it, then throws it away into the darkness)* But I ain't scared! *(his voice beginning to grow vacant and dreamy)* I'd begun to see something. Aw, Christ, it's gone again. I'm all mixed up, but I ain't scared now.

CLARA Maybe you ought to be scared—Scared maybe 'cause you ain't scared.

BIGGER Huh? Aw, to hell with it.

CLARA What you gonna do?

BIGGER *(with sudden rage)* Gonna scram, I tell you. Goddamit! *(with rough brutality)* And I don't need you now.

CLARA I know—all last night and today. Don't do no good now—nothing do any good. Your eyes so cold, your face so hard—like you want to kill me. And my heart's all heavy like a lump of lead—and dead.

BIGGER Yeh. Anything get in my way now, I kill it. *(another siren sounds in the streets below, and now, faintly comes the sound of a mumbling multitude.* BIGGER *darts back into the shadow and stops)* Listen there! *(again as if from an unseen brilliant eye, the ruined room is illuminated in a white light reflected in a million diamond facets from the icicles, snow and ice.* BIGGER *draws his gun)* Goddamn, they got a spotlight somewhere. They found me. *(whirling on* CLARA *and seizing her by the throat)* They seen you coming back. *(hissing)* I ought to kill you. You tell 'em.

CLARA Naw! Naw! Bigger! Bigger!

BIGGER *(his lips snarled back, his eyes cold as a snake's)* Yeh, weak, blind—couldn't do without you. Tell 'em where I am. *(he shakes her like a rag-doll. He hurls her from him against the ruined wall at the right. She lies still in the darkness, shivering and gasping. A low, dog-like whimper rises from her. He rushes over and kicks her)* Goddamit, stop that whining. *(she crawls toward him)* Don't you come toward me. I'll kill you. *(the noise in the streets below has increased in volume)*

CLARA *(now clinging to his feet)* Go ahead. Shoot me. Kill us both—and then, no more worry . . . no more pain—Do it, Bigger.

(He jerks his foot loose from her. She falls forward on her face and lies still. The brilliant light floods into the scene again from the faraway hidden spot, and BIGGER *stands, naked and alone, outlined in it. He whirls around him as if trying to beat it from him. He runs to the window and looks out. Suddenly the electric-sign falters in its cycle of going on and off—then goes out entirely—A clock is heard striking one. In a convulsive gesture, his hand rises to his lips, then drops to his side)*

BIGGER Yeh, you done it. They coming along that roof over there with their saw-off guns. *(he rushes to the right, starts to unbar the door when a heavy pounding sets up below. He springs back)* They coming up there, too. *(he runs over and jerks* CLARA *violently from the floor, an ooze of blood is seeping from her mouth)* You set 'em on me, you bitch! *(her head sways weakly from side to side, saying "no." He throws her from him. She stands tottering and about to fall. He runs out on the balcony at the rear. The powerful light remains on him. He starts back with an oath, then runs wildly along the balcony toward the left. The sound of the mob rises more loudly)*

CLARA They kill you! Kill you! *(she moves blindly toward the rear. A shot rings out.* BIGGER *ducks back into the room behind the piece of ruined wall. Another shot barks, and the sound of breaking glass is heard)*

BIGGER *(yelling)* Shoot! Shoot! *(the pounding at the right increases and shouts are heard near at hand off at the left. He grabs* CLARA *and holds her in front of him, moving swiftly over to the right rear)*

VOICES *(at the left)* There he is! Let him have it! We got him!

*(*BIGGER *whirls now, holding* CLARA *protectingly in front of him with one hand. Her arms go up and about him in an impulsive gesture of love. Another shot rings out and she sags down in his arms. He looks at her, then lets her slide out of his arm onto the floor)*

BIGGER Yeh. In front of me, and they shot you—All right, goddamit, I killed you. *(wagging his head)* Yeh. I said I would. I said so.

A VOICE *(beyond the door at the right)* Come on out of there, nigger!

*(*BIGGER *fires at the door, and now the air is permeated with voices, as if an invisible ring of persons were squeezing the scene in a tightening circle. A voice at the left calls out)*

VOICE Come on out if you're alive!

SECOND VOICE You're going to wish you was dead! *(the sound of horns, sirens, and voices from the distance have grown to a roaring volume. Above the tumult,* BIGGER*'s voice lashes out, high and clear)*

BIGGER Yeh, white boys! Come on and get me! You ain't scared of me, is you? Ain't nobody but Bigger in here—*(he shoots at the door)* Bigger! Bigger! Bigger standing against the lot of you! Against your thousand . . . two thousand . . . three thousand . . .

(He fires again and a volley of shots answers him. He is hit, tumbled completely over by the impact of the bullet. His gun flies from his hands and he falls back against the wall. Mouthing and snarling, he crawls toward the pistol, then collapses over CLARA*'s body. The door at the right is kicked in, and a policeman steps swiftly out of the shadow, his gun drawn. A second policeman runs in along the balcony from the left rear, his gun also drawn. Through the open door, two plainclothesmen enter behind the policemen)*

FIRST MAN *(bending over* CLARA*'s dead body)* Uhm, bullet went clean through her.

FIRST POLICEMAN The sonofabitch—killed her too. Just let that mob get at him!

SECOND POLICEMAN Come on, get him downstairs. They'll fix 'im! *(he seizes* BIGGER*'s heels and lifts them up. Walking into the scene at the right comes an elderly man in an enveloping overcoat. An old plug hat is pulled low over his forehead hiding the ringlets of his gray hair. He stops and stares down at* BIGGER*)*

FIRST POLICEMAN *(looking around)* Hum—better be law and order, boys—Here's old Max.

SECOND POLICEMAN *(hurriedly)* Try the back way, fellows. *(the sound of the sirens rises and continues. Fadeout)*

Scene Nine

(The sound of the mob dies away and the curtain goes up on the court room, two weeks later.

Behind the desk, on an imposing dais at the rear, sits the JUDGE*, draped in a long black gown, and with a gray and heavy juridical face. Hanging directly above him, and behind, is the picture of an eighteenth century statesman resembling the like-*

ness of Thomas Jefferson and surmounted by the graceful folds of the Stars and Stripes. Down in front of the JUDGE's *desk is an oblong table. Between the desk and the table sit the Sheriff, the Clerk, and the Court stenographer. To the right and left rear, somewhat framing the scene, stand two Militiamen at stiff attention, their bayoneted rifles held straight by their sides. At the right front sit* HANNAH THOMAS, VERA *and* BUDDY. BUDDY *is holding tightly to his mother's hand. In the same positions at the left sit the* DALTONS *and* PEGGY. *The two women wear veils and are in deep mourning.* BUCKLEY, *the Prosecuting Attorney, is sitting to the right of* DALTON. *At the table, with his back to the audience is* BIGGER. *He seems to pay no attention to what is going on around him. The scene is in darkness as the curtain rises, and out of this darkness comes the deep tumult of many voices, and then other voices raised in argument. As if in rhythm to the banging of the* JUDGE's *gavel the light comes swiftly up on the scene, showing* EDWARD MAX *and* BUCKLEY, *both on their feet, in front of the* JUDGE's *stand.*

MAX, *now that we see him in the light, is a big, flabby, kindly-faced man, with something sad and tragic in the pallid whiteness of his skin and the melancholy depths of his eyes. His hair is silvery white. There is a general air of poverty and yet of deep abiding peace about him.* BUCKLEY *is a suave, well-built man of about 40, with the florid, commanding face of the American business executive. He wears a carnation in the lapel of his morning coat)*

BUCKLEY *(shouting)* Your Honor!

MAX *(quietly)* I am not out of order, your Honor.

BUCKLEY The counsel for the defense cannot plead this boy both guilty and insane!

MAX I have made no such plea.

BUCKLEY If you plead him insane, the State will demand a jury trial.

JUDGE Go on, Mr. Max.

MAX Your Honor, I am trying to make the Court understand the true nature of this case—I want the mind of the Court to be free and clear—And then if the Court says death, let it mean death. And if the Court says life, let it mean that too. But whatever the Court says, let it know upon what ground its verdict is being rendered. *(glancing at his notes)* Night after night I have lain without sleep trying to think of a way to picture to you, and to the world, the causes, the reasons, why this Negro boy sits here today—a self-confessed murderer—and why this great city is boiling with a fever of excitement and hate. And yet how can I, I ask myself, make the picture of what has happened to this boy show plain and powerful upon a screen of sober reason, when a thousand newspaper and magazine artists have already drawn it in lurid ink upon a million sheets of public print? I have pled the cause of other criminal youths in this court as his Honor well knows. And when I took this case I thought at first it was the same old story of a boy run afoul of the law. But it is more terrible than that—with meaning more far-reaching. Where is the responsibility? Where is the guilt? For there is guilt in the rage that demands that this man's life be stamped out! There is guilt and responsibility in the hate that inflames that mob gathered in the streets below these windows! What is the atmosphere that surrounds this trial? Are the citizens intent upon seeing that the majesty of the Law is upheld? That retribution be dealt out in measure with the facts? That the guilty, and only the guilty, be caught and punished? No!

BUCKLEY I object, your Honor!

MAX *(continuing)* The hunt for Bigger Thomas has served as a political excuse, not only to terrorize the entire Negro population of this city, but also to arrest hundreds of members of suspect organizations, to raid labor union headquarters and workers' gatherings!

BUCKLEY Objection!

JUDGE Objection sustained! Strike all that from the record. You will confine your remarks to the evidence in the case.

MAX Your Honor, for the sake of this boy, I wish I could bring to you evidence of a morally worthier nature. I wish I could say that love, or ambition, or jealousy, or the quest for adventure, or any of the more romantic emotions were back of this case. But I cannot. I have no choice in the matter. Life has cut this cloth, not I. Fear and hate and guilt are the keynotes of this drama. You see, your Honor, I am not afraid to assign the blame, for thus I can the more honestly plead for mercy! I say that this boy is the victim of a wrong that has grown, like a cancer, into the very blood and bone of our social structure.

Bigger Thomas sits here today as a symbol of that wrong. And the judgment that you will deliver upon him is a judgment delivered upon ourselves, and upon our whole civilization. The Court can pronounce the sentence of death and that will end the defendant's life—but it will not end this wrong!

BUCKLEY Your Honor, I object—

JUDGE The Court is still waiting for you to produce mitigating evidence, Mr. Max!

MAX Very well. Let us look back into this boy's childhood. On a certain day, he stood and saw his own father shot down by a Southern mob—while trying to protect one of his own kind from violence and hate—the very violence and hate represented in the mob gathered around this court-house today. With his mother and sister and little brother, Bigger Thomas fled North to this great city, hoping to find here a freer life for himself and those he loved. And what did he find here? Poverty, idleness, economic injustice, race discrimination and all the squeezing and oppression of a ruthless world—our world, your Honor—yours and mine! Here again he found the violence and the degradation from which he had fled. Here again he found the same frustrated way of life intensified by the cruelty of a blind and enslaving industrial mechanism. It is that way of life that stands on trial today, your Honor, in the person of Bigger Thomas! Like his forefathers, he is a slave. But unlike his forefathers there is something in him that refuses to accept this slavery. And why does he refuse to accept it? Because through the very teachings of our schools and educational system he was led to believe that in this land of liberty men are free. With one part of his mind, he believed what we had taught him—that he was a free man! With the other he found himself denied the right to accept that truth. In theory he was stimulated by every token around him to aspire to be a free individual. And in practice by every method of our social system, he was frustrated in that aspiration. Out of this confusion, fear was born. And fear breeds hate, and hate breeds guilt, and guilt in turn breeds the urge to destroy—to kill. *(the* JUDGE *is now listening intently to* MAX*)*

BUCKLEY *(shouting out)* I object! All this is merely an attempt to prove the prisoner insane—

JUDGE *(rapping with his gavel)* Objection over-ruled.

MAX *(turning toward* MR. *and* MRS. DALTON*)* Consider these witnesses for the State, Mr. and Mrs. Dalton. I have only sympathy for these poor grieving parents. You have heard their testimony and you have heard them plead for leniency toward this boy. *(pause)* Well may they plead for leniency for perhaps they are as guilty of this crime as he is!

BUCKLEY Your Honor—

MAX Unconsciously, and against their will, they are partners in this drama of guilt and blood. They intended no evil—yet they produced evil.

BUCKLEY *(furiously)* I object. He is impugning the character of my witnesses.

MAX *(quietly)* I am not. I have only sympathy for them. But I am trying to state the facts, and these are the facts. This man rents his vast real estate holdings to many thousands of Negroes, and among these thousands is the family of this boy, Bigger Thomas. The rents in those tenements are proportionately the highest, and the living conditions the worst of any in this city. Yet this man is held in high esteem. Why? Because out of the profits he makes from those rents, he turns around and gives back to the Negroes a small part as charity. For this he is lauded in the press and held up as an example of fine citizenship. But where do the Negroes come in? Nowhere. What do they have to say about how they live? Nothing. Around the whole vicious circle they move and act at this man's behest, and must accept the crumbs of their own charity as Mr. Dalton wills, or wills not. It is a form of futile bribery that continues, and will continue, until we see the truth and stop it. For corpses cannot be bribed—And such living corpses as Bigger Thomas here, are warnings to us to stop it, and stop it now before it is too late—

BUCKLEY Your Honor! *(the* JUDGE *waves him down, and* MAX *goes on)*

MAX One more word, your Honor, and I am done. *(pointing towards the portrait on the wall at the rear)* There, under that flag, is the likeness of one of our forefathers—one of the men who came to these strange shores hundreds of years ago in search of freedom. Those men, and we who followed them, built here a nation mighty and powerful, the most powerful nation on earth! Yet to those who, as much as any others, helped us build this nation, we have said, and we continue to say, "This is a white man's country!" Night and day, millions of souls, the souls of our black people, are crying out, "This is our country too. We helped build it—helped defend it. Give us a part in it, a part free and hopeful and wide as the everlasting horizon." And in this fear-crazed, guilt-ridden body of Bigger Thomas that vast multitude cries out to you now in a mighty voice, saying, "Give us our freedom, our chance, and our hope to be men." Can we ignore this cry? Can we continue to boast through every medium of public utterance—through literature, newspapers, radio, the pulpit—that this is a land of freedom and opportunity, of liberty and justice for all—and in our behavior deny all these precepts of charity and enlightenment? Bigger Thomas is a symbol of that double-dealing, an organism which our political and economic hypocrisy has bred. Kill him, burn the life out of him, and still the symbol of his living death remains. And you cannot kill Bigger Thomas, for he is already dead. He was born dead—born dead among the wild forests of our cities, amid the rank and choking vegetation of our slums—in the Jim Crow corners of our buses and trains—in the dark closets and corridors and rest rooms marked off by the finger of a blind and prejudiced law as Black against White. And who created that law? We did. And while it lasts we stand condemned before mankind—Your Honor, I beg you, not in the name of Bigger Thomas but in the name of ourselves, spare this boy's life! *(he turns to his seat at the table beside* BIGGER. *Immediately the roar of the crowd outside swells in upon the scene. The* JUDGE *bangs with his gavel again and the lights dim down. For a moment the noise continues and then dies away as the lights come up again.* BUCKLEY *is now addressing the* JUDGE. *His manner is earnest, kindly and confident)*

BUCKLEY The counsel for the defense may criticize the American nation and its methods of government. But that government is not on trial today. Only one person, the defendant, Bigger Thomas, is on trial. He pleads guilty to the charges of the indictment. The rest is simple and brief. Punishment must follow—punishment laid down by the sacred laws of this Commonwealth—laws created to protect that society and that social system of which we are a part! A criminal is one who goes against those laws. He attacks the laws. Therefore the laws must destroy him. If thine eye offend thee, pluck it out; and if the branch of a tree withers and dies, it must be cut off lest it contaminate the rest of the tree. Such a tree is the State through whose flourishing and good health we ourselves exist and carry on our lives. The ruined, the rotten and degraded must be cut out, cleansed away so that the body politic itself may keep its health. I sympathize with the counsel for the defense. I understand his point of view, his persuasive argument. But the simple truth is, your Honor, he is deluded. His thinking, his arguments, run contrary to the true course of man's sound development. Yes, if the Defense wishes, let us speak not in terms of crime, but in terms of disease. I pity this diseased and ruined defendant. But as a true surgeon, looking to the welfare of the organic body of our people, I repeat that it is necessary this diseased member be cut off—cut out and obliterated—lest it infect us all unto death. Your Honor, I regret that the Defense has raised the viperous issue of race and class hatred in this trial. Justice should, and must be, dispensed fairly and equally, in accordance with the facts, and not with theories—and justice is all I ask. And what are the facts? That this Bigger Thomas is sane and is responsible for his crimes—And all the eloquent tongues of angels or men cannot convince this honorable court that it and I and others gathered here are the guilty ones. Bigger Thomas is guilty and in his soul he knows it. Your Honor, in the name of the people of this city, in the name of truth and Almighty God, I demand that this Bigger Thomas justly die for the brutal murder of Mary Dalton!

(Through the whole scene, the spectators have remained motionless, and even BUDDY *has sat like a little Black statue, his eyes fastened straight on the bowed figure of his brother. As* BUCKLEY *takes his seat, the lights begin to dim on the scene, and once again the sound of the great mob outside permeates the room in a heavy, undulating drone. The scene seems to recede from us, and now, out of the thickening gloom, comes the voice of the* JUDGE*)*

JUDGE'S VOICE Bigger Thomas, stand up.

(The murmur of the mob continues. Blackout)

Scene Ten

(The sound of the mob dies away and the curtain goes up on the death cell. It is a few weeks later.

Directly across and separated by only a few feet of corridor is the death chamber, its heavy iron door closed. There is a barred door in the left wall of the cell, and on the wall at the right a porcelain wash basin is fastened, sticking out like a frozen lip. Along the wall at the right rear is an iron cot covered with a white morgue-like sheet. The atmosphere is one of scientific anaesthesia and deathly cleanliness.

Seen through the slanting bars at the left rear are two uniformed guards seated at a little table playing rummy. One is an elderly man, the other much younger. The cell is lighted by a single electric bulb on the ceiling, and the streaking shadows of the bars cut across the figures of the two guards behind.

When the curtain rises, BIGGER *is standing against the wall by the door, looking out to the front, with his body half turned towards the rear. He is dressed in a white short-sleeved shirt open at the throat, and dark gray flannel trousers, one leg of which is slit open from the knee down. His head is shaved, and he is staring out after the retreating forms of his mother, sister and brother. Sobbing, the mother tries to go back to* BIGGER, *but is restrained by the younger guard who rises to meet her)*

HANNAH My boy, my poor boy—

BUDDY Ma, don't do that! Ma—*(*HANNAH *is led away and her sobs die out.* BIGGER *continues to stare after her without a sound)*

FIRST GUARD *(in a quiet voice laying down a card)* That old woman takes it hard.

SECOND GUARD *(coming back)* It's her son.

FIRST GUARD *(jerking his head towards* BIGGER*)* He don't seem to care though.

SECOND GUARD Since that time he cried all night long, he don't say much.

FIRST GUARD And how he cried—But reckon that old water hose stopped him—*(there is a rush at the left and* BUDDY *runs up to the cell bars and grips them in an agony of grief)*

BUDDY Ma says don't you worry—we gonna take care of you—later.

SECOND GUARD Go on, sonny.

BUDDY And it gonna be at Reverend Hammond's church, Bigger. And plenty of flowers—and folks, Bigger. *(at a gesture from the first guard, the second guard leads* BUDDY *off.* BIGGER *has stood motionless.* BUDDY *goes away, straining his eyes on* BIGGER *to the last)*

BIGGER *(calling quietly)* Tell Vera good-by.

BUDDY'S VOICE *(brokenly)* Yeh, yeh. Good-by—ee—*(his voice dies away)*

FIRST GUARD *(with meaningless comfort calling toward* BIGGER*)* I know—Time passes slow. Ten more minutes, boy, that's all.

SECOND GUARD *(returning)* Then eight seconds after that you won't worry. Just take a deep breath—eight seconds! Go ahead and talk, son. Make it easier, maybe. *(but* BIGGER *remains silent)*

FIRST GUARD Your lawyer's here—*(*BIGGER *shakes his head)*

SECOND GUARD He'll wanta walk with you in case—

BIGGER Don't need nobody—

SECOND GUARD *(admiringly)* Got iron in his blood, all right, I'll say that. *(he seats himself at the table again)* Damn, he's tough! *(they resume their card playing. A third guard comes up to the door out of the darkness, followed by* MAX. *He goes back the way he came. The second guard lets* MAX *into the cell and then reseats himself, his face still caught in its look of hurt and nauseous pain.* MAX *stands mopping his brow, his face flabby and old)*

MAX No word yet, son. I'm sorry.

BIGGER *(in a muffled voice)* That's okay, Mr. Max.

MAX We're doing all we can. Mrs. Dalton's with the Governor now. There's maybe still a chance—

BIGGER *(with an odd touch of shame as he suddenly indicates his shaved head)* They changed my looks.

MAX Mr. Dalton too. He's got power. I'm still hoping—

BIGGER I'm all right, Mr. Max. You ain't to blame for what's happened to me. *(his voice drops to a low, resigned and melancholy note)* I reckon—uh—I—uh—I just reckon I had it coming. *(he stands with his lips moving, shaking his head, but no words come)*

MAX *(leaning forward)* What is it, Bigger?

BIGGER *(in a heavy expiring breath)* Naw.

MAX Talk to me, Bigger. You can trust me, you know that.

BIGGER Trust or don't trust, all the same. Ain't nobody can help me now. *(he sits down, his lips moving inaudibly again)*

MAX *(quietly)* What are you trying to say, Bigger?

BIGGER *(after a moment, shouting)* I—I just want to say maybe I'm glad I got to know you before I go!

MAX I—I'm glad I got to know you too, Bigger. I'll soon be going, son. I'm old. But others will carry on our fight—

BIGGER What I got to do with it?

MAX And because of you—whether you live or die, Bigger, we will be nearer the victory—justice and freedom for men. I want you to know that.

BIGGER *(his voice dropping down)* Ain't nobody ever talked to me like you before. *(he breaks off and turns distractedly about him)* How come you do it—and you being a white man? *(with wild impulsiveness)* You oughta left me alone. How come you want to help me in the first place, and me Black and a murderer maybe ten times over?

MAX *(placing his hand on* BIGGER*'s shoulder as he pulls away)* Bigger, in my work—and the work the world has ahead—there are no whites and Blacks—only men. And you make me feel, Bigger, and others feel it—how badly men want to live in this world—to say here is where I once was. This was me, big and strong . . . till the years quit falling down. You feel like that, don't you, Bigger? You felt like that?

BIGGER Sometimes I wish you wouldn't ask me all them questions, Mr. Max. Goddamit, I wish you wouldn't. *(he chokes on his words in regret and impotent despair, and then regains his voice)* I was all set to die maybe. I was all right. Then you come and start talking, digging into me, opening up my guts.

MAX I want to understand you, get near to you, Bigger.

BIGGER *(almost whispering)* Understand me. She said that—understand me—*(his voice dies out. The guards now sit muffled and motionless in the gloom)*

MAX And she was trying to help you, wasn't she? *(pause)* Don't you know she was trying to help you?

BIGGER She made me feel like a dog! Yeah, that's the way all of 'em made me feel. In their big house I was all trembling and afraid. *(his voice trails off again)*

MAX *(suddenly)* Didn't you ever love anybody, Bigger?

BIGGER Maybe I loved my daddy. Long time ago. They killed him. *(suddenly shouting as he springs up and begins to pace the cell)* Goddamn it, there you start again. You mix me all up! *(with a wild moan)* You make me feel something could happen—something good maybe—*(frenziedly)* You creep in on me, crowd me to the wall, smother me and I want my breath, right up till that lightning hits me. Go away, Mr. Max.

MAX That day I said we had made you what you were, a killer—maybe I was wrong—I want to know I was wrong—*(he gazes at* BIGGER *with white pained face)*

BIGGER *(softly, half to himself)* His po' face like the face of Jesus hanging on that wall—like her face too.

MAX You killed Clara. Why? She loved you, she was good. You say you killed her.

BIGGER *(stopping his pacing)* Yeh, I killed her—

MAX You're not crazy, and there's not that kind of crazy logic in this world. I ask you and all the time you say, "I just did." That's not it, not it.

BIGGER Then I didn't kill her. They said I shot her. I didn't. Wasn't no use talking 'bout it. She didn't count. I just let 'em say it.

MAX *(an uncertain joy in his voice)* You didn't shoot her?

BIGGER One their bullets went clean through her. I had her in my arms, I let her fall down—

MAX *(with a shout)* We could have proved it. It might have—Thank God. *(he sinks down on the cot, staring at* BIGGER*)*

BIGGER But I killed her just the same. All the time I'd been killing her the way I'd been killing myself. She'd suffered for me, followed me, and I didn't want it—wanted to be free to walk wild and free with steps a mile long—over the houses, over the rivers, and straddling the mountains and on—something in me—

MAX And you didn't want to be hindered—you'd kill anything that got in your way—

BIGGER Reckon so. But I wasn't thinking of that then.

MAX *(watching him)* And would you kill again, Bigger, if you could?

BIGGER *(quieting down)* I dunno—Naw—Yessuh, I dunno. Sometimes I feel like it.

Maybe you're wrong now and I am bad and rotten the way you thought at the trial—made bad, and like that other man said. I dunno what I am—got no way to prove it. *(wetting his lips)* All the time I lie here thinking, beating my head against a wall, trying to see through, over it, but can't. Maybe 'cause I'm gonna die makes me want to see—know what I am maybe. How can I die like that, Mr. Max?

MAX If we knew how to live, Bigger, we'd know how to die.

BIGGER Yeh, people can live together but a man got to die by himself. That don't make sense—He needs something to die by more than to live by. *(as* MAX *is silent)* I ain't trying to dodge what's coming. But, Mr. Max, maybe I ain't never wanted to hurt nobody—for real I ain't, maybe. *(his eyes are wide as he stares ahead, straining to feel and think his way through the darkness)*

MAX Go on, Bigger.

BIGGER Seem like with you here try to help me—you so good and kind—I begin to think better. *(shaking his head again)* Uh, but why the folks who sent me here hate me so? That mob—I can hear 'em still—'Cause I'm Black?

MAX *(with gentle, yearning comfort)* No, that's not it, Bigger. Your being Black just makes it easier to be singled out in a white man's world. That's all. What they wanted to do to you they do to each other every day. They don't hate you and they don't hate each other. They are men like you, like me, and they feel like you. They want the things of life just as you do, their own chance. But as long as these are denied them—just so long will those millions keep groping around frightened and lost—angry and full of hate—the way you were, Bigger. *(he pauses)* Bigger, the day these millions—these millions of poor men—workers, make up their minds—begin to believe in themselves—

BIGGER Yeh, reckon the workers believe in themselves all right. Try to get into one them labor unions. Naw, Mr. Max. Everywhere you turn they shut the door in your face, keep you homeless as a dog. Never no chance to be your own man. That's what I always wanted to be—my own man—*(staring at* MAX*)* Honest to God, Mr. Max, I never felt like my own man till right after that happened—till after I killed her.

MAX *(fiercely)* No, Bigger.

BIGGER Yeh—and all the peoples and all the killings and the hangings and the burnings inside me, kept pushing me on—up and on to do something big—have money like that kidnap note—power—something great—to keep my head up—to put my name on the hot wires of the world—big—And, yeh, and all the bad I done, it seemed was right—and after they caught me I kept saying it was right and I was gonna stand on it, hold it—walk that long road down to that old chair—look at it, say, "Do your worst! Burn me. Shoot your juice, and I can take it. You can kill me but can't hurt me—can't hurt me—It's the truth, Mr. Max, after I killed that white girl, I wasn't scared no more—for a little while. *(his voice rises with feverish intensity)* I was my own man then, I was free. Maybe it was 'cause they was after my life then. They made me wake up. That made me feel high and powerful—free! *(with growing vehemence)* That day and night after I done killed her—when all of them was looking for me—hunting me—that day and night for the first time I felt like a man. *(shouting)* I was a man!

MAX *(loudly)* You don't believe that, Bigger.

BIGGER Yeah, yeah, I felt like a man—when I was doing what I never thought I'd do—something I never wanted to do. And it was crazy—wrong and crazy. *(with a piteous childlike cry)* Why, Mr. Max? Why?

MAX That's the answer men must find, Bigger.

BIGGER *(lowering his head)* I'm all right now, Mr. Max—I'm all right. Don't be scared of me. I'm all right. You go on. I don't feel that way now. It didn't last.

MAX It never lasts, Bigger.

(The dynamo in the death chamber at the left begins to hum, and the light in the ceiling of BIGGER*'s cell dims down and then regains its brilliance. The humming dies away)*

BIGGER They 'bout ready now. *(whispering queerly)* And that midnight mail is flying late.

MAX Hold onto yourself, son. There's still a chance—

BIGGER They ready but I can't see it clear yet. *(licking his lips)* But I be all right, Mr. Max. Just go and tell Ma I was all right and not to worry none—see? Tell her I was all right and not crying none.

MAX *(his words almost inaudible now)* Yes, Bigger.

BIGGER Yeh, I'm going now and ain't done it, ain't done it yet.

MAX What, Bigger?

BIGGER *(panting and beating his fists together)* Nothing really right yet—like what I wanted to do. Living or dead, they don't give me no chance—I didn't give myself no chance. *(the two guards rise from the table. They look off and up at the left rear)*

FIRST GUARD Well—

SECOND GUARD Yeh.

(A low mournful harmony, hardly heard at first, begins among the prisoners in the cells stretching away to the rear. The third guard comes swiftly up out of the darkness. He hands a telegram to MAX *who seizes it.* BIGGER *begins gazing up at the ceiling of his cell, as if listening for a sound afar off)*

MAX *(in a low voice)* Bigger. *(he opens the telegram—For an instant he looks at it and then his shoulders sag slowly down. He murmurs)* Want to read it, son—*(but* BIGGER *does not answer.* MAX *sticks out his hand in farewell, his face old and broken, then lets it fall)*

FIRST GUARD One minute past midnight.

SECOND GUARD All right, son. *(they start moving toward the cell.* BIGGER *still stands with his face lifted and set in its tense concentration)*

BIGGER *(in a fierce conclusive whisper)* There she comes—Yeh, I hear you. *(far above in the night the murmuring throb of an airplane motor is audible.* BIGGER*'s voice bursts from him in a wild frenzied call)* Fly them planes, boys—fly 'em!—riding through—riding through. I'll be with you! I'll—

FIRST GUARD Come on, he's going nuts! *(he quickly unlocks the cell and they enter)*

BIGGER *(yelling, his head wagging in desperation)* Keep on driving!—To the end of the world—smack into the face of the sun! *(gasping)* Fly 'em for me—for Bigger—*(the sound of the airplane fades away and now the death chant of the prisoners comes more loudly into the scene. In the dim corridor at the rear the white surplice of a priest is discerned)*

SECOND GUARD *(touching* BIGGER *on the arm)* This way, son.

(They start leading him from the cell. As if of its own volition the door to the little death house opens and a flood of light pours out. BIGGER*, with his eyes set and his shoulders straight, moves toward its sunny radiance like a man walking into a deep current of water. The guards quietly follow him, their heads bent down)*

MAX *(staring after him, his white face wet with tears)* Good-by, Bigger. *(*BIGGER *enters the door)*

PRIEST'S VOICE *(intoning from the shadows)* I am the resurrection and the life.

(The death chant of the prisoners grows louder. The door to the death house closes, cutting off the light. The end)

FAMILY LIFE

Louis Peterson • Lorraine Hansberry • Lonne Elder III • Thomas Pawley

When slaves were first brought to this country, they were divided and shipped in small numbers, often one or two at a time, to different plantations. Separating them from their kinsmen made them easier to handle. The slaves' owners attempted to strip the Africans of their language, culture and religion, but did not entirely succeed. On some plantations, slaves were occasionally permitted to marry, although the duration of the marriage was subject to the will of the masters. The precarious position of the male slave, who could be sold to another owner at any time, and the uncertainty of the duration of these marriages, resulted in the slave mother becoming the most important and dependable figure in the family.

Following the Civil War, freedmen throughout the South began a frantic search for family members, loved ones, and friends separated by slavery or by war. They legalized their marriages and took surnames different from their former owners. A large number of the women refused to work under white overseers. They sought land on which to live and farm in order to ensure their independence and solidify their families. They also sought educations for their children. By 1890, more than 90 percent of African families lived in the South, the majority of them farmers. At the center of these large extended families were married couples, with other relatives in close proximity. These units were augmented by family members related by marriage. This way of life was disrupted when the nation's economy shifted from agriculture to industry. Less than a hundred years later, 90 percent of all African American families lived in urban areas scattered in all parts of the country. This change altered the family structure from large extended ones to smaller ones consisting of husband, wife, and children. From the end of the Civil War up to 1960, there was a remarkable degree of stability in the structure of Black family life. Divorce was rare, and 78 percent of the homes were headed by married couples.

The shift from industry to technology had a disrupting effect on the Black family. Unskilled industrial workers were being replaced by machine technology, and Black employees were among the first to be replaced. With no jobs available in industry, and little formal education, Black men were forced to accept low-paying, menial jobs—when they were available. Too often they were not. The frustration of losing a job, inability to pay bills, and loss of self-esteem resulted in an increase in the number of working mothers, single parent households, divorces, teen pregnancies, substance abuse, unemployment, homelessness. There was a steady decline in married couple households from 64 percent in 1970 to 39 percent in 1990, and this decline is continuing. Single parent households headed by women escalated from 20 percent in 1960 to 57 percent in 1990.

In spite of this, 70 percent of the total population of all Blacks lived in families and were related to the people with whom they lived—by marriage, blood, or adoption—in 1990. This evidence demonstrates that marriage and family life are still important characteristics of the African American community regardless of political and media messages to the contrary.

The Tumult and the Shouting takes place between 1918 and 1948, a period covering almost the entire span of African American involvement in the industrial job market. Prior to 1915, industry employed European immigrant laborers and did not begin hiring Blacks until the onset of World War I. These job opportunities resulted in a mass migration of African Americans from the South to cities in the North, East, and West. The Younger family in *A Raisin in the Sun* was part of the migration to Chicago. A steady income provided some of these families with a kind of stability that allowed them to improve their status, as the Scotts in *Take a Giant Step* had done, from lower to middle class. The Scotts have the education and skills necessary to hold white-collar jobs, as does Pawley's character, David Sheldon, Sr. On the other hand, Walter Lee Younger and the Parker brothers in *Ceremonies in Dark Old Men* represent the 45 percent of Black unskilled laborers in the country at that time. Job opportunities are more difficult for the Parker brothers because by the mid-1960s, when *Ceremonies* unfolds, America was well into the technological age and employees were expected to be knowledgeable in either telecommunications or computers.

The Tumult and the Shouting and *A Raisin in the Sun* depict African American families as cohesive units pursuing the American dream: security, respectability, and the admiration of their loved ones. The paths they take to fulfill their dreams vary drastically. David Sheldon, Sr., a man of integrity, selects an admirable path, teaching, but is betrayed and defeated in the end; Walter Lee Younger falls victim to swindlers in his haste to become an entrepreneur, but rises from his defeat and becomes a man. In both instances, the family unit remains solid, as it does in *Take a Giant Step.* Spencer Scott matures with a new sense of direction and greater perception of his parents. The Parkers resort to illegal means to achieve their dream, which brings about the disintegration of the family. In each case, these families' lives are complicated by racism, but racism is not the primary concern of these playwrights.

TAKE A GIANT STEP
1953

Louis Peterson (1922–   )

African American artists are in a rather precarious position since what they produce is often interpreted as representative of the entire race rather than as an individual's personal expression. This has plagued the Black playwright for decades. Should he write for the commercial theatre or for Black audiences? Should his characters be drawn from the lower or the middle class? Should certain aspects of African American life be avoided, certain subjects rejected? Can the playwright afford to merely entertain, or does he have a duty to be didactic? Does writing for commercial theatre mean that the writer is selling out? Should he restrict himself to subject matter and characters deemed suitable and acceptable to white audiences? Do white and Black audiences have different expectations? If he writes for Black audiences, should the emphasis be on race problems and the struggle for equality, or can it simply be a personal problem of the protagonist?

While these questions continue to spark interesting debate, most playwrights know that if a work is to have any validity, each writer must write what he must write—what is most important and meaningful to that artist. Often what is most important is what the playwright has lived and feels in his heart. Such was the case with Louis Peterson's autobiographical first play, *Take a Giant Step*. Peterson's concern is with the frustrations of growing up, and the steps that his young protagonist, Spencer Scott, must take toward maturity. The author and his protagonist are cut from the same fabric; both are from middle-class backgrounds, were raised in white communities, attended white public schools, and had white playmates. Peterson no doubt experienced the same loneliness and rejection that Spencer does once his white friends begin to date and feel that he cramps their style.

Take a Giant Step, which opened in New York on September 24, 1953, to favorable reviews and much discussion, was different from the typical folksy or exotic African American Broadway fare. White audiences and critics were amazed to discover that the Scott family was just like them. They had the same middle-class aspirations—a decent home in a safe neighborhood, good schools for their children, and a quality of life conducive to progress. The play was hailed for its universality, since Peterson's portrayal of problems is common to both races. The agony of growing up, discovering sex, confronting the death of a loved one, and other adolescent crises are situations that most young people experience. Spencer's problems, however, are intensified because of his race. At school he is offended by a white teacher's condescending remarks about slaves during the Civil War, then by his white friends who are beginning to distance themselves from him because of their interest in girls, and finally by his parents' willingness to accept racial intolerance rather than speak up.

Spencer's language and actions are the same as his white friends, prompting some critics to refer to him as an African American Andy Hardy, and to compare him to Richard in Eugene O'Neill's *Ah, Wilderness!* He and Richard do have some things in common; both run away from home, become sexually aware, and mature at the conclusion of the plays. Richard, it appears, will live happily ever after, but Spencer's maturation is much more painful. He faces the realization that, as a Black person, the American melting pot is not eager to absorb him. Spencer confronts this first by rejecting his friends before they reject him, then by finishing high school, entering college, and rather than becoming the conformist that his parents are, would probably take that giant step becoming an activist in the movement for civil rights.

Despite excellent reviews, *Take a Giant Step* ran for only eight weeks. It was revived Off Broadway in 1956 and ran for 264 peformances. A film version of the play was released in 1960.

Louis Peterson has written for television and film. His television drama, *Class of 1958,* is considered a sequel to *Take a Giant Step* and concerns the difficulties that a young man experiences in college. It was produced by the *Goodyear Television Playhouse* with an all-white cast in 1954.

Take a Giant Step

Cast of Characters

SPENCER SCOTT
GRANDMOTHER
TONY
IGGIE
FRANK
MAN
VIOLET
POPPY
ROSE
CAROL
LEM SCOTT
MAY SCOTT
CHRISTINE
GUSSIE
JOHNNY REYNOLDS
BOBBY REYNOLDS

Act One

Scene One

(If you walked down a rather shady, middle class street in a New England town, you would probably find a house very similar to the one in which the Scotts live. It was a rather ordinary house when it was built and it is a rather ordinary house now, but it has been well cared for, devotedly watched and cared for, and it gives off an aura of good health and happiness if houses can ever know such things. The house has been cut away to expose to view to the audience the back entrance hall, a kitchen up left, a dining room left, a living room and a hall right in which there is a front door and a staircase leading to the upstairs. At the very top of the stairs, there is a little chair almost like a child's chair. If the house has any character at all it should resem-

ble a fat old lady who has all the necessary equipment of living about her person.

If you walked down a rather shady, middle class street in a New England town you would probably hear the same sounds that you are hearing when the curtain rises. The sounds of boys playing baseball in the lot across the street. SPENCER SCOTT *enters from right into his own yard. He is a Negro boy of seventeen years. He has a croquet stake in one hand that he has pulled up out of the ground, and books in his other hand. He is hitting the side of his leg with the stake. The time is the present—Fall—late October. It is a fine day—a golden warm day which is typical of New England at this time of year. After a moment* SPENCE, *still carrying the stake, walks into the hall. He slams the front door. On the door slam off-stage noises stop.* GRANDMA immediately calls offstage)

GRANDMA *(in bedroom upstairs)* Spence. Spence. Is that you?

SPENCE Yes, it's me, Gram. Who the hell does she think it is—Moses? *(jacket and books on sofa)*

GRANDMA Where have you been?

SPENCE No place.

GRANDMA Well, why are you so late coming home?

SPENCE No reason in particular, Gram. I just took my time. You know how that is—don't you, Gram—when you just want to take your time coming home? *(sits on sofa. Takes off shoes)*

GRANDMA Just a minute—I can't hear you. I'll be right down.

SPENCE If you do—I'll tell Mom that you've been horsing around again today.

GRANDMA Just you be quiet and come up and help me.

SPENCE *(gets up, goes upstairs)* You know you haven't got any business coming downstairs. Mom told you to stay up. Not only am I going to tell Mom, but when the doctor comes, I'm going to tell him too.

GRANDMA *(appears at door)* Tell him. You think I care. Now come up and help me.

SPENCE *(goes all the way upstairs and helps her)* Just lean on me, and hold right to the railing, and I think we'll make it.

GRANDMA *(comes downstairs)* I don't know why I can't come downstairs if I want to. *(pauses as she labors down the stairs)* And you keep your mouth shut about it, too.

SPENCE *(coming downstairs)* I've already told you what I'm going to do. I'm going to spill the beans all over the house.

GRANDMA You do and I'll tell your mother you were late coming home from school and that you haven't practiced yet.

SPENCE You'd better put all your concentration on getting down the steps, Gram, or you're gonna fall and break your behind.

GRANDMA Now you stop that kind of talk—you hear me?

SPENCE Now be careful, Gram—and don't get excited.

GRANDMA Well then—you stop it—you hear me?

SPENCE All right, Gram. All right. Just stop hopping around like a sparrow.

GRANDMA I never thought I'd live to see the day when my own daughter's child was cursing like a trooper.

SPENCE Haven't said anything yet, Gram. All I said was if you weren't careful you'd fall down and break your behind. And you will, too.

GRANDMA Take your hands off me. I can do the rest myself. *(crosses down stage toward kitchen. She notices the stake)* What are you doing with that dirty thing in the house?

SPENCE I wanted it. Something to bang around.

GRANDMA You're banging dirt all over the rug. *(she is going into the kitchen.* SPENCE *is going toward the living room)* Where are you going?

SPENCE I'm going in and practice. *(crosses to piano)*

GRANDMA Wouldn't you like something to eat first?

SPENCE No, I wouldn't. You think you can trick me—don't you? *(crosses down center to* GRANDMA, *crosses to piano)* I'm going in and practice and then you won't have a thing to tell Mom when she gets home.

GRANDMA Suit yourself. *(she sits on sofa. He sits down and begins practicing scales. There is a pause)* Spencer, would you get me a glass of water? I'm so out of breath.

SPENCE *(still practicing)* You mooched down all those stairs without batting an eye. You can get your own water. *(piano starts)*

GRANDMA You're a mean little beggar.

SPENCE I know it.

GRANDMA Well, come out and talk to me. I won't tell her.

SPENCE You're sure?

GRANDMA You don't take my word?

SPENCE I took your word the day before yesterday, and as a result I had to practice two hours in the morning.

GRANDMA Well go get it and stop that racket.

SPENCE *(gets up, crosses to bookcase for book)* You know, sometimes Gram, I think that you're uncultured and have no respect for art. *(crosses to sofa with book)* Put your right hand on this. Now repeat after me.

GRANDMA I'll do no such thing.

SPENCE *(taking the book)* O.K. then—don't. *(moves right)*

GRANDMA What do you want me to say?

SPENCE *(coming back, sits on sofa)* I swear and promise that—no matter what happens—I will not tell anybody that Spencer Scott did not practice this afternoon—and if asked I will lie and say that he did.

GRANDMA I swear and promise that—no matter what happens—I will not tell anybody that Spencer Scott did not practice this afternoon—and if asked I will lie and say that he did.

SPENCE Telling also includes writing notes to said parties.

GRANDMA Telling also includes writing notes to said parties.

SPENCE I swear and promise under fear of death.

GRANDMA I swear and promise under fear of death.

SPENCE Amen.

GRANDMA *(starts to answer, changes her mind)* No—I'm not—*(he puts her hand on book)* Amen.

SPENCE Kiss the book.

GRANDMA I'll do no such thing. It's dirty.

SPENCE Just one more time, Gram. Kiss the book.

GRANDMA *(she kisses and notices)* This isn't the Bible.

SPENCE *(gets up. Puts the book on TV)* It's "Crime and Punishment." Don't try welching. *(crosses toward kitchen)* What do you want to eat?

GRANDMA Anything will do.

SPENCE We'll have some crackers and cheese. *(gets cheese out of refrigerator)* Gram—now there's just one more thing. I won't tell Mom about your coming downstairs if you'll—

GRANDMA *(crossing for shoes at window right)* No—I'm not going to do it. I'll be a party to no such thing.

SPENCE O.K., Gram. It's your funeral. You don't even know what kind of a bargain I was going to strike up with you.

GRANDMA Yes, I do. You want a bottle of your father's beer.

SPENCE *(closes refrigerator)* All right, Gram. Fine. When you're taking twice as many of those ugly, nasty tasting pills—don't say I didn't try to be a good sport.

GRANDMA *(gets shoes at window)* One glass.

SPENCE *(opens refrigerator)* It's a deal. One glass. *(to kitchen)* What shall I do with the rest of the bottle? (GRANDMA *crosses left)* If he sees half a bottle he'll know right away.

GRANDMA Pour it down the sink *(crosses to right of table)*

SPENCE Good idea. *(he opens the bottle and pours a glass)*

GRANDMA *(as he starts to pour the rest out)* How much is left?

SPENCE Not much.

GRANDMA Well bring it here. Shame to let it go to waste.

SPENCE *(as he brings another glass over to the table)* You know, Gram. You ought to be in politics. You sure strike a hard bargain. *(sits left of table)*

GRANDMA *(sits right of table)* If I didn't you'd walk all over me. *(pouring beer)* This is nice—isn't it?

SPENCE Sure is. *(he picks up the stake again and starts hitting his leg)*

GRANDMA Put that dirty thing down. Stop hitting yourself with it. Where have you been?

SPENCE *(still hitting himself)* Well I suppose I might as well tell you. Mom's probably going to hear it coming up the street.

GRANDMA Well—what is it?

SPENCE What could you possibly imagine as being just about the worst thing that could happen to me?

GRANDMA You haven't gotten any little girls in trouble—have you?

SPENCE Nothing like that, Gram. Worse.

GRANDMA What have you done? Will you stop hitting yourself with that thing.

SPENCE Well, Gram, I just went and got my ass kicked out of school today.

GRANDMA Spencer Scott! What were you doing?

SPENCE Nothing much. Just smoking in the john.

GRANDMA Smoking! Where?

SPENCE In the john—the can, Gram. The Men's Room.

GRANDMA Well that's a pretty nasty place to be smoking if you ask me. What were you smoking?

SPENCE A cigar.

GRANDMA A cigar. Cigarettes are not dirty enough, I suppose. You have to start smoking cigars.

SPENCE What are you getting so excited for? I took one of Pop's.

GRANDMA Well you ought to be ashamed of yourself. Disgracing yourself in school.

SPENCE *(gets up, crossing right)* Well I sure loused myself up proper this time.

GRANDMA Where are you going?

SPENCE To see if there's any mail. *(at piano. Takes mail)*

GRANDMA There's none for you.

SPENCE Well, you don't mind my looking anyhow, do you? *(he goes through the mail)*

GRANDMA You come right back here. I want to know more about this.

SPENCE Just a second, Gram. Be patient—will you? *(pause)* I sure think that's a crummy way to behave. *(crosses down)* I've written him three letters now—the least he could do is answer one of them. *(puts letters on TV)*

GRANDMA Who are you talking about now?

SPENCE Mack—I'm talking about Mack.

GRANDMA Your brother's probably busy with his lessons. You know what college is like.

SPENCE No, I don't know what college is like. He's probably busy with the broads. The last letter I wrote him was about some damn important problems I got. He'll answer soon enough when he finds out they've shoved me into some loony bin. *(crosses back to left of table, hitting himself with stake)*

GRANDMA What's the matter with you, Spence?

SPENCE Aw! I don't know, Gram.

GRANDMA Stop hitting yourself with that thing.

SPENCE Will you leave me alone? Don't you understand that when a guy's upset he's got to hit himself with something? You gotta do something like that.

GRANDMA *(softly)* What's the matter, Spence?

SPENCE Aw, Gram. Cut out the sympathy please. Go on and finish your beer and get back upstairs before Mom catches you.

GRANDMA Tell me about it, Spence?

SPENCE *(pause)* There's nothing to tell. What's there to it. *(pause)* If you're gonna sit there and look at me that way I'm gonna start feeling sorry for myself and then I'm gonna start bawling—and then you'll start bawling and we won't get anywhere.

GRANDMA What do you want me to do?

SPENCE Keep eating.

GRANDMA All right, I'm eating.

SPENCE *(pause)* Well—from the very beginning of school I could've told you that that Miss Crowley and I weren't going to see eye to eye.

GRANDMA Who's Miss Crowley?

SPENCE The history teacher, Gram. The one that thinks she's cute. She's always giving the guys a preview of the latest fashions in underwear.

GRANDMA Nasty little hussy.

SPENCE That's the one. Well, today they started talking about the Civil War and one of the smart little skirts at the back of the room wanted to know why the Negroes in the South didn't rebel against slavery. Why did they wait for the Northerners to come down and help them? And this Miss Crowley went on to explain how they were stupid and didn't have sense enough to help themselves. *(crosses chair left of table; sits)* Well, anyway, Gram, when she got through talking they sounded like the worst morons that ever lived and I began to wonder how they'd managed to live a few thousand years all by themselves in Africa with nobody's help. I would have let it pass—see—except that the whole class was whispering and giggling and turning around and looking at me—so I got up and just stood next to my desk looking at her. She looked at me for a couple of minutes and asked me if perhaps I had something to say in the discussion. I said I might have a lot of things to say if I didn't have to say them in the company of such dumb jerks. Then I asked her frankly what college she went to.

GRANDMA What did she say?

SPENCE She told me I was being impudent. I told her it was not my intention to be impudent but I would honestly like to know. So she puts one hand on her hip—kinda throwing the other hip out of joint at the same time—and like she wants to spit on me she says "Scoville." Then I says, "And they didn't teach you nothing about the *up*rising of the slaves during the Civil War—or Frederick Douglass?" she says, "No—they didn't." "In that case," I said, "I don't want to be in your crummy history class." And I walk out of the room. When I get out in the hall, Gram, I'm shaking, I'm so mad—and I had this cigar I was going to sell for a sundae. I knew I couldn't eat a sundae now 'cause it would just make me sick so—I just had to do something so I went into the Men's Room and smoked the cigar. I just had about two drags on the thing when in comes the janitor and hauls me down to old Hasbrook's office—and when I get down there—there's Miss Crowley and old Hasbrook talking me over in low tones—and in five short minutes he'd thrown me out of school.

GRANDMA I should've thought he would've given you another chance.

SPENCE He's given me many other chances, Gram. I guess I'm just a chronic offender.

GRANDMA How long are you out for?

SPENCE It would've been one week, but since we have a week's vacation next week, he made it two weeks. Then I'm supposed to come back dragging Pop behind me like a tail. Is he going to be burned! *(pause)* Do you suppose Mom will go for the story, Gram?

GRANDMA I'm not sure.

SPENCE You mean she's not going to go for it at all.

GRANDMA I'm afraid that you're going to get what you rightfully deserve.

SPENCE That's a nasty thing to say—considering the fact that I was justified.

GRANDMA There are ways and ways of being justified.

SPENCE You mean that I shouldn't have gotten sassy with the fruit cake.

GRANDMA Spencer, I'm not going to say one more word to you if you don't stop using language like that—and put that stick down.

SPENCE *(gets ups, throwing the stake on the floor)* God—you're getting to be a crumb—just like the rest of the whole crummy world.

GRANDMA Where are you going?

SPENCE No place. Where in hell is there to go?

GRANDMA You ought to be thrashed with a stick for using that kind of language to me.

SPENCE Listen—are you my friend or not? *(crosses back to* GRANDMA*)*

GRANDMA No—I'm not—not when you talk like that.

SPENCE *(closer to* GRANDMA*)* Well—thanks for that. Thanks. You're a real good Joe. You're a psalm singer—just like the rest of them, Gram. Love me when I'm good—hate me when I'm bad. Thanks. *(crosses right)*

GRANDMA Don't mention it.

SPENCE You're welcome. *(sits in armchair right)*

GRANDMA The pleasure was all mine.

SPENCE For an old lady—you can sure be plenty sarcastic when you want to be. *(pause)*

GRANDMA These will be exactly the last words I will say to you today, Master Scott.

(From outside a voice begins calling SPENCE*. Softly at first, and then more loudly)*

TONY Spence.

GRANDMA Who's that calling you?

SPENCE Tony.

TONY Hey—Spence!

GRANDMA Well—what does he want?

SPENCE I don't know, Gram. I haven't asked him yet.

TONY Spencer!

GRANDMA Well, why don't you answer him?

SPENCE Let him wait—let him wait—it won't hurt him. He likes to holler like that anyway—he has to use his voice some place. No one could ever accuse him of speaking up while he's in school. *(rises)*

TONY Spencer!

GRANDMA *(gets up)* Spencer Scott—if you don't answer him—I will.

SPENCE All right. *(he starts for the door and opens it)* What're you doing there? *(*TONY *bounces in. He is a young Italian boy)* Rehearsing for the Metropolitan or something? Come on in. *(crosses to* GRANDMA *left)*

TONY *(crosses to center)* Hi, Spence. Hello, Mrs. Scott.

GRANDMA Tony—since the first day you could talk—*(sits)* I've told you that I'm not Mrs. Scott. I'm Mrs. Martin. How long are you going to keep doing that?

TONY I forget, Mrs. Martin *(front of sofa)*

SPENCE You forget lots of things—don't you, pal. *(pause. Back of chair)* Well—you got a week's vacation so it certainly can't be because you want me to help you with your algebra—besides I won't be doing algebra for a while. I got the heave-ho as you well know.

TONY Thrown out?

SPENCE Yep.

TONY For how long? *(crosses to right)*

SPENCE Not counting vacation—for a week.

TONY Gee!

SPENCE You can say that again. *(crosses to below table left)*

TONY Gee!

SPENCE Well—you said it. Thanks, pal. *(pause. Sits left of table)* Well, Tony—what little favor can I do you?

TONY Gee, Spence. I'm sure sorry. All the guys were talking about it on the way home from school.

SPENCE Yeh! Yeh! I know. I caught their sympathy when Miss Crowley was bitching me out.

GRANDMA I'm going to tell your mother.

SPENCE *(looking at* GRANDMA*)* Gram.

TONY That's not the way it was at all. *(pause)* What could we say?

SPENCE Exactly what you did. It was fine. What'd I call you when you came in—a pal? That's what you all were. *(*GRANDMA *goes into kitchen)* Two hundred carat, solid gold plate pals. *(to piano. Sits)*

TONY *(crosses right)* Geez—Spence—I'm sorry you feel that way about it.

SPENCE *(gets up)* Ah! you're scratching my back with a rake, Tony. Remember the time the cop had you for stealing apples down at Markman's?

TONY Sure I remember.

SPENCE Did I or did I not shoot him with my slingshot? Remember the time Mrs. Donahue comes out of her house and calls you a dirty wop?

TONY Well, hell, this was in school. *(*GRANDMA *crosses to sink with glass)*

SPENCE Did I stand there and let her get away with it? I did not. That night, as nice as you please, I throw a nest of caterpillars through her window.

TONY *(to center)* Yeah! And when she found out who did it—I cut your telephone wires for three nights running so she couldn't get to your mother.

GRANDMA *(enters room)* I think I should warn you both now—that everything you're saying is going to be used against you—because I'm going to tell all of it.

SPENCE *(crossing to* GRANDMA*)* Oh! No, you won't. If you so much as open your craw, Gram, I'll spill everything—and I'll really spill. I'm desperate. *(crosses to* TONY*)* So there's a big difference about whether it's in school or not. Has that ever made any difference to me?

TONY Naw!

SPENCE Naw! Is that all you've got to say?

TONY No—it isn't.

SPENCE You're a crumb, Tony—just like the rest of them. *(crosses to right)* And another thing—I dunno—maybe I'm getting deaf and need a hearing aid or something, but I don't hear you guys calling me for school any more in the morning.

TONY *(crosses to* SPENCE*)* Ah, Spence—how many times do I have to tell you. I'm taking Marguerite to school in the morning.

SPENCE And where are you taking her at night when you mozey past the house with her curled around your arm like a snake?

TONY We're doing our home work together.

SPENCE It's a little dark up in the park for home work.

TONY Spence—cut it out—your grandmother.

SPENCE My grandmother knows what the score is. She's been knowing it an awful long time now. She's going on eighty-three years old. You can talk freely in front of her.

TONY Lay off—will you?

SPENCE I'll lay off, Tony. I'll lay off plenty. You and that Marguerite Wandalowski. Two crumbs together. That don't even make a damn saltine.

TONY *(close to* SPENCE*)* It's not her fault. I told you before. *(*SPENCE *crosses to center)* She likes you. She thinks you're a nice kid. *(crosses; sits on ottoman)* It's her father—he—well he just doesn't like colored people. I'm sorry, Mrs. Martin. But that's the damn truth. Spence—he just doesn't like them. *(*SPENCE *goes to piano)*

GRANDMA Well, I don't like Polish people either. Never have—never will. They come over here—haven't been over, mind you, long enough to know "and" from "but"—and that's the first thing they learn. Sometimes I think Hitler was right—

SPENCE *(down two steps)* You're talking off the top of your head, Gram. You know he wasn't right. What've you got to say that for?

GRANDMA I don't care—I don't like them. Never have—never will.

SPENCE *(crosses to* GRANDMA*)* You say "them" as though it was some kind of bug or something. *Will* you do me a favor like a real pal, Gram? Quit trying to mix in things that you don't understand. *(to* TONY*)* O.K., Friend—you've said your piece—what did you come over for? *(crosses down to* TONY*)*

TONY Nothing—I didn't want nothing.

SPENCE Aw—cut the bull, Tony. You must've come over here for something. You just don't come here for nothing any more. What do you *want? (*TONY *crosses to TV set.* SPENCE *crosses to above chair right)* You feel uncultured—you want to hear a little Bach or something? You want to see a little television—borrow a book? I just read a good one—all about the causes and preventions of syphilis.

GRANDMA Spencer Scott!

SPENCE *(turns to* GRANDMA*)* That's what the book said, Gram. Bring it out in the open—so I'm bringing it out.

GRANDMA I'm going to tell your mother about that.

SPENCE *(crosses left)* I'll betcha I'll tell her about it before you do. *(to* TONY*)* So what'd you come over for? *(no answer)* Maybe I can guess. You're playing baseball over in the lot. You haven't got enough equipment. You thought maybe I'd be willing to lend some of mine. Right, Tony?

TONY The guys asked me. I didn't want to.

SPENCE Aw!—why didn't you want to? You're my friend, aren't you? Just because I'm sore at you? Damn sore at you?

TONY Cut it out now, Spence. I did the best I could.

SPENCE There's no doubt—and I'm a bum to be mad at you—*(crosses to kitchen)* So I'll tell you what I'm going to do. *(he goes out into the back hall off kitchen and comes back with a baseball glove)* Who's the pitcher?

TONY Gussie.

SPENCE *(back to* TONY*. Throws glove)* Give this to Gussie with my regards. *(crosses to kitchen)*

TONY Give it to him?

SPENCE *(crossing back to living room with mask and mitts)* As a gift—you know what I mean—like Christmas—give it to him. And here's a catcher's mitt and mask for you. *(crosses to kitchen)*

GRANDMA What on earth are you doing? Are you drunk, Spencer?

SPENCE They're mine—aren't they—well, I don't want them any more. *(crosses to* TONY*)* And here's a bat I'm contributing to the game. I think that's just about everything.

TONY *(picks up stuff)* You're sure you won't be wanting these back?

SPENCE Geez—the things you can't understand. I'm giving them to you because you've been such good friends to me—one and all.

TONY *(starts to pick up equipment. Starting to go)* Well thanks, Spence—thanks.

SPENCE Think nothing of it. But there's just one more thing I want you to know. If I couldn't do any better than Marguerite Wandalowski and her old man I'd cram my head into a bucket of horse manure.

GRANDMA Now see here—

TONY *(crosses to* SPENCE*)* See—that's the way you are. You can't do one nice thing without a dirty dig at the end. I ought to throw these things in your puss—

SPENCE You won't though—will you?

GRANDMA *(gets up)* Take 'em back, Spence. Take them right back.

TONY Somebody—some day is going to take a poke at you.

GRANDMA *(takes swing)* If he hits you, Spence—hit him right back.

SPENCE *(crosses up)* He's not going to hit anyone, Gram. He's just talking to be sure he hasn't lost his mouth some damned place. *(throws* TONY *to door)* Now scram the hell out of my house before I beat you and your whole team over the head. Get out! *(*TONY *exits quickly)* Well, I sure went and milked myself in public that time. *(sits on chair right)*

GRANDMA What are you talking about now?

SPENCE Aw, Gram—I just went and did it again. You think I wanted that crumb to know how he hurt me?

GRANDMA *(crosses to* SPENCE*)* Come on, Spence, let's you and I go watch television.

SPENCE Sometimes, Gram—you get the most disgusting ideas.

GRANDMA Well, then I'm going back upstairs. I don't understand what's wrong with you. You're just no fun to be with any more—cussing and ripping and tearing. Won't even watch a little television with me.

SPENCE *(gets up, crosses to ottoman)* Go on in and watch it by yourself then—go on. Spend the rest of life with your head stuck in front of an old light bulb. *(sits)*

GRANDMA What on earth is wrong with you, Spencer?

SPENCE *(rises)* Gram—you've been sitting down here listening all afternoon. Don't you see that I'm an outcast? *(sits on ottoman)*

GRANDMA How?

SPENCE They don't want me around any more, Gram. I cramp their style with the broads.

GRANDMA Why?

SPENCE Why! That's a stupid question. Because I'm Black—that's why.

GRANDMA Well, it's a good thing if they don't want you around. *(turns right to window)* I told your mother years and years ago, "May—stay out of the South End, 'cause mark my words there's nothing down there, nothing *(SPENCE crosses to kitchen)* but Wops and Germans and Lord knows what else they'll get in the future." And what did they get—more Wops and Germans and a few Polacks thrown in for good measure and not one self-respecting colored family in the whole lot.

SPENCE *(crosses to sofa)* Cut out that kind of talk. Sometimes, Gram—you're no help at all. I tell you my troubles and you tell me how we shouldn't have moved here in the first place. *(sits sofa)* But we're here, Gram—right here—and I was born here—and they're all the friends I've got—and it makes me damned unhappy, Gram.

GRANDMA *(crosses close to SPENCE)* Now—now—don't cry. Don't cry, Spencer. Everything's going to be all right.

SPENCE I had it all planned how I was going to make Tony feel like two cents the next time I saw him—and I had to go and get mad.

GRANDMA Your father is going to get you a new bicycle.

SPENCE Shove the bicycle.

GRANDMA Now why would you want to do that? The best thing to do, I should think, would be to get on it and ride it. *(crosses to ottoman with pillow)* Go and get the hairbrush, Spencer. Your hair's a mess.

SPENCE I don't want you messing around with my hair. That's sissy.

GRANDMA Suit yourself. *(sits on ottoman)*

SPENCE *(rises, crosses to kitchen)* If I get the hair brush you've got to promise to help me.

GRANDMA All right. *(he exits left in kitchen for the hairbrush)* Spence, you don't suppose you could go back up to school and tell them you were eating one of those chocolate cigars, could you?"

SPENCE *(returns; sits down at GRANDMA's feet; gives her brush)* I got a feeling that those things don't light too well, Gram. *(pause)* What am I going to do, Gram?

GRANDMA *(brushing his hair)* Well, now—I'm not sure—but one thing I am sure of. I don't know why you gave that boy all of your things. I think that's silly—damn silly if I might say so.

SPENCE Do you suppose this happens to everyone, Gram?

GRANDMA I suppose so. *(pause)* We haven't done this in a long time—have we?

SPENCE What?

GRANDMA Don't you remember when you were a little boy I used to do this every day. You'd stand—you were much shorter than you are now—and I'd brush and comb your hair. I used to do that for all my boys. They'd sit and tell me all their troubles while I combed and brushed their hair.

SPENCE One dumb crummy girl at school the other day asked me if we had to comb and brush our hair.

GRANDMA What did you tell her?

SPENCE I told her we very seldom bothered until the bugs got so fierce they started falling into food and things like that—then it was an absolute necessity.

GRANDMA Spencer—you didn't?

SPENCE I would've if I'd thought of it in time. *(pause)* Gram—if you take the bus down at the corner and stay on it when it gets to Main Street—it will take you right out to the colored section, won't it?

GRANDMA Well, it used to. I don't know if it still does or not. Why?

SPENCE I was just wondering. It's getting late, Gram. Mom will be home in about a half hour. You'd better get back upstairs.

GRANDMA *(putting down the brush)* Yes—hurry—come on and help me. *(gets up, crosses to stairs)*

SPENCE *(stays seated)* Gram—I don't suppose you could lend me five dollars, could you?

GRANDMA *(at foot of stairs)* What on earth do you need that much money for?

SPENCE Well, Gram—you and I know that an hour from now I'm going to be about the smallest thing crawling on two legs. The Old Lady is sure going to give me hell.

GRANDMA You shouldn't talk about your mother that way.

SPENCE *(rises, crosses to stairs)* I know, Gram—I know. It's easy for you to say—but it's true. And then I'm going to get cussed out. Pop is going to say that I'm no good and I'm no son of his. In short—he's going to call me a bastard.

GRANDMA That isn't what he means.

SPENCE *(helping* GRANDMA *upstairs)* It's sure the hell what it sounds like. In other words, Gram—if you'd lend me five dollars—I could go out and get some flowers for Mom and some cigars for Pop and begin by telling them how sorry I am, and it might take the edge off what is going to be at best a hell of an evening. *(*GRANDMA *on landing)* What do you say, Gram?

GRANDMA Well—all right. You go back downstairs and I'll get it for you.

*(*SPENCE *helps her off. Pause. Then he runs to kitchen, gets suitcase and clothes. Doorbell rings)*

SPENCE Dear, dear God—if that's my mother, just kill me as I open the door. *(crosses to door. He hides suitcase left of piano. Opens door)* Hi! Iggie—did you give me a scare!

IGGIE Hiya, Spence.

SPENCE I'm in a terrible hurry, Iggie. What do you want?

IGGIE I just came over to see if you have any stamps to trade.

SPENCE *(crosses left, gets shoes)* I haven't got much time. Come on in—but you can't stay long. I've got to go somewhere.

IGGIE *(comes in)* Where are you going?

SPENCE No place. *(pause)* You sure you came over to trade stamps?

IGGIE *(at sofa)* Sure—that's what I came over for. I finished my home work early—and so I thought I might—

SPENCE *(sits in chair left of table)* You know, Iggie—you're going to be out of school for a week. You didn't have to get your home work done so soon. That's the most disgusting thing I ever heard.

IGGIE *(crosses to table)* Now look, if I want to get my home work done—that's my business. I don't tell you it's disgusting when you don't get yours done at all, do I?

SPENCE *(crosses back to sofa)* O.K.—O.K., Iggie. I only thought you came over because you heard I got kicked out of school.

IGGIE No, Spence—I hadn't heard.

SPENCE You're sure?

IGGIE I told you I hadn't heard, didn't I? *(sits right of table)*

SPENCE *(crosses right to close door)* That kind of news has a way of getting around. *(looking at him)* Well, what are you thinking about? *(crosses back to sofa)*

IGGIE Nothing. I was just thinking that if I got kicked out of school, I guess I'd just as soon I dropped dead right there on the floor in the principal's office.

SPENCE O.K., Iggie. You don't need to rub it in. I get the picture. *(looks upstairs)*

IGGIE I'm sorry, Spence. Is there anything I can do?

SPENCE Now, Iggie—pardon me for being so damn polite—but what in the hell could you do about it?

IGGIE I only want to help, Spence.

SPENCE *(crosses left to below table)* Well, you can't—so let's drop it, shall we?'

IGGIE I didn't mean that business about dropping dead. I probably wouldn't drop dead anyway. There's nothing wrong with my heart.

SPENCE *(sits sofa)* Iggie—will you please cut it out.

IGGIE Anything you say. I didn't mean to offend you.

SPENCE You didn't offend me, Iggie. You just talk too much—that's all.

IGGIE I'll try to do better in the future.

SPENCE Look, Iggie—I've gone and hurt your feelings—haven't I? Hell—I'm sorry. I've always liked you, Iggie. You're a good kid. I'm apologizing, Iggie.

IGGIE It's O.K., Spence. I know you're upset.

SPENCE *(crosses down left)* I know how sensitive you are and all that and I just mow into you like crazy. I wish someone would tell me to shut my mouth. *(he walks to the stairs)* Gram—hurry up with that dough, will you. Iggie—look—I'll tell you what I'm going to do for you. *(he goes over to the piano and comes back with his stamp album)* Here—Iggie—it's yours. I want you to have it—because you're my friend.

IGGIE Your album! But don't you want it, Spence?

SPENCE No, Iggie. I don't want it.

IGGIE But why? I think you must be crazy. *(stands)*

SPENCE Hell, Iggie—because I'm growing up. I'm becoming a man, Iggie. And since I'm going out in just a few minutes with my girl friend—you know it's time for me to quit fooling around with stuff like that.

IGGIE Have you got a girl friend?

SPENCE Yeh! Yes—I have—as a matter of fact I might get married soon. Forget all about school and all.

IGGIE Really. Who is the girl, Spence?

SPENCE Just a girl—that's all. And if everything works out O.K., I won't be coming back. You know, I'll have to get a job and stuff like that. Now you've got to go, Iggie, cause I've got to finish packing and get dressed. *(leads* IGGIE *center)*

IGGIE Where are you going, Spence?

SPENCE I can't tell you, Iggie.

IGGIE Are you sure you're feeling all right?

SPENCE Yes, Iggie, I'm feeling all right.

IGGIE *(crossing to door)* Thank you for the gift. I appreciate it.

SPENCE Forget it.

IGGIE It's a beautiful album.

SPENCE It certainly is.

IGGIE *(crosses to center)* Hey, I was just thinking—maybe I could go up and talk to old Hasbrook. It might do some good.

SPENCE *(crosses to door)* I don't care about that any more, Iggie. I'm pretty sure I won't be coming back to school.

IGGIE Are you sure you want me to have this, Spence?

SPENCE Yes, Iggie, I want you to have it.

IGGIE *(crossing to door)* Well—I hope I'll see you soon. *(he is opening the door)*

SPENCE *(at door)* Hey, Iggie! You won't mind if just once in a while—I come over and see how you're doing with it?

IGGIE I hope you will. Goodbye. *(exits)*

SPENCE Geez—I don't know what's wrong with me. I think maybe my brains are molding or something. *(gets suitcase, shoves clothes inside and runs upstairs)* Hey, Gram—will you hurry up with that five bucks so I can get the hell out of here before I really do something desperate!

(Curtain)

Scene Two

(The curtain rises on a bar and restaurant. It is a very small bar with very few bottles. The bottles that are there are mostly of blended whiskey and rum. A woman stands at the telephone which is on the right wall. There is one table and a booth at left; a table and chairs down center, table up center; juke box left. The bartender, FRANK, *stands behind the bar, getting it ready for the evening.* ROSE *and* POPPY *are seated at the center table, and* CAROL *sits at the table in the left corner.* VIOLET, *the woman at the telephone, is speaking.* FRANK *and a man are arguing loudly at the bar.*

VIOLET *(at phone)* Hello. Hello. Is Lonny there? What's that you say? Hey, Frank, I can't hear a god damned thing.

FRANK Aw, shut up.

VIOLET What's that you said to me?

FRANK I said "Aw, shut up." Now shut up.

VIOLET Listen, Frank, don't you be jumping salty with me.

POPPY *(at center table)* Hey Violet—cut the crap, will you, and get back on the phone.

FRANK Comes in here, spends the whole damn afternoon, and buys two bottles of ginger ale. Cheap—*(he smothers the last word under his breath)*

ROSE *(gets up)* What's that you called us?

FRANK You didn't hear it, did you?

ROSE It's just as well I didn't—cause if I'd heard it—*(sits)*

VIOLET Hey! All of you—shut up. I can't hear a word. *(returns to the phone)* I said is Lonny there? He's not. Well, Sugar, could you tell me when you expect him? What? Would you mind telling me for how long? What in hell did he do? Lonny did that? Well, ain't that something. Well, if you happen to see him on visiting days—just tell him Violet called. Violet—roses are red—you know. That's right—thank you. *(hangs up)* Well, Poppy, you can scratch Lonny's name out of the book. *(sits stool, faces right)*

POPPY Hell, Violet—by the time we're through today—you're going to have more scratched-out names than anything else in this book. What happened to him?

VIOLET *(faces center)* You remember reading in the paper about that girl—in the three paper bags at the railroad station—in the locker?

POPPY *(nods)* Yeh.

VIOLET Lonny!

ROSE Girl—are you kidding?

VIOLET *(crosses to table, sits back of it)* Frank, bring us another bottle of ginger ale.

FRANK What do you want in it?

VIOLET We still have whiskey of our own—thank you.

FRANK Then it'll be fifteen cents a bottle.

(Man crosses to right of juke box. SPENCE *enters down right. He is carrying some books. He stands by the door looking left at* CAROL *at the corner table)*

ROSE Fifteen cents?

FRANK Either put your money where your mouth is or shut up.

VIOLET Well—give us the bottle and some ice.

FRANK The ice will cost you a dime. *(crosses to* CAROL *with drink)*

POPPY Damn—let's get the hell out of here before he begins charging for sitting down.

VIOLET It's all right, Poppy. Pay the man.

POPPY *(to* FRANK*)* Well, bring it on over—you chinchy skunk.

FRANK Call me names like that—you can come over and get it yourselves. *(*FRANK *notices* SPENCE *at bar)* Can I help you, pal? *(*SPENCE *doesn't hear at first. Everyone turns around)* Hey! You—over there.

SPENCE You talking to me?

FRANK Yeh. What do you want?

SPENCE Nothing. It's kind of warm outside—and I kind of came in here to get cool.

FRANK Out.

SPENCE *(with great discomfort)* I'm cool now. So—I'll be going. *(looks at* CAROL. *He hovers about door back of bar and finally exits.* FRANK *crosses back to bar)*

POPPY *(after a pause)* Well—do we get our stuff or don't we?

FRANK I told you—get it yourselves.

ROSE *(rising)* Let's get the hell out of this dump.

VIOLET It's all right—I'll get it. *(goes to bar and picks up the bottle of ginger ale and the ice)* And here's a quarter tip for you, Frank, for being so gracious.

POPPY All right, Violet—don't be going crazy over there now. Every little bit helps, and if we don't raise the money for the rent, we'll be out in the street tomorrow.

VIOLET *(ignoring her)* Thank you, Frank. You're a real gentleman. I'm going to tell all my friends to come over and trade with you. *(crosses to table with glasses and ice)*

FRANK You can tell those whores that I don't want them in my place.

POPPY Aw man—shut up.—Who else is left in that book of yours, Violet?

VIOLET I don't know—let me see. Well, there's Sidney. We haven't called Sidney.

POPPY What's his number? *(gets up)*

VIOLET Two—eight nine two seven. Whose turn is it?

POPPY *(crosses to phone)* Mine. Why in hell you think I'm getting up?

FRANK And don't be coming in here with food. This ain't no lousy picnic grove.

VIOLET Well, it's lousy.

POPPY Shh.

FRANK *(throws rag at her)* You heard what I said. Just be sure you clean up that mess before you leave.

VIOLET *(throws rag back)* I ain't no janitor.

POPPY *(on phone)* Hello, Sidney. This is Poppy. One and the same. Haven't seen you lately. Well that's too bad. *(pause)* Sugar, we're in a bad spot 'cause tomorrow the rent man is coming around, an—*(*VIOLET *crosses to phone)* Well now, Sugar, Violet is sitting right here and she's upset about the rent too. Do you remember the time you took Violet down to New York and registered in that hotel as Mr. and Mrs.? *(*ROSE *crosses to bar above* POPPY*)* Well now—Honey—to get down to New York, you had to cross a state line. Now have you ever heard of the Mann Act? Well, Violet has. Well—I don't know all the details of it, but it seems you can get into about ten or fifteen years worth of trouble for carrying girls over state lines for the kind of purposes you had in mind. *(man crosses to bar)* Now all Violet is asking for is about ten dollars—that roughly comes out to seventy-five cents a year, and she wants it tonight—at Carter's drug store—or else the F.B.I. Now have you got all that, Sugar? Fine—we'll be looking for you, hear? *(she hangs up, crosses back to her chair)*

Well, Sidney suddenly decided he had ten loose dollars around some place. We're supposed to meet him in Carter's in fifteen minutes. *(sits in her chair.* VIOLET *follows, sits above table)*

ROSE *(crosses back to her chair, sits)* Girl! I ain't never seen anything like you in my whole life.

POPPY How much more we got to raise, Violet?

VIOLET Let's see—that's Sidney—ten dollars! *(gets up, crosses up to rear table)* All we need is fifteen more.

FRANK —Coming in here—blackmailing people on my telephone.

POPPY We ain't blackmailing anybody. We're just keeping ourselves available. There's no telling—next week sometime—one of those boys might be glad that we're still here.

MAN *(at the bar)* I can't see why.

ROSE Why don't you shut up?

MAN This is a place of business. Man comes in here to have a quiet drink. If it ain't a bunch of whores, it's a television set.

POPPY Mister—don't you be calling us whores, hear—or I'm liable to come over there and knock you breathless.

ROSE Come on, Poppy. Don't pay no attention to him.

VIOLET Coming in here for a quiet drink—he calls it. I seen you lamping the little girl over in the corner. You ought to be ashamed of yourself. *(crosses to* CAROL*)* Baby, if he bothers you—just come over and tell me and I'll knock his brains out. Hear? *(*CAROL *says nothing.* VIOLET *returns to center table.* SPENCE *appears down right, outside door; carries books)*

ROSE Violet—come on and get your book out. We ain't got all night.

POPPY I don't know why in hell we ain't got all night. We haven't got anything else to do. *(they look at her)* Well—have we?

VIOLET No—we haven't, stupid. *(*SPENCE *enters, sits stool below bar, puts books on bar)* But you don't have to say it in here—do you? Hell—you have to keep up some pretenses, Poppy. *(crosses up stage; sits in chair)*

SPENCE *(knocking on the bar)* How about a little service here—sport? *(*ROSE *crosses to* VIOLET*)*

FRANK *(eyeing him)* What do you want now?

SPENCE A glass of beer. *(*FRANK *laughs, still eyes him)* I said a glass of beer.

FRANK How old are you?

SPENCE *(pointing at the man)* Did you ask him how old he was?

FRANK No—I didn't.

SPENCE Then why in hell are you asking me?

FRANK I know him. He comes in here all the time. *(man crosses left to juke box)*

SPENCE Well, my name is Spencer Scott—so now you know me. Give me a glass of beer.

FRANK What're you—just coming from school with all those books? The teacher didn't keep you after school all this time, did she? *(he laughs. He reaches for a book)* What's this? *(reading the title)* The Interpretation of Dreams by Sigmund—*(*SPENCE *gets up, grabs book)* You don't believe in that stuff, do you?

SPENCE Hey—do you run a quiz show or something? You know there are other joints on this street that probably got colder beer than you got anyway. *(pause)* I've been to the library, see. And inside this book is my library card. They have pink cards for children and yellow cards for adults. This is a yellow card. Now as to more personal things—I've been walking a hell of a long way and I've got a headache—now will you please give me a glass of beer. I've got money for it—see—I can pay for it. I'm not drunk already. What do you say?

FRANK How old are you?

SPENCE Twenty-one.

FRANK When were you born?

SPENCE *(without batting an eye)* January 20, 1932.

FRANK *(getting a piece of paper)* Let's see. Yep. *(figuring it out)* That makes you—twenty-one.

SPENCE That's what I said.

FRANK You look mighty young to be twenty-one.

SPENCE Beer—Hah? A nice tall one.

FRANK We got a special on whiskey today.

SPENCE You know—hot shot—you got remarkable powers of persuasion there. But I asked you for a beer.

POPPY That's right, Sugar—don't drink none of that man's whiskey. He ferments it himself.

VIOLET. You sure are right, Frank—that whiskey is special. Specially awful. *(*THREE FLOWERS *laugh uproariously)*

FRANK Quiet over there. I'm minding my business.

POPPY Say, Sugar—did I hear you say something about a dream book?

SPENCE Yeh—I found it in the library. *(man blows smoke at* CAROL*)* It's supposed to be pretty sexy.

VIOLET Come on over and sit down with us.

SPENCE Sure. *(crosses to center table)*

POPPY Does that book say anything about umbrellas? I keep having the damndest dreams with umbrellas in them.

SPENCE I don't know. I've just glanced through it. *(sits left chair)*

POPPY Do you mind if I take a look? (ROSE *crosses down, sits center)*

SPENCE Help yourself. *(looks at* CAROL*)*. You girls hang around here a lot?

ROSE No, this isn't one of our usual hangouts. We come here about once a month to take care of a financial transaction. Do you live around here?

SPENCE Yeh—around here. *(pause)* Say—do any of you know the girl over in the corner? *(man crosses to bar)*

ROSE No—we don't know her at all. Mousey little thing—ain't she?

SPENCE No, I don't think she's mousey at all.

POPPY Hell, I can't find a thing about umbrellas in this book. This is the damndest dream book I ever saw.

SPENCE Give it to me—Here I'll find it for you. *(he takes the book)*

VIOLET *(gets up, crosses to* ROSE. *Looking at her book)* Whose turn is it next?

ROSE Mine. *(gets up, starts for phone)*

VIOLET You call Homer. The number is two—five eight seven six.

ROSE Two—five eight—

VIOLET Seven six—and here's the dime. *(both cross to phone.* ROSE *dials.* VIOLET *at bar)*

SPENCE Did you say a cane or an umbrella?

POPPY An umbrella, Sugar. *(moves to center chair)* Hell—there ain't much difference between canes and umbrellas, is there? What does it say about canes? (VIOLET *turns to center)*

SPENCE It doesn't say much. It just says that a woman dreams about a man carrying a cane. It must mean you're plenty batty because they got her whole case history written up here.

POPPY Well, I didn't say I dreamed of canes, did I? Don't be trying to push her dreams off on me. Look for umbrellas—and don't be looking in those crazy people's dreams either. Look for some nice person that dreams of umbrellas.

ROSE Nobody answers.

VIOLET Well, keep ringing—his mother is always home.

ROSE Well, what will I say if his mother answers?

VIOLET Just ask for Homer, stupid.

ROSE *(in phone)* Hello, Homer? This is Rose. Well, I know an awful lot of Homers, too, and I know which one you are. Rose Thompson. How you been? Haven't seen you in a month of Sundays.

SPENCE Wouldn't that be a hell of a thing—a month with only Sundays in it? You'd spend your whole life in church.

VIOLET Ssh.

POPPY Shut up.

ROSE *(in phone)* Well, Sugar, I was calling you because we are kind of in a jam. Violet—Poppy and me. That's right—the three flowers. We need money for the rent. I don't know—I guess everyone is trying to save money what with Christmas coming and all and they must be cutting down on the little luxuries. Oh! Homer—you say the most terrible things. *(putting her hand over the mouthpiece)* The son of a bitch *(she takes her hand off)* Well, how about it? Well, I guess we'll just have to talk to your wife, Sugar. No, I don't think I want to talk to her tonight. You'd never. Well just thanks for nothing, Homer. The same to you quartetted. *(hangs up and sits on stool)* Can you beat that? He said he didn't give a damn whether his wife knew or not. There's something terrible immoral about that.

POPPY You're damn right. It's getting to the point where no one has any respect for marriage these days. I just wish somebody would ask me to marry them. I'd split their heads wide open.

SPENCE *(putting down the book)* Hey! Pardon me, are you girls prostitutes or something? (ALL *turn to him)*

POPPY Honey—we try to be.

SPENCE You know—I've never met any real prostitutes before. You wouldn't mind if I asked you a couple of questions—would you?

VIOLET Well, Honey—right now we're in a little hot water—and we also got to go out and pick up a little something down at Carter's drug store. *(at table down center)* But as soon as we come back we'll answer all your questions. Why don't you go over and talk to the little girl over there until we come back? *(crosses back to table up center)*

SPENCE Are you sure she wouldn't mind my bargin' over there like that?

POPPY What if she does? You can sit anywhere you want in this place. Go over there and sit down *(gets up)*

VIOLET *(crossing down to table)* Let's go, girls.

ROSE I don't see why all of us have to go to get a little ten dollars from Sidney.

POPPY Because in union there is strength. *(crosses to* ROSE*)* Now get the hell off that stool and let's go. I assume that none of us have any more names in our books? *(exits up right)*

VIOLET Your assumption is absolutely correct. *(*VIOLET *and* ROSE *exit up right.* FRANK *crosses table center, gets bottles, cleans table, returns to bar)*

SPENCE *(who has been going over to the left table very slowly—has just arrived—and is standing undecided right of booth)* Do you mind if I sit down? *(*CAROL *shakes her head.* SPENCE *sits down. He sits looking at her for a time)* You're sure I'm not bothering you or anything, 'cause if I am, I can get the hell up and go someplace else.

CAROL These tables aren't reserved. You can sit anywhere you please. If you bother me I can get up and get the hell out of here, that's all.

SPENCE *(rises, crosses right)* I'm sorry.

CAROL Where are you going?

SPENCE I guess—

CAROL Sit down, kid. I didn't mean to scare you away.

SPENCE *(looks at man)* I suppose a nice girl does have to be careful about who she talks to in a joint like this. *(crosses back to booth)* You don't need to be afraid of me, though.

CAROL What makes you think that I'm such a nice girl?

SPENCE *(sits right in booth)* You can just tell—that's all.

CAROL What makes you think that I'm not like Violet, Rose, and Poppy?

SPENCE Aw! Quit your kidding.

CAROL Well, thanks for thinking that I'm different from Violet, Rose, and Poppy.

SPENCE Well, you are—aren't you?

CAROL Yeh—in one or two respects I guess I am.

SPENCE *(relieved)* I thought you were. *(pause. Gets closer—hand out)* My name's Spencer Scott. Everybody calls me Spence.

CAROL *(takes hand)* I know. I heard you when you came in.

SPENCE. Yeh. That's because I've got such a damn big mouth. I've got a theory as to why I talk so loud. I think it's because of my youth. I guess as I get older like Mack maybe—I won't talk so loud. *(pause)* Mack is my brother. *(pause)* He used to talk loud when he was a kid.

CAROL You're not really twenty-one, are you?

SPENCE I was lying then. See, I've got to lie about my age until I get to be twenty-one. Since I lie about that, as you can guess, I lie about other things too. But as soon as I get to be twenty-one not another goddamn lie is going to pass my lips.

CAROL That's very sweet.

SPENCE I really honestly mean it.

CAROL I really honestly believe you. *(she takes a sip of her drink and then nervously bangs the drink down on the table. Looks at man)* Damn it. Who in the hell does he think he's looking at?

SPENCE Who?

CAROL That guy over there. He keeps staring at me.

SPENCE You want me to go over and speak to him?

CAROL *(restraining him)* No! No! Don't bother. *(pause. Man sits at chair up stage, reads paper.* FRANK *has fallen asleep, his head on the bar)*

SPENCE Well, now that we know each other—would you mind telling me your name?

CAROL My name's Carol—Carol Pearson.

SPENCE Is that Carol spelt with an "e" or with the "e" left off?

CAROL That's Carol with the "e" left off.

SPENCE I never knew a Carol with the "e" left off before except in a book I used to read as a kid. It was called "The Birds' Christmas Carol." Did you ever read it?

CAROL No, I don't think I ever did.

SPENCE I know you'd never believe it to look at me—but I read that book around ninety times I guess. That book used to make me cry like a baby. It was about a little girl named Carol who was doomed to die—and finally at the end, she dies—on the same day she was born—Christmas Day. Well, the last time I read that book I expected to cry again. I grabbed the old box of Kleenex and opened the book, and as I was reading, it was like me and the author had a big fight. She was trying to make me cry and I was damned if I was going to do her the favor. The whole book, believe it or not, was set up to make you cry. I gave the book to Iggie the next day.

CAROL *(after a pause)* So—what about it?

SPENCE Iggie's a friend of mine. He's kind of hard to talk to because he's real shy. You know what I mean? But he knows I like him and I think he's getting a lot better. I got a theory about that. Would you like to hear it?

CAROL I can hardly wait.

SPENCE Well—it's this. My theory is that everybody needs somebody else. What do you think about that?

CAROL I think you've got something.

SPENCE I kind of thought that you'd think so. *(pause)* I need somebody too, I guess. I know you wouldn't believe it to look at me but you're looking at one of the most friendless persons in the whole United States.

CAROL Aw! Come on—

SPENCE Well, I guess that that wasn't exactly the truth—because you see there's my Gram. She's the only pal I got left—I guess.

CAROL *(pulling out a cigarette)* Have you got a match, kid? *(*SPENCE *pulls out matches.* CAROL *takes them)* Thanks. So your Mom and Pop don't trust you, is that it?

SPENCE They'd like to—but I sure as hell think they're not so sure that I'm not going to turn out the family skeleton.

CAROL So what makes you think that you're so friendless? *(crosses to juke box)*

SPENCE Well, that's a story and a half. You see I live—I mean used to live down at the South End. *(turns right)* There aren't many colored families down there; in fact; there are about two. So Mack and I grew up with the white kids who lived on our street. We had lots of good times together—and it wasn't until the kids started getting interested in sex that my troubles began.

CAROL How do you mean?

SPENCE Well, actually it started happening last summer. For weeks they wouldn't call me. To be frank with you—I thought it was because my personality wasn't so hot maybe. You see—I'm a real guy *(*CAROL *has put a nickel in juke box which doesn't work. She gives up and returns to booth. Sits)* I play the piano—but not enough for the guys to think I'm a sissy. I'm a little thin but I got a build that would knock you out to be perfectly honest with you—but I still thought that something was wrong with me—

CAROL That's an old, old story, kid.

SPENCE What do you mean?

CAROL I can finish it for you. You're pretty fed up with the whole business, aren't you? You don't know what the hell to do because you're lonely. It's a hell of a feeling. So you start smoking, drinking beer. You want to be a real grown up guy before your time. The only thing you know is that this kid stuff is for the birds—so you're going to run away from it—get to be an adult because maybe being an adult will bring a couple of things with it. Happiness—a nice girl—maybe—

SPENCE Yes, I guess that's it. But all the kids my age are interested in the broads now. So I was passing by here—saw you in the window—and decided to give it a whirl.

CAROL *(laughs)* Thanks—for seeing me in the window.

SPENCE I know you think it sounds pretty silly because I know how girls are about going around with boys that are younger than they are—but have you ever gotten a really good look at the Kinsey report?

CAROL No, I'm afraid I don't read much.

SPENCE Well—I'm honestly not one to boast—but it says in that book that boys my age are usually pretty sexy. In fact, they're sexier at my age than they ever will be again in their whole goddamn lives. And what with my other qualifications that I told you about, I should be a pretty good boy friend to have.

CAROL You know—I'd almost bet that that was the truth.

SPENCE Well, what do you say? I know I started off all wrong. I should have started off by shooting you the old bull about how lovely you are and all that stuff, but I figured that if I asked you to be my girl friend you'd know that I thought you were pretty and all that because I really couldn't be interested in a lemon. I also want you to know that if everything goes right between me and you and we decide that we love each other, I'm perfectly willing to get married. *(*CAROL *moves down stage on bench)* My father wants me to go to college but I'd be perfectly willing to forego that if everything works out okay. How about it?

CAROL Spence, you're a sweet kid and that was about the sweetest proposal I've ever had. *(she watches* SPENCE *who has pressed glass to forehead)* Is there something wrong?

SPENCE Naw—just a headache. Too much beer, I guess.

CAROL *(taking glass from him)* You know what you ought to do? Go on home and let your grandmother give you a great big kiss and tuck you in.

SPENCE Don't you understand? I won't be going home. I've got to look for a job. What do you say?

CAROL I've already told you what I say. Go on home. I don't want to hear any more of your troubles. I've got troubles of my own. You talk about getting a job. What in hell could you do? You couldn't do any better than my husband.

SPENCE Your husband?

CAROL Yes. He works all day and he works all night and we've still got nothing. He's what is commonly known as unskilled labor. I guess you know what that means. *(pause)* I'm sorry, kid.

SPENCE You should have told me you were married in the first place. I feel like a great big can of garbage. *(turns away)*

CAROL You didn't hear a word I said, did you, kid? *(gathers her purse. Man crosses bar)* I've got to go now.

SPENCE Where are you going?

CAROL You see that guy in the corner of the bar? Well, he's been staring at me all night. I hope he has some money. I hope he has a car—a nice car with a top that goes down. I can go for a drive in the country and for maybe two hours I can have some fun.

SPENCE I think that's terrible.

CAROL So do I—so there's two of us. *(finishes drink)* And if my husband ever finds out, he'd kill me, so I guess there's three of us. But I'm going anyway because I've got to. I can't go home to that lousy one-room flat and wait all night. It's too quiet there. There's nobody to talk to. It's just no fun—that's all.

SPENCE *(pause)* If you're going—why don't you go?

CAROL It's funny how when you're young you can be so selfish about your feelings, isn't it? Thank you for the proposal. *(rises, crosses right of table)* Please don't be sore. I tried to help you, Spence. There's a nursery rhyme I used to know. It goes,

> Merry have we met, and merry have we been,
> Merry let us part, and merry meet again.

Let's not part angrily. *(he doesn't answer)* Spence! *(she walks over and kisses him squarely on the mouth)* Good luck, kid. *(she walks over to the man at the bar. He pays for her, and they leave together up right. The* THREE FLOWERS *re-enter up right.* VIOLET *enters first)*

VIOLET *(offstage)* I don't care what you say, it's a stinking way to behave. *(sees money man has left on bar, picks it up, crosses to center table, sits)* Standing us up like that.

POPPY Every little bit helps.

ROSE *(crosses to juke box, puts nickel in)* And then not answering the phone is the rudest thing I ever heard of

POPPY *(crosses to right of table, sits)* I told you to stop worrying about it. Tomorrow morning, on his way to work, I'll get him. And he'll either cough up that ten bucks or I'll snatch him baldheaded. That ten-spot is as good as got—so stop worrying about it. *(juke box starts playing)*

VIOLET Hey! Spence. We're through with our business. You can come over now if you want to. *(*SPENCE *doesn't move)*

ROSE *(crossing to center table, sits left)* Well as far as I can see we might just as well be dead. We might just as well amble on over to the graveyard and lie down.

*(*SPENCE *sits for one more moment, with his head hidden from them, and then he rises, crosses in)*

SPENCE Hey! Violet—is there any lipstick on my mouth to speak of?

VIOLET There sure is, Honey.

POPPY What're you doing smearing lipstick all over your mouth like that? You queer or something?

SPENCE Cut the comedy. Did you see that girl over there in the corner?

ROSE You mean she kissed you?

SPENCE Yeh. I guess I'm what you call a pretty fast worker, huh?

VIOLET How would you like to come with me? *(gets up)*

SPENCE Where are we going?

VIOLET You said you wanted to talk to me, didn't you? I just thought we could go some place where we could be alone—a quieter place.

SPENCE Sure—that's okay with me.

VIOLET Let's go, Sugar—I know just the place. (SPENCE *leans against booth)* What's the matter, Honey?

SPENCE Nothing. Been drinking too much, I guess.

VIOLET Well, come on, Sugar—You got enough money to buy me a sandwich or something?

SPENCE *(as he exits up right,* VIOLET *following)* Sure—I got two dollars and thirty-nine cents.

VIOLET *(coming back to table down center)* That sounds like the price of something in a fire sale—doesn't it? Well, Hell—*(exits up right)*

(Curtain)

Scene Three

*(*VIOLET*'s room.* VIOLET *is turning the key in the lock as the curtain rises.* SPENCE *is behind her. When they enter there is the distinct sound of muffled voices)*

SPENCE What's that?

VIOLET *(sits chair right, takes off shoes)* The two men next door. Don't worry about them—they're deaf.

SPENCE *(standing center)* It sounded like they were in the next room.

VIOLET They are. The walls here are very thin.

SPENCE Thin is hardly the word. You might say they are put together with spitballs. You been away or something?

VIOLET *(crossing left to drapes)* No, why?

SPENCE Nothing except that it looks like you've put everything to bed for the night.

VIOLET *(crosses to bed, takes off cover, folds it, puts it behind curtain)* Oh, those are my covers. It keeps things neat and clean.

SPENCE Say, I thought you wanted to go to another restaurant where we could talk?

VIOLET It's much more comfy to talk here. We can have something sent in if we want it. Don't you want to take your jacket off? It's pretty warm in here. *(turns on light above bureau)*

SPENCE *(crossing chair right)* Thanks—I guess I will. You wouldn't happen to have something to eat hanging around, would you? *(*VIOLET *crosses behind drapes)* I'm feeling pretty groggy. I think perhaps it's because I haven't had any supper.

VIOLET There's some crackers up there. *(she points to the bureau. Crosses to bureau—then behind drapes)*

SPENCE Thanks. *(crosses to bureau, gets crackers and starts eating them)* What kind of radio is this?

VIOLET It's a short wave radio. It gets the police calls. *(takes clothes off line, crosses behind drapes)*

SPENCE Why would anyone want the crummy police calls?

VIOLET For a number of reasons.

SPENCE What ever happens in this crumby town that should interest anybody?

VIOLET *(crossing to him)* Sugar—that radio is like a husband to me. Now why don't you stop worrying about the radio and take off your tie and get comfortable so we can talk.

SPENCE *(at bureau)* I can talk with my tie on. That's never been one of my difficulties.

VIOLET Would you like to hear a little music?

SPENCE That would be nice.

VIOLET *(turns on the radio. Crosses back of drapes)* You wouldn't mind if I changed into something a little more comfortable, would you?

SPENCE Not at all.

VIOLET I won't be a minute.

SPENCE You wouldn't have a little cheese to go with these crackers, would you? *(radio plays Chopin Sonata in B flat minor. Opus 35. Funeral March)*

VIOLET Look around and see.

SPENCE Any place in particular? *(looks in sink)*

VIOLET Just look around. I seem to remember seeing some cheese around here a couple of days ago. What's that they're playing?

SPENCE It's Chopin.

VIOLET Is he playing or being played?

SPENCE He's being played. Chopin's dead.

VIOLET Recently?

SPENCE *(crossing right)* Not too recently. Over a hundred years ago.

VIOLET Isn't that sad?

SPENCE *(looking on bed table and under bed)* I guess it was when it happened. Well—I don't seem to find any cheese around here at all.

VIOLET I guess Poppy must've taken it for the trap. *(re-enters)* Now—how do I look? *(she has emerged in a bronze satin negligee with maribou around the collar and down the front)*

SPENCE Do you honestly feel more comfortable in that?

VIOLET Oh! Much much more. *(she moves over to the bed, sits)* Now come on and let's sit down over here so we can talk.

SPENCE *(sits in chair right)* I should think that it would tickle the back of your neck something awful. What shall we talk about?

VIOLET Why I thought you wanted to talk to me. *(pause)* Do you have to listen to that?

SPENCE Not necessarily. *(rises and switches radio off)* These crackers don't seem to be doing a damn bit of good.

VIOLET Come on back.

SPENCE Sure. *(he sits back down on the chair right)*

VIOLET Come on closer.

SPENCE What for? I can hear you from here.

VIOLET *(crawling over bed)* Aw! Come on, Sugar. Stop being so bashful.

SPENCE I'm not being bashful. *(she pulls* SPENCE *by the hand)* All right, I'll come. You don't have to pull me. *(he sits on bed)*

VIOLET *(puts her arms around his neck)* Now tell Violet all about it.

SPENCE All about what?

VIOLET What's troubling you.

SPENCE Nothing's troubling me.

VIOLET Supposing you give Violet a little kiss. That might make you feel better.

SPENCE I honestly don't see how a kiss is going to do anything for my hunger.

VIOLET Well, try it, baby, and see. *(*SPENCE *gives her an experimental peck on the cheek)* Oh! Come on, Sugar. You can do better than that. *(she grabs* SPENCE*, pulls him back on the bed and kisses him)*

SPENCE *(after some time breaks away, crosses right)* God damn it.

VIOLET What's the matter?

SPENCE *(gets jacket from chair and starts to put it on)* I left my books over in the bar.

VIOLET Well—what about it?

SPENCE They're library books. If they were my books I wouldn't care.

VIOLET *(gets up, stands left of bed)* Say—what's the matter with you anyway?

SPENCE I told you. My books are over there.

VIOLET So let them stay there. No one's going to run away with them.

SPENCE How can you be so sure of that?

VIOLET Listen, Sugar—no one that ever goes in Frank's ever reads nothing. Take my word for it.

SPENCE I'd better go.

VIOLET *(jumps onto bed, runs over it, and holds door)* Hey! Are you trying to run out on me?

SPENCE Why would I do a thing like that?

VIOLET *(still standing on bed)* Well that's sure as hell what it looks like. *(pause)* What happened to all those questions you had to ask me? What happened to all that big talk you were throwing around in the bar?

SPENCE Nothing happened to it. I got a headache and I'm hungry—at least I think I'm hungry.

VIOLET I think you're just plain scared.

SPENCE Scared of who?

VIOLET Scared of me—that's who. *(a thought dawning on her, gets down from bed)* Hey! How old are you anyway?

SPENCE I told you—twenty-one.

VIOLET *(sits on bed)* If you're twenty-one, I'm sweet sixteen. Come over here. *(*SPENCE *sits in chair)* You've never been in a place like this before—have you? You're kind of scared aren't you?

SPENCE Well—to be perfectly honest with you, I guess I am kind of scared. I guess I just want to go and get my books—if you don't mind. *(crosses to door)*

VIOLET *(crossing to door)* Look, kid—I most certainly do mind. *(*SPENCE *sits chair)* Let me tell you how this mess works. You've taken me out of circulation for roughly fifteen minutes now—fifteen minutes in which anything could happen—and if you think that you're just going to put your coat on and walk out of here—you've got another thought coming. I want my two dollars and thirty-nine cents.

SPENCE But that's all the money I have.

VIOLET I know it's all the money you have. You think if you had more I'd be asking for two dollars and thirty-nine cents? What do you take me for anyway? It ain't that I don't understand, Sugar, it's just that business is business.

SPENCE *(reaching into his pocket)* Is it all right if I keep a half a dollar for supper?

VIOLET You can take the crackers as you leave. I want my two thirty-nine. *(taking it, crossing to bureau, puts money away)* Thank you. And another thing—if you ever tell anybody that all you paid me was two thirty-nine I'll have your head on a platter. You hear me? *(sits on bed, leans back)*

SPENCE I understand. Is it all right if I go now?

VIOLET Suit yourself. *(puts key on bed table* SPENCE *starts to go, then stops)* What's the matter—did you lose something?

SPENCE I was just thinking.

VIOLET Thinking what?

SPENCE Well—if I go back to that bar—Poppy and Rose are still there—aren't they?

VIOLET They'd better be.

SPENCE Well—I was just thinking—if I go back over there in such a short time they'll know that—

VIOLET You was a bust? They sure will.

SPENCE I was just wondering—if you'd mind terribly if I stayed about fifteen minutes more.

VIOLET Help yourself.

SPENCE *(goes over and sits stiffly in down right chair)* You wouldn't tell them—would you?

VIOLET Tell them what?

SPENCE That I was such a—bust?

VIOLET If you can keep my secret I can keep yours. *(they sit in silence for some time)* You know—if you're going to sit there—I'm afraid that you're going to have to say something. If there's one thing I can't stand it's silence.

SPENCE What do you want me to say?

VIOLET I don't want you to say anything that you don't want to say. Just talk. *(gets pillows and doll from behind drapes)*

SPENCE What time is it?

VIOLET The fifteen minutes ain't passed yet. You know the old saying about a watched pot never boiling. *(sits back on bed, arranges doll's dress)*

SPENCE Would you like me to read to you for a while?

VIOLET Do I look like an old lady to you?

SPENCE No.

VIOLET Well I can see to read to myself, thank you very much.

SPENCE I'm sorry. I'm—

VIOLET Forget it. Just forget it.

SPENCE I wonder—if you'd do me a favor?

VIOLET As long as there's no money involved—yes.

SPENCE Well—there is. I was wondering if you'd loan me a dime for bus fare. I want to go home.

VIOLET Well, can't you walk?

SPENCE It's down at the South End.

VIOLET Well that's what I get for playing around with kids. Just reach in and take a dime—and only a dime. *(*SPENCE *walks over to the bureau and opens it and takes a dime.* VIOLET *watches carefully, lying on her stomach, head down stage. He closes it and then stops and leans on it)* What's the matter with you, anyway?

SPENCE Nothing—I just don't feel good. *(starts for the door)* Thanks for the dime.

VIOLET Don't bother thanking me. It hurts me to give it to you.

SPENCE *(at door)* Well—thanks anyway. But there's one thing I want you to know.

VIOLET What's that?

SPENCE I think that's one of the ugliest bath robes I've ever seen in my life! *(he walks out the door as—)*

(Curtain)

Act Two

Scene One

(As the curtain rises on SPENCE*'s home—there is one light on—the light over* LEM SCOTT*'s chair. He is in it. He is asleep with a newspaper in his lap. The rest of the house is quiet—superficially at least. It is later the same evening. Someone passes in the street outside—they are whistling. It wakes* LEM*)*

LEM *(half-asleep)* May—we got to—*(rises, crosses to center below stairs)* Well, I'll be damned. May! May!

MAY *(upstairs)* What do you want?

LEM What time is it?

MAY Five minutes have passed since you asked me that the last time. It's ten minutes after ten.

LEM *(yawns)* Well—where the hell is he?

MAY Daddy—I don't know. I've told you that over and over again. I haven't got one idea left.

LEM Well, how can you be up there asleep—when for all you know he could be dead some place? *(crosses down right)*

MAY If he's dead, Daddy—there's nothing we can do about it until we know. I'm not asleep.

LEM Is that mother of yours asleep?

MAY I don't see how she could be.

LEM *(picks up more newspapers)* I think she knows more than she's letting on.

MAY Well, there's a five hundred watt light downstairs in the pantry. Why don't you bring it up along with your rubber hose and give her the third degree?

LEM Why don't you cut out being so smart. That's the trouble with your whole family—they think they're smart. *(kicks stool)*

MAY *(appears at head of stairs)* Why don't you just go back to your paper, Daddy—or watch the television for a while?

LEM When I get my hands on that little bastard I'll break every bone in his body.

MAY *(coming down the stairs to left side of sofa, sits)* Now that's no way to talk, Daddy.

GRANDMA *(offstage)* It most certainly is not. It's disgraceful.

MAY Mama—will you please keep out of it? *(turns on lamp by sofa)*

GRANDMA The truth is the truth and should be spoken at all times.

MAY Mother, please!

GRANDMA *(enters, sits landing)* Don't please Mother me. The truth is the truth. It's disgraceful. If there are any bastards around—it's you who've sired them. My May is a good girl.

LEM Would you please tell her to stay out of it?

MAY Mother, please.

GRANDMA—Well, speak up to him. Don't let him get away with talk like that. Just speak up.

MAY I'd speak up, Mama, if you'd give me half a chance.

GRANDMA Calling your husband "Daddy" all the time. If that isn't the silliest thing I ever heard.

MAY Mother, if you don't keep out of this, I'll come upstairs and give you a pill and shut your door.

GRANDMA And I'll spit out the pill and open the door. So there.

LEM *(gets up—crosses to foot of stairs)* Will you two stop that bickering and let's get down to the point at hand. *(calling up to* GRANDMA*)* Do you know where he is? *(no answer)* Hey! Old lady—I'm talking to you.

GRANDMA If you're talking to me—my name is Mrs. Martin, and I'd thank you to remember that. No—I don't know where he is, and if I did I wouldn't tell you. (LEM *turns away)*

MAY Would you tell me, Mama?

GRANDMA Tell you?—after your telling me to shut up? I wouldn't tell you a thing.

MAY I didn't tell you to shut up, Mama.

GRANDMA Well, you said "Mother please," which is the same thing.

LEM There's no use talking to her. *(sits in his chair, takes up paper)*

GRANDMA Calling your son a bastard—the very idea. No wonder he uses such terrible language. No wonder he's in trouble down there at—*(she stops)*

LEM Where is he in trouble? *(no answer)*

MAY Mama—what trouble is Spence in?

GRANDMA *(rising)* I'm a little tired. If you don't mind I think I'll go to bed now. *(from arch)* Good night.

LEM *(rises, crosses to stairs. On stairs)* I'm gonna—

MAY It's no use, Lem. She won't tell you. She's as stubborn as an old mule.

GRANDMA I heard that—and I'll remember it.

LEM *(from stairs)* What are we going to do?

MAY We'll sit here and wait for him—that's all. (LEM *crosses right to chair)* I'm a little worried now, Lem.

LEM It's about time.

MAY Oh, don't be silly. I was worried before. You don't suppose we should call the police, Lem?

LEM What for? We haven't done anything—have we?

MAY They'd help us find him.

LEM There'll be no police in this house—ever—for any reason.

MAY Now you're being silly.

LEM You heard what I said. I don't want any police in this.

MAY *(rises; crosses right to window)* Ssh! He's coming up the steps—and he's carrying a bag, Lem.

LEM *(crosses to center)* A bag? Well, I'll be damned!

MAY Now don't holler at him until we find out what's wrong.

LEM Don't worry. I'll handle this. You just stay out of it. (SPENCE *enters right.* LEM *lights cigar)*

GRANDMA *(as* SPENCE *shuts door)* Spence—is that you?

SPENCE *(takes off coat; crosses to foot of stairs)* Yes, it's me, Gram.

GRANDMA Would you come right upstairs, please. I've dropped my glasses and can't seem to find them.

SPENCE I'll be right up, Gram.

LEM You'll come in this house and sit down, young man. I want to talk to you.

SPENCE It'll just take a second, Pop.

LEM A second too long. Sit down now. The traitor upstairs can wait for her glasses. She can't read in the dark, anyhow. *(*SPENCE *sits on stool)*

MAY *(crosses to left of* SPENCE*)* Spence—you don't look well. Where have you been?

SPENCE To the library.

GRANDMA Spence—I haven't told them a thing. If they say I have they're lying.

LEM *(crossing down to* SPENCE*)* Will you shut her up?

MAY *(to center)* Mother, please.

GRANDMA Oh! Shut up, yourself. Mother please—Mother please. Why don't you tell me to shut up and be done with it?

LEM *(over* GRANDMA*'s last sentence)* I can't even think with her carrying on up there. So—you were at the library and you brought a suitcase to carry home a couple of books. *(*MAY *crosses to* SPENCE*)*

SPENCE Well—I had a tough time finding the books.

LEM I get it. You knew you were going to have a tough time finding the books so you just packed an overnight bag in case you had to spend the night.

MAY Have you had anything to eat, Spence?

SPENCE As a matter of fact I haven't.

LEM Will you please stop interrupting?

MAY I'll go and heat up something. *(goes into the kitchen, turns on kitchen light)*

LEM Do you think I'm crazy, Spence?

SPENCE I honestly don't think you're crazy, Pop.

LEM Well you must think something like that. Don't you think I know what time the library closes?

SPENCE What times does the library close, Pop?

LEM *(a pause)* May! *(crosses to arch up left center)*

MAY Yes?

LEM You'd better come in here and talk to this little bastard before I break his neck.

GRANDMA There he goes again. It's disgraceful. *(*MAY *comes in with saucepan and ladle.* LEM *crosses up right)*

MAY *(to* GRANDMA*)* All right now. Spence, where have you been?

SPENCE I told you—to the library. I got the books to prove it.

MAY I think it's been pretty well settled, Spence—that you did go to the library. The point is, where did you go after that? *(he doesn't answer)* It isn't like you Spence, not to answer. *(they wait.* MAY *puts pan on dining table, crosses to* SPENCE*)* Very well, Spence. When you came in I smelled beer on your breath. Have you been drinking beer?

SPENCE Yes.

LEM Well, I'll be damned.

MAY Daddy—please.

GRANDMA Don't be calling that man "Daddy." He's no husband of mine.

MAY Who have you been drinking beer with, Spence?

SPENCE I'd rather not say.

MAY Why not, Spence?

SPENCE *(gets up, crosses to TV)* Well, Mom, to be frank with you, I don't honestly think that you'd know any of them.

MAY I'd still like to know.

SPENCE Mom, I'm trying to be honest with you. If you keep asking me I'm going to lie about it—and I'd rather not lie about it, Mom.

MAY *(crosses to* SPENCE*)* Very well, Spence—we'll let that pass for now. A few minutes ago your Grandmother said that you were in some kind of trouble.

GRANDMA I didn't quite hear that. What's that you said I said?

MAY Are you in trouble, Spence?

SPENCE I sure am.

MAY What happened?

SPENCE I—got kicked out of school.

LEM *(crosses to left)* Well, I'll be good and goddamned.

MAY Do you know what you did that was wrong?

LEM *(crossing to right)* The little genius gets kicked out of school.

SPENCE I don't think that I honestly did anything that was wrong.

LEM That cinches it. He gets kicked out of school for doing nothing.

SPENCE I didn't mean that, Pop. I didn't mean that I didn't do anything. I just felt that I was justified.

MAY What happened, Spence?

SPENCE Look, Mom—I don't want to go through all that again. I don't feel like it. *(crosses to ottoman down stage of* MAY*)* The teacher, Miss Crowley, that is, said something about Negroes. I was sitting there. I told her she was wrong. She got mad—I got mad. I walked out of her room and went into the Men's Room. I was mad so I smoked a cigar. *(sits on ottoman)* They caught me and brought me down to the principal. They threw me out of school for a week. That's all there was to it.

LEM *(moves to* SPENCE*)* What are you talking about—that's all there was to it? We got a genius on our hands, May. He knows more than the teacher. What do you think of that? *(turning on* SPENCE*)* Where did you get that cigar?

SPENCE Out of your box.

LEM *(to* MAY*)* There you are!

MAY In other words you stole cigars from your father?

SPENCE I wouldn't exactly call it that.

LEM Well, that's damn well what I'd call it. *(crosses to above chair right)*

MAY You and I will go back to school Monday, Spence, and you will apologize to Miss Crowley and be reinstated in school.

SPENCE There's a week's vacation.

MAY Then we will go up on the following Monday.

SPENCE I don't think I can see my way clear to doing that, Mom.

MAY *(crosses sofa table for knitting)* There will be no more discussion about it, Spence. A week from Monday—and it's settled.

SPENCE I'm not going up to school with you, Mom. I'm going to stay out for the week. I won't go back to school and apologize to anyone.

MAY You want to disobey both your father and me?

SPENCE I don't want to disobey either of you. I kind of felt that you'd be on my side.

LEM You'll do what you're told. *(comes down stage)*

SPENCE I suppose you can make me go up there with you—but I won't apologize to anyone.

LEM Stop talking back to your mother.

SPENCE I'm not talking back to her. I just want her to understand how I feel. *(*MAY *is above* SPENCE*)*

LEM *(crossing to* SPENCE*)* We don't care how you feel. Now, what do you think of that? You talk about what you'll do and what you won't do. We do things we don't like to do every day of our lives. I hear those crumbs at the bank talking about niggers and making jokes about niggers every day—and I stay on—because I need the job—so that you can have the things that you need. And what do you do? You get your silly little behind kicked out of school. And now you're too proud to go back. *(crosses up right)*

GRANDMA Will you listen to him running his big mouth.

MAY *(crossing down)* Mama. We've given you boys everything that you could possibly want. You've never been deprived of anything, Spence. I don't need to tell you how hard we both work, and the fact that I'm in pain now doesn't seem to make any difference to you. I have arthritis in my wrist now, so badly that I can barely stand it, and it certainly doesn't help it any to hear you talk like this.

SPENCE I'm sorry your wrist hurts, Mom. *(*LEM *is at piano)*

MAY *(crosses right)* You're not sorry at all. If you were, you'd do something about it. We've bent every effort to see that you were raised in a decent neighborhood and wouldn't have to live in slums because we always wanted the best for you. But now I'm not so sure we haven't made a terrible mistake—because you seem not to realize what you are. You're a little colored boy—that's what you are—and you have no business talking back to white women, no matter what they say or what they do. If you were in the South you could be lynched for that and your father and I couldn't do anything about it. So from now on my advice to you is to try and remember your place.

SPENCE You'll pardon me for saying so—but that's the biggest hunk of bull I've ever heard in my whole life.

LEM *(crossing down to him)* What's that you said?

SPENCE *(rises)* You both ought to be shamed to talk to me that way.

LEM *(walks over and slaps him full across the face)* Now go upstairs and don't come down until you can apologize to both of us. Go on.

SPENCE *(crosses to foot of stairs, stops second step.* MAY *crosses down right)* I'll go upstairs, Pop, because you're my father and I still have to do what you tell me. But I'm still ashamed of you and I want you both to know it. *(he is walking upstairs)*

LEM *(crossing to foot of stairs)* That smart mouth of yours is going to get you into more trouble if you don't watch out. *(*SPENCE *has disappeared.* LEM *crosses down right)* It's those damn books you've been reading—that's the trouble with you.

MAY I don't think you should have slapped him, Lem.

LEM What was I supposed to do? Let the little skunk stand there and cuss us both out? *(going over to the stairs)* And be sure you go straight upstairs. Don't be stopping in the traitor's room.

GRANDMA He can stop in my room if he wants to. Who's to stop him, I'd like to know?

LEM *(starts upstairs, holding paper)* I will.

GRANDMA If you come into my room with your nasty mouth I'll bat you on the head with my cane.

LEM *(returns to room, moves paper)* It's a fine thing when a man can't get a little respect in his own house.

GRANDMA What have either of you done to get respect, I'd like to know? Nothing but bully the boy.

MAY All right, Mother—now you keep out of it.

GRANDMA *(on stairs)* I'll not keep out of it. When I've got something to say, I say it, and you know it, so don't try to hush me up.

MAY *(crossing to foot of stairs)* Mother, if you come down those stairs I'm going to tell the doctor.

GRANDMA *(comes downstairs.* MAY *crosses to piano)* Oh! Tell him, smell him, knock him down and sell him. What you think I care? All this slapping and going on.

LEM Where did Spence go? *(sits on his chair)*

GRANDMA *(at banister, crossing to sofa)* He went to his room. Where do you suppose he would go? He still does what you tell him, though why I'll never know.

MAY Mother—please.

LEM Oh! Let her go ahead and run herself down. It won't take long.

GRANDMA That's where you're wrong. I have no intention of running down. I've got a few things to say and I'm going to say them. *(picks papers off sofa, throws them at* LEM*)*

LEM Well, hurry up and say them and let's get it over with.

GRANDMA I will. Don't you worry your head about that. I'm going to sit down first. *(*GRANDMA *sits sofa.* MAY *crosses to piano)* Now, in the first place—that nasty little hussy that's teaching history in that school deserves exactly what she got—and the only thing that I think is that Spence didn't tell her enough.

MAY He can't go around talking to people like that.

GRANDMA That's a lot of twaddle and you know it. *(*MAY *crosses left to kitchen arch)* Now, in the second place—when you moved down here, did you ever stop to take into consideration that something like this was bound to happen sooner or later, and that the most important thing might be just having your love and company? You did not. You kept right on working—and instead of your company, they got a book or a bicycle or an electric train. Mercy—the stuff that came in this house was ridiculous.

LEM *(gets up, crosses to piano)* That's none of your—

GRANDMA Will you let me finish? Well, I don't agree with that kind of raising one bit—and allow me to be the first to tell you both. You got away with it with Mack because Mack had Spence. But do you know that that boy is absolutely alone? He hasn't a friend in the world. You didn't know, did you, that all his little pals around here have taken to the girls and the little girls' mothers don't want their little daughters going around with a colored boy. Did you know that there was a dance up at school last week and Spence couldn't go because he didn't have anybody to take? Well, whether you know it or not, he's alone. And now you want to desert him completely by not backing him up. You moved him out of a slum and taught him to think of himself as something to be respected—and now you get mad when he does the things that you made it possible for him to do. That bull—as he called it about staying in his place. I'm ashamed of you both and I want you to know it. I've said what I came down here to say—now help me out of this sofa. Well, don't just stand there like a dumb ox—help me up. *(*LEM *moves over, helps her)*

MAY You hadn't ought to come downstairs, Mother. You know that.

GRANDMA I'll come downstairs when I want to. Now—what do you think of that? *(shoves* LEM *away)* The trouble with you two is that you're too careful. I'm an old lady and I haven't got much longer to live one way or the other. I'll come downstairs when I want to. *(crosses to stairs)*

MAY Did Spence tell you all this? *(crosses right)*

GRANDMA Well, I certainly didn't find it out by talking to the neighbors.

LEM *(crosses to sofa, sits)* Well—why in hell didn't he say so when we were talking to him?

GRANDMA How could he? You attacked him like a rattlesnake the minute he came in the door.

LEM I did not.

GRANDMA You laid in wait and attacked him just like a rattlesnake. I heard you. *(she is staring up the stairs)* I'm going to send him downstairs. *(she is slowly mounting the stairs)* Talk to him. Be nice to him. *(on landing)* Don't be crumbs all your lives. *(she disappears)*

MAY *(starting to go to kitchen)* I'd better go and put the food on again.

LEM *(gets up, follows her)* You'll stay right here.

MAY He's hungry, Lem.

LEM You can do all of that when we're through. You're not going to leave me here by myself. What will I say to him?

MAY I don't know.

LEM Why didn't you tell me all this was going on anyway?

MAY Because I didn't know, Daddy.

LEM It's a mother's place to know what's happening to her son—isn't it?

MAY *(crossing to* LEM*)* You know—I didn't know how it was going to take place, but somehow I knew it would turn out to be my fault.

LEM *(moves right)* I didn't say—

MAY Oh! Shut up.

LEM *(turns to her)* What did you say to me?

MAY *(moves right)* I said "Shut up." I told you not to hop on him the minute he came into the house. Maybe if you'd asked him questions instead of calling him names you would've found all this out and you wouldn't have to stand here looking so foolish now.

LEM You were just as bad as I was.

MAY I'm going out in the kitchen. You can talk to him by yourself. *(she starts to exit as* SPENCE *starts down the stairs)*

LEM *(sotto voce)* You stay in here.

MAY I will not. So there. *(she exits into kitchen)*

LEM *(his back to stairway, pretends not to notice* SPENCE*; gets up his nerve and then)* Come on down, Spence. *(*SPENCE *starts down again.* LEM *crosses right)* We're going to have a little talk. *(*SPENCE *comes into the room)* Sit down—Son.

SPENCE *(walking over to the chair right)* Thanks, Pop. *(sits on stool)*

LEM Are you comfortable?

SPENCE Yes, Pop.

LEM *(at right of* SPENCE*)* How do you feel?

SPENCE I feel all right, Pop. I'm a little groggy, but I guess that's from the—*(he pauses)* stuff I've been drinking.

LEM *(moves close to* SPENCE*)* Serves you right. Now you gotta stop going around doing things like that. You hear? And another thing—You've got to stop talking back to me. If there's one thing that makes me good and damned mad it's talking back. I can't stand it and I won't stand it. *(crossing left)* It don't show the proper respect. You got that?

SPENCE Yes, Pop.

LEM *(after a glance into the kitchen)* You heard from Mack lately?

SPENCE No, I haven't, Pop.

LEM *(crossing right)* Well, I guess he's busy. You know how it is when you go to college.

SPENCE Yes, I guess he is busy.

LEM And that's what you've got to start thinking about—because you'll be busy, too, when you get to college. And you're going to college—you know that, don't you?

SPENCE Yes, Pop—I do.

LEM Well—just be sure. Now you go on and forget these little bastards around here. Don't pay any attention to them. *(crosses chair right)* You've got bigger things to think about—and if they won't play with you—you just tell them to go to hell—because you're better than any ten of them put together. All right. Now—you got your books and you've got your music—and if there's anything you want—you just tell me about it and I'll get it for you. Understand? (LEM *sits*)

SPENCE Yes. Pop.

LEM *(rises, crosses up)* And don't mind what these lousy teachers say either. The big thing is for you to graduate and get the hell out of that lousy school. And if they say anything you don't like—just forget it—'cause you're going to college—and you can't afford to get your butt thrown out of school too often. You understand?

SPENCE Yes, Pop.

LEM All right then *(crosses to chair, sits)* It's all settled. Now just forget the whole business. And if anything else happens—you just come to us and we'll take care of it. Understand?

SPENCE Yes, Pop.

LEM All right then. *(*LEM *returns to paper. Pause)* Your mother's fixing you something to eat. You'd better go out and get it.

SPENCE If you don't mind, Pop, I don't feel like eating. I think I'll just go to bed now.

LEM Now—that's what I'm talking about. It's silly to go around moping.

SPENCE *(rises, crosses to stairs)* I know it's silly, Pop. I know that. I'm going to try to do what you told me, but I want to go to bed now—that's all. *(he is on the stairs)* Goodnight, Pop. *(he turns)* And thanks for helping me, Pop. *(starts up)*

LEM It's all right. *(he is sitting down with the paper. From upstairs a voice—muffled and rather terrified, cries)*

GRANDMA Spence! Spence! *(*SPENCE *pauses for a moment and then rushes upstairs)*

LEM *(jumping from the chair and running upstairs)* May! Come up here.

MAY *(from the kitchen)* What? What's the matter? *(she comes out)* Where are you?

LEM Up here—come up here quickly. *(*MAY *runs up the stairs. There is the sound of* LEM*'s voice)* Now that's right—up here on the bed. There. Go down and call the doctor; tell him to get here as soon as he can. The number is on the pad.

MAY Mama! Mama!

LEM Get out of the way, May.

SPENCE *(rushes downstairs, goes to the telephone and dials the number. He waits)* Hello! Is Doctor Sloane there? This is Dr. Sloane? This is Spencer Scott. You've got to come over as soon as you can. It's my Grandmother. I don't know what's the matter with her. You've got to come—

MAY *(enters from the top of the stairs)* Spence! *(*SPENCE *puts his hand over the mouthpiece and waits)* Tell him he doesn't have to hurry. She's dead. *(*SPENCE *hangs up the phone without telling him.* MAY *keeps coming down the stairs and down right; sits in chair)* She didn't have to suffer, Spence, and she died quickly. We can thank God for that. *(*SPENCE *starts for the stairs as* LEM *starts down. He meets his father, who holds him)*

LEM Where are you going?

SPENCE Let me go—Pop, I said let me go. Damn it, Pop—take your hands off me.

MAY *(rising)* Let him go, Lem.

*(*LEM *releases him.* SPENCE *goes off as* LEM *comes down the stairs.* MAY *sits down and* LEM *stands silent, above her.* SPENCE *comes down the stairs again and goes into the kitchen. He doesn't notice his father or mother and goes quickly to get his coat, off left in kitchen)*

LEM Where are you going, Spence?

SPENCE *(putting on coat)* Out—outside for a while.

LEM *(crosses to center)* I think you'd better stay here with your mother, Spence. She needs you.

SPENCE I can't. She's got you anyway.

LEM I don't think you'd better go out now.

SPENCE Leave me alone! Will you?

LEM How can you be so selfish? Your mother needs you. *(he starts right.* LEM *holds him)* What's the matter with you anyway? You've got a fever. You'd better go to bed.

SPENCE I'm not going to bed. I want to go out for a few minutes. That's all. I want to be by myself for a few minutes.

MAY You don't have to go outside to cry, Spence. You don't have to be ashamed before us. *(*SPENCE *begins to sob incoherently, his head on* LEM*'s shoulder; breaks away from his father and runs out of the house.* LEM *starts after him)* Let him go, Lem.

LEM *(stopping at front door)* But he's got a fever. He can't—

MAY Let him alone, Lem.

LEM *(crosses down right to her)* I'll call the doctor. You go and rest. He can have a look at Spence while he's here.

MAY You'd better call Mack too, Lem. He's

so far away. I don't think he'll be able to come home.

LEM I'll call him.

MAY What's Spence doing, Lem?

LEM He's standing over in the lot—that's all.

(Curtain)

Scene Two

(At the curtain's rise, SPENCE*'s room is in semi-darkness because the shades are drawn. The door is shut. On the chair by* SPENCE*'s bed stands a tray of food. On the bureau is a decanter of water, a bottle of pills and medicine.* SPENCE *is in bed—asleep to all obvious intents. A woman appears climbing the stairs outside of the room and enters. She is carrying a clean pillow slip, which she places on the chair right. She glances over at the bed and then begins to pull the shades. Sun springs into the room as she does so. She is a woman perhaps in her late twenties, good-looking and trim. It is two weeks later—early afternoon)*

CHRISTINE You know, I've met many a mulish critter in my day, but you're the worst mule I've ever met. Now you ain't asleep because I heard you tipping around up here not ten minutes ago. Now open your eyes and eat your lunch.

SPENCE I don't want it.

CHRISTINE *(crosses with tray to bureau)* You know you don't have to eat it? You know that, don't you? But don't blame anyone but yourself when your bones are rattling around inside of your skin like two castanets hit together—you understand? I suppose you don't want your medicine either. *(crosses up of bed)* Boy, you sure do beat all. You're the stubbornest cus I ever met. I'll ask you one more time. Are you going to take this medicine or aren't you? Speak up, 'cause I don't have all day.

SPENCE No.

CHRISTINE I didn't quite catch that. Don't be mumbling at me, boy. Was it "Yes" or "No" that you said?

SPENCE I said "No."

CHRISTINE Boy, you know you're going to make some girl a pretty miserable husband one of these days. Course, you know, I don't believe you're not eating. *(crosses to bureau)* I think you sneak downstairs after I leave and eat everything in sight. *(pause)* Did you hear me? *(no answer. Crosses to bed)* Spence, won't you please sit up and eat something? Anything? Crust of bread? You know it kills me when folks don't eat. *(no answer)* I never knew anybody who could pick out just the right way to worry somebody. Won't you eat just a little bit?

SPENCE *(head up in bed)* I said "No."

CHRISTINE *(crosses to chair for pillowslip, returns)* Well, I guess that settles it—don't it? Then you can get out of bed so I can make it.

SPENCE You don't need to make it today.

CHRISTINE The devil you say. I've taken enough from you today already. Now just get out of that bed before I pick you up and throw you out of it. You're not supposed to stay in bed all day anyway. The doctor said to get up and walk around and to get some air if you felt like it.

SPENCE Don't you get sick of repeating yourself?

CHRISTINE *(crosses to bureau, returns with decanter)* You've got 'til I count three. One—two—three—*(throws water)*

SPENCE *(throwing the covers off and laughing in spite of himself)* All right—all right. I'm getting up now. *(he goes right and sits in chair)* You make me sick.

CHRISTINE The feeling is oh so mutual. *(she begins to make the bed—stands above it)* I've seen a mess of mourning in my day, but if the mourning you do don't beat anything I've ever seen yet, I don't want a nickel. But at the rate you're going you're not going to have much longer to mourn. You're going to be joining them that you're mournin' for if you don't watch your step.

SPENCE What do you say to my making a little bargain with you?

CHRISTINE What is it?

SPENCE I'll eat that slop that you brought up here if as soon as that bed is made you get the hell out of here and leave me alone.

CHRISTINE *(takes food tray from chair to bureau)* There ain't no call to be rude and nasty. All I'm saying is that you look like a bag of bones and you do.

SPENCE I've always been skinny.

CHRISTINE *(pours medicine in soup)* It's humanly impossible for somebody to be as skinny as you are and live. Consumption is chasing you in one direction and pneumonia is chasing you in the other—and when they meet with you in the middle, it's sure going to be a mess.

SPENCE Why don't you shut up?

CHRISTINE *(moves to above bed, continues making it)* Why don't you eat your lunch instead of sitting up there looking like death warmed over?

SPENCE *(gets out of the chair and viciously picks up the tray from the bureau; brings it back, sits down with it and begins to eat)* Now will you let me alone?

CHRISTINE *(crosses to bureau, gets out socks)* Who's bothering you?

SPENCE You are.

CHRISTINE *(crosses to him, puts wrapper around shoulders)* Aw! Go on, boy. You know you love it.

SPENCE *(tasting the soup)* What kind of soup is this?

CHRISTINE *(putting on left sock)* What'd you say?

SPENCE I said, "What kind of soup is this?"

CHRISTINE Chicken.

SPENCE Well, it tastes damn peculiar. *(tasting it again)* What's in it?

CHRISTINE Nothing.

SPENCE What's in this soup? *(pause)* You put the medicine in the soup.

CHRISTINE Does it taste awful?

SPENCE It tastes just like hell. You sure are a lousy cook. No wonder you can't keep a husband.

CHRISTINE I'll have you know that I've only had one husband—and he died.

SPENCE I'm not surprised.

CHRISTINE *(throws socks down, rises, crosses to bed, works on sheet)* I'm not speaking to you again today. And that's final.

SPENCE You're not really mad, are you, Christine? *(pause)* Christine, I was just kidding. *(pause)* Aw! Come on, Christine. You know I don't really think that you killed your husband.

CHRISTINE *(laughing. Crosses to* SPENCE*)* Boy, you sure are a mess. *(they look at one another)* You feel better now—don't you?

SPENCE I guess so.

CHRISTINE *(puts on right sock)* You're getting some color in your cheeks.

SPENCE Don't you think that you're hurrying things a little, Christine? I haven't finished eating yet.

CHRISTINE If there's one thing I can't stand it's skinny men around me. Never could stand skinny men since I can first remember. You wouldn't be a bad-looking boy if you just weren't so skinny.

SPENCE Thanks, Christine. Thanks. You're a real tin pitcher full of complaints today. You're as generous with the old complaints as Gram. *(he stops eating)*

CHRISTINE *(rises, stands over* SPENCE *left of him)* Now what's the matter? What've you stopped eating for?

SPENCE You know what's the matter.

CHRISTINE *(fixes something on tray)* Now there isn't any point in thinking about that now.

SPENCE I know there isn't, but I can't help it.

CHRISTINE Just don't think about it.

SPENCE That's a very stupid thing to say. You can't just stop thinking about someone because they're dead, can you?

CHRISTINE Yes, yes you can if you want to. You just don't open the door and let yourself in, that's all.

SPENCE What are you talking about?

CHRISTINE Nothing. Now eat your lunch. *(to above bed)*

SPENCE *(begins eating again)* You know, it's funny. I got expelled from school—Gram died—and I got sick—and so I couldn't go to school anyway—even if they hadn't kicked me out. Funny the way things turn out.

CHRISTINE Yes, it is—isn't it? *(she stops work, listens)*

SPENCE You know, Christine, I was just thinking. Course last week was the funeral and I figure maybe the guys didn't want to come and see me then. But I've been home all this week. *(*CHRISTINE *crosses to him, gets tray)* Wouldn't you have thought that one of them would have come over to see me by now?

CHRISTINE *(putting tray on bureau)* Nothing surprises me any more.

SPENCE What do you mean by that?

CHRISTINE Nothing. *(feels his head)* I don't think you have any more fever. You want to take your temperature?

SPENCE Naw! *(pause)* Your hands are very warm, Christine.

CHRISTINE Warm hands—warm heart.

SPENCE That would be fine except that that's not the way it goes.

CHRISTINE *(crossing to bed)* It goes that way for me and that's what matters.

SPENCE *(rises, crosses to right of bureau)* Were you born here, Christine?

CHRISTINE No, I was born in Alabama. Birmingham, Alabama, in Ensley, near the steel mills.

SPENCE I'll bet you didn't like it much down there, did you?

CHRISTINE No, I didn't like it much down there.

SPENCE Is your family still there?

CHRISTINE *(crosses down to front of bed. Changes pillow slip)* My father was killed in the mills when I was a little girl. My Ma died a couple of years ago. I had two brothers and two sisters. I don't know where they are now.

SPENCE *(crosses to bed, sits)* What made you come way the hell up here by yourself?

CHRISTINE *(laughing)* I wanted something better, I guess. I decided I was coming up North to try my luck. I worked for a whole year before I'd saved the money, and the day I had what I thought was enough, I went down to the railroad station. *(stops work)* Boy was that some day! The sun was shining and I felt real good like you feel maybe once or twice in your whole life. When I got to the ticket window, the man had a calendar, and it had an advertisement for a big insurance company on it. So I looked at the name of the town and then I told him that that's where I wanted my ticket to take me. Then I went home and packed my mama's cardboard suitcase, and that same night I caught the train. And that's the last I ever saw of my mother and my brothers and sisters and Rusty.

SPENCE Who the hell was Rusty?

CHRISTINE *(sits at head of bed.* SPENCE *sits in middle)* Rusty was my dog. Well, I didn't go to work for the insurance company. I went into service for a while and then I got married. And that's what I meant when I was telling you about the doors. See, my husband died about two years after that and about two months after he died, I had a baby and he was born dead.

SPENCE Christine!

CHRISTINE Well, I tell you for a while I felt like all I wanted to do was die myself. Then I realized that you just can't go on like that. It's like your mind is divided into little rooms and each time you go back into one of those rooms your heart likes to break in two. So all you do is shut the doors—and lock them—to those little rooms in your mind and never let yourself in them again. So I've got two little locked rooms in my mind. One for Bert, my husband, and one for my baby that never had a name. Do you want some more to eat?

SPENCE No, Christine, I don't think so. You sure do make me feel crumby, Christine.

CHRISTINE Why?

SPENCE Well, I've been giving you a pretty hard time about what's been happening to me. *(pause)* I'm sorry, Christine.

CHRISTINE That's all right, boy. You're just unhappy—that's all. But you'll get used to that. Pretty soon you'll be able to laugh a little bit and make jokes, even while you're unhappy. It won't be this bad forever. *(rises)* Well, the bed's made, the house is clean, and you've had your lunch. So—

SPENCE Don't go, Christine. Stay with me.

CHRISTINE *(crossing to bureau for tray)* I've got another cleaning job, Boy.

SPENCE Just for a little while longer. *(pause)* If you have to go, well then I guess you have to, but if you could stay just a little while longer it would mean a lot to me. It isn't that I'm afraid of anything, but I get to thinking about all the things I've got to do.

CHRISTINE What have you got to do?

SPENCE Well, I've got to really get well—first of all. I'll take the medicine and I'll take a hell of a lot of vitamins and I figure that'll fix me up all right.

CHRISTINE *(crossing to him with pills)* There's no time like the present to begin.

SPENCE Honest, Christine.

CHRISTINE A little water? *(she gets water glass from the tray)*

SPENCE *(takes the pill)* I know what you're going to say. "You're beginning to look fatter already." *(she laughs merrily and hugs him)* You're going to make me spill the water.

CHRISTINE *(releases him. Takes glass and puts it on tray)* What else?

SPENCE Well, I'm going to cut out the damn smoking and drinking and that ought to fix up the old body. *(rises, crosses right)* Then I've got to go up to school and make peace with old Hasbrook and Crowley. But the other things are going to be a hell of a lot harder to do.

CHRISTINE What are they?

SPENCE *(sits chair right)* I've got to do something about the guys and my Gram, Christine.

I'm going to be honest with you about Gram—it's going to be hard. I miss her a hell of a lot. But she's dead, Christine. She's dead—and you can tell yourself that and you can accept it, and maybe I'm a little selfish about it, but you know that no other living soul is talking with her or having fun with her. She didn't ditch you. She died. But the guys are different, Christine. They're not dead. They're over in the lot playing baseball. They're still horsing around up in the park. I don't suppose they can really help what's happened because that's the way it is. I've said some pretty lousy things to them, Christine, and I don't want it to be that way. *(he pauses. He is near tears)* God damn it—I hate being Black, Christine. I hate it. I hate it. I hate the hell out of it.

CHRISTINE *(crosses to him, holds him)* Ssh!

SPENCE I'm sorry I said that, Christine.

CHRISTINE It's all right, Spence. You don't have to explain to me. *(she releases him, but still holds his hand)*

SPENCE And I've got to cut out this goddamn crying. Everything makes me cry. I don't understand it. I was watching television the other day—a damn soap opera—and started crying like a baby. That's damn peculiar.

CHRISTINE It's not so peculiar as you think.

SPENCE There's just one more thing, Christine.

CHRISTINE What is it?

SPENCE I don't know whether I should tell you or not.

CHRISTINE Sure you can tell me.

SPENCE How are you so sure? You don't even know what it is yet.

CHRISTINE I'll take the risk.

SPENCE You promise you won't say anything about it to anybody?

CHRISTINE I won't mention it to a soul.

SPENCE No matter what it is?

CHRISTINE I've already said I won't tell it, haven't I?

SPENCE Well. I want to sleep with a girl, Christine. *(CHRISTINE turns away laughing)* What's the matter with you?

CHRISTINE Nothing. I just swallowed wrong.

SPENCE Yeh!

CHRISTINE *(turns to him)* Yeh! And many more of them right back at you. Who's the lucky girl?

SPENCE Aw! Christine. You know I haven't got any girl in mind. I think about it quite often, but I can't think of anybody. I suppose you think that sounds pretty horny to be thinking of it all the time?

CHRISTINE *(turns away)* No, I wouldn't say that.

SPENCE You wouldn't?

CHRISTINE No, I wouldn't.

SPENCE You know, Christine. You're a funny Joe. To look at you no one would think that somebody could talk to you like this.

CHRISTINE *(quite dryly, turns to him)* Thanks.

SPENCE Have you had much experience, Christine?

CHRISTINE Enough.

SPENCE Off hand—how much experience would you say you've had?

CHRISTINE Now that's the kind of question it's every woman's right to leave unanswered.

SPENCE You think that's a pretty nosey question?

CHRISTINE I not only think it's a nosey question. I know it is.

SPENCE O.K. *(rises. Crosses to below bed. CHRISTINE sits chair right. Pause)* Would you say, off hand, that I was trying to rush things, Christine?

CHRISTINE How do you mean?

SPENCE *(crossing down right)* You'd just as soon we talked about something else, wouldn't you?

CHRISTINE I just didn't understand what you meant, that's all.

SPENCE *(crossing to center)* Well, I mean about my age and all. Do you realize that I'm going on eighteen and have never slept with a girl?

CHRISTINE That's terrible—isn't it? *(turns away)*

SPENCE It sure as hell is. Hell. I'm practically a virgin. And you know I was thinking when I was sick, supposing I died. Supposing I just passed out now and died. *(indicates imaginary body on floor)* Why, I'd regret that I hadn't slept with anybody for the rest of my life practically.

CHRISTINE I guess that would be pretty terrible—wouldn't it?

SPENCE I think that you're having a hell of a good time laughing at me.

CHRISTINE I most certainly am not.

SPENCE You sure as hell are. You've got a sneaky laugh line around your whole mouth.

CHRISTINE *(turns to him)* Spence—I'm not laughing. I wouldn't laugh at you when you're telling me things like this. If I'm doing anything I'm remembering, and I might be just smiling a little bit at the memory, but I'm not laughing at you.

SPENCE You really honestly don't think that it's peculiar or anything?

CHRISTINE How could anything so natural be peculiar?

SPENCE That's a funny thing for you to say.

CHRISTINE Why is it so funny, might I ask?

SPENCE *(sits on foot of bed)* Well, I'm pretty sure, although I've never asked her, that Mom would give me a swat for my pains if—

CHRISTINE *(rises, crosses to him)* And what makes you think that your mother and I should have the same ideas?

SPENCE Well—you're both older than I am.

CHRISTINE Well, I'm not anywhere near as old as your mother. I might be a widow, but I'm a young widow, and I'm not through yet by a long shot.

SPENCE I didn't mean—

CHRISTINE I know exactly what you meant. Just remember you're no Tiny Tim yourself.

SPENCE I didn't mean what you thought I meant at all. I just meant that you seem to understand a lot of things. Aw! Hell—I don't mean that. I mean you seem to understand me—and I'm grateful. That's all.

CHRISTINE *(crosses to chair left. After a pause)* Well, we've done enough talking for one afternoon. I've got to go.

SPENCE Christine!

CHRISTINE *(turning around)* What is it now?

SPENCE *(pause)* Nothing.

CHRISTINE *(crossing to center)* Nothing is what you ask for, nothing is what you'll get.

SPENCE *(rises)* Christine!—*(she stops)* I'd appreciate it if you didn't turn around.

CHRISTINE Why?

SPENCE *(standing behind her)* Because I'm going to ask you something and if you're going to laugh at me I'd just as soon you weren't laughing in my face.

CHRISTINE I won't laugh.

SPENCE Well, would you mind not turning around just the same?

CHRISTINE All right.

SPENCE Well—I don't know quite how to say it. *(pause)* Do you like me, Christine?

CHRISTINE I certainly do.

SPENCE No kidding?

CHRISTINE No kidding.

SPENCE I was sure hoping you weren't. Because I like you too, Christine.

CHRISTINE Thank you.

SPENCE Well, I know that liking doesn't mean loving—but I kind of thought—that since—well—you're lonely, aren't you, Christine?

CHRISTINE I've been lonely for a long time now, Boy.

SPENCE Well—in case you didn't know, I'm lonely too, Christine—and I know that you're older than I am and I know it makes a lot of difference.

CHRISTINE I have to go, Spence.

SPENCE But what I'm lacking in age, Christine, I sure make up for in loneliness, and so we do have that much in common. Don't we, Christine?

CHRISTINE Yes.

SPENCE So maybe—if you stayed, Christine—since things are like I said they were—we might find a little happiness together. I don't mean for forever or anything like that—but could you call and say that you couldn't make it?

CHRISTINE You know you're very young, Spence, and you could be very foolish too. You know that—don't you?

SPENCE Yes, Christine. I know.

CHRISTINE And I could be very foolish to listen to you.

SPENCE I know, Christine.

CHRISTINE *(turns to him)* It's funny. I have to look at you, because I can't believe that you said what you just said. You said, that since we were both lonely maybe—just for an afternoon—we could find happiness together. You know that so soon?

SPENCE Yes, Christine.

CHRISTINE You see, I didn't laugh. I ain't laughing at all. I'll try to come back. I'll try. *(she gets the tray from the bureau and goes to the door)*

SPENCE You know where the phone is. If you can't come back, Christine, you don't need to come up and tell me. Just go. But if you can, there's a bell downstairs on the table that Mother uses to call us to meals. Would you ring it—if you can?

CHRISTINE I'll try. *(she exits)*

SPENCE *(crossing down right, then to door; listens)* Why in hell is she taking so long?

(Sound of hand bell off right. SPENCE *crosses slowly to window, pulls shade down as lights fade. Curtain)*

Scene Three

(The scene is the same as scene one. As the curtain rises, MAY *is coming out of the kitchen. She walks over to the piano and rings the bell. It is the following afternoon—Saturday)*

MAY Spence! Spence! Are you asleep?

SPENCE *(upstairs)* No.

MAY Well, suppose you come downstairs and get lunch. Hurry up now. I have a lot of work to do, and you're holding me up.

SPENCE What's the big hurry?

MAY *(crosses to dining room, gets fruit salad and milk from refrigerator)* Never mind. Just come downstairs and don't ask so many silly questions.

SPENCE *(appears at head of stairs)* O.K. So I'm coming. You sure do get yourself upset about nothing at all. Why don't you take it easy? *(makes basketball throw with sweater from stairs onto armchair right)*

MAY Have you gotten your clothes together yet?

SPENCE *(coming downstairs, crossing to dining table)* What clothes?

MAY *(counting groceries on shelf)* Your school clothes. I told you to get them ready and I'd have them pressed this afternoon.

SPENCE *(sits right of table, starts eating)* They're all right.

MAY I'm not going to have you going to school looking like a tramp.

SPENCE You sure got peculiar notions of what a tramp looks like.

MAY Never mind the sass. Did you get them ready?

SPENCE They're hanging up in the closet—just waiting to be taken off the hangers and brought down to the tailor's. How much more ready could they be?

MAY I told you to bring them down. You know you could cooperate a little bit more. Now I suppose I'm going to have to climb upstairs and bring them down. I told you my knee—

SPENCE All right. All right. I'll get them—*(gets up, crosses to stairs)*

MAY You're hollering at me, Spencer. *(pause)* You can't get them now. Just sit down and eat your lunch.

SPENCE *(crosses back to chair)* You know, Mom, I got to give it to you. You sure do know how to fix a guy's stomach for this lunch. *(pause as he sits again)* You know, I could wear my Sunday suit to school Monday and Chris could take these clothes. I don't want you to strain your knee any more than you have to. Or I could take them down myself?

MAY *(turns to shelf)* Chris? Christine won't be back Monday or any other day.

SPENCE *(pushes chair back)* What are you talking about?

MAY Christine will not be back. You're no longer ill. There's no need for Christine any longer.

SPENCE *(rises, crosses to* MAY*)* But I thought you said—

MAY I changed my mind. I called her and told her this morning.

SPENCE What did you tell her?

MAY I told her that her services were no longer needed by me. I decided that there was no need to spend that money since I could do the things myself. I've been doing them myself anyway.

SPENCE But you said you were too tired when you got home.

MAY Well, I've changed my mind. Why all this interest in Christine?

SPENCE *(crossing back to table)* Nothing. I just thought—

MAY I know what you just thought, young man, and don't think I don't.

SPENCE Now what are you talking about?

MAY You know my eyes weren't put on—

SPENCE The way they were put on for nothing. I know.

MAY All that pampering and coddling she did with you makes me sick to my stomach.

SPENCE *(crossing to her)* Will you please explain what you mean by that?

MAY I don't know. What should I mean by that? Maybe you can tell me. Well, I've heard those stories about maids being left alone in houses with boys before. I'm not saying it's gone that far yet. But an ounce of prevention is worth a pound of anybody's cure.

SPENCE *(crossing down)* You know, you sure have got a dirty mind.

MAY Don't be so sure that it's I that have a dirty mind. And if you say that to me again you'll get a good slap for your pains.

SPENCE How in hell—

MAY Don't use that kind of language before me.

SPENCE All I did was come down to eat lunch and then you start on me about a suit of clothes. *(crosses right)* I'll take the suit down to the tailor myself. I wouldn't have you strain yourself. As far as Christine is concerned, if she pampered and coddled me—then I'm grateful to her. And you promised her a job after I was sick and I think you're damned dirty—

MAY Spencer!

SPENCE *(crossing to table)* Yes, I think you're damned dirty to get rid of her. Now—that's all I've got to say and you can take this food away now because I can't eat it. *(crosses right)*

MAY *(taking glass away)* Suit yourself. No one is going to beg you to eat, young man.

SPENCE Mom—no one had to beg me to eat. All I wanted was a little peace to eat. I was perfectly willing to eat *(crosses to stairs)*

MAY Where are you going?

SPENCE *(climbing stairs)* To the tailor. Where did you think I was going?

MAY You haven't got time.

SPENCE What do you mean I haven't got time? All in hell—

MAY *(crosses to living room)* Be careful.

SPENCE All in hell I got left in the world is time—time for everything. If there's any little thing you want done from now on—just let me know.

MAY *(crosses to table, takes plate away)* You haven't got time to go to the tailor's now.

SPENCE *(on landing)* Why not?

MAY Because I asked some of your friends over this afternoon.

SPENCE You did what?

MAY *(turning to shelf)* I asked some of your friends over for ice cream and cake this afternoon.

SPENCE *(coming downstairs)* Are you kidding?

MAY I'm perfectly serious.

SPENCE *(in center)* Why didn't you make a little pink punch to go with it?

MAY I did.

SPENCE Well, you can call them the hell back up and tell them to stay home.

MAY *(turns, crosses to him)* Spence—don't you dare.

SPENCE You heard what I said. You can call them up and tell them to stay home. (MAY *crosses left.* SPENCE *follows her)* What right did you have to do that? It's none of your business. It's my business and you stay out of it. I'm not bribing those kids with ice cream, cake or pink punch. I'm never going to bribe anyone to be my friend.

MAY You'll do what you're told and you'll stop being so fresh. Do you understand that? *(*SPENCE *crosses to below table)* And I don't want to hear another word out of you about what you'll do and what you won't do. When you start talking like that it's about time you went out and got a job of your own and bought a house of your own (SPENCE *tucks in shirt-tails)* but as long as you're under this roof, you will do what you're told. (SPENCE *turns to go to front door)* Where are you going?

SPENCE I'm going to get the hell out of here. That's where I'm going.

MAY *(following him)* Go ahead—and see how far you get acting the way you act. *(both at front door)* Your father's right about you. You're too proud. You think you can go through life being proud, don't you? Well, you're wrong. You're a little Black boy—and you don't seem to understand it. But that's what you are. You think this is bad; well, it'll be worse. You'll serve them pink punch and ice cream—and you'll do a lot worse. You'll smile when you feel like crying. *(she begins to cry)* You'll laugh at them when you could put knives right into their backs without giving it a second thought—and you'll never do what you've done and let them know that they've hurt you. They never forgive you for that. So go on out and learn the lesson. Now get out of here. Get out of here and don't ever come back. (MAY *crosses to sofa, sits. Pause)* You think it's easy for me to tell my son to crawl when I know he can walk and walk well? I'm sorry I ever had children. I'm sorry you didn't die when you were a baby. Do you hear that? I'm sorry you didn't die. *(she is completely overcome)*

SPENCE *(crossing down)* Don't cry, Mom. I'm sorry. I'm sorry I've made it so difficult. I didn't mean to hurt you, Mom. *(pause)* What time did you tell them to be here?

MAY Around one.

SPENCE Well, they'll be here any minute. Is everything ready.

MAY It's in the pantry. The ice cream is in the refrigerator. *(*TONY *and* GUSSIE *enter outside the door)*

SPENCE Don't cry, Mom, I'm sorry. It seems to me that for the past two weeks all I've done is apologize to people. I seem to be apologizing for trying to be a human being. *(the bell rings)* That must be some of them now.

MAY Do you want me to stay?

SPENCE No. You can go out if you want to.

MAY *(crosses to stairs, starts up)* I have some shopping to do. *(stops on landing, turns)* Spence, don't be rude to them. *(*SPENCE *opens the door)*

GUSSIE Hi, Spence!

SPENCE Hi, Gussie! Hi, Tony! *(*TONY *and* GUSSIE *enter.* GUSSIE *first. He crosses to right of sofa)* What's the matter, Tony? You're not speaking or something?

TONY Hi, Spence! I'm sorry about your grandmother. *(crosses to below armchair right)*

SPENCE Thanks. Where are the rest of the guys?

GUSSIE They'll be around. *(pause)* You going back to school Monday?

SPENCE Yeh! I'm going back Monday. It's kind of creepy having a party for no reason— isn't it? See—I've been sick—you probably didn't know—my Mom thought it would be a big surprise if the gang came in today. That's all. Sit down.

TONY *(sits on stool)* We didn't see you around. We wondered what was wrong.

GUSSIE *(sits right arm of sofa)* You're better now—ain't you?

SPENCE Yeh! I'm better now. *(pause)* What you guys been doing?

GUSSIE Knocking around. That's all. *(pause)*

SPENCE You been playing baseball lately?

TONY Not much—No. We've had too much homework lately.

SPENCE *(crosses left)* Oh! I thought I heard you guys a couple of times but it was probably somebody else.

GUSSIE Yeh! It must have been somebody else.

SPENCE—Would you like some ice cream or anything? *(*MAY *appears at head of stairs. They rise)*

MAY *(coming downstairs)* Don't get up. It's nice seeing all of you again.

TONY and GUSSIE How do you do, Mrs. Scott!

MAY Just stay where you are. I'm going down to the grocer's. Haven't seen you in a long time, Tony.

TONY I've been pretty busy lately.

MAY Well, don't be such a stranger. We miss you.

SPENCE *(crosses to kitchen)* I'll get the ice cream.

GUSSIE Yeah. We've been pretty busy.

*(*IGGIE *enters right, crosses to door, followed by* JOHNNY *and* BOBBY REYNOLDS*)*

MAY Well, any time you want to come over and watch television—come. Spence will be very glad to see you. *(bell rings)* I'll get it.

SPENCE *(puts ice cream, plates and spoons on table as* MAY *opens door.* Well, here you are. Help yourselves.

*(*TONY *crosses to table, sits left of it.* GUSSIE *crosses to left of table)*

MAY Hello, boys. Come on in.

IGGIE Hello, Mrs. Scott. *(crosses left)*

JOHNNY Hello, Mrs. Scott. *(*MAY *is at door.* IGGIE *crosses left to table.* JOHNNY *is right of* BOBBY*)* My brother and I were very sad to hear of your recent—

BOBBY —death in your family.

MAY Thank you, boys. I have to go now. Spence will entertain you. I'll be back in a little while. *(exits.* BOBBY *and* JOHNNY *cross left)*

SPENCE *(crosses to them)* Well, if it isn't the Reynolds boys. Come on in.

IGGIE *(above table, his rear in* TONY*'s ice cream)* Hey, Spence. I didn't come to see you, because I thought maybe you wouldn't want any visitors, but I kept asking your mother about you.

SPENCE *(crossing to* IGGIE*)* Well—thanks, Iggie. Thanks.

TONY Hey, Iggie, will you get your ass out of my ice cream?

IGGIE I'm sorry. *(crosses to ottoman, sits.* SPENCE *is just about to tell* TONY *off)*

TONY Nothing to be sorry about. Just get out of it is all.

GUSSIE *(interrupting impending fight between*

TONY *and* SPENCE, *crosses in. Nervously)* This is fun—ain't it, Spence?

SPENCE Yeah! *(crosses* REYNOLDS BOYS *in living room)* Come on, you guys. Get yours while the getting is good. *(*BOBBY *and* JOHNNY *cross to table.* GUSSIE *crosses right)*

GUSSIE Hey! Spence. This is fun. We ain't had so much fun since we made that party that time—stealing off Mr. Markman. Remember that? *(*IGGIE *rises, crosses to dining room shelf for cake)*

SPENCE I sure do. I was responsible for getting dill pickles. What did you have to get?

GUSSIE The ice cream. I had to get the ice cream.

JOHNNY *(crosses to ottoman, sits)* How did you do it?

GUSSIE *(to center)* Gee, you guys are new around here. Well, Tony here—was the onliest one of us that had any money. He had a lousy dime—a lousy dime—so we all goes into Sam Markman's store big as you please and tells him we want a ten-cent guinea grinder. *(puts ice cream on sofa)* Can you imagine—that fat Jew bastard with a damn Jew store making guinea grinders.

TONY *(crosses right to* GUSSIE, *then to stool, sits)* For Christ sake. Will you cut it out? Iggie's here.

GUSSIE *(turns left)* Who? Oh! Iggie—I didn't even see you, Iggie. Geez—I'm sorry. No offense meant, Iggie.

IGGIE *(by refrigerator)* It's all right.

GUSSIE *(with rising intensity)* Yeh! Well, there we all were. So while he's cutting the damn bread in two, I'm practically falling into his ice cream freezer. I'm pulling the pints of ice cream out as fast as a son of a bitch and throwing them out the door. Tony is behind the candy counter stuffing his pocket with chocolate bars. *(*IGGIE *crosses to center)* And old Spence is in the barrel with the pickles. They're way down at the bottom, see, and he can't reach them—so there he is practically swimming in the pickle juice when Old Markman turns around and sees him. So he pulls his arm out, and he's got a pickle in his hand, and he says without blinking an eyelash, "Looks like you'd better be ordering some more pickles, Mr. Markman. They're getting pretty damn hard to reach." Remember that, Spence? *(sits right end of sofa)*

SPENCE Sure—I remember. You want some more cake, Iggie?

IGGIE No thanks, Spencer. *(sits left end of sofa)*

SPENCE Well, if you want more just reach for it. *(sits piano chair)*

BOBBY What happened after that, Gussie?

GUSSIE *(rises, crosses down)* What do you mean what happened? We goes up to the park with a guinea grinder, six quarts of ice cream, twelve chocolate bars, and a big loaf of cake that Spence finally got under his sweater. Geez—did he look funny. He looked like he had eight babies in there. *(sits sofa)* Boy, did we have fun. *(*JOHNNY *crosses to table)* Got any more of the cake, Spence? Goddamit your mother sure does make good cake.

SPENCE Sure! *(he takes the plate. Crosses to shelf for cake)*

GUSSIE Gee, I don't know why we been staying away from here so long. I've been missing that good stuff your Mom dishes out. *(pause)*

SPENCE *(at shelf)* That was the day Tony broke his arm, remember?

GUSSIE *(taking the cake)* Geez, that's right.

JOHNNY *(crosses to ottoman, sits)* How did that happen?

GUSSIE Geez, you guys are new around here, ain't you? *(rises, crosses to* JOHNNY*)* Well after we'd stuffed with all that food, we decided to play Tarzan. So, you know that big oak tree over near the golf course? We decides to play in that. We're all leaping for the branches and making the ape call—*(he imitates it)* then it gets to be Tony's turn—so Tony makes with the ape call and jumps for the branch, and the next thing you know he's falling right through the goddamn tree, hitting his head on one branch, his can on the next, and finally VOOM he hits the ground with the damndest noise I've ever heard. I'm convinced that he's dead. We're both honestly convinced that he's dead, he's so still. We're both scared to go near him so we keep calling from a distance—*(calling to* TONY *who sits on stool right)* "Tony! Tony!" Finally we notice his stomach moving, so we goes over, and son of a bitch if there ain't a big piece of bone sticking right through his damn shirt. What the hell did they call that, Tony?

TONY A compound fracture.

GUSSIE Yeh! That's right. We sure did have fun that summer. *(sits sofa)* Remember, Spence? *(*TONY *crosses to table, sits)*

SPENCE Yeh! I remember.

GUSSIE Those sure were the good old days. *(pause)* Hey! As a matter of fact we're going up to the park tonight. We're going on a hay ride. You're all better, ain't you Spence?

SPENCE Yes.

GUSSIE Well, why in hell don't you come along?

TONY *(puts down his plate sharply on the table, rises. Everybody reacts to the slip)* You did say you were coming back to school Monday, didn't you, Spence?

SPENCE Yes, Tony. Monday I'm coming back to school.

TONY *(crosses to living room)* Well, I guess we gotta be going. *(*BOBBY *rises)* Why don't we call you for school on Monday?

SPENCE *(rises)* Well, as a matter of fact my father is going to be driving me up to school on Monday. He's got to come with me—so we'll go up together.

TONY Yeh! Well, Gus and me gotta be going. *(*GUSSIE *rises)*

SPENCE *(crosses down right)* As a matter of fact, you know, I said when you first came in there was no damn reason for this party. Well, actually there is.

TONY *(crosses down right to* SPENCE*)* Yeh! What? It ain't your birthday. I know when your birthday is.

SPENCE Well, you know, I've been doing a hell of a lot of fooling around and I've been neglecting my lessons, not practicing, and all manner of things like that. And if you're going to college you got to be a little more serious about things than I've been. So from now on I've got to buckle down to the old books and concentrate on things of the mind.

GUSSIE Yeh! I guess you're right.

SPENCE So I've got a little schedule made out for myself. In the morning before school I've got to practice. And in the afternoon after school I've got my homework to do. So you see I'm going to be pretty busy.

GUSSIE Geez, Spence. You sure do play the piano damn good. You know that? Are you going to be a musician or something?

SPENCE I don't know. Maybe. I haven't given it too much thought. So I had all you guys over to kind of say goodbye and all 'cause I don't think I'm going to have much time for playing around. 'Course, it's going to be a little hard at first 'cause I'm not used to it, so all you guys could help me if you just kind of let me alone and let me get my work done.

TONY Sure, we'll do that, Spence.

GUSSIE Sure. Sure, Spence. *(*GUSSIE *crosses to left of piano)*

SPENCE Thanks—you're real pals.

TONY Thanks for the ice cream. *(he exits front door)*

SPENCE It's O.K. It was fun.

JOHNNY *(on exit)* Sure. Geeze, you guys sound like you must've been pretty crazy in those days. See you, Spence. *(*IGGIE *rises also)*

SPENCE Stay a second, Iggie. I want to talk to you.

BOBBY *(on exit)* Thanks for the party, Spence.

GUSSIE *(crosses down to* SPENCE*)* Hey, Spence! Geez, I can't get over that summer. We really did have a hell of a lot of fun, didn't we?

SPENCE *(with a hand on* GUSSIE*'s shoulder)* Yeh! We sure did. It was the best summer I ever had.

GUSSIE Goodbye, Spence. *(they shake hands. General ad libs from* BOYS *off right)*

SPENCE *(crosses left to* IGGIE*)* Hey! Iggie, I'm sorry for what happened—I mean Gussie's talking that way. He's just dumb and he needs a good paste in the jaw for his pains, but I couldn't do it. I'm sorry, Iggie.

IGGIE I understand.

SPENCE Then O.K., Iggie. That's all I wanted to talk to you about. Thanks for coming to my party. *(crosses to ottoman, sits)*

IGGIE Sure. *(starts to go, stops)* Did you really mean it, Spencer, about going to college?

SPENCE Yeh! Yeh, I did. That is something, isn't it? *(live ad libs blend into recorded baseball game)*

IGGIE You don't know which one?

SPENCE No, no, not yet.

IGGIE Well *(pause)* I'd better be going. *(he starts for the door)*

SPENCE Iggie! *(*IGGIE *turns)* Look, I know you're busy and all that but would you mind if I came over and looked at the old stamp collection?

IGGIE Do you want it back, Spencer?

SPENCE No, I don't want it back. I'd just like to see what you've added to it—that's all.

IGGIE Come over any time.

SPENCE Thanks, Iggie. Thanks.

IGGIE *(on exit)* Goodbye, Spence. *(pause.* IGGIE *has exited, leaving front door open)*

SPENCE Goodbye, Iggie. (SPENCE *rises, crosses to table to get plates as* MAY *enters up left, crosses to kitchen door and enters. She carries a full shopping bag)*

MAY Where is everyone?

SPENCE Gone.

MAY They didn't stay long.

SPENCE No, they didn't.

MAY *(puts bag on dining table)* What happened?

SPENCE *(center. Stopping)* Nothing—nothing. I just told them that I didn't want to see them anymore. That's all. I just said it to them before they said it to me.

MAY You'll never learn, will you?

SPENCE Mom, you've just got to believe that I'm trying to learn. I'm trying as hard as I know how. I might be wrong, but if I am, I think I'd like to find that out for myself.

MAY What are you going to do?

SPENCE I don't know, Mom. I don't know.

MAY *(crosses in)* Spence, look at me—You're not running away, are you?

SPENCE No, Mom, I'm not running away—and if you don't mind, Mom, let's not talk about it any more—I did the right thing. So let's just both try to forget it happened and go on to something else. Okay? *(he walks to piano, starts to sit, then walks to front door and closes it, shutting out the baseball sounds. He sits at piano and starts to play "Praeludium")*

MAY *(after a few bars)* Spence.—I love you very much. (MAY *picks up bag, crosses to kitchen.* SPENCER *watches her, surprised, then turns back to the piano. As he resumes playing,* MAY *crosses to dining table and starts collecting dishes)*

(Slow curtain)

A RAISIN IN THE SUN
1959

Lorraine Hansberry (1930–1965)

Lorraine Hansberry, disturbed by the depiction of African Americans in Broadway plays and musicals, decided to counter these stereotypes by writing her own play. Her intent was to write a social drama about believable characters who happened to be Black, rather than a "Negro play." She also wanted to create a work of art. She accomplished her goals with her first and most famous play, *A Raisin in the Sun.*

The critics, with few exceptions, were unanimous in their praise of the work. It was reminiscent of *Take a Giant Step* in that white audiences recognized similarities between themselves and Hansberry's characters—just as they had done with Peterson's 1953 drama. The Youngers' values, dreams, and aspirations were basically the same as theirs. Mama Younger wants a decent home, her daughter, Beneatha, wants to become a doctor, and her son, Walter Lee, wants to become a prosperous businessman. Like Willie Loman, the tragic protagonist in Arthur Miller's *Death of a Salesman,* Walter Lee believes in and pursues the American dream. Both men want to become capitalists, believing that wealth will solve their problems and bring them happiness. When they realize too late that these values are false ones, Willie Loman commits suicide, but Walter Lee retrieves his dignity and becomes the man that he has always wanted to be.

A Raisin in the Sun was written during the turbulent fifties when the Civil Rights Movement was well under way. The tactic employed by most activists was peaceful civil disobedience as advocated by Dr. Martin Luther King. They agreed with playwrights like Hansberry who believed that African Americans deserved their share of the American dream. More militant activists, on the other hand, found the play to be the perfect integrationist piece. Integration, they thought, was trivial and not the concern of poor African Americans who wanted *power*—the power to earn equal wages, to be politically active at all levels of government, and to enjoy the rights and privileges accorded other citizens. Harold Cruse, the noted African

American scholar and critic, was of the same opinion. He dismissed the play as "glorified soap opera." The Youngers, he felt, were "tidied up" with middle-class "values, sentiments and strivings," making them acceptable to Broadway, and that Hansberry and other Black playwrights misrepresented the poor Black majority by using them to promote their own cause: the integration of the Black middle class.

But are the Youngers' values limited to the middle class? The idea that poor Blacks would not have dreams and ambitions like the Youngers seems absurd. Why wouldn't a family living in a leaking apartment with rats and roaches want to move into a decent home? And where would you find affordable, decent homes? In white neighborhoods. The Youngers moved, not to be *with* whites, but to improve their condition; to live in a home that would provide them comfort and privacy.

When Hansberry was eight years old, her family purchased a home in a middle-class white section of Chicago where they were threatened and harassed by hostile neighbors. She narrowly escaped serious injury when a brick was thrown through their window. This experience, and her deep concern with the struggles of her people, served in part as impetus for *A Raisin in the Sun.*

A Raisin in the Sun is a landmark drama for a number of reasons: it was the first play written by an African American woman to be produced on Broadway; Lorraine Hansberry became the first African American and the youngest to win the New York Drama Critics Award; Lloyd Richards, the director, was the first African American to direct a Broadway show in over fifty years.

The Broadway opening was on March 11, 1959, where it ran for 530 performances. It is one of the most performed plays by an African American playwright. In less than a quarter of a century it became an American classic. Large numbers of whites were introduced to modern African American characters and life for the first time through Hansberry's play, which paved the way for the wider acceptance of other works by Black playwrights who followed, such as Lonne Elder, Charles Fuller, Adrienne Kennedy, and August Wilson. The movie adaption of the play featuring the Broadway cast, won the Cannes Film Festival Award in 1961. *Raisin,* a musical version of the play with book by Robert Nemiroff and Charlotte Zaltzberg, music by Judd Woldin, and lyrics by Robert Brittan, won Tony and Grammy Awards as Best Musical Comedy in 1974.

There were numerous cuts made in the original production, some having to do with plot and others with characters. The original ending, for example, was changed from one in which the Youngers waited in their new home for their neighbors to attack it, to the present, happier ending. The script that appears here is from the original Broadway production.

Lorraine Hansberry was born in Chicago, the daughter of a prosperous real estate broker. She attended segregated schools on the South Side where she made friends with students whose families were less fortunate than hers. After graduation from Englewood High School in 1948, she attended the University of Wisconsin studying art and stage design. There she developed an appreciation for the plays of Ibsen, Strindberg, and O'Casey. After her sophomore year she moved to New York, becoming active with little theatre groups, and working as a journalist for the African American publication, *Freedom.* She was on friendly terms with Paul Robeson, chairman of the editorial board, W.E.B. DuBois, and Langston Hughes. She met and married Robert Nemiroff, a music publisher, in 1953, who encouraged her to pursue her interest in playwriting. *A Raisin in the Sun* was the result. In 1963 she was diagnosed as having cancer and spent the next two years in and out of hospitals. She died on January 12, 1965. Nemiroff, her literary executor, compiled fragments from her plays, stories and letters into a biographical play celebrating her life and spirit which he called, *To Be Young, Gifted and Black*. It was the longest running Off-Broadway play during the 1969 season.

A Raisin in the Sun

A RAISIN IN THE SUN *was first presented by Philip Rose and David J. Cogan at the Ethel Barrymore Theatre, New York City, March 11, 1959, with the following cast:*

(In order of appearance)

RUTH YOUNGER *Ruby Dee*
TRAVIS YOUNGER *Glynn Turman*
WALTER LEE YOUNGER (BROTHER) *Sidney Poitier*
BENEATHA YOUNGER *Diana Sands*
LENA YOUNGER (MAMA) *Claudia McNeil*
JOSEPH ASAGAI *Ivan Dixon*
GEORGE MURCHISON *Louis Gossett*
KARL LINDNER *John Fiedler*
BOBO *Lonne Elder III*
MOVING MEN *Ed Hall, Douglas Turner*

Directed by Lloyd Richards

Designed and lighted by Ralph Alswang

Costumes by Virginia Volland

The action of the play is set in Chicago's Southside, sometime between World War II and the present.

ACT ONE
SCENE 1. Friday morning.
SCENE 2. The following morning.
ACT TWO
SCENE 1. Later, the same day.
SCENE 2. Friday night, a few weeks later.
SCENE 3. Moving day, one week later.
ACT THREE
An hour later.

What happens to a dream deferred?
Does it dry up
Like a raisin in the sun?
Or fester like a sore—
And then run?
Does it stink like rotten meat?
Or crust and sugar over—
Like a syrupy sweet?

Maybe it just sags
Like a heavy load.

Or does it explode?

—Langston Hughes

ACT ONE

Scene One

(The YOUNGER *living room would be a comfortable and well-ordered room if it were not for a number of indestructible contradictions to this state of being. Its furnishings are typical and undistinguished and their primary feature now is that they have clearly had to accommodate the living of too many people for too many years—and they are tired. Still, we can see that at some time, a time probably no longer remembered by the family (except perhaps for* MAMA*), the furnishings of this room were actually selected with care and love and even hope—and brought to this apartment and arranged with taste and pride.*

That was a long time ago. Now the once loved pattern of the couch upholstery has to fight to show itself from under acres of crocheted doilies and couch covers, which have themselves finally come to be more important than the upholstery. And here a table or a chair has been moved to disguise the worn places in the carpet; but the carpet has fought back by showing its weariness, with depressing uniformity, elsewhere on its surface.

Weariness has, in fact, won in this room. Everything has been polished, washed, sat on, used, scrubbed too often. All pretenses but living itself have long since vanished from the very atmosphere of this room.

Moreover, a section of this room, for it is not really a room unto itself, though the landlord's lease would make it seem so, slopes backward to provide a small kitchen area, where the family prepares the meals that are eaten in the living room proper, which must also serve as dining room. The single window that has been provided for these "two" rooms is located in this kitchen area. The sole natural light the family may enjoy in the course of a day is only that which fights its way through this little window.

At left, a door leads to a bedroom, which is shared by MAMA *and her daughter,* BENEATHA. *At right, opposite, is a second room (which in the beginning of the life of this apartment was probably a breakfast room), which serves as a bedroom for* WALTER *and his wife,* RUTH.

TIME *Sometime between World War II and the present.*

PLACE *Chicago's Southside.*

AT RISE *It is morning dark in the living room.* TRAVIS *is asleep on the make-down bed at center. An alarm clock sounds from within the bedroom at right, and presently* RUTH *enters from that room and closes the door behind her. She crosses sleepily toward the window. As she passes her sleeping son she reaches down and shakes him a little. At the window she raises the shade and a dusky Southside morning light comes in feebly. She fills a pot with water and puts it on to boil. She calls to the boy, between yawns, in a slightly muffled voice.*

RUTH *is about thirty. We can see that she was a pretty girl, even exceptionally so, but now it is apparent that life has been little that she expected, and disappointment has already begun to hang in her face. In a few years, before thirty-five even, she will be known among her people as a "settled woman."*

(She crosses to her son and gives him a good, final, rousing shake)

RUTH Come on now, boy, it's seven thirty! *(her son sits up at last, in a stupor of sleepiness)* I say hurry up, Travis! You ain't the only person in the world got to use a bathroom! *(the child, a sturdy, handsome little boy of ten or eleven, drags himself out of the bed and almost blindly takes his towels and "today's clothes" from drawers and a closet and goes out to the bathroom, which is in an outside hall and which is shared by another family or families on the same floor.* RUTH *crosses to the bedroom door at right and opens it and calls in to her husband)* Walter Lee! . . . It's after seven thirty! Lemme see you do some waking up in there now! *(she waits)* You better get up from there, man! It's after seven thirty I tell you. *(she waits again)* All right, you just go ahead and lay there and next thing you know Travis be finished and Mr. Johnson'll be in there and you'll be fussing and cussing round here like a mad man! And be late too! *(she waits, at the end of patience) Walter Lee*—it's time for you to get up!

(She waits another second and then starts to go into the bedroom, but is apparently satisfied that her husband has begun to get up. She stops, pulls the door to, and returns to the kitchen area. She wipes her face with a moist cloth and runs her fingers through her sleep-disheveled hair in a vain effort and ties an apron around her housecoat. The bedroom door at right opens and her husband stands in the doorway in his pajamas, which are rumpled and mismated. He is a lean, intense young man in his middle thirties, inclined to quick nervous movements and erratic speech habits—and always in his voice there is a quality of indictment)

WALTER Is he out yet?

RUTH What you mean *out*? He ain't hardly got in there good yet.

WALTER *(wandering in, still more oriented to sleep than to a new day)* Well, what was you doing all that yelling for if I can't even get in there yet? *(stopping and thinking)* Check coming today?

RUTH They *said* Saturday and this is just Friday and I hopes to God you ain't going to get up here first thing this morning and start talking to me 'bout no money—'cause I 'bout don't want to hear it.

WALTER Something the matter with you this morning?

RUTH No—I'm just sleepy as the devil. What kind of eggs you want?

WALTER Not scrambled. *(*RUTH *starts to scramble eggs)* Paper come? *(*RUTH *points impatiently to the rolled up* Tribune *on the table, and he gets it and spreads it out and vaguely reads the front page)* Set off another bomb yesterday.

RUTH *(maximum indifference)* Did they?

WALTER *(looking up)* What's the matter with you?

RUTH Ain't nothing the matter with me. And don't keep asking me that this morning.

WALTER Ain't nobody bothering you. *(reading the news of the day absently again)* Say Colonel McCormick is sick.

RUTH *(affecting tea-party interest)* Is he now? Poor thing.

WALTER *(sighing and looking at his watch)* Oh, me. *(he waits)* Now what is that boy doing in that bathroom all this time? He just going to have to start getting up earlier. I can't be being late to work on account of him fooling around in there.

RUTH *(turning on him)* Oh, no he ain't going to be getting up no earlier no such thing! It ain't his fault that he can't get to bed no earlier nights 'cause he got a bunch of crazy good-for-nothing clowns sitting up running their mouths in what is supposed to be his bedroom after ten o'clock at night . . .

WALTER That's what you mad about, ain't it? The things I want to talk about with my friends just couldn't be important in your mind, could they?

(He rises and finds a cigarette in her handbag on the table and crosses to the little window and looks out, smoking and deeply enjoying this first one)

RUTH *(almost matter of factly, a complaint too automatic to deserve emphasis)* Why you always got to smoke before you eat in the morning?

WALTER *(at the window)* Just look at 'em down there . . . Running and racing to work . . . *(he turns and faces his wife and watches her a moment at the stove, and then, suddenly)* You look young this morning, baby.

RUTH *(indifferently)* Yeah?

WALTER Just for a second—stirring them eggs. It's gone now—just for a second it was—you looked real young again. *(then, drily)* It's gone now—you look like yourself again.

RUTH Man, if you don't shut up and leave me alone.

WALTER *(looking out to the street again)* First thing a man ought to learn in life is not to make love to no colored woman first thing in the morning. You all some evil people at eight o'clock in the morning.

*(*TRAVIS *appears in the hall doorway, almost fully dressed and quite wide awake now, his towels and pajamas across his shoulders. He opens the door and signals for his father to make the bathroom in a hurry)*

TRAVIS *(watching the bathroom)* Daddy, come on!

*(*WALTER *gets his bathroom utensils and flies out to the bathroom)*

RUTH Sit down and have your breakfast, Travis.

TRAVIS Mama, this is Friday. *(gleefully)* Check coming tomorrow, huh?

RUTH You get your mind off money and eat your breakfast.

TRAVIS *(eating)* This is the morning we supposed to bring the fifty cents to school.

RUTH Well, I ain't got no fifty cents this morning.

TRAVIS Teacher say we have to.

RUTH I don't care what teacher say. I ain't got it. Eat your breakfast, Travis.

TRAVIS I *am* eating.

RUTH Hush up now and just eat!

(The boy gives her an exasperated look for her lack of understanding, and eats grudgingly)

TRAVIS You think Grandmama would have it?

RUTH No! And I want you to stop asking your grandmother for money, you hear me?

TRAVIS *(outraged)* Gaaaleee! I don't ask her, she just gimme it sometimes!

RUTH Travis Willard Younger—I got too much on me this morning to be—

TRAVIS Maybe Daddy—

RUTH *Travis!*

(The boy hushes abruptly. They are both quiet and tense for several seconds)

TRAVIS *(presently)* Could I maybe go carry some groceries in front of the supermarket for a little while after school then?

RUTH Just hush, I said. *(*TRAVIS *jabs his spoon into his cereal bowl viciously, and rests his head in anger upon his fists)* If you through eating, you can get over there and make up your bed.

(The boy obeys stiffly and crosses the room, almost mechanically, to the bed and more or less carefully

folds the covering. He carries the bedding into his mother's room and returns with his books and cap)

TRAVIS *(sulking and standing apart from her unnaturally)* I'm gone.

RUTH *(looking up from the stove to inspect him automatically)* Come here. *(he crosses to her and she studies his head)* If you don't take this comb and fix this here head, you better! *(*TRAVIS *puts down his books with a great sigh of oppression, and crosses to the mirror. His mother mutters under her breath about his "slubbornness")* 'Bout to march out of here with that head looking just like chickens slept in it! I just don't know where you get your stubborn ways . . . And get your jacket, too. Looks chilly out this morning.

TRAVIS *(with conspicuously brushed hair and jacket)* I'm gone.

RUTH Get carfare and milk money—*(waving one finger)*—and not a single penny for no caps, you hear me?

TRAVIS *(with sullen politeness)* Yes'm.

(He turns in outrage to leave. His mother watches after him as in his frustration he approaches the door almost comically. When she speaks to him, her voice has become a very gentle tease)

RUTH *(mocking; as she thinks he would say it)* Oh, Mama makes me so mad sometimes, I don't know what to do! *(she waits and continues to his back as he stands stock-still in front of the door)* I wouldn't kiss that woman good-bye for nothing in this world this morning! *(the boy finally turns around and rolls his eyes at her, knowing the mood has changed and he is vindicated; he does not, however, move toward her yet)* Not for nothing in this world! *(she finally laughs aloud at him and holds out her arms to him and we see that it is a way between them, very old and practiced. He crosses to her and allows her to embrace him warmly but keeps his face fixed with masculine rigidity. She holds him back from her presently and looks at him and runs her fingers over the features of his face. With utter gentleness—)* Now—whose little old angry man are you?

TRAVIS *(the masculinity and gruffness start to fade at last)* Aw gaalee—Mama . . .

RUTH *(mimicking)* Aw—gaaaaalleeeee, Mama! *(she pushes him, with rough playfulness and finality, toward the door)* Get on out of here or you going to be late.

TRAVIS *(in the face of love, new aggressiveness)* Mama, could I *please* go carry groceries?

RUTH Honey, it's starting to get so cold evenings.

WALTER *(coming in from the bathroom and drawing a make-believe gun from a make-believe holster and shooting at his son)* What is it he wants to do?

RUTH Go carry groceries after school at the supermarket.

WALTER Well, let him go . . .

TRAVIS *(quickly, to the ally)* I *have* to—she won't gimme the fifty cents . . .

WALTER *(to his wife only)* Why not?

RUTH *(simply, and with flavor)* 'Cause we don't have it.

WALTER *(to* RUTH *only)* What you tell the boy things like that for? *(reaching down into his pants with a rather important gesture)* Here, son—

(He hands the boy the coin, but his eyes are directed to his wife's. TRAVIS *takes the money happily)*

TRAVIS Thanks, Daddy.

(He starts out. RUTH *watches both of them with murder in her eyes.* WALTER *stands and stares back at her with defiance, and suddenly reaches into his pocket again on an afterthought)*

WALTER *(without even looking at his son, still staring hard at his wife)* In fact, here's another fifty cents . . . Buy yourself some fruit today—or take a taxi cab to school or something!

TRAVIS Whoopee—

(He leaps up and clasps his father around the middle with his legs, and they face each other in mutual appreciation; slowly WALTER LEE *peeks around the boy to catch the violent rays from his wife's eyes and draws his head back as if shot)*

WALTER You better get down now—and get to school, man.

TRAVIS *(at the door)* O.K. Good-bye. *(he exits)*

WALTER *(after him, pointing with pride)* That's *my* boy. *(she looks at him in disgust and turns back to her work)* You know what I was thinking 'bout in the bathroom this morning?

RUTH No.

WALTER How come you always try to be so pleasant!

RUTH What is there to be pleasant 'bout!

WALTER You want to know what I was thinking 'bout in the bathroom or not!

RUTH I know what you was thinking 'bout.

WALTER *(ignoring her)* 'Bout what me and Willy Harris was talking about last night.

RUTH *(immediately—a refrain)* Willy Harris is a good-for-nothing loud mouth.

WALTER Anybody who talks to me has got to be a good-for-nothing loud mouth, ain't he? And what you know about who is just a good-for-nothing loud mouth? Charlie Atkins was just a "good-for-nothing loud mouth" too, wasn't he! When he wanted me to go in the dry-cleaning business with him. And now—he's grossing a hundred thousand a year. A hundred thousand dollars a year! You still call *him* a loud mouth!

RUTH *(bitterly)* Oh, Walter Lee . . . *(she folds her head on her arms over on the table)*

WALTER *(rising and coming to her and standing over her)* You tired, ain't you? Tired of everything. Me, the boy, the way we live—this beat-up hole—everything. Ain't you? *(she doesn't look up, doesn't answer)* So tired—moaning and groaning all the time, but you wouldn't do nothing to help, would you? You couldn't be on my side that long for nothing, could you?

RUTH Walter, please leave me alone.

WALTER A man needs for a woman to back him up . . .

RUTH Walter—

WALTER Mama would listen to you. You know she listen to you more than she do me and Bennie. She thinks more of you. All you have to do is just sit down with her when you drinking your coffee one morning and talking 'bout things like you do and—*(he sits down beside her and demonstrates graphically what he thinks her methods and tone should be)*—you just sip your coffee, see, and say easy like that you been thinking 'bout that deal Walter Lee is so interested in, 'bout the store and all, and sip some more coffee, like what you saying ain't really that important to you— And the next thing you know, she be listening good and asking you questions and when I come home—I can tell her the details. This ain't no fly-by-night proposition, baby. I mean we figured it out, me and Willy and Bobo.

RUTH *(with a frown)* Bobo?

WALTER Yeah. You see, this little liquor store we got in mind cost seventy-five thousand and we figured the initial investment on the place be 'bout thirty thousand, see. That be ten thousand each. Course, there's a couple of hundred you got to pay so's you don't spend your life just waiting for them clowns to let your license get approved—

RUTH You mean graft?

WALTER *(frowning impatiently)* Don't call it that. See there, that just goes to show you what women understand about the world. Baby, don't *nothing* happen for you in this world 'less you pay *somebody* off!

RUTH Walter, leave me alone! *(she raises her head and stares at him vigorously—then says, more quietly)* Eat your eggs, they gonna be cold.

WALTER *(straightening up from her and looking off)* That's it. There you are. Man say to his woman: I got me a dream. His woman say: Eat your eggs. *(sadly, but gaining in power)* Man say: I got to take hold of this here world, baby! And a woman will say: Eat your eggs and go to work. *(passionately now)* Man say: I got to change my life, I'm choking to death, baby! And his woman say—*(in utter anguish as he brings his fists down on his thighs)*—Your eggs is getting cold!

RUTH *(softly)* Walter, that ain't none of our money.

WALTER *(not listening at all or even looking at her)* This morning, I was lookin' in the mirror and thinking about it . . . I'm thirty-five years old; I been married eleven years and I got a boy who sleeps in the living room—*(very, very quietly)*—and all I got to give him is stories about how rich white people live . . .

RUTH Eat your eggs, Walter.

WALTER *Damn my eggs . . . damn all the eggs that ever was!*

RUTH Then go to work.

WALTER *(looking up at her)* See—I'm trying to talk to you 'bout myself—*(shaking his head with the repetition)*—and all you can say is eat them eggs and go to work.

RUTH *(wearily)* Honey, you never say nothing new. I listen to you every day, every night and every morning, and you never say nothing new. *(shrugging)* So you would rather *be* Mr. Arnold than be his chauffeur. So—I would *rather* be living in Buckingham Palace.

WALTER That is just what is wrong with the colored woman in this world . . . Don't understand about building their men up and making 'em feel like they somebody. Like they can do something.

RUTH *(drily, but to hurt)* There *are* colored men who do things.

WALTER No thanks to the colored woman.

RUTH Well, being a colored woman, I guess I can't help myself none.

(She rises and gets the ironing board and sets it up and attacks a huge pile of rough-dried clothes, sprinkling them in preparation for the ironing and then rolling them into tight fat balls)

WALTER *(mumbling)* We one group of men tied to a race of women with small minds.

(His sister BENEATHA *enters. She is about twenty, as slim and intense as her brother. She is not as pretty as her sister-in-law, but her lean, almost intellectual face has a handsomeness of its own. She wears a bright-red flannel nightie, and her thick hair stands wildly about her head. Her speech is a mixture of many things; it is different from the rest of the family's insofar as education has permeated her sense of English—and perhaps the Midwest rather than the South has finally—at last—won out in her inflection; but not altogether, because over all of it is a soft slurring and transformed use of vowels, which is the decided influence of the Southside. She passes through the room without looking at either* RUTH *or* WALTER *and goes to the outside door and looks, a little blindly, out to the bathroom. She sees that it has been lost to the Johnsons. She closes the door with a sleepy vengeance and crosses to the table and sits down a little defeated)*

BENEATHA I am going to start timing those people.

WALTER You should get up earlier.

BENEATHA *(her face in her hands. She is still fighting the urge to go back to bed)* Really—would you suggest dawn? Where's the paper?

WALTER *(pushing the paper across the table to her as he studies her almost clinically, as though he has never seen her before)* You a horrible-looking chick at this hour.

BENEATHA *(drily)* Good morning, everybody.

WALTER *(senselessly)* How is school coming?

BENEATHA *(in the same spirit)* Lovely. Lovely. And you know, biology is the greatest. *(looking up at him)* I dissected something that looked just like you yesterday.

WALTER I just wondered if you've made up your mind and everything.

BENEATHA *(gaining in sharpness and impatience)* And what did I answer yesterday morning—and the day before that?

RUTH *(from the ironing board, like someone disinterested and old)* Don't be so nasty, Bennie.

BENEATHA *(still to her brother)* And the day before that and the day before that!

WALTER *(defensively)* I'm interested in you. Something wrong with that? Ain't many girls who decide—

WALTER *and* BENEATHA *(in unison)* —"to be a doctor."

(Silence)

WALTER Have we figured out yet just exactly how much medical school is going to cost?

RUTH Walter Lee, why don't you leave that girl alone and get out of here to work?

BENEATHA *(exits to the bathroom and bangs on the door)* Come on out of there, please! *(she comes back into the room)*

WALTER *(looking at his sister intently)* You know the check is coming tomorrow.

BENEATHA *(turning on him with a sharpness all her own)* That money belongs to Mama, Walter, and it's for her to decide how she wants to use it. I don't care if she wants to buy a house or a rocket ship or just nail it up somewhere and look at it. It's hers. Not ours—*hers*.

WALTER *(bitterly)* Now ain't that fine! You just got your mother's interest at heart, ain't you, girl? You such a nice girl—but if Mama got that money she can always take a few thousand and help you through school too—can't she?

BENEATHA I have never asked anyone around here to do anything for me!

WALTER No! And the line between asking and just accepting when the time comes is big and wide—ain't it!

BENEATHA *(with fury)* What do you want from me, Brother—that I quit school or just drop dead, which!

WALTER I don't want nothing but for you to stop acting holy 'round here. Me and Ruth done made some sacrifices for you—why can't you do something for the family?

RUTH Walter, don't be dragging me in it.

WALTER You are in it—Don't you get up

and go work in somebody's kitchen for the last three years to help put clothes on her back?

RUTH Oh, Walter—that's not fair . . .

WALTER It ain't that nobody expects you to get on your knees and say thank you, Brother; thank you, Ruth; thank you, Mama—and thank you, Travis, for wearing the same pair of shoes for two semesters—

BENEATHA *(dropping to her knees)* Well—I *do*—all right?—thank everybody . . . and forgive me for ever wanting to be anything at all . . . forgive me, forgive me!

RUTH Please stop it! Your mama'll hear you.

WALTER Who the hell told you you had to be a doctor? If you so crazy 'bout messing 'round with sick people—then go be a nurse like other women—or just get married and be quiet . . .

BENEATHA Well—you finally got it said . . . It took you three years but you finally got it said. Walter, give up; leave me alone—it's Mama's money.

WALTER *He was my father, too!*

BENEATHA So what? He was mine, too—and Travis' grandfather—but the insurance money belongs to Mama. Picking on me is not going to make her give it to you to invest in any liquor stores—*(underbreath, dropping into a chair)*—and I for one say, God bless Mama for that!

WALTER *(to* RUTH*)* See—did you hear? Did you hear!

RUTH Honey, please go to work.

WALTER Nobody in this house is ever going to understand me.

BENEATHA Because you're a nut.

WALTER Who's a nut?

BENEATHA You—you are a nut. Thee is mad, boy.

WALTER *(looking at his wife and his sister from the door, very sadly)* The world's most backward race of people, and that's a fact.

BENEATHA *(turning slowly in her chair)* And then there are all those prophets who would lead us out of the wilderness—*(*WALTER *slams out of the house)*—into the swamps!

RUTH Bennie, why you always gotta be pickin' on your brother? Can't you be a little sweeter sometimes?

(Door opens. WALTER *walks in)*

WALTER *(to* RUTH*)* I need some money for carfare.

RUTH *(looks at him, then warms; teasing, but tenderly)* Fifty cents? *(she goes to her bag and gets money)* Here, take a taxi.

*(*WALTER *exits.* MAMA *enters. She is a woman in her early sixties, full-bodied and strong. She is one of those women of a certain grace and beauty who wear it so unobtrusively that it takes a while to notice. Her dark-brown face is surrounded by the total whiteness of her hair, and, being a woman who has adjusted to many things in life and overcome many more, her face is full of strength. She has, we can see, wit and faith of a kind that keep her eyes lit and full of interest and expectancy. She is, in a word, a beautiful woman. Her bearing is perhaps most like the noble bearing of the women of the Hereros of Southwest Africa—rather as if she imagines that as she walks she still bears a basket or a vessel upon her head. Her speech, on the other hand, is as careless as her carriage is precise—she is inclined to slur everything—but her voice is perhaps not so much quiet as simply soft)*

MAMA Who that 'round here slamming doors at this hour?

(She crosses through the room, goes to the window, opens it, and brings in a feeble little plant growing doggedly in a small pot on the window sill. She feels the dirt and puts it back out)

RUTH That was Walter Lee. He and Bennie was at it again.

MAMA My children and they tempers. Lord, if this little old plant don't get more sun than it's been getting it ain't never going to see spring again. *(she turns from the window)* What's the matter with you this morning, Ruth? You looks right peaked. You aiming to iron all them things? Leave some for me. I'll get to 'em this afternoon. Bennie honey, it's too drafty for you to be sitting 'round half dressed. Where's your robe?

BENEATHA In the cleaners.

MAMA Well, go get mine and put it on.

BENEATHA I'm not cold, Mama, honest.

MAMA I know—but you so thin . . .

BENEATHA *(irritably)* Mama, I'm not cold.

MAMA *(seeing the make-down bed as* TRAVIS *has left it)* Lord have mercy, look at that poor bed. Bless his heart—he tries, don't he? *(she moves to the bed* TRAVIS *has sloppily made up)*

RUTH No—he don't half try at all 'cause he knows you going to come along behind him and fix everything. That's just how come he don't know how to do nothing right now—you done spoiled that boy so.

MAMA Well—he's a little boy. Ain't supposed to know 'bout housekeeping. My baby, that's what he is. What you fix for his breakfast this morning?

RUTH *(angrily)* I feed my son, Lena!

MAMA I ain't meddling—*(underbreath; busy-bodyish)* I just noticed all last week he had cold cereal, and when it starts getting this chilly in the fall a child ought to have some hot grits or something when he goes out in the cold—

RUTH *(furious)* I gave him hot oats—is that all right!

MAMA I ain't meddling. *(pause)* Put a lot of nice butter on it? *(*RUTH *shoots her an angry look and does not reply)* He likes lots of butter.

RUTH *(exasperated)* Lena—

MAMA *(to* BENEATHA. MAMA *is inclined to wander conversationally sometimes)* What was you and your brother fussing 'bout this morning?

BENEATHA It's not important, Mama.

(She gets up and goes to look out at the bathroom, which is apparently free, and she picks up her towels and rushes out)

MAMA What was they fighting about?

RUTH Now you know as well as I do.

MAMA *(shaking her head)* Brother still worrying hisself sick about that money?

RUTH You know he is.

MAMA You had breakfast?

RUTH Some coffee.

MAMA Girl, you better start eating and looking after yourself better. You almost thin as Travis.

RUTH Lena—

MAMA Un-hunh?

RUTH What are you going to do with it?

MAMA Now don't you start, child. It's too early in the morning to be talking about money. It ain't Christian.

RUTH It's just that he got his heart set on that store—

MAMA You mean that liquor store that Willy Harris want him to invest in?

RUTH Yes—

MAMA We ain't no business people, Ruth. We just plain working folks.

RUTH Ain't nobody business people till they go into business. Walter Lee say colored people ain't never going to start getting ahead till they start gambling on some different kinds of things in the world—investments and things.

MAMA What done got into you, girl? Walter Lee done finally sold you on investing.

RUTH No. Mama, something is happening between Walter and me. I don't know what it is—but he needs something—something I can't give him any more. He needs this chance, Lena.

MAMA *(frowning deeply)* But liquor, honey—

RUTH Well—like Walter say—I spec people going to always be drinking themselves some liquor.

MAMA Well—whether they drinks it or not ain't none of my business. But whether I go into business selling it to 'em *is*, and I don't want that on my ledger this late in life. *(stopping suddenly and studying her daughter-in-law)* Ruth Younger, what's the matter with you today? You look like you could fall over right there.

RUTH I'm tired.

MAMA Then you better stay home from work today.

RUTH I can't stay home. She'd be calling up the agency and screaming at them, "My girl didn't come in today—send me somebody! My girl didn't come in!" Oh, she just have a fit . . .

MAMA Well, let her have it. I'll just call her up and say you got the flu—

RUTH *(laughing)* Why the flu?

MAMA 'Cause it sounds respectable to 'em. Something white people get, too. They know 'bout the flu. Otherwise they think you been cut up or something when you tell 'em you sick.

RUTH I got to go in. We need the money.

MAMA Somebody would of thought my children done all but starved to death the way they talk about money here late. Child, we got a great big old check coming tomorrow.

RUTH *(sincerely, but also self-righteously)* Now that's your money. It ain't got nothing to do with me. We all feel like that—Walter and Bennie and me—even Travis.

MAMA *(thoughtfully, and suddenly very far away)* Ten thousand dollars—

RUTH Sure is wonderful.

MAMA Ten thousand dollars.

RUTH You know what you should do, Miss Lena? You should take yourself a trip somewhere. To Europe or South America or someplace—

MAMA *(throwing up her hands at the thought)* Oh, child!

RUTH I'm serious. Just pack up and leave! Go on away and enjoy yourself some. Forget about the family and have yourself a ball for once in your life—

MAMA *(drily)* You sound like I'm just about ready to die. Who'd go with me? What I look like wandering 'round Europe by myself?

RUTH Shoot—these here rich white women do it all the time. They don't think nothing of packing up they suitcases and piling on one of them big steamships and—swoosh!—they gone, child.

MAMA Something always told me I wasn't no rich white woman.

RUTH Well—what are you going to do with it then?

MAMA I ain't rightly decided. *(thinking. She speaks now with emphasis)* Some of it got to be put away for Beneatha and her schoolin'—and ain't nothing going to touch that part of it. Nothing. *(she waits several seconds, trying to make up her mind about something, and looks at* RUTH *a little tentatively before going on)* Been thinking that we maybe could meet the notes on a little old two-story somewhere, with a yard where Travis could play in the summertime, if we use part of the insurance for a down payment and everybody kind of pitch in. I could maybe take on a little day work again, few days a week—

RUTH *(studying her mother-in-law furtively and concentrating on her ironing, anxious to encourage without seeming to)* Well, Lord knows, we've put enough rent into this here rat trap to pay for four houses by now . . .

MAMA *(looking up at the words "rat trap" and then looking around and leaning back and sighing—in a suddenly reflective mood—)* "Rat trap"—yes, that's all it is. *(smiling)* I remember just as well the day me and Big Walter moved in here. Hadn't been married but two weeks and wasn't planning on living here no more than a year. *(she shakes her head at the dissolved dream)* We was going to set away, little by little, don't you know, and buy a little place out in Morgan Park. We had even picked out the house. *(chuckling a little)* Looks right dumpy today. But Lord, child, you should know all the dreams I had 'bout buying that house and fixing it up and making me a little garden in the back— *(she waits and stops smiling)* And didn't none of it happen. *(dropping her hands in a futile gesture)*

RUTH *(keeps her head down, ironing)* Yes, life can be a barrel of disappointments, sometimes.

MAMA Honey, Big Walter would come in here some nights back then and slump down on that couch there and just look at the rug, and look at me and look at the rug and then back at me—and I'd know he was down then . . . really down. *(after a second very long and thoughtful pause; she is seeing back to times that only she can see)* And then, Lord, when I lost that baby—little Claude—I almost thought I was going to lose Big Walter too. Oh, that man grieved hisself! He was one man to love his children.

RUTH Ain't nothin' can tear at you like losin' your baby.

MAMA I guess that's how come that man finally worked hisself to death like he done. Like he was fighting his own war with this here world that took his baby from him.

RUTH He sure was a fine man, all right. I always liked Mr. Younger.

MAMA Crazy 'bout his children! God knows there was plenty wrong with Walter Younger—hard-headed, mean, kind of wild with women—plenty wrong with him. But he sure loved his children. Always wanted them to have something—be something. That's where Brother gets all these notions, I reckon. Big Walter used to say, he'd get right wet in the eyes sometimes, lean his head back with the water standing in his eyes and say, "Seem like God didn't see fit to give the black man nothing but dreams—but He did give us children to make them dreams seem worth while." *(she smiles)* He could talk like that, don't you know.

RUTH Yes, he sure could. He was a good man, Mr. Younger.

MAMA Yes, a fine man—just couldn't never catch up with his dreams, that's all.

*(*BENEATHA *comes in, brushing her hair and looking up to the ceiling, where the sound of a vacuum cleaner has started up)*

BENEATHA What could be so dirty on that woman's rugs that she has to vacuum them every single day?

RUTH I wish certain young women 'round

here who I could name would take inspiration about certain rugs in a certain apartment I could also mention.

BENEATHA *(shrugging)* How much cleaning can a house need, for Christ's sakes.

MAMA *(not liking the Lord's name used thus)* Bennie!

RUTH Just listen to her—just listen!

BENEATHA Oh, God!

MAMA If you use the Lord's name just one more time—

BENEATHA *(a bit of a whine)* Oh, Mama—

RUTH Fresh—just fresh as salt, this girl!

BENEATHA *(drily)* Well—if the salt loses its savor—

MAMA Now that will do. I just ain't going to have you 'round here reciting the scriptures in vain—you hear me?

BENEATHA How did I manage to get on everybody's wrong side by just walking into a room?

RUTH If you weren't so fresh—

BENEATHA Ruth, I'm twenty years old.

MAMA What time you be home from school today?

BENEATHA Kind of late. *(with enthusiasm)* Madeline is going to start my guitar lessons today.

*(*MAMA *and* RUTH *look up with the same expression)*

MAMA Your *what* kind of lessons?

BENEATHA Guitar.

RUTH Oh, Father!

MAMA How come you done taken it in your mind to learn to play the guitar?

BENEATHA I just want to, that's all.

MAMA *(smiling)* Lord, child, don't you know what to do with yourself? How long it going to be before you get tired of this now—like you got tired of that little play-acting group you joined last year? *(looking at Ruth)* And what was it the year before that?

RUTH The horseback-riding club for which she bought that fifty-five-dollar riding habit that's been hanging in the closet ever since!

MAMA *(to* BENEATHA*)* Why you got to flit so from one thing to another, baby?

BENEATHA *(sharply)* I just want to learn to play the guitar. Is there anything wrong with that?

MAMA Ain't nobody trying to stop you. I just wonders sometimes why you has to flit so from one thing to another all the time. You ain't never done nothing with all that camera equipment you brought home—

BENEATHA I don't flit! I—I experiment with different forms of expression—

RUTH Like riding a horse?

BENEATHA —People have to express themselves one way or another.

MAMA What is it you want to express?

BENEATHA *(angrily)* Me! *(*MAMA *and* RUTH *look at each other and burst into raucous laughter)* Don't worry—I don't expect you to understand.

MAMA *(to change the subject)* Who you going out with tomorrow night?

BENEATHA *(with displeasure)* George Murchison again.

MAMA *(pleased)* Oh—you getting a little sweet on him?

RUTH You ask me, this child ain't sweet on nobody but herself—*(underbreath)* Express herself! *(they laugh)*

BENEATHA Oh—I like George all right, Mama. I mean I like him enough to go out with him and stuff, but—

RUTH *(for devilment)* What does *and stuff* mean?

BENEATHA Mind your own business.

MAMA Stop picking at her now, Ruth. *(a thoughtful pause, and then a suspicious sudden look at her daughter as she turns in her chair for emphasis)* What *does* it mean?

BENEATHA *(wearily)* Oh, I just mean I couldn't ever really be serious about George. He's—he's so shallow.

RUTH Shallow—what do you mean he's shallow? He's *Rich!*

MAMA Hush, Ruth.

BENEATHA I know he's rich. He knows he's rich, too.

RUTH Well—what other qualities a man got to have to satisfy you, little girl?

BENEATHA You wouldn't even begin to understand. Anybody who married Walter could not possibly understand.

MAMA *(outraged)* What kind of way is that to talk about your brother?

BENEATHA Brother is a flip—let's face it.

MAMA *(to* RUTH*, helplessly)* What's a flip?

RUTH *(glad to add kindling)* She's saying he's crazy.

BENEATHA Not crazy. Brother isn't really crazy yet—he—he's an elaborate neurotic.

MAMA Hush your mouth!

BENEATHA As for George. Well. George looks good—he's got a beautiful car and he takes me to nice places and, as my sister-in-law says, he is probably the richest boy I will ever get to know and I even like him sometimes—but if the Youngers are sitting around waiting to see if their little Bennie is going to tie up the family with the Murchisons, they are wasting their time.

RUTH You mean you wouldn't marry George Murchison if he asked you someday? That pretty, rich thing? Honey, I knew you was odd—

BENEATHA No I would not marry him if all I felt for him was what I feel now. Besides, George's family wouldn't really like it.

MAMA Why not?

BENEATHA Oh, Mama—the Murchisons are honest-to-God-real-*live*-rich colored people, and the only people in the world who are more snobbish than rich white people are rich colored people. I thought everybody knew that. I've met Mrs. Murchison. She's a scene!

MAMA You must not dislike people 'cause they well off, honey.

BENEATHA Why not? It makes just as much sense as disliking people 'cause they are poor, and lots of people do that.

RUTH *(a wisdom-of-the-ages manner. To* MAMA*)* Well, she'll get over some of this—

BENEATHA Get over it? What are you talking about, Ruth? Listen, I'm going to be a doctor. I'm not worried about who I'm going to marry yet—if I ever get married.

MAMA *and* RUTH *If!*

MAMA Now, Bennie—

BENEATHA Oh, I probably will . . . but first I'm going to be a doctor, and George, for one, still thinks that's pretty funny. I couldn't be bothered with that. I am going to be a doctor and everybody around here better understand that!

MAMA *(kindly)* 'Course you going to be a doctor, honey, God willing.

BENEATHA *(drily)* God hasn't got a thing to do with it.

MAMA Beneatha—that just wasn't necessary.

BENEATHA Well—neither is God. I get sick of hearing about God.

MAMA Beneatha!

BENEATHA I mean it! I'm just tired of hearing about God all the time. What has He got to do with anything? Does he pay tuition?

MAMA You 'bout to get your fresh little jaw slapped!

RUTH That's just what she needs, all right!

BENEATHA Why? Why can't I say what I want to around here, like everybody else?

MAMA It don't sound nice for a young girl to say things like that—you wasn't brought up that way. Me and your father went to trouble to get you and Brother to church every Sunday.

BENEATHA Mama, you don't understand. It's all a matter of ideas, and God is just one idea I don't accept. It's not important. I am not going out and be immoral or commit crimes because I don't believe in God. I don't even think about it. It's just that I get tired of Him getting credit for all the things the human race achieves through its own stubborn effort. There simply is no blasted God—there is only man and it is he who makes miracles!

*(*MAMA *absorbs this speech, studies her daughter and rises slowly and crosses to* BENEATHA *and slaps her powerfully across the face. After, there is only silence and the daughter drops her eyes from her mother's face, and* MAMA *is very tall before her)*

MAMA Now—you say after me, in my mother's house there is still God. *(there is a long pause and* BENEATHA *stares at the floor wordlessly.* MAMA *repeats the phrase with precision and cool emotion)* In my mother's house there is still God.

BENEATHA In my mother's house there is still God.

(A long pause)

MAMA *(walking away from* BENEATHA*, too disturbed for triumphant posture. Stopping and turning back to her daughter)* There are some ideas we ain't going to have in this house. Not long as I am at the head of this family.

BENEATHA Yes, ma'am.

*(*MAMA *walks out of the room)*

RUTH *(almost gently, with profound understanding)* You think you a woman, Bennie—but you still a little girl. What you did was childish—so you got treated like a child.

BENEATHA I see. *(quietly)* I also see that everybody thinks it's all right for Mama to be a tyrant. But all the tyranny in the world will never put a God in the heavens! *(she picks up her books and goes out)*

RUTH *(goes to* MAMA'S *door)* She said she was sorry.

MAMA *(coming out, going to her plant)* They frightens me, Ruth. My children.

RUTH You got good children, Lena. They just a little off sometimes—but they're good.

MAMA No—there's something come down between me and them that don't let us understand each other and I don't know what it is. One done almost lost his mind thinking 'bout money all the time and the other done commence to talk about things I can't seem to understand in no form or fashion. What is it that's changing, Ruth?

RUTH *(soothingly, older than her years)* Now . . . you taking it all too seriously. You just got strong-willed children and it takes a strong woman like you to keep 'em in hand.

MAMA *(looking at her plant and sprinkling a little water on it)* They spirited all right, my children. Got to admit they got spirit—Bennie and Walter. Like this little old plant that ain't never had enough sunshine or nothing—and look at it . . .

(She has her back to RUTH, *who has had to stop ironing and lean against something and put the back of her hand to her forehead)*

RUTH *(trying to keep* MAMA *from noticing)* You . . . sure . . . loves that little old thing, don't you? . . .

MAMA Well, I always wanted me a garden like I used to see sometimes at the back of the houses down home. This plant is close as I ever got to having one. *(she looks out of the window as she replaces the plant)* Lord, ain't nothing as dreary as the view from this window on a dreary day, is there? Why ain't you singing this morning, Ruth? Sing that "No Ways Tired." That song always lifts me up so—*(she turns at last to see that* RUTH *has slipped quietly into a chair, in a state of semiconsciousness)* Ruth! Ruth honey—what's the matter with you . . . Ruth!

(Curtain)

Scene Two

(It is the following morning; a Saturday morning, and house cleaning is in progress at the YOUNGERS. *Furniture has been shoved hither and yon and* MAMA *is giving the kitchen-area walls a washing down.* BENEATHA, *in dungarees, with a handkerchief tied around her face, is spraying insecticide into the cracks in the walls. As they work, the radio is on and a Southside disk-jockey program is inappropriately filling the house with a rather exotic saxophone blues.* TRAVIS, *the sole idle one, is leaning on his arms, looking out of the window)*

TRAVIS Grandmama, that stuff Bennie is using smells awful. Can I go downstairs, please?

MAMA Did you get all them chores done already? I ain't seen you doing much.

TRAVIS Yes'm—finished early. Where did Mama go this morning?

MAMA *(looking at* BENEATHA*)* She had to go on a little errand.

TRAVIS Where?

MAMA To tend to her business.

TRAVIS Can I go outside then?

MAMA Oh, I guess so. You better stay right in front of the house, though . . . and keep a good lookout for the postman.

TRAVIS Yes'm. *(he starts out and decides to give his* AUNT BENEATHA *a good swat on the legs as he passes her)* Leave them poor little old cockroaches alone, they ain't bothering you none.

(He runs as she swings the spray gun at him both viciously and playfully. WALTER *enters from the bedroom and goes to the phone)*

MAMA Look out there, girl, before you be spilling some of that stuff on that child!

TRAVIS *(teasing)* That's right—look out now! *(he exits)*

BENEATHA *(drily)* I can't imagine that it would hurt him—it has never hurt the roaches.

MAMA Well, little boys' hides ain't as tough as Southside roaches.

WALTER *(into phone)* Hello—Let me talk to Willy Harris.

MAMA You better get over there behind the bureau. I seen one marching out of there like Napoleon yesterday.

WALTER Hello, Willy? It ain't come yet. It'll be here in a few minutes. Did the lawyer give you the papers?

BENEATHA There's really only one way to get rid of them, Mama—

MAMA How?

BENEATHA Set fire to this building.

WALTER Good. Good. I'll be right over.

BENEATHA Where did Ruth go, Walter?

WALTER I don't know. *(he exits abruptly)*

BENEATHA Mama, where did Ruth go?

MAMA *(looking at her with meaning)* To the doctor, I think.

BENEATHA The doctor? What's the matter? *(they exchange glances)* You don't think—

MAMA *(with her sense of drama)* Now I ain't saying what I think. But I ain't never been wrong 'bout a woman neither.

(The phone rings)

BENEATHA *(at the phone)* Hay-lo . . . *(pause, and a moment of recognition)* Well—when did you get back! . . . And how was it? . . . Of course I've missed you—in my way . . . This morning? No . . . house cleaning and all that and Mama hates it if I let people come over when the house is like this . . . You *have*? Well, that's different . . . What is it—Oh, what the hell, come on over . . . Right, see you then. *(she hangs up)*

MAMA *(who has listened vigorously, as is her habit)* Who is that you inviting over here with this house looking like this? You ain't got the pride you was born with!

BENEATHA Asagai doesn't care how houses look, Mama—he's an intellectual.

MAMA *Who?*

BENEATHA Asagai—Joseph Asagai. He's an African boy I met on campus. He's been studying in Canada all summer.

MAMA What's his name?

BENEATHA Asagai, Joseph. Ah-sah-guy . . . He's from Nigeria.

MAMA Oh, that's the little country that was founded by slaves way back . . .

BENEATHA No, Mama—that's Liberia.

MAMA I don't think I never met no African before.

BENEATHA Well, do me a favor and don't ask him a whole lot of ignorant questions about Africans. I mean, do they wear clothes and all that—

MAMA Well, now, I guess if you think we so ignorant 'round here maybe you shouldn't bring your friends here—

BENEATHA It's just that people ask such crazy things. All anyone seems to know about when it comes to Africa is Tarzan—

MAMA *(indignantly)* Why should I know anything about Africa?

BENEATHA Why do you give money at church for the missionary work?

MAMA Well, that's to help save people.

BENEATHA You mean save them from *heathenism*—

MAMA *(innocently)* Yes.

BENEATHA I'm afraid they need more salvation from the British and the French.

(RUTH *comes in forlornly and pulls off her coat with dejection. They both turn to look at her)*

RUTH *(dispiritedly)* Well, I guess from all the happy faces—everybody knows.

BENEATHA You pregnant?

MAMA Lord have mercy, I sure hope it's a little old girl. Travis ought to have a sister.

(BENEATHA *and* RUTH *give her a hopeless look for this grandmotherly enthusiasm)*

BENEATHA How far along are you?

RUTH Two months.

BENEATHA Did you mean to? I mean did you plan it or was it an accident?

MAMA What do you know about planning or not planning?

BENEATHA Oh, Mama.

RUTH *(wearily)* She's twenty years old, Lena.

BENEATHA Did you plan it, Ruth?

RUTH Mind your own business.

BENEATHA It is my business—where is he going to live, on the *roof*? *(there is silence following the remark as the three women react to the sense of it)* Gee—I didn't mean that, Ruth, honest. Gee, I don't feel like that at all. I—I think it is wonderful.

RUTH *(dully)* Wonderful.

BENEATHA Yes—really.

MAMA *(looking at* RUTH, *worried)* Doctor say everything going to be all right?

RUTH *(far away)* Yes—she says everything is going to be fine . . .

MAMA *(immediately suspicious)* "She"— What doctor you went to?

(RUTH *folds over, near hysteria)*

MAMA *(worriedly hovering over* RUTH*)* Ruth honey—what's the matter with you—you sick?

(RUTH *has her fists clenched on her thighs and is fighting hard to suppress a scream that seems to be rising in her)*

BENEATHA What's the matter with her, Mama?

MAMA *(working her fingers in* RUTH's *shoulder to relax her)* She be all right. Women gets right depressed sometimes when they get her way. *(speaking softly, expertly, rapidly)* Now you just relax. That's right . . . just lean back, don't think 'bout nothing at all . . . nothing at all—

RUTH I'm all right . . .

(The glassy-eyed look melts and then she collapses into a fit of heavy sobbing. The bell rings)

BENEATHA Oh, my God—that must be Asagai.

MAMA *(to* RUTH*)* Come on now, honey. You need to lie down and rest awhile . . . then have some nice hot food.

(They exit, RUTH's *weight on her mother-in-law.* BENEATHA, *herself profoundly disturbed, opens the door to admit a rather dramatic-looking young man with a large package)*

ASAGAI Hello, Alaiyo—

BENEATHA *(holding the door open and regarding him with pleasure)* Hello . . . *(long pause)* Well—come in. And please excuse everything. My mother was very upset about my letting anyone come here with the place like this.

ASAGAI *(coming into the room)* You look disturbed too . . . Is something wrong?

BENEATHA *(still at the door, absently)* Yes . . . we've all got acute ghetto-itus. *(she smiles and comes toward him, finding a cigarette and sitting)* So—sit down! How was Canada?

ASAGAI *(a sophisticate)* Canadian.

BENEATHA *(looking at him)* I'm very glad you are back.

ASAGAI *(looking back at her in turn)* Are you really?

BENEATHA Yes—very.

ASAGAI Why—you were quite glad when I went away. What happened?

BENEATHA You went away.

ASAGAI Ahhhhhhhh.

BENEATHA Before—you wanted to be so serious before there was time.

ASAGAI How much time must there be before one knows what one feels?

BENEATHA *(stalling this particular conversation. Her hands pressed together, in a deliberately childish gesture)* What did you bring me?

ASAGAI *(handing her the package)* Open it and see.

BENEATHA *(eagerly opening the package and drawing out some records and the colorful robes of a Nigerian woman)* Oh, Asagai! . . . You got them for me! . . . How beautiful . . . and the records too! *(She lifts out the robes and runs to the mirror with them and holds the drapery up in front of herself)*

ASAGAI *(coming to her at the mirror)* I shall have to teach you how to drape it properly. *(he flings the material about her for the moment and stands back to look at her)* Ah—*Oh-pay-gay-day, oh-gbah-mu-shay. (a Yoruba exclamation for admiration)* You wear it well . . . very well . . . mutilated hair and all.

BENEATHA *(turning suddenly)* My hair—what's wrong with my hair?

ASAGAI *(shrugging)* Were you born with it like that?

BENEATHA *(reaching up to touch it)* No . . . of course not. *She looks back to the mirror, disturbed)*

ASAGAI *(smiling)* How then?

BENEATHA You know perfectly well how . . . as crinkly as yours . . . that's how.

ASAGAI And it is ugly to you that way?

BENEATHA *(quickly)* Oh, no—not ugly . . . *(more slowly, apologetically)* But it's so hard to manage when it's, well—raw.

ASAGAI And so to accommodate that—you mutilate it every week?

BENEATHA It's not mutilation!

ASAGAI *(laughing aloud at her seriousness)* Oh . . . please! I am only teasing you because you are so very serious about these things. *(he stands back from her and folds his arms across his chest as he watches her pulling at her hair and frowning in the mirror)* Do you remember the first time you met me at school? . . . *(he laughs)* You came up to me and you said—and I thought you were the most serious little thing I had ever seen—you said: *(he imitates her)* "Mr. Asagai—I want very much to talk with you. About Africa. You see, Mr. Asagai, I am looking for my *identity!*" *(he laughs)*

BENEATHA *(turning to him, not laughing)* Yes—*(her face is quizzical, profoundly disturbed)*

ASAGAI *(still teasing and reaching out and taking her face in his hands and turning her profile to him)* Well . . . it is true that this is not so much a profile of a Hollywood queen as perhaps a queen of the Nile—*(a mock dismissal of the importance of the question)* But what does it matter? Assimilationism is so popular in your country.

BENEATHA *(wheeling, passionately, sharply)* I am not an assimilationist!

ASAGAI *(the protest hangs in the room for a moment and* ASAGAI *studies her, his laughter fading)* Such a serious one. *(there is a pause)* So—you like the robes? You must take excellent care of them—they are from my sister's personal wardrobe.

BENEATHA *(with incredulity)* You—you sent all the way home—for me?

ASAGAI *(with charm)* For you—I would do much more . . . Well, that is what I came for. I must go.

BENEATHA Will you call me Monday?

ASAGAI Yes . . . We have a great deal to talk about. I mean about identity and time and all that.

BENEATHA Time?

ASAGAI Yes. About how much time one needs to know what one feels.

BENEATHA You never understood that there is more than one kind of feeling which can exist between a man and a woman—or, at least, there should be.

ASAGAI *(shaking his head negatively but gently)* No. Between a man and a woman there need be only one kind of feeling. I have that for you . . . Now even . . . right this moment . . .

BENEATHA I know—and by itself—it won't do. I can find that anywhere.

ASAGAI For a woman it should be enough.

BENEATHA I know—because that's what it says in all the novels that men write. But it isn't. Go ahead and laugh—but I'm not interested in being someone's little episode in America or—*(with feminine vengeance)*—one of them! *(*ASAGAI *has burst into laughter again)* That's funny as hell, huh!

ASAGAI It's just that every American girl I have known has said that to me. White—black—in this you are all the same. And the same speech, too!

BENEATHA *(angrily)* Yuk, yuk, yuk!

ASAGAI It's how you can be sure that the world's most liberated women are not liberated at all. You all talk about it too much!

*(*MAMA *enters and is immediately all social charm because of the presence of a guest)*

BENEATHA Oh—Mama—this is Mr. Asagai.

MAMA How do you do?

ASAGAI *(total politeness to an elder)* How do you do, Mrs. Younger. Please forgive me for coming at such an outrageous hour on a Saturday.

MAMA Well, you are quite welcome. I just hope you understand that our house don't always look like this. *(chatterish)* You must come again. I would love to hear all about—*(not sure of the name)*—your country. I think it's so sad the way our American Negroes don't know nothing about Africa 'cept Tarzan and all that. And all that money they pour into these churches when they ought to be helping you people over there drive out them French and Englishmen done taken away your land. *(The mother flashes a slightly superior look at her daughter upon completion of the recitation)*

ASAGAI *(taken aback by this sudden and acutely unrelated expression of sympathy)* Yes . . . yes . . .

MAMA *(smiling at him suddenly and relaxing and looking him over)* How many miles is it from here to where you come from?

ASAGAI Many thousands.

MAMA *(looking at him as she would* WALTER*)* I bet you don't half look after yourself, being away from your mama either. I 'spec you better come 'round here from time to time and get yourself some decent home-cooked meals . . .

ASAGAI *(moved)* Thank you. Thank you very much. *(they are all quiet, then—)* Well . . . I must go. I will call you Monday, Alaiyo.

MAMA What's that he call you?

ASAGAI Oh—"Alaiyo." I hope you don't mind. It is what you would call a nickname, I think. It is a Yoruba word. I am a Yoruba.

MAMA *(looking at* BENEATHA*)* I—I thought he was from—

ASAGAI *(understanding)* Nigeria is my country. Yoruba is my tribal origin—

BENEATHA You didn't tell us what Alaiyo means . . . for all I know, you might be calling me Little Idiot or something . . .

ASAGAI Well . . . let me see . . . I do not know how just to explain it . . . The sense of a thing can be so different when it changes languages.

BENEATHA You're evading.

ASAGAI No—really it is difficult . . . *(thinking)* It means . . . it means One for Whom Bread—Food—Is Not Enough. *(he looks at her)* Is that all right?

BENEATHA *(understanding, softly)* Thank you.

MAMA *(looking from one to the other and not understanding any of it)* Well . . . that's nice . . . You must come see us again—Mr.—

ASAGAI Ah-sah-guy . . .

MAMA Yes . . . Do come again.

ASAGAI Good-bye. *(he exits)*

MAMA *(after him)* Lord, that's a pretty thing just went out here! *(insinuatingly, to her daughter)* Yes, I guess I see why we done commence to get so interested in Africa 'round here. Missionaries my aunt Jenny! *(she exits)*

BENEATHA Oh, Mama! . . .

(She picks up the Nigerian dress and holds it up to her in front of the mirror again. She sets the headdress on haphazardly and then notices her hair again and clutches at it and then replaces the headdress and frowns at herself. Then she starts to wriggle in front of the mirror as she thinks a Nigerian woman might. TRAVIS *enters and regards her)*

TRAVIS You cracking up?

BENEATHA Shut up.

(She pulls the headdress off and looks at herself in the mirror and clutches at her hair again and squinches her eyes as if trying to imagine something. Then, suddenly, she gets her raincoat and kerchief and hurriedly prepares for going out)

MAMA *(coming back into the room)* She's resting now. Travis, baby, run next door and ask Miss Johnson to please let me have a little kitchen cleanser. This here can is empty as Jacob's kettle.

TRAVIS I just came in.

MAMA Do as you told. *(he exits and she looks at her daughter)* Where you going?

BENEATHA *(halting at the door)* To become a queen of the Nile!

(She exits in a breathless blaze of glory. RUTH *appears in the bedroom doorway)*

MAMA Who told you to get up?

RUTH Ain't nothing wrong with me to be lying in no bed for. Where did Bennie go?

MAMA *(drumming her fingers)* Far as I could make out—to Egypt. (RUTH *just looks at her)* What time is it getting to?

RUTH Ten twenty. And the mailman going to ring that bell this morning just like he done every morning for the last umpteen years.

(TRAVIS *comes in with the cleanser can)*

TRAVIS She say to tell you that she don't have much.

MAMA *(angrily)* Lord, some people I could name sure is tight-fisted! *(directing her grandson)* Mark two cans of cleanser down on the list there. If she that hard up for kitchen cleanser, I sure don't want to forget to get her none!

RUTH Lena—maybe the woman is just short on cleanser—

MAMA *(not listening)* —Much baking powder as she done borrowed from me all these years, she could of done gone into the baking business!

(The bell sounds suddenly and sharply and all three are stunned—serious and silent—mid-speech. In spite of all the other conversations and distractions of the morning, this is what they have been waiting for, even TRAVIS, *who looks helplessly from his mother to his grandmother.* RUTH *is the first to come to life again)*

RUTH *(to* TRAVIS*)* Get down them steps, boy!

(TRAVIS *snaps to life and flies out to get the mail)*

MAMA *(her eyes wide, her hand to her breast)* You mean it done really come?

RUTH *(excited)* Oh, Miss Lena!

MAMA *(collecting herself)* Well . . . I don't know what we all so excited about 'round here for. We known it was coming for months.

RUTH That's a whole lot different from having it come and being able to hold it in your hands . . . a piece of paper worth ten thousand dollars . . . (TRAVIS *bursts back into the room. He holds the envelope high above his head, like a little dancer, his face is radiant and he is breathless. He moves to his grandmother with sudden slow ceremony and puts the envelope into her hands. She accepts it, and then merely holds it and looks at it)* Come on! Open it . . . Lord have mercy, I wish Walter Lee was here!

TRAVIS Open, it Grandmama!

MAMA *(staring at it)* Now you all be quiet. It's just a check.

RUTH Open it . . .

MAMA *(still staring at it)* Now don't act silly . . . We ain't never been no people to act silly 'bout no money—

RUTH *(swiftly)* We ain't never had none before—*open it!*

*(*MAMA *finally makes a good strong tear and pulls out the thin blue slice of paper and inspects it closely. The boy and his mother study it raptly over* MAMA'*s shoulders)*

MAMA *Travis! (she is counting off with doubt)* Is that the right number of zeros.

TRAVIS Yes'm . . . ten thousand dollars. Gaalee, Grandmama, you rich.

MAMA *(she holds the check away from her, still looking at it. Slowly her face sobers into a mask of unhappiness)* Ten thousand dollars. *(she hands it to* RUTH*)* Put it away somewhere, Ruth. *(she does not look at* RUTH*; her eyes seem to be seeing something somewhere very far off)* Ten thousand dollars they give you. Ten thousand dollars.

TRAVIS *(to his mother, sincerely)* What's the matter with Grandmama—don't she want to be rich?

RUTH *(distractedly)* You go on out and play now, baby. *(*TRAVIS *exits.* MAMA *starts wiping dishes absently, humming intently to herself.* RUTH *turns to her, with kind exasperation)* You've gone and got yourself upset.

MAMA *(not looking at her)* I spec if it wasn't for you all . . . I would just put that money away or give it to the church or something.

RUTH Now what kind of talk is that. Mr. Younger would just be plain mad if he could hear you talking foolish like that.

MAMA *(stopping and staring off)* Yes . . . he sure would. *(sighing)* We got enough to do with that money, all right. *(she halts then, and turns and looks at her daughter-in-law hard;* RUTH *avoids her eyes and* MAMA *wipes her hands with finality and starts to speak firmly to* RUTH*)* Where did you go today, girl?

RUTH To the doctor.

MAMA *(impatiently)* Now, Ruth . . . you know better than that. Old Doctor Jones is strange enough in his way but there ain't nothing 'bout him make somebody slip and call him "she"—like you done this morning.

RUTH Well, that's what happened—my tongue slipped.

MAMA You went to see that woman, didn't you?

RUTH *(defensively, giving herself away)* What woman you talking about?

MAMA *(angrily)* That woman who—

*(*WALTER *enters in great excitement)*

WALTER Did it come?

MAMA *(quietly)* Can't you give people a Christian greeting before you start asking about money?

WALTER *(to* RUTH*)* Did it come? *(*RUTH *unfolds the check and lays it quietly before him, watching him intently with thoughts of her own.* WALTER *sits down and grasps it close and counts off the zeros)* Ten thousand dollars—*(he turns suddenly, frantically to his mother and draws some papers out of his breast pocket)* Mama—look. Old Willy Harris put everything on paper—

MAMA Son—I think you ought to talk to your wife . . . I'll go on out and leave you alone if you want—

WALTER I can talk to her later—Mama, look—

MAMA Son—

WALTER WILL SOMEBODY PLEASE LISTEN TO ME TODAY!

MAMA *(quietly)* I don't 'low no yellin' in this house, Walter Lee, and you know it—*(*WALTER *stares at them in frustration and starts to speak several times)* And there ain't going to be no investing in no liquor stores. I don't aim to have to speak on that again.

(A long pause)

WALTER Oh—so you don't aim to have to speak on that again? So *you* have decided . . . *(crumpling his papers)* Well, *you* tell that to my boy tonight when you put him to sleep on the living-room couch . . . *(turning to* MAMA *and speaking directly to her)* Yeah—and tell it to my wife, Mama, tomorrow when she has to go out of here to look after somebody else's kids. And tell it to *me,* Mama, every time we need a new pair of curtains and I have to watch *you* go out and work in somebody's kitchen. Yeah, you tell me then! *(*WALTER *starts out)*

RUTH Where you going?

WALTER I'm going out!

RUTH Where?

WALTER Just out of this house somewhere—

RUTH *(getting her coat)* I'll come too.

WALTER I don't want you to come!

RUTH I got something to talk to you about, Walter.

WALTER That's too bad.

MAMA *(still quietly)* Walter Lee—*(she waits and he finally turns and looks at her)* Sit down.

WALTER I'm a grown man, Mama.

MAMA Ain't nobody said you wasn't grown. But you still in my house and my presence. And as long as you are—you'll talk to your wife civil. Now sit down.

RUTH *(suddenly)* Oh, let him go on out and drink himself to death! He makes me sick to my stomach! *(She flings her coat against him)*

WALTER *(violently)* And you turn mine too, baby! (RUTH *goes into their bedroom and slams the door behind her)* That was my greatest mistake—

MAMA *(still quietly)* Walter, what is the matter with you?

WALTER Matter with me? Ain't nothing the matter with *me!*

MAMA Yes there is. Something eating you up like a crazy man. Something more than me not giving you this money. The past few years I been watching it happen to you. You get all nervous acting and kind of wild in the eyes—(WALTER *jumps up impatiently at her words)* I said sit there now, I'm talking to you!

WALTER Mama—I don't need no nagging at me today.

MAMA Seem like you getting to a place where you always tied up in some kind of knot about something. But if anybody ask you 'bout it you just yell at 'em and bust out the house and go out and drink somewheres. Walter Lee, people can't live with that. Ruth's a good, patient girl in her way—but you getting to be too much. Boy, don't make the mistake of driving that girl away from you.

WALTER Why—what she do for me?

MAMA She loves you.

WALTER Mama—I'm going out. I want to go off somewhere and be by myself for a while.

MAMA I'm sorry 'bout your liquor store, son. It just wasn't the thing for us to do. That's what I want to tell you about—

WALTER I got to go out, Mama—*(he rises)*

MAMA It's dangerous, son.

WALTER What's dangerous?

MAMA When a man goes outside his home to look for peace.

WALTER *(beseechingly)* Then, why can't there never be no peace in this house then?

MAMA You done found it in some other house?

WALTER No—there ain't no woman! Why do women always think there's a woman somewhere when a man gets restless. *(coming to her)* Mama—Mama—I want so many things . . .

MAMA Yes, son—

WALTER I want so many things that they are driving me kind of crazy . . . Mama—look at me.

MAMA I'm looking at you. You a good-looking boy. You got a job, a nice wife, a fine boy and—

WALTER A job. *(looks at her)* Mama, a job? I open and close car doors all day long. I drive a man around in his limousine and I say, "Yes, sir; no, sir; very good, sir; shall I take the Drive, sir?" Mama, that ain't no kind of job . . . that ain't nothing at all. *(very quietly)* Mama, I don't know if I can make you understand.

MAMA Understand what, baby?

WALTER *(quietly)* Sometimes it's like I can see the future stretched out in front of me—just plain as day. The future, Mama. Hanging over there at the edge of my days. Just waiting for me—a big, looming blank space—full of *nothing.* Just waiting for *me. (pause)* Mama—sometimes when I'm downtown and I pass them cool, quiet-looking restaurants where them white boys are sitting back and talking 'bout things . . . sitting there turning deals worth millions of dollars . . . sometimes I see guys don't look much older than me—

MAMA Son—how come you talk so much 'bout money?

WALTER *(with immense passion)* Because it is life, Mama!

MAMA *(quietly)* Oh—*(very quietly)* So now it's life. Money is life. Once upon a time freedom used to be life—now it's money. I guess the world really do change . . .

WALTER No—it was always money, Mama. We just didn't know about it.

MAMA No . . . something has changed. *(she*

looks at him) You something new, boy. In my time we was worried about not being lynched and getting to the North if we could and how to stay alive and still have a pinch of dignity too . . . Now here come you and Beneatha—talking 'bout things we ain't never even thought about hardly, me and your daddy. You ain't satisfied or proud of nothing we done. I mean that you had a home; that we kept you out of trouble till you was grown; that you don't have to ride to work on the back of nobody's streetcar— You my children—but how different we done become.

WALTER You just don't understand, Mama, you just don't understand.

MAMA Son—do you know your wife is expecting another baby? *(*WALTER *stands, stunned, and absorbs what his mother has said)* That's what she wanted to talk to you about. *(*WALTER *sinks down into a chair)* This ain't for me to be telling—but you ought to know. *(she waits)* I think Ruth is thinking 'bout getting rid of that child.

WALTER *(slowly understanding)* No—no—Ruth wouldn't do that.

MAMA When the world gets ugly enough—a woman will do anything for her family. *The part that's already living.*

WALTER You don't know Ruth, Mama, if you think she would do that.

*(*RUTH *opens the bedroom door and stands there a little limp)*

RUTH *(beaten)* Yes I would too, Walter. *(pause)* I gave her a five-dollar down payment.

(There is total silence as the man stares at his wife and the mother stares at her son)

MAMA *(presently)* Well—*(tightly)* Well—son, I'm waiting to hear you say something . . . I'm waiting to hear how you be your father's son. Be the man he was . . . *(pause)* Your wife say she going to destroy your child. And I'm waiting to hear you talk like him and say we a people who give children life, not who destroys them—*(she rises)* I'm waiting to see you stand up and look like your daddy and say we done give up one baby to poverty and that we ain't going to give up nary another one . . . I'm waiting.

WALTER Ruth—

MAMA If you a son of mine, tell her! *(*WALTER *turns, looks at her and can say nothing. She continues, bitterly)* You . . . you are a disgrace to your father's memory. Somebody get me my hat.

(Curtain)

ACT TWO

Scene One

TIME *Later the same day.*

AT RISE RUTH *is ironing again. She has the radio going. Presently* BENEATHA'S *bedroom door opens and* RUTH'S *mouth falls and she puts down the iron in fascination)*

RUTH What have we got on tonight!

BENEATHA *(emerging grandly from the doorway so that we can see her thoroughly robed in the costume Asagai brought)* You are looking at what a well-dressed Nigerian woman wears—*(she parades for* RUTH, *her hair completely hidden by her headdress; she is coquettishly fanning herself with an ornate oriental fan, mistakenly more like Butterfly than any Nigerian that ever was)* Isn't it beautiful? *(she promenades to the radio and, with an arrogant flourish, turns off the good loud blues that is playing)* Enough of this assimilationist junk! *(*RUTH *follows her with her eyes as she goes to the phonograph and puts on a record and turns and waits ceremoniously for the music to come up. Then, with a shout—)* OCOMOGOSIAY!

*(*RUTH *jumps. The music comes up, a lovely Nigerian melody.* BENEATHA *listens, enraptured, her eyes far away—"back to the past." She begins to dance.* RUTH *is dumfounded)*

RUTH What kind of dance is that?

BENEATHA A folk dance.

RUTH *(Pearl Bailey)* What kind of folks do that, honey?

BENEATHA It's from Nigeria. It's a dance of welcome.

RUTH Who you welcoming?

BENEATHA The men back to the village.

RUTH Where they been?

BENEATHA How should I know—out hunting or something. Anyway, they are coming back now . . .

RUTH Well, that's good.

BENEATHA *(with the record)*

Alundi, alundi
Alundi alunya
Jop pu a jeepua
Ang gu soooooooooo

Ai yai yae . . .
Ayehaye—alundi . . .

*(*WALTER *comes in during this performance; he has obviously been drinking. He leans against the door heavily and watches his sister, at first with distaste. Then his eyes look off—"back to the past"—as he lifts both his fists to the roof, screaming)*

WALTER YEAH . . . AND ETHIOPIA STRETCH FORTH HER HANDS AGAIN! . . .

RUTH *(drily, looking at him)* Yes—and Africa sure is claiming her own tonight. *(she gives them both up and starts ironing again)*

WALTER *(all in a drunken, dramatic shout)* Shut up! . . . I'm digging them drums . . . them drums move me! . . . *(he makes his weaving way to his wife's face and leans in close to her)* In my heart of hearts *(he thumps his chest)* I am much warrior!

RUTH *(without even looking up)* In your heart of hearts you are much drunkard.

WALTER *(coming away from her and starting to wander around the room, shouting)* Me and Jomo . . . *(intently, in his sister's face. She has stopped dancing to watch him in this unknown mood)* That's my man, Kenyatta. *(shouting and thumping his chest)* FLAMING SPEAR! HOT DAMN! *(he is suddenly in possession of an imaginary spear and actively spearing enemies all over the room)* OCOMOGOSIAY . . . THE LION IS WAKING . . . OWIMOWEH! *(he pulls his shirt open and leaps up on a table and gestures with his spear. The bell rings.* RUTH *goes to answer)*

BENEATHA *(to encourage* WALTER*, thoroughly caught up with this side of him)* OCOMOGOSIAY, FLAMING SPEAR!

WALTER *(on the table, very far gone, his eyes pure glass sheets. He sees what we cannot, that he is a leader of his people, a great chief, a descendant of Chaka, and that the hour to march has come)* Listen, my black brothers—

BENEATHA OCOMOGOSIAY!

WALTER —Do you hear the waters rushing against the shores of the coastlands—

BENEATHA OCOMOGOSIAY!

WALTER —Do you hear the screeching of the cocks in yonder hills beyond where the chiefs meet in council for the coming of the mighty war—

BENEATHA OCOMOGOSIAY!

WALTER —Do you hear the beating of the wings of the birds flying low over the mountains and the low places of our land—

*(*RUTH *opens the door.* GEORGE MURCHISON *enters)*

BENEATHA OCOMOGOSIAY!

WALTER —Do you hear the singing of the women, singing the war songs of our fathers to the babies in the great houses . . . singing the sweet war songs? OH, DO YOU HEAR, MY BLACK BROTHERS!

BENEATHA *(completely gone)* We hear you, Flaming Spear—

WALTER Telling us to prepare for the greatness of the time—*(to* GEORGE*)* Black Brother! *(he extends his hand for the fraternal clasp)*

GEORGE Black Brother, hell!

RUTH *(having had enough, and embarrassed for the family)* Beneatha, you got company—what's the matter with you? Walter Lee Younger, get down off that table and stop acting like a fool . . .

*(*WALTER *comes down off the table suddenly and makes a quick exit to the bathroom)*

RUTH He's had a little to drink . . . I don't know what her excuse is.

GEORGE *(to* BENEATHA*)* Look honey, we're going *to* the theatre—we're not going to be *in* it . . . so go change, huh?

RUTH You expect this boy to go out with you looking like that?

BENEATHA *(looking at* GEORGE*)* That's up to George. If he's ashamed of his heritage—

GEORGE Oh, don't be so proud of yourself, Bennie—just because you look eccentric.

BENEATHA How can something that's natural be eccentric?

GEORGE That's what being eccentric means—being natural. Get dressed.

BENEATHA I don't like that, George.

RUTH Why must you and your brother make an argument out of everything people say?

BENEATHA Because I hate assimilationist Negroes!

RUTH Will somebody please tell me what assimila-whoever means!

GEORGE Oh, it's just a college girl's way of calling people Uncle Toms—but that isn't what it means at all.

RUTH Well, what does it mean?

BENEATHA *(cutting* GEORGE *off and staring at him as she replies to* RUTH*)* It means someone who is willing to give up his own culture and submerge himself completely in the dominant, and in this case, *oppressive* culture!

GEORGE Oh, dear, dear, dear! Here we go! A lecture on the African past! On our Great West African Heritage! In one second we will hear all about the great Ashanti empires; the great Songhay civilizations; and the great sculpture of Bénin—and then some poetry in the Bantu—and the whole monologue will end with the word *heritage! (nastily)* Let's face it, baby, your heritage is nothing but a bunch of raggedy-assed spirituals and some grass huts!

BENEATHA *Grass huts! (*RUTH *crosses to her and forcibly pushes her toward the bedroom)* See there . . . you are standing there in your splendid ignorance talking about people who were the first to smelt iron on the face of the earth! *(*RUTH *is pushing her through the door)* The Ashanti were performing surgical operations when the English—*(*RUTH *pulls the door to, with* BENEATHA *on the other side, and smiles graciously at* GEORGE. BENEATHA *opens the door and shouts the end of the sentence defiantly at* GEORGE*)*—were still tattooing themselves with blue dragons . . . *(she goes back inside)*

RUTH Have a seat, George. *(they both sit.* RUTH *folds her hands rather primly on her lap, determined to demonstrate the civilization of the family)* Warm, ain't it? I mean for September. *(pause)* Just like they always say about Chicago weather: If it's too hot or cold for you, just wait a minute and it'll change. *(she smiles happily at this cliché of clichés)* Everybody say it's got to do with them bombs and things they keep setting off. *(pause)* Would you like a nice cold beer?

GEORGE No, thank you. I don't care for beer. *(he looks at his watch)* I hope she hurries up.

RUTH What time is the show?

GEORGE It's an eight-thirty curtain. That's just Chicago, though. In New York standard curtain time is eight forty. *(he is rather proud of this knowledge)*

RUTH *(properly appreciating it)* You get to New York a lot?

GEORGE *(offhand)* Few times a year.

RUTH Oh—that's nice. I've never been to New York.

*(*WALTER *enters. We feel he has relieved himself, but the edge of unreality is still with him)*

WALTER New York ain't got nothing Chicago ain't. Just a bunch of hustling people all squeezed up together—being "Eastern." *(he turns his face into a screw of displeasure)*

GEORGE Oh—you've been?

WALTER *Plenty* of times.

RUTH *(shocked at the lie)* Walter Lee Younger!

WALTER *(staring her down)* Plenty! *(pause)* What we got to drink in this house? Why don't you offer this man some refreshment. *(to* GEORGE*)* They don't know how to entertain people in this house, man.

GEORGE Thank you—I don't really care for anything.

WALTER *(feeling his head; sobriety coming)* Where's Mama?

RUTH She ain't come back yet.

WALTER *(looking* MURCHISON *over from head to toe, scrutinizing his carefully casual tweed sports jacket over cashmere V-neck sweater over soft eyelet shirt and tie, and soft slacks, finished off with white buckskin shoes)* Why all you college boys wear them fairyish-looking white shoes?

RUTH Walter Lee!

*(*GEORGE MURCHISON *ignores the remark)*

WALTER *(to* RUTH*)* Well, they look crazy as hell—white shoes, cold as it is.

RUTH *(crushed)* You have to excuse him—

WALTER No he don't! Excuse me for what? What you always excusing me for! I'll excuse myself when I needs to be excused! *(a pause)* They look as funny as them black knee socks Beneatha wears out of here all the time.

RUTH It's the college *style,* Walter.

WALTER Style, hell. She looks like she got burnt legs or something!

RUTH Oh, Walter—

WALTER *(an irritable mimic)* Oh, Walter! Oh, Walter! *(to* MURCHISON*)* How's your old man making out? I understand you all going to buy that big hotel on the Drive? *(he finds a* *beer in the refrigerator, wanders over to* MURCHISON, *sipping and wiping his lips with the back of his hand, and straddling a chair backwards to talk to the other man)* Shrewd move. Your old man is all right, man. *(tapping his head and half winking for emphasis)* I mean he knows how to operate. I mean he thinks *big,* you know what I mean, I mean for a *home,* you know? But I think he's kind of running out of ideas now. I'd like to talk to him. Listen, man, I got some plans that could turn this city upside down. I mean I think like he does. *Big.* Invest big, gamble big, hell, lose *big* if you have to, you know what I mean. It's hard to find a man on this whole Southside who understands my kind of thinking—you dig? *(he scrutinizes* MURCHISON *again, drinks his beer, squints his eyes and leans in close, confidential, man to man)* Me and you ought to sit down and talk sometimes, man. Man, I got me some ideas . . .

MURCHISON *(with boredom)* Yeah—sometimes we'll have to do that, Walter.

WALTER *(understanding the indifference, and offended)* Yeah—well, when you get the time, man. I know you a busy little boy.

RUTH Walter, please—

WALTER *(bitterly, hurt)* I know ain't nothing in this world as busy as you colored college boys with your fraternity pins and white shoes . . .

RUTH *(covering her face with humiliation)* Oh, Walter Lee—

WALTER I see you all all the time—with the books tucked under your arms—going to your *(British A—a mimic)* "clahsses." And for what! What the hell you learning over there? Filling up your heads—*(counting off on his fingers)*—with the sociology and the psychology—but they teaching you how to be a man? How to take over and run the world? They teaching you how to run a rubber plantation or a steel mill? Naw—just to talk proper and read books and wear white shoes . . .

GEORGE *(looking at him with distaste, a little above it all)* You're all wacked up with bitterness, man.

WALTER *(intently, almost quietly, between the teeth, glaring at the boy)* And you—ain't you bitter, man? Ain't you just about had it yet? Don't you see no stars gleaming that you can't reach out and grab? You happy?—you contented son-of-a-bitch—you happy? You got it made? Bitter? Man, I'm a volcano. Bitter? Here I am a giant—surrounded by ants! Ants who can't even understand what it is the giant is talking about.

RUTH *(passionately and suddenly)* Oh, Walter—ain't you with nobody!

WALTER *(violently)* No! 'Cause ain't nobody with me! Not even my own mother!

RUTH Walter, that's a terrible thing to say!

(BENEATHA *enters, dressed for the evening in a cocktail dress and earrings)*

GEORGE Well—hey, you look great.

BENEATHA Let's go, George. See you all later.

RUTH Have a nice time.

GEORGE Thanks. Good night. *(to* WALTER, *sarcastically)* Good night, *Prometheus.*

(BENEATHA *and* GEORGE *exit)*

WALTER *(to* RUTH*)* Who is Prometheus?

RUTH I don't know. Don't worry about it.

WALTER *(in fury, pointing after* GEORGE*)* See there—they get to a point where they can't insult you man to man—they got to go talk about something ain't nobody never heard of!

RUTH How you know it was an insult? *(to humor him)* Maybe Prometheus is a nice fellow.

WALTER Prometheus! I bet there ain't even no such thing! I bet that simple-minded clown—

RUTH Walter—*(she stops what she is doing and looks at him)*

WALTER *(yelling)* Don't start!

RUTH Start what?

WALTER Your nagging! Where was I? Who was I with? How much money did I spend?

RUTH *(plaintively)* Walter Lee—why don't we just try to talk about it . . .

WALTER *(not listening)* I been out talking with people who understand me. People who care about the things I got on my mind.

RUTH *(wearily)* I guess that means people like Willy Harris.

WALTER Yes, people like Willy Harris.

RUTH *(with a sudden flash of impatience)* Why don't you all just hurry up and go into the banking business and stop talking about it!

WALTER Why? You want to know why? 'Cause we all tied up in a race of people that don't know how to do nothing but moan, pray and have babies! *(the line is too bitter even for him and he looks at her and sits down)*

RUTH Oh, Walter . . . *(softly)* Honey, why can't you stop fighting me?

WALTER *(without thinking)* Who's fighting you? Who even cares about you? *(this line begins the retardation of his mood)*

RUTH Well—*(she waits a long time, and then with resignation starts to put away her things)* I guess I might as well go on to bed . . . *(more or less to herself)* I don't know where we lost it . . . but we have . . . *(then, to him)* I—I'm sorry about this new baby, Walter. I guess maybe I better go on and do what I started . . . I guess I just didn't realize how bad things was with us . . . I guess I just didn't really realize—*(she starts out to the bedroom and stops)* You want some hot milk?

WALTER Hot milk?

RUTH Yes—hot milk.

WALTER Why hot milk?

RUTH 'Cause after all that liquor you come home with you ought to have something hot in your stomach.

WALTER I don't want no milk.

RUTH You want some coffee then?

WALTER No, I don't want no coffee. I don't want nothing hot to drink. *(almost plaintively)* Why you always trying to give me something to eat?

RUTH *(standing and looking at him helplessly)* What else can I give you, Walter Lee Younger?

(She stands and looks at him and presently turns to go out again. He lifts his head and watches her going away from him in a new mood which began to emerge when he asked her "Who cares about you?")

WALTER It's been rough, ain't it, baby? *(she hears and stops but does not turn around and he continues to her back)* I guess between two people there ain't never as much understood as folks generally thinks there is. I mean like between me and you—*(she turns to face him)* How we gets to the place where we scared to talk softness to each other. *(he waits, thinking hard himself)* Why you think it got to be like that? *(he is thoughtful, almost as a child would be)* Ruth, what is it gets into people ought to be close?

RUTH I don't know, honey. I think about it a lot.

WALTER On account of you and me, you mean? The way things are with us. The way something done come down between us.

RUTH There ain't so much between us, Walter . . . Not when you come to me and try to talk to me. Try to be with me . . . a little even.

WALTER *(total honesty)* Sometimes . . . sometimes . . . I don't even know how to try.

RUTH Walter—

WALTER Yes?

RUTH *(coming to him, gently and with misgiving, but coming to him)* Honey . . . life don't have to be like this. I mean sometimes people can do things so that things are better . . . You remember how we used to talk when Travis was born . . . about the way we were going to live . . . the kind of house . . . *(she is stroking his head)* Well, it's all starting to slip away from us . . .

*(*MAMA *enters, and* WALTER *jumps up and shouts at her)*

WALTER Mama, where have you been?

MAMA My—them steps is longer than they used to be. Whew! *(she sits down and ignores him)* How you feeling this evening, Ruth?

*(*RUTH *shrugs, disturbed some at having been prematurely interrupted and watching her husband knowingly)*

WALTER Mama, where have you been all day?

MAMA *(still ignoring him and leaning on the table and changing to more comfortable shoes)* Where's Travis?

RUTH I let him go out earlier and he ain't come back yet. Boy, is he going to get it!

WALTER Mama!

MAMA *(as if she has heard him for the first time)* Yes, son?

WALTER Where did you go this afternoon?

MAMA I went down town to tend to some business that I had to tend to.

WALTER What kind of business?

MAMA You know better than to question me like a child, Brother.

WALTER *(rising and bending over the table)* Where were you, Mama? *(bringing his fists down and shouting)* Mama, you didn't go do something with that insurance money, something crazy?

(The front door opens slowly, interrupting him, and TRAVIS *peeks his head in, less than hopefully)*

TRAVIS *(to his mother)* Mama, I—

RUTH "Mama I" nothing! You're going to

get it, boy! Get on in that bedroom and get yourself ready!

TRAVIS But I—

MAMA Why don't you all never let the child explain hisself.

RUTH Keep out of it now, Lena. (MAMA *clamps her lips together, and* RUTH *advances toward her son menacingly)* A thousand times I have told you not to go off like that—

MAMA *(holding out her arms to her grandson)* Well—at least let me tell him something. I want him to be the first one to hear . . . Come here, Travis. *(the boy obeys, gladly)* Travis—*(she takes him by the shoulders and looks into his face)*—you know that money we got in the mail this morning?

TRAVIS Yes'm—

MAMA Well—what you think your grandmama gone and done with that money?

TRAVIS I don't know, Grandmama.

MAMA *(putting her finger on his nose for emphasis)* She went out and she bought you a house! *(the explosion comes from* WALTER *at the end of the revelation and he jumps up and turns away from all of them in a fury.* MAMA *continues, to* TRAVIS*)* You glad about the house? It's going to be yours when you get to be a man.

TRAVIS Yeah—I always wanted to live in a house.

MAMA All right, gimme some sugar then—(TRAVIS *puts his arms around her neck as she watches her son over the boy's shoulder. Then, to* TRAVIS, *after the embrace)* Now when you say your prayers tonight, you thank God and your grandfather—'cause it was him who give you the house—in his way.

RUTH *(taking the boy from* MAMA *and pushing him toward the bedroom)* Now you get out of here and get ready for your beating.

TRAVIS Aw, Mama—

RUTH Get on in there—*(closing the door behind him and turning radiantly to her mother-in-law)* So you went and did it!

MAMA *(quietly, looking at her son with pain)* Yes, I did.

RUTH *(raising both arms classically)* *Praise God! (looks at* WALTER *a moment, who says nothing. She crosses rapidly to her husband)* Please, honey—let me be glad . . . you be glad too. *(she has laid her hands on his shoulders, but he shakes himself free of her roughly, without turning to face her)* Oh, Walter . . . a home . . . *a home. (She comes back to* MAMA*)* Well—where is it? How big is it? How much it going to cost?

MAMA Well—

RUTH When we moving?

MAMA *(smiling at her)* First of the month.

RUTH *(throwing back her head with jubilance)* *Praise God!*

MAMA *(tentatively, still looking at her son's back turned against her and* RUTH*)* It's—it's a nice house too . . . *(she cannot help speaking directly to him. An imploring quality in her voice, her manner, makes her almost like a girl now)* Three bedrooms—nice big one for you and Ruth . . . Me and Beneatha still have to share our room, but Travis have one of his own—and—*(with difficulty)* I figures if the—new baby—is a boy, we could get one of them double-decker outfits . . . And there's a yard with a little patch of dirt where I could maybe get to grow me a few flowers . . . And a nice big basement . . .

RUTH Walter honey, be glad—

MAMA *(still to his back, fingering things on the table)* 'Course I don't want to make it sound fancier than it is . . . It's just a plain little old house—but it's made good and solid—and it will be *ours*. Walter Lee—it makes a difference in a man when he can walk on floors that belong to *him* . . .

RUTH Where is it?

MAMA *(frightened at this telling)* Well—well—it's out there in Clybourne Park—

(RUTH'S *radiance fades abruptly, and* WALTER *finally turns slowly to face his mother with incredulity and hostility)*

RUTH Where?

MAMA *(matter-of-factly)* Four o six Clybourne Street, Clybourne Park.

RUTH Clybourne Park? Mama, there ain't no colored people living in Clybourne Park.

MAMA *(almost idiotically)* Well, I guess there's going to be some now.

WALTER *(bitterly)* So that's the peace and comfort you went out and bought for us today!

MAMA *(raising her eyes to meet his finally)* Son—I just tried to find the nicest place for the least amount of money for my family.

RUTH *(trying to recover from the shock)* Well—well—'course I ain't one never been 'fraid of no crackers, mind you—but—well, wasn't there no other houses nowhere?

MAMA Them houses they put up for colored in them areas way out all seem to cost twice as much as other houses. I did the best I could.

RUTH *(struck senseless with the news, in its various degrees of goodness and trouble, she sits a moment, her fists propping her chin in thought, and then she starts to rise, bringing her fists down with vigor, the radiance spreading from cheek to cheek again)* Well—well!—All I can say is—if this is my time in life—*my time*—to say good-bye—*(and she builds with momentum as she starts to circle the room with an exuberant, almost tearfully happy release)*—to these God-damned cracking walls!—*(she pounds the walls)*—and these marching roaches!—*(she wipes at an imaginary army of marching roaches)*—and this cramped little closet which ain't now or never was no kitchen! . . . then I say it loud and good, *Hallelujah! and good-bye misery . . . I don't never want to see your ugly face again! (she laughs joyously, having practically destroyed the apartment, and flings her arms up and lets them come down happily, slowly, reflectively, over her abdomen, aware for the first time perhaps that the life therein pulses with happiness and not despair)* Lena?

MAMA *(moved, watching her happiness)* Yes, honey?

RUTH *(looking off)* Is there—is there a whole lot of sunlight?

MAMA *(understanding)* Yes, child, there's a whole lot of sunlight.

(Long pause)

RUTH *(collecting herself and going to the door of the room* TRAVIS *is in)* Well—I guess I better see 'bout Travis. *(to* MAMA*)* Lord, I sure don't feel like whipping nobody today! *(she exits)*

MAMA *(the mother and son are left alone now and the mother waits a long time, considering deeply, before she speaks)* Son—you—you understand what I done, don't you? *(*WALTER *is silent and sullen)* I—I just seen my family falling apart today . . . just falling to pieces in front of my eyes . . . We couldn't of gone on like we was today. We was going backwards 'stead of forwards—talking 'bout killing babies and wishing each other was dead . . . When it gets like that in life—you just got to do something different, push on out and do something bigger . . . *(she waits)* I wish you say something, son . . . I wish you'd say how deep inside you you think I done the right thing—

WALTER *(crossing slowly to his bedroom door and finally turning there and speaking measuredly)* What you need me to say you done right for? *You* the head of this family. You run our lives like you want to. It was your money and you did what you wanted with it. So what you need for me to say it was all right for? *(bitterly, to hurt her as deeply as he knows is possible)* So you butchered up a dream of mine—you—who always talking 'bout your children's dreams . . .

MAMA Walter Lee—

(He just closes the door behind him. MAMA *sits alone, thinking heavily. Curtain)*

Scene Two

TIME *Friday night. A few weeks later.*

AT RISE: *Packing crates mark the intention of the family to move.* BENEATHA *and* GEORGE *come in, presumably from an evening out again)*

GEORGE O.K. . . . O.K., whatever you say . . . *(they both sit on the couch. He tries to kiss her. She moves away)* Look, we've had a nice evening; let's not spoil it, huh? . . .

(He again turns her head and tries to nuzzle in and she turns away from him, not with distaste but with momentary lack of interest; in a mood to pursue what they were talking about)

BENEATHA I'm *trying* to talk to you.

GEORGE We always talk.

BENEATHA Yes—and I love to talk.

GEORGE *(exasperated; rising)* I know it and I don't mind it sometimes . . . I want you to cut it out, see— The moody stuff, I mean. I don't like it. You're a nice-looking girl . . . all over. That's all you need, honey, forget the atmosphere. Guys aren't going to go for the atmosphere—they're going to go for what they see. Be glad for that. Drop the Garbo routine. It doesn't go with you. As for myself, I want a nice—*(groping)*—simple—*(thoughtfully)*—sophisticated girl . . . not a poet—O.K.?

(She rebuffs him again and he starts to leave)

BENEATHA Why are you angry?

GEORGE Because this is stupid! I don't go out with you to discuss the nature of "quiet desperation" or to hear all about your thoughts—because the world will go on thinking what it thinks regardless—

BENEATHA Then why read books? Why go to school?

GEORGE *(with artificial patience, counting on his fingers)* It's simple. You read books—to learn facts—to get grades—to pass the course—to get a degree. That's all—it has nothing to do with thoughts.

(A long pause)

BENEATHA I see. *(a longer pause as she looks at him)* Good night, George.

*(*GEORGE *looks at her a little oddly, and starts to exit. He meets* MAMA *coming in)*

GEORGE Oh—hello, Mrs. Younger.

MAMA Hello, George, how you feeling?

GEORGE Fine—fine, how are you?

MAMA Oh, a little tired. You know them steps can get you after a day's work. You all have a nice time tonight?

GEORGE Yes—a fine time. Well, good night.

MAMA Good night. *(he exits.* MAMA *closes the door behind her)* Hello, honey. What you sitting like that for?

BENEATHA I'm just sitting.

MAMA Didn't you have a nice time?

BENEATHA No.

MAMA No? What's the matter?

BENEATHA Mama, George is a fool—honest. *(she rises)*

MAMA *(hustling around unloading the packages she has entered with. She stops)* Is he, baby?

BENEATHA Yes. *(*BENEATHA *makes up* TRAVIS' *bed as she talks)*

MAMA You sure?

BENEATHA Yes.

MAMA Well—I guess you better not waste your time with no fools.

*(*BENEATHA *looks up at her mother, watching her put groceries in the refrigerator. Finally she gathers up her things and starts into the bedroom. At the door she stops and looks back at her mother)*

BENEATHA Mama—

MAMA Yes, baby—

BENEATHA Thank you.

MAMA For what?

BENEATHA For understanding me this time.

(She exits quickly and the mother stands, smiling a little, looking at the place where BENEATHA *just stood.* RUTH *enters)*

RUTH Now don't you fool with any of this stuff, Lena—

MAMA Oh, I just thought I'd sort a few things out.

(The phone rings. RUTH *answers)*

RUTH *(at the phone)* Hello—Just a minute. *(goes to door)* Walter, it's Mrs. Arnold. *(waits. Goes back to the phone, tense)* Hello. Yes, this is his wife speaking . . . He's lying down now. Yes . . . well, he'll be in tomorrow. He's been very sick. Yes—I know we should have called, but we were so sure he'd be able to come in today. Yes—yes, I'm very sorry. Yes . . . Thank you very much. *(she hangs up.* WALTER *is standing in the doorway of the bedroom behind her)* That was Mrs. Arnold.

WALTER *(indifferently)* Was it?

RUTH She said if you don't come in tomorrow that they are getting a new man . . .

WALTER Ain't that sad—ain't that crying sad.

RUTH She said Mr. Arnold has had to take a cab for three days . . . Walter, you ain't been to work for three days! *(this is a revelation to her)* Where you been, Walter Lee Younger? *(*WALTER *looks at her and starts to laugh)* You're going to lose your job.

WALTER That's right . . .

RUTH Oh, Walter, and with your mother working like a dog every day—

WALTER That's sad too—Everything is sad.

MAMA What you been doing for these three days, son?

WALTER Mama—you don't know all the things a man what got leisure can find to do in this city . . . What's this—Friday night? Well—Wednesday I borrowed Willy Harris' car and I went for a drive . . . just me and myself and I drove and drove . . . Way out . . . way past South Chicago, and I parked the car and I sat and looked at the steel mills all day long. I just sat in the car and looked at them big black chimneys for hours. Then I drove back and I went to the Green Hat. *(pause)* And Thursday—Thursday I borrowed the car again and I got in it and I pointed it the other way and I drove the other way—for hours—way, way up to Wisconsin, and I looked at the farms. I just drove and looked at the farms. Then I drove back and I went to the Green Hat. *(pause)* And today—today I didn't get the car. Today I just walked. All over the Southside. And I looked at the Negroes and they looked at me and finally I just sat down on the curb at Thirty-ninth and South Parkway and I just sat there and watched the Negroes go by. And then I went to the Green Hat. You all sad? You all depressed? And you know where I am going right now—

(RUTH goes out quietly)

MAMA Oh, Big Walter, is this the harvest of our days?

WALTER You know what I like about the Green Hat? *(he turns the radio on and a steamy, deep blues pours into the room)* I like this little cat they got there who blows a sax . . . He blows. He talks to me. He ain't but 'bout five feet tall and he's got a conked head and his eyes is always closed and he's all music—

MAMA *(rising and getting some papers out of her handbag)* Walter—

WALTER And there's this other guy who plays the piano . . . and they got a sound. I mean they can work on some music . . . They got the best little combo in the world in the Green Hat . . . You can just sit there and drink and listen to them three men play and you realize that don't nothing matter worth a damn, but just being there—

MAMA I've helped do it to you, haven't I, son? Walter, I been wrong.

WALTER Naw—you ain't never been wrong about nothing, Mama.

MAMA Listen to me, now. I say I been wrong, son. That I been doing to you what the rest of the world been doing to you. *(she stops and he looks up slowly at her and she meets his eyes pleadingly)* Walter—what you ain't never understood is that I ain't got nothing, don't own nothing, ain't never really wanted nothing that wasn't for you. There ain't nothing as precious to me . . . There ain't nothing worth holding on to, money, dreams, nothing else—if it means—if it means it's going to destroy my boy. *(she puts her papers in front of him and he watches her without speaking or moving)* I paid the man thirty-five hundred dollars down on the house. That leaves sixty-five hundred dollars. Monday morning I want you to take this money and take three thousand dollars and put it in a savings account for Beneatha's medical schooling. The rest you put in a checking account—with your name on it. And from now on any penny that come out of it or that go in it is for you to look after. For you to decide. *(she drops her hands a little helplessly)* It ain't much, but it's all I got in the world and I'm putting it in your hands. I'm telling you to be the head of this family from now on like you supposed to be.

WALTER *(stares at the money)* You trust me like that, Mama?

MAMA I ain't never stop trusting you. Like I ain't never stop loving you.

(She goes out, and WALTER sits looking at the money on the table as the music continues in its idiom, pulsing in the room. Finally, in a decisive gesture, he gets up and, in a furious action, flings the bedclothes wildly from his son's makeshift bed to all over the floor—with a cry of desperation. Then he picks up the money and goes out in a hurry. Curtain)

Scene Three

TIME *Saturday, moving day, one week later.*

Before the curtain rises, RUTH's voice, a strident, dramatic church alto, cuts through the silence.

It is, in the darkness, a triumphant surge, a penetrating statement of expectation: "Oh, Lord, I don't feel no ways tired! Children, oh, glory hallelujah!"

As the curtain rises we see that RUTH is alone in the living room, finishing up the family's packing. It is moving day. She is nailing crates and tying cartons. BENEATHA enters, carrying a guitar case, and watches her exuberant sister-in-law)

RUTH Hey!

BENEATHA *(putting away the case)* Hi.

RUTH *(pointing at a package)* Honey—look in that package there and see what I found on sale this morning at the South Center. *(RUTH gets up and moves to the package and draws out some curtains)* Lookahere—hand-turned hems!

BENEATHA How do you know the window size out there?

RUTH *(who hadn't thought of that)* Oh—Well, they bound to fit something in the whole house. Anyhow, they was too good a bargain to pass up. *(RUTH slaps her head, suddenly remembering something)* Oh, Bennie—I meant to put a special note on that carton over there. That's your mama's good china and she wants 'em to be very careful with it.

BENEATHA I'll do it. (BENEATHA *finds a piece of paper and starts to draw large letters on it)*

RUTH You know what I'm going to do soon as I get in that new house?

BENEATHA What?

RUTH Honey—I'm going to run me a tub of water up to here . . . *(with her fingers practically up to her nostrils)* And I'm going to get in it—and I am going to sit . . . and sit . . . and sit in that hot water and the first person who knocks to tell *me* to hurry up and come out—

BENEATHA Gets shot at sunrise.

RUTH *(laughing happily)* You said, it, sister! *(noticing how large* BENEATHA *is absent-mindedly making the note)* Honey, they ain't going to read that from no airplane.

BENEATHA *(laughing herself)* I guess I always think things have more emphasis if they are big, somehow.

RUTH *(looking up at her and smiling)* You and your brother seem to have that as a philosophy of life. Lord, that man—done changed so 'round here. You know—you know what we did last night? Me and Walter Lee!

BENEATHA What?

RUTH *(smiling to herself)* We went to the movies. *(looking at* BENEATHA *to see if she understands)* We went to the movies. You know the last time me and Walter went to the movies together?

BENEATHA No.

RUTH Me neither. That's how long it been. *(smiling again)* But we went last night. The picture wasn't much good, but that didn't seem to matter. We went—and we held hands.

BENEATHA Oh, Lord!

RUTH We held hands—and you know what?

BENEATHA What?

RUTH When we come out of the show it was late and dark and all the stores and things was closed up . . . and it was kind of chilly and there wasn't many people on the streets . . . and we was still holding hands, me and Walter.

BENEATHA You're killing me.

*(*WALTER *enters with a large package. His happiness is deep in him; he cannot keep still with his new-found exuberance. He is singing and wiggling and snapping his fingers. He puts his package in a corner and puts a phonograph record, which he has brought in with him, on the record player. As the music comes up he dances over to* RUTH *and tries to get her to dance with him. She gives in at last to his raunchiness and in a fit of giggling allows herself to be drawn into his mood and together they deliberately burlesque an old social dance of their youth)*

BENEATHA *(regarding them a long time as they dance, then drawing in her breath for a deeply exaggerated comment which she does not particularly mean)* Talk about—olddddddddd-fashioned-dddddd—Negroes!

WALTER *(stopping momentarily)* What kind of Negroes?

(He says this in fun. He is not angry with her today, nor with anyone. He starts to dance with his wife again)

BENEATHA Old-fashioned.

WALTER *(as he dances with* RUTH*)* You know, when these *New Negroes* have their convention—*(pointing at his sister)*—that is going to be the chairman of the Committee on Unending Agitation. *(he goes on dancing, then stops)* Race, race, race! . . . Girl, I do believe you are the first person in the history of the entire human race to successfully brainwash yourself. *(*BENEATHA *breaks up and he goes on dancing. He stops again, enjoying his tease)* Damn, even the N double A C P takes a holiday sometimes! *(*BENEATHA *and* RUTH *laugh. He dances with* RUTH *some more and starts to laugh and stops and pantomimes someone over an operating table)* I can just see that chick someday looking down at some poor cat on an operating table before she starts to slice him, saying . . . *(pulling his sleeves back maliciously)* "By the way, what are your views on civil rights down there? . . ."

(He laughs at her again and starts to dance happily. The bell sounds)

BENEATHA Sticks and stones may break my bones but . . . words will never hurt me!

*(*BENEATHA *goes to the door and opens it as* WALTER *and* RUTH *go on with the clowning.* BENEATHA *is somewhat surprised to see a quiet-looking middle-aged white man in a business suit holding his hat and a briefcase in his hand and consulting a small piece of paper)*

MAN Uh—how do you do, miss. I am looking for a Mrs.—*(he looks at the slip of paper)* Mrs. Lena Younger?

BENEATHA *(smoothing her hair with slight embarrassment)* Oh—yes, that's my mother. Excuse me. *(She closes the door and turns to quiet the other two)* Ruth! Brother! Somebody's here. *(then she opens the door. The man casts a curious quick glance at all of them)* Uh—come in please.

MAN *(coming in)* Thank you.

BENEATHA My mother isn't here just now. Is it business?

MAN Yes . . . well, of a sort.

WALTER *(freely, the Man of the House)* Have a seat. I'm Mrs. Younger's son. I look after most of her business matters.

*(*RUTH *and* BENEATHA *exchange amused glances)*

MAN *(regarding* WALTER*, and sitting)* Well— My name is Karl Lindner . . .

WALTER *(stretching out his hand)* Walter Younger. This is my wife—*(*RUTH *nods politely)*—and my sister.

LINDNER How do you do.

WALTER *(amiably, as he sits himself easily on a chair, leaning with interest forward on his knees and looking expectantly into the newcomer's face)* What can we do for you, Mr. Lindner!

LINDNER *(Some minor shuffling of the hat and briefcase on his knees)* Well—I am a representative of the Clybourne Park Improvement Association—

WALTER *(pointing)* Why don't you sit your things on the floor?

LINDNER Oh—yes. Thank you. *(he slides the briefcase and hat under the chair)* And as I was saying—I am from the Clybourne Park Improvement Association and we have had it brought to our attention at the last meeting that you people—or at least your mother—has bought a piece of residential property at—*(he digs for the slip of paper again)*—four o six Clybourne Street . . .

WALTER That's right. Care for something to drink? Ruth, get Mr. Lindner a beer.

LINDNER *(upset for some reason)* Oh—no, really. I mean thank you very much, but no thank you.

RUTH *(innocently)* Some coffee?

LINDNER Thank you, nothing at all.

*(*BENEATHA *is watching the man carefully)*

LINDNER Well, I don't know how much you folks know about our organization. *(he is a gentle man; thoughtful and somewhat labored in his manner)* It is one of these community organizations set up to look after—oh, you know, things like block upkeep and special projects and we also have what we call our New Neighbors Orientation Committee . . .

BENEATHA *(drily)* Yes—and what do they do?

LINDNER *(turning a little to her and then returning the main force to* WALTER*)* Well—it's what you might call a sort of welcoming committee, I guess. I mean they, we, I'm the chairman of the committee—go around and see the new people who move into the neighborhood and sort of give them the lowdown on the way we do things out in Clybourne Park.

BENEATHA *(with appreciation of the two meanings, which escape* RUTH *and* WALTER*)* Un-huh.

LINDNER And we also have the category of what the association calls—*(he looks elsewhere)*—uh—special community problems . . .

BENEATHA Yes—and what are some of those?

WALTER Girl, let the man talk.

LINDNER *(with understated relief)* Thank you. I would sort of like to explain this thing in my own way. I mean I want to explain to you in a certain way.

WALTER Go ahead.

LINDNER Yes. Well. I'm going to try to get right to the point. I'm sure we'll all appreciate that in the long run.

BENEATHA Yes.

WALTER Be still now!

LINDNER Well—

RUTH *(still innocently)* Would you like another chair—you don't look comfortable.

LINDNER *(more frustrated than annoyed)* No, thank you very much. Please. Well—to get right to the point I—*(a great breath, and he is off at last)* I am sure you people must be aware of some of the incidents which have happened in various parts of the city when colored people have moved into certain areas—*(*BENEATHA *exhales heavily and starts tossing a piece of fruit up and down in the air)* Well—because we have what I think is going to be a unique type of organization in American community life—not only do we deplore that kind of thing—but we are trying to do something about it. *(*BENEATHA *stops tossing and turns with a new and quizzical interest to the man)* We feel—*(gaining confidence in his mission because of the interest in the faces of the people he is talking to)*—we feel that most of the trouble in this world, when you come right down to it—*(he hits his knee for emphasis)*—most of the trouble exists because people just don't sit down and talk to each other.

RUTH *(nodding as she might in church, pleased with the remark)* You can say that again, mister.

LINDNER *(more encouraged by such affirmation)* That we don't try hard enough in this world to understand the other fellow's problem. The other guy's point of view.

RUTH Now that's right.

*(*BENEATHA *and* WALTER *merely watch and listen with genuine interest)*

LINDNER Yes—that's the way we feel out in Clybourne Park. And that's why I was elected to come here this afternoon and talk to you people. Friendly like, you know, the way people should talk to each other and see if we couldn't find some way to work this thing out. As I say, the whole business is a matter of *caring* about the other fellow. Anybody can see that you are a nice family of folks, hard working and honest I'm sure. *(*BENEATHA *frowns slightly, quizzically, her head tilted regarding him)* Today everybody knows what it means to be on the outside of *something.* And of course, there is always somebody who is out to take advantage of people who don't always understand.

WALTER What do you mean?

LINDNER Well—you see our community is made up of people who've worked hard as the dickens for years to build up that little community. They're not rich and fancy people; just hard-working, honest people who don't really have much but those little homes and a dream of the kind of community they want to raise their children in. Now, I don't say we are perfect and there is a lot wrong in some of the things they want. But you've got to admit that a man, right or wrong, has the right to want to have the neighborhood he lives in a certain kind of way. And at the moment the overwhelming majority of our people out there feel that people get along better, take more of a common interest in the life of the community, when they share a common interest in the life of the community, when they share a common background. I want you to believe me when I tell you that race prejudice simply doesn't enter into it. It is a matter of the people of Clybourne Park believing, rightly or wrongly, as I say, that for the happiness of all concerned that our Negro families are happier when they live in their *own* communities.

BENEATHA *(with a grand and bitter gesture)* This, friends, is the Welcoming Committee!

WALTER *(dumfounded, looking at* LINDNER*)* Is this what you came marching all the way over here to tell us?

LINDNER Well, now we've been having a fine conversation. I hope you'll hear me all the way through.

WALTER *(tightly)* Go ahead, man.

LINDNER You see—in the face of all things I have said, we are prepared to make your family a very generous offer . . .

BENEATHA Thirty pieces and not a coin less!

WALTER Yeah?

LINDNER *(putting on his glasses and drawing a form out of the briefcase)* Our association is prepared, through the collective effort of our people, to buy the house from you at a financial gain to your family.

RUTH Lord have mercy, ain't this the living gall!

WALTER All right, you through?

LINDNER Well, I want to give you the exact terms of the financial arrangement—

WALTER We don't want to hear no exact terms of no arrangements. I want to know if you got any more to tell us 'bout getting together?

LINDNER *(taking off his glasses)* Well—I don't suppose that you feel . . .

WALTER Never mind how I feel—you got any more to say 'bout how people ought to sit down and talk to each other? . . . Get out of my house, man. *(he turns his back and walks to the door)*

LINDNER *(looking around at the hostile faces and reaching and assembling his hat and briefcase)* Well—I don't understand why you people are reacting this way. What do you think you are going to gain by moving into a neighborhood where you just aren't wanted and where some elements—well—people can get awful worked up when they feel that their whole way of life and everything they've ever worked for is threatened.

WALTER Get out.

LINDNER *(at the door, holding a small card)* Well—I'm sorry it went like this.

WALTER Get out.

LINDNER *(almost sadly regarding* WALTER*)* You just can't force people to change their hearts, son.

(He turns and puts his card on a table and exits. WALTER *pushes the door to with stinging hatred, and stands looking at it.* RUTH *just sits and* BENEATHA *just stands. They say nothing.* MAMA *and* TRAVIS *enter)*

MAMA Well—this all the packing got done since I left out of here this morning? I testify before God that my children got all the energy of the dead. What time the moving men due?

BENEATHA Four o'clock. You had a caller, Mama. *(she is smiling, teasingly)*

MAMA Sure enough—who?

BENEATHA *(her arms folded saucily)* The Welcoming Committee.

*(*WALTER *and* RUTH *giggle)*

MAMA *(innocently)* Who?

BENEATHA The Welcoming Committee. They said they're sure going to be glad to see you when you get there.

WALTER *(devilishly)* Yeah, they said they can't hardly wait to see your face.

(Laughter)

MAMA *(sensing their facetiousness)* What's the matter with you all?

WALTER Ain't nothing the matter with us. We just telling you 'bout the gentleman who came to see you this afternoon. From the Clybourne Park Improvement Association.

MAMA What he want?

RUTH *(in the same mood as* BENEATHA *and* WALTER*)* To welcome you, honey.

WALTER He said they can't hardly wait. He said the one thing they don't have, that they just *dying* to have out there is a fine family of colored people! *(to* RUTH *and* BENEATHA*)* Ain't that right!

RUTH *and* BENEATHA *(mockingly)* Yeah! He left his card in case—

(They indicate the card, and MAMA *picks it up and throws it on the floor—understanding and looking off as she draws her chair up to the table on which she has put her plant and some sticks and some cord)*

MAMA Father, give us strength. *(knowingly—and without fun)* Did he threaten us?

BENEATHA Oh—Mama—they don't do it like that any more. He talked Brotherhood. He said everybody ought learn how to sit down and hate each other with good Christian fellowship.

(She and WALTER *shake hands to ridicule the remark)*

MAMA *(sadly)* Lord, protect us . . .

RUTH You should hear the money those folks raised to buy the house from us. All we paid and then some.

BENEATHA What they think we going to do—eat 'em?

RUTH No, honey, marry 'em.

MAMA *(shaking her head)* Lord, Lord, Lord . . .

RUTH Well—that's the way the crackers crumble. Joke.

BENEATHA *(laughingly noticing what her mother is doing)* Mama, what are you doing?

MAMA Fixing my plant so it won't get hurt none on the way . . .

BENEATHA Mama, you going to take *that* to the new house?

MAMA Un-huh—

BENEATHA That raggedy-looking old thing?

MAMA *(stopping and looking at her)* It expresses *me*.

RUTH *(with delight, to* BENEATHA*)* So there, Miss Thing!

*(*WALTER *comes to* MAMA *suddenly and bends down behind her and squeezes her in his arms with all his strength. She is overwhelmed by the suddenness of it and, though delighted, her manner is like that of* RUTH *with* TRAVIS*)*

MAMA Look out now, boy! You make me mess up my thing here!

WALTER *(his face lit, he slips down on his knees beside her, his arms still about her)* Mama . . . you know what it means to climb up in the chariot?

MAMA *(gruffly, very happy)* Get on a way from me now . . .

RUTH *(near the gift-wrapped package, trying to catch* WALTER'*s eye)* Psst—

WALTER What the old song say, Mama . . .

RUTH Walter— Now? *(she is pointing at the package)*

WALTER *(speaking the lines, sweetly, playfully, in his mother's face)*

I got wings . . . you got wings . . .
All God's children got wings . . .

MAMA Boy—get out of my face and do some work . . .

WALTER

When I get to heaven gonna put on my wings,
Gonna fly all over God's heaven . . .

BENEATHA *(teasingly, from across the room)* Everybody talking 'bout heaven ain't going there!

WALTER *(to* RUTH, *who is carrying the box across to them)* I don't know, you think we ought to give her that . . . Seems to me she ain't been very appreciative around here.

MAMA *(eying the box, which is obviously a gift)* What is that?

WALTER *(taking it from* RUTH *and putting it on the table in front of* MAMA*)* Well—what you all think. Should we give it to her?

RUTH Oh—she was pretty good today.

MAMA I'll good you—*(she turns her eyes to the box again)*

BENEATHA Open it, Mama.

(She stands up, looks at it, turns and looks at all of them, and then presses her hands together and does not open the package)

WALTER *(sweetly)* Open it, Mama. It's for you. *(*MAMA *looks in his eyes. It is the first present in her life without its being Christmas. Slowly she opens her package and lifts out, one by one, a brand-new sparkling set of gardening tools.* WALTER *continues, prodding)* Ruth made up the note—read it . . .

MAMA *(picking up the card and adjusting her glasses)* "To our own Mrs. Miniver—Love from Brother, Ruth and Beneatha." Ain't that lovely . . .

TRAVIS *(tugging at his father's sleeve)* Daddy, can I give her mine now?

WALTER All right, son. *(*TRAVIS *flies to get his gift)* Travis didn't want to go in with the rest of us, Mama. He got his own. *(somewhat amused)* We don't know what it is . . .

TRAVIS *(racing back in the room with a large hatbox and putting it in front of his grandmother)* Here!

MAMA Lord have mercy, baby. You done gone and bought your grandmother a hat?

TRAVIS *(very proud)* Open it!

(She does and lifts out an elaborate, but very elaborate, wide gardening hat, and all the adults break up at the sight of it)

RUTH Travis, honey, what is that?

TRAVIS *(who thinks it is beautiful and appropriate)* It's a gardening hat! Like the ladies always have on in the magazines when they work in their gardens.

BENEATHA *(giggling fiercely)* Travis—we were trying to make Mama Mrs. Miniver—not Scarlett O'Hara!

MAMA *(indignantly)* What's the matter with you all! This here is a beautiful hat! *(absurdly)* I always wanted me one just like it! *(she pops it on her head to prove it to her grandson, and the hat is ludicrous and considerably oversized)*

RUTH Hot dog! Go, Mama!

WALTER *(doubled over with laughter)* I'm sorry, Mama—but you look like you ready to go out and chop you some cotton sure enough!

(They all laugh except MAMA, *out of deference to* TRAVIS' *feelings)*

MAMA *(gathering the boy up to her)* Bless your heart—this is the prettiest hat I ever owned— *(*WALTER, RUTH *and* BENEATHA *chime in—noisily, festively and insincerely congratulating* TRAVIS *on his gift)* What are we all standing around here for? We ain't finished packin' yet. Bennie, you ain't packed one book.

(The bell rings)

BENEATHA That couldn't be the movers . . . it's not hardly two yet—

*(*BENEATHA *goes into her room.* MAMA *starts for door)*

WALTER *(turning, stiffening)* Wait—wait—I'll get it. *(he stands and looks at the door)*

MAMA You expecting company, son?

WALTER *(just looking at the door)* Yeah—yeah . . .

*(*MAMA *looks at* RUTH, *and they exchange innocent and unfrightened glances)*

MAMA *(not understanding)* Well, let them in, son.

BENEATHA *(from her room)* We need some more string.

MAMA Travis—you run to the hardware and get me some string cord.

*(*MAMA *goes out and* WALTER *turns and looks at* RUTH. TRAVIS *goes to a dish for money)*

RUTH Why don't you answer the door, man?

WALTER *(suddenly bounding across the floor to her)* 'Cause sometimes it hard to let the future begin! *(stooping down in her face)*

I got wings! You got wings!
All God's children got wings!

(He crosses to the door and throws it open. Standing there is a very slight little man in a not too prosperous business suit and with haunted, frightened eyes and a hat pulled down tightly, brim up, around his forehead. TRAVIS *passes between the men and exits.* WALTER *leans deep in the man's face, still in his jubilance)*

When I get to heaven gonna put on my wings,
Gonna fly all over God's heaven . . .

(The little man just stares at him)

Heaven—

(Suddenly he stops and looks past the little man into the empty hallway) Where's Willy, man?

BOBO He ain't with me.

WALTER *(not disturbed)* Oh—come on in. You know my wife.

BOBO *(dumbly, taking off his hat)* Yes—h'you, Miss Ruth.

RUTH *(quietly, a mood apart from her husband already, seeing* BOBO*)* Hello, Bobo.

WALTER You right on time today . . . Right on time. That's the way! *(he slaps* BOBO *on his back)* Sit down . . . lemme hear.

*(*RUTH *stands stiffly and quietly in back of them, as though somehow she senses death, her eyes fixed on her husband)*

BOBO *(his frightened eyes on the floor, his hat in his hands)* Could I please get a drink a water, before I tell you about it, Walter Lee?

*(*WALTER *does not take his eyes off the man.* RUTH *goes blindly to the tap and gets a glass of water and brings it to* BOBO*)*

WALTER There ain't nothing wrong, is there?

BOBO Lemme tell you—

WALTER Man—didn't nothing go wrong?

BOBO Lemme tell you—Walter Lee. *(looking at* RUTH *and talking to her more than to* WALTER*)* You know how it was, I got to tell you how it was. I mean first I got to tell you how it was all the way . . . I mean about the money I put in, Walter Lee . . .

WALTER *(with taut agitation now)* What about the money you put in?

BOBO Well—it wasn't much as we told you—me and Willy—*(he stops)* I'm sorry, Walter. I got a bad feeling about it. I got a real bad feeling about it . . .

WALTER Man, what you telling me about all this for? . . . Tell me what happened in Springfield . . .

BOBO Springfield.

RUTH *(like a dead woman)* What was supposed to happen in Springfield?

BOBO *(to her)* This deal that me and Walter went into with Willy— Me and Willy was going to go down to Springfield and spread some money 'round so's we wouldn't have to wait so long for the liquor license . . . That's what we were going to do. Everybody said that was the way you had to do, you understand, Miss Ruth?

WALTER Man—what happened down there?

BOBO *(a pitiful man, near tears)* I'm trying to tell you, Walter.

WALTER *(Screaming at him suddenly)* THEN TELL ME, GODDAMNIT . . . WHAT'S THE MATTER WITH YOU?

BOBO Man . . . I didn't go to no Springfield, yesterday.

WALTER *(halted, life hanging in the moment)* Why not?

BOBO *(the long way, the hard way to tell)* 'Cause I didn't have no reasons to . . .

WALTER Man, what are you talking about!

BOBO I'm talking about the fact that when I got to the train station yesterday morning—eight o'clock like we planned . . . Man—*Willy didn't never show up.*

WALTER Why . . . where was he . . . where is he?

BOBO That's what I'm trying to tell you . . . I don't know . . . I waited six hours . . . I called his house . . . and I waited . . . six hours . . . I waited in that train station six hours . . . *(breaking into tears)* That was all the extra money I had in the world . . . *(looking up at*

WALTER *with the tears running down his face)* Man, *Willy is gone.*

WALTER Gone, what you mean Willy is gone? Gone where? You mean he went by himself. You mean he went off to Springfield by himself—to take care of getting the license—*(turns and looks anxiously at* RUTH*)* You mean maybe he didn't want too many people in on the business down there? *(looks to* RUTH *again, as before)* You know Willy got his own ways. *(looks back to* BOBO*)* Maybe you was late yesterday and he just went on down there without you. Maybe—maybe—he's been callin' you at home trying' to tell you what happened or something. Maybe—maybe—he just got sick. He's somewhere—he's got to be somewhere. We just got to find him—me and you got to find him. *(grabs* BOBO *senselessly by the collar and starts to shake him)* We got to!

BOBO *(in sudden angry, frightened agony)* What's the matter with you, Walter! *When a cat take off with your money he don't leave you no maps!*

WALTER *(turning madly, as though he is looking for* WILLY *in the very room)* Willy! . . . Willy . . . don't do it . . . Please don't do it . . . Man, not with that money . . . Man, please, not with that money . . . Oh, God . . . Don't let it be true . . . *(he is wandering around, crying out for Willy and looking for him or perhaps for help from God)* Man . . . I trusted you . . . Man, I put my life in your hands . . . *(he starts to crumple down on the floor as* RUTH *just covers her face in horror.* MAMA *opens the door and comes into the room, with* BENEATHA *behind her)* Man . . . *(he starts to pound the floor with his fists, sobbing wildly) That money is made out of my father's flesh . . .*

BOBO *(standing over him helplessly)* I'm sorry, Walter . . . *(Only* WALTER*'s sobs reply.* BOBO *puts on his hat)* I had my life staked on this deal, too . . . *(he exits)*

MAMA *(to* WALTER*)* Son—*(she goes to him, bends down to him, talks to his bent head)* Son . . . Is it gone? Son, I gave you sixty-five hundred dollars. Is it gone? All of it? Beneatha's money too?

WALTER *(lifting his head slowly)* Mama . . . I never . . . went to the bank at all . . .

MAMA *(not wanting to believe him)* You mean . . . your sister's school money . . . you used that too . . . Walter? . . .

WALTER Yessss! . . . All of it . . . It's all gone . . .

(There is total silence. RUTH *stands with her face covered with her hands;* BENEATHA *leans forlornly against a wall, fingering a piece of red ribbon from the mother's gift.* MAMA *stops and looks at her son without recognition and then, quite without thinking about it, starts to beat him senselessly in the face.* BENEATHA, *goes to them and stops it)*

BENEATHA Mama!

*(*MAMA *stops and looks at both of her children and rises slowly and wanders vaguely, aimlessly away from them)*

MAMA I seen . . . him . . . night after night . . . come in . . . and look at that rug . . . and then look at me . . . the red showing in his eyes . . . the veins moving in his head . . . I seen him grow thin and old before he was forty . . . working and working and working like somebody's old horse . . . killing himself . . . and you—you give it all away in a day . . .

BENEATHA Mama—

MAMA Oh, God . . . *(she looks up to Him)* Look down here—and show me the strength.

BENEATHA Mama—

MAMA *(folding over)* Strength . . .

BENEATHA *(plaintively)* Mama . . .

MAMA Strength!

(Curtain)

ACT THREE

(An hour later.

At curtain, there is a sullen light of gloom in the living room, gray light not unlike that which began the first scene of Act One. At left we can see WALTER *within his room, alone with himself. He is stretched out on the bed, his shirt out and open, his arms under his head. He does not smoke, he does not cry out, he merely lies there, looking up at the ceiling, much as if he were alone in the world.*

In the living room BENEATHA *sits at the table, still surrounded by the now almost ominous packing crates. She sits looking off. We feel that this is a mood struck perhaps an hour before, and it lingers now, full of the empty sound of profound disappointment. We see on a line from her brother's bed-*

room the sameness of their attitudes. Presently the bell rings and BENEATHA *rises without ambition or interest in answering. It is* ASAGAI, *smiling broadly, striding into the room with energy and happy expectation and conversation)*

ASAGAI I came over . . . I had some free time. I thought I might help with the packing. Ah, I like the look of packing crates! A household in preparation for a journey! It depresses some people . . . but for me . . . it is another feeling. Something full of the flow of life, do you understand? Movement, progress . . . It makes me think of Africa.

BENEATHA Africa!

ASAGAI What kind of a mood is this? Have I told you how deeply you move me?

BENEATHA He gave away the money, Asagai . . .

ASAGAI Who gave away what money?

BENEATHA The insurance money. My brother gave it away.

ASAGAI Gave it away?

BENEATHA He made an investment! With a man even Travis wouldn't have trusted.

ASAGAI And it's gone?

BENEATHA Gone!

ASAGAI I'm very sorry . . . And you, now?

BENEATHA Me? . . . Me? . . . Me I'm nothing . . . Me. When I was very small . . . we used to take our sleds out in the wintertime and the only hills we had were the ice-covered stone steps of some houses down the street. And we used to fill them in with snow and make them smooth and slide down them all day . . . and it was very dangerous you know . . . far too steep . . . and sure enough one day a kid named Rufus came down too fast and hit the sidewalk . . . and we saw his face just split open right there in front of us . . . And I remember standing there looking at his bloody open face thinking that was the end of Rufus. But the ambulance came and they took him to the hospital and they fixed the broken bones and they sewed it all up . . . and the next time I saw Rufus he just had a little line down the middle of his face . . . I never got over that . . .

ASAGAI What?

BENEATHA That that was what one person could do for another, fix him up—sew up the problem, make him all right again. That was the most marvelous thing in the world . . . I wanted to do that. I always thought it was the one concrete thing in the world that a human being could do. Fix up the sick, you know—and make them whole again. This was truly being God . . .

ASAGAI You wanted to be God?

BENEATHA No—I wanted to cure. It used to be so important to me. I wanted to cure. It used to matter. I used to care. I mean about people and how their bodies hurt . . .

ASAGAI And you've stopped caring?

BENEATHA Yes—I think so.

ASAGAI Why?

BENEATHA Because it doesn't seem deep enough, close enough to the truth.

ASAGAI Truth? Why is it that you despairing ones always think that only you have the truth? I never thought to see *you* like that. You! Your brother made a stupid, childish mistake—and you are grateful to him. So that now you can give up the ailing human race on account of it. You talk about what good is struggle; what good is anything? Where are we all going? And why are we bothering?

BENEATHA *And you cannot answer it!* All your talk and dreams about Africa and Independence. Independence and then what? What about all the crooks and petty thieves and just plain idiots who will come into power to steal and plunder the same as before—only now they will be Black and do it in the name of the new Independence— You cannot answer that.

ASAGAI *(shouting over her)* *I live the answer! (pause)* In my village at home it is the exceptional man who can even read a newspaper or who ever *sees* a book at all. I will go home and much of what I will have to say will seem strange to the people of my village . . . But I will teach and work and things will happen, slowly and swiftly. At times it will seem that nothing changes at all . . . and then again . . . the sudden dramatic events which make history leap into the future. And then quiet again. Retrogression even. Guns, murder, revolution. And I even will have moments when I wonder if the quiet was not better than all that death and hatred. But I will look about my village at the illiteracy and disease and ignorance and I will not wonder long. And perhaps . . . perhaps I will be a great man . . . I mean perhaps I will hold on to the substance of truth and find my way always with the right course . . . and perhaps for it I will be butchered in my bed some night by the servants of empire . . .

BENEATHA *The martyr!*

ASAGAI . . . or perhaps I shall live to be a very old man, respected and esteemed in my new nation . . . And perhaps I shall hold office and this is what I'm trying to tell you, Alaiyo; perhaps the things I believe now for my country will be wrong and outmoded, and I will not understand and do terrible things to have things my way or merely to keep my power. Don't you see that there will be young men and women, not British soldiers then, but my own Black countrymen . . . to step out of the shadows some evening and slit my then useless throat? Don't you see they have always been there . . . that they always will be. And that such a thing as my own death will be an advance? They who might kill me even . . . actually replenish me!

BENEATHA Oh, Asagai, I know all that.

ASAGAI Good! Then stop moaning and groaning and tell me what you plan to do.

BENEATHA Do?

ASAGAI I have a bit of a suggestion.

BENEATHA What?

ASAGAI *(rather quietly for him)* That when it is all over—that you come home with me—

BENEATHA *(slapping herself on the forehead with exasperation born of misunderstanding)* Oh—Asagai—at this moment you decide to be romantic!

ASAGAI *(quickly understanding the misunderstanding)* My dear, young creature of the New World—I do not mean across the city—I mean across the ocean; home—to Africa.

BENEATHA *(slowly understanding and turning to him with murmured amazement)* To—to Nigeria?

ASAGAI Yes! . . . *(smiling and lifting his arms playfully)* Three hundred years later the African Prince rose up out of the seas and swept the maiden back across the middle passage over which her ancestors had come—

BENEATHA *(unable to play)* Nigeria?

ASAGAI Nigeria. Home. *(coming to her with genuine romantic flippancy)* I will show you our mountains and our stars; and give you cool drinks from gourds and teach you the old songs and the ways of our people—and, in time, we will pretend that—*(very softly)*—you have only been away for a day—

(She turns her back to him, thinking. He swings her around and takes her full in his arms in a long embrace which proceeds to passion)

BENEATHA *(pulling away)* You're getting me all mixed up—

ASAGAI Why?

BENEATHA Too many things—too many things have happened today. I must sit down and think. I don't know what I feel about anything right this minute. *(she promptly sits down and props her chin on her fist)*

ASAGAI *(charmed)* All right, I shall leave you. No—don't get up. *(touching her, gently, sweetly)* Just sit awhile and think . . . Never be afraid to sit awhile and think. *(he goes to door and looks at her)* How often I have looked at you and said, "Ah—so this is what the New World hath finally wrought . . ."

(He exits. BENEATHA *sits on alone. Presently* WALTER *enters from his room and starts to rummage through things, feverishly looking for something. She looks up and turns in her seat)*

BENEATHA *(hissingly)* Yes—just look at what the New World hath wrought! . . . Just look! *(she gestures with bitter disgust)* There he is! *Monsieur le petit bourgeois noir*—himself! There he is—Symbol of a Rising Class! Entrepreneur! Titan of the system! *(*WALTER *ignores her completely and continues frantically and destructively looking for something and hurling things to floor and tearing things out of their place in his search.* BENEATHA *ignores the eccentricity of his actions and goes on with the monologue of insult)* Did you dream of yachts on Lake Michigan, Brother? Did you see yourself on that Great Day sitting down at the Conference Table, surrounded by all the mighty baldheaded men in America? All halted, waiting, breathless, waiting for your pronouncements on industry? Waiting for you—Chairman of the Board? *(*WALTER *finds what he is looking for—a small piece of white paper—and pushes it in his pocket and puts on his coat and rushes out without ever having looked at her. She shouts after him)* I look at you and I see the final triumph of stupidity in the world!

(The door slams and she returns to just sitting again. RUTH *comes quickly out of* MAMA'*s room)*

RUTH Who was that?

BENEATHA Your husband.

RUTH Where did he go?

BENEATHA Who knows—maybe he has an appointment at U.S. Steel.

RUTH *(anxiously, with frightened eyes)* You didn't say nothing bad to him, did you?

BENEATHA Bad? Say anything bad to him? No—I told him he was a sweet boy and full of dreams and everything is strictly peachy keen, as the ofay kids say!

*(*MAMA *enters from her bedroom. She is lost, vague, trying to catch hold, to make some sense of her former command of the world, but it still eludes her. A sense of waste overwhelms her gait; a measure of apology rides on her shoulders. She goes to her plant, which has remained on the table, looks at it, picks it up and takes it to the window sill and sits it outside, and she stands and looks at it a long moment. Then she closes the window, straightens her body with effort and turns around to her children)*

MAMA Well—ain't it a mess in here, though? *(a false cheerfulness, a beginning of something)* I guess we all better stop moping around and get some work done. All this unpacking and everything we got to do. *(*RUTH *raises her head slowly in response to the sense of the line; and* BENEATHA *in similar manner turns very slowly to look at her mother)* One of you all better call the moving people and tell 'em not to come.

RUTH Tell 'em not to come?

MAMA Of course, baby. Ain't no need in 'em coming all the way here and having to go back. They charges for that too. *(she sits down, fingers to her brow, thinking)* Lord, ever since I was a little girl, I always remembers people saying, "Lena—Lena Eggleston, you aims too high all the time. You needs to slow down and see life a little more like it is. Just slow down some." That's what they always used to say down home—"Lord, that Lena Eggleston is a high-minded thing. She'll get her due one day!"

RUTH No, Lena . . .

MAMA Me and Big Walter just didn't never learn right.

RUTH Lena, no! We gotta go. Bennie—tell her . . . *(She rises and crosses to* BENEATHA *with her arms outstretched.* BENEATHA *doesn't respond)* Tell her we can still move . . . the notes ain't but a hundred and twenty five a month. We got four grown people in this house—we can work . . .

MAMA *(to herself)* Just aimed too high all the time—

RUTH *(turning and going to* MAMA *fast—the words pouring out with urgency and desperation)* Lena—I'll work . . . I'll work twenty hours a day in all the kitchens in Chicago . . . I'll strap my baby on my back if I have to and scrub all the floors in America and wash all the sheets in America if I have to—but we got to move . . . We got to get out of here . . .

*(*MAMA *reaches out absently and pats* RUTH'*s hand)*

MAMA No—I sees things differently now. Been thinking 'bout some of the things we could do to fix this place up some. I seen a second-hand bureau over on Maxwell Street just the other day that could fit right there. *(she points to where the new furniture might go.* RUTH *wanders away from her)* Would need some new handles on it and then a little varnish and then it look like something brand-new. And—we can put up them new curtains in the kitchen . . . Why this place be looking fine. Cheer us all up so that we forget trouble ever came . . . *(to* RUTH*)* And you could get some nice screens to put up in your room round the baby's basinet . . . *(she looks at both of them, pleadingly)* Sometimes you just got to know when to give up some things . . . and hold on to what you got.

*(*WALTER *enters from the outside, looking spent and leaning against the door, his coat hanging from him)*

MAMA Where you been, son?

WALTER *(breathing hard)* Made a call.

MAMA To who, son?

WALTER To The Man.

MAMA What man, baby?

WALTER The Man, Mama. Don't you know who The Man is?

RUTH Walter Lee?

WALTER *The Man.* Like the guys in the streets say—The Man. Captain Boss—Mistuh Charley . . . Old Captain Please Mr. Bossman . . .

BENEATHA *(suddenly)* Lindner!

WALTER That's right! That's good. I told him to come right over.

BENEATHA *(fiercely, understanding)* For what? What do you want to see him for!

WALTER *(looking at his sister)* We going to do business with him.

MAMA What you talking 'bout, son?

WALTER Talking 'bout life, Mama. You all always telling me to see life like it is. Well—I laid in there on my back today . . . and I figured it out. Life just like it is. Who gets and who don't get. *(he sits down with his coat on and laughs)* Mama, you know it's all divided up. Life is. Sure enough. Between the takers and the "tooken." *(he laughs)* I've figured it out finally. *(he looks around at them)* Yeah. Some of us always getting "tooken." *(he laughs)* People like Willy Harris, they don't never get "tooken." And you know why the rest of us do? 'Cause we all mixed up. Mixed up bad. We get to looking 'round for the right and the wrong; and we worry about it and cry about it and stay up nights trying to figure out 'bout the wrong and the right of things all the time . . . And all the time, man, them takers is out there operating, just taking and taking. Willy Harris? Shoot—Willy Harris don't even count. He don't even count in the big scheme of things. But I'll say one thing for old Willy Harris . . . he's taught me something. He's taught me to keep my eye on what counts in this world. Yeah—*(shouting out a little)* Thanks, Willy!

RUTH What did you call that man for, Walter Lee?

WALTER Called him to tell him to come on over to the show. Gonna put on a show for the man. Just what he wants to see. You see, Mama, the man came here today and he told us that them people out there where you want us to move—well they so upset they willing to pay us not to move out there. *(he laughs again)* And—and oh, Mama—you would of been proud of the way me and Ruth and Bennie acted. We told him to get out . . . Lord have mercy! We told the man to get out. Oh, we was some proud folks this afternoon, yeah. *(he lights a cigarette)* We were still full of that old-time stuff . . .

RUTH *(coming toward him slowly)* You talking 'bout taking them people's money to keep us from moving in that house?

WALTER I ain't just talking 'bout it, baby—I'm telling you that's what's going to happen.

BENEATHA Oh, God! Where is the bottom! Where is the real honest-to-God bottom so he can't go any farther!

WALTER See—that's the old stuff. You and that boy that was here today. You all want everybody to carry a flag and a spear and sing some marching songs, huh? You wanna spend your life looking into things and trying to find the right and the wrong part, huh? Yeah. You know what's going to happen to that boy someday—he'll find himself sitting in a dungeon, locked in forever—and the takers will have the key! Forget it, baby! There ain't no causes—there ain't nothing but taking in this world, and he who takes most is smartest—and it don't make a damn bit of difference *how.*

MAMA You making something inside me cry, son. Some awful pain inside me.

WALTER Don't cry, Mama. Understand. That white man is going to walk in that door able to write checks for more money than we ever had. It's important to him and I'm going to help him . . . I'm going to put on the show, Mama.

MAMA Son—I come from five generations of people who was slaves and sharecroppers—but ain't nobody in my family never let nobody pay 'em no money that was a way of telling us we wasn't fit to walk the earth. We ain't never been that poor. *(raising her eyes and looking at him)* We ain't never been that dead inside.

BENEATHA Well—we are dead now. All the talk about dreams and sunlight that goes on in this house. All dead.

WALTER What's the matter with you all! I didn't make this world! It was give to me this way! Hell, yes, I want me some yachts someday! Yes, I want to hang some real pearls 'round my wife's neck. Ain't she supposed to wear no pearls? Somebody tell me—tell me, who decides which women is suppose to wear pearls in this world. I tell you I am a *man*—and I think my wife should wear some pearls in this world!

(This last line hangs a good while and WALTER *begins to move about the room. The word "Man" has penetrated his consciousness; he mumbles it to himself repeatedly between strange agitated pauses as he moves about)*

MAMA Baby, how you going to feel on the inside?

WALTER Fine! . . . Going to feel fine . . . a man . . .

MAMA You won't have nothing left then, Walter Lee.

WALTER *(coming to her)* I'm going to feel fine, Mama. I'm going to look that son-of-a-bitch in the eyes and say—*(he falters)*—and say, "All right, Mr. Lindner—*(he falters even more)*—that's your neighborhood out there. You got the right to keep it like you want. You got the right to have it like you want. Just write the check and—the house is yours." And, and I am going to say—*(his voice almost breaks)* And you—you people just put the money in my hand and you won't have to live next to this bunch of stinking niggers! . . . *(he straightens up and moves away from his mother, walking around the room)* Maybe—maybe I'll just get down on my Black knees . . . *(he does so;* RUTH *and* BENNIE *and* MAMA *watch him in frozen horror)* Captain, Mistuh, Bossman. *(he starts crying)* A-hee-hee-hee! *(wringing his hands in profoundly anguished imitation)* Yassss-suh! Great White Father, just gi' ussen de money, fo' God's sake, and we's ain't gwine come out deh and dirty up yo' white folks neighborhood . . . *(he breaks down completely, then gets up and goes into the bedroom)*

BENEATHA That is not a man. That is nothing but a toothless rat.

MAMA Yes—death done come in this here house. *(she is nodding, slowly, reflectively)* Done come walking in my house. On the lips of my children. You what supposed to be my beginning again. You—what supposed to be my harvest. *(to* BENEATHA*)* You—you mourning your brother?

BENEATHA He's no brother of mine.

MAMA What you say?

BENEATHA I said that that individual in that room is no brother of mine.

MAMA That's what I thought you said. You feeling like you better than he is today? *(*BENEATHA *does not answer)* Yes? What you tell him a minute ago? That he wasn't a man? Yes? You give him up for me? You done wrote his epitaph too—like the rest of the world? Well, who give you the privilege?

BENEATHA Be on my side for once! You saw what he just did, Mama! You saw him—down on his knees. Wasn't it you who taught me—to despise any man who would do that. Do what he's going to do.

MAMA Yes—I taught you that. Me and your daddy. But I thought I taught you something else too . . . I thought I taught you to love him.

BENEATHA Love him? There is nothing left to love.

MAMA There is always something left to love. And if you ain't learned that, you ain't learned nothing. *(looking at her)* Have you cried for that boy today? I don't mean for yourself and for the family 'cause we lost the money. I mean for him; what he been through and what it done to him. Child, when do you think is the time to love somebody the most; when they done good and made things easy for everybody? Well then, you ain't through learning—because that ain't the time at all. It's when he's at his lowest and can't believe in hisself 'cause the world done whipped him so. When you starts measuring somebody, measure him right, child, measure him right. Make sure you done taken into account what hills and valleys he come through before he got to wherever he is.

*(*TRAVIS *bursts into the room at the end of the speech, leaving the door open)*

TRAVIS Grandmama—the moving men are downstairs! The truck just pulled up.

MAMA *(turning and looking at him)* Are they, baby? They downstairs?

(She sighs and sits. Lindner appears in the doorway. He peers in and knocks lightly, to gain attention, and comes in. All turn to look at him)

LINDNER *(hat and briefcase in hand)* Uh—hello . . .

*(*RUTH *crosses mechanically to the bedroom door and opens it and lets it swing open freely and slowly as the lights come up on* WALTER *within, still in his coat, sitting at the far corner of the room. He looks up and out through the room to* LINDNER*)*

RUTH He's here.

(A long minute passes and WALTER *slowly gets up)*

LINDNER *(coming to the table with efficiency, putting his briefcase on the table and starting to unfold papers and unscrew fountain pens)* Well, I certainly was glad to hear from you people. *(*WALTER *has begun the trek out of the room, slowly and awkwardly, rather like a small boy, passing the back of his sleeve across his mouth from time to time)* Life can really be so much simpler than people let it be most of the time. Well—with whom do I negotiate? You, Mrs. Younger, or your son here? *(*MAMA *sits with her hands folded on her lap and her eyes* *closed as* WALTER *advances.* TRAVIS *goes close to* LINDNER *and looks at the papers curiously)* Just some official papers, sonny.

RUTH Travis, you go downstairs.

MAMA *(opening her eyes and looking into* WALTER's*)* No. Travis, you stay right here. And you make him understand what you doing, Walter Lee. You teach him good. Like Willy Harris taught you. You show where our five generations done come to. Go ahead, son—

WALTER *(looks down into his boy's eyes.* TRAVIS *grins at him merrily and* WALTER *draws him beside him with his arm lightly around his shoulder)* Well, Mr. Lindner. (BENEATHA *turns away)* We called you—*(there is a profound, simple groping quality in his speech)*—because, well, me and my family *(he looks around and shifts from one foot to the other)* Well—we are very plain people . . .

LINDNER Yes—

WALTER I mean—I have worked as a chauffeur most of my life—and my wife here, she does domestic work in people's kitchens. So does my mother. I mean—we are plain people . . .

LINDNER Yes, Mr. Younger—

WALTER *(really like a small boy, looking down at his shoes and then up at the man)* And—uh—well, my father, well, he was a laborer most of his life.

LINDNER *(absolutely confused)* Uh, yes—

WALTER *(looking down at his toes once again)* My father almost beat a man to death once because this man called him a bad name or something, you know what I mean?

LINDNER No, I'm afraid I don't.

WALTER *(finally straightening up)* Well, what I mean is that we come from people who had a lot of pride. I mean—we are very proud people. And that's my sister over there and she's going to be a doctor—and we are very proud—

LINDNER Well—I am sure that is very nice, but—

WALTER *(starting to cry and facing the man eye to eye)* What I am telling you is that we called you over here to tell you that we are very proud and that this is—this is my son, who makes the sixth generation of our family in this country, and that we have all thought about your offer and we have decided to move into our house because my father—my father—he earned it. (MAMA *has her eyes closed and is rocking back and forth as though she were in church, with her head nodding the amen yes)* We don't want to make no trouble for nobody or fight no causes—but we will try to be good neighbors. That's all we got to say. *(he looks the man absolutely in the eyes)* We don't want your money. *(he turns and walks away from the man)*

LINDNER *(looking around at all of them)* I take it then that you have decided to occupy.

BENEATHA That's what the man said.

LINDNER *(to* MAMA *in her reverie)* Then I would like to appeal to you, Mrs. Younger. You are older and wiser and understand things better I am sure . . .

MAMA *(rising)* I am afraid you don't understand. My son said we was going to move and there ain't nothing left for me to say. *(shaking her head with double meaning)* You know how these youngs folks is nowadays, mister. Can't do a thing with 'em. Good-bye.

LINDNER *(folding up his materials)* Well—if you are that final about it . . . There is nothing left for me to say. *(he finishes. He is almost ignored by the family, who are concentrating on* WALTER LEE. *At the door* LINDNER *halts and looks around)* I sure hope you people know what you're doing. *(he shakes his head and exits)*

RUTH *(looking around and coming to life)* Well, for God's sake—if the moving men are here—LET'S GET THE HELL OUT OF HERE!

MAMA *(into action)* Ain't it the truth! Look at all this here mess. Ruth put Travis' good jacket on him . . . Walter Lee, fix your tie and tuck your shirt in, you look just like somebody's hoodlum. Lord have mercy, where is my plant? *(she flies to get it amid the general bustling of the family, who are deliberately trying to ignore the nobility of the past moment)* You all start on down . . . Travis child, don't go empty-handed . . . Ruth, where did I put that box with my skillets in it? I want to be in charge of it myself . . . I'm going to make us the biggest dinner we ever ate tonight . . . Beneatha, what's the matter with them stockings? Pull them things up, girl . . .

(The family starts to file out as two moving men appear and begin to carry out the heavier pieces of furniture, bumping into the family as they move about)

BENEATHA Mama, Asagai—asked me to marry him today and go to Africa—

MAMA *(in the middle of her getting-ready activ-*

ity) He did? You ain't old enough to marry nobody—*(Seeing the moving men lifting one of her chairs precariously)* Darling, that ain't no bale of cotton, please handle it so we can sit in it again. I had that chair twenty-five years . . .

(The movers sigh with exasperation and go on with their work)

BENEATHA *(girlishly and unreasonably trying to pursue the conversation)* To go to Africa, Mama—be a doctor in Africa . . .

MAMA *(distracted)* Yes, baby—

WALTER Africa! What he want you to go to Africa for?

BENEATHA To practice there . . .

WALTER Girl, if you don't get all them silly ideas out your head! You better marry yourself a man with some loot . . .

BENEATHA *(angrily, precisely as in the first scene of the play)* What have you got to do with who I marry!

WALTER Plenty. Now I think George Murchison—

(He and BENEATHA *go out yelling at each other vigorously;* BENEATHA *is heard saying that she would not marry* GEORGE MURCHISON *if he were Adam and she were Eve, etc. The anger is loud and real till their voices diminish.* RUTH *stands at the door and turns to* MAMA *and smiles knowingly)*

MAMA *(fixing her hat at last)* Yeah—they something all right, my children . . .

RUTH Yeah—they're something. Let's go, Lena.

MAMA *(stalling, starting to look around at the house)* Yes—I'm coming. Ruth—

RUTH Yes?

MAMA *(quietly, woman to woman)* He finally come into his manhood today, didn't he? Kind of like a rainbow after the rain . . .

RUTH *(biting her lip lest her own pride explode in front of* MAMA*)* Yes, Lena.

*(*WALTER'S *voice calls for them raucously)*

MAMA *(waving* RUTH *out vaguely)* All right, honey—go on down. I be down directly.

*(*RUTH *hesitates, then exits.* MAMA *stands, at last alone in the living room, her plant on the table before her as the lights start to come down. She looks around at all the walls and ceilings and suddenly, despite herself, while the children call below, a great heaving thing rises in her and she puts her fist to her mouth, takes a final desperate look, pulls her coat about her, pats her hat and goes out. The lights dim down. The door opens and she comes back in, grabs her plant, and goes out for the last time. Curtain)*

CEREMONIES IN DARK OLD MEN

1965

Lonne Elder III (1931 -)

Ceremonies in Dark Old Men examines the disintegration of an African American family living in Harlem. Elder's concern is with the men in the family, Russell B. Parker and his sons, Theopolis and Bobby. Parker, a vaudeville dancer, was forced to retire early due to an injury. He has refused to work "downtown" because he does not want to be humiliated and degraded by white employers, so his wife must work to support the family. Following her death, Parker's daughter, Adele, assumes the role of materfamilias. As sole supporter of her father and two grown brothers, she issues an ultimatum: either find jobs or leave. Parker pretends to be a barber but has no customers, Theo is a hustler, and Bobby, a petty thief. Parker idles his time away playing a game of checkers with his friend, Jenkins, although he never wins. He is warned that the day he wins will be the most unlucky day of his life.

With Adele's deadline for jobs approaching, Theo sets his plan in motion; the family will go into business selling corn whiskey, which Theo will make. The business will be backed by an underworld figure named Blue Haven, the leader of a revolutionary organization designed to drive white businesses out of Harlem. The backroom of Parker's shop will be headquarters, where they will also operate a numbers game racket, and fence stolen items. Parker agrees to participate and by doing so begins a new and most dangerous game. A series of lies are set into motion that harm the family individually and collectively. Blue Haven lies to Theo, promising to provide a helper, which he does not, and vowing not to use Bobby as one of his thieves. Theo, in turn, lies to Blue after fixing the books to cover the money that Parker has stolen from the cash drawer. Parker is lied to and betrayed by his young girlfriend, who claims that she loves him and is faithful to him. Adele is used and lied to by her new boyfriend, Wilmer, who is notorious for abusing women. As dishonesty mounts, the foundation of the Parker household begins to crumble. Theo finds himself a prisoner to his business, Parker is locked out of his girlfriend's apartment and her life, and Adele is physically abused by Wilmer. The blow that topples the home, however, is the death of Bobby, who is killed during a robbery with the Blue Haven gang. Elder brings the game full circle by having Parker force Jenkins into a final game of checkers, which he wins, confirming the prophesy that winning would occur on the worst day of his life.

Lonne Elder was born in Americus, Georgia, and raised in Jersey City, New Jersey. He attended Jersey City State Teachers College, continuing his studies at the Jefferson School, the New School for Social Research, and the Yale University School of Drama. After his discharge from the army, he returned to Harlem, where he joined the Harlem Writers Guild and was encouraged to write fiction and poetry. His interest in playwriting developed after he met Douglas Turner Ward, with whom he shared an apartment. Elder is an actor, playwright, screenwriter, and has written for television. His television credits include scripts for the *N.Y.P.D.* and *McCloud* series. His best-known filmscript is *Sounder*, for which he received the Writers Guild of America Award, the Atlanta Film Festival Silver Award, the Christophers Award, the NAACP Image Award, the Stanley Drama Award, and the Los Angeles Drama Critics Award. It was also nominated for an Academy Award. *Ceremonies in Dark Old Men* won the Outer Drama Critics Circle Award, the Vernon Rice Drama Desk Award, the Stella Holt Memorial Playwrights Award, the Stanley Drama Award, the Los Angeles Drama Critics Award, and was nominated for a Pulitzer Prize. The 1975 ABC television production of the play won the Christophers Award that year.

Ceremonies in Dark Old Men

Cast

MR. RUSSELL B. PARKER
MR. WILLIAM JENKINS
THEOPOLIS PARKER
BOBBY PARKER
ADELE ELOISE PARKER
BLUE HAVEN
YOUNG GIRL

(Early spring, about 4:30 in the afternoon, now.

A small, poverty-stricken barbershop on 126th Street between Seventh and Lenox Avenues, Harlem, U.S.A.

There is only one barber's throne in this barbershop. There is a not-too-lengthy mirror along the wall, and a high, broad shelf in the immediate area of the throne. There are two decks of shelves of equal width projecting just below the main shelf. These shelves are covered by small sliding panels. On the far left corner of the shop is the street door, and on the far right corner is a door leading to a back room. Just to the right of the door, flush against the wall, is a card table and two chairs. Farther right is a clothes rack. Against the wall to the far left of the shop, near the door, are four chairs lined up uniformly.

The back room is like any back room in a poverty-stricken barbershop. It has an old refrigerator, an even older antique-type desk, and a medium-size bed. On the far right is a short flight of stairs leading up. A unique thing about this room: a door to stairs coming up from a small basement.

The action of the play takes place in the barbershop and the back room)

ACT ONE

Scene One

(As the curtain rises, MR. RUSSELL B. PARKER *is seated in the single barber's throne, reading the* Daily News. *He is in his early or middle fifties. He rises nervously, moves to the window, and peers out, his right hand over his eyebrows. He returns to the chair and continues to read. After checking his watch, he rises again and moves to the window for another look. Finally he sees the right person coming and moves to the door to open it.* MR. WILLIAM JENKINS *enters: early fifties, well dressed in a complete suit of clothes, and carrying a newspaper under his arm)*

MR. PARKER Where have you been?

MR. JENKINS Whatcha mean? You know where I was.

MR. PARKER You want to play the game or not?

MR. JENKINS That's what I came here for.

MR. PARKER *(slides open a panel in the counter)* I wanted to get in at least three games before Adele got home, but this way we'll be lucky if we get in one.

MR. JENKINS Stop complaining and get the board out—I'll beat you, and that will be that.

MR. PARKER I can do without your bragging. *(pulls out a checkerboard and a small can, quickly places them on the table, then shakes up the can)* Close your eyes and take a man.

MR. JENKINS *(closing his eyes)* You never learn. *(reaches into the can and pulls out a checker)* It's red.

MR. PARKER All right, I get the black. *(sits at the table and rushes to set up his men)* Get your men down, Jenkins!

MR. JENKINS *(sits)* Aw, man, take it easy, the checkers ain't gon' run away! *(setting his men up)* If you could play the game I wouldn't mind it—but you can't play!—Your move.

MR. PARKER I'll start here—I just don't want Adele to catch us here playing checkers. She gave me and the boys a notice last week that we had to get jobs or get out of the house.

MR. JENKINS Don't you think it's about time you got a job? In the five years I've been knowing you, I can count the heads of hair you done cut in this shop on one hand.

MR. PARKER This shop is gon' work yet; I know it can. Just give me one more year and you'll see . . . Going out to get a job ain't gon' solve nothing—all it's gon' do is create a lot of bad feelings with everybody. I can't work! I don't know how to! *(moves checker)*

MR. JENKINS I bet if all your children were living far from you like mine, you'd know how to. That's one thing I don't understand about you, Parker. How long do you expect your daughter to go on supporting you and those two boys?

MR. PARKER I don't expect that! I just want some time until I can straighten things out. My dear Doris understood that. She understood me like a book. *(makes another move)*

MR. JENKINS You mean to tell me your wife enjoyed working for you?

MR. PARKER Of course she didn't, but she never worried me. You been married, Jenkins: you know what happens to a man when a woman worries him all the time, and that's what Adele been doing, worrying my head off! *(makes another move)*

MR. JENKINS Whatcha gon' do about it?

MR. PARKER I'm gon' get tough, evil and bad. That's the only sign a woman gets from a man. *(makes move)*

*(*THEOPOLIS PARKER *enters briskly from street. He is in his twenties, of medium height, and has a lean, solid physique. His younger brother,* BOBBY, *follows, carrying a huge paper bag whose contents are heavy and fragile)*

THEO That's the way I like to hear you talk, Pop, but she's gon' be walking through that door soon, and I wants to see how tough you gon' be.

MR. PARKER Leave me alone, boy.

THEO Pop, we got six more days. You got to do something!

MR. PARKER I'll do it when the time comes.

THEO Pop, the time is *now.*

MR. PARKER And right now I am playing a game of checkers with Mr. Jenkins, so leave me alone!

THEO All right—don't say I didn't warn you when she locks us out of the house!

*(*THEO *and* BOBBY *rush through the back room.* BOBBY *places the brown bag in the old refrigerator as they dart up the stairs leading to the apartment.* PARKER *makes another move)*

MR. PARKER *You're trapped, Jenkins!*

(Pause)

MR. JENKINS *(pondering)* Hmmmmmm . . . It looks that way, don't it?

MR. PARKER *(moves to the door)* While you're moaning over the board, I'll just make a little check to see if Adele is coming . . . Don't cheat now! *(he backs toward the window, watching that his adversary does not cheat. He quickly looks out the window)* Uh-uh! It's Adele! She's in the middle of the block, talking to Miss Thomas! *(rushes to take out a towel and spreads it over the checkerboard)* Come on, man! *(drags* MR. JENKINS *by the arm toward the back room)*

MR. JENKINS *What are you doing, Parker!*

MR. PARKER You gon' have to hide out in the back room, 'cause if Adele comes in here and sees you, she'll think that we been playing checkers all day!

MR. JENKINS I don't care about that!

MR. PARKER You want to finish the game, don't you?

MR. JENKINS Yeah, but—

MR. PARKER All you have to do, Jenks, is lay low for a minute, that's all. She'll stop in and ask me something about getting a job, I'll tell her I got a good line on one, and then she'll go on upstairs. There won't be nobody left here but you and me. Whatcha say, Jenks?

MR. JENKINS *(pause)* All right, I'll do it. I don't like it, but I'll do it, and you better not mention this to nobody, you hear!

MR. PARKER Not a single soul in this world will know but you and me.

MR. JENKINS *(moves just inside the room and stands)* This is the most ridiculous thing I ever heard of, hiding in somebody's back room just to finish up a checker game.

MR. PARKER Stop fighting it, man!

MR. JENKINS All right!

MR. PARKER Not there!

MR. JENKINS What in the hell is it now!

MR. PARKER *You've got to get under the bed!*

MR. JENKINS No, I'm not gettin' under nobody's bed!

MR. PARKER Now look . . . Adele never goes through the front way. She comes through the shop and the back room, up the basement stairs to the apartment. Now you want her to catch you hiding in there, looking like a fool?

MR. JENKINS No, I can take myself out of here and go home!

MR. PARKER *(pushes* JENKINS *over to the table and uncovers the checkerboard)* Look at this! Now you just take a good look at this board! *(releases him)*

MR. JENKINS I'm looking, so what?

MR. PARKER *So what?* I got you and you know it! There ain't no way in the world you'll ever get out of that little trap I got you in. *And it's your move.* How many years we been playing against each other?

MR. JENKINS Three.

MR. PARKER Never won a game from you in all that time, have I?

MR. JENKINS That ain't the half of it. You ain't gon' win one either.

MR. PARKER Now that I finally got you, that's easy talk, comin' from a running man. All right, go on. Run. *(moves away)*

MR. JENKINS Go on, hell! All I gotta do is put my king here, give you this jump here, move this man over there, and you're dead!

MR. PARKER *(turns to him)* Try me then. Try me, or are you scared at last I'm gon' beat you?

MR. JENKINS I can't do it now, there ain't enough time!

MR. PARKER *(strutting like a sport)* Run, rabbit, run . . .

MR. JENKINS All right! I'll get under the bed. But I swear, Parker, I'm gon' beat you silly! *(they move into the back room)*

MR. PARKER Hurry it up then. We ain't got much time.

(As MR. PARKER *struggles to help* MR. JENKINS *get under the bed in the back room,* ADELE *comes in from the street. She is in her late twenties, well dressed in conventional New York office attire. She is carrying a smart-looking handbag and a manila envelope. She stops near the table on which checkerboard is hidden under towel.* MR. PARKER *enters from the back room)*

MR. PARKER Hi, honey.

(She doesn't answer, instead busies herself putting minor things in order)

ADELE You looked for work today?

MR. PARKER All morning . . .

(Pause)

ADELE No luck in the morning, and so you played checkers all afternoon.

MR. PARKER No, I've been working on a few ideas of mine. My birthday comes up the tenth of the month, and I plan to celebrate it with an idea to shake up this whole neighborhood, and then I'm gon' really go to the country!

ADELE Don't go to the country—go to work, huh? *(moves toward back room)* Oh, God, I'm tired!

MR. PARKER *(rushing to get her away from bed)* Come on and let me take you upstairs. I know you must've had yourself a real tough day at the office . . . and you can forget about cooking supper and all of that stuff.

ADELE *(breaks away, moves back into shop toward counter)* Thank you, but I've already given myself the privilege of not cooking your supper tonight.

MR. PARKER You did?

ADELE The way I figure it, you should have my dinner waiting for me.

MR. PARKER But I don't know how to cook.

ADELE *(turns sharply)* You can learn.

MR. PARKER Now look, Adele, if you got something on your mind, say it, 'cause you know damn well I ain't doin' no cooking.

ADELE *(pause)* All right, I will. A thought came to me today as it does every day, and I'm damn tired of thinking about it—

MR. PARKER What?

ADELE —and that is, I've been down at that motor-license bureau so long, sometimes I forget the reasons I ever took the job in the first place.

MR. PARKER Now look, everybody knows you quit college and came home to help your mama out. Everybody knows it! What you want me to do? Write some prayers to you?

(The two boys enter the back room from upstairs)

ADELE I just want you to get a job!

(The boys step into shop and stand apart from each other)

BOBBY Hey, Adele.

ADELE Well! From what cave did you fellows crawl out of? I didn't know you hung around barbershops . . . Want a haircut, boys?

THEO For your information, this is the first time we been in this barbershop today. We been upstairs thinking.

ADELE With what?

THEO With our *minds*, baby!

ADELE If the two of you found that house upstairs so attractive to keep you in it all day, then I can think of only three things: the telephone, the bed, and the kitchen.

BOBBY The kitchen, that's it: we been washing dishes all day!

ADELE I don't like that, Bobby!

THEO And I don't like your attitude!

ADELE Do you like it when I go out of here every morning to work?

THEO There you go again with that same old tired talk: work! Mama understood about us, I don't know why you gotta give everybody a hard time . . .

ADELE That was one of Mama's troubles: understanding everybody.

THEO Now don't start that junk with me!

ADELE I have got to start that, *Mr. Theopolis Parker!*

MR. PARKER Hold on now, there's no need for all this . . . Can't we settle this later on, Adele . . .

ADELE We settle it now. You got six days left, so you gotta do something, and quick. I got a man coming here tomorrow to change the locks on the door. So for the little time you have left, you'll have to come by me to enter this house.

THEO Who gives you the right to do that?

ADELE Me, Adele Eloise Parker, Black, over twenty-one, and the only working person in this house! *(pause)* I am not going to let the three of you drive me into the grave the way you did Mama. And if you really want to know how I feel about that, I'll tell you: Mama killed herself because there was no kind of order in this house. There was nothing but her old-fashion love for a bum like you, Theo—and this one *(points to* BOBBY*)* who's got nothing better to do with his time but to shoplift every time he walks into a department store. And you, Daddy, you and those fanciful stories you're always ready to tell, and all the talk of the good old days when you were the big vaudeville star, of hitting the numbers big. How? How, Daddy? The money you spent on the numbers you got from Mama . . . In a way, you let Mama make a bum out of you—you let her kill herself!

MR. PARKER That's a terrible thing to say, Adele, and I'm not going to let you put that off on me!

ADELE But the fact remains that in the seven years you've been in this barbershop you haven't earned enough money to buy two hot dogs! Most of your time is spent playing checkers with that damn Mr. Jenkins.

THEO *(breaks in)* Why don't you get married or something! We don't need you—Pop is here, it's HIS HOUSE!

ADELE You're lucky I don't get married and—

THEO Nobody wants you, baby!

ADELE (THEO*'s remark stops her for a moment. She resettles herself)* All right, you just let someone ask me, and I'll leave you with *Pop,* to starve with Pop. Or, there's another way: why don't the three of you just leave right now and try making it on your own? Why don't we try that!

MR. PARKER What about my shop?

ADELE Since I'm the one that has to pay the extra forty dollars a month for you to keep this place, there's going to be no more shop. It was a bad investment and the whole of Harlem knows it!

MR. PARKER *(grabbing her by the arm, in desperation)* I'm fifty-four years old!

ADELE *(pulling away)* Don't touch me!

MR. PARKER You go ahead and do what you want, but I'm not leaving this shop! *(crosses away from her)*

ADELE Can't you understand, Father? I can't go on forever supporting three grown men! *That ain't right!*

(Long pause)

MR. PARKER *(shaken by her remarks)* No, it's not right—it's not right at all.

ADELE —It's going to be *you* or *me.*

BOBBY *(after a pause)* I'll do what I can, Adele.

ADELE You'll do *more* than you can.

BOBBY I'll do more than I can.

ADELE Is that all right by you, Mr. Theopolis?

THEO Yes.

(Pause)

ADELE That's fine. Out of this house tomorrow morning—before I leave here, or with me—suit your choice. And don't look so mournful *(gathers up her belongings at the shelf)*, smile. You're going to be happier than you think, earning a living for a change. *(moves briskly through the back room and up the stairs)*

BOBBY You do look pretty bad, Theo. A job might be just the thing for you.

(MR. JENKINS *comes rushing from the bed into the shop)*

MR. PARKER Jenkins! I plumb forgot—

MR. JENKINS I let you make a fool out of me, Parker!

MR. PARKER We can still play!

MR. JENKINS *(gathering his jacket and coat)* We can't play nothing, I'm going home where I belong!

MR. PARKER Okay, okay, I'll come over to your place tonight.

MR. JENKINS That's the only way. I ain't gon' have my feelings hurt by that daughter of yours.

MR. PARKER I'll see you tonight—about eight.

MR. JENKINS *(at the door)* And, Parker, tell me something?

MR. PARKER Yeah, what, Jenks?

MR. JENKINS Are you positively sure Adele is your daughter?

MR. PARKER Get out of here! (MR. JENKINS *rushes out)* Now what made him ask a silly question like that?

THEO I think he was trying to tell you that you ain't supposed to be taking all that stuff from Adele.

BOBBY Yeah, Pop, he's right.

(MR. PARKER *starts putting his checker set together.)*

THEO *(to* BOBBY*)* I don't know what you talking about—you had your chance a few minutes ago, but all you did was poke your eyes at me and nod your head like a fool.

BOBBY I don't see why you gotta make such a big thing out of her taking charge. Somebody's gotta do it. I think she's right!

THEO I know what she's up to. She wants us to get jobs so she can fix up the house like she always wanted it, and then it's gon' happen.

BOBBY What's that?

THEO She gon' get married to some konkhead out on the Avenue, and then she gon' throw us out the door.

BOBBY She wouldn't do that.

THEO She wouldn't, huh? Put yourself in her place. She's busting thirty wide open.

Thirty years old—that's a lot of years for a broad that's not married.

BOBBY I never thought of it that way . . .

THEO *(in half confidence)* And you know something else, Pop? I sneaked and peeped at her bank book, and you know what she got saved?

MR. PARKER and BOBBY *(simultaneously, turning their heads)* How much!?

THEO Two thousand two hundred and sixty-five dollars!

BOBBY WHAT!!!

MR. PARKER I don't believe it!

THEO You better—and don't let her hand you that stuff about how she been sacrificing all these years for the house. The only way she could've saved up that kind of money was by staying right here!

MR. PARKER Well, I'll be damned—two thousand dollars!

THEO She better watch out is all I gotta say, 'cause I know some guys out there on that Avenue who don't do nothing but sit around all day figuring out ways to beat working girls out of their savings.

MR. PARKER You oughta know, 'cause you're one of them yourself. The way I figure it, Theo, anybody that can handle you the way she did a few minutes ago can very well take care of themselves. *(he occupies himself putting checkers and board away and cleaning up)*

THEO That's mighty big talk coming from you, after the way she treated you.

MR. PARKER Lay off me, boy.

THEO You going out to look for a job?

MR. PARKER I'm giving it some serious thought.

THEO Well, I'm not. I ain't wasting myself on no low, dirty, dead-end job. I got my paintings to think about.

BOBBY Do you really think you're some kind of painter or something?

THEO You've seen them.

BOBBY Yeah, but how would I know?

THEO *(rushes into the back room, takes paintings from behind the refrigerator)* All right, look at 'em.

BOBBY Don't bring that stuff in here to me—show it to Pop!

*(*THEO *holds up two ghastly, inept paintings to his brother.* MR. PARKER, *sweeping the floor, pays no attention)*

THEO Look at it! Now tell me what you see.

BOBBY Nothing.

THEO You've got to see something—even an idiot has impressions.

BOBBY I ain't no idiot.

THEO All right, fool then.

BOBBY Now look, you better stop throwing them words "fool" and "idiot" at me any time you feel like it. I'm gon' be one more fool, and then my fist is gonna land right upside your head!

THEO Take it easy now—I tell you what: try to see something.

BOBBY Try?

THEO Yeah, close your eyes and really try.

BOBBY *(closes his eyes)* Okay, I'm trying, but I don't know how I'm gon' see anything with my eyes closed!

THEO Well, open them!

BOBBY They open.

THEO Now tell me what you see.

BOBBY I see paint.

THEO I know you see paint, stupid.

BOBBY *(slaps him ferociously across the face)* Now I told you about that! Every time you call me out of my name, you get hit!

THEO You'll never understand!

BOBBY All I know is that a picture is supposed to be pretty, but I'm sorry, that mess you got there is downright ugly!

THEO You're hopeless—You understand this, don't you, Pop? *(holding the painting for him to see)*

MR. PARKER *(not looking at the painting)* Don't ask me—I don't know nothing about no painting.

THEO You were an artist once.

MR. PARKER That was a different kind.

THEO Didn't you ever go out on the stage with a new thing inside of you? One of them nights when you just didn't want to do that ol' soft-shoe routine? You knew you had to do it—after all, it was your job—but when you did it, you gave it a little bite here, a little acid there, and still, with all that, they laughed at you anyway. Didn't that ever happen to you?

MR. PARKER More than once . . . But you're BSn', boy, and you know it. You been something new every year since you quit school. First you was going to be a racing-car driver, then a airplane pilot, then a office big shot, and now it's a painter. As smart a boy as you is, you should've stayed in school, but who do you think you're fooling with them pictures?—It all boils down to one thing: you don't want to work. But I'll tell you something, Theo: time done run out on you. Adele's not playing, so you might as well put all that junk and paint away.

THEO Who the hell is Adele? You're my father, you're the man of the house.

MR. PARKER True, and that's what I intend to be, but until I get a job, I'm gon' play it cool.

THEO You're going to let her push you out into the streets to hustle up a job. You're an old man. You ain't used to working, it might kill you.

MR. PARKER Yeah, but what kind of leg do I have to stand on if she puts me out in the street?

THEO She's bluffing!

MR. PARKER A buddy of mine who was in this same kind of fix told me exactly what you just said. Well, the last time I saw him, he was standing on the corner of Eighth Avenue and 125th Street at four o'clock in the morning, twenty-degree weather, in nothing but his drawers, mumbling to himself, "I could've sworn she was bluffing!"

THEO Hey, Pop! Let me put it to you this way: if none of us come up with anything in that two-week deadline she gave us—none of us, you hear me?

MR. PARKER I hear you and that's just about all.

THEO Don't you get the point? That's three of us—you, me, and Bobby. What she gon' do? Throw the three of us out in the street? I tell you, she ain't gon' do that!

MR. PARKER If you want to take that chance, that's your business, but don't try to make me take it with you. Anyway, it ain't right that she has to work for three grown men. It just ain't right.

THEO Mama did it for you.

MR. PARKER *(sharply)* That was different. She was my wife. She knew things about me you will never know. We oughtn' talk about her at all.

THEO I'm sorry, Pop, but ever since Mama's funeral I've been thinking. Mama was the hardest-working person I ever knew, and it killed her! Is that what I'm supposed to do? No, that's not it, I know it's not. You know what I've been doing? I've been talking to some people, to a very important person right here in Harlem, and I told him about this big idea of mine—

MR. PARKER You're loaded with ideas, boy—*bad ideas! (puts broom away)*

THEO WHY DON'T YOU LISTEN TO WHAT I HAVE TO SAY!

MR. PARKER Listen to you for what? Another con game you got up your sleeve because your sister's got fed up with you lying around this house all day while she's knocking herself out. You're pulling the same damn thing on me you did with those ugly paintings of yours a few minutes ago.

THEO Okay, I can't paint. So I was jiving, but now I got something I really want to do—something I got to do!

MR. PARKER If you're making a point, Theo, you've gotta be smarter than you're doing to get it through to me.

THEO *(goes to back room, opens refrigerator, and takes out brown-paper bag, then comes back into the shop)* Pop, I got something here to show how smart I really am. *(lifts an old jug out of the bag)* Check this out, Pop! Check it out!

MR. PARKER What is it?

THEO Whiskey—corn whiskey—you want some?

MR. PARKER *(hovers)* Well, I'll try a little bit of it out, but we better not let Adele see us.

THEO *(starts unscrewing cork from jug)* That girl sure puts a scare in you, Pop, and I remember when you wouldn't take no stuff off Mama, Adele, or nobody.

MR. PARKER God is the only person I fear.

THEO *(stops unscrewing the jug)* God! Damn, you're all alike!

MR. PARKER What are you talking about, boy?

THEO You, the way Mama was—ask you any question you can't answer, and you throw that Bible stuff at us.

MR. PARKER I don't get you.

THEO For instance, let me ask you about the Black man's oppressions, and you'll tell me about some small nation in the East rising one day to rule the world. Ask you about pain and dying, and you say, "God wills it." . . . Fear?—and you'll tell me about Daniel, and how Daniel wasn't scared of them lions. Am I right or wrong?

MR. PARKER It's all in the book and you can't dispute it.

THEO You wanta bet? If that nation in the

East ever do rise, how can I be sure they won't be worse than the jokers we got running things now?—Nobody but nobody wills me to pain and dying, not if I can do something about it. That goes for John, Peter, Mary, J.C., the whole bunch of 'em! And as for ol' Daniel: sure, Daniel didn't care nothing about them lions—*but them lions didn't give a damn about him either! They tore him into a million pieces!*

MR. PARKER That's a lie! That's an ungodly, unholy lie! *(takes his Bible from the shelf)* And I'll prove it!

THEO What lie?

MR. PARKER *(moving from the counter, thumbing through Bible)* You and those bastard ideas of yours. Here, here it is! *(reading from Bible)* "And when he came near unto the den to Daniel, he cried with a pained voice; The King spoke and said to Daniel: 'O Daniel, servant of the living God, is thy God, whom thou servest continually, able to deliver thee from the lions?' Then said Daniel unto the King: 'O King, live forever! My God hath sent his angel, and hath shut the lions' mouths, and they have not hurt me; for as much as before him innocence was found in me, and also before thee, O King, have I done no hurt.' Then was the King exceeding glad, and commanded that they should take Daniel up out of the den. So Daniel was taken up out of the den, and no manner of hurt was found upon him, because he trusted his God!!!" *(slams the book closed, triumphant)*

THEO Hollywood, Pop, Hollywood!

MR. PARKER Damn you! How I ever brought something like you into this world, I'll never know! You're no damn good! Sin! That's who your belief is! Sin and corruption! With you, it's nothing but women! Whiskey! Women! Whiskey! *(while he is carrying on,* THEO *pours out a glass of corn and puts it in* MR. PARKER*'s hand)* Women! Whiskey! *(takes a taste)* Whisk— Where did you get this from? *(sits on throne)*

THEO *(slapping* BOBBY*'s hand)* I knew you'd get the message, Pop—I just knew it!

MR. PARKER Why, boy, this is the greatest corn I ever tasted!

BOBBY And Theo puts that stuff together like he was born to be a whiskey maker!

MR. PARKER Where did you learn to make corn like this?

THEO Don't you remember? You taught me.

MR. PARKER By George, I did! Why, you weren't no more'n nine years old—

THEO Eight. Let's have another one. *(pours another for* PARKER*)* Drink up. Here's to ol' Daniel. You got to admit one thing—he had a whole lot of heart!

MR. PARKER *(drinks up and puts his hand out again)* Another one, please . . .

THEO *(pouring)* Anything you say, Pop! *You're the boss of this house!*

MR. PARKER Now that's the truth if you ever spoke it. *(drinks up)* Whew! This is good! *(putting his glass out again, slightly tipsy)*

THEO About this idea of mine, Pop: well, it's got something to do with this corn.

MR. PARKER *(drinks up)* Wow! Boy, people oughta pay you to make this stuff.

THEO Well, that's what I kinda had in mind. I tested some of it out the other day, and I was told this corn liquor could start a revolution—that is, if I wanted to start one. I let a preacher taste some, and he asked me to make him a whole keg for him.

MR. PARKER *(pauses. Then, in a sudden change of mood)* God! Damnit!

BOBBY What's wrong, Pop?

MR. PARKER I miss her, boy, I tell you, I miss her! Was it really God's will?

THEO Don't you believe that—*don't you ever believe that!*

MR. PARKER But I think, boy—I think hard!

THEO That's all right. We think hard too. We got it from you. Ain't that right, Bobby?

BOBBY Yeah.

MR. PARKER *(pause)* You know something? That woman was the first woman I ever got close to—your mama . . .

BOBBY *How old were you?*

MR. PARKER Twenty.

BOBBY Aw, come on, Pop!

MR. PARKER May God wipe me away from this earth . . .

THEO Twenty years old and you had never touched a woman? You must've been in bad shape.

MR. PARKER I'll tell you about it.

THEO Here he goes with another one of his famous stories!

MR. PARKER I can always go on upstairs, you know.

THEO No, Pop, we want to hear it.

MR. PARKER Well, I was working in this circus in Tampa, Florida—your mother's hometown. You remember Bob Shepard—well, we had this little dance routine of ours we used to do a sample of outside the tent. One day we was out there doing one of our numbers, when right in the middle of the number I spied this fine, foxy-looking thing, blinking her eyes at me. 'Course ol' Bob kept saying it was him she was looking at, but I knew it was *me*—'cause if there was one thing that was my specialty, it was a fine-looking woman.

THEO You live twenty years of you life not getting anywhere near a woman, and all of a sudden they become *your specialty?*

MR. PARKER Yeah, being that—

THEO Being that you had never had a woman for all them terrible years, naturally it was on your mind all the time.

MR. PARKER That's right.

THEO And it being on your mind so much, you sorta became a specialist on women?

MR. PARKER Right again.

THEO *(laughs)* I don't know. But I guess you got a point there!

MR. PARKER You want to hear this or not!?

BOBBY Yeah, go on, Pop. *I'm* listening.

MR. PARKER Well, while I was standing on the back of the platform, I motions to her with my hand to kinda move around to the side of the stand, so I could talk to 'er. She strolled 'round to the side, stood there for a while, and you know what? Ol' Bob wouldn't let me get a word in edgewise. But you know what she told him; she said Mister, you talk like a fool! *(all laugh)*

BOBBY That was Mama, all right.

MR. PARKER So I asked her if she would like to meet me after the circus closed down. When I got off that night, sure enough, she was waiting for me. We walked up to the main section of town, off to the side of the road, 'cause we had a hard rain that day and the road was full of muddy little ponds. I got to talking to her and telling her funny stories and she would laugh—boy, I'm telling you that woman could laugh!

THEO That was your technique, huh? Keep 'em laughing!

MR. PARKER Believe it or not, it worked—'cause she let me kiss her. I kissed her under this big ol' pecan tree. She could kiss too. When that woman kissed me, somethin' grabbed me so hard and shook me so, I fell flat on my back into a big puddle of water! *And that woman killed herself laughing! (pause)* I married her two weeks later.

THEO And then you started making up for lost time. I'm glad you did, Pop—'cause if you hadn't, I wouldn't be here today.

MR. PARKER If I know you, you'd have made some kind of arrangement.

BOBBY What happened after that?

MR. PARKER We just lived and had fun—and children, too, that part you know about. We lived bad and we lived good—and then my legs got wobbly, and my feet got heavy, I lost my feeling, and everything just stayed as it was. *(pause)* I only wish I had been as good a haircutter as I was a dancer. Maybe she wouldn't have had to work so hard. She might be living today.

THEO Forget it, Pop—it's all in the gone by. Come on, you need another drink. *(pouring)*

MR. PARKER Get me to talking about them old days. It hurts, I tell you, it—

THEO Pop, you have got to stop thinking about those things. We've got work to do!

MR. PARKER You said you had an idea . . .

THEO Yes—you see, Pop, this idea has to do with Harlem. It has to do with the preservation of Harlem. That's what it's all about. So I went to see this leader, and I spoke to him about it. He thought it was great and said he would pay me to use it!

MR. PARKER Who wants to preserve this dump! Tear it down, is what I say!

THEO But this is a different kind of preserving. Preserve it for Black men—preserve it for men like you, me, and Bobby. That's what it's all about.

MR. PARKER That sounds good.

THEO Of course, I told this leader I couldn't promise to do anything until I had spoken to my father. I said, after straightening everything out with you I would make arrangements for the two of you to meet.

MR. PARKER Meet him for what?

THEO For making money! For business! *This man knows how to put people in business!*

MR. PARKER All right, I'll meet him. What's his name?

THEO —But first you gotta have a showdown with Adele and put her in her place once and for all.

MR. PARKER Now wait just a minute. You didn't say Adele would have anything to do with this.

THEO Pop, this man can't be dealing with men who let women rule them. Pop, you've got to tell that girl off or we can't call ourselves men!

MR. PARKER *(pause)* All right. If she don't like it, that's too bad. Whatever you have in mind for us to do with this leader of yours, we'll do it.

THEO Now that's the way I like to hear my old man talk! Take a drink, Pop! *(starts popping his fingers and moves dancing about the room)*

We're gonna show 'em now
We're gonna show 'em how
All over
This ol' Harlem Town!

*(*THEO *and* BOBBY *start making rhythmic scat sounds with their lips as they dance around the floor)*—Come on, Pop, show us how you used to cut one of them things!

BOBBY *(dancing)* This is how he did it!

THEO Nawwww, that's not it. He did it like this!

MR. PARKER *(rising)* No, no! Neither one of you got it! Speed up that riff a little bit . . . *(the two boys speed up the riff, singing, stomping their feet, clapping their hands. Humped over,* MR. PARKER *looks down on the floor concentrating)* Faster! *(they speed it up more)*

THEO Come on now, Pop—let 'er loose!

MR. PARKER Give me time . . .

BOBBY *Let that man have some time!*

*(*MR. PARKER *breaks into his dance)*

THEO Come on, Pop, take it with you!

BOBBY Work, Pop!

THEO DOWNTOWN!

*(*MR. PARKER *does a coasting "camel walk")*

BOBBY NOW BRING IT ON BACK UPTOWN!

*(*MR. PARKER *really breaks loose: a rapid series of complicated dance steps)*

THEO YEAHHHHHHH!

BOBBY That's what I'm talkin' about!

*(*ADELE *enters, stops at the entrance to the shop, observes the scene, bemused.* PARKER, *glimpsing her first, in one motion abruptly stops dancing and reaches for the broom.* BOBBY *looks for something to busy himself with.* THEO *just stares)*

ADELE Supper's ready, fellows!

(Curtain)

Scene Two

(Six days later. Late afternoon.

BOBBY *is seated in the barber's throne, munching on a sandwich.* THEO *enters from the front of the shop)*

THEO Did Pop get back yet? *(*BOBBY *shrugs shoulders)* You eating again? Damn. *(calling upstairs)* Pop! *(No answer.* THEO *checks his watch, steps back into shop, looks through window, then crosses to* BOBBY *and snatches the sandwich from his mouth)* You eat too damn much!

BOBBY What the fuck you do that for?

THEO *(handing the sandwich back)* 'Cause you always got a mouth full of peanut butter and jelly!

BOBBY I'm hungry! And let me tell you something: don't you *ever* snatch any food from my mouth again.

THEO You'll hit me—you don't care nothing about your brother. One of these days, I'm gon' hit back.

BOBBY *Nigger!* The day you swing your hand at me, you'll draw back a nub.

THEO You see! That's exactly what I mean. Now when Blue gets here tonight, I don't want you talking like that, or else you gon' blow the whole deal.

BOBBY I know how to act. I don't need no lessons from you.

THEO Good. I got a job for you.

BOBBY A job? Shit!

THEO Don't get knocked out now—it ain't no real job. I just want you to jump over to Smith's on 125th Street and pick me up a portable typewriter.

BOBBY Typewriter—for what?

THEO Don't ask questions, just go and get it.

BOBBY Them typewriters cost a lotta money.

THEO You ain't gon' use money.

BOBBY You mean—

THEO —I mean you walk in there and take one.

BOBBY Naw, you don't mean I walk into nowhere and take nothing!

THEO Now, Bobby.

BOBBY No!

THEO Aw, come on, Bobby. You the one been bragging about how good you are, how you can walk into any store and get anything you wanted, provided it was not too heavy to carry out.

BOBBY I ain't gon' do it!

THEO You know what day it is?

BOBBY Thursday.

THEO That's right. Thursday, May 10th.

BOBBY What's that suppose to mean, Thieves' Convention on 125th Street?

THEO It's Pop's birthday!

BOBBY I didn't know he was still having them.

THEO Well, let me tell you something: Adele remembered it and she's planning on busting into this shop tonight with a birthday cake to surprise him.

BOBBY She suppose to be throwing us out today. That don't make no sense with her buying him a birthday cake.

THEO He's been looking for work, I guess she changed her mind about him. Maybe it's gon' be just me and you that goes.

BOBBY *(pause)* What's he gon' type?

THEO Them lies he's always telling—like the one about how he met Mama. Pop can tell some of the greatest lies you ever heard of and you know how he's always talking about writing them down.

BOBBY Pop don't know nothing 'bout writing—specially no typewriting!

THEO *(takes out his father's notebook)* Oh no? Take a look at this. *(hands book to* BOBBY*)* All he has to do is put it down on paper the way he tells it. Who knows, somebody might get interested in it for television or movies, and we can make ourselves some money, and besides, I kinda think he would get a real charge out of you thinking about him that way—don't you?

BOBBY *(pause)* Well, ain't no use in lettin' you go over there, gettin' yourself in jail with them old clumsy fingers of yours.

THEO Good boy, Bobby! *(*MR. PARKER *enters the shop)* Hey, Pop! Did you get that thing straightened out with Adele yet?

MR. PARKER What?

THEO *Adele?*

MR. PARKER Oh, yeah, I'm gon' take care of that right away. *(shoves* BOBBY *out of throne and sits)*

THEO Where you been all day?

*(*BOBBY *moves into back room)*

MR. PARKER Downtown, seeing about some jobs.

THEO You sure don't care much about yourself.

MR. PARKER I can agree with you on that, because lookin' for a job can really hurt a man. I was interviewed five times today, and I could've shot every last one of them interviewers—the white ones and the colored ones too. I don't know if I can take any more of this.

THEO Yeah, looking for a job can be very low-grading to a man, and it gets worse after you get the job. Anyway, I'm glad you got back here on time, or you would've missed your appointment. *(no response from* PARKER*)* Now don't tell me you don't remember! The man, the man that's suppose to come here and tell you how life in Harlem can be profitable.

MR. PARKER *(steps out of throne, edging toward back room)* Oh, that.

THEO *(following him)* Oh, that—my foot! Today is the day we're suppose to come up with those jobs, and you ain't said one word to Adele about it—not one single word! All you do is waste your time looking for work! Now that don't make no sense at all, Pop, and you know it.

MR. PARKER Look, son. Let me go upstairs now and tell her about all the disappointments I suffered today, soften her up a bit, and then I'll come on back down here to meet your man. I promise, you won't have to worry about me going downtown any more—not after what I went through today. And I certainly ain't giving up my shop for nobody! *(exits upstairs)*

THEO *(turns to* BOBBY*, who's at the mirror)* Now that's the way I like to hear my old man talk! Hey, baby, don't forget that thing. It's late, we ain't got much time.

BOBBY All right!

(A jet-black-complexioned young man comes in. He is dressed all in blue and wears sunglasses. He carries a gold-top cane and a large salesman's valise. He stops just inside the door)

THEO Blue, baby!

BLUE Am I late?

THEO No, my father just walked in the door. He's upstairs now, but he'll be right back down in a few minutes. Let me take your things. *(takes* BLUE*'s cane and valise)* Sit down, man, while I fix you a drink. *(places* BLUE*'s things on the table and moves into back room.* BOBBY *enters shop)*

BLUE Hey, Bobby. How's the stores been treating you?

BOBBY I'm planning on retiring next year. *(laughs)*

THEO *(returning with jug and two glasses. Moves to the table and pours)* I was thinking, Blue—we can't let my old man know about our "piano brigade." I know he ain't going for that, but we can fix it where he will never know a thing.

BLUE You know your father better than I do. *(takes a drink)*

BOBBY What's the "piano brigade"?

THEO Blue here has the best thieves and store burglars in this part of town, and we plan to work on those businesses over on 125th Street until they run the insurance companies out of business.

BOBBY You mean breaking into people's stores at night and taking their stuff?

THEO That's right, but not the way you do it. We'll be organized, we'll be revolutionary.

BOBBY If the police catch you, they ain't gon' care what you is, and if Pop ever finds out, the police gon' seem like church girls! *(slips out the front door)*

THEO *(after him)* You just remember that the only crime you'll ever commit is the one you get caught at! *(pause)* Which reminds me, Blue—I don't want Bobby to be a part of that "piano brigade."

BLUE If that's the way you want it, that's the way it shall be, Theo. How's your sister?

THEO You mean Adele?

BLUE You got a sister named Mary or something?

THEO What's this with Adele?

BLUE I want to know, how are you going to get along with her, selling bootleg whiskey in this place?

THEO This is not her place, it's my father's. And once he puts his okay on the deal, that's it. What kind of house do you think we're living in, where we gon' let some woman tell us what to do? Come here, let me show you something. *(moves into back room.* BLUE *follows)* How you like it—ain't it something?

BLUE *(standing in doorway)* It's a back room.

THEO Yeah, I know. But I have some great plans for reshaping it by knocking down this wall, and putting—

BLUE Like I said, it's a back room. All I wanta know is, will it do the job? It's a good room. You'll do great with that good-tasting corn of yours. You're going to be so busy here, you're going to grow to hate this place—you might not have any time for your love life, Theopolis!

THEO *(laughing)* Don't you worry about that—I can manage my sex life!

BLUE Sex! Who's talking about sex? You surprise me, Theo. Everyone's been telling me about how you got so much heart, how you so deep. I sit and talk to you about life, and you don't know the difference between sex and love.

THEO Is it that important?

BLUE Yes, it is, ol' buddy, if you want to hang out with me, and you do want to hang out with me, don't you?

THEO That depends—

BLUE It depends upon you knowing that sex's got nothing to do with anything but you and some woman laying up in some funky bed, pumping and sweating your life away all for one glad moment—you hear that, *one moment!*

THEO I'll take that moment!

BLUE With every woman you've had?

THEO One out of a hundred!

BLUE *(laughing, and moving back into shop)* One out of a hundred! All that sweat! All that pumping and grinding for the sake of one little dead minute out of a hundred hours!

*(*MR. PARKER *comes in from upstairs.)*

THEO *(pause. Stopping* PARKER*)* Pop, you know who this is?

MR. PARKER I can't see him.

THEO This is Blue!

MR. PARKER Blue who?

THEO The man I was telling you about . . . *Mr. Blue Haven.*

MR. PARKER *(extends his hand to shake* BLUE*'s)* Please to make your acquaintance, Mr. Haven.

BLUE *(shaking* MR. PARKER*'s hand)* Same to you, Mr. Parker.

THEO You sure you don't know who Blue Haven is, Pop?

MR. PARKER I'm sorry, but I truly don't know you, Mr. Haven. If you're a celebrity, you must accept my apology. You see, since I got out of the business, I don't read the *Variety* any more.

THEO I'm not talking about a celebrity.

MR. PARKER Oh, no?

THEO He's the leader!

MR. PARKER Ohhhhh!

THEO Right here in Harlem.

MR. PARKER Where else he gon' be but in Harlem? We got more leaders within ten square blocks of this barbershop than they got liars down in City Hall. That's why you dressed up that way, huh, boy? So people can pick you out of a crowded room?

THEO Pop, this is serious!

MR. PARKER All right, go on, don't get carried away—there are some things I don't catch on to right away, Mr. Blue.

THEO Well, get to this: I got to thinking the other day when Adele busted in here shoving everybody around—I was thinking about this barbershop, and I said to myself: Pop's gon' lose this shop if he don't start making himself some money.

MR. PARKER Now tell me something I don't know. *(sits on throne)*

THEO Here I go. What would you say if I were to tell you that Blue here can make it possible for you to have a thriving business going on, right here in this shop, for twenty-four hours a day?

MR. PARKER What is he—some kind of hair grower!

THEO Even if you don't cut but one head of hair a week!

MR. PARKER Do I look like a fool to you?

THEO *(holds up his jug)* *Selling this!*

MR. PARKER *(pause)* Well, well, well. I knew it was something like that. I didn't exactly know what it was, but I knew it was something. And I don't want to hear it!

THEO Pop, you've always been a man to listen—even when you didn't agree, even when I was wrong, you listened! That's the kind of man you are! You—

MR. PARKER Okay, okay, I'm listening!

THEO *(pause)* Tell him who you are, Blue.

BLUE I am the Prime Minister of the Harlem De-Colonization Association.

MR. PARKER *(pause)* Some kind of organization?

BLUE Yes.

MR. PARKER *(as an aside, almost under his breath)* They got all kinds of committees in Harlem. What was that name again, "De"?

THEO De-Colo-ni-zation! Which means that Harlem is owned and operated by Mr. You-Know-Who. Let me get this stuff—we gon' show you something . . . *(moves to the table and opens* BLUE*'s valise)*

BLUE We're dead serious about this project, Mr. Parker. I'd like you to look at this chart.

THEO And you'll see, we're not fooling. *(hurriedly pins charts taken from* BLUE*'s valise on wall out in the shop)*

MR. PARKER *(reading from center chart)* The Harlem De-Colonization Association, with Future Perspective for Bedford Stuyvesant. *(turns to* BLUE*)* All right, so you got an organization. What do you do? I've never heard of you.

BLUE The only reason you've never heard of us is because we don't believe in picketing, demonstrating, rioting, and all that stuff. We always look like we're doing something that we ain't doing, but we are doing something—and in that way nobody gets hurt. Now you may think we're passive. To the contrary, we believe in direct action. We are doers, enterprisers, thinkers—and most of all, we're businessmen! Our aim is to drive Mr. You-Know-Who out of Harlem.

MR. PARKER Who's that Mr. You-Know-Who?

THEO Damn, Pop! The white man!

MR. PARKER Oh, himmm!

BLUE We like to use that name for our members in order to get away from the bad feelings we have whenever we use the word "white." We want our members to always be objective and in this way we shall move forward. Before we get through, there won't be a single Mr. You-Know-Who left in this part of town. We're going to capture the imagination of the people of Harlem. And that's never been done before, you know.

MR. PARKER Now, tell me how?

BLUE *(standing before the charts, pointing with his cane)* You see this here. This is what we call a "brigade." And you see this yellow circle?

MR. PARKER What's that for?

BLUE My new and entertaining system for playing the numbers. You do play the numbers, Mr. Parker?

MR. PARKER I do.

BLUE You see, I have a lot of colors in this system and these colors are mixed up with a whole lot of numbers, and the idea is to catch the right number with the right color. The right number can be anything from one to a hundred, but in order to win, the color must always be black. The name of this game is called "Black Heaven." It's the color part that gives everybody all the fun in playing this game of mine.

MR. PARKER Anybody ever catch it?

BLUE Sure, but not until every number and every color has paid itself off. The one thing you'll find out about my whole operation: you can't lose. *(pauses for effect)*

MR. PARKER Keep talking.

BLUE Now over here is the Red Square Circle Brigade, and this thing here is at the heart of my dream to create here in Harlem a symbolic life-force in the heart of the people.

MR. PARKER You don't say . . .

BLUE Put up that target, Theo. *(*THEO *hurriedly pins on wall a dart target with the face of a beefy, Southern-looking white man as bull's-eye)*

MR. PARKER Why, that's that ol' dirty sheriff from that little town in Mississippi!

BLUE *(taking a dart from* THEO*)* That's right—we got a face on a target for every need. We got governors, mayors, backwood crackers, city crackers, Southern crackers, and Northern crackers. We got all kinds of faces on these targets that any good Harlemite would be willing to buy for the sake of slinging one of these darts in that bastard's throat! *(throws dart, puncturing face on board)*

MR. PARKER Let me try it one time. *(Rising, takes dart from* BLUE *and slings it into the face on the target)* Got him! *(a big laugh)*

BLUE It's like I said, Mr. Parker: the idea is to capture the imagination of the people!

MR. PARKER You got more? Let me see more!

BLUE Now this is our green circle—that's Theo and his corn liquor—for retail purposes will be called "Black Lightning." This whiskey of Theo's can make an everlasting contribution to this life-force I've been telling you about. I've tested this whiskey out in every neighborhood in Harlem, and everybody claimed it was the best they ever tasted this side of Washington, D.C. You see, we plan to supply every after-hours joint in this area, and this will run Mr. You-Know-Who and his bonded product out of Harlem.

THEO You see, Pop, this all depends on the barbershop being open night and day so the people can come and go as they please, to pick up their play for the day, to get a bottle of corn, and to take one of them targets home to the kiddies. They can walk in just as if they were getting a haircut. In fact, I told Blue that we can give a haircut as a bonus for anyone who buys two quarts.

MR. PARKER What am I suppose to say now?

THEO You're suppose to be daring. You're suppose to wake up to the times, Pop! These are urgent days—a man has to stand up and be counted!

MR. PARKER The police might have some counting of their own to do.

THEO Do you think I would bring you into something that was going to get us in trouble? Blue has an organization! Just like Mr. You-Know-Who. He's got members on the police force! In the city government, the state government.

BLUE Mr. Parker, if you have any reservations concerning the operation of my association, I'd be only too happy to have you come to my summer home, and I'll let you in on everything—especially our protective system against being caught doing this thing.

THEO Did you hear him, Pop, *he's got a summer home!*

MR. PARKER Aw, shut up, boy! Let me think! *(turns to* BLUE*)* So you want to use my place as a headquarters for Theo's corn, the colored numbers, and them targets?

BLUE Servicing the area of 125th to 145th, between the East and West rivers.

MR. PARKER *(pause)* I'm sorry, fellows, but I can't do it. *(moves into back room)*

THEO *(following* MR. PARKER*)* Why?

MR. PARKER It's not right.

THEO Not right! What are you talking about? Is it right that all that's out there for us is to go downtown and push one of them carts? I have done that, and I ain't gon' do it no more!

MR. PARKER That still don't make it right.

THEO I don't buy it! I'm going into this thing with Blue, with or without you!

MR. PARKER Go on, I don't care! You quit school, I couldn't stop you! I asked you to get a job, you wouldn't work! You have never paid any attention to any of my advice, and I don't expect you to start heeding me now!

THEO Remember what you said to me about them paintings, and being what I am—

well, this is me! At last I've found what I can do, and it'll work—I know it will. Please, Pop, just—

MR. PARKER Stop begging, Theo. *(crosses back into shop, looks at* BLUE*)* Why?

BLUE I don't get you.

MR. PARKER What kind of boy are you that you went through so much pain to dream up this cockeyed, ridiculous plan of yours?

BLUE Mr. Parker, I was born about six blocks from here, and before I was ten I had the feeling I had been living for a hundred years. I got so old and tired I didn't know how to cry. Now you just think about that. But now I own a piece of this neighborhood. I don't have to worry about some bastard landlord or those credit crooks on 125th Street. Beautiful, Black Blue—they have to worry about me! *(reaches into his pocket and pulls out a stack of bills. Places them in* PARKER*'s hands)* Can't you see, man—I'm here to put you in business! *(*MR. PARKER *runs his fingers through the money.)* Money, Mr. Parker—brand-new money . . .

(After concentrated attention, MR. PARKER *drops money on table and moves into back room.* THEO *hurriedly follows.* MR. PARKER *sits on bed, in deep thought)*

THEO That's just to get us started. And if we can make a dent into Mr. You-Know-Who's going-ons in Harlem, nobody's going to think of us as crooks. We'll be heroes from 110th Street to Sugar Hill. And just think, Pop, you won't have to worry about jobs and all that. You'll have so much time for you and Mr. Jenkins to play checkers, your arms will drop off. You'll be able to sit as long as you want, and tell enough stories and lies to fit between the cover of a 500-page book. That's right! Remember you said you wanted to write all them stories down! Now you'll have time for it! You can dress up the way you used to. And the girls—remember how you used to be so tough with the girls before you got married? All that can come back to you, and some of that you never had. It's so easy! All you have to do is call Adele down those stairs and let her know that you're going into business and if she don't like it she can pack up and move out, because you're not going to let her drive you down because you're a man, and—

MR. PARKER All right! *(moves back into shop, where* BLUE *is putting away his paraphernalia)* I'll do it! *(pause)* I'll do it under one condition—

BLUE And that is?

MR. PARKER If my buddy Jenkins wants to buy into this deal, you'll let him.

BLUE Theo?

THEO It's all right.

MR. PARKER *(extending his hand to* BLUE*)* Then you got yourself some partners, Mr. Haven!

BLUE Welcome into the association, Mr. Parker.

MR. PARKER Welcome into my barbershop!

THEO *(jubilantly)* Yehhhhhhhhhh!

*(*BLUE *checks his watch.* ADELE *comes into the back room)*

BLUE Well, I have to check out now, but I'll stop over tomorrow and we will set the whole thing up just as you want it, Mr. Parker. See you later, Theo.

MR. PARKER *(to* BLUE *as he is walking out the front door)* You should stick around awhile and watch my polish!

THEO Pop, don't you think it would be better if you would let me give the word to Adele?

MR. PARKER No. If I'm going to run a crooked house, *I'm* going to run it, and that goes for you as well as her.

THEO But, Pop, sometimes she kinda gets by you.

MR. PARKER Boy, I have never done anything like this in my life, but since I've made up my mind to it, you have nothing to say—not a word. You have been moaning about me never making it so you can have a chance. Well, this time you can say I'm with you. But let me tell you something: I don't want no more lies from you, and no more conning me about painting, airplane piloting, or nothing. If being a crook is what you want to be, you're going to be the best crook in the world—even if you have to drink mud to prove it.

THEO *(pause)* Okay, Pop.

MR. PARKER *(moves toward back room)* Well, here goes nothing. Adele! *(just as he calls,* ADELE *steps out of the back room, stopping him in his tracks)*

ADELE Yes, Father.

MR. PARKER Oh, you're here already. Well, I want to talk to—well, I, er—

ADELE What is it?

MR. PARKER *(pause)* Nothing. I'll talk to you later. *(He spots* BOBBY *entering from the outside with a package wrapped in newspaper)* What you got there?

BOBBY Uh . . . uh . . . —fish!

MR. PARKER Well, you better get them in the refrigerator before they stink on you.

THEO *(going over to* BOBBY *and taking package from him)* No, no. Now, Bobby, I promised Pop we would never lie to him again. It ain't fish, Pop. We've got something for you. *(puts the package on the table and starts unwrapping it. The two boys stand over the table, and as the typewriter is revealed, both turn to him)*

THEO and BOBBY Happy Birthday!

MR. PARKER Birthday? Birthday?

THEO and BOBBY Yes, Happy Birthday!

MR. PARKER Now hold on just a minute!

BOBBY What are we holding on for, Pop?

MR. PARKER *(pause)* That's a good question, son. We're—we're holding on for a celebration! *(laughs loudly)* Thanks, fellows! But what am I going to do with a typewriter! I don't know nothing about no typing!

ADELE I would like to know where they got the money to buy one!

THEO *(ignoring her)* You know what you told me about writing down your stories—now you can write them down three times as fast!

MR. PARKER But I don't know how to type!

THEO With the money we're gonna be having, I can hire somebody to teach you!

ADELE What money you going to have?

THEO We're going into business, baby—right here in this barbershop!

MR. PARKER Theo—

THEO *(paying no attention)* We're going to sell bootleg whiskey, numbers, and—

ADELE You're what!?

MR. PARKER Theo—

THEO You heard me, and if you don't like it you can pack your bags and leave!

ADELE Leave? I pay the rent here!

THEO No more! I pay it now!

MR. PARKER Shut up, Theo!

THEO We're going to show you something, girl. You think—

MR. PARKER *I said shut up!*

ADELE Is he telling the truth?

MR. PARKER Yes, he is telling the truth.

ADELE You mean to tell me you're going to turn this shop into a bootleg joint?

MR. PARKER I'll turn it into anything I want to!

ADELE Not while I'm still here!

MR. PARKER The lease on this house has my signature, not yours!

ADELE I'm not going to let you do this!

MR. PARKER You got no choice, Adele. *You don't have a damn thing to say!*

ADELE *(turns sharply to* THEO*)* You put him up to this!

MR. PARKER Nobody puts me up to anything I don't want to do! These two boys have made it up in their minds they're not going to work for nobody but themselves, and the thought in my mind is *why should they!* I did like you said, I went downtown, and it's been a long time since I did that, but *you're* down there every day, and you oughta know by now that I am too old a man to ever dream I . . . could overcome the dirt and filth they got waiting for me down there. I'm surprised at you, that you would have so little care in you to shove me into the middle of that mob.

ADELE You can talk about caring? What about Mama? She *died* working for you! Did you ever stop to think about that! In fact, *did you ever love her?* No!!!

MR. PARKER That's a lie!

ADELE I hope that one day you'll be able to do one good thing to drive that doubt out of my mind. *But this is not it!* You've let this hoodlum sell you his twisted ideas of making a short cut through life. But let me tell you something—this bastard is going to ruin you!

THEO *(into her face)* Start packing, baby!

ADELE *(strikes him across the face)* Don't you talk to me like that!

(He raises his hand to strike her back)

MR. PARKER Drop your hand, boy! *(*THEO *does not respond)* I said, drop your goddamn hand!

THEO She hit me!

MR. PARKER I don't care if she had broken your jaw. If you ever draw your hand back to hit this girl again—*as long as you* live! You better not be in my hand reach when you do, 'cause *I'll split your back in two!* (to ADELE) We're going into business, Adele. I have come to that and I have come to it on my own. I am going to stop worrying once and for all whether I live naked in the cold or whether I die like an animal, unless I can live the best way I know how to. I am getting old and I oughta have some fun. I'm going to get me some money, and I'm going to spend it! I'm going to get drunk! I'm going to dance some more! *I'm getting old! I'm going to fall in love one more time before I die!* So get to that, girl, and if it's too much for you to bear, I wouldn't hold it against you if you walked away from here this very minute—

ADELE *(opens the door to the back room to show him the birthday surprise she has for him)* Happy birthday!

MR. PARKER *(goes into the room and stands over table where birthday cake is)* I guess I fooled all of you. Today is not my birthday. It never was. *(moves up the stairs)*

ADELE It's not going to work! You're going to cut your throat—you hear me! You're going to rip yourself into little pieces! *(turns to* THEO*)* It's not going to be the way you want it—because I know Mr. Blue Haven, and he is not a person to put your trust in. *(*THEO *turns his back on her, heads for the shop door)* . . . I am talking to you!

THEO *(stops and turns)* Why don't you leave us alone. You're the one who said we had to go out and do something. Well, we did, but we're doing it our way. Me and Bobby, we're men—if we lived the way you wanted us to, we wouldn't have nothing but big fat veins popping out of our heads.

ADELE I'll see what kind of men you are every time a cop walks through that door, every time a stranger steps into this back room and you can't be too sure about him, and the day they drag your own father off and throw him into a jail cell.

THEO But, tell me, what else is there left for us to do. You tell me and I'll do it. You show me where I can go to spin the world around before it gets too late for somebody like Mama living fifty years just to die on 126th Street! *You tell me of a place where there are no old crippled vaudeville men!*

ADELE There is no such place. *(pause)* But you don't get so hung up about it you have to plunge a knife into your own body. You don't bury yourself here in this place; you climb up out of it! Now that's something for you to wonder about, boy.

THEO I wonder all the time—how you have lived here all your whole life on this street, and you haven't seen, heard, learned, or felt a thing in all those years. I wonder how you ever got to be such a damn fool!

(Curtain)

Act Two

Scene One

(Two months later. It is about 9 P.M.

As the curtain rises, the lights come up in the back room. BOBBY *is there, listening to a record of James Brown's "Money Won't Change You, But Time Will Take You On." As he is dancing out to the shop,* THEO *appears from the cellar, which has been enlarged by taking out a panel in the lower section of the wall and houses the whiskey-making operation.* THEO *brings in two boxes filled with bottles of corn whiskey and shoves them under the bed.*

BOBBY *moves past* THEO *into the shop, carrying a target rolled up in his hand, and two darts. He is wearing a fancy sports shirt, new trousers, new keen-toed shoes, and a stingy, diddy-bop hat. He pins the target up on the wall of the shop. In the center of the target is the face of a well-known American racist)*

BOBBY *(moves away from the target, aims and hurls the dart)* That's for Pop! Huh! *(throws another)* And this is for me! Huh! *(moves to the target to pull darts out.* THEO *cuts record off abruptly. A knock at the door)*

THEO *(calling out to* BOBBY *from the back room)* Lock that door!

BOBBY Lock it yourself!

THEO *(with quick but measured steps moves toward front door)* I'm not selling another bottle, target, or anything, till I get some help! *(Locks door in spite of persistent knocking)* We're closed!

BOBBY I don't think Blue is gon' like you turning customers away. *(sits in barber chair, lighting up cigar)*

THEO You can tell Blue I don't like standing over that stove all day, that I don't like him promising me helpers that don't show up. There are a lot of things I don't go for, like Pop taking off and not showing up for two days. I make this whiskey, I sell it, I keep books. I peddle numbers and those damn targets. *And*

I don't like you standing around here all day not lifting a finger to help me!

BOBBY *(taking a big puff on his cigar)* I don't hear you.

THEO Look at you—all decked out in your new togs. Look at me: I haven't been out of these dungarees since we opened this place up.

BOBBY *(jumps out of chair)* I don't wanta hear nothing! You do what you wanta do, and leave me alone!

THEO What am I supposed to be, a work mule or something?

BOBBY You're the one that's so smart—you can't answer your own stupid questions?

THEO You done let Blue turn you against me, huh?

BOBBY You ask the questions, and you gon' answer them—but for now, stop blowing your breath in my face!

THEO You make me sick. *(moves into back room. Sits on bed)*

ADELE *(enters from upstairs, dressed in a smart Saks Fifth Avenue outfit)* Getting tired already, Theo?

THEO No, just once in a while I'd like to have some time to see one of my women!

ADELE You being the big industrialist and all that, I thought you had put girls off for a year or two!

THEO Get away from me. *(crosses to desk and sits)*

ADELE I must say, however—it is sure a good sight to see you so wrapped up in work. I never thought I'd live to see the day, but—

THEO Don't you ever have anything good to say?

ADELE I say what I think and feel. I'm honest.

THEO Honest? You're just hot because Pop decided to do something my way for a change.

ADELE That's a joke, when you haven't seen him for two whole days. Or, *do* you know where he has gone to practically every night since you opened up this little store.

THEO He's out having a little sport for himself. What's wrong with that? He hasn't had any fun in a long time.

ADELE Is fun all you can think of? When *my* father doesn't show up for two days, I worry.

THEO You're not worried about nobody but yourself—I'm on to your game. You'd give anything in the world to go back just the way we were, because you liked the idea of us being dependent on you. Well, that's all done with, baby. We're on our own. So don't worry yourself about Pop. When Blue gets here tonight with our money, he'll be here!

ADELE If my eyes and ears are clear, then I would say that Father isn't having the kind of money troubles these days that he must rush home for your pay day.

THEO What do you mean by that?

ADELE I mean that he has been dipping his hands into that little drawer of yours at least two or three times a week.

THEO You ain't telling nothing I don't know.

ADELE What about your friend Blue?

THEO I can handle him.

ADELE I hope so, since it is a known fact that he can be pretty evil when he thinks someone has done him wrong—and it happened once, in a bar uptown, he actually killed a man.

THEO You're lying. *(he moves quickly to shop entrance)* Bobby, have you heard anything about Blue killing a man? *(*BOBBY*, seated in the barber's chair, looks at him, then turns away, not answering.* THEO *returns to the back room)*

ADELE Asking him about it is not going to help you. Ask yourself a few questions and you will know that you are no better than Blue—because it is you two who are the leaders of those mysterious store raids on 125th Street, and your ace boy on those robberies is no one other than your brother, Bobby Parker!

THEO Bobby!

ADELE I don't know why that should surprise you, since he is known as the swiftest and coolest young thief in Harlem.

THEO I didn't know about Bobby—*who told you!*

ADELE As you well know by now, I've been getting around lately, and I meet people, and people like to have something to talk about, and you know something: this place is becoming the talk along every corner and bar on the Avenue!

THEO You're just trying to scare me.

ADELE I wish to God I was. *(Starts out)*

THEO Where are you going?

ADELE *(stops, turns abruptly)* Out. Do you mind?

THEO *That's all you ever do!*

ADELE Yes, you're right.

THEO They tell me you're going with Wilmer Robinson?

ADELE Yes, that's true. *(moving through shop toward door.* BOBBY *doesn't move from the barber's throne and buries his nose in a comic book)*

THEO *(following behind her)* He's a snake.

ADELE No better or worse than someone like you or Blue.

THEO He'll bleed you for every dime you've got!

ADELE So what. He treats me like a woman, and that's more than I can say for any man in this house!

THEO He'll treat you like a woman until he's gotten everything he wants, and then he's gon' split your ass wide open!

ADELE *(turns sharply at door)* Theoooooooooooo! *(pause)* You talk like that to me because you don't know how to care for the fact that I am your sister.

THEO But why are you trying to break us up? Why?

ADELE I don't have to waste that kind of good time. I can wait for you to bust it up yourself. Good night! *(slams the door behind herself)*

*(*THEO *stands with a long, deep look in his eyes, then goes down cellar.* MR. PARKER *steps into the shop, all dapper, dressed up to a fare-thee-well, holding a gold-top cane in one hand and a book in the other.* BOBBY *stares at him, bewildered)*

BOBBY What's that you got on?

MR. PARKER What does it look like?

BOBBY Nothing.

MR. PARKER You call this nothing!

BOBBY Nothing—I mean, I didn't mean nothing when I asked you that question.

MR. PARKER Where's Theo?

BOBBY In the back, working.

MR. PARKER Good! Shows he's got his mind stretched out for good and great things. *(hangs up hat and puts away cane)*

BOBBY He's been stretching his mind out to find out where you been.

MR. PARKER Where I been is none of his business, Blue is the man to think about. It's pay day, and I wanta know, where the hell is he! *(checks his watch, taps* BOBBY, *indicating he should step down from chair)*

BOBBY *(hops down from chair.* PARKER *sits)* Whatcha reading?

MR. PARKER A book I picked up yesterday. I figured since I'm in business I might as well read a businessman's book.

BOBBY Let me see it. *(takes the book in his hand) The Thief's Journal,* by Jean Gin-nett. *(fingering through pages)* Is it a good story?

MR. PARKER So far—

BOBBY *(hands it back)* What's it all about?

MR. PARKER A Frenchman who was a thief.

BOBBY Steal things?

MR. PARKER Uh-huh.

BOBBY Where did he get all that time to write a book?

MR. PARKER Oh, he had the time all right, 'cause he spent most of it in jail.

BOBBY Some thief!

MR. PARKER The trouble with this bird is that he became a thief and then he became a thinker.

BOBBY No shucking!

MR. PARKER No shucking. But it is my logicalism that you've got to become a thinker and then you become a crook! Or else, why is it when you read up on some of these politicians' backgrounds you find they all went to one of them big law colleges? That's where you get your start!

BOBBY Well, I be damned!

MR. PARKER *(jumps down out of the chair, moves briskly toward door)* Now where is Blue! He said he would be here nine-thirty on the nose! *(opens the door and* JENKINS *comes in)* Hey, Jenkins! What's up!

MR. JENKINS That Blue fellow show up yet?

MR. PARKER No, he didn't, and I'm gon' call him down about that too.

MR. JENKINS It don't matter. I just want whatever money I got coming, and then I'm getting out of this racket.

MR. PARKER Don't call it that, it's a committee!

MR. JENKINS This committee ain't no committee. It ain't nothing but a racket, and I'm getting out of it!

MR. PARKER You put your money into this thing, man. It ain't good business to walk out on an investment like that.

MR. JENKINS I can, and that's what I'm doing before I find myself in jail! Man, this thing you got going here is the talk in every bar in this neighborhood.

MR. PARKER There ain't nothing for you to be scared of, Jenkins. Blue guaranteed me against ever being caught by the police. Now that's all right by me, but I've got some plans of my own. When he gets here tonight, I'm gon' force him to make me one of the leaders in this group, and if he don't watch out, I just might take the whole operation over from him. I'll make you my right-hand man, and not only will you be getting more money, and I won't just guarantee you against getting caught, but I'll guarantee you against being scared!

MR. JENKINS There's nothing you can say to make me change my mind. I shouldn't've let you talk me into this mess in the first place. I'm getting out, and that's it! *(starts for the door)* And if he gets back before I do, you hold my money for me! *(exiting)*

MR. PARKER *(pursuing him to door)* Suit yourself, but you're cutting your own throat. This little set-up is the biggest thing to hit this neighborhood since the day I started dancing! *(slams door)* Fool! *(takes off coat, hangs it up. Goes to mirror to primp)*

BOBBY Going somewhere again?

MR. PARKER Got myself a little date to get to if Blue ever gets here with our money—*and he better gets here with our money!*

BOBBY You been dating a lot lately—night-time dates, and day ones too—and Theo's not happy about it. He says you don't stay here long enough to cut Yul Brynner's hair.

MR. PARKER He can complain all he wants to. I'm the boss here, and he better not forget it. He's the one that's got some explaining to do: don't talk to nobody no more, don't go nowhere, looking like he's mad all the time . . . I've also noticed that he don't get along with you any more.

BOBBY Well, Pop, that's another story.

MR. PARKER Come on, boy, there's something on his mind, and you know what it is.

BOBBY *(moving away)* Nothing, except he wants to tell me what to do all the time. But I've got some ideas of my own. I ain't no dumbbell; I just don't talk as much as he do. If I did, the people I talk to would know just as much as I do. I just want him to go his way, and I'll go mine.

MR. PARKER There's more to it than that, and I wanta know what it is.

BOBBY There's nothing.

MR. PARKER Come on now, boy.

BOBBY That's all, Pop!

MR. PARKER *(grabs him)* It's not, and you better say something!

BOBBY He—I don't know what to tell you, Pop. He just don't like the way things are going—with you, me—Adele. He got in a fight with her today and she told him about Blue killing a man.

MR. PARKER Is it true?

BOBBY Yeah. Blue killed this man one time for saying something about his woman, and this woman got a child by Blue but Blue never married her and so this man started signifying about it. Blue hit him, the man reached for a gun in his pocket, Blue took the gun from him, and the—man started running, but by that time Blue had fire in his eyes, and he shot the man three times.

MR. PARKER Well . . .

BOBBY Blue got only two years for it!

MR. PARKER Two years, hunh? That's another thing I'm gon' throw in his face tonight if he tries to get smart with me. Ain't that something. Going around bumping people off, and getting away with it too! What do he think he is, white or something! *(*THEO *comes in and sits at desk.* MR. PARKER *checks his watch)* I'm getting tired of this! *(moves into back room)* Where's that friend of yours!? I don't have to wait around this barbershop all night for him. It's been two months now, and I want my money! When I say be here at nine-thirty, I mean be here!

THEO *(rising from desk)* Where have you been, Pop?

MR. PARKER That's none of your business! Now where is that man with my money!

THEO Money is not your problem—you've been spending it all over town! And you've been taking it out of this desk!

MR. PARKER So? I borrowed a little.

THEO You call four hundred dollars a little! Now I've tried to fix these books so it don't show too big, and you better hope Blue don't notice it when he starts fingering through these pages tonight.

MR. PARKER To hell with Blue! It's been two months now, and he ain't shown us a dime!

THEO What are you doing with all that money, Pop?

MR. PARKER I don't have to answer to you! I'm the boss here. And another thing, there's a lot about Blue and this association I want to know about. I want a position! I don't have to sit around here every month or so, waiting for somebody to bring me *my* money.

THEO Money! Money! That's all you can think about!

MR. PARKER Well, look who's talking. You forget this was all your idea. Remember what I told you about starting something and sticking with it. What is it now, boy? The next thing you'll tell me is that you've decided to become a priest or something. What's the new plan, Theo?

THEO No new plans, Pop. I just don't want us to mess up. Don't you understand—things must be done right, or else we're going to get ourselves in jail. We have to be careful, we have to think about each other all the time. I didn't go into this business just for myself, I wasn't out to prove how wrong Adele was. I just thought the time had come for us to do something about all them years we laid around here letting Mama kill herself!

MR. PARKER I have told you a thousand times I don't wanta hear any talk about your mama. She's dead, damnit! So let it stay that way! *(moves toward shop)*

THEO All right, let's talk about Adele then.

MR. PARKER *(stopping at steps)* What about her?

THEO She's out of this house every night.

MR. PARKER Boy, you surprise me. What do you think she should do, work like a dog all day and then come to this house and bite her fingernails all night?

THEO She's got herself a boyfriend too, and—

MR. PARKER *(crossing to counter)* Good! I got myself a girlfriend, now that makes two of us!

THEO *(following him)* But he's—aw, what's the use. But I wish you'd stay in the shop more!

MR. PARKER That's too bad. I have things to do. I don't worry about where you're going when you leave here.

THEO I don't go anywhere and you know it. If I did, we wouldn't do an hour's business. *But we have been doing great business!* And you wanta know why? They love it! *Everybody* loves the way ol' Theo brews corn! Every after-hours joint is burning with it! And for us to do that kind of business, I've had to sweat myself down in this hole for something like sixteen hours a day for two whole months!

MR. PARKER What do you want from me?

THEO I just want you here in the shop with me, so at least we can pretend that this is a barbershop. A cop walked through that door today while I had three customers in here, and I had to put one of them in that chair and cut his hair!

MR. PARKER How did you make out?

THEO Pop, I don't need your jokes!

MR. PARKER All right, don't get carried away. *(goes to* THEO *and puts his arm around the boy's shoulders)* I'll make it my business to stay here in the shop with you more.

THEO And make Blue guarantee me some help.

MR. PARKER You'll get that too. But you've got to admit one thing, though—you've always been a lazy boy. I didn't expect you to jump and all of a sudden act like John Henry!

THEO I have never been lazy. I just didn't wanta break my back for the man!

MR. PARKER Well, I can't blame you for that. I know, because I did it. I did it when they didn't pay me a single dime!

BOBBY When was that?

MR. PARKER When I was on the chain gang!

BOBBY Now you know you ain't never been on no chain gang!

MR. PARKER *(holds up two fingers)* Two months, that's all it was. Just two months.

BOBBY Two months, my foot!

MR. PARKER I swear to heaven I was. It was in 19-something, I was living in Jersey City, New Jersey . . . *(crosses to throne and sits)*

BOBBY Here we go with another story!

MR. PARKER That was just before I started working as a vaudeville man, and there was this ol' cousin of mine we used to call "Dub," and he had this job driving a trailer truck from Jersey City to Jacksonville, Florida. One day he asked me to come along with him for company. I weren't doing nothing at the time, and—

BOBBY As usual.

MR. PARKER I didn't say that! Anyway, we drove along. Everything was fine till we hit Macon, Georgia. We weren't doing a thing, but before we knew it this cracker police stopped us, claiming we'd ran through a red light. He was yelling and hollering and, boyyy, did I get mad—I was ready to get a hold of that cracker and work on his head until . . .

BOBBY Until what?

MR. PARKER Until they put us on the chain gang, and the chain gang they put us on was a chain gang and a half! I busted some rocks John Wayne couldn't've busted! I was a rock-busting fool! *(rises and demonstrates how he swung the hammer)* I would do it like this! I would hit the rock, and the hammer would bounce—bounce so hard it would take my hand up in the air with it—but I'd grab it with my left hand and bring it down like this: Hunh! *(carried away by the rhythm of his story, he starts twisting his body to the swing of it)* It would get so good to me, I'd say: Hunh! Yeah! Hunh! I'd say, Ooooooooooweeeee! I'm wide open now! *(swinging and twisting)* Yeah, baby, I say, Hunh! Sooner or later that rock would crack! Old Dub ran into a rock one day that was hard as Theo's head. He couldn't bust that rock for nothing. He pumped and swung, but that rock would not move. So finally he said to the captain: "I'm sorry, Cap, but a elephant couldn't break this rock." Cap didn't wanna hear nothing. He said, "Well, Dub, I wanna tell you something—your lunch and your supper is in the middle of that rock." On the next swing of the hammer, Dub busted that rock into a thousand pieces! *(laughs)* I'm telling you, them crackers is mean. Don't let nobody tell you about no Communists, Chinese, or anything: there ain't nothing on this earth meaner and dirtier than an American-born cracker! We used to sleep in them long squad tents on the ground, and we was all hooked up to this one big long chain: the guards had orders to shoot at random in the dark if ever one of them chains would rattle. You couldn't even turn over in your sleep! *(sits on throne)*

BOBBY A man can't help but turn over in his sleep!

MR. PARKER Not on this chain gang you didn't. You turn over on this chain gang in your sleep and your behind was shot! But if you had to, you would have to wake up, announce that you was turning over, and then you go back to sleep!

BOBBY What!

MR. PARKER Just like this. *(illustrating physically)* "Number 4 turning over!" But that made all the chains on the other convicts rattle, so they had to turn over too and shout: "Number 5 turning over! Number 6 turning over! Number 7!"

THEO Why don't you stop it!

MR. PARKER I ain't lying!

BOBBY Is that all?

MR. PARKER Yeah, and I'm gon' get Adele to type that up on my typewriter! *(goes to the window)* Now where the hell is that Blue Haven!

MR. JENKINS *(rushing in)* Did he show up yet?

MR. PARKER Naw, and when he does, I'm—

MR. JENKINS I told you I didn't trust that boy—who knows where he is! Well, I'm going out there and get him! *(starts back out)*

MR. PARKER *(grabs him by the arm)* Now don't go out there messing with Blue, Jenkins! If there's anybody got a reason for being mad with him, it's me. Now take it easy. When he gets here, we'll all straighten him out. Come on, sit down and let me beat you a game one time. *(takes board out quickly)*

BOBBY Tear him up, Pop!

MR. JENKINS *(pause)* Okay, you're on. *(moves toward* MR. PARKER *and the table)* It's hopeless. I been playing your father for three solid years, and he has yet to beat me one game!

MR. PARKER Yeah! But his luck done come to past!

MR. JENKINS My luck ain't come to past, 'cause my luck is skill. *(Spelling the word out)* S-K-I-L-L.

MR. PARKER *(shakes up the can)* Come on now, Jenkins, let's play the game. Take one. *(*MR. JENKINS *pulls out a checker)* You see there, you get the first move.

MR. JENKINS You take me for a fool, Parker, and just for that I ain't gon' let you get a king.

MR. PARKER Put your money where your lips is. I say I'm gon' win this game!

MR. JENKINS I don't want your money, I'm just gon' beat you!

MR. PARKER I got twenty dollars here to make a liar out of you! *(slams down a twenty-dollar bill on the table)* Now you doing all the bragging about how I never beat you, but I'm valiant enough to say that, from here on in, you can't win air, and I got twenty dollars up on the table to back it up.

MR. JENKINS Oh, well, he ain't satisfied with me beating him all the time for sport. He wants me to take his money too.

MR. PARKER But that's the difference.

MR. JENKINS What kind of difference?

MR. PARKER We're playing for money, and I don't think you can play under that kind of pressure. You do have twenty dollars, don't you?

MR. JENKINS I don't know what you're laughing about, I always keep some money on me. *(pulls out change purse and puts twenty dollars on the table)* You get a little money in your pocket and you get carried away.

MR. PARKER It's your move.

MR. JENKINS Start you off over here in this corner.

MR. PARKER Give you that little ol' fellow there.

MR. JENKINS I'll take him.

MR. PARKER I'll take this one.

MR. JENKINS I'll give you this man here.

MR. PARKER I'll jump him—so that you can have this one.

MR. JENKINS I'll take him.

MR. PARKER Give you this man here.

MR. JENKINS All right. *(he moves)*

MR. PARKER I'll take this one. *(series of grunts and groans as they exchange men)* And I'll take these three. *(jumping* MR. JENKINS'*s men and laughing loud)* Boom! Boom! Boom! *(the game is now definitely in favor of* MR. PARKER. MR. JENKINS *is pondering over his situation. Relishing* MR. JENKINS'*s predicament)* Study long, you study wrong. I'm afraid that's you, ol' buddy . . . I knew it, I knew it all the time—I used to ask myself: I wonder how ol' Jenks would play if he really had some pressure on him? You remember how the Dodgers used to raise hell every year until they met the Yankees in the World Series, and how under all that pressure they would crack up? *(laughs)* That pressure got him!

MR. JENKINS Hush up, man. I'm trying to think!

MR. PARKER I don't know what you could be thinking about, 'cause the rooster done came and wrote, skiddy biddy!

MR. JENKINS *(finally makes a move)* There!

MR. PARKER *(in sing-song)* That's all—that's all . . . *(makes another jump)* Boom! Just like you say, Bobby—"tear him up!" *(rears his head back in ecstatic laughter)*

MR. JENKINS *(makes a move)* It's your move.

MR. PARKER *(his laughter trails off sickly as he realizes that the game is now going his opponent's way)* Well, I see. I guess that kinda changes the color of the game . . . Let me see now . . .

MR. JENKINS *(getting his revenge)* Why don't you laugh some more? I like the way you laugh, Parker.

MR. PARKER Shut up, Jenkins. I'm thinking!

MR. JENKINS Thinking? Thinking for what? The game is over! *(now he is laughing hard.* MR. PARKER *ruefully makes his move)* Uh-uh! Lights out! *(still laughing, answers* PARKER'*s move)* Game time, and you know it! Take your jump! *(*MR. PARKER *is forced to take his jump.* JENKINS *takes his opponent's last three men)* I told you about laughing and bragging in my game! Boom! Boom! Boom!

MR. PARKER *(rises abruptly from the table and dashes to coat rack)* DAMNIT!!!

MR. JENKINS Where you going—ain't we gon' play some more?

MR. PARKER *(putting on coat)* I don't wanta play you no more. You too damn lucky!

MR. JENKINS Aw, come on, Parker. I don't want your money, I just want to play!

MR. PARKER You won it, you keep it—I can *afford* it! But one of these days you're going to leave that voodoo root of yours home, and that's gonna be the day—you hear me, you sonofabitch!

BOBBY Pop!

MR. PARKER I don't want to hear nothing from you!

MR. JENKINS *(realizing that* PARKER *is really upset)* It's only a game—and it don't have nothing to do with luck . . . But you keep trying, Parker, and one of these days you're going to beat me. And when you do, it won't have nothing to do with luck—it just might be the unluckiest and worst day of your life. You'll be champion checker player of the world. Meanwhile, I'm the champ, *and you're gonna have to live with it.*

MR. PARKER *(smiling, grudgingly moves toward him with his hand extended)* All right, Jenkins! You win this time, but I'm gon' beat you yet. I'm gon' whip your behind until it turns white!

BOBBY That's gon' be some strong whipping! *(there's a tap at the door)* That must be Blue. *(rushes to the door and opens it)*

MR. PARKER About time. *(*BLUE *enters)* Hey, boy, where have you been?

BLUE *(moves in, carrying an attaché case)* I got stuck with an emergency council meeting.

MR. PARKER What kind of council?

BLUE The council of the Association. I see

you're sporting some new clothes there, Mr. P. You must be rolling in extra dough these days.

MR. PARKER Just a little something I picked up the other day. All right, where is the money, Blue?

BLUE You'll get your money, but first I want to see those books. *(moves to the desk in the back room and starts going over the books. In the shop an uneasy silence prevails.* JENKINS, *out of nervousness, sets up the checkers for another game)*

BLUE I see. *(takes out pencil and pad and starts scribbling on a sheet of paper)* Uh-huh. Uh-huh . . . *(re-enters shop)*

MR. PARKER Well?

BLUE Everything seems to be okay.

MR. PARKER Of course everything is all right. What did you expect? *(angry, impatient)* Now come on and give me my money.

BLUE Take it easy, Mr. Parker! *(takes a white envelope from his case and passes it on to* PARKER*)* Here's your money.

MR. PARKER Now this is what I like to see!

BLUE *(passes some bills to* MR. JENKINS*)* And you, Mr. Jenkins.

MR. JENKINS Thank you, young man. But from here on in, you can count me out of your operation.

BLUE What's the trouble?

MR. JENKINS No trouble at all. I just want to be out of it.

BLUE People and headaches—that's all I ever get from all the Mr. Jenkinses in this world!

MR. JENKINS Why don't you be quiet sometimes, boy.

MR. PARKER I'm afraid he's telling you right, Blue.

BLUE *He's telling me that he is a damn idiot, who can get himself hurt!*

THEO Who's going to hurt him?

(They all stare at BLUE.*)*

BLUE *(calming down)* I'm sorry. I guess I'm working too hard these days. I got a call today from one of them "Black committees" here in Harlem . . .

THEO What did they want?

BLUE They wanted to know what we did. They said they had heard of us, but they never see us—meaning they never see us picketing, demonstrating, and demanding something all the time.

MR. PARKER So?

BLUE They want us to demonstrate with them next Saturday, and I have decided to set up a demonstrating committee, with you in charge, Mr. Parker.

MR. PARKER You what!

BLUE You'd be looking good!

MR. PARKER You hear that! *(cynical laughter) I'd be looking good!* Count me out! When I demonstrate, it's for real!

BLUE You demonstrate in front of any store out there on that street, and you'll have a good sound reason for being there!

MR. PARKER I thought you said we was supposed to be different, and we was to drive out that Mr. You-Know-Somebody—well, ain't that what we doing? Two stores already done put up "going out of business" signs.

BLUE That's what we started this whole thing for, and that's what we're doing.

MR. PARKER I got some questions about that, too. I don't see nothing that we're doing that would cause a liquor store, a clothing store, and a radio store to just all of a sudden close down like that, unless we've been raiding and looting them at night or something like that.

*(*BOBBY *quickly moves out of the shop into the back room and exits upstairs)*

BLUE It's the psychological thing that's doing it, man!

MR. PARKER Psychological? Boy, you ain't telling me everything, and anyway I wanta know who made this decision about picketing.

BLUE The council!

MR. PARKER Who is on this council?

BLUE You know we don't throw names around like that!

MR. PARKER I don't get all the mystery, Blue. This is my house, and you know everything about it from top to bottom. I got my whole family in this racket!

BLUE You're getting a good share of the money—ain't that enough?

MR. PARKER Not when I'm dealing with you in the dark.

BLUE You're asking for something, so stop beating around corners and tell me what it is you want!

MR. PARKER All right! You been promising my boy some help for two months now, and he's still waiting. Now I want you to give him that help starting tomorrow, and I want you to put somebody in this shop who can cut hair to relieve me when I'm not here. And from here on in, I want to know everything that's to be known about this "de-colonization committee"—how it works, who's in it, who's running it—*and I want to be on that council you was talking about!*

BLUE NO!

MR. PARKER Then I can't cooperate with you any more!

BLUE What does that mean?

MR. PARKER It means we can call our little deal off, and you can take your junk out of here!

BLUE Just like that?

MR. PARKER Just any ol' way you want it. I take too many risks in this place, not to know where I stand.

BLUE Mr. Parker—

MR. PARKER All right, let me hear it and let me hear it quick!

BLUE There is an opening on our council. It's a—

MR. PARKER Just tell me what position is it!

BLUE President.

MR. PARKER President?

BLUE The highest office on our council.

MR. PARKER Boy, you're gonna have to get up real early to get by an old fox like me. A few minutes ago you offered me nothing, and now you say I can be president—that should even sound strange to *you!*

BLUE There's nothing strange. A few minutes ago you weren't ready to throw me out of your place, but now *I've got no other choice!*

MR. PARKER *(pointing his finger at him and laughing)* That's true! You don't! All right, I'll give you a break—I accept! Just let me know when the next meeting is. *(checks watch and grabs his hat)* Come on, Jenkins, let's get out of here! *(starts out with* MR. JENKINS*)*

THEO Hey, Pop—you're going out there with all that money in your pocket.

MR. PARKER Don't worry about it. I'm a grown man, I can take care of myself.

THEO But what about our part of it?

MR. PARKER Look, son, he held me up—I'm late already. You'll get yours when I get back.

THEO But, Pop—

MR. PARKER Good night, Theo! *(bolts out the door, with* MR. JENKINS *following)*

THEO *(rushes to the door)* Pop, you better be careful! I'll be waiting for you! I don't care if it's till dawn!

BLUE You're becoming a worrier, Theo! *(pause)* But that's the nature of all things . . . I'm forever soothing and pacifying someone. Sometimes I have to pacify myself. You don't think that president stuff is going to mean anything, do you? He had me up-tight, so what I did was to bring him closer to me so I would be definitely sure of letting him know less and having more control over him—and over you, too.

THEO What do you mean by that?

BLUE It didn't take me more than one glance into those books to know that he's been spending money out of the box. And to think—you didn't bother to tell me about it.

THEO Why should I? I trust your intelligence.

BLUE Please don't let him do it any more.

THEO Why don't you hire your own cashier and bookkeeper? *(he goes into back room)*

BLUE *(following him)* That's an idea! What about Adele! Now that was a thought in the back of my mind, but I'm putting that away real quick. Seems this sweet, nice-girl sister of yours has took to partying with the good-time set and keeping company with a simple-ass clown like Wilmer Robinson. No, that wouldn't work, would it? I'd have more trouble with her than I'm having with you. When a girl as intelligent as your sister, who all of a sudden gets into things, and hooked up to people who just don't go with her personality, that could mean trouble. To be honest with you, I didn't think this thing was going to work, but *it is working,* Theo! I've got three places just like this one, and another on the way. A man has to care about what he does. Don't you want to get out of this place?

THEO Yes, but lately I've been getting the feeling that I'm gonna have to hurt someone.

BLUE I see.

THEO You think the old man was asking you those questions about stores closing down as a joke or something?

BLUE He asks because he thinks, but he is still in the dark!

THEO He was playing with you! And when my father holds something inside of him and plays with a man, he's getting meaner and more dangerous by the minute.

BLUE I don't care what he was doing—he is messing with my work! He has gotten himself into a "thing" with one of the rottenest bitches on the Avenue, who happens to be tight with a nigger who is trying to fuck up my business. Now that's something you had better get straight: it's your turn to soothe and pacify!

THEO Why should I do anything for you when you lied to me and sent my brother out with that band of thieves of yours?

BLUE He said he needed the money, and I couldn't stop him.

THEO But I told you I didn't want that!

BLUE Let's face it, baby! Bobby's the greatest thief in the world! He's been prancing around stores and stealing all of his life! And I think that's something to bow down to—because he's Black and in trouble, just like you and me. So don't ride me so hard, Theo! *(they cross back into shop. He picks up attaché case, preparing to leave)*

THEO Blue! Now I don't care what kind of protection you got, but I say those store raids are dangerous and I don't want my brother on them, and I mean it!

BLUE When we first made our plans, you went along with it—you knew somebody had to do it. What makes you and your brother so special?

THEO Well, you better—

BLUE *To hell with you, Theo!* I could take this hand and make you dead! You are nothing but what I make you be!

THEO *(pause)* That just might be. But what if tomorrow this whole operation were to bust wide open in your face because of some goof-up by my father or sister—something that would be just too much for you to clean up. What would you do? Kill them?

BLUE *(pause. Then calmly and deliberately)* The other day I went up on the hill to see my little boy. I took him out for a ride and as we were moving along the streets he asked me where all the people were coming from. I said from work, going home, going to the store, and coming back from the store. Then we went out to watch the river and then he asked me about the water, the ships, the weeds—everything. That kid threw so many questions at me, I got dizzy—I wanted to hit him once to shut him up. He was just a little dark boy discovering for the first time that there are things in the world like stones and trees . . . It got late and dark, so I took him home and watched him fall asleep. Then I took his mother into my arms and put her into bed. I just laid there for a while, listening to her call me all kinds of dirty mother-fuckers. After she got that out of her system, I put my hands on her and before long our arms were locked at each other's shoulders and then my thighs moved slowly down between her thighs and then we started that sweet rolling until the both of us were screaming as if the last piece of love was dying forever. After that, we just laid there, talking soft up into the air. I would tell her she was the loveliest bitch that ever lived, and all of a sudden she was no longer calling me a dirty mother-fucker, she was calling me a sweet mother-fucker. It got quiet. I sat up on the edge of the bed with my head hanging long and deep, trying to push myself out of the room and back into it at one and the same time. She looked up at me and I got that same question all over again. Will you marry me and be the father of your son! I tried to move away from her, but she dug her fingernails into my shoulders. I struck her once, twice, and again and again—with this hand! And her face was a bloody mess! And I felt real bad about that. I said, I'll marry you, *Yes! Yes! Yes! (pause)* I put my clothes on and I walked out into the streets, trembling with the knowledge that now I have a little boy who I must walk through the park with every Sunday, who one day just may blow my head off—and an abiding wife who on a given evening may get herself caught in the bed of some other man, and I could be sealed in a dungeon until dead! I was found lying in a well of blood on the day I was born! But I have been kind! I have kissed babies for the simple reason they were babies! I'm going to get married to some bitch and that gets me to shaking all over! *(he moves close to* THEO*)* The last time I trembled this way *I killed a man! (quickly and rhythmically takes out a long, shiny switchblade knife. It pops open just at* THEO's *neck.* BLUE *holds it there for a moment, then withdraws and closes it. Puts it away. Then he collects his belongings, then calmly addresses* THEO*)* Things are tight and cool on my end, Theo, and that's how you should keep it here. If not, everything gets messy and I find myself acting like a policeman, keeping order. I don't have the time for that kind of trick. (BLUE *exits)*

THEO *(after a moment of silent thought, moves decisively to the back-room stairs and calls)* Bobby! *(BOBBY comes downstairs)*

THEO I want you to stay away from those store raids, Bobby.

BOBBY Not as long as I can get myself some extra money. *(moving close to him)* You didn't say nothing to me before, when I was stealing every other day and giving you half of everything I stole. You didn't think nothing that day you sent me for that typewriter!

THEO I don't know what you're going to do from here on in, because I'm calling the whole affair off with Blue.

BOBBY That won't stop me, and you know it!

THEO What is it, Bobby—we used to be so close! Bobby, don't get too far away from me!

BOBBY *(heatedly)* What do you want me to do? Stick around you all the time? Hell, I'm tired of you! I stick by you and I don't know what to do! I steal and that puts clothes on my back and money in my pockets! *That's* something to do! But I sit here with you all day just thinking about the next word I'm going to say—I'm not stupid! I sit here all day thinking about what I'm going to say to you. I stuck by you and I hoped for you because whatever you became, I was gonna become. I thought about that, and that ain't shit! *(he leaves the shop. THEO is alone with his troubled thoughts. Suddenly he rushes into back room, gets hat and shirt, puts them on, and goes out into the street)*

MR. PARKER *(stepping down into the back room from the apartment upstairs.)* Come on, girl! *(a very attractive, well-dressed YOUNG GIRL in her early twenties follows him into the shop)*

MR. PARKER You wanted to see it. Well, here it is.

GIRL *(looking about the place)* So this is where you do your business. Like I keep asking you, Russell, what kind of business is it for you to make all that money you got?

MR. PARKER *(heading toward the refrigerator in the back room)* Come on in here, sweetheart. I'll fix us a drink!

GIRL *(moves briskly after him)* I asked you a question, Russell.

MR. PARKER *(still ignoring her question, he takes a jug out of refrigerator and grabs two glasses)* I'm going to make you a special drink, made from my own hands. It's called "Black Lightning."

GIRL *(surveys the room as PARKER pours drink)* That should be exciting.

MR. PARKER Here you go. *(hands her the drink) Toujours l'amour!*

GIRL *(gasping from the drink)* What the fuck is this! What *is* this, Russell?

MR. PARKER *(patting her on the back)* Knocks the tail off of you, don't it! But it gets smoother after the second swallow . . . Go on, drink up!

GIRL Okay. *(tries it again and scowls. Moves away as he sits on bed)*

MR. PARKER Now, did you think about what I asked you last night?

GIRL About getting married?

MR. PARKER Yes.

GIRL Why do you want to marry me, Russell?

MR. PARKER Because I love you, and I think you could make me happy.

GIRL Well, I don't believe you. When I asked you a question about your business, you deliberately ignored me. It was like you didn't trust me, and I thought that love and trust went together.

MR. PARKER I'm not so sure about that. My son Theo, I'm wild about him, but I wouldn't trust him no farther 'n I could throw a building.

GIRL I'm not your son!

MR. PARKER What is it you wanta know?

GIRL Where you gettin' all that money from?

MR. PARKER Oh, that. That's not for a girl to know, baby doll.

GIRL Then it's time for me to go. I'm not gettin' myself hooked up with no mystery man! *(moves as if to leave. PARKER stops her, then pauses for a moment)*

MR. PARKER All right, I'll tell you. I'm partners in a big business, which I'm the president of.

GIRL Partners with who, Russell?

MR. PARKER That's not important, baby.

GIRL Partners with who, Russell?

MR. PARKER Mr. Blue Haven.

GIRL *Blue Haven!* Then it's crooked business.

MR. PARKER Oh no, baby, it's nothing like that. It's real straight.

GIRL What does that mean?

MR. PARKER That what we're doing is right!

GIRL Tell me about it, then.

MR. PARKER I've said enough. Now let's leave it at that! *(tries to embrace her)*

GIRL *(wards him off, sits on bed)* All you take me for is something to play with.

MR. PARKER That's not true, I wanna marry you. *(sits beside her)*

GIRL You say you want to marry me, but how do you expect me to think about marrying somebody who won't confide in me about what they're doing. How do I know I'm not letting myself in for trouble.

MR. PARKER *(ponders for a moment, then rises.)* All right, I'll tell you! We peddle a variety of products to the community and we sell things to people at a price they can't get nowhere else in this city. Yes, according to the law it's illegal, but we help our people, our own people. We take care of business and at the same time we make everybody happy. We take care of our people. Just like I been taking care of you.

GIRL You take care of me? How? You've never given me more than ten dollars in cash since I've known you.

MR. PARKER Well, I've got a big present for you coming right out of this pocket and I'm gon' take you downtown tomorrow and let you spend till the store runs out.

GIRL Taking me to a store and giving me spending change makes me feel like a child and I don't like it and I'm not gonna stand for it any more.

MR. PARKER Then take this and you do whatever you want with it.

GIRL *(taking the money and putting it away)* Now don't get the idea I'm just in love with your money.

MR. PARKER Now I want you to stop talking to me about money. I've got *plenty* of it! You've got to understand—I'm the most different man you ever met. I've been around this world, I danced before the King and Queen of England. I've seen and heard many a thing in my lifetime—and you know what: I'm putting it all down on paper—my story!

GIRL Your story!

*(*MR. PARKER *moves into shop, gets notebook from behind one of the sliding panels. During his absence* GIRL *checks under the bed)*

MR. PARKER *(re-enters)* Here it is, right here. *(sits next to her on the bed, giving her the notebook)*

GIRL *(thumbing through the pages)* You write things too?

MR. PARKER I certainly do—and I've been thinking about writing a poem about you.

GIRL A poem about me!

MR. PARKER *(taking book from her and dropping it on floor)* I'm gon' do it tonight before I go to sleep. *(he kisses her neck and reaches for the hem of her dress)*

GIRL *(breaking out of his embrace)* No, Russell, not here!

MR. PARKER Why not?

GIRL Just because there's a bed wherever we go don't mean that we have to jump into it. You don't understand, Russell! You've got to start treating me the same as if I was your wife.

MR. PARKER *That's exactly what I'm trying to do!*

GIRL *(rising)* Don't yell at me!

MR. PARKER All right. I tell you what: I'm kinda tired, let's just lie down for a while and talk. I ain't gon' try nothing.

GIRL Russell—

MR. PARKER May the Lord smack me down this minute into hell—I swear I won't do nothing.

GIRL What are the three biggest lies men tell to women, Russell?

MR. PARKER I ain't just any man—I'm the man you gon' spend your life with.

GIRL Okay, Russell, we'll lie down, but you've got to keep your word. If I'm the girl you want to marry, you've got to learn to keep your word. *(they lie on bed. To her surprise,* PARKER *is motionless, seemingly drifting off to sleep. After a moment she takes the initiative and begins love-making. He responds, and once his passion has reached an aggressive peak she breaks off abruptly)* Where do you get these things you sell to people?

MR. PARKER What are you talking about?

GIRL You know what I'm saying. I overheard you tell Mr. Jenkins you suspected your son was robbing stores.

MR. PARKER You heard no such thing!

GIRL *(desperately)* Where do they keep the stuff?

MR. PARKER Now, baby, you've got to relax and stop worrying about things like that! *(pulls her by the shoulders. She does not resist.)* Come here. *(he pulls her down to the bed, takes her into his arms and kisses her, reaching again for the hem of her dress)*

GIRL *(struggling, but weakening to his ardor)* Russell, you said you wouldn't do nothing!

MR. PARKER I ain't! I just want to get a little closer to you!

GIRL Russell, not here!

MR. PARKER Just let me feel it a little bit!

GIRL You swore to God, Russell! *(*THEO *comes in the front door and heads toward back room)*

MR. PARKER I ain't gon' do nothing!

GIRL *(hears* THEO*)* Russell! Russell! Somebody is out there!

MR. PARKER *(jumps up quickly.* THEO *stands before him)* What are you doing here?

THEO The question is, *what are you doing!*

MR. PARKER I have been having a private talk with a good friend of mine. Now get out of here!

*(*GIRL *jumps up, moving past* MR. PARKER*)*

MR. PARKER *(stopping her)* Where are you going?

GIRL Home!

MR. PARKER Hold it now, honey!

GIRL I never should have come here in the first place!

MR. PARKER No, you're not going anywhere. This is my place and you don't have to run off because of this Peeping Tom!

THEO Pop, it's time to give us our money.

MR. PARKER You'll get your share tomorrow and not before!

THEO I want it now before you give it all to that girl. Pop, cut that broad loose!

MR. PARKER What was that?

THEO I said, cut her loose! She don't need an old man like you, she's just pumping you for information. That bitch is a hustler!

MR. PARKER *(slaps* THEO *with the back of his hand)* Bite your tongue!

GIRL I think I better go, Russell. *(heads for the front door)*

MR. PARKER *(following her)* Okay, but I'll be right with you as soon as I get things straight here. You will be waiting for me, won't you?

GIRL Sure!

MR. PARKER You run along now and I'll be right over there. *(*GIRL *exits.* PARKER *whirls back into shop)* What do you think you're doing, boy?

THEO Just be careful, Pop. Please be careful.

MR. PARKER If there's anybody I got to be careful of, it's you! You lying selfish sonofabitch! You think I don't know about you and Blue running that gang of thieves—about you sending your own brother out there with them?

THEO I didn't do that!

MR. PARKER If Bobby gets hurt out on them streets, I'm gonna kill you, boy! I'm gonna kill you. *(hurriedly collects hat and coat)*

THEO You're not worried about Bobby! All you can think of is the money you're rolling in. The clothes. And that stupid outfit you've got on.

*(*ADELE *comes in from the street, obviously distraught)*

MR. PARKER What's wrong with you? Are you drunk? *(moves in.* ADELE *doesn't answer, so he moves off)*

THEO Of course she's drunk. What did you expect—did you think everything would stop and stand still while you were being reborn again!

MR. PARKER What do you want from me? Call this whole thing off? It was your idea, not mine! But now that I've got myself something—I'm not going to throw it away for nobody!

THEO But can't you see what's happening here?

MR. PARKER If she wants to be a drunken wench, let her! I'm not going to take the blame. And as for you—*(fumbles in his coat pocket)* If you want this money, you can take it from me—I can throw every dollar of it into the ocean if I want to! You can call me a fool too, but I'm a *burning fool!* I'm going to marry that little girl. She is not a whore! She is a woman! And I'm going to marry her! And if the two of you don't like it, you can kiss my ass! *(bolts out into the street)*

THEO You're not drunk. What happened?

ADELE *(heading for the back room)* What does it look like? Wilmer hit me.

THEO *(following)* Why?

ADELE *(sits on bed)* He caught me in Morgan's with a friend of his after I had lied about going bowling with the girls. He just walked in and started hitting me, over and over again.

His friend just stood there pleading with him not to hit me, but he never did anything to stop him. I guess he figured, "Why should I risk getting myself killed over just another piece of ass?" I thought he was going to kill me but then Blue came in with some of his friends and they just grabbed him by the arms and took him away.

THEO Was Bobby with them?

ADELE I couldn't tell.

THEO Damnit! Everything gets fucked up!

ADELE It had to, because you don't think. If you're going to be a crook, you don't read a comic book for research, you don't recruit an old Black man that's about to die!

THEO No matter what you do, he's gon' die anyway. This whole place was built for him to die in—so you bite, you scratch, you kick: you do anything to stay alive!

ADELE Yes, you bite! You scratch, you steal, you kick, and you get killed anyway! Just as I was doing, coming back here to help Momma.

THEO Adele, I'm sick and tired of your talk about sacrifices. You were here because you had no other place to go. You just got scared too young and too soon.

ADELE You're right. All I was doing was waiting for her to die so I could get on with what I thought I wanted to do with myself. But, God, *she took so long to die!* But then I found myself doing the same things she had done, taking care of three men, trying to shield them from the danger beyond that door, *but who the hell ever told every Black woman she was some kind of goddamn savior!* Sure, this place was built for us to die in, but if we aren't very careful, Theo—that can actually happen. Good night. *(heads for the stairs)*

THEO Adele— *(she stops in her tracks and turns)* I've decided that there's going to be no more of Blue's business here. It's over. We're getting out.

ADELE *(after a long pause)* Theo, do you really mean it? *(*THEO *nods yes)* What about Daddy?

THEO He will have to live with it. This set-up can't move without me.

ADELE And Bobby?

THEO I'll take care of him.

ADELE That's fine, Theo. We'll throw the old things into the river—and we'll try something new: I won't push and you won't call me a bitch! *(goes upstairs.* THEO *picks up his father's notebook from the floor beside the bed. A knock at the door)*

THEO We're closed!

(The knocking continues)

THEO WE'RE CLOSED!

(The knocking turns to banging and a voice calls out to THEO*. He rushes to the door and opens)*

THEO I SAID WE'RE CLOSED! Oh, I'm sorry, Mr. Jenkins, I didn't know that was you . . . What are you doing here this time of night?

MR. JENKINS I want to speak to Parker.

THEO You know him—he's been keeping late hours lately . . .

MR. JENKINS I'll wait for him.

THEO Suit yourself, but don't you have to work tomorrow?

MR. JENKINS I have something to tell him, and I'll wait if it takes all night.

THEO In that case, you can tell me about it.

*(*ADELE *comes downstairs and stops on steps leading to shop, looking about confusedly. She has a deadly, almost blank look on her face)*

THEO What's wrong with you?

ADELE *(pause)* Some—somebody just called me.

THEO What did they call you about? *(she does not answer.* JENKINS *rises and seats her gently on bed)* Didn't you hear me—what about? *(she still does not respond)* WHAT IS IT, ADELE!!!

MR. JENKINS THEO!!! *(*THEO *turns to* MR. JENKINS*)* I think she probably just heard that your brother Bobby has been killed in a robbery by a night watchman.

THEO Uh-uh, nawww, nawww, that's not true.

MR. JENKINS Yes, it is, son.

ADELE Yes.

THEO No.

MR. JENKINS Yes! *(moves toward the shop door)*

THEO *I don't believe you!*

MR. JENKINS I saw him, boy, I saw him. *(dead silence as* MR. JENKINS *slowly moves toward the street exit)*

THEO You should've seen this dude I caught the other day on Thirty-second Street. He had on a bright purple suit, gray shirt, yellow tie, and his hair was processed with bright purple color. What a sight he was! But I have to say one thing for him—he was clean. *(the lights are slowly dimming)* Used to be a time when a dude like that came in numbers, but you don't see too many of them nowadays. I have to say one thing for him—he was clean. You don't see too many like—he was clean. He was—he was clean—

(Blackout)

Scene Two

(About two hours later, in the shop.

MR. PARKER *and* MR. JENKINS *enter the shop.* MR. PARKER *is drunk, and* MR. JENKINS *helps him walk and finally seats him on the barber's throne)*

MR. PARKER Thank you, Jenkins. You are the greatest friend a man can have. They don't make 'em like you any more. You are one of the last of the great friends, Jenkins. Pardon me, Mister Jenkins. No more will I ever call you Jenks or Jenkins. From now on, it's Mister Jenkins!

MR. JENKINS Thank you, but when I ran into Theo and Adele tonight, they said they had something important to say to you, and I think you oughta see them.

MR. PARKER I know what they want. They want to tell me what an old fool I am.

MR. JENKINS I don't think that's it, and you should go on upstairs and—

MR. PARKER Never! Upstairs is for the people upstairs!

MR. JENKINS Russell, I—

MR. PARKER I am downstairs people! You ever hear of downstairs people?

MR. JENKINS *(pause)* No.

MR. PARKER Well, they're the people to watch in this world.

MR. JENKINS If you say so.

MR. PARKER *Put your money on 'em!*

MR. JENKINS Come on, Mister Parker: why don't you lie down in the back room and—

MR. PARKER Oh! No—you don't think I'd have you come all the way over here just for me to go to bed, do you? I wouldn't do a thing like that to you, Jenkins. I'm busy—Mister Jenkins. Just stay with me for a little while . . . *(his tone changes)* Why did that girl lock me out? She said she would be waiting for me, but she locked me out. Why did she do a thing like that? I give her everything—money, clothes, pay her rent. I even love her!

MR. JENKINS Russell—

MR. PARKER *(rising precariously)* Tell me something, Mister Jenkins—since you are my friend—why do you think she locked me out?

MR. JENKINS *(steadying him)* I don't know.

MR. PARKER I'll tell you why. I'm an old man, and all I've got is a few dollars in my pocket. Ain't that it?

MR. JENKINS I don't know . . . Good night, Parker. *(starts out)*

MR. PARKER *(grabs his arm)* You think a man was in that room with my girl?

MR. JENKINS *Yes!*

MR. PARKER *Goddamnit! Goddamnit!*

MR. JENKINS Russell—

MR. PARKER I don't believe it! When I love 'em, they stay loved!

MR. JENKINS Nobody's got that much love, man!

MR. PARKER *(pause)* No, no—you're wrong. My wife—my dear Doris had more love in her than life should've allowed. A hundred men couldn't have taken all that love.

MR. JENKINS We ain't talking about Doris, Russell.

MR. PARKER Aw, forget it! *(crossing toward table) Goddamnit!* You stumble around like an old black cow and you never get up again . . .

> I have had my fun!
> If I don't get well no more!
> I have had my fun!
> If I—

*(*PARKER *falls down)* Get up, old bastard! Get up! *(rises to his feet, aided by* JENKINS*)* Get up and fall back down again. Come on, Mister Jenkins, let's play ourselves a game of checkers.

MR. JENKINS I don't want to play no damn checkers.

MR. PARKER Why do you curse my home, Mister Jenkins?

MR. JENKINS *(pause)* I apologize for that.

MR. PARKER Come on, have a game of checkers with your good friend. *(sits at table)*

MR. JENKINS *(moves to the table)* All right, one game and then I'm going home.

MR. PARKER One game.

MR. PARKER *(pausing while* JENKINS *sits down)* I said a lot of dirty things to my children tonight—the kind of things you have to live a long time to overcome.

MR. JENKINS I know exactly what you mean. *(*JENKINS *sets up jumps for* PARKER.

PARKER *seems unaware of it. They play briefly.* PARKER *stops)*

MR. PARKER Theo is a good boy, and a smart one too, but he lets people push him around. That's because he's always trying to con somebody out of something—you know the kind: can't see for looking. And Bobby? He wouldn't hurt a flea. A lot of people think that boy is dumb, but just let somebody try to trick or fool him if they dare! *(begins a series of checker jumps. Pause)* Got a story for you.

MR. JENKINS No stories tonight, Parker . . .

MR. PARKER Mister Parker. *(the last move is made, the game is over. His conquest slowly sinks in. And* MR. PARKER *is at long last the victor. Rising from the table)* Call me champ! *(*THEO *and* ADELE *enter shop from outside, and stand just inside the door.* PARKER *is laughing)* You're beat! I beat you! I beat you! *(*MR. PARKER *throws his arm around* MR. JENKINS*'s waist and holds him from behind)* . . . You fall down and you never get up! *(still laughing)* Fall down, old man! Fall down! *(releases* JENKINS *upon seeing* ADELE *and* THEO*)* You hear that, children, I beat him! I beat him! *(his laughter subsides as he realizes they are not responding to him. Guilt-ridden, he approaches* THEO*, looks at him intently, then reaches into his inside coat pocket and pulls out the money)* Here, Theo, here's the money, here's all of it. Take it, it's yours. Go out and try to get happy, boy. *(*THEO *does not move or take the money from his father's outstretched hand. He turns to* ADELE*. Her face is almost a blank)* WHY DON'T SOMEBODY SAY SOMETHING! *(*ADELE *attempts to speak but* PARKER *cuts her off)* I know you have some trouble with me . . . *(*PARKER *spies the notebook in the throne, takes it in his hand, and approaches* ADELE*)* You have a woman, you love her, you stop loving her, and sooner or later she ups and dies and you sit around behaving like you was a killer. I didn't have no more in me. I just didn't have no more in me! *(pause)* I know you don't believe I ever loved your mother, but it's here in this book—read it . . . *(she does not respond)* You wanta read something, boy! *(*THEO *turns away.* PARKER *slowly crosses, hands the book to* MR. JENKINS*, and addresses his remarks to him)* I got sour the day my legs got so trembly and sore on the stage of the Strand Theatre—I couldn't even walk out to take a proper bow. It was then I knew nobody would ever hire me to dance again. I just couldn't run downtown to meet the man the way she did—not after all those years of shuffling around like I was a dumb clown, with my feet hurting and aching the way they did, having my head patted as if I was some little pet animal: back of the bus, front of the train, grinning when I was bleeding to death! . . . After all of that I was going to ask for more by throwing myself into the low drag of some dusty old factory in Brooklyn. All I could do was to stay here in this shop with you, my good friend. And we acted out the ceremony of a game. And you, boy— *(turns to* THEO*)* . . . You and Blue with your ideas of overcoming the evil of white men. To an old man like me, it was nothing more than an ounce of time to end my dragging about this shop. All it did was to send me out into those streets to live a time—and I did live myself a time for a while. I did it amongst a bunch of murderers—all kinds of 'em—where at times it gets so bad till it seems that the only thing that's left is for you to go out there and kill somebody before they kill you. That's all—that's out there! *(goes to* ADELE*)* Adele, as for that girl that was here tonight, she's probably no good, but if at my age I was stupid enough to think that I could have stepped out of here and won that little girl, loved her, and moved through the rest of my days without killing anybody, that was a victory! *(moves to center stage, stands silently, then does a little dance)* Be a dancer—any kind of dancer you wanta be—but dance it! *(tries out a difficult step, but can't quite make it)* Uh-uhhh! Can't make that one no more. *(continues to dance)* Be a singer—sing any song you wanta sing, but sing! *(stops in his tracks)* And you've got enough trouble to take you to the graveyard! *(pause)* But think of all that life you had before they buried you. *(breaks into a frantic dance, attempting steps that just cross him up. He stumbles about until he falls. Everyone in the room rushes to help him up)* . . . I'm okay, I'm okay . . . *(he rises from the floor, slowly)* I'm tired, I'm going to bed and by the time tomorrow comes around, let's see if we can't all throw it into the river. *(moves into the back room, singing)*

I have had my fun!
If I don't get well no more
I have had my fun
If I don't get well no more—

(a thought strikes him. He turns and moves back to where JENKINS *is standing at the entrance to the back room)* Jenkins, you said that the day I beat you playing checkers, you said it could be the unluckiest day of my life. But after all that's happened today—I'm straight—I feel just great! *(moves to the stairs leading up, suddenly stops, turns and briskly moves back to the doorway leading to the shop)* Say, where's Bobby?

(Curtain)

THE TUMULT AND THE SHOUTING
1969

Thomas Pawley (1917-)

Among the immediate priorities of slaves once they were freed was obtaining an education, an essential step, they believed, in their adjustment to freedom. Private agencies in the North began educating freed slaves in 1861, when the American Missionary Society opened day schools in several Virginia communities. By the last year of the Civil War, more than 1,000 Northern white men and women joined white southerners and African Americans in the South to teach and care for ex-slaves.

School attendance was sporadic in some areas because most of the students were required to work on the family farm during planting and harvesting seasons. Students who could attend class regularly and progressed to upper grades assisted the instructor by teaching beginners. Gifted students were encouraged to continue their education, as was the case with Mary McLeod Bethune, George Washington Carver, and Booker T. Washington, all of whom worked their way through college, Bethune and Carver in the North and Washington at Hampton Institute in Virginia. They dedicated their lives to educating African American students in the South. Mrs. Bethune, with one dollar and fifty cents in her purse and six students, established a school in Daytona Beach, Florida, which became Bethune-Cookman College. Booker T. Washington was selected to run Tuskegee Institute in Tuskegee, Alabama, and became the foremost African American educator of his day. Dr. Carver, who taught at Tuskegee, became an internationally recognized and respected scientist.

The Tumult and the Shouting is about a pioneer African American teacher who dreams of freeing Black children from ignorance and preparing them to survive in a cruel and hostile world. David Sheldon, Sr., the teacher, dedicates his life to this mission, believing that it will provide security for his family, make him a respected member of the community, and shelter him to some degree from racism, since the college campus is generally free of whites. Educated men like Sheldon were restricted to a limited number of jobs and professions. They could become doctors (but could not practice in white hospitals), lawyers (but were not allowed to practice in court), dentists, ministers, businessmen (if they could raise the capital), or teachers. Because there were a limited number of teaching positions available for African Americans, it was common to find degreed persons earning their living as postal workers, Pullman porters, redcaps, elevator operators, janitors, or waiters. African American school teachers were paid far less than their white counterparts, and their teaching facilities, of course, were vastly inferior. It was common practice that used textbooks and outdated lab equipment (and at the college level, even discarded beds and mattresses) from white schools be passed on to Black schools. Sheldon is fortunate; he finds work in his profession, but not the respect and honor that a lifetime of committed work deserves. Pawley shows very clearly that those who wish to lead respectful and respected lives may perish if they are at the bottom of a capitalist ladder that has no room for them in white America.

The Tumult and the Shouting is the first play to examine middle-class African American life from the perspective of a Black teacher in a southern Black college. It was first produced at the Institute of Dramatic Arts, Lincoln University, in 1969, and has since been performed at Jackson State University; Langston University in Oklahoma; Tennessee Technological University; Rhein Main Air Force Base, Frankfurt, Germany; the Afro-American Research Society, Bronx, New York; and most recently at Clark Atlanta University.

Dr. Pawley is the retired Dean of the College of Arts and Sciences at Lincoln University, Jefferson City, Missouri, and is the author of a number of articles, essays, poems, and plays. Born in Jackson, Mississippi, he received his A.B. degree from Virginia State College, his A.M. and Ph.D. degrees from the University of Iowa, and has done postdoctoral study at the University of Missouri at Columbia. He has taught at Atlanta University and at Prairie View A & M College in Texas. In 1986, the National Conference on African American Theatre honored Dr. Pawley by making him their "Mister Brown Recipient," an award presented annually for distinguished work in theatre.

The Tumult and the Shouting

CAST OF CHARACTERS

DAVID SHELDON
DAVID SHELDON, SR., *his father*
WILLA SHELDON, *his mother*
BILLY SHELDON } *his brothers*
JULIAN SHELDON }
HARRIET SHELDON, *his sister*
JOHN CRENSHAW, *a farmer*
MR. BLANKENSHIP, *a grocer*
EMMA, *a young white woman*
MAMIE TOWNES, *the college librarian*
LAWYER CLARK
DR. BOWEN, *a physician*
DR. WALKER, *president of the college*
MISS JACKSON, *a secretary*
A VOICE
TAXI DRIVER
STUDENTS

Act One

Scene One

Processional

SCENE *The façade of a two-story brick house cut away to reveal the interior: a living room, kitchen, dining room on the first floor and two bedrooms upstairs. The house remains on stage always in the background throughout the play.*

TIME *1918-1948. The action is continuous.*

PLACE *A Negro college in the town of Warwick, Virginia.*

(The musical overture fades into the Recessional theme as DAVID *enters)*

DAVID Recognize that tune? They used to play it quite a lot at college commencements when I was a kid around here. It's called "The Recessional." Students used to march out to it after getting their diplomas. Nowadays there's little or no music. They just walk in very casually and walk out. You've probably guessed that this is a college play. Actually it's the story of a college teacher—a man who gives thirty years of his life to a single institution of higher learning as they say in the jargon and then suddenly finds himself retired—a condition for which he is totally unprepared. I know. You see, this man, this teacher was my father. I hope this does not confuse you because I am both a character in this play and yet I stand outside of it, watching the events as they move irresistibly toward a climax. This gives me an advantage over you. I know what's coming. I saw it happen. My father was an amazing person—an orphan at two, raised by his older sisters, educated in the North, he returned to his native South to Mississippi at thirty-five, just before the great war broke out, with his brand new Bachelor of Arts degree. When most men his age were becoming established he was just getting started. He intended to remain "down home" only long enough to earn money for divinity school, but he never made it. He remained a teacher all of his life. Why? That's what this play is all about.

(The lights fade. In the darkness a newsboy is heard shouting)

NEWSBOY Allies start big push! Extra! Marines go over the top! Extra! Extra!

(The lights come up on a spot set: a piano and a divan on the forestage. DAVID SHELDON *and his young wife* WILLA *are playing a duet. She plays the piano and sings. He accompanies her on the violin. The song is "O Promise Me." Suddenly* SHELDON *stops)*

WILLA What's the matter, Mister?

SHELDON Thought I heard the mailman.

WILLA At this time of day? It's only your imagination.

SHELDON No. I'm sure I heard something on the porch.

WILLA The evening paper. Come on. Let's start again. *(she resumes playing)*

SHELDON It's no use, Willa. I can't keep my mind on it.

WILLA If that college is going to hire you it'll hire you.

SHELDON But there's so little time left. I can't hold off signing my contract much longer.

WILLA Then sign it. You can resign later if the offer comes.

SHELDON I can't do that. Once I sign it I'll have to stay on for another year.

WILLA You and your scruples.

SHELDON After you've been at a place five years you owe something to the people. And when I leave—*if* I leave—I want to leave on good terms with everybody, especially President Adams.

WILLA I don't see how anybody could become attached to these rundown buildings on fifty dollars a month. *(closing the piano)* Well, I guess that ends the music for today.

SHELDON Sorry, Willa.

WILLA That's all right. *(she kisses him)* It's time to start dinner anyway. And I've got to heat the baby's bottle.

SHELDON *(putting the violin in the case)* Why don't we run up to Yazoo City this weekend?

WILLA What'll we use for train fare?

SHELDON Then let's take in the concert tomorrow night. It's free.

WILLA One of those student recitals. No, thank you. We've already been to three.

SHELDON It'd be something to do.

WILLA Mister, if you are really serious about doing something we can ask some people over for five hundred.

SHELDON But you just said we're broke.

WILLA It won't cost anything. I've got some

Jell-O and I can make some cookies and punch.

SHELDON Oh, I don't know.

WILLA Why not? Don't tell me you've lost interest in cards?

SHELDON Not exactly.

WILLA What's the matter then?

SHELDON It's the people we play with.

WILLA What's wrong with them? They're all faculty members and their wives.

SHELDON It's the way they gossip.

WILLA But harmless gossip.

SHELDON And when they're not gossiping, it's nonsense, trivialities.

WILLA Serious conversation and five hundred don't mix. It's not relaxing.

SHELDON Well, I can't relax around them.

WILLA But they're our friends. We've got nobody else to associate with. And they're good people even if they're not intellectuals.

SHELDON Let's not argue, Willa.

WILLA But you've become so grouchy the last few weeks—ever since you wrote to that college in Virginia.

SHELDON It'll be better for us up there, Willa. Better salary, better schools, better white people and better—

WILLA Negroes? They're the same everywhere.

SHELDON I was going to say race relations. *(he starts toward an imaginary door)*

WILLA Where are you going?

SHELDON To get the paper.

WILLA Before you get settled, I want you to go to the store. I'm out of corn meal.

SHELDON *(pulls out his empty pockets)* I'll have to charge it.

WILLA Our credit's good.

SHELDON I don't know for how long. Mr. Blankenship's been very patient. If he takes a notion to cut us off—

WILLA We'll take our business elsewhere. *(she hands him his hat and jacket)* And please don't let him start a conversation.

SHELDON That's how I keep our credit going. I'm about the only one from the Institute who'll listen to the old geezer. *(he goes out)*

(The light fades on the living room and comes up on the store—a counter with shelves of groceries behind. MR. BLANKENSHIP, *the proprietor, is a kindly looking and loquacious white man. He is waiting on a customer.* SHELDON enters*)*

BLANKENSHIP And what else'll it be, John?

JOHN How much this come to?

BLANKENSHIP *(figuring)* Sixty-five cents.

JOHN That'll leave me twenty-five out of a dollar, won't it?

BLANKENSHIP Thirty-five.

JOHN Slice me up thirty-five cents of bacon.

BLANKENSHIP Sure thing, John.

JOHN How much that gon weigh?

BLANKENSHIP Bout a pound and a half. *(*BLANKENSHIP *takes down a slab of bacon and puts it on the machine)*

JOHN Don't make 'em too thick, Mr. Blankenship.

BLANKENSHIP Bout medium?

JOHN Yes, sir.

BLANKENSHIP *(noticing* SHELDON*)* Oh, hello, Professor. Be with you in just a minute.

JOHN Howdy, Professor.

SHELDON *(nodding)* Mr. Crenshaw. How's your boy?

JOHN Doing just fine, Professor. We hear from him regular. Says he got awful sick on the boat going over but he likes it fine there in France.

SHELDON Glad to hear it.

BLANKENSHIP Well, he can have it. I'm going to stay as far away from the shooting as I can.

JOHN Oh, he ain't in the front lines. At least he ain't doing no shootin. He's in one of them labor batallions.

BLANKENSHIP He's lucky. He'll come back in one piece.

JOHN Well, I don't know, Mr. Blankenship. He might not never come home. Says he might stay over there after the war.

BLANKENSHIP Oh—?

JOHN Yessir. *(there is an awkward pause)*

BLANKENSHIP Well, that'll be exactly one dollar, John. *(he wraps the bacon and ties it.* JOHN *pulls out an old change purse and extracts a wrinkled dollar bill and hands it to* BLANKENSHIP*)*

JOHN Thank you, Mr. Blankenship. *(he starts out)*

BLANKENSHIP Oh, John—*(*JOHN *stops)*

JOHN Yes sir.

BLANKENSHIP When you write to Lon tell him I'm holding his delivery job for him.

JOHN I'll do that, sir. *(he goes)*

BLANKENSHIP Now then, Professor, what's for you?

SHELDON I need half-pound of corn meal, Mr. Blankenship.

BLANKENSHIP Charge or cash?

SHELDON Charge.

BLANKENSHIP *(opens a gray ledger and consults it)* That'll bring your account to just over eighteen dollars. Twenty dollars the limit on credit, you know.

SHELDON *(swallowing hard)* Yes, sir.

BLANKENSHIP Which reminds me. Something ought to be done about the salaries they pay you teachers at the Institute. You doing a fine job with our boys and girls around here.

SHELDON Thank you, Mr. Blankenship.

BLANKENSHIP Yes, sir. I've heard my father say how years ago folks was dead set against setting up an Institute for colored in this town. But it's done a world a good. I'm all for it.

SHELDON *(resigned to a long discourse)* Yes, sir.

BLANKENSHIP Now you take John Crenshaw. Known his family for years. Didn't get past the fourth grade but he's getting to educate all his children. *(he starts for the corn meal bin)* Why you spose Lon don't want to come home? He owes something to his daddy, don't you reckon?

SHELDON *(trying to avoid conversation)* Yes, sir.

BLANKENSHIP Then why you spose he ain't coming back?

SHELDON It's probably his being away from home for the first time and seeing how different things can be.

BLANKENSHIP Hum—I spose. But he could do a lot of good around here for his folks—the colored people, I mean.

SHELDON That's true. *(he sees that* BLANKENSHIP *has forgotten about the corn meal)*

BLANKENSHIP Now take you for instance. You're from South Carolina, ain't you?

SHELDON Yes.

BLANKENSHIP How come you come back to the South?

SHELDON This was the only place I could find a job teaching in college.

BLANKENSHIP That's what I mean. Folks was afraid you wouldn't fit. Said as much to Principal Adams. You know, you being educated up East. But he said they ought to give you a chance, by George, he was dead right. Folks like you Sheldon. You might even be the head some day.

SHELDON Thank you.

BLANKENSHIP But you can't keep good people if you don't pay 'em. And I'm going to say as much to Professor Adams the next time he's in here. Now what was it you wanted?

SHELDON Corn meal, Mr. Blankenship.

BLANKENSHIP Right away. *(at this moment a young white woman enters the store)* Excuse me a moment.

SHELDON Yes, sir. *(he steps to one side)*

BLANKENSHIP Afternoon, Miss Emma. What can I do for you?

EMMA *(noticing* SHELDON*)* I can wait.

BLANKENSHIP Oh, he don't mind waiting, do you, Professor?

SHELDON Well, I am in a hurry, Mr. Blankenship.

BLANKENSHIP It'll only take a minute. Miss Emma?

EMMA Mamma says to send her two quarts of your best snap beans, Mr. Henry.

BLANKENSHIP All right, little lady. *(he proceeds to ladle out huge handfuls of stringbeans.* EMMA *turns to* SHELDON*)*

EMMA You from the normal school?

SHELDON Yes, ma'm.

EMMA I thought so—how you dress an all. You all sure do ave a wonderful choir.

SHELDON Yes, ma'm. *(pause)*

EMMA Are you in the choir?

SHELDON No, ma'm. I don't sing.

EMMA Well, what do you do?

SHELDON I'm an English teacher.

EMMA Oh, how nice. But I'm sprised to hear you don't sing.

SHELDON I play the violin occasionally.

EMMA Oh, a fiddler! How wonderful. Do you play for parties?

BLANKENSHIP Here you are, Miss Emma. He ain't got time to play for no parties. He's a teacher.

EMMA Well, that's a shame. I know he could pick up right smart on the side if he'd a mind to. Charge this, will you, Mr. Blankenship.

BLANKENSHIP Right now, Miss Emma. *(she leaves)* Better write this down before I forget it. *(he licks the end of the pencil and writes laboriously.* SHELDON *fidgets)* All right, now let's see. Corn meal wasn't it, Professor?

SHELDON *(brusquely)* Yes. (BLANKENSHIP *looks at him sharply)*

BLANKENSHIP *(ladling out the corn meal into a sack on the scales)* One half-pound of corn meal. Good measure. Never short change my customers. There you are. *(he folds and wraps the sack tying it with a piece of string)* Charge, wasn't it? (SHELDON *nods.* BLANKENSHIP *writes after wetting the pencil)* Corn meal, twenty cents. D. Sheldon. All right, Professor, here you are. (SHELDON *starts out)* Oh, Professor.

SHELDON Yes. *(he stops. At the same time a middle-aged white woman enters.* SHELDON *does not see her. She pauses in the door)*

BLANKENSHIP Sorry you had to wait. *(pause)* But you know how it is.

SHELDON Yes. I know how it is. (SHELDON *turns, almost bumps into the woman)*

WOMAN Here, boy, why don't you look where you're going?

SHELDON *(stiffly)* Pardon me, madam.

WOMAN You almost bumped into me.

SHELDON I'm sorry.

WOMAN That all you got to say? (SHELDON *starts to reply but leaves abruptly)* What's the matter with that boy? He better mind his manners.

BLANKENSHIP He apologized, Sally.

WOMAN Funny way of apologizing. He speaks awful proper. Can't be from round here.

BLANKENSHIP South Carolina.

WOMAN He don't talk like it.

BLANKENSHIP He teaches at the Institute.

WOMAN Well, now that explains it. His airs and all . . .

BLANKENSHIP Oh, come on, Sally. He didn't touch you.

WOMAN Well, I just can't stand an uppity nigger. *(the light fades on the store)*

(SHELDON *enters the living room)*

WILLA What took you so long?

SHELDON He made me wait while he served some white woman.

WILLA Well, I forgive you then. Beggars can't be choosers.

SHELDON *(angrily)* I'm no beggar. I pay my bills like anyone else.

WILLA Don't shout at me—I didn't make you wait. Tell him.

SHELDON But I can't tell him. I don't dare tell him. As decent as he has been, he'd say I was forgetting my place and cut off our credit.

WILLA Why are you getting so upset? This isn't the first time this has happened.

SHELDON I'm fed up. I've got to get away from this town. It's hard to keep your self-respect on fifty dollars a month and always having to remember your place. That's why I've got to get that job in Virginia. Down here I'm just an underpaid nigger teacher.

WILLA And up there you'll still be underpaid and you'll still be a nigger teacher.

SHELDON But they even got a law against lynching up there. And that college is an oasis. Everything's right there on the campus. We won't even have to come in contact with white people.

WILLA I wouldn't be too hopeful.

(The lights fade and the music rises)

Scene Two

DAVID That's how we came to this house. I don't remember anything about it since I was barely a year old. But the salary was seventy-five dollars a month and Virginia *was* an improvement over Mississippi. This is quite a big house as houses go. It's got four bedrooms, a living room, dining room, kitchen and a room my mother called the pantry where she kept the food, the icebox, and her dishes. Just the kind of house for raising a family like ours. And the rent was only twenty-five dollars a month, including utilities. You didn't even have to pay for gas unless you exceeded the maximum. Imagine. Twenty-five dollars a month for a house like this. And never once did they raise the rent in thirty years. Right on campus too. Just a short distance from Old Main. You see, the college used this as inducement to get teachers. They couldn't afford to pay much in salaries directly, so this kind of made up for it. Trouble with this was it made you accustomed to good living and it didn't encourage you to own your own home. And then it kind of left people at the mercy of the administration, which was beholden only to the white folks in Richmond. *(pause)* By 1923 I had a brother and another was on his way. Coming to Virginia had isolated the family from the race problem but hadn't solved the financial one. Dad was under pressure to get his Master's degree so he had to go to school every summer. This only increased the financial strain and it didn't help the marriage—tensions began to develop. Of course there had been a couple of small salary raises. But after ten years of teaching he was making less than a hundred dollars a month.

(The lights fade on the forestage and rise on the interior of the house)

WILLA David, you stay out of Mr. Townes' toolshed. *(she is on the porch)*

DAVID *(off)* Yes'm.

WILLA Come on around this side where I can watch you.

DAVID *(off)* Oh, mama.

WILLA Right now. Do you hear?

DAVID *(off)* Yes'm.

(MAMIE TOWNES, *a tall spare woman with a pleasant disposition, comes up on the porch and knocks on the front door)*

MAMIE Willa, it's me. Mamie.

WILLA Come on in, Mamie. I'm in the kitchen. (MAMIE *enters)* You're home early.

MAMIE We've started closing at five for supper. Nobody uses the library then anyhow.

WILLA I know you can use the rest. I don't see how you can stand on your feet all day.

MAMIE It's an occupational hazard. Show me a librarian and I'll show you a case of varicose veins.

WILLA Why do you do it, Mamie? You don't need to work. Your husband's perfectly able to take care of you.

MAMIE True. But I don't know of anybody around here who's got too much money. Besides, I'd go stark, raving mad if I had to sit in that house all day while Jim's at school Now if I had children like you—

WILLA You'd be looking forward to the day when they were grown. And I'm looking forward to their being old enough for me to get a job. The president's promised me work. God knows we need the money.

MAMIE Can't you get someone to take care of the children? So you could work now, I mean?

WILLA Mister wouldn't hear of it.

MAMIE Old fashioned, eh?

WILLA I guess. But you know he was raised by his sisters and he says even that is not like being raised by your mother and father.

MAMIE Obviously you agree with him.

WILLA I suppose I do.

MAMIE Well, I've only got a minute. What I stopped by to ask is what are you wearing to the faculty social Friday evening?

WILLA Social?

MAMIE Yes. The invitation said semi-formal. For the life of me I never know what to wear when I get that kind of invitation. I wish they'd just say formal and get it over with.

WILLA Well, I don't know.

MAMIE You mean you haven't even thought about it?

WILLA Well, I've been so busy with the house and children—

MAMIE But you're going, aren't you?

WILLA I don't know—we haven't decided.

MAMIE Haven't decided? But Jim said those that were going had to respond by last Friday.

MAMIE Oh?—

MAMIE *(suddenly)* Willa, didn't you know about the dance? Didn't Sheldon tell you?

WILLA It must have slipped his mind.

MAMIE Like fun it did.

WILLA Oh, you don't know him. He gets so absorbed in his work he hardly knows the time of day. He's teaching five courses this quarter plus the debating team. He's dead tired when he gets home evenings. Yes, I'm sure it just slipped his mind.

MAMIE Then all you have to do is ask him.

WILLA But isn't it too late now? You just said—

MAMIE Oh, come on. They always expect somebody to change his mind at the last minute. That's no problem.

WILLA It'll mean buying a new dress.

MAMIE No, it won't. I'll lend you one of mine.

WILLA *(laughing)* I'd never get in it.

MAMIE *(laughing)* Then borrow one from Susie Parker. You and she are an exact match.

WILLA Oh, no, Mamie.

MAMIE Why not? Susie won't mind.

WILLA It's like accepting charity and I know Mister won't like it.

MAMIE You're crazy. Why everybody borrows from everybody else on this campus. You know that.

WILLA I get tired of borrowing from people, Mamie. And Mister would be furious if I did it again.

MAMIE Tell a lie then. Say you made it or your sister sent it to you.

WILLA That's the last thing on earth I'd say. He doesn't like them sending me things either.

MAMIE Poor but proud, huh?—But you need to get out together, you two. When you first came you were going all the time. But now—people will soon get the notion you've gone high hat and stop inviting you out.

WILLA I guess so.

MAMIE Don't you really want to go?

WILLA I'd love to.

MAMIE Then tell him.

WILLA I'll mention it to him after supper.

*(*SHELDON *enters, crosses to the porch and opens the door)*

MAMIE Good. I've got to run now and heat up the leftovers. I'm due back at six-thirty.

SHELDON *(entering and going to the hall tree)* Willa, I'm home.

MAMIE Seems to me there was something else I wanted to ask—oh, well, it couldn't have been important. *(she goes into the hall)* Hello, Professor.

SHELDON Oh, hello, Mamie.

MAMIE I'm afraid I've kept Willa from finishing your supper.

SHELDON Oh, that's all right. She likes to talk to you.

MAMIE Well, I've got to run. *(she goes out of the front door)*

SHELDON *(proceeding to the kitchen)* Mamie quit her job?

WILLA Un-unh. Library's closing for meals. Started today.

SHELDON *(shaking his head)* A shame. *(*WILLA *starts to protest)* I know—not many students use the library between meals but then that's the only time some can.

WILLA Librarians need a break too. It's a long day for them.

SHELDON Yes. They're pretty much overworked like the rest of us. And I'm afraid there's not much can be done about it till those people in Richmond have a change of heart. I'm going upstairs and catch a few winks before supper. Prudential committee meets tonight.

WILLA All right, dear. Any mail?

SHELDON On the hall table. Nothing much except bills.

(He ascends the stairs to the bedroom. WILLA *waits until she hears the door close then she goes into the hall and thumbs through the mail on the table. Finding nothing, she pulls out the drawer and rummages through the letters there. Not finding what she's looking for she goes to the hall tree and searches the pockets of* SHELDON*'s overcoat. She finally gives up and returns to the kitchen where she sits deep in thought. After a moment she lifts her head as if staring through the ceiling. She rises and goes up the stairs to the bedroom and pauses at the door)*

WILLA Mister, are you still awake? *(receiving no answer she enters softly.* SHELDON *is asleep, fully clothed. She goes to the bureau and thumbs through the letters there. Seeing* SHELDON*'s coat on the back of a chair, she crosses to it and searches the pockets carefully. Then she replaces the coat and crosses to the door. She is about to leave when she turns and faces the bed. She pauses and coughs gently.* SHELDON *stirs)*

SHELDON That you, Willa? What time is it?

WILLA Mister, can I talk to you for a minute?

SHELDON *(sitting up)* What's the matter? Something wrong? Don't you feel well?

WILLA I'm all right.

SHELDON You sure?

WILLA I'm sure.

SHELDON I thought maybe the baby was acting up again.

WILLA *(placing her hand on her stomach)* No. He's behaving himself.

SHELDON *He?* But it's going to be a girl.

WILLA It's too early to tell. I'll let you know when I'm about six months.

SHELDON *(laughing)* How'll you know?

WILLA By the way it kicks.

SHELDON You mean you can tell the difference between a football player and a ballet dancer? *(he is laughing)*

WILLA I can.

SHELDON *(lying back)* I'm glad you're all right, Willa. *(pause)*

WILLA Mister?

SHELDON Yes?

WILLA Are we going to the dance?

SHELDON What?

WILLA Are we going to the dance—Did we get an invitation to the faculty social?

SHELDON Oh, that?

WILLA Well, did we?

SHELDON Yes.

WILLA Where is it? Why haven't you told me about it?

SHELDON I left it at the office.

WILLA Why didn't you bring it home?

SHELDON I didn't want you to get excited about going.

WILLA *(not understanding)* What?

SHELDON You know—in your condition—

WILLA My condition? Being pregnant doesn't mean I'm dead. *(she is angry)* Besides the doctor hasn't said I shouldn't go out.

SHELDON That's not what I mean.

WILLA I don't understand.

SHELDON I don't think expectant mothers should go to dances.

WILLA Who's going to know I'm pregnant? The baby won't come for another seven months. I'm not showing at all.

SHELDON I guess I'm old fashioned.

WILLA Women don't go into seclusion any more because they're pregnant.

SHELDON Well, my mother did. And I'm sure your mother did.

WILLA I don't know about your mother but my mother did not. She went right ahead doing exactly what she did before and that's exactly what I intend to do.

SHELDON *(falling back on the bed)* All right, Willa.

WILLA Then we're going?

SHELDON I don't know.

WILLA But why don't you know? You've had the invitation for over a week.

SHELDON It'll mean new clothes, for you at least.

WILLA If I can arrange to get a dress, will you go?

SHELDON You mean borrow one? I don't think we should advertise our poverty.

WILLA Mamie will help me find one.

SHELDON So that's what Mamie was doing doing here. I wish she'd keep her mouth shut.

WILLA I'd have heard about it sooner or later, you know that. Besides she came over to ask what I was wearing. She assumed I already knew.

SHELDON Well, she needn't go around offering you dresses. I've got some pride, you know.

WILLA I'm the one who'll be wearing the dress.

SHELDON And I'm the one who couldn't afford to buy you one.

WILLA Have I ever complained?

SHELDON No, you haven't. You've been wonderful.

WILLA If I had known soon enough, I could have made a dress.

SHELDON *(abruptly)* What about the boys? Who'll stay with them?

WILLA I can get one of the girls out of the dormitory.

SHELDON Who?

WILLA I'll ask Miss Lillian to recommend someone. It won't be a problem. Girls like to have an excuse to get out of the dormitory to eat some home-cooked food.

SHELDON She'd stay overnight?

WILLA Why not?

SHELDON Oh, I don't know. We've got a case before the Prudential tonight. Some girl slipped out of the dormitory to meet her boyfriend.

WILLA Don't be ridiculous. She wouldn't meet him here. *(pause)*

SHELDON How much do they charge?

WILLA They usually leave it up to you.

SHELDON You have to be careful whom you leave with young children.

WILLA *(exasperated)* One night, Mister.

SHELDON Willa, would you go to the party without me?

WILLA You mean go by myself?

SHELDON Well, with Jim and Mamie.

WILLA No, I wouldn't. Besides that's the whole point, for us to go out together.

SHELDON I really don't want to go, Willa. I'm just not in a dancing mood.

WILLA And you haven't been for some time now.

SHELDON No, I haven't.

WILLA You're beginning to show your age.

SHELDON Willa, please—let's not argue.

WILLA It's what my friends warned me about before we got married, your being so much older than me.

SHELDON And you believed them?

WILLA Would I have married you if I had believed them? *(pause)* You used to be so gay, so debonair—wearing the latest styles and all. All the boys at the Institute tried to dress like you. I would never have believed you'd go into retirement so soon.

SHELDON It's this damned poverty.

WILLA But we don't have to give up everything. We're not that poor.

SHELDON Once we pay our bills there's nothing left for parties.

WILLA Your salary's the same as the others around here. And they manage to do things.

SHELDON But their wives are working.

WILLA Well, I could work too if you weren't so squeamish about the boys. So afraid someone is going to poison their little minds. It's your attitude that's keeping us back, not your salary.

SHELDON I don't think a husband should have to rely on his wife to make ends meet. And I won't have to after I get my degree.

WILLA What's that got to do with our going out this weekend?

SHELDON Everything. We'll be able to go out on weekends.

WILLA What about *this* weekend?

SHELDON *(wearily)* Willa, I'm tired. I'd like to get a little rest before debate practice. Please.

WILLA Then you won't go?

SHELDON No, Willa.

*(*WILLA *rushes out of the room slamming the door. She pauses at the head of the stairs and cries. Composing herself she descends to the kitchen where she begins setting the table. After a moment she slumps into a chair and buries her head on the table and sobs uncontrollably. There is a knock at the kitchen door which she does not hear. A second knock and she raises her head and wipes her eyes on her apron)*

WILLA Who is it?

MAMIE *(off, rear)* It's me. Mamie.

WILLA Just a minute. *(she wipes her eyes again, arranges her hair then moves to the back door)*

MAMIE What took you so long? *(looking around)* You and Sheldon down here smooching? I'm out of butter. Can you lend me some until I can get to the grocery?

WILLA Sure. How much do you need? *(goes to ice box)*

MAMIE One stick will do.

WILLA Oh.

MAMIE What's the matter? You out too?

WILLA No, but *(removing butter dish)* we buy it this way. *(she reveals a solid block of butter)* It's cheaper. You'll have to slice it.

MAMIE What's the difference? It all comes from the same cows.

WILLA *(laughing and relieved)* Take as much as you want. There's a knife in the drawer. I'll get something for you to wrap it in. *(she goes to the cabinet and removes wax paper, while* MAMIE *slices away)*

MAMIE I meant to borrow some on my way home just now but I clean forgot until we were ready to sit down to the table.

WILLA It's no trouble. We hadn't started. Mister's resting.

MAMIE Have you asked him about the social?

WILLA Yes—but nothing's definite—yet.

MAMIE *(staring at her)* Have you been crying?

WILLA *(surprised)* What?

MAMIE I heard you through the door.

WILLA Oh.

MAMIE You've had an argument.

WILLA *(reluctantly)* Yes.

MAMIE And he's refused to go. *(*WILLA *does not answer)* Well, it's none of my business but if it were me I'd go anyhow.

*(*SHELDON *sits up on the bed upstairs, rises, stretches, and crosses to the stairs. He pauses when he reaches the bottom)*

WILLA I won't go by myself.

MAMIE Then come with Jim and me. *(*WILLA *shakes her head)* Why not? And you don't need to worry about being a wallflower. I'll see to it that all the husbands dance with you.

WILLA Mister already suggested that.

MAMIE Then what's stopping you?

WILLA I don't want to get started going out by myself.

MAMIE Suit yourself. But look at it this way. You're young for only a little while. When you get older like Sheldon naturally you won't want to go as much.

*(*SHELDON *enters the kitchen)*

SHELDON Mamie, your butter's getting warm.

MAMIE What? Oh, yes. Excuse me. *(she heads quickly for the back door)*

SHELDON And Mamie—why don't you mind your own business? *(* MAMIE *exits)*

WILLA You've got no right to talk to her like that.

SHELDON I've got every right when she starts meddling in my affairs.

WILLA She invited me to go along with Jim and her. Is there anything wrong with that?

SHELDON No. But when she begins to discuss the differences in our ages, she's meddling.

WILLA *(defensively)* Well, she's my friend. One of the few people I ever see and I won't have you talking to her like that.

SHELDON Won't "have" me?

WILLA Don't threaten me.

SHELDON I'm not threatening you. *(he starts out)*

WILLA You are. And just for that I am going to that social! *(SHELDON stops)* And what's more I'm going to all the other socials from now on. You stay here and dry rot if you want to but not me! *(SHELDON goes out quietly. WILLA follows to the entry door, pauses then leans against the door jamb and weeps softly. The lights fade and the music swells)*

DAVID But she didn't go to the dance. She never really meant to. She was a faithful and dutiful wife with the highest of scruples.—But to get on. The baby was born—another boy, Billy—a sickly little fellow from the instant of his birth. Soon there would be a girl and the family, my family, will be complete. It's 1928 now and time for me to join the story.

Scene Three

(WILLA is in the upstairs bedroom sitting in a rocker. She is in labor. Every once in a while as the pains strike she moans softly. Outside the house JULIAN and DAVID are playing catch with a tennis ball. In the living room the younger boy, BILLY, is lying on the floor reading. SHELDON sits nearby grading papers. He continues for a moment, finishes a paper and enters a grade in his rollbook. Then he gathers all the papers and puts a rubber band around them. He rises and puts on his coat)

SHELDON *(glancing at his pocket watch)* Nearly four. I'd better hurry or I'll be late for class. *(as he passes BILLY)* What're you reading, Billy?

BILLY Nothing.

SHELDON Aren't those the comics?

BILLY Yep. But I've finished them. I'm thinking.

SHELDON Oh. *(pause)* Why don't you go outside and play?

BILLY I don't want to. It tires me out. Can I go with you?

SHELDON *May* I go with you.

BILLY Well, may I?

SHELDON I'm going to class.

BILLY At four o'clock? Why?

SHELDON Because it's my job.

BILLY Why is it so late? David and Julian are home from school.

SHELDON College is different. You go to school all day.

BILLY Oh *(pause)* Daddy—

SHELDON Yes.

BILLY I don't want to go to college.

SHELDON *(smiling)* All right. I'm going up to look in on your mother. I'll be back in a minute.

BILLY Okay. *(as SHELDON ascends the stairs BILLY crosses to the porch)*

JULIAN Hey, Billy, want to catch?

BILLY No, thank you.

DAVID Oh, come on.

BILLY Nope.

JULIAN Why not?

BILLY I'd rather watch.

(SHELDON enters the room upstairs)

SHELDON How's it going?

WILLA They're about a half hour apart now.

SHELDON That's getting close. I'll send David for Dr. Bowen.

WILLA It's still an hour or so away.

SHELDON Maybe. You sure you don't want to go to the hospital?

WILLA No. It'd mean another doctor since Dr. Bowen isn't allowed to practice there. I'll be all right. Everything's ready. I've even got water on the stove ready to heat. *(she winces)* That was a sharp one.

SHELDON I'll dismiss my class and come right back. I hate to leave you alone.

WILLA No, don't do that. The boys will be here. I'm sure you'll get back before anything happens. I'll send for you if I need you.

SHELDON Promise?

WILLA Promise.

SHELDON *(reluctantly)* All right. *(he kisses her on the forehead and descends the stairs. BILLY hears him and moves to the front)*

BILLY You going to class now?

SHELDON Yes.

BILLY Why? It's past four o'clock.

SHELDON Yes. I'm late.

BILLY Won't your students be gone?

SHELDON *(patting him on the head)* I wouldn't be surprised. *(he goes out on the porch. BILLY follows)*

SHELDON David, you and Julian come here. *(the boys stop playing and come up on the porch)*

SHELDON I'm going to class now. I want you to stay close by and do whatever your mother tells you.

BILLY What's the matter with mama?

JULIAN Nothing. She's having a baby.

DAVID How do you know?

SHELDON *(interrupting)* All right, all right. David, I want you to go to the infirmary the moment she tells you. And then come to my class and get me.

DAVID Where is your class?

SHELDON Old Main, second floor. Room 212. Okay?

DAVID Okay.

SHELDON Be good now and look after your little brother.

JULIAN He don't need to look after me.

SHELDON I'm talking about Billy.

(As SHELDON *leaves the porch,* WILLA *is struck by another sharp pain. She arches backward stifling an outcry. The lights dim up on the classroom)*

RUSSELL I tell you, man, he ain't coming.

CANDY He never misses.

SNEAD Well, it's five minutes after.

CANDY The rule says you got to wait ten minutes.

VIVIAN I sure hope he misses today.

RUSSELL Let's go.

*(*WILLA *is suddenly convulsed with pain and screams aloud. The boys hear her and stop playing.* DAVID *rushes inside.* BILLY *starts after him but is held back by* JULIAN. DAVID *enters the bedroom.* WILLA *indicates he should go get the doctor. The scene in the classroom continues)*

SNEAD I hear his old lady is expecting again.

SHIELDS Then that's what's keeping him.

RUSSELL I don't care what's keeping him. But being as how I got a report to make and I ain't ready, I move we cut.

CANDY You better be glad he didn't hear you say that. He'd flunk your behind sure.

NELLIE What are we going to name the new baby?

SHIELDS Well, now let's see. The oldest boy is Noun, the brother is Pronoun and the baby is Participle. I move we name the new one Conjunction.

HELEN Shame!

NELLIE We don't mean any harm.

GRIFFIN Here he comes!

RUSSELL Nine minutes past four. Made it with a minute to spare, Goddammit.

CANDY What did I tell you?

(There is a general scrambling around for seats)

RUSSELL What the hell are you so happy about?

CANDY *(grinning)* I'm anxious to hear your report, daddio. *(*SHELDON *enters in a hurry. He crosses to his desk)*

SHELDON I must apologize for being late and I want to thank you for waiting. This shows that you are really interested in getting an education. I realize we've lost nearly ten minutes but perhaps you won't mind staying a little longer and making it up. *(there is a groan)* I beg your pardon. Did someone say something? *(silence)* As you know, Mrs. Sheldon is—uh—not feeling well. *(someone snickers)* And I may have to leave suddenly. *(the class brightens perceptibly)* Meanwhile let us turn to the lesson for today which is *(consulting his notes)* the subjunctive mode. Oh, yes, we're to be favored by a report on the subject from Mr. Russell. Mr. Russell? *(silence)* Is Mr. Russell present?

RUSSELL Yes, sir.

SHELDON *(sitting)* You may come forward, Mr. Russell, and proceed.

RUSSELL *(rising wearily)* Professor, I don't have my report. I'm not prepared.

SHELDON Eh, what's that?

RUSSELL I said I'm not prepared.

SHELDON Why not?

RUSSELL I—I didn't understand the assignment.

SHELDON Why didn't you come in and see me about it then?

RUSSELL See you?

SHELDON Yes. You know where my office is, don't you?

RUSSELL Oh, yes, sir.

SHELDON Well?

RUSSELL I don't know, Professor, I just can't seem to get interested in grammar.

SHELDON Earlier in the year you told me English is your favorite subject.

RUSSELL Oh, yes, sir. English is my favorite subject but not grammar English.

SHELDON *(after the laughter subsides)* Hum. *(pause)* You don't really like it, do you?

RUSSELL Oh, yes, sir. I like stories and stuff like that. *(someone laughs)*

SHELDON Don't laugh. He's simply saying what most of you feel. *(loud protests)* I know, I know. There are one or two exceptions but most of you would rather you didn't have to be bothered.

RUSSELL I'm sorry, Professor Sheldon.

SHELDON *(closing his book and putting up his notes)* Let's forget today's lesson for the moment. Anyone have any ideas why we're studying grammar?

HELEN It's a requirement. *(laughter)*

SHELDON Yes, Miss Quander, it is. But why is it?

SPENCER Because we need to be able to speak and write correctly.

SHELDON All right. That's one reason. College graduates need to know how to write and speak correctly. Any others?

HAZEL *(lisping)* Well, I don'th know, thir. But it theems to me that no matter what we want to be we've goth to be able to communicate.

SHELDON *(smiling)* Very good. Someone else? *(silence)* Can't anyone think of a special reason why *we* need to study English?

SNEAD By *we,* do you mean colored people?

SHELDON Exactly.

A VOICE So we can talk like white people.

SHELDON Right church, wrong pew. *(there is a buzz)*

CANDY Is that the reason? Is he right, Professor?

SHELDON Have you ever been to a minstrel show? *(murmurs of affirmation including:* "Florida Blossoms, Georgia Peaches, Silas Green from New Orleans")

SHELDON What's it like?

SNEAD A lot of Negroes in blackface running around singing plantation songs and telling darky jokes.

SHELDON Yes, and using a dialect so thick you could cut it with a knife. You and I know we don't talk like that but that's the stereotype the average white person has of us. They're shocked and surprised when they're confronted with someone who doesn't say, "Here, ah is." But that's the stereotype we've helped to build for ourselves. And that's why "Amos and Andy" has made millionaires out of Freeman and Gosden. The whole thing's a burlesque, a caricature. But it's also true that after fifty years of education many of us are still illiterate, unable to read and write or spell our own name. And we rationalize it and say it's not important and go on perpetuating illiteracy. And it's being constantly used as an argument against a college education. "They can't learn English," they say. "Listen at the way they talk." Now I don't give a tinker's damn about sounding like white people or being accepted by them. But I do want to be able to communicate with them and with my own people. And there are limitations to what I can do with the language that's used on Old Street.

RUSSELL *(protesting)* But grammar, Professor.

SHELDON I know. It seems so pointless. But let's think of it as a tool, Russell, as a means to an end so that you can say what you want to say. Take tense for example. We'd all be pretty confused if we didn't have past, present, and future to indicate when something happened.

RUSSELL You got a point, Professor. But since so many of us don't talk the way they do, wouldn't it be easier for us to make our own grammar? How about them learning to talk like us?

SHELDON That's a very interesting point. But I'm willing to bet my meager salary that if the federal government decreed that our speech—the so called Negro dialect—would become the official language and we started teaching it in the schools and requiring it to be used, most of you would start complaining it was too difficult.

SHIELDS But how could that be?

SHELDON As an experiment I want each of you to write a short essay using jive language. There is only one requirement. You must communicate an idea.

RUSSELL But how can we? Professor, you don't know jive talk.

SHELDON Try me, *(he pauses)* "Jack." *(the class howls)* Mr. Russell, I know what the problem is, really I do. But we can lick this thing—I know we can. The trouble is formal English is so far removed from our experience—that is, for most of us. That's why I'm writing a new grammar based upon our needs, upon the language as it is used today. It will be quite practical. In fact I call it Practical English Grammar. It will stress the kinds of errors which our students make.

SPENCER When is it going to be published?

(The lights come up on the bedroom. The doctor and nurse are there. The baby has been delivered. The doctor comes downstairs and calls DAVID. *He talks to him for a moment after which* DAVID *runs off)*

SHELDON I don't have a publisher yet.

SNEAD Do you think you can get one? You a Negro college professor?

SHELDON Of course.

RUSSELL Professor, you know, I might really start studying if I had a book like that. And I ain't jiving.

(David appears in the doorway and attempts to signal his father)

SHELDON That's an encouraging sign.

HELEN Professor?

SHELDON Yes? *(*HELEN *indicates* DAVID *who is standing nervously at the door)* All right son. *(as he begins to gather his books and papers together)* I've got to go. My wife's having a baby. Class dismissed. *(he stops at the doorway)* Mr. Russell?

RUSSELL Yes, sir.

SHELDON I'll expect your report next time.

RUSSELL Oh, yes, sir. I'll be ready, sir.

SHELDON Hum. *(he goes)*

A VOICE Hey, Russell, I know what we can name the baby.

RUSSELL What?

VOICE Subjunctive mode!

(The lights fade)

Scene Four

DAVID It happened in October, 1929—black Tuesday, or was it Thursday? By the fall of the next year the breadlines stretched from New York to California. On the campus we didn't see the breadlines but we knew they were there. Fewer students were coming to college and those that came were begging for jobs. At the opening faculty meeting the President announced that the college had suffered a ten per cent cut—ten per cent from their already meager resources. This would mean cutting salaries for everybody. It was hoped that by the end of the year things would be better so that the salaries could be restored. Families like our neighbors with both husband and wife working didn't feel the pinch so badly. But in ours it was another story.

(As the lights rise SHELDON *is seated in the living room reading the Richmond News Leader.* WILLA *is in the kitchen mixing oleomargarine. A pause. Then shouts from outside the house and the three boys enter the kitchen from the rear door)*

JULIAN How long before supper?

WILLA Soon.

BILLY What are you doing?

WILLA Mixing oleo.

BILLY Can I help?

WILLA No. I want all three of you to get your hands washed.

DAVID Last one up is a dirty dog. *(they race for the stairs with loud shouts.* BILLY *is knocked down in the scuffle but gets up and runs manfully after his older brothers. As they reach the stairs,* SHELDON *puts down his paper)*

SHELDON Boys! *(they stop) Walk* up the stairs. You'll wake the baby.

DAVID Yes, sir. *(they resume the ascent, walking but with* JULIAN *trying to get by* DAVID *As they reach the second floor the race is resumed.* SHELDON *puts down his paper in disgust. Shouts from upstairs mark the battle for position around the washbowl. Suddenly the door is closed with a loud slam. Silence.* SHELDON *resumes his reading as* WILLA *begins to set the supper table in the dining room. She places a cereal bowl, a knife, spoon, and glass beside each plate. Then she gets a box of shredded wheat biscuits, breaks them in half and places a half in each bowl. Suddenly the door to the bathroom swings open. A water fight is in progress)*

BILLY Mama, David and Julian throwin water on me.

WILLA Mister, see after them, won't you?

SHELDON *(crossing to the bottom of the stairs)* David! *(the fighting stops)*

DAVID *(off)* Yes, sir.

SHELDON If I have to come upstairs, I'm bringing my razor strap. Understand?

DAVID *(off)* Yes, sir.

BILLY Daddy, Julian's shaking his fist at me.

SHELDON David, you come down here and wash your hands in the kitchen.

DAVID I've finished, Daddy.

SHELDON Come on down anyway. *(pause)* Did you hear me?

DAVID Yes, sir. I'm coming. *(*DAVID *appears at the head of the staircase)*

SHELDON And don't sulk.

DAVID I'm not sulking.

SHELDON You go sit at the table. And I don't want to hear another peep out of you.

DAVID Yes, sir. *(*DAVID *enters the kitchen.* SHELDON *resumes his seat.* WILLA *is now removing a can of evaporated milk from the cabinet. She punches holes in both ends with a can opener then pours the contents into a glass pitcher)*

WILLA David, get me the ice water.

(DAVID *goes into the pantry, opens the icebox and removes a green water bottle which he gives to* WILLA)

DAVID Don't put too much water in it mama. I don't like it when it's watery.

WILLA All right. *(she pours the water and stirs it)*

DAVID When we going to start using bottle milk again?

WILLA Soon I hope. *(she now removes a loaf of whole wheat bread and begins to slice it)* Go call the others. I'm just about ready.

DAVID Yes'm. *(he crosses to the foot of the stairs and shouts)* Supper's ready! *(to* SHELDON*)* Supper's ready, Daddy.

SHELDON You all go ahead. I'll eat later.

DAVID Yes, sir. *(he returns to the kitchen)* Daddy says he'll eat later. (WILLA *comes into the living room)*

WILLA Mister, what's the matter? You haven't eaten with us all week.

SHELDON I'm not hungry.

WILLA Then come and sit with us. Are you angry with me about something?

SHELDON No.

WILLA There's something troubling you, I know. Whenever you start acting like a hermit. Won't you tell me what it is?

SHELDON Later. (WILLA *shrugs her shoulders and turns to the stairs)*

WILLA Julian, you and Billy, come on. *(she goes into the kitchen. The bathroom door swings open and another race begins.* BILLY *and* JULIAN *are met at the foot of the stairs by* SHELDON*)*

SHELDON This ripping and tearing about the house has got to stop!

(DAVID *hearing the lecture appears in the door behind* SHELDON *grinning and poking fun at his helpless brothers)*

SHELDON You act more like wild savages than the sons of a college professor. Cultured and refined people do not yell and shout all over the house. Do you understand?

JULIAN Yes, sir.

BILLY *(blameless but manfully imitating his brother)* Yes, sir.

SHELDON Now go and get your supper. (DAVID *ducks out of sight.* JULIAN *and* BILLY *walk meekly to the table.* SHELDON *shakes his head, resumes his seat and picks up the paper)*

WILLA Whose turn is it to say grace?

JULIAN It ain't mine.

BILLY Isn't.

JULIAN Well, it ain't.

BILLY It's David's.

DAVID I said it this morning.

WILLA All right. We'll all say it together. Let's bow our heads. *(they do so.* WILLA *leads off with the Grace. The others chime in)* "Thank thee, Lord, for all these blessings. Amen."

DAVID I don't like our grace. It's too short.

JULIAN Well, why don't you find another one?

DAVID I already know one.

JULIAN Aw, you don't.

DAVID I do. Can I say it, Mama?

WILLA If you wish.

BILLY But we already said one. I'm hungry!

DAVID Let us bow our heads. "Lord make us truly thankful for these and all other blessings. Amen." There!

JULIAN *(counting)* It's only four words longer.

BILLY Pass the bread, please.

WILLA *(pouring milk in each bowl of cereal)* Eat your cereal first.

JULIAN I want mine with my cereal so I can dunk it.

WILLA All right. (JULIAN *reaches for the bread and margarine simultaneously)* Ask for things to be passed.

JULIAN Pass the bread and butter, please. *(after receiving them he proceeds to apply the margarine liberally)*

BILLY May I have a glass of milk, please? (WILLA *pours milk for him)* It tastes funny. (WILLA *pats his head and puts a tiny bit of sugar into the glass)*

WILLA Try it now.

BILLY *(grinning)* Fine.

JULIAN Butter dish is almost empty. (WILLA *takes the butter dish and begins to refill it with margarine)*

DAVID It's not butter. It's margarine.

JULIAN Same thing.

DAVID No, it isn't. Butter's made from milk and oleo's made from vegetables, ain't it, mama.

WILLA Yes.

JULIAN Well, they look alike. You can't tell the difference.

DAVID I can.

BILLY Mama, why does butter from cows and butter from vegetables both come out yellow?

WILLA They aren't. Margarine's white. I mix it with coloring so it'll look yellow.

BILLY Why are we eating vegetable butter instead of real butter?

WILLA It's cheaper.

DAVID Don't you know there's a depression on?

JULIAN Mama, can I go to the movies tomorrow?

WILLA I don't know.

JULIAN Please, Mama. There's a cowboy picture and a serial.

WILLA You'll have to ask your father for the money.

JULIAN It'll only cost me five cents.

WILLA I thought it was ten.

JULIAN Well, it is. But I can get in for five.

WILLA How?

JULIAN I saw a boy do it. He had only five cents and he asked Mr. Goldstein to let him in. So Mr. Goldstein asked him about the other five cents and the boy said he'd pay him later. Mr. Goldstein said, "I don't allow credit. You'll have to pay me now. Come here." So he took the boy by the nose and whacked him on his head and said, "Okay, you can go in."

WILLA He didn't?

DAVID We do it all the time.

JULIAN *(brightly)* Yeah. We Jew him down.

WILLA *(sharply)* Where did you hear that?

JULIAN Hear what?

WILLA That expression. What you just said.

JULIAN All the kids say it.

WILLA Well, I don't want you saying it. It isn't nice.

JULIAN But—

WILLA Mr. Goldstein can't help it because he's a Jew.

JULIAN I didn't mean any harm.

DAVID What's wrong with it, Mama?

WILLA Just don't let me hear you say it again—ever. Why aren't you eating, David?

BILLY It's those candy bars. *(*DAVID *signals him to be quiet)*

WILLA What candy bars?

BILLY The candy he was eating outside.

WILLA David, where did you get money for candy bars?

DAVID Working—

WILLA For whom?

DAVID For Miss Fannie in the bookstore.

WILLA And she paid you in candy bars?

BILLY She gave him a whole box.

WILLA I don't believe it. David, tell me the truth. Where did you get that candy? *(silence)* David? *(he does not answer)* Julian, do you know where he got them? *(silence)* Well, I guess I'll have to tell your father.

DAVID *(blurting it out)* I took 'em.

WILLA Where?

DAVID At school.

WILLA You took candy at school? How? Why?

DAVID We're supposed to sell it to raise money for our trip.

WILLA Yes?

DAVID One day last week after school we were playing football behind the school when one boy got the idea to go inside. He found the supply closet unlocked and all the candy in it. Then he called us and gave each of us a box.

WILLA Oh, David.

BILLY I'm going to tell Daddy.

WILLA *(grabbing him)* Sit down, Billy. David, why did you do this? Why? Don't you know that's stealing?

DAVID Well, it wasn't really stealing, Mama—

WILLA It is and you know it. Why, David? Why did you do it? Haven't we taught you right from wrong?

DAVID *(breaking down)* I'm sorry, Mama. I'm sorry. I won't do it again. I promise.

WILLA But why did you do it, David?

DAVID I overheard you and Daddy talking one night about his salary cut—I knew you were having a hard time so I didn't want to ask you for the money for the show and stuff like that—so I thought I could sell the candy.

WILLA But stealing, David—

DAVID *(breaking down again)* I'm sorry, Mama. I'm sorry. Please don't tell Daddy, please.

WILLA That money will have to be repaid. And we'll have to tell Miss Butler.

DAVID She'll put me out of school.

WILLA We'll have to take that chance. I don't want any of you to say a word of this to anyone. Is that clear? Billy?

BILLY Yes, Mama.

JULIAN Yes'm.

WILLA *(sternly)* Finish your supper and then go upstairs. And I don't want a peep out of any of you. I'll have to tell your father about this.

DAVID Mama, please—

WILLA No, David. He'll have to know.

DAVID He'll whip me.

WILLA I wouldn't be at all surprised. (WILLA *rises, closes the door, and enters the living room. The lights dim on the kitchen)*

WILLA Mister, you said that after supper you'd tell me what's the matter.

SHELDON *(putting down his paper)* Where are the boys?

WILLA Still eating. What is it?

SHELDON There's going to be a second salary cut.

WILLA Oh, no.

SHELDON *(nodding)* Starting the first of January. Another ten per cent.

WILLA But what are we going to do?

SHELDON I don't know. I honestly don't know.

WILLA Mister, I'll have to go to work.

SHELDON Now let's not start that.

WILLA But we can't live on your salary after another cut.

SHELDON I know.

WILLA Then what are we going to do?

SHELDON The book'll be published soon. That'll make up the difference.

WILLA But how can you be sure?

SHELDON Both Hampton and Virginia Union are going to adopt it.

WILLA But twelve hundred copies have to be sold before your royalties start.

SHELDON Yes, I know.

WILLA And God knows how long that'll take. Mister, you've got to let me go to work.

SHELDON *(wearily)* There may not be any work now, Willa.

WILLA The President's told me any time I want to—

SHELDON That was *before.*

WILLA Before—

SHELDON They're eliminating some jobs, consolidating others. Business manager and cashier are going to have the same secretary.

WILLA What?

SHELDON So you see even if I say yes your chances are slim.

WILLA Then I'll try the city. I'm a good practical nurse.

SHELDON No. It'll mean leaving the children all day.

WILLA It's the children I'm thinking about.

SHELDON You mean the money?

WILLA Of course I mean the money. They all need new shoes and Billy ought to have his tonsils removed. You know the doctor's warned that if they don't come out soon, it might lead to serious trouble. We had to take him out of school for the last two winters.

SHELDON All the more reason for you to be at home.

WILLA *(abruptly)* There's another reason.

SHELDON What?

WILLA David took a box of candy from the school.

SHELDON Took? You mean he stole it?

WILLA Yes.

SHELDON *(rising)* I'll give him the whipping of his life.

WILLA I think you'd better listen to me first.

SHELDON I'm not raising any thieves.

WILLA That's exactly what you *are* doing.

SHELDON You're crazy. What're you talking about?

WILLA Will you please listen to me? (SHELDON *sits down startled)* David has overheard us talking. He knows we've been having a hard time.

SHELDON So he decided to steal?

WILLA He didn't want to bother us about money.

SHELDON Couldn't he do without? He's almost fourteen. I did without when I was his age and I didn't steal either. And I didn't have a father or mother to guide me.

WILLA This constant talk of money. Children are impressionable.

SHELDON I'm sorry but I don't agree. He knows right from wrong. And if he doesn't I'm going to teach him.

WILLA We are to blame. Telling him that he had to set an example for the other children by doing without things.

SHELDON What kind of example has he set by stealing?

WILLA He's sorry—he's genuinely sorry. He broke down and cried just now telling me about it. I don't know when I've seen him do that.

SHELDON David cried?

WILLA He's tried to be a man because we asked him to. But after all he's only a child.

SHELDON Yes, he is a child. And that's why you must stay home with him and the others. If he's done this with you here there's no telling what notions he might develop with both of us gone all day.

WILLA They'll be at school. Mrs. Givens can take care of the baby. I'll be home at five. Mrs. Givens is a good woman. Raised six children. She won't let them go astray.

SHELDON My job is to earn the money to keep the family going. Yours is to make a home for them.

WILLA You'll never change, will you? I'll bet that if we were actually starving and living in a hovel, you'd say my place was by the hearth.

SHELDON I can't help being what I am.

WILLA *(quietly)* And I can't help being what I am. Mister, I'm going to work if I can find a job.

SHELDON Even if I say no?

WILLA Yes.

SHELDON Then there's nothing more I can say. I'll have my supper now. *(he turns and enters the kitchen as the lights fade and the music swells)*

Scene Five

DAVID She tried but there were no jobs. And the breadlines in the cities grew longer. Soon the Black masses would abandon the Grand Old Party for the man in the wheelchair—the great white father who would assuage their hunger. But the W.P.A. and P.W.A. were still letters in the alphabet. Grand Central Station was overflowing with Black M.A.'s and Ph.D.'s moonlighting to make ends meet. And with increasing frequency white faces began to appear beneath the red cap. The first of the year came and with it the second salary cut. As winter closed in on the campus Billy began having asthmatic attacks and had to be taken out of school for the third straight year. He was slowly falling behind in school, a fact which later on made him want to quit. As the attacks grew worse he was put to bed.

(The lights come up on the bedroom. BILLY *is in bed sleeping.* SHELDON *sits nearby reading. He has on his eye shade. Occasionally he glances toward the bed.* BILLY *begins to toss fitfully.* SHELDON *puts the book aside and goes to the bed. He takes* BILLY'S *hands then feels his forehead. His face shows alarm. He crosses quickly to the door and calls)*

SHELDON Willa. *(no answer)* Willa.

WILLA Yes.

SHELDON Come quickly. *(he turns to the bed)*

WILLA *(entering)* What is it?

SHELDON The fever seems to be getting worse. Feel his head.

WILLA *(after doing so)* Yes, he's burning up.

SHELDON Stay here. I'm going to call the doctor.

WILLA Try the infirmary. He's usually there this time of evening.

SHELDON I'll be back as quickly as I can. *(He grabs his coat on the run and dashes out of the house)*

BILLY Mama.

WILLA Yes, baby.

BILLY I'm hot. Can I have some water?

WILLA All right. *(she pours out a glass)* Here you are. *(*BILLY *sits up.* WILLA *holds the glass to his mouth and puts her arm around his back.* BILLY *drains the glass)*

BILLY More!

WILLA No. That's enough. Lie back and go to sleep.

BILLY I can't—it's too hot. *(he throws off the bedcover)* Can't you open a window?

WILLA *(covering him)* No. I'd create a draft. Lie back now and try to sleep till the doctor comes. He'll give you something that'll make you feel better.

BILLY I'll try. *(he lies back.* WILLA *straightens the cover.* DAVID *and* JULIAN *stick their heads in the door)*

JULIAN How's Billy?

WILLA Ssh—*(she motions them to keep quiet and go into the hall. She follows. In the hallway)* His temperature's up.

DAVID Much?

WILLA A whole lot.

DAVID What you going to do?

WILLA Your father's gone for Dr. Bowen.

JULIAN Is Billy ever going to get well? Seems like he gets sick every winter.

DAVID Well, at least he gets to miss school.

JULIAN What's he got, Mama?

WILLA Asthma and his tonsils are bad.

JULIAN Can't they cure it?

WILLA Sometimes. But mostly people have to grow out of it.

DAVID I wish we could do something for him.

WILLA You can—pray. *(*JULIAN *and* DAVID *look at each other)*

DAVID Yes'm.

WILLA It's time you were doing your homework. Go into your room and no fighting tonight, please.

JULIAN Okay.

(They go into their room across the hall. The light comes on. We see them going about the routine of getting school books, notes, etc. and settling down at their desk. WILLA *goes back into the sick room and settles into a rocker. For a moment all is quiet, broken only by the soft squeak of the rocker.* WILLA *closes her eyes and hums softly to herself)*

JULIAN David—you going to pray for Billy?

DAVID I spose. You?

JULIAN *(nods)* What you going to say?

DAVID I don't know.

JULIAN It's kind of hard, ain't it.

DAVID Isn't it.

JULIAN *(starts to argue but remembers his promise)* Isn't it? To pray I mean?

DAVID Awfully hard.

JULIAN *(after a pause)* You spose it'll really help?

DAVID Mama thinks it will—but I don't know. Seems like that's all our folks do—is pray.

JULIAN I don't guess it'd do no harm. *(pause)* Would the Lord's prayer do?

DAVID We say that every night.

JULIAN *(helplessly)* Yeah—*(pause)*

DAVID But I spose it's better'n nothing. At the end you could add a couple of lines like "an please help our little brother to get well."

JULIAN *(repeating)* "an please help our little brother get well"—Thanks, David.

DAVID That's okay. *(they resume their studies.* BILLY *has begun to toss fitfully. Suddenly he starts to scream)*

BILLY Mama, mama.

WILLA *(putting her arms around him)* Here I am, baby. I'm right here with you.

BILLY Mama, mama.

WILLA I'm here, Billy, here. *(*BILLY *tries to force his way out of bed, screaming and waving his arms.* DAVID *and* JULIAN *are on their feet)*

BILLY Save them! Save them! They're drowning!

WILLA No one's drowning, baby. You're here with mama.

BILLY Save David—save Julian. They're in the river. Don't let them drown.

WILLA They're in their room, Billy. They're here with us.

BILLY No. They've gone swimming again. Down in the river. Down in the Appomatox.

WILLA David, Julian, come here! *(*DAVID *and* JULIAN *enter the room)*

WILLA Here they are, Billy. Here they are. See they're safe. They're right here.

BILLY *(suddenly sobbing)* Ohhhh—Ohhhh—they're gone.

WILLA No, baby, they're here. Can't you see them?

BILLY *(moaning)* They're gone—they're gone.

WILLA Oh, my god.

DAVID He's out of his head, mama. He's delirious from the fever.

JULIAN *(becoming frightened)* He's gonna die. He's gonna die!

WILLA *(sharply)* Don't talk like that.

BILLY Miss Phillips—Miss Phillips!

JULIAN He's calling his teacher.

BILLY Miss Phillips—Miss Phillips.

DAVID Mama, what are we going to do?

WILLA *(struggling to contain* BILLY*)* Julian, run to the infirmary. Get your father. Hurry! *(*JULIAN *hurries out of the room)* Help me, David. Help me to hold him. *(*DAVID *goes to the bed)*

BILLY David, David! Save Miss Phillips. Save Miss Phillips.

DAVID *(starting to cry)* I'll save her, Billy—I'll save her.

BILLY Ohhhh—ohhhh—

WILLA Go to the bathroom. Bring me a wet cloth. *(*DAVID *runs down the hall and returns almost immediately)* Put it on his forehead. *(he does so.* BILLY *continues to sob. Below,* SHELDON, *the* DOCTOR, *and* JULIAN *enter)*

SHELDON Upstairs, doctor. *(the three of them ascend the stairs to the bedroom)*

WILLA *(as they enter)* He's delirious, doctor.

(The doctor makes a quick examination feeling BILLY'S *hands and forehead)*

SHELDON David, you and Julian wait outside. *(*DAVID *and* JULIAN *leave, go down the hall and enter their room)*

DOCTOR Hand me my bag, Mrs. Sheldon. *(*WILLA *hands him the bag. The* DOCTOR *removes a hypodermic needle)* I'm going to give him a sedative. *(he holds the syringe up to the light, squeezes it, then places it on the table in a piece of cotton. He then removes a bottle of alcohol and a swab of cotton and begins to clean* BILLY'S *arm. He then makes the injection.* BILLY *flinches slightly)* Now he'll sleep. *(he puts the cotton, alcohol and hypodermic needle back into the bag)*

WILLA Doctor, what's wrong with him?

DOCTOR Tonsillitis and he's got a very high fever, Mrs. Sheldon. His tonsils are badly infected as I told you. They'll have to come out soon or his heart may be damaged. I just hope we haven't put it off too long.

SHELDON Will that stop the asthma too?

DOCTOR That I can't say. But it certainly won't make it any worse. I'm going to give you a prescription for the fever and something to reduce the inflammation. Where can I write?

SHELDON Downstairs in the living room, doctor. *(*JULIAN *and* DAVID *appear in the hallway. The* DOCTOR *goes down)*

DAVID Daddy?

SHELDON Yes, David.

DAVID Can we go in?

SHELDON No. You'd better not. *(he starts down)*

JULIAN Daddy?

SHELDON Yes *(a bit impatient)*

JULIAN How is he?

SHELDON Don't bother me now, boys. I'm busy.

DAVID *(calling after him)* Is he going to be all right? *(*SHELDON *does not answer.* JULIAN *and* DAVID *turn and go back down the hall.* SHELDON *enters the living room)*

DOCTOR He'll be all right now, Professor. *(hands him the prescription)* Here you are. Have this filled right away. I think he'll be all right now but if you need me, don't hesitate to call. *(glancing around)* You have a telephone, don't you?

SHELDON There's a pay phone in Old Main. I can get the night watchman to let me in.

DOCTOR Fine. *(he shakes hands with* SHELDON *and leaves.* SHELDON *accompanies him to the front door)* Uh, Professor.

SHELDON Yes, doctor.

DOCTOR I mean it.

SHELDON What will an operation cost?

DOCTOR Let's not talk about that now. The main thing is Billy's health.

SHELDON Thank you, doctor.

DOCTOR Well, good night. *(he goes.* SHELDON *stands there examining the two prescriptions as* WILLA *comes down the stairs)*

WILLA He's asleep.

SHELDON *(showing her the prescriptions)* I'm going to get these filled.

WILLA Mister—

SHELDON Yes?

WILLA What about the operation?

SHELDON I don't know—

WILLA *(exasperated)* You don't know what?

SHELDON I don't know where the money's coming from—that's all.

(He puts on his hat and coat and goes out the front door as the lights fade)

Scene Six

END OF THE PROCESSIONAL

DAVID Somehow Billy survived and somehow money was found for the operation. I didn't know it at the time but they cashed in an insurance policy. Things didn't get better. They got worse. By my senior year in high school the biggest bank in the city had closed and the teachers had received still another salary cut. Things were at rock bottom. I knew my dream of going away to college was impossible. I would have to remain at home. In March the Squire of Hyde Park moved into the White House and the fireside chats began. Abroad rumblings and flashes of lightning along the Rhine.

JULIAN *(off)* Hey, David!

DAVID And now it's time for me to become an active part of the story.

(The lights dim. JULIAN *continues to call in the darkness)*

JULIAN Hey, David. David!

DAVID Yeah!

JULIAN Where are you?

DAVID Upstairs.

(The lights dim up and JULIAN *is seen bounding up the stairs, two at a time)*

DAVID *(as* JULIAN *enters the bedroom)* What's up?

JULIAN Mutt Johnson's recruiting guys for summer work.

DAVID Virginia Beach?

JULIAN Yeah.

DAVID How much?

DOCTOR Fifteen dollars a month, room and board.

DAVID What the hell—that ain't no money.

JULIAN Waiting table or hoppin bells—He says you'll pick up a hundred a month in tips.

DAVID I'm still for going to Atlantic City or Asbury Park.

JULIAN Man, you sure are on that up north kick. Why?

DAVID You can make more.

JULIAN Says who?

DAVID Pretty Boy Jones.

JULIAN You believe him? He's the biggest damn liar in school.

DAVID And then there's more to do when you're off work. The Beach hasn't got more'n a couple places where colored can go and they're dumps.

JULIAN That's true.

DAVID And in upstate Jersey you can tell a paddy to go to hell. On the beach, those peckerwoods will climb up side your head in a minute.

JULIAN But what'll the old man say? It's pretty far from home.

DAVID He won't like the idea.

JULIAN I'm for going anyhow.

DAVID You mean just up and leave?

JULIAN Sure. He'll get over it.

DAVID Man, there ain't nothin to do around this place in the summer. No decent jobs *or* chicks. Nothin. I sure am fed up with staying here year around.

JULIAN Me, too. *(pause)* Well, what we going to do?

DAVID Let's talk it over with Mama. Maybe she'll talk to Daddy.

JULIAN What the hell makes you think she'll approve?

DAVID She's more realistic. Always was.

JULIAN And if she says no?

DAVID Don't count your chickens—

JULIAN Well, I can tell you what I'm going to do—I'm going someplace upstate or downstate—I ain't spending the summer here.

DAVID *(uncertainly)* Aunt Mamie has promised me a job in the library.

JULIAN How much can you draw out?

DAVID Nothing til next year's tuition is paid.

JULIAN How you going to get any new togs?

DAVID Daddy will have to buy 'em.

JULIAN With what?

DAVID Damn if I know.

JULIAN Well then?

DAVID Okay, you win.

JULIAN Where's Mama?

DAVID In the kitchen.

JULIAN Okay, let's go. *(they descend the stairs in silence and enter the kitchen)*

WILLA Too soon for dinner, boys.

JULIAN Mama, can we talk to you?

WILLA Something wrong?

JULIAN No, ma'm. We just want to talk.

DAVID Sit down, Mama. You look tired.

WILLA What are you two up to?

DAVID Go ahead, Julian.

DOCTOR Huh?

DAVID Go ahead. Tell her.

JULIAN I thought you were going to do the talking.

WILLA Look. Your father will be coming home soon. *(starts to rise)* I've got to finish supper.

DAVID Wait, Mama. It'll only take a minute.

WILLA *(resuming her seat)* Well—

DAVID Mama, Julian and I want to go off this summer.

WILLA Off? Where?

DAVID Some place to work.

WILLA But you've already got a job. *(silence)* Where do you want to go?

JULIAN To the beach.

WILLA I see. *(pause)* You'll have to ask your father.

JULIAN That's just it, Mama. We want you to ask him.

WILLA What makes you think *I* approve of you going? *(silence)* Why do you want to go?

DAVID To make some real dough. I need clothes when I enter college next fall.

JULIAN And I need clothes period.

WILLA I see—

JULIAN Will you do it, Mama?

WILLA I'll have to think about it.—You're both so young.

DAVID Oh, Mama, don't start that. That's why we've got to get away. People around here treat us like children. Little David and Little Julian. We'll never grow up if we stay here.

JULIAN Yeah, I can't even walk a girl home from school before some old bat is over here tattling to you.

DAVID And then you and Daddy are always telling us to remember that we are a college professor's sons. We can never relax.

JULIAN And then look at it this way, Mama. With me and David gone you won't have to have as many mouths to feed for a couple of months.

WILLA *(smiling)* Well—

DAVID Please, Mama—

WILLA *(sighing)* All right. *(the boys are elated)* It's hard for me to realize you're growing up. And three months isn't such a long time. I'll speak to him as soon as he comes home.

JULIAN Thanks, Mama.

DAVID Thanks, Mama.

WILLA You'd better hold your thanks until after.

DAVID Thanks anyhow.

WILLA Now I've got to finish dinner. *(she goes back into the kitchen)*

JULIAN That was easy.

DAVID What'd I tell you?

JULIAN Solid, Jack, solid. *(they shake hands)*

DAVID And she'll handle daddy, too.

JULIAN *(as they go upstairs)* Boardwalk here I come!

(They disappear down the hall chattering. A pause. SHELDON *enters the front door. He looks old and tired. He carries a briefcase bulging with papers. He removes his hat and coat and hangs them on the hall tree)*

SHELDON Willa, I'm home.

WILLA Supper'll be ready soon.

SHELDON There's no hurry. I'm not going out tonight.

WILLA There's a telegram on the table. Came about three o'clock.

SHELDON I suspect it's from my publisher. *(he opens the telegram, reads it several times, then slumps on the divan)*

WILLA *(entering)* Bad news?

SHELDON *(nodding)* From the publisher. They're going out of business. The company which bought them out has declined to handle my book so they're shipping me the balance of the printing. Eight hundred and fifty copies.

WILLA Too bad.

SHELDON *(wearily)* I've been expecting it. Oh, well—at least the college will continue to use it. Maybe I can find another publisher before the supply is exhausted.

WILLA Do you really think you can?

SHELDON I don't know, Willa. I don't know.

WILLA Well, at least I've got some good news.

SHELDON What's that?

WILLA I've got a job.

SHELDON Where?

WILLA Here on the campus as assistant house director of Craig Hall.

SHELDON You're going to be a dormitory matron?

WILLA Yes. At seventy dollars a month. They couldn't find a replacement for Mrs. Billings so—

SHELDON Mrs. Billings—you're going to be a night matron.

WILLA From four until closing time.

SHELDON That's hard work, Willa, hard work, running up and down those steps, answering calls, keeping the girls quiet.

WILLA We need the money. And it may lead to something better.

SHELDON Yes, we need the money and it'll be a long time before I get my salary back, not to speak of a raise.

WILLA Mrs. Givens will come in each afternoon at three-thirty.

SHELDON *(wearily)* All right. *(silence)*

WILLA Mister, what do you think of the boys going off to work this summer?

SHELDON Going off?

WILLA Yes.

SHELDON David's got a job in the library and Julian doesn't need to work. He'll have to go to summer school if he's to graduate with his class next year.

WILLA They're set on doing it.

SHELDON Why? Why are they so anxious to leave home?

WILLA They're at that stage.

SHELDON But they're too young. And they've lived on the campus all their lives. They don't know anything about the outside world.

WILLA Maybe it's time for them to find out.

SHELDON They'll find out soon enough. *(silence)* Where do they want to go?

WILLA The Beach.

SHELDON Which beach?

WILLA I don't know. You'll have to ask them.

SHELDON I will not ask them. They should have come to me directly anyhow instead of bothering you.

WILLA To tell you the truth, Mister, I think they're afraid of you.

SHELDON Afraid of me? Why? Haven't I been a good father—a good provider?

WILLA *(nodding)* Of course you have. But

you haven't spent much time with them in recent years.

SHELDON I haven't had much time to spend.

WILLA When you come home you go directly to your room. And after dinner you go back to the office.

SHELDON But I've always been here when they really needed me.

WILLA That's just it. Their problems are not really big problems, but it's awfully important to be able to talk to someone. That's why they always come to me first. *(pause)* What shall I tell them?

SHELDON Tell them—No. I'll tell them. *(he crosses to the stairs)*

WILLA Don't lose your temper. *(she goes into the kitchen.* SHELDON *ascends the stairs and enters the boys' bedroom)*

SHELDON *(entering)* May I come in?

DAVID Hello, Daddy. Sure.

SHELDON May I sit down? I've been on my feet all day.

JULIAN Sure. Sit here. *(he dumps clothes from a chair)*

SHELDON You really should hang them up.

JULIAN *(picking up clothes)* Yes, sir.

SHELDON Your mother tells me you want to leave us this summer. That right?

DAVID We want to work—yes, sir.

SHELDON What's the matter? Don't you like your home? Getting tired of us?

DAVID Oh, no, sir.

SHELDON Why then?

DAVID We need clothes, Daddy.

SHELDON What's the matter with the clothes you have?

DAVID They're out of style, everybody's wearing English togs now.

SHELDON That why you want to go off, Julian?

JULIAN Yes, sir. And this campus is a pretty dead place in summer after you've been here all the year round. It's not like living in Richmond or Norfolk.

SHELDON This is your home.

JULIAN Yes, sir. But we never get to go any place. We stay here year in and year out—we don't even take vacations.

SHELDON I can't afford them.

JULIAN I'm not blaming you. We know you're doing the best you can.

SHELDON What do you know about working? Have you ever waited table? Worked in a hotel?

DAVID We can learn quickly enough. There's nothing complicated about it. And there'll be enough guys from the college around to show us the ropes.

SHELDON It's not the kind of life for sixteen- and seventeen-year-old boys.

JULIAN I don't mind hard work.

DAVID Neither do I.

JULIAN If you stood it when you were our age, we can too.

SHELDON It's not a decent life either. All kinds of immoral things go on at those beach hotels, bootlegging, prostitution, gambling—

JULIAN You saw them didn't you?

SHELDON Yes.

JULIAN Well, it didn't make you immoral.

SHELDON I was older, much older. And I had to do it. There were my sisters and brothers who relied on me.

DAVID You've always said that nothing could overcome good home training. Why are you so afraid that we'll go astray?

SHELDON I didn't say that.

DAVID But you implied it.

SHELDON I'm only trying to suggest that it's not so glamorous as you've been made to believe.

JULIAN I'm not going for glamour. I'm going for money.

SHELDON Watch your tone, young man.

JULIAN *(defensively)* Well, I mean it.

SHELDON Now, I've had about enough of this. I'm trying to reason with you but if you won't listen to reason so be it. You're not going to the beach or any place else to work next summer. You, David, are going to work in the library. And you, Julian, are going to summer school to remove those deficiencies you've been piling up for the last three years.

JULIAN Oh, no I'm not.

SHELDON What did you say?

JULIAN Tell him, David.

SHELDON David?

DAVID We want to help, Daddy, in our own way.

SHELDON You mean you're going without my approval?

DAVID I'm sorry, Daddy, but that's the way we see it.

SHELDON You go and you're gone for good.

JULIAN That's all right with me.

DAVID Shut up, Julian!

SHELDON That's the way you feel, is it?

DAVID I just don't see why we've got to argue about it. That's all.

SHELDON *(strangely calm)* Arguing? I'm not arguing. I'm still your father and as long as you're in this house, I expect you to obey. When the day comes that you can't, you're welcome to leave.

DAVID *(after looking at* JULIAN*)* We're still going, Daddy.

*(*SHELDON *looks at them for a moment, starts to speak but suppresses the impulse. He goes out quietly, slowly pausing at the door to look at them once more. He descends the stairs slowly, thoughtfully.* WILLA *is waiting)*

WILLA Supper is ready. *(*SHELDON *passes without speaking and enters the living room)* Mister, supper is ready. *(*SHELDON *does not respond)* What happened?

SHELDON My own sons are defying me.

WILLA Oh.

SHELDON They can go if they like, I'm through with them, for good.

WILLA You don't mean that.

SHELDON I do mean it. And as long as I'm supporting them they'll do as I say. When they don't, they go.

WILLA You can't dictate their lives.

SHELDON Am I wrong in wanting them here at home?

WILLA I didn't say that. But you've got to begin to treat them as men. They'll be leaving us for good in a few years anyhow. I'm just trying to face reality.

SHELDON And what is the reality?

WILLA That they're men—that they're grown up right under your nose without you realizing it. I tried to warn you. I begged you to spend more time with them.

SHELDON So what am I to do? Go back up there? Beg their pardon? Tell them I didn't mean what I said?

WILLA Tell them the truth.

SHELDON What truth?

WILLA That you want them here at home with you. That you want them to continue to lean on you. That you don't want them to grow up.

SHELDON But I do.

WILLA Do you? I don't. I dread the day they'll leave this house for good. But I know it's coming. So I want them here with me as long as possible.

SHELDON Must I eat crow?

WILLA You'll lose them for good if you don't.

(After a long pause SHELDON *walks slowly to the staircase)*

SHELDON Willa, there are times when I feel as if I've never known you.

WILLA Mister, there are times when I think you never have.

(The lights fade and the curtain closes)

Act Two

Scene One

THE RECESSIONAL

(Music rises with the curtain and continues until DAVID *appears)*

DAVID The war came. Julian and I were drafted. Billy tried to join up but was rejected. He stayed home, finished college, and got a job as a mail carrier. Lots of college grads did that. It beat teaching and there wasn't much else a Black man could do in those days. Somehow my mother and father had stuck it out. He is now seventy, still vigorous but seventy. Mother, fifteen years his junior, is a beautiful middle-aged woman. There is a great serenity about their lives. Having grown tired of fighting, they take each other for granted. There are still occasional flareups but they don't mean anything. But now, two years after the war they are going to face the greatest crisis of their lives.

(The lights come up on the house. WILLA *is busy preparing the evening meal. The* PROFESSOR *enters slowly, stopping in the hallway to remove his coat and hat)*

WILLA That you, Mister?

SHELDON Yes.

WILLA Supper'll be ready in a little while. I just got in.

SHELDON Something the matter?

WILLA No. Relief was late coming on. Any mail for me?

SHELDON Yes one. I'll leave it on the table. *(he drops the letter on the hall table and continues upstairs, carrying his briefcase and other mail. He sits down in the rocking chair and begins thumbing through the letters. One catches his attention. He holds it up to the light, carefully tears it open and reads it slowly. Shock, dismay, and disbelief creep into his face. Finally, he rises in anger)* Willa!

WILLA *(downstairs)* What is it?

SHELDON Come here, please. *(*WILLA *wipes her hand on her apron, leaves the kitchen and ascends the stairs)*

WILLA *(entering the bedroom)* Something wrong?

SHELDON *(handing her the letter)* Read this. *(he crosses to the front window and stares out)*

WILLA *(glancing at the signature)* From the President. *(*SHELDON *does not answer.* WILLA *reads)*

WILLA *(as she finishes)* It's come.

SHELDON You were expecting this? *(*WILLA *nods)*

WILLA Mrs. Willis received her retirement notice this morning. It upset her so she couldn't come to work. Notices went out yesterday following the Board meeting. You didn't pick up your mail this morning?

SHELDON No.

WILLA It's been there all day—*(silence)*

SHELDON What am I to do?

WILLA Do?

SHELDON Yes. I can't retire now. I've nothing to retire on.

WILLA You'll have your pension.

SHELDON Eighty-five dollars a month. We can't live on that. I've got no savings.

WILLA I'll still be working.

SHELDON *(slowly)* That's right. They're not firing you, are they?

WILLA *(trying to be pleasant)* I've a little while longer.

SHELDON Fifteen years. A whole lifetime. *(pause)* So now you're going to take care of me.

WILLA I wish you wouldn't look at it that way.

SHELDON How should I look at it?

WILLA We should both be grateful that I can still work.

SHELDON So can I work—I'm not an invalid.

WILLA I didn't mean it that way. *(pause)* They want the house in August.

SHELDON Yes. The job and the house, just like that.

WILLA We've known it was coming—ever since the college joined the Retirement System.

SHELDON Somehow I couldn't believe it. Somehow I just couldn't believe they'd retire me—after all these years of not caring what went on over here—just as they do at the other state colleges. Time was you could teach here until you dropped.

WILLA You thought they'd let you go on teaching past seventy?

SHELDON Why not? The least I expected was the same treatment as Dr. Stanley. He's still living on campus and has an office in the library.

WILLA But after all, he was the president for more than thirty years.

SHELDON Don't we count? We teachers?

WILLA You know the answer to that.

SHELDON No, I don't. They buy us for a dime a dozen. Then when they're through with us they kick us out no matter how much service we've given—or how unprepared we are for it.

WILLA *(after a pause)* Well, we'd better start looking.

SHELDON For what?

WILLA A house. It'll take some doing to find one. A decent one.

SHELDON You mean accept this? *(pointing to the letter)*

WILLA What else can you do? You *are* seventy.

SHELDON I'm not so sure.

WILLA But the law is specific, optional retirement at sixty-five, compulsory at seventy.

SHELDON I'm talking about *my* age.

WILLA *(perplexed)* What?

SHELDON You remember I've always had some doubt about how old I actually am.

WILLA *(nodding)* Yes.

SHELDON And I indicated as much at the time I filled out the retirement forms?

WILLA I don't remember.

SHELDON That'll give me a fighting chance—perhaps as much as two more years.

WILLA I doubt it.

SHELDON At least it's worth a try. They owe me that much after thirty years.

WILLA Mister, those white people on the Board don't care about you.

SHELDON Perhaps not. But they'll listen to the President. They'll do anything he says—or almost anything.

WILLA I don't know—

SHELDON Why else would they have made him President—an ignorant, unknown, itinerant teacher-trainer, elevated to the presidency of a college?

WILLA That's why.

SHELDON What?

WILLA He follows orders.

SHELDON But he knows how to get what he wants. If he'd been a general during the war the Germans wouldn't have had a chance. He may be an Uncle Tom but he's a shrewd one.

WILLA You mean you would go to him? Ask his help?

SHELDON Yes.

WILLA A man you despise?

SHELDON Yes.

WILLA I can't believe it. He'll make you crawl. He knows what you think of him.

SHELDON Yes.

WILLA What makes you think he'd want to fight for you?

SHELDON I don't. I think he'll be flattered I've come to him at all. I never have before.

WILLA *(slowly)* He'll make you lick his boots.

SHELDON *(desperately)* I know it. But I can't retire now. I simply can't afford to retire now.

WILLA And I simply can't believe it. I simply can't believe it. A man whose pride made him leave Mississippi. *(pause)* If it's money you're worried about, Julian and David will help.

SHELDON They've got their own families—and I've always promised myself that I would never be a burden to them.

WILLA Billy will help.

SHELDON What's he got? A monthly paycheck which he spends on liquor and women.

WILLA But we don't need much. My salary and your pension will take care of us.

SHELDON For how long? Will it buy us a house?

WILLA *(quietly)* Does teaching mean so much to you?

SHELDON It means a great deal.

WILLA Then apply to one of the private colleges. I'm sure you could get on at one of them.

SHELDON I don't want to get on at one of them. I'm needed here.

WILLA All right, Mister, do what you want to do. I just don't think it'll do much good.

SHELDON Thanks for encouraging me.

WILLA *(starts to answer then changes her mind)* I've got to finish supper.

(She goes out and down the stairs. SHELDON *goes to his bureau and opens the bottom drawer. He removes a small black strong box which he places on the bed. Opening the box with a key on his chain, he hurriedly rifles through the contents. Finally he discovers what he is looking for and his face lights up. He moves quickly to his desk and proceeds to write a letter. The lights fade on him and come up on the kitchen below as* HARRIET *enters)*

HARRIET Mama, guess what?

WILLA What?

HARRIET Guess?

WILLA I've no idea.

HARRIET I've been invited to Roanoke for a party.

WILLA That's nice. By whom?

HARRIET Bobby's mother and father. I'm dying to go. Can I?

WILLA Ask your father.

HARRIET Right away. *(she starts out)*

WILLA Harriet, I don't think right now is a good time.

HARRIET Why?

WILLA Your father's being retired.

HARRIET Oh?

WILLA He's awfully upset.

HARRIET Doesn't he want to retire? He's worked so hard all his life.

WILLA No.

HARRIET Why? Isn't he seventy?

WILLA Yes and no.

HARRIET *(puzzled)* What?

WILLA He's never really known his age. Birth records of colored people weren't kept in South Carolina when he was born.

HARRIET What about Aunt Thelma? Wouldn't she know?

WILLA Yes but then it would be hard to prove. All the old records, the family Bible and papers were lost—burned in a fire years ago. It'd be guesswork.

HARRIET That's too bad.

WILLA We've never been able to save much on the little he's made—never even bought a home. We couldn't. I tried to warn him several times we should get ready but he wouldn't listen to me. And now it's come. We've got to give up the house by August. I just don't know what we're going to do.

HARRIET Don't you think after the shock's worn off he'll be all right?

WILLA No. He's going to appeal.

HARRIET But that'll only postpone it for a year or so even if he wins.

WILLA I know. *(pause)* So you see, I don't think you'd better ask him about Roanoke right now. Maybe tomorrow or the next day—

HARRIET *(disappointed)* I'll tell Bobby I can't go.

WILLA No, don't do that. When's it to be?

HARRIET A week from next Friday.

WILLA How soon must he know?

HARRIET He didn't say.

WILLA Then let's wait a day or two. If you must, explain to Bobby why you have to wait.

HARRIET Okay.

WILLA Set the table for me, will you baby, while I get your father.

HARRIET Will Billy be home?

WILLA I don't know. Haven't seen him all day. But you might as well set a place for him although I suspect he's at Mary Kay's.

HARRIET Lord, what he sees in that girl I don't know.

WILLA Now, baby—

HARRIET She's nothing but a tramp.

WILLA *(gently)* Go ahead and set the table.

*(*WILLA *leaves the kitchen and ascends the stairs.* HARRIET *proceeds to set the table. The lights come on in the bedroom.* WILLA *enters)*

SHELDON *(looking)* Oh, Willa, I was just getting ready to call you.

WILLA Supper's ready.

SHELDON Listen to this. It'll only take a minute. *(*WILLA *sits on the bed)* "Dear Doctor *(clearing his throat contemptuously)* hunh—Walker: I am writing to ask reconsideration of the action taken on yesterday by the Board of Visitors, placing me on permanent retirement as of August 1 of this year. Five years ago at the time of our joining the State Retirement System I indicated that I was uncertain of the exact year of my birth. The age which I listed on the membership application was a guess. Therefore, in view of the uncertainty concerning my age, I respectfully request that any action regarding my retirement be delayed until I can appear before the Board. Please consider this letter a formal request for a hearing on the matter. *(he swallows)* Knowing that you will be sympathetic to my position, I will greatly appreciate anything you can do to assist me. Very respectfully yours, David Sheldon, Senior."

WILLA All right—I suppose—

SHELDON Well, is it or isn't it?

WILLA It must have hurt you to write the last line, didn't it?

SHELDON It doesn't hurt to be courteous.

WILLA I remember when you would call it something else.

SHELDON What's the matter? You sound as if you want me to be retired?

WILLA No, I'd like to see you go on for as long as you want. But I hate to see you beat your head against a stone wall. Come on, supper's ready.

SHELDON Go ahead. I want to address the envelope. *(*WILLA *starts out but stops in the doorway)*

WILLA Oh, by the way—

SHELDON Yes? *(he's writing)*

WILLA Harriet has an invitation to spend next weekend in Roanoke with the Nelsons. *(*SHELDON *nods)* What do you think? *(he doesn't answer)* Mister?

SHELDON Yes—what?

WILLA What do you think?

SHELDON About what?—Oh, the invitation. Do what you think best.

WILLA You really mean that?

SHELDON *(looking up)* Why shouldn't I mean it?

WILLA Why, no reason at all. *(She leaves the room, pauses at the head of the stairs and looks back. The lights come up in the kitchen.* HARRIET *is seated at the table reading.* WILLA *descends the stairs thoughtfully and enters the kitchen.* HARRIET *puts the books aside)*

HARRIET Where's Daddy? Isn't he going to eat?

WILLA Yes.

HARRIET What's the matter, Mama, don't you feel well?

WILLA I'm all right. *(pause)* You can go.

HARRIET Hunh?

WILLA You can go—to Roanoke.

HARRIET *(delighted)* You mean *you* asked him? *(*WILLA *nods)* And he said yes?

WILLA *I* said yes. He left it up to me. He actually left it up to me.

HARRIET *(overjoyed)* Wonderful.

WILLA He's worried—that man's worried.

HARRIET Then maybe I oughtn't to go.

WILLA His whole nature's changing—giving up his pride and his parental authority—

HARRIET Maybe I shouldn't—

WILLA Don't you want to go?

HARRIET Yes, but it'll cost. And we don't have money to throw around.

WILLA Going to Roanoke is throwing money around?

HARRIET Well—*(pause. Then suddenly)*—I know, I'll get the money from Billy.

WILLA I wouldn't count on it. He's always broke.

HARRIET But he gets paid next week. I'll be right there when he cashes his check.

WILLA I wish Billy would pull himself together—go back to school or get married. He just doesn't seem to have any ambition. When he was little even though he was sickly he was the one who showed more promise than the others. But now—*(she gestures hopelessly)* I wonder what's keeping your father?

(The lights come up on the staircase. SHELDON *is descending the stairs the letter in his hand. As he passes the hall table he drops the letter on it. He stands there for a moment then picks the letter up, reopens it and reads. When he finishes he slowly tears it to pieces and drops it on the table. He enters the kitchen)*

WILLA *(after he sits)* Will you say the grace, Mister?

SHELDON I tore it up.

WILLA You what?

SHELDON The letter. I tore it up.

WILLA You've decided not to appeal.

SHELDON No, not at all. It's just easier to deny a written request. I'm going in to see Walker in person. I'm going in with my hat in my hand and my pride in my hip pocket. But I'm going.

HARRIET Daddy—

WILLA Mister—

SHELDON Let us bow our heads. Gracious Lord . . .

(The lights fade)

Scene Two

DAVID He begged and won a year's reprieve. I can only imagine what must have occurred. A man who had never begged for anything. How he was able to humble himself and contain that fierce pride is something I'll never understand. Originally I had planned to describe what happened but since it happens again I've decided against it. You see, my father blindly believed that he was right and he was prepared to reenact the scene as often as necessary. Six months later he had done absolutely nothing about his retirement. In spite of the entreaties of Willa and inflated by his temporary victory, he ignored the omens and portents around him.

(As the lights rise WILLA *and* BILLY *are in the kitchen.* WILLA *is putting a meat loaf in the oven.* BILLY *is "high")*

WILLA But why must you stay out all night, Billy?

BILLY I don't mean to, Mama, the time just flies. *(he gestures like a bird flying)*

WILLA *(sitting)* Where do you go? What do you do?

BILLY *(smiling)* I visit—people—and places—

WILLA *(insistently)* But there's no place to visit in Warwick. (BILLY *gestures vaguely)* Don't you know what people are saying, baby?

BILLY What people?

WILLA People on the campus.

BILLY I thought so. Well, I don't give a damn what they're saying—snoopin, prying busybodies.

WILLA They're saying all sorts of nasty things.

BILLY Like what?

WILLA That you stay drunk most of the time—that you're even drunk on the job.

BILLY It's true. They're threatening to fire me.

WILLA And that you're spending your nights at Mary Kay's—

BILLY How would they know that? What are they doing in that part of town—slumming?

WILLA Is it true, Billy? About Mary Kay, I mean?

BILLY *(nodding)* Yes.

WILLA Oh, my god.

BILLY I'm sorry, Mama. I can't help myself.

WILLA Why don't you marry the girl since you're sleeping with her?

BILLY Is that all there is to marriage, Mama?

WILLA Answer me.

BILLY She wants me to.

WILLA Then why don't you?

BILLY I don't know—I wouldn't make a good husband—for Mary Kay or anybody for that matter.

WILLA Why not?

BILLY Look at me. I'm an alcoholic—I've got chronic asthma—and I've got a father to worry about.

WILLA He's not your responsibility.

BILLY Honor thy father and mother—that's what you taught us.

WILLA If you want to honor your father, you'd think about yourself. Do you think your carousing and whoring is making it any easier for him during his last year?

BILLY No, I don't suppose it is.

WILLA Well then?

BILLY But then we've heard that all of our lives, haven't we? Think about your father, remember his position. Well, I have thought about it. I acted like a little gentleman—we all did. And what good's it done him. Here he is old, an old, old, man and nothing to show for it. No home, no savings, no nothing.

WILLA Think about your sister.

BILLY What about her?

WILLA What kind of example are you setting for her?

BILLY *(musing)* Dear, sweet little Harriet. Pretty innocent little Harriet.

WILLA She knows what's going on, Billy.

BILLY Only on the outside—not what's here. *(he touches his heart)* None of you do.

WILLA We all love you, Billy. Your life is your life. But living here we do worry about you.

BILLY Maybe I ought to move.

WILLA You still need someone to look after you, to fix your meals, to wash your clothes. You know you've got to be careful, very careful. *(pause)* When have you seen the doctor?

BILLY I—I can't remember.

WILLA There you are. And with your constitution. Oh, Billy, I'm so worried about you.

BILLY And I'm worried about you. What's going to happen to you when Dad—What's going to happen to Dad when he's no longer working? And what's going to happen to Harriet?

WILLA Baby, baby—you're not to think about us. You must begin to think about yourself.

(HARRIET enters from the outside carrying a load of school books)

HARRIET *(in the hall)* Anybody home?

WILLA *(calling)* Back here.

(HARRIET drops her books in the living room and enters the kitchen)

HARRIET The closer I get to finishing, the more I wonder if it's worth it.

WILLA What's the matter?

HARRIET Another term paper. Durn it—that makes four. I think all my teachers have gone stark, raving mad. I might as well move into the library.

BILLY Want me to do a couple for you?

HARRIET Aw, cut it out, Billy. It's not funny.

BILLY I'm not kidding. I'll just dust off a couple of my old ones and give them to you.

HARRIET I'll have you know I do my own work.

BILLY My idealistic little sister.

WILLA Children, children. *(she rises)* I've got to get dressed. Go on duty soon. Don't let the meat loaf burn. *(she leaves the kitchen and goes upstairs)*

BILLY Hey, little sister, want a drink? *(he reaches inside his jacket)*

HARRIET No, thank you.

BILLY *(after taking a swig)* Harriet, are you still a virgin?

HARRIET *(shocked)* Billy!

BILLY Well, are you?

HARRIET What business is it of yours?

BILLY *(harshly)* Are you?

HARRIET *(startled)* Yes.

BILLY I don't believe you.

HARRIET What you believe is your business.

BILLY You don't drink, you don't smoke, and you don't screw. Beautiful.

HARRIET You're drunk.

BILLY *(nodding)* I am.

HARRIET Do you have to get that way in front of Mama?

BILLY Nooo—I don't have to—in fact, I didn't intend to. It just happened.

HARRIET Oh, Billy, Mama and Daddy are worried to death about you.

BILLY And I'm worried to death about you, little sister.

HARRIET I can take care of myself.

BILLY Crap.

HARRIET Well, I can.

BILLY You're so idealistic. You've grown up so protected more so than we were—the wolves will eat you up alive.

HARRIET I know a thing or two.

BILLY I'll bet. Book learning and Mama's lectures. Some of these cats on the outside make a specialty of your type—pigmeat.

HARRIET What do you want me to do? Become a sybarite so that I can be "hep?"

BILLY That's an idea, but you'd never make it.

HARRIET Well, what are you talking about?

BILLY About life, little sister, about life. You're going to graduate next year and you'll be on your own. No mother and father to look after you. No profligate brother to embarrass you.

HARRIET Billy, I—

BILLY Don't be afraid of life, Harriet. Get away from this place. Don't stay here.

HARRIET I intend to help Mama all I can.

BILLY Do so but do so away from here—from this campus—from these—these niggers! They'll destroy you if you stay around here. This place is insidious—evil—it gets inside of you—turns you into the very devil and it'll destroy you—like it's destroying me.

HARRIET Billy, what on earth are you talking about?

BILLY About us—about our lives, we campus brats. David and Julian got away but I didn't. I couldn't. Innocent little kids, growing up in a fairyland—away from reality—protected from dirt and filth—living in a dream world where we don't even realize that we are Black and despised. I was unprepared for the outside—the great beyond. It's mean and ugly. And it's full of lustful men *and* women waiting to sap up little lambs like you and me.

HARRIET I feel sorry for you, Billy.

BILLY Don't, little sister. Don't feel sorry for me—just get away—leave.

HARRIET Just like that.

BILLY As soon as you can.

HARRIET And the family?

BILLY We'll survive and if we don't—who cares?

HARRIET You've got me all confused. *(pause)* I want to leave when I finish, but when I think of Mama and Daddy and the struggle they've had—

BILLY They'll go on struggling—

HARRIET It just doesn't seem right. A lifetime of giving—and they don't even have a home to go to in their old age. What's it all about, Billy? What's it all mean? I've been protected as you say and I don't understand things like that.

BILLY It means life's miserable, rotten rat race. Some make it, some don't. It means those that *can,* look out for number one and they survive. It means you can't give everything to everybody and keep nothing for yourself. Only God can do that and even he was crucified.

HARRIET So what am I to do?

BILLY Marry and be happy. Try to be happy. I wish I could love somebody enough to get married but sick as I am it wouldn't be fair to the girl. I'm practically a walking corpse. I'm no good to anybody—

HARRIET But there are things you could do—there are people who could help you.

BILLY But first I must admit I need help, right?

HARRIET Yes.

BILLY If I thought it was worth it, I'd go up to Burkeville this minute. If I thought it could help the folks I'd do it. But what's the use? They prop me up—rehabilitate me—and I'd still be Billy Sheldon, A.B., mail carrier.

HARRIET Is being a mail carrier that bad?

BILLY When you've dreamed of reaching the stars and your feet are mired in clay? All those years I had to stay home, you know, each winter when I had those attacks and they'd take me out of school? How I dreamed of becoming a great artist—a painter. I built another fairyland within the one in which we were living. Shimmering crystal palaces where all of us would live—Mama, Daddy, David, Julian, you, and me. Then the coughing would begin and the palaces would crumble, year after year until I was four years behind my class.

HARRIET I remember.

BILLY So many times I thought how nice it must be in heaven—I figured that I'd surely go there since I hadn't done anything wrong—and Mama was constantly praying over me. Many times as I crossed the Campbell Street bridge I'd stand looking at the water remembering Langston Hughes' poem: "The cool, calm face of the river, asked me for a kiss."

HARRIET No, Billy, don't ever do that.

BILLY But then when I'd look down expecting to see my reflection, I'd see that the waters were dirty and muddy and I'd remember all the filth and sewage that comes into the river below the bridge and I couldn't do it. I'm a coward, little sister. Along with everything else, your brother is a coward.

HARRIET Oh, my brother, how I wish I could help you.

BILLY Just move away from here, little sister. Don't let yourself get trapped the way I am.

(The PROFESSOR trudges wearily on from the direction of the campus. At the same time the lights come on in the upstairs bedroom. WILLA has finished dressing)

SHELDON *(as he enters)* Willa? Willa, where are you?

WILLA I'm upstairs, Mister.

(HARRIET crosses to BILLY, stands behind him with a hand on his shoulder. He takes the hand without looking up. The lights fade on the kitchen. The PROFESSOR enters the bedroom)

SHELDON Here, read this.

WILLA What is it?

SHELDON Another notice that I'll have to vacate the house—that the one year extension of my contract will not be renewed.

WILLA Then we'd better start looking.

SHELDON What?

WILLA I said we'd better start looking for a house.

SHELDON I'm going to see a lawyer.

WILLA There's nothing for you to see a lawyer about.

SHELDON It's entirely possible that I can establish a legal age which will allow me to continue to work.

WILLA Oh, Mister, we went through that before. That's why the Board gave you another year.

SHELDON But it's not fair.

WILLA I think they've been very fair.

SHELDON I'm not talking about my age. I'm talking about what they've done for Stanley.

WILLA He was the President.

SHELDON That's what I mean. Why should an exception be made for him?

WILLA *(shrugging)* Because he was the President.

SHELDON I don't begrudge him the house. Stanley is a grand old man, a real educator. But they have an obligation to me too. I've given just as much as he has.

WILLA Apparently they don't see it that way. Apparently that's not the way it's going to be.

SHELDON It's not right, I tell you, tossing a man aside like an old hat just because he's seventy. What's age got to do with how good a teacher you are? Some teachers ought to be retired when they're thirty.

WILLA But the system doesn't work that way.

SHELDON I don't feel seventy. Do I look seventy? My mind's clear, my heart's good. And I've got offers from several of the private schools.

WILLA Then take one.

SHELDON But don't you see, if I'm good enough to teach elsewhere then I'm good enough to teach here. Why should I move to Harper's Ferry or Lawrenceville when they need me here?

WILLA But it's no use protesting any more, Mister, believe me. We'd do better to get ready to move.

SHELDON You give in too easily, Willa.

WILLA Lawyers cost money—and you still have to pay even when you lose. *(she starts to leave)*

SHELDON I haven't finished. Where are you going?

WILLA Time to go on duty.

SHELDON Oh. Yes. How late will you be tonight?

WILLA Usual time, I hope. Dormitory closes at eleven. Don't wait up for me.

SHELDON I've got some papers to grade.

WILLA The meat loaf should be ready now. Harriet will serve you when you're ready.

SHELDON *(almost timidly)* Can—can't you eat with us?

WILLA No, I'm late. Don't want to keep the day hostess waiting.

SHELDON All right. *(he turns away)*

WILLA Goodnight. *(pause)*

SHELDON Goodnight, Willa.

(The lights fade and the music rises)

Scene Three

(A few days later. A storm is threatening. Heavy masses of dark storm clouds have blotted out the sun. A steady wind is blowing. There is the sound of an automobile. It stops. A car door slams. LAWYER CLARK *appears from the rear of the house and crosses to the front door. He rings the bell.* WILLA *appears from the kitchen)*

WILLA Oh, Lawyer Clark, come in. You needn't have come out with a storm threatening. And it's likely to be a cloudburst. The radio says we may get a little hail.

CLARK Well, I didn't want to keep the Professor waiting. *(he stamps his feet and enters the house)*

WILLA *(taking his coat and hat and putting them on the hall tree)* Go on in, Lawyer Clark, and have a seat. I'll get Mister.

*(*CLARK *enters the living room and sits.* WILLA *goes half way up the stairs and calls)*

WILLA Lawyer Clark is here.

SHELDON I'll be right down.

*(*WILLA *returns to the living room)*

WILLA Well, how is your family?

CLARK Fine, Miz Sheldon. They're all going just fine.

WILLA Let's see, the oldest boy finishes high school this year, doesn't he?

CLARK Yes, ma'm, he does.

WILLA How nice. And is he going to be a lawyer too?

CLARK I hope not, Miz Sheldon. I hope not. I'd rather he become a doctor or a dentist. Our people will get sick and call the doctor and if their teeth hurt they'll go to a dentist. But most of 'em don't know what a lawyer's for.

WILLA Well, I declare.

CLARK Yes, ma'm. Most of my work is in buying and selling real estate now. I don't get many cases to speak of.

*(*SHELDON *enters from above)*

SHELDON *(profusely)* Lawyer! Good to see you. *(*CLARK *rises)* Sit down. Can I get you something? Coffee? Tea?

CLARK No, thank you, Professor. It's started to rain and it may hail too. So I'd like to get off the streets since my tires—well, the treads are kinda thin.

SHELDON Of course.

CLARK I finally got an answer from the city clerk in Georgetown. Here it is.

SHELDON I don't have my glasses. What does it say?

CLARK Well, in brief, they have no record of your birth—no record of your family either.

SHELDON What about property—deeds, etc.

CLARK Nothing there either.

SHELDON But my parents and grandparents did own property. I know that.

CLARK Someone would have to go through the records. That'd mean employing a local lawyer. I couldn't go down there myself. It would be quite expensive and time consuming.

SHELDON I suppose it would.

CLARK The clerk suggests that most of the old families in South Carolina kept pretty careful records of births and deaths in the family Bible.

SHELDON Ours was lost in all the moving about and the church we attended was destroyed in a fire.

CLARK Sometimes the plantation owners kept records of their people.

SHELDON I wouldn't know where to begin.

CLARK That's too bad. Without any supporting evidence, Professor, I would advise against going to court. Without the records of someone we don't have much chance of establishing a younger age for you.

SHELDON But we do have a chance.

CLARK Is there anyone down there who knew your family—who knew you?

SHELDON *(shaking his head)* They're either dead or moved away long ago.

CLARK Then our chances are practically nil.

SHELDON So what am I to do?

CLARK Professor Sheldon, you still have a good many years left and you're a good teacher—I ought to know—you taught me.

*(*BILLY *comes to the front door, realizes that there are people in the living room and goes around to the back of the house)*

SHELDON Thank you.

CLARK I understand you've got some offers to teach. Why don't you take one?

SHELDON It would mean moving away, separating from my family.

CLARK You could commute to Richmond if you got on there.

SHELDON No.

CLARK Why not?

SHELDON At my age driving the round trip every day over the turnpike would leave me a nervous wreck. That highway traffic terrifies me. And I'd have to leave at daybreak to make an eight o'clock class.

CLARK Why?

SHELDON Thirty miles an hour is my speed limit.

CLARK *(laughing)* I see what you mean.

(BILLY *enters the kitchen, sits and listens)*

CLARK You'll need a house, won't you?

SHELDON If they make me give up this one. Yes.

CLARK How many rooms?

SHELDON Well, there's four of us—about the size of this one. We're accustomed to space.

CLARK As houses go this is a pretty big house. It'd be quite expensive even if you rent.

SHELDON But I can't afford to buy.

CLARK On the other hand you won't be getting any equity if you rent. It would be better in the long run to buy, Professor, and a small cottage.

SHELDON No, I'll need a big house so we won't get in each other's way.

CLARK The kids will all move away eventually—they always do. I was telling my wife the other day—

SHELDON Not Billy. He isn't well, as you know. (BILLY *reacts to this)* And what about the boys when they come to visit with their families? Where'll we put them?

CLARK You can always double up for a couple of weeks. I would strongly suggest that you buy a small house for you and Miz Sheldon. If you like I'll try to find one for you and we'll forget about my commission. I owe you that much.

SHELDON I'm very grateful to you, Lawyer Clark, and I'm very proud to have been your teacher. But I can't accept charity. *(he goes upstairs)*

CLARK Miz Sheldon, did I say something wrong? Wouldn't hurt the Professor's feelings for anything in the world. If I did I'll apologize.

WILLA He's naturally disappointed and a little sensitive right now. You were his last hope. But he'll get over it. No need to apologize—he's very fond of you.

CLARK I wish I could help him but—*(he gestures hopelessly)*

WILLA Don't blame yourself. He knows you've done everything you could.

CLARK Why won't he accept one of those teaching offers, Miz Sheldon?

WILLA He just can't believe that the college can get along without him after nearly thirty years. He wants to stay here where he can watch over things, be available should they ever need him.

CLARK It's an admirable thought—self sacrificial and all that—not many of the old teachers left like the Professor. But he's going to have to face up to it. They can and they will get along without him.

WILLA It's something that we've all got to face some day—isn't it?

CLARK Yes, ma'm. *(pause)* Well, I've got to go. *(he starts for the hall)* Shall I try to find a cottage?

WILLA Yes. I'll talk to Mister. I'm sure he'll appreciate what you're trying to do. *(she helps him with his overcoat)*

CLARK I'll get started on it right away.

(SHELDON *reappears)*

WILLA And thank you for coming out. Be careful, now, driving home.

CLARK Yes, ma'm. Goodnight. *(he goes)*

SHELDON What's he going to get started on?

WILLA A cottage.

SHELDON You told him to go ahead?

WILLA Yes.

SHELDON Well, you just tell him you've changed your mind—I'm not leaving here. They'll have to carry me out. And I'll get another lawyer if need be. *(he disappears slamming the bedroom door)*

WILLA Oh, Mister. *(she shakes her head and wearily ascends the stairs to the bedroom. She pauses then enters the room)*

WILLA Mister, why won't you be reasonable? *(the door closes and the lights fade, shutting off the argument)*

(HARRIET *enters the front door. She goes immediately to the hall tree, removes her overcoat and hat. Entering the kitchen she sees* BILLY *sitting at the table staring into space)*

HARRIET Hi, Billy boy. *(he does not answer)* You passing? *(pause)* Billy, you all right? *(she crosses to him)*

BILLY What?

HARRIET Are you all right?

BILLY Yeah, I'm okay—just hungry. *(he shivers)* Is there a door open somewhere? It's chilly in here. I think there's a draft.

SHELDON I'm not blaming Clark. I'm sure he's done his best.

WILLA Then why?

SHELDON Because I'm not ready to give up.

HARRIET Billy, are you sure you're okay? *(he nods vaguely)*

BILLY I'll be all right when I get some food in me. I haven't eaten all day. *(he shivers)*

HARRIET No wonder. *(feeling his forehead)* Hey, you've got a fever.

BILLY You're crazy.

HARRIET Yes, you have. And you're probably coming down with something.

BILLY *(a little irritated)* I'm all right, I tell you.

WILLA You're just being stubborn—obstinate.

SHELDON I have other reasons.

WILLA What, for example?

HARRIET Why don't you go lie down on the sofa? I'll call you when supper's ready.

BILLY All right. *(he rises, staggers slightly)*

HARRIET I'm going to call the doctor.

BILLY No, no don't. Just let me lie down.

(He moves slowly into the living room and eases on to the sofa. HARRIET *watches at the door for a moment then returns to the kitchen. A pause, then the bedroom door opens and* WILLA *comes out into the hallway)*

WILLA I can't understand this sudden concern over Billy. (BILLY *sits up)*

SHELDON It's not so sudden.

WILLA He's a grown man.

SHELDON He's a sick man.

WILLA But he'll have to face the fact that we won't always be around to look after him.

(BILLY *sobs, rises, almost falls, and stumbles out the front door. He staggers off the* PORCH *and collapses in front of the house)*

SHELDON But where will he live?

WILLA I don't know—I just don't know. *(she descends the stairs into the hallway)* That's funny—I'm sure I closed that door. *(she closes the door and enters the kitchen)* Hello, baby, when did you come?

HARRIET Just now.

WILLA What're you doing?

HARRIET Fixing dinner for Billy.

WILLA Oh, will he be home tonight?

HARRIET He's in the living room.

WILLA Oh, then he must have left the front door open.

HARRIET What?

WILLA The front door was open just now. I closed it.

HARRIET No—he was here when I got home.

WILLA Well, I declare—

HARRIET I wonder? *(She hurries into the living room followed by* WILLA*)*

WILLA What's the matter?

HARRIET *(in the living room)* He's gone.

WILLA And without closing the door—that boy.

HARRIET He's sick, Mama—he's got a fever.

WILLA And he went outside in this snow? What do you suppose?—*(they go out on the porch. As they reach the front steps* BILLY *groans.* WILLA *screams)* There he is. He's fallen. *(the two women rush to* BILLY. SHELDON *appears at the upstairs window)*

SHELDON What's going on out there?

HARRIET It's Billy, Daddy, he's collapsed.

SHELDON I'll be right down. *(he disappears from the window. The two women pick* BILLY *up laboriously between them and half carry, half drag him toward the porch)*

BILLY *(screaming)* No, no—leave me here. I want to die. I want to die.

(Blackout)

Scene Four

DAVID They took Billy to the hospital. He had come down with double pneumonia. Afterwards they took him to Burkeville when it was discovered that he had a spot on his lungs. *(musing)* Burkeville Sanatorium—the State Hospital for colored T.B. patients. Like Billy said, once you stepped off the campus you discovered you were Black. In the spring I got an urgent letter from Mama asking me to come home—Daddy was deteriorating rapidly she said—had begun to drink. It made me miserable but I couldn't go. I promised I'd spend the month of August with them before going on my leave of absence from Douglass U. I had decided it was time to start on my Ph.D. What happened during the ensuing months I'll never know. When I arrived in August things were in a bad way—Mama looked twenty years older. My father had written to the Board over the President's objection. Of course they turned him down. The President was so incensed he threatened to take Mama's job but later he recanted when she assured him there would be no repetition of the incident. Daddy's occasional drinking had increased and he was no longer rational about his inevitable retirement although he was perfectly lucid about other things. When I arrived he insisted that I go in to see the President with him. Somehow he had gotten the notion that I could work a miracle. He was sadly mistaken. Against my better judgment I consented. I wish now I hadn't.

(The lights fade. In the darkness SHELDON'S *voice is heard)*

SHELDON David, David.

DAVID I'm on the porch, Dad.

SHELDON *(entering)* It's awfully hot, isn't it?

DAVID Yes.

SHELDON And those fans inside don't seem to help at all.

DAVID No. August is always fierce.

SHELDON They tell me that some people are beginning to use air conditioning in their homes.

DAVID Yes.

SHELDON How the world has changed—is changing—I almost feel lost. *(pause)* Would you like a little something before we go?

DAVID Something to drink you mean?

SHELDON No thanks. *(pause)* Well, shall we plan our strategy?

DAVID What?

SHELDON Our strategy.

DAVID What strategy?

SHELDON Well, I didn't exactly mean that. But if you're going to change his mind—

DAVID Change whose mind, Dad? About what?

SHELDON The President, Dr. Walker. About my retirement, about giving me another year.

DAVID Dad, I only agreed to see him because you insisted.

SHELDON I know—I know. But the President has great respect for you. He might just possibly ask the Board to give me another year if you were to ask him to.

DAVID Please don't ask me to do that.

SHELDON *(angrily)* Why do you think I wanted you to go? To pay a social call?

DAVID You said you wanted me to hear the President's explanation.

SHELDON Yes, and show him that he's wrong.

DAVID No, I won't. And if you insist I won't go at all.

SHELDON All right, all right. No need to get angry. *(pause)* I'll go upstairs and change my shirt and tie, then I'll be ready. *(he goes inside)*

WILLA *(after a pause, entering from the house)* It's warm.

DAVID It's hot.

WILLA Yes. *(pause)*

DAVID I dread this interview.

WILLA I know.

DAVID It won't do a bit of good.

WILLA Do it to please him, David. If you don't he'll spend the rest of his life blaming you.

DAVID That doesn't make sense. When we were little he was too busy to talk to us and now he's relying on me. I don't understand him. I guess I never will.

WILLA He loves you, David. You're the apple of his eye. He believes you can do anything.

DAVID That's crazy.

WILLA Try to control your temper and don't become upset.

DAVID Oh, I'll play it cool. *(glancing at his wristwatch)* What's keeping him?

WILLA Probably bolstering his courage.

DAVID With whiskey you mean?

WILLA Vodka. You can't smell it. But don't let on. He's been very careful with his drinking since you've been here. He'd be mortified if he thought you knew.

DAVID Why, Mama? Why'd he *start* drinking?

WILLA Why do any of us do what we do? I don't know, David. I suppose it's partly an escape, partly the result of the insecurity he feels now that he's to be retired.

DAVID He could write all those books he's wanted to.

WILLA *(shaking her head)* It's not enough. When you've been as active as he has, when you've been in the thick of things and suddenly you're put out to pasture like an old stud horse, it's not enough even to graze knee-deep in clover. And when there is no clover—*(she gestures hopelessly)*

DAVID But we all love him.

WILLA But we don't have to depend on him anymore. He'll be dependent on us.

DAVID What the hell are we going to do, Mama?

WILLA I just don't know.

*(*SHELDON *enters holding his coat)*

SHELDON I'll carry this. I'll put it on when we get there. *(*DAVID *rises)*

WILLA Well, good luck, you two.

SHELDON *(jovially)* Oh, don't worry, Mama. Everything's going to be all right. *(they go out.* HARRIET *comes out on the porch)*

HARRIET Daddy seemed very happy.

WILLA He always is when David's home.

HARRIET What do you think?

WILLA I think you and I'd better get inside and start dinner. *(she crosses to the front door)*

HARRIET *(following)* But the kitchen's like an oven.

WILLA We'll make a tuna salad and some iced tea so we won't have to light the stove.

(They enter the house as the lights fade on the porch and rise on the office. DR. WALKER, *a genial looking gentleman who looks like the man in the whiskey ads, is dictating to his secretary)*

DR. WALKER The Honorable Garland Claytor, Holly Tree Lane Farms, Sussex County, Virginia. Dear Mr. Claytor *(pause)* We are extremely gratified that our esteemed governor has selected you to serve on our Board of Visitors. I know of no one in the state who is better qualified for this appointment than you. Your keen interest in our *little* college *(pause)* over the years *(pause)* and the generous contributions you have made through the Claytor Scholarships *(pause)* have established you as one who is deeply interested in the higher education of Negroes. I am especially pleased because of our *long, personal* friendship which has transcended the barriers of race and because I know that this augurs well for the continued progress of this institution. Welcome to the college family. Very respectfully yours, H. Sam Walker. How's that, Miss Jackson?

SECRETARY A bit thick, isn't it?

DR. WALKER He'll love it.

SECRETARY *(as* SHELDON *and* DAVID *enter)* That's probably Professor Sheldon. Can you see him now?

DR. WALKER Send him in. *(the* SECRETARY *crosses to the outer office)*

SECRETARY Go right in, gentlemen. *(she pretends to hold open a door and closes it after they enter)*

DR. WALKER *(rising)* Come right in, gentlemen. *(he approaches* SHELDON, *extending his hand)* How are you, Professor?

SHELDON Oh, I'm bearing up, thank you.

DR. WALKER David, it's good to see you.

DAVID *(shaking hands)* It's good to see you, Dr. Walker.

DR. WALKER How's your family?

DAVID They're fine. They stopped off in Roanoke with Julian and his family.

DR. WALKER And how are things at Douglass?

DAVID We're managing to survive.

DR. WALKER And my friend Dr. Carroll?

DAVID Oh, the President's doing very well. He asked to be remembered to you.

DR. WALKER Fine man—fine man. He's president of our land grant college association, you know.

DAVID Yes, sir. *(there is a pause.* SHELDON *fidgets)*

DR. WALKER And Professor, how are your plans coming along?

SHELDON We're still looking around, Mr. President.

DR. WALKER Oh?

SHELDON I had no idea how difficult finding a house would be.

DR. WALKER I see.

SHELDON I guess I've been blessed living all these years in a campus home.

DR. WALKER Does Douglass provide faculty housing, David?

DAVID No, sir. Only the President lives on campus.

DR. WALKER Faculty all own their homes?

DAVID Some. But mostly they rent. It's pretty tough to find what you want. Good property for our people's scarce.

DR. WALKER Yes, I suppose that's true everywhere. That's been one of our big problems—housing and salaries. We've been fortunate here in Warwick in being able to provide homes for our staff as a part of their salary. But then that has limitations as well as advantages. Take a man like your father. When it comes time to retire, he's got to start from scratch.

SHELDON I'm glad you understand, Mister President.

DR. WALKER Oh, yes, I understand. That's why when you requested a delay I was only too glad to go before the Board. But it wasn't easy, I tell you. Those white people in Richmond believe in the letter of the law. The days when we could do just about as we pleased are over, Professor.

SHELDON Times are changing—I was just saying so to David.

DR. WALKER Yes, indeed.

SHELDON But the Board was also kind to Dr. Stanton—

DR. WALKER That's what they call good public relations—

SHELDON Pardon—?

DR. WALKER A man who'd been president for more than thirty years and a teacher for fifteen before that—but he didn't have a dime. If he'd been turned out there'd been hollering from all over the state from both white and colored. Oh, these white people are smart all right.

SHELDON But haven't they set a precedent? Won't that permit them to do the same things for others?

DR. WALKER For you, you mean.

SHELDON I don't have a dime either.

DR. WALKER *(sadly)* I'm afraid not, Professor.

SHELDON Why not?

DR. WALKER *(impatiently)* Oh, now, Sheldon, let's stop playing games. You know how the system operates.

SHELDON No—I'm afraid I don't. I'm a department head or *was,* it's true. But I have very little contact with the Board. They were just so many names to me. What little information I got came from the Dean. And he didn't know much either. We were all in the dark about what the Board did or thought about the college.

DR. WALKER Then I'll tell you. There's one person whom they all respect and that's the President—sometimes it's the fiscal officer. It doesn't matter—whoever's in charge gets their respect. So now I'm the one they look up to. What about Missouri, David?

DAVID Same thing. From what I've observed it's true in every Negro college—in every community.

DR. WALKER Yes, the Black overseer or as they say on the street, H.N.I.C.

SHELDON I beg your pardon.

DR. WALKER Head nigger in charge.

DAVID It's funny but they don't know anybody but him. Take Dr. Young—he's always the Negro representative on any civic committee. They even call him up if we try to make a loan or buy a suit of clothes.

SHELDON Are you trying to tell me—

DR. WALKER Stanley *was* the H.N.I.C. He rendered faithful service for years. He didn't make too many demands, made do with what he had. And for that he was rewarded.

SHELDON And so you, too, will be rewarded?

DR. WALKER No—times are changing. NAACP is giving 'em hell in the courts. I don't think the Gaines decision will hold up much longer. Time will come when we'll have to desegregate. When that happens, goodbye H.N.I.C.

SHELDON You're not even willing to try?

DR. WALKER No. Because I had to play the Uncle Tom to get you the one year postponement. I explained your thirty years of devoted service, teaching five and six classes a quarter, coaching debate, directing plays, and raising a family of four. You should have seen me. I put on quite a show for you. I had 'em sniffling and the women actually weeping. But I can't do it again.

SHELDON I've got no place to go.

DR. WALKER Even if I were inclined to help I couldn't.

SHELDON Why not?

DR. WALKER The house, you see. It's already been promised to your replacement.

SHELDON *(after a pause)* My replacement?

DR. WALKER Yes. And we promised him to have it renovated, you know, repainted, floors done, etc. And that'll take a little while.

SHELDON *(shocked)* Who is my replacement?

DR. WALKER A young fellow just got his Ph.D. from Wisconsin. Comes highly recommended. He'll carry on the Sheldon tradition of excellence.

SHELDON *(emotionally)* But what am I going to do? What am I going to do?

DR. WALKER Perhaps David can help.

SHELDON No, he's on his way to school—to start on his degree.

DR. WALKER Then I don't know.

SHELDON That's all you've got to say?

DR. WALKER What do you want from me, Sheldon, blood?

SHELDON I'd die of anemia. *(*WALKER *is stung)* I'll tell you what I want. I want thirty-five years of my life back. I want the dignity and respect of my beloved teachers at Amherst and Harvard when *they* retired. I want you—I want *somebody* to assure me that it's all been worth it—spending a lifetime trying to help the children and grandchildren of slaves "lift the veil of ignorance." Because I've begun to wonder. I'm not so sure anymore. I think somebody sold me a bill of goods. Education may not be the answer. Whoever said, "You shall know the truth and the truth shall make you free" told a *god damn lie!*

DR. WALKER Professor, this is doing no good. I think you'd better go.

SHELDON You'll have to put me out of the house.

DR. WALKER Oh, now, Sheldon, that's ridiculous.

SHELDON I mean it. You'll have to carry me out.

DAVID Dad, stop it.

SHELDON Don't you yell at me.

DAVID *(approaching)* Dad, I think we'd better go. *(he reaches out for him)*

SHELDON Keep your hands off me. I can walk. I'm not an invalid. *(he breaks down and sobs violently)*

SECRETARY *(entering in a hurry)* Dr. Walker, is there anything wrong?

DR. WALKER Everything's all right, Miss Jackson. Professor Sheldon's been overcome by the heat. I'd appreciate you bringing him a glass of water.

SECRETARY Yes, sir. *(she goes quickly to the water fountain in the outer office, fills a paper cup and returns.* SHELDON *has begun to control himself)*

SECRETARY *(handing him the cup)* Professor Sheldon—

SHELDON Thank you. *(he sips)*

SECRETARY Dr. Walker, we'll just have to do something about cooling this office. It's just like an oven. You can't expect elderly people to bear up under it like you do.

DR. WALKER Yes, Miss Jackson, we'll look into it. *(she leaves)* Let's see, it's the middle of August now. If a two week extension will help you, you can have it. Don't know how I'll explain the delay to the new Ph.D. but I'll do it. We'll put 'em in the guest house. *(pause)*

DAVID Thank you, Dr. Walker, and goodbye. *(he crosses to his father and speaks gently)* Dad?

*(*SHELDON *looks up as if in a coma, sees* DAVID*'s extended hand which he rejects and rises slowly)*

SHELDON *(stiffly)* I'm all right, thank you. *(he moves toward the door)*

DR. WALKER Goodbye, Professor.

SHELDON Goodbye, Mister President. *(he goes out, followed by* DAVID. HARRIET *comes out on the porch)*

WILLA *(inside)* Can you see them?

HARRIET *(looking off)* No. Yes, they're just coming out of Old Main.

WILLA *(entering)* Does he seem pleased?

HARRIET They don't seem to be talking.

WILLA They never did talk much to each other, those two.

HARRIET I guess I'd better go inside.

WILLA Yes—no. You stay here. Whatever is said I want you to hear it. *(*SHELDON *and* DAVID *appear. They cross the stage in silence)* How did it go? *(*SHELDON *says nothing. He trudges wearily into the house and upstairs to the bedroom. After watching* SHELDON *disappear)* David?

DAVID It was awful—whimpering and begging the president to intercede for him. It was awful. I felt so ashamed.

WILLA It was that bad—you felt ashamed of your father?

DAVID Yes. And all he got for it was a two week reprieve.

WILLA He's not himself any more, David. He hasn't been for a long time now.

DAVID But where is his pride?

WILLA I don't know. I just don't know.

DAVID What do we do now?

WILLA We start packing and looking for a room for your father.

DAVID Room? Aren't you going with him?

WILLA No—I've got to live in the dormitory if I want to keep my job. New regulation. Besides we can't find a cottage that quickly.

DAVID What about Harriet?

WILLA She'll live in the senior dorm next year. That'll give me a whole year to find a place for Billy when he comes home from the sanatorium.

DAVID He'll be by himself.

WILLA It can't be helped.

DAVID Alone.

WILLA We'll be close by. I'll visit him every day.

DAVID My god. What a comedown.

(The lights fade and music is heard)

Scene Five

END OF THE PROCESSIONAL

(The lights rise. Two men, professional movers, come out of the house carrying a divan. Another enters as they disappear around the house. DAVID *comes out dressed for travel. He puts his luggage on the porch and saunters back and forth gazing at the house. The movers continue to come back and forth)*

DAVID It's all over now. Movers are here and the house is all but empty. Just a few pieces left. Some Mama will take with her to the dormitory to fix up her room and make it homey. Dad rejected the two week extension. Said *he'd* decide the time of his departure. He's upstairs now in the bedroom. Won't come down he says till we're all gone—like the captain of a sinking ship. Up there with his rocking chair and his Bible. He's taking the chair with him. That's all he'll have to remind him of this house. In a few minutes now I'll be on my way. I'm to meet my family in Roanoke and from there we'll take the Norfolk and Western and head back into the midwest for the great University of Iowa. I'm off to school again—going to start on my meal ticket—my Ph.D. Kids joke about the letters. Say it stands for phenomenally dumb. But I've got to get it if I'm going to make it in this racket—that's the only way you can beat the system. And that's what they're paying for nowadays—looks good in the catalogue. Nobody cares very much about teaching. It's the degree that counts. *(pause)* Dad's got a room in a boarding house just across from the campus. He'll take his meals there, too. It's not so bad—small but comfortable. *(pause)* No, that's a goddam lie. It's tiny, cramped and no place for a man who's lived in a big roomy house with children romping about. *(the last of the movers come out)* Well, that should do it. It's bare and empty—a house that's seen so much of joy and sorrow, happiness, sickness, and death. Oh yes, I didn't tell you about that—but there was another birth—a stillborn. They might have saved it in the hospital. But Mom wouldn't go—didn't trust 'em she said where our people were concerned. *(pause)* I hate to go back in there but I've got to say goodbye. *(he enters the house. The lights come up in the bedroom.* SHELDON *sits alone reading. He looks up as he hears* DAVID*'s footsteps echoing on the stairs.* DAVID *enters. For a moment neither speaks)*

SHELDON I didn't hear the taxi.

DAVID It hasn't come. But they said ten minutes so I thought I'd better come up now.

SHELDON Well, you've a few minutes. Here, take my chair.

DAVID No thanks, Dad. I won't have time.

SHELDON Well, keep in touch. And come see us whenever you can.

DAVID Okay.

SHELDON *(almost too confidently)* I'll be buying a place soon. And don't worry about your mother and Harriet. We'll make out. Got several teaching offers, you know.

DAVID *(softly)* That's fine, Dad. *(*WILLA *and* HARRIET *appear from around the rear of the house)*

SHELDON Now you go ahead and get that degree and don't stop until you've finished. Don't make the mistake I did of assuming that a Master of Arts represented security. And if you get in a jam financially let me know. My credit's good.

DAVID All right. *(a long pause, then a taxi horn)*

HARRIET *(downstairs)* David, taxi's here.

DAVID I'll be right down. *(to* SHELDON*)* Got to go now, Dad. *(He holds out his hand.* SHELDON *grasps it firmly rising as he does so.* DAVID *leaves and* SHELDON *goes to the window. Downstairs* DAVID *embraces* HARRIET *and then* WILLA*)*

WILLA Take care of yourself. Write often and give our love to Connie.

DAVID Sure, Mom. *(He embraces her again, picks up his bags and hurries to the left. He is met by the taxi driver who takes his bags)*

DRIVER Got to hurry, sir. We're a little late and train's on time.

DAVID Right. *(he turns, waves to* WILLA *and* HARRIET *on the porch and* SHELDON *at the upstairs window. The lights fade as the music of the Recessional rises. When the lights are completely down except for a spot on* DAVID, *he turns and faces the audience)*

DAVID *(listening)* They're getting ready for the summer commencement exercises. It'll be as hot as hell in the auditorium. *(listening)* "The tumult and the shouting die, the captains and the kings depart, still *stands* our ancient sacrifice"—*(he turns, back to the audience and stares at the dim outline of the house)* We're done. The story's finished. And now, my story begins. *(he jams his hands into his pockets and strolls into the darkness. The music swells)*

(The Recessional ends)

COMEDY AND SATIRE

Langston Hughes • Abram Hill • Douglas Turner Ward

African American folklore is filled with stories of slaves who outwitted the master as the legendary rabbit outwitted the fox. The master, when seeing his slaves falling into gales of laughter, would shake his head: "Them darkies are like children. They'll laugh at anything." But as Ralph Ellison phrased it, the slaves had changed the joke, and slipped the yoke.[1]

When the Emperor suppresses jokes, he drives ridicule underground. "This story will kill you!" whispers one. "I thought I'd die laughing," responds another. "We wear the mask," wrote Paul Laurence Dunbar, and the Black comic mask has shown many faces—some healthy and heart-warming; some pernicious and deadly. Through jokes, people express their fears and hatred. They use code words and find subtle ways to speak the unmentionable, because laughter can be a dangerous blade if it cuts too deeply, especially when aimed at the Emperor's new clothes. African American comics have always known this; for example, when Black comics like Bert Williams and George Walker played before white audiences, their humor appeared to mock themselves; nonetheless, if one reads carefully, satirical barbs are subtilely aimed at white society. (See the song "Vassar Girl" in *In Dahomey*).

The Emperor, in old clothes or new, enjoyed laughing at others. Often used as a form of social control, laughter polices the people's behavior. Comedy may sometimes mock the overly serious, the vain, the pompous, the ugly, the stupid, the eccentric, even the vicious and the mean, but at other times, the laughter of the Emperor may mock skin color, hair texture, lip size, and speech, creating anger and resentment, as whites did in minstrelsy, America's first mass family entertainment.

1. Ralph Ellison, "Change the Joke and Slip the Yoke," *Partisan Review* (Spring 1958).

Minstrelsy, as a commercial entertainment, lasted sixty years (1830s–1890s). As political jokes are popular in fascist states, jokes about race and sex were popular in American folklore, evoking emotions too deep and too unsettling to be spoken directly. The blackfaced, burnt-cork mask allowed white men to express all the things they themselves feared: the new immigrants, homosexuality, women, the wealthy, and Negro sexuality. Their own dangerous emotions—suppressed and secure behind the disguise of the burnt-cork mask, like a jack out-of-the-box—leapt clear and free onto the minstrel stage.

As white fears traveled the twisted comic roads of minstrelsy, Black humor for African Americans traveled via the Theatre Owners Booking Association (TOBA). Black vaudeville circuits booked into nightclubs and cabarets where comedians played exclusively to Black audiences. As late as the 1930s, Langston Hughes could send African Americans into waves of laughter with his satires of popular white movies like *Imitation of Life* or plays like *Scarlet Sister Mary.* His parodies did not reach white audiences, or if they did, they were not appreciated.

In the 1950s and 1960s, stand-up comics like Dick Gregory, Moms Mabley, Shelley Berman, Redd Foxx, Lenny Bruce, and later Richard Pryor, brought race and sex out of the toilets and into nightclubs, onto records, and finally into television. To hear the forbidden spoken aloud in mixed audiences was shocking enough to evoke laughter in both whites and Blacks.

Racial laughter as a weapon against racial injustice in the mainstream theatres is a recent sound, arriving only after the Supreme Court decision on segregation, the Birmingham bus strike, the Greensboro sit-ins, the success of *A Raisin in the Sun,* and the provocative speech of Dick Gregory and Malcolm X. Racial oppression in America had lifted to the degree that humor could come off the streets, out of the pool halls, bars, and beauty salons, up from the kitchen and into the theatre. Although musicals like *Finian's Rainbow* (1947) had used laughter to ridicule white superiority, Black playwrights did not make wide use of the device in commercial theatre until the 1960s with *Purlie Victorious, Fly Blackbird, Jerico-Jim Crow,* and *Day of Absence.* By the latter half of the 1960s, a large Black audience began to attend the theatre and pay for the pleasure of publicly laughing at the absurdity of race politics and at the whites and Blacks who had developed unproductive ways of dealing with that system.

In this section, the three plays raise the questions: What does their racial humor depend on, and is it still funny today? The main thrust of *Limitations of Life* (1938) is mocking white ignorance; *On Strivers Row* (1939) ridicules Black vanity, and *Day of Absence* (1965) reverses the minstrel images for the racially mixed audiences of the sixties.

LIMITATIONS OF LIFE
1938

Langston Hughes (1902–1967)

In the 1930s, Langston Hughes wrote four skits to satirize the American motion pictures produced by an industry that perpetuated the concept of white superiority. Over the next two decades, the negative stereotypes of Italians, Jews, Spaniards, Irish, Asians, and even Native Americans were ameliorated in favor of more representative human beings; only the Black stereotypes, while undergoing many transformations, remained locked into variations on roles established in nineteenth-century minstrelsy: buffoons, primitives, and loyal servants. Not until the 1980s and 1990s with films made by African American directors—Charles Burnett, Spike Lee, Julie Dash, William Greaves, and Camille Billops—did Black Americans see images that reflected their own reality.

In 1934, Fanny Hurst's novel, *Imitation of Life,* was adapted to the screen. "Passing" may have been a fresh subject in Hollywood, but as Sterling Brown pointed out in his reivew, the "old stereotype Mammy and the tragic mulatto, and the ancient ideas about the mixture of the races" still existed.[1] This crazy-quilt pattern, one that the motion picture industry helped mold and perpetuate, was firmly embedded in the consciousness of an extremely large portion of American whites as absolute truth.

Langston Hughes agreed with Brown and reversed the roles of the characters as they appeared in *Imitation of Life,* enabling him to point out the silliness of the stories. No white reader could identify with Audette Aubert and her motives in Hughes's skit—anymore than a Black could identify with Delilah in the film. (It is not necessary to have seen the film to get the point of the play.)

Mr. Hughes's satiric skit is no less applicable to the 1959 remake of the film, even though there was an attempt in the later film to add dignity to the roles of Blacks by eliminating the dialect and plac-

1. Sterling Brown, "Literary Scene—Chronicle and Comment," *Opportunity* (April 1935).

ing more emphasis on the mulatto problem. Still, the movie remains a romantic concept based on white attitudes about what Black Americans ought to think, feel, and be, rather than a realism relevant to the times.

Just as the Great Depression of the thirties transformed the art theatre movement into one of social problems and leftist politics, Langston Hughes's four skits, which seem to date from 1938 when he put them in circulation, in reality stem from earlier inspirations. For example, *Scarlet Sister Barry* took its origin from a Pulitzer Prize novel, *Scarlet Sister Mary* (1928). In 1930, Ethel Barrymore appeared on Broadway in the play adapted by Julia Peterkin from her novel. In blackface makeup, Barrymore played Mary, a "scarlet" Negro woman who bears eight illegitimate children. In a few short pages, Hughes lashes Peterkin's play and Ethel Barrymore's performance, and he even gets in a dig or two at *Showboat* (1927).

Hughes fashioned *The Em-Fuehrer Jones* into a double satire: the first on Eugene O'Neill's *The Emperor Jones* (1920); the second on Adolf Hitler's embarrassment at Jesse Owens's triumph over the Aryan race at the Berlin Olympics in 1936, followed two years later by Joe Louis flooring the German boxer Max Schemling three times in the first round for the world's heavyweight boxing match.

Uncle Tom's Cabin, a story known to most Americans of the 1930s, gave Hughes material for the fourth skit, *Little Eva,* which mocked the dog-faithful image of Uncle Tom. With the same blow, *Little Eva* also mocked two Hollywood spin-offs: *The Little Colonel* (1935) and *The Little Rebel* (1936) starring Shirley Temple in Little Eva roles, with her own congenial Uncle Tom, Bill Robinson.

At various times during the run of the Harlem Suitcase Theatre production of *Don't You Want To Be Free?* (see that play's introduction), *Limitations of Life* was performed. Hughes included two movie skits in his musical revue entitled *Run, Ghost, Run*—the title, a metaphor for his exorcism of false images that dominated the theatre. His revue, perhaps too radical for the racial climate of that day, was never produced, and the ghosts still haunt our attics.

Limitations of Life

CAST OF CHARACTERS

MAMMY WEAVERS
AUDETTE AUBERT
ED STARKS

PLACE *Harlem.*

TIME *Right now.*

SCENE *A luxurious living room. Swell couch and footstool. At right, electric stove, griddle, pancake turner, box of pancake flour (only Aunt Jemima's picture is white), and a pile of paper plates. Also a loaf of white bread.*

(AUDETTE AUBERT, *pretty blond maid, is busy making pancakes on the stove. Enter* MAMMY WEAVERS, *a colored lady, in trailing evening gown, with tiara and large Metropolitan Opera program, speaking perfect English with Oxford accent)*

AUDETTE *(taking* MAMMY'*s ermine)* Mammy Weavers, ah been waitin' up for you-all. Ah thought you might like some nice hot pancakes before you-all went to bed.

MAMMY You shouldn't have waited up for me, my dear.

AUDETTE Aw, chile!

MAMMY Besides, I don't want any pancakes, Audette. I've just had lobster à la Newburg at the Mimo Club.

AUDETTE Well, now! How did you-all like the opera, Mammy Weavers?

MAMMY Flagstad was divine tonight, but Melchior was a wee bit hoarse.

AUDETTE Oh, ah'ms so sorry, Mammy Weavers! Maybe Melchior ought to use Vicks like Nelson Eddy.

MAMMY *(sighing)* I'm just a little tired, Audette.

AUDETTE Oh, Mammy Weavers, set right down and rest your feet. I'll run fetch your slippers, honey.

MAMMY I don't know what I'd do without you, Audette.

AUDETTE I'll never leave you, Mammy Weavers. *(runs and gets slippers)* Just lemme put your carpet slippers on. *(kneels)* I'll rub your feet a little first.

MAMMY *(relaxing)* Oh, that feels so good!

AUDETTE *(looking up like a faithful dog)* Do it, Mammy Weavers?

MAMMY Tell me, Audette, where is your little Riola tonight?

AUDETTE Lawd, Mammy Weavers, ma little daughter's tryin' so hard to be colored. She just loves Harlem. She's lyin' out in de backyard in de sun all day long tannin' herself, every day, tryin' so hard to be colored.

MAMMY What a shame, the darling's so fair and blue-eyed! Even though her father was an Eskimo, you'd never know it. Never.

AUDETTE He wooed me on a dog sled when I were on that Re-Settlement Project in Alaska. How romantic it were! But he melted away after Riola was born. Then I started workin' for you, Mammy Weavers.

(Enter ED STARKS, *a sleek-headed jigaboo in evening clothes)*

ED Delilah, here's your car keys, my dear. *(to the maid)* Audette, why don't you go to bed?

AUDETTE I can't sleep till Mammy Weavers gets home.

MAMMY Darling Audette! I want to do something nice for you, my sweet. Try to think of something you want more than anything else in the world.

AUDETTE All I wants, Mammy Weavers, is a grand funeral when I die.

MAMMY Darling! But don't you want a nice home of your own?

AUDETTE No, Mammy Weavers, that little room down in your basement's all right for me! *(jumping up)* I gwine make Mr. Ed Starks some nice pancakes right now. Don't you want some, Mr. Ed?

ED You know I like your pancakes, Audette. But if it's all the same with you tonight, give me some of that fine white bread.

MAMMY No, Ed! No! Pancakes will do! I got a patent on that flour so we get it free. Bread's too high.

ED O.K.

AUDETTE *(turning pancakes)* Does you want butter, 'lasses, or honey on your pancakes, Mr. Ed?

ED I want jelly on mine!

AUDETTE Then I'll run downstairs to the pantry and get you some, Mr. Ed.

MAMMY Oh, Audette, you shouldn't do so much for us.

AUDETTE I never gets tired doin' for you and Mr. Ed, Mammy Weavers. I like colored folks!

MAMMY I like white folks, too, my dear. *(musing)* I was raised by the sweetest old white mammy! When I remember all my dear old New England mammy did for me, I want to do something for you, Audette. Something you'll never forget. *(with great generosity)* Darling, maybe you'd like a day off?

AUDETTE *(flipping a pancake)* Not even a day off, Mammy Weavers! Ah wouldn't know what to do with it. *(exits, head down)*

ED *(throwing up hands)* Once a pancake, always a pancake! *(picks up Jemima box with white auntie on it, and shakes his head)*

(Curtain)

ON STRIVERS ROW
1939

Abram Hill (1911–1986)

The theatre, in its fullest sense, is created from the lives of the people and expresses the very foundation upon which the life is built. Each nation and each people has a contribution to make such a theatre of the people.

—American Negro Theatre Constitution

In 1940, Abram Hill and Frederick O'Neal, in the basement of the library on 135th Street in Harlem, founded the most renowned theatre group of the forties—the American Negro Theatre (ANT), which trained over 200 people and attracted 50,000 patrons to witness 325 performances.[1] Hill's inspiration came in great part from the collapse of the Federal Theatre Project (see introductions to *Liberty Deferred* and *Big White Fog*), where he had worked in the Living Newspaper unit with John Silvera while writing *Liberty Deferred.*

Hill surrounded himself with talents who shared his vision: James Jackson, Frederick O'Neal, Austin Briggs Hall, and others. They conceived a nonprofit, cooperative acting company "deriving its own theatre craft and acting style by combining all standard forms, putting to artful use the fluency and rhythm that lie in the Negro's special gifts." The plays they would choose would be contemporary and, if possible, would deal with issues that concerned the Harlem community.

During the nine years of ANT's existence, Hill remained its driving and unifying force. Their successful productions in the small theatre of the 135th Street library included Theodore Browne's *Natural Man* (1941), Abram Hill's *Walk Hard* (1944), and Owen Dodson's *Garden of Time* (1945). An impressive list of distinguished actors trained and taught at ANT: Harry Belafonte, Helen Martin, Sidney Poitier, Claire Leyba, Alice and Alvin Childress, Osceola Archer, Ruby Dee, Earle Hyman, Hilda Simms, and many others. ANT's greatest success contributed to the group's demise. *Anna Lucasta* (1944), the

1. Ethel Pitts Walker, "The American Negro Theatre," in *The Theatre of Black Americans: A Collection of Critical Essays,* edited by Errol Hill (New York: Applause Theatre Book Publishers, 1987).

story of an immigrant Polish family, which Hill adapted for African Americans, created an excitement that moved it to Broadway and then to London. The result: the best actors left ANT for commercial work.

Hill himself had a long apprenticeship in theatre. Born in 1911, the son of a railway fireman in Atlanta, Georgia, at age seven Hill appeared in a Morehouse College Theatre production. In 1925, the family moved to New York City where Hill graduated from De Witt Clinton High School and attended the City College of New York for two years. In 1936, he secured a job in drama with the CCC (Civilian Conservation Corps) where he directed plays with young men ages sixteen to twenty-five. For the next two years, Hill shuttled between his job directing for the CCC and working for his B.A. at Lincoln University in Pennsylvania, where he studied theatre under J. Newton Hill. After graduation in 1938, Hill returned to New York and joined the Federal Theatre as a script reader. While serving in this capacity, he wrote two plays (*Stealing Lightning* and *Hell's Half Acre*), the latter produced by the Unity Players of the Bronx. This helped him obtain a Theresa Helbrun Scholarship at the New School for Social Research to study playwriting with John Gassner and Erwin Piscator. Within a year, Hill completed a social satire, which he gave to actor/director Dick Campbell of the Rose McClendon Players. With some revision, *On Strivers Row,* ran for sixteen performances. With the founding of ANT in 1940, Hill became its director and produced his play as the theatre's first major effort; it ran for a 101 performances. So popular did *Strivers Row* become that ANT revived it twice, once as a musical.

Hill's comedy, with its theme similar to Moliere's *Bourgeois Gentleman,* has continued to delight college and community audiences. Although it is doubtful that Hill had read *In Dahomey* (1902), the Van Striven family members of *On Strivers Row* are dramatically "kissing cousins" to the Lightfoot family of *In Dahomey.* They both live in a chichi neighborhood; they both have a daughter they wish to place in high society; they both are surrounded by a greedy entourage, and both party-crashing Joe Smothers of *On Strivers Row* and jive-talking Hustling Charlie of *In Dahomey* embarrass the families by their low-class behavior. Finally, in both plays, young, true love wins out over family pretense, demonstrating to the audience that all's well that ends well.

On Strivers Row
A SATIRE

CHARACTERS

SOPHIE
DOLLY VAN STRIVEN
PROFESSOR HENNYPEST
TILLIE PETUNIA
CHUCK
COBINA
MRS. PACE
OSCAR VAN STRIVEN
LILY LIVINGSTON
ROWENA
ED TUCKER
LOUISE DAVIS
DR. LEON DAVIS
RUBY JACKSON
BEULAH
JOE SMOTHERS

SCENES

The action takes place in the reception room and foyer of the Van Striven Home in Harlem.

Act I	Scene 1	A morning in the fall of the 1940s
	Scene 2	Nine P.M., the same day
Act II	Scene 1	A few minutes later
	Scene 2	Later, the same evening

BACKGROUND

The Van Strivens' residence stands high and mighty in the heart of Harlem on West 139th Street between Seventh and Eighth Avenues. In bygone days when this and similar homes in the block were built, (circa 1913), they became the town homes for upper-class whites. As the complexion of Harlem later changed, the noire bourgeoisie, especially the socially inclined ones, purchased these properties.

By the 1920s, the block had become known as Strivers Row, a trim, tree-dotted, exclusive community of "society" Blacks. Fearing slum encroachment, affluent lawyers, doctors, teachers, real estate brokers, business people, and renowned celebrities established a rigid pattern of disciplined living, guarded orderliness, and more than a hint of luxury.

Striving to set an exclusive and fashionable way of living became the order of the day. Neighbor competed with neighbor to outdo one another. Meanwhile less fortunate Blacks developed varying degrees of mockery and hostility. *It is no mere coincidence that our story deals with a family by the name of Van Striven.*

Musicales, teas, and soirees set the social vogue in these homes; whereas yacht parties, theater-concert-opera attending, weekend retreats at resorts and summer homes, motor trips in high-powered cars, and trips abroad added additional luster to the doings of this tribe.

The Van Strivens consider themselves socially miles above their neighbors. Though their home is a four-story dwelling—the same as the others in the block—Van Strivens have engineered themselves into a position of "second to none." The first floor of the home includes an entrance, sitting room, den, dining room, kitchen, pantry, maid's room, and bath. The second floor includes a foyer, reception room, back parlor, and family room. The third and fourth floors have baths and bedrooms.

SCENE

The scene of the play is the large reception room (front parlor) and the foyer, an elevated entrance area further upstage. Here, the Van Strivens entertain small and informal gatherings. The back parlor off left is reserved for larger and more formal affairs.

An arch in the center of the upstage wall of the reception room, three steps, flanking wrought-iron rails and an accompanying balustrade separate the room from the foyer. The foyer floor is about two feet above the level of the parlor floor. The walls of the room, heightened by the sunken floor and a spectacular chandelier, enhance a quiet elegance and a hint of pretentiousness.

Upstage off right leads to the front door. It cannot be seen, but it frequently can be heard to slam. Upstage off left leads to the stairwell, the hall, back parlor, and a den. Along the right wall is a pair of French doors, leading to a veranda overlooking the street. Partially drawn drapes and venetian blinds encase the French doors. This wall is indented, allowing a three-quartered viewing of the doors by the audience. Downstage of the left wall is a doorway leading to a passageway to the back parlor. Double swivel doors are suggested for the area, thus allowing easy-flowing exits and entrances.

Clusters of furniture are arranged for easy conversation. Right of center is a stylish loveseat with a small table above holding a lamp. An upholstered armchair down left, a cocktail table in front of the loveseat, and a stool extremely down right complete this grouping. A console table with a vase and a French phone plus a radio and record-playing combination along the left wall add luster.

Right and left of the arch are single antique chairs. A classy painting and a delicately carved bench dominate the foyer. Other paintings, furnishings, and minutiae are strategically placed, including rugs and candlelight wall fixtures.

The setting is very prim, proper, and affluent. One has to wonder why there is a sign tucked in the French door that makes one *wonder* about the Van Strivens. The sign reads: ROOM TO RENT.

ACT I

Scene 1

(Before the curtain rises, appropriate music—classical, please—sets the high and mighty tone of Strivers Row. The music is emanating from a radio. Since the blinds are drawn, very little light illuminates the room. Entering from the left foyer is SOPHIE, *a rather chic, casual, and extremely informal maid. She is wearing the customary maid's uniform and is carrying a dust mop and a basket of cleaning paraphernalia. She adjusts the venetian blinds; light filters the room. She is humming "When the Saints Go Marching In" and is deliberately drowning out the radio music. Her cleaning begins with her feathered duster and cleaning cloth taking a stroke at the furniture. Shutting off the radio, she sings, synchronizing her strokes with the song)*

SOPHIE:

Lord, I want to be in that number;
When the saints go marching in.
Oh, when the saints go marching in;
Oh, when the saints go marching in,

(almost prayerfully)

Lord, I sure wish I'd hit a number—

DOLLY *(offstage)* Good morning, Sophie.

SOPHIE *(now, very busy)* Morning, Ma'am.

DOLLY You sound as if you attended a revival meeting last night instead of a dance. *(entering from left foyer)*

SOPHIE Ain't no difference. At one you dance with your man. At the other, you dance with the Holy Ghost.

(Now within full view, DOLLY *is dressed in a Dior housecoat and is strikingly handsome, well-bred, youthfully fortyish matron of the Afro-American elite that descended from pre-Civil War Black and white Romeos and Juliets in downstate New York. Though totally confident of the supremacy of her social status, there is a slight edge of uncertainty—"a hidden dissuader"—that creeps into her manner. She masks this dissuader with wit, but at times frustration makes her a bit daffy. She is carrying a pair of slippers)*

DOLLY You must have had fun. You didn't get in until the wee hours this morning. Break these in again for me, please.

SOPHIE *(taking the slippers)* What again! I crucified my feet last night at the Bellhops Ball. I don't feel—

DOLLY *(embracing her)* You also wore my mink cape. Am I annoyed! No!

SOPHIE *(changing to slippers)* When I first took the job, having access to your wardrobe was part of the deal.

DOLLY *(very lightly)* My jewelry and cape were the exceptions. Let's remember not to forget that. (SOPHIE *winces, her feet hurt)* It's that left one that pinches, isn't it?

SOPHIE It's the left side of my face that's screwed up, ain't it? In the Flip Flop Boogie we danced, the action was on the right foot.

DOLLY Where was the left foot?

SOPHIE In the air, like this—*(rises, does the Flip Flop Boogie on the right foot, the left stabbing the air)*

DOLLY Get the mail. That's no dance. That's some new version of a fit. (SOPHIE *shuf-*

fles toward the foyer) Stop, Sophie! I'll get it. You shuffle like Uncle Tom after he has swallowed ten beers. *(she goes off foyer right)*

SOPHIE *(sitting on chair arm)* It's beyond me why some colored people—even "the well-bred ones"—have such unbred feet.

DOLLY *(entering with mail and a newspaper)* Lovely! Lovely! Scores of people have R-S-V-Peed! *(examining the mail)*

SOPHIE Any mail for me?

DOLLY No, dear. Nobody wrote to you. *(opening mail)*

SOPHIE Who cares. The only male I'm interested in wears pants.

DOLLY A reply from Dr. Leon Davis and his wife, Louise.

SOPHIE His hands stray too much on foreign territory. *(smacks her buttocks)*

DOLLY How nice! Judge and Mrs. Tucker, true born aristocrats.

SOPHIE They may be aristocrats, but that son is a acrobat. He—

DOLLY And George P. Muzzumer, the undertaker tycoon. Why, the money he has!

SOPHIE You know, when my fourth husband died, he wouldn't let him down in his grave until I paid a deposit on his funeral.

DOLLY *(puzzled at the letter)* Rita Richpot—Rita Richpot—?

SOPHIE That's the former Rita Kale. You see, Dr. Kale ain't filling her perscription no more.

DOLLY What's that?

SOPHIE He pulled that mink coat off her and put her tail out on the turf.

DOLLY Heavens! *(throws reply into waste basket)* Then I must retract my invitation. I'll telephone her—make some excuse for her not to come. When people drop their morals, I drop them from my guest book. *(picks up book and scratches name from book)* Couples are so dizzy nowadays. They change one another faster than you can change the bed linen.

SOPHIE *(impertinently)* That do'd it! My salary, please.

DOLLY *(sitting* SOPHIE *down)* Oh—come now, Sophie—there's something between us bigger than salaries.

SOPHIE It sure is. And that's my bill.

DOLLY *(rising)* Come, Sophie, we have plenty to do.

SOPHIE *(rallying)* We! That bunch of snobs coming here can't appreciate the fact that I've lost ten pounds in ten days getting this house in shape for them tonight.

DOLLY 'Tis not in vain, Sophie. Cobina Van Striven's debut will be the debut of the season.

SOPHIE That child don't want no debut.

DOLLY But, my dear, debutantes at eighteen always make their bows before society.

SOPHIE *(resuming dusting)* I nearly busted my corset when I debuted.

DOLLY Hahahahaha—you bowing before society—at eighteen, I suppose!

SOPHIE What old society at eighteen! I was bowing before the Captain at Precinct 32, explaining!

DOLLY Sophie, you're impossible. But, what would I ever do without you?

SOPHIE That's what *he* wants to know.

DOLLY He?

SOPHIE Joe.

DOLLY Joe who? Has he no last name?

SOPHIE *(gloatingly)* Ain't nothin' in a name.

DOLLY You would love a man without knowing whether he was good or not?

SOPHIE And will you tell me what a good man can do?

DOLLY Well, what do you expect in a man?

SOPHIE Excitement!

DOLLY *(disdainfully)* Oh! Such talk! I hope mother nor Cobina has ever heard you talking like this.

SOPHIE Cobina would surprise you.

DOLLY *(puzzled)* What do you mean?

SOPHIE Nothing.

DOLLY *(she strolls to the window)* You will see some fine young men here tonight. Unfortunately, one or two have kinky hair.

SOPHIE Ma Pace ain't gonna have them.

DOLLY Mother, well—yes—she can be made to—That sign. That awful sign! *(going to window)* Why Oscar insists upon putting it there—he is so uncommonly common.

SOPHIE You know Mr. Van Striven ain't gonna have you taking that thing down.

DOLLY *(coming down center with sign "Room For Rent")* I cannot have it up now. What will people say? *(lays it on table near sofa)* The Van Strivens' palatial residence is *not* a rooming house.

SOPHIE Mr. Van Striven's more interested in getting it paid for than he is in getting it palatial. Besides, four people don't need no fourteen rooms.

(Door slams offstage)

DOLLY Get my foot into your shoe—I mean get your foot into my shoe. Hurry!

SOPHIE *(rising slowly)* They seen feet b'fore.

DOLLY *(threatening* SOPHIE*)* One of these days—

*(*HENNYPEST *enters through hall door. He is a humble little fat man with a bald head. Somewhere between forty and fifty, he has traded his youth for wisdom—he has gained more than he has lost in the bargain. The apex of his stomach puffs out between a wrinkled vest and his baggy pants)*

DOLLY Good morning, Professor—always full of smiles.

HENNYPEST Smiles—Madame—at home they say, I grin like a "Chessy" cat.

SOPHIE *(slyly)* Well, Professor, down home we still grin, but up North we smile.

DOLLY That will do, Sophie.

HENNYPEST *(folding his hands)* You have one beautiful home, and a beautiful maid.

SOPHIE *(coquettishly)* Aw, gone.

DOLLY I say—you catch New York's flattering habit in your first three days. You're quite apt, Professor. How was your morning stroll?

HENNYPEST I didn't stroll this morning—I was basking in the sunshine out in the backyard . . .

DOLLY *(correcting)* You mean *court!*

HENNYPEST Oh, yes, court. Someone across the way hung out a blanket and blocked out the sunshine.

DOLLY *(abruptly)* You mean in the next block?

HENNYPEST Yes, Madame.

DOLLY *(with a feeling of difference)* Those common hookies are such an envious bunch of hoodlums.

SOPHIE *(defensively)* Hey, my brother lives in that block.

DOLLY *(gently)* Oh, but your brother is different.

SOPHIE He's an Elk.

DOLLY I mean that crowd that curses from Monday to Friday, throws those noisy Saturday night gin parties, and cooks pig's feet all day Sunday.

HENNYPEST You wouldn't happen to have any now, would you?

DOLLY Heavens, no! Why Professor Hennypest, pig's feet come from the lowest part of the pig. People of class simply do not partake.

HENNYPEST But, Madame, what I cast into my stomach has nothing to do with class distinction.

DOLLY Appetites and attitudes will at times get confused. However, Oscar telephoned that you had breakfast at the Hotel Clarissa.

HENNYPEST *(sadly)* Exactly three orders, Madame, and I regret to say that what you New Yorkers call a meal is a gross overstatement.

DOLLY I am so sorry. Sophie, prepare a big breakfast for Professor Hennypest. A glass of orange juice—an egg and some toast.

SOPHIE *(to* HENNYPEST*)* Two eggs wouldn't kill you, would they?

HENNYPEST Physically, Sophie, no. Socially, I hope not.

DOLLY Good gracious, no! This isn't Sugar Hill. Why, fix him as many as—three eggs if you like.

(The doorbell rings)

HENNYPEST Thank you, Madame.

DOLLY Answer the door!

SOPHIE *(at second ring,* SOPHIE *rises slowly)* Take it easy, I'm coming!

DOLLY Hurry!

HENNYPEST I will answer it.

DOLLY Of course not, Professor. Let her do something. *(pauses—sees her feet)* Look at her feet! *(rises)* Never mind, I will—

SOPHIE *(bangs into both from her tilted position)* Will you make up your

DOLLY *(screams)* Ouch! Get off my foot! *(crossing down right)*

SOPHIE *(exiting right)* This ain't no time for no visitors!

DOLLY Such a maid.

SOPHIE *(off right as doorbell rings again)* Keep down your dandruff!

TILLIE *(offstage)* Please stay in your place! Such horrible manners!

(Entering from right in a huff, stopping down center, SOPHIE *enters, stops and leans nonchalantly against archway.* TILLIE, *dressed fashionably in mink stole and mink hat, is a high-powered forty-ish, uppity "do wager" with an SS figure—somewhat like a drunken dollar sign. She radiates a*

disarming superiority that is more calculated than real)

TILLIE Dolly—that maid! Such impertinence. Such undiluted insolence.

DOLLY What did you say to Mrs. Petunia?

SOPHIE That her big, white Cadillac looks like a pregnant Frigidaire.

DOLLY *(bangs into* HENNYPEST, *both dashing to window right)* New Cadillac. Tillie, it's magnificent. It must be twenty feet long.

TILLIE Twenty-two.

SOPHIE Honey, you could paste a vacancy sign on your bumper and rent that thing out as a floating motel.

TILLIE And the sign on your bumper should read MAD, not MAID.

DOLLY Take her stole, Sophie.

*(*TILLIE *sits upper end of sofa)*

SOPHIE *(takes stole)* I wonder how many animals would be wearing their own furs this season if it wasn't for the installment . . . plan?

DOLLY Suppose you let the skunks do their own worrying and bring tea for us.

*(*SOPHIE *flings stole on foyer table, exits left after a mean look at* TILLIE.*)*

TILLIE Did you say she was from Newark or Noah's Ark?

DOLLY *(sitting opposite* TILLIE*)* Mrs. Petunia, I want you to meet Professor Hennypest.

HENNYPEST How are you, Mrs. Petunia?

TILLIE *(sizes him up)* You're not one of these root doctors or numerologists?

DOLLY Don't mind her, Professor. *(to* TILLIE*)* He occupies the Chair of Zoology at Buskeegee University.

TILLIE *(aside)* No doubt, uncomfortably. *(direct)* How nice. I wonder if you get as tired of meeting trash as I do. I cannot risk introductions anywhere in Harlem. You never know whether you're meeting a deacon or a devil. Dolly's house is different, thank God.

HENNYPEST And she is a most congenial hostess.

TILLIE Have you been here long?

HENNYPEST No, Madame—just for the annual meeting of the American Zoological Society, at the Bronx Zoo.

DOLLY My house guest for three days.

TILLIE House guests are like fish.

HENNYPEST Fish?

TILLIE They smell after three days. But, of course, Professor Hennypest, you are a celebrity.

HENNYPEST No, Madame, Baptist.

TILLIE What—oh yes, related to the Kings County Hennypests?

HENNYPEST No, Madame.

TILLIE The North Jersey Hennypests?

HENNYPEST No, Madame.

TILLIE Certainly the Philadelphia, everybody is related to them.

HENNYPEST Sorry, Madame. I am not.

TILLIE Surely you have some relations. They are a bore, but they do give you a sort of family tree, if you get what I mean.

HENNYPEST I guess mine was chopped down. That makes me something of a stump.

TILLIE How *very* true. Those things do happen.

DOLLY You are matched against a man with two Ph.D.'s, Tillie.

TILLIE Where'd he steal them?

DOLLY Northwestern and University of Pennsylvania. He's a little short on front—

TILLIE I'd say he has a lot of *front.*

DOLLY Don't let her frighten you, Professor.

HENNYPEST Saepe satins fuit dissimulare quam ulcisci. *(*TILLIE *gawks, he translates)* It is better not to see an insult than avenge it. *(exiting)*

TILLIE Leaving?

HENNYPEST Immediately after breakfast. I'm going up to the Bronx Zoo.

TILLIE Visiting relatives?

HENNYPEST No, Madame, animals.

TILLIE Homo sapiens and animals are both living beings. *(smiling triumphantly)*

HENNYPEST Them I *am* visiting relatives—our relatives. *(pauses, then exiting)* I suppose I'll see you at the party.

TILLIE Me?? I never visit zoos.

DOLLY He means Cobina's party tonight.

TILLIE *(to* HENNYPEST *with disbelief)* *You'll* be at the party?

HENNYPEST Yes, Madame, do save a dance for me.

TILLIE I'm not good at dancing.

HENNYPEST You'll be good with me. Just hold tight and let me lead.

TILLIE Hold tight? I'm allergic to bay windows.

HENNYPEST Then we'll just hold hands.

TILLIE Holding hands with strange men makes me nervous.

HENNYPEST I'll have my tranquilizer.

TILLIE I have an aversion to tranquilizers.

HENNYPEST How do you relax, Madame?

TILLIE *(conclusively)* Through meditation; *very private and personal!* Any companionship there would provoke a saint!

HENNYPEST *(crossing to foyer, pauses)* Amen, Madame. Perhaps at benediction you'll join me in prayer. *(stumbles, smiles apologetically, turns up his nose and exits left)*

DOLLY I find him so amusing.

TILLIE *(somewhat miffed)* More of a peasant than a professor. Unbutton his vest and the whole man will tumble out.

DOLLY Well, he is a heavy eater—

TILLIE And a heavyweight nuisance!

SOPHIE *(entering with tea on tray, tarries on stairs)* Come and get it.

DOLLY Right here, dear.

SOPHIE Lord, today!

(She reluctantly places the tray on the coffee table, then pours a cup. As TILLIE *reaches for the cup, thinking it is for her,* SOPHIE *gobbles down a drink and exits nonchalantly as the two ladies sit dumbfounded)*

TILLIE Well—I never!

DOLLY *(readying tea)* That girl! That girl! She's like driving a car. When I see the red in her eyes, I jam on the brakes.

TILLIE As long as there's one ounce of vitamin "I" in your face, they will insult us.

DOLLY Vitamin "I"?

TILLIE Ink, Dolly, ink. *(touching her face—colorwise)*

DOLLY Tillie, you are a scream. *(serving tea, airishly)*

TILLIE By the way, Dolly. Why don't you move out to Brooklyn? Harlem has gotten to be such a cesspool of nobodies. *(sipping, equally airishly)*

DOLLY Oh, I'm holding my ground on Strivers Row.

TILLIE Why the hoi polloi has invaded and ruined Harlem.

DOLLY *(defensively)* True, we all live in the same area, but we don't travel in the same circle.

TILLIE You may, but what about Cobina?

DOLLY My daughter never associates with anyone without my approval. *(both sipping à la grande dames)*

TILLIE Then what was she doing at the benefit party at the Savoy Ballroom last week—slumming?

DOLLY I tell you, we did not participate. I purchased tickets, but when I found out the affair was unrestricted, I gave my tickets to the grocery boy.

TILLIE I could have sworn I saw that child with some moonfaced boy—looking as brown and broke as Haile Selassie.

DOLLY And what were *you* doing there?

TILLIE Only to cover the event for my newspaper. My social reporter was ill because she didn't want to become a mother. But her ordeal was nothing compared to those nobodies. That awful Dr. Davis swung me around doing the Atomic Flop. *(dramatizes Atomic Flop)*

DOLLY Oh—you're too rigid.

TILLIE Will he be here tonight?

DOLLY Of course, he and his wife.

TILLIE I'll join you for a headache when they arrive.

DOLLY Listen, I'm having a debutante party—not a jamboree.

TILLIE If it's all you say it will be, then I'll carry it in the front page of the *Black Dispatch* next week.

DOLLY *(annoyed)* Which will be far better than this week's headline—"Three in Bed Causes Divorce."

TILLIE People like dirt—and I believe in digging deep into it for them.

DOLLY You should elevate their readership.

TILLIE What else is there to print besides news about these charitable affairs! If someone is born, marries, or dies, he's given a benefit. Only other event is news about the antics of these dizzy debs.

DOLLY Charity is for the devil's poor. Society is for God's chosen few. Debs do silly things, mixing society and charity. But they aren't half as bad as these roué widows clinging to these chippy boys.

TILLIE *(strangling)* Er—er—well a modern woman must have an escort.

DOLLY Be thankful that you still have your reputation.

TILLIE Reputation is only what your worst enemy thinks!

(The doorbell rings. DOLLY *rises)*

DOLLY True—true—*(calling)* Sophie—Sophie—the door—Sophie . . . *(she hides her limp as she walks toward the hall door)*

TILLIE Down there drunk, I bet.

SOPHIE *(passing down the hall)* I ain't gonna have that. *(going toward arch door)* I'm comin! Keep your boots laced. *(the bell rings again)*

DOLLY Hurry—hurry.

SOPHIE *(exits)* Plague take it!

DOLLY Hurry—hurry.

TILLIE *(having peeped at the pad)* I see you've invited old Tyler Beecher, the old robust beer barrel. He squeezes so hard, it causes my stockings to run.

DOLLY But he's gentle and nice.

TILLIE The man isn't wood!

DOLLY All men like to go on a little spree. But they always come back.

TILLIE Yes, slightly soiled.

SOPHIE *(in the door)* A boy is heah—wanna know if you got any work he kin do.

TILLIE *(incredulously)* A boy looking for work!

DOLLY No snow outside. The windows are cleaned. No, I guess not, dear. *(trying to think of something)*

SOPHIE He's a nice boy.

DOLLY Tell him Father Divine has a Sunday School in the next block.

SOPHIE The back parlor needs waxing.

DOLLY Haven't you done that yet?

SOPHIE I ain't getting down on these knees. He tole me not to git no cones on 'em.

DOLLY All right, show him down to the kitchen—

SOPHIE Now you talking—come on, Sonny.

TILLIE *(informatively)* Dolly—is he trustworthy?

DOLLY *(excitedly)* Sophie—

SOPHIE I know—come, Sonny.

*(*CHUCK *enters through arch door. A bashful boy about twenty, he walks in timidly. He fingers a crushed hat in his hands. His clothes are aged but clean.* TILLIE*'s haughty manner frightens him. He steps behind the sofa)*

SOPHIE Meet the *dark* Daughters of the American Revolution.

DOLLY Sophie!

CHUCK *(anxiously)* I'll do anything, Miss. Fire the furnace—

DOLLY Have you any reference?

CHUCK Yessum! U.S. Government Conservation Agency, stocking ponds with baby fish.

TILLIE A fish planter!

CHUCK Then I went into the army—

DOLLY *(to* CHUCK*)* Oh a war veteran—a real hero. *(to* TILLIE*)*

CHUCK Not exactly. I was stationed on Marshall Island where the biggest battle I had was with the gallinippers.

TILLIE I suppose you slew them.

CHUCK Yessum—by the hundreds.

DOLLY *(seriously)* Oh you are a real hero, killing hundreds of gallinippers.

TILLIE Ts-sk! Yes, with a spray.

DOLLY I guess he'll do, Tillie.

SOPHIE *(to* DOLLY*)* After all who's paying him—if he gets paid.

CHUCK I'll work for whatever you're willing to pay.

TILLIE Unbelievably generous! Was Bellevue one pond where you planted fish?

CHUCK Ma'am?

SOPHIE Somebody got to wax the floors.

DOLLY Yes—yes—*(to* CHUCK*)* Do a good job now.

CHUCK Yessum. I sure will. Thank you, Ma'am.

SOPHIE Pick up your cross and follow me.

*(*SOPHIE *and* CHUCK *exit through hall door)*

DOLLY He is safe, I hope.

TILLIE Looked pretty anxious to get in.

DOLLY But his face, did you notice that round and handsome face?

TILLIE Humph! Plain as the Ethiopian moon! Where is Rowena? She said she would be here in ten minutes. *(rising—observing her wristwatch)* I must go.

DOLLY *(moving tray to table near steps)* Now you have plenty of time—no need to whiz off.

TILLIE I have a meeting at the YWCA. The Ad Hoc Committee for Retarded Prostitutes is meeting. First, I must pick up Rowena.

DOLLY Where did Rowena stop?

TILLIE At Brenda's. Just had to chat with her. Brenda married Ben, you know.

DOLLY *(surprised)* No—clever girl indeed.

TILLIE In spite of those knock-knees, too. She snatched him right out from under Cobina, eh?

DOLLY *(indifferently)* Who cares? He's too old for her anyway.

TILLIE *(moving close to* DOLLY*)* Will you tell me just whom are you landing for Cobina?

DOLLY *(laughing)* I knew at the time you popped in here, that's what you were after. *(*TILLIE *sitting next to her)* Well, there's Charlie—

TILLIE *(scoffing)* Some deb is always on his lap.

DOLLY Yes, but not on his mind. Then there's Roy Tomkinson.

TILLIE *(derisively)* The C.P.A.! He's a constant pain in the tootsie.

DOLLY Mother doesn't like him anyway. There's Ed—

TILLIE Judge Tucker's son?

DOLLY *(brightening)* Yes—now, he—

TILLIE But I thought—that is—oh, he is real quality.

DOLLY Then there is—

TILLIE Judge Tucker said—

DOLLY What?

TILLIE Well—I heard that Ed is out for someone else.

DOLLY That's ridiculous. He's been here every night during Cobina's vacation from school.

TILLIE Every night?

DOLLY At least every other night. Harlem sees him plenty.

TILLIE No doubt slumming! Brooklyn girls are his favorites!

DOLLY *(mounting indignation)* I bet you right now, he is down there in Central Park, horseback riding with Cobina.

TILLIE He takes Rowena to the formal dances.

DOLLY Is that so? He never mentions her. He avoids her—

TILLIE Only occasionally because of her bright mind.

DOLLY *(rising)* Bright? That's an inflated statement! *(walking toward the window)*

TILLIE Cobina is cute as a button, but Ed doesn't like buttons.

DOLLY *(turning)* You'll need more than that *Black Dispatch* to make him your nephew!

TILLIE I didn't say that. My niece will choose whom she pleases—

DOLLY You said enough! *(coming D.C. thundering as* TILLIE *backs away)* You've been running all up and down Strivers Row trying to find out who—

*(*COBINA *comes stamping into the room through the arch door. She is followed by* MRS. PACE *and* OSCAR VAN STRIVEN. OSCAR *stops confused at the door.* MRS. PACE *follows* COBINA *to the upper end of the sofa.* COBINA *is eighteen, wears riding habit. She is bubbling over with rage. Crossing* DOLLY *without saying a word, she stops next to the chair extreme left and flings her coat in it)*

COBINA Oh, let me alone!

DOLLY *(going to* COBINA*)* Have you no manners?

COBINA *(boisterously)* I checked them in the hall!

*(*MRS. PACE, *a very cold and stately woman of sixty, stares at* COBINA. *She is extremely correct in her costume. Her mixed gray hair gives her an air of distinction. She wears a tailored winter suit with a cape. Her mouth is a thin line of depression. The little furrow in her forehead, her black eyes piercing from underneath her brows, one usually cocked, have a disarming effect. People say her eyebrows are optical wings of social deportment)*

MRS. PACE Stop wobbling! Stop swagging like a bag of wet dough. The idea! *(to* TILLIE*)* Hello, Petunia!

*(*OSCAR *is a businesslike man about forty-five years of age. Though he speaks with absolute sincerity, his mind seems to be somewhere else. Acknowledges* TILLIE*'s presence by nodding)*

OSCAR She was slouching against a lamp post on the corner of 133rd Street and Lenox Avenue!

TILLIE What kind of horse riding is that? *(slyly)* Do—tell—I never!

DOLLY Cobina, what about the horse you phoned for?

MRS. PACE *(walks down left)* The horse didn't answer the phone!

OSCAR *(to* COBINA*)* I have asked you to explain.

COBINA *(turning in wrath)* Let me alone!

MRS. PACE *(fiercely)* Waiting for someone on that corner.

OSCAR A pack of noisy brats, winking at you.

COBINA They were playground kids.

MRS. PACE What time was the strip tease to begin?

OSCAR *(moves left to* COBINA*)* I won't have it. You know I won't. I will pack you up and drive you back to Radcliffe, before you can bat your eye. Whom were you waiting for, I ask you?

MRS. PACE In Washington, you would be positively disgraced.

TILLIE *(chirping)* And in Brook—

MRS. PACE Yes, Brooklyn. I know, Tillie. What are you doing here, digging up dirt before the party begins?

TILLIE Why, Mrs. Pace.

DOLLY *(to* COBINA*)* If it weren't for your party tonight, I would—

COBINA I told you I didn't want any party.

MRS. PACE Stop twisting! All my efforts wasted. When will you learn poise?

COBINA I don't give a hoot about phonies and stuffed shirts—

DOLLY *(shakes pad in* COBINA*'s face)* Don't speak like that about my guests, child.

COBINA I'm not a child. I'm now eighteen.

DOLLY Well, ex-child. Only my funeral could stop this party.

COBINA Is it my party or your coronation? *(waving)*

MRS. PACE Keep your hands still. I ought to have you in Washington.

OSCAR We're going to settle this thing . . .

COBINA *(verging on tears)* Daddy—

MRS. PACE Stop taxing your face! You'll look like a hag tonight.

COBINA *(plaintively)* I am unhappy. I'd rather spend my birthday in bed. Who needs to be stuck in a receiving line to meet a bunch of phony bolonies. Society, my foot! They've all just escaped from poverty and spend their time gossiping against being overtaken. I didn't ask to be born into society. I didn't even ask to be born!

OSCAR *(disgustedly)* Radcliffe!

MRS. PACE I told you to send her to me in Washington. Why, there—

TILLIE *(beaming)* This is Harlem, Mrs. Pace.

MRS. PACE I can smell it.

TILLIE You can't raise a rose in a junkyard.

MRS. PACE Is the fertilizer of Brooklyn any different?

COBINA *(crossing to* OSCAR*)* Dad, please cancel it. You know you don't care for all this social nonsense.

OSCAR Go to your room at once!

*(*COBINA *exits center à la waddling duck)*

MRS. PACE Stop walking like a duck! I shall put a prop behind you tonight. *(following the exiting* COBINA*)* Don't bend your knees. *(offstage)* Curve them in line with your body. You ought to stay off horses. Let go that balustrade! *(offstage, a tumbling noise)* Look out!

DOLLY *(exiting, followed by* OSCAR*)* Oh!

COBINA *(offstage)* Make her stop shouting at me!

*(*TILLIE *grabs pad from table, studies it religiously)*

MRS. PACE *(offstage)* Please! Please!

COBINA *(offstage)* No, I'm not hurt!

DOLLY *(offstage)* Thank God, she isn't hurt.

MRS. PACE *(offstage)* She fell with the grace of a feeble cow.

TILLIE *(has returned pad to table as* DOLLY *returns)* Dear Mrs. Pace, so completely put out. *(*TILLIE *is leaving, but hesitates)*

DOLLY *(reassuringly)* Mother will make a lady out of her yet.

TILLIE Perhaps through hypnosis.

DOLLY *(arms* TILLIE*, nudging her exit)* You aren't going?

TILLIE Yes, dear, I must. And have I got a story! Tell Rowena to meet me at the YWCA. The meeting has certainly started—

OSCAR *(entering)* Mrs. Petunia, wait a minute, please.

TILLIE *(led forward by* OSCAR*)* Of course, Oscar.

DOLLY *(skeptically, moving up)* What is it, Oscar?

OSCAR *(heavily)* Something I must tell you. I know you will need Mrs. Petunia's advice.

DOLLY *(crossing, turning* TILLIE *to leave)* Tillie has an engagement, Oscar.

TILLIE *(unyieldingly)* Oh, but Dolly—Oscar looks so grave.

DOLLY *(softly)* That's what I'm afraid of. What is it, Oscar?

OSCAR You know those lots, the Jamaica lots?

DOLLY Do I—with them on our hands for five years?

TILLIE Your property near the city dump?

OSCAR *(smiling)* Yes—that is—yes.

DOLLY What about it?

OSCAR I have a buyer for them.

DOLLY *(a smile brightens her face)* You don't say. Oscar, I—

TILLIE *(carelessly, disappointed)* Do tell!

DOLLY *(happily)* I told you all we had to do was wait. It is a miracle. *(talking to* TILLIE*)*

OSCAR A lady is going to build a twelve-room house and develop a lawn, tennis courts, and swimming pool—

TILLIE *(eagerly)* This is news. Who?

OSCAR Miss Ruby Jackson.

TILLIE *(searchingly)* Jackson . . . Jackson? Not the insurance Jacksons? They went into bankruptcy after paying me my husband's premiums on his life insurance policy.

OSCAR This Jackson only came into money recently and—

DOLLY Recently, of course, then we wouldn't know her.

TILLIE Jackson—Jackson—wait, you mean the maid or cook who won a large sum of money from the sweepstakes?

OSCAR That's her.

DOLLY Why Oscar, that's nothing to be so tragic about. I think she is very wise. What a break for us!

TILLIE You hardly need my advice on that.

OSCAR Oh! I do—there is something else.

DOLLY *(lightly)* Now what could it be?

OSCAR Sure you won't get angry?

DOLLY Oscar, just like a child. No, dear.

OSCAR *(mildly)* She wants to meet society.

TILLIE *(sitting)* That's nothing. Tell her to join the Elks.

OSCAR I mean the razzle dazzle set.

DOLLY *(suspiciously)* So?

OSCAR *(in a humble manner)* I invited her—to Cobina's debut.

DOLLY *(swooning against the sofa, she is caught by* OSCAR*)* W-w-w-what!

TILLIE *(jumps up and runs to her)* Don't let her fall! Dolly, if you faint, I'll join you. *(they get her on the sofa)* You what?

DOLLY Are you crazy? What do you mean to make me, the laughingstock of the season? My daughter's debut—a sideshow for some ambitious scrub woman. Her eyes flaming with social suds!

OSCAR But, Dolly, just this once—I *must* I tell you. The woman is a first-class cook for a Forest Hills family. Her pies won prizes—

DOLLY A plain, common, shabby cook. How could you? That woman will not enter this house. I will not have her. Self-rising flour has inflated her brain. The woman is sick. Have her here! No! Most emphatically, NO! *(pounds the sofa three beats)*

OSCAR *(pleadingly)* It is business. She told me she only wants to get an introduction. She knows you can do it for her. She has read about you. That is all I need to clinch the deal. It won't hurt. You will introduce her, and then it will all be over.

DOLLY What am I, the promoter for some social striver? Tillie, tell him how silly it would be. Oh, for Pete's sake, I'm sick of this. *(stretching out on sofa)*

TILLIE *(unimpressively)* Now, Mr. Van Striven, there must be some other way.

DOLLY What will people say? The Smiths—the Davies—the Judge and— *(rising quickly)*

TILLIE *(clicking)* What will people say—er-er— *(exiting)* Dolly, I must be going. I must.

DOLLY I am afraid. I have planned—planned—and planned. *(thinking)*

OSCAR *(coming down to sofa)* Miss Jackson cannot do that much harm in one night.

DOLLY That's out. No sir! One moment of unwise benevolence can tear down a lifetime of prominence. You would dare mention this right to Tillie Petunia. That heckler, always trying to outshine me.

OSCAR I figured both of you would agree. Who could think of laughing with you and Tillie backing up Miss Jackson.

DOLLY *(resentfully crossing)* Tillie! Who do you think is the leading socialite in this neck of the woods? I need no one to help me say No! No! No! *(punctuates "NO" by tapping his chest)*

OSCAR I have invited her. She may bring a friend. I don't know what I can tell her now.

DOLLY Tell her it is off. Tell her anything. She *cannot* come here. That's that!

OSCAR *(angered)* I will not.

DOLLY *(stunned)* Oscar!

OSCAR I was hoping I wouldn't have to tell you this. But if that deal doesn't go through, if I don't sell Miss Jackson those lots, we will lose this house.

DOLLY *(irritated)* Now that wasn't very bright.

OSCAR Doubt it, huh? Well, notes on the mortgage have been mounting. They have not been paid for months. Slipping because I have not had the money.

DOLLY *(casually)* You have the money. You should have paid them. You keep reinvesting the profits.

OSCAR You guzzle the bulk of every dollar I make.

DOLLY Me?

OSCAR Yes you! Who must keep up with Tillie and the rest of those greenback burners. From one resort to another—Atlantic City, Saratoga, Martha's Vineyard—a roving band of gypsies cannot keep pace with you. Clothes, clothes, enough to supply the Ethiopian Army. Money, more money! Radcliffe itself, costing me a Scotch fortune! Where do you think it is coming from? I ain't Father Divine!

DOLLY *(to* OSCAR*)* You are exaggerating. *(quickly)*

OSCAR I most certainly am. This party, almost two thousand dollars. More gowns, band—liquor for a bunch of beer drinkers. I got to pay for it. All this for you. Yet you accuse me of throwing—*(spots the vacancy sign—blasting)* and that sign! (DOLLY *jumps)* I told you to keep that sign in the window. How can I rent those rooms upstairs? I have to have some money. I told you. What do you reserve them for—guests? Guests who don't pay. (DOLLY *moves toward the sofa)* I'll show you, I will put a turnstile to the third floor, and your guests will have to drop a silver dollar in it before they go up there and pile on one of those idle beds.

DOLLY Oscar, my friends!

OSCAR *(his voice rises, forcefully)* Shut up! Your vanity has run me into a hole. Your vanity is going to pull me out or it'll crack like the walls of Jericho. (MRS. PACE *enters from hall. She stares at* OSCAR *like he is a raging maniac)* You shall pave the way for Miss Jackson or move into the Harlem River Flats—and like it—the F.H.A. is doing all the real estate business, anyway.

MRS. PACE *(huffing)* What in the devil is this? (OSCAR *stares at her disgustedly)*

DOLLY *(goes pleading to* MRS. PACE, *who is now in front of the sofa.* OSCAR *moves over to the vase of flowers)* Mother—Oscar invited a cook to the party. *(childlike)*

MRS. PACE *(adroitly)* The caterer has already—

SOPHIE *(enters through arch door)* I need some more money for— *(freezes, then edges to the right as* OSCAR *gives her a mean look)*

DOLLY *(helplessly)* Not to cook, but as a guest. He says it is business.

(SOPHIE, *feeling the tension, works her way around to the chair facing the sofa)*

MRS. PACE *(her lips tighten. Her brow cocks. The words flow fast and tingling)* Business! The mantle with which a man can cover his vices as well as his virtues. Business, a concealing, conniving word!

DOLLY I will have to accept her. *(tearfully)*

MRS. PACE Some silly, stupid striver!

DOLLY What shall I do?

MRS. PACE *(tilting her chin)* Pray, if you know how. *(turning)* Sophie, pack my bag! I am going to Washington!

(DOLLY *opens her mouth to speak.* SOPHIE *looks puzzled.* MRS. PACE *stands rigid and firm.* OSCAR *blasts)*

OSCAR Sit down!

MRS. PACE *(stepping up to* OSCAR*)* To whom are you talking?

OSCAR Sit down!

(As if he had jerked a string that held them up, MRS. PACE *and* DOLLY *flop on the sofa.* SOPHIE *flops in the chair.* OSCAR *towers over them. They sit frightened, stiff as dummies. Curtain)*

Scene 2

(It is evening. The reception room is warm and cozy. The soft lights and vases of cut flowers in abundance add luster to the room. Soft music from an orchestra in the back parlor trails in. At the rise of the curtain, SOPHIE, *in a more frilly cap and apron, moves about adding another flower from her arm to the several vases, counting each placement.)*

SOPHIE One hundred and seventeen, one hundred and eighteen, one—

CHUCK *(appearing from left foyer, wearing a short white waiter's jacket armed with flowers and a covered bird cage)* Sophie, who is Fred?

SOPHIE What's that?

CHUCK Over and over, this parrot's been saying, "Hey, Fred, drop dead."

SOPHIE *(continuing her placements)* You do look a lot like Fred, but you don't have his dull disposition.

CHUCK *(leaving cage, he crosses and bows)* Thank you, Your Grace.

SOPHIE *(twirls around, freezes into a pose and curtsies)* You are welcome, Sir Chuck.

CHUCK See you later. *(exiting, resuming the cage)*

SOPHIE Where are you going?

CHUCK *(stalling)* To the garbage can.

SOPHIE Getting into the trash can is your affair, but the flowers?

CHUCK Mrs. Van Striven ordered me to remove them from the den and discard them.

SOPHIE *(stopping her chores)* Wait a minute! No complaint's been filed with me. *(crosses, inspecting* CHUCK's *flowers)*

CHUCK I must get fresh ones from the florist. I have to hurry before it closes.

SOPHIE I see nothing wrong with these flowers.

CHUCK The rejection comes not from sight, but from smell.

SOPHIE *(after a whiff)* They do have the strangest stink!

CHUCK The parrot vomited on them.

SOPHIE *(lifting the cage cover)* Why, you feather-faced bonehead!

CHUCK She's asleep. According to Mrs. Van Striven, she'll sleep as long as her cage is covered.

SOPHIE Asleep, my foot! She's drunk!

PARROT *(well, her voice, anyway)* Hey Fred, drop dead! QQQUUUUAAAARRRRKKKK!

CHUCK She's had much more than a swig of whiskey.

SOPHIE Not whiskey! I gave her *gin.*

CHUCK Why?

SOPHIE She hates flowers! Whenever flowers get more attention than her, she squawks, scratches, and bites them. Gin usually calms her down. This time—with such a flower overload—instead of protesting, she just puked!

CHUCK For the duration of the party, she is now confined to the cellar.

SOPHIE That's too doggone much. Covering her cage is enough. Place her in my room.

CHUCK Won't Mrs. Van Striven—

SOPHIE In *my* room! I got the only pad in the house that's without two or three dozen roses making faces at you.

CHUCK As you say, Madame. *(leaving)*

SOPHIE And don't go buy no more flowers. We can't afford them. *(*CHUCK *stops)* Lord! You should have heard Papa Van Striven this morning, blasting the budget.

CHUCK I heard him.

SOPHIE *(suspiciously)* Nothing seems to get past you. What is your story anyway?

CHUCK *(impulsively drops the cage)* Can I trust you?

PARROT *(reacting to the drop, loudly)* HEY, FRED, DROP DEAD! HEY, FRED, DROP DEAD!!!

SOPHIE *(topping him)* Get him out of here before he wakes up the dead! *(the* PARROT *continues as* CHUCK *grabs the cage and exits foyer left as the* PARROT's *voice trails off)* A bird in hand is worth two in the bush. A parrot in your fist, twist and don't miss. *(resumes placing cut flowers, pauses, trying to recall her count)* One hundred and—one hundred and—oh, what the hell! *(jams the remaining flowers into a vase already loaded)* Two hundred!

HENNYPEST *(appears in foyer, from left, dressed in a tuxedo and focusing his camera on* SOPHIE*)* Focus, please.

SOPHIE *(with a rose, she strikes a Statue of Liberty pose)* Cheeze. *(he snaps)* You should be sick of taking my picture by now.

HENNYPEST I photograph my wife every day—

SOPHIE and HENNYPEST *(this is old hat)* "You remind me of her."

HENNYPEST You'll even perform like her if you'll assist me. My cummerbund is shrinking.

SOPHIE *(missing it)* Your—

HENNYPEST *(from pocket, he reveals his cummerbund)* Here, Sophie—

SOPHIE Oh—your vest! Looking like your wife and *acting* in her place is two— *(she gets it on him but not with ease)* Different things!

HENNYPEST *(innocently)* Why, Sophie—

OSCAR *(offstage)* Forward, MARCH! One, two, three, four—*(in a single-file line, the family marches in, led by* COBINA*. They stop center awaiting orders from the commanding* OSCAR*)* One, two, three, HALT! It may not be the grand march of the ball, but it will do. Take your positions. At ease!

(Yes, HENNYPEST *snaps the family, gestures approvingly, and exits right. They form a receiving line at a right angle to the arch doorway so that* OSCAR *will be the first to greet the guests.* DOLLY *second, and* COBINA *third.* MRS. PACE *is opposite of them, sustaining a detachment. They are most properly dressed in evening clothes and jewelry.* COBINA *wears the traditional deb white and holds a bouquet of flowers in her hands.* DOLLY*, her feet hurting and no guests having arrived, poses uncomfortably.* OSCAR *and* MRS. PACE *exchange an-*

gry glances. SOPHIE *gives a last-minute touch to the flowers.*

DOLLY If I ever get out of this alive, I shall never stop thanking God.

MRS. PACE Nobody ever gives God a thought except for about a half-hour on Sundays and fifteen minutes prior to their demise.

OSCAR It is nine-fifteen. Where are the people?

MRS. PACE If anybody shows up besides this Miss Jackson, we're lucky. *(the music grows softer)*

DOLLY I wish I could be calm. Mother, if you just hadn't insisted on this debut.

MRS. PACE You should have been calm when you married that. Matchmaking is as old as the hills. My mother's husband was picked. Mine was picked. You became restless and picked that thing out of the woodpile!

OSCAR There is nothing wrong with my family.

MRS. PACE Just the one idiot on your father's side.

*(*DOLLY *goes to the window)*

COBINA Stop worrying, Mother.

MRS. PACE *(crossing, correcting bouquet)* Cobina, hold that bouquet exactly sixteen inches below the chin. NOW KEEP IT THERE. *(returning to her post)*

SOPHIE *(swaying with sudden inspiration)* Joe brought me some flowers once.

COBINA Were they orchids?

SOPHIE Naw—honeysuckles.

MRS. PACE This is no time to discuss flowers with servants!

SOPHIE Did anybody ever bring you any flowers?

MRS. PACE Be quiet! I was showered with flowers?

SOPHIE What, poison ivy?

COBINA *(seeing* CHUCK *was in the hall)* Chu—Chu—

MRS. PACE What's wrong with you, Cobina? It's only the boy hired to serve.

COBINA *(sneezing, faking)* Awchu—awchu—was just sneezing.

DOLLY *(returning from the window)* Not a single car out there. The Van Strivens entertaining and not a block of cars.

MRS. PACE Cobina, stop twisting your neck! You are not a turtle! What are *you* limping for?

DOLLY I'm walking all right.

MRS. PACE You ever see a three-legged bear in a swamp?

DOLLY My foot hurts.

MRS. PACE Wait until the misery climbs up. You will have plenty time to complain then. *(the doorbell rings)* Someone's coming!

DOLLY *(rushes up to the window)* I bet it's a Packard. No, it's just a cut-rate cab.

*(*SOPHIE *goes through arch door)*

MRS. PACE In line, Dolly.

OSCAR *(to* MRS. PACE*)* Will you relax?

MRS. PACE *(whispering quickly)* Remember, Cobina, shoulders kept straight, with all movements from the waist down. Swaying the hips is not permissible. So don't jiggle them like your mother.

(The VAN STRIVENS *are ready)*

LILY *(offstage)* My dear Sophie, am I late?

SOPHIE Naw, chile, you is first. I was gitting scared nobody was coming.

LILY *(sweeps into the room like a breeze. She is somewhere between twenty and thirty, exotic and glamorous in a sort of theatrical way with hair in an upsweep. She speaks in a deep-throated voice, soft and warm)* Cobina! My child, how perfectly sweet!

*(*COBINA *smiles and curtsies in her best manner.* LILY *kisses* COBINA, SOPHIE *waits at the door.* OSCAR *bows)*

LILY Mr. and Mrs. Van Striven, how do you do? *(tapping the* VAN STRIVENS' *palms lightly)*

DOLLY *(raising her elbows)* Hello, Lily—we are glad you came.

OSCAR Indeed we are. Miss Livingston—you are more pretty than ever.

LILY Regardless how bad we women may look in the morning, Oscar, we never wake up needing a shave.

*(*OSCAR *laughs)*

MRS. PACE Hello, Lily.

LILY *(swaying from* DOLLY *across the floor)* Mrs. Pace, how charming. Everything is so exquisite. Cobina, just like a bride. Aren't you happy?

MRS. PACE *(batting her eyes rapidly)* Indeed, Lily—and you are on time as usual.

LILY *(she holds a pose, exactly like a dancer from the court of King Tut)* How could I ever miss this party! Late, no such word in the theater. Punctuality, darling, punctuality! *(*SOPHIE *has moved in.* LILY *locks her fingers underneath her chin and sways about the room)* What a paradise! Mrs. Pace, the most charming flower in this whole Garden of Eden.

MRS. PACE Oh—Lily, a Harlem garden, but a garden just the same.

LILY Exactly like the last scene in "Gal of Charleston"—the ideal home, the perfect family, and the maid—

DOLLY Now, Lily, you will spoil Sophie. Take her wrap, Sophie.

SOPHIE If she ever stops fluttering like a butterfly.

LILY My wrap—eh—yes, take it, Sophie.

*(*LILY*'s gown is a low-back affair with two panels attached to her shoulders. They beat and fan the air)*

SOPHIE What a pretty frock! Where'd you git it?

LILY Fifth Avenue.

SOPHIE Ain't it gorgeous? Mine is like that.

LILY Sophie—

LILY Have no fear. I know Sophie. It comes from Lord and Taylor's.

SOPHIE Mine came from Lord and Numbers.

LILY Really?

*(*DOLLY *nudges* SOPHIE*)*

SOPHIE I prayed to the Lord that night before I got it. He gimmie the figuh in my dream. Next day I went right down an bought that frock and—

DOLLY *(shoving* SOPHIE*)* I know you want to powder up a bit, Lily. What would a party be without you?

LILY *(exiting with* DOLLY*)* Me miss this! Not for the world—Dolly, you are limping!

DOLLY *(bracing)* Rheumatism, darling— *(exits with* LILY *via arch)*

SOPHIE *(examining the wrap)* Ain't this elegant?

MRS. PACE *(harshly)* You get out of here!

SOPHIE Lay it on me, Mr. Striven. Lay it on me!

OSCAR If you persist in addressing the guests, I'll deduct a fine from your salary.

SOPHIE *(sincerely)* My dough? I'm leaving.

MRS. PACE Get down in the kitchen with the skillets where you belong! Such decorum for a maid. Why, in Washington—

OSCAR Never mind, Mother.

MRS. PACE Why don't you make that maid stay in her place? You addressed like that—get below!

OSCAR Take the wrap to the ladies lounge, Sophie. And you had better stay down on the floor below.

SOPHIE *(going toward the arch door)* All right. I'm leaving tomorrow. *(exits)*

COBINA She means it, too.

MRS. PACE Good riddance.

(The orchestra plays)

OSCAR *(direct)* This party is costing me too much to have it spoiled by you. I shall do my best to stay out of your way the remainder of the evening.

MRS. PACE Good!

OSCAR Do me a favor?

MRS. PACE *(coming center)* I make no promise, but what is it?

OSCAR The ribbon around your neck is loose. Tighten it.

MRS. PACE *(reaching the back of her neck)* It's—It's not loose.

OSCAR Yes, yes, I know, I know. *(exits left)*

MRS. PACE *(dawning, then violently)* Why you insulting Jackson—you *(exits after* OSCAR*)*

COBINA *(laying flowers on the table)* I'll be glad when this party is over.

CHUCK *(peeping in from the arch door)* Cobina!

COBINA *(happily, surprised)* Chuck!

CHUCK *(they go toward each other)* Honey!

SOPHIE *(passing in the hall, interrupts)* Hey now!

*(*CHUCK *and* COBINA *stand wanting but frightened)*

CHUCK Oh she knows, honey—she knows.

SOPHIE Umm hmm.

COBINA You won't tell, Sophie.

SOPHIE Who me—gwan girlie. *(winks and exits left)*

COBINA Oh Chuck! Darling! You scared me nearly to death, when you passed in the hall. Why didn't you warn me?

CHUCK *(whispering)* I tried to. I had to come. I couldn't take a chance.

COBINA But Mother and Grandmother—Chuck, you shouldn't have come.

CHUCK Oh they think I just came to do some work. Darling, I missed you on the corner, this morning I came here—I—

COBINA Dad came along in the car, he and Granny. They brought me home. What happened?

CHUCK I went downtown to see about a job.

COBINA You get it?

CHUCK No—and after making me wait an hour. I came back up to our meeting place. No sign of you. I said I was going to be right here, tonight. I made up a tale. I thought sure your mother wouldn't hire me. Sophie made her. Here I am. I am going to serve and see that none of those other guys get you, even Ed—

COBINA Oh, him—

CHUCK Yeah, has he come yet?

COBINA No.

CHUCK Well, give him your hand, but give me your kisses.

COBINA Not one, just to be formal?

CHUCK None. You don't want to, do you?

COBINA *(reluctantly)* I have once.

CHUCK Oh.

COBINA But kissing him is like scratching a place that doesn't itch.

CHUCK Try mine again. *(they kiss)*

COBINA Oh, Chuck—I'm afraid.

(Music swells)

CHUCK But, darling, this is your debut.

COBINA I don't want any debut. I want you.

CHUCK May I have the first dance? *(they dance)*

(The doorbell rings)

COBINA The door!

CHUCK *(dashing about)* Where's my tray?

COBINA *(excitedly)* You didn't have any. Hurry! Hurry!

(CHUCK exits through arch door. OSCAR enters from salon)

OSCAR You seem nervous.

(She gathers her bouquet. OSCAR goes to the door. MRS. PACE enters from the salon)

MRS. PACE Places! Where's Dolly? Where is—Soph—no, that boy? *(DOLLY enters from hall)* It is about time you got here.

DOLLY Oh—I hope it's Judge and Mrs. Tucker.

OSCAR *(offstage)* Well well well—Brooklyn at her best. Come right in, Ed.

(TILLIE enters the arch door, arm in arm with ROWENA. ED follows, talking in pantomime with OSCAR. TILLIE is well-gowned and jeweled. She wears a high-powered society smile. ROWENA is an attractive girl of nineteen or twenty, with a searching stare in her eyes. She's dressed with impeccable care. ED is a young man of about twenty-five. He wears full dress clothes and carries his top hat with a dash of urbanity. TILLIE speaks with a gloating suspicion)

TILLIE Cobina—Mrs. Van Striven—and of course, Mrs. Pace.

COBINA Hello, Rowena.

ROWENA Hello, Cobina. I know exactly how you feel. Shift into your half squat, child. Get high like I did, bow at nine, out at ten.

ED Cobina—what an angel you would make!

TILLIE Ed, how could you! Cobina wouldn't think of Father Divine. *(sitting on sofa)*

ED I didn't mean that— *(shaking hands with MRS. PACE)*

MRS. PACE We are pleased that you came.

ED Where there is a debut, you will always find Ed Tucker.

COBINA What will we debs do to ever win you, Ed?

ED Just trust in God and keep your powder dry.

TILLIE Isn't that cute? Ed has a brand of humor all of his own. Where there's life there's still hope, Cobina.

DOLLY *(to CHUCK)* Take their wraps. Chunk—I mean Chuck!

TILLIE Aren't you the porter who transplants fish?

CHUCK *(taking her coat)* Yes, Madame.

ED *(amused)* Well, porter, trot me out some trout!

CHUCK Right this way, please. *(CHUCK exits)*

ROWENA Auntie—isn't Cobina stunning?

TILLIE White is always pretty, Rowena. It does make one look so plain, like you were when you were confirmed.

OSCAR The bar is wide open, Ed.

ED Bar—you say—liquor.

OSCAR And how.

(The orchestra plays)

ED Liquor does different things to different people. But it only makes me drunk. *(teams up with* ROWENA*)*

ROWENA Whatever it does to you, it does twice as much to me. Oh sinner, lead me on. *(they tango a few steps and exit off left followed by* OSCAR*)*

*(*DOLLY *peeps out of the window)*

TILLIE Looking for someone, Dolly?

DOLLY *(coming down center)* I don't mind telling you, Tillie, I'm worried. The people, where are they?

TILLIE I don't know—I thought the place was packed by now. Where's Miss Jackson?

DOLLY Who knows—after all, you'll be rubbing elbows with her.

TILLIE There are times when we simply must condescend. If well-bred must rub elbows with the gutter-bred, where else should it be—but in Harlem.

DOLLY *(exiting into salon)* Sometimes, Tillie, I wonder how you and I manage to live on the same globe. *(exiting)*

TILLIE You're feeling all right, Mrs. Pace?

MRS. PACE *(frigidly)* Yes, Petunia, steaming like a kettle.

OSCAR *(enters)* Give your old dad the first dance, Cobina.

COBINA Certainly, Dad—*(they exit into salon)*

MRS. PACE *(moves to center)* I see you brought him.

TILLIE Oh—oh—and such a swell boy. Mrs. Tucker says every deb in New York is after him.

MRS. PACE Now that's tragic.

TILLIE Isn't it?

MRS. PACE Where are Judge and Mrs. Tucker?

TILLIE Ed said if they approve of a girl, they go to her debut! If not, they stay away, very cordially, of course. So far my niece's debut has been the only one they've attended. Now isn't that strange?

MRS. PACE You think you'll take him back?

TILLIE What do you mean?

MRS. PACE You know what I mean.

TILLIE That isn't a very friendly question.

MRS. PACE *(cuttingly)* I can tell my friends from my enemies by their emotional vibrations.

TILLIE Pray tell, what are mine?

MRS. PACE Positively negative.

LILY *(outside)* Come on now. *(*LILY *swings in from doorway left, dancing the "La Congo."* HENNYPEST, *in a tuxedo, attempts the difficult steps in following her)* That's it! Hello, Mrs. Petunia, look what I found.

HENNYPEST *(to* TILLIE*)* How do you do—this time?

TILLIE The same as I was this morning.

LILY *(dancing down center)* We are doing the La Congo!

TILLIE Bring him back alive!

HENNYPEST *(winking)* Even otherwise, Mrs. Petunia—I must have a dance with you.

TILLIE It will be a pleasure.

LILY *(stopping)* You're cute. As D.W. said, "Gal, this is a story of savage love. Feel the heathen in the part. Let yourself go. Let loose every limb." A-a-a-hh *(she and* HENNYPEST *glide off)*

TILLIE She took him right into her bosom.

MRS. PACE That's New York for you. Now, Washington

TILLIE *(quickly)* And Brooklyn—

MRS. PACE *(lecturing like)* In Boston, they say "Has he manners?" In Brooklyn, "How much money has he got?" And New York—they say "Let's take the sucker!"

TILLIE That may be true about New York, but Brooklyn—

MRS. PACE *(quickly)* Just a petticoat for New York's gaudy frock.

TILLIE *(rising)* You don't know Brooklyn—you never came over there.

MRS. PACE Oh, yes I do. I frequent it.

TILLIE To visit?

MRS. PACE Yes, my father's grave.

TILLIE There's something else in Brooklyn besides graveyards.

MRS. PACE Yes, churches.

TILLIE *(huffing)* Humph! *(exiting into salon)*

ROWENA *(passing from hall to veranda)* My, it's stuffy in here. How about some fresh air on the veranda, Aunt Tillie?

MRS. PACE *(cutting in)* Your aunt is full of air! All hot!

*(*ROWENA *exits to veranda. Bell rings)*

MRS. PACE Where's that boy?

OSCAR *(entering from salon)* I'll answer it.

LILY *(entering from hall)* This must be something real. Where is Cobina?

MRS. PACE She's with Ed.

DOLLY Oh! Cobina should be right here in the line.

MRS. PACE Never mind, she's got Ed cornered. It's you the one who's spoiling everything—with your silly manners.

OSCAR *(offstage)* Go right in, Leon!

MRS. PACE *(quickly)* Stop grinning. You'll scare the daylights out of them.

*(*LOUISE *and* LEON *enter. They are both in their thirties.* LOUISE *is the older of the two. Both wear evening clothes with taste.* LOUISE *may be a bit overdressed to compensate for her unattractiveness.* LEON'S *attraction to women is magnetic. His hands are unable to resist female contact.*

DOLLY *(very pretentious)* Dr. and Mrs. Davis, so glad you came. Louise, that coat, those lines.

LOUISE *(in a high-pitched irritated voice)* Good evening, Dolly.

DOLLY *(flattering)* You look like a dark-souled villainess. That coat!

LOUISE It ought to. It cost enough. *(*DOLLY *goes blank)*

MRS. PACE Dr. Davis, we were afraid you wouldn't get out of that old hospital.

LEON *(going over to* MRS. PACE*)* Couldn't keep me from this party. I do believe you are getting younger. *(*MRS. PACE *actually blushes)*

DOLLY *(scrutinizing* LOUISE'S *coat)* How do you do it, Leon?

LEON *(glancing at* DOLLY*)* What, Mrs. Van Striven?

DOLLY *(helplessly)* I'm so happy you came, I don't know what to say.

LEON *(smiling)* Anything you say is all right as long as it is accompanied with your lovely smile.

DOLLY *(befuddled)* Isn't he simply a darling? Where does he learn such lovely things?

LOUISE I wish I knew. The only times he says them things to me is in his sleep.

MRS. PACE Dolly is already gitting tipsy. Now you go and try to catch up.

LEON *(removing his coat)* Now you just wait for me, Van Striven. All these attractive ladies. Hmm, as I always say, women grow old from neglect and not from age, eh, Oscar?

OSCAR Oh yes—oh yes.

LOUISE That's why I love him so. Who else can phrase a lie so beautifully?

OSCAR Come on, Leon. I think I have what you need.

LOUISE *(nervously)* Any strange women down there?

DOLLY No, dear—

LOUISE He's safe then. Take my wrap. *(*LEON *reaches for it)* No, wait— *(searching her wrap)* Where is it? Where is my—here it is all right, darling. Take it now.

*(*LEON *exits with* OSCAR. LOUISE *reveals the objects, her refuge powder puff and lipstick, etc.)*

DOLLY *(coming down center)* Louise, I'm proud of the way your career and marriage succeeded.

LOUISE Under the circumstances, everything is so-so, except every week our names lead off the squabble column. That *Black Dispatch* prints it even if I just pinch the man.

DOLLY *(sits on the sofa)* Ignore it. One of these days I am going to sue that scandal sheet.

MRS. PACE *(sits in the chair facing the sofa)* Bravo. Now Dolly, let her enjoy herself.

LOUISE I always do at the Van Strivens'. Excuse me while I check this map I call a face. I surely have to watch out.

DOLLY You're looking like a peach.

LOUISE As long as there is a beauty parlor and a monthly check, I will feel well armed. I'm not giving up, though. He runs around, but after he gets through chasing Diana around the woods, he always comes back. If he should ever fail to come back—

DOLLY Divorce?

LOUISE Not as simple as that. *(with deep feeling)* Dolly, be sure Cobina marries a man older than herself. It is no fun to see a man grow robust and handsome while you fight like the very devil to sugarcoat the waning forties. Life begins at forty—huh! What a lie. Always there is just one affair after another. I can't make them. I just can't. They wear you down so. He never gets tired.

DOLLY There are plenty other affairs besides these strenuous dances, Louise.

LOUISE They're pretty much the same. Take the art exhibit night before last. A Bohemian atmosphere, they call it. All the guests piled up on Bloomstein's bargain pillows, smoking and drinking, low lights and shocking music.

MRS. PACE *(seconding)* A society pledged to primitive discipline.

DOLLY Then there are those endless ofay affairs!

LOUISE The whole of the village—ultra modern!

DOLLY So many of us prefer them.

LOUISE Yes, especially those that—pass.

MRS. PACE *(tactfully)* You can't escape God and Africa.

LOUISE Don't I know it! I will not attend another on Sugar Hill or anywheres else. Leon might as well let that soak through his plastered head. I get tired of straining my ears trying to hear what he is saying to some doll-faced model!

DOLLY You still have the upper hand. A doll face is a handicap. It distracts from the curves.

LEON *(enters from the hall)* There you are, my little sugar lump. Let's dance.

LOUISE *(rises)* No more liquor for you. *(taking his arm)*

LEON But I had no more than a thimble full. *(after a reproachful glare from her)* All right, my sweet, just as you say. *(*LEON *and* LOUISE *exit to left)*

MRS. PACE She loves the ground he staggers on.

DOLLY *(again at the window)* Three lousy cars! Look, mama, look! The neighbors are peeping at our house, the jealous Peeping Toms.

MRS. PACE And this is a Van Striven affair.

DOLLY Here I was afraid too many people would come, and instead there is hardly any at all.

MRS. PACE You sure they were received?

DOLLY Of course they were. Because they all responded in writing. The Tuckers—they all did. I knew something would happen. I told you this debut would not go over. I knew it. Maybe they think it will be too stiff. Oh, the devil, where is Oscar?

MRS. PACE Drowned in his martini.

ROWENA *(entering from veranda)* And whom may I ask do you wish such a fate?

MRS. PACE Oh, Rowena, why your fate will lead directly to the island, if you don't stop parading on the veranda without a coat.

ROWENA There's such a lovely breeze sweeping up the street.

MRS. PACE You will catch your death of cold in that thin dress.

ROWENA *(sitting on sofa)* It doesn't bother me. Winter or summer, I take my dip. I'm mad about the water. I just can't resist it. *(lights cigarette)* Aunt Tillie knows exactly where to find me when I'm missing. Out at the beach home on the sound.

MRS. PACE I imagine you have quite a time keeping up with her.

ROWENA In a way. Auntie gets about more than I do. Yesterday, she was in New Rochelle, Mt. Vernon, and then down to East Orange, all in the space of two short hours.

MRS. PACE *(sits in chair facing her)* She has an abundance of energy.

ROWENA And how! When she got home this afternoon, she had been to a dozen places, then phoned an army of people—

MRS. PACE *(carefully)* But weren't you with her this morning and the balance of the day?

ROWENA To keep up with that human rocket! No, I missed her at the trade building. Mind you, there only ten minutes and was gone. She travels like a gale of wind.

MRS. PACE *(nodding)* And she called a number of people?

ROWENA Oh yes, quick calls. All of them but Mrs. Tucker. She talked for hours—

MRS. PACE *(smelling a rat)* Mrs. Tucker?

ROWENA Yes, Ed's mother. *(*MRS. PACE *snaps her fingers)* Why, Mrs. Pace, you look so queer. What—

MRS. PACE *(rising)* Excuse me, Rowena.

ROWENA Must you go?

MRS. PACE I am going to do a bit of phoning myself.

ROWENA *(crossing to phone)* May I dial for you? I'd simply love to.

MRS. PACE *(going toward hall door)* That phone there is a little too public. The one upstairs is much more suitable for dishing dirt.

ROWENA See you later. *(thinking aloud)* I wonder what I said? *(wanders toward hall door)* Young man—I say, hey you—*(*CHUCK *enters nervously)* Well, if you don't mind. Pardon me for the interruption—

CHUCK I— I wasn't doing anything.

ROWENA *(walking down center coyly)* Oh, but you were. How can I spoil your moment of ecstasy. It was all about you like a veil.

CHUCK Is there something I can do for you, Miss?

ROWENA Do for me—oh yes—I would like for you to get a drink.

CHUCK Yes, Miss, what kind?

ROWENA Oh some of that bull shot.

CHUCK *(puzzled)* Bull—I ain't—I—that is—I'm working for Mr. Van Striven. Just for the party, you know. Nice gentleman, Mr. Van Striven.

ROWENA *(shrewdly)* And a nice daughter?

CHUCK What you mean, Miss—er—Cobina is a very beautiful, that is—

ROWENA Sweet?

CHUCK I think so. I guess so—

ROWENA You should know. I saw you kiss her.

CHUCK *(amazed)* You hadn't come. Where were you?

ROWENA Oh, tonight, too—dear, dear. I meant last Wednesday, the actors' benefit at the Savoy.

CHUCK *(seizing her)* Why—er—you—you didn't tell? You can't. You'll spoil everything. Please, Rowena, please! Please don't. Promise me? *(COBINA enters from the left)* Promise me! You must! You must!

COBINA *(dumbfounded)* Chuck!

(Doorbell rings)

CHUCK *(whirling around)* I was just—er—er—

COBINA *(she looks at ROWENA and bites her lip. The bell rings. She braces angrily)* The doorbell is ringing!

CHUCK *(pleadingly)* But Cobina, I can explain everything.

COBINA The doorbell is ringing!

(CHUCK rushes out into the hall)

ROWENA *(pointing)* Aha. I thought you were coming from the weekends just a little too often.

COBINA What are you talking about?

(OSCAR and DOLLY enter from salon)

ROWENA I understand, kiddo, as a servant he looks about as much at home as a bear in a penthouse.

(The orchestra plays)

DOLLY *(excitedly)* Where is your nosegay? Where is mother? Where is Sophie? Get set!

COBINA *(studying)* Were they kissing?

DOLLY What—who—where—who's kissing?

OSCAR *(booms)* Relax, for God's sakes!

CHUCK *(offstage)* Yes Ma'am, come right in, Ma'am.

(COBINA gets in line, breathlessly, after getting her nosegay. RUBY enters from arch door, happy and smiling. She is a woman of thirty-nine, dressed in an ostentatious outfit with a feather sticking straight up in her hair. She walks with an exaggerated restraint. Her mouth is filled with gold. She speaks anxiously and hopefully)

RUBY Good evening.

DOLLY *(opens her mouth, but is unable to speak. She is shocked. She sways slightly and catches herself again as OSCAR tries to smile with exasperation)* Good heavens!

COBINA *(curtsying)* How do you do?

OSCAR Miss Jackson—my wife, Mrs. Van Striven—my daughter, Cobina.

RUBY *(to COBINA, grinning)* Hello, baby. You're cute as a chorus girl. *(coming down center timidly)* You all can come on in, Beulah, I guess.

(BEULAH cuts in from the arch door, as if she has just finished the final step in the lindy hop. She is a loose swaying girl of twenty-two. She has a mass of curled hair, pigeon toes and a dissipating face. She wears a tight coat, split skirt, and a tam. She walks an arresting switch, with her hands stuck in her sides)

BEULAH Hi, everybody—the stuff is heah.

DOLLY *(gasping)* Pinch me, Cobina, am I breathing?

BEULAH Bring me a pint of gin and sixteen glasses. Ouch!

COBINA *(curtsying)* Glad you came.

BEULAH *(to COBINA)* I'm Beulah—whatcha squattin' foh?

(DOLLY starts forward. OSCAR restrains her)

COBINA It's the vogue.

BEULAH Thought you'd done got too tight under the belt.

DOLLY *(blasting)* Oscar!

OSCAR Yes, dear, of course. *(to RUBY)* Miss Jackson, after all—you understand that—

RUBY Shore, honey—I know, but Beulah and Joe fell in for a little snack an' I jus' had to bring 'em with me. It was that or I would have to stay away.

DOLLY You should have done the latter.

OSCAR *(with a saving grace)* We will go right in and rest your things.

(BEULAH moves in on OSCAR and squeezes his hand, flinging her fur piece in his arm)

BEULAH Rest the mink, papa. You an' me is gonna have heaps of fun. *(DOLLY steps in and gets a whiff of BEULAH's breath and stumbles back)* Just gin chile. *(laughing)* The old dame busted her kickers.

DOLLY Miss—please!

BEULAH *(shifting her weight)* I'm Beulah.

RUBY Yes mum, Mrs. Van Striven, that's my friend Beulah. Joe's comin—

DOLLY *(angrily)* So what?

BEULAH So I'm Beulah!

OSCAR *(going toward hall door)* This way, please.

BEULAH *(shouting)* Wait for Joe!

(JOE is heard entering offstage. Music fades)

JOE *(offstage)* Scram, Sam. Get lost! You nickel snatching taxi driver!

(JOE enters archway from right. He is about twenty-five. A man about town, anyway a man about certain towns, or if you will, certain parts of all towns. His associates call him a "hepped cat." Togged out in a draped coat that pinches in shapely at the waist and then blossoms about his hips and ends with a snazzy flare. His britches stand way up about under his arm pits and are hitched even higher by his gaudy braces over the shoulders. His pants peg down to the top of his shoes, ballooning a bit at the knees. His hat of a Tyrolean version shades his features in the best tin-horn gangster manner. He speaks to CHUCK behind him)

JOE Hi, folks, I'm Joe the Jiver. *(freezes, posing the hep cat's stance—his arms down, his fists tight, his forefingers pointing outward from the sides)*

OSCAR That's er—er—Joe—Joe—

JOE *(bending and bracing up, he is all over the room in a showoff manner)* What a dommy from pistromy. Dig the layout. It's a solid killer from maniller. Get off that pillar.

RUBY *(tickled high-pitched laughter)* Joe keeps me laffing all the time.

BEULAH Fall in, Joe. The joint is jumping.

COBINA *(curtsying)* How are you?

(DOLLY yanks COBINA backward)

JOE *(to COBINA)* Lamp the chick. Mellow as a chellow. She lays that thing. Same as I was a king.

OSCAR *(indignantly)* That's my daughter.

JOE Dig pop's gait sharp as a tack, hard as a nail. Them powerful tails dangle like a whale. *(OSCAR walks away)* Some vine, pop. Dig mine. *(lifting the lapels of his coat)*

DOLLY Mr.—

JOE Smothers, Joe Smothers!

DOLLY As this is a formal affair—

JOE *(advances on DOLLY, she walks away, half frightened)* Don't play cheap, I ain't no bo peep. Let me get you straight. 'Fore it is too late. I'm here to stay, so on your way. *(turning away from her)* That chick comes on like an Eskimo.

DOLLY *(hatefully)* I would like to speak to you alone!

JOE Come 'round any day but Thursdays. That's when sud-busters git their pay. I'll 'spect you around. So don't let me down. I'll lay some spiel that'll bust your heel!

OSCAR *(with an effort)* Mr. Smothers, you'll find the bar downstairs. I'm sure you are more interested in that!

JOE *(snappingly)* Right, Jack Lark! That's where I park with a fine skin in the dark.

BEULAH *(snapping her fingers, she jumps back and wiggles. Gazing to the back parlor)* Whoo-ie—that's Tom Wild and his Wildcats playing. Look at them broads struggling.

DOLLY Struggling?

BEULAH Dancing, dame, dancing!

JOE That's nothin', they's shuffle and mug like they've been drugged. Let me light up and cut some rug.

(Music reaches crescendo)

BEULAH This ball is a slight drag.

JOE Don't whine, wait'll I put up my sign. Look out biffers' 'um coming on like the March of Time, yippee! *(JOE rushes center, bending and bracing up in rhythm with the music. BEULAH raises and flaps her arms as she begins the break in the lindy hop. They dance wildly. The music comes up in full. They make the place jump. DOLLY swoons against OSCAR in exasperation. OSCAR tries to get things under control again. COBINA is amused. She snaps her fingers and sways as* CHUCK *looks about helplessly)* Ain't this a killer—hey hey! *(*JOE *swings around with* BEULAH *who hops back, runs toward him as he swings her around)*

DOLLY *(screaming in exasperation with her hand raised high)* Stop the wildcats! *(as she stops within* JOE's *dance range,* BEULAH's *swinging leg hits* DOLLY's *foot.* DOLLY *screams in pain)* My foot!

(Music blasting)

OSCAR *(rushing to* DOLLY, *upsets* COBINA, *bouquet and all)* My wife!

COBINA *(excitedly)* My flowers!

(Complete freeze of action and music)

BEULAH *(being dropped to the floor, sits rubbing her side)* My ass! *(*RUBY *does not say a word)*

(Curtain)

ACT II

Scene 1

SCENE *The same as Act II, Scene 1.*

TIME *A few minutes later.*

SUSTAIN *At the rise of the curtain,* OSCAR *is sitting on the sofa. He is mopping his brow and trying very hard to get over the recent escapade. He talks to* RUBY, *who sits near him. The orchestra plays.*

RUBY *(pathetically)* I know Joe would be sort of out of place, but he is so full of life, usually people beg me to bring him along. These—that is, your kind don't understand him.

OSCAR That's all right, Miss Jackson. Forget them.

RUBY Yes suh, but Mrs. Van Striven's foot, oh, I'm so sorry 'bout that.

OSCAR *(clearing his throat)* That's nothing. She'll be all right. Now this dump—er, this piece of ground is right in the heart of the new upcoming community. Five lots and—

RUBY Well—that is, I only want to entertain the best. Are there any high-toned folks out there?

OSCAR Just as grand as these are here, if not better.

RUBY Does Mrs. Van Striven know them?

OSCAR I believe she knows some very fine Long Island families.

RUBY Then she'll introduce me sorter formal-like to them? You know, all elegant with a lot of noise. I'll throw a house-warming out there that'll be heard from here to Krum Elbow!

OSCAR *(scratching his head)* I think we'd better dance. *(rises and offers his arm)*

COBINA *(enters from hall door)* Dad, Mother says will she have to send down here for you again?

OSCAR Someone has to stay down here and take care of the guests. Is she any better?

COBINA Her foot is better, but her grandiloquence still pains.

OSCAR That will heal in due time. Tell her I will be up shortly.

COBINA But, Dad, she won't come down until you—

OSCAR Shortly, Cobina, shortly!

TILLIE *(entering from salon)* Isn't this a lovely ball, Miss Jackson?

RUBY As rambunctious as Park Avenue. We is class, ain't we?

*(*OSCAR *and* RUBY *exit into salon)*

TILLIE *(ironically)* Aren't we though! *(noticing* COBINA*)* Some debut, isn't it, Cobina?

COBINA I wish Mama thought so. Excuse me, as I have to tell her what Dad said. *(exits through hall door.* TILLIE *tips to salon door and calls* LOUISE*)*

TILLIE H-s-s-s-st!

LOUISE *(backing in, talking to* LEON*)* I said dance, not squeeze the life out of her.

LEON *(entering from salon)* I am, Louise, I am.

LOUISE Why do you hold her so tight? You don't hold me that way.

LEON Now, Louise—

ROWENA *(enters from salon and slips her hand under his arm)* All right, Dr. Davis—we can finish now.

LEON *(watching* LOUISE*)* Oh yes—oh yes!

LOUISE *(to* ROWENA*)* Be sure it's the dance you mean.

ROWENA *(chiding)* Oh my—my—

*(*ROWENA *and* LEON *exit into salon)*

LOUISE *(watching them)* I hope I don't have to break his neck before twelve o'clock.

TILLIE You don't think Leon and Rowena—

LOUISE *(suggestively)* She's woman—

TILLIE You know Rowena better than that.

LOUISE Oh, it isn't just for her, everybody he dances with. You wait until I get him home. Tillie, you ought to be glad your husband is dead. *(sits on the sofa powdering her face)*

TILLIE Safe in heaven, thank God—er— You'll have something on your hands soon as that Joe and Beulah get together again.

LOUISE Attractive?

TILLIE You heard of a face that would stop a clock? Well, Beulah would silence a telephone.

LOUISE Not one iota of difference to Leon, he never looks that high. If I catch him near her—why did I come. Honestly, I should have taken your advice this afternoon.

TILLIE You see the inner circle stayed at home . . .

LOUISE Just why did you put in an appearance, after what you said?

TILLIE Oh, well, I have a score to settle.

LOUISE But I do believe you've gone too far.

ED *(enters from salon, he staggers a bit)* Where's that little imp, Cobina. If she can't duck down to that bar more than anything I have ever seen.

TILLIE Ed is so handsome when he is mad, isn't he?

LOUISE *(indifferently)* A handsome lover is one thing. (ED *exits through hall door,* LOUISE *leans over to* TILLIE) A good husband is another. I pity Cobina if she gets him.

TILLIE *(quickly)* Or Rowena—

LOUISE *(bewildered)* What?

TILLIE *(softly)* Didn't you know—

LOUISE But Dolly said—

TILLIE That's what she thinks.

LOUISE I believe in fighting in the open.

TILLIE Maybe you'd better change your technique.

LOUISE *(efficiently)* I haven't done so badly. Standing on my feet seven hours a day, singing out verbs to a bunch of dumb brats, getting by on a bowl of chili and cut-rate frock, all to put him through medical school. Now, he's all rosy and popular. Debonair, they say. Well, I'm fattening no frogs for any snakes. He knows I'm not going to keep on fighting in the dark or otherwise—he's mine and the female creature that tries to really take him from me will gaze up at the Harlem moon underneath six feet of woodlawn dirt!

TILLIE Woodlawn?

LOUISE Cemetery. He winks at every young thing he sees now. I'm not jealous, but—

TILLIE Well, you take a woman like that Ruby Jackson.

LOUISE So the Ruby Jackson came.

TILLIE What a headline! "Pimp and Pal Wreck Society Gal."

LOUISE Now, Tillie, that's what I have been wanting to talk to you about. That *Black Dispatch* is—

ED *(enters with* COBINA *from hall)* I found her at the bar guzzling as usual.

COBINA *(halting to powder her nose)* Wait— let me get this shine off.

TILLIE *(enviously)* Cobina, you seem a bit limited in your selections tonight!

COBINA I have what I want.

LOUISE *(happily)* Is that so—oh, Ed is—

COBINA They didn't have to give this party for me. I had him all the time.

ED *(with self-esteem)* Don't be too sure.

COBINA *(brusquely)* What—you—what sparrow pecked that into your head?

ED *(abashed, he takes her arm)* I don't get you. Lower that mirror so I can see your face.

COBINA *(jerking away)* Wait—wait—

ED *(to* TILLIE*)* I get tired of these girls with their five-and-ten faces. They listen to you with one hand, touching up a string of hair, while holding a mirror with the other.

(HENNYPEST *enters from salon)*

COBINA A woman's prerogative.

LOUISE And a final refuge.

(HENNYPEST *gestures to* TILLIE)

TILLIE *(to* HENNYPEST*)* One moment, Professor. We can't miss this.

ED *(avoiding)* You put your entire trust in physical manifestations. You are perfectly confident in the right shade of nail polish, the perfect number of oily curls, lips of a shady red ink. Don't they, Professor?

HENNYPEST Well, now, that is—

COBINA *(interrupting)* A lecture on the philosophy of woman. You are becoming serious. *(she winks at* TILLIE *and* LOUISE*)* Before you go too deep, what do you expect in the fairer sex?

ED Something pretty scarce around here, brains!

COBINA Oh be still! Brains, that's just a camouflage for your overweening arrogance. Take us for what we are. Not for what you want us to be in your narrow little heart. What sort of an opinion is that?

ED Mine! The sensible one, the one of any real man.

COBINA Real man? You mean an impetuous youth. Surely, Professor, you do not agree with him?

HENNYPEST *(moves down center)* I am not sure it would be wise for me to get into this.

COBINA Name me just one man, one great man, who hasn't had the love of a woman to push him on—to just—

ED Just so much dead weight.

HENNYPEST *(to* ED*)* I don't think so. The heart of a woman does more to mankind than all the gold and silver that ever has been mined. She has a smile for every joy, a tear for every sorrow, a consolation for every grief—for every fault, a tolerant forgiveness, and a prayer for every hope.

ED It doesn't matter. I understand them perfectly.

HENNYPEST Then go to the head of the class. Ahead of the philosophers, scientists, poets, musicians, and psychologists who have fallen in their zest to analyze woman. The fact is that woman doesn't understand herself. She has yet to be solved. The few men who have been silly enough to think that, they had either learned of their mistake before they died, or passed into eternity as congenital idiots.

COBINA *(coy)* Idiots!

TILLIE *(directly to* HENNYPEST*)* That could have been left out.

ED *(touching his moustache lightly)* Aw—anyway, they're made to love, not to understand. Their charm, their beauty, their glory has all been reduced to a price—

HENNYPEST Of all other attributes of vices, the personal piety born of chastened love is woman's crowning charm. Can there be love without understanding?

ED But you said they are not understandable—

HENNYPEST Indeed, indeed, like the stars and flowers, her presence imparts warmth and life-giving energy to hearts bowed down. Her influence bends earth to heaven and heaven to earth. Do we understand the universe? (LOUISE *nods with affirmation*). No. (LOUISE *relaxes innocently)* We only think we do. Does the universe understand us? *(*LOUISE *looks askingly)* I believe it does. Such is the position of woman. You give her the proper love. I am sure the understanding will come about in due time.

LOUISE *(exuberant)* Professor Hennypest, that is beautiful. Isn't it, Mrs. Petunia?

TILLIE *(casually)* I have heard it before.

(The orchestra plays)

COBINA And you will forever. Truth withstands both the tide and the times.

ED *(unaffected)* If a woman can't tell me she loves me first, then she can use the first door out. This chivalry stuff is just so much nonsense. I can get along without her very well.

TILLIE Don't let them get the best of you, Ed.

COBINA *(in praise)* Oh, Professor, what an intricate mechanism we women are. Really, it's—it—Louise, aren't you glad you are a woman?

TILLIE *(rises and goes to* ED*)* Ed, you know you can't judge us here. This is Harlem. There are women—that is, girls—well, you know. Now you take Brooklyn. We have—

CHUCK *(enters from hall door. He carries a drink on the tray)* Bull shot!

TILLIE *(whirling to* CHUCK*)* What?

(COBINA *laughs.* LOUISE *sits dreamingly on the sofa)*

CHUCK *(looking about)* Re—er, Miss Rowena called for—bull shot.

(ED *moves toward* CHUCK*)*

ED *(to* CHUCK*)* You might have called for her first.

CHUCK I'm sorry. Will you have one?

ED I don't drink this Harlem hootch.

(TILLIE *smiles at* COBINA*)*

COBINA Give it to me. *(she takes the drink before* ED *can stop her. Sits on chair at right)*

ED *(both rivals on either side of* COBINA*)* That's the third time I have seen you carry a glass to your lips. (COBINA *gulps the drink down)*

LEON *(enters followed by* HENNYPEST. LEON *very carefully removes from his shoulder a string of hair, looks to see if* LOUISE *saw it. He throws it away quickly, then goes to her)* Our dance, Louise.

LOUISE *(looking up at him with a marked dumbness)* Oh Leon, do you know what an intricate mechanism woman is?

LEON *(mysteriously)* What the Sam Hill are you talking about?

LOUISE *(hunching him with her elbow)* You would! Come on.

LEON But baby—

LOUISE *(on her way out)* That's nice what you say, but to hold him you have to wake up what's worse in him.

*(*LOUISE *and* LEON *exit into salon)*

HENNYPEST *(to* TILLIE*)* Madame Petunia, will you—

TILLIE *(disgustedly)* Good grief. I might as well get it over with. *(exits into salon with* HENNYPEST*)*

COBINA *(returning glass to* CHUCK*)* It was swell.

CHUCK I mixed it.

ED Who asked you?

CHUCK No one.

ED Well, mix them, but don't mix in.

COBINA *(to* ED*)* You are going too far. You stop bulldozing him. He's working for Dad.

CHUCK *(starts away)* I must get back to the bar.

ED *(to* CHUCK*)* Come back here!

CHUCK *(stopping)* Listen, pal—

ED Pal?

CHUCK *(with force)* As man to man. Maybe you don't like me. Well, I don't like you either.

ED If you were swinging that tray for ofays, you wouldn't be talking like you are.

CHUCK That has nothing to do with it.

COBINA Daddy will not tolerate you speaking to him in that manner.

CHUCK *(giving* ED *a coin)* No, thank you—I'm paid.

COBINA *(to* ED*)* You're making me sick! Chuck is just as good as you are. He's a member of Alpha Beta Zeta, the same as you are.

ED What?

COBINA Yes, and—

ED What chapter?

CHUCK *(to* ED*)* Aida Chapter—snake! *(both do a razzle-dazzle handshake and a frat gesture)*

ED They're letting in anything now. *(to* COBINA*)* Are you dancing or not?

COBINA I've changed my mind. They're dying for you in there.

*(*ED *exits into salon)*

CHUCK And that's what they want to put off on you.

COBINA Darling—I gave him a look that hasn't been washed in years. You know I wouldn't have him with a down payment on a radio.

JOE *(swings in from salon with* BEULAH, *both slightly drunk)* Old Jim Pool from Liverpool. Cut that powerful muggin' and gruggin'.

BEULAH *(clapping her hands)* Come on, you dicties. Swing out. Di-di-di-dum-dum.

JOE *(snapping his fingers. Jumping back,* LILY *appears just inside the room)* What's your story, Morning Glory? Git off the shelf. Swing yourself.

LILY *(moves in nearer)* Aha!

*(*LILY *swings a couple of times)*

JOE Come on, Garbo, blow your top.

(She stops dead still)

LILY I beg your pardon.

JOE Don't start puffin'. You ain't done nothin'.

TILLIE *(peeps in from the hall)* What is this?

JOE If you can't fall, stick to the wall. Joe is takin' charge. *(*TILLIE *emerges)* Git back, granny-hep-hep. You're too large. *(*TILLIE *recedes)*

BEULAH Here I come, Papa. On your mark.

JOE *(to* CHUCK*)* Stack some ham on that platter. Tray away, what's the matter?

CHUCK Food is served on the floor below.

JOE *(stopping the strutting)* I ain't no square from Delaware, nor bloke from Idaho. Grab that platter. Take some air. Who's gwine eat on any flooh?

COBINA *(to* CHUCK *quickly)* Wait on the veranda for me, Chuck.

*(*CHUCK *exits through French doors)*

JOE Say chick, you're crumpy as a Uneeda biscuit.

LILY Cobina, who is this man?

COBINA Mr. Smothers, Joe Smothers.

LILY Delighted, I'm sure.

JOE Send my brown body to the morgue.

BEULAH You kill me with that drawl. Where's Professor Chickenbreast? *(exits into salon)*

LILY I'm not the slightest bit amused.

JOE You let me down to the ground. Let me show you the town. *(*LILY *smiles)*

COBINA I believe you can take care of yourself. *(exits through French doors)*

JOE *(getting close to* LILY*)* Them big black eyebrows. Them long lashes. They flop a breeze that causes me to squeeze. A fine feeling shakes my frame. Gosh, ain't this a shame!

LILY *(crossing)* Ha-ha-ha-ha-ha-ha—

JOE *(right on* LILY*)* Getcha! Hoi! Hoi! There's plenty squares who can slave. But a hard-cuttin' lover is in the rave.

LILY With whom did you come?

JOE *(sing-song)* Ruby—Ruby Tutti-fruity.

LILY Now I understand.

JOE Don't jump in the amen row. Ruby's jus' lousy with dough.

LILY *(a new interest)* From the sweepstakes?

JOE A hundred and fifty grand. Old slick Joe is the man. Swing out with me a while. I'll tog you out in style.

LILY Listen, big boy, don't jive me now.

JOE Believe me if I sing you in praise—a half a hundred tender ways. Believe me if I still repeat that you are glamorous and sweet. But if you see my glances stray, just shrug and look the other way. And don't believe, dear, nor weep if I tell my secrets in my sleep.

*(*COBINA *and* CHUCK *enter from veranda.* CHUCK *exits down hall.* COBINA *watches* JOE *and* LILY*)*

LILY I'm a woman of the stage, you know.

COBINA Lily, do you know what you are doing?

LILY Aw, does anyone?

JOE *(elated)* Lily, your wit, your repartee, good God, you knock a hole in me. Dazzle me! Send me! Leave me a perfect wreck!

SOPHIE *(dashes in from foyer left)* Joe, Joe, I—

JOE *(whirls around startled)* Sophie Slow, ready as a radio!

SOPHIE *(leaps into his arms.* LILY *is indignant)* Bust me, Joe. Bust me! My Joe. Good ole Joe. Sharp as a tack. Ain't them the togs I brought cha?

LILY *(looking around helplessly, tosses her head back)* That took the starch out of him.

COBINA Sophie, is that your he?

SOPHIE In the flesh. My Joe, ain't he cute?

JOE I thought you pulled your slave act in the Bronx.

SOPHIE Naw, babe, I cut out. No more of that fifteen cents an hour for me. Up there they nelly starved me to death with that cheese and pumpinicker bread. I like here better. I kin fuss all I wants. Boy, that drape hugs you tight as your skin. You been jiving Lily? *(crosses to* LILY*)*

LILY No, he amused me.

SOPHIE I know. Different name but same feelin'! Come on up to my room, Joe.

*(*LILY *hustles into parlor)*

JOE Naw, honey, don't be funny. I got to stash down here.

SOPHIE I nevah knowed you hung out with the swanks, you and your pranks.

COBINA Sophie, if Mother sees you—

SOPHIE That's right. Say, Joe, I got to git below.

JOE You fall on down. I got to kill some wine an' be right down in a half of chime.

*(*SOPHIE *exits foyer left)*

COBINA Mr. Smothers, you seem completely put out.

JOE *(sitting on sofa)* Listen chile, out, out awhile. None of your jinks, I got to think.

RUBY *(enters from back parlor)* Miss Cobina, kin you tell me where your mama is?

COBINA Up in her room, I think. I'll try to find her.

RUBY Never mind, maybe she's busy.

COBINA I don't mind *(exits through foyer left)*

RUBY Joe, has you been smokin' any marianna weeds? *(sits beside* JOE*)*

JOE Cut out that innocent act. I'm gittin' outah this shack. *(*RUBY *takes his arm)*

RUBY But babe, I'm having a ball. You must be, too. You wanted to come so bad.

JOE I just wanna leave. Let go my sleeve!

RUBY What done happen? 'Course you should nah come on so hard.

JOE That ain't it atall. I'm leaving, that's all. One thing I don't do. Cross my chicks, they git me blue.

RUBY I ain't crossed you. I let you jive them biggies.

*(*TILLIE *enters from parlor)*

JOE I ain't callin' no name. *(sees* TILLIE*)* Cut out. I gotta spiel to this dame. *(*RUBY *rises and exits slowly foyer left.* JOE *urges her on. He shouts at her)* Beat it stuff. I don't wanna git rough *(sits on sofa)*

TILLIE Mr. Smothers—

JOE Can it!

TILLIE S-s-s-sh.

JOE *(boisterously)* None of that high-falutin' junk. What the hell you take me for, a chump?

TILLIE What, Joe—what's the matter?

JOE You got me on the run, woman. She knocked me for my fun.

TILLIE Who, Mrs. Van Striven? You do just what I told you—

JOE When I fell in through that door, I didn't 'spect to see Sophie Slow.

TILLIE Will you stop that silly rhyme and tell me just what is—

JOE Just this. You done run me into a chick of mine who's worse than a nest of starving monkeys when she's riled. How can I wreck this joint with her—

TILLIE You mean that awful maid?

JOE Better say that when she's out of sight. She swings a mean fist when she fights.

TILLIE Is she one of—

JOE Yeah, what of it?

TILLIE I gave you credit for having better use of your talents. *(sits close to* JOE*)* But listen, don't let me down now. Make everybody miserable. Start a fight or something. Ruin them. Give them a pain in the neck. That dancing was great stuff. Raise the tin roof off this stable. *(marked bitterness)* These Van Strivens and their uppish ways!

JOE I don't know. They seem sorter nice.

TILLIE Nice—they're mean little people who'll shrink up and die from one good scandal.

JOE But Ruby wants to be a muckitymuck. I have to—

TILLIE You do your job. When Ruby wants to meet society, I'll give her a sendoff. These jittery quacks do nothing but try to impress their neighbors and live in constant agitation and comparison with me. *(walks down center)* Me, Tillie Petunia!

JOE What about the old dame with the ramrod up her back? She passed me like greased lightning.

TILLIE *(turns, coming center)* That imitation of a Victorian. She's the sharpest-tongued one of these strivers. Don't let her scare you. She'll fidget and squirm if you blow your nose hard. Rip all the sham off all of them. *(*LILY *enters from parlor.* TILLIE *rises quickly)* Oh, Lily—we were just talking about you.

LILY That shows importance. Importance is quite essential, you know. *(*LILY *relaxes on sofa.* TILLIE *snaps the wall lights off, darkening the room with the exception of a beam light.* TILLIE *exits left)*

JOE *(easing up behind* LILY*)* Do you dig, do you dig? Let *this* pig fit your jig.

LILY No, thank you!

JOE *(easing around edge of sofa, creeping closer to* LILY*)* Light up and grow limp, Lily.

LILY I want to enjoy a moment of solitude. Miss Livingston to you.

JOE *(beside* LILY*)* Lemme stash my frame on that freakish lounge, while that glimmer beats down on my woolly-kong and tickle out the Romeo in me.

LILY The Smothers technique is back.

JOE Never got out from my chest, just a short recess.

LILY I'm a wicked woman.

(The orchestra plays)

JOE Wickedness is for a lady, goodness for a hag. The first sends me. The last one is a drag.

LILY What do you want me to do?

JOE Bust me with your beauty. You're such a cutie.

LILY I'm not that beautiful.

JOE Enough for me, babe, you seem so true. I gotta lay this hard love on you.

LILY If you love like you lie, you're good.

JOE I'm better than that, I'm a hepped cat. *(*JOE *leans over* LILY, *who squirms)* Easy—easy, don't start wringling. Watch your skin start tingling. *(*LILY *kisses* JOE *quickly.* JOE *kicks and jumps up in delight)* Whooie! Bo-peep, come and git your sheep!

OSCAR *(rushes in from parlor)* Miss Livingston, what are you doing?

LILY *(jumping up quickly)* Just—just a scene, Mr. Van Striven!

OSCAR *(turning up the lights)* A scene—a scene—these lights.

JOE *(all over the room)* Yeah, Jack, the mad scene from Gimbels' basement.

BEULAH *(enters from parlor)* Say, Papa, let's finish our dance.

OSCAR Sorry—I must see my wife. *(exits through arch door left)*

BEULAH *(scornfully)* The guy has to git permission from his dame.

CHUCK *(rushes in from foyer left)* Where is Miss—Cobina?

LILY I—I don't know.

(ED enters from parlor)

ED Oh—pardon me! *(turns)*

JOE *(to ED with a purpose)* Say, Jim—Cobina—you seen her?

ED *(reproachfully)* What—and you too?

JOE What's that?

ED *(points to CHUCK)* Him—and now you?

CHUCK I don't get you, pal.

ED I thought you weren't playing that role for nothing. What a damn cheap trick!

JOE *(raising his fist)* Don't bite off too much.

LILY Ed Tucker, you'd better—

JOE *(CHUCK and ED face to face)* Easy, honey, this is funny. The well-bred and the gutter-bred gonna bust heads.

CHUCK *(to ED)* I ain't looking for no trouble.

ED Plenty nerve. Who do you think you are fooling, anyway?

(JOE encircles CHUCK and ED)

BEULAH Look out—let me git a ringside special. *(stands up in a chair)*

ED So you took Cobina to the actors' benefit.

(JOE edges them out)

LILY Is that the fellow she was with?

ED *(swearing at him)* You're the guy who's been taking up all her time, the reason why she breaks all her dates with me. You upstart. Why don't you stay in the alley with the rest of—

COBINA *(dashes in from parlor)* What is this?

ED What's the idea going around with him pretending you like me?

COBINA What are you talking about?

CHUCK *(quickly)* Rowena just told him. He knows, Cobina.

COBINA *(to ED)* Well—well, it's my business. You might as well know now—

ED I'll see what Mrs. Van Striven has to say.

COBINA Well, go ahead!

JOE He's gonna run and tell Mama.

CHUCK Now listen—

ED Take your filthy hands off me—

(JOE pushes CHUCK)

BEULAH *(slugging the air)* Pile drive him. Break down his bridge work!

ED You—

(JOE steps in to push CHUCK into ED. At this moment, ED ducks. COBINA screams. The blow catches JOE in the face. JOE knocks ED down near the sofa. BEULAH leaps up and down in the chair up left)

BEULAH Plaster him in the kisser. This is a killer, just like a Saturday night at the Hole-in-the-wall.

COBINA *(screaming)* Stop it—stop it!

CHUCK *(to JOE)* What did you do that for? This is my affair.

LILY Mrs. Van Striven—

JOE *(tapping his thumb with his tongue)* Come one—come all.

(DOLLY enters at arch door)

CHUCK *(lets loose a lightning blow. JOE spins around—staggers blindly—stumbles and falls at BEULAH's feet)* You started it.

COBINA Chuck—Chuck—don't! Papa—Mama—somebody!

TILLIE *(rushes in from the parlor. She sees ED knocked out on the floor. She runs over to him, screaming hysterically. ROWENA stops in the door)* Ed, darling—oh, his face is bruised. *(she kisses him tenderly)* Ed—oh, Ed—*(shouting at CHUCK)* You dare strike him—you—

CHUCK I didn't do it.

COBINA Joe did it. Joe, it was he.

(BEULAH lifts JOE to his feet)

TILLIE *(screaming at JOE)* You Lenox Avenue lizard. I'll have you put in jail.

JOE You said wreck it, start a fight—

TILLIE *(holding ED's head in her arms)* Not him— *(ED is coming to)* Ed, darling— *(to JOE)* You fool—you backdoor pimp!

DOLLY *(confused with anger)* Wreck it—wreck what?

(TILLIE rises slowly. DOLLY is right in back of her. TILLIE's eyes blink)

TILLIE *(trembling)* Nothing, I—

JOE *(angrily)* What the hell, she told me to wreck your party. Make it a scandal.

DOLLY Scandal—my party—my greatest party— *(DOLLY swings TILLIE around, facing her)*

JOE Sure she did. Ask her. Told me to come along with Ruby. Get some hoodlums, like Beulah, and make the ball a flop.

TILLIE That's a lie.

BEULAH *(to TILLIE)* You beefy hussy!

TILLIE *(pleading)* He's lying, Dolly. I never saw him before in my—

JOE Ask Ruby. She knows I begged her to bring me. *(to TILLIE)* Pimp, am I?

(ROWENA turns tearfully in the door)

MRS. PACE *(rushes in from the arch door)* The police are coming!

(JOE makes a dash to exit. He stumbles, but dashes out wildly)

BEULAH Me and cops don't mix! *(makes a dash for the door, knocking TILLIE off balance. TILLIE tumbles into DOLLY, who lands on the sofa. All the guests converge around the sofa)*

SOPHIE *(dashing in with a trail of policy slips following)* The cops coming. Git them policy slips out!

MRS. PACE Dolly, what are you doing?

DOLLY *(holding fast to sprawling TILLIE, she takes off her shoe)* I'm going to put some misery where it belongs.

TILLIE Don't you put your hands on me!

HENNYPEST *(dashing in with his camera, focusing from a downstage vantage point)* Focus, please.

(All freeze just as DOLLY raises her slipper above TILLIE's posterior. Curtain)

Scene 2

(TIME *Later that evening.*

PLACE *Same.*

At the rise of the curtain, ROWENA paces the floor, excited over the recent happenings. ED is sitting in the chair at left, nursing his right eye.)

ROWENA You ought to be ashamed of yourself!

ED I, ashamed? What about your aunt and her rummies spoiling the party? Just like her, always messing up— *(gestures, exposing a black eye, a real mouser)*

ROWENA Get my wrap. I'm going home.

ED Don't shout at me! I only dance to my own music. I'm sick and tired of both of you trying to make small of other people and end up stuck with the dummy cap yourselves.

ROWENA Stop talking about her!

ED *(rising)* Stop the world! Her majesty, party-nuisance number one. Same thing at Small's last night, got high and pushed me off a stool, splashing rum all over—

ROWENA Aunt Tillie was in Corona last night.

ED Maybe her spirit was, but her body was with me at Small's Paradise and as high as a kite.

ROWENA You took her there?

ED *(crossing to right)* Let us say she took me there.

ROWENA *(crossing to ED)* You're a conceited liar!

ED And for a grand finale, we shacked up at the Hotel Theresa.

ROWENA What are you saying? *(her eyes glued on him)*

DOLLY *(enters via foyer in a huff)* You, assassins, still here? Get going!

ROWENA *(to ED, undistracted)* You *are* lying!

DOLLY *(missing the point)* Lying? You're as welcome here as a bastard at a family reunion. *(crosses, snatches wrap from sofa, flings it at her)*

MRS. PACE *(enters from left, steaming)* Where is Tillie? Where is that horrible creature?

DOLLY Denture hunting. She lost her partials during the melee.

MRS. PACE I have been on the phone and—

ROWENA *(finally with realization to ED)* You—you—drip! You dripping drip. *(crosses, slaps him and picks up her wrap and flees thru foyer and off right. ED instinctively pursues her, but pauses and calmly picks up his hat, faces MRS. PACE and DOLLY)*

ED *(scornfully, conclusively)* So long, social coolies!

DOLLY *(crossing to him, gracefully, bowing regally and joined by MRS. PACE)* Adios ameba! *(both arm and oust him before he knows what is happening. After a pause, DOLLY collapses on the sofa)* Oh, Mother, I feel like the last drip from a faucet!

MRS. PACE *(crossing behind sofa)* I found out that—

RUBY *(enters from left with* LOUISE, *both in their wraps)* Mrs. Van Striven, I can't tell you how sorry I is.

MRS. PACE My daughter wants to be alone.

RUBY Yessum, I was just leaving and—

MRS. PACE Leave by the lower floor then.

(RUBY *exits left via foyer after a sad glance at* DOLLY)

LOUISE Dolly, I had a perfectly delightful time.

MRS. PACE This is one time that lie is not in order!

LOUISE I did. Didn't we, Leon? *(looking back)* Where is that man? Leon?

LEON *(entering from left)* Coming, honey.

LOUISE You're not going to take her home with you, are you?

LEON *(now pretty high, he makes a production out of getting on his scarf and coat)* Who—who—who?

LOUISE Look at him—who—who? Wait until I get you home.

LEON I have to speak before the Medical Association tomorrow. *(his scarf now is like a lasso around his neck)* You're not going to scratch up my face tonight.

LOUISE *(jerking* LEON's *scarf)* It won't be your face!

MRS. PACE Louise!!!

LOUISE I'm sorry, Mrs. Pace. *(sits next to* DOLLY*)*

MRS. PACE We saw you come up from that 134th Street railroad flat up on Sugar Hill. Dolly sponsored you in and made you what you are today.

LOUISE She did, and I would cut off my right arm for her.

MRS. PACE (LEON *still entangling the scarf)* You had better save your arm for him. *(referring to* LEON) Tillie told you not to come to our party, didn't she?

LOUISE Yes, Mrs. Pace—

DOLLY What's this?

LEON *(crossing to* DOLLY, *his hand tracing her spine)* I told Louise that she should have phoned you—hic—hic— (DOLLY *disassociates his hand)*

LOUISE I didn't mean to hide it. You and Tillie both have been nice to me.

DOLLY I am convinced that *you* wouldn't want to hurt me.

LOUISE Never! Never! Never! It's that man's womanizing escapades. He keeps my mind boggled up! If it just weren't for this man, I would be a full-time lady instead of a part-time hag!

MRS. PACE Leon! *(he crosses to her, pinching her cheek affectionately. She distances herself)* When are you going to stop playing cupid to every young creature you see?

LEON *(staggers)* I guess it's the African in me, a woman for every mood.

LOUISE Get going! I'm going to start *de-mooding* you tonight. *(pushing him out)*

LEON Now, honey, it's you I love. I don't mismeasure your treasure. What are you going to do to your papa-wappa?

LOUISE I'm putting you on a diet.

LEON *(at the foyer exit)* Oh, I don't mind my weight going down.

LOUISE It won't be your weight. The diet is saltpeter! (LEON *swoons as* LOUISE *waves good-bye and shoves him off right, following him)*

CHUCK *(entering from left)* Mrs. Van Striven, I apologize for striking that—

MRS. PACE Get your pay and leave by the lower floor.

CHUCK There is something else—

MRS. PACE Please take it up with Mr. Van Striven!

(CHUCK *moves down right)*

LILY *(enters from left foyer, posing dramatically with her wrap draped over her left shoulder, acting out a scene with* HENNYPEST, *who follows her. She projects a Jamaican accent)* Ha-ha-ha, then I say, "The quality of mercy is not strained; it droppeth, as the gentle rain from heaven."

HENNYPEST *(throwing kisses)* Bravo—bravo. Yum—um.

LILY "It is an attribute to God Himself; and earthly power doth show likest God's, when mercy seasons justice. Therefore, Jew—"

HENNYPEST That's I.

MRS. PACE Stop it! The masquerade is over!

LILY *(descending into room)* I simply had to do that scene. I'm rehearsing "The Merchant of Venice"—to be *laid* in Jamaica. (MRS. PACE *gawks)* I mean the setting of the play is *laid* in Jamaica. Instead of Portia, I'm called Portiaette.

MRS. PACE You have 'et too much already. You are drunk!

DOLLY Good night, Lily.

HENNYPEST *(glowing)* I'm escorting her home.

DOLLY Don't lose your way back, Professor.

(Backing out, HENNYPEST *collides with* LILY, *posturing another fight)*

LILY Goodnight reminds me of last season's African version of "Romeo and Juliet." *(crossing down center)* "Good night, Good night. Parting is such sweet sorrow. Good night 'til it be morrow." *(flings her wrap over her right shoulder, whirls and exits via foyer to the right. Two beats behind her,* HENNYPEST *waves a cuppish farewell and pursues* LILY*)*

CHUCK *(impatiently)* Mrs. Van Striven, I must talk to you.

MRS. PACE *(quickly)* You still here! *(crossing to left entrance)* Oscar! Oscar! Come and show this person out!

OSCAR *(enters from parlor with* RUBY*)* One minute. I must pay the orchestra.

MRS. PACE The boy is annoying Dolly.

CHUCK Honest, sir, it's about—

MRS. PACE Pay him and get rid of him!

OSCAR *(exploding)* This is a union band. Every minute counts. Come, young man, I will give you your money. Wait here, Miss Jackson. No doubt, tomorrow I shall be applying for welfare.

*(*CHUCK *follows* OSCAR *off left)*

RUBY *(crossing to chair left)* I'll just sit right here. *(sits)*

MRS. PACE *(after a long pause that discomforts* RUBY, *she stiffens)* For the past half-hour, I have been trying to converse with my daughter.

RUBY Please don't let me stop you.

MRS. PACE I am not encouraging conversation with you, but you do figure prominently in what concerns me.

DOLLY *(coldly, turning away)* Her presence is part of a total design to embarrass me.

MRS. PACE Why did you bring this rowdy Mr. Smothers into this house?

RUBY Because he asked me to.

MRS. PACE What if you had refused his request?

RUBY He'd probably come on, on his own. Men like Joe is heaps of fun and heaps of risk. You don't refuse them anything.

MRS. PACE How did he come to know Petunia so well?

RUBY He *hangs* out at the Blue Ball Poolroom. Her paper business is just next door. I didn't know she told him to funk up your party. 'Course, I don't know the tricks of you high-toned folks. Bringing him here was surely a miscarriage.

MRS. PACE You have met our upper class. I hope you are satisfied.

RUBY I am, but—

MRS. PACE But what?

RUBY I'm going to buy that big mansion on Long Island. 'Course you all will be my house guests and—

*(*DOLLY *crosses stage)*

MRS. PACE *(tensely)* Don't lose your dignity. Dolly!

DOLLY *(exploding with laughter above couch)* Ha-ha-ha-ha—

*(*RUBY *rises, goes toward hall)*

RUBY It's just that I want to be in society.

DOLLY The word swims before my eyes.

MRS. PACE Keep your dignity—

DOLLY Come here, Miss Jackson. *(*RUBY *picks up stool at right and down center, sits hopefully center)* What a blind and silly woman you are.

RUBY *(disappointedly)* My Madame, the one I use to work for, says I have the makings of a lady.

*(*MRS. PACE *sits on sofa)*

DOLLY *(severely)* A lady! Such a superficial term. Is your life position one of distinct advantage? Do you dress correctly? That rooster feather in your hair, positively nauseating. This being a lady is a complicated thing! It requires development, step by step. You are not even in the kindergarten. What do you possess that might make you worthy?

RUBY Goodness.

DOLLY *(she almost whispers)* And what do you think I possess?

RUBY *(firm but kind)* Snobbishness! Vanity! Pride!

MRS. PACE And I?

RUBY Meanness! Stiffness! It all amounts to just being snobbish.

MRS. PACE *(with modest condescension)* She's a snob. I am a snob. Well, who isn't? Snobbery is a universal failing—or maybe it's a virtue. It is the art of rubbing it in the other person. And it isn't peculiar to our smart set either.

RUBY I wouldn't be one for—

MRS. PACE But you are. You are a snob of humility and modesty. Now, are you not sorry for what you have said?

RUBY No'm.

DOLLY If you think so lightly of us, why have you selected us?

RUBY I know every rich cultured woman ain't a lady. Still, every ten-dollar scrub woman ain't a saint. God is funny. He mixed them up. When you work all your days, suddenly you git powerfully rich, ain't much else to do but show off and git talked about.

DOLLY *(as an equal)* Money can buy you all the publicity you need, but not breeding. Now, Grandfather was an original settler in Rockland County and an Episcopalian minister. Dad became president of Skidwell College—

MRS. PACE Where I was dean of women until I retired and moved to Washington.

DOLLY Oscar's background is equally outstanding.

MRS. PACE Though a far lesser eclipse of Anglo-Saxon sunshine with the African moon. We overlook one Dutch ancestor who went to the debtor's jail—

DOLLY But a good name, Van Striven! Does that mean anything to you?

RUBY Yessum.

DOLLY Indeed, what?

RUBY That the line between you and me is very thin.

DOLLY *(indignantly)* I am trying to rationalize this thing with you. If you are capable of speaking with sense.

MRS. PACE What was your father?

RUBY A dog ketcher.

DOLLY You couldn't be satirizing?

RUBY Who?

DOLLY Skip it. What did your grandfather do?

RUBY He ran aroun' lak a blind mule in a hailstorm because Culnal Cheatum tricked him outah his farm. Five little devils use to break loose in his brain, he said, so he'd go aroun' buttin' his head against pine trees. I was a little mite of a gal when he used to say, "Dad-bobbit, naow I'se too pooh to gie you the upbringing you deserve."

DOLLY Then you admit you lack breeding?

RUBY Maybe I does, but the hoss that won me this money shore had plenty.

DOLLY What I can't understand is why are you struggling to get into my social set and away from your own, such as Joe or Beulah.

RUBY I like you better.

DOLLY Is there any difference between you and Beulah?

RUBY Yessum, in a way.

DOLLY Then everybody isn't the same breed?

RUBY Well, er—

DOLLY Are they, Miss Jackson? (RUBY *is confused)* Are they, Miss Jackson?

RUBY I mean—the difference between me and Beulah is just like the difference between you and Miss Petunia.

MRS. PACE A matter of attitude?

RUBY Yessum, that's it, that's just what I mean—a attitude is what I got that they don't have and don't want.

DOLLY *(resigning)* I see. Is that all you have to offer for your social ambitions?

RUBY Skersely much more, Mrs. Van Striven.

DOLLY *(conclusively, rising)* I am afraid the price you are willing to pay will not purchase you a ticket into the inner circle. *(strolls left, looking off)*

RUBY *(meditatively)* I—get—you. My mistake.

*(*MRS. PACE *rises. Exiting right.* RUBY, *thoroughly dejected, comes to put chair back to table—pauses.* DOLLY *crosses as* MRS. PACE *stands rigidly.* RUBY *comes down center)*

RUBY I have stood over a hot greasy stove, rolling out biscuits, peeling onions 'til my eyes turned red. I never want to see another roasting pot! Have you ever had hot grease pop on you on a sizzling morning in August? And home to sit out on a stinking stoop—with a pile of cussing sickly men, lousing around like lizards in a pile of rotten logs! Aw, what's the use—*(exits to parlor)*

DOLLY That's over—thank heaven. *(sits on sofa)*

MRS. PACE May it never be repeated. *(hears voices in the hall)*

COBINA *(offstage)* And I think I ought to know!

OSCAR *(offstage)* Go on inside!

MRS. PACE *(as* COBINA *enters from foyer left followed by* CHUCK *and* OSCAR*)* You want Dolly to explode? Speak up!

COBINA No, I'm not ashamed! And I don't care!

OSCAR I just learned why Cobina can't stay at college over the weekends. *(he comes down center.* CHUCK *stands nearby)*

MRS. PACE Running down here for those stupid swing sessions. Swing! That horrible noise called music.

OSCAR No! *(indicates* CHUCK*)* He's the reason.

DOLLY *(with a toss of her head)* Him? That person. That boy! This—Cobina—

MRS. PACE W-w-w-what?

DOLLY *(going over to her)* What's been going on? What do you mean? Cobina, where do you know this person from?

COBINA The Village.

MRS. PACE *(cocking her brows)* Dolly, you permit Cobina to be seen with such people! How long have you known this this—nobody?

*(*OSCAR *sits on sofa rubbing his hands)*

COBINA About a year.

DOLLY *(to* COBINA*)* Where have you been seeing him?

OSCAR She said they have been going to the park.

DOLLY *(wincing)* My daughter in a public park. Cobina, I don't understand! Jeepers creepers! Did he make love to you?

COBINA Aw, Mother!

MRS. PACE Hold yourself together, Dolly! Keep your dignity! *(steps on* DOLLY*'s foot)*

DOLLY Ouch! Get off my foot! *(flops on sofa)* What have I done to deserve this? Och, it's too much, much too much. My poor aching feet.

MRS. PACE *(to* CHUCK*)* Do you realize what an uncouth thing you've done?

CHUCK I tried to tell all of you. I didn't mean to be sly or—

OSCAR *(interrupting)* They have been out evenings *together.*

MRS. PACE *(incensed)* Evening, a sheltering veil for promiscuity. *Black* evil night! And why have you seen her at night?

CHUCK I worked during the day.

MRS. PACE Then I suppose you have something in your pocket besides a pair of dice.

OSCAR He is not working now. He was discharged.

MRS. PACE If you think Cobina is endowed to support you—

CHUCK I love Cobina. I love her with all my soul.

DOLLY But what could you offer her?

CHUCK My youth—my—

MRS. PACE What can she do with that?

OSCAR I have explained to Chuck. Such a thing is utterly impossible, completely out of the question—*(rises, crosses to* CHUCK*)*

COBINA *(defiantly)* I'm sick of being led around by the nose.

OSCAR Cobina, I seldom interfere in your affairs. I allow you to your own judgment. You are eighteen. This is a big thing. Too big for you to decide alone.

MRS. PACE This is most unhealthy or—something.

COBINA I don't care. I love him.

DOLLY What do you see in this boy?

COBINA See—see—probably no more than you, but I feel different.

MRS. PACE Keep your remarks out of the gutter.

COBINA What difference does it make? Mother ran away to marry Dad and—

MRS. PACE And she has been regretting it ever since.

COBINA Nobody is going to pick out my boyfriend. I'm sick of these jaded jerks. With their swell heads, they're on the painful side of the absurd. They love only themselves.

OSCAR We know what's good for you.

COBINA I don't want what's good!

DOLLY *(going over to* CHUCK*)* You have been listening to Sophie. And you, young man—you know what you've done? You have pulled a sneaking, unmanly trick! The idea of seeing my daughter in the park—in the Village—with those kooks.

CHUCK We went other places—shows, bus riding, fights—

MRS. PACE Fights?

CHUCK Yessum, prize fights at Madison Square Garden.

COBINA Chuck can fight, too.

OSCAR *(gladly—drawn to* CHUCK*)* Oh, he can?

DOLLY *(interrupting)* A prize fighter! What is your name?

CHUCK Chuck Reynolds.

DOLLY Mrs. Chuck Reynolds! How lacking in lyricism!

OSCAR I've always wanted to manage a boxer—

CHUCK Boxing ain't my calling.

DOLLY Why did you decide to come here?

CHUCK I didn't want you all to engage Cobina to anyone else.

DOLLY And if we had?

CHUCK I am not ready to marry, but we would have eloped.

OSCAR *(crossing to* CHUCK*)* And I would have had it annulled.

CHUCK We would have kept it a secret.

MRS. PACE Her mother hid her elopement. But she did not hide the results.

DOLLY Mother! *(truly embarrassed)*

OSCAR As you see, Chuck, your way of life is different. Though you say you have been to college.

MRS. PACE *(to* OSCAR*)* Collge, where?

OSCAR *(explodes)* Aw, Bugalu College or something—

MRS. PACE You mean *institution!*

OSCAR There are plenty of Harlem business men who would have gladly given you a job.

CHUCK They must be hiding somewhere.

OSCAR Jobs just don't fall out of the tree of hope.

CHUCK I came here with a letter of introduction from college to the Reverend Cooke. He was glad to see me. He invited me to hear him preach the following Sunday.

OSCAR The Reverend Cooke gave you no assistance?

CHUCK He was kind. He gave me a copy of the New Testament. Next I went to Gotsby Employment Agency.

OSCAR I know, recently opened.

CHUCK I told Mr. Gotsby I needed a job. He said he couldn't find one himself. That's why he opened his agency.

OSCAR There is a wide gap between you and my daughter. What I mean is, there is a lot of difference between you and me, and—

CHUCK We do belong to the same sex.

COBINA Score one for Chuck. Hooray!

OSCAR Putting it as politely as I can, permission to see my daughter is denied.

CHUCK I didn't ask *your* permission, sir.

OSCAR You didn't, but—

DOLLY Did you come here to win our friendship or *extract* it?

CHUCK I have *Cobina's* consent. She's eighteen now.

COBINA Both of you may have been kidding me when you told me that a girl of eighteen can make her own decisions, but I believed you. So please shut up!

OSCAR *(crossing to* COBINA*))* What will it be? Shell steaks or chopped chuck?

COBINA Chopped chuck with CHUCK!

DOLLY Name the first offspring Groundmeat!

RUBY *(stepping up to* CHUCK*)* Sonny, I sure like the way you talk.

OSCAR Oh, Miss Jackson, I'll be with you in a minute.

RUBY What would you do if you had my money?

CHUCK Madame, education isn't a bad investment. A sharp mind deters chiselers and—

OSCAR *(blustering)* Now just a minute—

MRS. PACE Keep your dignity.

OSCAR *(evenly)* A few minutes ago, before my daughter's declaration of chop meat independence, I was about to offer you a job—

CHUCK As a panic peddler?

OSCAR Come again.

CHUCK Panic peddlers, blockbusting goons—hired by real estate dealers to funk up neighborhoods.

*(*DOLLY *looks askance at* MRS. PACE *and mimes "Language?"* MRS. PACE *mimes "Funk is proper")*

CHUCK Johnny Whiteface flees the neighborhood, taking everything except his cemetery.

OSCAR *(not with pride)* Business is business.

CHUCK That's what's wrong with it.

OSCAR No, you certainly won't fit into my stable.

CHUCK Thank you for including me out.

OSCAR There are times when the end justifies the means. If the end is a good one, you bend the moral code a little—

CHUCK Or bust it.

OSCAR Show me a business strictly on the up and up, and I'll show you where it is coasting on eggs. Such is the fashion and pattern of our time. Anybody in this business who doesn't earn fifty thousand a year is loafing. Sure, I trigger the whole busting sequence. Blockbusting is an odious name for my craft. Real estate speculator, yes. But as long as we have the average American with his average prejudice, we blockbusting bastards will be in business. *And* nothing you can say will release any ants in my conscience!

DOLLY *(she's had it)* Enough! Absolutely enough! This talk of business—flavored with nasty words—does not belong in our home!

CHUCK I think—

DOLLY Enough, damnit, enough. *(tearfully regretting)*

COBINA Chuck isn't as impractical as you think. He has already taken the civil service exam for recreation director.

DOLLY *(with new interest)* Did he pass?

CHUCK I made the second highest mark.

(The VAN STRIVENS, *glaciers melt. All are drawn to* CHUCK*)*

OSCAR *(putting his arm around* CHUCK*)* Well, tell me something. You will be appointed?

CHUCK I guess I will unless something better turns up.

MRS. PACE Civil service *is* civil service.

CHUCK It can be a dead end.

DOLLY Mother, what about his background?

MRS. PACE Some people have backgrounds. Others have *backbone*.

OSCAR *(to* MRS. PACE*)* Do you mean *you* accept him?

MRS. PACE When I objected to you twenty years ago, I did so in vain.

COBINA Thank you, Granny. *(kisses her)*

(Commotion off upper left stage: dog barking, tumbling footsteps on the stairs, and TILLIE*'s frantic voice)*

TILLIE Let go! Let go! Do you hear me? *(dog growls, cries and whines.* TILLIE, *in her wrap, enters from left foyer all shaky and disheveled)* That damn dog of yours had my bridge work down there in his kennel.

COBINA *(alarmed, dashes out, followed by* CHUCK, OSCAR, MRS. PACE, *and* RUBY*)* Oh, is he hurt?

TILLIE He wouldn't let go until I stuck him with a hair pin.

DOLLY Now, will you get the hell out of here?

TILLIE I can't get out of here fast enough. Where's my niece? Where's Ed?

DOLLY They left long ago.

TILLIE *(recapturing her composure)* How dare they leave me!

DOLLY When ordered out, *they* obeyed!

TILLIE You'll have to explain to my lawyer how that mutt got my partial!

DOLLY Get out! Let the doorknob bang your backside! *(steps toward her)*

TILLIE Don't you touch me again!

MRS. PACE *(enters from left, stops center)* Touch you! Why, you deceiving, calculating wench! I knew when you came flying by here this morning that you were up to nothing good. You should have been spanked in Macy's window!

DOLLY She has been ding-donging with Ed Tucker.

MRS. PACE *(with asperity)* That's it! That's why this old bag was sinking us and at the same time securing Ed Tucker tightly to her monstrous bosom! Thanks gossip-monger for telling our guests not to come.

DOLLY What's this?

MRS. PACE I have been trying to tell you for the last half-hour that I phoned our guests. Some tried to lie out of it. Others admitted that Petunia warned them that the party was going to be a disaster. That this scrub-woman Jackson was coming and others who are more at home in jail.

TILLIE What if I did! Who do you think you are? Van Strivens—VAN SKUNKS! You dare lay your filthy hands on me. I'm not afraid of you. I'll show you. I'm going to sue you. I will make you the biggest goats of the season. I shall smear your names in the biggest and boldest letters on the front page of the *Black Dispatch*. You little upstarts. You scheming, broke climbers. As long as you give parties, I don't need any comic section in my newspaper!

DOLLY So you will, eh?

TILLIE B-e-l-i-e-v-e me!

DOLLY *(fiercely)* You back-biting, two-faced hussy!

MRS. PACE Don't spare the rod, but keep your dignity.

DOLLY Nothing that you can print can scandalize me more than I can discredit you! The mud you fling on me will splatter back into the map you call a face!

TILLIE *(most gratified)* Seeing you socially dead is worth any price. I'm glad I fouled up your party.

DOLLY Rejoice, evil child! But exactly what poison did you sprinkle among my friends?

TILLIE I told them that the creeps and

floozies crashing the party were bound to cause a riot.

MRS. PACE *That* would deter God Himself. *(sits chair down left)*

TILLIE They realized something that you don't.

DOLLY And that is?

TILLIE That without the press, all of you are papier mâché.

DOLLY The press be damned. *I know who I am.* I've been middle-class for three generations.

TILLIE You're still just another face in the Harlem coal bin.

MRS. PACE Rumors persist that your grandmother was a slut!

TILLIE That's a lie!

MRS. PACE And that your membership in every committee for fallen girls is an act of repentance.

TILLIE Grandma was the *owner* of the best whorehouse in downtown Brooklyn, regardless of race, creed, or need. Slut *herself,* she was not.

MRS. PACE Your credentials for the underclass are excellent. You are vulgar and gauche. Your disgraceful ancestors and unrefined instincts add up to zero. Why my daughter tolerates you is—

TILLIE *(angrily)* Tolerate me! People fear me. Had your guests come here tonight, my press would have blackballed their names. Their fear of me outweighed their loyalty to you. With that kind of clout, I need no ancestor. I am my own ancestor.

DOLLY Fear is a weapon that can work for you or against you. *(takes photo film from desk drawer, crosses, showing it to* TILLIE*)* Won't your butt look swell on the front pages of the *Amsterdam News?*

TILLIE *(stunned, grabs at it.* MRS. PACE *grabs it first and clears)* You're . . . you're lying—

DOLLY After it's developed, I'm giving it to the *Amsterdam News.* Hennypest snapped it just as I was spanking you. Oh, what a front-page feature that will make!

TILLIE *(painfully)* They would print it—with monstrous glee.

DOLLY No doubt at all. And with a little retouch that would expose your nude bottom. Remember, Mother, the picture of the Baptist minister with his leading soprano, both nude?

MRS. PACE *(claps her hands, unnerving* TILLIE*)* Halleluiah! Halleluiah!

TILLIE That picture will scandalize us both. Please give me that film.

DOLLY I will give you nothing.

TILLIE How much do you want for it?

DOLLY It is not for sale.

TILLIE You'll ruin my reputation. You'll ruin our reputation.

DOLLY It's too late for salvation.

TILLIE I promise not to print anything about you and what has happened.

DOLLY And what about that disaster zone you call a mouth?

TILLIE In my mouth your name will no longer find comfort.

DOLLY Bless you. Now, get out!

MRS. PACE She said get out!

*(*TILLIE *crosses to arch)*

DOLLY Just a minute. *(tears up negative and gives it to* TILLIE*)*

TILLIE You did this because you think you are the better person.

DOLLY *(firmly)* Good night, Tillie.

TILLIE At best, we were stepfriends. I'm going to miss that.

DOLLY Now we're close enemies.

TILLIE Sometimes your worst enemy is your best friend.

(She has gone. DOLLY *sits on sofa.* MRS. PACE *crosses behind sofa and presses* DOLLY*'s shoulders reassuringly)*

DOLLY *(soul searching)* I should have destroyed her.

MRS. PACE You stayed within the bounds of decency.

DOLLY She will destroy herself.

RUBY *(entering with* OSCAR*)* So, you just expect me in your office at nine tomorrow morning.

MRS. PACE You mean you will buy anyway?

RUBY Why, surely, I ain't changed my mind.

DOLLY *(stunned)* Why, Miss Jackson!

RUBY Never you mind, honey. Forget the sendoff. I need a good place to live. The razzle dazzle can come later.

MRS. PACE *(coaxing)* Having such a nice home, you will want to have nice friends.

DOLLY *(crossing to* MRS. PACE*)* Mother, are we to accept her?

MRS. PACE *(whispering to* DOLLY*)* How much did you say that sweepstake was?

DOLLY Two hundred and fifty thousand dollars.

MRS. PACE Well then—

DOLLY Of course.

RUBY Don't you bother, child. You all seem to do 'bout the same thing I do.

MRS. PACE Now, Miss Jackson, it ain't what you do. It's the way how you do it. *(braces herself)*

RUBY Well, all right then.

DOLLY Miss Jackson, please forgive me. If I have made you unhappy, then let me show you how happy I can make you. You must for there is something that you can teach me.

RUBY But what can I teach you 'doubt it's how to pick a lucky horse?

DOLLY You can teach me to have a heart as big as yours. I am beginning to think my way of doing things is somewhat phony.

RUBY Why, Mrs. Van Striven.

DOLLY Will you?

RUBY Sakes alive . . . I sure will.

DOLLY *(crossing, embracing her)* Thank you, my dear. Why don't you stay overnight?

OSCAR Yes, do. I might change my mind about putting a turnstile to that third floor. Uhem—we can get right down to business the first thing in the morning.

RUBY That's right nice of you all.

DOLLY Mother, show Miss Jackson to the Booker T. Washington bedroom.

MRS. PACE Come, Miss Jackson. *(crosses to arch and waits)*

RUBY Ain't she sweet. *(struts toward archway, totally lacking in grace)*

MRS. PACE *(stopping her)* Miss Jackson, please. The first lesson in social deportment is not to walk like a duck. Walk this way. *(braces and strolls through archway, pauses, looks back and exits)*

RUBY She walks like she's leading me to Jesus at the second coming. *(assuming an exact carbon copy of* MRS. PACE *she exits after pausing and winking)*

*(*DOLLY *quickly closes the window, takes* ROOM FOR RENT *sign and tucks it neatly in the window as* OSCAR *embraces her agreeably. Curtain)*

DAY OF ABSENCE
1965

Douglas Turner Ward (1930–)

African American periodicals generally have used Black critics because they understood the material. In the 1920s, the best known were Theophilus Lewis, Tony Langston, J.A. Jackson, Romeo Doughtery, and Lester Walton. White critics on the major papers, who besides dispensing the usual bits of lemon with sugar, often felt compelled to wax authoritatively on what African American Theatre should be.

This condescension was relieved by three developments: the use of Black theatre critics in the late 1960s, such as Clayton Riley and Larry Neal; the development of a Black audience who bought tickets in increasing numbers; and a developing sensitivity on the part of white critics, who had realized that their judgments were biased by ignorance of the Black experience, their own commitment to traditional white aesthetics, and (in some cases) by their own overt racial prejudices.

By 1970, if a white critic didn't like a Black play, he wrote long and circuitous passages to let the reader know that he intended to be fair. Usually these passages boiled down to either: "I don't care if he's brown, black, green, or pink, theatre must . . ." or, "Maybe I'm ignorant of the Black experience and missing the point, but theatre must . . ."

Some of the newspaper critics who reviewed *Happy Ending* and *Day of Absence* when they premiered Off Broadway on November 15, 1965, were becoming aware that traditional criticisms did not always apply. Michael Smith of the *Village Voice* noted that in Black plays, "their content is all important . . ." and that "Douglas Turner Ward is writing for a Black audience." Such observations may seem elementary now, but compare them to Martin Gottfried's comments in *Women's Wear Daily:*

> Douglas Turner Ward's first plays . . . are in turn derivative, contradictory, childish, dull and silly. . . . Mr. Ward's best interests are not really being served in the production of his fledgling creations.
>
> The theatrical thematic affect of a Negro in white face is enormous and could only be conceived by a royal artist like Genet. Ward's borrowing of it was presumptuous and his application of it to a play whose at-

titude basically is peevish, makes it obscene. *Day of Absence* is an elaborate pout.

Putting Mr. Gottfried's anger aside, he expresses three traditional white viewpoints. First, his standard of judgment is based on Jean Genet (substitute "Shakespeare" or "the Greeks"). Second, he purports to know Mr. Ward's best interest. Third, he finds the work "dull," and "contradictory," although he acknowledges in the same review that the plays were "designed for the special taste and background of the Negro, as in 'race records.'" Several other critics also noted that the Negroes in the audience "were knocking themselves out with laughter while the whites sat stone faced."

Nothing succeeds like success—especially in the commercial theatre. Mr. Ward's plays were vindicated by a run of 504 performances, and it has been widely produced in schools and colleges. Ward had realized that some lessons are more easily absorbed through humor than through serious drama—particularly if the author wishes to avoid the appearance of preaching. James Baldwin, for example, used stark drama in *Blues for Mister Charley* to point out racial inequities. White audiences felt uncomfortable, which was Baldwin's intent. Critics gave the play mixed reviews. On the other hand, shows such as *Fly Blackbird* and *The Colored Museum*, which approach the same theme with humor, were more warmly received. *Day of Absence* announced the arrival of new southern African Americans, ones who were attuned to the times. The play sent a message to America: We are an integral part of this society, and you must accept us as equals. In 1969, a Day of Absence was declared in New York City, a day in which all Black people were to stay home from work.

The man who created the stir and who is sometimes referred to as the "Father" of the modern Black theatre, was born on a plantation near the small town of Burnside, Louisiana, in 1930. He attended Wilberforce and Michigan Universities, discovered radical politics, and left college at age nineteen for New York City. In 1951, during the Korean War, he was arrested for alleged draft evasion and spent two months in prison. The Supreme Court eventually threw out the case against him. Ward studied acting with Paul Mann and secured the role of understudy to Sidney Poitier in *A Raisin in the Sun*. He had also begun writing plays, which he showed to his friend Robert Hooks. In 1965, they produced *Day of Absence* and *Happy Ending* at the St. Marks Place Theatre. The following year, Ward wrote an article for the *New York Times* about the need for a Black theatre in America. This article changed his life as well as the history of Black theatre because it was read by George McBundy of the Ford Foundation, which soon granted Ward, Hooks, and producer Gerald Krone a three-year grant of $1,200,000 to found the Negro Ensemble Company. (Ward insisted on retaining the word "Negro" because "it had a long, honored history, and I didn't like the posturing that went with the total put-down of the word.")

Except for its first production, *Song of the Lusitanian Bogey)* (1967) by Peter Weiss, all of the scripts staged by NEC over the next twenty years would be by Blacks—American, Caribbean, and African. Some became critical successes: *The River Niger* (1972) by Joseph Walker won a Tony Award for the best play on Broadway; *The First Breeze of Summer* (1975) by Leslie Lee won an Obie as the best Off-Broadway drama; and *A Solder's Play* (1981) by Charles H. Fuller, Jr., won the Pulitzer Prize. Phillip Hayes Dean's *The Sty of the Blind Pig* (1971) won the Drama Desk Award. The company trained and provided work for hundreds of actors including Frances Foster, Roscoe Lee Brown,

Rosalind Cash, Cleavon Little, Roxie Roker, Ron O'Neal, Glynn Turman, Al Freeman, Jr., Esther Rolle, and dozens more. However, NEC failed to purchase a building, and in the second decade, as government and foundation support lessened, the cost of maintaining a producing company became impossible. By 1992, the company was homeless and stopped all production soon after. Nonetheless, the Negro Ensemble Company had made the world conscious of the variety of Black theatre and the high quality of writing, acting, and production it had attained.

Day of Absence

CAST OF CHARACTERS

The play is conceived for performance by a Black cast, a reverse minstrel show done in white face.

CLEM, *a country cracker*
LUKE, *another*
MARY, *young white mother*
JOHN, *young white father*
FIRST OPERATOR
SECOND OPERATOR
THIRD OPERATOR
SUPERVISOR
MAYOR, *a small town official*
JACKSON, *his assistant*
MEN FROM THE TOWN
BUSINESSMAN
CLUBWOMAN
COURIER
CLAN, *as in* KKK
ANNOUNCER
AIDE
REB PIOUS, *a religious man*
RASTUS, *the missing man*

SCENE *Street*

TIME *Early morning*

CLEM *(sitting under a sign suspended by invisible wires and bold-printed with the lettering: "STORE")* 'Morning, Luke . . .

LUKE *(sitting a few paces away under an identical sign)* 'Morning, Clem . . .

CLEM Go'n' be a hot day.

LUKE Looks that way . . .

CLEM Might rain though . . .

LUKE Might.

CLEM Hope it does . . .

LUKE Me, too . . .

CLEM Farmers could use a little wet spell for a change . . . How's the Missis?

LUKE Same.

CLEM 'N' the kids?

LUKE Them, too . . . How's yourns?

CLEM Fine, thank you . . . *(they both lapse into drowsy silence, waving lethargically from time to time at imaginary passersby)* Hi, Joe . . .

LUKE Joe . . .

CLEM . . . How'd it go yesterday, Luke?

LUKE Fair.

CLEM Same wit' me . . . Business don't seem to git no better or no worse. Guess we in a rut, Luke, don't it 'pear that way to you?—Morning, ma'am.

LUKE Morning . . .

CLEM Tried display, sales, advertisement, stamps—everything, yet merchandising stumbles 'round in the same old groove . . . But—that's better than plunging downwards, I reckon.

LUKE Guess it is.

CLEM Morning, Bret. How's the family? . . . That's good.

LUKE Bret—

CLEM Morning, Sue.

LUKE How do, Sue.

CLEM *(staring after her)* . . . Fine hunk of woman.

LUKE Sure is.

CLEM Wonder if it's any good?

LUKE Bet it is.

CLEM Sure like to find out!

LUKE So would I.

CLEM You ever try?

LUKE Never did . . .

CLEM Morning, Gus . . .

LUKE Howdy, Gus.

CLEM Fine, thank you. *(they lapse into silence again.* CLEM *rouses himself slowly, begins to look around quizzically)* Luke . . . ?

LUKE Huh?

CLEM Do you . . . er, er—feel anything—funny . . . ?

LUKE Like what?

CLEM Like . . . er—something—strange?

LUKE I dunno . . . haven't thought about it.

CLEM I mean . . . like something's wrong—outta place, unusual?

LUKE I don't know . . . What you got in mind?

CLEM Nothing . . . just that—just that—like somp'ums outta kilter. I got a funny feeling somp'ums not up to snuff. Can't figger out what it is . . .

LUKE Maybe it's in your haid?

CLEM No, not like that . . . Like somp'ums happened or happening gone haywire, loony.

LUKE Well, don't worry 'bout it, it'll pass.

CLEM Guess you're right. *(attempts return to somnolence but doesn't succeed)* . . . I'm sorry, Luke, but you sure you don't feel nothing peculiar . . . ?

LUKE *(slightly irked)* Toss it out your mind, Clem! We got a long day ahead of us. If something's wrong, you'll know 'bout it in due time. No use worrying about it 'till it comes and if it's coming, it will. Now, relax!

CLEM All right, you right . . . Hi, Margie . . .

LUKE Marge.

CLEM *(unable to control himself)* Luke, I don't give a damn what you say. Somp'ums topsy-turvy, I just know it!

LUKE *(increasingly irritated)* Now look here, Clem—it's a bright day, it looks like it's go'n' git hotter. You say the wife and kids are fine and the business is no better or no worse? Well, what else could be wrong? . . . If somp'ums go'n' happen, it's go'n' happen anyway and there ain't a damn fool thing you kin do to stop it! So you ain't helping me, yourself or nobody else by thinking 'bout it. It's not go'n' be no better or no worse when it gits here. It'll come to you when it gits ready to come and it's go'n' be the same whether you worry about it or not. So stop letting it upset you! *(*LUKE *settles back in his chair.* CLEM *does likewise.* LUKE *shuts his eyes. After a few moments, they reopen. He forces them shut again. They reopen in greater curiosity. Finally, he rises slowly to an upright position in the chair, looks around frowningly. Turns slowly to* CLEM*)* . . . Clem? . . . You know something? . . . Somp'um is peculiar . . .

CLEM *(vindicated)* I knew it, Luke! I just knew it! Ever since we been sitting here, I been having that feeling!

(Scene is blacked out abruptly. Lights rise on another section of the stage where a young couple lie in bed under an invisible-wire-suspension-sign lettered: "HOME." Loud insistent sounds of baby yells are heard. JOHN*, the husband, turns over trying to ignore the cries,* MARY*, the wife, is undisturbed.* JOHN*'s efforts are futile, the cries continue until they cannot be denied. He bolts upright, jumps out of bed and disappears offstage. Returns quickly and tries to rouse* MARY*)*

JOHN Mary . . . *(nudges her, pushes her, yells into her ear, but she fails to respond)* Mary, get up . . . Get up!

MARY Ummm . . . *(shrugs away, still sleeping)*

JOHN GET UP!

MARY UMMMMMMMMM!

JOHN Don't you hear the baby bawling! . . . NOW GET UP!

MARY *(mumbling drowsily)* . . . What baby . . . whose baby . . . ?

JOHN Yours!

MARY Mine? That's ridiculous . . . what'd you say . . . ? Somebody's baby bawling? . . . How could that be so? *(hearing screams)* Who's crying? Somebody's crying! . . . What's crying? . . . WHERE's LULA?!

JOHN I don't know. You better get up.

MARY That's outrageous! . . . What time is it?

JOHN Late 'nuff! Now rise up!

MARY You must be joking . . . I'm sure I still have four or five hours sleep in store—even more after the head-splittin' blow-out last night . . . *(tumbles back under covers)*

JOHN Nobody told you to gulp those last six bourbons—

MARY Don't tell me how many bourbons to swallow, not after you guzzled the whole stinking bar! . . . Get up? . . . You must be cracked . . . Where's Lula? She must be here, she always is . . .

JOHN Well, she ain't here yet, so get up and muzzle that brat before she does drive me cuckoo!

MARY *(springing upright, finally realizing gravity of situation)* Whaddaya mean Lula's not here? She's always here, she must be here . . . Where else kin she be? She supposed to be . . . She just can't *not* be here—CALL HER!

(Blackout as JOHN *rushes offstage. Scene shifts to a trio of* TELEPHONE OPERATORS *perched on stools before imaginary switchboards. Chaos and bedlam are taking place to the sound of buzzes. Effect of following dialogue should stimulate rising pandemonium)*

FIRST OPERATOR The line is busy—
SECOND OPERATOR Line is busy—
THIRD OPERATOR Is busy—
FIRST OPERATOR Doing best we can—
SECOND OPERATOR Having difficulty—
THIRD OPERATOR Soon as possible—
FIRST OPERATOR Just one moment—
SECOND OPERATOR Would you hold on—
THIRD OPERATOR Awful sorry, madam—
FIRST OPERATOR Would you hold on, please—
SECOND OPERATOR Just a second, please—
THIRD OPERATOR Please hold on, please—
FIRST OPERATOR The line is busy—
SECOND OPERATOR The line is busy—
THIRD OPERATOR The line is busy—
FIRST OPERATOR Doing best we can—
SECOND OPERATOR Hold on please—
THIRD OPERATOR Can't make connections—
FIRST OPERATOR Unable to put it in—
SECOND OPERATOR Won't plug through—
THIRD OPERATOR Sorry madam—
FIRST OPERATOR If you'd wait a moment—
SECOND OPERATOR Doing best we can—
THIRD OPERATOR Sorry—
FIRST OPERATOR One moment—
SECOND OPERATOR Just a second—
THIRD OPERATOR Hold on—
FIRST OPERATOR YES—
SECOND OPERATOR STOP IT!—
THIRD OPERATOR HOW DO I KNOW—
FIRST OPERATOR YOU ANOTHER ONE!
SECOND OPERATOR HOLD ON DAMMIT!
THIRD OPERATOR UP YOURS, TOO!
FIRST OPERATOR THE LINE IS BUSY
SECOND OPERATOR THE LINE IS BUSY—
THIRD OPERATOR THE LINE IS BUSY—

(The switchboard clamors a cacophony of buzzes as OPERATORS *plug connections with the frenzy of a Chaplin movie. Their replies degenerate into a babble of gibberish. At the height of frenzy, the* SUPERVISOR *appears)*

SUPERVISOR WHAT'S THE SNARL-UP???!!!

FIRST OPERATOR Everybody calling at the same time, ma'am!

SECOND OPERATOR Board can't handle it!

THIRD OPERATOR Like everybody in big New York City is trying to squeeze a call through to li'l' ole us!

SUPERVISOR God! . . . Somp'un terrible musta happened! . . . Buzz the emergency frequency hookup to the Mayor's office and find out what the hell's going on!

(Scene blacks out quickly to CLEM *and* LUKE*)*

CLEM *(something slowly dawning on him)* Luke . . . ?

LUKE Yes, Clem?

CLEM *(eyes roving around in puzzlement)* Luke . . . ?

LUKE *(irked)* I said what, Clem!

CLEM Luke . . . ? Where—where is—the—the—?

LUKE THE WHAT?!

CLEM Nigras . . . ?

LUKE ?????What . . . ?

CLEM Nigras . . . Where is the Nigras, where is they, Luke . . . ? ALL THE NIGRAS! . . . I don't see no Nigras . . . ?!

LUKE Whatcha mean . . . ?

CLEM *(agitatedly)* Luke, there ain't a darkey in sight . . . And if you remember, we ain't spied a nappy hair all morning . . . The Nigras, Luke! We ain't laid eyes on nary a coon this whole morning!!!

LUKE You must be crazy or something, Clem!

CLEM Think about it, Luke, we been sitting here for an hour or more—try and recollect if you remember seeing jist *one* go by?!!!

LUKE *(confused)* . . . I don't recall . . . But . . . but there musta been some . . . The heat musta got you, Clem! How in hell could that be so?!!!

CLEM *(triumphantly)* Just think, Luke! . . .

Look around ya . . . Now, every morning mosta people walkin' 'long this street is colored. They's strolling by going to work, they's waiting for the buses, they's sweeping sidewalks, cleaning stores, starting to shine shoes and wetting the mops—right?! . . . Well, look around you, Luke—where is they? *(*LUKE *paces up and down, checking)* I told you, Luke, they ain't nowheres to be seen.

LUKE ???? . . . This . . . this . . . some kind of holiday for 'em—or something?

CLEM I don't know, Luke . . . but . . . but what I do know is they ain't here 'n' we haven't seen a solitary one . . . It's scaryfying, Luke . . . !

LUKE Well . . . maybe they's jist standing 'n' walking and shining on other streets.—Let's go look!

(Scene blacks out to JOHN *and* MARY. *Baby cries are as insistent as ever)*

MARY *(at end of patience)* SMOTHER IT!

JOHN *(beyond his)* That's a hell of a thing to say 'bout your own child! You should know what to do to hush her up!

MARY Why don't you try?!

JOHN You had her!

MARY You shared in borning her!!

JOHN Possibly not!

MARY Why, you lousy—!

JOHN What good is a mother who can't shut up her own daughter?!

MARY I told you she yells louder every time I try to lay hands on her.—Where's Lula? Didn't you call her?!

JOHN I told you I can't get the call through!

MARY Try ag'in—

JOHN It's no use! I tried numerous times and can't even git through to the switchboard. You've got to quiet her down yourself. *(firmly)* Now, go in there and clam her up 'fore I lose my patience! *(*MARY *exits. Soon, we hear the yells increase. She rushes back in)*

MARY She won't let me touch her, just screams louder!

JOHN Probably wet 'n' soppy!

MARY Yes! Stinks something awful! Phoooooey! I can't stand that filth and odor!

JOHN That's why she's screaming! Needs her didee changed.—Go change it!

MARY How you 'spect me to when I don't know how?! Suppose I faint?!

JOHN Well let her blast away. I'm getting outta here.

MARY You can't leave me here like this!

JOHN Just watch me! . . . See this nice split-level cottage, peachy furniture, multi-colored teevee, hi-fi set 'n' the rest? . . . Well, how you think I scraped 'em together while you curled up on your fat li'l' fanny? . . . By gitting outta here—not only *on time* . . . but EARLIER!—Beating a frantic crew of nice young executives to the punch—gitting there fustest with the mostest brown-nosing you ever saw! Now if I goof one day—just ONE DAY!—You reckon I'd stay ahead? NO! . . . There'd be a wolf-pack trampling over my prostrate body, racing to replace my smiling face against the boss' left rump! . . . NO, MAM! I'm zooming outta here on time, just as I always have and what's more—you go'n' fix me some breakfast, I'M HUNGRY!

MARY But—

JOHN No buts about it! *(flash blackout as he gags on a mouthful of coffee)* What you trying to do, STRANGLE ME!!! *(jumps up and starts putting on jacket)*

MARY *(sarcastically)* What did you expect?

JOHN *(in biting fury)* That you could possibly boil a pot of water, toast a few slices of bread and fry a coupler eggs! . . . It was a mistaken assumption!

MARY So they aren't as good as Lula's!

JOHN That is an overstatement. Your efforts don't result in anything that could possibly be digested by man, mammal, or insect! . . . When I married you, I thought I was fairly acquainted with your faults and weaknesses—I chalked 'em up to human imperfection . . . But now I know I was being extremely generous, over-optimistic and phenomenally deluded!—You have no idea how useless you really are!

MARY Then why'd you marry me?!

JOHN Decoration!

MARY You shoulda married Lula!

JOHN I might've if it wasn't 'gainst the segregation law! . . . But for the sake of my home, my child and my sanity, I will even take a chance on sacrificing my slippery grip on the status pole and drive by her shanty to find out whether she or someone like her kin come over here and prevent some ultimate disaster. *(storms toward door, stopping abruptly at exit)* Are you sure you kin make it to the bathroom wit'out Lula backing you up?!!!

(Blackout. Scene shifts to MAYOR's *office where a cluttered desk stands center amid papered debris)*

MAYOR *(striding determinedly toward desk, stopping midways, bellowing)* WOODFENCE! . . . WOODFENCE! . . . WOODFENCE! *(receiving no reply, completes distance to desk)* JACKSON! . . . JACKSON!

JACKSON *(entering worriedly)* Yes, sir . . . ?

MAYOR Where's Vice-Mayor Woodfence, that no-good brother-in-law of mine?!

JACKSON Hasn't come in yet, sir.

MAYOR HASN'T COME IN?!!! . . . Damn bastard! Knows we have a crucial conference. Soon as he staggers through that door, tell him to shoot in here! *(angrily focusing on his disorderly desk and littered surroundings)* And git Mandy here to straighten up this mess—Rufus too! You know he shoulda been waiting to knock dust off my shoes soon as I step in. Get 'em in here! . . . What's the matter wit' them lazy Nigras? . . . Already had to dress myself because of JC, fix my own coffee without May-Belle, drive myself to work 'counta Bubber, feel my old Hag's tits after Sapphi—NEVER MIND!—Git 'em in here—QUICK!

JACKSON *(meekly)* They aren't . . . they aren't here, sir . . .

MAYOR Whaddaya mean they aren't here? Find out where they at. We got important business, man! You can't run a town wit' laxity like this. Can't allow things to git snafued jist because a bunch of lazy Nigras been out gitting drunk and living it up all night! Discipline, man, discipline!

JACKSON That's what I'm trying to tell you, sir . . . they didn't come in, can't be found . . . none of 'em.

MAYOR Ridiculous, boy! Scare 'em up and tell 'em scoot here in a hurry befo' I git mad and fire the whole goddamn lot of 'em!

JACKSON But we can't find 'em, sir.

MAYOR Hogwash! Can't nobody in this office do anything right?! Do I hafta handle every piddling little matter myself?! Git me their numbers, I'll have 'em here befo' you kin shout to—*(three men burst into room in various states of undress)*

ONE Henry—they vanished!

TWO Disappeared into thin air!

THREE Gone wit'out a trace!

TWO Not a one on the street!

THREE In the house!

ONE On the job!

MAYOR Wait a minute!! . . . Hold your water! Calm down—!

ONE But they've gone, Henry—GONE! All of 'em!

MAYOR What the hell you talking 'bout? Gone? Who's gone—?

ONE The Nigras, Henry! They gone!

MAYOR Gone? . . . Gone where?

TWO That's what we trying to tell ya—they just disappeared! The Nigras have disappeared, swallowed up, vanished! All of 'em! Every last one!

MAYOR Have everybody 'round here gone batty? . . . That's impossible, how could the Nigras vanish?

THREE Beats me, but it's happened!

MAYOR You mean a whole town of Nigras just evaporate like this—poof!—Overnight?

ONE Right!

MAYOR Y'all must be drunk! Why, half this town is colored. How could they just sneak out!

TWO Don't ask me, but there ain't one in sight!

MAYOR Simmer down 'n' put it to me easy-like.

ONE Well . . . I first suspected somp'um smelly when Sarah Jo didn't show up this morning and I couldn't reach her—

TWO Dorothy Jane didn't 'rive at my house—

THREE Georgia Mae wasn't at mine neither—and SHE sleeps in!

ONE When I reached the office, I realized I hadn't seen nary one Nigra all morning! Nobody else had either—wait a minute—Henry, have you?!

MAYOR ???Now that you mention it . . . no, I haven't . . .

ONE They gone, Henry . . . Not a one on the street, not a one in our homes, not a single, last living one to be found nowheres in town. What we gon' do?!

MAYOR *(thinking)* Keep heads on your shoulders 'n' put clothes on your back . . . They can't be far . . . Must be 'round somewheres . . . Probably playing hide 'n' seek, that's it! . . . JACKSON!

JACKSON Yessir?

MAYOR Immediately mobilize our Citizens Emergency Distress Committee!—Order a fleet of sound trucks to patrol streets urging the population to remain calm—situation's not as bad as it looks—everything's under control! Then, have another squadron of squawk buggies drive slowly through all Nigra alleys, ordering them to come out wherever they are. If that don't git 'em, organize a vigilante search-squad to flush 'em outta hiding! But most important of all, track down that lazy goldbricker, Woodfence and tell him to git on top of the situation! By God, we'll find 'em even if we hafta dig 'em outta the ground!

(Blackout. Scene shifts back to JOHN *and* MARY *a few hours later. A funereal solemnity pervades their mood.* JOHN *stands behind* MARY *who sits, in a scene duplicating the famous "American Gothic" painting)*

JOHN . . . Walked up to the shack, knocked on door, didn't git no answer. Hollered: "LULA? LULA . . . ?—Not a thing. Went 'round the side, peeped in window—nobody stirred. Next door—nobody there. Crossed other side of street and banged on five or six other doors—not a colored person could be found! Not a man, neither woman or child—not even a little black dog could be seen, smelt or heard for blocks around . . . They've gone, Mary.

MARY What does it all mean, John?

JOHN I don't know, Mary . . .

MARY I always had Lula, John. She never missed a day at my side . . . That's why I couldn't accept your wedding proposal until I was sure you'd welcome me and her together as a package. How am I gonna git through the day? My baby don't know *me,* I ain't acquainted wit' *it.* I've never lifted cover off pot, swung a mop or broom, dunked a dish or even pushed a dustrag. I'm lost wit'out Lula, I need her, John, I need her. *(begins to weep softly.* JOHN *pats her consolingly)*

JOHN Courage, honey . . . Everybody in town is facing the same dilemma. We mustn't crack up . . .

(Blackout. Scene shifts back to MAYOR*'s office later in day. Atmosphere and tone resembles a wartime headquarters at the front.* MAYOR *is poring over huge map)*

INDUSTRIALIST Half the day is gone already, Henry. On behalf of the factory owners of this town, you've got to bail us out! Seventy-five per cent of all production is paralyzed. With the Nigra absent, men are waiting for machines to be cleaned, floors to be swept, crates lifted, equipment delivered and bathrooms to be deodorized. Why, restrooms and toilets are so filthy until they not only cannot be sat in, but it's virtually impossible to get within hailing distance because of the stench!

MAYOR Keep your shirt on, Jeb—

BUSINESSMAN Business is even in worse condition, Henry. The volume of goods moving 'cross counters has slowed down to a trickle—almost negligible. Customers are not only not purchasing—but the absence of handymen, porters, sweepers, stock-movers, deliverers and miscellaneous dirty-work doers is disrupting the smooth harmony of marketing.

CLUB WOMAN Food poisoning, severe indigestitis, chronic diarrhea, advanced diaper chafings and a plethora of unsanitary household disasters dangerous to life, limb and property! . . . As a representative of the Federation of Ladies' Clubs, I must sadly report that unless the trend is reversed, a complete breakdown in family unity is imminent . . . Just as homosexuality and debauchery signalled the fall of Greece and Rome, the downgrading of Southern Bellesdom might very well prophesy the collapse of our indigenous institutions . . . Remember—it has always been pure, delicate, lily-white images of Dixie femininity which provided backbone, inspiration and ideology for our male warriors in their defense against the on-rushing Black horde. If our gallant men are drained of this worship and idolatry—God knows! The cause won't be worth a Confederate nickel!

MAYOR Stop this panicky defeatism, y'all hear me! All machinery at my disposal is being utilized. I assure you wit' great confidence the damage will soon repair itself.—Cheerful progress reports are expected any moment now.—Wait! See, here's Jackson . . . Well, Jackson?

JACKSON *(entering)* As of now, sir, all efforts are fruitless. Neither hide nor hair of them has been located. We have not unearthed a single one in our shack-to-shack search. Not a single one has heeded our appeal. Scoured every crick and cranny inside their hovels, turning furniture upside down and inside out, breaking down walls and tearing through ceilings. We made determined efforts to discover where 'bouts of our faithful Uncle Toms and informers—but even they have vanished without a trace . . . Searching squads are on the verge of panic and hysteria, sir, wit' hotheads among 'em campaigning for scorched earth policies. Nigras on a whole lack cellars, but there's rising sentiment favoring burning to find out whether they're underground—DUG IN!

MAYOR Absolutely counter such foolhardy suggestions! Suppose they are tombed in? We'd only accelerate the gravity of the situation using incendiary tactics! Besides, when they're rounded up where will we put 'em if we've already burned up their shacks—IN OUR OWN BEDROOMS?!!!

JACKSON I agree, sir, but the mood of the crowd is becoming irrational. In anger and frustration, they's forgetting their original purpose was to FIND the Nigras!

MAYOR At all costs! Stamp out all burning proposals! Must prevent extremist notions from gaining ascendancy. Git wit' it . . . Wait—'n' for Jehovah's sake, find out where the hell is that trifling slacker, WOODFENCE!

COURIER *(rushing in)* Mr. Mayor! Mr. Mayor! . . . We've found some! We've found some!

MAYOR *(excitedly)* Where?!

COURIER In the—in the—*(can't catch breath)*

MAYOR *(impatiently)* Where, man? Where?!

COURIER In the colored wing of the city hospital!

MAYOR The hos—? The hospital? I shoulda known! How could those helpless, crippled, cut and shot Nigras disappear from a hospital! Shoulda thought of that! . . . Tell me more, man!

COURIER I—I didn't wait, sir . . . I—I ran in to report soon as I heard—

MAYOR WELL GIT BACK ON THE PHONE, YOU IDIOT, DON'T YOU KNOW WHAT THIS MEANS!

COURIER Yes, sir. *(races out)*

MAYOR Now we gitting somewhere! . . . Gentlemen, if one sole Nigra is among us, we're well on the road to rehabilitation! Those Nigras in the hospital must know somp'um 'bout the others where'bouts . . . Scat back to your colleagues, boost up their morale and inform 'em that things will zip back to normal in a jiffy! *(they start to file out, then pause to observe the* COURIER *reentering dazedly)* Well . . . ? Well, man . . . ? WHAT'S THE MATTER WIT' YOU, NINNY, TELL ME WHAT ELSE WAS SAID?!

COURIER They all . . . they all . . . they all in a —in a—a coma, sir . . .

MAYOR They all in a what . . . ?

COURIER In a coma, sir . . .

MAYOR Talk sense, man! . . . Whaddaya mean, they all in a coma?

COURIER Doctor says every last one of the Nigras are jist laying in bed . . . STILL . . . not moving . . . neither live or dead . . . laying up there in a coma . . . every last one of 'em . . .

MAYOR *(splutters, then grabs phone)* Get me Confederate Memorial . . . Put me through to the Staff Chief . . . YES, this is the Mayor . . . Sam? . . . What's this I hear . . . But how could they be in a coma, Sam? . . . You don't know! Well, what the hell you think the city's paying you for! . . . You've got 'nuff damn hacks and quacks there to find out! . . . How could it be somp'um unknown? You mean Nigras know somp'um 'bout drugs your damn butchers don't?! . . . Well, what the crap good are they! . . . All right, all right, I'll be calm . . . Now, tell me . . . Uh huh, uh huh . . . Well, can't you give 'em some injections or somp'um . . . ?—You did . . . uh huh . . . DID YOU TRY A LI'L' ROUGH TREATMENT?—that too, huh . . . All right, Sam, keep trying . . . *(puts phone down delicately, continuing absently)* Can't wake em' up. Just lay there. Them that's sick won't git no sicker, them that's half-well won't git no better, babies that's due won't be born and them that's come won't show no life. Nigras wit' cuts won't bleed and them which needs blood won't be transfused . . . He say dying Nigras is even refusing to pass away! *(is silently perplexed for a moment, then suddenly breaks into action)* JACKSON?! . . . Call up the police—THE JAIL! Find out what's going on there! Them Nigras are captives! If there's one place we got darkies under control, it's there! Them sonsabitches too onery to act right either for colored or white! *(*JACKSON *exits. The* COURIER *follows)* Keep your fingers crossed, citizens, them Nigras in jail are the most important Nigras we got! *(All hands are raised conspicu-*

ously aloft, fingers prominently ex-ed. Seconds tick by. Soon JACKSON *returns crestfallen)*

JACKSON Sheriff Bull says they don't know whether they still on premises or not. When they went to rouse Nigra jailbirds this morning, cell-block doors refused to swing open. Tried everything—even exploded dynamite charges—but it just wouldn't budge . . . Then they hoisted guards up to peep through barred windows, but couldn't see good 'nuff to tell whether Nigras was inside or not. Finally, gitting desperate, they power-hosed the cells wit' water but had to cease 'cause Sheriff Bull said he didn't wanta jeopardize drowning the Nigras since it might spoil his chance of shipping a record load of cotton pickers to the State Penitentiary for cotton-snatching jubilee . . . Anyway—they ain't heard a Nigra-squeak all day.

MAYOR ???That so . . . ? WHAT 'BOUT TRAINS 'N' BUSSES PASSING THROUGH? There must be some dinges riding through?

JACKSON We checked . . . not a one on board.

MAYOR Did you hear whether any other towns lost their Nigras?

JACKSON Things are status-quo everywhere else.

MAYOR *(angrily)* Then what the hell they picking on us for!

COURIER *(rushing in)* MR. MAYOR! Your sister jist called—HYSTERICAL! She says Vice-Mayor Woodfence went to bed wit' her last night, but when she woke up this morning he was gone! Been missing all day!

MAYOR ???Could Nigras be holding brother-in-law Woodfence hostage?!

COURIER No, sir. Besides him—investigations reveal that dozens or more prominent citizens—two City Council members, the chairman of the Junior Chamber of Commerce, our City College All-Southern halfback, the chair-lady of the Daughters of the Confederate Rebellion, Miss Cotton-Sack Festival of the Year and numerous other miscellaneous nobodies—are all absent wit'out leave. Dangerous evidence points to the conclusion that they have been infiltrating!

MAYOR Infiltrating???

COURIER Passing all along!

MAYOR ???PASSING ALL ALONG???

COURIER Secret Nigras all the while!

MAYOR NAW! (CLUB WOMAN *keels over in faint.* JACKSON, BUSINESSMAN *and* INDUSTRIALIST *begin to eye each other suspiciously)*

COURIER Yessir!

MAYOR PASSING???

COURIER Yessir!

MAYOR SECRET NIG—!???

COURIER Yessir!

MAYOR *(momentarily stunned to silence)* The dirty mongrelizers! . . . Gentlemen, this is a grave predicament indeed . . . It pains me to surrender priority of our states' right credo, but it is my solemn task and frightening duty to inform you that we have no other recourse but to seek outside help for deliverance.

(Blackout. Lights re-rise on Huntley-Brinkley-Murrow-Sevareid-Cronkite-Reasoner-type Announcer grasping a hand-held microphone [imaginary] a few hours later. He is vigorously, excitedly mouthing his commentary, but no sound escapes his lips . . . During this dumb wordless section of his broadcast, a bedraggled assortment of figures marching with picket signs occupy his attention. On their picket signs are inscribed various appeals and slogans. "CINDY LOU UNFAIR TO BABY JOE" . . . "CAP'N SAM MISS BIG BOY" . . . "RETURN LI'L BLUE TO MARSE JIM" . . . "INFORMATION REQUESTED 'BOUT MAMMY GAIL" . . . "BOSS NATHAN PROTEST TO FAST LEROY." Trailing behind the marchers, forcibly isolated, is a woman dressed in widow-black holding a placard which reads: "WHY DIDN'T YOU TELL US—YOUR DEFILED WIFE AND TWO ABSENT MONGRELS")

ANNOUNCER *(who has been silently mouthing his delivery during the picketing procession, is suddenly heard as if caught in the midst of commentary)* . . . Factories standing idle from the loss of non-essential workers. Stores shuttered from the absconding of uncrucial personnel. Uncollected garbage threatening pestilence and pollution . . . Also, each second somewheres in this former utopia below the Mason and Dixon, dozens of decrepit old men and women usually tended by faithful nurses and servants are popping off like flies—abandoned by sons, daughters and grandchildren whose refusal to provide their doddering relatives with bedpans and other soothing necessities result in their hasty, nasty, messy corpus delicties . . . But most critically affected of all by this complete drought of Afro-American resources are policemen and other public safety guardians denied their daily quota of Negro arrests. One officer known affectionately as "TWO-A-DAY-PETE" because of his unblemished record of TWO Negro headwhippings per day has already been carted off to the County Insane Asylum—straight-jacketed, screaming and biting, unable to withstand the shock of having his spotless slate sullied by interruption . . . It is feared that similar attacks are soon expected among municipal judges prevented for the first time in years of distinguished bench-sitting from sentencing one single Negro to a hoosegow or pokey . . . Ladies and gentlemen, as you trudge in from the joys and headaches of workday chores and dusk begins to descend on this sleepy Southern hamlet, we REPEAT—today—before early morning dew had dried upon magnolia blossoms, your comrade citizens of this lovely Dixie village awoke to the realization that some—pardon me! Not some—but ALL OF THEIR NEGROES were missing . . . Absent, vamoosed, departed, at bay, fugitive, away, gone and so-far unretrieved . . . In order to dispel your incredulity, gauge the temper of your suffering compatriots and just possibly prepare you for the likelihood of an equally nightmarish eventuality, we have gathered a cross-section of this city's most distinguished leaders for exclusive interviews . . . First, Mr. Council Clan, grand-dragoon of this area's most active civic organizations and staunch bellwether of the political opposition . . . Mr. Clan, how do you ACCOUNT for this incredible disappearance?

CLAN A PLOT, plain and simple, that's what it is, as plain as the corns on your feet!

ANNOUNCER Whom would you consider responsible?

CLAN I could go on all night.

ANNOUNCER Cite a few?

CLAN Too numerous.

ANNOUNCER Just one?

CLAN Name names when time comes.

ANNOUNCER Could you be referring to native Negroes?

CLAN Ever try quaranteening lepers from their spots?

ANNOUNCER Their organizations?

CLAN Could you slice a nose off a mouth and still keep a face?

ANNOUNCER Commies?

CLAN Would you lop off a titty from a chest and still have a breast?

ANNOUNCER Your city government?

CLAN Now you talkin'!

ANNOUNCER State administration?

CLAN Warming up!

ANNOUNCER Federal?

CLAN Kin a blind man see?!

ANNOUNCER The Court?

CLAN Is a pig clean?!

ANNOUNCER Clergy?

CLAN Do a polecat stink?!

ANNOUNCER Well, Mr. Clan, with this massive complicity, how do you think the plot could've been prevented from succeeding?

CLAN If I'da been in office, it never woulda happened.

ANNOUNCER Then you're laying major blame at the doorstep of the present administration?

CLAN Damn tooting!

ANNOUNCER But from your oft-expressed views, Mr. Clan, shouldn't you and your followers be delighted at the turn of events? After all—isn't it one of the main policies of your society to *drive* the Negroes away? *Drive* 'em back where they came from?

CLAN DRIVVVE, BOY! DRIIIIVVVE! That's right! . . . When we say so and not befo'. Ain't supposed to do nothing 'til we tell 'em. Got to stay put until we exercise our God-given right to tell 'em when to git!

ANNOUNCER But why argue if they've merely jumped the gun? Why not rejoice at this premature purging of undesirables?

CLAN The time ain't ripe yet, boy . . . The time ain't ripe yet.

ANNOUNCER Thank you for being so informative, Mr. Clan—Mrs. Aide? Mrs. Aide? Over here, Mrs. Aide . . . Ladies and gentlemen, this city's Social Welfare Commissioner, Mrs. Handy Anna Aide . . . Mrs. Aide, with all your Negroes *AWOL*, haven't developments alleviated the staggering demands made upon your Welfare Department? Reduction of relief requests, elimination of case loads, removal of chronic welfare dependents, et cetera?

AIDE Quite the contrary. Disruption of our pilot projects among Nigras saddles our white community with extreme hardship . . . You see, historically, our agencies have always been foremost contributors to the Nigra Git-A-Job movement. We pioneered in enforcing social welfare theories which oppose coddling the fakers. We strenuously believe in helping Nigras help themselves by participating in meaningful labor. "Relief is Out, Work is In," is our motto. We place them as maids, cooks, butlers, and breast-feeders, cesspool-diggers, wash-basin maintainers, shoe-shine boys, and so on—mostly on a volunteer self-work basis.

ANNOUNCER Hired at prevailing salaried rates, of course?

AIDE God forbid! Money is unimportant. Would only make 'em worse. Our main goal is to improve their ethical behavior. "Rehabilitation Through Positive Participation" is another motto of ours. All unwed mothers, loose-living malingering fathers, bastard children and shiftless grandparents are kept occupied through constructive muscle-therapy. This provides the Nigra with less opportunity to indulge his pleasure-loving amoral inclinations.

ANNOUNCER They volunteer to participate in these pilot projects?

AIDE Heavens no! They're notorious shirkers. When I said the program is voluntary, I meant white citizens in overwhelming majorities do the volunteering. Placing their home, offices, appliances, and persons at our disposal for use in "Operation Uplift." . . . We would never dare place such a decision in the hands of the Nigra. It would never get off the ground! . . . No, they have no choice in the matter. "Work or Starve" is the slogan we use to stimulate Nigra awareness of what's good for survival.

ANNOUNCER Thank you, Mrs. Aide, and good luck . . . Rev? . . . Rev? . . . Ladies and gentlemen, this city's foremost spiritual guidance counselor, Reverend Reb Pious . . . How does it look to you, Reb Pious?

PIOUS *(continuing to gaze skyward)* It's in *His* hands, son, it's in *His* hands.

ANNOUNCER How would you assess the disappearance, from a moral standpoint?

PIOUS An immoral act, son, morally wrong and ethically indefensible. A perversion of Christian principles to be condemned from every pulpit of this nation.

ANNOUNCER Can you account for its occurrence after the many decades of the Church's missionary activity among them?

PIOUS It's basically a reversion of the Nigra to his deep-rooted primitivism . . . Now, at last, you can understand the difficulties of the Church in attempting to anchor God's kingdom among ungratefuls. It's a constant, unrelenting, no-holds-barred struggle against Satan to wrestle away souls locked in his possession for countless centuries! Despite all our aid, guidance, solace and protection, Old BeezleBub still retains tenacious grips upon the Nigras' childish loyalty—comparable to the lure of bright flames to an infant.

ANNOUNCER But actual physical departure, Reb Pious? How do you explain that?

PIOUS Voodoo, my son, voodoo . . . With Satan's assist, they have probably employed some heathen magic which we cultivated, sophisticated Christians know absolutely nothing about. However, before long we are confident about counteracting this evil witch-doctory and triumphing in our Holy Savior's name. At this perilous juncture, true believers of all denominations are participating in joint, 'round-the-clock observances, offering prayers for our Master's swiftest intercession. I'm optimistic about the outcome of his intervention . . . Which prompts me—if I may, sir—to offer these words of counsel to our delinquent Nigras . . . I say to you without rancor or vengeance, quoting a phrase of one of your greatest prophets, Booker T. Washington: "Return your buckets to where they lay and all will be forgiven."

ANNOUNCER A very inspirational appeal, Reb Pious. I'm certain they will find the tug of its magnetic sincerity irresistible. Thank you, Reb Pious . . . All in all—as you have witnessed, ladies and gentlemen—this town symbolizes the face of disaster. Suffering as severe a prostration as any city wrecked, ravaged and devastated by the holocaust of war. A vital, lively, throbbing organism brought to a screeching halt by the strange enigma of the missing Negroes . . . We take you now to offices of the one man into whose hands has been thrust the final responsibility of rescuing this shuddering metropolis from the precipice of destruction . . . We give you the honorable Mayor, Henry R. E. Lee . . . Hello, Mayor Lee.

MAYOR *(jovially)* Hello, Jack.

ANNOUNCER Mayor Lee, we have just concluded interviews with some of your city's leading spokesmen. If I may say so, sir, they don't sound too encouraging about the situation.

MAYOR Nonsense, Jack! The situation's well-in-hand as it could be under the circumstances. Couldn't be better in hand. Underneath every dark cloud, Jack, there's always a ray of sunlight, ha, ha, ha.

ANNOUNCER Have you discovered one, sir?

MAYOR Well, Jack, I'll tell you . . . Of course we've been faced wit' a little crisis, but look at it like this—we've faced 'em befo': Sherman marched through Georgia—ONCE! Lincoln freed the slaves—MOMENTARILY! Carpetbaggers even put Nigras in the Governor's mansion, state legislature, Congress and the Senate of the United States. But what happened?—Ole Dixie bounced right on back up . . . At this moment the Supreme Court's trying to put Nigras in our schools and the Nigra has got it in his haid to put hisself everywhere . . . But what you 'spect go'n' happen?—Ole Dixie will kangaroo back even higher. Southern courage, fortitude, chivalry and superiority always wins out . . . SHUCKS! We'll have us some Nigras befo' daylight is gone!

ANNOUNCER Mr. Mayor, I hate to introduce this note, but in an earlier interview, one of your chief opponents, Mr. Clan, hinted at your own complicity in the affair—

MAYOR A LOT OF POPPYCOCK! Clan is politicking! I've beaten him four times outta four and I'll beat him four more times outta four! This is not time for partisan politics! What we need now is level-headedness and across-the-board unity. This typical, rash, mealy-mouth, shooting-off-at-the-lip of Clan and his ilk proves their insincerity and voters will remember that in the next election! Won't you, voters?! *(has risen to the height of campaign oratory)*

ANNOUNCER Mr. Mayor! . . . Mr. Mayor! . . . Please—

MAYOR . . . I tell you, I promise you—

ANNOUNCER PLEASE, MR. MAYOR!

MAYOR Huh? . . . Oh—yes, carry on.

ANNOUNCER Mr. Mayor, your cheerfulness and infectious good spirits lead me to conclude that startling new developments warrant fresh-found optimism. What concrete, declassified information do you have to support your claim that Negroes will reappear before nightfall?

MAYOR Because we are presently awaiting the pay-off of a masterful five-point supra-recovery program which can't help but reap us a bonanza of Nigras 'fore sundown! . . . First: Exhaustive efforts to pinpoint the where'bouts of our own missing darkies continue to zero in on the bullseye . . . Second: The President of the United States, following an emergency cabinet meeting, has designated us the prime disaster area of the century—National Guard is already on the way . . . Third: In an unusual, but bold maneuver, we have appealed to the NAACP 'n' all other Nigra conspirators to help us git to the bottom of the vanishing act . . . Fourth: We have exercised our non-reciprocal option and requested that all fraternal Southern states express their solidarity by lending us some of their Nigras temporarily on credit . . . Fifth and foremost: We have already gotten consent of the Governor to round up all stray, excess and incorrigible Nigras to be shipped to us under escort of the State Militia . . . That's why we've stifled pessimism and are brimming wit' confidence that this fullscale concerted mobilization will ring down a jackpot of jigaboos 'fore light vanishes from sky!—

ANNOUNCER Congratulations! What happens if it fails?

MAYOR Don't even think THAT! Absolutely no reason to suspect it will . . . *(peers over shoulder, then whispers confidentially while placing hand over mouth by* ANNOUNCER*'s imaginary mike)* . . . But speculating on the dark side of your question—if we don't turn up some by nightfall, it may be all over. The harm has already been done. You see the South has always been glued together by the uninterrupted presence of its darkies. No telling how unstuck we might git if things keep on like they have.—Wait a minute, it musta paid off already! Mission accomplished 'cause here's Jackson head a time wit' the word . . . Well, Jackson, what's new?

JACKSON Situation on the home front remains static, sir—can't uncover scent or shadow. The NAACP and all other Nigra front groups 'n' plotters deny any knowledge or connection wit' the missing Nigras. Maintained this even after appearing befo' a Senate Emergency Investigating Committee which subpoenaed 'em to Washington post haste and threw 'em in jail for contempt. A handful of

Nigras who agreed to make spectacular appeals for ours to come back to us, have themselves mysteriously disappeared. But, worst news of all, sir, is our sister cities and counties, inside and outside the state, have changed their minds, fallen back on their promises and refused to lend us any Nigras, claiming they don't have 'nuff for themselves.

MAYOR What 'bout Nigras promised by the Governor?!

JACKSON Jailbirds and vagrants escorted here from chain-gangs and other reservations either revolted and escaped enroute or else vanished mysteriously on approaching our city limits . . . Deterioration rapidly escalates, sir. Estimates predict we kin hold out only one more hour before overtaken by anarchistic turmoil . . . Some citizens seeking haven elsewheres have already fled, but on last report were being forcibly turned back by armed sentinels in other cities who wanted no parts of 'em—claiming they carried a jinx.

MAYOR That bad, huh?

JACKSON Worse, sir . . . we've received at least five reports of plots on your life.

MAYOR What?!—We've gotta act quickly then!

JACKSON Run out of ideas, sir.

MAYOR Think harder, boy!

JACKSON Don't have much time, sir. One measly hour, then all hell go'n' break loose.

MAYOR Gotta think of something drastic, Jackson!

JACKSON I'm dry, sir.

MAYOR Jackson! Is there any planes outta here in the next hour?

JACKSON All transportation's been knocked out, sir.

MAYOR I thought so!

JACKSON What were you contemplating, sir?

MAYOR Don't ask me what I was contemplating! I'm still boss 'round here! Don't forgit it!

JACKSON Sorry, sir.

MAYOR . . . Hold the wire! . . . Wait a minute . . . ! Waaaaait a minute—GODAMMIT! All this time crapping 'round, diddling and fotsing wit' puny li'l' solutions—all the while neglecting our ace in the hole, our trump card! Most potent weapon for digging Nigras outta the woodpile!!! All the while right befo' our eyes . . . Ass! Why didn't you remind me?!!!

JACKSON What is it, sir?

MAYOR . . . ME—THAT'S WHAT! ME! A personal appeal from ME! *Directly to them!* . . . Although we wouldn't let 'em march to the polls and express their affection for me through the ballot box, we've always known I'm held highest in their esteem. A direct address from their beloved Mayor! . . . If they's anywheres close within the sound of my voice, they'll shape up! Or let us know by a sign they's ready to!

JACKSON You sure *that'll* turn the trick, sir?

MAYOR As sure as my ancestors befo' me who knew that when they puckered their lips to whistle, ole Sambo was gonna come a-lickety-splitting to answer the call! . . . That same chips-down blood courses through these Confederate gray veins of Henry R. E. Lee!

JACKSON I'm delighted to offer our network's facilities for such a crucial public interest address, sir. We'll arrange immediately for your appearance on an international hookup, placing you in the widest proximity to contact them wherever they may be.

MAYOR Thank you, I'm very grateful . . . Jackson, re-grease the machinery and set wheels in motion. Inform townspeople what's being done. Tell 'em we're all in this together. The next hour is countdown. I demand absolute cooperation, city-wide silence and inactivity. I don't want the Nigras frightened if they's nearby. This is the most important hour in town's history. Tell 'em if one single Nigra shows up during hour of decision, victory is within sight. I'm gonna git 'em that one—maybe all! Hurry and crack to it! (ANNOUNCER *rushes out, followed by* JACKSON. *Blackout. Scene re-opens, with* MAYOR *seated, eyes front, spotlight illuminating him in semi-darkness. Shadowy figures stand in the background, prepared to answer phones or aid in any other manner.* MAYOR *waits patiently until "GO!" signal is given. Then begins, his voice combining elements of confidence, tremolo and gravity)* Good evening . . . Despite the fact that millions of you wonderful people throughout the nation are viewing and listening to this momentous broadcast—and I thank you for your concern and sympathy in this hour of our peril—I primarily want to concentrate my attention and address these remarks solely for the benefit of our departed Nigra friends who may be listening somewheres in our farflung land to the sound of my voice . . . If you are—it is with heart-felt emotion and fond memories of our happy association that I ask—"Where are you . . . ?" Your absence has left a void in the bosom of every single man, woman and child of our great city. I tell you—you don't know what it means for us to wake up in the morning and discover that your cheerful, grinning, happy-go-lucky faces are missing! . . . From the depths of my heart, I can only meekly, humbly suggest what it means to me personally. . . . You see—the one face I will never be able to erase from my memory is the face—not of my Ma, not of Pa, neither wife or child—but the image of the first woman I came to love so well when just a wee lad—the vision of the first human I laid clear sight on at childbirth—the profile—better yet, the full face of my dear old . . . Jemimah—God rest her soul . . . Yes! My dear ole mammy, wit' her round ebony moon-beam gleaming down upon me in the crib, teeth shining, blood-red bandana standing starched, peaked and proud, gazing down upon me affectionately as she crooned me a Southern lullaby . . . OH! It's a memorable picture I will eternally cherish in permanent treasure chambers of my heart, now and forever always . . . Well, if this radiant image can remain so infinitely vivid to me all these many years after her unfortunate demise in the Po' folks home—THINK of the misery the rest of us must be suffering after being *freshly* denied your soothing presence?! We need ya. If you kin hear me, just contact this station 'n' I will welcome you back personally. Let me just tell you that since you eloped, nothing has been the same. How could it? You're part of us, you belong to us. Just give us a sign and we'll be contented that all is well . . . Now if you've skipped away on a little fun-fest, we understand, ha, ha. We know you like a good time and we don't begrudge it to ya. Hell—er, er, we like a good time ourselves—who doesn't? . . . In fact, think of all the good times we're had together, huh? We've had some real fun, you and us, yesiree! . . . Nobody knows better than you and I what fun we've had together. You singing us those old Southern coon songs and dancing those Nigra jigs and us clapping, prodding 'n' spurring you on! Lots of fun, huh?! . . . OH BOY! The times we've had together . . . If you've snucked away for a bit of fun by yourself, we'll go 'long wit' ya—long as you let us know where you at so we won't be worried about you . . . We'll go 'long wit' you long as you don't take the joke too far. I'll admit a joke is a joke and you've played a LULU! . . . I'm warning you, we can't stand much more horsing 'round from you! Business is business 'n' fun is fun! You've had your fun so now let's get down to business! Come on back, YOU HEAR ME!!! . . . If you been hoodwinked by agents of some foreign government, I've been authorized by the President of the United States to inform you that this liberty-loving Republic is prepared to rescue you from their clutches. Don't pay no 'tention to their sireen songs and atheistic promises! You better off under our control and you know it! . . . If you been bamboozled by rabble-rousing nonsense of your own so-called leaders, we prepared to offer same protection. Just call us up! Just give us a sign! . . . Come on, give us a sign . . . give us a sign—even a teeny-weeny one . . . ??!! *(glances around checking on possible communications. A bevy of headshakes indicate no success.* MAYOR *returns to address with desperate fervor.)* Now look—you don't know what you doing! If you persist in this disobedience, you know all too well the consequences! We'll track you to the end of the earth, beyond the galaxy, across the stars! We'll capture you and chastise you with all the vengeance we command! 'N' you know only too well how stern we kin be when double-crossed! The city, the state and the entire nation will crucify you for this unpardonable defiance! *(checks again)* No call . . . ? No sign . . . ? Time is running out! Deadline slipping past! They gotta respond! They gotta! *(resuming)* Listen to me! I'm begging y'all, you've gotta come back . . . ! LOOK, GEORGE! *(waves dirty rag aloft)* I brought the rag you wax the car wit'. . . . Don't this bring back memories, George, of all the days you spent shining that automobile to shimmering perfection . . . ? And you, Rufus?! . . . Here's the shoe polisher and the brush! . . . 'Member, Rufus? . . . Remember the happy mornings you spent popping this rag and whisking this brush so furiously 'till it created music that was sympho-nee to the ear . . . ? And you—MANDY? . . . Here's the waste-basket you didn't dump this morning. I saved it just for you! . . . LOOK, all y'all out there . . . ? *(signals and a three-person procession parades one after the other before the imaginary camera)*

DOLL WOMAN *(brandishing a crying baby [doll] as she strolls past and exits)* She's been crying ever since you left, Caldonia . . .

MOP MAN *(flashing mop)* It's been waiting in the same corner, Buster . . .

BRUSH MAN *(flagging toilet brush in one hand and toilet plunger in other)* It's been dry ever since you left, Washington . . .

MAYOR *(jumping in on the heels of the last exit)* Don't these things mean anything to y'all? By God! Are your memories so short?! Is there nothing sacred to ya? . . . Please come back, for my sake, please! All of you—even you questionable ones! I promise no harm will be done to you! Revenge is disallowed! We'll forgive everything. Just come on back and I'll git down on my knees—*(immediately drops to knees)* I'll be kneeling in the middle of Dixie Avenue to kiss the first shoe of the first one 'a you to show up . . . *I'll smooch any other spot you request* . . . Erase this nightmare 'n' we'll concede any demand you make, just come on back—please???!! . . . PLEEEEEEEZE?!!!

VOICE *(shouting)* TIME!!!

MAYOR *(remaining on knees, frozen in a pose of supplication. After a brief, deadly silence, he whispers almost inaudibly)* They wouldn't answer . . . they wouldn't answer . . .

(Blackout as bedlam erupts offstage. Total blackness holds during a sufficient interval where offstage sound-effects create the illusion of complete pandemonium, followed by a diminution which trails off into an expressionistic simulation of a city coming to a strickened standstill: industrial machinery clanks to halt, traffic blares to silence, etc. . . . The stage remains dark and silent for a long moment, then lights re-arise on the ANNOUNCER*)*

ANNOUNCER A pitiful sight, ladies and gentlemen. Soon after his unsuccessful appeal, Mayor Lee suffered a vicious pummeling from the mob and barely escaped with his life. National Guardsmen and State Militia were impotent in quelling the fury of a town venting its frustration in an orgy of destruction—a frenzy of rioting, looting and all other aberrations of a town gone beserk . . . Then—suddenly—as if a magic wand had been waved, madness evaporated and something more frightening replaced it: Submission . . . Even whimperings ceased. The city: exhausted, benumbed.—Slowly its occupants slinked off into shadows, and by midnight, the town was occupied exclusively by zombies. The fight and life had been drained out . . . Pooped . . . Hope ebbed away as completely as the beloved, absent Negroes . . . As our crew packed gear and crept away silently, we treaded softly—as if we were stealing away from a mausoleum . . . The Face Of A Defeated City.

(Blackout. Lights rise slowly at the sound of rooster-crowing, signalling the approach of a new day, the next morning. Scene is same as opening of play. CLEM *and* LUKE *are huddled over dazedly, trancelike. They remain so for a long count. Finally, a figure drifts on stage, shuffling slowly)*

LUKE *(gazing in silent fascination at the approaching figure)* . . . Clem . . . ? Do you see what I see or am I dreaming . . . ?

CLEM It's a . . . a Nigra, ain't it, Luke . . . ?

LUKE Sure looks like one, Clem—but we better make sure—eyes could be playing tricks on us . . . Does he still look like one to you, Clem?

CLEM He still does, Luke—but I'm scared to believe—

LUKE . . . Why . . . ? It looks like Rastus, Clem!

CLEM Sure does, Luke . . . but we better not jump to no hasty conclusion . . .

LUKE *(in timid softness)* That you, Rastus . . . ?

RASTUS *(Stepin Fetchit, Willie Best, Nicodemus, B. McQueen and all the rest rolled into one)* Why . . . howdy . . . Mr. Luke . . . Mr. Clem . . .

CLEM It is him, Luke! It is him!

LUKE Rastus?

RASTUS Yeas . . . sah?

LUKE Where was you yesterday?

RASTUS *(very, very puzzled)* Yes . . . ter . . . day? . . . Yester . . . day . . . ? Why . . . right . . . here . . . Mr. Luke . . .

LUKE No you warn't, Rastus, don't lie to me! Where was you yestiddy?

RASTUS Why . . . I'm sure I was . . . Mr. Luke . . . Remember . . . I made . . . that . . . delivery for you . . .

LUKE That was MONDAY, Rastus, yestiddy was TUESDAY.

RASTUS Tues . . . day . . . ? You don't say . . . Well . . . well . . . well . . .

LUKE Where was you 'n' all the other Nigras yesterday, Rastus?

RASTUS I . . . thought . . . yestiddy . . . was . . . Monday, Mr. Luke—I coulda swore it . . . ! . . . See how . . . things . . . kin git all mixed up? . . . I coulda swore it . . .

LUKE TODAY is WEDNESDAY, Rastus. Where was you TUESDAY?

RASTUS Tuesday . . . huh? That's somp'um . . . I . . . don't . . . remember . . . missing . . . a day . . . Mr. Luke . . . but I guess you right . . .

LUKE Then where was you!!!???

RASTUS Don't rightly know, Mr. Luke. I didn't know I had skipped a day.—But that jist goes to show you how time kin fly, don't it, Mr. Luke . . . Uuh, uuh, uuh . . . *(he starts shuffling off, scratching head, a flicker of a smile playing across his lips.* CLEM *and* LUKE *gaze dumbfoundedly as he disappears)*

LUKE *(eyes sweeping around in all directions)* Well . . . There's the others, Clem . . . Back jist like they useta be . . . Everything's same as always . . .

CLEM ??? . . . . Is it . . . Luke . . . !

(Slow fade. Curtain)

CHURCH AND GOD

James Baldwin • Owen Dodson

The first Africans imported to this country as slaves in the seventeenth century were not allowed to practice their own religion—nor were many allowed to convert to Christianity because whites feared that baptism would give them a claim to freedom. After 1700, it was decided that slaves could legally become Christians and that converting them had several advantages. Piety not only increased their value, but the services allowed them to release their frustrations and taught them to serve and obey.

On some plantations Blacks and whites attended church together, the Blacks seated either in the rear or in the balcony. Other plantations held separate services for slaves, with a white or sometimes a Black minister officiating. When Black ministers were allowed to preach, a white man was always present to observe—unless these services were secret ones. Secret, unsupervised services allowed slaves to express themselves freely and engage in social intercourse, as well as be spiritually uplifted—at least for the moment. Even in the North, Blacks were not equal in the Lord's house. In 1786, Richard Allen, a Northern minister and former slave, was invited to preach at St. George's Methodist Episcopal church in Philadelphia. Other freed Blacks attended this service, and when they continued attending services at the church, they were segregated in seats along the wall. Allen and several of his friends knelt and prayed in the gallery reserved for whites, but were snatched from their knees and told to sit in the rear. Rather than do this, they walked out with other Blacks attending the service. Not welcome in the white church, Allen and his companion, Absalom Jones, established the Free African Society, a self-help group that opposed slavery, with the intent of building a church. This plan was curtailed when a serious yellow fever epidemic hit the city. When the epidemic ended, Allen purchased a lot and began construction on his church. The Bethel African Methodist Episcopal Church was founded in 1794. It cut its ties to the Methodist Church in 1816, uniting with other African Methodist churches to become one of the largest denominations of African American churches in the country today. Over time, other Black churches were organized in the North, and in the South, by free Blacks. These churches were often actively involved in abolitionist activities, and sometimes served as "stations" in the underground railroad.

The African American church became the first social institution in the country totally controlled by Blacks. These churches provided opportunities for developing leadership skills, and many of their ministers were among the first African American politicians and liaisons between Black and white communities. Black churches sought to improve social and moral conditions; they promoted education and provided material relief in their communities. Day nurseries, kindergartens, and employment agencies were sometimes established for their congregations. The Black church has been a leader in the Civil Rights Movement and in the fight against social and political injustice, poverty, hunger, crime, drugs, disease, alcoholism, teenage pregnancy, juvenile delinquency, divorce, and gangs.

Since religion has played such a prevalent role in the lives of African Americans, Black playwrights would naturally be drawn to this subject. Neither *A Raisin in the Sun* nor *The Tumult and the Shouting* are plays about religion, yet the ethical fiber that governs the lives of both families is built on religious principles.

James Baldwin and Owen Dodson were raised in religious families in New York—Baldwin in Harlem, where he and his stepfather preached in storefront churches, and Dodson in Brooklyn, where he attended Concord Baptist Church with his family. The impact of religion on these men is reflected in their writing. Baldwin's observations of the church are recorded in his novel, *Go Tell It on the Mountain,* and in his play, *The Amen Corner.* Dodson reflects his religious experiences in his novel, *The Boy at the Window* and in *The Confession Stone.*

THE AMEN CORNER
1954

James Baldwin (1924–1987)

James Baldwin learned very early in his quest to become a writer that if he was to succeed he would have to use his own experiences as subject matter. His first novel, *Go Tell It on the Mountain*, was not only autobiographical but also therapeutic in that it allowed Baldwin to free himself of his burning hatred of his stepfather. Once the novel was completed, he decided to write a play based on his experiences in the Pentecostal Church. At fourteen he had been engaged in an inner tug-of-war between good and evil. He was afraid and consumed with guilt and was seeking direction, but found none in sight. He feared that he could be lured into the street life of Harlem—hustling and dealing like so many of his acquaintances and classmates had done; that he could easily become a victim of the streets or a criminal. During this difficult phase in his life, his best friend took him to his church, Mount Calvary Pentecostal, and introduced him to the pastor, Mother Horn. He recalled that

> . . . one night, when this woman had finished preaching, everything came roaring, screaming, crying out, and I fell on the ground before the altar. It was the strangest sensation I have ever had in my life—up to that time, or since . . . I was on the floor all night. Over me, to bring me "through," the saints sang and rejoiced and prayed. And in the morning, when they raised me, they told me that I was "saved."
>
> . . . I was utterly drained and exhausted, and released, for the first time, from all my guilty torment.[1]

Baldwin joined the church and, at fourteen, became a "young minister," preaching regularly at the Fireside Pentecostal Assembly for the next three years.

The Amen Corner is about his experiences in this church. Mother Horn was the model for Sister Margaret, and the conflict centers around her relationship with her rebellious son, David. When Baldwin told his agent, Helen Strauss, his intent, she attempted to discourage him, believing that the theatre was not interested in a play

1. James Baldwin, *The Price of the Ticket* (New York: St. Martin's/Marek, 1985), pp. 343–344.

about obscure facets of Negro life, especially by a virtually unknown author. His publisher, Knopf, was of the same opinion; that such a play would not appeal to white audiences. But *The Amen Corner* did appeal to Black audiences—first at Howard University, where it premiered in 1954 under the direction of Owen Dodson, and later in Los Angeles, where Frank Silvera's production became an instant hit—first in the eighty-seat Robertson Playhouse, and then at the larger Coronet Theatre, where it played eight performances a week for over a year.

The Los Angeles Company of *The Amen Corner* opened on Broadway in April 1965 and ran for twelve weeks. The critics were unanimous in their condemnation of the play's turgidity. Black audiences and critics apparently saw something in the play that white critics did not. They could empathize with Sister Margaret and her desperate struggle to hold on to the last remanent of her family, David. And, of course, they knew that religion often brings out the best and the worst in people. They had either lived it or witnessed it.

It is this difference in perception that led African American artists and critics to demand that Black drama critics be used to judge the validity of the Black experience, an experience that rests not only on the script and its theatrical production but also in the eye, ear, and life of the beholder.

One final first should be noted about *The Amen Corner*'s New York run. The entire production—set, lights, costumes—was designed by a Black man, Vantile Whitfield. Although Whitfield was not the first to design on Broadway (Perry Watkins did the set for *Mamba's Daughters* in 1939), he may have been the first to do an entire production design for a Black show on the Great White Way. Despite his accomplishments, the Scenic Designers Guild never invited Whitfield to become a member. It may be that Whitfield holds the second distinction of being the first production designer on Broadway who was not first required to join the union.

The Amen Corner

Act I A Sunday morning in Harlem
Act II The following Saturday afternoon
Act III The next morning

All the action takes place on a unit set which is the church and home of MARGARET ALEXANDER.

CAST OF CHARACTERS

MARGARET ALEXANDER, *pastor of the church*
ODESSA, *Margaret's older sister*
IDA JACKSON, *a young woman*
SISTER MOORE, SISTER BOXER, BROTHER BOXER — *elders of the church*
DAVID, *Margaret's 18-year-old son*
LUKE, *her husband*
SISTER SALLY, SISTER DOUGLASS, SISTER RICE, BROTHER DAVIS, BROTHER WASHINGTON — *members of the congregation*
WOMAN
OTHER MEMBERS OF CONGREGATION

ACT ONE

We are facing the scrim wall of the tenement which holds the home and church of SISTER MARGARET ALEXANDER.

It is a very bright Sunday morning.

Before the curtain rises, we hear street sounds, laughter, cursing, snatches of someone's radio; and under everything, the piano, which DAVID *is playing in the church.*

When the scrim rises we see, stage right, the church, which is dominated by the pulpit, on a platform, upstage. On the platform, a thronelike chair. On the pulpit, an immense open Bible.

To the right of the pulpit, the piano, the top of which is cluttered with hymnbooks and tambourines.

Just below the pulpit, a table, flanked by two plain chairs. On the table two collection plates, one brass, one straw, two Bibles, perhaps a vase of artificial flowers. Facing the pulpit, and running the length of the church, the camp chairs for the congregation.

To the right, downstage, the door leading to the street.

The church is on a level above the apartment and should give the impression of dominating the family's living quarters.

The apartment is stage left. Upstage, the door leading to the church; perhaps a glimpse of the staircase. Downstage, the kitchen, cluttered: a new Frigidaire, prominently placed, kitchen table with dishes on it, suitcase open on a chair.

Downstage, left, LUKE*'s bedroom. A small, dark room with a bed, a couple of chairs, a hassock, odds and ends thrown about in it as though it has long been used as a storage room. The room ends in a small door which leads to the rest of the house.*

Members of the congregation almost always enter the church by way of the street door, stage right. Members of the family almost always enter the church by way of the inside staircase. The apartment door is stage left of the kitchen.

At rise, there is a kind of subdued roar and humming, out of which is heard the music prologue, "The Blues Is Man," which segues into a steady rollicking beat, and we see the congregation singing.)

All

One day I walked the lonesome road
The spirit spoke unto me
And filled my heart with love—
Yes, he filled my heart with love,
Yes, he filled my heart with love,
And he wrote my name above,
And that's why I thank God I'm in His care.

[CHORUS]
Let me tell you now
Whilst I'm in His care,
I'm in my Saviour's care,
Jesus got His arms wrapped around me,
No evil thoughts can harm me
'Cause I'm so glad I'm in His care.

Contralto

I opened my Bible and began to read
About all the things He's done for me;
Read on down about Chapter One
How He made the earth then He made the sun.
Read on down about Chapter Two
How He died for me and He died for you.
Read on down about Chapter Three
How He made the blind, the blind to see.
Read on down about Chapter Four
How He healed the sick and blessed the poor.
Read on down about Chapter Five
How it rained forty days and Noah survived.
Six, seven, about the same
Just keep praising my Jesus' name.
Read on down about Chapter Eight,
The golden streets and the pearly gates.
Read on down about Chapter Nine
We all get to heaven in due time.
Read on down about Chapter Ten
My God's got the key and He'll let me in.
When I finish reading the rest
I'll go to judgment to stand my test.
He'll say come a little higher, come a little higher,
He'll say come a little higher and take your seat.

All

Let me tell you now
Whilst I'm in His care,
I'm in my Saviour's care,
Jesus got His arms wrapped around me,
No evil thoughts can harm me
'Cause I'm so glad I'm in His care.

MARGARET Amen! Let the church say amen!

ALL Amen! Hallelujah! Amen!

MARGARET And let us say amen again!

ALL Amen! Amen!

MARGARET Because the Lord God Almighty—the King of *Kings*, amen!—had sent out the word, "Set thine house in order, for thou shalt die and not live." And King Hezekiah turned his face to the wall.

ODESSA Amen!

SISTER MOORE Preach it, daughter! Preach it this morning!

MARGARET Now, when the king got the message, amen, he didn't do like some of us do today. He didn't go running to no spiritualists, no, he didn't. He didn't spend a lot of money on no fancy doctors, he didn't break his neck trying to commit himself to Bellevue Hospital. He sent for the prophet, Isaiah. Amen. He sent for a saint of God.

SISTER BOXER Well, amen!

MARGARET Now, children, you know this king had a mighty kingdom. There were many souls in that kingdom. He had rich and poor, high and low, amen! And I believe he had a lot of preachers around, puffed up and riding around in chariots—just like they is today, bless God—and stealing from the poor.

ALL Amen!

MARGARET But the king didn't call on none of them. No. he called on Isaiah. He called on Isaiah, children, because Isaiah lived a holy life. He wasn't one of them always running in and out of the king's palace. When the king gave a party, I doubt that he even thought of inviting him. You know how people do, amen: Well, let's not have him. Let's not have her. They too sanctified. They too holy. Amen! They don't drink, they don't smoke, they don't go to the movies, they don't curse, they don't play cards, they don't covet their neighbor's husband or their neighbor's wife—well, amen! They just holy. If we invite that sanctified fool they just going to make everybody else feel uncomfortable!

ALL Well, bless the Lord! Amen!

MARGARET But let the trouble come. Oh, let the trouble come. They don't go to none of them they sees all the time, amen. No, they don't go running to the people they was playing cards with all night long. When the trouble comes, look like they just can't stand none of their former ways—and they go a-digging back in their minds, in their memories, looking for a saint of God. Oh, yes! I've seen it happen time and time again and I know some of you out there this morning, you've seen it happen too. Sometimes, bless the Lord, you be in the woman's kitchen, washing up her cocktail glasses, amen, and maybe singing praises to the Lord. And pretty soon, here she come, this woman who maybe ain't said two words to you all the time you been working there. She draw up a chair and she say, "Can I talk to you, sister?" She got a houseful of people but she ain't gone to them. She in the kitchen, amen, talking to a saint of God. Because the world is watching you, children, even when you think the whole world's asleep!

ALL Amen! Amen!

MARGARET But, dearly beloved, she can't come to you—the world can't come to you—if you don't live holy. This way of holiness is a hard way. I know some of you think Sister Margaret's too hard on you. She don't want you to do this and she won't let you do that. Some of you say, "Ain't no harm in reading the funny papers." But children, *yes,* there's harm in it. While you reading them funny papers, your mind ain't on the Lord. And if your mind ain't stayed on Him, every hour of the day, Satan's going to cause you to fall. Amen! Some of you say, "Ain't no harm in me working for a liquor company. I ain't going to be drinking the liquor, I'm just going to be driving the *truck!*" But a saint of God ain't got no business delivering liquor to folks all day—how you going to spend all day helping folks into hell and then think you going to come here in the evening and help folks into heaven? It can't be done. The Word tells me, No man can serve two masters!

ALL Well, the Word *do* say it! Bless the Lord!

MARGARET Let us think about the Word this morning, children. Let it take root in your hearts: "Set thine house in order, for thou shalt die and not live."

(MARGARET *begins to sing and instantly* DAVID *strikes up another "shout" song and the congregation sings—loud, violent, clapping of hands, tambourines, etc.* MARGARET *rises and sits)*

Margaret

I got the holy spirit
To help me run this race.
I got the holy spirit,
It appointed my soul a place.
My faith looks up to heaven,
I know up there I'll see
The Father, the Son, the Holy Spirit
Watching over me.

Baritone

Once I was a sinner
Treading a sinful path;
Never thought about Jesus
Or the fate of His wrath.
Then I met the Saviour
And ever since that day
I been walking my faith,
Praying with love,
Looking up above.
With His arms around me,
I'm just leaning on Him.
For there is no other
On Him I can depend.
When my life is ended
And I lay these burdens down
I'm gonna walk with faith,
Pray with love,
Looking from above.

All

I got the holy spirit
To help me run this race.
I got the holy spirit,
It appointed my soul a place.
My faith looks up to heaven,
I know up there I'll see
The Father, the Son, the Holy Spirit
Watching over me.

*(*SISTER MOORE *comes forward. The excitement begins to subside)*

SISTER MOORE Well, I know our souls is praising God this morning!

ALL Amen!

SISTER MOORE It ain't every flock blessed to have a shepherd like Sister Margaret. Let's praise God for her!

ALL Amen! Amen!

SISTER MOORE Now, I ain't here to take up a lot of your time, amen. Sister Margaret's got to go off from us this afternoon to visit our sister church in Philadelphia. There's many sick up there, amen! Old Mother Phillips is sick in the body and some of her congregation is sick in the soul. And our pastor done give her word that she'd go up there and try to strengthen the feeble knees. Bless God! *(music begins and underlines her speech)* Before we close out this order of service, I'd like to say, I praise the Lord for being here, I thank Him for my life, health and strength. I want to thank Him for the way He's worked with me these many long years and I want to thank Him for keeping me *humble!* I want to thank Him for keeping me pure and set apart from the lusts of the flesh, for protecting me—hallelujah!—from all carnal temptation. When I come before my Maker, I'm going to come before Him *pure.* I'm going to say "Bless your name, Jesus, no man has ever touched me!" Hallelujah! *(congregation begins to sing)*

All

Come to Jesus, come to Jesus,
Come to Jesus, just now.
Come to Jesus, come to Jesus just now.
He will save you, He will save you,
He will save you, just now.
He will save you, He will save you just now.

SISTER MOORE Now before we raise the sacrifice offering, the Lord has led *me,* amen, to ask if there's a soul in this congregation who wants to ask the Lord's especial attention to them this morning? Any sinners, amen, any backsliders? Don't you be ashamed, you just come right on up here to the altar. *(tentative music on the piano)* Don't hold back, dear ones. Is there any sick in the building? The Lord's hand is outstretched. *(silence)* Come, dear hearts, don't hold back. *(toward the back of the church, a young woman, not dressed in white, rises. She holds a baby in her arms)* Yes, honey, come on up here. Don't be ashamed. *(the congregation turns to look at the young woman. She hesitates.* MARGARET *rises and steps forward)*

MARGARET Come on, daughter! *(the young woman comes up the aisle. Approving murmurs come from the congregation.* SISTER MOORE *steps a little aside)* That's right, daughter. The Word say, If you make one step, He'll make two. Just step out on the promise. What's your name, daughter?

YOUNG WOMAN Jackson. Mrs. Ida Jackson.

SISTER MOORE *(to the congregation)* Sister Ida Jackson. Bless the Lord!

ALL Bless her!

MARGARET And what's the name of that little one?

MRS. JACKSON His name is Daniel. He been sick. I want to pray for him. *(she begins to weep)*

MARGARET Dear heart, don't you weep this morning. I know what that emptiness feel like. What's been ailing this baby?

MRS. JACKSON I don't know. Done took him to the doctor and the doctor, he don't know.

He can't keep nothing in his little stomach and he cry all night, every night, and he done got real puny. Sister, I done lost one child already, please pray the Lord to make this baby well!

MARGARET *(steps down and touches* MRS. JACKSON*)* Don't fret, little sister. Don't you fret this morning. The Lord is mighty to save. This here's a Holy Ghost station. *(to the congregation)* Ain't that so, dear ones?

ALL Amen!

MARGARET He a right fine little boy. Why ain't your husband here with you this morning?

MRS. JACKSON I guess he at the house. He done got so evil and bitter, looks like he don't never want to hear me mention the Lord's name. He don't know I'm here this morning. *(sympathetic murmurs from the congregation.* MARGARET *watches* MRS. JACKSON*)*

MARGARET You poor little thing. You ain't much more than a baby yourself, is you? Sister, is you ever confessed the Lord as your personal Saviour? Is you trying to lead a life that's pleasing to Him?

MRS. JACKSON Yes, ma'am. I'm trying every day.

MARGARET Is your husband trying as hard as you?

MRS. JACKSON I ain't got no fault to find with him.

MARGARET Maybe the Lord wants you to leave that man.

MRS. JACKSON No! He don't want that! *(smothered giggles among the women)*

MARGARET No, children, don't you be laughing this morning. This is serious business. The Lord, He got a road for each and every one of us to travel and we is got to be saying amen to Him, no matter what sorrow He cause us to bear. *(to* MRS. JACKSON*)* Don't let the Lord have to take another baby from you before you ready to do His will. Hand that child to me. *(takes the child from* MRS. JACKSON*'s arms)*

SISTER MOORE Kneel down, daughter. Kneel down there in front of the altar. (MRS. JACKSON *kneels)*

MARGARET I want every soul under the sound of my voice to bow his head and pray silently with me as I pray. *(they bow their heads.* MARGARET *stands, the child in her arms, head uplifted, and congregation begins to hum "Deep River")* Dear Lord, we come before you this morning to ask you to look down and bless this woman and her baby. Touch his little body, Lord, and heal him and drive out them tormenting demons. Raise him up, Lord, and make him a good man and a comfort to his mother. Yes, we know you can do it, Lord. You told us if we'd just call, trusting in your promise, you'd be sure to answer. And all these blessings we ask in the name of the Father—

ALL In the name of the Father—

MARGARET And in the name of the Son—

ALL And in the name of the Son—

MARGARET And in the name of the blessed Holy Ghost—

ALL And in the name of the blessed Holy Ghost—

MARGARET Amen.

ALL Amen.

MARGARET *(returning the child)* God bless you, daughter. You go your way and trust the Lord. That child's going to be all right.

MRS. JACKSON Thank you, sister. I can't tell you how much I thank you.

MARGARET You ain't got me to thank. You come by here and let us know that child's all right, that's what'll please the Lord.

MRS. JACKSON Yes. I sure will do that.

MARGARET And bring your *husband* with you.

MRS. JACKSON Yes, sister. I'll bring him.

MARGARET Amen!

(MRS. JACKSON *returns to her seat.* MARGARET *looks at her watch, motions to* ODESSA, *who rises and leaves. In a moment, we see her in the apartment. She exits through* LUKE*'s room, returns a moment later without her robe, puts coffee on the stove, begins working.* SISTER MOORE *comes forward)*

SISTER MOORE Well now, children, without no more ado, we's going to raise the sacrifice offering. And when I say sacrifice, I *mean* sacrifice. Boxer, hand me that basket. (BROTHER BOXER *does so.* SISTER MOORE *holds a dollar up before the congregation and drops it in the plate)* I know you don't intend to see our pastor walk to Philadelphia. I want every soul in this congregation to drop just as much money in the plate as I just dropped, or *more,* to help with the cost of this trip. Go on, Brother Boxer, they going to give it to you, I know they is.

(The congregation, which has been humming throughout all this, begins singing slightly more

strongly as BROTHER BOXER *passes around the plate, beginning at the back of the church)*

All

Glory, glory, hallelujah, since I laid my burdens down,
Glory, glory, hallelujah, since I laid my burdens down.
I feel better, so much better, since I laid my burdens down,
I feel better, so much better, since I laid my burdens down,
Glory, glory, hallelujah, since I laid my burdens down.

*(*MARGARET *leaves the pulpit and comes downstairs. The lights dim in the church; the music continues, but lower, and the offering is raised in pantomime)*

ODESSA Well! My sister sure walked around Zion this morning! *(*MARGARET *sits at the table.* ODESSA *pours coffee, begins preparing something for* MARGARET *to eat)*

MARGARET It ain't me, sister, it's the Holy Ghost. Odessa—? I been thinking I might take David with me to Philadelphia.

ODESSA What you want to take him up there for? Who's going to play for the service down here?

MARGARET Well, old Sister Price, she can sort of stand by—

ODESSA She *been* standing by—but she sure can't play no piano, not for me she can't. She just ain't got no *juices,* somehow. When that woman is on the piano, the service just gets so dead you'd think you was in a Baptist church.

MARGARET I'd like Mother Phillips to see what a fine, saved young man he turned out to be. It'll make her feel good. She told me I was going to have a hard time raising him—by myself.

(Service is over, people are standing about chatting and slowly drifting out of the church)

ODESSA Well, if he want to go—

MARGARET David's got his first time to disobey me. The Word say, Bring up a child in the way he should go, and when he is old he will not depart from it. Now. That's the Word. *(at the suitcase)* Oh Lord, I sure don't feel like wasting no more time on Brother Boxer. He's a right sorry figure of a man, you know that?

ODESSA I hope the Lord will forgive me, but, declare, I just can't help wondering sometimes who's on top in that holy marriage bed.

MARGARET *(laughs)* Odessa!

ODESSA Don't waste no time on him. He knows he ain't got no right to be driving a liquor truck.

MARGARET Now, what do you suppose is happened to David? He should be here.

ODESSA He's probably been cornered by some of the sisters. They's always pulling on him.

MARGARET I praise my Redeemer that I got him raised right—even though I didn't have no man—you think David missed Luke? *(*DAVID *enters the apartment)* Ah, there you are.

DAVID Morning, Aunt Odessa. Morning, Mama. My! You two look—almost like two young girls this morning.

ODESSA That's just exactly the way he comes on with the sisters. I reckon you know what you doing, taking him to Philadelphia.

DAVID No, I mean it—just for a minute there. You both looked—different. Somehow—what about Philadelphia?

MARGARET I was just asking your Aunt Odessa if she'd mind me taking you with me.

DAVID Mama, I don't want to go to Philadelphia. Anyway—who's going to play for the service down here?

ODESSA Sister Price can play for us.

DAVID That woman can't play no piano.

MARGARET Be careful how you speak about the saints, honey. God don't love us to speak no evil.

DAVID Well, I'm sure she's sanctified and all that, but she *still* can't play piano. Not for *me,* she can't. She just makes me want to get up and leave the service.

MARGARET Mother Phillips would just love to see you—

DAVID I don't hardly remember Mother Phillips at all.

MARGARET You don't remember Mother Phillips? The way you used to follow her around? Why, she used to spoil you something awful—you was always up in that woman's face—when we—when we first come north—when Odessa was still working down home and we was living in Mother Phillips' house in Philadelphia. Don't you remember?

DAVID Yeah. Sort of. But, Mama, I don't want to take a week off from music school.

MARGARET Is the world going to fall down because you don't go to music school for a week?

DAVID Well, Mama, music is just like everything else, you got to keep at it.

MARGARET Well, you keeping at it. You playing in service all the time. I don't know what they can teach you in that school. You got a *natural* gift for music, David—*(a pause. They stare at each other)*—the Lord give it to you, you didn't learn it in no school.

DAVID The Lord give me eyes, too, Mama, but I still had to go to school to learn how to read.

MARGARET I don't know what's got into you lately, David.

DAVID Well, Mama, I'm getting older. I'm not a little boy anymore.

MARGARET I know you is getting older. But I hope you still got a mind stayed on the Lord.

DAVID Sure. Sure, I have.

MARGARET Where was you last night? You wasn't out to tarry service and don't nobody know what time you come in.

DAVID I had to go—downtown. We—having exams next week in music school and—I was studying with some guys I go to school with.

MARGARET Till way late in the morning?

DAVID Well—it's a pretty tough school.

MARGARET I don't know why you couldn't have had them boys come up here to *your* house to study. Your friends is always welcome, David, you know that.

DAVID Well, this guy's got a piano in his house—it was more convenient.

*(*BROTHER *and* SISTER BOXER *and* SISTER MOORE *leave the church and start downstairs. The church dims out.)*

MARGARET And what's wrong with that piano upstairs?

DAVID Mama, I can't practice on that piano—

MARGARET You can use that piano anytime you want to—

DAVID Well, I couldn't have used it last night! *(the* BOXERS *and* SISTER MOORE *enter.* DAVID *turns away)*

SISTER MOORE I come down here to tell Sister Margaret myself how she blessed my soul this morning! Praise the Lord, Brother David. How you feel this morning?

DAVID Praise the Lord.

SISTER BOXER Your mother sure preached a sermon this morning.

BROTHER BOXER Did my heart good, amen. Did my heart *good.* Sister Odessa, what you got cool to drink in that fine new Frigidaire? *(opens the Frigidaire)* You got any Kool-aid?

SISTER BOXER You know you ain't supposed to be rummaging around in folks' ice-boxes, Joel.

BROTHER BOXER This ain't no icebox, this is a *Frigidaire.* Westinghouse. Amen! You don't mind my making myself at home, do you, Sister Odessa?

MARGARET Just make yourself at home, Brother Boxer. I got to get ready to go. David, you better start packing—don't you make me late. He got any clean shirts, Odessa?

ODESSA I believe so—I ironed a couple last night—he uses them up so fast.

SISTER MOORE Why, is you going to Philadelphia with your mother, son? Why, that's just lovely!

DAVID Mama—I got something else to do—this week—

MARGARET You better hurry.

*(*DAVID *goes into* LUKE*'s bedroom, pulls a suitcase from under the bed)*

BROTHER BOXER I believe David's sweet on one of them young sisters in Philadelphia, that's why he's so anxious to go. *(*DAVID *re-enters the kitchen)* How about it, boy? You got your eye on one of them Philadelphia saints? One of them young ones?

MARGARET David's just coming up with me because I asked him to come and help me.

SISTER MOORE Praise the Lord. That's sweet. The Lord's going to bless you, you hear me, David?

BROTHER BOXER Ain't many young men in the Lord like David. I got to hand it to you, boy. I been keeping my eye on you and you is—all right! *(He claps* DAVID *on the shoulder)*

SISTER BOXER How long you figure on being gone, Sister Margaret?

MARGARET I ain't going to be gone no longer than I have to—this is a mighty sad journey. I don't believe poor Mother Phillips is long for this world. And the way her congregation's behaving—it's just enough to make you weep.

ODESSA I don't know what's got into them

folks up there, cutting up like they is, and talking about the Lord's anointed. I guess I *do* know what's got into them, too—ain't nothing but the Devil. You know, we is really got to watch and pray.

SISTER MOORE They got more nerve than I got. You ain't never going to hear me say nothing against them the Lord is set above me. No sir. That's just asking for the wrath.

ODESSA It'll fall *on* you, too. You all is seen the way the Lord is worked with Sister Margaret right here in this little tabernacle. You remember all those people tried to set themselves up against her—? Where is they now? The Lord is just let every one of them be dispersed.

SISTER BOXER Even poor little Elder King is in his grave.

BROTHER BOXER I sort of liked old Elder King. The Lord moved him right out just the same.

SISTER MOORE He'd done got too *high*. He was too set in his ways. All that talk about not wanting women to preach. He didn't want women to do nothing but just sit quiet.

MARGARET But I remember, Sister Moore, you wasn't so much on women preachers, neither, when I first come around.

SISTER MOORE The Lord opened my eyes, honey. He opened my eyes the first time I heard you preach. Of course, I ain't saying that Elder King couldn't preach a sermon when the power was on him. And it *was* under Elder King that I come into the church.

BROTHER BOXER You weren't sweet on Elder King, were you, Sister Moore?

SISTER MOORE I ain't never been sweet on no man but the Lord Jesus Christ.

SISTER BOXER You remember Elder King, son? You weren't nothing but a little bundle in them days.

DAVID I was reading and writing already. I was even playing the piano already. It was him had this church then and we was living down the block.

BROTHER BOXER I reckon you must have missed your daddy sometimes, didn't you, son?

SISTER MOORE If he'd stayed around his daddy, I guarantee you David wouldn't be the fine, saved young man he is today, playing piano in church, would you, boy?

DAVID No'm, I reckon I wouldn't. Mama, if I'm going to be gone a whole week, there is something I've got to—

BROTHER BOXER He better off without the kind of daddy who'd just run off and leave his wife and kid to get along the best they could. That ain't right. I believe in a man doing *right*, amen!

MARGARET You hear him, don't you? *He* know—miss his daddy? The Lord, He give me strength to be mother and daddy both. Odessa, you want to help me with my hair? *(they start out)*

DAVID Mama—I!

MARGARET What is it, son?

DAVID There is something I got to get down the block. I got to run down the block for a minute.

MARGARET Can't it wait till you come back?

DAVID No. I want to—borrow a music score from somebody. I can study it while I'm away.

MARGARET Well, you hurry. We ain't got much time. You put something on. You act like you catching cold. (ODESSA *and* MARGARET *exit through* LUKE*'s room)*

BROTHER BOXER You got to say goodbye to some little girl down the block?

DAVID I'll be right back. *(he rushes into the street, vanishes in the alley)*

BROTHER BOXER Hmmph! I wonder what kind of business he got down the block. I guarantee you one thing—it ain't sanctified business.

SISTER BOXER The Word say we ain't supposed to think no evil, Joel.

BROTHER BOXER I got news for you folks. You know what I heard last night?

SISTER BOXER Don't you come on with no more foolishness, Joel. I'm too upset. I can't stand it this morning.

SISTER MOORE Don't you be upset, sugar. Everything's going to turn out all right—what did you hear, Brother Boxer?

BROTHER BOXER That boy's daddy is back in New York. He's working in a jazz club downtown.

SISTER MOORE A *jazz* club?

SISTER BOXER How come you know all this?

BROTHER BOXER Heard it on the job, honey. God don't want us to be ignorant. He want us to know what's going on around us.

SISTER MOORE Do Sister Margaret know this?

BROTHER BOXER I bet you David, *he* know it—he been keeping bad company. Some young white boy, didn't have nothing better to do, went down yonder and drug his daddy up to New York—for a comeback. Last time anybody heard about him, he was real sick with TB. Everybody thought he was dead.

SISTER MOORE Poor Sister Margaret! A jazz club!

SISTER BOXER Poor Sister Margaret! She ain't as poor as I am.

BROTHER BOXER You ain't poor, sugar. You got me. And I ain't going to stay poor forever.

SISTER MOORE I'm going to talk to her about that job business now. She reasonable. She'll listen.

SISTER BOXER She ain't going to listen.

SISTER MOORE Of course she's going to listen. Folks is got a right to make a living.

BROTHER BOXER Uh-huh. Folks like us ain't got nothing and ain't never supposed to have nothing. We's supposed to live on the joy of the Lord.

SISTER MOORE It ain't like Brother Boxer was going to become a drunkard or something like that—he won't even *see* the liquor—

SISTER BOXER He won't even be selling it.

SISTER MOORE He just going to be driving a truck around the city, doing hard work. I declare, I don't see nothing wrong with that.

SISTER BOXER Sister Moore, you know that woman I work for, sometime she give a party and I got to serve them people cocktails. I *got* to. Now, I don't believe the Lord's going to punish me just because I'm working by the sweat of my brow the only way I *can*. He say, "Be in the world but not of it." But you got to be *in* it, don't care how holy you get, you got to *eat*.

BROTHER BOXER I'm glad Sister Boxer mentioned it to you, Sister Moore. I wasn't going to mention it to you myself because I was sure you'd just take Sister Margaret's side against us.

SISTER MOORE Ain't no taking of sides in the Lord, Brother Boxer. I'm on the Lord's side. We is all sinners, saved by grace. Hallelujah!

*(*MARGARET *and* ODESSA *re-enter. The* BOXERS *and* SISTER MOORE *begin to sing.)*

Sister Moore
What a mighty God we serve!

Sister and Brother Boxer
What a mighty God we serve!

Together
Angels around the throne,
'Round the throne of God,
Crying, what a mighty God we serve!

MARGARET Bless your hearts, children, that sure done my spirit good. You all ain't like them wayward children up in Philadelphia. It sure is nice to be here with my real faithful children.

*(*DAVID *enters the alley, slowly, looking back; enters the apartment)*

BROTHER BOXER Oh, we's faithful, Sister Margaret.

(Jazz version of "Luke's Theme" begins)

SISTER MOORE Yes, I'm mighty glad you said that, Sister Margaret. I'm mighty glad you *knows* that. Because the Lord's done laid something on my heart to say to you, right here and now, and you going to take it in the proper spirit, I know you is. I know you know I ain't trying to find fault. Old Sister Moore don't mean no wrong.

MARGARET What is it, Sister Moore?

DAVID Mama, can I see you for a minute?

MARGARET In a minute, son.

SISTER MOORE Why, Brother and Sister Boxer here, they just happened to mention to me something about this job you don't think Brother Boxer ought to take. I don't mean no wrong, Sister Margaret, and I know you the pastor and is set above me, but I'm an older woman than you are and, I declare, I don't see no harm in it.

MARGARET You don't see no harm in it, Sister Moore, because the Lord ain't placed you where he's placed me. Ain't no age in the Lord, Sister Moore—older or younger ain't got a thing to do with it. You just remember that I'm your pastor.

SISTER MOORE But, Sister Margaret, can't be no harm in a man trying to do his best for his family.

MARGARET The Lord comes before all things, Sister Moore. All things. Brother Boxer's supposed to do his best for the Lord.

SISTER MOORE But, Sister Margaret—

MARGARET I don't want to hear no more about it.

(SISTERS MOORE *and* BOXER *exchange a bitter look and they begin singing a church tune.* ODESSA *closes* MARGARET'S *suitcase and puts it on the floor.* LUKE *appears in the alley, walking very slowly.)*

Sisters Moore and Boxer

'Bye and 'bye when the morning comes
All the saints of God are gathering home,
We will tell the story how we overcome,
And we'll understand it better 'bye and 'bye.

(LUKE *climbs the stairs into the church, walks through it slowly; finally enters the apartment as they finish the song)*

LUKE Good morning, folks. *(silence. Everyone stares, first at* LUKE, *then at* MARGARET. MARGARET *stands perfectly still)* Maggie, you ain't hardly changed a bit. You *still* the prettiest woman I ever laid eyes on.

MARGARET Luke.

LUKE Don't look at me like that. I changed that much? Well, sure, I might of lost a little weight. But you gained some. You ever notice how men, they tend to lose weight in later life, while the women, they gain? You look good, Maggie. It's good to see you.

MARGARET Luke—

LUKE *(to* ODESSA*)* Hey, you look good too. It's mighty good to see you again. You didn't think I'd come to New York and not find you? Ain't you going to say nothing, neither?

ODESSA Ah. You bad boy.

LUKE I bet my son is in this room somewhere. He's got to be in this room somewhere—*(to* BROTHER BOXER*)*—but I reckon it can't be you. I know it ain't been that long. *(to* DAVID*)* You come downtown last night to hear my play, didn't you?

DAVID Yes. Yes, sir. I did.

LUKE Why didn't you come up and say hello? I saw you, sitting way in the back, way at the end of the bar. I knew right away it was you. And, time I was finished, you was gone. *(a pause)* Cat got your tongue, Maggie? *(to* DAVID*)* I never knowed that to happen to your mama before.

MARGARET I never knowed my son to lie to me, neither. God don't like liars.

DAVID I was going to tell you.

MARGARET Luke, how'd you find us?

LUKE I had to find you. I didn't come to cause you no trouble. I just come by to say hello.

ODESSA Luke, sit down! I can't get overseeing you, right here in this room. I can't get over it. I didn't reckon on never seeing you no more—

LUKE In life. I didn't neither. But here I am—

ODESSA With your big, black, no-count self. You hungry?

LUKE Odessa, you ain't never going to change. Everytime you see a man, you think you got to go digging for some pork chops. No, I ain't hungry. I'm tired, though. I believe I'll sit down. *(he sits.* ODESSA *and* DAVID *glance at each other quickly)*

MARGARET How long you going to be in New York, Luke? When did you get here? Nobody told me—*(she looks at* DAVID*)*—nobody told me—you was here—

LUKE A couple of weeks is all. I figured I'd find you somewhere near a church. And you a pastor now? Well, I guess it suits you. She a good pastor?

SISTER MOORE Amen!

LUKE What do you think, David? (DAVID *is silent)* Well, she sure used to keep on at me about my soul. Didn't you, Maggie? Of course, that was only toward the end, when things got to be so rough. In the beginning—well, it's always different in the beginning.

MARGARET You ain't changed, have you? You still got the same carnal grin, that same carnal mind—you ain't changed a bit.

LUKE People don't change much, Maggie—

MARGARET Not unless the Lord changes their hearts—

LUKE You ain't changed much, neither—you dress a little different.

MARGARET Why did you come here? You ain't never brought me nothing but trouble, you come to bring me more trouble? Luke—I'm glad to see you and all but—I got to be going away this afternoon. I stay busy all the time around this church. David, he stays busy too—and he's coming with me this afternoon.

LUKE Well, honey, I'm used to your going. I done had ten years to get used to it. But, David—David, you can find a couple of minutes for your old man, can't you? Maybe you'd like to come out with me sometime—we could try to get acquainted—

DAVID You ain't wanted to get acquainted all this time—

LUKE Yes, I did. It ain't my fault—at least it ain't *all* my fault—that we ain't acquainted.

ODESSA Luke!

DAVID You run off and left us.

LUKE Boy, your daddy's done a lot of things he's ashamed of, but I wouldn't never of run off and left you and your mother. Your mama knows that. *(a pause)* You tell him, Maggie. Who left? Did I leave you or did you leave me?

MARGARET It don't make no difference now.

LUKE Who left? Tell him.

MARGARET When we was living with you, I didn't know half the time if I had a husband or not, this boy didn't know if he had a father!

LUKE That's a goddam lie. *You* knew you had a husband—this boy knew he had a father. Who left the house—who left?

MARGARET You was always on the road with them no-count jazz players—

LUKE But who *left?*

MARGARET I ain't going to stand here arguing with you—I got to go—David—

LUKE *Who left?*

MARGARET *I* did! *I* left! To get away from the stink of whisky—to save my baby—to find the Lord!

LUKE I wouldn't never of left you, son. Never. Never in this world.

MARGARET Leave us alone, Luke. Go away and leave us alone. I'm doing the Lord's work now—

DAVID Mama—you just said—God don't like liars.

MARGARET Your daddy weren't hardly ever home. I was going to explain it all to you—when you got big.

LUKE I done spent ten years wishing you'd leave the Lord's work to the Lord. *(he rises slowly)* You know where I'm working, boy. Come on down and see me. Please come on down and see me.

MARGARET Luke, he ain't going down there. You want to see him, you come on up here.

LUKE He's big enough to find his way downtown.

MARGARET I don't want him hanging around downtown.

LUKE It ain't no worse down there than it is up here.

MARGARET I ain't going to fight with you—not now—in front of the whole congregation. Brother Boxer, call me a taxi. David, close that suitcase and get yourself a coat. We got to go. *(*BROTHER BOXER *hesitates, rises, leaves)*

ODESSA Maggie, he's sick.

*(*LUKE *sways, falls against the table.* SISTER BOXER *screams.* DAVID *and* ODESSA *struggle to raise him)*

SISTER MOORE Try to get him back here in this little room. Back here, in this bed, in this little room.

*(*DAVID *and the women struggle with* LUKE *and get him to the bed.* DAVID *loosens his father's collar and takes off his shoes)*

LUKE *(moans)* Maggie.

SISTER BOXER We better send that man to a hospital.

MARGARET This here's a Holy Ghost station. The Lord don't do nothing without a purpose. Maybe the Lord wants to save his soul.

SISTER MOORE Well, amen.

MARGARET And Luke, if he want to keep on being hardhearted against the Lord, his blood can't be required at our hands. I got to go.

DAVID Mama, I'm going to stay here. *(a pause)* Mama, couldn't you write or telephone or something and let them folks know you can't get up there right now?

SISTER BOXER Yes, Sister Margaret, couldn't you do that? I don't believe that man is long for this world.

SISTER MOORE Yes, Sister Margaret, everybody understands that when you got trouble in the home, the home comes first. Send a deputy up there. I'll go for you.

MARGARET In this home, Sister Moore, the Lord comes first. The Lord made me leave that man in there a long time ago because he was a sinner. And the Lord ain't told me to stop doing my work just because he's come the way all sinners come.

DAVID But, Mama, he's been calling you, he going to keep on calling you! What we going to do if he start calling for you again?

MARGARET Tell him to call on the Lord! It ain't me can save him, ain't nothing but the Lord can save him!

ODESSA But you might be able to help him, Maggie—if you was here.

DAVID Mama, you don't know. You don't know if he be living, time you get back. *(the taxi horn is heard)* But I reckon you don't care, do you?

MARGARET Don't talk to your mother that way, son. I don't want to go. I got to go.

SISTER BOXER When a woman make a vow to God, she got to keep it.

MARGARET You folks do what you can for him, pray and hold onto God for him. *(to* ODESSA*)* You send me a telegram if—if anything happens. *(to the others)* You folks got a evening service to get through. Don't you reckon you better run, get a bite to eat, so you can get back here on time?

BROTHER BOXER *(off stage)* Sister Margaret!

MARGARET Go, do like I tell you. David, see if you can find a doctor. You ain't going to do no good, standing there like that. Praise the Lord.

ODESSA Praise the Lord.

MARGARET *(to the others, dangerously)* Praise the Lord, I say.

SISTERS MOORE *and* BOXER *(dry)* Praise the Lord. *(*MARGARET *goes through the church into the street)*

LUKE Maggie. Maggie. Oh, Maggie

ODESSA Children, let us pray.

(Slowly, all except DAVID, *go to their knees. They begin singing)*

If Jesus had to pray, what about me?
If Jesus had to pray, what about me?
He had to fall down on His knees,
Crying Father, help me if you please,
If Jesus had to pray, what about me?

In the garden Jesus prayed
While night was falling fast.
He said Father, if you will,
Let this bitter cup be past
But if not I am content,
Let my will be lost in Thine.
If Jesus had to pray, what about me?

(Curtain)

END OF ACT ONE

ACT TWO

(Late afternoon the following Saturday. The sun is bright-red, the street is noisy. Cries of children playing, blaring radios and jukeboxes, etc.

LUKE's *room is dark, the shades drawn. He is still.*

ODESSA, SISTER BOXER *and* SISTER MOORE *are in the kitchen)*

SISTER MOORE *(to* ODESSA*)* We all loves Sister Margaret, sugar, just as much as you do. But we's supposed to bear witness, amen, to the truth. Don't care *who* it cuts.

SISTER BOXER She been going around all these years acting so *pure.*

SISTER MOORE Sister Margaret ain't nothing but flesh and blood, like all the rest of us. And she is got to watch and pray—like all the rest of us.

ODESSA Lord, honey, Sister Margaret, *she* know that.

SISTER BOXER She don't act like she know it. She act like she way above all human trouble. She always up there on that mountain, don't you know, just a-chewing the fat with the Lord.

SISTER MOORE That poor man!

ODESSA Sister Moore, you ain't never had no use for men all your life long. Now, how come you sitting up here this afternoon, talking about that *poor* man and talking against your pastor?

SISTER MOORE Don't you try to put words in my mouth, Sister Odessa, don't you do it! I ain't talking against my pastor, no, I ain't. I ain't doing a thing but talking like a Christian.

SISTER BOXER Last Sunday she acted like she didn't think that man was good enough to touch the hem of that white robe of her'n. And, you know, that ain't no way to treat a man who knowed one *time* what you was like with no robe on.

SISTER MOORE Sister Boxer!

SISTER BOXER Well, it's the truth. I'm bearing witness to the truth. I reckon I always thought of Sister Margaret like she'd been born holy. Like she hadn't never been a young girl or nothing and hadn't never had no real temptations.

*(*BROTHER BOXER *enters)*

ODESSA I don't know how you could of thought that when everybody knowed she's been married—and she had a son.

BROTHER BOXER Praise the Lord, holy sisters, can a man come in?

ODESSA Come on in the house, Brother Boxer. *(to the others)* You be careful how you talk about your sister. The Lord ain't *yet* taken away His protecting arm.

BROTHER BOXER Look like it might rain this evening.

ODESSA Yes. The sky is getting mighty low.

SISTER BOXER Oh, sure, I knowed she'd been married and she had this boy. But, I declare, I thought that that was just a mistake and she couldn't wait to get away from her husband. There's women like that, you know, ain't got much nature to them somehow.

SISTER MOORE Now, you be careful, Sister Boxer, you know I ain't never been married, nor *(proudly)* I ain't never knowed no man.

SISTER BOXER Well, it's different with you, Sister Moore. You give your life to the Lord right quick and you ain't got nothing like that to remember. But, you take me now, I'm a married woman and the Lord done blessed me with a real womanly nature and, I tell you, honey, you been married once, it ain't so easy to get along single. 'Course, I know the Holy Ghost is mighty and *will* keep—but, I declare, I wouldn't like to try it. No *wonder* that woman make so much noise when she get up in the pulpit.

BROTHER BOXER She done gone too far, she done rose too *high.* She done forgot it ain't the woman supposed to lead, it's the man.

ODESSA Is you done forgot your salvation? Don't you know if she'd followed that man, he might have led her straight on down to hell?

SISTER BOXER That ain't by no means certain. If she'd done her duty like a wife, she might have been able to lead that man right straight to the throne of grace. I led *my* man there.

BROTHER BOXER Well, you's a woman, sugar, and, quite natural, you want your man to come to heaven. But I believe in Sister Margaret's heaven, ain't going to be no men allowed. When that young woman come to the altar last Sunday morning, wanted the saints to pray for her baby, the first words out of Sister Margaret's mouth was "You better leave your husband."

SISTER BOXER Amen! The *first* words.

ODESSA Children, you better be careful what you say about a woman ain't been doing nothing but trying to serve the Lord.

SISTER MOORE Is she been trying to serve the Lord? Or is she just wanted to put herself up over everybody else?

BROTHER BOXER Now, that's what I'm talking about. The Word say, You going to know a tree by its fruit. And we ain't been seeing such good fruit from Sister Margaret. I want to know, how come she think she can rule a church when she can't rule her own house? That husband of hers is in there, dying in his sins, and that half-grown, hypocrite son of hers is just running all roads to hell.

ODESSA Little David's just been a little upset. He ain't thinking about going back into the world, he see what sin done for his daddy.

BROTHER BOXER I got news for you, Sister Odessa. Little David ain't so little no more. I stood right in this very room last Sunday when we found out that boy had been lying to his mother. That's *right.* He been going out to *bars.* And just this very evening, not *five* minutes ago, I seen him down on 125th Street with some white horn player—the one he say he go to *school* with—and two other boys and three girls. Yes sir. They was just getting into a car.

ODESSA It's just natural for David to be seeing folks his own age every now and then. And they just might be fixing to drop him at this very doorstep, you don't know. He might be here in time for tarry service.

BROTHER BOXER I don't hear no cars drawing up in front of this door—no, I don't. And I bet you prayer meeting ain't what David had on his mind. That boy had a cigarette between his lips and had his hand on one of them girls, a real common-looking, black little thing, he had his hand on her—well, like he knowed her pretty *well* and wasn't expecting her to send him off to no prayer meeting.

SISTER MOORE The Lord sure has been causing the scales to fall from the eyes of His servant this week. Thank you, Jesus!

ODESSA You ought to be ashamed of yourselves! You ought to be ashamed of your Black, deceitful hearts. You's liars, every one of you, and the truth's not in you! *(a pause)* Brother Boxer, Sister Boxer, Sister Moore. Let's go upstairs and pray.

SISTER MOORE Yes, we *better* go upstairs and pray. The Lord's been working in the hearts of some other folks in this church and they's going to be along presently, asking the elders of this church to give them an accounting—amen!—of their spiritual leader.

ODESSA What kind of accounting, Sister Moore?

SISTER MOORE Well, I just happened to be talking to some of the saints the other day and while we was talking some of them got to wondering just how much it cost to get to Philadelphia. Well, I said I didn't know because the Lord, He keep *me* close to home. But I said it couldn't cost but *so* much, ain't like she was going on a great long trip. Well—we got to talking about other things and then we just decided we'd come to church this evening and put our minds together. Amen. And let everybody say his piece and see how the Lord, *He* wanted us to move.

ODESSA Was you there, too, Brother Boxer?

BROTHER BOXER Naturally I was there too. I'm one of the elders of the church.

ODESSA I'm one of the elders, too. But *I* wasn't there—wherever it was.

SISTER MOORE We wasn't planning to shut you out, Sister Odessa. Some folks just happened to drop by the house and we got to talking. That's all.

ODESSA Is folks thinking that Margaret's stealing their money?

SISTER BOXER That ain't no way to talk, Sister Odessa. Before God, ain't nobody said a word about stealing.

SISTER MOORE Ain't nobody accusing Margaret of *nothing.* Don't you let the Devil put that idea in your mind. Sister Margaret's been blessed with a real faithful congregation. Folks just loves Sister Margaret. Just the other day one of the saints—was it you, Sister Boxer?—one of the saints was saying to me how much trouble she have with her old refrigerator and she say it sure done her heart good to know her pastor had a nice, new Frigidaire. Amen. She said it done her heart good.

(They exit into the church. The lights go up slightly as they enter and sit. The church blacks out.

For a moment the stage is empty. Then DAVID *appears, enters the house. He is very tired and nervous. He wanders about the kitchen; goes to* LUKE'*s room, looks in. He is about to turn away when* LUKE *speaks)*

LUKE Hello, there.

DAVID I thought you was asleep.

LUKE I ain't sleepy. Is it nighttime yet?

DAVID No, not yet.

LUKE Look like it's always nighttime in this room. You want to come in, pull up the shade for me? *(*DAVID *does so. A faint sound of singing is heard from the church upstairs)* Ain't you going to play piano for them tonight?

DAVID I don't much feel like playing piano right now. *(he is flustered; reaches in his pocket, takes out a pack of cigarettes, realizes his mistake too late)*

LUKE Didn't know you was smoking already. Let's have a cigarette.

DAVID You ain't suppose to be smoking. The doctor don't want you smoking.

LUKE The doctor ain't here now. (DAVID *gives* LUKE *a cigarette, lights it, after a moment lights one for himself)*

DAVID Look like you'd of had enough of smoking by now.

LUKE Sit down. We got a minute. (DAVID *sits on the hassock at the foot of* LUKE'*s bed)* Didn't I hear you playing piano one night this week?

DAVID No.

LUKE Boy, I'm sure I heard you playing *one* night—at the beginning of the service?

DAVID Oh, Yes, I guess so. I didn't stay. How did you know it was me?

LUKE You play piano like I dreamed you would.

DAVID I been finding out lately you was pretty good. Mama never let us keep a phonograph. I just didn't never hear any of your records—until here lately. You was right up there with the best, Jellyroll Morton and Louis Armstrong and cats like that.

LUKE You fixing to be a musician?

DAVID No.

LUKE Well, it ain't much of a profession for making money, that's the truth.

DAVID There were guys who did.

LUKE There were guys who didn't.

DAVID You never come to look for us. Why?

LUKE I started to. I wanted to. I thought of it lots of times.

DAVID Why didn't you never do it? Did you think it was good riddance we was gone?

LUKE I was hoping you wouldn't never think that, never.

DAVID I wonder what you expected me to think. I remembered you, but couldn't never talk about you. I used to hear about you sometime, but I couldn't never say, That's my daddy. I was too ashamed. I remembered how you used to play for me sometimes. That was why I started playing the piano. I used to go to sleep dreaming about the way we'd play together one day, me with my piano and you with your trombone.

LUKE David. David.

DAVID You never come. You never come when you could do us some good. You come now, now when you can't do nobody any good. Every time I think about it, think about *you,* I want to break down and cry like a baby. You make me—ah! You make me feel so bad.

LUKE Son—don't try to get away from the things that hurt you. The things that hurt you—sometimes that's all you got. You got to learn to live with those things—and—use them. I've seen people—put themselves through terrible torture—and die—because they was afraid of getting hurt. *(he wants to get rid of his cigarette.* DAVID *takes it from him. They stare at each other for a moment)* I used to hold you on my knee when you weren't nothing but a little—you didn't have no teeth then. Now I reckon you's already started to lose them. I reckon I thought we was a-going to bring down the moon, you and me, soon as you got a little bigger. I planned all kinds of things for you—they never come to pass.

DAVID You ain't never been saved, like Mama. Have you?

LUKE Nope.

DAVID How come Mama, she got saved?

LUKE I reckon she thought she better had—being married to me. I don't know. Your mama's kind of proud, you know, proud and silent. We had us a little trouble. And she wouldn't come to me. That's when she found the Lord.

DAVID I remember. I remember—that was when the baby was born dead. And Mama was in the hospital—and you was drunk, going to that hospital all the time—and I used to hear you crying, late at night. *Did* she find the Lord?

LUKE Can't nobody know but your mama, son.

DAVID A few months ago some guys come in the church and they heard me playing piano and they kept coming back all the time. Mama said it was the Holy Ghost drawing them in. But it wasn't.

LUKE It was your piano.

DAVID Yes. And I didn't draw them in. They drew me out. They setting up a combo and they want me to come in with them. That's when I stopped praying. I really began to think about it hard. And, Daddy—things started happening inside me which hadn't ever happened before. It was terrible. It was wonderful. I started looking around this house, around this church—like I was seeing it for the first time. Daddy—that's when I stopped believing—it just went away. I got so I just hated going upstairs to that church. I hated coming home. I hated lying to Mama all the time—and—I knew I had to do something—and that's how—I was scared, I didn't know what to do. I didn't know how to stay here and I didn't know how to go—and—there wasn't anybody I could talk to—I couldn't do—nothing! Every time I—even when I tried to make it with a girl—something kept saying, Maybe this is a sin. I hated it! *(he is weeping)* I made Mama let me go to music school and I started studying. I got me a little part-time job. I been studying for three months now. It gets better all the time—you know? I don't mean *me*—I got a long way to go—but *it* gets better. And I was trying to find some way of preparing Mama's mind—

LUKE When you seen me. And you got to wondering all over again if you wanted to be like your daddy and end up like your daddy. Ain't that right?

DAVID Yeah, I guess that's right.

LUKE Well, son, tell you one thing. Wasn't music put me here. The most terrible time in a man's life, David, is when he's done lost everything that held him together—it's just gone and he can't find it. The whole world just get to be a great big empty basin. And it just as hollow as a basin when you strike it with your fist. Then that man start going down. If don't no hand reach out to help him, that man goes under. You know, David, it don't take much to hold a man together. A man can lose a whole lot, might look to everybody else that he done lost so much that he ought to want to be dead, but he can keep on—he can even die with his head up, hell, as long as he got that one thing. That one thing is *him,* David, who he is inside—and, son, I don't believe no man ever got to that without somebody loved him. Somebody *looked* at him, looked *way* down in him and spied him way down there and showed him to himself—and then started pulling, a-pulling of him up—so he could live. *(exhausted)* Hold your head up, David. You'll have a life. Tell me there's all kinds of ways for ruined men to keep on living. You hears about guys sometimes who got a bullet in their guts and keeps on running—running—spilling blood every inch, keeps running a long time—before they fall. I don't know what keeps them going. Faith—or something—something—something I never had. *(a pause)* So don't you think you got to end up like your daddy just because you want to join a band.

DAVID Daddy—weren't the music enough?

LUKE The music. The music. Music is a moment. But life's a long time. In that moment, when it's good, when you really swinging—then you joined to everything, to everybody, to skies and stars and every living thing. But music ain't kissing. Kissing's what you want to do. Music's what you *got* to do, *if* you got to do it. Question is how long you can keep up with the music when you ain't got nobody to kiss. You know, the music don't come out of the air, baby. It comes out of the man who's blowing it.

DAVID You must have had a time.

LUKE I had me a time all right.

DAVID Didn't you never call on God?

LUKE No. I figured it was just as much His fault as mine.

DAVID Didn't you never get scared?

LUKE Oh yes.

DAVID But you're not scared now?

LUKE Oh yes.

*(*DAVID *goes off, stage left. The lights come up in the church, dim down in the apartment.* SISTER MOORE, SISTER BOXER, BROTHER BOXER, *along with some members of the congregation seen in the First Act, are grouped together in camp chairs.* ODESSA *sits a little away from them.* SISTER RICE, *fortyish,* SISTER SALLY, *extremely young and voluptuous,* SISTER DOUGLASS, *quite old and slow and Black)*

SISTER SALLY Why, a couple of months ago, just after we got married? Why, Herman and I, we had to go to Philadelphia *several* times and it don't cost no forty some odd dollars to get there. Why, it don't cost *that* much round trip.

SISTER DOUGLASS It ain't but up the road a ways, is it? I used to go up there to see my nephew, he stay too busy to be able to get to New York much. It didn't seem to me it took so long. 'Course, I don't remember how much it cost.

ODESSA I don't know why you folks don't just call up Pennsylvania Station and just *ask* how much it costs to get to Philadelphia.

BROTHER BOXER Most folks don't go to Philadelphia by train, Sister Odessa. They takes the bus because the bus is cheaper.

SISTER MOORE Now, of course ain't nothing these days what you might call really *cheap.* Brother Boxer, you remember when Sister Boxer had to go down home to bury her sister? You was going up to Philadelphia quite regular there for a while. You remember how much it cost?

SISTER BOXER You ain't never mentioned you knew anybody in Philadelphia.

SISTER SALLY Men don't never tell women nothing. Look like you always finding out something new.

BROTHER BOXER Man better not tell a woman everything he know, not if he got good sense. *(to* SISTER MOORE*)* It didn't cost no more'n about three or four dollars.

SISTER BOXER That round trip or one way?

SISTER DOUGLASS How much you folks say you raised on the offering last Sunday?

SISTER MOORE Brother Boxer and me, we counted it, and put it in the envelope. It come to—what did it come to altogether, Brother Boxer? Give us the *exact* figure, amen.

BROTHER BOXER It come to forty-one dollars and eighty-seven cents.

SISTER RICE Don't seem to me we ought to be sitting here like this, worrying about the few pennies we give our pastor last Sunday. We been doing it Sunday after Sunday and ain't nobody never had nothing to say against Sister Margaret. She's our pastor, we ain't supposed to be thinking no evil about her.

SISTER MOORE That's what I say, amen. Sister Margaret our pastor and the few pennies we scrapes together by the sweat of our brow to give her she got a right to do with as she see *fit,* amen! And I think we ought to stop discussing it right here and now and just realize that we's blessed to have a woman like Sister Margaret for our shepherd.

ODESSA You folks sound like a church don't have to pay no rent, and don't never pay no bills and nothing in a church don't never wear out. Them chairs you got your behinds on right now, they have to keep on being replaced—you folks is always breaking them during the service, when you gets happy. Those of you what wears glasses, though, I notice you don't never break them. You holds yourself together somehow until somebody comes and takes them off'n you. Rugs on the floor cost money, robes cost money—and you people is just murder on hymnbooks, tambourines and Bibles. Now, Margaret don't use hardly none of that money on herself—ain't enough money *in* this church for nobody to be able to live off it.

BROTHER BOXER You folks got a new Frigidaire, though. I ain't saying nothing, but—

ODESSA That Frigidaire is in *my* name, Brother Boxer—it's the first new thing I bought for that house in I don't know how many years—with money *I* made from scrubbing white folks' floors. Ain't a one of you put a penny in it. Now. You satisfied?

SISTER MOORE How's your mother getting along, Sister Rice? I hope she feeling better. We ain't seen her for a long time.

SISTER RICE We's holding onto God for her. But she been doing poorly, poor thing. She say she sure do miss not being able to come out to service.

SISTER MOORE But Sister Margaret's been there, praying for her, ain't she?

SISTER RICE No, Sister Margaret ain't got there yet. She say she was going to make it last Sunday, but then she had to go to Philadelphia—

SISTER MOORE Poor Sister Margaret. She sure has had her hands full.

SISTER BOXER She got her hands full right down there in her own house. Reckon she couldn't get over to pray for your mother, Sister Rice, she couldn't stay here to pray for her own husband.

SISTER DOUGLASS The Word say we ain't supposed to think no evil, Sister Boxer. Sister Margaret have to go the way the Lord leads her.

SISTER BOXER I ain't thinking no evil. But the Word *do* say, if you don't love your brother who you can see, how you going to love God, who you ain't seen?

SISTER SALLY That is a *true* saying, bless the Lord.

SISTER DOUGLASS How is that poor, sin-sick soul?

SISTER BOXER He ain't long for this world. He lying down there, just rotten with sin. He dying in his sins.

SISTER MOORE He real pitiful. I declare, when you see what sin can do it make you stop and think.

SISTER RICE Do David spend much time with him, Sister Odessa? I reckon it must make him feel real bad to see his father lying there like that.

ODESSA Luke so sick he do a lot of sleeping, so David can't really be with him so much.

SISTER DOUGLASS Oh. We ain't seen David hardly at all this week and I just figured he was downstairs with his father.

BROTHER BOXER Little David—I'm mighty afraid little David got other fish to fry. The Lord has allowed me to see, with my *own* eyes, how David's done started straying from the Word. I ain't going to say no more. But the brother needs prayer. Amen. Sister Moore, do you recollect how much it cost us to get that there window painted?

SISTER MOORE Why, no, Brother Boxer, I don't. Seem to me it cost about fifty dollars.

SISTER BOXER It cost fifty-three dollars. I remember because Sister Margaret weren't here when the work was finished and I give the man the money myself.

SISTER DOUGLASS It a mighty pretty window. Look like it make you love Jesus even more, seeing Him there all in the light like that.

BROTHER BOXER You remember who she got to do it?

SISTER BOXER Why, she got one of them folks from Philadelphia to do it. That was before we was even affiliated with that church.

BROTHER BOXER I believe we could of got it done for less, right down here among our own.

SISTER RICE I don't know, Brother Boxer, that's fine work. You got to have *training* for that. People think you can just get up and draw a picture, but it ain't so.

SISTER DOUGLASS That's the truth, Sister Rice. My nephew, he draws, and he all the time telling me how hard it is. I have to help him out all the time, you know, 'cause it ain't easy to make a living that way—

SISTER BOXER I don't know why your nephew couldn't of drew it for us. I bet you he wouldn't of charged no fifty-three dollars, either.

SISTER SALLY My mother, she go to Bishop William's church up there on 145th Street, you know, and she was saying to me just the other day she don't see why, after all these years, Sister Margaret couldn't move her congregation to a better building.

SISTER MOORE Sister Margaret ain't worried about these buildings down here on earth, daughter. Sister Margaret's working on another building, hallelujah, in the *heavens*, not made with hands!

SISTER SALLY Why, that's what my mother's doing, too, Sister Moore. But she say she don't see why you got to be in dirt all the time just because you a Christian.

ODESSA If anybody in this church is in dirt, it ain't the dirt of this church they's in. I know this ain't no palace, but it's the best we can do right now. Sister Margaret's been doing her best for every one of us and it ain't right for us to sit up here this evening, back-biting against her.

SISTER MOORE Sister Odessa, I told you downstairs it ain't nothing but the Devil putting them thoughts in your head. Ain't nobody back-biting against your sister. We's just discussing things, the Lord, He give us eyes to see and understanding to understand.

SISTER BOXER Amen!

SISTER MOORE I got yet to say my first word against your sister. I know the Lord is seen fit, for reasons *I* ain't trying to discover, to burden your sister with a heavy burden. I ain't sitting in judgment. I ain't questioning the ways of the Lord. I don't know what that half-grown son of hers done seen to cause him to backslide this-a-way. *I* don't know why that man of hers is down there, dying in his sins—just rotting away, amen, before her eyes. I ain't asking no questions. I'm just waiting on the Lord because He say He'll reveal all things. In His own good time.

SISTER BOXER Amen! and I believe He's going to use us to help Him reveal.

*(*SISTER MOORE *begins singing)*

ODESSA Sister Moore!

Sister Moore

You can run on for a long time,
You can run on for a long time,
You can run on for a long time,
I tell you the great God Almighty gonna cut you down.

Contralto

Some people go to church just to signify
Trying to make a date with their neighbor's wife.
Brother, let me tell you just as sure as you're born
You better leave that woman, leave her alone.
One of these days, just mark my word,
You'll think your neighbor has gone to work,
You'll walk right up and knock on the door—
That's all, brother, you'll knock no more.
Go tell that long-tongued liar, go tell that midnight rider,
Go tell the gambler, rambler, backslider,
Tell him God Almighty's gonna cut you down.

(During the last line of song MARGARET *enters)*

MARGARET Praise the Lord, children. I'm happy to see you's holding the fort for Jesus.

SISTER MOORE Praise the *Lord*, Sister Margaret! We was just wondering if you was *ever* coming back here!

SISTER BOXER Praise the Lord, Sister Margaret, we sure is glad you's back. Did you have a good trip?

MARGARET Praise the Lord, children. It sure is good to be back here. The Lord, He give us the victory in Philadelphia, amen! He just worked and uncovered sin and put them children on their knees!

All

What a wonder, what a marvel,
And I'm glad that I can tell
That the Lord saved me and He set me free,
He endowered me with power,
And gave me the victory.

What a wonder, what a marvel,
And I'm glad that I can tell
That the Lord saved me and He set me free,
He endowered me with power,
And gave me the victory.

What a wonder, what a marvel,
And I'm glad that I can tell
That the Lord saved me and He set me free,
He endowered me with power,
And gave me the victory.

SISTER MOORE When it come time for the Lord to uncover, He sure do a mighty uncovering!

MARGARET *(to* ODESSA*)* Has everything been all right, sugar?

ODESSA Yes, Maggie. Everything's been fine.

SISTER BOXER How did you come down, Sister Margaret? Did you take the train or the bus?

MARGARET Honey, one of the Philadelphia saints drove me down.

SISTER BOXER *Drove* you down! I reckon you *did* get the victory. *(laughter)*

SISTER MOORE Well, bless the Lord, that's real nice. I reckon they was trying to help you cut down on expenses.

MARGARET Children, tomorrow is going to be a mighty big Sunday. The Philadelphia church is coming down here, all of them, for the evening service. Even Mother Phillips might be coming, she say she's feeling so much better. You know, this church is going to be packed. *(to* BROTHER BOXER*)* Brother Boxer, you going to have to clear a little space around that piano because they bringing their drums down here. *(to the others)* They got drums up there, children, and it help the service a whole lot, I wouldn't have believed it. *(the merest pause)* They even got a man up there making a joyful noise to the Lord on a trumpet!

BROTHER BOXER He coming down here, too?

MARGARET Oh, yes, he'll be here. Children, I want you all to turn out in full force tomorrow and show them Philadelphia saints how to praise the Lord.

SISTER DOUGLASS Look like they going to be able to teach us something, they got them drums and trumpets and all—

SISTER MOORE That don't make no difference. We been praising the Lord without that all this time, we ain't going to let them show us up.

MARGARET You better *not* let them show you up. You supposed to be an example to the *Philadelphia* church.

SISTER RICE But, Sister Margaret, you think it's right to let them come down here with all that—with drums and trumpets? Don't that seem kind of worldly?

MARGARET Well, the evil ain't in the drum, Sister Rice, nor yet in the trumpet. The evil is in what folks do with it and what it leads them to. Ain't no harm in praising the Lord with anything you get in your hands.

BROTHER BOXER It'll bring Brother David out to church again, I guarantee you that. That boy loves music.

MARGARET I hope you don't mean he loves music more than he loves the Lord.

BROTHER BOXER Oh, we all know how much he loves the Lord. But he got trumpets or *some* kind of horn in his *blood.*

ODESSA I reckon you going to have to speak to David, Maggie. He upset about his daddy and he ain't been out to service much this week.

SISTER MOORE When you upset, that's the time to come to the Lord. If you believe He loves you, you got to trust His love.

MARGARET Poor David. He don't talk much, but he feel a whole lot.

SISTER BOXER How is his daddy, Sister Margaret? You been downstairs to look at him yet?

ODESSA We ain't allowed to break his rest.

MARGARET I pray the Lord will save his soul.

SISTER MOORE Amen. And, church, we got to pray that the Lord will draw our David back to Him, so he won't end up like his daddy. Our pastor, she got a lot to bear.

MARGARET David ain't foolish, Sister Moore, and he done been well raised. He ain't going back into the world.

SISTER MOORE I hope and pray you's right, from the bottom of my soul I do. But every living soul needs prayer, Sister Margaret, every living soul. And we's just trying to hold up your hand in this time of trouble.

SISTER BOXER Sister Margaret, I ain't trying to dig up things what buried. But you told Joel and me he couldn't take that job driving that truck. And now you bringing down drums and trumpets from Philadelphia because you say the evil ain't in the thing, it's in what you do with the thing. Well, ain't that truck a *thing?* And if it's all right to blow a trumpet in church, why ain't it all right for Joel to drive that truck, so he can contribute a little more to the house of God? This church is *poor,* Sister Margaret, we ain't got no cars to ride you around in, like them folks in Philadelphia. But do that mean we got to *stay* poor?

MARGARET Sister Boxer, you know as well as me that there's many a piano out in them night clubs. But that ain't stopped us from using a piano in this church. And there's all the difference in the world between a saint of God playing music in a church and helping to draw people in and a saint of God spending the whole day driving a liquor truck around. Now I know you got good sense and I know you see that, and I done already told you I don't want to talk no more about it.

SISTER BOXER It don't seem to me you's being fair, Sister Margaret.

MARGARET When is I ain't been fair? I been doing my best, as the Lord led me, for all of you, for all these years. How come you to say I ain't been fair? You sound like you done forget your salvation, Sister Boxer.

*(*DAVID *reappears, carrying a phonograph and a record. He enters* LUKE*'s bedroom.* LUKE*'s eyes are closed. He goes to the bed and touches him lightly and* LUKE *opens his eyes)*

LUKE What you got there?

DAVID You going to recognize it. Be quiet, listen. *(he plugs in the phonograph)*

SISTER MOORE Now the Word say Blessed is the peacemaker, so let me make peace. This ain't no way to be behaving.

MARGARET Sister Moore, I'm the pastor of this church and I don't appreciate you acting as though we was both in the wrong.

SISTER MOORE Ain't nobody infallible, Sister Margaret. Ain't a soul been born infallible.

ODESSA We better all fall on our knees and pray.

MARGARET Amen.

*(*DAVID *has turned on the record, watching* LUKE*. The sound of* LUKE*'s trombone fills the air)*

SISTER MOORE Where's that music coming from?

ODESSA It must be coming from down the street.

MARGARET *(recognition)* Oh, my God.

SISTER MOORE It coming from your house, Sister Margaret.

MARGARET Kneel down. *(they watch her)* Kneel *down*, I say!

*(*LUKE *takes his mouthpiece from his pajama pocket and pantomimes a phrase, then stops, his mouthpiece in his hand, staring at his son. In the church, slowly, they kneel)*

MARGARET Pray. Every single one of you. Pray that God will give you a clean heart and a clean mind and teach you to obey. *(she turns and leaves the pulpit. Upstairs, they turn and look at each other and slowly rise from their knees. The church dims out.* MARGARET *stands for a moment in the door of* LUKE*'s bedroom)* David!

DAVID Mama—I didn't hear you come in!

MARGARET I reckon you didn't hear me come in. The way that box is going, you wouldn't of hear the Holy *Ghost* come in. Turn it off! Turn it off! *(*DAVID *does so)* You ain't supposed to let your daddy come here and lead you away from the Word. You's supposed to lead your daddy to the Lord. *(to* LUKE*)* It seems to me by this time the very sound of a horn would make you to weep or pray.

DAVID It's one of Daddy's old records. That you never let me play.

MARGARET Where'd that box come from? What's it doing in this house?

DAVID I borrowed it.

MARGARET Where'd you get that record?

DAVID It's mine.

LUKE That's right. It's his—now. *(a pause)*

MARGARET I ain't trying to be hard on you, son. But we's got to watch and pray. We's got to watch and pray.

DAVID Yes, Mama. Mama, I got to go now.

MARGARET Where you going, son?

LUKE Maggie, he ain't five years old, he's eighteen. Let him alone.

MARGARET You be quiet. You ain't got nothing to say in all this.

LUKE That's a lie. I got a lot to say in all this. That's my son. Go on, boy. You remember what I told you.

DAVID I'm taking the record player back where I got it. *(at the door)* So long—Daddy—

LUKE Go on, boy. You all right?

MARGARET David—

DAVID I'm all right, Daddy. *(*DAVID *goes)*

LUKE So long, son.

MARGARET Luke, ain't you never going to learn to do right? Ain't you learned nothing out all these years, all this trouble?

LUKE I done learned a few things. They might not be the same things you wanted me to learn. Hell, I don't know if they are the same things *I* wanted me to learn.

MARGARET I ain't never wanted you to learn but one thing, the love of Jesus.

LUKE You done changed your tune a whole lot. That ain't what we was trying to learn in the beginning.

MARGARET The beginning is a long time ago. And weren't nothing but foolishness. Ain't nothing but the love of God can save your soul.

LUKE Maggie, don't fight with me. I don't want to fight no more. We didn't get married because we loved God. We loved each other. Ain't that right?

MARGARET I sure can't save your soul, Luke.

LUKE There was a time when I believed you could.

MARGARET Luke. That's all past. *(she sits on the edge of the bed)* Luke, it been a long time we ain't seen each other, ten long years. Look how the Lord done let you fall. Ain't you ready to give up to Him and ask Him to save you from your sins and bring peace to your soul?

LUKE Is you got peace in your soul, Maggie?

MARGARET Yes! He done calmed the waters, He done beat back the powers of darkness, He done made me a new woman!

LUKE Then that other woman—that funny, fast-talking, fiery little thing I used to hold in my arms—He done done away with her?

MARGARET *(rises)* All that's—been burned out of me by the power of the Holy Ghost.

LUKE Maggie, I remember you when you didn't hardly know if the Holy Ghost was something to drink or something to put on your hair. I know we can't go back, Maggie. But you mean that whole time we was together, even with all our trouble, you mean it don't mean nothing to you now? You mean—you don't remember? I was your *man,* Maggie, we was everything to each other, like that Bible of yours say, we was one flesh—we used to get on each other's nerves something *awful*—you mean that's all dead and gone?

MARGARET You is still got that old, sinful Adam in you. You's thinking with Adam's mind. You don't understand that when the Lord changes you He makes you a new person and He gives you a new mind.

LUKE Don't talk at me like I was a congregation. I ain't no congregation. I'm your husband, even if I ain't much good to you no more.

MARGARET Well, if it's all dead and gone—you killed it! Don't you lay there and try to make me feel accused. If it's all dead and gone, you did it, you did it!

LUKE Ah. Now we coming. At least it wasn't the Holy Ghost. Just how did I do it, Maggie? How did I kill it?

MARGARET I never knew why you couldn't be like other men.

LUKE I was the man you married, Maggie. I weren't supposed to be like other men. When we didn't have nothing, I made it my business to find something, didn't I? Little David always had shoes to his feet when I was there and you wasn't never dressed in rags. And anyway—you want me to repent so you can get me into heaven, or you want me to repent so you can keep David home?

MARGARET Is David been talking about leaving home?

LUKE Don't you reckon he going to be leaving home one day?

MARGARET David going to work with me in these here churches and he going to be a pastor when he get old enough.

LUKE He got the call?

MARGARET He'll *get* the call.

LUKE You sure got a lot of influence with the Holy Ghost.

MARGARET I didn't come in here to listen to you blaspheme. I just come in here to try to get you to think about your soul.

LUKE Margaret, once you told me you loved me and then you jumped up and ran off from me like you couldn't stand the smell of me. What you think *that* done to my soul?

MARGARET I had to go. The Lord told me to go. We'd been living like—like two animals, like two children, never thought of nothing but their own pleasure. In my heart, I always knew we couldn't go on like that—we was too happy—

LUKE Ah!

MARGARET And that winter—them was terrible days, Luke. When I'd almost done gone under, I heard a voice. The voice said, Maggie, you got to find you a hiding place. I knowed weren't no hiding place to be found in you—not in no man. And you—you cared more about that trombone than you ever cared about me!

LUKE You ought to of tried me, Maggie. If

you had trusted me till then, you ought to have trusted me a little further.

MARGARET When they laid my baby in the churchyard, that poor little baby girl what hadn't never drawn breath, I knowed if we kept on a-going the way we'd been going, He weren't going to have no mercy on neither one of us. And that's when I swore to my God I was going to change my way of living.

LUKE Then that God you found—He just curse the poor? But He don't bother nobody else? Them big boys, them with all the money and all the manners, what let you drop dead in the streets, watch your blood run all over the gutters, just so they can make a lousy dime—He get along fine with them? What the hell had we done to be cursed, Maggie?

MARGARET We hadn't never thought of nothing but ourself. We hadn't never thought on God!

LUKE All we'd done to be cursed was to be poor, that's all. That's why little Margaret was laid in the churchyard. It was just because you hadn't never in your whole life had enough to eat and you was sick that winter and you didn't have no strength. Don't you come on with me about no judgment, Maggie. That was my baby, too.

MARGARET *Your* baby, yours! I was the one who carried it in my belly, *I* was the one who felt it starving to death inside me. *I* was the one who had it, in the cold and dark alone! You wasn't nowhere to be found, you was out drunk.

LUKE I was *there*. I was *there*. Yes, I was drunk, but I was sitting at your bedside every day. Every time you come to yourself you looked at me and started screaming about how I'd killed our baby. Like I'd taken little Margaret and strangled her with my own two hands. *Yes*, I was drunk but I was waiting for you to call me. You never did. You never did.

MARGARET I reckon the Lord was working with me, even then.

LUKE I reckon so.

MARGARET Luke. Luke, it don't do to question God.

LUKE No, it don't. It sure as hell don't.

MARGARET Don't let your heart be bitter. You'd come way down, Luke, bitterness ain't going to help you now. Let Him break your heart, let the tears come, ask Him to forgive you for your sins, call on Him, call on Him!

LUKE Call on Him for what, Maggie?

MARGARET To save your soul. To keep you from the fires of hell. So we can be together in glory.

LUKE I want to be together with you now.

MARGARET Luke. You ain't fighting with men no more. You's fighting with God. You got to humble yourself, you got to bow your head.

LUKE It ain't going to be like that, Maggie. I ain't going to come crawling to the Lord now, making out like I'd do better if I had it all to do over. I ain't going to go out, screaming against hell-fire. It would make *you* right. It would prove to David you was right. It would make me nothing but a dirty, drunk old man didn't do nothing but blow music and chase the women all his life. I ain't going to let it be like that. That ain't all there was to it. You know that ain't all there was to it.

MARGARET Stubborn, stubborn, stubborn Luke! You like a little boy. You think this is a game? You think it don't hurt me to my heart to see you the way you is now? You think my heart ain't black with sorrow to see your soul go under?

LUKE Stop talking about my soul. It's me, Maggie—*me!* Don't you remember *me?* Don't you care nothing about *me?* You ain't never stopped loving me. Have you, Maggie? Can't you tell me the truth?

MARGARET Luke—we ain't young no more. It don't matter no more about us. But what about our boy? You want him to live the life you've lived? You want him to end up—old and empty-handed?

LUKE I don't care what kind of life he lives—as long as it's *his* life—not mine, not his mama's, but his own. I ain't going to let you make him safe.

MARGARET I can't do no more. Before God, I done my best. Your blood can't be required at my hands.

LUKE I guess I could have told you—it weren't *my* soul we been trying to save.

(Low, syncopated singing from the church begins)

MARGARET Luke. You's going to die. I hope the Lord have mercy on you.

LUKE I ain't asking for no goddam mercy. *(he turns his face to the wall)* Go away.

MARGARET You's going to die, Luke. *(she moves slowly from the bedroom into the kitchen.*

ODESSA *enters from the church, goes to* MARGARET*)*

ODESSA Honey—they's going to have a business meeting upstairs. You hear me? You know what that means? If you want to hold onto this church, Maggie—if you do—you better get on upstairs. *(*MARGARET *is silent)* Where's David? He ought to be here when you need him.

MARGARET I don't know.

ODESSA I'll go and see if I can find him. You all right?

MARGARET It looks like rain out there. Put something on. *(after a moment,* ODESSA *goes.* MARGARET *walks up and down the kitchen. Her tears begin)* Lord, help us to stand. Help us to stand. Lord, give me strength! Give me strength!

(Curtain)

END OF ACT TWO

ACT THREE

(Music is heard offstage, a slow, quiet sound. Early the following morning. A bright, quiet day. Except for LUKE*, the stage is empty. His room is dark. He is sleeping.*

The light comes up very slowly in the church. After a moment, MRS. JACKSON *enters. She is wearing a house dress and slippers. She puts her hands to her face, moaning slightly, then falls heavily before the altar.*

MARGARET *enters through* LUKE's *bedroom. She pauses a moment at the foot of* LUKE's *bed, then enters the kitchen, then slowly mounts to the church.*

As she enters, MRS. JACKSON *stirs. They stare at each other for a moment.*

MRS. JACKSON *is weeping)*

MRS. JACKSON Sister Margaret, you's a woman of the Lord—you say you in communion with the Lord. Why He take my baby from me? Tell me why He do it? Why He make my baby suffer so? Tell me why He do it!

MARGARET Sister—we got to trust God—somehow. We got to bow our heads.

MRS. JACKSON My head is bowed. My head been bowed since I been born. His daddy's head is bowed. The Lord ain't got no right to make a baby suffer so, just to make me bow my head!

MARGARET Be careful what you say, daughter. Be careful what you say. We can't penetrate the mysteries of the Lord's will.

MRS. JACKSON *(moves away)* Why I got to be careful what I say? You think the Lord going to do me something else? I ain't got to be careful what I say no more. I sit on the bench in the hospital all night long, me and my husband, and we waited and we prayed and we wept. I said, Lord, if you spare my baby, I won't never take another drink, I won't do nothing, nothing to displease you, if you only give me back my baby, safe and well. He was such a nice baby and just like his daddy, he liked to laugh already. But I ain't going to have no more. Such a nice baby, I don't see why he had to get all twisted and curled up with pain and scream his little head off. And couldn't nobody help him. He hadn't never done nothing to nobody. Ain't nobody never done nothing bad enough to suffer like that baby suffered.

MARGARET Daughter, pray with me. Come, pray with me.

MRS. JACKSON I been trying to pray. Everytime I kneel down, I see my baby again—and—I can't pray. I can't get it out of my head, it ain't right, even if He's God, it ain't right.

MARGARET Sister—once I lost a baby, too. I know what that emptiness feel like, I declare to my Saviour I do. That was when I come to the Lord. I wouldn't come before. Maybe the Lord is working with you now. Open your heart and listen. Maybe, out of all this sorrow, He's calling you to do His work.

MRS. JACKSON I ain't like you, Sister Margaret. I don't want all this, all these people looking to me. I'm just a young woman, I just want my man and my home and my children.

MARGARET But that's all I wanted. That's what I wanted! Sometimes—what we want—and what we ought to have—ain't the same. Sometime, the Lord, He take away what we want and give us what we need.

MRS. JACKSON And do I need—that man sitting home with a busted heart? Do I need—two children in the graveyard?

MARGARET I don't know, I ain't the Lord, I don't know what you need. You need to pray.

MRS. JACKSON No, I'm going home to my husband. He be getting worried. He don't know where I am. *(she starts out)*

MARGARET Sister Jackson! (MRS. JACKSON *turns)* Why did you say you ain't going to have no more babies? You still a very young woman.

MRS. JACKSON I'm scared to go through it again. I can't go through it again.

MARGARET That ain't right. That ain't right. You ought to have another baby. You ought to have another baby right away. *(a pause)* Honey—is there anything you want me to do for you now, in your time of trouble?

MRS. JACKSON No, Sister Margaret, ain't nothing you can do. *(she goes.* MARGARET *stands alone in the church)*

MARGARET Get on home to your husband. Go on home, to your man.

(Downstairs, ODESSA *enters through* LUKE*'s room; pauses briefly at* LUKE*'s bed, enters the kitchen. She goes to the stove, puts a match under the coffeepot.* MARGARET *stares at the altar; starts downstairs)*

Odessa *(sings, under her breath)*

Some say the rose of Sharon,
Some say the Prince of Peace.
But I call Jesus my rock!

(MARGARET *enters)*

ODESSA How long you been up, Maggie?

MARGARET I don't know. Look like I couldn't sleep.

ODESSA You got a heavy day ahead of you.

MARGARET I know it. David ain't come in yet?

ODESSA No, but don't fret. He's all right. He'll be along. It's just natural for young boys to go a little wild every now and again. Soon this'll all be over, Maggie, and when you look back on it it won't be nothing more than like you had a bad dream.

MARGARET A bad dream!

ODESSA They ain't going to turn you out, Maggie. They ain't crazy. They know it take a *long* time before they going to find another pastor of this church like you.

MARGARET It won't take them so long if Sister Moore have her way. She going to be the next pastor of this church. Lord, you sure can't tell what's going on in a person's heart.

ODESSA The Bible say the heart is deceitful above all things. And desperately wicked.

MARGARET Who can know it? I guess whoever wrote that wasn't just thinking about the hearts of other people.

ODESSA Maggie, you better go on in the front and lie down awhile. You got time. Sunday school ain't even started yet. I'll call you in time for you to get dressed for service.

MARGARET I reckon I better. *(she starts out, stops)* They talk about me letting my own house perish in sin. The Word say if you put father or mother or brother or sister or husband—or *anybody*—ahead of Him, He ain't going to have nothing to do with you on the last day.

ODESSA Yes. The Word do say so.

MARGARET I married that man when I weren't hardly nothing but a girl. I used to know that man, look like, just inside *out*, sometime I knowed what he was going to do before he knowed it himself. Sometime I could just look up, look up at that face, and just—*know*. Ain't no man never made me laugh the way Luke could. No, nor cry neither. I ain't never held no man until I felt his pain coming into me like little drops of acid. Odessa, I bore that man his only son. Now, you know there's still something left in my heart for that man.

ODESSA Don't think on it, honey. Don't think on it so. Go on in front and lie down.

MARGARET Yes. *(she starts out, stops)* Odessa—you know what amen means?

ODESSA Amen means—*amen*.

MARGARET Amen means Thy will be done. Amen means So be it. I been up all morning, praying—and—I couldn't say amen. *(she goes)*

ODESSA Lord, have mercy. Have mercy, Lord, this morning. *(sings, under her breath)* Some say the Rose of Sharon, some say the Prince of Peace. But I call Jesus my rock! *(she goes to the door of* LUKE*'s room.* BROTHER *and* SISTER BOXER *and* SISTER MOORE *enter the church. The two women are all in white)* Yes, Lord. Every time a woman don't know if she coming or going, every *time* her heart get all swelled up with grief, there's a man sleeping somewhere close by. (SISTER BOXER *crosses the church and comes down the stairs)*

SISTER BOXER Praise the Lord, Sister Odessa. You all alone this morning?

ODESSA I didn't know you folks was upstairs. How long you been there?

SISTER BOXER We just this minute come in.

ODESSA You all mighty early, seems to me.

SISTER BOXER Well, Sister Moore, she thought if we got here early we might be able to see Sister Margaret before anybody else come in.

ODESSA Sister Margaret ain't ready to see nobody yet.

SISTER BOXER It almost time for Sunday school.

ODESSA Sister Boxer, you know right well that Sister Margaret don't hardly never come to Sunday school. She got to save her strength for the morning service. You know that.

SISTER BOXER Well, Sister Moore thought—maybe *this* morning—

ODESSA Sister Boxer—don't you think enough harm's been done with all them terrible things was said last night?

SISTER BOXER Ain't nobody said nothing last night that wasn't the gospel truth.

ODESSA I done heard enough truth these last couple of days to last me the rest of my life.

SISTER BOXER The truth is a two-edged sword, Sister Odessa.

ODESSA It ain't never going to cut you down. You ain't never going to come that close to it.

SISTER BOXER Well—do Jesus! Soon as something happens to that sister of yours you forgets all about your salvation, don't you? You better ask the Lord to watch your tongue. The tongue is a *unruly* member.

ODESSA It ain't as unruly as it's going to get. *(a pause)* Sister Boxer, this ain't no way for us to be talking. We used to be *friends.* We used to have right *good* times together. How come we got all this bad feeling all of a sudden? Look like it come out of nowhere, overnight.

SISTER BOXER I ain't got no bad feeling toward *you,* Sister Odessa. *(after a moment,* SISTER BOXER *turns and mounts to the church.* ODESSA *follows)*

SISTER MOORE Praise the Lord, Sister Odessa. How you this Lord's day morning?

ODESSA I'm leaning on the Lord, Sister Moore. How you feeling?

BROTHER BOXER Praise the Lord, Sister Odessa. I'm mighty glad to hear you say that. We needs the Lord this morning. We needs to hear Him speak peace to our souls.

ODESSA How come you folks want to see Sister Margaret so early in the morning?

SISTER BOXER Well, we ain't really got to see Sister Margaret, not now that you're here, Sister Odessa. You is still one of the elders of this church.

SISTER MOORE We want to do everything we got to do in front, amen. Don't want nobody saying we went around and done it in the dark.

ODESSA You's doing it in front, all right. You's supposed to do it in front of the whole congregation this afternoon.

BROTHER BOXER Well, the Lord's done led us to do a little different from the way we was going to do last night.

ODESSA How's that, Brother Boxer? *(a pause)* Well, now, the way I understood it last *night*—you folks say that Margaret ain't got no right to call herself a spiritual leader. *You* folks say that Margaret done let her own household perish in sin and—you folks say—that all these things is a sign from the Lord that He ain't pleased with Margaret and you was going to put all that in front of this church and the church from Philadelphia and see what *they* thought. Ain't that right?

SISTER BOXER We done already spoken to the members of this church. Margaret's as good as read out of this church already, ain't hardly no need for her to come to service.

SISTER MOORE I spoke to them myself. I been up since early this morning, bless the Lord, just ringing doorbells and stirring up the people against sin.

ODESSA You must of got up mighty early.

SISTER MOORE When the Lord's work is to be done, I gets up out of my bed. God don't love the slothful. And, look like the more I do, the more He gives me strength to do.

BROTHER BOXER We thought it might be easier on Sister Margaret if we done it this way. Ain't no need for folks to know all of Sister Margaret's personal business. So we ain't said nothing about Brother Luke. Folks is bound to try and put two and two together—but *we* ain't said nothing. We ain't said nothing about Brother David. We is just told the congregation that the Lord's done revealed to the elders of this church that Sister Margaret ain't been leading the life of a holy woman, especially a holy woman in *her* position, is supposed to lead. That's all. And we said we weren't sitting in *judgment* on Sister Margaret.

We was leaving it up to her conscience, amen, and the Lord.

BROTHER BOXER But we did say—since we're the elders of the church and we got a responsibility to the congregation, too—that the Lord ain't pleased at Margaret sitting in the seat of authority.

SISTER MOORE It's time for her to come down.

ODESSA And how did folks take it when you told them all this?

BROTHER BOXER Well, folks ain't in this church to worship Sister Margaret. They's here to worship the Lord.

ODESSA Folks thought Margaret was good enough to be their pastor all these years, they ain't going to stop wanting her for pastor overnight.

BROTHER BOXER She rose overnight. She can fall overnight.

SISTER BOXER I tell you, Sister Odessa, like the song says: "You may run on a great, long time but great God Almighty going to cut you down." Yes, indeed, He going to let the truth be known one *day.* And on that day, it's just too bad *for* you. Sister Margaret done had a lot of people fooled a long time, but now, bless God forever, the truth is out.

ODESSA What truth? What is that woman done to make you hate her so? Weren't but only yesterday you was all saying how wonderful she was, and how blessed we was to have her. And now you can't find nothing bad enough to say about her. Don't give me that stuff about her letting her household perish in sin. Ain't a one of you but ain't got a brother or a sister or somebody on the road to hell right now. I want to know what is she *done?* What is she done to you, Sister Moore?

SISTER BOXER *I* ain't got no brothers or sisters on the road to hell. Only sister I *had* is waiting for me in glory. And every *soul* I come in contact with is saved—except of course for them people I work for. And I got no trombone-playing husband dying in my house and I ain't got no half-grown son out fornicating in the wilderness.

SISTER MOORE Don't you come up here and act like you thought we was just acting out of spite and meanness. Your sister ain't done nothing to me; she *can't* do nothing to me because the Lord holds me in His hands. All we's trying to do is the Lord's will—you ought to be trying to do it, too. If we want to reign with him in glory, we ain't supposed to put nobody before Him. Amen! We ain't supposed to have no other love but Him.

SISTER BOXER I looked at that man and I says to myself, How in the *world* did Sister Margaret ever get herself mixed up with a man like that?

ODESSA Ain't no mystery how a woman gets mixed up with a man, Sister Boxer, and you sure ought to know that, even if poor Sister Moore here *don't.*

SISTER MOORE Don't you poor-Sister-Moore *me.* That man put a demon inside your sister and that demon's walking up and down inside her still. You can see it in her eyes, they done got all sleepy with lust.

ODESSA Sister Moore, I sure would like to know just how come *you* know so much about it.

SISTER BOXER Sister Odessa, ain't no sense to you trying to put everybody in the wrong because Sister Margaret is falling. That ain't going to raise her back up. It's the Lord's *will* she should come down.

ODESSA I don't understand how you can take her part against my sister. *You* ought to know how much Sister Margaret's suffered all these years by herself. *You* know it ain't no easy thing for a woman to go it alone. She done spent more'n ten years to build this up for herself and her little boy. How you going to throw her out now? What's she going to do, where's she going to go?

BROTHER BOXER She didn't worry about Elder King when she took over this church from him.

SISTER MOORE I think you think I hates your sister because she been married. And I ain't never been married. I ain't questioning the Lord's ways. He done kept me pure to Himself for a purpose, and that purpose is working itself out right here in this room this morning—right here in this room, this upper room. It make your sister look double-minded, I do declare it do, if she done tried, one time, to bring peace to one man, and failed, and then she jump up and think she going to bring peace to a whole lot of people.

ODESSA Sister Margaret done give good

service all those years. She ain't been acting like she was double-minded.

BROTHER BOXER But I bet you—she is double-minded *now.*

*(*DAVID *enters the apartment. He is suffering from a hang-over, is still a little drunk. He goes to the sink and splashes cold water on his face. He moves with both bravado and fear and there is a kind of heartbreaking humor in his actions)*

SISTER BOXER Odessa, a church can't have no woman for pastor who done been married once and then decided it didn't suit her and then jump up and run off from her husband and take a seat in the pulpit and act like she ain't no woman no more. That ain't no kind of example to the young. The Word say the marriage bed is holy.

ODESSA I can't believe—I can't *believe* you really going to do it. We been friends so long.

*(*DAVID *dries his face. He goes to the door of* LUKE*'s room, stands for a moment looking at his father. He turns back into the kitchen. At this moment,* MARGARET *enters, dressed in white. She and* DAVID *stare at each other)*

SISTER BOXER You the one I'm sorry for, Sister Odessa. You done spent your life, look like, protecting that sister of yours. And now you can't protect her no more.

ODESSA It ain't been me protecting Sister Margaret. It been the Lord. And He ain't yet withdrawed His hand. He ain't never left none of His children alone. *(she starts for the rear door of the church)*

SISTER BOXER How come you ain't never been married, Sister Odessa?

ODESSA Suppose we just say, Sister Boxer, that I never had the time.

SISTER BOXER It might have been better for you if you'd taken the time.

ODESSA I ain't got no regrets. No, I ain't. I ain't claiming I'm pure, like Sister Moore here. I ain't claiming that the Lord had such special plans for me that I couldn't have nothing to do with men. Brothers and sisters, if you knew just a little bit about folks' lives, what folks go through, and the low, black places they finds their feet—you *would* have a meeting here this afternoon. Maybe I don't know the Lord like you do, but I know something else. I know how men and women can come together and change each other and make each other suffer, and make each other glad. If you putting my sister out of this church, you putting me out, too. *(she goes out through the street door. The church dims out)*

MARGARET Where you been until this time in the morning, son?

DAVID I was out visiting some people I know. And it got to be later than I realized and I stayed there overnight.

MARGARET How come it got to be so late before you realized it?

DAVID I don't know. We just got to talking.

MARGARET Talking? *(she moves closer to him)* What was you talking about, son? You stink of whiskey! *(she slaps him.* DAVID *sits at the table)*

DAVID That ain't going to do no good, Ma. *(she slaps him again.* DAVID *slumps on the table, his head in his arms)*

MARGARET Is that what I been slaving for all these long, hard years? Is I carried slops and scrubbed floors and ate leftovers and swallowed bitterness by the gallon jugful—for this? So you could walk in here this Lord's-day morning stinking from whiskey and some no-count, dirty, Black girl's sweat? Declare, I wish you'd died in my belly, too, if I been slaving all these years for this!

DAVID Mama. Mama. Please.

MARGARET Sit up and look at me. Is you too drunk to hold up your head? Or is you too ashamed? Lord knows you ought to be ashamed.

DAVID Mama, I wouldn't of had this to happen this way for nothing in the world.

MARGARET Was they holding a pistol to your head last evening? Or did they tie you down and pour the whiskey down your throat?

DAVID No. No. Didn't nobody have no pistol. Didn't nobody have no rope. Some fellows said, Let's pick up some whiskey. And I said, Sure. And we all put in some money and I went down to the liquor store and bought it. And then we drank it. (MARGARET *turns away)*

MARGARET David, I ain't so old. I know the world is wicked. I know young people have terrible temptations. Did you do it because you was afraid them boys would make fun of you?

DAVID No.

MARGARET Was it on account of some girl?

DAVID No.

MARGARET Was it—your daddy put you up to it? Was it your daddy made you think it was manly to get drunk?

DAVID Daddy—I don't think you can blame it on Daddy, Mama.

MARGARET Why'd you do it, David? When I done tried so hard to raise you right? Why'd you want to hurt me this way?

DAVID I didn't want to hurt you, Mama. But this day has been coming a long time. Mama, I can't play piano in church no more.

MARGARET Is it on account of your daddy? Is it your daddy put all this foolishness in your head?

DAVID Daddy ain't been around for a long time, Mama. I ain't talked to him but one time since he been here.

MARGARET And that one time—he told you all about the wonderful time he had all them years, blowing out his guts on that trombone.

DAVID No. That ain't exactly what he said. That ain't exactly what we talked about.

MARGARET What *did* you talk about?

(A sound of children singing "Jesus Loves Me" comes from the church)

DAVID Well—he must have been talking about you. About how he missed you, and all.

MARGARET Sunday school done started. David, why don't you go upstairs and play for them, just this one last morning?

DAVID Mama, I told you. I can't play piano in church no more.

MARGARET David, why don't you feel it no more, what you felt once? Where's it gone? Where's the Holy Ghost gone?

DAVID I don't know, Mama. It's empty. *(he indicates his chest)* It's empty here.

MARGARET Can't you pray? Why don't you pray? If you pray, pray hard, He'll come back. The Holy Ghost will come back. He'll come down on heavenly wings, David, and *(she touches his chest)* fill that empty space, He'll start your heart to singing—singing again. He'll fill you, David, with a mighty burning fire and burn out *(she takes his head roughly between her palms)* all that foolishness, all them foolish dreams you carries around up there. Oh, David, David, pray that the Holy Ghost will come back, that the gift of God will come back!

DAVID Mama, if a person don't feel it, he just don't feel it.

MARGARET David, I'm older than you. I done been down the line. I know ain't no safety nowhere in this world if you don't stay close to God. What you think the world's got out there for you but a broken heart?

*(*ODESSA*, unnoticed, enters)*

ODESSA You better listen to her, David.

MARGARET I remember boys like you down home, David, many years ago—fine young men, proud as horses, and I seen what happened to them. I seen them go down, David, until they was among the lowest of the low. There's boys like you down there, today, breaking rock and building roads, they ain't never going to hold up their heads up on this earth no more. There's boys like you all over this city, filling up the gin mills and standing on the corners, running down alleys, tearing themselves to pieces with knives and whiskey and dope and sin! You think I done lived this long and I don't know what's happening? Fine young men and they're lost—they don't know what's happened to their life. Fine young men, and some of them dead and some of them dead while they living. You think I want to see this happen to you? You think I want you one day lying where your daddy lies today?

ODESSA You better listen to her, David. You better listen.

MARGARET No. He ain't going to listen. Young folks don't never listen. They just go on, headlong, and they think ain't nothing ever going to be too big for them. And, time they find out, it's too late then.

DAVID And if I listened—what would happen? What do you think would happen if I listened? You want me to stay here, getting older, getting sicker—hating you? You think I want to hate you, Mama? You think it don't tear me to pieces to have to lie to you all the time. Yes, because I been lying to you, Mama, for a long time now! I don't want to tell no more lies. I don't want to keep on feeling so bad inside that I have to go running down them alleys you was talking about—that alley right outside this door!—to find something to help me hide—to hide—from what I'm feeling. Mama, I want to be a man. It's time you let me be a man. You got to let me go. *(a pause)* If I stayed here—I'd end up worse than Daddy—because I wouldn't be doing what I know I got to do—I *got* to do! I've seen your life—and now I see Daddy—and I love you, I love you both!—but I've got my work to do, something's happening in the world out there, I got to go! I know you think I don't know what's happening, but I'm beginning to see—something. Every time I play, every time I listen, I see Daddy's face and yours, and so many faces—who's going to speak for all that, Mama? Who's going to speak for all of us? I can't stay home. Maybe I can say something—one day—maybe I can say something in music that's never been said before. Mama—*you* knew this day was coming.

MARGARET I reckon I thought I was Joshua and could make the sun stand still.

DAVID Mama, I'm leaving this house tonight. I'm going on the road with some other guys. I got a lot of things to do today and I ain't going to be hanging around the house. I'll see you before I go. *(he starts for the door)*

MARGARET David—?

DAVID Yes, Mama?

MARGARET Don't you want to eat something?

DAVID No, Mama. I ain't hungry now. *(he goes)*

MARGARET Well. There he go. Who'd ever want to love a man and raise a child! Odessa—you think I'm a hard woman?

ODESSA No. I don't think you a hard woman. But I think you's in a hard place.

MARGARET I done something, somewhere, wrong.

ODESSA Remember this morning. You got a awful thing ahead of you this morning. You got to go upstairs and win them folks back to you this morning.

MARGARET My man is in there, dying, and my baby's in the world—how'm I going to preach, Odessa? How'm I going to preach when I can't even pray?

ODESSA You got to face them. You got to think. You got to pray.

MARGARET Sister, I can't. I can't. I can't.

ODESSA Maggie. It was you had the vision. It weren't me. You got to think back to the vision. If the vision was for anything, it was for just this day.

MARGARET The vision. Ah, it weren't yesterday, that vision. I was in a cold, dark place and I thought it was the grave. And I listened to hear my little baby cry and didn't no cry come. I heard a voice say, Maggie. Maggie. You got to find you a hiding place. I wanted Luke. *(she begins to weep)* Oh, sister, I don't remember no vision. I just remember that it was dark and I was scared and my baby was dead and I wanted Luke, I wanted Luke, I wanted Luke!

ODESSA Oh, honey. Oh, my honey. What we going to do with you this morning? (MARGARET *cannot stop weeping)* Come on, honey, come on. You got them folks to face.

MARGARET All these years I prayed as hard as I knowed how. I tried to put my treasure in heaven where couldn't nothing get at it and take it away from me and leave me alone. I asked the Lord to hold my hand. I didn't expect that none of this would ever rise to hurt me no more. And all these years it just been waiting for me, waiting for me to turn a corner. And there it stand, my whole life, just like I hadn't never gone nowhere. It's a awful thing to think about, the way love never dies!

ODESSA You's got to pull yourself together and think how you can *win.* You always been the winner. Ain't no time to be a woman *now.* You can't let them throw you out of this church. What we going to do then? I'm getting old, I can't help you. And you ain't young no more, neither.

MARGARET Maybe we could go—someplace else.

ODESSA We ain't got no money to go no place. We ain't paid the rent for this month. We ain't even finished paying for this Frigidaire.

MARGARET I remember in the old days whenever Luke wanted to spend some money on foolishness, that is exactly what I would have to say to him: "Man, ain't you got good sense? Do you know we ain't even paid the rent for this month?"

ODESSA Margaret. You got to think.

MARGARET Odessa, you remember when we was little there was a old blind woman lived down the road from us. She used to live in this house all by herself and you used to take me by the hand when we walked past her house because I was scared of her. I can see her, just as plain somehow, sitting on the porch, rocking in that chair, just looking out over them roads like she could see something. And she used to hear us coming, I guess, and she'd shout out, "How you this Lord's-day morning?" Don't care what day it was, or what time of day it was, it was always the Lord's-day morning for her. Daddy used to joke about her, he used to say, "Ain't no man in that house. It's a mighty sad house." I reckon this going to be a mighty sad house before long.

ODESSA Margaret. You got to think.

MARGARET I'm thinking. I'm thinking. I'm thinking how I throwed away my life.

ODESSA You can't think about it like that. You got to remember—you gave your life to the Lord.

MARGARET I'm thinking now—maybe Luke needed it more. Maybe David could of used it better. I know. I got to go upstairs and face them people. Ain't nothing else left for me to do. I'd like to talk to Luke.

ODESSA I'll go on up there.

MARGARET The only thing my mother should have told me is that being a woman ain't nothing but one long fight with men. And even the Lord, look like, ain't nothing but the most impossible kind of man there is. Go on upstairs, sister. Be there—when I get there.

(After a moment, ODESSA *goes. Again, we hear the sound of singing: "God be with you till we meet again."* MARGARET *walks into* LUKE*'s bedroom, stands there a moment, watching him.* BROTHER BOXER *enters the kitchen, goes to the Frigidaire, pours himself a Kool-aid.)*

MARGARET *(turns)* What are you doing down here, Brother Boxer? Why ain't you upstairs in the service?

BROTHER BOXER Why ain't *you* upstairs in the service, Sister Margaret? We's waiting for you upstairs.

MARGARET I'm coming upstairs! Can't you go on back up there now and ask them folks to be—a little quiet? He's sick, Brother Boxer. He's sick!

BROTHER BOXER You just finding that out? He *been* sick, Sister Margaret. How come it ain't never upset you until now? And how you expect me to go upstairs and ask them folks to be quiet when you been telling us all these years to praise the Lord with fervor? Listen! They got fervor. Where's all your fervor done gone to, Sister Margaret?

MARGARET Brother Boxer, even if you don't want me for your pastor no more, please remember I'm a woman. Don't talk to me this way.

BROTHER BOXER A woman? Is *that* where all your fervor done gone to? You trying to get back into that man's arms, Sister Margaret? What you want him to do for you—you want him to take off that long white robe?

MARGARET Be careful, Brother Boxer. It ain't over yet. It ain't over yet.

BROTHER BOXER Oh, yes it is, Sister Margaret. It's over. You just don't know it's over. Come on upstairs. Maybe you can make those folks keep quiet. *(the music has stopped)* They's quiet now. They's waiting for you.

MARGARET You hate me. How long have you hated me? What have I ever done to make you hate me?

BROTHER BOXER All these years you been talking about how the Lord done called you. Well, you sure come running, but I ain't so sure you was called. I seen you in there, staring at that man. You ain't no better than the rest of them. You done sweated and cried in the nighttime, too, and you'd like to be doing it again. You had me fooled with that long white robe but you ain't no better. You ain't as good. You been sashaying around here acting like weren't nobody good enough to touch the hem of your garment. You was always so pure, Sister Margaret, you made the rest of us feel like dirt.

MARGARET I was trying to please the Lord.

BROTHER BOXER And you reckon you did? Declare, I never thought I'd see you so quiet. All these years I been running errands for you, saying, Praise the Lord, Sister Margaret. That's *right,* Sister Margaret! Amen, Sister Margaret! I didn't know if you even knew what a man was. I never thought I'd live long enough to find out that Sister Margaret weren't nothing but a woman who run off from her husband and then started ruling other people's lives because she didn't have no man to control her. I sure hope you make it into heaven, girl. You's too late to catch any other train.

MARGARET It's not over yet. It's not over.

BROTHER BOXER You coming upstairs?

MARGARET I'm coming.

BROTHER BOXER Well. We be waiting.

(He goes. MARGARET *stands alone in the kitchen. As* BROTHER BOXER *enters, the lights in the church go up. The church is packed. Far in the back* SISTER ODESSA *sits.* SISTER MOORE *is in the pulpit, and a baritone soloist is singing)*

Baritone

Soon I'll be done with the troubles of the world,
Troubles of the world, troubles of the world,
Soon I'll be done with the troubles of the world,
Going home to live with my Lord.

Soon I'll be done with the troubles of the world,
Troubles of the world, troubles of the world,
Soon I'll be done with the troubles of the world,
Going home to live with my Lord.

Soon I'll be done with the troubles of the world,
Troubles of the world, troubles of the world,
Soon I'll be done with the troubles of the world,
Going home to live with my Lord.

SISTER MOORE *(reads)* For if after they have escaped the pollution of the world through the knowledge of the Lord and Saviour Jesus Christ they are again entangled therein and overcome, the latter end is worse with them than the beginning.

ALL Amen!

SISTER MOORE *(reads)* For it had been better for them not to have known the way of righteousness than after they had known it to turn away from the holy commandment delivered unto them. Amen! Sister Boxer, would you read the last verse for us? Bless our God!

SISTER BOXER *(reads)* But it is happened unto them according to the true proverb, the dog is turned to his own vomit again and the sow that was washed to her wallowing in the mire.

(The church dims out. MARGARET *walks into the bedroom)*

MARGARET Luke?

LUKE Maggie. Where's my son?

MARGARET He's gone, Luke. I couldn't hold him. He's gone off into the world.

LUKE He's gone?

MARGARET He's gone.

LUKE He's gone into the world. He's into the world!

MARGARET Luke, you won't never see your son no more.

LUKE But I seen him one last time. He's in the world, he's living.

MARGARET He's gone. Away from you and away from me.

LUKE He's living. He's living. Is you got to see your God to know he's living.

MARGARET Everything—is dark this morning.

LUKE You all in white. Like you was the day we got married. You mighty pretty.

MARGARET It were a sunny day. Like today.

LUKE Yeah. They used to say, "Happy is the bride the sun shines on."

MARGARET Yes. That's what they used to say.

LUKE Was you happy that day, Maggie?

MARGARET Yes.

LUKE I loved you, Maggie.

MARGARET I know you did.

LUKE I love you still.

MARGARET I know you do. *(they embrace and singing is heard from the darkened church: "The Old Ship of Zion")* Maybe it's not possible to stop loving anybody you ever really loved. I never stopped loving you, Luke. I tried. But I never stopped loving you.

LUKE I'm glad you's come back to me, Maggie. When your arms was around me I was always safe and happy.

MARGARET Oh, Luke! If we could only start again! *(his mouthpiece falls from his hand to the floor)* Luke? *(he does not answer)* My baby. You done joined hands with the darkness. *(she rises, moving to the foot of the bed, her eyes on* LUKE. *She sees the mouthpiece, picks it up, looks at it)* My Lord! If I could only start again! If I could only start again!

(The light comes up in the church. All, except ODESSA, *are singing, "I'm Gonna Sit at the Welcome Table," clapping, etc.* SISTER MOORE *leads the service from the pulpit. Still holding* LUKE'S *mouthpiece clenched against her breast,* MARGARET *mounts into the church. As she enters, the music dies)*

MARGARET Praise the Lord!

SISTER MOORE You be careful, Sister Margaret. Be careful what you say. You been uncovered.

MARGARET I come up here to put you children on your knees! Don't you know the Lord is displeased with every one of you? Have every one of you forgot your salvation? Don't you know that it is *forbidden*—amen!—to talk against the Lord's anointed? Ain't a soul under the sound of my voice—bless God!—who has the right to sit in judgment on my life! Sister Margaret, this woman you see before you, has given her life to the Lord—and you say the Lord is displeased with me because ain't a one of you willing to endure what I've endured. Ain't a one of you willing to go—the road I've walked. This way of holiness ain't no joke. You can't love the Lord and flirt with the Devil. The Word of God is right and the Word of God is plain—and you can't love God unless you's willing to give up everything for Him. Everything. I want you folks to pray. I want every one of you to go down on your knees. We going to have a tarry service here tonight. Oh, yes! David, you play something on that piano—*(she stops, stares at the piano, where one of the saints from Philadelphia is sitting)* David—David—*(she looks down at her fist)* Oh, my God.

SISTER BOXER Look at her! *Look* at her! The gift of God has left her!

MARGARET Children. I'm just now finding out what it means to love the Lord. It ain't all in the singing and the shouting. It ain't all in the reading of the Bible. *(she unclenches her fist a little)* It ain't even—it ain't even—in running all over everybody trying to get to heaven. To love the Lord is to love all His children—all of them, everyone!—and suffer with them and rejoice with them and never count the cost! *(Silence. She turns and leaves the pulpit)*

SISTER MOORE Bless our God! He give us the victory! I'm gonna feast on milk and honey. *(she is joined by the entire congregation in this final song of jubilation)*

(MARGARET *comes down the stairs. She stands in the kitchen.* ODESSA *comes downstairs. Without a word to* MARGARET, *she goes through* LUKE'*s room, taking off her robe as she goes. The lights dim down in the church, dim up on* MARGARET, *as* MARGARET *starts toward the bedroom, and falls beside* LUKE'*s bed. The scrim comes down. One or two people pass in the street)*

(Curtain)

END OF ACT THREE

THE CONFESSION STONE
1960

Owen Dodson (1914–1983)

At first glance, *The Confession Stone* appears to be a poem, but a closer examination will reveal that it has many elements of compelling drama. The characters all speak from great passion, emerging as well-rounded, believable individuals. We get to know them, understand them, identify with them, empathize with them. They are not staid biblical characters with halos; they are real, down-to-earth people recognizable as family, friends, neighbors.

The Confession Stone needs no set and would no doubt be most effective if performed on an empty stage with lighting to capture the moods of the songs. The shadow of a cross might be projected from downstage across the stage floor so that a portion of it is cast into the upstage section of the cyclorama. Lighting would define the limits of the space used for each song. The only furniture would be a chair or stool, and a table. The costumes should be timeless and dateless, not biblical—simple peasant clothing in muted colors.

The plays opens with the lights picking up Mary seated cradling an imaginary child. She is a mother in mourning, confronting her pain through activity and memories. At first she is serene with her baby, Jesus, then abruptly she is thrust into the future with her son admonishing the money lenders in the temple. Her mood changes from song to song. She is filled with wonderment over Lazarus's resurrection, and in the fourth song, with despair stemming from her premonition of impending danger as she recalls her feelings the night of the Last Supper. Her emotional plea to God to save her son is perhaps the most dramatic of the poems in this section, while her following poem to Martha is the most interesting and challenging. Dodson approaches this poem on three levels: (1) we must continually bear in mind that Mary is in deep mourning and that her underlying pain is what she is struggling to suppress; (2) her conversation with Martha is an attempt to carry on as usual, thus keeping her mind off her sorrow; and (3) the complex task of knitting, which gives her something to do, is an additional attempt to conceal her hurt. But nothing works. She cannot concentrate, not knowing when Martha left or if she was even there; she is unable to complete the task of knitting—her pain is too deep. The scene concludes just as it began, with Mary seated in a pool of light, her arms cradling her imaginary son—a return to that secure state of innocence and happiness when a mother could hold and protect her child, when she truly possessed him.

After the lights dim, a table might be placed before the chair where Joseph is discovered composing his telegram to his sister-in-law. His grief is a lingering one that is with him as he ages, approaching his own death. Unlike Mary, who finds solace in charitable work and is able to go on with her life, Joseph is isolated, alone with nothing but his recurring melancholy. He has never reconciled with God because he has never fully understood God's relationship with Mary. He knows that he is dealing with a force far greater than he, yet in his momentary surge of anger he can assert that "He should be in when I called!"—suggesting a classical father-son conflict.

The lights now pick up Mary, the Magdalene, age eighty-six and still haunted by memories of Christ. Her entries in her journal characterize a tormented, senile old soul in physical pain and at the point of lunacy. Picture this scene expressionistically, that is, movement and color used to symbolically reflect what she is feeling inside. An eerie burnt-orange with deep shadows might fill the entire stage, decreasing in dimension with each of her songs until, at the conclusion, she is in a spot of light that fades to black.

The Judas scene could be confined to a relatively small area of light suggesting isolation or a tomb. Like the other characters, there is a madness in Judas allowing his personality to fluctuate from one extreme to another. He repents in one breath, then arrogantly demands that Jesus free him in the next. Again a variation of the classical father-son confrontation, but this time the disciple must slay the leader.

In the next scene we are introduced to Jesus, who, instead of being at peace, is wrought with despair over the evil and corruption engulfing the world. He believes that his death for the redemption of mankind was in vain. He impatiently begs to return to earth; begs for answers from God, and when they are not immediately forthcoming, his final plea is for God to act. His inner storm subsides and he implores God to "talk to me" as fathers talk to sons. These poems expressed the problems that Dodson had with his father and with God.

The Confession Stone places Dodson in the ranks of other playwrights who have used religion as the springboard for their plays: Hall Johnson (*Run, Little Childun*), Langston Hughes (*Tambourines to Glory* and *Black Nativity*), Willa Sanders Jones (*Black Passion Play*), Clifton Lamb (*Roughshod up the Mountain*), Vinnette Carroll and Micki Grant (*Your Arms Too Short to Box with God*), and Glenda Dickerson (*Jesus Christ—Lawd Today*) are but a few of the Black writers to examine this theme.

Owen Dodson was born in Brooklyn, New York, in 1914. After attending P.S. 64, Thomas Jefferson High School, and Bates College, he received a scholarship to Yale to begin work on his M.F.A. degree in playwriting. His first job following graduation in 1939 was at Spelman College in Atlanta, Georgia, teaching three classes and assisting with dramatics. In 1941, he was hired to teach drama at Hampton Institute in Virginia. After enlisting in the navy during World War II, he was assigned to write and produce weekly shows based on the lives of naval heroes. He accepted a position at Howard University in 1948, where he became head of the Drama Department. In 1970, Dodson resigned and returned to New York, where he taught and directed plays at the Harlem School of the

Arts, lectured and conducted workshops, and continued to write.

His first play, *Gargoyles in Florida,* was written at Yale. It was an adaptation of Langston Hughes's short story, *Red-Headed Baby.* His major play at Yale, *Divine Comedy,* premiered there on February 16, 1938, to favorable reviews. It was based on Father Divine, a popular Black minister during the Depression, who proclaimed himself God.

Dodson has published three volumes of poetry, *Powerful Long Ladder, The Confession Stone,* and *The Harlem Book of the Dead* (with Camille Billops and James Van Der Zee); two novels, *Boy at the Window* and *Come Home Early, Child,* and numerous poems, short stories, plays, and essays, which have appeared in periodicals and anthologies. He has written librettos for the operas *A Christmas Miracle* and *Till Victory Is Won,* directed more than 125 plays, acted, and designed stage scenery.

Three directors who worked with Owen Dodson were asked how they would stage *The Confession Stone.* Dodson's work allows the director to be as imaginative and creative as he likes, as the ideas of Robert West, Thomas Pawley (see *The Tumult and the Shouting*), and Whitney LeBlanc will attest.

Robert West recently retired from the University of the District of Columbia where he served as Assistant Dean of the College of Liberal and Fine Arts. He studied with Dodson at Howard University and has since worked professionally as a lighting and scenic designer and as a director. At present he is Executive Director/Treasurer of the National Conference on African American Theatre.

Whitney LeBlanc has designed scenery and directed plays for theatres across the country. He has also worked in television, directing episodes of shows such as *Benson, Marblehead Manor, Generations, The Young and the Restless,* and *The Robert Guillaume Show.* In addition to teaching at Antioch College and Howard University, he has written for the stage and for television.

On reading *The Confession Stone* I was immediately struck with the poetry's crying pain of loneliness. Desperate claims for and against religion are central to the work and must be conveyed in any production.

The stage should be quite open, with the largest cyclorama possible. I would use a unit setting with either ramps or stairways in the form of a "lazy" crucifix. The structure must be skeletal so that the audience can see underneath the setting.

Music, live music, is a must! A group of very skilled African percussionists, three to four, and a flutist would be a great ensemble. There are several songs that would be enhanced by dancers, but this is not essential. The music must constantly show the struggle between that of a High Mass, Gospel, and African tribal ritual. The actors should be of good voice, but their singing will be a reactionary and "Amen Corner"–like response. Considerable time has to be spent on vocal coaching to ensure the clarity of the text.

Casting must be done very selectively, choosing at minimum three women and three men. One woman and man must be young of spirit and in their twenties. The second man and woman must be in the fifty age bracket, and the third pair must be capable of representing the seventy-to-eighty age bracket. Color of skin is not important.

There should be very few props used and the action should be continuous. Projections will be used during the work dealing with contemporary issues to illustrate the struggles of the characters. It would be particularly effective during the Judas songs to have slides and video footage showing the wrongs of the world.

The lighting has to be precise and exquisite. Some events require high contrast directional side lighting, while others require tight head spots. All of this has to work with the projections, music, and movements of the actors.

This represents a beginning of my thought processes on developing a "point of view" or director's theme for *The Confession Stone.* My next task would be to develop thorough characterizations for each character. One way to do this would be to share songs among two or more performers in an attempt to deal with the duality or multicharacteristics of humankind. There is a particular beauty in the ending song that would lend itself to this technique.

—*Robert West*

The Confession Stone Song Cycles lend themselves to the staging techniques of Readers and Chamber Theatre and the choral speaking methods espoused by Mona Swann and Marjory Gullan in the 1930s. The cycles are in fact a verse drama not unlike the Book of Job in the Old Testament, describing the agonies and sufferings of persons intimately involved in the Passion of Christ. It concludes with God's reassurance to Jesus that despite humankind's continuing profligacy following the Crucifixion, He will not desert him or mankind.

Death and dying constitute the central theme as they relate to the sorrowing and sorrowful Mother of God, the aging Joseph, they dying Magdalene, the tormented Iscariot, and a depressed Christ. Their laments are presented in seven episodes, two of which (five and six) viewed dramatically constitute a single unit. An undefined space, with levels and ramps and specific areas highlighted with pools of light should constitute the *mise-en-scène,* the whole to be surrounded by a sky cyclorama. Characters should be robed in stylized biblical dress, with long flowing lines and colors symbolic of their historic roles. Each scene should be underscored by music enhancing the prevailing mood. A single female dancer in "The Confession Stone" and "Journals of the Magdalene," and a male dancer in "Your Servant: Judas" during "Voice-Over" narration would illuminate the dramatic action.

—*Thomas Pawley*

Metaphor: The soul-image of truth is the mother of our beliefs.

The last rays of sunlight stream down from the broken stained-glass rose window above the altar of an abandoned Catholic Church, which now resembles a junk heap. Trash and the remains of former church activity is everywhere. The pews have been stacked in pyramids right and left of the center area. A cold wind is blowing outside and evidence of the breeze can be felt and seen inside. The atmosphere of the interior is covered with a fine powdery dust, which the fading light cuts through like shafts of illumination. All creates a world of former promise and salvation that is now forlorn, desolate, and abandoned. It is the place of the forgotten—the cast aside—place that causes one to ask, "Where is God now?"

The fading sunlight is replaced by rays of light that precede a frail, cold figure who enters from a broken door upstage right of the altar. The figure is an aged woman of dignity wearing a shawl that covers her body like a shroud. The Woman moves down center and looks around at the crumbling edifice. She lights one of the large candles standing to one side of the altar. For several moments The Woman looks up at the crucifix that has fallen askew. Christ's left arm is broken and it would seem that the body would fall from the wooden cross if not held by the nail in the right palm. The Woman lowers the shawl to her shoulders, shakes her head, turns and begins to search the debris. She finds a broken baptismal fount, drags it left of center and then looks around for material to build a fire. She finds the remains of a Christmas crib and uses the straw and wood from the manger to feed her fire. She also finds a statue of the baby Jesus and lays it gently down near her activities. When the fire is ablaze, she takes a sausage out of her coat pocket along with a silver plate and silverware. She prepares her feast and in the process, she stumbles over the baby Jesus, picks it up, and with tears in her voice and eyes, begins,

Song Cycle I: The Woman wanders the space, talking to the baby gently held in her arms, bathed in rays of light that cut through the dusty interior. By the time she gets to

Song Cycle IV: her voice has awakened the form asleep on the pews. We are able to perceive the shadowy figure of a man stirring out of a blanket of rags. He sits up and listens. He moves several feet away and shakes another blanket of rags. Another homeless man emerges. The First Man points to his head and twirls his finger in a "she's crazy" motion. The Second Man furtively crosses the church to pews on the other side and rouses yet another blanket of rags. He puts his finger to his lips for silence and gives the "crazy" gesture. The Three Men, wrapped in strips of tattered bands of dirty cloth, observe the action of The Woman.

Song Cycle VI: The Woman is so involved in the illusion of her new-found world that she is unaware of The Men who have now quietly moved on hands and knees to form a circle around the fire. The First Man finds, and begins roasting, the abandoned sausage. All three focus their full attention on the antics and words of The Woman, as they hungrily devour the meal. By the time The Woman gets to

Song Cycle VII: she is standing on the altar. At the beginning of

Song Cycle VIII: The Three Men slowly approach. The Woman is totally unaware of their presence. At the end of the song, she lays the baby gently down in the center of the altar. She then becomes aware of The Men, who are staring at her from the perimeter of the altar. The Men reach in attempting to grab her by the ankles. She skillfully avoids their grasps with an agility that belies her advanced age. She proceeds to kick and throw the various items on the altar, which they duck and dodge. The Second Man catches a box as it sails in his direction. He looks inside and beckons the attention of the other two. Their curiosity is now focused on a bundle of letters tied with a ribbon. Unnoticed by The Men, The Woman quickly climbs down from the altar and hides among the pews. The Third Man opens one of the letters and begins to read. Each in turn reads

Mary Passed This Morning, Songs I thru X: When they are finished, there is silence. The Woman appears clothed in flowing white gossamer with a grotesque hump on her back. She sings

Journals of the Magdalene, Songs I thru VII: The Three Men remain as statues—immobile. They are seen in silhouette against a background of light. The Woman addresses each of the statues in turn and then all. They show no life or response. By the time Song VII is finished, The Woman is sitting next to the fire. A grotesque light shines up from below, which brings the Third Man to life. He begins,

Your Servant: Judas, Song I: At the end, he vanishes in hell fire and smoke. A grotesque light shines up from below, which brings the Second Man to life. He begins,

Your Servant: Judas, Song II: At the end, he vanishes in hell fire and smoke. A grotesque light shines up from below, which brings the First Man to life. He begins,

Your Servant: Judas, Song III: At the end, he vanishes in hell fire and smoke.

Your Servant: Judas, Song IV: The figures of the First, Second, and Third Man appear through the fire and smoke which engulf them as the song ends. A Voice, seeming to emanate from the Crucifix, comes out of the air. The Voice begins,

Father, I Know You're Lonely, Songs I thru IV: The Woman takes a sausage from the folds of her garment and cooks it over the fire. She consumes her meal from the silver service during the songs. A deeper and more dominant Voice comes out of the air. The Voice begins,

Dear, My Son: Near the end, The Woman makes her way to the altar. By the time the song is finished, The Woman has picked up the baby Jesus and is cradling it in her arms. She leaves the altar and makes her way out of the edifice while singing,

Oh My Boy Jesus: The candle and the fire are the only remaining light.

—*Whitney J. LeBlanc*

The Confession Stone

A Song Cycle

The Confession Stone
Sung by Mary about Jesus

I
Oh my boy: Jesus,
my first and only son,
rock on my breast,
my first and only one.
My first and only son.
Oh my Jesus:
my first and only one:
born of God and born near His sun:
oh my boy Jesus rest—
Shusshh, you need the rest.

II
Don't pay attention
to the old men in the Temple:
they have given up.
Tell them what you told me:
cast the sinners out.
Clean the house of God.
Load the rich with grief,
prepare the poor with hope . . .
. . . and Jesus,
don't stop to play
with Judas and his friends
along the way.

III
Jesus, did you know
that Lazarus is back?
Jesus, are you listening:
Lazarus has come back.
His grave is still open
and Martha tell she heard
three angels singing
with three birds:
their feathers brushed together.
Jesus, are you hearing:
Lazarus has returned
to Bethany.
Jesus, won't you answer:
Lazarus has come back
and he's calling for you.
He says that death was gentle
and woke him up early.
Jesus, are you praying:
Lazarus has returned.

IV
There's a supper in Jerusalem tonight
and I wish that I was there,
I'd journey anywhere
to be with Jesus:
to stroke his hair,
remind him, oh my baby dear,
I'd journey anywhere
to be with Jesus tonight.
There's that supper in Jerusalem
tonight
and I could be right there.
But I don't dare
to venture to Jerusalem tonight,
and I wish I was there.
Oh my boy take care
at that supper in Jerusalem tonight.

V
Cold and icy in my bed:
laid on the ground of Jerusalem:
every flower is withered,
the birds have left their song,
the sun wears a twisted eye.
I'm alone with your dreams of
redemption
my Lord . . . save him, save our son.
I'm his mother: save him:
Let me rock him again in my trembling
arms.
Save him. I'll receive the silver from
Judas.
Help him. Your word is all my word.
I'll receive the silver from Judas' hand
and spend it on . . . nothing . . .
Save him . . . Jehovah
Help him . . . my God
Bless him . . . my Lord
Redeem him . . . my Husband.
Oh save him, save him, save him,
save him, save our boy!

VI

Bring me those needles, Martha,
I believe I'll knit Jesus a scarf.
Go on snapping those butterbeans . . .
What time is it?
Let me see now: knit one . . .
You say it's twelve o'clock?
Snap enough for Joseph and Lazarus:
They'll be home before you're through.
Martha, what time is it? Purl two . . .
Purl one,
Knit one,
Purl two . . .
If I had the star of Bethlehem . . .
I'd knit three . . .
. . . and light his sky . . .
Where was I, Martha?
Oh yes: knit one,
Purl seven . . .
What time is it, Martha?
Knit three . . . purl ten . . .
It can't be near three o'clock.
Where was I? Knit . . . purl twelve . . .
Purl nothing . . .
Martha, don't leave me alone.
Where are you, Martha?
Martha, where are you, Martha?
Martha!

VII

Mary,

When I got home, chile
I was so hot. It was just
after three P.M.

I called you from Sister
Eliza's next door.
I called you, you seemed
so nervous. The phone
kept ringing: Busy, busy,
busy. So I hung up, after
I gave the operator a
piece of my mind. When
she sassed me I told her
to shut her mouth and went about
scraping the fish
scales clean.

Martha

P.S. I mean scraping the scales from
off the fish.

VIII

Everything is black:
air, water, sun, moon,
all light . . . dirt is black.
Heaven is in mourning for our son.
The earth is dead:
it will light again
almighty God.
Now I understand
what light is:
It is our Son.
It is Jesus, no longer trembling
in my arms: It is THE CHRIST.
(Oh my boy Jesus,
my first and only one.)
Now on my knees, with Joseph at my
side.
I ask thee: send the resurrection now.
Give the air and the water and the sun
and the moon and the dirt Thy light
again.
Send the presence, almighty God,
send it even to evil men.

I see Jesus in the clouds,
oh oh oh oh ohoh oh oh ohooo,
free Him from death to life:
we must be free to sing:
loose the birds for their songs,
light Martha, whose brother came back
from death, light Mary Magdalene,
light Gethsemane's gardens:
light those walkways with lillies,
and heal the seven wounds of Christ.
Let me rise up into your starry sky
and love our Son.
AND PRAISE THEE
AND PRAISE THEE.

. . . Ah comfort me in Paradise.

IX

Mary dear,

They told me about Jesus
at the market today. I couldn't make
it to Jerusalem yesterday because
my corns were hard as nails. (Chile,
I'm sorry I said that.) When they
take him from off the cross I'll be
there if I can make it. Supreme sorrow.

Martha

X
I am sending you the seized
Properties of your son.
My soldiers rounded up the thieves
who gambled for them after he died.

One day walking in my garden
I touched and smelled a red rose.
My nose and hands were
Full of blood. Before I could wash
A man approached me saying he was
John.
He spat at my feet. Instead of calling
my bodyguard
I demanded he explain himself.
He stared at me as if I were a leper.
Then said he was a follower of Jesus,
That I had not saved the Master.
I asked him to come once a week
And speak of the lessons the Master
taught.
He did not return.
I feel haunted now.

It is hard for me to sleep.
I feel some danger in the garden
And would not go there.
Once I approached my pool,
I saw your son walking the water.
I see him everywhere.
He has forgiven me.
I feel dead with shame.
Send me some grace
So I can rest.
Your taxes will be paid as long as you
live.
My hair turned all white last night.

Pontius Pilate, Governor.

XI
Oh my boy: Jesus,
my first and only son,
rock on my breast,
my first and only one.
My first and only son.
Oh my Jesus:
my first and only one:
born of God and born near His sun:
bright boy: my only one:
oh my Jesus,
rest on my breast,
my first and only son:
Oh my boy Jesus: rest—
Shushhh, you need the rest.

. . . .

Mary Passed This Morning:
Letters from Joseph to Martha,
From Martha to Joseph.

I
Martha
Mary passed this morning
funeral this evening stop
Near six o'clock
tell the others stop
Raising bus fare for you
stop

signed Joseph

II
Dear Martha,

I'm sorry you missed the bus
for the funeral and what not.
I had raised the fare.

Mary didn't look dead
as we took her out to go . . .
Peter began to sing:
'Leaving for home,
leaving for home,
Mary's going home . . .'
I felt like crying,
but I wept. Oh Martha.
Peter kept singing:
'Leaving for home,
leaving for home.
Mary's going home,
Mary's almost there . . .'

It was dark twilight
and the sun came out
to go back in again
and hide us all.
'Leaving for home . . .'

Then John joined Peter:
'Going to home,
Mary's almost there,'
Oh Martha

signed Joseph

III

Dear Martha,

We laid her flat in the earth
where lillies of the valley
and poppies grew with grass;

then there was the laying on
of hands; Peter's touched Mary's
face, then the disciples kissed
his hand in equal turn like prayer;
then in equal turn they bowed to me.
Mary seemed to smile.
A hallelujah crossed the air.
Some bird began to cry.
I picked some poppies and some lillies:
It was all I could do,
to sprinkle over her.
The bird wept on like a child.
We left her lying there.
Oh oh Martha.

signed Joseph

IV
Joseph

Supreme sorrow to you about
Mary. They surely sent her
off in style. Now Joseph
hitch your horse sense
to a plow and get over her
absence.
If you had started the
storefront church we planned
it might have been a cathedral by now.

Martha

V
Dear Martha,

Mary just finished
baking sesame biscuits
for the poor
before she passed.
Can't find my way clear
to take them out of the oven,
they smell so fresh and good.
Ah Martha . . .

signed Joseph

VI
Dear Martha,

After Mary passed
I carried out her orders:
I dialed her friend
(that I never saw):
his secretary said
he was not in . . .
out somewhere looking at
Sunday for a while.
I thought he should be present
to view the remains and make
remarks. When I called again
she said he was still out there
Looking at lillies and the birds.
He should have been in when I called!

signed Joseph

VII
Dear Martha,

I don't know Lazarus' address
so I am sending these to you.
Mary said Jesus wanted him
to have these garments:
here they are. Tell him
to keep warm and what not.

signed Joseph

VIII
Dear Martha,

You asked how it happened—
from the beginning. Well, when Mary
was sixteen, I noticed her.
Then I had to move away
to carve some Roman crosses
for a time. When I came back
some years ahead, I courted her;
we were married before Jesus came.

signed Joseph

IX
Dear Martha,

I thought Judas had killed himself.
I strolled in the cool gardens
last night to get cool,
to take a stroll.
The darkness was thick
as a wailing wall:
Then the moon appeared:
sitting on the wall,
under a tree
smelling a flower,
I saw a man the spit
and image of Judas.
He began to cry at me,
then ran up the hill.
I thought Judas had killed himself!
Burn this letter.

signed Joseph

X
Dear Martha,

I'm glad you have the copy of
the Beatitudes which Jesus wrote
in his own hand. I'm happy Paul
was in your neighborhood.
He tells me you have
rheumatism and arthritis
at the same time . . . (smile)
Walk in the sun
to bake them out.
The weather here is chancey.

signed Joseph

XI
Dear Martha,

I don't write so much now these days:
my hands are getting shaky.
I must be getting old.
I sat at her grave tonight
just to linger there with her.
I wanted to talk with her:
about our life together
and the son. She answered me
in tongues when I whispered
to the grave. I only spoke
the words I knew: 'Mene, mene
teckel upharsin.'
When I got them out
she ceased to speak.
What do these words mean?
Oh Martha, answer me. You're wise.
What do these words mean?
What do these words mean?
What did I say?

I'm weary now, I'm tired out.
So I sign my friend to thee,
so I sign my life to her,
so I sign my love to her.
I must be getting old.
Goodnight, goodnight.

signed Joseph

XII
Joseph,

Do be careful. It did take me a time to
read your last letter. Life has been
battering at you from Egypt to the
cross. I wish I could take care of you.
But Joseph, I can barely move—the
arthritis, rheumatism and what not.
Wish I could walk through the sand
and bush to comfort you. Please wear
a bag of assofetti around your neck.
It might help.

(Joseph, remember there by the willow
tree.)
If you feel the trip you indicate—
please see all the sights so you can
show me around. Jerusalem is a desert.
Give my best to Jesus, Mary and
Lazarus if you get there.

(Joseph, remember there by the willow
tree.)

I said that before. Forgive my forgetting mind.

Martha

. . . .

Journals of the Magdalene
The Last Entries

I
I'm eighty-six years old:
short of breath,
short of time.
I have no teeth to bite my enemies.
It is time to munch
up time, memories, enemies,
letters, crosses: repair my soul,
by drinking his water I washed
His feet in. Ahahaaaahhhaah!
Give me dandelions,
fresh potatoes, grapes
to make my wine for drink,
before my hair falls out.

Oh God, mend the scratches
in my mind:
I want Jesus to know me
as I was.
Oh god, heal my humpback,
clear my eyes of rheum,
grow my hair to red—
reverse me.

I want Jesus to know me
as I was.

Vanity is my grace: I wish to enter
Heaven whole!
If Jesus is not there
I'll fall away.
Aaahaaahaaaaaah.

Old lady cease.
Old, ugly lady, cease.
If I fall, will he follow?
If I fall, will he raise me up?
If mirrors are in Heaven,
I'll crack quicksilver
and wound myself,
Will he heal that wound?
aaaaaaaaaaaaaaaaaaaAAAAAhhh!
Old lady cease.

II
I've been rendered by light.
I'm exhausted with memories.
Of His sun and moon,
lakes of Galilee.
I'm an old moth:
all my bright colors
are black and gray.
The cocoon of Jerusalem
dried when He was thirty-three:
I was forty-two.
The sexton in the Temple
swept it up.
I'm a cobweb now
in the old places where the world
changed faces:
a cross for
the frog look
of Pilate, and the Hill:
When he washed his hands
That day
He washed the tongues
of sin and let
Christ happen
to the world.

If I put out this
candle tonight, tomorrow
will happen to me:
the sorrow in my fingernails
(when your fingernails crack
you're going mad!)
this is pronounced by seers!
Aaaaaaaaaahhhaaaaaaaaaahhh!

III
Journal, remember
I am The Magdalene.
I'll crawl the air
to Heaven to kiss
His feet again.
Stigmata is my
way of mind.
I'll crucify myself
to be with him. Amen.

IV
My bedclothes
are real noisy.
John and Paul
are stirring up.
Jesus help me.
They are writing letters
to the world:
I wish to sleep.
I've got work to do:
curl my hair and die:
I crucified myself
you know.
Martha was nowhere
to be seen:
I did it by myself,
in agony.

V
I can say this about Martha:
her food is not well cooked:
if you do not cook in copper
the flavor will not hold.
This is especially true
of manna, milk and honey.
Aaaaaaaaaaaahhhaaaha. Old lady,
cease. Martha can't hammer straight,
but I can.

VI
Only two Marys and Martha
were there when
He passed away.
He wept from
three o'clock to the tomb.
He witnessed a thief die:
one eye fell out
to look at God.
It cried out to Him:
I witnessed the Calvary
sunset. It was a fire
in the clouds like war:
it burnt up stars.

VII
I've got his chalice
in my room. I've drunk wine
from it forty-four years.
Now I make my will:
to John, who is Divine:
lessons in love.
To Paul, who writes letters:

a broken quill.
To Peter, who is ambitious:
an edifice.
To Luke, who is meek:
tears and handkerchiefs.
To Matthew, who grazes land:
a cup of soil.
To Thomas, who doubted Him:
a glass of shame.
To Judas, who is dead,
I leave my Hell.

Please, please, Jesus, please:
I have ceased
I sign in blood
Mary, The Magdalene.

. . . .

Your Servant: Judas
Sung by Judas

I

Did Christ ever tell a joke?
Bless me, how should I know.
Here in dirt
I, I saw Lazarus raised.
Raised like Spring
To be praised
From a tomb.
Who wrought that?

Bow down to scabcloths
The knowledge of dirt's infinities,
Bow down and weep to dirt.

Where shall we worship
But at the feet.
Bless us in this unregular hour.

Jokes in the dirt house?

Help me to laugh, Christ,
Help me to your better land.
I've used the silver
In confusion
I've got lonely bones;
Let me recognize Thy apex mirth,
Thy miracle purpose,
Since everything is burdens
Helping Simon up your hill.

II

Dear Jesus, I killed myself last night.
I drank the hemlock like Golgotha wine.
I am not fit for Heaven or for Hell.
Before I left I cried into The Magdalene
because she loved you . . . too, I wept,
I slept, I died.
Now nothing will have me but worms.
Misery, misery, misery . . . misery
dead.
My heart is all mouldy, broken bread.
My cross is made of worms, my Jesus.
Dear Jesus, beloved brother, I am dead.
Judas, the betrayer, from Iscariot,
is ashamed.

III

Dear Jesus, I want to tell you how
the thieves who hung beside you on the
hill
climbed down and dug my grave.
They tore their arms and feet
from out the nails to bury me;
they dripped with the blood into the
grave.
Then they heaped olive leaves
into my final home.
Then your lonely Judas was alone.
I am scorching in this cold,
I am plunged into eternity.
When those worms get to my bones . . .
I do not know . . . I do not know,
if I can bear the biting of their teeth.
Judas, your friend, in agony, alone.

IV

Salvation Jesus . . . if Jesus is your
name!
Get me out of here. I suffocate.
I think I cannot die and I am dead.
I have fits.
Worms are at my armpits.
Now they eat my pubic hair.
They ate all other hair:
I am already bald.
Now my flesh
now my flesh
(smile, haha).
Don't burn my letters, Jesus
(smile, haha).
Call your Father on the telephone:
you tell Him I'm alone.
Help me, help me, free me, get me out!
He begged me to commit you to the
cross:
use your mercy, plead for me:
we can row together
on the sea of Galilee

when I am free:
plead for me.
I made your creed
an immortality.
Call Your Father to release these
worms,
free my body plus my eaten soul.
Get me out of here!
This is no blackmail to the Godhead
. . . (smile, haha)
but get me out of here—Judas
Jesus, I am Judas, Jesus—Judas

Father, I Know You're Lonely
Sung by Jesus

I
Dear Father:
In the world today
our name is constant mockery,
Father I refuse my name:
point me on the way
to go again and change
the image carved by men.
Point me the way
to change the daggers
to wonder and surprise:
map me down to earth:
there are trapdoors,
there are nooses,
in hallways
broken steps seem whole.
Calvary was a long way up,
how do I go down?
I dreamed: hoot owls
haunted me down the steps:
they've sold every nail in my cross.
I dreamed I heard
your nightingales
sing flat and out of tune.
I dreamed: night is not dark,
all flowers have turned black,
even my lillies.
I dreamed morning was tired,
noon was midnight.
I dreamed: angels are not safe.
I dreamed: Lucifer whispers
from Hell.
I dreamed: constellations
are not whole.
Release me from my name,
let me return.
It is time to make a time again.
I sign me,

Jesus

II
Dear Father:

Leaning out my window
I can vaguely see
the restless lakes of Galilee,
the gardens of Gethsemane:
you, Father, fashioned these for me.

Give me back that lost country.
Heaven is so high:
I cannot closely see
neglected lakes of Galilee,
gardens of Gethsemane.

My Mother rented me a star:
I want to see that rented star
shine in lakes of Galilee,
shine in walks of Gethsemane.

Yes, Father, you gave a world to me—
now I ask again to see
the bright world that you gave to me.
This is all I ask of thee:
the restless lakes of Galilee,
the gardens of Gethsemane—
the bright world that you gave to me.
I sign me in sincerity,

Jesus

III
Father,

I am no longer disappointed.
Somehow I have found peace
in denial.
I asked for the presence of John, The
Divine:
I was denied.
I asked for the presence of Mary, The
Magdalene:
I was denied.
I asked for the presence of Mary, My
Mother:
I was denied.
I asked for peace
among all men:
not to be Prince of Peace—
I was denied.

There have been wars:
my credos were denied,

the Saints distorted me.
Hell is in rebellion
with all of us. It acts
through batallions of sin.
Heaven is an Indian Summer
day still. Father,
resurrection will break
to annihilation unless you act:
the faith we stand on
will splinter to disaster
and little children will
catch odema, erosyphillis and death
unless You act.

In these fat centuries
everything has dwindled
to the widow's mite
of mercy. If you have
power, act. I drove the
evil from the Temple on
my own years ago. Father, act!
I have only a symbol cross
left me now:
men have torn my name to pieces:
they eat silver instead of Holy Bread:
they drink waters of Gomorrah
instead of Holy Wine.
If I fast and pray much longer, I will
surely die.

I sign me, Your Son, Jesus

IV
Father, I know you're lonely:
talk to me, talk to me.
We need not speak of Calvary
of the lakes of Galilee:
as my Father, talk to me.
Notify my soul where
You will be,
send some message:
answer me.

I sign me, your son,

Jesus

. . . .

Dear, My Son
Sung by God

Dear my Son,
my One, my constant One:
only men
can free us
from prisons
of Heaven and
give us back
our names again—
we left our souls
on earth for men.
We cannot have them back again.
Heaven is no shame
because they stomp our name.

The Kingdom is in men:
I rented it to them.
The winds still blow
torrents in the sea
for mankind to remember me:
the stars still shine,
for they are mine.
I pitched the tent of Heaven
so cunningly
no child on earth can live
without the sight of me.
I am with them constantly.
They might sin and they might shame
but they know my mighty name.
The stars are the tears I weep,
the sun is my sleep.
Your Father has not deserted Thee
to gardens of Gethsemane.
The stars are the tears we weep,
the sun is Our Mercy,
the moon is Our slumber.
Sleep Jesus, sleep.
Sleep, Jesus, sleep.
Your Father first, then God!

Oh My Boy Jesus
Sung by Mary

Oh my boy: Jesus,
my first and only son,
rock on my breast
my first and only one.
My first and only son.
Oh my Jesus:
my first and only one:
born of God and born near His sun:
bright boy: my only one:
oh my Jesus
rest on my breast
my first and only son:
oh my boy Jesus: rest—
Shusshhh, you need the rest.

MODERN WOMEN WRITING ON WOMEN

Adrienne Kennedy • Alice Childress • Ntozake Shange • Robbie McCauley

Although women had been writing and directing since the nineteenth century (Pauline Hopkins, the Hyers sisters), the professional Black theatre, like white theatre, has suffered from male domination in playwriting and directing except on educational or amateur stages, which women dominated in the 1920s. Beginning in the forties and fifties, Shirley Graham (*I Gotta Home,* and *It's Morning*) along with Alice Childress (*Trouble in Mind* and *Wine in the Wilderness*) established themselves as professional craftswomen; yet no play by a Black woman was produced on or off Broadway until *Gold Through the Trees* by Alice Childress won an Obie as the Best Off Broadway play in 1952. Seven years later, Lorraine Hansberry's *A Raisin in the Sun* became the first play to break the color barrier on Broadway.

Males continued to dominate the militant sixties and seventies, but a handful of women demanded attention. Some women turned to directing—Shauneille Perry, Glenda Dickerson, Tisch Jones—while others founded their own theatre groups—Rosetta LeNoire's AMAS; Vinnette Carroll's Urban Art Corp; Hazel Bryant's Richard Allen Center; Barbara Ann Teer's National Black Theatre; Val Grey Ward's Kuumba Workshop Theatre; Gertrude Jeanette's Hadley Players; and Marjorie Moon's Billie Holiday Theatre.

At the same time, a few women playwrights won their place on the stage. Adrienne Kennedy, with *Funnyhouse of a Negro* (1962), won an Obie and established herself as one of the very few poets in the theatre. Sonia Sanchez came to attention with two militant one acts: *The Bronx Is Next* (1968) and *Sister Son/ji* (1969). J.E. Franklin's *Black Girl* (1969) toured eighty-five universities and colleges. Micki Grant's musical revue *Don't Bother Me I Can't Cope* (1970) won two Drama Desk Awards. Ntozake Shange's *For Colored Girls Who Commit Sui-*

cide\When the Rainbow Is Enuf (1976) created a gender storm. Aishah Rahman's *The Mojo and the Sayso* (1989) won the Doris Abramson Award.

Addressing race, gender, and class through deconstruction of incident, the playwrights of the 1990s reflected diverse styles. Suzan-Lori Parks seized upon the assassination of Lincoln for *The American Play* (1993), using a musical structure of theme and variation in lieu of plot development. In *Fires in the Mirror* (1992), Anna Deveare Smith, after the Crown Heights riots in Brooklyn, impersonated multiple characters based on her own interviews with Blacks and Jews. Robbie McCauley's *Sally's Rape* (1992) uses "personal" document to address violation of person and soul.

The four plays in this section reflect radically different styles—the realism of *Wine in the Wilderness*, the surrealism of *Funnyhouse of a Negro,* the choreopoem of *For Colored Girls . . .* , and the personal duolog of *Sally's Rape*—yet all four plays address problems of identity and self-respect, important concerns for African American women.

FUNNYHOUSE OF A NEGRO
1962

Adrienne Kennedy (1931-)

No script in this volume is as dense with images as *Funnyhouse of a Negro*. Without an actual theatrical production, the play may seem to be a nightmare, and in a sense, it is. Objects and characters may have many meanings, sometimes simultaneously. But like a dream, there is a suggested literal story behind the kaleidoscopic visions, and that story is a surrealistic version of the tragic mulatto; Kennedy has reversed the racial images of Langston Hughes's play *Mulatto*.

This time the mulatto is a woman. Her mother is light, her father black and African; her mother had status, her father, none. Her loyalty to her European heritage, represented by Queen Victoria and the Duchess of Hapsburg, forces her to hate and deny her African heritage, forces her to murder her father, much as the Europeans murdered Patrice Lumumba because he threatened European dominance. All of these conflicts rage inside Sarah's mind, which is the funnyhouse, the madhouse. The two characters outside Sarah's head—Raymond, her Jewish lover, and her landlady—contribute to her anguish through mockery. For the reader who is fascinated by the beauty, the tenderness, the horror, reading and rereading the play (in the absence of a production) will be a pleasurable frustration.

Born in Pittsburgh in 1931, Kennedy's father was a social worker, her mother a school teacher. When she was four, the family moved to Cleveland, where her father became secretary to the colored YMCA. She attended unsegregated, predominately Jewish schools. Although she enjoyed working on the school paper, her journalism teacher discouraged her from pursuing a career in news writing. Upon graduation, she enrolled at Ohio State University, lived in a segregated dormitory, and suffered racial ridicule on campus. As a major in psychiatric social work, she never studied theatre. Two weeks after graduation, she married.

At age twenty-two, while pregnant with her first child, she wrote her first play based on Elmer Rice's *Street Scene*. She wrote *Pale Flowers* (1955) in imitation of Tennessee Williams's *Glass Menagerie*, an influence that can still be detected in her plays. She followed her husband to Africa and then to Rome where, in 1961, she began *Funnyhouse.* When they returned to New York (her husband was teaching at Hunter College), she joined Edward Albee's workshop at the Circle in the Square Theatre, where her play received a workshop production. In January, Edward Albee produced *Funnyhouse* Off Broadway, with Billie Allen as Sarah, the young girl. The play shared an Obie Award (1964) with *Dutchman* by LeRoi Jones, as the best Off Broadway play.

Kennedy reported in an interview that the cast, director, and Albee liked the play very much, but the audiences, particularly the Black audiences, did not like it, and a controversy broke out in the Black press.[1] Some considered *Funnyhouse* a laundering of "dirty linen" because the racism of lighter Blacks against darker African Americans should not be aired in public. In 1964, to express her emerging African awareness, Kennedy stopped straightening her hair and wore an Afro cut, something very few Black women were doing and something she was criticized for. In *Funnyhouse,* Sarah loses her hair (symbolically her European identity), but she is unable to identify herself as an African; hence, in the madhouse of racism, she has neither straight nor kinky hair—she is bald.

Many helpful clues to interpret her symbolism can be found by studying Ms. Kennedy's other plays. Her three best-known one-act plays—*Funnyhouse of a Negro, The Rat's Mass,* and *The Owl Answers*—all center around a young girl who is torn between the paradoxes of Spirit and Flesh, Black and White, Past and Present. They should be read as an Adrienne Kennedy trilogy, the story of a poet writing one long, surreal fantasy about herself.

Beginning September 24, 1995, the New York Public Theater presented a series of seven Kennedy plays. *Funnyhouse of a Negro,* which opened the program, received elaborate praise from *New York Times* critic Ben Brantley—"Ms. Kennedy has carefully forged an emotional bridge that one cannot avoid crossing, regardless of race, age or sex. She is unmistakably the real thing: a strong utterly individual voice in American theater."

1. Adrienne Kennedy interviewed by James V. Hatch, January 25, 1978.

Funnyhouse of a Negro

CHARACTERS

NEGRO SARAH
DUCHESS OF HAPSBURG, One of herselves
QUEEN VICTORIA REGINA, One of herselves
JESUS, One of herselves
PATRICE LUMUMBA, One of herselves
SARAH'S LANDLADY, Funnyhouse Lady
RAYMOND, Funnyhouse Man
THE MOTHER

AUTHOR'S NOTE

Funnyhouse of a Negro is perhaps clearest and most explicit when the play is placed in the girl Sarah's room. The center of the stage works well as her room, allowing the rest of the stage as the place for herselves. Her room should have a bed, a writing table, and a mirror. Near her bed is the statue of Queen Victoria; other objects might be her photographs and her books. When she is placed in her room with her belongings, then the director is free to let the rest of the play happen around her.

BEGINNING: *Before the closed curtain, a woman dressed in a white nightgown walks across the stage carrying before her a bald head. She moves as one in a trance and is mumbling something inaudible to herself. Her hair is wild, straight, and black and falls to her waist. As she moves, she gives the effect of one in a dream. She crosses the stage from right to left. Before she has barely vanished, the curtain opens. It is a white satin curtain of a cheap material and a ghastly white, a material that brings to mind the interior of a cheap casket; parts of it are frayed and look as if it has been gnawed by rats.*

SCENE TWO WOMEN *are sitting in what appears to be a Queen's chamber. It is set in the middle of the stage in a strong white light, while the rest of the stage is in unnatural blackness. The quality of the white light is unreal and ugly. The Queen's chamber consists of a dark monumental bed resembling an ebony tomb, a low, dark chandelier with candles, and wine-colored walls. Flying about are great black ravens.* QUEEN VICTORIA *is standing before her bed holding a small mirror in her hand. On the white pillow of her bed is a dark, indistinguishable object. The* DUCHESS OF HAPSBURG *is standing at the foot of the bed. Her back is to us as is the* QUEEN'S. *Throughout the entire scene, they do not move. Both women are dressed in royal gowns of white, a white similar to the white of the curtain, the material cheap satin. Their headpieces are white and of a net that falls over their faces. From beneath both their headpieces springs a headful of wild kinky hair. Although in this scene we do not see their faces, I will describe them now. They look exactly alike and will wear masks or be made up to appear a whitish yellow. It is an alabaster face, the skin drawn tightly over the high cheekbones, great dark eyes that seem gouged out of the head, a high forehead, a full red mouth, and a head of frizzy hair. If the characters do not wear a mask, then the face must be highly powdered and possess a hard expressionless quality and a stillness as in the face of death. We hear knocking.*

VICTORIA *(listening to the knocking)* It is my father. He is arriving again for the night. *(The* DUCHESS *makes no reply)*. He comes through the jungle to find me. He never tires of his journey.

DUCHESS How dare he enter the castle, he who is the darkest of them all, the darkest one? My mother looked like a white woman, hair as straight as any white woman's. And at least I am yellow, but he is black, the blackest one of them all. I hoped he was dead. Yet he still comes through the jungle to find me.

(The knocking is louder)

VICTORIA He never tires of the journey, does he, Duchess? *(looking at herself in the mirror)*

DUCHESS How dare he enter the castle of Queen Victoria Regina, Monarch of England? It is because of him that my mother died. The wild black beast put his hands on her. She died.

VICTORIA Why does he keep returning? He keeps returning forever, coming back ever and keeps coming back forever. He is my father.

DUCHESS He is a black Negro.

VICTORIA He is my father. I am tied to the black Negro. He came when I was a child in the south; before I was born he haunted my conception, diseased my birth.

DUCHESS Killed my mother.

VICTORIA My mother was the light. She was the lightest one. She looked like a white woman.

DUCHESS We are tied to him unless, of course, he should die.

VICTORIA But he is dead.

DUCHESS And he keeps returning.

(The knocking is louder; blackout. The lights go out in the chamber. Onto the stage from the left comes the figure in the white nightgown carrying the bald head. This time we hear her speak)

MOTHER Black man, Black man, I never should have let a Black man put his hands on me. The wild Black beast raped me and now my skull is shining. *(she disappears to the right)*

(Now the light is focused on a single white square wall that is to the left of the stage, that is suspended and stands alone, of about five feet in dimension and width. It stands with the narrow part facing the audience. A character steps through. She is a faceless, dark character with a hangman's rope about her neck and red blood on the part that would be her face. She is the NEGRO. *The most noticeable aspect of her looks is her wild kinky hair. It is a ragged head with a patch of hair missing from the crown, which the* NEGRO *carries in her hand. She is dressed in black. She steps slowly through the wall, stands still before it and begins her monologue)*

NEGRO Part of the time I live with Raymond, part of the time with God, Maxmillian, and Albert Saxe Coburg. I live in my room. It is a small room on the top floor of a brownstone in the West Nineties in New York, a room filled with my dark old volumes, a narrow bed, and on the wall old photographs of castles and monarchs of England. It is also Victoria's chamber. Queen Victoria Regina's. Partly because it is consumed by a gigantic plaster statue of Queen Victoria who is my idol and partly for other reasons; three steps that I contrived out of boards lead to the statue, which I have placed opposite the door as I enter the room. It is a sitting figure, a replica of one in London, and a thing of astonishing whiteness. I found it in a dusty shop on Morningside Heights. Raymond says it is a thing of terror, possessing the quality of nightmares, suggesting large and probable deaths. And of course he is right. When I am the Duchess of Hapsburg I sit opposite Victoria in my headpiece and we talk. The other time I wear the dress of a student, dark clothes and dark stockings. Victoria always wants me to tell her of whiteness. She wants me to tell her of a royal world where everything and everyone is white and there are no unfortunate Black ones. For as we of royal blood know, black is evil, and has been from the beginning. Even before my mother's hair started to fall out. Before she was raped by a wild Black beast. Black was evil.

As for myself, I long to become even a more pallid Negro than I am now; pallid like Negroes on the covers of American Negro magazines; soulless, educated, and irreligious. I want to possess no moral value, particularly value as to my being. I want not to be. I ask nothing except anonymity. I am an English major, as my mother was when she went to school in Atlanta. My father majored in social work. I am graduated from a city college and have occasional work in libraries, but mostly spend my days preoccupied with the placement and geometric position of words on paper. I write poetry, filling white page after white page with imitations of Edith Sitwell. It is my dream to live in rooms with European antiques and my Queen Victoria, photographs of Roman ruins, walls of books, a piano, oriental carpets, and to eat my meals on a white glass table. I will visit my friends' apartments which will contain books, photographs of Roman ruins, pianos and oriental carpets. My friends will be white.

I need them as an embankment to keep me from reflecting too much upon the fact that I am a Negro. For, like all educated Negroes—out of life-and-death essential—I find it necessary to maintain a stark fortress against recognition of myself. My white friends, like myself, will be shrewd, intellectual, and anxious for death. Anyone's death. I will mistrust them, as I do myself, waver in their opinion of me, as I waver in the opinion of myself. But if I had not wavered in my opinion of myself, then my hair would never have fallen out. And if my hair hadn't fallen out, I wouldn't have bludgeoned my father's head with an ebony mask.

In appearance I am good-looking in a boring way; no glaring Negroid features, medium nose, medium mouth, and pale yellow skin. My one defect is that I have a head of frizzy hair, unmistakably Negro kinky hair; and it is indistinguishable. I would like to lie and say I love Raymond. But I do not. He is a poet and is Jewish. He is very interested in Negroes.

(The NEGRO *stands by the wall and throughout her following speech, the following characters come through the wall, disappearing off into varying directions in the darkened night of the stage:* DUCHESS, QUEEN VICTORIA, JESUS, PATRICE LUMUMBA. JESUS *is a hunch-back, yellow-skinned dwarf, dressed in white rags and sandals.* PATRICE LUMUMBA *is a Black man. His head appears to be split in two with blood and tissue in eyes. He carries an ebony mask)*

SARAH (NEGRO) The rooms are my rooms; a Hapsburg chamber, a chamber in a Victorian castle, the hotel where I killed my father, the jungle. These are the places myselves exist in. I know no places. That is, I cannot believe in places. To believe in places is to know beauty. It links us across a horizon and connects us to the world. I find there are no places, only my funnyhouse. Streets are rooms, cities are rooms, eternal rooms. I try to create a space for myselves in cities, New York, the midwest, a southern town, but it becomes a lie. I try to give myselves a logical relationship but that too is a lie. For relationships was one of my last religions. I clung loyally to the lie of relationships, again and again seeking to establish a connection between my characters. Jesus is Victoria's son. Mother loved my father before her hair fell out. A loving relationship exists between myself and Queen Victoria, a love between myself and Jesus, but they are lies.

(Then to the right front of the stage comes the white light. It goes to a suspended stairway. At the foot of it, stands the LANDLADY. *She is a tall, thin, white woman dressed in a black-and-red hat and appears to be talking to someone in a suggested open doorway in a corridor of a rooming house. She laughs like a mad character in a funnyhouse throughout her speech)*

LANDLADY *(who is looking up the stairway)* Ever since her father hung himself in a Harlem hotel when Patrice Lumumba was murdered, she hides herself in her room. Each night she repeats: He keeps returning. How dare he enter the castle walls, he who is the darkest of them all, the darkest one? My mother looked like a white woman, hair as straight as any white woman's. And I am yellow but he, he is Black, the blackest one of them all. I hoped he was dead. Yet he still comes through the jungle.

I tell her: Sarah, honey, the man hung himself. It's not your blame. But, no, she stares at me: No, Mrs. Conrad, he did not hang himself, that is only the way they understand it, they do, but the truth is that I bludgeoned his head with an ebony skull that he carries about with him. Wherever he goes, he carries Black masks and heads.

She's suffering so till her hair has fallen out. But then she did always hide herself in that room with the walls of books and her statue. I always did know she thought she was somebody else, a Queen or something, somebody else.

(Blackout)

SCENE *Funnyman's place.*

(The next scene is enacted with the DUCHESS *and* RAYMOND. RAYMOND'*s place is suggested as being above the* NEGRO'*s room and is etched in with a prop of blinds and a bed. Behind the blinds are mirrors and when the blinds are opened and closed by* RAYMOND *this is revealed.* RAYMOND *turns out to be the funnyman of the funnyhouse. He is tall, white, and ghostly thin and dressed in a black shirt and black trousers in attire suggesting an artist. Throughout his dialogue he laughs. The* DUCHESS *is partially disrobed and it is implied from their attitudes of physical intimacy—he is standing and she is sitting before him clinging to his leg. During the scene* RAYMOND *keeps opening and closing the blinds)*

DUCHESS *(carrying a red paper bag)* My father is arriving and what am I to do?

(RAYMOND *walks about the place opening the blinds and laughing)*

FUNNYMAN He is arriving from Africa, is he not?

DUCHESS Yes, yes, he is arriving from Africa.

FUNNYMAN I always knew your father was African.

DUCHESS He is an African who lives in the jungle. He is an African who has always lived in the jungle. Yes, he is a nigger who is an African who is a missionary teacher and is now dedicating his life to the erection of a Christian mission in the middle of the jungle. He is a Black man.

FUNNYMAN He is a Black man who shot himself when they murdered Patrice Lumumba.

DUCHESS *(goes on wildly)* Yes, my father is a Black man who went to Africa years ago as a missionary teacher, got mixed up in politics, was revealed, and is now devoting his foolish life to the erection of a Christian mission in the middle of the jungle in one of those newly freed countries. Hide me. *(clinging to his knees)* Hide me here so the nigger will not find me.

FUNNYMAN *(laughing)* Your father is in the jungle dedicating his life to the erection of a Christian mission.

DUCHESS Hide me here so the jungle will not find me. Hide me.

FUNNYMAN Isn't it cruel of you?

DUCHESS Hide me from the jungle.

FUNNYMAN Isn't it cruel?

DUCHESS No, no.

FUNNYMAN Isn't it cruel of you?

DUCHESS No. *(she screams and opens her red paper bag and draws from it her fallen hair. It is a great mass of dark wild hair. She holds it up to him. He appears not to understand. He stares at it)* It is my hair. *(he continues to stare at her)* When I awakened this morning it had fallen out, not all of it but a mass from the crown of my head that lay on the center of my pillow. I arose and in the greyish winter morning light of my room I stood staring at my hair, dazed by my sleeplessness, still shaken by nightmares of my mother. Was is true? Yes. It was my hair. In the mirror I saw that, although my hair remained on both sides, clearly on the crown and at my temples my scalp was bare. *(she removes her black crown and shows him the top of her head)*

FUNNYMAN *(staring at her)* Why would your hair fall out? Is it because you are cruel? How could a Black father haunt you so?

DUCHESS He haunted my very conception. He was a wild Black beast who raped my mother.

FUNNYMAN He is a black Negro. *(Laughing)*

DUCHESS Ever since I can remember he's been in a nigger pose of agony. He is the wilderness. He speaks niggerly, groveling about wanting to touch me with his black hand.

FUNNYMAN How tormented and cruel you are.

DUCHESS *(as if not comprehending)* Yes, yes, the man's dark, very dark-skinned. He is the darkest, my father is the darkest, my mother is the lightest. I am in between. But my father is the darkest. My father is a nigger who drives me to misery. Any time spent with him evolves itself into suffering. He is a Black man and the wilderness.

FUNNYMAN How tormented and cruel you are.

DUCHESS He is a nigger.

FUNNYMAN And your mother, where is she?

DUCHESS She is in the asylum. In the asylum, bald. Her father was a white man. And she is in the asylum.

(He takes her in his arms. She responds wildly)

(Blackout)

(Knocking is heard; it continues, then somewhere near the center of the stage a figure appears in the darkness, a large, dark faceless MAN *carrying a mask in his hand)*

MAN It begins with the disaster of my hair. I awaken. My hair has fallen out, not all of it, but a mass from the crown of my head that lies on the center of my white pillow. I arise and in the greyish winter morning light of my room I stand staring at my hair, dazed by sleeplessness, still shaken by nightmares of my mother. Is it true? Yes. It is my hair. In the mirror I see that, although my hair remains on both sides, clearly on the crown and at my temples my scalp is bare. And in my sleep I had been visited by my bald crazy mother who comes to me crying, calling me to her bedside. She lies on the bed watching the strands of her own hair fall out. Her hair fell out after she married, and she spent her days lying on the bed watching the strands fall from her scalp, covering the bedspread until she was bald and admitted to the hospital. Black man, Black man, my mother says, I never should have let a Black man put his hands on me. She comes to me, the bald skull shining. Black diseases, Sarah, she says. Black diseases. I run. She follows me, her bald skull shining. That is the beginning.

(Blackout)

SCENE: *Queen's Chamber.*

(Her hair is in a small pile on the bed and in a small pile on the floor. Several other small piles of hair are scattered about her and her white gown is covered with fallen-out hair. QUEEN VICTORIA *acts out the following scene: She awakens [in pantomime] and discovers her hair has fallen. It is on her pillow. She arises and stands at the side of the bed with her back toward us, staring at the hair. The* DUCHESS *enters the room, comes around, standing behind* VICTORIA, *and they stare at the hair.* VICTORIA *picks up a mirror. The* DUCHESS *then picks up a mirror and looks at her own hair. She opens the red paper bag that she is carrying and takes out her hair, attempting to place it back on her head [for unlike* VICTORIA, *she does not wear her headpiece now]. The lights remain on. The unidentified* MAN *returns out of the darkness and speaks. He carries the mask)*

MAN *(Patrice Lumumba)* I am a nigger of two generations. I am Patrice Lumumba. I am a nigger of two generations. I am the black shadow that haunted my mother's conception. I belong to the generation born at the turn of the century and the generation born before the depression. At present I reside in New York City in a brownstone in the West Nineties. I am an English major at a city college. My nigger father majored in social work, so did my mother. I am a student and have occasional work in libraries. But mostly I spend my vile days preoccupied with the placement and geometric position of words on paper. I write poetry, filling white page after white page with imitations of Sitwell. It is my vile dream to live in rooms with European antiques and my statue of Queen Victoria, photographs of Roman ruins, walls of books, a piano and oriental carpets, and to eat my meals on a white glass table. It is also my nigger dream for my friends to eat their meals on white glass tables and to live in rooms with European antiques, photographs of Roman ruins, pianos and oriental carpets. My friends will be white. I need them as an embankment to keep me from reflecting too much upon the fact that I am Patrice Lumumba who haunted my mother's conception. They are necessary for me to maintain recognition against myself. My white friends, like myself, will be shrewd intellectuals and anxious for death. Anyone's death. I will despise them as I do myself. For if I did not despise myself, then my hair would not have fallen, and if my hair had not fallen then I would not have bludgeoned my father's face with the ebony mask.

(The light remains on him. Before him a bald head is dropped on a wire, someone screams. Another wall is dropped, larger than the first one was. This one is near the front of the stage facing thus. Throughout the following monologue, the characters, DUCHESS, VICTORIA, JESUS, *go back and forth. As they go in, their backs are to us but the* NEGRO *faces us, speaking)*

NEGRO I always dreamed of a day when my mother would smile at me. My father . . . his mother wanted him to be Christ. From the beginning in the lamp of their dark room she said—I want you to be Jesus, to walk in Genesis and save the race. You must return to Africa, find revelation in the midst of golden savannas, nim and white frankopenny trees, white stallions roaming under a blue sky. You must walk with a white dove and heal the race, heal the misery, take us off the cross. She stared at him anguished in the kerosene light . . . At dawn he watched her rise, kill a hen for him to eat at breakfast, then go to work down at the big house till dusk, till she died.

His father told him the race was no damn good. He hated his father and adored his mother. His mother didn't want him to marry my mother and sent a dead chicken to the wedding. I DON'T want you marrying that child, she wrote. She's not good enough for you. I want you to go to Africa. When they first married they lived in New York. Then they went to Africa, where my mother fell out of love with my father. She didn't want him to save the black race and spent her days combing her hair. She would not let him touch her in their wedding bed and called him black. He is black of skin with dark eyes and a great dark square brow. Then in Africa he started to drink and came home drunk one night and raped my mother. The child from the union is me. I clung to my mother. Long after she went to the asylum I wove long dreams of her beauty, her straight hair and fair skin and grey eyes, so identical to mine. How it anguished him. I turned from him, nailing him on the cross, he said, dragging him through grass and nailing him on a cross until he bled. He pleaded with me to help him find Genesis, search for Genesis in the midst of golden savannas, nim and white frankopenny trees and white stallions roaming under a blue sky, help him search for the white doves. He wanted the Black man to make a pure statement, he wanted the Black man to rise from colonialism. But I sat in the room with my mother, sat by her bedside and helped her comb her straight black hair and wove long dreams of her beauty. She had long since begun to curse the place and spoke of herself trapped in Blackness. She preferred the company of night owls. Only at night did she rise, walking in the garden among the trees with owls. When I spoke to her she saw I was a Black man's child and she preferred speaking to owls. Nights my father came from his school in the village struggling to embrace me. But I fled and hid under my mother's bed while she screamed of remorse. Her hair was falling badly and after a while we had to return to this country.

He tried to hang himself once. After my mother went to the asylum he had hallucinations, his mother threw a dead chicken at him, his father laughed and said the race was no damn good, my mother appeared in her nightgown screaming she had trapped herself in Blackness. No white doves flew. He had left Africa and was again in New York. He lived in Harlem and no white doves flew. Sarah, Sarah, he would say to me, the soldiers are coming and a cross they are placing high on a tree and are dragging me through the grass and nailing me upon the cross. My blood is gushing. I wanted to live in Genesis in the midst of golden savannas, nim and white frankopenny trees and white stallions roaming under a blue sky. I wanted to walk with a white dove. I wanted to be a Christian. Now I am Judas. I betrayed my mother. I sent your mother to the asylum. I created a yellow child who hates me. And he tried to hang himself in a Harlem hotel.

(Blackout)

(A bald head is dropping on a string. We hear laughing)

SCENE *Duchess's place.*

(The next scene is done in the DUCHESS OF HAPSBURG*'s place, which is a chandeliered ballroom with snow falling, a black-and-white marble floor, a bench decorated with white flowers. All of this can be made of obviously fake materials as they would be in a funnyhouse. The* DUCHESS *is wearing a white dress and, as in the previous scene, a white headpiece with her kinky hair springing out from under it. In the scene are the* DUCHESS *and* JESUS. JESUS *enters the room, which is at first dark, then suddenly brilliant. He starts to cry out at the* DUCHESS, *who is seated on a bench under the chandelier, and pulls his hair from the red paper bag holding it up for the* DUCHESS *to see)*

JESUS My hair. *(the* DUCHESS *does not speak,* JESUS *again screams)* My hair. *(holding the hair up, waiting for a reaction from the* DUCHESS*)*

DUCHESS *(as if oblivious)* I have something I must show you. *(she goes quickly to shutters and darkens the room, returning, standing before* JESUS. *She then slowly removes her headpiece and from under it takes a mass of her hair)* When I awakened I found it fallen out, not all of it but a mass that lay on my white pillow. I could see, although my hair hung down at the sides, clearly on my white scalp it was missing. *(her baldness is identical to* JESUS'*)*

(Blackout)

(The lights come back up. They are both sitting on the bench examining each other's hair, running it through their fingers, then slowly the DUCHESS *disappears behind the shutters and returns with a long red comb. She sits on the bench next to* JESUS *and starts to comb her remaining hair over her baldness. (this is done slowly)* JESUS *then takes the comb and proceeds to do the same to the* DUCHESS OF HAPSBURG*'s hair. After they finish, they place the* DUCHESS*'s headpiece back on and we can see the strands of hair falling to the floor.* JESUS *then lies down across the bench while the* DUCHESS *walks back and forth. The knocking does not cease. They speak in unison as the* DUCHESS *walks about and* JESUS *lies on the bench in the falling snow, staring at the ceiling.*

DUCHESS and JESUS *(their hair is falling more now. They are both hideous)* My father isn't going to let us alone. *(knocking)* Our father isn't going to let us alone, our father is the darkest of us all, my mother was the fairest, I am in between, but my father is the darkest of them all. He is a Black man. Our father is the darkest of them all. He is a Black man. My father is a dead man.

(Then they suddenly look up at each other and scream, the lights go to their heads and we see that they are totally bald. There is a knocking. Lights go to the stairs and the LANDLADY.*)*

LANDLADY He wrote to her saying he loved her and asked her forgiveness. He begged her to take him off the cross *(he had dreamed she would)*, stop them from tormenting him, the one with the chicken and his cursing father. Her mother's hair fell out, the race's hair fell out because he left Africa, he said. He had tried to save them. She must embrace him. He said his existence depended on her embrace. He wrote her from Africa where he is creating his Christian center in the jungle and that is why he came here. I know that he wanted her to return there with him and not desert the race. He came to see her once before he tried to hang himself, appearing in the corridor of my apartment. I had let him in. I found him sitting on a bench in the hallway. He put out his hand to her, tried to take her in his arms, crying out—Forgiveness, Sarah, is it that you never will forgive me for being Black? Sarah, I know you were a child of torment. But forgiveness. That was before his breakdown. Then, he wrote her and repeated that his mother hoped he would be Christ but he failed. He had married her mother because he could not resist the light. Yet, his mother from the beginning in the kerosene lamp of their dark rooms in Georgia said: I want you to be Jesus, to walk in Genesis and save the race, return to Africa, find revelation in the Black. He went away.

But Easter morning, she got to feeling badly and went into Harlem to see him; the streets were filled with vendors selling lilies. He had checked out of that hotel. When she arrived back at my brownstone he was here, dressed badly, rather drunk. I had let him in again. He sat on a bench in the dark hallway, put out his hand to her, trying to take her in his arms, crying out—forgiveness, Sarah, forgiveness for my being Black, Sarah. I know you are a child of torment. I know on dark winter afternoons you sit alone weaving stories of your mother's beauty. But Sarah, answer me, don't turn away, Sarah. Forgive my Blackness. She would not answer. He put out his hand to her. She ran past him on the stairs, left him there with his hand out to me, repeating his past, saying his mother hoped he would be Christ. From the beginning in the kerosene lamp of their dark rooms, she said, "Wally, I want you to be Jesus, to walk in Genesis, and save the race. You must return to Africa, Wally, find revelation in the midst of golden savannas, nim and white frankopenny trees and white stallions roaming under a blue sky. Wally, you must find the white dove and heal the pain of the race, heal the misery of the Black man, Wally, take us off the cross, Wally." In the kerosene light she stared at me anguished from her old Negro face—but she ran past him leaving him. And now he is dead, she says, now he is dead. He left Africa and now Patrice Lumumba is dead.

(The next scene is enacted back in the DUCHESS OF HAPSBURG*'s place.* JESUS *is still in the* DUCHESS*'s chamber. Apparently he has fallen asleep and as we see him he awakens with the* DUCHESS *by his side, and sits there as in a trance. He rises terrified and speaks)*

JESUS Through my apocalypses and my raging sermons I have tried so to escape him, through God Almighty I have tried to escape being Black. *(he then appears to rouse himself from his thoughts and calls)* Duchess, Duchess. *(he looks about for her; there is no answer. He gets up slowly, walks back into the darkness, and there we see that she is hanging on the chandelier, her bald head suddenly drops to the floor and she falls upon* JESUS*. He screams)* I am going to Africa and kill this Black man named Patrice Lumumba. Why? Because all my life I believe my Holy Father to be God, but now I know that my father is a Black man. I have no fear for whatever I do, I will do in the name of God, I will do in the name of Albert Saxe Coburg, in the name of Victoria, Queen Victoria Regina, the monarch of England, I will.

(Blackout)

SCENE: *In the jungle, red sun, flying things, wild black grass. The effect of the jungle is that it, unlike the other scenes, is over the entire stage. In time, this is the longest scene in the play and is played the slowest, as the slow, almost standstill stages of a dream. By lighting, the desired effect would be—suddenly the jungle has overgrown the chambers and all the other places with a violence and a dark brightness, a grim yellowness.*

*(*JESUS *is the first to appear in the center of the jungle darkness. Unlike in previous scenes, he has a nimbus above his head. As they each successively appear, they all to have nimbuses atop their heads in a manner to suggest that they are saviours)*

JESUS I always believed my father to be God.

(Suddenly they all appear in various parts of the jungle. PATRICE LUMUMBA, *the* DUCHESS, VICTORIA, *wandering about speaking at once. Their speeches are mixed and repeated by one another)*

ALL He never tires of the journey, he who is the darkest one, the darkest one of them all. My mother looked like a white woman, hair as straight as any white woman's. I am yellow but he is Black, the darkest one of us all. How I hoped he was dead, yet he never tires of the journey. It was because of him that my mother died because she let a Black man put his hands on her. Why does he keep returning? He keeps returning forever, keeps returning and returning and he is my father. He is a black Negro. They told me my Father was God but my father is Black. He is my father. I am tied to a black Negro. He returned when I lived in the south back in the twenties, when I was a child, he returned. Before I was born at the turn of the century, he haunted my conception, diseased my birth . . . killed my mother. He killed the light. My mother was the lightest one. I am bound to him unless, of course, he should die.

But he is dead.

And he keeps returning. Then he is not dead. Then he is not dead.

Yet, he is dead, but dead he comes knocking at my door.

(This is repeated several times, finally reaching a loud pitch and then ALL *rushing about the grass. They stop and stand perfectly still, speaking tensely at various times in a chant)*

ALL I see him. The Black ugly thing is sitting in his hallway, surrounded by his ebony masks, surrounded by the Blackness of himself. My mother comes into the room. He is there with his hand out to me, groveling, saying—Forgiveness, Sarah, is it that you will never forgive me for being Black.

Forgiveness, Sarah, I know you are a nigger of torment.

Why? Christ would not rape anyone.

You will never forgive me for being Black.

Wild beast. Why did you rape my mother? Black beast, Christ would not rape anyone.

He is in grief from that Black anguished face of his. Then at once the room will grow bright and my mother will come toward me smiling while I stand before his face and bludgeon him with an ebony head.

Forgiveness, Sarah, I know you are a nigger of torment.

(Silence. Then they suddenly begin to laugh and shout as though they are in victory. They continue for some minutes, running about laughing and shouting)

(Blackout)

(Another wall drops. There is a white plaster statue of Queen Victoria, which represents the NEGRO'*s room in the brownstone. The room appears near the staircase highly lit and small. The main prop is the statue, but a bed could be suggested. The figure of Victoria is a sitting figure, one of astonishing repulsive whiteness, suggested by dusty volumes of books and old yellowed walls.*

The NEGRO-SARAH *is standing perfectly still. We hear the knocking, the lights come on quickly, her* FATHER'*s black figure with bludgeoned hands rushes upon her, the light goes black, and we see her hanging in the room.*

Lights come on the laughing LANDLADY *and at the same time remain on the hanging figure of the* NEGRO.*)*

LANDLADY The poor bitch has hung herself. *(*FUNNYMAN RAYMOND *appears from his room at the commotion)* The poor bitch has hung herself.

RAYMOND *(observing her hanging figure)* She was a funny little liar.

LANDLADY *(informing him)* Her father hung himself in a Harlem hotel when Patrice Lumumba died.

RAYMOND Her father never hung himself in a Harlem hotel when Patrice Lumumba was murdered. I know the man. He is a doctor, married to a white whore. He lives in the city in rooms with European antiques, photographs of Roman ruins, walls of books and oriental carpets. Her father is a nigger who eats his meals on a white glass table.

(End)

WINE IN THE WILDERNESS
1969

Alice Childress (1916–1994)

From 1940 to 1948, Alice Childress worked as an actor, a technician, a teacher with the American Negro Theatre in Harlem (see introduction to *On Strivers Row*). She later declared that those years were "the greatest experience of my life," for there she learned her craft as a writer. From her grandmother, with whom she lived as a child, she acquired an appetite for education (reading two books a day in the library) and a passion for integrity. "I will never cut my conscience to fit the fashion of the day," might have been her motto as it was Lillian Hellman's.[1] In later years, producers offered her contracts "under the table," if she would ignore her union contract with the Dramatists Guild, which she refused to do. She said that if her plays were to have misrepresentations of society and humanity in them, the errors would be her own mistakes and not those of producers. Eleven times, her plays were optioned for Broadway, and each time, never performed because she would not compromise. These options included *Wedding Band* (1966), a play about a Black/white love affair based on her ancestors in South Carolina. When some found the subject "offensive," she replied, "If a racist society cannot stand what its playwrights have to say, it will suffer for it." In later decades, *Wedding Band* became her most produced play.

She observed that the theatre rarely represented the people she respected most—ordinary people. "I always deal with those who know the condition they're in, who don't like it, but cope on a day-to-day basis. These people have been missing from drama." These are the people she writes about in *Wine in the Wilderness.*

To understand the transformation that Bill Jameson undergoes in this play requires some review of the evolution of the Black middle class in America. In his book *Black Bourgeoisie* (1957), E. Franklin Frazier traces the origins of this class from slavery through the mid-twentieth century, when "society" in the Black, segregated communities flaunted "conspicuous

1. Spoken by Lillian Hellman before the House Committee on Un-American Activities when summoned to testify against her friends and colleagues in 1952.

consumption" by lavish living and entertainment (see *On Strivers Row*). In the 1950s, with the advent of the Civil Rights Movement, this social striving began to diminish; emphasis shifted from desire to be "socially elite" to the desire for unity of all Blacks. Older members of the middle class put aside their martinis and marched along with the young; those who did not march, cheered from the sidelines.

As Childress reveals in *Wine in the Wilderness*, however, class consciousness is not easily ignored or erased. Bill Jameson, Sonny-Man, and Cynthia are also victims of the old Black bourgeois values. They are empty, artificial people, preaching Blackness, brotherhood, and love simply because it is in vogue; they remain self-centered individuals who reflect the values of the old slave masters. They accept Oldtimer (they don't even know his name) because they find him amusing, and Tommy only because she is useful to them. They consciously and unconsciously label themselves "better" than the "street people," Tommy and Oldtimer, the "real" people of the play; they are honest. The beauty of *Wine in the Wilderness* is in part due to the author's sensitive treatment of Tommy, "a poor, dumb chick that had her behind kicked until it's numb," but whose warmth, compassion, inner dignity, and pride make her more of a woman than Cynthia will ever be. Tommy is the source of inspiration that they all so desperately need to find themselves and their Blackness.

In Tommy, Alice Childress created a powerful, *new* Black heroine who emerges from the depths of the community, offering a sharp contrast to the typical strong "Mama-on-the-couch" figure who dominates the plays George C. Wolfe will mock in *The Colored Museum*.

Lillian Hellman, an immaculate theatre artist, once said she had learned her craft by copying with a pen, line by line, the plays of Ibsen. One might do the same with *Wine in the Wilderness*. Childress has placed every character, every line, every word, for a purpose. Writing over twenty plays, she remains among the finest artists in the American theatre.

Wine in the Wilderness

CAST OF CHARACTERS

BILL JAMESON, *an artist aged thirty-three*
OLDTIMER, *an old roustabout character in his sixties*
SONNY-MAN, *a writer aged twenty-seven*
CYNTHIA, *a social worker aged twenty-five; she is Sonny-man's wife*
TOMMY, *a woman factory worker aged thirty*

TIME *The summer of 1964. Night of a riot.*

PLACE *Harlem, New York City, New York, U.S.A.*

SCENE: *A one room apartment in a Harlem tenement. It used to be a three room apartment but the tenant has broken out walls and is half finished with a redecorating job. The place is now only partly reminiscent of its past tawdry days, plaster broken away and lathing exposed right next to a new brick-faced portion of wall. The kitchen is now a part of the room. There is a three-quarter bed covered with an African throw, a screen is placed at the foot of the bed to ensure privacy when needed. The room is obviously Black dominated, pieces of sculpture, wall hangings, paintings. An artist's easel is standing with a drapery thrown across it so the empty canvas beneath it is hidden. Two other canvases the same size are next to it, they too are covered and conceal paintings. The place is in a beautiful, rather artistic state of disorder. The room also reflects an interest in other darker peoples of the world . . . A Chinese incense-burner Buddha, an American Indian feathered war helmet, a Mexican serape, a Japanese fan, a West Indian travel poster. There is a kitchen table, chairs, floor cushions, a couple of box crates, books, bookcases, plenty of artist's materials. There is a small raised platform for model posing. On the platform is a backless chair.*

The tail end of a riot is going on out in the street. Noise and screaming can be heard in the distance, . . . running feet, voices shouting over loudspeakers)

OFFSTAGE VOICES Off the street! Into your homes! Clear the street! *(the whine of a bullet is heard)* Cover that roof! It's from the roof!

*(*BILL *is seated on the floor with his back to the wall, drawing on a large sketch pad with charcoal pencil. He is very absorbed in his task but flinches as he hears the bullet sound, ducks and shields his head with upraised hand, . . . then resumes sketching. The telephone rings, he reaches for phone with caution, pulls it toward him by the cord in order to avoid going near window or standing up)*

BILL Hello? Yeah, my phone is on. How the hell I'm gonna be talkin' to you if it's not on? *(sound of glass breaking in the distance)* I could lose my damn life answerin' the phone. Sonny-man, what the hell you callin' me up for! I thought you and Cynthia might be downstairs dead. I banged on the floor and hollered down the air-shaft, no answer. No stuff! Thought yall was dead. I'm sittin' here drawin' a picture in your memory. In a bar! Yall sittin' in a bar? See there, you done blew the picture that's in your memory . . . No kiddin', they wouldn't let you in the block? Man, they can't keep you outta your own house. Found? You found who? Model? What model? Yeah, yeah, thanks, . . . but I like to find my own models. No! Don't bring nobody up here in the middle of a riot . . . Hey, Sonny-man! Hey! *(sound of yelling and rushing footsteps in the hall)*

WOMAN'S VOICE *(offstage)* Dammit, Bernice! The riot is over! What you hidin' in the hall for? I'm in the house, your father's in the house, . . . and you out here hidin' in the hall!

GIRL'S VOICE *(offstage)* The house might burn down!

BILL Sonny-man, I can't hear you!

WOMAN'S VOICE *(offstage)* If it do burn down, what the hell you gon' do, run off and leave us to burn up by ourself? The riot is over. The police say it's over! Get back in the house! *(sound of running feet and a knock on the door)*

BILL They say it's over. Man, they oughta let you on your own block, in your own house . . . Yeah, we still standin', this seventy year old house got guts. Thank you, yeah, thanks but I like to pick my own models. You drunk? Can't you hear when I say not to . . . Okay, all right, bring her . . . *(frantic knocking at the door)* I gotta go. Yeah, yeah, bring her. I gotta go . . . *(hangs up phone and opens the door for* OLDTIMER. *The old man is carrying a haul of loot . . . two or three bottles of liquor, a ham, a salami and a suit with price tags attached)* What's this! Oh, no, no, no, Oldtimer, not here . . . *(faint sound of a police whistle)* The police after you? What you bring that stuff in here for?

OLDTIMER *runs past* BILL *to center as he looks for a place to hide the loot)* No, no, they not really after me but . . . I was in the basement so I could stash this stuff, . . . but a fella told me they pokin' round down there . . . in the back yard pokin' round . . . the police doin' a lotta pokin' round.

BILL If the cops are searchin' why you wanna dump your troubles on me?

OLDTIMER I don't wanna go to jail. I'm too old to go to jail. What we gonna do?

BILL We can throw it the hell outta the window. Didn't you think of just throwin' it away and not worry 'bout jail?

OLDTIMER I can't do it. It's like . . . I'm Oldtimer but my hands and arms is somebody else that I don't know-a-tall. *(*BILL *pulls stuff out of* OLDTIMER*'s arms and places loot on the kitchen table.* OLDTIMER*'s arms fall to his sides)* Thank you, son.

BILL Stealin' ain't worth a bullet through your brain, is it? You wanna get shot down and drown in your own blood, . . . for what? A suit, a bottle of whiskey? Gonna throw your life away for a damn ham?

OLDTIMER But I ain't really stole nothin', Bill, cause I ain' no thief. Them others, . . . they smash the windows, they run in the stores and grab and all. Me, I pick up what they left scatter in the street. Things they drop . . . things they trample underfoot.

What's in the street ain' like stealin'. This is leavin's. What I'm goin' do if the police come?

BILL *(starts to gather the things in the tablecloth that is on the table)* I'll throw it out the air-shaft window.

OLDTIMER *(places himself squarely in front of the air-shaft window)* I be damn. Un-uh, can't let you do it, Billy-Boy. *(grabs the liquor and holds on)*

BILL *(wraps the suit, the ham and the salami in the tablecloth and ties the ends together in a knot)* Just for now, then you can go down and get it later.

OLDTIMER *(getting belligerent)* I say I ain' gon' let you do it.

BILL Sonny-man calls this "The people's revolution." A revolution should not be looting and stealing. Revolutions are for liberation. *(*OLDTIMER *won't budge from before the window)* Okay, man, you win, it's all yours. *(walks away from* OLDTIMER *and prepares his easel for sketching)*

OLDTIMER Don't be mad with me, Billy-Boy, I couldn't help myself.

BILL *(at peace with the old man)* No hard feelin's.

OLDTIMER *(as he uncorks bottle)* I don't blame you for bein' fed up with us, . . . fella like you oughta be fed up with your people sometime. Hey, Billy, let's you and me have a little taste together.

BILL Yeah, why not.

OLDTIMER *(at table pouring drinks)* You mustn't be too hard on me. You see, you talented, you got somethin' on the ball, you gonna make it on past these white folk, . . . but not me, Billy-Boy, it's too late in the day for that. Time, time, time, . . . time done put me down. Father Time is a bad white cat. Whatcha been paintin' and drawin' lately? You can paint me again if you wanta, . . . no charge. Paint me 'cause that might be the only way I get to stay in the world after I'm dead and gone. Somebody'll look up at your paintin' and say, . . . "Who's that?" And you say, . . . "That's Oldtimer." *(*BILL *joins* OLDTIMER *at table and takes one of the drinks)* Well, here's lookin' at you and goin' down me. *(gulps drink down)*

BILL *(raising his glass)* Your health, oldtimer.

OLDTIMER My day we didn't have all this grants and scholarship like now. Whatcha been doin'?

BILL I'm working on the third part of a triptych.

OLDTIMER A what tick?

BILL A triptych.

OLDTIMER Hot-damn, that call for another drink. Here's to the trip-tick. Down the hatch. What is one-a-those?

BILL It's three paintings that make one work . . . three paintings that make one subject.

OLDTIMER Goes together like a new outfit . . . hat, shoes and suit.

BILL Right. The title of my triptych is . . . "Wine In The Wilderness" . . . Three canvases on black womanhood. . . .

OLDTIMER *(eyes light up)* Are they naked pitchers?

BILL *(crosses to paintings)* No, all fully clothed.

OLDTIMER *(wishing it was a naked picture)* Man, ain' nothin' dirty 'bout naked pitchers. That's art. What you call artistic.

BILL Right, right, right, but these are with clothes. That can be artistic too. *(uncovers one of the canvases and reveals painting of a charming little girl in Sunday dress and hair ribbon)* I call her . . . "Black girlhood."

OLDTIMER Awwwww, that's innocence! Don't know what it's all about. Ain't that the little child that live right down the street? Yeah. That call for another drink.

BILL Slow down, Oldtimer, wait till you see this. *(covers the painting of the little girl, then uncovers another canvas and reveals a beautiful woman, deep mahogany complexion, she is cold but utter perfection, draped in startling colors of African material, very "Vogue" looking. She wears a golden head-dress sparkling with brilliants and sequins applied over the paint)* There she is . . . "Wine In The Wilderness" . . . Mother Africa, regal, black womanhood in her noblest form.

OLDTIMER Hot damn. I'd die for her, no stuff, . . . oh, man. "Wine In The Wilderness."

BILL Once, a long time ago, a poet named Omar told us what a paradise life could be if a man had a loaf of bread, a jug of wine and . . . a woman singing to him in the wilderness. She is the woman, she is the bread, she is the wine, she is the singing. This Abyssinian maiden is paradise, . . . perfect Black womanhood.

OLDTIMER *(pours for* BILL *and himself)* To our Abyssinian maiden.

BILL She's the Sudan, the Congo River, the Egyptian Pyramids . . . Her thighs are African Mahogany . . . she speaks and her words pour forth sparkling clear as the waters . . . Victoria Falls.

OLDTIMER Ow! Victoria Falls! She got a pretty name.

BILL *(covers her up again)* Victoria Falls is a waterfall not her name. Now, here's the one that calls for a drink. *(snatches cover from the empty canvas)*

OLDTIMER *(stunned by the empty canvas)* Your . . . your pitcher is gone.

BILL Not gone, . . . she's not painted yet. This will be the third part of the triptych. This is the unfinished third of "Wine In the Wilderness." She's gonna be the kinda chick that is grass roots, . . . no, not grass roots, . . . I mean she's underneath the grass roots. The lost woman, . . . what the society has made out of our women. She's as far from my African queen as a woman can get and still be female, she's as close to the bottom as you can get without crackin' up . . . she's ignorant, unfeminine, coarse, rude . . . vulgar . . . a poor, dumb chick that's had her behind kicked until it's numb . . . and the sad part is . . . she ain't together, you know, . . . there's no hope for her.

OLDTIMER Oh, man, you talkin' 'bout my first wife.

BILL A chick that ain't fit for nothin' but to . . . to . . . just pass her by.

OLDTIMER Yeah, later for her. When you see her, cross over to the other side of the street.

BILL If you had to sum her up in one word it would be nothin'!

OLDTIMER *(roars with laughter)* That call for a double!

BILL *(beginning to slightly feel the drinks. He covers the canvas again)* Yeah, that's a double! The kinda woman that grates on your damn nerves, and Sonny-man just called to say he found her runnin' round in the middle-a this riot, Sonny-man say she's the real thing from underneath them grass roots. A back-country chick right outta the wilds of Mississippi, . . . but she ain' never been near there. Born in Harlem, raised right here in Harlem, . . . but back country. Got the picture?

OLDTIMER *(full of laughter)* When . . . when . . . when she get here let's us stomp her to death.

BILL Not till after I paint her. Gonna put her right here on this canvas. *(pats the canvas, walks in a strut around the table)* When she gets put down on canvas, . . . then triptych will be finished.

OLDTIMER *(joins him in the strut)* Trip-tick will be finish . . . trip-tick will be finish . . .

BILL Then "Wine In The Wilderness" will go up against the wall to improve the view of some post office . . . or some library . . . or maybe a bank . . . and I'll win a prize . . . and the queen, my Black queen will look down from the wall so the messed-up chicks in the neighborhood can see what a woman oughta be . . . and the innocent child on one side of her and the messed-up chick on the other side of her . . . MY STATEMENT.

OLDTIMER *(turning the strut into a dance)* Wine in the wilderness . . . up against the wall . . . wine in the wilderness . . . up against the wall . . .

WOMAN FROM UPSTAIRS APT *(offstage)* What's the matter! The house on fire?

BILL *(calls upstairs through the air-shaft window)* No, baby! We down here paintin' pictures! *(sound of police siren in distance)*

WOMAN FROM UPSTAIRS APT *(offstage)* So much-a damn noise! Cut out the noise! *(to her husband, hysterically)* Percy! Percy! You hear a police siren! Percy! That a fire engine?!

BILL Another messed up chick. *(gets a rope and ties it to Oldtimer's bundle)* Got an idea. We'll tie the rope to the bundle, . . . then . . . *(lowers bundle out of window)* lower the bundle outta the window . . . and tie it to this nail here behind the curtain. Now! Nobody can find it except you and me . . . Cops come, there's no loot. *(ties rope to nail under curtain)*

OLDTIMER Yeah, yeah, loot long gone 'til I want it. *(makes sure window knot is secure)* It'll be swingin' in the breeze free and easy. *(there is knocking on the door)*

SONNY-MAN Open up! Open up! Sonny-man and company.

BILL *(putting finishing touches on securing knot to nail)* Wait, wait, hold on. . . .

SONNY-MAN And-a here we come! *(pushes the door open. Enters room with his wife* CYNTHIA *and* TOMMY. SONNY-MAN *is in high spirits. He is in his late twenties, his wife* CYNTHIA *is a bit younger. She wears her hair in a natural style, her clothing is tweedy and in good, quiet taste.* SONNY-MAN *is wearing slacks and a dashiki over a shirt.* TOMMY *is dressed in a mis-matched skirt and sweater, wearing a wig that is not comical, but is wiggy looking. She has the habit of smoothing it every once in a while, patting to make sure it's in place. She wears sneakers and bobby sox, carries a brown paper sack)*

CYNTHIA You didn't think it was locked, did you?

BILL Door not locked? *(looking over* TOMMY*)*

TOMMY You oughta run him outta town, pushin' open people's door.

BILL Come right on in.

SONNY-MAN *(standing behind* TOMMY *and pointing down at her to draw* BILL*'s attention)* Yes, sireeeeee.

CYNTHIA Bill, meet a friend-a ours . . . This is Miss Tommy Fields. Tommy, meet a friend-a ours . . . this is Bill Jameson . . . Bill, Tommy.

BILL Tommy, if I may call you that . . .

TOMMY *(likes him very much)* Help yourself, Bill. It's a pleasure. Bill Jameson, well, all right.

BILL The pleasure is all mine. Another friend-a ours, Oldtimer.

TOMMY *(with respect and warmth)* How are you, Mr. Timer?

BILL *(laughs along with others,* OLDTIMER *included)* What you call him, baby?

TOMMY Mr. Timer, . . . ain't that what you say? *(they all laugh expansively)*

BILL No, sugar pie, that's what everybody call him . . .

OLDTIMER Yeah, they all call me that . . . everybody say that . . . OLDTIMER.

TOMMY That's cute, . . . but what's your name?

BILL His name is . . . er . . . er . . . What *is* your name?

SONNY-MAN Dog-bite, what's your name, man? *(there is a significant moment of self-consciousness as* CYNTHIA, SONNY *and* BILL *realize they don't know* OLDTIMER*'s name)*

OLDTIMER Well, it's . . . Edmond L. Matthews.

TOMMY Edmond L. Matthews. What's the L for?

OLDTIMER Lorenzo, . . . Edmond Lorenzo Matthews.

BILL *and* SONNY-MAN Edmond Lorenzo Matthews.

TOMMY Pleased to meetcha, Mr. Matthews.

OLDTIMER Nobody call me that in a long, long time.

TOMMY I'll call you Oldtimer like the rest but I like to know who I'm meetin'. *(*OLDTIMER *gives her a chair)* There you go. He's a gentleman too. Bet you can tell my feet hurt. I got one corn . . . and that one is enough. Oh, it'll ask you for somethin'. *(general laughter.* BILL *indicates to* SONNY-MAN *that* TOMMY *seems right.* CYNTHIA *and* OLDTIMER *take seats near* TOMMY*)*

BILL You rest yourself, baby, er . . . er . . . Tommy. You did say Tommy.

TOMMY I cut it to Tommy . . . Tommy-Marie, I use both of 'em sometime.

BILL How 'bout some refreshment?

SONNY-MAN Yeah how 'bout that. *(pouring drinks)*

TOMMY Don't yall carry me too fast, now.

BILL *(indicating liquor bottles)* I got what you see and also some wine . . . couple-a cans-a beer.

TOMMY I'll take the wine.

BILL Yeah, I knew it.

TOMMY Don't wanta start nothin' I can't keep up. *(*OLDTIMER *slaps his thigh with pleasure)*

BILL That's all right, baby, you just a wine-o.

TOMMY You the one that's got the wine, not me.

BILL I use this for cookin'.

TOMMY You like to get loaded while you cook? *(*OLDTIMER *is having a ball)*

BILL *(as he pours wine for* TOMMY*)* Oh, baby, you too much.

OLDTIMER *(admiring* TOMMY*)* Oh, Lord, I wish, I wish, I wish I was young again.

TOMMY *(flirtatiously)* Lively as you are, . . . I don't know what we'd do with you if you got any younger.

OLDTIMER Oh, hush now!

SONNY-MAN *(whispering to* BILL *and pouring drinks)* Didn't I tell you! Know what I'm talkin' about. You dig? All the elements, man.

TOMMY *(worried about what the whispering means)* Let's get somethin' straight I didn't come bustin' in on the party, . . . I was asked. If you married and any wives or girlfriends round here . . . I'm innocent. Don't wanta get shot at, or jumped on. Cause I wasn't doin' a thing but mindin' my business! . . . *(saying the last in loud tones to be heard in other rooms)*

OLDTIMER Jus' us here, that's all.

BILL I'm single, baby. Nobody wants a poor artist.

CYNTHIA Oh, honey, we wouldn't walk you into a jealous wife or girlfriend.

TOMMY You paint all-a these pitchers? *(*BILL *and* SONNY-MAN *hand out drinks)*

BILL Just about. Your health, baby, to you.

TOMMY *(lifts her wine glass)* All right, and I got one for you . . . Like my grampaw used-ta say, . . . Here's to the men's collars and the women's skirts, . . . may they never meet. *(general laughter)*

OLDTIMER But they ain't got far to go before they do.

TOMMY *(suddenly remembers her troubles)* Niggers, niggers . . . niggers, . . . I'm sick-a niggers, ain't you? A nigger will mess up everytime . . . Lemmie tell you what the niggers done . . .

BILL Tommy, baby, we don't use that word around here. We can talk about each other a little better than that.

CYNTHIA Oh, she doesn't mean it.

TOMMY What must I say?

BILL Try Afro-Americans.

TOMMY Well, . . . the Afro-Americans burnt down my house.

OLDTIMER Oh, no they didn't!

TOMMY Oh, yes they did . . . it's almost burn down. Then the firemen nailed up my door . . . the door to my room, nailed up shut tight with all I got in the world.

OLDTIMER Shame, what a shame.

TOMMY A *damn* shame. My clothes . . . Everything gone. This riot blew my life. All I got is gone like it never was.

OLDTIMER I know it.

TOMMY My transistor radio . . . that's gone.

CYNTHIA Ah, gee.

TOMMY The transistor . . . and a brand new pair-a shoes I never had on one time . . . *(raises her right hand)* If I never move, that's the truth . . . new shoes gone.

OLDTIMER Child, when hard luck fall it just keep fallin'.

TOMMY And in my top dresser drawer I got a my-on-ase jar with forty-one dollars in it. The fireman would not let me in to get it . . . And it was a Afro-American fireman, don'tcha know.

OLDTIMER And you ain't got no place to stay. *(*BILL *is studying her for portrait possibilities)*

TOMMY *(rises and walks around room)* That's a lie. I always got some place to go. I don't wanta boast but I ain't never been no place that I can't go back the second time. Woman I use to work for say . . . "Tommy, any time, any time you want a sleep-in place you come right here to me." . . . And that's Park Avenue, my own private bath and T.V. set . . . But I don't want that . . . so I make it on out here to the dress factory. I got friends . . . not a lot of 'em . . . but a few *good* ones. I call my friend—girl and her mother . . . they say . . . "Tommy, you come here, bring yourself over here." So Tommy got a roof with no sweat. *(looks at torn walls)* Looks like the Afro-Americans got to you too. Breakin' up, breakin' down, . . . that's all they know.

BILL No, Tommy, . . . I'm re-decorating the place . . .

TOMMY You mean you did this to yourself?

CYNTHIA It's gonna be wild . . . brick-face walls . . . wall to wall carpet.

SONNY-MAN She was breakin' up everybody in the bar . . . had us all laughin'—crackin' us up. In the middle of a riot . . . she's gassin' everybody!

TOMMY No need to cry, it's sad enough. They hollerin' whitey, whitey . . . but who they burn out? Me.

BILL The brothers and sisters are tired, weary of the endless get-no-where struggle.

TOMMY I'm standin' there in the bar . . . tellin' it like it is . . . next thing I know they talkin' bout bringin' me to meet you. But you know what I say? Can't nobody pick nobody for nobody else. It don't work. And I'm standin' there in a mis-match skirt and top and these sneaker-shoes. I just went to put my dresses in the cleaner . . . Oh, Lord, wonder if they burn down the cleaner. Well, no matter, when I got back it was all over . . . They went in the grocery store, rip out the shelves, pull out all the groceries . . . the hams . . . the . . . the . . . the can goods . . . everything . . . and then set fire . . . Now who you think live over the grocery? Me, that's who. I don't even go to the store lookin' this way . . . but this would be the time, when . . . folks got a fella they want me to meet.

BILL *(suddenly self-conscious)* Tommy, they thought . . . they thought I'd like to paint you . . . that's why they asked you over.

TOMMY *(pleased by the thought but she can't understand it)* Paint me? For what? If he was gonna paint somebody seems to me it'd be one of the pretty girls they show in the beer ads. They even got colored on television now, . . . brushin' their teeth and smokin' cigarettes, . . .

some of the prettiest girls in the world. He could get them, . . . couldn't you?

BILL Sonny-man and Cynthia were right. I want to paint you.

TOMMY *(suspiciously)* Naked, with no clothes on?

BILL No, baby dressed just as you are now.

OLDTIMER Wearin' clothes is also art.

TOMMY In the cleaner I got a white dress with a orlon sweater to match it, maybe I can get it out tomorrow and pose in that. *(*CYNTHIA, OLDTIMER *and* SONNY-MAN *are eager for her to agree)*

BILL No, I will paint you today, Tommy, just as you are, holding your brown paper bag.

TOMMY Mmmmmm, me holdin' the damn bag. I don' know 'bout that.

BILL Look at it this way, tonight has been a tragedy.

TOMMY Sure in hell has.

BILL And so I must paint you tonight, . . . Tommy in her moment of tragedy.

TOMMY I'm tired.

BILL Damn, baby, all you have to do is sit there and rest.

TOMMY I'm hongry.

SONNY-MAN While you're posin' Cynthia can run down to our house and fix you some eggs.

CYNTHIA *(gives her husband a weary look)* Oh, Sonny, that's such a lovely idea.

SONNY-MAN Thank you, darlin', I'm in there, . . . on the beam.

TOMMY *(ill at ease about posing)* I don't want no eggs. I'm goin' to find me some Chinee food.

BILL I'll go. If you promise to stay here and let me paint you, . . . I'll get you anything you want.

TOMMY *(brightening up)* Anything I want. Now, how he sound? All right, you comin' on mighty strong there. "Anything you want." When last you heard somebody say that? . . . I'm warnin' you, now, . . . I'm free, single and disengage, . . . so you better watch yourself.

BILL *(keeping her away from ideas of romance)* Now this is the way the program will go down. First I'll feed you, then I'll paint you.

TOMMY Okay, I'm game, I'm a good sport. First off, I want me some Chinee food.

CYNTHIA Order up, Tommy, the treat's on him.

TOMMY How come it is you never been married? All these girls runnin' round Harlem lookin' for husbands. *(to* CYNTHIA*)* I don't blame 'em, 'cause I'm looking for somebody myself.

BILL I've been married, married and divorced, she divorced me, Tommy, so maybe I'm not much of a catch.

TOMMY Look at it this-a-way. Some folks got bad taste. That woman had bad taste. *(all laugh except* BILL *who pours another drink)* Watch it, Bill, you gonna rust the linin' of your stomach. Ain't this a shame? The riot done wipe me out and I'm sittin' here havin' me a ball. Sittin' here ballin' *(as* BILL *refills her glass)* Hold it, that's enough. Likker ain' my problem.

OLDTIMER I'm havin' me a good time.

TOMMY Know what I say 'bout divorce. *(slaps her hands together in a final gesture)* Anybody don' wantcha, . . . later, let 'em go. That's bad taste for you.

BILL Tommy, I don't wanta ever get married again. It's me and my work. I'm not gettin' serious about anybody . . .

TOMMY He's spellin' at me, now. Nigger, . . . I mean Afro-American . . . I ain' ask you nothin'. You hinkty, I'm hinkty too. I'm independent as a hog on ice, . . . and a hog on ice is dead, cold, well-preserved . . . and don't need a mother-grabbin' thing. *(all laugh heartily except* BILL *and* CYNTHIA*)* I know models get paid. I ain' no square but this is a special night and so this one'll be on the house. Show you my heart's in the right place.

BILL I'll be glad to pay you, baby.

TOMMY You don't really like me, do you? That's all right, sometime it happen that way. You can't pick for *nobody*. Friends get to matchin' up friends and they mess up everytime. Cynthia and Sonny-man done messed up.

BILL I like you just fine and I'm glad and grateful that you came.

TOMMY Good enough. *(extends her hand. They slap hands together)* You'n me friends?

BILL Friends, baby, friends. *(putting rock record on)*

TOMMY *(trying out the model stand)* Okay, Dad! Let's see 'bout this *anything I want* jive. Want me a bucket-a Egg Foo Yong, and you get you a shrimp-fry rice, we split that and each have some-a both. Make him give you the soy sauce, the hot mustard and the duck sauce too.

BILL Anything else, baby?

TOMMY Since you ask, yes. If your money hold out, get me a double order egg roll. And a half order of the sweet and sour spare ribs.

BILL *(to* OLDTIMER *and* SONNY-MAN*)* Come on, come on. I need some strong men to help me bring back your order, baby.

TOMMY *(going into her dance . . . simply standing and going through some boo-ga-loo motions)* Better go get it 'fore I think up some more to go 'long with it. *(the men laugh and vanish out of the door. Steps heard descending stairs)* Turn that off. (CYNTHIA *turns off record player)* How could I forget your name, good as you been to me this day. Thank you, Cynthia, thank you. I *like* him. Oh, I *like* him. But I don't wanta push him too fast. Oh, I got to play these cards right.

CYNTHIA *(a bit uncomfortable)* Oh, Honey, . . . Tommy, you don't want a poor artist.

TOMMY Tommy's not lookin' for a meal ticket. I been doin' for myself all my life. It takes two to make it in this high-price world. A Black man see a hard way to go. The both of you gotta pull together. That way you accomplish.

CYNTHIA I'm a social worker . . . and I see so many broken homes. Some of these men! Tommy, don't be in a rush about the marriage thing.

TOMMY Keep it to yourself, . . . but I was thirty my last birthday and haven't ever been married. I coulda been. Oh, yes, indeed, coulda been. But I don't want any and everybody. What I want with a no-good piece-a nothin'? I'll never forget what the Reverend Martin Luther King said . . . "I have a dream." I liked him sayin' it 'cause truer words have never been spoke. *(straightening the room)* I have a dream, too. Mine is to find a man who'll treat me just half-way decent . . . just to meet me half-way is all I ask, to smile, to be kind to me. Somebody in my corner. Not to wake up by myself in the mornin' and face this world all alone.

CYNTHIA About Bill, it's best not to ever count on anything, anything at all, Tommy.

TOMMY *(this remark bothers her for a split second but she shakes it off)* Of course, Cynthia, that's one of the foremost rules of life. Don't count on *nothin'!*

CYNTHIA Right, don't be too quick to put your trust in these men.

TOMMY You put your trust in one and got yourself a husband.

CYNTHIA Well, yes, but what I mean is . . . Oh, you know. A man is a man and Bill is also an artist and his work comes before all else and there are other factors . . .

TOMMY *(sits facing* CYNTHIA*)* What's wrong with me?

CYNTHIA I don't know what you mean.

TOMMY Yes you do. You tryin' to tell me I'm aimin' too high by lookin' at Bill.

CYNTHIA Oh, no, my dear.

TOMMY Out there in the street, in the bar, you and your husband were so sure that he'd *like* me and want to paint my picture.

CYNTHIA But he does want to paint you, he's very eager to . . .

TOMMY But why? Somethin' don't fit right.

CYNTHIA *(feeling sorry for* TOMMY*)* If you don't want to do it, just leave and that'll be that.

TOMMY Walk out while he's buyin' me what I ask for, spendin' his money on me? That'd be too dirty. *(looks at books. Takes one from shelf)* Books, books, books everywhere. "Afro-American History." I like that. What's wrong with me, Cynthia? Tell me, I won't get mad with you, I swear. If there's somethin' wrong that I can change, I'm ready to do it. Eighth grade, that's all I had of school. You a social worker, I know that mean college. I come from poor people. *(examining the book in her hand)* Talkin' 'bout poverty this and poverty that and studyin' it. When you *in* it you don' be studyin' 'bout it. Cynthia, I remember my mother tyin' up her stockin's with strips-a-rag 'cause she didn't have no garters. When I get home from school she'd say, . . . "Nothin' much here to eat." Nothin' much might be grits, or bread and coffee. I got sick-a all that, got me a job. Later for school.

CYNTHIA The Matriarchal Society.

TOMMY What's that?

CYNTHIA A Matriarchal Society is one in which the women rule . . . the women have the power . . . the women head the house.

TOMMY We didn't have nothin' to rule over, not a pot nor a window. And my papa picked hisself up and run off with some finger-poppin' woman and we never hear another word 'til ten, twelve years later when a undertaker call up and ask if Mama wanta come claim his body. And don'cha know, Mama went on over and claim it. A woman need a man to claim, even if it's a dead one. What's wrong with me? Be honest.

CYNTHIA You're a fine person . . .

TOMMY Go on, I can take it.

CYNTHIA You're too brash. You're too used to looking out for yourself. It makes us lose our femininity . . . It makes us hard . . . it makes us seem very hard. We do for ourselves too much.

TOMMY If I don't, who's gonna do for me?

CYNTHIA You have to let the Black man have his manhood again. You have to give it back, Tommy.

TOMMY I didn't take it from him, how I'm gonna give it back? What else is the matter with me? You had school, I didn't. I respect that.

CYNTHIA Yes, I've had it, the degree and the whole bit. For a time I thought I was about to move into another world, the so-called "integrated" world, a place where knowledge and know-how could set you free and open all the doors, but that's a lie. I turned away from that idea. The first thing I did was give up dating white fellas.

TOMMY I never had none to give up. I'm not soundin' on you. White folks, nothin' happens when I look at 'em. I don't hate 'em, don't love 'em, . . . just nothin' shakes a-tall. The dullest people in the world. The way they talk . . . "Oh, hooty, hooty, hoo" . . . Break it down for me to A, B, C's. That Bill . . . I like him, with his Black, uppity, high-handed ways. What do you do to get a man you want? A social worker oughta tell you things like that.

CYNTHIA Don't chase him . . . at least don't let it look that way. Let him pursue you.

TOMMY What if he won't? Men don't chase me much, not the kind I like.

CYNTHIA *(rattles off instructions glibly)* Let him do the talking. Learn to listen. Stay in the background a little. Ask his opinion . . . "what do *you* think, Bill?"

TOMMY Mmmmm, "Oh, hooty, hooty, hoo."

CYNTHIA But why count on him? There are lots of other nice guys.

TOMMY You don't think he'd go for me, do you?

CYNTHIA *(trying to be diplomatic)* Perhaps you're not really his type.

TOMMY Maybe not, but he's mine. I'm so lonesome . . . I'm *lonesome* . . . I want somebody to love. Somebody to say . . . "That's all-right," when the world treats me mean.

CYNTHIA Tommy, I think you're too good for Bill.

TOMMY I don't wanta hear that. The last man that told me I was too good for him . . . was tryin' to get away. He's good enough for me. *(straightening room)*

CYNTHIA Leave the room alone. What we need is a little more sex appeal and a little less washing, cooking and ironing. *(*TOMMY *puts down the room straightening)* One more thing, . . . do you have to wear that wig?

TOMMY *(a little sensitive)* I like how *your* hair looks. But some of the naturals I don't like. Can see all the lint caught up in the hair like it hasn't been combed since know not when. You a Muslim?

CYNTHIA No.

TOMMY I'm just sick-a hair, hair, hair. Do it this way, don't do it, leave it natural, straighten it, process, no process. I get sick-a hair and talkin' 'bout it and foolin' with it. That's why I wear the wig.

CYNTHIA I'm sure your own must be just as nice or nicer than that.

TOMMY It oughta be. I only paid nineteen ninety five for this.

CYNTHIA You ought to go back to usin' your own.

TOMMY *(tensely)* I'll be givin' that some thought.

CYNTHIA You're pretty nice people just as you are. Soften up, Tommy. You might surprise yourself.

TOMMY I'm listenin'.

CYNTHIA Expect more. Learn to let men open doors for you . . .

TOMMY What if I'm standin' there and they don't open it?

CYNTHIA *(trying to level with her)* You're a fine person. He wants to paint you, that's all. He's doing a kind of mural thing and we thought he would enjoy painting you. I'd hate to see you expecting more out of the situation than what's there.

TOMMY Forget it, sweetie-pie, don' nothin' that's not suppose to. *(sound of laughter in the hall.* BILL, OLDTIMER *and* SONNY-MAN *enter)*

BILL No Chinese restaurant left, baby! It's wiped out. Gone with the revolution.

SONNY-MAN *(to* CYNTHIA*)* Baby, let's move, split the scene, get on with it, time for home.

BILL The revolution is here. Whatta you do with her? You paint her!

SONNY-MAN You write her . . . you write the revolution into a novel nine hundred pages long.

BILL Dance it! Sing it! "Down in the cornfield hear dat mournful sound . . . *(*SONNY-MAN *and* OLDTIMER *harmonize.)* Dear old Massa am-a sleepin' in the cold, cold ground." Now for "Wine In The Wilderness!" Triptych will be finished.

CYNTHIA *(in* BILL*'s face)* "Wine In The Wilderness," huh? Exploitation!

SONNY-MAN Upstairs, all out, come on, Oldtimer. Folks can't create in a crowd. Cynthia, move it, baby.

OLDTIMER *(starting toward the window)* My things! I got a package.

SONNY-MAN *(heads him off)* Up and out. You don't have to go home, but you have to get outta here. Happy paintin', yall. *(one backward look and they are all gone)*

BILL Whatta night, whatta night, whatta night, baby. It will be painted, written, sung and discussed for generations.

TOMMY *(notices nothing that looks like Chinese food. He is carrying a small bag and a container)* Where's the Foo-Yong?

BILL They blew the restaurant, baby. All I could get was a couple-a franks and a orange drink from the stand.

TOMMY *(tersely)* You brought me a frankfooter? That's what you think-a me, a frankfooter?

BILL Nothin' to do with what I think. Place is closed.

TOMMY *(quietly surly)* This is the damn City-a New York, any hour on the clock they sellin' the chicken in the basket, barbecue ribs, pizza pie, hot pastrami samitches; and you brought me a frank-footer?

BILL Baby, don't break bad over somethin' to eat. The smart set, the jet set, the beautiful people, kings and queens eat frankfurters.

TOMMY If a queen sent you out to buy her a bucket-a Foo-yung, you wouldn't come back with no lonely-ass frank-footer.

BILL Kill me 'bout it, baby! Go 'head and shoot me six times. That's the trouble with our women, yall always got your mind on food.

TOMMY Is that our trouble? *(laughs)* Maybe you right. Only two things to do. Either eat the frankfooter or walk outta here. You got any mustard?

BILL *(gets mustard from the refrigerator)* Let's face it, our folks are not together. The brothers and sisters have busted up Harlem, . . . no plan, no nothin'. There's your Black revolution, heads whipped, hospital full and we still in the same old bag.

TOMMY *(seated at the kitchen table)* Maybe what everybody need is somebody like you, who know how things oughta go, to get on out there and start some action.

BILL You still mad about the frankfurter?

TOMMY No. I keep seein' pitchers of what was in my room and how it all must be spoiled now. *(sips the orange drink)* A orange never been near this. Well, it's cold. *(looking at an incense burner)* What's that?

BILL An incense burner, was given to me by the Chinese guy, Richard Lee. I'm sorry they blew his restaurant.

TOMMY Does it help you to catch the number?

BILL No, baby, I just burn incense sometime.

TOMMY For what?

BILL Just 'cause I feel like it. Baby, ain't you used to nothin'?

TOMMY Ain't used to burnin' incent for nothin'.

BILL *(laughs)* Burnin' what?

TOMMY That stuff.

BILL What did you call it?

TOMMY Incent.

BILL It's not incent, baby. It's incense.

TOMMY Like the sense you got in your head. In-sense. Thank you. You're a very correctable person, ain't you?

BILL Let's put you on canvas.

TOMMY *(stubbornly)* I have to eat first.

BILL That's another thing 'bout Black women, they wanta eat 'fore they do anything else. Tommy, . . . Tommy, . . . I bet your name is Thomasina. You look like a Thomasina.

TOMMY You could sit there and guess til your eyes pop out and you never would guess my first name. You might could guess the middle name but not the first one.

BILL Tell it to me.

TOMMY My name is Tomorrow.

BILL How's that?

TOMMY Tomorrow, . . . like yesterday and *tomorrow,* and the middle name is just plain

Marie. That's what my father name me, Tomorrow Marie. My mother say he thought it had a pretty sound.

BILL Crazy! I never met a girl named Tomorrow.

TOMMY They got to callin' me Tommy for short, so I stick with that. Tomorrow Marie, . . . Sound like a promise that can never happen.

BILL *(straightens chair on stand. He is very eager to start painting)* That's what Shakespeare said, . . . "Tomorrow and tomorrow and tomorrow." Tomorrow, you will be on this canvas.

TOMMY *(still uneasy about being painted)* What's the hurry? Rome wasn't built in a day, . . . that's another saying.

BILL If I finish in time, I'll enter you in an exhibition.

TOMMY *(loses interest in the food. Examines the room. Looks at portrait on the wall)* He looks like somebody I know or maybe saw before.

BILL That's Frederick Douglass. A man who used to be a slave. He escaped and spent his life trying to make us all free. He was a great man.

TOMMY Thank you, Mr. Douglass. Who's the light colored man? *(indicates a frame next to the Douglass)*

BILL He's white. That's John Brown. They killed him for tryin' to shoot the country outta the slavery bag. He dug us, you know. Old John said, "Hell no, slavery must go."

TOMMY I heard all about him. Some folks say he was crazy.

BILL If he had been shootin' at *us* they wouldn't have called him a nut.

TOMMY School wasn't a great part-a my life.

BILL If it was you wouldn't-a found out too much 'bout Black history cause the books full-a nothin' but whitey, . . . all except the white ones who dug us, . . . they not there either. Tell me, . . . who was Elijah Lovejoy?

TOMMY Elijah Lovejoy, . . . Mmmmmmm. I don't know. Have to do with the Bible?

BILL No, that's another white fella, . . . Elijah had a printin' press and the main thing he printed was "Slavery got to go." Well the man moved in on him, smashed his press time after time . . . but he kept puttin' it back together and doin' his thing. So, one final day, they came in a mob and burned him to death.

TOMMY *(blows her nose with sympathy as she fights tears)* That's dirty.

BILL *(as* TOMMY *glances at titles in bookcase)* Who was Monroe Trotter?

TOMMY Was he white?

BILL No, soul brother. Spent his years tryin' to make it all right. Who was Harriet Tubman?

TOMMY I heard-a her. But don't put me through no test, Billy. *(moving around studying pictures and books)* This *room* is full-a things I don' know nothin' about. How'll I get to know?

BILL Read, go to the library, book stores, ask somebody.

TOMMY Okay, I'm askin'. Teach me things.

BILL Aw, baby, why torment yourself? Trouble with our women, . . . they all wanta be great brains. Leave somethin' for a man to do.

TOMMY *(eager to impress him)* What you think-a Martin Luther King?

BILL A great guy. But it's too late in the day for the singin' and prayin' now.

TOMMY What about Malcolm X.?

BILL Great cat . . . but there again . . . Where's the program?

TOMMY What about Adam Powell? I voted for him. That's one thing 'bout me. I vote. Maybe if everybody vote for the right people . . .

BILL The ballot box. It would take me all my life to straighten you on that hype.

TOMMY I got the time.

BILL You gonna wind up with a king size headache. The Matriarchy gotta go. Yall throw them suppers together, keep your husband happy, raise the kids.

TOMMY I don't have a husband. Course, that could be fixed. *(leaving the unspoken proposal hanging in the air)*

BILL You know the greatest thing you could do for your people? Sit up there and let me put you down on canvas.

TOMMY Bein' married and havin' a family might be good for your people as a race, but I was thinkin' bout myself a little.

BILL Forget yourself sometime, sugar. On that canvas you'll be givin' and givin' and givin' . . . That's where you can do your thing best. What you stallin' for?

TOMMY *(returns to table and sits in chair)* I . . . I don't want to pose in this outfit.

BILL *(patience is wearing thin)* Why, baby, why?

TOMMY I don't feel proud-a myself in this.

BILL Art, baby, we talkin' art. Whatcha want . . . Ribbons? Lace? False eyelashes?

TOMMY No, just my white dress with the orlon sweater, . . . or anything but this what I'm wearin'. You oughta see me in that dress with my pink linen shoes. Oh, hell, the shoes are gone. I forgot 'bout the fire . . .

BILL Oh, stop fightin' me! Another thing . . . our women don't know a damn thing bout bein' feminine. *Give in* sometime. It won't kill you. You tellin' me how to paint? Maybe you oughta hang out your shingle and give art lessons! You too damn opinionated. You gonna pose or you not gonna pose? Say somethin'!

TOMMY You makin' me nervous! Hollerin' at me. My mama never holler at me. Hollerin'.

BILL I'll soon be too tired to pick up the brush, baby.

TOMMY *(eye catches picture of white woman on the wall)* That's a white woman! Bet you never hollered at her and I bet she's your girlfriend . . . too, and when she posed for her pitcher I bet yall was laughin' . . . and you didn't buy her no frankfooter!

BILL *(feels a bit smug about his male prowess)* Awww, come on, cut that out, baby. That's a little blonde, blue-eyed chick who used to pose for me. That ain't where it's at. This is a new day, the deal is goin' down different. This is the Black moment, doll. Black, Black, Black, is bee-yoo-tee-full. Got it? *Black is beautiful.*

TOMMY Then how come it is that I don't *feel* beautiful when you *talk* to me?!!

BILL That's your hang-up, not mine. You supposed to stretch forth your wings like Ethiopia, shake off them chains that been holdin' you down. Langston Hughes said let 'em see how beautiful you are. But you determined not to ever be beautiful. Okay, that's what makes you Tommy.

TOMMY Do you *have* a girlfriend? And who is she?

BILL *(now enjoying himself to the utmost)* Naw, naw, naw, doll. I *know* people, but none-a this "tie-you-up-and-I-own-you" jive. I ain't mistreatin' nobody and there's enough-a me to go around. That's another thing with our women, . . . they want a *latch* on. Learn to play it by ear, roll with the punches, cut down on some-a this "got-you-to-the-grave" kinda relationship. Was today all right? Good, be glad, . . . take what's at hand because tomorrow never comes, it's always today. *(she begins to cry)* Awwww, I didn't mean it that way . . . I forgot your name. *(he brushes her tears away)* You act like I belong to you. You're jealous of a picture?

TOMMY That's how women are, always studyin' each other and wonderin' how they look up 'gainst the next person.

BILL *(a bit smug)* That's human nature. Whatcha call healthy competition.

TOMMY You think she's pretty?

BILL She was, perhaps still is. Long, silky hair. She could sit on her hair.

TOMMY *(with bitter arrogance)* Doesn't *everybody?*

BILL You got a head like a rock and gonna have the last word if it kills you. Baby, I bet you could knock out Mohamud Ali in the first round, then rare back and scream like Tarzan . . . "Now, I am the greatest!" *(he is very close to her and is amazed to feel a great sense of physical attraction)* What we arguin' bout? *(looks her over as she looks away. He suddenly want to put the conversation on a more intimate level. His eye is on the bed)* Maybe tomorrow would be a better time for paintin'. Wanna freshen up, take a bath, baby? Water's nice n' hot.

TOMMY *(knows the sound and turns to check on the look. Notices him watching the bed. Starts weeping)* No, I don't, Nigger!

BILL Was that nice? What the hell, let's paint the picture. Or are you gonna hold that back too?

TOMMY I'm posin'. Shall I take off the wig?

BILL No, it's a part of your image, ain't it? You must have a reason for wearin' it. *(*TOMMY *snatches up her orange drink and sits in the model's chair)*

TOMMY *(with defiance)* Yes, I wear it cause you and those like you go for long, silky hair, and this is the only way I can have some without burnin' my mother-grabbin' brains out. Got it? *(she accidently knocks over container of orange drink into her lap)* Hell, I can't wear this. I'm soaked through. I'm not gonna catch no double pneumonia sittin' up here wringin' wet while you paint and holler at me.

BILL Bitch!

TOMMY You must be talkin' bout your mama!

BILL Shut up! Aw, shut-up! *(phone rings. He finds a African throw-cloth and hands it to her)*

Put this on. Relax, don't go way mad, and all the rest-a that jazz. Change, will you? I apologize. I'm sorry. *(he picks up phone)* Hello, survivor of a riot speaking. Who's calling? *(*TOMMY *retires behind the screen with the throw. During the conversation she undresses and wraps the throw around her. We see* TOMMY *and* BILL*, but they can't see each other)* Sure, told you not to worry. I'll be ready for the exhibit. If you don't dig it, don't show it. Not time for you to see it yet. Yeah, yeah, next week. You just make sure your exhibition room is big enough to hold the crowds that's gonna congregate to see this fine chick I got here. *(this perks* TOMMY*'s ears up)* You oughta see her. The finest Black woman in the world . . . This gorgeous satin chick is . . . is . . . black velvet moonlight . . . an ebony queen of the universe . . . *(*TOMMY *can hardly believe her ears)* One look at her and you go back to Spice Islands . . . She's Mother Africa . . . You flip, double flip. She has come through everything that has been put on her . . . *(he unveils the gorgeous woman he has painted . . . "Wine In The Wilderness."* TOMMY *believes he is talking about her)* Regal . . . grand . . . magnificent, fantastic . . . You would vote her the woman you'd most like to meet on a desert island, or around the corner from anywhere. She's here with me now . . . and I don't know if I want to show her to you or anybody else . . . I'm beginnin' to have this deep attachment . . . She sparkles, man, Harriet Tubman, Queen of the Nile . . . sweetheart, wife, mother, sister, friend . . . The night . . . a black diamond . . . A dark, beautiful dream . . . A cloud with a silvery lining . . . Her wrath is a storm over the Bahamas. "Wine In the Wilderness" . . . The memory of Africa . . . The *now* of things . . . but best of all and most important . . . She's tomorrow . . . she's my tomorrow . . . *(*TOMMY *is dressed in the African wrap. She is suddenly awakened to the feeling of being loved and admired. She removes the wig and fluffs her hair. Her hair under the wig must not be an accurate, well-cut Afro . . . but should be rather attractive natural hair. She studies herself in a mirror. We see her taller, more relaxed and sure of herself. Perhaps braided hair will go well with Afro robe)* Aw, man, later. You don't believe in nothin'! *(he covers "Wine In The Wilderness." Is now in a glowing mood)* Baby, whenever you ready. *(she emerges from behind the screen. Dressed in the wrap, sans wig. He is astounded)* Baby, what . . . ? Where . . . where's the wig?

TOMMY I don't think I want to wear it, Bill.

BILL That is very becoming . . . the drape thing.

TOMMY Thank you.

BILL I don't know what to say.

TOMMY It's time to paint. *(steps up on the model stand and sits in the chair. She is now a queen, relaxed and smiling her appreciation for his last speech to the art dealer. Her feet are bare)*

BILL *(mystified by the change in her. Tries to do a charcoal sketch)* It is quite late.

TOMMY Makes me no difference if it's all right with you.

BILL *(wants to create the other image)* Could you put the wig back on?

TOMMY You don't really like wigs, do you?

BILL Well, no.

TOMMY Then let's have things the way you like.

BILL *(has no answer for this. He makes a haphazard line or two as he tries to remember the other image)* Tell me something about yourself, . . . anything.

TOMMY *(now on sure ground)* I was born in Baltimore, Maryland and raised here in Harlem. My favorite flower is "Four O'clocks," that's a bush flower. My wearin' flower, corsage flower, is pink roses. My mama raised me, mostly by herself, God rest the dead. Mama belonged to "The Eastern Star." Her father was a "Mason." If a man in the family is a "Mason" any woman related to him can be an "Eastern Star." My grandfather was a member of "The Prince Hall Lodge." I had a uncle who was an "Elk," . . . a member of "The Improved Benevolent Protective Order of Elks of the World": "The Henry Lincoln Johnson Lodge." You know, the white "Elks" are called "The Benevolent Protective Order of Elks" but the Black "Elks" are called "The *Improved* Benevolent Protective Order of Elks of *the World.*" That's because the Black "Elks" got the copyright first but the white "Elks" took us to court about it to keep us from usin' the name. Over fifteen hundred Black folk went to jail for wearin' the "Elk" emblem on their coat lapel. Years ago, . . . that's what you call history.

BILL I didn't know about that.

TOMMY Oh, it's understandable. Only way I heard bout John Brown was because the

Black "Elks" bought his farmhouse where he trained his men to attack the government.

BILL The Black "Elks" bought the John Brown Farm? What did they do with it?

TOMMY They built a outdoor theater and put a perpetual light in his memory, . . . and they buildin' cottages there, one named for each state in the union and . . .

BILL How do you know about it?

TOMMY Well, our "Elks" helped my cousin go through school with a scholarship. She won a speaking contest and wrote a composition titled "Onward and Upward, O, My Race." That's how she won the scholarship. Coreen knows all that Elk history.

BILL *(seeing her with new eyes)* Tell me some more about you, Tomorrow Marie. I bet you go to church.

TOMMY Not much as I used to. Early in life I pledged myself in the A.M.E. Zion Church.

BILL *(studying her face, seeing her for the first time)* A.M.E.

TOMMY A.M.E. That's African Methodist Episcopal. We split off from the white Methodist Episcopal and started our own in the year Seventeen hundred and ninety six. We built our first buildin' in the year 1800. How 'bout that?

BILL That right?

TOMMY Oh, I'm just showin' off. I taught Sunday School for two years and you had to know the history of A.M.E. Zion . . . or else you couldn't teach. My great, great grandparents was slaves.

BILL Guess everybody's was.

TOMMY Mine was slaves in a place called Sweetwater Springs, Virginia. We tried to look it up one time but somebody at Church told us that Sweetwater Springs had become a part of Norfolk . . . so we didn't carry it any further . . . As it would be a expense to have a lawyer trace your people.

BILL *(throws charcoal pencil across room)* No good! It won't work! I can't work anymore.

TOMMY Take a rest. Tell me about you.

BILL *(sits on bed)* Everybody in my family worked for the Post Office. They bought a home in Jamaica, Long Island. Everybody on that block bought an aluminum screen door with a duck on it, . . . or was it a swan? I guess that makes my favorite flower crab grass and hedges. I have a lot of bad dreams. *(*TOMMY *massages his temples and the back of his neck)* A dream like suffocating, dying of suffocation. The worst kinda dream. People are standing in a weird looking art gallery, they're looking and laughing at everything I've ever done. My work begins to fade off the canvas, right before my eyes. Everything I've ever done is laughed away.

TOMMY Don't be so hard on yourself. If I was smart as you I'd wake up singin' every mornin'. *(there is the sound of thunder. He kisses her)* When it thunders that's the angels in heaven playin' with their hoops, rollin' their hoops and bicycle wheels in the rain. My Mama told me that.

BILL I'm glad you're here. Black *is* beautiful, you're beautiful, A.M.E. Zion, Elks, pink roses, bush flower, . . . blooming out of the slavery of Sweetwater Springs, Virginia.

TOMMY I'm gonna take a bath and let the riot and the hell of living go down the drain with the bath water.

BILL Tommy, Tommy, Tomorrow Marie, let's save each other, let's be kind and good to each other while it rains and the angels roll those hoops and bicycle wheels.

(They embrace. The sound of rain. Music in as lights come down. As lights fade down to darkness, music comes in louder. There is a flash of lightning. We see TOMMY *and* BILL *in each other's arms. It is very dark. Music up louder, then softer and down to very soft. Music is mixed with the sound of rain beating against the window. Music slowly fades as gray light of dawn shows at window. Lights go up gradually. The bed is rumpled and empty.* BILL *is in the bathroom.* TOMMY *is at the stove turning off the coffee pot. She sets table with cups and saucers, spoons.* TOMMY*'s hair is natural, she wears another throw [African design] draped around her. She sings and hums a snatch of a joyous spiritual)*

TOMMY "Great day, Great day, the world's on fire, Great day . . ." *(calling out to* BILL *who is in the bath)* Honey, I found the coffee, and it's ready. Nothin' here to go with it but a cucumber and a Uneeda biscuit.

BILL *(offstage. Joyous yell from offstage)* Tomorrow and tomorrow and tomorrow! Good mornin', Tomorrow!

TOMMY *(more to herself than to* BILL*)* "Tomorrow and tomorrow." That's Shakespeare. *(calls to* BILL*)* You say that was Shakespeare?

BILL *(offstage)* Right, baby, right!

TOMMY I bet Shakespeare was Black! You know how we love poetry. That's what give him away. I bet he was passin'. *(laughs)*

BILL *(offstage)* Just you wait, one hundred years from now all the honkeys gonna claim our poets just like they stole our blues. They gonna try to steal Paul Laurence Dunbar and LeRoi and Margaret Walker.

TOMMY *(to herself)* God moves in a mysterious way, even in the middle of a riot. *(a knock on the door)* Great day, great day the world's on fire . . . *(opens the door,* OLDTIMER *enters. He is soaking wet. He does not recognize her right away)*

OLDTIMER "Scuse me, I must be in the wrong place.

TOMMY *(patting her hair)* This is me. Come on in, Edmond Lorenzo Matthews. I took off my hair-piece. This is me.

OLDTIMER *(very distracted and worried)* Well, howdy-do and good mornin'. *(he has had a hard night of drinking and sleeplessness)* Where Billy-boy? It pourin' down some rain out there. *(makes his way to the window)*

TOMMY What's the matter?

OLDTIMER *(raises the window and starts pulling in the cord, the cord is weightless and he realizes there is nothing on the end of it)* No, no, it can't be. Where is it? It's gone! *(looks out the window)*

TOMMY You gonna catch your death. You wringin' wet.

OLDTIMER Yall take my things in? It was a bag-a loot. A suit and some odds and ends. It was my loot. Yall took it in?

TOMMY No. *(realizes his desperation. She calls to* BILL *through the closed bathroom door)* Did you take in any loot that was outside the window?

BILL *(offstage)* No.

TOMMY He said "no."

OLDTIMER *(yells out window)* Thieves, . . . dirty thieves . . . lotta good it'll do you . . .

TOMMY *(leads him to a chair, dries his head with a towel)* Get outta the wet things. You smell just like a whiskey still. Why don't you take care of yourself. *(dries off his hands)*

OLDTIMER Drinkin' with the boys. Likker was everywhere all night long.

TOMMY You got to be better than this.

OLDTIMER Everything I ever put my hand and mind to do, it turn out wrong, . . . Nothin' but mistakes . . . When you don' know, you don' know. I don' know nothin'. I'm ignorant.

TOMMY Hush that talk . . . You know lotsa things, everybody does. *(helps him remove wet coat)*

OLDTIMER Thanks. How's the trip-tick?

TOMMY The what?

OLDTIMER *Trip-tick.* That's a paintin'.

TOMMY See there, you know more about art than I do. What's a trip-tick? Have some coffee and explain me a trip-tick.

OLDTIMER *(proud of his knowledge)* Well, I tell you, . . . a trip-tick is a paintin' that's in three parts . . . but they all belong together to be looked at all at once. Now . . . this is the first one . . . a little innocent girl . . . *(unveils picture)*

TOMMY She's sweet.

OLDTIMER And this is "Wine In The Wilderness" . . . The Queen of the Universe . . . the finest chick in the world.

TOMMY *(*TOMMY *is thoughtful as he unveils the second picture)* That's not me.

OLDTIMER No, you gonna be this here last one. The worst gal in town. A messed-up chick that—that—*(he unveils the third canvas and is face to face with the almost blank canvas, then realizes what he has said. He turns to see the stricken look on* TOMMY*'s face)*

TOMMY The messed-up chick, *that's* why they brought me here, ain't it? That's why he wanted to paint me! Say it!

OLDTIMER No, I'm lyin', I didn't mean it. It's the society that messed her up. Awwwwww, Tommy, don't look that-a-way. It's art, . . . it's only art . . . He couldn't mean you . . . it's art . . . *(the door opens.* CYNTHIA *and* SONNY-MAN *enter)*

SONNY-MAN Anybody want a ride down . . . down . . . down . . . downtown? What's wrong? Excuse me . . . *(starts back out)*

TOMMY *(blocking the exit to* CYNTHIA *and* SONNY-MAN*)* No, come on in. Stay with it . . . "Brother" . . . "Sister." Tell 'em what a trip-tick is, Oldtimer.

CYNTHIA *(very ashamed)* Oh, no.

TOMMY You don't have to tell 'em. They already know. The messed-up chick! How come you didn't pose for that, my sister? The messed-up chick lost her home last night, . . . burnt out with no place to go. You and Sonny-man gave me comfort, you cheered me up and took me in, . . . *took me in!*

CYNTHIA Tommy, we didn't know you, we didn't mean . . .

TOMMY It's all right! I was lost but now I'm found! Yeah, the blind can see! *(she dashes behind the screen and puts on her clothing, sweater, skirt etc.)*

OLDTIMER *(goes the to bathroom door)* Billy, come out!

SONNY-MAN Billy, step out here, please! *(BILL enters shirtless, wearing dungarees)* Oldtimer let it out 'bout the triptych.

BILL The rest of you move on.

TOMMY *(looking out from behind screen)* No, don't go a step. You brought me here, see me out!

BILL Tommy, let me explain it to you.

TOMMY *(coming out from behind screen)* I gotta check out my apartment, and my clothes and money. Cynthia, . . . I can't wait for anybody to open the door or look out for me and all that kinda crap you talk. A bunch-a liars!

BILL Oldtimer, why you . . .

TOMMY Leave him the hell alone. He ain't said nothin' that ain' so!

SONNY-MAN Explain to the sister that some mistakes have been made.

BILL Mistakes have been made, baby. The mistakes were yesterday, this is today . . .

TOMMY Yeah, and I'm Tomorrow, remember? Trouble is I was Tommin' to you, to all of you, . . . "Oh, maybe they gon' like me." . . . I was your fool, thinkin' writers and painters know moren' me, that maybe a little bit of you would rub off on me.

CYNTHIA We were wrong. I knew it yesterday. Tommy, I told you not to expect anything out of this . . . this arrangement.

BILL This is a relationship, not an arrangement.

SONNY-MAN Cynthia, I tell you all the time, keep outta other people's business. What the hell you got to do with who's gonna get what outta what? You and Oldtimer, yakkin' and hakkin'. *(to OLDTIMER)* Man, your mouth gonna kill you.

BILL It's me and Tommy. Clear the room.

TOMMY Better not. I'll kill him! The "Black people" this and the "Afro-American" . . . that . . . You ain' got no use for none-a us. Oldtimer, you their fool too. 'Til I got here they didn't even know your damn name. There's something inside-a me that says I ain' suppose to let *nobody* play me cheap. Don't care how much they know! *(she sweeps some of the books to the floor)*

BILL Don't you have any forgiveness in you? Would I be beggin' you if I didn't care? Can't you be generous enough . . .

TOMMY Nigger, I been too damn generous with you, already. All-a these people know I wasn't down here all night posin' for no pitcher, nigger!

BILL Cut that out, Tommy, and you not going anywhere!

TOMMY You wanna bet? Nigger!

BILL Okay, you called it, baby, I did act like a low, degraded person . . .

TOMMY *(combing out her wig with her fingers while holding it)* Didn't call you no low, degraded person. Nigger! *(to CYNTHIA who is handing her a comb)* "Do you have to wear a wig?" Yes! To soften the blow when yall go up side-a my head with a baseball bat. *(going back to taunting BILL and ignoring CYNTHIA's comb)* Nigger!

BILL That's enough-a that. You right and you're wrong too.

TOMMY Ain't a-one-a us you like that's alive and walkin' by you on the street . . . you don't like flesh and blood niggers.

BILL Call me that, baby, but don't call yourself. That what you think of yourself?

TOMMY If a Black somebody is in a history book, or printed on a pitcher, or drawed on a paintin', . . . or if they're a statue, . . . dead, and outta the way, and can't talk back, then you dig 'em and full-a so much-a damn admiration and talk 'bout *"our"* history. But when you run into us livin' and breathin' ones, with the life's blood still pumpin' through us, . . . then you comin' on 'bout how we ain' never together. You hate us, that's what! *You hate Black me!*

BILL *(stung to the heart, confused and saddened by the half truth which applies to himself)* I never hated you, I never will, no matter what you or any of the rest of you do to *make* me hate you. I won't! Hell, woman, why do you say that! Why would I hate you?

TOMMY Maybe I look too much like the mother that gave birth to you. Like the Ma and Pa that worked in the post office to buy you a house and a screen door with a damn duck on it. And you so ungrateful you didn't even like it.

BILL No, I didn't, baby. I don't like screen doors with ducks on 'em.

TOMMY You didn't like who was livin' behind them screen doors. Phoney Nigger!

BILL That's all! Damnit! don't go there no more!

TOMMY Hit me, so I can tear this place down and scream bloody murder.

BILL *(somewhere between laughter and tears)* Looka here, baby, I'm willin' to say I'm wrong, even in fronta the room fulla people . . .

TOMMY *(through clenched teeth)* Nigger.

SONNY-MAN The sister is upset.

TOMMY And you stop callin' me "the" sister, . . . if you feelin' so brotherly why don't you say "*my*" sister? Ain't no we-ness in your talk. "The" Afro-American, "the" black man, there's no we-ness in you. Who you think *you* are?

SONNY-MAN I was talkin' in general er . . . *my* sister, 'bout the masses.

TOMMY There he go again. "The" masses. Tryin' to make out like we pitiful and you got it made. You the masses your damn self and don't even know it. *(another angry look at* BILL*)* Nigger.

BILL *(pulls dictionary from shelf)* Let's get this ignorant "nigger" talk squared away. You can stand some education.

TOMMY You *treat* me like a nigger, that's what. I'd rather be called one than treated that way.

BILL *(questions* TOMMY*)* What is a nigger? *(talks as he is trying to find word)* A nigger is a low, degraded person, *any* low degraded person. I learned that from my teacher in the fifth grade.

TOMMY Fifth grade is a liar! Don't pull that dictionary crap on me.

BILL *(pointing to the book)* Webster's New World Dictionary of The American Language, College Edition.

TOMMY I don't need to find out what no college white folks say nigger is.

BILL I'm telling you it's a low, degraded person. Listen. *(reads from the book)* Nigger, N-i-g-g-e-r, . . . A Negro . . . A member of any dark-skinned people . . . Damn. *(amazed by dictionary description)*

SONNY-MAN Brother Malcolm *said* that's what they meant, . . . nigger is a Negro, Negro is a nigger.

BILL *(slowly finishing his reading)* A vulgar, offensive term of hostility and contempt. Well, so much for the fifth grade teacher.

SONNY-MAN No, they do not call low, degraded white folks niggers. Come to think of it, did you ever hear whitey call Hitler a nigger? Now if some whitey digs us, . . . the others might call him a nigger-*lover*, but they don't call him no nigger.

OLDTIMER No, they don't.

TOMMY *(near tears)* When they say "nigger," just dry-long-so, they mean educated you and uneducated me. They hate you and call you "nigger," I called you "nigger" but I love you. *(there is dead silence in the room for a split second)*

SONNY-MAN *(trying to establish peace)* There you go. There you go.

CYNTHIA *(cautioning* SONNY-MAN*)* Now is not the time to talk, darlin'.

BILL You love me? Tommy, that's the greatest compliment you could . . .

TOMMY *(sorry she said it)* You must be runnin' a fever, nigger, I ain' said nothin' 'bout lovin' you.

BILL *(in a great mood)* You did, yes, you did.

TOMMY Well, you didn't say it to *me*.

BILL Oh, Tommy, . . .

TOMMY *(cuts him off abruptly)* And don't you dare say it now. I'm tellin' you, . . . it ain't to be said now. *(checks through her paper bag to see if she has everything. Starts to put on the wig, changes her mind, holds it to end of scene. Turns to the others in the room)* Oldtimer, . . . my brothers and my sister.

OLDTIMER I wish I was a thousand miles away, I'm so sorry. *(he sits at the foot of the model stand)*

TOMMY I don't stay mad, it's here today and gone tomorrow. I'm sorry your feelin's got hurt, . . . but when I'm hurt I turn and hurt back. Somewhere, in the middle of last night, I thought the old me was gone, . . . lost forever, and gladly. But today was flippin' time, so back I flipped. Now it's "turn the other cheek" time. If I can go through life other-cheekin' the white folk, . . . guess yall can be other-cheeked too. But I'm goin' back to the nitty-gritty crowd, where the talk is we-ness and us-ness. I hate to do it but I have to thank you 'cause I'm walkin' out with much more than I brought in. *(goes over and looks at the queen in the "Wine In The Wilderness" painting)* Tomorrow-Marie had such a lovely yesterday. *(*BILL *takes her hand, she gently removes it from his grasp)* Bill, I don't have to wait for anybody's by-your-leave to be a "Wine In The Wilderness" woman. I can be it if I wanta, . . . and I *am.* I am. I am. I'm not the one you made up and painted, the very pretty lady who can't talk back, . . . but I'm "Wine In The Wilderness" . . . alive and kickin', me . . . Tomorrow-Marie, cussin' and fightin' and lookin' out for my damn self 'cause ain' nobody else 'round to do it, dontcha know. And, Cynthia, if my hair is straight, or if it's natural, or if I wear a wig, or take it off, . . . that's all right; because wigs . . . shoes . . . hats . . . bags . . . and even this . . . *(she picks up the African throw she wore a few moments before . . . fingers it)* They're just what what you call . . . access . . . *(fishing for the word)* . . . like what you wear with your Easter outfit . . .

CYNTHIA Accessories.

TOMMY Thank you, my sister. Accessories. Somethin' you add or take off. The real thing is takin' place on the inside . . . that's where the action is. That's "Wine In The Wilderness," . . . a woman that's a real one and a good one. And yall just better believe I'm it. *(she proceeds to the door)*

BILL Tommy. *(she turns. He takes the beautiful queen, "Wine In The Wilderness" from the easel)* She's not it at all, Tommy. This chick on the canvas, . . . nothin' but accessories, a dream I drummed up outta the junk room of my mind. *(places the "queen" to one side) You* are and . . . *(points to* OLDTIMER*)* . . . Edmund Lorenzo Matthews . . . the real beautiful people, . . . Cynthia . . .

CYNTHIA *(bewildered and unbelieving)* Who? Me?

BILL Yeah, honey, you and Sonny-man, don't know how beautiful you are. *(indicates the other side of the model stand)* Sit there.

SONNY-MAN *(places cushions on the floor at the foot of the model stand)* Just sit here and be my beautiful self. *(to* CYNTHIA*)* Turn on, baby, we gonna get our picture took. *(*CYNTHIA *smiles)*

BILL Now there's Oldtimer, the guy who was here before there were scholarships and grants and stuff like that, the guy they kept outta the schools, the man the factories wouldn't hire, the union wouldn't let him join . . .

SONNY-MAN Yeah, yeah, rap to me. Where you goin' with it, man? Rap on.

BILL I'm makin' a triptych.

SONNY-MAN Make it, man.

BILL *(indicating* CYNTHIA *and* SONNY-MAN*)* On the other side, Young Man and Woman, workin' together to do our thing.

TOMMY *(quietly)* I'm goin' now.

BILL But you belong up there in the center, "Wine In The Wilderness" . . . that's who you are. *(moves the canvas of "the little girl" and places a sketch pad on the easel)* The nightmare, about all that I've done disappearing before my eyes. It was a good nightmare. I was painting in the dark, all head and no heart. I couldn't see until you came, baby. *(to* CYNTHIA, SONNY-MAN *and* OLDTIMER*)* Look at Tomorrow. She came through the biggest riot of all, . . . somethin' called "Slavery," and she's even comin' through the "now" scene, . . . folks laughin' at her, even her own folks laughin' at her. And look *how* . . . with her head high like she's poppin' her fingers at the world. *(takes up charcoal pencil and tears old page off sketch pad so he can make a fresh drawing)* Aw, let me put it down, Tommy. "Wine In The Wilderness," you gotta let me put it down so all the little boys and girls can look up and see you on the wall. And you know what they're gonna say? "Hey, don't she look like somebody we know?" *(*TOMMY *slowly returns and takes her seat on the stand.* TOMMY *is holding the wig in her lap. Her hands are very graceful looking against the texture of the wig)* And they'll be right, you're somebody they know . . . *(he is sketching hastily. There is a sound of thunder and the patter of rain)* Yeah, roll them hoops and bicycle wheels. *(music is low. Music up higher as* BILL *continues to sketch. Curtain)*

FOR COLORED GIRLS WHO HAVE CONSIDERED SUICIDE/ WHEN THE RAINBOW IS ENUF

1976

Ntozake Shange (1948–)

Twenty poems serve as content for Ntozake Shange's *for colored girls who have considered suicide when the rainbow is enuf,* a choreopoem exploring the mean realities of life for seven African American women who have given their love unconditionally to men who degrade and abuse them. The first poem, *dark phases,* reveals the anguish of Black women who have been relegated to silence and are taken for granted by their men. United, they decry their condition, pleading for the respect that is their due. *graduation nite,* the second poem, depicts the tender joy, fun, and abandonment of youth—that final phase of a carefree existence coming to an end as the harsh responsibilities of adulthood rapidly approach. This special night for the lady in yellow marks her first sexual experience, which she recalls years later as being memorable and beautiful, sharply contrasting her present relationship. The third poem, *now i love somebody more than,* begins a series of encounters between Black men and their mistreated women who find relief from their troubled lives through poetry and dance. The lady in red, having debased herself by loving a demanding man who gives nothing in return, decides now to leave him. Rape, the women proclaim, is committed by men they know—friends who betray them. These men are not prosecuted because no one—not even close relatives believe that they are capable of committing such an act. In *abortion cycle #1* the lady in blue describes the horror, shame and pain of abortion. Shange's ninth poem, *toussaint,* takes us back into the past as an eight-year-old schoolgirl explains the impact that Toussaint L'Ouverture had on her life because "he didnt 'low no white man to tell him nothin." The living conditions in African American ghettos are vividly described in *i used to live in the world* by the lady in blue, whose universe is now six blocks of squalor in

Harlem. Three women allude to the shortage of Black men in *pyramid,* and in *no more love poems #l, #2, #3,* and *#4,* four of the women explain what they desire in a relationship. The lady in orange seeks a love free of vulgarity, cruelty, and degradation, where there is no suppressed hurt and abuse. The lady in purple desperately needs love despite the mistreatment that it brings. The lady in blue wants a love where there are no pretenses, only truth from someone who truly loves her. The lady in yellow has concluded that love is complicated. She wants a sensitive lover rather than the one exerting physical force and violence upon her. *somebody almost walked off wid alla my stuff* is the lady in green's plea to be allowed to come into her own as a woman instead of being taken body and soul by a man who reduces her to a nonentity. The eighteenth poem, *sorry,* is the lady in blue's rejection of the apologies that men are constantly making after some offense against women, and in poem twenty, *a laying on of hands,* the women unite in strength and sisterhood, discovering who they are and their worth—a ritual of self-realization freeing them from the subjugation of the Black male.

Since the publisher of *for colored girls . . .* would not allow the complete work to be printed in this anthology, only the nineteenth poem, *a nite wid beau willie brown,* is included here. This poem is the most dramatic and controversial piece in the choreopoem. It is the graphic and moving story of an African American man who murders his children as their mother implores him for mercy. His powerful characterization makes him a prototype for African American males and a dangerous stereotype for unknowledgeable whites who want to believe that all Black men are like beau willie. He is the product of the system in which he lives; a system where he has been disenfranchised socially, politically, and economically. He was a school dropout because he found nothing there relevant to him or his needs. He was forced to fight a war to liberate the Vietnamese while his brothers and sisters back home were fighting to liberate themselves from America's racial oppression. He cannot find a job that will allow him to support his family or afford him some dignity. He is forced into a corner by racism and has no self-esteem. His frustrations mount and are relieved through drink and drugs. His need for crystal, the mother of his children—his *love* for her, his masculinity, is defined through his strength, that is, through his violence. Shange does not ask us to forgive beau willie, but she does want us to understand and judge him in terms of the conditions that shaped him.

for colored girls . . . was first presented in a woman's bar outside Berkeley called the Bacchanal. Subsequent performances with the addition and deletion of poems allowed the author to further develop her piece until it was ready for performance at the Studio Rivbea in New York. Oz Scott offered his assistance in restaging the work so that it would appeal to New Yorkers. Shange accepted his offer, and Scott eventually assumed the role of director. It was optioned by Woodie King, Jr., who produced it with set, lighting, and two additional actresses at the Henry Street Settlement's New Federal Theatre in April, 1976. That June, Joseph Papp transferred it to his New York Shakespeare Festival's Public Theatre, and in September it opened at the Booth Theatre on Broadway, co-produced by King and Papp, where it ran for 876 performances. In celebration of its twentieth anniversary, King revived the play at the Henry Street Settlement in 1995 with Shange as director. She made subtle changes in the production, discarding the bold colors of the costumes worn originally in favor of softer shades like aqua, rose, and mint, and introducing timely subjects like AIDS.

Ntozake Shange (Paulette Williams), the daughter of a surgeon and a psychiatric social worker, was born in Trenton, New Jersey, and raised in upstate New York and St. Louis. She graduated with honors from Barnard College in 1970 with a B.A. in American Studies and received her M.A. in that field from the University of Southern California in 1973. She took her African name in 1971, which in Zulu means "she who comes with her own thing [Ntosake]," and "one who walks like a lion [Shange]." Her volumes of poetry include *Nappy Edges, A Daughter's Geography, Ridin' the Moon in Texas,* and *From Okra to Greens.* She has written novels: *Sassafras, Cypress and Indigo,* and *The Resurrection of the Daughter: Liliane,* and has had numerous short stories, articles and poems published in a wide variety of magazines and anthologies. Aside from her work as a poet, playwright, and novelist, she is an actress, dancer, teacher, and is in great demand around the country as a director. She is the recipient of two Obie Awards, one for her adaptation of Bertolt Brecht's *Mother Courage and Her Children,* and the other for *for colored girls.* In addition she received the Outer Critic's Circle, AUDELCO, and *Mademoiselle* Awards for *for colored girls,* which was nominated for a Tony and a Grammy Award.

for colored girls who have considered suicide/ when the rainbow is enuf

LADY IN RED

there waz no air / the sheets made ripples under
his body like crumpled paper napkins in a summer park / & lil
specks of somethin from tween his toes or the biscuits
from the day before ran in the sweat that tucked the sheet
into his limbs like he waz an ol frozen bundle of chicken /
& he'd get up to make coffee drink wine drink water / he
wished one of his friends who knew where he waz wd come by
with some blow or some shit / anythin / there waz no air /
he'd see the spotlights in the alleyways downstairs movin
in the air / cross his wall over his face / & get under the
covers & wait for an all clear or til he cd hear traffic
again /
there waznt nothin wrong with him / there waznt nothin wrong
with him / he kept tellin crystal /
any niggah wanna kill vietnamese children more n stay home
& raise his own is sicker than a rabid dog /
that's how their thing had been goin since he got back /
crystal just got inta sayin whatta fool niggah beau waz
& always had been / didnt he go all over uptown sayin the
child waznt his / waz some no counts bastard / & any ol city
police cd come & get him if they wanted / cuz as soon as
the blood type & shit waz together / everybody wd know that
crystal waz a no good lyin whore / and this after she'd been
his girl since she waz thirteen / when he caught her
on the stairway /

he came home crazy as hell / he tried to get veterans benefits
to go to school & they kept right on puttin him in
remedial classes / he cdnt read wortha damn / so beau
cused the teachers of holdin him back & got himself
a gypsy cab to drive / but his cab kept breakin
down / & the cops was always messin wit him / plus not
gettin much bread /

& crystal went & got pregnant again / beau most beat
her to death when she tol him / she still gotta scar
under her right tit where he cut her up / still crystal
went right on & had the baby / so now beau willie had
two children / a little girl / naomi kenya & a boy / kwame beau
willie brown / & there waz no air /

how in the hell did he get in this mess anyway / somebody
went & tol crystal that beau waz spendin alla his money
on the bartendin bitch down at the merry-go-round cafe /
beau sat straight up in the bed / wrapped up in the sheets
lookin like john the baptist or a huge baby wit stubble
& nuts / now he hadta get alla that shit outta crystal's
mind / so she wd let him come home / crystal had gone &
got a court order saying beau willie brown had no access
to his children / if he showed his face he waz subject
to arrest / shit / she'd been in his ass to marry her
since she waz 14 years old & here when she 22 / she wanna
throw him out cuz he say he'll marry her / she burst
out laughin / hollerin whatchu wanna marry me for now /
so i can support yr
ass / or come sit wit ya when they lock yr behind
up / cause they gonna come for ya / ya goddamn lunatic /
they gonna come / & i'm not gonna have a thing to do
wit it / o no i wdnt marry yr pitiful black ass for
nothin & she went on to bed /

the next day beau willie came in blasted & got ta swingin
chairs at crystal / who cdnt figure out what the hell
he waz doin / til he got ta shoutin bout how she waz gonna
marry him / & get some more veterans benefits / & he cd
stop drivin them crazy spics round / while they tryin
to kill him for $15 / beau waz sweatin terrible / beatin
on crystal / & he cdnt do no more with the table n chairs /
so he went to get the high chair / & lil kwame waz in it /
& beau waz beatin crystal with the high chair & her son /
& some notion got inta him to stop / and he run out /

crystal most died / that's why the police wdnt low
beau near where she lived / & she'd been tellin the kids
their daddy tried to kill her & kwame / & he just wanted
to marry her / that's what / he wanted to marry her / &
have a family / but the bitch waz crazy / beau willie
waz sittin in this hotel in his drawers drinkin
coffee & wine in the heat of the day spillin shit all
over hisself / laughin / bout how he waz gonna get crystal
to take him back / & let him be a man in the house / & she
wdnt even have to go to work no more / he got dressed
all up in his ivory shirt & checkered pants to go see
crystal & get this mess all cleared up /
he knocked on the door to crystal's rooms / & she
didnt answer / he beat on the door & crystal & naomi
started cryin / beau gotta shoutin again how he wanted

to marry her / & waz she always gonna be a whore / or
did she wanna husband / & crystal just kept on
screamin for him to leave us alone / just leave us
alone / so beau broke the door down / crystal held
the children in fronta her / she picked kwame off the
floor / in her arms / & she held naomi by her shoulders /
& kept on sayin / beau willie brown / get outta here /
the police is gonna come for ya / ya fool / get outta here /
do you want the children to see you act the fool again /
you want kwame to brain damage from you throwin him
round / niggah / get outta here / get out & dont show yr
ass again or i'll kill ya / i swear i'll kill ya /
he reached for naomi / crystal grabbed the lil girl &
stared at beau willie like he waz a leper or somethin /
dont you touch my children / muthafucker / or i'll kill
you /

beau willie jumped back all humble & apologetic / i'm
sorry / i dont wanna hurt em / i just wanna hold em &
get on my way / i dont wanna cuz you no more trouble /
i wanted to marry you & give ya things
what you gonna give / a broken jaw / niggah get outta here /
he ignored crystal's outburst & sat down motionin for
naomi to come to him / she smiled back at her daddy /
crystal felt naomi givin in & held her tighter /
naomi / pushed away & ran to her daddy / cryin / daddy, daddy
come back daddy / come back / but be nice to mommy /
cause mommy loves you / and ya gotta be nice /
he sat her on his knee / & played with her ribbons &
they counted fingers & toes / every so often he
looked over to crystal holdin kwame / like a statue /
& he'd say / see crystal / i can be a good father /
now let me see my son / & she didnt move / &
he coaxed her & he coaxed her / tol her she waz
still a hot lil ol thing & pretty & strong / didnt
she get right up after that lil ol fight they had
& go back to work / beau willie oozed kindness &
crystal who had known so lil / let beau hold kwame /

as soon as crystal let the baby outta her arms / beau
jumped up a laughin & a gigglin / a hootin & a hollerin /
awright bitch / awright bitch / you gonna marry me /
you gonna marry me . . .
i aint gonna marry ya / i aint ever gonna marry ya /
for nothin / you gonna be in the jail / you gonna be
under the jail for this / now gimme my kids / ya give
me back my kids /

he kicked the screen outta the window / & held the kids
offa the sill / you gonna marry me / yeh i'll marry ya /
anything / but bring the children back in the house /
he looked from where the kids were hangin from the
fifth story / at alla the people screamin at him / &
he started sweatin again / say to alla the neighbors /
you gonna marry me /

i stood by beau in the window / with naomi reachin
for me / & kwame screamin mommy mommy from the fifth
story / but i cd only whisper / & he dropped em.

SALLY'S RAPE
1989

Robbie McCauley (1942–)

The form and flow of McCauley's performance pieces stem from music; the process of her work stems from her experience as an actor—she played the Lady in Red in *for colored girls . . .* Joan Little in Ed Bullins's *The Taking of Miss Janie,* as well as roles in Adrienne Kennedy's *Cities in Bezique* and with the Negro Ensemble Company. She describes her creative process:

> I write on my feet. I dance and move around. I sit down and I talk to myself, do scenes. I do it until I feel like writing. I become the audience. I become the story. I ask myself what happens next? That opens up a process.[1]

Beginning as a "work-in-progress" at P.S. 122 in New York City in December 1989, *Sally's Rape* evolved through performances at The Kitchen in Soho, New York, at Lincoln Center, at the Studio Museum of Harlem, and at the Davis Center at City College of New York. It received the Obie Award in 1992 for Best American Play. In a real sense, *Sally's Rape* is still "in progress" because McCauley invites those who perform the play to improvise, to make it their own. This openness, this freedom to "happen" and to carry on a conversation with the audience, makes *Sally's Rape* a grandchild of the "happenings" of the sixties, when many theatre performances were not locked into a scripted text but flowed with whatever was "happening."[2]

Printed here is a dialogue scenario, an outline for what occurred in performance. McCauley uses "Sally" [Hemmings], who was Thomas Jefferson's slave mistress, as the generic name for all women without social, economic, political, or physical power, who are therefore available to be raped. The play begins with lessons in proper manners for young ladies—how to drink tea, how to cross the ankles. Circling like a conjurer who's raising spirits from the dead, McCauley's performance moves carefully around rape; it does not present one, nor is one described in specific detail,

1. Vicki Patraka, "Robbie McCauley, Observing in Public," *The Drama Review,* Summer 1993.

2. The Open Theatre developed its plays, including Claude Van Italie's *America Hurrah* and Megan Terry's *Calm Down Mother,* by this method.

yet the audience is witness to rape's resonance.

Born in Norfolk, Virginia, and growing up in Georgia, Robbie McCauley had heard the tales of Black women being dragged out of their cabins into the dirt and "being done it to" by slave masters as a ritual passage into white manhood. Through suggestion and a seeming simplicity of style, McCauley immerses us in male brutality, a Bosnia-of-the-mind.[3] Her works are informed by history and by the range of specific ways that rape is related to race, class, and gender.

The three performers in the play are two women (one white, one Black) and the audience (divided into three groups), which serves as a chorus. The audience is encouraged to enter the magic circle and experience in some empathic way "the tightness of the thighs." McCauley believes that the best performance of *Sally's Rape*, happened at Crossroads Theater, a Black theatre in New Jersey where "the audience really enacted the role of group number three, whose function was to comment. They also did the slave ritual, the auction block ritual, with relish."[4]

McCauley's performance works, which often include slides, live music, video, and film, can be divided into four genres: Site-Specific Pieces Involving Community Collaboration—works centering around the history of three different city communities; Collaborations with Thought Music—five pieces that work with poets, dancers, visual artists, and musicians; Sedition Ensemble Pieces—five works cowritten with musican Ed Montgomery; The Family Series—four pieces, including *Sally's Rape,* that use McCauley's personal family stories.

A shibboleth for McCauley's performance pieces might be taken from her own testimony: "I like the concept of speaking the unspeakable . . . I prefer when people say, 'You made me think; I disagreed with you, but I was moved to think.'"

Sally's Rape

A bench up right. A piano up left. A large, sturdy square table up center and two chairs. All are set at angles. Rocks are lying about the space. General lighting. Audience enters, sits.

Prologue: Talking About What It Is About

ROBBIE *and* JEANNIE *enter with cups of tea on saucers. They walk to a space down left in conversation between themselves, aware of Audience. Easy talk.*

ROBBIE Somebody said it was about cups.

JEANNIE Somebody else said it was about language.

ROBBIE What do you think it's about?

JEANNIE Well, that one person said it was about you and me. And I know it's not about me but it's about you and I'm in it.

ROBBIE It's my story and you're in it because I put you in it.

JEANNIE Fair enough.

ROBBIE It *is* about cups.

JEANNIE It's about getting culture.

ROBBIE Cup says culture.

JEANNIE Comportment.

3. In the war following the breakup of Yugoslavia, the Bosnian Serbs raped thousands of Muslim women as an act of terrorism.

4. Patraka, "Robbie McCauley."

ROBBIE Commonality. Well actually where I come from cups and saucers were like. . . . We had to learn about these things. I mean we went from jars to cups and saucers . . . nothing in between. I once went to a class in tea pouring. . . . It was Japanese but it was about containment . . . proper . . . deportment.

JEANNIE Doing the . . . proper . . .

ROBBIE AND JEANNIE . . . right . . . thing.

ROBBIE Like my Aunt Nell said: If you do the wrong thing you could get your ass killed, so it was more like a matter of life and death.

JEANNIE You know we had cups and saucers. I even think we had six that matched. But mostly we used mugs.

ROBBIE Mugs?

JEANNIE Because they hold a little more, and they have a bigger bottom, so they don't tip. The only disadvantage of a mug is after you use a spoon you have to just kind of put it on the table, and it leaves a little mark.

ROBBIE I think sometimes we did this for the sake of itself. Cups and saucers. Charm school. White gloves.

JEANNIE But that's South, too. I mean, that's southern stuff. The one girl that was like that I knew . . . she had gone to charm school, she was being groomed to be a Southern Belle. She had monogrammed sweaters. She went to charm school one summer in junior high, and she learned to walk like this . . . *(does the walk)* with a book on her head. And we all tried.

ROBBIE We didn't worry about books on our heads. We already had this *up* thing. I guess that was the African in us before I even knew it. But we *(walking,* JEANNIE *following)* had to contain our hips. To keep tucked up. Slightly seductive but not too much . . . *(at the bench)* and when you sit . . . you know this part.

JEANNIE Yeah, you touch the front of the seat with the back of the calf, and then you descend without bending at the waist.

(They sit together; JEANNIE *crosses her legs*

ROBBIE Now you can—no! *(hits* JEANNIE*'s knee away)* Don't do that. *((*JEANNIE *corrects) Now* you can drink your tea. *(they sip simultaneously)* My Aunt Nell would have *died* if she saw you—

JEANNIE —cross my legs like that.

ROBBIE That's it. Put your feet just so, or slightly cross at the ankle.

JEANNIE Why was that?

1. Confessing About Family and Religion and Work in Progress

ROBBIE Almost everybody in my mother's family was half white. But that wasn't nothing but some rape. These confessions are like a mourning for the lost connections.

ROBBIE *starts singing and* JEANNIE *joins in.*

ROBBIE AND JEANNIE

"I'm going there to meet my mother
I'm going there no more to roam
I'm just a-going over Jordan
I'm just a-going over home . . . "

ROBBIE *continues humming like in church*

JEANNIE That was the only thing that would make it worth going to church for me, to sing those songs. But I didn't really have a religion, so that's why I invented one. When I was about seven, I invented a religion, and it was all about rocks, and trees and leaves, and nature and so forth, everything that I knew. And I tried to convert my best friend, Eileen, who was Catholic. It ended up just being mine.

ROBBIE I envy that. To have a religion that you find where you are was something I couldn't even conceive of until Africa. Before that, of course, it was the big white god up there. . . . If oppression is at the core, if there must be one at the top and others on the bottom . . . the struggle will always be . . . *(gesture of pushing and straining)* You know, I mean the way I dealt with religion was to be a Marxist . . .

JEANNIE AND ROBBIE . . . another . . . big white god . . .

JEANNIE What was it your Aunt Nell said when you said you were a Marxist?

ROBBIE "Well, at least you're *sumpthin'*." If this . . . *(same gesture)* kind of struggle, if oppression is at the core, then this work will never end. It's a work in progress . . .

JEANNIE Well, *if* you can dialogue, you can get rid of some of that.

ROBBIE Well, *if* you can weed it out. *If* it's about something else, then—

JEANNIE *Then* it's a work in progress . . .

ROBBIE . . . a dialogue . . .

JEANNIE Otherwise, there is no progress.

JEANNIE AND ROBBIE *(to audience, alternating the lines between them)* And we can't have a dialogue by ourselves. So you're in it. Don't worry I won't jump in your face or down your throat. We'll feed you. *(They pass out cookies and apples, improvising about "fishes and loaves" and about how food eases tension, may help you talk)* We'll use hand signals, lead like camp directors, divide you into groups. One . . . *(one of them points out sections of the audience)* Two . . . Three. Well, it doesn't matter what section you're in, it just matters who you are, and you can change your opinion as time goes on.

Group One will be the agreeable ones. When we signal like this *(two fingers up)* you say "That's right!," "Yes indeed" or "I'm telling you." Any short sentence of agreement. Let's practice. *(they lead responses with Group One)* Good . . . !

Group Two will be the bass line. You just go "uh huh," "umm humm," or "yeah, yeah." Here's your signal . . . *(one finger pointed out)* Let's try it. *(Group Two practices with sounds)* Very nice.

(talking fast) Group Three is the dialogue group, people who have something to add, to disagree with, who like to talk.

ROBBIE Don't worry, I'm in control. Your signal is two hands out flat like this . . . . Dialogue!

JEANNIE Let's practice with something from the context of the piece. Lights!

Lights on ROBBIE *and* JEANNIE *in two house aisles. Stage black.*

2. Stating the Context

ROBBIE I believe white is a condition that anyone can take in. It causes one to feel superior in order to be okay.

(They signal to Groups. Groups respond. In this improvisation with the AUDIENCE, *when* ROBBIE *feels someone makes a strong point, agreeable to her or not, she impulsively stomps her feet. Stage lights up. Aisle lights off.* JEANNIE *moves among rocks.*

(walking in 6/8 time) It's about my great-great-grandmother Sally who was a young woman with children when official slavery ended. And she's in me. She was house but *field.*

My Aunt Jessie who died at the age of ninety-three—

JEANNIE Ninety-six.

ROBBIE She always put her age back. She said we was bad off in Harris County 'cause the white folks wasn't doing too good, and we were brought up to believe that, that our well-being depended on white people being well-off. You know how families can raise you with counterrevolutionary ideas in order to survive.

They call for Audience response. ROBBIE *waves off dialogue.*

We don't hafta discuss *that.*

JEANNIE *moves among the rocks.* ROBBIE *continues in 6/8 rhythm.*

It wasn't *fine* like the gone-with-the-wind-type house-nigger mythology. Sally did the housework and the cooking, and she tended to Mistress when some really fine white folks come to visit. They say that day might not a been really rich white folks anyhow. They say Sally had them chillun by the master like that was supposed to a been something. They say Massa was mean and nasty. You know how white folks gets when they ain't doin' good. Word was freedom was coming, everybody know what happen on that day freedom come when we follow Uncle Buck—I believe that was his name—

JEANNIE Yeah, Uncle Buck.

ROBBIE —up to the Massa porch. *(sudden anger)* But back up in *heah* 'fore freedom they say po' citter white folks was buying us ignorant! No telling what woulda happen! *(she pauses)*

3. Trying to Transform

ROBBIE *(upset, she moves over left):* I I I become others inside me, standing at the bus stop with my socks rolled down screaming things I shoulda said, "Just because people are crazy don't mean they can't think straight!" Hollering periodically at white men "YOU RAPED ME! GODDAMN MOTHERFUKA! YOU RAPED ME!" *(reaching out, gathering air)* Sometimes I'll gather and push away the wall of vibrations that make walls between us . . . *(throws air to* JEANNIE*)* Black

JEANNIE *(catching, molding the bunch of air):* Black

ROBBIE Women

JEANNIE Women

ROBBIE Get

JEANNIE Get

ROBBIE AND JEANNIE Bitter.

JEANNIE Black women get bitter. Scared somebody gonna look at them run and search for the wind, look at them go to the bottom of the pain and sadness, looking for breezes. You know how Black folks gets when they ain't doing good.

ROBBIE It's a journey of chains.

JEANNIE I latched on, crawled in like a spider clinging to the walls, looking for light in tunnels of despair. I wanted to go deeper, darker, never to remember the empty days. I wanted to be . . . Billie Holiday.

ROBBIE I wanted to be Rosa Luxemburg!

JEANNIE Rosa Luxemburg?

ROBBIE Poland.

JEANNIE That's so idealistic.

ROBBIE *(aside)* So was Billie Holiday.

JEANNIE *(responding to aside)* I didn't have to know that to want to be her.

ROBBIE *(does dance kicks)* Poland. She liked Poland. Communism wasn't even a word back then. The main deity in Poland is a Black Madonna. In Eastern Europe women were more revered, more venerated.

JEANNIE Do you have proof? Who told you that?

ROBBIE A woman from Eastern Europe.

JEANNIE Well, a woman from Turkey told me there was no racism in Turkey.

ROBBIE Well, from her point of view, there probably wasn't.

JEANNIE Why are you so understanding, so generous toward people in another part of the world?

ROBBIE I was listening to a woman who had pride in her ancestors and that turned me on.

JEANNIE That's very nice.

ROBBIE Socialism goes way back. Way back women gathered in groups to pick. And Africa. Let's do 1964.

Light change: a pool of light center. They stand in it. Other areas dim.

ROBBIE In 1964 at the library job a U.S. history major who'd graduated from Smith College said—

JEANNIE I never knew white men did anything with colored women on plantations.

ROBBIE I said, "It was rape." Her eyes turned red. She choked on her sandwich and quit the job.

JEANNIE *(pointing at each Audience group in turn)* Was the Smith College graduate denying . . . ? lying . . . ? or dumb? *(Audience response)* Yeah she was dumb. I keep telling you that.

They cross past each other. Light change.

ROBBIE Why do I feel like crying . . . because she went to Smith College. . . . I think of the dumb educated bourgeois thing in me . . .

JEANNIE You have this thing that an Ivy League education could prevent her dumbness about that, and there's nothing that can prevent that.

ROBBIE Right, I do have a thing that an Ivy League education oughta prevent that. I mean, look, okay. I wanted to go to Barnard, and they didn't let me in . . . a rejection letter . . .

JEANNIE And you're bitter.

ROBBIE Bitterness about Barnard I admit. But when I'm sitting around my grandmother's breakfast table, and she's telling me something that this woman who went to Smith College didn't know, a U.S. history major—

JEANNIE *(overlap)* Well, aren't you more fortunate then, that you learned so much more through your grandmother?

ROBBIE The point is that Smith College, all those colleges, are places that people should go to learn things that help the world. All right? And if she went there and studied U.S. history and comes out sounding dumb about what went on during slavery time, I don't understand. I can't give her no credit for just being dumb. I mean my grandmother would also teach us that. . . . You know, we lived in a neighborhood back then down south that had Black people and white people, back when they had signs that said *white* and *colored* to separate bathrooms and stuff. Well, back then there were white people who lived down the street from us because that was where they had to live. And we played together till we were about ten. After ten back then we couldn't speak to each other. Even back then my grandmother taught us that white people were not genetically evil or anything, they were just dumb, and when they learned something, they would be smarter about us . . .

JEANNIE *starts to do folk-dance steps in 3/4 time.* ROBBIE *joins in. . . .*

. . . and we could get together and change the world.

JEANNIE Rosa Luxemburg had no patience for bourgeois women who didn't work. She called them—

ROBBIE Co-consumptive.

JEANNIE More parasitic than the parasites. She was a small, powerful woman.

ROBBIE Zaftig.

JEANNIE When she talked, people listened. I believe she would have marched with us.

JEANNIE AND ROBBIE *(they stop dancing)* She was murdered by men who would later be Nazis.

ROBBIE *(turning, kicking, squatting)* Dancing in half circles. Trying to connect. She was internationalist—so far ahead of her time—we haven't begun to get there yet.

JEANNIE *(overlap)* —as opposed to nationalist.

ROBBIE *(still dancing)* In Pennsylvania a town with the Black Madonna and the little brown Jesus. A Polish town. In Eastern Europe way back . . . women more venerated . . .

JEANNIE There's one in Texas too. I sent you the postcard. The shrine to Our Lady of Czestochowa.

ROBBIE Not long ago in Poland a pilgrimage to her.

JEANNIE But you've never explained why in Poland there'd be a Black Madonna.

Pause.

ROBBIE Socialism goes way back.

JEANNIE But a burned statue or anything, there's no explanation for it?

ROBBIE Way back, way back! Women gathered in groups to pick and hunt.

JEANNIE Did they really hunt? That's unsubstantiated.

Pause.

ROBBIE *(stops dancing)* Of *course* they hunted. And of course it's unsubstantiated. And Africa.

JEANNIE Old memories. Ancient stuff. We all come from one African woman. Dancing in circles, pushing walls. I was underneath him in the dirt too—he doesn't want to hear this, he thinks he civilized the world! I sold slaves when I worked at the Welfare Department. Did you put them on the ship?

JEANNIE *puts her hands on* ROBBIE*'s hair. Pause.* ROBBIE *lifts them.*

4. Moment in the Chairs

They set up the two chairs. Light changes. One bright circle. Other areas dark. They sit in the light, face each other, hold hands and move their arms to and fro, as if giving and receiving dialogue.

They improvise on why they are angry with each other. The differences go deep. JEANNIE *thinks* ROBBIE *can see through her to something she can't admit. She thinks their idealism is similar.* ROBBIE *thinks admitting the differences in their histories is more important.* JEANNIE *is concerned that she can't win. They try to reveal something to each other as if they are alone and honest about their differences. The following is an example of the dialogue that has resulted in performance.*

JEANNIE Your hands are like ice.

ROBBIE What upsets me is language. I can't win in your language.

JEANNIE You're going to win anyway. What upsets me is there's an underlying implication that you're gonna unmask me. That you're gonna get underneath something and pull it out. That you can see it and I can't.

ROBBIE What do you think it is? I mean, it's better if you say it.

JEANNIE Some kind of delusion, self-deception.

ROBBIE About what? I mean, what's the content of it?

JEANNIE About my idealism. I have some idea of . . . humanism, something that we share, more important than our differences. Of greater. . . . Of greater value.

ROBBIE Let me see if I can use the language to say what I feel about your idealism. I think it covers over something in your history that makes your idealism still a whim. It angers me that even though your ancestors might have been slaves— because they did have white slaves . . . only made Black slavery mandatory for economic reasons, so they could catch us when we ran away—that history has given you the ability to forget your shame about being oppressed by being ignorant, mean or idealistic . . . which makes it dangerous for me. *(stands)*

JEANNIE I have the same thing about education you were talking about. I mean I believed that through education, if I could change my thinking, that anything would be possible. And it just sounds so stupid.

ROBBIE *may use this moment to say something more to Audience.* JEANNIE *takes chairs away, joins* ROBBIE *facing Audience. Beat. They go stand in front of bench, pick up cups and drink tea.*

5. Sally's Rape

ROBBIE
Do you think Thomas
took his Sally to European tea rooms?
And what did she wear?
And what do you think Mrs. J. thought?

ROBBIE AND JEANNIE That musta been some business huh?

They take their cups to piano. JEANNIE *first sings with* ROBBIE, *then becomes* MRS. J *and does the dance of the frail white lady.*

ROBBIE *(plays piano and sings)*
Grandma Sally had two children
by the master. One of 'em
was my Grandma Alice, my mother's
grandmother, where my mother got her name.

ROBBIE *continues to play.* MRS. J. *speaks, conscious of the music.*

JEANNIE
In the woods . . .
I immediately become Harriet
in the woods.
Swamps are my memory.
ROBBIE *(coaching)* Shoot.
JEANNIE
Shoot, how you gonna be scared of freedom?
Some teachers don't know nothing.
ROBBIE Once.
JEANNIE
Once somebody I almost married
said I was too scared of dogs.
I said I'm scared of slavery.
I wanted to be . . . darker . . . deeper.
These are dreams but the wounds remain
and there are no meetings of ourselves
at these crossroads.

Lights change. The Auction Block. JEANNIE *moves bench center to be the auction block, but then improvises with* ROBBIE, *deciding to move big table there instead.* JEANNIE *takes bench down left.* ROBBIE *steps onto auction block, takes off her sack dress, drops it on the block. She is naked.* JEANNIE *starts to chant, "Bid 'em in," coaxing the Audience, taking time to thank them for joining in. It should be a moment of communion.*

ROBBIE
On the auction block. With my socks rolled down
I take off my sack dress. Mistress? Come on.
This is what they brought us here for.
On the auction block. They put their hands all down our bodies
to sell you, for folks to measure you smeltcha . . .
They say in Ecuador where 40% of the population is African,
that Jesuits heaped us into huts by the hundreds
and listened while we bred.
JEANNIE That's what they brought us here for.

Auction block light is blue. JEANNIE *circles down near Audience, leading the chant, and back to dim light up right.*

ROBBIE *(still naked)* Aunt Jessie said that's how they got their manhood on the plantations. They'd come down to the quarters and do it to us and the chickens.
A TIGHTNESS BETWEEN HER THIGHS. WHEN IT LETS GO SHE SCREAMS WITH TERROR. AND THEN TIGHTENS AGAIN. WHY DOES SHE KEEP COMING TO ME IN THESE NIGHTMARES? THEY SAY SALLY WAS TOUGH. BOUGHT A HOUSE AFTER SLAVERY TIME. TAUGHT HER DAUGHTERS TO BE LADIES. ASKED THE WHITE MAN, HOW MUCH WAS THE HOUSE ON 23RD STREET. HE TOLD HER AND LAUGHED. LIVING IN ONE OF THE RED HOUSES, PAYING BY THE MONTH, TOOK IN WASHING, CLEANED UP THEIR HOUSES FOR MONEY. SHE ALWAYS SAID FOR MONEY. TOOK $750 TO THE

BANK WHICH IS WHERE THE COLORED HAD TO GO TO GET THE PAPER FOR PROPERTY. SAID SHE DID ALL THAT AND NONE OF US EVER HAD TO BE WHORES.

JEANNIE *ends chant, signaling with her hands like a conductor.* ROBBIE *asks the light board operator to bring up the lights as she picks up the sack dress and holds it in front of her.*

(to audience) I wanted to do this—stand naked in public on the auction block. I thought somehow it could help free us from *this. (refers to her naked body)* Any old socialist knows one can't be free till all are free.

Lights back to auction-block blue. ROBBIE *curls down onto block.*

In the dream I. I am Sally being *(an involuntary sound of pain)* b'ah. Bein' bein' I . . . I being bound down I didn't I didn't wanna be in the dream, bound down in the dream I am I am Sally being done it to I am down on the groundbeing done it to bound down didn't wanna be bound down on the ground. In the dream I am Sally down on the ground being done it to. In the dream I am Sally being done it to bound down on the ground.

JEANNIE *moves auction block back, places chairs down right and crosses past* ROBBIE *to bench.* ROBBIE, *carrying dress, goes to* JEANNIE'*s light.*

6. *In a Rape Crisis Center*

ROBBIE *(putting on dress)* Before they changed the Bill of Rights / Constitution/Articles of Confederation—whatever it was for white men before they changed it—it said they all had a right to land, cattle, Negroes, and other livestock . . . pigs . . . dogs . . .

JEANNIE *(curled up on bench)*

To be raped is not to scream
but to whimper and lock and never to remember
but feel the closing in the thighs
between the legs locking up everything
biting lips, the teeth bleed.

ROBBIE

On the plantation you hafta stay tough and tight
no matter how many times they come down there.
Sally stayed down there with us in the quarters
and at night they pulled us out in the dirt.

JEANNIE *crosses to chairs, stands.* ROBBIE *crosses to bench, sits.*

Wasn't nothing to it. You just stay tight till they finish. Sally worked in the house, but she stayed down in the quarters with us. He took Sally out on the ground.

JEANNIE In a rape crisis center, your wounds are fresh. They can put warm cloths on you, tell you it's not your fault.

ROBBIE

Wadn't nuthin' to it. The others watched.
Sometimes they did it too.

Pause. She crosses and stands down left of JEANNIE.

They say Sally had
dem chillun by the massa like it was supposed
to a been something. Shit Thomas' Sally was just as
much a slave as our grandma and it was just as much a rape.
One Sally's rape by the massa no gooder n'an n'othern.

JEANNIE All anyone would have to do is keep you warm.

ROBBIE After slaverytime, say Sally married Gilford, a Black man, and they had two boys. And nobody, not even them two chillun she had by the massa—which is what everybody called 'em like that was supposed to a been something—nobody ever blamed Sally for calling them two *boys* her real chillun.

JEANNIE There's no reason to feel that cold all the time.

ROBBIE COLD. VERY COLD. VERY VERY VERY COLD.

JEANNIE Someone would give you a cup of tea. Hot chocolate. Warm milk.

ROBBIE These new ones with the alligators act like they wadn't born with no memory. I don't know what all went on underneath those houses of women and silent men.

JEANNIE Herb tea.

ROBBIE You . . . let the cabs roll by . . . let shit roll off your back . . . *stay* . . . ain't no rape crisis center on the plantation.

JEANNIE Then what do you do about it?

7. Talking About Different Schools and How to Do

Pause. ROBBIE *crosses over to chairs. They both sit.*

ROBBIE My Ma Willie and my Aunt Jessie had a school. It was called—well, their school, I don't remember what it was called. But they had gone to Mr. Pierce's school. Now Mr. Pierce's father or grandfather was—

JEANNIE I think it was his grandfather.

ROBBIE But Mr. Pierce himself had taught my grandmother and them, so it must have been his father who had been a slave and had worked in the big house and looked in and learned how the white folks do. So his son had a school called Mr. Pierce's School where the girls, and I reckon some of the boys, went to learn how to do. Now when my Ma Willie and Aunt Jessie opened their school it wasn't just for how to do. It was for reading, writing, and numbers, and Aunt—

JEANNIE Tell them about the motto.

ROBBIE Jeannie likes this. Back then they said, "Each one teach one." And that's how the learning was transmitted. My Aunt Jessie could name the capital and the river it was on of every state in the United States.

JEANNIE Alphabetically.

ROBBIE Alphabetically. One of the first words they learned was *garage*. It was a new word back then. Garage—a building in which you place an automobile.

JEANNIE What about rhetoric?

ROBBIE Oh yes, they learned rhetoric. My mother said rhetoric was learning to tell the truth over and over.

JEANNIE You know we had classes in a garage, too. But I think they were opposite. The whole idea was wild abandon. This was about a year before I invented the religion. But the whole thing was nature. My teacher had a long red ponytail and a drum under her arm, and we'd go running across the room. We were about six years old, all girls. Some forest . . . some beast . . . some storm . . . you know the whole thing—wild, free, running!

ROBBIE *runs across the space and back.*

Yeah, we were freer than that.

ROBBIE *(in her own world)*

What difference it a been, it a been by the master?

They all come down there. They all do it to you.

And do it to the chickens too.

What difference it a been?

JEANNIE What do you do about it? See, this section to me is where everything is clear. The difference in weight. I say the word "free," and what do you think of? A feather, or a butterfly. You say the word "free," it's totally different. It's light . . . substantial, flimsy . . . weighty . . .

ROBBIE Come, let's do this.

ROBBIE *and* JEANNIE *get the auction block.*

JEANNIE I thought we weren't going to do this. It's so . . . art.

ROBBIE Get up there. *(to light board operator)* Put the auction block lights on, please. *(to* JEANNIE*)* Take off your dress. *(to Audience)* Let's do it for her, please . . . . Bid 'em in. Bid 'em in.

JEANNIE *takes down one strap*

(to JEANNIE*)* Do you have something to say? *(*JEANNIE *shakes her head "no")* That's something right there.

JEANNIE *gets down and moves block back.*

8. The Language Lesson

ROBBIE *holds* JEANNIE *by her shoulders from behind.*

ROBBIE Everybody know how on the day freedom come, we followed Uncle Buck up to the massa porch. And Uncle Buck said,

JEANNIE Massa is we free?

ROBBIE And that white man took out his shotgun, and said "Yeah nigger, you free" and shot Uncle Buck dead.

JEANNIE Massa is we free?

ROBBIE Shot Uncle Buck dead.

JEANNIE Massa is we free?

ROBBIE Say it again.

JEANNIE Is we free?

ROBBIE *(to audience)* They say Massa was mean and nasty. He was all dressed up, and the ladies too, and they all came back to the kitchen. And one of the uncles took the blame for stealing the bucket of fatback and greens that Sally was gon' bring down to the quarters for us. And they made him eat the whole bucket of fatback and greens, until he commenced to rolling on the floor and passing gas, and they laughed and laughed . . . and the ladies too.

JEANNIE Is that it?

ROBBIE *(aside)* They say that day might not a been really rich white folks anyhow. *(to Audience)* On the day the really rich white folks came, they dressed up Sally and one of the uncles like staff, like house staff, so Massa and them would seem richer than they were and so we'd seem more profitable. They were figna sell us! Figna sell us further down south Georgia! If the war hadn't a come, no telling what woulda happened. *(pause)* I reckon we'd a never been here to tell y'all this.

They call for AUDIENCE *response.* ROBBIE *waves off dialogue.* JEANNIE *sits on bench*

JEANNIE But you were already in south Georgia. How much further down could you go?

ROBBIE *(sits next to* JEANNIE*)* They say Sally had them children by the master to save us. How come they thought she had a choice? Survival is luck. Or unlucky.

They improvise. The following is an example of the dialogue that has resulted in performance.

You wanna try the language lesson?

JEANNIE Okay. . . . They was from south o' Albany way down Seminole or Decatur.

ROBBIE That's sort of—

JEANNIE Jimmy Carter.

ROBBIE Sort of a bad imitation of a white southerner.

JEANNIE I'm not trying . . .

ROBBIE As I've said before, try to know, like actors do, what you're talking about.

JEANNIE Further south?

ROBBIE Where slaves were sent, couldn't get back from, way away from their loved ones. It resonated dread. See it, know it, feel the dread when you say where that place was. *(doing it)* They's from souf a Allbeny way down Semino o' De kaytuh.

JEANNIE They's from south o' Al bany way down Semino o' Decatur.

ROBBIE Better. When we learned the English language, we had to learn the English culture. I only learned later that iambic pentameter was street language . . . like rap . . . "To be or not to be, that is the question." Deep ambivalence. I could play Hamlet.

JEANNIE If they let you.

ROBBIE If I wanted to.

They sit quiet. Lights out. Applause.

Epilogue: Leaving the Audience Talking.

Lights up. JEANNIE *and* ROBBIE *get their cups of tea.*

JEANNIE There's a part we sort of want to do to involve the audience, but we get more involved . . .

ROBBIE It has to do with talking to people, even if you already know 'em, and especially if you don't, how a lot of people in different cultures greet each other, I know some Native American cultures do: "Who are you and who are your people?" And where I come from, African-American folk be like, "Who children you?"

JEANNIE So our idea was that you were going to turn to somebody else and find out something.

ROBBIE Which you can do.

ROBBIE *and* JEANNIE *walk off.*

BLACK THEATRE FOR BLACK PEOPLE

Amiri Baraka • Ed Bullins • Ben Caldwell • Ted Shine • Kalamu ya Salaam

Between 1816 and 1817, a Mr. Brown (purported to be William A. Brown) opened a tea garden in lower Manhattan and, in doing so, launched a series of firsts in African American theatre. The popularity of the entertainment that Brown provided for his African American customers—songs, poetry, dramatic monologues—led to the formation of the African Company, a performing troupe of Black actors. On September 21, 1821, they presented Shakespeare's *Richard III* at the African Grove tea garden. This was the first play performed by Blacks in America. When Brown converted the upstairs apartments of the African Grove into a theatre seating 300 to 400 people, he established the first Black theatre in the country. A play written by Brown, *The Drama of King Shotaway*, about an insurrection on the island of St. Vincent in which he participated, was the first drama written by a Black American. Brown seems to have been moving his theatre in the direction that African American critics and artists were demanding a century later—a theatre by, about, and for Blacks. Although Brown's theatre was opened to serve Black performers and audiences, whites attended out of curiosity and to mock the players. Their behavior ultimately caused the demise of the theatre.

In 1915, the Lafayette Players were organized in Harlem for basically the same reasons that led to the establishment of the African Company: African American actors needed a place to work and master their craft, and Black audiences needed a theatre and drama in their community. Harlem critics were pleased with the performers but disappointed because the Lafayette Players were presenting Black actors in white Broadway plays, rather than developing Black playwrights. It was not until 1925, when W.E.B. Du Bois initiated the Krigwa Playwriting Contest, that young African American playwrights were introduced to the nation through the publication of their prize-winning plays in *Crisis,* the NAACP magazine that Dr. Du Bois edited. The following year, Du Bois organized the Krigwa Little Theatre to produce plays *about, by, for,* and *near* African Americans. The white mass media did not attack it and white America remained unthreatened by a separatist movement.

In 1965, LeRoi Jones demanded a theatre *about, with, for* Black people—and *only* black people. This time caucasians rose up righteously to denounce "reverse racism." There were reasons for the backlash: the ungrateful Jones (who was soon to abandon his "slave" name) was biting the hand that had given him the awards (see *Dutchman*). Also, the nation had just survived the "separatist threat" of Malcolm X and the Black Muslims. Finally, white America had made reluctant gestures toward integration. For a supplicant to spurn the majority was too much.

The authors in this section are speaking primarily to their own people in their own idiom. A white may read the plays, attend the performances, be hip to in-group life and language, but must finally remain outside the total experience of the play because, as Woodie King, Jr., founder of the New Federal Theatre at the Henry Street Settlement, put it, "White values are not Black values."[1]

Each play in this section is concerned with some aspect of the African American experience. Jones's avant-garde allegory warns his audience of the danger and destructiveness of attempting to assimilate into white society. Shine, too, is concerned with Black and white relationships, but uses humor as a means of exploring America's racial problem. *Blk Love Song #1* is ritual theatre depicting negative and positive images of African Americans in order to raise the consciousness of Black audiences. Bullins shows us characters attempting to make it in a capitalistic society, where betrayal and corruption are acceptable means of achieving one's end.

1. Woodie King, Jr., *Black Theatre Present Condition* (New York: Publishing Center for Cultural Resources, 1981), p. 10.

DUTCHMAN

1964

LeRoi Jones (Amiri Baraka)

(1934–   )

"One night I sat up all night and wrote a play I called *Dutchman*. I had gotten the title from *The Flying Dutchman* but abstracted it, because . . . It didn't quite serve my purpose. . . ."[1]

LeRoi Jones draws on several historical and literary sources for his play. Jones's title brings to mind the Dutch slave ships that transported human cargo to the Americas. The title also suggests the Flying Dutchman maritime legend and Wagnerian opera about a ship that haunted the seas around the Cape of Good Hope, luring other ships to their destruction. One legend has it that a Dutch captain insisted on sailing around the Cape during a violent storm against the protests of his passengers and crew. When a vision of God appeared on deck, the captain not only refused to acknowledge it but drew his pistol, fired, and cursed the image. His punishment was to wander the seas tormenting sailors until Judgment Day.

Richard Wagner's opera gives the captain an escape route—the curse can be lifted if he finds a woman who will love and be faithful to him unto death. For Wagner, the woman means redemption; for Jones, death. The characters in *Dutchman* are linked symbolically to the legend, Clay representing the God figure and Lula, the captain.

The Biblical story of Adam and Eve is also incorporated into Jones's play—Clay being Adam and Lula, Eve. Jones's Flying Dutchman is a subway train speeding through the innards of New York City. Within this underground serpent, Clay, a middle-class, naive, African American intellectual, encounters Lula, an apple-eating "nutty" and dangerous bohemian white woman. Lula sets out to seduce Clay, but to accomplish this she must first mold him into the image that she desires—the stereotypical Black figure whom whites create and demand. She taunts Clay about

1. Amiri Baraka, *The Autobiography of LeRoi Jones/Amiri Baraka* (New York: Freundlich Books, 1984), p. 187.

those things that single him out as middle-class, igniting his anger. Lula eventually discovers that gentle, "complaisant" Blacks can also be threatening and dangerous.

Jones uses the white myth of Black male sexuality to expose the systematic and deliberate annihilation of African Americans. Headlines in newspapers from around the country have described the horrors of lynching from the late nineteenth until well into the twentieth century: "Two Blacks Strung Up: Grave Doubt of Their Guilt," "Negro Lynched to Avenge Assault on White Woman," "An Innocent Man Lynched," "Lynch Mob May Have Erred," "Lynched Despite Protests of Rape Victim's Parents," "Doubt Bludgeoned Negro Was Accoster of Girls."[2] A large percentage of these lynchings were responses to allegations of rape, others to minor offenses. One of the most heinous lynchings occurred near Money, Mississippi, in 1955, when Emmett Till, a fourteen-year-old boy from Chicago, was abducted, beaten, and shot in the head, and his body thrown into the Tallahatchie River, for allegedly whistling at a white woman. James Baldwin used this tragedy as the basis for his play *Blues for Mister Charlie*. For Jones, Clay's murder becomes the symbolic lynching of all African Americans.

Jones was born in Newark, New Jersey. He attended Rutgers University in 1951 and transferred to Howard University, where he majored in English. He is a poet, playwright, author, and educator. He was founder-director of the Black Arts Repertory Theatre and School in Harlem in 1964, and later founder-director of Spirit House in Newark, where young African American playwrights' works were performed by the African Revolutionary Movers repertory theatre company. In addition to plays, he has published more than two dozen books, including poetry, fiction, and nonfiction. He has been the recipient of numerous grants, fellowships, and awards, and in 1972 was awarded a Doctor of Humane Letters degree by Malcolm X College in Chicago. Jones is hailed as the leader of the revolutionary Black Arts and Black Theatre movements of the 1960s. *Dutchman* won the Obie Award for best Off Broadway play in 1964.

Dutchman

CHARACTERS

CLAY, a twenty-year-old Negro
LULA, thirty-year-old white woman
RIDERS OF COACH, white and Black
YOUNG NEGRO
CONDUCTOR

In the flying underbelly of the city. Steaming hot, and summer on top, outside. Underground. The subway heaped in modern myth.

Opening scene is a man sitting in a subway seat, holding a magazine but looking vacantly just above its wilting pages. Occasionally he looks blankly toward the window on his right. Dim lights and darkness whistling by against the glass. (Or paste the lights, as admitted props, right on the subway windows. Have them move, even dim and flicker. But give the sense of speed. Also stations, whether the train is stopped or the glitter and activity of these stations merely flashes by the windows.)

The man is sitting alone. That is, only his seat is visible, though the rest of the car is outfitted as a complete subway car. But only his seat is shown.

2. Ralph Ginzburg, *100 Years of Lynching* (New York: Lancer Books, 1962).

There might be, for a time, as the play begins, a loud scream of the actual train. And it can recur throughout the play, or continue on a lower key once the dialogue starts.

The train slows after a time, pulling to a brief stop at one of the stations. The man looks idly up, until he sees a woman's face staring at him through the window; when it realizes that the man has noticed the face, it begins very premeditatedly to smile. The man smiles too, for a moment, without a trace of self-consciousness. Almost an instinctive though undesirable response. Then a kind of awkwardness or embarrassment sets in, and the man makes to look away, is further embarrassed, so he brings back his eyes to where the face was, but by now the train is moving again, and the face would seem to be left behind by the way the man turns his head to look back through the other windows at the slowly fading platform. He smiles then; more comfortably confident, hoping perhaps that his memory of this brief encounter will be pleasant. And then he is idle again.

Scene I

Train roars. Lights flash outside the windows.

LULA *enters from the rear of the car in bright, skimpy summer clothes and sandals. She carries a net bag full of paper books, fruit, and other anonymous articles. She is wearing sunglasses, which she pushes up on her forehead from time to time.* LULA *is a tall, slender, beautiful woman with long red hair hanging straight down her back, wearing only loud lipstick in somebody's good taste. She is eating an apple, very daintily. Coming down the car toward* CLAY.

She stops beside CLAY'*s seat and hangs languidly from the strap, still managing to eat the apple. It is apparent that she is going to sit in the seat next to* CLAY, *and that she is only waiting for him to notice her before she sits.*

CLAY *sits as before, looking just beyond his magazine, now and again pulling the magazine slowly back and forth in front of his face in a hopeless effort to fan himself. Then he sees the woman hanging there beside him and he looks up into her face, smiling quizzically.*

LULA Hello.

CLAY Uh, hi're you?

LULA I'm going to sit down. . . . O.K.?

CLAY Sure.

LULA *(swings down onto the seat, pushing her legs straight out as if she is very weary)* Oooof! Too much weight.

CLAY Ha, doesn't look like much to me. *(leaning back against the window, a little surprised and maybe stiff)*

LULA It's so anyway. *(And she moves her toes in the sandals, then pulls her right leg up on the left knee, better to inspect the bottoms of the sandals and back of her heel. She appears for a second not to notice that* CLAY *is sitting next to her or that she has spoken to him just a second before.* CLAY *looks at the magazine, then out the black window. As he does this, she turns very quickly toward him)* Weren't you staring at me through the window?

CLAY *(wheeling around and very much stiffened)* What?

LULA Weren't you staring at me through the window? At the last stop?

CLAY Staring at you? What do you mean?

LULA Don't you know what staring means?

CLAY I saw you through the window . . . if that's what it means. I don't know if I was staring. Seems to me you were staring through the window at me.

LULA I was. But only after I'd turned around and saw you staring through that window down in the vicinity of my ass and legs.

CLAY Really?

LULA Really. I guess you were just taking those idle potshots. Nothing else to do. Run your mind over people's flesh.

CLAY Oh boy. Wow, now I admit I was looking in your direction. But the rest of that weight is yours.

LULA I suppose.

CLAY Staring through train windows is weird business. Much weirder than staring very sedately at abstract asses.

LULA That's why I came looking through the window . . . so you'd have more than that to go on. I even smiled at you.

CLAY That's right.

LULA I even got onto this train, going some other way than mine. Walked down the aisle . . . searching you out.

CLAY Really? That's pretty funny.

LULA That's pretty funny. . . . God, you're dull.

CLAY Well, I'm sorry, lady, but I really wasn't prepared for party talk.

LULA No, you're not. What are you prepared for? *(wrapping the apple core in a Kleenex and dropping it on the floor)*

CLAY *(takes her conversation as pure sex talk. He turns to confront her squarely with this idea)* I'm prepared for anything. How about you?

LULA *(laughing loudly and cutting it off abruptly)* What do you think you're doing?

CLAY What?

LULA You think I want to pick you up, get you to take me somewhere and screw me, huh?

CLAY Is that the way I look?

LULA You look like you been trying to grow a beard. That's exactly what you look like. You look like you live in New Jersey with your parents and are trying to grow a beard. That's what. You look like you've been reading Chinese poetry and drinking lukewarm sugarless tea. *(laughs, uncrossing and recrossing her legs)* You look like death eating a soda cracker.

CLAY *(Cocking his head from one side to the other, embarrassed and trying to make some comeback, but also intrigued by what the woman is saying . . . even the sharp city coarseness of her voice, which is still a kind of gentle sidewalk throb)* Really? I look like all that?

LULA Not all of it. *(she feigns a seriousness to cover an actual somber tone)* I lie a lot. *(smiling)* It helps me control the world.

CLAY *(relieved and laughing louder than the humor)* Yeah, I bet.

LULA But it's true, most of it, right? Jersey? Your bumpy neck?

CLAY How'd you know all that? Huh? Really, I mean about Jersey . . . and even the beard. I met you before? You know Warren Enright?

LULA You tried to make it with your sister when you were ten.

(CLAY leans back hard against the back of the seat, his eyes opening now, still trying to look amused)

But I succeeded a few weeks ago. *(she starts to laugh again)*

CLAY What're you talking about? Warren tell you that? You're a friend of Georgia's?

LULA I told you I lie. I don't know your sister. I don't know Warren Enright.

CLAY You mean you're just picking these things out of the air?

LULA Is Warren Enright a tall skinny black black boy with a phony English accent?

CLAY I figured you knew him.

LULA But I don't. I just figured you would know somebody like that. *(laughs)*

CLAY Yeah, yeah.

LULA You're probably on your way to his house now.

CLAY That's right.

LULA *(putting her hand on CLAY's closest knee, drawing it from the knee up to the thigh's hinge, then removing it, watching his face very closely, and continuing to laugh, perhaps more gently than before)* Dull, dull, dull. I bet you think I'm exciting.

CLAY You're O.K.

LULA Am I exciting you now?

CLAY Right. That's not what's supposed to happen?

LULA How do I know? *(she returns her hand, without moving it, then takes it away and plunges it in her bag to draw out an apple)* You want this?

CLAY Sure.

LULA *(she gets one out of the bag for herself)* Eating apples together is always the first step. Or walking up uninhabited Seventh Avenue in the twenties on weekends. *(bites and giggles, glancing at CLAY and speaking in loose sing-song)* Can you get involved . . . boy? Get us involved. Um-huh. *(mock seriousness)* Would you like to get involved with me, Mister Man?

CLAY *(trying to be as flippant as LULA, whacking happily at the apple)* Sure. Why not? A beautiful woman like you. Huh, I'd be a fool not to.

LULA And I bet you're sure you know what you're talking about. *(taking him a little roughly by the wrists, so he cannot eat the apple, then shaking the wrist)* I bet you're sure of almost everything anybody ever asked you about . . . right? *(shakes his wrist harder)* Right?

CLAY Yeah, right. . . . Wow, you're pretty strong, you know? Whatta you, a lady wrestler or something?

LULA What's wrong with lady wrestlers? And don't answer because you never knew any. Huh. *(cynically)* That's for sure. They don't have any lady wrestlers in that part of Jersey. That's for sure.

CLAY Hey, you still haven't told me how you know so much about me.

LULA I told you I didn't know anything about *you* . . . you're a well-known type.

CLAY Really?

LULA Or at least I know the type very well. And your skinny English friend too.

CLAY Anonymously?

LULA *(settles back in seat, single-mindedly finishing her apple and humming snatches of rhythm and blues song)* What?

CLAY Without knowing us specifically?

LULA Oh boy. *(looking quickly at* CLAY*)* What a face. You know, you could be a handsome man.

CLAY I can't argue with you.

LULA *(vague, off-center response)* What?

CLAY *(raising his voice, thinking the train noise has drowned part of his sentence)* I can't argue with you.

LULA My hair is turning gray. A gray hair for each year and type I've come through.

CLAY Why do you want to sound so old?

LULA But it's always gentle when it starts. *(attention drifting)* Hugged against tenements, day or night.

CLAY What?

LULA *(refocusing)* Hey, why don't you take me to that party you're going to?

CLAY You must be a friend of Warren's to know about the party.

LULA Wouldn't you like to take me to the party? *(imitates clinging vine)* Oh, come on, ask me to your party.

CLAY Of course I'll ask you to come with me to the party. And I'll bet you're a friend of Warren's.

LULA Why not be a friend of Warren's? Why not? *(taking his arm)* Have you asked me yet?

CLAY How can I ask you when I don't know your name?

LULA Are you talking to my name?

CLAY What is it, a secret?

LULA I'm Lena the Hyena.

CLAY The famous woman poet?

LULA Poetess! The same!

CLAY Well, you know so much about me . . . what's my name?

LULA Morris the Hyena.

CLAY The famous woman poet?

LULA The same. *(laughing and going into her bag)* You want another apple?

CLAY Can't make it, lady. I only have to keep one doctor away a day.

LULA I bet your name is . . . something like . . . uh, Gerald or Walter. Huh?

CLAY God, no.

LULA Lloyd, Norman? One of those hopeless colored names creeping out of New Jersey. Leonard? Gag. . . .

CLAY Like Warren?

LULA Definitely. Just exactly like Warren. Or Everett.

CLAY Gag. . . .

LULA Well, for sure, it's not Willie.

CLAY It's Clay.

LULA Clay? Really? Clay what?

CLAY Take your pick. Jackson, Johnson, or Williams.

LULA Oh, really? Good for you. But it's got to be Williams. You're too pretentious to be a Jackson or Johnson.

CLAY Thass right.

LULA But Clay's O.K.

CLAY So's Lena.

LULA It's Lula.

CLAY Oh?

LULA Lula the Hyena.

CLAY Very good.

LULA *(starts laughing again)* Now you say to me, "Lula, Lula, why don't you go to this party with me tonight?" It's your turn, and let those be your lines.

CLAY Lula, why don't you go to this party with me tonight, Huh?

LULA Say my name twice before you ask, and no huh's.

CLAY Lula, Lula, why don't you go to this party with me tonight?

LULA I'd like to go, Clay, but how can you ask me to go when you barely know me?

CLAY That is strange, isn't it?

LULA What kind of reaction is that? You're supposed to say, "Aw, come on, we'll get to know each other better at the party."

CLAY That's pretty corny.

LULA What are you into anyway? *(looking at him half sullenly but still amused)* What thing are you playing at, Mister? Mister Clay Williams? *(grabs his thigh, up near the crotch)* What are *you* thinking about?

CLAY Watch it now, you're gonna excite me for real.

LULA *(taking her hand away and throwing her apple core through the window)* I bet. *(she slumps in the seat and is heavily silent)*

CLAY I thought you knew everything about me? What happened?

*(*LULA *looks at him, then looks slowly away, then over where the other aisle would be. Noise of the train. She reaches in her bag and pulls out one of the paper books. She puts it on her leg and thumbs*

the pages listlessly. CLAY *cocks his head to see the title of the book. Noise of the train.* LULA *flips pages and her eyes drift. Both remain silent)*

Are you going to the party with me, Lula?

LULA *(bored and not even looking)* I don't even know you.

CLAY You said you know my type.

LULA *(strangely irritated)* Don't get smart with me, Buster. I know you like the palm of my hand.

CLAY The one you eat the apples with?

LULA Yeh. And the one I open doors late Saturday evening with. That's my door. Up at the top of the stairs. Five flights. Above a lot of Italians and lying Americans. And scrape carrots with. Also . . . *(looks at him)* the same hand I unbutton my dress with, or let my skirt fall down. Same hand. Lover.

CLAY Are you angry about anything? Did I say something wrong?

LULA Everything you say is wrong. *(mock smile)* That's what makes you so attractive. Ha. In that funnybook jacket with all the buttons. *(more animate, taking hold of his jacket)* What've you got that jacket and tie on in all this heat for? And why're you wearing a jacket and tie like that? Did your people ever burn witches or start revolutions over the price of tea? Boy, those narrow-shoulder clothes come from a tradition you ought to feel oppressed by. A three-button suit. What right do you have to be wearing a three-button suit and striped tie? Your grandfather was a slave, he didn't go to Harvard.

CLAY My grandfather was a night watchman.

LULA And you went to a colored college where everybody thought they were Averell Harriman.

CLAY All except me.

LULA And who did you think you were? Who do you think you are now?

CLAY *(laughs as if to make light of the whole trend of the conversation)* Well, in college I thought I was Baudelaire. But I've slowed down since.

LULA I bet you never once thought you were a Black nigger.

(Mock serious, then she howls with laughter. CLAY *is stunned but after initial reaction, he quickly tries to appreciate the humor.* LULA *almost shrieks)*

A Black Baudelaire.

CLAY That's right.

LULA Boy, are you corny. I take back what I said before. Everything you say is not wrong. It's perfect. You should be on televiion.

CLAY You act like you're on television already.

LULA That's because I'm an actress.

CLAY I thought so.

LULA Well, you're wrong. I'm no actress. I told you I always lie. I'm nothing, honey, and don't you ever forget it. *(lighter)* Although my mother was a Communist. The only person in my family ever to amount to anything.

CLAY My mother was a Republican.

LULA And your father voted for the man rather than the party.

CLAY Right!

LULA Yea for him. Yea, yea for him.

CLAY Yea!

LULA And yea for America where he is free to vote for the mediocrity of his choice! Yea!

CLAY Yea!

LULA And yea for both your parents who even though they differ about so crucial a matter as the body politic still forged a union of love and sacrifice that was destined to flower at the birth of the noble Clay . . . what's your middle name?

CLAY Clay.

LULA A union of love and sacrifice that was destined to flower at the birth of the noble Clay Clay Williams. Yea! And most of all yea yea for you, Clay Clay. The Black Baudelaire! Yes. *(and with knifelike cynicism)* My Christ. My Christ.

CLAY Thank you, ma'am.

LULA May the people accept you as a ghost of the future. And love you, that you might not kill them when you can.

CLAY What?

LULA You're a murderer, Clay, and you know it. *(her voice darkening with significance)* You know goddamn well what I mean.

CLAY I do?

LULA So we'll pretend the air is light and full of perfume.

CLAY *(sniffing at her blouse)* It is.

LULA And we'll pretend the people cannot see you. That is, the citizens. And that you are free of your own history. And I am free of my history. We'll pretend that we are both anonymous beauties smashing along through the city's entrails. *(she yells as loud as she can)* GROOVE!

Black

Scene II

Scene is the same as before, though now there are other seats visible in the car. And throughout the scene other people get on the subway. There are maybe one or two seated in the car as the scene opens, though neither CLAY *nor* LULA *notices them.* CLAY*'s tie is open.* LULA *is hugging his arm.*

CLAY The party!

LULA I know it'll be something good. You can come in with me, looking casual and significant. I'll be strange, haughty, and silent, and walk with long low strides.

CLAY Right.

LULA When you get drunk, pat me once, very lovingly on the flanks, and I'll look at you cryptically, licking my lips.

CLAY It sounds like something we can do.

LULA You'll go around talking to young men about your mind, and to old men about your plans. If you meet a very close friend who is also with someone like me, we can stand together, sipping our drinks and exchanging codes of lust. The atmosphere will be slithering in love and half-love and very open moral decision.

CLAY Great. Great.

LULA And everyone will pretend they don't know your name, and then . . . *(she pauses heavily)* later, when they have to, they'll claim a friendship that denies your sterling character.

CLAY *(kissing her neck and fingers)* And then what?

LULA Then? Well, then we'll go down the street, late night, eating apples and winding very deliberately toward my house.

CLAY Deliberately?

LULA I mean, we'll look in all the shopwindows, and make fun of the queers. Maybe we'll meet a Jewish Buddhist and flatten his conceits over some very pretentious coffee.

CLAY In honor of whose God?

LULA Mine.

CLAY Who is . . . ?

LULA Me . . . and you?

CLAY A corporate Godhead.

LULA Exactly. Exactly. *(notices one of the other people entering)*

CLAY Go on with the chronicle. Then what happens to us?

LULA *(a mild depression, but she still makes her description triumphant and increasingly direct)* To my house, of course.

CLAY Of course.

LULA And up the narrow steps of the tenement.

CLAY You live in a tenement?

LULA Wouldn't live anywhere else. Reminds me specifically of my novel form of insanity.

CLAY Up the tenement stairs.

LULA And with my apple-eating hand I push open the door and lead you, my tender big-eyed prey, into my . . . God, what can I call it . . . into my hovel.

CLAY Then what happens?

LULA After the dancing and games, after the long drinks and long walks, the real fun begins.

CLAY Ah, the real fun. *(embarrassed, in spite of himself)* Which is . . . ?

LULA *(laughs at him)* Real fun in the dark house. Hah! Real fun in the dark house, high up above the street and the ignorant cowboys. I lead you in, holding your wet hand gently in my hand . . .

CLAY Which is not wet?

LULA Which is dry as ashes.

CLAY And cold?

LULA Don't think you'll get out of your responsibility that way. It's not cold at all. You Fascist! Into my dark living room. Where we'll sit and talk endlessly, endlessly.

CLAY About what?

LULA About what? About your manhood, what do you think? What do you think we've been talking about all this time?

CLAY Well, I didn't know it was that. That's for sure. Every other thing in the world but that. *(notices another person entering, looks quickly, almost involuntarily up and down the car, seeing the other people in the car)* Hey, I didn't even notice when those people got on.

LULA Yeah, I know.

CLAY Man, this subway is slow.

LULA Yeah, I know.

CLAY Well, go on. We were talking about my manhood.

LULA We still are. All the time.

CLAY We were in your living room.

LULA My dark living room. Talking endlessly.

CLAY About my manhood.

LULA I'll make you a map of it. Just as soon as we get to my house.

CLAY Well, that's great.

LULA One of the things we do while we talk. And screw.

CLAY *(trying to make his smile broader and less shaky)* We finally got there.

LULA And you'll call my rooms black as a grave. You'll say, "This place is like Juliet's tomb."

CLAY *(laughs)* I might.

LULA I know. You've probably said it before.

CLAY And is that all? The whole grand tour?

CLAY Not all. You'll say to me very close to my face, many, many times, you'll say, even whisper, that you love me.

CLAY Maybe I will.

LULA And you'll be lying.

CLAY I wouldn't lie about something like that.

LULA Hah. It's the only kind of thing you will lie about. Especially if you think it'll keep me alive.

CLAY Keep you alive? I don't understand.

LULA *(bursting out laughing, but too shrilly)* Don't understand? Well, don't look at me. It's the path I take, that's all. Where both feet take me when I set them down. One in front of the other.

CLAY Morbid. Morbid. You sure you're not an actress? All that self-aggrandizement.

LULA Well, I told you I wasn't an actress . . . but I also told you I lie all the time. Draw your own conclusions.

CLAY Morbid. Morbid. You sure you're not an actress? All scribed? There's no more?

LULA I've told you all I know. Or almost all.

CLAY There's no funny parts?

LULA I thought it was all funny.

CLAY But you mean peculiar, not ha-ha.

LULA You don't know what I mean.

CLAY Well, tell me the almost part then. You said almost all. What else? I want the whole story.

LULA *(searching aimlessly through her bag. She begins to talk breathlessly, with a light and silly tone)* All stories are whole stories. All of 'em. Our whole story . . . nothing but change. How could things go on like that forever? Huh? *(slaps him on the shoulder, begins finding things in her bag, taking them out and throwing them over her shoulder into the aisle)* Except I do go on as I do. Apples and long walks with deathless intelligent lovers. But you mix it up. Look out the window, all the time. Turning pages. Change change change. Till, shit, I don't know you. Wouldn't, for that matter. You're too serious. I bet you're even too serious to be psychoanalyzed. Like all those Jewish poets from Yonkers, who leave their mothers looking for other mothers, or others' mothers, on whose baggy tits they lay their fumbling heads. Their poems are always funny, and all about sex.

CLAY They sound great. Like movies.

LULA But you change. *(blankly)* And things work on you till you hate them.

(More people come into the train. They come closer to the couple, some of them not sitting, but swinging drearily on the straps, staring at the two with uncertain interest)

CLAY Wow. All these people, so suddenly. They must all come from the same place.

LULA Right. That they do.

CLAY Oh? You know about them too?

LULA Oh yeah. About them more than I know about you. Do they frighten you?

CLAY Frighten me? Why should they frighten me?

LULA 'Cause you're an escaped nigger.

CLAY Yeah?

LULA 'Cause you crawled through the wire and made tracks to my side.

CLAY Wire?

LULA Don't they have wire around plantations?

CLAY You must be Jewish. All you can think about is wire. Plantations didn't have any wire. Plantations were big open whitewashed places like heaven, and everybody on 'em was grooved to be there. Just strummin' and hummin' all day.

LULA Yes, yes.

CLAY And that's how the blues was born.

LULA Yes, yes. And that's how the blues was born.

(Begins to make up a song that becomes quickly hysterical. As she sings she rises from her seat, still throwing things out of her bag into the aisle, beginning a rhythmical shudder and twistlike wiggle, which she continues up and down the aisle, bumping into many of the standing people and tripping over the feet of those sitting. Each time she runs

into a person she lets out a very vicious piece of profanity, wiggling and stepping all the time)

And that's how the blues was born. Yes. Yes. Son of a bitch, get out of the way. Yes. Quack. Yes. Yes. And that's how the blues was born. Ten little niggers sitting on a limb, but none of them ever looked like him. *(points to* CLAY, *returns toward the seat, with her hands extended for him to rise and dance with her)* And that's how blues was born. Yes. Come on, Clay. Let's do the nasty. Rub bellies. Rub bellies.

CLAY *(waves his hand to refuse. He is embarrassed, but determined to get a kick out of the proceedings)* Hey, what was in those apples? Mirror, mirror on the wall, who's the fairest one of all? Snow White, baby, and don't you forget it.

LULA *(grabbing for his hands, which he draws away)* Come on, Clay. Let's rub bellies on the train. The nasty. The nasty. Do the gritty grind, like your ol' rag-head mammy. Grind till you lose your mind. Shake it, shake it, shake it, shake it! OOOOweeee! Come on, Clay. Let's do the choo-choo train shuffle, the navel scratcher.

CLAY Hey, you coming on like the lady who smoked up her grass skirt.

LULA *(becoming annoyed that he will not dance, and becoming more animated as if to embarrass him still further)* Come on, Clay . . . let's do the thing. Uhh! Uhh! Clay! Clay! You middle-class Black bastard. Forget your social-working mother for a few seconds and let's knock stomachs. Clay, you liver-lipped white man. You would-be Christian. You ain't no nigger, you're just a dirty white man. Get up, Clay. Dance with me, Clay.

CLAY Lula! Sit down, now. Be cool.

LULA *(mocking him, in wild dance)* Be cool. Be cool. That's all you know . . . shaking that wildroot cream-oil on your knotty head, jackets buttoning up to your chin, so full of white man's words. Christ. God. Get up and scream at these people. Like scream meaningless shit in these hopeless faces. *(she screams at people in train, still dancing)* Red trains cough Jewish underwear for keeps! Expanding smells of silence. Gravy snot whistling like sea birds. Clay. Clay, you got to break out. Don't sit there dying the way they want you to die. Get up.

CLAY Oh, sit the fuck down. *(he moves to restrain her)* Sit down, goddamn it.

LULA *(twisting out of his reach)* Screw yourself, Uncle Tom. Thomas Woolly-head. *(begins to dance a kind of jig, mocking* CLAY *with loud forced humor)* There is Uncle Tom . . . I mean Uncle Thomas Woolly-Head. With old white matted mane. He hobbles on his wooden cane. Old Tom. Old Tom. Let the white man hump his ol' mama, and he jes' shuffle off in the woods and hide his gentle gray head. Ol' Thomas Woolly-Head.

(Some of the other riders are laughing now. A drunk gets up and joins LULA *in her dance, singing, as best he can, her "song."* CLAY *gets up out of his seat and visibly scans the faces of the other riders)*

CLAY Lula! Lula!

(She is dancing and turning, still shouting as loud as she can. The drunk too is shouting, and waving his hands wildly)

Lula . . . you dumb bitch. Why don't you stop it?

(He rushes half stumbling from his seat, and grabs one of her flailing arms)

LULA Let me go! You Black son of a bitch. *(she struggles against him)* Let me go! Help!

*(*CLAY *is dragging her towards her seat, and the drunk seeks to interfere. He grabs* CLAY *around the shoulders and begins wrestling with him.* CLAY *clubs the drunk to the floor without releasing* LULA, *who is still screaming.* CLAY *finally gets her to the seat and throws her into it)*

CLAY Now you shut the hell up. *(grabbing her shoulders)* Just shut up. You don't know what you're talking about. You don't know anything. So just keep your stupid mouth closed.

LULA You're afraid of white people. And your father was Uncle Tom Big Lip!

CLAY

(Slaps her as hard as he can, across the mouth. LULA*'s head bangs against the back of the seat. When she raises it again,* CLAY *slaps her again)*

Now shut up and let me talk.

(He turns toward the other riders, some of whom are sitting on the edge of their seats. The drunk is on one knee, rubbing his head, and singing softly the same song. He shuts up too when he sees CLAY

watching him. The others go back to newspapers or stare out the windows)

Shit, you don't have any sense, Lula, nor feelings either. I could murder you now. Such a tiny ugly throat. I could squeeze it flat, and watch you turn blue, on a humble. For dull kicks. All all these weak-faced ofays squatting around here, staring over their papers at me. Murder them too. Even if they expected it. That man there . . . *(points to well-dressed man)* I could rip that *Times* right out of his hand, as skinny and middle-classed as I am, I could rip that paper out of his hand and just as easily rip out his throat. It takes no great effort. For what? To kill you soft idiots? You don't understand anything but luxury.

LULA You fool!

CLAY *(pushing her against the seat)* I'm not telling you again, Tallulah Bankhead! Luxury. In your face and your fingers. You telling me what I ought to do. *(sudden scream frightening the whole coach)* Well, don't! Don't you tell me anything! If I'm a middle-class fake white man . . . let me be. And let me be in the way I want. *(through his teeth)* I'll rip your lousy breasts off! Let me be who I feel like being. Uncle Tom. Thomas. Whoever. It's none of your business. You don't know anything except what's there for you to see. An act. Lies. Device. Not the pure heart, the pumping Black heart. You don't ever know that. And I sit here, in this buttoned-up suit, to keep myself from cutting all your throats. I mean wantonly. You great liberated whore! You fuck some Black man, and right away you're an expert on Black people. What a lotta shit that is. The only thing you know is that you come if he bangs you hard enough. And that's all. The belly rub? You wanted to do the belly rub? Shit, you don't even know how. You don't know how. That ol' dipty-dip shit you do, rolling your ass like an elephant. That's not my kind of belly rub. Belly rub is not Queens. Belly rub is dark places, with big hats and overcoats held up with one arm. Belly rub hates you. Old bald-headed four-eyed ofays popping their fingers . . . and don't know yet what they're doing. They say, "I love Bessie Smith." And don't even understand that Bessie Smith is saying, "Kiss my ass, kiss my black unruly ass." Before love, suffering, desire, anything you can explain, she's saying and very plainly, "Kiss my black ass." And if you don't know that, it's you that's doing the kissing.

Charlie Parker? Charlie Parker. All the hip white boys scream for Bird. And Bird saying, "Up your ass, feeble-minded ofay! Up your ass." And they sit there talking about the tortured genius of Charlie Parker. Bird would've played not a note of music if he just walked up to East Sixty-seventh Street and killed the first ten white people he saw. Not a note! And I'm the great would-be poet. Yes. That's right! Poet. Some kind of bastard literature . . . all it needs is a simple knife thrust. Just let me bleed you, you loud whore, and one poem vanished. A whole people of neurotics, struggling to keep from being sane. And the only thing that would cure the neurosis would be your murder. Simple as that. I mean if I murdered you, then other white people would begin to understand me. You understand? No. I guess not. If Bessie Smith had killed some white people she wouldn't have needed that music. She could have talked very straight and plain about the world. No metaphors. No grunts. No wiggles in the dark of her soul. Just straight two and two are four. Money. Power. Luxury. Like that. All of them. Crazy niggers turning their backs on sanity. When all it needs is that simple act. Murder. Just murder! Would make us all sane. *(suddenly weary)* Ahhh. Shit. But who needs it? I'd rather be a fool. Insane. Safe with my words, and no deaths, and clean, hard thoughts, urging me to new conquests. My people's madness. Hah! That's a laugh. My people. They don't need me to claim them. They got legs and arms of their own. Personal insanities. Mirrors. They don't need all those words. They don't need any defense. But listen, though, one more thing. And you tell this to your father, who's probably the kind of man who needs to know at once. So he can plan ahead. Tell him not to preach so much rationalism and cold logic to these niggers. Let them alone. Let them sing curses at you in code and see your filth as simple lack of style. Don't make the mistake, through some irresponsible surge of Christian charity, of talking too much about the advantages of Western rationalism, or the great intellectual legacy of the white man, or maybe they'll begin to listen. And then, maybe one day, you'll find they actually do understand exactly what you are talking about, all these fantasy people. All these blues people. And on that day, as sure as shit, when you really believe you can "accept" them into your fold, as half-white trusties late of the subject peoples. With no more blues, except the very old ones, and not a watermelon in sight, the great missionary heart will have triumphed, and all of those ex-coons will be stand-up Western men, with eyes for clean hard useful lives, sober, pious and sane, and they'll murder you. They'll murder you, and have very rational explanations. Very much like your own. They'll cut your throats, and drag you out to the edge of your cities so the flesh can fall away from your bones, in sanitary isolation.

LULA *(her voice takes on a different, more businesslike quality)* I've heard enough.

CLAY *(reaching for his books)* I bet you have. I guess I better collect my stuff and get off this train. Looks like we won't be acting out that little pageant you outlined before.

LULA No. We won't. You're right about that, at least. *(she turns to look quickly around the rest of the car)* All right!

(The others respond)

CLAY *(bending across the girl to retrieve his belongings)* Sorry, baby, I don't think we could make it.

(As he is bending over her, the girl brings up a small knife and plunges it into CLAY*'s chest. Twice. He slumps across her knees, his mouth working stupidly)*

LULA Sorry is right.

(Turning to the others in the car who have already gotten up from their seats)

Sorry is the rightest thing you've said. Get this man off me! Hurry, now!

(The others come and drag CLAY*'s body down the aisle)*

Open the door and throw his body out.

(They throw him off)

And all of you get off at the next stop.

*(*LULA *busies herself straightening her things. Getting everything in order. She takes out a notebook and makes a quick scribbling note. Drops it in her bag. The train apparently stops and all the others get off, leaving her alone in the coach.*

Very soon a young Negro of about twenty comes into the coach, with a couple of books under his arm. He sits a few seats in back of LULA*. When he is seated she turns and gives him a long slow look. He looks up from his book and drops the book on his lap. Then an old Negro conductor comes into the car, doing a sort of restrained soft shoe, and half mumbling the words of some song. He looks at the young man, briefly, with a quick greeting)*

CONDUCTOR Hey, brother!
YOUNG MAN Hey.

(The conductor continues down the aisle with his little dance and the mumbled song. LULA *turns to stare at him and follows his movements down the aisle. The conductor tips his hat when he reaches her seat, and continues out the car)*

(Curtain)

GOIN' A BUFFALO

1966

Ed Bullins (1935–)

Goin' a Buffalo is a play about the wretched of the earth: little men and women with big dreams trying to make it in a capitalistic system that equates money with success. As the savings-and-loans scandals of the 1980s revealed, even the most trusted and respected members of our society are capable of cruel and unscrupulous measures in their search for the almighty dollar. Bullins's characters are no different. They are poor, corrupt, underworld creatures, surviving as best they can through prostitution, pimping, dealing drugs, hustling, and whatever other vice is at hand. Pandora, for example, is unable to earn a living as a singer because the owner of the club, Deeny, exploits the entertainers working for him. Her husband, Curt, allows Pandora to support him through prostitution. Curt realizes that, as a Black man, he is an outcast, and therefore he makes no apology for his behavior: "This ain't a world we built," he says, "so why should we try to fit in?" He masterminds one big drug deal in Los Angeles so that he and his entourage can move to Buffalo, where they will reestablish themselves as criminals. Art is a observer who describes himself as a "taker." He betrays and then deserts his best friend, and uses violence and drugs to induce Pandora and Mama Too Tight to accompany him to Buffalo, where they will be forced to work as his prostitutes. Motivated by money, all the characters operate on the assumption that one big score will provide them with the financing to fulfill their dreams.

Bullins's characters are not admirable people but they are to be pitied. Curt, Pandora, and Art are intelligent individuals with potential that they are not allowed to fulfill. Despite Curt's business acumen, he has no means with which to establish a business. Pandora sings, but is too busy trying to survive to pursue this as a career. Art is not only smart but clever, yet his motivations are all misdirected. These characters are familiar figures in African American communities. In a society with high unemployment, vice becomes an avenue to success, allowing you to make money and flaunt it in the form of dress, jewelry, cars, and cash, and often to become an idol and role model for impoverished youth. Death or imprisonment is a risk you take—since life itself is a risk in the ghetto.

Bullins's play speaks to African Americans specifically, but has significance for all audiences. *Goin' a Buffalo* is an indictment of a corrupt America that enslaved a race; permitted a system of sharecropping that dehumanized the poor; tolerates substandard housing and landlord absenteeism; allows industry to contaminate the soil and atmosphere in minority communities, resulting in deformities and death; allows farmers to exploit migrant workers; and permits the confiscation of farmland by denying seasonal loans—all for profit.

Ed Bullins is a prolific playwright, editor, essayist, filmmaker, novelist, poet, and teacher. He was born in Philadelphia, Pennsylvania. He attended Los Angeles City College and San Francisco State College. During the 1950s, he was a leader of the Black Arts movement in California and founder of Black Arts/West, an experimental theatre company in San Francisco. Bullins moved to New York City in 1967, subsequently becoming playwright-in-residence and associate director of the New Lafayette Theatre in Harlem. With Richard Wesley, he founded and edited *Black Theatre* magazine and he organized the Surviving Theatre in the Bronx. Bullins has taught English and writing at universities around the country. In 1971, he won the Obie Award for his play *The Fabulous Miss Marie* and the Drama Critics Award for *The Taking of Miss Janie*, which was voted the best play of the 1974–75 season. Bullins currently is playwright-in-residence at Northeastern University in Boston.

Goin' a Buffalo

Cast of Characters

CURT, *29 years old*
RICH, *28 years old*
PANDORA, *22 years old. Curt's wife*
ART, *23 years old*
MAMMA TOO TIGHT, *20 years old*
SHAKY, *36 years old. Mama Too Tight's man*
PIANO PLAYER
BASS PLAYER
DRUMMER
BARTENDER
DEENY
BOUNCER
CUSTOMERS
SHOWGIRL
VOICE

Act 1

Scene 1

This play is about some Black people: CURT, PANDORA, ART, RICH *and* SHAKY, *though* MAMMA TOO TIGHT *is white. The remainder of the cast is interracial, but two of the musicians are Black and if* DEENY, *the* BOUNCER *and one of the customers are white, there might be added tensions. But it is left to the director's imagination to match the colors to the portrayals.*

TIME: *Early 1960's late evening in January.*

SCENE: *A court apartment in Los Angeles in the West Adams district. The room is done in white: white ceiling, white walls, white overly elaborate furniture, but a red wall-to-wall carpet covers the floor. A wall bed is raised. Upstage, two doorless entrances stand on each side of the head of the bed. The right entrance is to the kitchen; the backstage area that represents the kitchen is shielded by a filmy curtain and the actors' dim silhouettes are seen when the area is lighted. The left entrance will be raised and offstage right at the head of a short flight of stairs and a platform which leads into the combination bathroom-dressing room-closet. When the actors are within this area their shadows will be cast upon the wall fronting the stairs. And when the bed is lowered a scarlet spread is shown.*

Within the interior of the front room the light is a mixture of red, blues, and violet with crimson shadows bordering the edges of the stage to create the illusion of a world afire with this pocket of atmosphere an oasis.

A Telefunken, turned very low, plays the local jazz station, and CURT *and* RICH *lean over a chess board.* CURT *squats upon a stool, and facing him across the coffee table and chess board,* RICH, *a stocky brooding man, studies his next move, seated on the edge of the couch. Each has an empty beer bottle and a glass close at hand.*

CURT I just about have you up tight, Rich.

RICH *(annoyed)* Awww . . . Curt, man . . . don't try and hustle me!

CURT *(looks at him)* Did I say somethin' to upset you, man? *(*RICH *shakes his head and curses to himself. A shadow appears at head of stairs and pauses as if the figure is listening for conversation, then* PANDORA *enters, a beautiful Black girl wearing tight white pants, a crimson blouse and black boots, and slowly descends the stairs while looking at the men. She crosses behind them and walks toward the kitchen.* RICH *looks a second at her behind, but drops his gaze when* CURT *begins tapping the chess board with a fingernail.* CURT *gives no discernible attention to* PANDORA. *She enters the kitchen; a light goes on.* CURT *stares at* RICH*)* This game's somethin' else . . . man.

RICH *(studies board, looks up at* CURT *and concentrates upon the board again. Mutters to himself)* Ain't this somethin' else, though . . . *(looking up)* You almost got my ass, man.

CURT *(mocking)* I have got your ass, Rich.

RICH *(half-hearted)* Awww . . . man . . . why don't you go fuck yourself? *(he places hand upon a piece)*

CURT *(warning and placing hand upon one of his pieces)* Wouldn't do that if I were you, good buddy.

RICH *(frowns and takes hand from board; he shakes head and mumbles, then curses his own caution)* Sheeet! *(he makes move)* Lets see what you're goin' ta do with that, man!

CURT *(deliberately)* Checkmate!

RICH *(half-rising)* What you say, Curt?

CURT *(toneless)* Checkmate, man. *(*CURT *looks toward the rear of the apartment; the faucet has been turned on, and in the kitchen* PANDORA *leisurely crosses the entrance doorway)* WE'RE READY FOR ANOTHER ONE, PANDORA!

PANDORA *(off)* Already!

CURT That's what I said, baby!

PANDORA *(re-crosses doorway)* Okay.

RICH *(mumbles and studies chess board)* Well . . . I'll be goddamned. *(faucet sound goes off)*

PANDORA *(off)* You don't need fresh glasses, do ya? *(sound of refrigerator opening)*

CURT *(surly)* NO, PANDORA, JUST THE BEER!

PANDORA *(raising voice)* Okay . . . Okay . . . wait a fuckin' minute, will ya? Be right there! *(rattles of bottles)*

CURT *(glowering toward the kitchen, then staring at* RICH *who sits stoop-shouldered)* How 'bout another one, Rich?

RICH *(reaches into pocket and brings out a small roll and pulls off two bills and places them beside* CURT*'s glass. He mutters to himself)* I wonder why in the fuck I didn't see that?

PANDORA *(with a cross expression enters carrying two bottles of Miller's Highlife)* Just because you're pissed off at the world, don't take it out on me! What'ta hell ya think ya got 'round here, maid service? *(*CURT *stands to meet her; she slows. Whining)* Awww . . . Curt . . . *(a knock comes from backstage; relieved she looks at* CURT*)* I wonder who would be knocking at the kitchen door, honey?

CURT *(reaches down, palms and pockets the money)* There's only one way to be sure, sugar. *(sits down, looks at* RICH*)* You clean, man?

RICH *(nods)* Yeah . . . Curt.

CURT *(nods to* PANDORA *as the knock sounds again)* Just watch your mouth, pretty baby . . . it's goin' ta get you in trouble one of these days, ya know. *(*PANDORA *places bottles on the edge of the table and briskly goes to open back door)*

PANDORA Maybe it's little Mamma already.

CURT *(mostly to himself)* She wouldn't come around to the back door for nobody. *(*CURT *disregards the noise of the kitchen door's lock snap-*

ping back and the rattle of the night chain being fixed in its hasp) I have the blackmen this time, right, Rich?

RICH *(reaching for the beer)* Yeah.

ART *(off)* Hello, is Curt home? My name's Art. I ran into Curt this afternoon and he told me to drop by.

PANDORA *(off)* Just a minute . . . I'll see. *(the sound of the door closing is heard, and* PANDORA *returns to the main room)* Curt . . . Curt?

CURT *(setting up his chess pieces; in a bored voice)* Yeah, baby?

PANDORA There's a guy named Art out here who says you told him to drop around.

CURT *(not looking at her but down at the board)* Invite him in, baby. *(*PANDORA *exits)*

RICH Is this the guy?

CURT *(nods, in low voice)* Never a dull moment . . . right, Rich?

RICH *(sarcastic)* Yeah. We're really in ta somethin', man.

(The music changes during the remainder of this scene. "Delilah" and "Parisian Thoroughfare" as recorded by Max Roach and Clifford Brown play. These will be the theme for the scenes between ART *and* PANDORA*, except when other music is necessary to stress altering moods. If act one extends long enough, "Sketches in Spain" by Miles Davis is to be played also, but "Delilah" should be replayed during* PANDORA*'s box scene*

(Offstage, PANDORA *says)*

PANDORA Just a minute. *(and the noise of the lock and chain is followed by* ART*)*

ART Good evening.

(She leads him into the living room. RICH *has poured beer for* CURT *and himself; he stands and saunters to the radio as if to change stations, but turns after* ART *has passed behind him and sizes up the stranger from the rear)*

CURT *(stands)* Hey, good buddy! You found the place okay, huh?

ART *(pleased by greeting)* Yeah, it wasn't so hard to find but I guess I came around to the wrong door.

CURT *(with a wave)* Awww . . . that's okay. One's good as the other. It's better to come in that way if you're walkin' from Washington Boulevard. You live somewhere 'round there, don't ya?

ART *(hesitant)* Well . . . I did.

CURT *(gesturing)* Here, I want you to meet my wife and a buddy of mine. *(introducing* PANDORA*)* This is my wife, Pandora . . . and . . .

PANDORA *(smiles brightly)* We already met, kinda. He told me his name at the door.

CURT *(ignoring* PANDORA*)* . . . and this is Rich.

RICH *(remains in same spot.* ART *turns and* RICH *gives him a casual salute)* What's happen'n, brother?

CURT *(to* PANDORA *and* RICH*)* This is a guy I met in jail. *(introduces* ART*)* Art Garrison. *(shows* ART *a seat on the couch, downstage from* RICH*)* Yeah, Art was one of the best young cons on Tier Three . . . *(to* PANDORA*)* Get my boy here a drink, baby.

PANDORA *(starts for kitchen)* You drink beer, Art?

ART Sure . . . that sounds great.

PANDORA *(over her shoulder)* We got some scotch, if you want it.

ART No, thanks. *(*RICH *sits, makes opening move, not looking at* ART*)*

CURT *(to* RICH*)* Yeah, if it wasn't for Art here I wouldn't be sittin' here.

RICH *(bored)* Yeah?

CURT This is the kid who banged Scooter aside the jaw during the riot last summer in the joint.

RICH *(sounding more enthused)* Yeah . . . you were doin' a stretch down at county jail when that happened, weren't you?

CURT Yeah, man. I was there bigger den shit. *(takes a seat)* Yeah, that paddy mathafukker, Scooter, was comin' down on me with an ice pick, man . . . we had all been rumblin' up and down the cell block and I slipped on somethin' wet . . . I think it was Cory's blood 'cause Miles and his boys had stomped that mathafukker so good . . . *(during the telling of the incident,* PANDORA *stands framed in the kitchen doorway, watching the men)* And I went to look up and all I could see was that grey-eyed mathafukkin' Scooter comin' at me with that ice pick of his . . . He reached down and grabbed my shirt front and drew back his arm and WHAMMO . . . *(indicating* ART*)* . . . just like a bat out'ta hell my boy here had scored on the sucker's jaw.

ART *(pleased)* Well . . . I wouldn't let that white sonna bitch do you in, man.

RICH *(dryly)* What was the beef about, man?

CURT Well you know Miles goes for the Muslims though he ain't one hisself. Now the Muslims were in a hassle at the joint with the guards and the big people up top because of their religious beliefs, dig?

RICH *(interested)* What do you mean?

CURT Well, the guards didn't want them havin' their meetin's 'cause they said they were organizin' and plottin'. And the Muslims wanted some of the chow changed 'cause they don't eat the same kind'a food that we do.

RICH Yeah!

CURT So while this was all goin' on, Cory . . . a young, wise nigger who thinks he's in ta somethin' . . . well he started agitatin' and signifyin' 'bout who the Muslims think they was. And what made it so rank was a lot of the ofays, ya know, Charles, the white man, start in sayin' things they had held back before, so Miles and some of the boys got together one day and caught that little jive sucker Cory outside his cell block and stomped him so bad the deck was greasy wit' his blood, man. That's when the shit started really goin' down, right there, man. Bumpy, Cory's cousin, come runnin' up, man, and that big nigger kicked Miles square in the nuts and laid out two of his boys before the rest of them got themselves together. By that time some of the whiteys come runnin' up and a few more of Miles' boys. Yeah, the whole shit started right there where Cory lay almost done in . . .

RICH Yeah . . . I heard a couple of cats got stabbed, man.

CURT Yeah, man, it was pretty scary for a while, mostly Black cons against white ones except for the studs who just tried to stay out of the shit and the Uncle Toms . . . those Toms we were really out to cool.

RICH *(heated)* Yeah, you should have done those mathafukkers in!

CURT Even the guards wouldn't come into the cell block and break it up at first . . . a whole lot of shit went down that day. *(looking at* ART*)* I owe my boy here a lot for that day.

ART *(embarrassed)* Yeah, man, I would have liked to have stayed out of it but I couldn't.

CURT Yeah, Art, I us'ta wonder about that . . . *(a two beat pause)* . . . How could you just go about your business and stay in the middle all the time in that place when so much crap was goin' down?

ART I just stayed out of everything, that's all.

CURT But didn't you care about anything, man? Didn't you feel anything when that shit was happen'n to you?

ART Yeah, I cared but I just didn't let it bother me too much. I just froze up on everything that tried to git in and not too much touched me.

PANDORA *(from doorway)* Talk about somebody bein' cold!

CURT *(having noticed her in doorway for first time, stares at* ART*)* But you don't know how I appreciate what you did, man. It wasn't your fight, man. You weren't takin' sides. You were one of the quiet guys waitin' for trial who just kept his mouth shut and minded his own business.

ART I never do try and take sides in stir, just serve my time and forget about it, that's all. *(*PANDORA *has moved out of the doorway)*

CURT Well, I'm glad you did that time, man, and if there's anything I can ever . . . *(*RICH *interrupts)*

RICH What were you in for, Art? *(*CURT *takes a drink of his beer, lights a cigarette and blows smoke across the table above the two men's heads.* PANDORA *drops something made of glass in the kitchen and curses)*

ART Well . . . I was waiting for trial . . . attempted murder.

RICH That's a tough one to have on your rap sheet.

ART Yeah, it doesn't do your record or you any good, especially when it ain't for money.

CURT *(finally makes answering chess move)* It was over a broad, wasn't it?

ART *(lights a cigarette, offers* RICH *a light but is refused)* Yeah. I guess girls are my main weakness.

RICH *(with unlit cigarette dangling from his lips, makes move)* How much time did you do?

ART Waited on my trial for nine months at county when the husband of the girl dropped the charges and left town.

CURT *(replies to move)* That's who you shot, the girl's husband?

ART *(his eyes following game)* Yeah.

RICH *(moves quickly)* You pretty good with a gun?

ART *(caught up in game)* I can usually hold one without it blowing my foot off.

RICH *(sharply)* Any simple ass can do that! I asked you are you any good with one!

(The three men are fixed in tableau for a three beat interval; ART *strains forward from his seat and is about to speak)*

CURT *(to* RICH *as he makes his move)* This move's goin' ta show ya ta stop fuckin' with Curt the Kid, good buddy. *(noise of refrigerator opening and slamming, and* PANDORA *enters with a bottle and a glass. She pours beer for* ART *and sets the glass down beside him as the men all look at the chess board)*

PANDORA *(in a light mood)* Sorry I took so long, Art. I just dropped the supper. *(to* CURT*)* Honey, the beans are all messed up. Little Mamma won't have anything to eat 'cept eggs.

CURT *(not looking at her)* Didn't want no fuckin' beans anyhow! And I know Mamma Too Tight don't want any either . . . what kind'a shit is that . . . givin' that broad beans on her first night on the streets?

PANDORA *(defensively)* That's all we got, honey . . . You know we won't have any spendin' money until Deeny pays me.

RICH Why don't you have a seat, Pan?

PANDORA I gotta finish cleanin' the kitchen . . . I don't want no roaches 'round here. Last place we had we had to split 'cause the roaches took it over. The little matha-fukkers got mo' of the food than Curt or me. Soon as I bring in a little money to get some food with . . . *(*CURT *looks at her sharply but she is turned toward* RICH *and* ART*)* . . . there's mo' of them little mathafukkers there than your eyes could see. And I put too much time in fixin' this pad up nice the way it is to have them little mathafukkers move in on me and try to take it over.

CURT You better finish up, sweetcake, so I can take you to work. *(the use of the term "sweetcake" is done with derision and seldom with affection.* PANDORA *picks up* CURT*'s empty bottles and exits)* Your move, Richie.

RICH Are you sure, man?

CURT Just ask Art, he's been watchin' the game.

ART Well, I ain't in it, man.

RICH That's right, you ain't in it.

CURT *(watching* ART*'s face)* Yeah, it's your move, Richie, babe.

RICH *(to* ART*)* That was pretty nice of that girl's ole man to let you off, Art.

ART Nawh . . . he wanted his ole lady to leave the state with him so he had to drop the charges against me to let her off the hook too.

RICH She was in it too, huh?

ART She shot him with me.

CURT You play this game, Art?

ART Yeah, some. But I haven't had much practice lately.

CURT Well, this one's about over.

RICH *(snorts)* Sheeet!

CURT Maybe you'd like ta play the winner.

RICH *(grimacing before making hesitant move)* Where ya livin' now, Art?

ART I just got locked out of my room.

RICH Yeah, Curt said you wanted to make some money.

ART *(intensely)* I have to, man. I'm really on my ass.

CURT Check!

RICH *(makes move)* Not yet, sucker.

ART I gotta get out of this town.

RICH You got a car, ain't ya?

CURT *(moves)* Not long now, Rich.

ART Yeah, that's about all I got. A car and a suitcase. I've also gotten more jail time in this town than in my whole life, and I've been halfway round the world and all over this country.

RICH *(moves and acts angry)* Yeah, L.A.'s no fuckin' good, man. If I was off parole now I would get the first thing on wheels out of here. How 'bout you, Curt? If you weren't out on bail wouldn't you make it?

*(*CURT *doesn't answer. Stage left, a knock sounds and* PANDORA *comes out of the kitchen striding toward the entrance which serves as the front door to the apartment)*

PANDORA That must be little Mamma.

CURT Sure hope it is . . . I would really like ta see that little broad.

PANDORA *(peers through window)* Yeah, there's that chick. *(calling outside in jocular way:)* HEY, BROAD, WHAT THEY DOIN' LETTIN' YOU OUT'TA JAIL? *(an indistinct shout and a laugh comes from outside)*

RICH *(to* RICH*)* Checkmate, man!

(Lights lower to blacken the stage)

Scene 2

(When the lights go up MAMMA TOO TIGHT *and* SHAKY *sit upon the lowered bed. Faintly reflecting a glow, the bed spread gives them the appearance of sitting upon smoldering coals.* MAMMA TOO TIGHT*, a small, voluptuous girl, is dressed well. Her shift complements her creamy complexion and full-blown build.* SHAKY *is nondescript but dresses in expensive casual clothes.*

CURT, RICH *and* ART *sit in the same area, stage right, facing the bed, forming the lower lip of a half-moon, and* PANDORA *has changed to a black cocktail dress and sits upon the stairs to the bathroom. She faces front with a bit of red-ruffled slip peeking beneath and around her black-stockinged legs.*

They all eat chicken from cardboard containers and reach for beers and cigarettes. The light in the kitchen is off, and the radio plays.)

ART Thanks again, Curt . . . if you hadn't invited me to eat I don't know what I'd do . . . probably had to drive downtown on what little gas I got and eat at one of those Rescue Missions.

MAMA TOO TIGHT *(nudging* SHAKY *in the ribs)* Well, I'll be damned . . . Ole Curt done saved himself a soul.

SHAKY *(slow and languid)* Easy, baby, you gonna make me spill my beer.

MAMA TOO TIGHT What you know 'bout eatin' at Rescue Missions, boy?

PANDORA *(interjecting)* You better stop callin' that guy ah boy, Mamma . . . ha ha . . . girl . . . you got mo' gall.

RICH *(drinking beer)* Yeah, Mamma, how fuckin' big do boys grow where you come from?

CURT *(with food in mouth)* Forget about it, Art, glad to have ya. One more don't mean a thing.

PANDORA Listen ta that, Mamma Too Tight . . . *(mocking)* . . . "One mo' mouf don't mean a thing." . . . We eat beans all week and when you and Curt's friends come in we play big shit! . . . And call out for food and beer.

*(*CURT, SHAKY *and* ART *stop eating.* CURT *stares at* PANDORA *and* ART *holds his plate like it is hot and he is trying not to drop it on the floor.* SHAKY *eyes* MAMMA TOO TIGHT *and gives a mean scowl.* MAMMA *has seen the look on* CURT*'s face before.* RICH *goes on enjoying his meal)*

MAMMA *(in a jolly tone, to* PANDORA*)* Girl, you don't have ta tell me a thing . . . these here men think that money can be just picked up off'a them pavements out there like chewin' gum paper . . . until they got ta get out there for themselves. *(she swings off the bed and shows flashes of lingerie)* Like this pretty boy here with the fuzz on his face. *(she approaches* ART *and stands so her hips form a prominent profile to* CURT*'s line of vision)* He ain't even eatin' no mo' . . . and Curt's not either, honey. What I tell ya? These men are somethin' else. So weak from plottin' what we should be doin' to bring some money in that they can't eat themselves. *(puts her plate on coffee table)* I know that Curt is a big strong man . . . he's always lettin' Pan know. *(strong dialect)* . . . So he don't need no help from us frail ass women but maybe ole fuzzy wuzzy face here needs some help. *(her audience is in better humor once more. to* ART*)* You wants Mamma Too Tight to feeds him some food, baby boy?

SHAKY Cut out the Magnolia act. Everything wears thin, *Queenie!*

MAMMA *(sudden anger)* Don't you call me no fuckin' Queenie!

SHAKY *(sarcastic)* Anything you say, baby. *(*PANDORA *guffaws at* SHAKY*'s tone)*

PANDORA *(mimicking* MAMMA*'s drawl)* But ain't dat you name, hoon e e e?

*(*MAMMA *ignores* SHAKY *and* PANDORA*, picks drumstick from plate and offers it to* ART *who frowns, and she pulls it away and puts it to her mouth imitating a mother feeding a reluctant child. Finally,* ART *smiles at her as* SHAKY *speaks)*

SHAKY Why don'chou lighten up, woman!

MAMMA Lighten up? . . . Damn . . . man . . . I ain't here ten minutes befoe I see your face and you tell *me* to lighten up! I been with you since I hit the streets at noon and you still checkin' up on me . . . don't worry, man . . . I'm goin' ta get right ta work.

SHAKY *(slow and languid)* I know that, baby.

MAMMA *(to* PANDORA*)* Girl, you should of seen Shaky . . . ha ha ha . . . almost swept me off my feet, girl. Said he loved me and really missed me so much the last ninety days that he almost went out of his mind . . . ha ha . . . *(coyly)* I was so embarrassed and impressed, girl, I liked to have blushed and nearly peed on myself like a sixteen year old girl. *(change of voice)* But the ole sonna bitch didn't fool me none with that shit! . . . The only thing he missed was that good steady money!

CURT *(piqued)* Why don't you check yourself, Mamma?

MAMMA *(waving* CURT'*s threat off and returning to the edge of the bed)* But, girl, he sho threw some lovin' on me . . . he heee . . . sheeet, I should go away again after this afternoon. *(*PANDORA *laughs throughout)* Ummm . . . chile . . . I nearly thought I was on that honeymoon I never had.

PANDORA You should after that routine, baby.

MAMMA And then when the sun start goin' down and things got really gettin' romantic, girl . . . this mathafukker says . . . *(lights lower; spot on bed.* SHAKY *speaks the line)*

SHAKY I want you to bring in a yard tonight, baby. *(*MAMMA *resumes speech. Bed spot off; colored spot on* MAMMA*)*

MAMMA You what, man? *(colored spot off; bed spot on)*

SHAKY A hundred stone cold dollars, baby. Tonight, baby! *(spot off; lights go up)*

MAMMA *(to* PANDORA*)* And girl, do you know what I said?

PANDORA Yeah, I know what you said.

MAMMA That's right, baby, I said to Shaky, "How do you want them daddy . . . in fives or tens?" *(laughter halts the speeches and the glasses are filled and fingers cleaned of chicken grease and cigarettes are lit)*

CURT *(to* SHAKY*)* Don't let Mamma try and fool you . . . she wanted to see you so bad . . . everytime Pan us'ta go visit her she would say to Pan, "How's that ole dirty Shaky doin'?"

MAMMA Yeah, I'd ask . . . 'cause I'd be wonderin' why ain't the mathafukker down here.

SHAKY Now, let's not go into that again, baby.

CURT Yeah, Mamma . . . you know what's happen'n behind that. You know why Shaky didn't come down . . . you never can tell when they might have a warrant out on him or somethin' and keep him too. You remember what happened at court, don't cha?

MAMMA Yeah, I remember. How can I forget? The judge said for Shaky to leave the court 'cause everytime I'm on trial he's in the back row hangin' 'round and that last ole woman judge said she knew who Shaky was an' she'd like to put him behind bars instead of me . . . but comin' down to visit me in jail is different, Curt!

SHAKY *(pleading)* Now, baby . . .

CURT Listen, Mamma . . . how old are you?

MAMMA Twenty.

CURT That means you're a big girl now, a woman who should be able to understand things, right?

MAMMA Yeah, but . . .

CURT *(cutting)* Right! Now listen, baby . . . and listen hard . . . now how many times you been busted?

MAMMA Thirty-three times . . . but I only fell this once for more than ten days and that was because I got that new fuckin' woman judge. I got the best record in town of any broad on the block I know. Pandora's rap sheet is worst than mine and I was on the block two years before she was.

CURT Exactly, baby. Now if you didn't have an old man like Shaky out there workin' for you, you'd be out of business and servin' some big time . . . right? Wouldn't that be a drag to be servin' some grand theft time behind givin' up a little body! Pan ain't been snatched since before we were married . . . ain't that right, Pandora? See there? Now let me tell you, baby, and listen hard. *(intensely)* A self-respectin' man won't let this ole lady stay in jail. If he can't get the bail for her or the juice to pay off somebody downtown like Shaky done you to have your time cut to one-third . . . *(disgust)* . . . he's a punk! And any broad that even looks at the jive sucker should get her funky ass run into the ground like a piece of scum!

MAMMA *(on defensive)* I know all that, Curt, but I got so lonely down there. Nothin' down there but broads and most of them butches.

PANDORA Mamma . . . don't even talk about it. Makes cold chills run up my back just thinkin' 'bout it.

CURT Yeah, we know it was hard, baby, but you can't afford to lose your old man by his gettin' busted behind a jail visit. That would be a stone trick, Mamma. Nothin' but a hammer . . . Right?

MAMMA Awww . . . Curt, you try and make it sound so smooth.

PANDORA He can really make it do that, girl.

RICH *(finishes drinking the last of his beer)* Hey, Shaky, I want you to take a walk with me, okay?

SHAKY *(standing slowly and visibly rocking)* Yeah, man. *(to* MAMMA*)* I'll see you back at the house, baby. Watch yourself.

MAMMA I'll probably be in early, Shaky. Unless I catch somethin' good. *(*RICH *and* SHAKY *exit by the front door.* PANDORA *accompanies them and checks the outside before they step out)* Sheet, Pandora, I thought Shaky was the Chicken Delight man when he knocked. I wasn't here ten minutes before he was knockin' on the door to see if I had my ride to the club. Didn't even think about feedin' me. *(soulful)* Just give me some good lovin' ta show me where it's at.

PANDORA These men are somethin' else, girl . . . 'spect a girl to go out'ta here on an empty stomach and turn all kinds of tricks . . . but Curt and me did have some beans for you, girl, but I dropped them.

MAMMA Well, I'm glad you did.

CURT *(packing away chess board)* I told her you didn't want no beans, Mamma.

MAMMA I got too many beans in the joint.

PANDORA *(peeved)* Well, that's what I had for you, chick.

MAMMA *(to* ART*)* Hey, pretty baby, why you so quiet?

ART Oh, I ain't got much to say, I guess.

CURT This is my boy Art, Mamma. I introduced you when you came in.

MAMMA *(sultry)* I know his name . . . ha ha I just want to know his game, dat's all. Hey, fuzz face, what's yo game? Is you kinda fuzzy wuzzy 'round the edges?

ART I'm sorry . . . I don't know . . .

CURT Awww . . . he's okay, Mamma . . . he was in the joint with me. He's just quiet, that's all. Reads too much . . . somethin' you should do more of.

PANDORA Why should she? Ain't heard of nobody gettin' no money readin'.

MAMMA *(to* ART*)* Now I know your name, fuzzy boy, now you say my name.

ART *(surprise)* Your name?

MAMMA Yeah. Say MA-MA TOO TIGHT!

ART I know your name.

MAMMA But I want you to say it.

ART I don't have to with you broadcasting it all over the place ever since you been here.

MAMMA *(cross)* You must think you're wise, man.

ART *(in low, even voice)* I am, you big mouthed bitch, and I want you to stop jivin' with me. *(*PANDORA *giggles.* CURT *looks on enjoying the surprise showing on* MAMMA*'s face)*

MAMMA Well . . . 'scuse me, tiger. *(walks over to* ART *and sits beside him)* Awww . . . forget it. I always act this way, ask Pan and Curt. 'Specially when I'm ah little bit loaded . . . Hey, Pandora, your friend here ain't got no sense of humor.

PANDORA Nawh . . . he's too much like Curt. Serious. That's why they probably get along so good, girl . . . they probably made for each other. *(the girls laugh)*

CURT C'mon, Pan . . . it's almost time for you to go to work. Deeny will be callin' nex' thing and that's one mathafukker I don't even want to see much less talk to. Go and get the stuff. *(*PANDORA *exits through the bathroom door)*

MAMMA *(to* ART*)* You want to know why they call me Mamma Too Tight, pretty baby?

CURT If Shaky ever heard you callin' my boy that, he'd break your arm, Mamma.

MAMMA Yeah, he might. But Shaky ain't where nothin's shakin' at the moment . . . Just out givin' Rich a fix . . .

CURT Both of you bitches talk too much!

MAMMA *(to* ART*)* You know what, fuzz wuzz? I sho wish I had a lil fuzzy wuzzy like you up there some of those cold nights in the joint. *(she gets up and walks to stand before the men. She plays it strictly for laughs, swinging her hips to the radio music and singsongs in a hearty, brazen voice like one of the old time red hot mamma's. Singing)* Why do they call me what they call me, baby? When what they call me is my name.

ART *(dryly)* I have suspicions but I'm not positive.

MAMMA *(ridiculing, but friendly)* You have suspicions as every little fuzzy wuzzy does but let me tell you . . . because my real name is Queenie Mack! Queenie Bell Mack! Ain't that some shit? No self-respectin' whore in the world can go 'round with a name like that unless she's in Mississippi . . . sheeet . . . QUEENIE!

ART So you named yourself Mamma Too . . .

MAMMA *(cutting)* No! It just happened. I don't know how. I just woke up one day with my name that way . . . And I like it that way . . . it's me! *(turning toward* ART*)* Don't you think it fits, honey?

ART I think it really does.

MAMMA Damn right it does. It makes me feel so alive. That's why I'm glad to be out . . .

CURT *(yelling)* HEY, PANDORA!

MAMMA Man, but it's so good to be high again. It's so good to be free. *(*PANDORA *enters from the bathroom and descends the stairs and places a cardboard box on the table as the lights blacken briefly and the music rises)*

Scene 3

(As the lights go up and the music lowers, the scene has shifted. CURT *and* PANDORA *sit upon the couch, across from* ART*, and* MAMMA TOO TIGHT *has taken the stool* CURT *was seated on. Uncovered, the box waits in the center of the table.* CURT *is licking a brown cigarette as the theme plays)*

CURT Yeah. We want to make some money, Art, so we can get out of this hole. *(lights the cigarette and inhales fiercely. Drops head. Two beat pause. In strained voice, holding smoke back)* We're makin' it to Buffalo, man. You hip to Buffalo?

ART No, I don't think so . . .

CURT *(takes another drag)* It's a good little hustlin' town, I hear. I got a case comin' up here for passin' some bad paper, ya know, forgin' payroll checks . . . and when I get the money to make restitution and give the people downtown some juice, ya know, man, pay them off, I'm makin' it East. But I need some grand theft dough.

ART But won't you get some time with your record?

CURT Nawh. Probably not. You see, I'm a good thief. I take money by my wits . . . ya know, with a pen or by talkin' some sucker out of it. It's only seldom that I'm forced to really take any money by force. If I make full restitution for these checks and fix my lawyer up and the other people downtown, I'll get probation. They'll reduce it to a misdemeanor and breakin' probation for somethin' like that ain't nothin' . . . besides, Buffalo's a long way away, man.

PANDORA *(receiving cigarette from* CURT*)* It's supposed to be a good little town. A different scene entirely. I'm due for a good scene for a change.

CURT Yeah, but we have to get that juice money first, baby. We gotta get us some long money.

MAMMA Any place is better than L.A. but I heard that Buffalo is really boss.

PANDORA *(languid)* It sho is, baby.

MAMMA I wonder if I could get Shaky to go?

CURT Sure you could, Mamma. He can get connections to deal this stuff there just like here. That's the idea. When we make our hit and split out of here we're goin'a take as many as we can with us. You know, set up a kinda organization.

PANDORA *(passing cigarette to* MAMMA*)* They really got respect for cats from the coast back there.

ART *(getting caught up in the mood)* Yeah, they really do . . . when I . . .

PANDORA *(cutting speech)* With me workin' on the side and with Curt dealin' we'd be on our feet in no time.

CURT We want to be on our feet when we get there, baby.

ART And that's where I come in, right?

CURT Right, good buddy.

MAMMA *(handing cigarette to* ART*)* Here, baby.

ART *(waving it away)* So what's on your mind, Curt?

MAMMA *(extending cigarette)* I said here, baby, I just don't like to hold this thing and see all this bread go up in ashes.

ART I don't want any.

(A three beat stop, all caught in tableau staring at ART*, then* PANDORA *snickers and breaks into a tittering laugh, looking at* CURT*)*

PANDORA *(ridicule)* You and your friends, Curt . . . I thought . . .

CURT *(heated)* Shut up, bitch . . . you talk too much!

PANDORA *(rising anger)* Why shouldn't I when you bring some square-ass little . . . *(*CURT *slaps her; she jumps to her feet and spins to claw him but* CURT *lunges forward and slaps her again, causing her to trip backwards across the edge of the coffee table. From the floor, removing one of her shoes)* Goddamn you, Curt . . . *(she begins to crawl to her knees and* CURT *moves around the table after her. Then* ART *steps between them and pushes* CURT *backward on the couch. Surprise is upon* CURT*'s face and* MAMMA TOO TIGHT *seems frozen in place)*

CURT WHAT THE FUCK'S GOIN' ON, MAN?

ART *(low)* Don't hit her anymore, Curt.

CURT *(incredulous)* What? . . . Man, are you payin' this woman's bills . . . have you got any papers on her?

PANDORA *(to* CURT*)* ARE YOU PAYIN' MY BILLS, MATHAFUKKER?

CURT *(rising to attack* PANDORA*;* ART *blocks his way)* I've told you to keep your mouth . . . *(to* ART *when he won't let him pass)* Now listen, Art, you're like a brother to me but you don't know what's goin' down, man.

ART Why don't we all sit down and try and relax, Curt? Why don't you do it for me, huh? As a favor. I'm sorry for buttin' in to your business between you and your old lady but somethin' just happens to me, man, when I see a guy hit a girl. *(after a minute,* CURT *is soothed and sits upon the couch again, glaring at* PANDORA *who holds her shoe like a weapon)*

MAMMA *(partially recovered)* Oh, man, I just hit the streets and this is what I run into . . .

CURT *(intense, to* ART*)* What are you doin', man? Squarin' out on me? Man, I've went a long way . . .

ART *(leaning forward)* Well, look, Curt . . . I can split . . . *(*CURT *stands and looks down on* ART*. Changing expression,* PANDORA *makes a move for the box but* CURT *waves her hand away)*

CURT No, I don't think you better try that, Art. *(pause)* Tell me, Art. Why don't you want to smoke any marijuana?

ART Why don't . . . I don't understand why you should ask me that.

CURT Is your playin' hero for Pandora a game to cover up somethin', man? *(*MAMMA *is clutching herself as if she has returned to the womb)*

MAMMA Oh . . . shit shit shit . . . shit . . . just today . . . just today they cut me loose . . . just today.

PANDORA *(no longer angry, placing hand on* CURT*'s arm)* Easy, baby, I think he's okay.

CURT You would!

ART Now, look, man, I don't put down anybody for doin' what they want but just don't hassle me!

PANDORA *(hostile, to* ART*)* Cool it, baby, you're in some deep trouble now.

MAMMA Oh, goddamn . . . why can't I just be plain'ass Queenie Bell Mack?

CURT *(low)* What's happen'n, brother?

ART I just don't get high . . . that's all . . .

MAMMA *(nearly screaming)* Neither does J. Edgar Hoover, sucker, but he don't come in here pretend'n to be no friend!

PANDORA *(enraged, fearful of losing control, to* MAMMA*)* SHUT UP, BITCH! THIS IS CURT AND OUR PLACE. WE GOT MO' TO LOSE THAN JUST OUR ASS. JUST SHUT ON UP! *(*MAMMA *looks most like a small girl with wide, moist eyes)*

CURT For the last time, Art, tell me somethin'.

ART I just don't . . . *(*PANDORA *stands and moves in front of* CURT*. The coffee table separates them from* ART*, but she leans over)*

PANDORA *(to* CURT*, behind her)* He's alright, honey. If he were a cop he'd be smokin' stuff right along with us . . . you know that . . .

ART *(bewildered)* A cop! . . .

PANDORA *(sarcastic)* He's just a little square around the edges, Curt . . . *(silence, then: to* ART*)* But why, honey?

ART *(shrugging sheepishly)* I had a bad experience once behind pot, that's all. *(*MAMMA *chuckles until* CURT *stops her)*

MAMMA He had a bad experience . . . hee hee hee . . . ha ha ha . . . He had . . .

CURT *(menace)* Pan has already told you to check yourself, woman, he's still my friend.

PANDORA What was it all about, man . . . can you tell us about it?

ART I'd rather not . . .

CURT *(cutting)* We know you'd rather not but . . .

PANDORA *(cutting)* Now look, Art, you're not givin' us much of a break . . . we don't want to act like this but we got a lot of the future riding on what happens in the nex' few days. Why don't you tell us?

ART I would but it don't seem that much . . .

CURT *(not so threatening)* But it is, Art!

PANDORA C'mon, trust me. Can't you say anything? We've gone more than half- . . .

CURT Stop rankin' him, will ya!

PANDORA I'M ONLY DOIN' IT FOR YOU! *(silence as* CURT *and* PANDORA *stare at each other)*

ART Yeah, I'll talk about it . . . *(*CURT *sits.* PANDORA *moves around the table closer to* ART*. The cigarette has been dropped by* MAMMA *beside the box. "Delilah" plays)* You see . . . it was about three years ago. I shipped out on a freighter . . . ya know, one of those scows that fly the Panamanian or Liberian flag but don't really belong to any country . . .

MAMMA *(in small girl's voice)* Ain't they American?

ART Well, in a way. They belong to American corporations and the businessmen don't want to pay high taxes on 'em. They're pretty ratty. *(*PANDORA *makes a seat on the floor between the men)* Well, I went on a four month cruise, ya know, to ports around the West Indies and then to North Africa.

MAMMA Wow . . . that sounds gassy . . . I wish . . .

PANDORA *(cutting)* MAMMA!

ART Well, I been blowin' weed since I was about twelve . . .

MAMMA *(ridicule)* Ha ha ha . . . since he was twelve . . . *(*PANDORA *and* CURT *frown at her and she huddles in her seat and looks cold)*

ART . . . and everything was cool. I smoked it when I ran into it and never thought about it much unless someone turned me on. But in Tangier it was about as easy to get as a bottle of beer. Man, I had a ball all the while I was over there and before I left I bought a big bag. *(showing with his hands)* This big for about five bucks. All the way back on my night watches I just smoked grass and just thought of what the guys on my corner back home would say when I would pull out a joint or two and just give it to them. Prices back east are about triple what they are here, so you can guess what it was worth . . . And all the broads I would make . . . you know how it goes . . . take a broad up to your room and smoke a little weed and if you have anything goin' for you at all, man, that's it.

PANDORA *(disgust)* Yeah, there's a lot of stupid broads in this world.

ART *(sensing the reduced tension)* And I could still sell some when my money got low and come out beautiful. I was really feeling good about that grass, Curt. Well, this tub docks in Philly about 1 A.M. and I have to leave ship and when I get to the station I find that my train don't leave until 2 the next afternoon. I got my pay and my belongings, so I stash most of my bags in a locker at the station, a bag of weed is in one but I have about half a dozen joints on me. Now I know Philly a little. I know where there's an after-hour joint so I grab a cab and go over there. The place is jumpin' . . . they're havin' a fish fry, and I start in drinkin' and talkin' to girls but none of them are listen'n 'cept for seven bucks for them and three for the management for rentin' one of the upstairs rooms, and I ain't buyin' no cock . . . not in the States . . .

PANDORA Well, I'm glad of that. I can take squares but not tricks, baby.

CURT *(to* PANDORA*)* You still runnin' your mouth, ain't you?

ART So I start talkin' with some guy and he tells me of a place he knows 'cross town that's better than this one. He looks okay to me. A blood. Dressed real sharp with a little goatee and everything. I had been talkin' to him about bein' out to sea and since he don't try and con me into a crap game and is buyin' one drink for every one of mine, I don't give a damn where we go 'cause I got the whole night to kill.

MAMMA Oh wow . . . I know this is the bad part . . .

PANDORA Listen, Mamma.

MAMMA *(turning her face away)* I don't like to hear bad things.

ART So we drinkin' bottles of beer and drivin' up Broad Street in Philly in his old wreck of a Buick and I think how it would be nice to turn on and get really loaded before we get where we're goin'. So I reach for my pocket but it's wintertime and I got on a pea jacket and sweaters and I have trouble gettin' to my pocket. And while I was lookin' I start in laughin'.

CURT Laughin'?

ART Yeah, I start wonderin' what would happen if this was a cop I was with and the idea was just too much. So funny. So I started in laughin'. And the guy asks me what I was laughin' at and I said I was just laughin' about him bein' a cop. And he said that he was and how did I know. *(two beat pause)* I don't know how I got out of that car or away from him. But soon after I was pukin' my guts up, and I threw those joints into a sewer and they wouldn't go down 'cause snow and ice was cloggin' it up. And I was stompin' on 'em so they would go down and gettin' sick and after a while my feet were all covered with ice and snow and puke and marijuana . . . Ya know . . . I had nearly twenty bucks worth of dope frozen to the soles of my shoes.

MAMMA *(seriously)* Awww . . . no, man . . . I can't stand any more.

PANDORA *(giggling)* That's the best trip I've been on this week, Art.

ART Nawh, really . . . baby. And the bag . . . I left it in a locker. Not the one I used but another empty one.

MAMMA Those janitors must'a naturally been happy the next day.

ART Yeah, they must have been but I couldn't even think of the stuff for a long time without wanting to heave up my guts.

CURT That must'a been pretty scary, man. *(*PANDORA *has reached over and gotten the cigarette and re-lit it)*

PANDORA *(offering it to* ART*)* Now it's time to get back on the horse, cowboy.

ART *(placing hand on stomach)* I don't think I can.

MAMMA You'll never think about that time in Philly again after the first drag, baby.

CURT C'mon, man, you're already one of us. Do you think I'd bring you in if I thought you'd be a square?

PANDORA Don't say that, Curt. He's not. Somethin' like what happened to him can mess up your mind about things. *(she stands over him and puffs on the cigarette. Staring at him)* Now don't think about anything . . . just look into my eyes. *(she inhales once more and gives the cigarette to* ART*)* Now, here, put it in your mouth.

ART *(takes it and puts to lips)* I can do it all right but I just don't want to.

PANDORA *(staring)* Look into my eyes and inhale. Don't think about it being in your hand. *(*ART *inhales and looks at her)* All the way down now and hold it.

MAMMA Don't ever say you don't believe in witches, boy.

CURT Cool it, Mamma!

PANDORA Now one more drag, Art. *(*ART *takes another puff and hands the reefer to* CURT*.* ART *has a great grin on his face)*

ART So that's what's in Pandora's box? *(lights change)*

PANDORA *(fantasy)* Among other things, Art. Among other things. But those have been lies you've been told about bad things comin' out of Pandora's box.

MAMMA Most people think that a girl's box is in other places.

PANDORA Nothin' can be found bad in there either. People only bring evil there with them. They only look for evil there. The sick . . .

ART What do you mean by sick?

PANDORA The come freaks, that's who. The queers who buy sex from a woman.

MAMMA *(bitterly)* Yeah, they say we're wrong but they're the queers . . . payin' for another person's body.

CURT *(in euphoria, musing)* Art, my man, we're goin'a Buffalo . . . goin' one day real soon.

PANDORA *(repulsion)* Some of them are real nice lookin' cats. Not old with fat greasy bellies. Real nice lookin' studs. *(bitterly)* Those are the real queers you have ta watch. They want ta hurt women.

MAMMA You hip ta that, baby? Those muscle cats, you know, muscle queens . . . always wantin ta freak out on ya.

ART And that's all that comes out of Pandora's box? *(*CURT *pulls a nickel-plated revolver out of the box)*

CURT No. Right now this is the most important thing. There's always something new in there. *(handing gun to* ART*)* Feel it, brother. *(*ART *takes the gun. He is caught up in the music and with his new friends)*

ART It's a good one.

MAMMA Looks how it shines. *(lights change)*

ART *(dreamlike)* Yeah . . . like Pandora's eyes. *(lights change)*

PANDORA *(fantasy)* Nothin' bad comes out of me or from my box, baby. Nothin' bad. You can believe that. It's all in what you bring to us. *(lights change)*

MAMMA That's wha's happen'n baby.

CURT It's yours now, Art, as much yours as mine. Can you handle it, brother?

ART *(looking at* PANDORA *and taking a new reefer)* If that's my job, brother. *(the cigarette has been replaced by a new one and others are in the hands of the group;* PANDORA *drags in deeply)*

PANDORA Buffalo's goin'a be a gas. *(the phone rings from the dressing room and* CURT *goes to answer. His shadow can be seen upon the wall at the top of the stairs)*

CURT *(off)* Yeah, Deeny . . . yeah yeah yeah . . . yeah, man . . . yeah.

MAMMA Who ever heard of a telephone in the toilet?

PANDORA It's in the dressing room next to the bathroom, Mamma.

MAMMA Sho is strange . . . Hey, are you goin'a Buffalo too, fuzz wuzz?

ART It looks that way.

PANDORA *(smiling)* I think I'll like that, Art. I think that'll be nice. *(a knock sounds at the front door.* CURT*'s shadow hangs up the phone and retreats further into the area)*

CURT *(off)* PANDORA! MOVE! GOD-DAMN IT! GET A MOVE ON! *(*ART *stands as* PANDORA *jumps to her feet. He has a cross expression as he looks toward the dressing room entrance)*

ART *(to* PANDORA*)* Can I help you? *(*PANDORA *shakes her head)* Is there anything I can do?

PANDORA No, I don't think anybody can do anything, especially you. *(she places the gun and the marijuana in the box and hurries up the stairs. The knock comes again)*

MAMMA *(still seated, toward door)* JUST A MINUTE! *(*ART *watches* PANDORA *enter dressing room)* You want to get the door, Art?

ART I learned once never to open another man's door. *(*PANDORA *and* CURT, *in coats, come from the dressing room;* PANDORA *has her costumes in her arms.* MAMMA TOO TIGHT *gets up and walks downstage)*

CURT That fuckin' Deeny wants you to rehearse some new music before your act, Pan.

PANDORA Sonna bitch! Always late payin' somebody and always wantin' you to work your ass off.

CURT Is your car parked far, Art?

ART Not too far.

MAMMA *(looking out window)* It's only Rich.

CURT Good. He can stay here and watch the phone while we're at the club. First we'll stop and get you some gas, Art, and then you can take us to the Strip Club.

PANDORA Is your car big enough to get us all to the Strip Club on Western, Art?

ART It'll even get us as far as Buffalo, Pandora.

(They exit. RICH *enters, turns in doorway and is seen talking to someone outside. Then he shuts door, saunters gracefully across the room and turns the radio off. Lights dim out as he spreads upon the couch. Curtain)*

ACT 2

(The curtain opens showing the Strip Club, or rather, the suggested representation of a cheap night club in the Wilshire area of Los Angeles, featuring "Bronze" strip-teasers. But the effect should be directed toward the illusions of time, place and matter. Reality is questionable here. The set should be painted in lavish phony hues except for the bare brown floor. Seeing the set, the female audience should respond: "gorgeous, lovely, marvelous, delightful," and with similar banalities. The men should wonder if the habitat of whores is not indeed the same region as their creatures of private myth, dream and fantasy.

A rotating color-wheel, in front of the major lights, should turn constantly throughout this scene, giving an entire spectrum of altering colored shadows. Additional colored lights and spots should be used to stress mood changes and the violence of the ending scene.

A MUSICIAN *plays randomly at the piano. He is tall, wearing a dark suit with an open-necked dark shirt. The* BARTENDER, *wiry with his head shaven clean, sweeps the floor and empties ash trays. A few customers sit and watch the* MUSICIAN, *and later, the* GROUP, *as the show hasn't begun.*

The voice which is heard at the close of this act can be that of a customer.

Two other MUSICIANS *enter and climb upon the stage.*

PIANO PLAYER *(joking, to* BASS PLAYER *seated at piano)* Hey, man, they lookin' for bass players all up and down the street but you cats are all bangin' out chords on out of tune pianos.

BASS PLAYER What's happen'n, man? Say . . . listen to this . . . *(he plays a couple of frames)* What about that, man . . . huh?

PIANO PLAYER Man, like I said . . . you're a damn good bass man . . .

BASS PLAYER *(getting up)* What you say about somebody lookin' for bass men? . . . Man! Turn me on. I wouldn't be here in this trap if I knew where one of those gigs were.

DRUMMER *(seated, working up a beat)* Yeah, man, they need you like they need me.

PIANO *(wryly)* How's it feel to keep gettin' replaced by a juke box? *(*BASS PLAYER *begins working with* DRUMMER. PIANO PLAYER *strikes a few chords then lights a cigarette)*

BASS Hey, where's Stew and Ronny? I want to practice those new charts before Pandora gets in.

PIANO *(blowing smoke out)* They quit.

BASS *(halting)* What!

DRUMMER Deeny wouldn't pay them this afternoon and pushed the new charts on them. They didn't want to learn new scores, not getting paid the money owed them, so they quit.

BASS Just like that . . . they quit?

PIANO This is our last night here, too. Deeny's in trouble with the union. No more gigs here until the hearin'.

BASS Awww, man . . . there's always some shit with that jive-ass sucker. Is we gettin' our bread from Deeny tonight?

DRUMMER Who knows? He don't have to pay until the last performance, and the union says stay on the gig until tonight.

BASS We always gettin' put in some cross . . .

PIANO Yeah, man. But juke boxes don't go on strike and Deeny knows we know it, so let's take care of business.

BASS Man, don't tell me that . . . the broads can't dance to no juke box.

PIANO *(seriously)* Why not, man?

BASS It just ain't done, man. No machine ain't never goin'a take a musician's play from him when it comes to providin' music for shows.

PIANO Don't believe it, baby . . . in a couple of mo' years they'll find a way. Broads will be shakin' their cans to canned music just as good as to your playin' or mine and the customers will be payin' even higher prices . . . no body wins, man. Least of all us. C'mon, let's hit it . . . *(he begins playing "Delilah" as* PANDORA, MAMMA TOO TIGHT *and* CURT *make their entrances. The girls wave at the* MUSICIANS *and stop at the bar, then move to a table near the bandstand.* PANDORA *places her costumes on an empty chair of a nearby table.* CURT *stands with his back to the bar)* Okay. That's better . . . c'mon . . . Cook! . . .

BASS *(not enthused, to* MAMA *who waves again)* Hey, pretty girl . . . *(*ART *walks in, saunters to the cigarette machine;* CURT *joins the girls)*

CURT Hey, I wonder where everybody's at?

DRUMMER *(stopping, followed by others)* Hey . . . hey . . . what's the use of this fuckin' shit? . . .

PIANO What's happen'n now, man? *(*DRUMMER *hops from stage)*

MAMMA Damn . . . Stew and Ronny must be late, Pan.

PANDORA *(to* BARTENDER*)* What happened to your boss, Deeny, Chico? *(*BARTENDER *ignores her)*

DRUMMER *(to* PIANO PLAYER*)* Not a thing, man . . . everything's cool . . . *(goes to bar, to* BARTENDER*)* Hey, Chico. Give me a screwdriver and charge it to your boss.

BARTENDER Deeny ain't in the charity business, baby. *(*ART *sits down with his friends. One of the customers leaves)*

PANDORA *(to* BARTENDER*)* Yeah, baby, give me the usual and give my friends what they want. Put it on my tab.

DRUMMER *(to* BARTENDER*)* You let me and Deeny worry about that, cool breeze. Give me a screwdriver like I said. *(*BARTENDER *goes behind bar and begins mixing* DRUMMER*'s drink)*

BARTENDER *(sullenly to* PANDORA*)* When you gonna take care of that tab, sweetcake?

PANDORA *(angry)* When your fuckin' boss pays me, mister! Now get us our drinks, please!

CURT *(to* BASS PLAYER *who stands beside instrument)* Where's Deeny? *(*PIANO PLAYER *has gotten off of stage and talks to* DRUMMER *at the bar. A customer goes to jukebox and looks over the selections)*

PIANO What's happen'n, man? We got to make this gig . . . that's what the union says.

DRUMMER Fuck the union.

BASS *(to* CURT*)* It's a mystery to me, Curt.

MAMMA *(to* BASS PLAYER*)* That number's a gassy one, honey. Pan's gonna work by that, ain't she?

BASS Looks that way, Mamma, if anybody works at all tonight.

PIANO *(to* DRUMMER*)* Awww, man . . . you know I know how you feel . . .

DRUMMER Well, just don't run that crap down to me. I'm just fed up. The union screws you out of your dues and the clubs fuck you every chance they get . . .

PIANO It ain't exactly that way . . . now if . . .

MAMMA Don't you like Pan's new number, Art? *(*ART *doesn't answer. The Customer drops a coin into the jukebox and punches a selection: "Something Cool" sung by June Christie is played)*

PANDORA *(to* ART *and* MAMA*)* Can't come in here one day without some shit goin' down. Where's the brass so I can rehearse?

MAMMA They better get here soon, honey. It'll be too late after a while.

BASS *(to* PAN*)* Forget about it, Pan. They

ain't no brass tonight. *(to* PIANO PLAYER*)* Well I know all that, but it's no use rehearsin' without any brass and if this is our last night anyhow . . .

CURT *(rising and going to the bar)* You said this is the last night, man?

PANDORA *(to* BASS PLAYER*)* NO BRASS!

MAMMA *(to* ART*)* You hear what he said?

BASS *(putting down instrument)* Hey, fix me a C.C. and ginger ale, Chico! *(customer that played record goes to the bar and sits down)*

PANDORA *(to* BARTENDER*)* Hey, what about our drinks, man!

BARTENDER Okay, Pandora . . . just a minute.

CURT Hey, fellas . . . what's goin' down?

(The MUSICIANS *tell* CURT *about the trouble as the scene plays on in center stage at the table. The conversations should overlap as they have but become increasingly rapid and confusing if necessary.*

After the MUSICIANS *are served the* BARTENDER *takes the orders at* PANDORA*'s table as* CURT *continues to talk at the bar)*

PANDORA Shit . . . no brass . . . musicians quittin' . . . I ain't got no job no more.

MAMMA Yeah. It don't look so good but perhaps Deeny can do somethin' when he comes in . . .

PANDORA Deeny . . . shit . . . Deeny . . . all he can do! . . . *(furious, searching for words)* Why, shit, woman! Deeny can't even do numbers and shit cucumbers!

ART Thanks for the drink, Pan.

PANDORA Is that all you can do, man? Say thank you!

ART No. It's not the only thing.

*(*MAMMA *gets up and goes over to the* BASS PLAYER *who drops out of the conversation between* CURT*, the other two* MUSICIANS *and the* BARTENDER*.*

Another customer leaves, leaving only one sitting upon a stool, attempting to get the BARTENDER*'s attention)*

BARTENDER Well, look, man, I only work here. You better settle that with Deeny. *(behind the bar the phone rings. The* BARTENDER *answers)*

CURT If that's Deeny I want to talk to him.

BARTENDER Hey, man, I'm talkin' on the phone.

DRUMMER Let me talk to the mathafukker! *(he tries to reach across the bar)*

BARTENDER *(backing off)* Hey, cool it! Wait!

PIANO *(grabbing* DRUMMER*'s arm)* Hold it, man!

DRUMMER Take your fuckin' hands off me, baby!

BARTENDER Wait, I said.

CURT Tell Deeny I'm waitin' for him. *(*DRUMMER *breaks away from* PIANO PLAYER *and begins around the bar.* BARTENDER *reaches under bar for a weapon)*

BARTENDER *(shouts)* WAIT!!! *(the scene freezes in tableau except for the* BARTENDER, PANDORA *and* CURT*. Lights go down to purples and deep shadow shades as an eerie spot plays upon the table. Occasionally from the shadows voices are heard. In shadows)* Okay, Deeny. I'll be expectin' ya.

PANDORA *(to* ART*)* So he's comin'.

ART Yeah, no need to wait for very long now.

PANDORA What else can you do, Art?

ART What else can I do except say thank you, you mean?

PANDORA Yeah. That's what I mean.

ART I can wait, Pandora.

PANDORA *(jolly)* What the good of waitin' when things have ta be done? Is that why you have to eat at Rescue Missions and get favors from friends, baby? 'Cause you waitin'? Tell me. What are you waitin' on, Art?

ART Me? I'm just waitin' so I won't jump into somethin' too fast and I think you should do the same.

PANDORA I didn't know you gave out advice too. But I wish I could take some of it. Ya see, we're already in the middle of some deep shit . . . There just ain't time to sit back and cool it, honey . . .

ART *(disregarding the ridicule in her voice, soothing)* Yes you can . . . just sit back and look around and wait a while. You don't have to do anything . . . baby, the whole world will come to you if you just sit back and be ready for it.

PANDORA *(serious)* I wish I could. But so much has to be done and we keep fallin' behind.

BARTENDER *(in shadow)* Now what can I do, man? Deeny left with Pete and he said he'd be right back and for you guys to practice with the girls.

(One of the customers who walked out enters with a show girl. She is dark and thin and pretty in a tinseled way. They stop in the shadows and whisper and the girl separates from him, enters the light, passes through and heads toward the dressing rooms in the rear. The customer takes a seat at the bar. He is engulfed by shadows and becomes frozen in place like the others)

PANDORA *(nodding to show girl as she passes)* Hi, Cookie. I really dig that dress, baby.

ART Things can always get worst, Pan.

PANDORA Oh, you're one of those? How can they? Just lost my job. This was to keep us goin' until you guys turned up somethin' big and I didn't even get paid for the last two weeks so I know this just means another great big zero.

ART What do you think will happen now?

PANDORA I don't know . . . the job Curt's got planned can't be pulled off until three more days and in a week we got to have all our money together for the restitution and juice . . . not to mention the goin' away money. And I'm not even goin'a get paid for the gig.

ART Haven't you got any now?

PANDORA Just a couple of hundred but we can't go into that. Got to hold onto it. We wouldn't eat if we didn't have to. We got to hold on to every cent.

BARTENDER *(in shadows)* Do you want that scotch with anything? *(*DRUMMER *momentarily breaks out of position)*

DRUMMER I ain't finished talkin' yet, Chico.

BARTENDER Just a minute, man. *(*MAMMA *breaks out of position and goes to* PANDORA*)*

MAMMA Lend me a dime, Pan. I got to call Shaky.

PANDORA *(fishing in her outsized purse)* You got somethin' workin', baby?

MAMMA Yeah, Slim's gonna get somethin' from Shaky.

PANDORA That's workin'. *(she gives* MAMMA *a coin.* MAMMA *enters the shadows and walks to the rear of the club.* PANDORA *notices* ART *looking at her)* Forget about her. Shaky's got her up tight. All you could do is play young lover a little. You can't support her habit, Art.

ART She can't have a habit if she's just hit the street.

PANDORA She's got one. What do you think they came in high on? In a couple more days she'll be hooked as bad as before. Shaky'll see to that.

ART What does she do it for?

PANDORA What does . . . ? Awww, man . . . what kinda question is that? I thought you knew somethin', baby.

ART I tried to ask an honest question, Pan.

PANDORA Is it an honest question when you don't have anything to go by to compare her experience with yours?

ART I don't know. Is it?

PANDORA Do you know how it feels havin' somebody paw all over you everyday?

ART Well, no . . .

PANDORA Then you don't know that she has to use that stuff to put off the reality of it happen'n?

ART Oh, I see.

PANDORA *(bitter)* Yeah, you see. Do you see her givin' up her body everyday and murdering herself everyday? Is that what the world has brought to her, Art? That's all she can look forward to each day . . . killin' herself with that needle by inches. She has her fix, and maybe a bust and she has keepin' her man. She just takes her fixes to get through the day and Shaky keeps her on it so she'll need him more.

ART That's too bad.

PANDORA Wait a minute, Art. Don't sing no sad songs for that woman, you understand? She's not askin' for your pity. She's a real woman in some ways and she won't let you take it away from her by your pity. She'd spit on your pity.

ART *(annoyed)* And you? *(lights change)*

PANDORA *(fantasy)* And me? . . . Well I ain't no whore . . . I'm just makin' this money so Curt and me can get on our feet. One day we gonna own property and maybe some businesses when we get straight . . . and out of this town.

ART In Buffalo?

PANDORA Maybe if we decide to stay there but I'm really an entertainer. I'll show you my act one day and Curt's got a good mind. He's a good hustler but he's givin' that up after a while. He can be anything he wants. *(lights change)*

ART What does he want?

PANDORA He wants what I want.

ART How do you know?

PANDORA He tells me . . . We talk about it all the time.

ART Can you be sure?

PANDORA Sure?

ART Yeah . . . like Mamma's sure she'll always get her fix and her bail paid.

PANDORA You little smooth faced punk . . . wha . . .

ART *(cutting)* Some guys are really lucky.

PANDORA Kiss my ass, sucker!

ART Curt and Shaky are really into something.

PANDORA Yeah! Because they're men!

ART Is that what bein' a man is, bein' lucky?

PANDORA No. It's from gettin' what you want.

ART And how do you get what you want, Pan?

PANDORA You go after it.

ART And after you have it?

PANDORA Then maybe it's yours and you can do whatever you want with it.

ART And what if I wanted you, Pandora?

PANDORA *(three beat pause)* You don't have enough to give me, Art. What could you give me that would make things better for me?

ART I'm not a giver, Pan, I'm a taker.

(Lights go up evenly. Figures become animated and resume activities. The BARTENDER *pours drinks and nods to grumbling* MUSICIANS *and to* CURT. *A customer goes to jukebox and drops coin in. "Parisian Thoroughfare" plays. The show girl, in thin robe, revealing skimpy costume, walks from the rear and takes seat beside customer she entered with.* MAMMA TOO TIGHT *goes to the table and sits)*

MAMMA *(brightly)* What you guys been talkin' bout so long?

PANDORA Nothin' much, why?

MAMMA Oh nothin' . . . just thought I'd ask. But the way you and ole fuzz wuzz was goin' at it and lookin' at each other . . .

PANDORA Looks can't hurt you, Mamma, but your big mouth can.

MAMMA *(fake surprise)* Pan . . . I didn't mean . . .

PANDORA I'm sure you didn't, Mamma!

MAMMA *(now hurt)* Now listen, Pan. If you can't take a little teasin' . . . What's wrong with you? This is my first day home and you been on my ass all the time. Girl . . . you been the best friend I ever had, but lighten up.

PANDORA Awww, Mamma . . . let's not you and me start in actin' flaky . . .

ART Would you like a drink, Mamma?

MAMMA *(pleased)* Yeah . . . but you can't pry Chico from behind that bar. *(*ART *stands and places hand upon* MAMMA*'s shoulder)*

ART That's okay. Just sit. *(he goes to bar and stands beside* CURT *who has his back to him, drinking and brooding)*

MAMMA *(to* PANDORA*)* Hey, he's so nice.

PANDORA See . . . I told you I wasn't tryin' to steal your little playmate.

MAMMA *(serious)* If I didn't know you was kiddin' I wouldn't take that, Pan.

PANDORA You wouldn't? . . . Well, I wasn't kiddin', broad!

MAMMA *(half-rising)* Hey, check yourself, girl. This is me! Remember? Mamma Too Tight. Don't you know me? Lil ole Queenie Bell Mack from Biloxi, Mississippi.

PANDORA Okay, Sit down before you trip over yourself. I know who you are.

MAMMA *(sitting)* And I know you too, baby. Remember I was the one who was there those times so many yesterdays ago. Remember? I was there with you holding your hand in those dark, little lonely rooms all them nights that your man was out on a job . . . Remember how we shivered together, girl? Remember how we cried together each time he got busted and sent away again . . . I'm your friend, baby . . . and you actin' like this to me?

PANDORA *(genuine)* I'm sorry, Mamma. It's just that Art. He's different. Everything seems different when he's around.

MAMMA I think I know what you mean, Pan. I think I know . . .

(Lights dim; color-wheel still throws pastel shadows. CURT *and* ART *stand in spot at end of bar. In the shadows there are rustles from the other people and lighted cigarettes are through the gloom toward mouths which suck at them like spiders draining fireflies.* CURT *turns)*

CURT Hey, Art. Sorry to put you through all this hassle but some bad shit is goin' down, man. I'm really gettin' worried . . . If things keep breakin' bad like this . . .

ART Don't worry about me, Curt. I'm just along for the ride. Try and get yourself together. It don't matter to me what you have to go through to get yourself straight, man. Just work it on out. *(spot off* ART *and* CURT. *Spot on show girl and customer)*

CUSTOMER How 'bout it, sugar?

SHOW GIRL Are you kiddin', man?

CUSTOMER *(whining)* Well Christ . . . twenty-five bucks . . . what's it lined with . . . gold or somethin'?

SHOW GIRL You see those two broads over at that table? *(lights on* PANDORA *and* MAMMA*)*

CUSTOMER Yeah. You suggestin' that I hit on them?

SHOW GIRL Yeah. Do that. The one in the black dress won't even speak to you unless you're ready to leave a hundred or more . . . and besides . . . she has to like your type first. The other one might consider it for fifty.

CUSTOMER Who's the girl in the black dress?

SHOW GIRL That's *Pandora.* She headlines the Revue. You have to give her twenty bucks just to get her phone number. So why don't you go hit on her? *(lights off. Spot on* BARTENDER*)*

BARTENDER You call yourselves artists and then you want me to bleed for you? What kinda crap is that?

DRUMMER *(in shadows)* Listen you jive time whisky-pourer. We are artists and I don't care what you call us or how you bleed. It's cats like you and your boss who make us all the time have to act like thugs, pimps and leeches to just make it out here in this world.

BARTENDER So why ya tellin' me? So make it some other way?

PIANO PLAYER *(in shadows)* It's just impossible to talk to you people . . . it's just impossible to be heard anymore. *(spot off* BARTENDER. *Spot on* CURT *and* ART*)*

CURT Yeah . . . when I first met her, Art. You should of seen her. It was a joint somethin' like this . . . *(lights off; spot picks up* PANDORA *standing in the door looking younger, nervous.* CURT *crosses stage to meet her as he speaks. Entering light)* She was just eighteen . . . had the prettiest pair of tits poking right out at me . . . sharp enough to put your eyes out. *(he takes* PANDORA *in his arms and kisses her violently. She resists but he is overwhelming)*

PANDORA *(young voice)* I beg your pardon, mister.

CURT I said that you're beautiful . . . that I want you . . . that you are mine forever . . . that it will always be this way for you, for you are mine. *(he brutally subdues her. Her hair falls across her face. Her face has that expression that prisoners sometime have when they are shifted without prior explanation from an old cell to an unfamiliar cell, equally as old)*

PANDORA Are you the man I'm to love?

CURT *(dragging her into the shadows)* Don't talk of something you'll never know anything about . . . *(they speak from the shadows now, facing the audience)*

PANDORA I can't love you? I can't love you if I even wanted? . . .

CURT You are mine . . . my flesh . . . my body . . . you are in my keeping.

PANDORA Is it so much to ask for . . . just to be your woman?

CURT You will do as I say . . . your flesh, your soul, your spirit is at my command . . . I possess you . . .

PANDORA First there were others . . . now there is you . . . always always the same for me . . . *(lights change)*

CURT *(in shadows, walking toward* ART*)* Yeah . . . she was ready . . . has always been. *(spot on* ART. CURT *enters light)*

ART Pandora's a beautiful girl, Curt. You're lucky, man, to have her. I envy you.

CURT Thanks, Art.

ART Don't mention it, don't mention it at all. *(lights go down. Come up with* SHAKY *sitting at the table with* MAMMA *and* PANDORA*)*

SHAKY What's happen'n, baby?

MAMMA Nothin' yet, Shaky. Give me time. The joint ain't even open yet.

SHAKY Don't take too long, woman.

MAMMA Give me time, Shaky. Why you got to come on so strong, man? You know I always take care of business. You know I got to get used to it again. Didn't I set up that thing between you and Slim?

SHAKY Yeah, baby. But that's my department. You take care of business on your side of the street. *(the* BASS PLAYER *comes over to the table. To* BASS PLAYER*)* Let's take a walk, poppa.

BASS After you, Shake Shake.

MAMMA I'll be here, Shaky.

SHAKY Let's hope you're either here or there . . . okay?

MAMMA Shaky . . . you're goin' too fast. Don't push me so hard.

SHAKY *(leaving)* Tonight, baby. One hundred stone cold dollars, baby. *(light on show girl and customer)*

SHOW GIRL They're alone. Why not now?

CUSTOMER Okay . . . okay . . . twenty-five you get . . . after the show tonight. *(lights off; spot on* CURT *and* ART*)*

CURT When I saw you in action, Art. I said to myself I could really use that kid. Man, you're like a little brother to me now, man. I watch the way you act around people. You think on your feet and study them like a good gambler does. You're like me in a lot of ways. Man, we're a new breed, ya know. Renegades. Rebels. There's no rules for us . . . we make them as we break them.

ART Sounds kind'a romantic, Curt.

CURT And why shouldn't it? Man, this ain't a world we built so why should we try and fit in it? We have to make it over the best we can . . . and we are the ones to do it. We are, man, we are! *(spot on* MAMMA*)*

MAMMA I don't know why I'm this way . . . I just am. Is it because my name is different and I am different? Is it because I talk like a spade?

PANDORA *(from shadows)* Take a look at that! Just because this white broad's been hangin' out with us for a couple of years she's goin' ta blame that bad talk on us. *(light on table. To* MAMMA*)* When you brought your funky ass from Mississippi woman we couldn't even understand . . . sheet . . . we taught you how to speak if anything!

MAMMA *(out at audience)* All I know is that I'm here and that's where I'm at . . . and I'll be here until somethin' happens . . . I wish Shaky wouldn't push me so . . . I want to be good for him . . . I want him to be my man and care about me a little . . . *(*ART *brings* MAMMA *her drink.* CURT *sits with him at the table)*

CURT *(to* PANDORA*)* Don't look so pissed off, honey.

PANDORA Why shouldn't I? Everything's gone wrong. *(*CURT *stands and takes* PANDORA*'s arm)*

CURT C'mere, baby. Let me talk to you. *(they walk into the shadows)*

ART Just saw Shaky. He didn't stay long.

MAMMA Nawh. He's gone to take care of some business. Wants me to stay here and take care of mine.

ART I guess that's what you should do then.

MAMMA Should I? He's rushin' me too fast, that's what he's doin'. He knows I take a little time gettin' right inside before I can go back to work but he's pushin' me. It's Curt's and Pan's fault . . . they're desperate for money and they're pressin' Shaky.

ART Maybe you should try and talk to him or to Curt.

MAMMA It wouldn't do any good!

ART It wouldn't? If you were my girl I'd listen to what you had to say.

MAMMA Oh, man, knock off the bullshit!

ART But I would, really.

MAMMA *(hesitant)* You would? I bet you're full of shit.

ART Sure I would. I look younger but I know what you need . . . and I know what you want.

MAMMA *(giggling)* You do? *(peering over her glass)* What do I need and want, Fuzz Wuzz?

ART Understanding.

MAMMA What!

ART *(soft)* Understanding.

MAMMA Sheet . . .

ART *(softer)* Understanding. *(lights down; spot on* CURT *and* PANDORA*)*

PANDORA I'm gettin' fed up with all this shit, Curt. We seem to be goin' backwards not forward.

CURT I know that, baby. But things will get straightened out. You know it has to. When the job . . .

PANDORA *(cutting)* The job! Yeah . . . it better be somethin', Curt, or you're in some big trouble . . . We're both in some big trouble . . . what'd I do without you?

CURT If anything happens, baby . . . let Art take care of things . . .

PANDORA Art?

CURT Yeah.

PANDORA *(afraid)* But I'm your woman, remember?

CURT He's like a little brother to me. I've already spoken to him about it . . . you can get a real gig in a show or somethin' and share an apartment with him. He'll look out for you while I'm away. Go up to Frisco and wait for me . . . Art's got a head and he can look after things until I get out . . . then things will be okay again. But that's if the worst happens and we don't get the juice money . . .

PANDORA *(struck)* You think that much of him, Curt?

CURT I told you he's like my brother, baby. I've been waitin' a long time for a real cat to come along . . . we're on our way way now . . . *(lights lower; spot on the table as* SHAKY *enters)*

SHAKY *(to* ART*)* Hey, what you say your name was?

ART *(smiling, holding out his hand)* It's Art, Shaky, you know I met . . .

SHAKY *(cutting)* Yeah, I know . . . what you doin' takin' up my ole lady's time? *(*BASS PLAYER *enters)*

ART I was only sittin' here and bought her a drink. She rode over in my car with Curt and Pan.

SHAKY That's what I mean, man . . . takin' up her time.

MAMMA Shaky . . . stop it! He wasn't doin' nothin' . . . he's a friend of Curt's man . . .

SHAKY SHUT UP!

MAMMA You don't understand . . . *(he slaps her.* ART *grabs his arm and pushes him sprawling across a chair.* SHAKY *regains his balance and begins to lunge but is caught by* CURT*)*

CURT HEY, COOL IT, MAN! What's goin' on?

SHAKY This little punk friend of yours doesn't like what I do with my woman.

BASS PLAYER Why don't you forget it, Shaky. If it had been me I would of done the same thing. Forget it. It ain't worth it.

MAMMA *(scared)* He don't understand.

SHAKY You'll see what I understand when we get home, bitch!

ART *(putting out his hand)* I'm sorry, man. It was my fault. I had . . . *(*SHAKY *knocks* ART*'s hand aside and turns, being led toward the door by the* MUSICIAN*)*

SHAKY *(to* ART*)* I'll see you later.

CURT Hey, Shaky. C'mere, man. It don't mean nothin'.

(They exit. PANDORA *takes a seat.* CURT *goes to the bar and answers the questions of the* MUSICIANS *and the* BARTENDER*. The show girl goes to the rear of the club and the customer orders another drink)*

MAMMA He just don't understand . . . he can't understand and he can't give me any understanding . . .

PANDORA Who don't understand, Mamma?

MAMMA Shaky . . . he just don't understand . . . he should try and understand me more.

PANDORA Girl, you so stoned you're not makin' any sense. He understands, Mamma. He understands you perfectly.

MAMMA He can't, Pan. He can't or I wouldn't feel this way about him now.

ART Maybe you're changin'.

PANDORA Oh, man, you're full of it!

ART You're cynical but not that hard, Pandora.

PANDORA Man, I've seen it all. I don't have to be hard . . . I just use what I know.

ART Have you seen everything, Pan?

PANDORA Yes!

ART Then you've seen me before?

PANDORA *(staring)* Yeah . . . I've seen you before. There's a you standin' on every corner with his hands in his pockets and his fly half unzipped . . . there's a you in every drunk tank in every city . . . there's a you sniffin' around moochin' drinks and kissin' ass and thinkin' he's a make-out artist. Yeah . . . I've seen you before, punk!

MAMMA He just don't understand . . .

ART No, you've never seen me before, Pandora. I'm goin'a tell you something.

PANDORA *(sarcastic)* What are you goin'a tell me, Art?

ART That I'm goin'a change your life.

PANDORA WHAT!!!

(Lights go up with a startling flash. DEENY *and the bouncer,* PETE*, enter.* DEENY*, in black glasses, sports an ascot and a cummerbund under his sport coat. In the thin dress she entered in, the show girl walks from the rear and takes a seat beside the customer.* MAMMA TOO TIGHT *stands and* CURT *nearly bowls over a customer on his way to meet* DEENY *in center stage in front of* PANDORA*'s table.* PANDORA *jumps to her feet beside* MAMMA*, followed by* ART*)*

CURT Deeny!

(The BASS PLAYER *enters, and the* DRUMMER *and* PIANO PLAYER *hurry over. Behind the bar the* BARTENDER *stands tensed; the* BASS PLAYER *climbs upon the stage and begins zippering his bass fiddle into its cloth bag)*

DEENY Keep it, Curt! I don't want to hear it. I just came from the union and I've taken all the crap I'm gonna . . . the show's closed. *(chorus of yells)*

CURT Deeny, what you take us for?

PANDORA Hey, man . . . let's go in the back and talk . . .

DRUMMER *(pushing his way around the* PIANO PLAYER*)* Yeah, Deeny, I want to talk to you!

DEENY I just don't want to hear it from any of you. OKAY? . . . OKAY? Now everybody . . . this club is closin'. Ya hear? Everybody out inside of ten minutes . . . understand? This is my property. Get off it inside of ten minutes or I'm callin' the cops . . . your things and you out . . . hit the street . . . that means everybody! *(another chorus of yells from nearly everyone. The customers hurry out the exit and the show girl joins the group)*

BASS PLAYER *(to other* MUSICIANS*))* Hey, fellas, I'm splittin' . . . what about you? *(*MAMMA *turns and goes over to him)*

DRUMMER Man, what about my pay?

DEENY Take your bitchin' to the union, fellah. They instigated this hassle.

PANDORA We don't know nothin' bout no union, Deeny . . .

DEENY *(sarcastic)* I know you don't, sugar. But you girls should get organized . . . try to get paid hourly and get off the quota system and you'd . . .

CURT Watch your mouth, mathafukker!

BOUNCER You'd better watch yours!

DEENY *(to* BARTENDER*)* HEY, CHICO, CALL THE COPS! YOU JUST CAN'T REASON WITH SOME JERKS! CALL THEM NOW! *(the* BARTENDER *dials)*

PANDORA *(to* CURT*)* What we gonna do, baby? . . .

CURT Quiet!

PANDORA But your case, honey . . .

BARTENDER *(on phone)* Yeah . . . there's trouble at The Strip Club on Western . . . yeah . . .

*(*DEENY *tries to push his way past but* CURT *blocks him. The* BOUNCER *moves to shove* CURT *out of the way but* ART *steps in as the four confront each other, and the girls back off. The* PIANO PLAYER *has coaxed the* DRUMMER *to join the* BASS PLAYER *upon the stage, packing away his equipment. At a run, the show girl rushes to the rear of the club as the* BARTENDER *hangs up the phone. As the other* MUSICIANS *pack up, the* PIANO PLAYER *comes back to the group)*

PIANO Deeny, you just can't do this. This ain't right about us. We stuck by you for below scale wages, riskin' our own needs with the union to keep you in business, until you got on your feet. And still we never got paid on time. Now I hear you gonna put some names in here and clean up on the rep we made for you.

BOUNCER Shut up, mister. You're not supposed to be here right now, remember?

PANDORA *(furious)* You owe me for two and a half weeks, man!

DEENY *(trying to get by again)* Sorry, baby. Come around some time and maybe we can work out somethin'.

CURT I know why you doin' this, Deeny. Don't pull that union shit on me! You want all the girls to work for you . . . on the block like tramps for ten and fifteen dollars a trick. Pan, Mamma and all the other broads. I'd die before I'd let you put my woman on the street for ten tricks a day. Why you got to be so fuckin' greedy, man? You ain't right! You already got six girls now.

BOUNCER Just say he has taste and discrimination, Curt. You know he wants your old lady because . . .

DEENY *(cutting)* Shut up all of you! And are you goin' to get out of my way?

MAMMA *(from bandstand)* Deeny. Who you think you are?

DEENY *(to* MAMMA*)* You know who I am, you stupid country cunt. And if you want to stay on the streets and keep that junkie ole man of yours cool, just keep your mouth out of this! That way you won't get your legs broke and . . .

CURT *(cutting)* I know why you doin' this, Deeny. *(*SHAKY *enters. The show girl rushes from the rear with costumes in arms and exits, speaking to no one)*

SHAKY Did I hear somebody say they gonna break Mamma's legs? *(there is general bedlam with shouts and near screaming)*

DRUMMER *(exiting)* I'm goin' ta take this farther than to the union, Deeny!

BOUNCER You can take it to your mother, punk! *(*DRUMMER *drops equipment and lunges toward* BOUNCER *but* PIANO PLAYER *grabs him and holds.* BASS PLAYER *helps)*

BASS PLAYER *(exiting with* DRUMMER*)* Hey Deeny, you're wrong! You're dead wrong, man!

PIANO *(to* CURT *and* PANDORA*)* Cool it. Let's all split. This ain't nothin' but a big bust. *(it becomes suddenly quiet and the* BARTENDER*, a club in hand, comes around the bar and stands* *behind* CURT *and* ART. SHAKY *stands to the side of* DEENY *and the* BOUNCER. MAMMA *is on the bandstand, wide-eyed, and* PANDORA *is downstage glowering at her enemies. Leaving)* I'll see you guys. *(seeing* SHAKY*)* Hey, man. It ain't worth it.

SHAKY I'll get in touch with you, okay?

PIANO C'mon, man. I don't like what I see.

SHAKY Make it! Be a good friend and make it. (PIANO PLAYER *exits. It is even more quiet. Very low, from somewhere outside, the theme is heard as each group eyes the other and tenses)*

PANDORA *(spitting it out, violent as unsuspected spit splattering a face)* Fuck you, Deeny! Fuck you! Fuck you! FUCK YOU!

DEENY *(frenzied)* YOU LITTLE TRAMPY BITCH . . . YOU . . .

*(*CURT *smashes him in the mouth as he reaches for* PANDORA. DEENY *falls back beside the table, grabs a glass and hurls it into* CURT*'s face, shattering it.* CURT *launches himself upon him and pummels* DEENY *to the floor.*

Meanwhile, the BOUNCER *and* ART *fight in center stage.* SHAKY *is struck almost immediately from behind by the* BARTENDER*'s club.* ART, *seeing the* BARTENDER *advancing on* CURT*'s rear, breaks away and desperately kicks out at the* BARTENDER. *With a screech he doubles over and grabs his groin. The* BOUNCER *seizes* ART *from behind, about the throat, in an armlock, and begins strangling him.* PANDORA, *who has taken off her shoes after kicking* DEENY *several times as* CURT *beats him upon the floor, attacks the* BOUNCER *from behind and repeatedly strikes him about the head with her shoe heels. The* BOUNCER *loosens his grip on* ART *and grabs* PANDORA *and punches her. She falls.* ART, *gasping, reaches down for the* BARTENDER*'s dropped club, picks it up and turns and beats the* BOUNCER *to the floor.*

All the while MAMMA TOO TIGHT *screams.*

With face bloodied from splintered glass, CURT *has beaten* DEENY *into unconsciousness and staggers over and pulls* PANDORA *up.*

Sirens, screeches and slamming car doors are heard from outside. Shouts)

CURT *(towing* PANDORA*)* C'mon, Art! Pull yourself together. The cops are here. (ART *staggers over to* SHAKY *and tries to lift him but he is too weak.* MAMMA, *crying and screaming, jumps from the bandstand and pulls at* SHAKY. *Heading for the rear)* He's too heavy, Art. Leave him. Grab Mamma and let's get out the back way. MOVE! C'MON, MAN, MOVE! *(dazed, but following orders,* ART *grabs* MAMMA*'s arm and struggles with her)*

MAMMA *(resisting)* NO! NO! I CAN'T LEAVE HIM LIKE THAT!

CURT *(exiting)* Bring her, Art. Out the back way to the car.

MAMMA *(being dragged out by* ART*)* My first day out . . . my first day . . . *(They exit and immediately the stage blackens, then the tumble of running feet, then)*

VOICE CHRIST! *(more heavy running, then stop)* Hey, call a couple of ambulances . . . Emergency!

(Curtain)

ACT 3

Scene 1

TIME *three days later. Afternoon*

SCENE CURT*'s apartment. He and* RICH *play chess as in act one. The bed is lowered and* MAMMA TOO TIGHT *sleeps with the covers pulled up to her chin as if she is cold. The radio is off and the California sunshine glistens in the clean room. The room looks sterile, unlived in and motel-like without the lighting of the first act.*

CURT *wears two band-aids upon his face, one upon his forehead, the other on the bridge of his nose.*

CURT *(bored)* It'll be mate in two moves, Rich. Do you want to play it out?

RICH Nawh, man. I ain't up to it.

CURT *(sitting back)* The last three days have just taken everything out of me, man.

RICH Yeah. They been pretty rough. (CURT *stands, stretches and walks across the stage)* Hey, man. Is there any more beer?

CURT Nawh. Pan and Art's bringing some in with them when they come.

RICH *(muttering)* Yeah . . . when they get here.

CURT *(noticing* RICH*'s tone)* What did you say, man?

RICH Oh, Nothin', man.

CURT *(sharply)* You're a liar . . . I heard what you said!

RICH *(sullen)* I ain't goin'a be many more of them liars, Curt.

CURT *(gesturing)* Awww, man. Forget it . . . you know how I feel with Deeny in a coma from his concussion for the past three days and me not knowin' if he's goin' ta press charges finally or die.

RICH Yeah, man. I'm a bit edgy myself. Forget about what I said. *(*CURT *returns to the couch and sprawls back)*

CURT But I'd like to know what you meant by it, Rich.

RICH *(seeing no way out)* Now, Curt. You and I been friends since were young punks stealin' hub caps and tires together, right? Remember that time you, me and the guys gang banged that Pechuco broad? . . . And the Dog Town boys came up and we had that big rumble and they killed Sparky?

CURT *(sensing something coming)* How can I forget it . . . I served my first stretch behind it for stabbin' that Mexican kid, Manuel.

RICH Yeah. That was a good time ago and Manuel ain't no kid no more . . . he got killed in Korea.

CURT Yeah. But, tell me. What do you have to say, good buddy?

RICH *(pausing, then serious)* It's about this guy Art and Pandora, man.

CURT What do you mean, man?

RICH Man . . . I don't mean there's anything goin' on yet . . . but each afternoon he's taken Pandora out for the past three days they been gettin' back later . . . and . . .

CURT And what, Rich!

RICH And the way she looks at him, Curt.

CURT *(disgusted and angry)* Awww, man . . . I thought I knew you better.

RICH Well I told you that I didn't think that they were doin' anything really.

CURT But, what? That he drives her up to Sunset Strip to keep her dates with the big tricks . . . you know how much dough she brings back, man?

RICH *(resolutely)* Yeah, man. Sometimes over a hundred dollars for one trick.

CURT So you can't hurry those people for that kinda bread, man.

RICH *(trying to be understood)* But I wasn't talkin' about the tricks, Curt. I don't think they're holdin' back any money on you.

CURT Then what are you talkin' 'bout?

RICH About that little jive-ass square gettin' next to your woman, that's what!

CURT Now listen, Rich. We're friends and all that but that little jive-ass square as you call him is just like a brother to me . . . and we been in some tighter things than you and me will ever be in.

RICH *(obviously hurt)* Well, forget it!

CURT No, let's not forget it. You're accusing my wife of jivin' around on me. You know that Pan's the straightest broad you'll ever find. That's why I married her. You know if we couldn't have gotten another man that she would have gone on the job and been as good as most men. She and I are a team. What could she gain by messin' 'round on me with my ace buddy?

RICH Forget it, I said.

CURT Nawh, Rich. I don't want to. I know what's really buggin' you. Ever since Shaky got busted at the Club and they found all that smack on him you been buggin' Mamma to be your woman 'cause you know that with Shaky's record he won't be hittin' the streets again for at least ten years. But you're wrong on two counts 'cause we're bailin' out Shaky tonight and takin' him with us and Mamma don't want you 'cause she wants Art but he don't go for her.

RICH *(getting to his feet)* I'll see you, man. Between your broad and that cat you can't think any more! *(*CURT *reaches for* RICH*'s shirt front;* RICH *throws his hands off)* Take it easy, Curt. You already won a close one this week. And your guardian angel ain't around to sneak punch people. *(*CURT *stares at him and steps back)*

MAMMA *(from bag)* Hey, what's all that shoutin' about?

CURT Nothin', baby. Rich and I are just crackin' jokes.

MAMMA *(sitting up)* Curt, I wonder if . . .

CURT No, Mamma. You can't have no fix. Remember what I told you? You don't turn no tricks in town 'cause you're hot behind Shaky's bust so you don't need any heroin, right? You're on holiday and besides, you're full of codein now . . . that's enough . . .

MAMMA But I would be good if I could get some. I wouldn't worry about Shaky so much and I'd feel . . .

CURT You just come out of the joint clean, Mamma. You don't need anything but to keep cool.

MAMMA *(pouting)* But I got the sixteen hundred dollars that Shaky had stashed at our pad. I could buy it okay, Curt.

CURT Forget it. That money is with the other broad. We all takin' a trip with that. Besides . . . Shaky had over two thousand bucks worth of stuff in the pad and we sellin' it tonight so we can bail him out so he can leave with us . . . *(*MAMMA *jumps out of bed in a thin gown)*

MAMMA *(delighted)* You are? Then he'll be home soon?

CURT Yeah. Then we all make it before Deeny comes out his coma or croaks. Now get back in bed before Rich grabs you!

MAMMA *(playful)* Rich, you better not. Shaky will be home soon.

RICH *(teasing)* Sheet, woman. I don't care about old ass Shaky. C'mon, baby, why don't you get yourself a young stud?

MAMMA *(getting in bed)* When I get one it won't be you.

RICH *(serious)* Then who?

CURT *(mutters)* I told Art and Pan that we need the car this evening to drop off the stuff. After that it'll be time to get ready for the job.

RICH *(bitterly, to* MAMMA*)* So he's got to you, too.

MAMMA Nobody's got to me. What'chou talkin' 'bout, Rich? Art's been stayin' over to Shaky and my place for the last couple of nights while I stayed here. How can he get . . .

RICH *(cutting)* How did you know I was talkin' about Art?

MAMMA 'Cause you got Art on the brain, that's why!

CURT I thought we dropped that, Rich.

RICH *(to* MAMMA*)* If you're goin'a get somebody young . . . get a man . . . not some little book readin' faggot . . .

MAMMA *(red faced, to* RICH*)* Oh, go fuck yourself, man! *(she covers her head)*

RICH Okay, man. We got a lot to do tonight, so I'll lay off.

(Through the back curtain the outside kitchen door can be seen opening. Dusk is come and ART *enters first with a large bag.* PANDORA *follows, closes the door and purposely bumps against him as she passes. She wears dark glasses, her pants and boots)*

ART Hey, you almost made me drop this! Where should I put it? *(*PANDORA *enters front room smiling)*

PANDORA Hi, honey. Hello, Rich. *(She walks over to* CURT*, kisses him and places money in his hand)*

CURT Hey, pretty baby. *(he pulls her to him, gives her an extended kiss and breaks it, looking over* PANDORA*'s shoulders at* RICH *who looks away)* Everything okay?

PANDORA Smooth as Silky Sullivan.

(In the kitchen ART *is taking items from the bag.* CURT *hands back the money to* PANDORA*)*

CURT Here, Pan, put this in the box with the rest.

PANDORA Okay. *(she walks past bed and looks down)* What's wrong with Mamma?

CURT Rich's been tryin' to love her up.

RICH She won't go for my program, baby.

PANDORA *(entering the kitchen)* That's too bad . . . you better cultivate some charm, Rich.

RICH Yeah, that's what's happen'n. I'm not one of the lucky ones . . . some people don't need it.

PANDORA *(going to* ART*)* Let me take in the beer, Art. You put the frozen food in the refrigerator and the canned things in the cupboard. *)* ART *pulls her to him and kisses her. Taking breath)* Hand me the glasses, will ya? *(they kiss again, she responding this time, then she pushes him away and begins fixing beer for* CURT *and* RICH*)*

CURT Hey, Mamma. You want any beer?

MAMMA *(under the cover)* No, no. *(*PANDORA *serves* CURT *and* RICH *then climbs the stairs and enters the dressing room.* ART *comes out of the kitchen)*

RICH How you feel, Art?

ART Okay. Hollywood's an interesting place. First job I ever had just drivin' somebody around.

CURT Hope it's your last, Art. With this job tonight and my cut from sellin' Shaky's heroin we'll be just about in. Might even go into business back East.

ART Yeah? I hope so.

CURT We already got almost twenty-four hundred with Shaky's money we found at his place and the bread we've been able to hustle the last few days. After tonight we'll be set.

RICH Yeah. After tonight you'll be set.

CURT *(looking at* RICH*)* It's too bad you won't come with us, Rich. But your share will fix you up out here okay.

RICH Fix me up? Ha ha . . . I'll probably shoot that up in smack inside of several months . . . but if I make it I'll probably be lookin' you up in two more years when my probation's up. No use ruin'n a good thing. When I cut this town loose I want to be clean. I just hope all goes well with you.

ART *(smiling)* Why shouldn't it?

CURT Yeah, Rich, why shouldn't it?

RICH Funny things happen to funny-style people, ya know.

CURT Yeah. Too bad you won't be comin' along . . . we need a clown in our show. *(*RICH *watches* ART *studying the chess game)*

RICH Do you see anything I missed, good buddy?

ART Oh, I don't know.

RICH You know I seldom beat Curt. Why don't you play him?

ART *(still looking at board)* Maybe I will when we find time.

CURT What would you have done from there, Art?

ART It's according to what side I'm on.

CURT You have the black. White's going to mate you in two moves.

ART He is?

RICH Yeah. He is. *(*ART *reaches over and picks up the black king)*

ART Most kings need a queen to be most powerful but others do the best they can. *(he places the king upon another square)* That's what I'd do, Rich.

CURT *(perceiving)* Yeah. I see . . . I see . . .

RICH Say, why'd you move there? . . . He can't move now . . . he can't put himself in check.

ART *(as* RICH *stares at him)* Yeah, Rich?

CURT *(matter-of-factly)* A stalemate.

RICH *(muttering)* I should of seen that. *(to* ART*)* How did you . . . why . . .

ART When you play the game you look for any break you can make.

CURT We should play sometime, Art.

ART I'm looking forward to it, Curt. But you name the time.

CURT *(standing)* I'll do that. HEY, PANDORA! We got to go! *(*PANDORA *comes to the top of the stairs. She has changed into a simple dress)*

PANDORA We goin' some place?

CURT I got to drop Shaky's stuff off and go down to the bail bondsman and the lawyer. I want you to drive. C'mon, Rich. Pan will sit in the car down the street in the next block and you and me will walk up the street talkin' about baseball, understand? On the corner of Adams and Crenshaw we'll meet a man and hit a grand slam.

RICH Yeah, I hope so, brother.

CURT It's trip time from here on in, baby.

PANDORA *(excited)* Wait until I get my coat.

CURT *(in good humor)* Let's go, woman. It's eighty degrees outside and we might be the hottest thing in L.A. but it just ain't that warm. Let's go, now. See you, Art. *(going to* ART*)* Oh, I almost forgot the car keys.

ART *(handing him the keys)* See you guys.

CURT *(hands keys to* PANDORA*)* You'll watch the phone, okay?

ART Sure, good buddy, I'll see to the phone.

CURT If Mamma wakes up and wants a fix don't give in to her.

ART I'll try not to.

CURT *(serious)* I mean it, Art.

ART *(smiling)* I'm dead serious, man.

PANDORA See you later, Art.

ART See you later, Pan. Good-bye, Curt. Good-bye, Rich.

(The trio exit and ART *goes to the radio and switches it on. It plays the theme as he enters the kitchen and gets himself a beer. He comes from the kitchen drinking from the bottle and climbs the bathroom stairs. His shadow is seen lifting and then dialing. His voice is muffled by the music and by his whisper; nothing is understood.*

After the shadow hangs up, ART *returns to the living room and descends the stairs. He sits upon the bed and shakes* MAMMA TOO TIGHT*)*

MAMMA *(being shaken)* Huh! I don't want any beer. *(*ART *shakes her once more. She uncovers her head)* Oh, Art. It's you. Where's everybody? *(he doesn't answer, looks at her. Evening comes and the room blackens)* I'm glad you woke me. I always like to talk to you but I guess I bug you since you don't say too much to me. Why ain't you sayin' nothin' now? *(three beat pause)*

ART *(laughing)* Ha ha ha . . . ha ha . . . Mama Too Tight! . . . ha ha ha . . .

MAMMA You said it! Sometimes you have such a nice look on your face and now . . . you look different . . . *(pause)* . . . like you so happy you could scream . . . You never looked at me like this before, Art, never. *(in total blackness as the music plays)* You said Shaky wouldn't be back? . . . He won't? . . . I don't care as long as you don't go away . . . You know . . . you understand me. It's like you can look inside my head . . . Oh how did you know? Just a little bit? More? You say I can have a fix anytime I want? . . . Oh! . . . you understand me, don't cha? Don't let Curt know . . . you say don't worry about Curt . . . don't care what anybody thinks or says except you? . . . *(silence, pause)* Oh I feel so good now . . . I didn't know but I was hoping . . . I didn't know, honey . . . OH ART! . . . Ahhhh . . . now I can feel you oozing out of me . . . and I'm glad so glad . . . it's good . . .

Scene 2

PANDORA *leans against the kitchen door as the lights go up. The atmosphere of the first act is recreated by the lights and music. The bed has been put up and* ART *sits upon the couch.* PANDORA *has been crying and what can be seen of her face around her dark glasses appears shocked. She walks to the center of the room and faces* ART*)*

PANDORA Art . . . Art . . . they got them. They got Curt and Rich . . . with all that stuff on them. The cops were waitin' on them. They busted them with all those narcotics . . . we'll never see them again.

ART *(rising)* We're hot, Pandora. We got to get out of town.

PANDORA They got 'em, don't you hear me, Art? What can we do?

ART Nothin' . . . we got to make it before Curt or Rich break and the cops are kickin' that door in.

PANDORA You said nothin'? But we . . . what do you mean? We got to do somethin'! *(crying)* We can't just let it happen to them . . . we got to do somethin' like Curt would do if it was one of us . . . Art! Art! DON'T JUST STAND THERE! *(he slaps her viciously, knocking off her glasses, exposing her blackened eyes)*

ART *(commanding)* Get a hold of yourself, Pandora. You've had a bad experience. *(she holds her face and looks dazed)* Now listen to me. Mamma has gone over to her place to pack and as soon as she gets back we're all leaving.

PANDORA *(dazed)* Mamma is packin'? . . . Did Curt tell her to pack

ART You know he didn't. Now as soon as she gets here I want us to be packed, okay?

PANDORA But . . . Art . . . packed . . . where we goin'?

ART To Buffalo, baby. Where else?

PANDORA To Buffalo?

ART That's what I said. Now go up in your dressing room and get your case. *(a knock comes from the front door)* That's Mamma already . . . we're runnin' late, woman. C'mon, get a move on. *(he shoves her)* MOVE! GET A MOVE ON, PANDORA! *(she stumbles over the first step, catches her balance and begins climbing.* ART *looks after her)* Oh . . . Pandora . . . *(she turns and looks vacantly at him)* . . . Don't forget your box! *(as she turns and climbs the last steps,* ART *saunters to the radio as the knock sounds again. Instantaneously, as he switches the radio off, the stage is thrown in complete blackness)*

PRAYER MEETING: OR, THE FIRST MILITANT PREACHER[1]

1967

Ben Caldwell (1937–)

The seventh of nine children, Ben Caldwell was born in Harlem to parents who had migrated from the South two years before his birth. Demonstrating at an early age a talent for writing and drawing, he was encouraged to study at the School for Industrial Arts in New York City; however, in 1954, his father died, and Ben had to leave school to help support the family. In the 1960s, he met LeRoi Jones (later Amiri Baraka) who encouraged him to begin writing for the theatre.[1]

After the demise in 1965 of his Black Arts Theatre, Baraka left Harlem and Caldwell followed him to Spirit House, a new cultural center in Newark, New Jersey. *Prayer Meeting* is a product of that Newark period, a time when Caldwell wrote several "agitprop cartoons": *Hypnotism* reveals that "nonviolence" and "integration" are white hypnotic tricks to pacify Blacks; *Riot Sale* or, *Dollar Psyche Fake-Out*, shows how "revolutionary" Blacks can be bought out by poverty money; and *Family Portrait* or *My Son The Black Nationalist*, deals with the conflicting material/spiritual values of different generations.[2] In nearly all his plays, Caldwell's satiric darts were initially aimed at African Americans, to arouse them to racial awareness of what actions must be taken if their political status is to change. However, in ripping off the benign mask of white paternalism, Caldwell reveals its wearer to be a clever racist who is manipulating African Americans to exploit them.

In April 1969, in a program called "A Black Quartet," Woodie King, Jr., produced *Prayer Meeting* along with three other short plays (*The Warning—A Theme for Linda* by Ronald Milner, *The Gentleman Caller* by Ed Bullins, and *Great Goodness of Life* by LeRoi Jones). Black critic Clayton Riley described the seminal event: "The plays can serve well to define a mood and movement, an artistic motion to adjourn all former misunderstandings—histories of

1. "I am forever grateful to Amiri Baraka and Woodie King, Jr., for their inspiration, encouragement, and support."—Ben Caldwell. For information regarding performance rights, write to Ben Caldwell, POB 656, Morningside Station, New York 10026.

2. Robbie Jean Walker. "Ben Caldwell," in *Dictionary of Literary Biography* 38 (Detroit: Gale Research Company, 1985).

false assumptions. Plays designed to further a spirit of newness. Further it. Bring the thing down front where we all can see what it wants to mean. *Has* to mean." Riley went on to find Caldwell's work a "total commitment to the cause of Black Nationalism and the complete devotion to militancy that cause implies."[3]

Prayer Meeting: or, The First Militant Preacher

Cast

BURGLAR
MINISTER

The time is the late sixties. Black-white trouble in a large U.S. city. The scene is black. Someone is searching in this darkness with a flashlight. Talking to himself, angrily, in whispered tones. He bumps into an object and curses.

BURGLAR Damm! Where's a mother-fuckin' light switch? I can't find nothin' this way. Oh, here it is.

(He spots a lamp with his flashlight and turns it on. The scene is a bedroom, decorated in very expensive French Provincial. The room is semi-dark and eerie from just the light of the table lamp. He looks around appraisingly)

Mmmmmmmmm. Looks nice. Oughta be a lotta good shit in here.

(He starts to search in dresser drawers, closets, under the bed, etc. He examines small items and places some, upon approval, into the small canvas bag he's carrying. On the dresser is a picture of a serious looking minister. He picks it up, looks at it, puts it face-down on the dresser)

I shoulda known this was a preacher's pad. A nigger livin' like this, either a preacher, a politician, or a hustler. Really ain't no difference though. All of 'em got some kind of game to get your money!

(All the larger items he's selected, he places near the place of his entrance: a portable TV, a clock-radio, several suits)

Sho' is lotta good shit in here! *(still placing items into the bag)* When you get home tonight, Rev., you gon' find you've been un-blessed. Oh, oh! Somebody's comin'! *(he hides behind the dresser at the sound of someone approaching)*

MINISTER *(slowly coming, singing and humming)* What a friend we have in Jeee-sus. Jesus Christ! How many times have I told Ellen 'bout leavin' these lights on!

(Enters the room and drops wearily to a position of prayer at the bedside. Talking to himself; not really praying; so much on his mind that he doesn't notice the disarray of the room. There is no sincerity in his words. It's as though he's rehearsing a role he plays, checking to hear if he sounds convincing in this role. He sounds tired.)

Thank God this day is over! Lord! What a trying, troublesome day. Trying to console my people 'bout brother Jackson's death at the hands of that white po-liceman. I tried, Lord. I tried to keep them from the path of violence. I tried to show them where it was really brother Jackson's fault fo' provokin' that off'cer. There's a time for protest and a time for silence. They say the off'cer hit him a few times. Brother Jackson could've taken a *little* beatin'. It wouldn't be the first time he'd taken a beating. Now the people want to go downtown and raise hell, Lord. They talk of vengeance! We should leave such things in yo' hands. You said, Vengeance is Mine, Lord. *(pause; long sigh)* For the first time in all my years of delivering God's word they were unbelieving *(shaking his head in disbelief)* and beyond my control. What have I done wrong

3. Woodie King, Jr., ed., *Black Quartet* (New York: New American Library, 1970).

that has shaken their faith, Lord? *(he practices his most pitiful whine)* I'm trying to show them the right way. Your way, Lord. But I am truly perplexed. The mayor said if I can't stop them there'll be trouble . . . and more killing! What must I do, Lord? Tell me how I can save my people?

BURGLAR *(disgustedly)* Aw, man shut up and get up off your mother-fuckin' knees!

(The MINISTER *is shocked. He looks around, fear all over his face)*

MINISTER My God! What? Who's that?!

*(*BURGLAR *starts to come out of hiding and confront the* MINISTER *with his arguments, man to man. He suddenly realizes that the* MINISTER *believes he's been answered by God. The* MINISTER *hides his trembling face in his hands. The* BURGLAR *decides to elaborate on this deception)*

BURGLAR What do you mean, who? Who the hell was you talkin' to? Didn't you expect to get an answer?

(The MINISTER *rises slowly from his kneeling position and stands frozen in the middle of the room)*

That's right! Get up off your knees! And stop trying to bullshit me! You ain't worried 'bout what's gon' happen to your people. You worried 'bout what's gon' happen to you if something happens to your people. You so sure that if they go up 'gainst the white man they gon' lose and whitey won't need *you* no more. Or if they go up 'gainst whitey and win, then they won't need you. Either way yo' game is messed up. So you want things to stay just as they are. You tell them to do nothin' but wait. Wait and turn the other cheek. No matter what whitey do, always turn the other cheek. As long as you keep them off the white folks you alright with the white folks. MY PEOPLE got to keep catchin' hell so you can live like this! YOU STOP PREACHING AND TEACHING MY PEOPLE THAT SHIT! You better stop or I'll reveal myself and put somethin' on your cheeks!

MINISTER *(nervous and excited)* Lord, Lord! Believe me. Those were not my motives. I was only trying to bring them along in your righteous way. Didn't you say that . . .

BURGLAR Don't tell me what I said, DAMNIT! How in the hell you know I haven't changed my mind since then? How you know how I feel 'bout that violence-vengeance bullshit now? I haven't written anything since the Bible!

MINISTER But my people can't win with violence.

BURGLAR If you call what they doin' now, winnin', you the dumbest m.f. ever tried to interpret my word. My people can do anything if I am with them. I can do anything but fail. Do you remember that line?

MINISTER But there are men like the man who killed brother Jackson who are hoping such a thing will happen. They'll welcome the opportunity to come into the Black community and kill up a lot of inno—

BURGLAR So what! They got to bring some ass to get some ass! I want my people to BE READY whey they come. The shit you preachin' gon' get MY PEOPLE hurt!

MINISTER Lord, you keep saying "my people." Are black people your "chosen people?"

BURGLAR You goddamn right! and you and everybody else better ack like it!

MINISTER I, I, I can't accept that . . .

BURGLAR What! You questionin' me, man? I oughta come out from here and . . .

MINISTER I didn't mean that, Lord. I just thought . . .

BURGLAR Stop thinkin'. Especially for so many others. The only thing you better think about is how to tell my people the opposite of what you been tellin' them for so long. I *know* what's best. I made *all* this shit up. Y'all messed up. I'm tryin' to help straighten it out.

MINISTER Give me the strength, Lord, and I will try to do your bidding.

BURGLAR Try? Man, you better. Ain't nobody afraid of dyin' but you. And those like you who're so comfortable they've forgot they're victims. It's time to put a stop to this shit. Some of my people gon' have to die so the rest can live in peace.

MINISTER But . . .

BURGLAR But nothing! Tomorrow you'll lead a protest march to end all protest marches. I don't want this to be no damned "sing-along." I said a *protest* march! You'll demand justice. And if you don't get justice you'll raise hell. I want brother Jackson's death avenged. You tell my people to be ready. Ready for what ever might come. Tell them I don't want no more cheek turnin'. Tell them I will be with them. *(gestures menacingly with his blackjack)* And if you don't tell them, you will be the first one to feel my . . . wrath. Now pray that you don't forget to do anythin' I've told you to do.

MINISTER This is a heavy burden you place upon my shoulders, Lord.

BURGLAR I feel like I'm takin' some of your burdens away.

(He is passing some of the larger items out the window)

MINISTER But why? Why me, Lord?

BURGLAR Because I feel like it should be you. You don't question that white man's judgment, don't you dare question mine!

MINISTER *(dropping to his knees)* Yes, Lord! Thank You, Jesus!

BURGLAR And stop calling me Jesus! My name is God!

*(*MINISTER *begins a fervent, mumbled prayer. While he is so occupied, the* BURGLAR *gathers all he has selected and exits. The* MINISTER *finishes his prayer, gets up from his knees. He goes to the night table, picks up the Bible. He leafs through it till he finds the desired passage. He reads it aloud to himself)*

MINISTER "As I was with Moses, so I will be with thee; I will not fail thee, nor forsake thee. *(more searching)* An eye for an eye; tooth for tooth; hand for hand; foot for foot."

(He lays the Bible down, reaches into the drawer, takes out a revolver, checks it, places the Bible and gun atop the table. He walks to the dresser, stands before the mirror, and affects a pulpit pose)

Brothers and sisters, I had a talk with God last night. He told me to tell you that the time has come to put an end to this murder, suffering, oppression, exploitation to which the white man subjects us. The time has come to put an end to the fear which, for so long, suppressed our actions. The time has come . . .

(The lights fade out)

Curtain

CONTRIBUTION

1969

Ted Shine (1931–)

America was in the midst of racial turmoil when *Contribution* was written. African Americans were unified as never before in pursuit of a common goal—their full and equal rights as American citizens. Rosa Parks sparked the Civil Rights Movement by refusing to move to the rear of a bus in Montgomery, Alabama. The Supreme Court decreed that segregated schools were illegal, and Black children, protected by federal troops, began enrolling in white public schools. Medger Evers, an NAACP field worker in Mississippi, was assassinated. African Americans of all ages marched, picketed, and staged sit-ins, demonstrating for civil rights. Television coverage allowed the world to see men, women, and children being attacked with electric cattle prods, sprayed with fire hoses, and assaulted by police dogs. Vicious beatings were commonplace—as was murder. This was the atmosphere in which *Contribution* was born, and which it reflects.

The idea for *Contribution* derived from the anger of a few young Black militants. They were particularly annoyed by the positions that some Black presidents of state colleges in the South had taken regarding demonstrations. They were ordered by all-white school boards to end the demonstrations or expel the students involved. When the orders were carried out, the student militants felt betrayed and became distrustful not only of their college administration, but also of others in that age bracket.

Eugene, the grandson in the play, is a student at a Black southern college, and harbors this anger. Like many of his classmates, he is young, frequently unreasonable, and sometimes immature in his outlook. He sees the Civil Rights Movement as a youth movement that does not require older people.

Mrs. Love, on the other hand, takes the opposite stance. She wants to be a participant in their demonstration, but is rejected because of her age. Despite constant reminders of what is "appropriate" for someone her age, she refuses to be relegated to "place." She learned early in life to persevere—her survival depended on it. She has witnessed lynchings, has been subjected to the vilest indignities, and has reached a point in her life where she can no longer turn the other cheek.

Her position regarding the movement is contrary to that of her grandson. It is ironic their that positions are not reversed; he being the young militant and she the conservative. But Mrs. Love is not a conformist—nor does she fit a stereotype. She is a woman with depth and dimension. We see the real Mrs. Love, her capacity to love, to hurt, to endure, and to hate, in this scene with Eugene.

Contribution was first produced by the Negro Ensemble Company in 1969. It opened Off Broadway at Tambellini's Gate Theatre in March 1970 along with two other one-act plays by Shine, *Shoes* and *Plantation*, under the collective title *Contributions*.

Ted Shine was born in Baton Rouge, Louisiana, and raised in Dallas, Texas. He attended Howard University, where he studied playwriting with Owen Dodson. He received his M.A. degree from the University of Iowa and his Ph.D. degree from the University of California, Santa Barbara. He is currently teaching at Prairie View A&M University in Texas.

Contribution

CAST

MRS. GRACE LOVE, a Negro woman in her seventies

EUGENE LOVE, her grandson, a twenty-one year old college student

KATY JONES, her neighbor, thirty-eight

CONTRIBUTION

SCENE MRS. LOVE'S *kitchen. Clean, neatly furnished. A door U.C. leads into the backyard. A door, R., leads into the hall. In the C. of the room is an ironing board with a white shirt resting on it to be ironed.*

AT RISE KATY *sits at the table drinking coffee. She is ill at ease.* MRS. LOVE *stands beside her mixing cornbread dough. Now and then she takes a drink of beer from the bottle resting on the table.*

MRS. LOVE *(singing:)*
WHERE HE LEADS ME
IIIIII SHALL FOLLOW!
WHERE HE LEADS ME
IIIIII SHALL FOLLOW!
WWWWWWHERE HE LEADS ME
IIIIII SHALL FOLLOW!
IIIIII'LLLLL GO WITH HIM—

EUGENE *(offstage)* Grandma, please! You'll wake the dead!

MRS. LOVE I called you half an hour ago. You dressed?

EUGENE I can't find my pants.

MRS. LOVE I pressed them. They're out here. *(*EUGENE *enters in shorts and undershirt, unaware that* KATY *is present)*

EUGENE I just got those trousers out of the cleaners and they didn't need pressing! I'll bet you scorched them! *(He sees* KATY *and conceals himself with his hands)*

MRS. LOVE You should wear a robe around the house, boy. You never know when I'm having company. *(She tosses him the pants.)*

EUGENE I'm . . . sorry. 'Mornin', Miss Katy. *(he exits quickly)*

KATY Mornin', Eugene. *(to* MRS. LOVE*)* He ran out of here like a skint cat. Like I ain't never seen a man in his drawers before.

MRS. LOVE *(pouring cornbread into pan)* There. I'll put this bread in the oven and it'll be ready in no time. I appreciate your taking it down to the Sheriff for me. He'd bust a gut if he didn't have my cornbread for breakfast. *(sings)*

I SING BECAUSE I'M HAPPY—
I SING BECAUSE I'M FREE—

KATY I'm only doing it because I don't want to see a woman your age out on the streets today—

MRS. LOVE *(singing)*

HIS EYE IS ON THE SPARROW
AND I KNOW HE WATCHES ME!

KATY Just the same I'm glad you decided to take off. White folks have been coming into town since sun up by the truck loads. Mean white folks who're out for blood!

MRS. LOVE They're just as scared as you, Katy Jones.

KATY Ain't no sin to be scared. Ain't you scared for Eugene?

MRS. LOVE Scared of what?

KATY That lunch counter has been white for as long as I can remember—and the folks around here aim to keep it that way.

MRS. LOVE Let'em *aim* all they want to! The thing that tees me off is they won't let me march.

KATY Mrs. Love, your heart couldn't take it!

MRS. LOVE You'd be amazed at what my heart's done took all these years, baby.

EUGENE *(entering)* Where's my sport shirt? The green one?

MRS. LOVE In the drawer where it belongs. I'm ironing this white shirt for you to wear.

EUGENE A white shirt? I'm not going to a formal dance.

MRS. LOVE I want you neat when you sit down at that counter. Newspaper men from all over the country'll be there and if they put your picture in the papers, I want folks to say, "my, ain't that a nice looking, neat, young man."

EUGENE You ask your boss how long he'll let me stay neat?

MRS. LOVE I ain't asked Sheriff Morrison nothin'.

EUGENE He let you off today so you could nurse my wounds when I get back, huh?

MRS. LOVE You ain't gonna get no wounds, son, and you ain't gonna get this nice white shirt ruined either. What's wrong with you anyway? You tryin' to—what yawl say—"chicken out"?

EUGENE No, I'm not going to chicken out, but I am nervous.

KATY I'm nervous too—for myself and for all you young folks. Like the Mayor said on TV last night the whites and the colored always got on well here—

MRS. LOVE So long as "we" stayed in our respective places.

KATY He said if we want to eat in a drug store we ought to build our own.

EUGENE Then why don't you build a drug store on Main Street with a lunch counter in it?

KATY Where am I gonna get the money?

MRS. LOVE Where is any colored person in this town gonna get the money? Even if we got it, you think they'd let us lease a building—let alone buy property on Main Street.

KATY I know, Mrs. Love, but—

MRS. LOVE But nothin'! If I was a woman your age I'd be joinin' them children!

KATY I'm with yawl, Eugene, in mind—if not in body.

EUGENE Um-huh.

KATY But I have children to raise and I have to think about my job.

MRS. LOVE. Why don't you think about your children's future? Them few pennies you make ain't shit! And if things stay the same it'll be the same way for those children too, but Lord knows, if they're like the rest of the young folks today—they're gonna put you down real soon!

KATY I provide for my children by myself—and they love me for it! We have food on our table each and every day!

MRS. LOVE Beans and greens! When's the last time you had steaks?

KATY Well . . . at least we ain't starvin'!

EUGENE Neither is your boss lady!

KATY Mrs. Comfort says yawl are—*communists!*

MRS. LOVE I'll be damned! How come every time a Black person speaks up for himself he's got to be a communist?

KATY That's what the white folks think!

MRS. LOVE Well ain't that somethin'! Here I am—old black me—trying to get this democracy to working like it oughta be working, and the democratic white folks say wait. Now tell me, why the hell would I want to join another bunch of white folks that I don't know nothin' about and expect them to put me straight? *(to* EUGENE*)* Here's your shirt, son. Wear a tie and comb that natural! Put a part in your hair!

EUGENE Good gracious! *(he exits)*

KATY "Militant"! That's what Mrs. Comfort calls us—"militants"!

MRS. LOVE *(removing bread from oven)* What does that mean?

KATY Bad! That's what it means—bad folks!

MRS. LOVE I hope you love your children as much as you seem to love Miss Comfort.

KATY I hate that woman!

MRS. LOVE Why?

KATY I hate all white folks—don't you?

MRS. LOVE Katy Jones, I don't hate nobody. I get disgusted with 'em, but I don't hate 'em.

KATY Well, you're different from me.

MRS. LOVE Ummmmmmm, just look at my cornbread!

KATY It smells good!

MRS. LOVE *(buttering bread and wraps it)* Don't you dare pinch off it either!

KATY I don't want that white man's food! I hope it chokes the hell outta that mean bastard!

MRS. LOVE I see how come your boss lady is calling you militant, Katy.

KATY Well, I don't like him! Patting me on the behind like I'm a dog. He's got that habit bad.

MRS. LOVE You make haste with this bread. He likes it hot.

KATY Yes'em. I ain't gonna be caught dead in the midst of all that ruckus.

MRS. LOVE You hurry along now. *(gives* KATY *the bread and* KATY *exits.* MRS. LOVE *watches her from the back door.)* And don't you dare pinch off it! You'll turn to stone! *(She laughs to herself, turns and moves to the hall door)* You about ready, son?

EUGENE I guess so.

MRS. LOVE Come out here and let me look at you.

EUGENE Since when do I have to stand inspection?

MRS. LOVE Since *now!* (EUGENE *enters)* You look right smart. And I want you to stay that way.

EUGENE How? You know the Sheriff ain't gonna stop at nothing to keep us out of that drug store.

MRS. LOVE Stop worrying about Sheriff Morrison.

EUGENE He's the one who's raisin' all the hell! The mayor was all set to integrate until the Sheriff got wind of it.

MRS. LOVE Yes, I know, but—don't worry about him. Try to relax.

EUGENE How can I relax?

MRS. LOVE I thought most of you young cats had nerve today—

EUGENE And I wish you'd stop embarrassing me using all that slang!

MRS. LOVE I'm just tryin' to talk your talk, baby.

EUGENE There's something wrong with a woman eighty years old trying to act like a teenager!

MRS. LOVE What was it you was telling me the other day? 'Bout that gap—how young folks and old folks can't talk together?

EUGENE The generation gap!

MRS. LOVE Well, I done bridged it, baby! You dig?

EUGENE You are ludicrous!

MRS. LOVE Well, that's one up on me, but I'll cop it sooner or later.

EUGENE I know you'll try!

MRS. LOVE Damned right!

EUGENE That's another thing—all this swearing you've been doing lately—

MRS. LOVE Picked it up from you and your friends sitting right there in my living room under the picture of Jesus!

EUGENE I . . .

MRS. LOVE Don't explain. Now you know how it sounds to me.

EUGENE Why did you have to bring this up at a time like this?

MRS. LOVE You brought it up, baby.

EUGENE I wish you wouldn't call me baby—I'm a grown man.

MRS. LOVE Ain't I heard you grown men callin' each other baby?

EUGENE Well . . . that's different. And stop usin' 'ain't' so much. You know better.

MRS. LOVE I wish I was educated like you, Eugene, but I *aren't!*

EUGENE Good gracious!

MRS. LOVE Let me fix that tie.

EUGENE My tie is all right.

MRS. LOVE It's crooked.

EUGENE Just like that phoney sheriff that

you'd get up at six in the mornin' to cook cornbread for.

MRS. LOVE The sheriff means well, son, in his fashion.

EUGENE That bastard is one dimensional—all black!

MRS. LOVE Don't let him hear you call him black!

EUGENE What would he do? Beat me with his billy club like he does the rest of us around here?

MRS. LOVE You have to try to understand folks like Mr. Morrison.

EUGENE Turn the other cheek, huh?

MRS. LOVE That's what the Bible says.

EUGENE *(mockingly)* That's what the Bible says!

MRS. LOVE I sure do wish I could go with yawl!

EUGENE To eye-witness the slaughter?

MRS. LOVE You young folks ain't the only militant ones, you know!

EUGENE You work for the meanest paddy in town—and to hear you tell it, he adores the ground you walk on! Now you're a big militant!

MRS. LOVE I try to get along with folks, son.

EUGENE You don't have to work for trash like Sheriff Morrison! You don't have to work at all! You own this house. Daddy sends you checks which you tear up. You could get a pension if you weren't so stubborn—you don't have to work at your age! And you surely don't have to embarrass the family by working for trash!

MRS. LOVE What am I supposed to do? Sit here and rot like an old apple? The minute a woman's hair turns gray folks want her to take to a rockin' chair and sit it out. Not this chick, baby. I'm keepin' active. I've got a long way to go and much more to do before I go to meet my maker.

EUGENE Listen to you!

MRS. LOVE I mean it! I want to be a part of this 'rights' thing—but no, yawl say I'm too old!

EUGENE That's right, you are! Your generation and my generation are complete contrasts—we don't think alike at all! The grin and shuffle school is dead!

MRS. LOVE *(slaps him)* That's for calling me a "Tom"!

EUGENE I didn't call you a "Tom," but I have seen you grinning and bowing to white folks and it made me sick at the stomach!

MRS. LOVE And it put your daddy through college so he could raise you with comfort like he raised you—Northern comfort which you wasn't satisfied with. No, you had to come down here and "free" us soul brothers from bondage as if we can't do for ourselves! Now don't try to tell me that your world was perfect up there—I've been there and I've seen! Sick to your stomach! I'm sick to my stomach whenever I pick up a paper or turn on the news and see where young folks is being washed down with hoses or being bitten by dogs—even killed! I get sick to my stomach when I realize how hungry some folks are—and how disrespectful the world's gotten! I get sick to my stomach, baby, because the world is more messed up now than it ever was! You lookin' at me like that 'cause I shock you? *You* shock me! You know why? Your little secure ass is down here to make history in your own way—And you are scared shitless! I had dreams when I was your age too!

EUGENE Times were different then. I know that—

MRS. LOVE Maybe so, but in our hearts we knowed what was right and what was wrong. We knowed what this country was suppose to be and we knowed that we was a part of it—for better or for worse—like a marriage. We prayed for a better tomorrow—and that's why that picture of Jesus got dust on it in my front room right now—'cause the harder we prayed—the worser it got!

EUGENE Things are better now, you always say.

MRS. LOVE Let's hope they don't get no worse.

EUGENE Thanks to *us*.

MRS. LOVE If you don't take that chip off your shoulder I'm gonna blister your behind, boy! Sit down there and eat your breakfast!

EUGENE I'm not hungry.

MRS. LOVE Drink some juice then.

EUGENE I don't want anything!

MRS. LOVE Look at you—a nervous wreck at twenty-one—just because you've got to walk through a bunch of poor white trash and sit at a lunch counter in a musty old drug store!

EUGENE I may be a little tense—it's only natural—you'd be too!

MRS. LOVE I do my bit, baby, and it don't affect me in the least! I've seen the blazing cross and the hooded faces in my day. I've smelled black flesh burning with tar, and necks stretched like taffy.

EUGENE Seeing those things was your contribution, I guess?

MRS. LOVE You'd be surprised at *my* contribution!

EUGENE *Nothing* that you did would surprise me at all! You're a hard headed old woman!

MRS. LOVE And I'm *justified*—justified in whatever I do. *(sits)* Life ain't been pretty for me, son. Oh, I suppose I had some happiness like when I married your granddaddy or when I gave birth to your daddy, but as I watched him grow up I got meaner and meaner.

EUGENE You may be evil, but not mean.

MRS. LOVE I worked to feed and clothe him like Katy's doin' for her children, but I had a goal in mind. Katy's just doin' it to eat. I wanted something better for my son. They used to call me "nigger" one minute and swear that they loved me the next. I grinned and bore it like you said. Sometimes I even had to scratch my head and bow, but I got your daddy through college.

EUGENE I know and I'm grateful—he's grateful. Why don't you go and live with him like he wants you to?

MRS. LOVE 'Cause I'm stubborn and independent! And I want to see me some more colored mens around here with pride and dignity!

EUGENE So that Sheriff Morrison can pound the hell out of it every Saturday night with his billy club?

MRS. LOVE I've always worked for folks like that. I worked for a white doctor once, who refused to treat your granddaddy. Let him die because he hated Black folks. I worked for him and his family and they grew to love me like one of the family.

EUGENE You are the *true* Christian lady!

MRS. LOVE I reckon I turned the other cheek some—grinned and bowed, you call it. Held them white folks' hand when they was sick. Nursed their babies—and I sat back and watched 'em all die out year by year. Old Dr. Fulton was the last to go. He had worked around death all his life and death frightened him. He asked me—Black me—to sit with him during his last hours.

EUGENE Of course you did.

MRS. LOVE Indeed! And loved every minute of it! Remind me sometimes to tell you about it. It's getting late. I don't want you to be tardy.

EUGENE I bet you hope they put me under the jail so that you can Tom up to your boss and say, "I tried to tell him, but you know how—"

MRS. LOVE *(sharply)* I don't want to have to hit you again, boy!

EUGENE I'm sorry.

MRS. LOVE I've got my ace in the hole—and I ain't nervous about it either. You doin' all that huffin' and puffin'—the white folks' are apt to blow you down with a hard stare. Now you scoot. Us Loves is known for our promptness.

EUGENE If I die—remember I'm dying for Negroes like Miss Katy.

MRS. LOVE You musta got that inferior blood from your mama's side of the family. You ain't gonna die, boy. You're coming back here to me just as pretty as you left.

EUGENE Have you and the Sheriff reached a compromise?

MRS. LOVE Just you go on.

EUGENE *(starts to the door. He stops)* I'll be back home, Grandma.

MRS. LOVE I know it, hon. *(he turns to leave again)* Son!

EUGENE Ma'am?

MRS. LOVE The Bible says love and I does. I turns the other cheek and I loves 'til I can't love no more—*(*EUGENE *nods)* Well . . . I reckon I ain't perfect—I ain't like Jesus was, I can only bear a cross so long. I guess I've "had it" as you young folks say. Done been spit on, insulted, but I grinned and bore my cross for a while—then there was peace—satisfaction—sweet satisfaction. *(*EUGENE *turns to go again)* Son, you've been a comfort to me. When you get to be my age you want someone to talk to who loves you, and I loves you from the bottom of my heart.

EUGENE *(embarrassed)* Ahhh, Granny . . . I know . . . *(he embraces her tightly for a moment. She kisses him)* I'm sorry I said those things. I understand how you feel and I understand why you—

MRS. LOVE Don't try to understand me, son, 'cause you don't even understand yourself yet. Gon' out there and get yourself some dignity—be a man, then we can talk.

EUGENE I'll be damned, old lady—

MRS. LOVE Now git!

EUGENE *(exiting)* I'll be damned! (MRS. LOVE *watches him exit. She stands in the doorway for a moment, turns and takes the dishes to the sink. She takes another beer from her refrigerator and sits at the table and composes a letter)*

MRS. LOVE *(writing slowly)* "Dear Eugene, your son has made me right proud today. You ought to have seen him leaving here to sit-in at the drug store with them other fine young colored children." Lord, letter writin' can tire a body out! I'll let the boy finish it when he gets back.

KATY *(offstage)* Miss Love! Miss Love!

MRS. LOVE *(rising)* Katy? (KATY *enters. She has been running and stops beside the door to catch her breath)* What's wrong with you, child? They ain't riotin', are they? (KATY *shakes her head)* Then what's the matter? You give the sheriff his bread? *(she nods yes)*

KATY I poked my head in through the door and he says: "What you want, gal?" I told him I brought him his breakfast. He says, "all right, bring it here." His eyes lit up when he looked at your cornbread!

MRS. LOVE Didn't they!

KATY He told me to go get him a quart of buttermilk from the icebox, then he started eatin' that bread and he yelled at me—"Hurry up, gal, 'fore I finish!"

MRS. LOVE Then what happened?

KATY I got his milk and when I got back he was half-standin' and half-sittin' at his desk holding that big stomach of his'n, and cussin' to high heaven. "Gimme that goddamned milk! Can't you see these ulcers is killin' the hell outta me?"

MRS. LOVE He ain't got no ulcers.

KATY He had something all right. His ol' blue eyes was just dartin' about in what looked to be little pools of blood. His face was red as a beet—

MRS. LOVE Go on, child!

KATY He was panting and breathin' hard! He drank all that milk in one long gulp, then he belched and told me to get my Black ass outta his face. He said to tell all the Negroes that today is the be all and end all day!

MRS. LOVE Indeed!

KATY And he flung that plate at me! I ran across the street. The street was full of white folks with sticks and rocks and things—old white folks and young 'em—even children. My white folks was even there!

MRS. LOVE What was they doin'?

KATY Just standin'—that all. They wasn't sayin' nothin'—just staring and watching. They'd look down the street towards the drug store, then turn and look towards the Sheriff office. Then old Sheriff Morrison come out. He was sort of bent over in the middle. He belched and his stomach growled! I could hear it clear across the street.

MRS. LOVE Oh, I've seen it before, child! I've seen it! First Dr. Fulton a medical man who didn't know his liver from his kidney. He sat and watched his entire family die out—one by one—then let hisself die because he was dumb! Called me to his deathbed and asked me to hold his hand. "I ain't got nobody else to turn to now, Auntie." I asted him, "You related to me in some way?" He laughed and the pain hit him like an axe. "Sing me a spiritual," he told me. I told him I didn't know no spiritual. "Sing something holy for me, I'm dyin'!" he says. *(she sings)*

I'LL BE GLAD WHEN YOU'RE DEAD, YOU
RASCAL, YOU!
I'LL BE GLAD WHEN YOU'RE DEAD YOU
RASCAL, YOU—

Then I told him how come he was dyin'.

KATY He was a doctor, didn't he know?

MRS. LOVE Shoot! Dr. Fulton, how come you didn't treat my husband? How come you let him die out there in the alley like an animal? When I got through openin' his nose with what was happen', he raised up—red like the sheriff with his hands outstretched toward me and he fell right square off that bed onto the floor—dead. I spit on his body! Went down stairs, cooked me a steak, got my belongings and left.

KATY You didn't call the undertaker?

MRS. LOVE I left that bastard for the maggots. I wasn't his "auntie"!! The neighbors found him a week later stinking to hell. Oh, they came by to question me, but I was grieved, chile, and they left me alone. "You know how nigras is scared of death," they said. And now the sheriff. Oh, I have great peace of mind, chile, cause I'm like my grandson in my own fashion. I'm too old to be hit and wet up, they say, but I votes and does my bit.

KATY I reckon I'll get on. You think you oughta stay here by yourself?

MRS. LOVE I'll be all right. You run along now. Go tend to your children before they get away from you.

KATY Ma'am?

MRS. LOVE Them kids got eyes, Katy, and they know what's happenin' and they ain't gonna be likin' their mama's attitude that much longer. You're a young woman, Katy, there ain't no sense in your continuing to be a fool for the rest of your life.

KATY I don't know what you're talking about, Mrs. Love!

MRS. LOVE You'll find out one day—I just hope it ain't too late. I thank you for that favor.

KATY Yes 'em. *(she exits)*

EUGENE *(entering. He is dressed the same, but seems eager and excited now)* Grandma! They served us and didn't a soul do a thing! We've integrated!

MRS. LOVE Tell me about it.

EUGENE When I got there every white person in the county was on that street! They had clubs and iron pipes. There were dogs and firetrucks with hoses. When we reached the drugstore, Old man Thomas was standing in the doorway. "What yawl want?" he asked. "Service," someone said. That's when the crowd started yelling and making nasty remarks. None of us moved an inch. Then the Sheriff came down the street from his office. He walked slowly like he was sick—

MRS. LOVE Didn't he cuss none?

EUGENE He swore up and down! He walked up to me and said, "Boy, what you and them other niggers want here?" "Freedom, baby!" I told him. "Freedom my ass," he said. "Yawl get on back where you belong and stop actin' up before I sic the dogs on you." "We're not leaving until we've been served!" I told him. He looked at me in complete amazement—

MRS. LOVE Then he belched and started to foam at the mouth.

EUGENE He was *mad*, grandma! He said he'd die before a nigger sat where a white woman's ass had been. "God is my witness!" he shouted. "May I die before I see this place integrated!" Then he took out his whistle—

MRS. LOVE Put it to his lips and before he could get up the breath to blow, he fell on the ground—

EUGENE He rolled himself into a tight ball, holding his stomach. Cussing, and moaning and thrashing around—

MRS. LOVE And the foaming at the mouth got worse! He puked—a bloody puke, and his eyes looked like they'd popped right out of their sockets. He opened his mouth and gasped for breath.

EUGENE In the excitement some of the kids went inside the drug store and the girl at the counter says, "Yawl can have anything you want—just don't put a curse on me!" While Black faces were filling that counter, someone outside yelled—

MRS. LOVE "Sheriff Morrison is *dead!*"

EUGENE How do you know so much? You weren't there.

MRS. LOVE No, son, I wasn't there, but I've seen it before. I've seen—

EUGENE What?

MRS. LOVE Death in the raw. Dr. Crawford's entire family went that away.

EUGENE Grandma . . . ?

MRS. LOVE Some of them had it easier and quicker than the rest—dependin'.

EUGENE "Dependin'" on what?

MRS. LOVE How they had loved and treated their neighbor—namely *me. (unconsciously she fumbles with the bag dangling from around her neck, which she removes from her bosom)*

EUGENE What's in that bag you're fumbling with?

MRS. LOVE Spice.

EUGENE You're lying to me. What is it?

MRS. LOVE The spice of life, baby.

EUGENE Did you . . . Did you do something to Sheriff Morrison?

MRS. LOVE *(singing)*

IN THE SWEET BYE AND BYE
WE SHALLLLLLL MEET . . .

EUGENE What did you do to Sheriff Morrison!??!

MRS. LOVE I helped yawl integrate—in my own fashion.

EUGENE What did you do to that man?

MRS. LOVE I gave him peace! Sent him to

meet his maker! And I sent him in grand style too. Tore his very guts out with my special seasoning! Degrading me! Callin' me "nigger"! Beating my men folks!

EUGENE *(sinks into chair)* Why?

MRS. LOVE Because I'm a tired old Black woman who's been tired, and who ain't got no place and never had no place in this country. You talk about a "new Negro"—Hell, I was a new Negro seventy-six years ago. Don't you think I wanted to sip me a coke-cola in a store when I went out shopping? Don't you think I wanted to have a decent job that would have given me some respect and enough money to feed my family and clothe them decently? I resented being called "Girl" and "Auntie" by folks who weren't even as good as me. I worked for nigger haters—made 'em love me, and I put my boy through school—and then I sent *them* to eternity with flying colors. I got no regrets, boy, just peace of mind and satisfaction. And I don't need no psychiatrist—I done vented my pent-up emotions! Ain't that what you're always saying?

EUGENE You can be sent to the electric chair!

MRS. LOVE Who? Aunt Grace Love? Good old Black auntie? Shoot! I know white folks, son, and I've been at this business for a long time now, and they know I know my place.

EUGENE Oh, grandma . . .

MRS. LOVE Cheer up! I done what I did for all yawl, but if you don't appreciate it, ask some of the colored boys who ain't been to college and who's felt ol man Morrison's stick against their heads—they'd appreciate it. Literation! Just like the underground railroad—Harriett Tubman—that's me, only difference is I ain't goin' down in history. Now you take off them clothes before you get them wrinkled.

EUGENE Where're you going?

MRS. LOVE To shed a tear for the deceased and get me a train ticket.

EUGENE You're going home to daddy?

MRS. LOVE Your daddy don't need me no more, son. He's got your mama. No, I ain't going to your daddy.

EUGENE Then where're you going?

MRS. LOVE Ain't you said them college students is sittin' in Mississippi and they ain't makin' much headway 'cause of the governor? *(*EUGENE *nods)* Well . . . I think I'll take me a little trip to Mississippi and see what's happenin'. You wouldn't by chance know the governor's name, would you?

EUGENE What?

MRS. LOVE I have a feeling he just might be needing a good cook.

EUGENE Grandma!

MRS. LOVE Get out of those clothes now. *(she starts for the door)* And while I'm downtown I think I'll have me a cold ice cream soda at Mr. Thomas'! *(examining the bag)* Ain't much left, Lord . . . I wonder who'll be next? I'll put me an ad in the paper. Who knows, it may be you . . . or you . . . or you . . . *(sings as she exits)*

WHERE HE LEADS ME
I SHALLLLLL FOLLOW . . .
WHERE HE LEADS ME
I SHALLLLLL FOLLOW . . .

(Eugene sits stunned as the old woman's voice fades)

(Curtain)

BLK LOVE SONG #1
1969

Kalamu ya Salaam (1947–   )

From 1964 to 1974, before federal arts grants to small organizations began to dry up, Black theatre burgeoned across America; as many as 600 Black community and college theatre groups organized in major cities. Several of the most prominent of these were in Harlem, including Robert Macbeth's New Lafayette Theatre (1966), which had a rich repertory of actors and playwrights: Whitman Mayo, Richard Wesley, Sonny Jim Gaines, Martie Charles, and Ed Bullins. The National Black Theatre, founded in Harlem in 1968 by actor Barbara Ann Teer, sought to "raise the level of consciousness through liberating the spirits and strengthening the minds of its people." Other area theatres included Ernie McClintock's Afro-American Studio, Mical Whitaker's East River Players, as well as the New Heritage Repertory Theatre founded by Roger Furman and Gertrude Jeanette's Hadley Players.

Downtown, Vinnette Carroll created the Urban Arts Corps. Hazel Bryant established the Afro American Total Theatre, later renamed the Richard Allen Center. Bryant also served as secretary of the Black Theatre Alliance (1969–1982), a not-for-profit umbrella for struggling Black theatres. At one time, seventy-five Black theatre and dance companies belonged, fifty-two of them in New York City.

In Los Angeles, C. Bernard Jackson and Josie Dotson founded the Inner City Cultural Center in 1965. Vantile Whitfield established the Performing Arts Society of Los Angeles (PASLA); in Hollywood, Frank Silvera created the Theatre of Being. In 1968, Val and Francis Ward founded Kuumba on Chicago's South Side.

An important regional theatre grew out of the Tougaloo Drama Workshop in Jackson, Mississippi. Gilbert Moses, Doris Derby, and John O'Neal christened themselves the Free Southern Theatre (1964–1980); they toured Mississippi and Louisiana, performing original plays by John O'Neal, Tom Dent, Sharon Stockard Martin, and Kalamu ya Salaam. Most of these short and didactic skits contained messages of self-pride and liberation for rural audiences, many of whom were witnessing a live stage performance for the first time.

Playwright/activist Kalamu ya Salaam,

whose "slave name" was Vallery Ferdinand III, joined the Free Southern Theatre in 1968. He had attended Carlton College in Minnesota and Southern University, spent three years in the U.S. Army, married and fathered five children. He was director of Blkartsouth in New Orleans and coeditor of *Nkombo,* the quarterly journal of Blkartsouth. For thirteen years, he served as editor of *The Black Collegian Magazine.* His poetry books include *The Blue Merchant; Hofu Ni Kwenu (My Fear Is for You); Iron Flowers, a Poetic Report on a Visit to Haiti; Revolutionary Love;* and *Pamoja Tutashinda.* He was also coeditor of the Southern Literature issue of the African American Review. He has two books of essays, *Our Women Keep Our Skies from Falling* and *What Is Life?,* and two books for children, *Who Will Speak for Us: New African Folktales* and *Herufi: An Alphabet Reader.* He is past director of the New Orleans Jazz & Heritage Foundation and presently serves as executive director of the New Orleans Cultural Foundation.

Blk Love Song #1 is representative of a popular genre that was designed to raise race consciousness and create pride among young Blacks. A touring British production of the play by Temba Theatre Company won a "Best Off Fringe" award from the *Manchester Guardian.* The updated script presented here was used in that British production. The main difference between this version and the original are the discussion of the role of women at the end of the play and the improvised song that the woman sings.

Kalamu ya Salaam introduces his own play.

Blk Love Song #1

Free Southern Theatre, it's hard to really explain it. It's an idea about drama and black people's minds. An actuality sometimes. Sometimes, like when Amiri Baraka's *Slaveship* was performed in Greenville, Mississippi during the summer of 69 and literally sent the people out into the streets. Or sometimes, like when *Blkartsouth* upset the southern city of Little Rock by daring to infer that we African people were not only black and beautiful but were also now and should forever be preparing to make it on our own as a nation of black and beautiful people. It's hard to explain it. When it happens it really happens. When we get close to ourselves/our people and be for real the *Free Southern Theater* really exists. It exists when we do it. I said earlier, an idea, well . . . but not really, cause like nothing is an idea/an idea is nothing. Just nothing, not even occupying space, dreamstuff, hallucinations. An idea. No.

FST did a book that documented what FST was about for its first four years of existence. Dig that if you want to know what FST was and by extension may now be about. *FST By the FST* is a historical document. It's finished. But FST as a black theater is moving on. By the time this is in print FST (or some extension or offspring of it) will hopefully be into a better/blacker thing than we're now into. More pure. More actuality. Less ideas, theories. Real tangible alive living experiences.

We spent the first year of seventy just holding on for most of the year without funds making it totally on the voluntary commitment of a dedicated staff . . . (at times it was like voluntary slavery). The latter part of seventy was spent restructuring, evaluating, studying, and redefining. The following is from a staff paper, it explains what FST is trying to get into:

> Some define their objectives in terms of achievement in the ordinary or established realm of the theater as it exists and has existed in western culture. When we speak of Black Theater it is our intent to include only those whose primary commitment is to using the theater as an instrument to further the struggle for liberation of Black people rather than achievement in

> terms of traditional western or commercial theater.
>
> . . . FST is valid only in so far as it is a vehicle for our contribution to the struggle of our people for total liberation.

Like that don't have nothing to do with aesthetics. Just simply commitment, goals, aspirations, etc. But for some, that statement takes FST out of the realm of theater and sets us into something else. Which is cool. You don't really have to call what we're doing theater . . . you can call it construction work if you want to or ritual/propaganda drama or bullshit. It don't matter what you call it, not real/ity. But for sho it ain't somemore jive entertainment to win awards, we ain't just acting. We living for real.

The play you will read in here was written in *Blkartsouth,* FST's community writing/acting workshop. The audiences that saw it dug it and gave us indications of what more needed to be done. FST has a reputation of traveling around giving plays all over the south and so like even if this book sells out, more people will have seen the plays than will ever read them. And that's important to us. Frankly we hope that as a result of reading some of our work you might decide you want to perform them. That's more important than studying them for techniques and styles and methods (which is not to say that all of those things are not present). Besides you won't find even half of what we do with a play written in the script. There's hardly any of the staging we use, none of the movements hardly, not much sound, the script is a skeleton. It will give you some idea of what the play is like but only a hazy idea, a dull generality. It's left to the director and actors to put it out front, to get to the meanings. So understand that when you study say BLS #1 you won't see any stage directions or indications of who is doing what at what point. You have to do that. You got to do it to really find out what the play means. Really do it. If you are going to study this stuff at least read the play out loud, A/LOUD. Put it in the air, put some breath into it, use your muscles and your senses. Feel it, Do it like that, Study it like that. It makes a difference. Otherwise you going to miss what we're doing. You have to use more than your minds to understand/experience these plays.

We don't feel that there necessarily has to be an exact logic to what we're doing. In fact after all is said and done you *will not* really be able to get into what we're all about just by thinking about it. You might be able to catch all of the mental precepts and arguments we throw out but a lot of the stuff that hangs in the air during our performances can only be touched or felt, experienced. Much like dancing with a woman or group dancing to the other side of reality when the experience by its own weight flips the m in "me" and turns "me" into "WE!" That calls for spiritual/physical identification and tremendous releases of energy. Total acceptance. The closest thing that can be pointed to (that we know of) that will give you an idea of what black theater will be like once we get it together is negro down home church (and maybe certain black music shows, like JB or Pharoah). That's total spiritual/physical identification. The good sista sitting up and screaming in church, walking the pews, speaking in tongues and rejoicing. We want that energy/identification in our art. We want to couple that with a straight ahead pan african ideology to produce a *nation.* If a baptist preacher can build a church, buy a house and ride in a cadillac because of his ability to get people to release energy and identify then we black theater people can help build a nation.

Our writers are increasingly conscious of this direction and their work tries to move that way. We look at black people, our total make up. We try to appeal to black people, to every facet of our black peopleness. We try to fill our people's lives. Like a lot of so-called black writers aren't interested in writing about negroes or colored folks or whatever they term non-"B*L*A*C*K" black people. We feel that we have to be interested in all black people. Our motivations for writing are various but primarily we see ourselves as black artists contributing to the struggle for liberation that's trying to build a strong black nation. We know. It sounds more political than artistic . . . and a lot of it seems to be propaganda. We know. But see, drama, all art, but especially what you call drama, well that is (among other things) a very precise political/propaganda projection. Very precise. Shakespeare was an anglo-saxon english nationalist and one of the reasons they still teach his work in colleges and universities and schools period is to keep on projecting that nationalism. It don't really matter that they call it universal. That simply means that they want to be everywhere, want to push that shit on everybody regardless of whether people can identify with it or not. Cause it's universal. Like the english all ways usta say (or want to say): the sun never sets on the british empire; it was universal. But it wasn't necessarily of use to anybody but english people and people who wanted to be like them. You know like finally we believe if we be what we are, what ever we are, and be the best of it, well like that's enough.

Most of our artifacts are trivial. We can throw away statues and paintings and records. They ain't nothing but artifacts, leavings, residue. The art is in the doing, the living. And we can do it and do it and keep on doing it as long as we remain our true black selves. The impulses of creativity are even so strong in us that even in this western culture as slaves and the children of slaves (american negroes) we have been able to produce our art. See you can't equate our art with artifacts or art forms. That ain't where we at. But like that is usually where western critics look to base their arguments. Them artifacts and art forms. Them Mona Lisa's and music scores and other shit them critics and art lovers carry around in books, pictures, diagrams, and logically constructed heads. We carry ours around in our hearts. Miles shows up for a recording date with his horn. Coltrane played *kulu Se Mama* while Juno Lewis hummed it in his ear. It was transmitted like that. I mean there's a big difference.

Maybe we shouldn't use the word trivial, let's just say expendable. We don't mean to imply that the artifact is worthless, just simply that the artifact itself is not where the worth of our art resides. The essence of blackness resides in the black hearts of our people. The spiritual/physical forces that emanate from the heart. But we are conscious too that our minds have to come into play if we are to keep on keepin on, if we are to survive this western sojourn and once having survived it, journey to our nation and ensure that we are never separated again. We have to develop, redevelop some things that we once took for granted. We got to lay them out. And so like our art, its essence comes from the heart (along with all that implies) but in order for us to survive as a people in these times we must (at least some of us must) use our minds. Construct an ideology, a frame work to hang out on. Shakespeare didn't have to invent the kingship or any other social order as such, it was already invented, so he just went from within that framework. But we got to develop our own framework and at the same time that we work from within it. Many people don't understand that. We got to study ourselves, study ourselves. You can't just throw any idea out into space and say that this is a black concept, a black thing. See concepts follow actions and being. A thing is a thing. Black is a way of thing*ing* not a thing. Black is a way of arting not an art form or artifact. So the only way we can develop BLK ART concepts is to first be the concepts, is to first be the concepts we want to develop.

Something else too, we got to get our art forms and artifacts more together but we can only do this in terms of developing the artist so that the artist has capability, understanding, heart, soul, and technique enough to transmit whatever the artist wants to transmit. We don't have to work on forms no more. We got to work on the artists. If the artists feel the need for a heavier form they will create it. Witness Bird, witness Trane, Pharoah, all us can do it. An artifact can be said to be worthy based on several factors. One, that it says what the artists wants it to say; two that what it says is of some use to black people, meaning that the artifact is functional; and three that the artist had a purpose for doing it and wasn't just bullshitting. All three are important. The first is obvious. The second has to do with our particular hierarchy of values in terms of art. We're not trying to say that other people have to share this criterion. What does it matter to college english teachers (and plenty black ones for that matter) whether or not wordsworth or even ginsberg (even?) is creating an art form or artifact that is functional for black people? The third has to do with the fact that we feel that the artist can not disassociate his life as an artist from his life as a black person=people. It ain't enough to say black is beautiful. If you a black artist by what you say you are, what your art says you are, what you be telling others to be.

Now the other ways people judge art are purely subjective. They be matters of whether or not you (as an individual) agree or disagree with what is presented, how you react based on what you believe/think. The american people in general have no eye, ear, nose, heart for art. They don't know art from soup cans. They think pictures of naked ladies is art and get uptight behind African dancers. Playboy, Cavelier, et alla them is america's realest art magazines. They show what's really on the american man's mind. True confession, movie screen, mccalls, house & yard (garden), vogue, stuff like that along with some other tripe is what american art is about. The dead cemeteries called museums, the same notes over and over again in so-called concert halls, paintings old with age and the paint peeling off, some poems that were written two hundred years ago and run off in some book, that is what americans think art is. They do. Some of you probably think this book is art. An art book or something just cause it got writing in it. The american people are un-witting dupes of faggots and circus intellectuals who are passing deadness off as art. People produce art. People are art. People art ART! If they don't they'll have to lap up some deadness or steal it if they want art. If americans want music so much let them create some instead of copying and imitating and *stealing.* We don't mean to go into a diatribe against the american people here but damn, americanism is a dumb flat kind of consciousness that ain't connected to nuthing much except money, god, the president, and phoney history. And oh yeah landing on the moon. When we say american people, we mean all people who think as americans think which includes a whole lot of black people. But anyway, meanwhile some other kind of things are happening.

We do not happen as an opposite, or a reaction, we happen because we are. This art we are doing will be just as valid, just as functional, just as beautiful after the ways of the west have past on, after new york is dust, after the nation is erected. African drums and the black art of drumming is just as valid as when the first drumbeat was sounded in the chests and breasts of our original black ancestors. If you cover both of your ears tightly with your hands and lie still you just might hear it. If you're black it just might mean that your ancestors are calling. Heed that call brothers. Sisters. Heed that call. And come on let's live.

BLK LOVE SONG #1

A song. meditation. on possible movement. use music to the maximum stretches of your imagination/be sure to include a blues guitar, drums, flute, and some singers scatting on top of all of that.

CHARACTERS

BLK MAN dressed in blk dashiki suit, w/h liberation flag on his left shoulder like a patch

BLK WOMAN, dressed in long blk wrap or dress w/h liberation flag as head wrap

CHORUS, can be BM and BW speaking together, but preferably about six people dressed in liberation colors

JETHRO, 1st scene: old pants and torn shirt (slave); 2nd scene: army jacket w/h shades and boots (militant); 3rd scene: contemporary casual

SARAH, 1st scene: shapeless old-time dress w/h head rag (slave); 2nd scene: modern dress w/h wig; 3rd scene: contemporary casual, wears natural hair

PEACHES, extravagant wig (maybe blond or blond streaked), mod dress, wears bright red and boots

SLICK, flashy dresser wears silk scarf around his neck

BEAT, old blue suit w/h white shirt and white socks, a red tie, no shoes, wears glasses and has pencils sticking out of his front jacket pocket, holds a beat-up old black hat in his hands

Make use of mime and pantomime when CHORUS is singing/speaking to give the illusion that action is still going on among the other characters.

(Bareness. Open area. Use platforms or audience area for places for BLK MAN, BLK WOMAN, and the CHORUS. Use lights where possible and live music, although the musicians need not be visible.)

BLK WOMAN *(moves in slowly, semi-arcs of swaying loveliness)* Where is the seed of Africa? Where? Where are the first men who walked the earth? Have they vanished? Has the air sucked them up into the clouds? Has the wind shook them and hung them out to dry? Where has the seed of Africa gone? What lands, what homes, where are they gone? My brother, my brothers and my father. Our fathers. Where?
Where has the seed of Africa gone?

Chorus

(flute and drums in fast rocking sound)
They are gone to America
They are gone to the new world
They are gone to America
They are gone to the new world
They are gone to America
Into hell they have been hurled

SCENE 1

Blk Man

And they whipped us in America
And seized our bodies with terrible afflictions
And they whipped us in America
And made us do their bidding
And we died there, we died there in America

Sarah
(entering) Jethro . . . Jethro

Jethro
I am here Sarah

Sarah
Oh my man, I thought you were lost
I thought the paddy rollers done caught you sho
I heard the dogs moaning at the new risen moon
And I reached out for you
But you were gone from yo pallet on the flo
Your bed was empty and my heart became empty too
I cried. I cried and then I heard
The hound dogs baying
And I could imagine them snapping at your heels
I could imagine them dogs running dead in your tracks
Hunting you down like some wild game
And I could see you running Jethro
I could see you running
Running from the fields
Running through the thick swamps

Jethro
Sarah be quiet . . . the paddy rollers gone hear us sho

Sarah
Jethro is we flying to freedom
Is we gon follow the north star
Jethro is we going north

Jethro
Be quiet woman. Our home ain't north
neither is it south. Our home is in the east
Way east, way across the water

Sarah
Well what we gon do, Jethro
How we gon go home?

Jethro
We find a way, Sarah. We find a way.

Chorus
But is there a way for the black man
Is there a way back home
Is there a way for the black man
Is there a way back home
Is there a hope for the black man
Can someone guide him through this storm

Beat
Boy you remember this,
You is home now
Who in the hell you think you is
You young negroes

Jethro
Us young negroes, what?

Beat
Yeah, I don seen it all befo
I done seen many a young boy like you
This here world ain't big enuf to hold you
Is it boy?
Your mind is way off somewheres else

Jethro
I just ain't got no tentions of being
a slave all my life.
I got other ideas, I got other things to do

Beat
What they do to you boy?

Jethro
They whipped me. They whipped me til
they was tired.

Beat
What they do to you boy

Jethro
They hung me in a tree
and made me outta forbidden fruit
they stretched my body out
and ripped it open
they set me afire
and I blazed til my guts fell
out. And they left me
there, to rot. They left me there
until my burnt bones dropped.

Beat
And what they do to you boy?

Jethro
They stole my woman.

Sarah
(exiting. pantomine being pulled. quickly. from off-stage screaming). Jethro, help me!

Chorus
Can someone guide us through this storm?
Can we make it alone?

SCENE 2

Beat
What they do your woman boy?

Jethro

They . . . they

Sarah

They ain't did me a damn thing
you ain't let um do.
I remember you nigger.
I remember you
Can you look at me?
you half a man!
Where were you when I screamed
Where were you?
Where were you when the
horrible weight of that
pale beast weighted mightily upon my breasts? Where
were you my man?
Where were you when that pale beast stuck himself into me.
I called you.
I called you.
Where were you.
My belly was swelling and growing, the ugly pale
seed increasing daily in me.
How could you stand to look at me then?
Where were you.
My breasts grew larger each day
more full of my life giving milk,
they grow heavy with milk
and they sagged, my breasts
and my milk for my own pale bastards. My own.
Those children, our people. One son yours and
one son, the man's. One girl calls you daddy,
the other don't know your face.
Where were you nigger.
Parading around the streets in your sharp suits
or was you hiding somewhere
your knees shaking and cracking
where were you man?

Jethro

I was here Sarah. I been here all along.
I been here from the time he first grabbed you.
I been here and I have suffered for it.
I been here. You don't know. What can I tell you?
What can I say to you. Can I tell you how it feels?
Can I tell you how it feels to see someone else's baby
come shootin out your body? Can I tell you how it
feels to lay and listen
in the night waitin for you to return from the big house
can I tell you how it feels to not be able to protect you
to not be able to say: You leave my woman alone.
But I done all I could, I done all I could
and I fought and I fought and I fought even tho I knew
I wasn't goin na win. I fought all I could

Sarah

But it wasn't enuf
it didn't stop the white men from coming.
They came anyway. They came into me.
What you could, wasn't enuf

Jethro

I know.
I . . . so finally
I left *(he exits)*

Chorus

(flute and drums again)
Black men walk the streets alone
Black men walk the streets alone
Black men walk cause they ain't got no home
Some black folks call america home
Some black folks call america home
But if this is home, how come black men alone?

Scene 3

Beat

I don told these young negroes
that this here is our home
they need to get all that talk
about Africa out they head
they don't know nothing about Africa
They don't even know how to talk African
They don't know nothing
you see Africans don't no mo want to see
us then we wants to see them
cause they sold us to the white man
to get rid of us
they sold us children, yes sir
And don't nobody that care for nobody
be selling they own kin
now how I'ma love somebody who suppose to be my brother
and done went and sold me into slavery
why I says them Africans is as bad
as the white man, cept they don't know as much.

Blk Man

They have told us these lies and half truths about our mother

and we in turn have believed them all
They have told us these lies and we have come to live them
We have come to be the lies that they told us we are
Oh we are a sad people my brothers
We have denied our mother
We have refused the milk that we grow strong on
We have died the silly death
Our women lost, gone, taken from us
Raped and made over into the image
of filth, into the image of fairy tales,
into the image of a white lie
And our men, our men . . .

Jethro
Kill the silly dilly hunky motherfuckers
Stick telephone poles up between the legs of his women.
Kill them. Come on brothers. What we got to lose?
Come on! Now! Now!
Who are we to let the white man rule?
Where are we that we swim in this shitty cesspool?
Let us move. Let us be. Come. See.
There is truth somewhere there is beauty and wine and women and whatever else we talk about in our lives
There is all, come . . .

Sarah
You lie! You lie, man. There is only you
and the whiteman. You a cheap
cockhound freak and the whiteman,
the devil. That is all there is. There is no beauty.
There is no truth. No peace.

Jethro
Black is beautiful.

Sarah
You lie, if it is beautiful make it so.
Be that beauty. Be that beauty black . . .
no, but you lie . . .

Jethro
I do not lie. It is just
just that you are blind

Sarah
I see you! I see you, is that blindness.
But then maybe I am blind for I do
not see anything in you
no man actions, no nation, no nothing,
I do not see anything that you do.
Do you do anything?
Are you anything black man besides hot air,
broken dreams and invalid promises.
Are you anything or just a cheap 45 record
cracked and warped by the sun.

Jethro
I am your world

Sarah
Well be it!

Jethro
I speak of the beginning of how it was then,
of how it will be again, I speak . . .

Sarah
Speak of the end of those white devils
who invade our flesh. Speak of that . . .

Jethro
Tomorrow

Sarah
Tomorrow is now.
Tomorrow is here.

Jethro
Tomorrow. There is plenty time . . .
we are time we are the time of this planet . . .

Sarah
How many white bastards must I have
before you realize that time is
now for your seed to flow into me

Peaches (entering)
Give it up sista that nigger
ain't gonna marry you.
And that's all you doin
Really that's all.
Just trying to run a
so-fis-ti-cated game down on this man's head.
He don't want ta hear that.
He wants a piece of ass.
Doncha baby? Isn't that what you really want?
Me. You want me.
You want to get into me.
Doncha baby? Ain't you crazy about me . . .

Sarah
Black man hear me I am calling.
Don't listen to her foolish vulgarities.
Don't listen to her marilyn monroe dream dribblings.
I want only you. I want you to claim me.

Peaches
Yeah you sho do need a man.
Come clean bitch, admit you want a husband.

Blk Woman
And the world of personal encounters
becomes more and more the sordid history
of who can fuck who
Our encounters with one another become
sexual games and gains

Beat
Boy listen here!
Take that pussy and run.

Peaches
Buy me a drink, daddy.
Get me a mink, sugar.
Dress me in pink, honey . . .
And I'll give you all the love that a man can stand.

Sarah
My love is not for sale
My love is your love when you love me.

Slick (entering)
What's happenin yall?
My you women sho are looking good.
(coming close to Sarah)
That's a nice looking fro baby
and yo legs is nice too.

Peaches
She don't wanna hear that, man.
She trying to find her a husband.

Slick (laughing)
What for?

Peaches
So the nigger can stick it to her
and then run out on her ass
after the children come droppin out her belly.
I can see her now. Ten snotty nose
kids running around the welfare office . . .

Sarah
Why do you talk like that . . .

Peaches
Like what? Like "sticking it to ya"
Like that? Why? Cause I know.
I know nigger men. I know them.
I have held them close to me.
I have heard their promises
I have felt their hands on my body.
I have beared the pain of their children.
I have even washed the tears of their manhood from their eyes.
I know them. I speak from my experience. I speak from
lessons my life taught me.
I speak of nigger men and their incompetence.

Slick
We are good lovers . . .

Peaches
You a good lay. A wet dream.

Slick
You black bitch . . .

Peaches
Kiss my ass, Slick.

Slick
Ain't nobody in the world got to kiss the ass of a
funky scroungy nigger bitch . . .
you'd like me to do that.
You like that idea.
You want somebody to kiss your ass.
But you can hang that shit up.

Blk Woman
Why do we talk to each other like that?
We act like machines,
like some animal the white man
has invented. We act as if
we were made to hate each other . . .

Sarah
Why . . .

Slick
Shut up bitch. What you know about life?
You still thinking about getting married.

Beat
Man the only way to get a woman
like that to respect you is to go up side her head
ask me, man I been living a long time and
I done had to slap many a silly hoe

(SLICK slaps SARAH. She screams)

Slick
Shut up bitch. I'm just learnin you
how to be a woman.

Beat
Good work boy.

Peaches

Look at your *black man* now honey
just standing around
dumb like a manhole cover
dumb with shit in his pants
why he don't protect you?

Slick

Why I'd cut that nigger four ways twice if
he was so much as to say boo
See he don't understand, he don't understand that
if I don't hit her she'll forget that she's a
nigger bitch. If I don't hit her . . .

Sarah

You don't have to hit me,
I know what I am

Peaches

That bitch don't even make sense man.
I know what you talkin about
Will you beat me if I don't give you money?
Will you beat me when I come home late?
Will you beat me to show me your love?

Slick

I will beat you every day
in more ways than one.

Peaches

You are a true man.

Sarah

And you . . . are you a true woman?

Blk Woman

Are we true? Where are the seeds of Africa?
Are we true to ourselves? Are we true?
What are our lives . . .
sad twisted reflections . . . dead junk . . .
broken window dreams

Blk Man

Can we wake from this
and move into something else can we grow into the jungles
of life we were/we are
can we be vast sweeping plains of humanity
or is the weather too cold here for us to grow,
to grow, to grow
Let us turn to them. Let us see . . .

(Both the BLK MAN *&* BLK WOMAN *now step into the scene for the first time)*

Peace my brothers.

Peace my sisters.

Blk Woman

Peace.

Beat

More of this sickness!
What are you now
Afro-Americans for the glorious coming
back of ancient savage Africa
What are you
dream songs who call themselves
oog-la-boog-la and other good sambo ancestry names
What are you advertisements for instant blackness
What are you?

Blk Man

Be quiet old man.

Slick

Who you think you are?

Blk Man

I'm only a man.

Slick

Yeah, well me too.

Blk Woman

Hey my brother, how you do?
How you be? How are you?

Slick

You da one sound sick.

Blk Woman

Well cure me. Deal with me.
Nullify the poisons you think you see in me
with the sweet antidote of your
righteous manhood being

Slick

Bitch, I'll slap you down . . .
(SLICK *raises his hand and* BLK MAN *gestures and freezes* SLICK *in a sick motion of attempting to slap* BLK WOMAN)

Blk man

My brother, your actions mark you as negative.
You destroy our women with your false notions
of how to relate to them.
My brother we must stop you, we must be firm
enough to stand and say no to you & we will.
Leave us and return when you are willing to relate
to us as a brother to his people. Go now.

(BLK MAN *gestures.* SLICK *slinks off-stage in the still-frozen stance)*

Beat

Who you think you is to be coming here giving out orders?
You ain't nothing but a nigger, same as me . . .

Blk Man

I'm the same as you, same as you used to be but not
a nigger. Same as you could be, but not a nigger.
Just merely the more saner same than your craziness.

Peaches

You motherfuckers make me sick.

Blk Woman

Sister, your life too has to change
If you are ready to be a woman.

Peaches

Let me tell you something. My life is like it is
because of what men are, I'm like that cause they
been like that, cause if I wanted to survive
I had no choice but to be like that.
A man is a low down animal.

Blk Woman

No, my sister, a man is a wondrous creation,
a dawn, a deep night, a whole world.
A man is a life force born, a giver, a keeper, a seeker.
A man is our hope.

Peaches

The day I hope for a nigger to . . .

Blk Man

Submit to your true . . .

Peaches

Submit, shit! Submit to what
to your overblown talk
you call manhood. Submit
to a man, never. For what?
Man, I can do everything
you can do and most things
better. I can be everything
you can be.

Blk Man

Can you be a man?

Peaches

From what I done seen men be for most of my life
I can be that and more. I can't give myself
no baby but I damn sho can out fuck any man alive.

Blk Man

So be it. Go head on and out fuck any man alive.
Be that perversion you think is a woman.
You must submit to yourself of yourself, in yourself.
I can not force you to be better, but can only be the / betterness
I would like you to be. Go head on. Dance on sister.
Dance on to the rising tom-toms of your own death
throes. Dance on, dance the spastic dance of self
inflicted bareness. Dance my sister to the artificial
lights of the white world. Whirl and dance and jump.

(PEACHES *shakes lewdly to a gutbucket music, she is grinning wildly as she dances trying to entice a frozen* SLICK *into a warmness of desire for her body)*

Blk Man

Sister, no *man* wants a thing, a toy, a sex puppet.
Dance. You cannot warm him. Remember
your love is stronger than his. You said that.

Peaches

Come on nigger. Come on. Take me, put it in me.
Do it to me. Come on man.

Blk Man

If that is all you wish for in your life. Be gone.

(SLICK remains frozen and PEACHES falls at his feet, clutching his legs)

Blk Woman

Oh my sister, my sister, please rise out of
that filthiness. Be stronger than that.

Blk Man

Rise my sister. Rise.

Peaches

Slick, Slick, Slick, come on Slick,
these niggers, they crazy, you hit me Slick,
you wake me up. You beat me up. Come on Slick,
you give me money. You tell me what to do . . .

Blk Man

You turn to the frozen man now sister
but . . .

(BLK MAN *gestures and* PEACHES *freezes to* SLICK)

Beat

See, like I ain't been sayin nuthin all this time but I
believes that you niggers is witches and such
and that you is working hoo-doo magic on that
poor boy's head. You done fixed him and
spelled him and froze her up.

Blk Woman

Negro you are the worst invention of the centuries of
man's living. Your breath steals life from all
those around and near you. Negro.

Blk Man

I have no hoo-doo powers. It is simply the positive
assertion of all that I am that is freezing them.
They the pimps and whores of our life, they the simple
people who have been transfixed by the whites.
They are only frozen now. But if they want to
they can rise. They can be men and women. They
can be everything. They can be the original beginning.
It's there if they want it but you are
the one whom we can never cure.

Blk Woman

We cannot even call you brother.

Beat

Who are you niggers to be judging somebody.

Blk Man

We are not judging you but your life, your actions,
all that you have been, have done. Show us your best.
Show us that you have struggled, tried . . .

Sarah

Jethro, what is happening?

Blk Man

The day is dawning, my sister.

Jethro

Sarah . . .

Blk Woman

Do not be afraid, my brother. You are a ray of this new sun.
Your heart is part of this fire
You have struggled all you could
no one can fault you.

Blk Man

Come my brother and let us try to live our lives.
Let us try to get along with each other.
Let us be people, the people that we are.
Come my brother. The day is dawning and we've
much work to do. We have much sickness to look into
ourselves and extract. We have studying to do.
New ways to learn. Come my brother and walk
together with your woman along side this new day.

Jethro

What . . . what do I have to do?

Blk Woman

No matter what it is, you will be able to master it.
Do not be afraid my brother. You are the sun my brother
and we Black women, we are the earth. We've been waiting
a long, long winter season for your spring sun to shine
through the coldness which had captured you. Where's your
fire, bring your warmth, let us taste fire, nourish us
spread manness across our land. Plant seeds, tend fields,
be real. We await you. Been ready. We await your coming
Black man, brother, man. Come on. Don't stop. Come on
come on into yourself, into us, into us selves.

(BLK WOMAN *reaches out to* JETHRO. *She embraces him warmly)*

Blk Man

Come sister.

(BLK MAN *hugs* SARAH *briefly, steps back, holding her at arms' length, looking into her eyes. Silence. Turns to* JETHRO *and gives him a huge hug with both arms.* BLK WOMAN *embraces* SARAH, *stands close beside her, takes* SARAH*'s hand into her own)*

Beat
What kind of shit is this. What you niggers havin, a love in?

Blk Woman
You are a dream walker, a freak projection.
We are looking for men now. This is our search.
The sun. We need the warmth and fire and love
of the sun. Black suns. Black suns to end
this dead life we lead. What is this life,
if we do not have men, where are we to go and what are
we to do, without men. I live with a man.
Together we create new life.

Beat
You niggers is sick. Listen ain't no nigger
gon ever be free. And don't you forget that.
You can want all you want but baby the die has
been cast a long time ago. I know what you want
but baby the man knows too and like he's
not about to let you become free.

Blk Man
We can free ourselves . . .

Beat
We couldn't even make enough gas right now to
start a real big fire. All we got is
what the white man lets us have.

Blk Man
And most of what he has he got from us.

Beat
That may be but the point is, he got it
and we ain't got it and ain't bout to get it.
So you got to learn to get what you
can when you can't get what you want.

Blk Man
We can get what we want!

Blk Woman
Your silliness is a curse on our people. Your fear is the death of many of our brothers. Who are you, negro?

Beat
Rochester. Amos N'Andy. Mod Squad. Jim Brown.

Blk Woman
No those are white projections. What is your name?

Beat
The Temptations. The Supremes.

Blk Man
No. *Your* name.

Beat
I have no name.

Blk Man
Then give yourself a name. Name yourself.

Beat
Negro.

Blk Man
No, that is a name put on you.
Take a name if you have no name.

Beat
AMERICA!!!!!

*(*BEAT *pulls an American flag out of his jacket and begins waving it)*

AMERICANAMERICANAMERICANAMERICAN

Blk Woman
Stop. Here take this or some other warm colors. Make this your flag. Create your own flag. But please stop raising your own death notice.

*(*BLK WOMAN *unwraps her headwrap, offering it to* BEAT*)*

Beat
No, no, no, no, no, you crazy, you crazy, crazy, crazy.

Blk Man
You have become a creature, not a human. We must cast
you out from among us. Live as you will among the cold
ones whose frost you admire.

(In slow motion BLK MAN *casts* BEAT *off the stage)*

Jethro
Why did you do that, are we not all brothers, all one?

Blk Man
All of those who want to be one, all who want to live
in brotherhood. But because a man's skin is black that
does not mean that he is your brother. For when
a father refuses his child he is no longer a father
to that child even though he is still the father

of that child. My brother there are many among us
who play the role of brother but they are not brothers.
Do not accept an enemy as a friend simply because
he calls you brother.

Jethro
Then how are we to know who is who?

Blk Woman
Check their actions, their lives
The righteous are righteous in deed,
Indeed your friends will be friends
and your enemies will be enemies. That is how it
is no matter how they say they are.

Sarah
And what of them?

Blk Man
We shall see.

(BLK MAN *motions and* PEACHES *and* SLICK *are released from the freeze.* PEACHES *slowly climbs to her feet)*

Blk Woman
As salaam alaikum my brother, my sister.

Peaches
And salami to you too. Come on Slick
let's split this shit. This scene is strange.
Let's go somewhere and party. It's too
dead around here.

Blk Man (to JETHRO*)*
You see my brother, many
of us have no concern for liberation.

(PEACHES *and* SLICK *exit laughing loudly, strongly)*

Sarah
They act just like nothing has happened.

Blk Woman
Nothing has happened as far as they are concerned
their whole world never changes
Friday night negroes who live only to have
a good time, or what they think is a good time,
but we've other things to do.

Blk Man
Well, Jethro, Sarah, we must leave . . .

Blk Woman
Yes.

Jethro
But wait. You haven't told us what to do.
You haven't told us what must be done.
We want to be free but we don't know how to get free.
You must tell us.

Blk Woman
Here take this.
(holding out her headwrap)
Make a flag. Create and define space,
give beauty to empty air, give the wind
something to celebrate, something to wave, give
the birds something brilliant to sing about, take . . .

Jethro
A woman is not suppose to lead.
(turning to BLK MAN*)*
You're in charge here right. And after you're gone
then me. Right? It's man time now . . .

Blk Woman
If you were Harriet Tubman and I was man slave
you'd better believe I would follow and say
thanks for the woman pointing the way ahead,
If you were Nanny catching British bullets in
your teeth and I were warrior man I would
follow you into the hills,
when you get stronger in your manhood
then it will be easier for you to deal with others,
easier for you to understand women,
you are weak and afraid now, but go ahead, step
Jethro, claim your life, claim our lives

Sarah
You're telling him what to do.

Blk Woman
Shake the sun Black man!

Blk Man
(laughing)
Go for it. Shake the sun Black woman.
Don't wait. Shake the sun, Sarah. If I were
woman, I wouldn't wait. Shake the sun. Sing
that lyric, feel how the words sound in your
mouth, feel how the world responds, shake the sun . . .

(BLK WOMAN *and* BLK MAN *are laughing, happy)*

Jethro
I can't . . .

Sarah
Why don't yall lead us.

Blk Woman
We're only spirit. The world requires flesh
and spirit. We're history. You are now. We're
out of time. You are in time.
(laughing)
Sarah, all around the world people are making
sunshine. Sarah. Sha . . .

Sarah
Shake the sun.

Jethro
They will kill us. I know. I've died before.
They will kill us before they ever let us touch the sun . . .
They will ki . . .

Blk Man
They can not kill us all.

Jethro
They have the bomb.

Blk Man
It is only a projection of their death wishes.
They cannot destroy what they did not create.
They cannot kill human life. Human beings, yes.
But human life, no. People will survive.
In spite of the coldness of the west.
This is just another ice age. We can survive this.
Come on Black man. You are drugged.
Not listening to yourself, to inside yourself,
to all the selves that died striving to go beyond
the circumstances of your birth.
You speak and act as if you are in a stupor,
or an impotent dream. Wake on up. Wake up and sh . . .

Jethro
Shake the sun.

Blk Man
Yeah.

Jethro
Yeah.
(softly, almost to himself)
And, shake the sun.

Sarah
Tell us how, tell us what to do, how to reach
the rays.

Blk Woman
We can't. We don't really know.
You try, we do.

Blk Man
It is not really for any man to tell another what
really to do. Each man must do as he must to help
his brother to be. Each woman. Each child. Sarah
you can tell me. It's in you.
I will tell you this much:
If you do not become the teller, the one who says what
is, defines, bees, then others will, against your interest
They will define you out of human existence. You will
be lost. You must examine your life. You must
study yourself. You must be careful what you eat.
Be careful the friends you choose. In the
beginning you must do much of it alone. And slowly,
with laughter and humbleness . . .

Blk Woman
And know that you will fall
before you rise up full, but everytime you
fall, you can get up again . . .

Blk Man
And beware machines don't make you human . . .

Jethro
But you still ain't told . . .

Blk Woman
We must go. Jethro, remember Sarah always.
If you lose touch with her, you have lost yourself.
Lose sight of Sarah and you will never see yourself.
Let's sing something together.
Make a song.

Sarah
A what?

Blk Woman
A song.

Blk Man
Sing something.

Jethro
Sing something? Sing? What?

Sarah
Sing . . .

Blk Woman
Sing: Shake the sun.

Jethro
How does it go.

Blk Woman
Like however you sing it. Like however you shake
it. Sun don't care.
(BLK WOMAN *improvises a melody)*
However you shake it
Sun don't care.
Shake the sun Black man
And dance til day is done.
(laughs to herself)
And dance blood, dance til day is done.

*(*BLK WOMAN *and* BLK MAN *back away slowly.* BLK WOMAN *is still singing her melody. Laughing. Now the music, flute, and drums, and some real wild saxophone walking through the space, playing on* BLK WOMAN*'s melody is heard.*

JETHRO *and* SARAH *call out to* BLK MAN *and* BLK WOMAN *but their motions get slower and slower. Drums. Somebody is really singing "Shake the sun!" The saxophone rises in a cadenza long as the spirit lasts. Everything else stops. The horn is alone. The horn stops)*

Jethro
What has happened to us?

Sarah
I'm . . . I'm . . . I'm not sure. I thought . . . but then . . . Jethro.

Jethro
I know. I mean I don't know. But I know.

Sarah
We know. We know and we don't know.

Jethro
I feel it.

Sarah
Let's go.

Jethro
Where . . .

Sarah
Shake . . .
(SARAH *and* JETHRO *say it together)*
the sun!

(They exit. Together. Excited. Laughing)

(Flute and drums)

Chorus
Where is the seed of Africa? When will they come home? Where is the seed of Africa? When will they come home? How long before from the seeds a new Black nation shall bloom.
Let a new Black nation bloom
Let a new Black nation bloom
Let us a new Black nation bloom!

(Faintly at first, then slowly louder, we hear singing:

"Shake the sun")

(Lights up. End)

NEW PLAYS, NEW IDEAS, NEW FORMS

George C. Wolfe • Aishah Rahman • Anna Deavere Smith

While a Broadway show remains the goal of many playwrights, economics have rerouted the path to the Great White Way. Regional theatres now serve the function once performed by out-of-town tryouts. August Wilson achieved his initial recognition at Lou Bellamy's Penumbra Theatre in St. Paul, Minnesota, one of several vital regional African American theatres. Director Lloyd Richards at the Eugene O'Neill National Playwrights Conference has workshopped all of Wilson's plays prior to their opening on Broadway. Other regional theatres include Jomandi Productions in Atlanta, Black Repertory in St. Louis, and the Freedom Theatre in Philadelphia. The largest company, with a budget of nearly $3 million, is the Crossroads Theatre Company in New Brunswick, New Jersey, where George C. Wolfe's *The Colored Museum* began in 1986.

The playwrights of the 1980s reflect diverse styles. Anna Deavere Smith (*Fires in the Mirror*) uses documentary realism, as do P.J. Gibson (*Long Time Since Yesterday*) and J.e. *[sic]* Franklin (*The Gray Panthers*). Other plays address race, gender, and class through the deconstruction of incident and event. For example, Suzan-Lori Parks, who seizes upon the assassination of Lincoln for *The American Play* (1993), uses the traditional musical structure of theme and variation in lieu of plot development, much as she did in her previous play, *The Death of the Last Black Man in the Whole Entire World* (1990). In still another style, Robbie McCauley herself performed in her presentational play *Sally's Rape*—as did Vy Higginsen in *Mama I Want to Sing* (1980), which broke the record for the longest running gospel musical—eight years.

As African American theatre moved into the nineties, an old issue took on new energy—nonconventional casting, or casting roles for talent and not for color. The proargument asserted that a greater variety of parts would be available to Black actors, for example, the role of Pedro in the film *Much Ado about Nothing,* which was played by Denzel Washington. The other side argued that few directors would use cross-casting; additionally, Black actors could be replaced by members of other ethnic groups in the name of multiculturalism.

At the same time, Black artists made inroads in other previously closed arenas, with corresponding changes in racial imagery. Oprah Winfrey and Arsenio Hall hosted programs on national television. In Hollywood, Julie Dash, Spike Lee, and Bill Duke directed films. Whoopi Goldberg and Danny Glover starred in major movies. Theatre scholars Errol Hill, Winona Fletcher, and Margaret Wilkerson received tenure in "white" college theatre departments. While these prestigious names provide inspiration for younger African Americans, there are still relatively few professional Black costume and set designers, talent and publicity agents, play producers, house managers, or theatre owners.

THE COLORED MUSEUM

1988

George C. Wolfe (1954–)

George C. Wolfe was born on September 23, 1954, in Frankfurt, Kentucky. His father, Costello Wolfe, had been a writer for U.S. Army newspapers during World War II and later worked as a clerk at Kentucky State University. Wolfe's mother, Anna, taught school and earned a doctorate at Miami University. As a child, he enjoyed art and ceramics classes; he directed plays in high school and describes himself as " . . . probably a neurotic child, very spoiled. If I didn't want to do a thing, I wouldn't do it." The person young George revered was his grandmother, Addie Parker Lindsay President, who fired his imagination with her courage.[1]

Wolfe, anxious to know the larger world, found his way to Pomona College in Claremont, California, where he wrote *Up for Grabs,* a satire on television game shows. At Pomona in 1976, he took a class with Angela Davis. The paper he submitted on theatre stereotypes (she gave him an A+) was the seed concept for *The Colored Museum,* which he would write ten years later. In nearby Los Angeles, the directors of the Inner City Cultural Center, Bernard Jackson and Josie Dotson, recognized Wolfe's talents and provided him with a stage at the Center to write and direct his own plays.

In 1979, he elected to come to New York City and "starve" ("I had been practicing").[2] He enrolled in New York University's Dramatic Writing Program and after a year switched to NYU's Musical Theatre Program in order to meet the top producers and directors on Broadway. Wolfe supported himself by teaching acting at the Richard Allen Center and at the City College of New York, where he directed his own play, *The Coming of Nubuku* (1982), a "Japanese theatre-Caribbean cartoon." In 1985, Playwright's Horizons produced *Paradise,* a satire on the role Western colonial greed had played in destroying the beauty of the natural world, as well as its Third World cultures. The critics blasted the play

1. Interview with George C. Wolfe, *Artist and Influence* VII (New York: Hatch-Billops Collection, Inc., 1989), p. 116.

2. Ibid., p. 118.

as though they personally had been attacked.

From 1980, Wolfe worked part-time for four years as an assistant librarian at the Hatch-Billops Collection, an archive of African American theatre materials. Wolfe's exposure to documents and programs of Black drama history became the second inspiration for *The Colored Museum,* which in 1986 premiered at the Crossroads Theatre Company. Within six months, Joseph Papp brought the play to New York's Public Theatre, initiating a new era in African American performance. In the words of Frank Rich of *The New York Times,* "George C. Wolfe says the unthinkable, says it with uncompromising wit and leaves the audience, as well as a sacred target, in ruins. The devastated audience, one should note, includes both blacks and whites. Mr. Wolfe is the kind of satirist, almost unheard of in today's timid theater, who takes no prisoners."[3]

What had Wolfe done? In eleven "exhibits" he had attacked basketball stars, slavery, miscegenation, the mammy stereotype, *Ebony* magazine, the drug legacy of Vietnam, homophobia, Black hairstyles, *A Raisin in the Sun,* the trashing of Black popular culture, Josephine Baker's legend, and teenage pregnancy, to name only the most important. The most outrageous of his parodies came in the middle of the revue—a comic caricature of Black males who see themselves as victims of "the man" (Bigger Thomas in *Native Son,* Walter Lee Younger in *A Raisin in the Sun,* Beau Willie in *For Colored Girls . . .*). To add insult to injury, Wolfe satirized the most sacred image in African American theatre, the Black mother who holds the family together, referred to by Wolfe as "Mama-on-the-couch." For this, he was roundly abused; nonetheless, his wit and his theatrical inventiveness enabled his vision to triumph. African American theatre had been reborn with an edge, with no self-pity or stereotypes, and with a style that shunned realism.

The Colored Museum was followed by *Spunk* (1989), an adaptation of three stories by Zora Neale Hurston and *Jelly's Last Jam* (1991), a musical based on the life of New Orleans jazz musician Jelly Roll Morton. Finally, Wolfe was chosen to direct Tony Kushner's *Angels in America.* In 1993, Wolfe was appointed producer of the New York Shakespeare Festival\Joseph Papp Public Theatre, where he initiated a broad multicultural program of new plays, which included Anna Deavere Smith's *Fires in the Mirror* (1993) and *Twilight in Los Angeles, 1992* (1994).

The energy and the intense focus that brought Wolfe from an unknown to a premiere theatre artist can be glimpsed in this statement about himself:

> Nobody else can do George, so let me do it as fully as I possibly can, and that means knocking down and the hell out of my way anything that demands or that inhibits the process. Not recklessly, hopefully, but anything which stops me from getting in touch with the powers that have been passed onto me by my ancestors. Because it's their stories I'm trying to tell. I am so grateful for this energy. Humility, I think, is tremendously overrated. Reality and racism are gonna try and humble you, so there's absolutely no reason in the world for you to be humble.[4]

3. Frank Rich, "'Colored Museum,' Satire by George C. Wolfe," *New York Times,* November 3, 1986, p. C:4.

4. Interview with George C. Wolfe, p. 121.

The Colored Museum

THE CAST

*An ensemble of five, two men and three women, all Black, who perform all the characters that inhabit the exhibits.**

The Stage

White walls and recessed lighting. A starkness befitting a museum where the myths and madness of Black/Negro/colored Americans are stored.

Built into the walls are a series of small panels, doors, revolving walls, and compartments from which actors can retrieve key props and make quick entrances.

A revolve is used, which allows for quick transitions from one exhibit to the next.

Music

All of the music for the show should be prerecorded. Only the drummer, who is used in Git on Board, *and then later in* Permutations *and* The Party, *is live.*

THERE IS NO INTERMISSION

The Exhibits

GIT ON BOARD
COOKIN' WITH AUNT ETHEL
THE PHOTO SESSION
SOLDIER WITH A SECRET
THE GOSPEL ACCORDING TO MISS ROJ
THE HAIRPIECE
THE LAST MAMA-ON-THE-COUCH PLAY
SYMBIOSIS
LALA'S OPENING
PERMUTATIONS
THE PARTY

The Characters

Git on Board
MISS PAT
Cookin' with Aunt Ethel
AUNT ETHEL
The Photo Session
GIRL
GUY
Soldier with a Secret
JUNIE ROBINSON
The Gospel According to Miss Roj
MISS ROJ
WAITER
The Hairpiece
THE WOMAN
JANINE
LAWANDA
The Last Mama-on-the-Couch Play
NARRATOR
MAMA
WALTER-LEE-BEAU-WILLIE-JONES
LADY IN PLAID
MEDEA JONES
Symbiosis
THE MAN
THE KID
Lala's Opening
LALA LAMAZING GRACE
ADMONIA
FLO'RANCE
THE LITTLE GIRL
Permutations
NORMAL JEAN REYNOLDS
The Party
TOPSY WASHINGTON
MISS PAT
MISS ROJ
LALA LAMAZING GRACE
THE MAN *(from Symbiosis)*

*A LITTLE GIRL, seven to twelve years old, is needed for a walk-on part in *Lala's Opening.*

GIT ON BOARD

(Blackness. Cut by drums pounding. Then slides, rapidly flashing before us. Images we've all seen before, of African slaves being captured, loaded onto ships, tortured. The images flash, flash, flash. The drums crescendo. Blackout. And then lights reveal MISS PAT, *frozen. She is Black, pert, and cute. She has a flip to her hair and wears a hot pink mini-skirt stewardess uniform.)*

(She stands infront of a curtain which separates her from an offstage cockpit.)

(An electronic bell goes "ding" and MISS PAT *comes to life, presenting herself in a friendly but rehearsed manner, smiling and speaking as she has done so many times before.)*

MISS PAT Welcome aboard Celebrity Slaveship, departing the Gold Coast and making short stops at Bahia, Port Au Prince, and Havana, before our final destination of Savannah.

Hi. I'm Miss Pat and I'll be serving you here in Cabin A. We will be crossing the Atlantic at an altitude that's pretty high, so you must wear your shackles at all times.

(She removes a shackle from the overhead compartment and demonstrates.)

To put on your shackle, take the right hand and close the metal ring around your left hand like so. Repeat the action using your left hand to secure the right. If you have any trouble bonding yourself, I'd be more than glad to assist.

Once we reach the desired altitude, the Captain will turn off the "Fasten Your Shackle" sign . . . *(She efficiently points out the "FASTEN YOUR SHACKLE" signs on either side of her, which light up.)* . . . allowing you a chance to stretch and dance in the aisles a bit. But otherwise, shackles must be worn at all times.

(The "Fasten Your Shackles" signs go off.)

MISS PAT Also, we ask that you please refrain from call-and-response singing between cabins as that sort of thing can lead to rebellion. And, of course, no drums are allowed on board. Can you repeat after me, "No drums." *(she gets the audience to repeat)* With a little more enthusiasm, please. "No drums." *(after the audience repeats it)* That was great!

Once we're airborn, I'll be by with magazines, and earphones can be purchased for the price of your first-born male.

If there's anything I can do to make this middle passage more pleasant, press the little button overhead and I'll be with you faster than you can say, "Go down, Moses." *(she laughs at her "little joke")* Thanks for flying Celebrity and here's hoping you have a pleasant take off.

(The engines surge, the "Fasten Your Shackle" signs go on, and over-articulate Muzak voices are heard singing as MISS PAT *pulls down a bucket seat and "shackles-up" for takeoff.)*

VOICES

GET ON BOARD CELEBRITY SLAVESHIP
GET ON BOARD CELEBRITY SLAVESHIP
GET ON BOARD CELEBRITY SLAVESHIP
THERE'S ROOM FOR MANY A MORE

(The engines reach an even, steady hum. Just as MISS PAT *rises and replaces the shackles in the overhead compartment, the faint sound of African drumming is heard.)*

MISS PAT Hi. Miss Pat again. I'm sorry to disturb you, but someone is playing drums. And what did we just say . . . "No drums." It must be someone in Coach. But we here in Cabin A are not going to respond to those drums. As a matter of fact, we don't even hear them. Repeat after me. "I don't hear any drums." *(the audience repeats)* And "I will not rebel."

(The audience repeats. The drumming grows.)

MISS PAT *(placating)* OK, now I realize some of us are a bit edgy after hearing about the tragedy on board The Laughing Mary, but let me assure you Celebrity has no intention of throwing you overboard and collecting the insurance. We value you!

(She proceeds to single out individual passengers/ audience members.)

Why the songs *you* are going to sing in the cotton fields, under the burning heat and stinging lash, will metamorphose and give birth to the likes of James Brown and the Fabulous Flames. And you, yes *you*, are going to come up with some of the best dances. The best dances! The Watusi! The Funky Chicken! And just think of what *you* are going to mean to William Faulkner.

All right, so you're gonna have to suffer for a few hundred years, but from your pain will come a culture so complex. *And*, with this little item here . . . *(she removes a basketball from the overhead compartment)* . . . you'll become millionaires!

(There is a roar of thunder. The lights quiver and the "Fasten Your Shackle" signs begin to flash. MISS PAT *quickly replaces the basketball in*

the overhead compartment and speaks very reassuringly.)

MISS PAT No, don't panic. I'm here to take care of you. We're just flying through a little thunder storm. Now the only way you're going to make it through this one is if you abandon your God and worship a new one. So, on the count of three, let's all sing. One, two, three . . .

NOBODY KNOWS DE TROUBLE I SEEN

Oh, I forgot to mention, when singing, omit the T-H sound. "The" becomes "de". "They" becomes "dey". Got it? Good!

NOBODY KNOWS . . .

NOBODY KNOWS . . .

Oh, so you don't like that one? Well then let's try another—

SUMMER TIME

AND DE LIVIN' IS EASY

Gershwin. He comes from another oppressed people so he understands.

FISH ARE JUMPIN' . . . come on.

AND DE COTTON IS HIGH.

Sing, damnit!

(Lights begin to flash, the engines surge, and there is wild drumming. MISS PAT *sticks her head through the curtain and speaks with an offstage* CAPTAIN.*)*

MISS PAT WHAT?

VOICE OF CAPTAIN *(o.s.)* Time warp!

MISS PAT Time warp! *(she turns to the audience and puts on a pleasant face)* The Captain has assured me everything is fine. We're just caught in a little time warp. *(trying to fight her growing hysteria)* On your right you will see the American Revolution, which will give the U.S. of A. exclusive rights to your life. And on your left, the Civil War, which means you will vote Republican until F.D.R. comes along. And now we're passing over the Great Depression, which means everybody gets to live the way you've been living. *(there is a blinding flash of light, and an explosion. She screams)* Ahhhhhhhhh! That was World War I, which is not to be confused with World War II . . . *(there is a larger flash of light, and another explosion)* . . . Ahhhhh! Which is not to be confused with the Korean War or the Vietnam War, all of which you will play a major role in.

Oh, look, now we're passing over the sixties. Martha and Vandellas . . . Malcolm X. *(there is a gun shot)* . . . "Julia" with Miss Diahann Carroll . . . and five little girls in Sunday school . . . *(there is an explosion)* Martin Luther King . . . *(a gun shot)* Oh no! The Supremes just broke up! *(the drumming intensifies)* Stop playing those drums. I said, stop playing those damn drums. You can't stop history! You can't stop time! Those drums will be confiscated once we reach Savannah. Repeat after me. I don't hear any drums and I will not rebel. I will not rebel! I will not re—

(The lights go out, she screams, and the sound of a plane landing and screeching to a halt is heard. After a beat, lights reveal a wasted, disheveled MISS PAT, *but perky nonetheless.)*

MISS PAT Miss Pat here. Things got a bit jumpy back there, but the Captain has just informed me we have safely landed in Savannah. Please check the overhead before exiting as any baggage you don't claim, we trash.

It's been fun, and we hope the next time you consider travel, it's with Celebrity.

(Luggage begins to revolve onstage from offstage left, going past MISS PAT *and revolving offstage right. Mixed in with the luggage are two male slaves and a woman slave, complete with luggage and I.D. tags around their necks.)*

MISS PAT *(with routine, rehearsed pleasantness)*
Have a nice day. Bye bye.
Button up that coat, it's kind of chilly.
Have a nice day. Bye bye.
You take care now.
See you.
Have a nice day.
Have a nice day.
Have a nice day.

COOKIN' WITH AUNT ETHEL

(As the slaves begin to revolve off, a low-down gutbucket blues is heard. AUNT ETHEL, *a down-home Black woman with a bandana on her head, revolves to center stage. She stands behind a big black pot and wears a reassuring grin.)*

AUNT ETHEL Welcome to "Aunt Ethel's Down-Home Cookin' Show," where we explores the magic and mysteries of colored cuisine.

Today, we gonna be servin' ourselves up some . . . *(she laughs)* I'm not gonna tell you. That's right! I'm not gonna tell you what it is till after you done cooked it. Child, on "The Aunt Ethel Show" we loves to have ourselves some fun. Well, are you ready? Here goes.

(She belts out a hard-drivin' blues and throws invisible ingredients into the big, black pot.)

FIRST YA ADD A PINCH OF STYLE
AND THEN A DASH OF FLAIR
NOW YA STIR IN SOME PREOCCUPATION
WITH THE TEXTURE OF YOUR HAIR

NEXT YA ADD ALL KINDS OF RHYTHMS
LOTS OF FEELINGS AND PIZZAZ
THEN HUNNY THROW IN SOME RAGE
TILL IT CONGEALS AND TURNS TO JAZZ

NOW YOU COOKIN'
COOKIN' WITH AUNT ETHEL
YOU REALLY COOKIN'
COOKIN' WITH AUNT ETHEL, OH YEAH

NOW YA ADD A HEAP OF SURVIVAL
AND HUMILITY, JUST A TOUCH
ADD SOME ATTITUDE
OPPS! I PUT TOO MUCH

AND NOW A WHOLE LOT OF HUMOR
SALTY LANGUAGE, MIXED WITH SADNESS
THEN THROW IN A BOX OF BLUES
AND SIMMER TO MADNESS

NOW YOU COOKIN'
COOKIN' WITH AUNT ETHEL, OH YEAH!

NOW YOU BEAT IT—REALLY WORK IT
DISCARD AND DISOWN
AND IN A FEW HUNDRED YEARS
ONCE IT'S AGED AND FULLY GROWN
YA PUT IT IN THE OVEN
TILL IT'S BLACK
AND HAS A SHEEN
OR TILL IT'S NICE AND YELLA
OR ANY SHADE IN BETWEEN

NEXT YA TAKE 'EM OUT AND COOL 'EM
'CAUSE THEY NO FUN WHEN THEY HOT
AND WON'T YOU BE SURPRISED
AT THE CONCOCTION YOU GOT

YOU HAVE BAKED
BAKED YOURSELF A BATCH OF NEGROES
YES YOU HAVE BAKED YOURSELF
BAKED YOURSELF A BATCH OF NEGROES

(She pulls from the pot a handful of Negroes, Black dolls)

But don't ask me what to do with 'em now that you got 'em 'cause child, that's your problem *(she throws the dolls back into the pot)* But in any case, yaw be sure to join Aunt Ethel next week, when we gonna be servin' ourselves up some chitlin quiche . . . some grits-under-glass,

AND A SWEET POTATO PIE
AND YOU'LL BE COOKIN'
COOKIN' WITH AUNT ETHEL
OH YEAH!

(On AUNT ETHEL*'s final rift, lights reveal . . .)*

THE PHOTO SESSION

(. . . a very glamorous, gorgeous, Black couple, wearing the best of everything and perfect smiles. The stage is bathed in color and bright white light. Disco music with the chant: "We're fabulous" plays in the background. As they pose, larger-than-life images of their perfection are projected on the museum walls. The music quiets and the images fade away as they begin to speak and pose.)

GIRL The world was becoming too much for us.

GUY We couldn't resolve the contradictions of our existence.

GIRL And we couldn't resolve yesterday's pain.

GUY So we gave away our life and we now live inside *Ebony Magazine*.

GIRL Yes, we live inside a world where everyone is beautiful, and wears fabulous clothes.

GUY And no one says anything profound.

GIRL Or meaningful.

GUY Or contradictory.

GIRL Because no one talks. Everyone just smiles and shows off their cheekbones.

(They adopt a profile pose.)

Last month I was Black and fabulous while holding up a bottle of vodka.

GIRL This month we get to be Black and fabulous together.

(They dance/pose. The "We're fabulous" chant builds and then fades as they start to speak again.)

GIRL There are of course setbacks.

GUY We have to smile like this for a whole month.

GIRL And we have no social life.

GUY And no sex.

GIRL And at times it feels like we're suffocating, like we're not human anymore.

GUY And everything is rehearsed, including this other kind of pain we're starting to feel.

GIRL The kind of pain that comes from feeling no pain at all.

(They then speak and pose with a sudden burst of energy.)

GUY But one can't have everything.

GIRL Can one?

GUY So if the world is becoming too much for you, do like we did.

GIRL Give away your life and come be beautiful with us.

GUY We guarantee, no contradictions.

GIRL/GUY Smile/click, smile/click, smile/click.

GIRL And no pain.

(They adopt a final pose and revolve off as the "We're fabulous" chant plays and fades into the background.)

A Soldier with a Secret

(Projected onto the museum walls are the faces of Black soldiers—from the Spanish-American thru to the Vietnam War. Lights slowly reveal JUNIE ROBINSON, *a Black combat soldier, posed on an onyx plinth. He comes to life and smiles at the audience. Somewhat dim-witted, he has an easy-going charm about him.)*

JUNIE Pst. Pst. I know the secret. The secret to your pain. 'Course, I didn't always know. First I had to die, then come back to life, 'fore I had the gift.

Ya see the Cappin sent me off up ahead to scout for screamin' yella bastards. 'Course, for the life of me I couldn't understand why they'd be screamin', seein' as how we was tryin' to kill them and they us.

But anyway, I'm off lookin', when all of a sudden I find myself caught smack dead in the middle of this explosion. This blindin', burnin', scaldin' explosion. Musta been a booby trap or something, 'cause all around me is fire. Hell, I'm on fire. Like a piece of chicken dropped in a skillet of cracklin' grease. Why, my flesh was justa peelin' off my bones.

But then I says to myself, "Junie, if yo' flesh is on fire, how come you don't feel no pain!" And I didn't. I swear as I'm standin' here, I felt nuthin. That's when I sort of put two and two together and realized I didn't feel no whole lot of hurtin' cause I done died.

Well I just picked myself up and walked right on out of that explosion. Hell, once you know you dead, why keep on dyin', ya know?

So, like I say, I walk right outta that explosion, fully expectin' to see white clouds, Jesus, and my Mama, only all I saw was more war. Shootin' goin' on way off in this direction and that direction. And there, standin' around, was all the guys. Hubert, J.F., the Cappin. I guess the sound of the explosion must of attracted 'em, and they all starin' at me like I'm some kind of ghost.

So I yells to 'em, "Hey there Hubert! Hey there Capin!" But they just stare. So I tells 'em how I'd died and how I guess it wasn't my time 'cause here I am, "Fully in the flesh and not a scratch to my bones." And they still just stare. So I took to starin' back.

(The expression on JUNIE*'s face slowly turns to horror and disbelief.)*

Only what I saw . . . well I can't exactly to this day describe it. But I swear, as sure as they was wearin' green and holdin' guns, they was each wearin' a piece of the future on their faces.

Yeah. All the hurt that was gonna get done to them and they was gonna do to folks was right there clear as day.

I saw how J. F., once he got back to Chicago, was gonna get shot dead by this po-lice, and I saw how Hubert was gonna start beatin' up on his old lady which I didn't understand, 'cause all he could do was talk on and on about how much he loved her. Each and every one of 'em had pain in his future and blood on his path. And God or the Devil one spoke to me and said, "Junie, these colored boys ain't gonna be the same after this war. They ain't gonn have no kind of happiness."

Well right then and there it come to me. The secret to their pain.

Late that night, after the medics done checked me over and found me fit for fightin', after everybody done settle down for the night, I sneaked over to where Hubert was sleepin', and with a needle I stole from the medics . . . pst, pst . . . I shot a little air into his veins. The second he died, all the hurtin-to-come just left his face.

Two weeks later I got J.F. and after that Woodrow . . . Jimmy Joe . . . I even spent all night waitin' by the latrine 'cause I knew the Cappin always made a late night visit and pst . . . pst . . . I got him.

(smiling, quite proud of himself) That's how come I died and come back to life. 'Cause just like Jesus went around healin' the sick, I'm supposed to go around healin' the hurtin' all these colored boys wearin' from the war.

Pst, pst. I know the secret. The secret to your pain. The secret to yours, and yours. Pst. Pst. Pst. Pst.

(The lights slowly fade.)

The Gospel According to Miss Roj

(The darkness is cut by electronic music. Cold, pounding, unrelenting. A neon sign which spells out THE BOTTOMLESS PIT clicks on. There is a lone bar stool. Lights flash on and off, pulsating to the beat. There is a blast of smoke and, from the haze, MISS ROJ *appears. He is dressed in striped patio pants, white go-go-boots, a halter, and cat-shaped sunglasses. What would seem ridiculous on anyone else,* MISS ROJ *wears as if it were high fashion. He carries himself with total elegance and absolute arrogance.)*

MISS ROJ God created Black people and Black people created style. The name's MISS ROJ . . . that's R.O.J. thank you and you can find me every Wednesday, Friday, and Saturday nights at "The Bottomless Pit," the watering hole for the wild and weary which asks the question, "Is there life after Jherri-curl?"

(A waiter enters, hands MISS ROJ *a drink, and then exits.)*

Thanks, doll. *Yes,* if they be Black and swish, the B.P. has seen them, which is not to suggest the Pit is lacking in cultural diversity. Oh no. There are your dinge queens, white men who like their chicken legs dark. *(He winks/flirts with a man in the audience)* And let's not forget, "Los Muchachos de la Neighborhood." But the specialty of the house is The Snap Queens. *(he snaps his fingers)* We are a rare breed.

For, you see, when something strikes our fancy, when the truth comes piercing through the dark, well you just can't let it pass unnoticed. No darling. You must pronounce it with a snap. *(he snaps)*

Snapping comes from another galaxy, as do all snap queens. That's right. I ain't just your regular oppressed American Negro. No-no-no! I am an extraterrestrial. And I ain't talkin' none of that shit you see in the movies! I have real power.

(The waiter enters. MISS ROJ *stops him.)*

Speaking of no power, will you please tell Miss Stingy-with-the-rum, that if Miss Roj had wanted to remain sober, she could have stayed home and drank Kool-aid. *(he snaps)* Thank you.

(The waiter exits. MISS ROJ *crosses and sits on bar stool.)*

Yes, I was placed here on Earth to study the life habits of a deteriorating society, and child when we talkin' New York City, we are discussing the Queen of Deterioration. Miss New York is doing a slow dance with death, and I am here to warn you all, but before I do, I must know . . . don't you just love my patio pants? Annette Funicello immortalized them in "Beach Blanket Bingo," and I have continued the legacy. And my go-gos? I realize white after Labor Day is very gauche, but as the saying goes, if you've got it flaunt it, if you don't, front it and snap to death any bastard who dares to defy you. *(laughing)* Oh ho! My demons are showing. Yes, my demons live at the bottom of my Bacardi and Coke.

Let's just hope for all concerned I dance my demons out before I drink them out 'cause child, dancing demons take you on a ride, but those drinkin' demons just take you, and you find yourself doing the strangest things. Like the time I locked my father in the broom closet. Seems the liquor made his tongue real liberal and he decided he was gonna baptize me with the word "faggot" over and over. Well, he's just going on and on with "faggot this" and "faggot that," all the while walking toward the broom closet to piss. Poor drunk bastard was just all turned around. So the demons just took hold of my wedges and forced me to kick the drunk son-of-a-bitch into the closet and lock the door. *(laughter)* Three days later I remembered he was there. *(he snaps)*

(The waiter enters. MISS ROJ *takes a drink and downs it.)*

Another!

(The waiter exits.)

(dancing about) Oh yes-yes-yes! Miss Roj is quintessential style. I corn row the hairs on my legs so that they spell out M.I.S.S. R.O.J. And I dare any bastard to fuck with me because I will snap your ass into oblivion.

I have the power, you know. Everytime I snap, I steal one beat of your heart. So if you find yourself gasping for air in the middle of the night, chances are you fucked with Miss Roj and she didn't like it.

Like the time this asshole at Jones Beach decided to take issue with my coulotte-sailor ensemble. This child, this muscle-bound Brooklyn thug in a skin-tight bikini, very skin tight so the whole world can see that instead of a brain, God gave him an extra thick piece of sausage. You know the kind who beat up on their wives for breakfast. Well, he decided to blurt out when I walked by, "Hey look at da monkey coon in da faggit suit." Well, I walked up to the poor dear, very calmly lifted my hand, and. . . . *(he snaps in rapid succession)* A heart attack, right there on the beach. *(he singles out someone in the audience)* You don't believe it? Cross me! Come on! Come on!

(The waiter enters, hands MISS ROJ *a drink.* MISS ROJ *downs it. The waiter exits.)*

(looking around) If this place is the answer, we're asking all the wrong questions. The only reason I come here is to communicate with my origins. The flashing lights are signals from my planet way out there. Yes, girl, even further than Flatbush. We're talking another galaxy. The flashing lights tell me how much time is left before the end.

(very drunk and loud by now) I hate the people here. I hate the drinks. But most of all I hate this goddamn music. That ain't music. Give me Aretha Franklin any day. *(singing)* "Just a little respect. R.E.S.P.E.C.T." Yeah! Yeah!

Come on and dance your last dance with Miss Roj. Last call is but a drink away and each snap puts you one step closer to the end.

A high-rise goes up. You can't get no job. Come on everybody and dance. A whole race of people gets trashed and debased. Snap those fingers and dance. Some sick bitch throws her baby out the window 'cause she thinks it's the Devil. Everybody snap! *The New York Post.* Snap!

Snap for every time you walk past someone lying in the street, smelling like frozen piss and shit and you don't see it. Snap for every crazed bastard who kills himself so as to get the jump on being killed. And snap for every sick muthafucker who, bored with carrying around his fear, takes to shooting up other people.

Yeah, snap your fingers and dance with Miss Roj. But don't be fooled by the banners and balloons 'cause, child, this ain't no party going on. Hell no! It's a wake. And the casket's made out of stone, steel, and glass and the people are racing all over the pavement like maggots on a dead piece of meat.

Yeah, dance! But don't be surprised if there ain't no beat holding you together 'cause we traded in our drums for respectability. So now it's just words. Words rappin'. Words screechin'. Words flowin' instead of blood 'cause you know that don't work. Words cracklin' instead of fire 'cause by the time a match is struck on 125th Street and you run to midtown, the flame has been blown away.

So come on and dance with Miss Roj and her demons. We don't ask for acceptance. We don't ask for approval. We know who we are and we move on it!

I guarantee you will never hear two fingers put together in a snap and not think of Miss Roj. That's power, baby. Patio pants and all.

(The lights begin to flash in rapid succession.)

So let's dance! And snap! And dance! And snap!

(MISS ROJ *begins to dance as if driven by his demons. There is a blast of smoke and when the haze settles,* MISS ROJ *has revolved off and in place of him is a recording of Aretha Franklin singing "Respect."*)

The Hairpiece

(As "Respect" fades into the background, a vanity revolves to center stage. On this vanity are two wigs, an Afro wig, circa 1968, and a long, flowing wig, both resting on wig stands. A Black WOMAN *enters, her head and body wrapped in towels. She picks up a framed picture and after a few moments of hesitation, throws it into a small trash can. She then removes one of her towels to reveal a totally bald head. Looking into a mirror on the "fourth wall," she begins applying makeup.)*

(The wig stand holding the Afro wig opens her eyes. Her name is JANINE. *She stares in disbelief at the bald woman.)*

JANINE: *(calling to the other wig stand)* LaWanda. LaWanda girl, wake up.

(The other wig stand, the one with the long, flowing wig, opens her eyes. Her name is LAWANDA.*)*

LAWANDA What? What is it?

JANINE Check out girlfriend.

LAWANDA Oh, girl, I don't believe it.

JANINE *(laughing)* Just look at the poor thing, trying to paint some life onto that face of hers. You'd think by now she'd realize it's the hair. It's all about the hair.

LAWANDA What hair! She ain't go no hair! She done fried, dyed, de-chemicalized her shit to death.

JANINE And all that's left is that buck-naked scalp of hers, sittin' up there apologizin' for being odd-shaped and ugly.

LAWANDA *(laughing with* JANINE*)* Girl, stop!

JANINE I ain't sayin' nuthin' but the truth.

LAWANDA/JANINE The bitch is bald! *(they laugh)*

JANINE And all over some man.

LAWANDA I tell ya, girl, I just don't understand it. I mean, look at her. She's got a right nice face, a good head on her shoulders. A good job even. And she's got to go fall in love with that fool.

JANINE That political quick-change artist. Everytime the nigga went and changed his ideology, she went and changed her hair to fit the occasion.

LAWANDA Well at least she's breaking up with him.

JANINE Hunny, no!

LAWANDA Yes child.

JANINE Oh, girl, dish me the dirt!

LAWANDA Well, you see, I heard her on the phone, talking to one of her girlfriends, and she's meeting him for lunch today to give him the ax.

JANINE Well it's about time.

LAWANDA I hear ya. But don't you worry 'bout a thing, girlfriend. I'm gonna tell you all about it.

JANINE Hunny, you won't have to tell me a damn thing 'cause I'm gonna be there, front row, center.

LAWANDA You?

JANINE Yes, child, she's wearing me to lunch.

LAWANDA *(outraged)* I don't think so!

JANINE *(with an attitude)* What do you mean, you don't think so?

LAWANDA Exactly what I said, "I don't think so." Damn, Janine, get real. How the hell she gonna wear both of us?

JANINE She ain't wearing both of us. She's wearing me.

LAWANDA Says who?

JANINE Says me! Says her! Ain't that right, girlfriend?

(The WOMAN *stops putting on makeup, looks around, sees no one, and goes back to her makeup.)*

JANINE I said, ain't that right!

(The WOMAN *picks up the phone.)*

WOMAN Hello . . . hello . . .

JANINE Did you hear the damn phone ring?

WOMAN No.

JANINE Then put the damn phone down and talk to me.

WOMAN I ah . . . don't understand.

JANINE It ain't deep so don't panic. Now, you're having lunch with your boyfriend, right?

WOMAN *(breaking into tears)* I think I'm having a nervous breakdown.

JANINE *(impatient)* I said you're having lunch with your boyfriend, right!

WOMAN *(scared, pulling herself together)* Yes, right . . . right.

JANINE To break up with him.

WOMAN How did you know t hat?

LAWANDA I told her.

WOMAN *(stands and screams)* Help! Help!

JANINE Sit down. I said sit your ass down!

(The WOMAN *does.)*

JANINE Now set her straight and tell her you're wearing me.

LAWANDA She's the one that needs to be set straight, so go on and tell her you're wearing me.

JANINE No, tell her you're wearing me.

(There is a pause.)

LAWANDA Well?

JANINE Well?

WOMAN I ah . . . actually hadn't made up my mind.

JANINE *(going off)* What do you mean you ain't made up you mind! After all that fool has put you through, you gonna need all the attitude you can get and there is nothing like attitude and a healthy head of kinks to make his shit shrivel like it should!

That's right! When you wearin' me, you lettin' him know he ain't gonna get no sweet-talkin' comb through your love without some serious resistance. No-no! The kink of my head is like the kink of your heart and neither is about to be hot-pressed into surrender.

LAWANDA That shit is so tired. The last time attitude worked on anybody was 1968. Janine girl, you need to get over it and get on with it. *(to the* WOMAN*)* And you need to give the nigga a goodbye he will never forget.

I say give him hysteria! Give him emotion! Give him rage! And there is nothing like a toss of the tresses to make your emotional outburst shine with emotional flair.

You can toss me back, shake me from side to side, all the while screaming, "I want you out of my life forever!!!" And not only will I come bouncing back for more, but you just might win an Academy Award for best performance by a head of hair in a dramatic role.

JANINE Miss hunny, please! She don't need no Barbie doll dipped in chocolate telling her what to do. She needs a head of hair that's coming from a fo' real place.

LAWANDA Don't you dare talk about nobody coming from a "fo' real place," Miss Made-in-Taiwan!

JANINE Hey! I ain't ashamed of where I come from. Besides, it don't matter where you come from as long as you end up in the right place.

LAWANDA And it don't matter the grade as long as the point gets made. So go on and tell her you're wearing me.

JANINE No, tell her you're wearing me.

(The WOMAN *unable to take it, begins to bite off her fake nails as* LAWANDA *and* JANINE *go at each other.)*

LAWANDA Set the bitch straight. Let her know there is no way she could even begin to compete with me. I am quality. She is kink. I am exotic. She is common. I am class and she is trash. That's right. T.R.A.S.H. We're talking three strikes and you're out. So go on and tell her you're wearing me. Go on, tell her! Tell her! Tell her!

JANINE Who you callin' a bitch? Why, if I had hands I'd knock you clear into next week. You think you cute. She thinks she's cute just 'cause that synthetic mop of hers blows in the wind. She looks like a fool and you look like an ever bigger fool when you wear her, so go on and tell her you're wearing me. Go on, tell her! Tell her! Tell her!

(The WOMAN *screams and pulls the two wigs off the wig stands as the lights go to black on three bald heads.)*

The Last Mama-on-the-Couch Play

(A NARRATOR, *dressed in a black tuxedo, enters through the audience and stands center stage. He is totally solemn.)*

NARRATOR We are pleased to bring you yet another Mama-on-the-Couch play. A searing domestic drama that tears at the very fabric of racist America. *(he crosses upstage center and sits on a stool and reads from a playscript)* Act One. Scene One.

*(*MAMA *revolves on stage left, sitting on a couch reading a large, oversized Bible. A window is placed stage right.* MAMA'*s dress, the couch, and drapes are made from the same material. A doormat lays down center.)*

NARRATOR Lights up on a dreary, depressing, but with middle-class aspirations tenement slum. There is a couch, with a Mama on it. Both are well worn. There is a picture of Jesus on the wall . . . *(a picture of Jesus is instantly revealed)* . . . and a window which looks onto an abandoned tenement. It is late spring.

Enter Walter-Lee-Beau-Willie-Jones (SON *enters through the audience)* He is Mama's thirty-year-old son. His brow is heavy from three hundred years of oppression.

MAMA *(looking up from her Bible, speaking in a slow manner)* Son, did you wipe your feet?

SON *(an ever-erupting volcano)* No, Mama, I didn't wipe me feet! Out there, every day, Mama, is the Man. The Man, Mama. Mr. Charlie! Mr. Bossman! And he's wipin' his feet on me. On me, Mama, every damn day of my life. Ain't that enough for me to deal with? Ain't that enough?

MAMA Son, wipe your feet.

SON I wanna dream. I wanna be somebody. I wanna take charge of my life.

MAMA You can do all of that, but first you got to wipe your feet.

SON *(as he crosses to the mat, mumbling and wiping his feet)* Wipe my feet . . . wipe my feet . . . wipe my feet . . .

MAMA That's a good boy.

SON *(exploding)* Boy! Boy! I don't wanna be nobody's good boy, Mama. I wanna be my own man!

MAMA I know son, I know. God will show the way.

SON God, Mama! Since when did your God ever do a damn thing for the Black man. Huh, Mama, huh? You tell me. When did your God ever help me.

MAMA *(removing her wire-rim glasses)* Son, come here.

*(*SON *crosses to* MAMA*, who slowly stands and in an exaggerated stage slap, backhands* SON *clear across the stage. The* NARRATOR *claps his hands to create the sound for the slap.* MAMA *then lifts her clinched fists to the heavens.)*

MAMA Not in my house, my house, will you ever talk that way again!

(The NARRATOR*, so moved by her performance, erupts in applause and encourages the audience to do so.)*

NARRATOR Beautiful. Just stunning.

(He reaches into one of the secret compartments of the set and gets an award which he ceremoniously gives to MAMA *for her performance. She bows and then returns to the couch.)*

NARRATOR Enter Walter-Lee-Beau-Willie's wife, The Lady in Plaid.

(Music from nowhere is heard, a jazzy pseudoabstract intro as the LADY IN PLAID *dances in through the audience, wipes her feet, and then twirls about.)*

LADY She was a creature of regal beauty
who in ancient time graced the temples of the
Nile with her womanliness
But here she was, stuck being colored
and a woman in a world that valued neither.

SON You cooked my dinner?

LADY *(oblivious to* SON*)* Feet flat, back
broke, she looked at the man who, though he
be thirty, still ain't got his own apartment.
Yeah, he's still livin' with his Mama!
And she asked herself, was this the life
for a Princess Colored, who by the
translucence of her skin, knew the
universe was her sister.

(The LADY IN PLAID *twirls and dances.)*

SON *(becoming irate)* I've had a hard day of dealin' with the Man. Where's my damn dinner? Woman, stand still when I'm talkin' to you!

LADY And she cried for her sisters in
Detroit
Who knew, as she, that their souls belonged
in ancient temples on the Nile.
And she cried for her sisters in Chicago
who, like her, their life has become
one colored hell.

SON There's only one thing gonna get through to you.

LADY And she cried for her sisters in New
Orleans
And her sisters in Trenton and Birmingham,
and
Poughkeepsie and Orlando and Miami Beach
and
Las Vegas, Palm Springs.

(As she continues to call out cities, he crosses offstage and returns with two Black dolls and then crosses to the window.)

SON Now are you gonna cook me dinner?

LADY Walter-Lee-Beau-Willie-Jones, No! Not my babies.

(SON throws them out the window. The LADY IN PLAID then lets out a primal scream.)

LADY He dropped them!!!!

(The NARRATOR breaks into applause.)

NARRATOR Just splendid. Shattering.

(He then crosses and after an intense struggle with MAMA, he takes the award from her and gives it to the LADY IN PLAID, who is still suffering primal pain.)

LADY Not my babies . . . not my . . . *(upon receiving the award, she instantly recovers)* Help me up, sugar. *(she then bows and crosses and stands behind the couch)*

NARRATOR Enter Medea Jones, Walter-Lee-Beau-Willie's sister.

(MEDEA moves very ceremoniously, wiping her feet and then speaking and gesturing as if she just escaped from a Greek tragedy.)

MEDEA

Ah, see how the sun kneels to speak
her evening vespers, exalting all
in her vision, even lowly tenement
long abandoned.

Mother, wife of brother, I trust
the approaching darkness finds you
safe in Hestia's busom.

Brother, why wear the face of a man
in anguish. Can the garment of thine
feelings cause the shape of your
countenance to disfigure so?

SON *(at the end of his rope)* Leave me alone, Medea.

MEDEA *(to MAMA)*

Is good brother still going on and on and on about He and The Man.

MAMA/LADY What else?

MEDEA Ah brother, if with our thoughts and words
we could cast thine oppressors
into the lowest bowels of wretched
hell, would that make us more like the
gods or more like our oppressors.

No, brother, no, do not let thy rage
choke the blood which annoints thy
heart with love. Forgo thine darkened
humor and let love shine on your
soul, like a jewel on a young maiden's hand.

(Dropping to her knees.)

I beseech thee, forgo thine
anger and leave wrath to the gods!

SON Girl, what has gotten into you.

MEDEA Julliard, good brother. For I am no
longer bound by rhythms of race or
region. Oh, no. My speech, like my
pain and suffering, have become
classical and therefore universal.

LADY I didn't understand a damn thing she said, but girl you usin' them words.

(LADY IN PLAID crosses and gives MEDEA the award and everyone applauds.)

SON *(trying to stop the applause)* Wait one damn minute! This my play. It's about me and the Man. It ain't got nuthin' to do with no ancient temples on the Nile and it ain't got nuthin' to do with Hestia's busom. And it ain't got nuthin' to do with you slappin' me across no room. *(his gut-wrenching best)* It's about me. Me and my pain! My pain!

THE VOICE OF THE MAN Walter-Lee-Beau-Willie, this is the Man. You have been convicted of overacting. Come out with your hands up.

(SON starts to cross to the window.)

SON Well now that does it.

MAMA Son, no, don't go near that window. Son, no!

(Gun shots ring out and SON falls dead.)

MAMA *(crossing to the body, too emotional for words)* My son, he was a good boy. Confused. Angry. Just like his father. And his father's father. And his father's father's father. And now he's dead.

(Seeing she's about to drop to her knees, the NARRATOR rushes and places a pillow underneath her just in time.)

If only he had been born into a world better than this. A world where there are no well-worn couches and no well-worn Mamas and nobody over emotes.

If only he had been born into an all-Black musical.

(A song intro begins.)

Nobody ever dies in an all-Black musical.

*(*MEDEA *and* LADY IN PLAID *pull out church fans and begin to fan themselves)*

MAMA *(singing a soul-stirring gospel)*
OH WHY COULDN'T HE
BE BORN
INTO A SHOW WITH LOTS OF SINGING
AND DANCING

I SAY WHY
COULDN'T HE
BE BORN

LADY Go ahead hunny. Take your time.

MAMA
INTO A SHOW WHERE EVERYBODY
IS HAPPY

NARRATOR/MEDEA Preach! Preach!

MAMA
OH WHY COULDN'T HE BE BORN WITH
THE CHANCE
TO SMILE A LOT AND SING AND
DANCE
OH WHY
OH WHY

OH WHY
COULDN'T HE
BE BORN
INTO AN ALL-BLACK SHOW
WOAH-WOAH

(The CAST *joins in, singing do-wop gospel background to* MAMA*'s lament.)*

OH WHY
COULDN'T HE
BE BORN
(HE BE BORN)
INTO A SHOW WHERE EVERYBODY
IS HAPPY

WHY COULDN'T HE BE BORN WITH
THE CHANCE
TO SMILE A LOT AND SING AND
DANCE
WANNA KNOW WHY
WANNA KNOW WHY

OH WHY
COULDN'T HE
BE BORN
INTO AN ALL-BLACK SHOW
A-MEN

(A singing/dancing, spirit-raising revival begins.)

OH, SON, GET UP
GET UP AND DANCE
WE SAY GET UP
THIS IS YOUR SECOND CHANCE

DON'T SHAKE A FIST
JUST SHAKE A LEG
AND DO THE TWIST
DON'T SCREAM AND BEG
SON SON SON
GET UP AND DANCE

GET
GET UP
GET UP AND
GET UP AND DANCE—ALL RIGHT!
GET UP AND DANCE—ALL RIGHT!
GET UP AND DANCE!

*(*WALTER-LEE-BEAU-WILLIE *springs to life and joins in the dancing. A foot-stomping, hand-clapping production number takes off, which encompasses a myriad of Black-Broadwayesque dancing styles—shifting speeds and styles with exuberant abandonment.)*

MAMA *(bluesy)*
WHY COULDN'T HE BE BORN INTO AN
ALL-BLACK SHOW

CAST WITH SINGING AND DANCING

MAMA BLACK SHOW

*(*MAMA *scats and the dancing becomes manic and just a little too desperate to please.)*

CAST
WE GOTTA DANCE
WE GOTTA DANCE
GET UP GET UP GET UP AND DANCE
WE GOTTA DANCE
WE GOTTA DANCE
GOTTA DANCE!

(Just at the point the dancing is about to become violent, the cast freezes and pointedly, simply sings:)

IF WE WANT TO LIVE
WE HAVE GOT TO
WE HAVE GOT TO

DANCE . . . AND DANCE . . . AND DANCE . . .

(As they continue to dance with zombie-like frozen smiles and faces, around them images of coon performers flash as the lights slowly fade.)

Symbiosis

(The Temptations singing "My Girl" are heard as lights reveal a BLACK MAN *in corporate dress standing before a large trash can throwing objects from a Saks Fifth Avenue bag into it. Circling around him with his every emotion on his face is* THE KID, *who is dressed in a late-sixties street style. His moves are slightly heightened. As the scene begins the music fades.)*

MAN *(with contained emotions)*
My first pair of Converse All-stars. Gone.
My first Afro-comb. Gone.
My first dashiki. Gone.
My autographed pictures of Stokley Carmichael, Jomo Kenyatta, and Donna Summer. Gone.

KID *(near tears, totally upset)* This shit's not fair man. Damn! Hell! Shit! Shit! It's not fair!

MAN
My first jar of Murray's Pomade.
My first can of Afro-sheen.
My first box of curl relaxer. Gone! Gone! Gone!
Eldridge Cleaver's *Soul on Ice.*

KID Not *Soul on Ice!*

MAN It's been replaced on my bookshelf by *The Color Purple.*

KID *(horrified)* No!

MAN Gone!

KID But—

MAN
Jimi Hendrix's "Purple Haze." Gone.
Sly Stone's "There's A Riot Goin' On." Gone.
The Jackson Five's "I Want You Back."

KID Man, you can't throw that away. It's living proof Michael had a black nose.

MAN It's all going. Anything and everything that connects me to you, to who I was, to what we were, is out of my life.

KID You've got to give me another chance.

MAN *Fingertips Part 2.*

KID Man, how can you do that? That's vintage Stevie Wonder.

MAN You want to know how, Kid? You want to know how? Because my survival depends on it. Whether you know it or not, the Ice Age is upon us.

KID *(jokingly)* Man, what the hell you talkin' about. It's 95 damn degrees.

MAN The climate is changing, Kid, and either you adjust or you end up extinct. A sociological dinosaur. Do you understand what I'm trying to tell you? King Kong would have made it to the top if only he had taken the elevator. Instead he brought attention to his struggle and ended up dead.

KID *(pleading)* I'll change. I swear I'll change. I'll maintain a low profile. You won't even know I'm around.

MAN If I'm to become what I'm to become then you've got to go . . . I have no history. I have no past.

KID Just like that?

MAN *(throwing away a series of buttons)* Free Angela! Free Bobby! Free Huey, Duey, and Louie! U.S. out of Viet Nam. U.S. out of Cambodia. U.S. out of Harlem, Detroit, and Newark. Gone! . . . The Temptations Greatest Hits!

KID *(grabbing the album.)* No!!!

MAN Give it back, Kid.

KID No.

MAN I said give it back!

KID No. I can't let you trash this. Johnny man, it contains fourteen classic cuts by the tempting Temptations. We're talking, "Ain't Too Proud to Beg," "Papa was a Rolling Stone," "My Girl."

MAN *(warning)* I don't have all day.

KID For God's sake, Johnny man, "My Girl" is the jam to end all jams. It's what we are. Who we are. It's a way of life. Come on, man, for old times sake. *(singing)*

I GOT SUNSHINE ON A CLOUDY DAY
DUM-DA-DUM-DA-DUM-DA-DUM
AND WHEN IT'S COLD OUTSIDE

Come on, Johnny man, sing

I GOT THE MONTH OF MAY

Here comes your favorite part. Come on, Johnny man, sing.

I GUESS YOU SAY
WHAT CAN MAKE ME FEEL THIS WAY
MY GIRL, MY GIRL, MY GIRL
TALKIN' 'BOUT

MAN *(exploding)* I said give it back!

KID *(angry)* I ain't givin' you a muthafuckin' thing!

MAN Now you listen to me!

KID No, you listen to me. This is the kid you're dealin' with, so don't fuck with me!

(He hits his fist into his hand, and THE MAN *grabs for his heart.* THE KID *repeats with two more hits, which causes the man to drop to the ground, grabbing his heart.)*

KID Jai! Jai! Jai!

MAN Kid, please.

KID Yeah. Yeah. Now who's begging who. . . . Well, well, well, look at Mr. Cream-of-the-Crop, Mr. Colored-Man-on-Top. Now that he's making it, he no longer wants anything to do with the Kid. Well, you may put all kinds of silk ties 'round your neck and white lines up your nose, but the Kid is here to stay. You may change your women as often as you change your underwear, but the Kid is here to stay. And regardless of how much of your past that you trash, I ain't goin' no damn where. Is that clear? Is that clear?

MAN *(regaining his strength, beginning to stand)* Yeah.

KID Good. *(after a beat)* You all right man? You all right? I don't want to hurt you, but when you start all that talk about getting rid of me, well, it gets me kind of crazy. We need each other. We are one . . .

(Before THE KID *can complete his sentence,* THE MAN *grabs him around his neck and starts to choke him violently.)*

MAN *(as he strangles him)* The . . . Ice . . . Age . . . is . . . upon us . . . and either we adjust . . . or we end up . . . extinct.

*(*THE KID *hangs limp in* THE MAN's *arms.)*

MAN *(laughing)* Man kills his own rage. Film at eleven. *(he then dumps* THE KID *into the trash can, and closes the lid. He speaks in a contained voice)* I have no history. I have no past. I can't. It's too much. It's much too much. I must be able to smile on cue. And watch the news with an impersonal eye. I have no stake in the madness.

Being Black is too emotionally taxing; therefore I will be Black only on weekends and holidays.

(He then turns to go, but sees the Temptations album lying on the ground. He picks it up and sings quietly to himself.)

I GUESS YOU SAY
WHAT CAN MAKE ME FEEL THIS WAY

(He pauses, but then crosses to the trash can, lifts the lid, and just as he is about to toss the album in, a hand reaches from inside the can and grabs hold of THE MAN's *arm.* THE KID *then emerges from the can with a death grip on* THE MAN's *arm.)*

KID *(smiling)* What's happenin'?

Blackout

LALA'S OPENING

(Roving follow spots. A timpani drum roll. As we hear the voice of the ANNOUNCER, *outrageously glamorous images of* LALA *are projected onto the museum walls.)*

VOICE OF ANNOUNCER From Rome to Rangoon! Paris to Prague! We are pleased to present the American debut of the one! The only! The breathtaking! The astounding! The stupendous! The incredible! The magnificent! Lala Lamazing Grace!

(Thunderous applause as LALA *struts on, the definitive Black diva. She has long, flowing hair, an outrageous lamé dress, and an affected French accent which she loses when she's upset.)*

LALA

EVERYBODY LOVES LALA
EVERYBODY LOVES ME
PARIS! BERLIN! LONDON! ROME!
NO MATTER WHERE I GO
I ALWAYS FEEL AT HOME

OHHHH
EVERYBODY LOVES LALA
EVERYBODY LOVES ME
I'M TRES MAGNIFIQUE
AND OH SO UNIQUE
AND WHEN IT COMES TO GLAMOUR
I'M CHIC-ER THAN CHIC

(She giggles)

THAT'S WHY EVERYBODY
EVERYBODY

EVERYBODY-EVERYBODY-EVERYBODY
LOVES ME

(She begins to vocally reach for higher and higher notes, until she has to point to her final note. She ends the number with a grand flourish and bows to thunderous applause.)

LALA I-love-it-I-love-it-I-love-it!

Yes, it's me! Lala Lamazing Grace and I have come home. Home to the home I never knew as home. Home to you, my people, my blood, my guts.

My story is a simple one, full of fire, passion, magique. You may ask how did I, a humble girl from the backwoods of Mississippi, come to be the ninth wonder of the modern world. Well, I can't take all of the credit. Part of it goes to him. *(she points toward the heavens)*

No, not the light man, darling, but God. For, you see, Lala is a star. A very big star. Let us not mince words, I'm a fucking meteorite. *(she laughs)* But He is the universe and just like my sister, Aretha la Franklin, Lala's roots are in the black church. *(she sings in a showy gospel style)*

THAT'S WHY EVERYBODY LOVES
SWING LOW SWEET CHARIOT
THAT'S WHY EVERYBODY LOVES
GO DOWN MOSES, WAY DOWN IN
EGYPT LAND
THAT'S WHY EVERYBODY EVERYBODY
LOVES
ME!!!

(Once again she points to her final note and then basks in applause.)

Thank you. Thank you.

Now, before I dazzle you with more of my limitless talent, tell me something, America. *(musical underscoring)* Why has it taken you so long to recognize my artistry? Mother France opened her loving arms and Lala came running. All over the world Lala was embraced. But here, ha! You spat at Lala. Was I too exotic? Too much woman, or what?

Diana Ross you embrace. A too-bit nobody from Detroit, of all places. Now, I'm not knocking la Ross. She does the best she can with the little she has. *(she laughs)* But the Paul la Robesons, the James la Baldwins, the Josephine la Baker's, who was my godmother you know. The Lala Lamazing Grace's you kick out. You drive . . .

AWAY
I AM GOING AWAY
HOPING TO FIND A BETTER DAY
WHAT DO YOU SAY
HEY HEY
I AM GOING AWAY
AWAY

(LALA, caught up in the drama of the song, doesn't see ADMONIA, her maid, stick her head out from offstage.)

(Once she is sure LALA isn't looking, she wheels onto stage right FLO'RANCE, LALA's lover, who wears a white mask/blonde hair. He is gagged and tied to a chair. ADMONIA places him on stage and then quickly exits.*)*

LALA
AU REVOIR—JE VAIS PARTIER MAIN-
TENANT
JE VEUX DIRE MAINTENANT
AU REVOIR
AU REVOIR
AU REVOIR
AU REVOIR
A-MA-VIE

(On her last note, she sees FLO'RANCE and, in total shock, crosses to him.)

LALA Flo'rance, what the hell are you doing out here, looking like that. I haven't seen you for three days and you decide to show up now?

(He mumbles.)

I don't want to hear it!

(He mumbles.)

I said shut up!

(ADMONIA enters from stage right and has a letter opener on a silver tray.)

ADMONIA Pst!

(LALA, embarrassed by the presence of ADMONIA on stage, smiles apologetically at the audience.)

LALA Un momento.

(She then pulls ADMONIA to the side.)

LALA Darling, have you lost your mind coming onstage while I'm performing. And what have you done to Flo'rance? When I asked you to keep him tied up, I didn't mean to tie him up.

(ADMONIA *gives her the letter opener.)*

LALA Why are you giving me this? I have no letters to open. I'm in the middle of my American debut. Admonia, take Flo'rance off this stage with you! Admonia!

(ADMONIA *is gone.* LALA *turns to the audience and tries to make the best of it.)*

LALA That was Admonia, my slightly overweight Black maid, and this is Flo'rance, my amour. I remember how we met, don't you Flo'rance. I was sitting in a café on the Left Bank, when I looked up and saw the most beautiful man staring down at me.

"Who are you," he asked. I told him my name . . . whatever my name was back then. Yes, I told him my name and he said, "No, that cannot be your name. Your name should dance the way your eyes dance and your lips dance. Your name should fly, like Lala." And the rest is la history.

Flo'rance molded me into the woman I am today. He is my Svengali, my reality, my all. And I thought I was all to him, until we came here to America, and he fucked that bitch. Yeah, you fucked 'em all. Anything Black and breathing. And all this time, I thought you loved me for being me. *(she holds the letter opener to his neck)*

Well, you may think you made me, but I'll have you know I was who I was, whoever that was, long before you made me what I am. So there! *(she stabs him and breaks into song)*

OH, LOVE CAN DRIVE A WOMAN TO MADNESS
TO PAIN AND SADNESS
I KNOW
BELIEVE ME I KNOW
I KNOW
I KNOW

(LALA *sees what she's done and is about to scream but catches herself and tries to play it off.)*

LALA Moving right along.

(ADMONIA *enters with a telegram on a tray.)*

ADMONIA Pst.

LALA *(anxious/hostile)* What is it now?

(ADMONIA *hands* LALA *a telegram.)*

LALA *(excited)* Oh, la telegram from one of my fans and the concert isn't even over yet. Get me the letter opener. It's in Flo'rance.

(ADMONIA *hands* LALA *the letter opener.)*

LALA Next I am going to do for you my immortal hit song, "The Girl Inside." But first we open the telegram. *(she quickly reads it and is outraged)* What! Which pig in la audience wrote this trash? *(reading)* "Dear Sadie, I'm so proud. The show's wonderful, but talk less and sing more. Love, Mama."

First off, no one calls me Sadie. Sadie died the day Lala was born. And secondly, my Mama's dead. Anyone who knows anything about Lala Lamazing Grace knows that my mother and Josephine Baker were French patriots together. They infiltrated a carnival rumored to be the center of Nazi intelligence, disguised as Hottentot Siamese twins. You may laugh but it's true. Mama died a heroine. It's all in my autobiography, "Violá Lala!" So whoever sent this telegram is a liar!

(ADMONIA *promptly presents her with another telegram.)*

LALA No doubt an apology. *(reading)* "Dear Sadie, I'm not dead. P.S. Your child misses you." What? *(she squares off at the audience)* Well, now, that does it! If you are my mother, which you are not, and this alleged child is my child, then that would mean I am a mother and I have never given birth. I don't know nothin' 'bout birthin' no babies! *(she laughs)* Lala made a funny.

So whoever sent this, show me the child! Show me!

(ADMONIA *offers another telegram.)*

LALA *(to* ADMONIA*)* You know you're gonna get fired! *(she reluctantly opens it)* "The child is in the closet." What closet?

ADMONIA Pst.

(ADMONIA *pushes a button and the center wall unit revolves around to reveal a large black door.* ADMONIA *exits, taking* FLO'RANCE *with her, leaving* LALA *alone.)*

LALA *(laughing)* I get it. It's a plot, isn't it. A nasty little CIA, FBI kind of plot. Well let me tell you muthafuckers one thing, there is nothing in that closet, real or manufactured, that will be a dimmer to the glimmer of Lamé the star. You may have gotten Billie and Bessie and a little piece of everyone else who's come along since, but you won't get Lala. My clothes are too fabulous! My hair is too long! My accent too french. That's why I came home to America. To prove you ain't got nothing on me!

(The music for her next song starts, but LALA *is caught up in her tirade, and talks/screams over the music.)*

My mother and Josephine Baker were French patriots together! I've had brunch with the Pope! I've dined with the Queen! Everywhere I go I cause riots! Hunny, I am a star! I have transcended pain! So there! *(yelling)* Stop the music! Stop that goddamn music.

(The music stops. LALA *slowly walks downstage and singles out someone in the audience.)*

Darling, you're not looking at me. You're staring at that damn door. Did you pay to stare at some fucking door or be mesmerized by my talent?

(To the whole audience)

Very well! I guess I am going to have to go to the closet door, fling it open, in order to dispell all the nasty little thoughts these nasty little telegrams have planted in your nasty little minds. *(speaking directly to someone in the audience)* Do you want me to open the closet door? Speak up, darling, this is live. *(once she gets the person to say "yes")* I will open the door, but before I do, let me tell you bastards one last thing. To hell with coming home and to hell with lies and insinuations!

*(*LALA *goes into the closet and after a short pause comes running out, ready to scream, and slams the door. Traumatized to the point of no return, she tells the following story as if it were a jazz solo of rushing, shifting emotions.)*

LALA I must tell you this dream I had last night. Simply magnifique. In this dream, I'm running naked in Sammy Davis Junior's hair. *(crazed laughter)*

Yes! I'm caught in this larger than life, deep, dark forest of savage, nappy-nappy hair. The kinky-kinks are choking me, wrapped around my naked arms, thighs, breast, face. I can't breathe. And there was nothing in that closet!

And I'm thinking if only I had a machete, I could cut away the kinks. Remove once and for all the roughness. But then I look up and it's coming toward me. Flowing like lava. It's pomade! Ohhh, Sammy!

Yes, cakes and cakes of pomade. Making everything nice and white and smooth and shiny, like my Black/white/Black/white/Black behiney.

Mama no!

And then spikes start cutting through the pomade. Combing the coated kink. Cutting through the kink, into me. There are bloodlines on my back. On my thighs.

It's all over. All over . . . all over me. All over for me.

*(*LALA *accidentally pulls off her wig to reveal her real hair. Stripped of her "disguise" she recoils like a scared little girl and sings.)*

MOMMY AND DADDY
MEET AND MATE
THE CHILD THAT'S BORN
IS TORN WITH LOVE AND WITH HATE
SHE RUNS AWAY TO FIND HER OWN
AND TRIES TO DENY
WHAT SHE'S ALWAYS KNOWN
THE GIRL INSIDE

(The closet door opens. LALA *runs away, and a* LITTLE BLACK GIRL *emerges from the closet. Standing behind her is* ADMONIA.*)*

(The LITTLE GIRL *and* LALA *are in two isolated pools of light, and mirror each other's moves until* LALA *reaches past her reflection and the* LITTLE GIRL *comes to* LALA *and they hug.* ADMONIA *then joins them as* LALA *sings. Music underscored.)*

LALA

WHAT'S LEFT IS THE GIRL INSIDE
THE GIRL WHO DIED
SO A NEW GIRL COULD BE BORN

Slow Fade to Black

PERMUTATIONS

(Lights up on NORMAL JEAN REYNOLDS. *She is very Southern/country and very young. She wears a simple faded print dress and her hair, slightly mussed, is in plaits. She sits, her dress covering a large oval object.)*

NORMAL My mama used to say, God made the exceptional, then God made the special and when God got bored, he made me. 'Course she don't say too much of nuthin' no more, not since I lay me this egg.

(She lifts her dress to uncover a large, white egg laying between her legs.)

Ya see it all got started when I had me sexual relations with the garbage man. Ooowee, did he smell.

No, not bad. No! He smelled of all the good things folks never shoulda thrown away. His sweat was like cantaloupe juice. His neck was like a ripe-red strawberry. And the water that fell from his eyes was like a deep, dark, juicy-juicy grape. I tell ya, it was like fuckin' a fruit salad, only I didn't spit out the seeds. I kept them here, deep inside. And three days later, my belly commence to swell, real big like.

Well my mama locked me off in some dark room, refusin' to let me see light of day 'cause, "What would the neighbors think." At first I cried a lot, but then I grew used to livin' my days in the dark, and my nights in the dark. . . . *(she hums)* And then it wasn't but a week or so later, my mama off at church, that I got this hurtin' feelin' down here. Worse than anything I'd ever known. And then I started bleedin', real bad. I mean there was blood everywhere. And the pain had me howlin' like a near-dead dog. I tell ya, I was yellin' so loud, I couldn't even hear myself. Noooooooo! Noooooo! Carrying on something like that.

And I guess it was just too much for the body to take, 'cause the next thing I remember . . . is me coming to and there's this big white egg layin' 'tween my legs. First I thought somebody musta put it there as some kind of joke. But then I noticed that all 'round this egg were thin lines of blood that I could trace to back between my legs.

(laughing) Well, when my mama come home from church she just about died. "Normal Jean, what's that thing 'tween your legs? Normal Jean, you answer me, girl!" It's not a thing, Mama. It's an egg. And I laid it.

She tried separatin' me from it, but I wasn't havin' it. I stayed in that dark room, huggin', holdin' onto it.

And then I heard it. It wasn't anything that coulda been heard 'round the world, or even in the next room. It was kinda like layin' back in the bath tub, ya know, the water just coverin' your ears . . . and if you lay real still and listen real close, you can hear the sound of your heart movin' the water. You ever done that? Well that's what it sounded like. A heart movin' water. And it was happenin' inside here.

Why, I'm the only person I know who ever lay themselves an egg before, so that makes me special. You hear that, Mama? I'm special and so's my egg! And special things supposed to be treated like they matter. That's why everynight I count to it, so it knows nuthin' never really ends. And I sing it every song I know so that when it comes out, it's full of all kinds of feelings. And I tell it secrets and laugh with it and . . .

(She suddenly stops and puts her ear to the egg and listens intently.)

Oh! I don't believe it! I thought I heard . . . yes! *(excited)* Can you hear it? Instead of one heart, there's two. Two little hearts just pattering away. Boom-boom-boom. Boom-boom-boom. Talkin to each other like old friends. Racin' toward the beginnin' of their lives.

(listening) Oh, no, now there's three . . . four . . . five, six. More hearts than I can count. And they're all alive, beatin' out life inside my egg.

(We begin to hear the heartbeats, drums, alive inside NORMAL'*s egg.)*

Any day now, this egg is gonna crack open and what's gonna come out a be the likes of which nobody has ever seen. My babies! And their skin is gonna turn all kinds of shades in the sun and their hair a be growin' every which-a-way. And it won't matter and they won't care 'cause they know they are so rare and so special 'cause it's not everyday a bunch of babies break outta a white egg and start to live.

And nobody better not try and hurt my babies 'cause if they do, they gonna have to deal with me.

Yes, any day now, this shell's gonna crack and my babies are gonna fly. Fly! Fly!

(She laughs at the thought, but then stops and says the word as if it's the most natural thing in the world.)

Fly.

Blackout

The Party

(Before we know what's hit us, a hurricane of energy comes bounding into the space. It is TOPSY WASHINGTON. *Her hair and dress are a series of stylistic contradictions which are hip, Black, and unencumbered.)*

(Music, spiritual and funky, underscores.)

TOPSY *(dancing about)* Yoho! Party! Party! Turn up the music! Turn up the music!

Have yaw ever been to a party where there was one fool in the middle of the room, dancing harder and yelling louder than everybody in the entire place. Well, hunny, that fool was me!

Yes, child! The name is Topsy Washington and I love to party. As a matter of fact, when God created the world, on the seventh day, he didn't rest. No child, he partied. Yo-ho! Party! Yeah! Yeah!

But now let me tell you 'bout this function I went to the other night, way uptown. And baby when I say way uptown, I mean way-way-way-way-way-way-way-way uptown. Somewhere's between 125th Street and infinity.

Inside was the largest gathering of Black/Negro/colored Americans you'd ever want to see. Over in one corner you got Nat Turner sippin' champagne out of Eartha Kitt's slipper. And over in another corner, Bert Williams and Malcolm X was discussing existentialism as it relates to the shuffle-ball-change. Girl, Aunt Jemima and Angela Davis was in the kitchen sharing a plate of greens and just goin' off about South Africa.

And then Fats sat down and started to work them eighty-eights. And then Stevie joined in. And then Miles and Duke and Ella and Jimi and Charlie and Sly and Lightin' and Count and Louie!

And then everybody joined in. I tell you all the children was just all up in there, dancing to the rhythm of one beat. Dancing to the rhythm of their own definition. Celebrating in their cultural madness.

And then the floor started to shake. And the walls started to move. And before anybody knew what was happening, the entire room lifted up off the ground. The whole place just took off and went flying through space—defying logic and limitations. Just a spinning and a spinning and a spinning until it disappeared inside of my head.

*(*TOPSY *stops dancing and regains her balance and begins to listen to the music in her head. Slowly we begin to hear it, too.)*

That's right, girl, there's a party goin' on inside of here. That's why when I walk down the street my hips just sashay all over the place. 'Cause I'm dancing to the music of the madness in me.

And whereas I used to jump into a rage anytime anybody tried to deny who I was, now all I got to do is give attitude, quicker than light, and then go on about the business of being me. 'Cause I'm dancing to the music of the madness in me.

(As TOPSY *continues to speak,* MISS ROJ, LALA, MISS PAT, *and* THE MAN *from SYMBIOSIS revolve on, frozen like soft sculptures.)*

TOPSY And here, all this time I been thinkin we gave up our drums. But, naw, we still got 'em. I know I got mine. They're here, in my speech, my walk, my hair, my God, my style, my smile, and my eyes. And everything I need to get over in this world, is inside here, connecting me to everybody and everything that's ever been.

So, hunny, don't waste your time trying to label or define me.

(The sculptures slowly begin to come to "life" and they mirror/echo TOPSY's *words.)*

TOPSY/EVERYBODY . . . 'cause I'm not what I was ten years ago or ten minutes ago. I'm all of that and then some. And whereas I can't live inside yesterday's pain, I can't live without it.

(All of a sudden, madness erupts on the stage. The sculptures begin to speak all at once. Images of Black/Negro/colored Americans begin to flash—images of them dancing past the madness, caught up in the madness, being lynched, rioting, partying, surviving. Mixed in with these images are all the characters from the exhibits. Through all of this TOPSY *sings. It is a vocal and visual cacaphony which builds and builds.)*

LALA I must tell you about this dream I had last night. Simply magnifique. In this dream I'm running naked in Sammy Davis Junior's hair. Yes. I'm caught in this larger-than-life, deep, dark tangled forest of savage, nappy-nappy hair. Yes, the kinky kinks are choking me, are wrapped around my naked arms, my naked thighs, breast, and face, and I can't breathe and there was nothing in that closet.

MISS ROJ Snap for every time you walk past someone lying in the street smelling like frozen piss and shit and you don't see it. Snap for every crazed bastard who kills himself so as to get the jump on being killed. And snap for every sick muthafucker who, bored with carrying about his fear, takes to shooting up other people.

THE MAN I have no history. I have no past. I can't. It's too much. It's much too much. I must be able to smile on cue and watch the news with an impersonal eye. I have no stake in the madness. Being Black is too emotionally taxing, therefore I will be Black only on weekends and holidays.

MISS PAT Stop playing those drums. I said stop playing those damn drums. You can't stop history. You can't stop time. Those drums will be confiscated once we reach Savannah, so give them up now. Repeat after me: I don't hear any drums and I will not rebel. I will not rebel.

TOPSY *(singing)*
THERE'S MADNESS IN ME
AND THAT MADNESS SETS ME FREE
THERE'S MADNESS IN ME
AND THAT MADNESS SETS ME FREE
THERE'S MADNESS IN ME
AND THAT MADNESS SETS ME FREE
THERE'S MADNESS IN ME
AND THAT MADNESS SETS ME FREE
THERE'S MADNESS IN ME
AND THAT MADNESS SETS ME FREE

TOPSY My power is in my . . .

EVERYBODY *Madness!*

TOPSY And my colored contradictions.

(The sculptures freeze with a smile on their faces as we hear the voice of MISS PAT.*)*

VOICE OF MISS PAT Before exiting, check the overhead as any baggage you don't claim, we trash.

Blackout

THE MOJO AND THE SAYSO
1989

Aishah Rahman

Writers are sometimes moved by articles that they read in newspapers or magazines, or by stories featured on television. Current events often become subject matter for their plays. Maxwell Anderson's interest in the Sacco and Vanzetti case resulted in *Winterset,* which most critics consider his greatest achievement. Arthur Miller's *The Crucible* was the result of his reaction to Senator Joseph McCarthy's anticommunist "witchhunt." James Baldwin's anger over the Emmitt Till case (a fourteen-year-old Black boy was brutally murdered in Mississippi for allegedly whistling at a white woman, and his murderer acquitted) was the motivation for *Blues for Mister Charlie.* The killing of a ten-year-old boy, Clifford Glover, compelled Aishah Rahman to write *The Mojo and the Sayso.* In a case of mistaken identity, Glover was fatally shot by a policeman as he walked down a Queens, New York, street with his father. The city paid Glover's mother for the wrongful death of her son, but she was swindled out of the money by her minister. After some investigation, Rahman realized that the Glovers were voiceless people. *The Mojo and the Sayso* would give them voice.

The Mojo and the Sayso has been called avant-garde, absurd, surrealistic, allegorical, farce, ritual, and satire; perhaps it is all of these things. The play unfolds like a nightmare with characters floating like clouds in and out of reality. Their lives have been uprooted by a senseless tragedy that they cannot comprehend. They are grieving for their son, Linus, who was killed by an off-duty police officer. To retain some sanity they must embrace something or someone for momentary escape. In other words, they must have a mojo—some form of magic—that will enable them to survive this tragedy. Awilda's escape is the church and her pastor; Acts, her husband, is totally immersed in the restoration of automobiles; their son, Walter, acknowledges his manhood and his Blackness by aligning himself with those young African Americans who were "beyond fear" and not afraid to act—even if acting means death. He also changes his name to Blood. They survive but are unable to free themselves of the gloom that hangs over their home.

It is not until these characters participate in a ritual of exorcism, in which truths are revealed, that they are finally released from the darkness of despair and able to resume their normal lives. The scene unfolds like magic as Blood peels away the Pastor's facade layer by layer, exposing him for the vulture that he is. This transformation is both frightening and amusing, and is contrasted to Acts's automobile suddenly coming to life. Truth releases the family from darkness, and they are able to remove their garments of sorrow, replacing them with outfits symbolic of happier times. They sit in Acts's completed car and it drives them from darkness into light.

The nightmarish quality of *The Mojo and the Sayso* is enhanced by Rahman's use of the "jazz aesthetic." This " . . . aesthetic in drama expresses multiple ideas and experiences through language, movement, visual art and spirituality simultaneously." It "acknowledges the characters' various levels of reality."[1] We recognize this technique immediately in the opening conversation between Awilda and Acts. An idea is introduced just as a jazz musician might introduce a theme, then is abruptly dropped as the author seems to zoom into the mind of a character who speaks what is there, like a jazz improvisation might express what is on the musician's mind.

Rahman grew up in Harlem, where she attended public school. She began writing plays in the sixth grade. She has taught writing at Nassau Community College in New York and is currently teaching in Brown University's graduate creative writing program. She has received fellowships from the New York Foundation for the Arts and from the Rockefeller Foundation. In addition, she is director of the Playwriting Workshop at the New Federal Theatre and cofounder of Blackberry Productions Company. She won the Doris Abramson Playwriting Award for *The Mojo and the Sayso in 1989.* Her other plays include *Lady Day: A Musical Tragedy, Tale of Madam Zora,* a libretto, *Has Anybody Seen Marie Laveau?,* and two one acts, *Transcendental Blues* and *The Lady And The Tramp.* Among her numerous awards Miss Rahman was cited in 1989 by the Rockefeller Foundation for American Playwrights for "proven talent, sustained dedication to work in the theatre and current productivity." Her forthcoming novel, *Illegitimate Life,* stretches across the borders of autobiography, fiction and memoir.

1. Sydne' Mahone, ed., *Moon Marked & Touched By Sun* (New York: Theatre Communication Group, 1994), p. 283.

The Mojo and the Sayso

Author's Note

The Mojo and the Sayso is a story of a family: vulnerable human beings who sustain pain and love, hatreds, fears, joys, sorrows and degradation, and finally triumph.

The production style should serve and illuminate the absurdity, fantasy and magic mayhem that are intrinsic in this script.

Characters

AWILDA
ACTS
BLOOD
PASTOR

Time

Now. Sunday.

Place

The living room of the Benjamins' home.

The Mojo and the Sayso

[for Clifford Glover and all the others . . .]

> *O deliver not the soul of thy turtle-dove unto the multitude of the wicked . . .*
>
> PSALM 74:19

Act 1

Morning. Lights up on the Benjamins' living room. Stage left is a mantlepiece with a collection of various colored candles on it. Center stage, on a slightly raised platform, is a half-built car. Hubcaps, tires, fenders, etc. are scattered around. The rest of the room is neat: it is only the platform area that is disordered. AWILDA, *dressed entirely in white, is frantically searching for something among the mechanical automotive parts. Her voice is heard over the whir of an acetylene torch which* ACTS, *inside the car frame, is using.*

AWILDA *(searching frantically for something very important)* Ball joints, tires, shock absorbers, spark plugs, carburetors.

ACTS The treasures and dreams that's buried in a junkyard!

AWILDA *stares at him unbelievingly for a second then continues her search.*

Damn near tore my paws off trying to get to this baby but I got it. Knowed it was only a few left in the world. Never thought I'd own one but I do now. A Lycomen engine. They used to put it in only the best of machines back in '47. Used to put it in a deluxe car they called the Auborn Cord. It had an electric shift, front-wheel drive same as you got today. Car was so advanced, so ahead of its time they took it off the market. Man this engine was so bad they used to put her in aeroplanes. Now I'm gonna put her right in, Jim!

AWILDA Wrenches. hammers.

ACTS Soon I'll be finished the dream car of my mind.

AWILDA *(reacts to his last words by looking at him and shaking her head: she resumes her search)* Batteries, mufflers, spark coils, piston rings, radiator caps, gaskets, fenders, exhaust pipes. White gloves? No white gloves.

ACTS A chrome-plated masterpiece. Brown and gold-flecked with a classy body . . . built with my own hands.

AWILDA I can't find them.

ACTS' *only response is to continue working.*

I searched and looked and searched and still can't find them. I searched and looked and rummaged all through this mess and I still can't. . . . *(going to the mantelpiece)* Let's see. Orange. A good color for concentration. *(she lights the candle and is immediately soothed)* There. I've lit the way to my white gloves. I'll have them in time to go to church.

ACTS' *only response is to bang with his hammer.*

Pastor Delroy wants all us saints dressed in white. Pure white, from crown to toe.

ACTS What a beautiful engine. They don't come any better.

AWILDA Don't forget this Sunday is special.

ACTS A priceless engine. Tossed away in the junkyard.

AWILDA It happened three years ago today.

ACTS Been looking for this engine for three years.

AWILDA And Pastor is having a special memorial service today for Linus.

ACTS And what do you know? Boom! This morning out of all the hundreds of other mornings. This is the morning I find him.

AWILDA There's gonna be organ music.

ACTS Must be some kind of special sign . . . finding this engine this morning.

AWILDA And flowers. Gladiolas and carnations. Lovely church flowers.

ACTS Now that I got the engine I want, I can finish him. Finish him today. Three years is a long time.

AWILDA Our choir will sing "Sweet Lil' Jesus Boy."

ACTS Soon he'll be purring like a kitten. Soon every nut and bolt will be in place.

AWILDA And the congregation will bow their heads for a moment of silence. And think of Linus.

ACTS Shut up! I see no need to draw attention to the unfortunate by-products of your womb!

AWILDA Our children. What became of our children?

ACTS *(getting up suddenly and leaving the room)* We'll say no more about it. No more!

AWILDA *(hurling these words at his exiting back)* You never talk about anything! Especially not about Linus.

ACTS *(returns, carrying a steering wheel)* That's another thing. He's dead. Let the dead rest. I never mention the boy's name in this house since the funeral but just like a woman you just talk and talk and always call his name.

AWILDA LINUS IS NOT DEAD. I remember him. Every part. I remember his scalp, his bones, his smooth flesh, the bright color of his blood, his white teeth, his boy smell. As long as I remember him, Linus is alive.

ACTS Linus is dead. *(taking her in his arms)* But I'm here.

AWILDA *(pushing him away)* If Linus could run as fast as you did, he could be here too.

ACTS *recoils from her as if she had slapped him.*

AWILDA *(horrified at what has slipped out of her mouth)* "He that is cruel troubleth his own flesh." Book of Proverbs, 29th Chapter, 11th verse. I feel terrible. I hope you can forgive me.

ACTS *(returning to his car)* You know a junkyard is a funny place. Most of the cars are thrown in the scrap heap because of lots of wear and tear. Not because they are worthless. Not worthless at all.

AWILDA Forgive me. It's just that we used to have two boys and now there's only one.

ACTS *only response is the voice of his hammer.*

And that one floats around with a bomb in his heart.

ACTS *continues to pound away.*

While I dream of Linus every night.

ACTS' *hammer continues to be his only response.*

I did it again last night.

ACTS' *hammering begins to accelerate.*

The only way I can remember it is to tell it.

ACTS *continues to hammer away.*

It's always the same dream. Linus is still ten years old but yet he is older than all of us. You and Linus and I are strolling down the avenue. Suddenly, Aretha's voice is all around us. We breathe it in with our bodies. It is like a feeding. When all of a sudden the music changes and the sound of Monk's piano jumps in front of us. The boy and I jump into the chords, leaving our bodies like old clothes.

ACTS *stops working on the car, looks at her as if this is the first time he has ever heard this.*

A-n-d you . . . you steal our bodies and run!

ACTS I do not! I DO NOT!

AWILDA You run and run and run and run! *(in the voice of Linus)* "Daddy, Daddy. Please . . . don't . . . run."

ACTS *(yelling and screaming)* You are such a liar! Look at you with your face twisted like a peach pit. You are such a liar! If lies were brains you'd be smart. If lies were mountaintops you'd be way up. If I wasn't such a calm and gentle man I'd strangle you till you admit that I don't run away. That I rush to your side.

That I put your bodies in mine. I keep telling you that.

AWILDA I know. Maybe I'll get it right tonight.

ACTS If you could only go to sleep thinking, "He could never run away and leave us in danger."

AWILDA But when I'm awake, I tell you that I believe you. Besides, what do you care what I think as long as God knows the truth. Isn't God enough for you?

ACTS HELL NO! I need people. I need you. There are nights when I see myself all the way to my bones. Check out every corner of myself and feel strong about me. But come the morning . . . I look at you and the doubt I see in you makes me guilty.

AWILDA "Heal me O Lord, my bones are vexed. My soul is sore vexed." Clean my thoughts and keep the Devil out of them. I want to believe you. I have to believe you but . . . but . . . just give me another chance. I'll dream it right. I promise I'll wake myself up if I dream it wrong.

ACTS All of us have a dream world. Get in, my lady.

Reluctantly, AWILDA *climbs in the frame of the car and sits. He continues in the manner of a king showing his queen the castle.*

This is where the radio's gonna be. Soon you'll be able to flick the dial to your favorite music. Not none of them Jesus songs, honey. I mean give me a break. You should learn how to drive. Be good for you. Give you something else to think about. You comfortable? I'm gonna cover the seats with something soft. Mink maybe. Just for you. Gonna put a bar in the back. You can keep your ginger ale in there. If you want. Here we go sweetcakes. Past Jamaica Avenue. Mmmmmmm. Smell the air. Someone's barbecuing. On. Here we go. We're cruising up past Kissena Boulevard, down Sunset, past Jamaica Avenue. Mmmmmmmmm. Smell the air. Someone's barbecuing. Look at those old wooden frame houses next to the tall apartment buildings. See the churches. See the ladies in they pinks and yellows and whites and blues. See the folks hanging out. See them turn they heads as we go riding by. Whew! Hot, isn't it? Let's get a couple of beers and drive out to the beach, take off our clothes and lay in the sun—

AWILDA *(standing up, breaking the spell)* I'm late for church.

ACTS Shh. Don't be scared. Don't be nervous. You with me now. Sit back down!

AWILDA *(sitting down)* I can't help it.

ACTS I know. I know. Just get it together. Listen, don't you hear what people are saying? They are saying, "There goes the wizard of the automobile world. Acts Benjamin and his wife. See that car he's driving? He only builds them for the leading citizens of the world." *(sees* AWILDA *getting up and tries to pull her back)* Hey, where are you going? We're almost there. I'll park the car and we can lay in the sun—

AWILDA I want to get out. I need my white gloves! I'm late for church!

ACTS It's folks like you that give religion a bad name.

AWILDA *(escaping from the car)* Now you listen to me. I'd rather do what God tells me than listen to you. *(resuming her search for gloves)* All you do is rummage through junkyards, bringing scrap that been thrown away right here, in our living room, working on the car, in our living room, every hour, day or night, winter or summer, snowstorm or heat wave, in our living room!

ACTS That's just why I want it in the house—so that the weather don't matter.

AWILDA All the time, whacking, banging, drilling on that . . . that . . .

ACTS Car . . . it's a car. I've told you two hundred times before. Don't call my car out of its name. Please . . . don't . . . badmouth . . . my . . . car . . . !

AWILDA All the time working on that car. Something I always wanted to ask you. Tell me. Just what do you get out of it? What do you see in it?

ACTS Anything I want to.

AWILDA Just tell me what.

ACTS I'm glad you finally asked. When I look at this car I see lots of things.

AWILDA What things?

ACTS I see understanding. No worries. I see tittie-squeezing and pussy-teasing.

AWILDA It's no wonder that I turned to Christ.

ACTS No wonder.

AWILDA Pastor says that you . . .

ACTS If I didn't have firsthand personal knowledge that Jesus done locked your thighs and thrown the key away, that religion done stole your natural feelings. I'd be 'clined to think that you and that jackleg son of a bi—

AWILDA *(with religious fervor)* Jealous. That's what you are. Just plain jealous. Imagine being jealous of God. That's why you badmouth the messengers of God's word every chance you get. I used to have a hard heart like you till Pastor saved me. One day I was listening to him preach, my breath grew short, my throat closed up and I couldn't breathe. It was Pastor Delroy I was looking at but Jesus that I was seeing. "Lord," I said. "Lord, I am in your hands.

Her fervor has aroused ACTS. *He goes towards her and seriously tries to possess her.* AWILDA *struggles hard.*

ACTS I was once into that holiness bag and I know that trick. All them jackleg pastors and deacons and elders laughing at you and taking your money. All you women jumping up and down yelling, "Come sweet Jesus" need to stay home and say it to your husbands!

AWILDA You ain't nothing but the Devil!

ACTS *(suddenly disgusted, walks away from her, laughing harshly)* Forget about the Devil. Forget about the sign of the Cross. It is the sign of power *(holds up a dollar bill)* and the sign of the trick *(holds up a pair of soiled white gloves in the other hand)* that counts.

AWILDA You! You had them all the time.

ACTS *(returning to work on his car)* Maybe.

AWILDA *(snatching up the white gloves)* These white gloves are genuine brushed cotton. The other day I was downtown window-shopping, thinking about what I would wear in church today and suddenly I found myself in Bonwit's. I don't know how I got there. It was like my feet had grown a mind of they own. I wanted to turn around and run but something made me brazen it out. So I marched to the glove counter and stood there. Four detectives followed me. The salesgirl left the blue-haired, silver-foxed madame she was waiting on and rushed over to me. "Can I help you, Miss," she said. Imagine that. "Miss" to me though I am a married woman and had—at one time—two children. Then I told her, "I'm not a Miss. I'm a Mrs., and I'd like a pair of white gloves." "They start at fifty dollars, Miss," she snapped. And then I took my time and made her show me lace gloves, net gloves, nylon gloves, leather gloves, and I didn't like any of them until she showed me these. The most expensive ones and I said, "Oh, aren't they lovely. I'll take them." And so after all that aggravation I don't see why you would hide them from me unless you wanted to make me late for church and keep me here with you.

ACTS *(working on the car)* I'm getting kinda hungry, woman.

AWILDA Sure. What would you like. Spark plugs? Machine oil? Gasoline? *(*ACTS *ignores her)* I really think sometimes that you are turning into that car.

ACTS Honk honk!

AWILDA You could come with me if you wanted to. You could get dressed and come with me to church.

ACTS Don't get started on that again. Please.

AWILDA *(going toward the windows)* I'm opening up all the windows.

ACTS *(preoccupied)* Yeah, yeah, yeah, yeah.

AWILDA Every night I lay out your striped blue suit and your Van Heusen shirt with the rolled collar and your diamond stickpin and your patent-leather wing tips and your ribbed silk socks and your monogrammed hand-embroidered linen pocket handkerchief hoping that you will come to church with me.

ACTS Me? I keep telling you. I don't go for that bull. Besides, your beloved Pastor is there. You don't need me.

AWILDA Need? I need you to talk to me. What happened that night. . . .Tell me that. That's what I need.

Silence. ACTS *works on the car.*

See that? All the trouble we went through was for God but all you think about is that car. You can build me a Rolls Royce and say it's mine but it ain't. It's God's car.

The sound of ACTS *working is his only response.*

Mr. Benjamin. I'm a God-fearing woman and I'm opening all these windows wide so that He can come in here and fill your heart.

ACTS *(looking up from his car)* Stay away from the windows.

AWILDA *(running around, opening up windows)* Get him God. Get him God. Come in. Come in. Stab his soul. Pierce his stubborn heart!

ACTS *(enraged, runs around slamming windows)* Shutupshutup-shutup. Goddammit! *(he smashes all the windows with a tool)*

AWILDA *(singing at the top of her voice)*

I knit my world
With strong church yarn
With stitches even and unbroken
For God is my true husband
Who keeps me from harm
He is my only one.

As ACTS *finishes breaking the windows, they gaze at each other silently. The maniacal peal of church bells rushes through the broken windows.* AWILDA *goes over to the mantelpiece, fighting tears, tries to light a candle but the wind from the broken windows keeps extinguishing it.*

AWILDA Blue is for peace.

ACTS *stands there gazing at the broken glass.*

I . . . we . . . need a blue candle.

ACTS *(looking at the broken windows and glass)* I'll clean it up later. I'm going to finish that car tonight. *(returns to car)*

AWILDA We've got to take care of one another. Keep healthy. There's no one else to look after us. *(begins a frantic search for something)* Where is it? I know I put it here.

ACTS Where is what? You got the white gloves, don't you?

AWILDA YOU KNOW what I'm looking for.

ACTS I don't have anything to do with it. Ever since it come in the mail yesterday. I give it to you.

AWILDA I couldn't look at it. But I remember. I put it right here.

ACTS Then that's where it should be.

AWILDA It's not.

ACTS It should be right where you put it.

AWILDA It isn't.

ACTS Look. If it can't walk, if it ain't got legs of it own, then it's gotta be where you put it.

AWILDA *(discovering a check)* Aha! Here it is. And I didn't put it there. Why do you keep doing that?

ACTS What? Doing what?

AWILDA The check. Putting it near my candles. This is the second time I've moved it away from here.

ACTS I don't. I didn't.

AWILDA Then how did it get here next to my candles?

ACTS Don't ask me.

AWILDA *(gingerly taking up check and looking at it)* UGH. I hate to touch it. It feels . . . funny. It's got an awful smell too. It must be the paper they use nowadays to print these things. "Payment for Wrongful Death." Big digits. Now we got lots of money. Lots of money for the life of our boy. How do they figger? How do they know? How do they add up what a ten-year-old boy's life is worth to his parents? Maybe they have a chart or something. Probably feed it into a computer. Bzzzz. "One scrawny brown working-class boy. Enter. No wealthy relatives. Size 4 shoe. A chance of becoming rich in his lifetime if he plays Lotto regularly." How many dollars? How many cents? Do they know about the time I found out I was pregnant with him? My absolute joy that God has sent me this child. True. I already had Walter but that was before you. But you loved us anyhow and soon Linus was growing inside of me because we were in love. Yes, there was never enough money and we were always struggling but that's just the way life is. We knew we were supposed to have this baby. You took me to your mother and father and sisters and all your sisters, brothers, aunts and uncles. Your whole tribe. You told them. "This is my woman and she's going to have our child." They all hugged and kissed me. Do they know about the way you would put your head on my stomach and listen? Did they figger in the way you held my hand with tears in your eyes when I was in labor? When he was born the grandparents, aunts, uncles, neighbors and friends brought presents, ate and drank and danced and sang. Do they know about those moments? Did they add them in here? And what about Linus himself? He would make me throw out all my mean, petty, selfish parts and give him the best person I could be. Remember when he was good? Remember when he was bad? The times he was like us yet someone brand-new? And . . . what . . . about . . . what . . . he . . . might . . . have . . . been? How do they figger? How do they know?

ACTS Evil. Blood money. Payoff. Hush money. . . . Do what you want with it and don't tell me.

AWILDA No one could fault you if you put it in the bank or started your own something with it. Every worldly person has got some fantasy.

ACTS *glares angrily at her but doesn't answer.*

I understand. If you would only talk about that night. Tell someone what really happened. Somebody. Anybody. Especially me. (ACTS *continues to remain silent)* One thing for sure. It ain't ordinary money and I won't buy a car or a house or store up riches like a vain, greedy sinner.

ACTS: *(barely audible)* I tried to protect him.

AWILDA *(does not hear* ACTS *and continues)* I thought Walter would have taken over after Linus. Look after everything. Look after us. . . . After "the accident" I put all my hopes on Walter. He was always making something. He was smart! He was kind! He was tender! You remember?

ACTS *holds her.*

Now he's got a grenade for a soul. Guns. Knives. Before the "accident" there wasn't a mean bone in his body. He loved everybody. Everybody loved him. He used to sing and dance and laugh all the time. You remember?

ACTS Go to church. I think a storm is coming.

AWILDA: *(holding her arms as if cradling a child, singing a lullaby)*

> Go to sleep my little son.
> Snow is falling on the sun.
> Trees run blood and sidewalks grow
> Guns besides a dead boy child!

(suddenly walking away from ACTS*)* Don't worry about a storm. The sun will light my path all the way to church. When I get there I will just pay attention to the songs and sermons, the music and words, voices, faces and feelings that keep me going. I guess I just believe in spiritual things. Spiritual things is all.

ACTS Better go. It's getting late.

AWILDA: *(whirling around dervishlike in her agony)* Then you stop time. I want you to stop it. Stop . . . time . . . now. Turn time back in its track. Make time go back to when Linus was alive. Make time go back to when Walter was tender. He was gentle. He wouldn't hurt anybody. Turn back time! Stop! Time! Stop!

During AWILDA'*s monologue,* BLOOD *has stuck his face through one of the broken windows. While she is still speaking, he surreptitiously climbs through the window, registering fear and confusion.*

BLOOD *(at first in the voice of a terrified little child)* Mommy? Daddy? What's wrong? What happened? You aren't hurt are you? O GOD! MA? POPS? *(guns drawn, searching for imagined invaders)* ALL RIGHT. WHOEVER YOU ARE I KNOW YOU ARE HIDING IN THIS HOUSE. I KNOW YOU ARE HERE SOMEWHERE IN HERE. THROW OUT YOUR WEAPONS. GIVE YOURSELF UP. 'CAUSE I CAN BOMB YOU, SHOOT YOU OR CUT YOU. I DONE WARNED I AIN'T NO PUNK YOU DEALING WITH. THIS IS ME. BLOOD! *(he stalks around the room, searching for enemies)* Come on out. YA STUPID PUNK BASTIDS. I GOT YA COVERED FROM EVERY ANGLE. I WANT YOU ALIVE BUT I HAVE ENUF TO BLAST YA OUT! BETTER COME ON OUT NOW 'CAUSE YOU FOOLING WITH A MAN WHO IS NOT AFRAID OF DEATH!

ACTS FUCK YOU! This is our home. Put that gun down!

AWILDA This is our home!

BLOOD *(continuing his search)* I'LL BREAK YOUR NECKS. I'LL SMASH YOUR HEADS! I'LL BREAK YOUR BACKS!

AWILDA Walter! *(to* ACTS*)* Look at him! Imagine being afraid of my own son!

BLOOD It's okay Ma. Don't be afraid. COME ON OUT, GUYS. YOU DON'T HAVE A CHANCE!

ACTS Give . . . me . . . the . . . gun, Walter.

BLOOD GIVE IT UP! COME ON OUT! IT'S ALL OVER. I'LL BUST YOUR HEADS!

AWILDA A killer ain't a pretty sight.

BLOOD SHOW YOURSELVES NOW. HOW MANY OF THEM DID YOU SAY THERE ARE, POPS?

ACTS There's nobody in the house but us, punk, so . . . give . . . me . . . the gun!

BLOOD I'LL BLOW UP EVERY CORNER OF THIS HOUSE TILL THEY COME OUT WITH THEIR HANDS UP!

ACTS *has sneaked behind* BLOOD. *He knocks him down and gets the gun.*

ACTS *(pressing the gun right to* BLOOD'*s head)* You want to play crazy? I'll show you how! This is the lowdownest trick you've pulled yet. This tops all!

BLOOD You just can't sneak up from behind, knock me on the floor and take my piece.

ACTS I can't?

BLOOD You'd better give it back to me before I get mad.

ACTS You will?

AWILDA *(To* BLOOD *in a soft, terrified voice; she keeps on repeating the words underneath the following dialogue)* Don't run don't shoot don't run don't shoot don't run don't shoot.

ACTS *(touches* AWILDA *to reassure her)* Will snookums get sooo maddy mad and doo-doo all over hims diapers? SHITFACE. YA FUCKING DUMB-ASS KID.

BLOOD I'M NOT A KID. I'M A MAN.

ACTS Didn't I tell you to keep your behind parts away from here till you could stop acting like a hysterical female. Like a lady on the ra—

BLOOD I'M NO LADY, MISTER. I'M A MAN!

ACTS *(keeping the gun aimed at his head)* Then stand up . . . M-A-N.

BLOOD Why you putting that pistol at me? I'm your son.

ACTS Get up!

BLOOD *(getting up)* Listen to me. Quit pointing it at me. It's loaded. You never listen.

ACTS You busted into my house with a loaded gun and you want me to listen. Go ahead. Talk!

BLOOD I . . . I . . . just came to say goodbye.

ACTS *(pressing the gun right up against* BLOOD'*s temple)* Damn right you gonna say "goodbye."

Blood Easy. It's loaded. Let me explain.

ACTS Speak, liar.

BLOOD When I opened my eyes this morning I got that old feeling again. As I lay in my room, on my bed, I could see Lunus's blood on every street. The chalk outline of his body on every corner. I could see his brown leather jacket and his baseball cap tipped to the side. Once again this city was getting to me. I had to split. As I was coming down the street, walking to this house, I practiced saying goodbye. I knew you would be working on the car and when I told you I was leaving again you would grunt but not look at me. Mom would light a candle for me and look at me, accusing me, but not saying anything. As I come near the house I sense something isn't right. I creep up on the porch, afraid of my own eyes. Windows are busted. I hear Mom's voice. What's she saying? Sounds like crying. You are standing. Just standing in a river of broken glass. Staring. Staring out a busted window. What am I supposed to think? I stare in, thinking, "Don't worry Pops. Your son's here. I'll protect you."

ACTS Well, well, well. You protect me? What we have here is mighty Robin Hood. All you need is your pointed, upturned ballet slippers and your green tights!

BLOOD It's the truth.

ACTS You're a liar and this *(indicating gun)* is a lie.

BLOOD *just shakes his head from side to side.*

Never play with guns. Even if they aren't loaded. Didn't I always teach you that?

BLOOD You wanna kill me Pops? It's loaded.

ACTS Liar!

BLOOD Believe me. It is.

ACTS *pulls the trigger. It clicks empty. He looks at* BLOOD *with disgust and throws the empty gun at his feet.*

ACTS Get that thing away from around me!

BLOOD *(pleadingly)* So it wasn't loaded. Aren't you the one that always says, "Attitude is everything, Son"?

ACTS A bellowing bull never gets fat.

BLOOD *(walking and talking like a tough-guy gangster type)* You gotta be hard. Tough. Cold. Ice. Steel. Woof or be woofed at. Take no shit. Play with death. Learn to gamble. Learn to win. Learn to kill.

AWILDA Your brother wouldn't like to see you act this way. Especially today. Have some respect. I thought you were going to kill us.

BLOOD You afraid of me? O my God, Mom. I could never hurt you.

AWILDA *(begins to sweep the broken glass)* I mean there's all kinds of other ways to enter a house. You could have knocked on the door. Rang the bell . . . come through the front door. . . . A lot of other ways.

BLOOD I'm sorry.

AWILDA I remember the time you smashed the blue Mercury into the plate-glass window of Mr. Johnny's barbershop. Your father straightened out the motor bed, plugged the holes in the radiator, hammered out some of the dents and folds in the fender and taped a new light onto its front. It was one of the few times you helped him. Linus was always working on cars with him but you hardly did. You were different.

BLOOD *(taking broom from* AWILDA*)* You shouldn't do that. I'll do it.

AWILDA *(exiting)* Pastor's waiting for me. I'm late for church.

BLOOD *(goes over to* ACTS*)* Isn't there anything you can do?

ACTS *(working on the car)* Do? About what?

BLOOD Can't you get her away from that holy hustler? Can't you stop her from always going crosstown to his so-called "church"?

ACTS I tried, Walter.

BLOOD I keep telling you the name is "Blood."

Almost unconsciously, without being told, BLOOD *begins to hand* ACTS *tools that he needs. They pass the tools between them like a surgical team during the following monologue.*

ACTS I know why you doing all this. I know. I know why you so set to hurt me. It's your doubt about that night. Something you can never bring yourself to tell me. But the thought is always in you. I see it. I catch you looking at me wondering . . . and then turning away when I look at you. You think what people say about that night is true. I knew that soon as you went and changed your name. That wasn't right. You and I was real tight. Closer than father and son. We was Ace Boon Coons. 'Member the time I made a deluxe racer for you out of a rusty bicycle frame I found in the yard? We had a lot of nice years together before. . . . Why you wanna go and call yourself "Blood" when you got a perfectly good name like Walter Acts Benjamin the Second? There's a lot that goes into a name and you shouldn't just go and call yourself something else. A name belongs in a family. It was passed down to me and I take it and give it to you even though you ain't my flesh and blood directly. And you take it and throw it away. You shouldn't do that. I remember the first time I heard how good things were in New York. I decided to see for myself. I wasn't used to the cold and almost went back home but after a while I decided to stay. The first job I had in the city was driving a cab. Then I carted coal for a couple of years. After that I worked as a long-shoreman when I could. Then I went to work for a man named Quinn at the wrecking yard on Springfield Boulevard. And I worked many years as a garage handyman hoping one day to achieve the title of mechanic. I went near crazy from being alone until I met you and your ma. I first saw her in a little restaurant on South Road. The Silver Fly. I had to have her. We stayed up late talking and laughing. Soon we got married because after all that aloneness I been through she was having a kid for me. A baby with my eyes, my nose, my mouth and my name. Now I'm telling you straight, boy, what happened to your brother is done. I can't change it. Your mother can't change it and God won't. You ain't no different from any other person that something terrible has happened to. Don't let what happened to Linus madden or cheapen you. I bear a lot of pain but I bear it with expression. Just who in the hell do you think you are?

BLOOD *(walks away from him)* Who am I? I want to be a righteous gunman like George Jackson. Or his brother, Jonathan. I would have liked to walk in the courtroom where they acquitted the cop that shot my brother in the back with my guns drawn and announce, "All right, gentlemen, I'm taking over." Just like Jonathan did. Alone and armed. Righteous and tough. Beyond fear. He knew his fate and did not hesitate. A man evolved to the highest level. Now they mighta shot some bullets into Jonathan Jackson's brain that day but he ain't dead. I got to be him 'cause I sure ain't me. I should be the kind of man that pours down hot revenge on his enemies because I had a brother, once. A kid brother. Sometimes he used to pee in the bed. A scrawny, ash-brown kid, ninety-four pounds, about this high. He was always beating up on little girls 'cause he liked them. Used to be afraid of being weak and afraid. We used to arm-wrestle all the time and I'd let him win and then show him how I could beat him anytime I wanted to. He looked up to me and I liked that.

ACTS Tell you what. "Blood" or whatever you call yourself. We got some money now. Plenty of it with that "wrongful death" check from the city that come yesterday. Ask your mother for some. You'd be able to go anyplace.

BLOOD I don't want any of that money. I can get all kinds of bread.

ACTS Yeah?

BLOOD Yeah.

ACTS You called me on the phone and asked me for money, I remember.

BLOOD That was a long time ago.

ACTS When you gonna pay me back?

BLOOD Soon.

ACTS You need money. Ask your mother.

BLOOD You think I want to stand here and argue with you about that filthy blood money? I know the price we've all paid for it.

ACTS You sure you don't want to come sneaking up on us and knife us in the back?

BLOOD That's not funny, Pops. I hate that money much as you. It's no treasure. It's no pot of gold after the rainbow.

AWILDA *starts to enter and stops. Audience sees her standing and listening.* BLOOD *and* ACTS *are unaware of her presence.*

ACTS Money, money, money. It's the story of our lives. "Learn how to make you a dollar, boy. Earn some spending change and keep you some folding money and don't let anybody take your money from you," I used to preach to Linus. So he would get up every Saturday and go to the yard with me before dawn. That's when they shot him. Right before daybreak. And though everybody knew the truth, they said Police Officer Rhea was only doing his duty.

BLOOD In school he would tear up his work in a rage if he got a bad mark. At home, he was our mother's favorite child and I knew it. When he discovered he had a joint he used to go around touching it, looking at it, airing it out, seeing how far he could pee with it. What a little brat!

AWILDA *(entering the room, concentrating on her white-gloved hands)* Pastor said Linus would have turned out to be somebody. Somebody big. You know what Pastor says. Pastor says we should give Linus a special memorial. Something unusual and unselfish. That's what Pastor says.

Lights start to dim as AWILDA *continues to turn her hands inside out, stretching her arms toward the sky as if she were dancing.*

Ever notice how when you wash white gloves just one time all the life seems to go out of them? Suddenly they are old. Like faded bits of sunlight. Can you tell these are not fresh, pure, unwashed white gloves that I'm wearing to church this morning?

ACT 2

Scene 1

Evening. New windowpanes. Everything has been cleaned. BLOOD *is repairing the last window.* ACTS *is underneath his car, working.*

BLOOD *(talk-singing to himself as he hammers a nail in place and plays an imagined guitar)*:

And I said to myself
'Cause I'm always talking to me,
"Self," said I,
"We all must die
And darkness will soon surround us."

"Ohhhhhhhh NO!" self hollered.
"I don't want to be dead
Me, I ain't never gonna die
Gonna buy a car,
Gonna drive it far,
Gonna drive away from me, myself and I."

(steps back and surveys his work) Shall I paint them, stain them or what?

ACTS *(preoccupied)* Mmmmm. Yeah. Okay . . .

BLOOD Which one?

ACTS Whatever. Valves are slightly worn but that's light stuff.

BLOOD *(angrily)* How would you like the windows done up in red? Red paint?

ACTS Wrist pins and connecting rod bearings are in good condition.

BLOOD It must be hard on Mom.

ACTS She'll be glad you fixed them. Low oil consumption. This baby is practically brand-new.

BLOOD I'm not talking 'bout the windows. I mean her. My mother and your wife.

ACTS What about her? The flywheel is okay too. Hotdammit! It's gonna be something else when I finish.

BLOOD Nothing else matters to you. That's gotta be hard on her.

ACTS S'no difference between a car and a woman. Cool 'em. Ignite 'em. Give 'em plenty of lubrication. Keep their engine in good condition.

BLOOD *(as he speaks he writes red graffiti on the new windowpanes)* I had a woman once. She worked at the express counter in the supermarket. I used to make seven, eight shopping trips a day just to walk through her line. Every time she saw me she smiled and I was sure she really loved me. Whenever she asked me if I wanted a single or double bag I knew she was really pledging her love. And all those times I replied, "Single bag, thank you" I was really asking her to let me drink her bathwater.

Although I never knew her name, we were very happy. All over the city I drew red hearts for her. No clean space went unmarked. I even added some of my blood to the red paint. When I pricked all my fingers and toes I started on my knuckles and ankles. It hurt like hell!

One time I stayed up all night making hearts for her. Next morning I ran to our supermarket and got on her line. Some man was with her making her laugh. She didn't even know that I was there. I just stood there looking at her. I screamed at her silently, "You love him and not me. You want his low voice, his strong chest and his big thighs. Why can't you want me?" I was very angry.

ACTS *(surveying the windowpanes without ever stopping his work)* I know what you trying to do but it won't work. You striving to prevent me from getting my work done. You hate this car. You trying to keep it from being born. Now you can act a fool if you want but just don't get in my way.

BLOOD *(resignedly looking over the car)* It's state-of-the-art all right.

ACTS Damn straight.

BLOOD You sure ain't no "pliers-and-screwdriver" mechanic.

ACTS Never was. Never will be.

BLOOD *takes out a gleaming knife with a feather stuck in its handle and plays with it.*

What . . . is . . . that?

BLOOD It's a knife, man.

ACTS For what?

BLOOD *slowly takes out an orange and begins slowly to peel it as he looks at the car.*

BLOOD For peeling things. I like to peel things. Just like to see if with one slow continuous steady movement I can take the skin off anything in one, long, thin, graceful, piece.

ACTS Hope you can handle a knife better than you can a gun.

BLOOD I can do a lot of things. *(holding up the entire orange peel in one piece)*

ACTS What about important things? You remember the first time I put you underneath a car?

BLOOD No. I don't remember.

ACTS You need to kneel down beside me again and take another look. Give you a different perspective when you laying on your back flat out, looking up inside the belly of a car.

BLOOD No thanks. All you do is wake up thinking about your car and sleep dreaming about it. No thank you. What about me? You never really talk to me. And when you talk you never really say anything.

ACTS Okay, you been after me all this time so I'm gonna talk. Gonna tell you something. So listen real good.

As ACTS *speaks* BLOOD *keeps peeling, letting the peelings and fruit pile up on the floor. Every once in a while he seems to nick himself accidentally.*

In this world, in order to survive, you gotta have a little gris-gris to depend on. It could be anything. A prayer, a saying, a rabbit foot, a horseshoe, a song. A way of looking at life, a way of doing things, a way of understanding the world you find yourself in. Something that will never fail to pull you through the hard times. Now I see you got no formula for survival, no magic, no juju, so let me give you a very important piece of mojo right now. Always remember that the secret of a car is its engine. The engine is the car's heart. Treat it right and you can trust it. The trick is you gotta take your time and learn it. Study it inside out. Most folks abuse the engine by racing it when it's cold. How would you like to be waked up in the morning by someone shouting and screaming at you while you're still yawning and under the covers? You couldn't respond even if you wanted to. It takes time to fully warm up. And you gotta give it good fuel.

Then you gotta inspire it. Set it on fire. Ignite the bad boy. Then he's gotta be stroked and lubricated real good. Now don't forget there's plenty of fire and heat inside so you gotta cool him off, too. Learn the engine, boy. Understand the heart. It's the secret of life.

BLOOD Is that all you can talk about? Cars? Is that all?

ACTS Fool! Is that all you think I'm talking about? *(he grimaces in sudden pain)*

BLOOD What is it . . . what's wrong?

ACTS *(a gesture of weariness)* Nothing. I ache all over.

BLOOD What do you expect, hunched over that car all day and night? A good massage will fix you up. *(he begins to massage* ACTS' *shoulders, gently at first and then with increasing violence)*

ACTS Ahhhhhh. That feels good. Ouch. Not so rough.

A look passes between BLOOD *and* ACTS *which establishes the element of distrust between them.*

BLOOD *(continuing the massage)* Is this where the pain is? *(gives him a powerful whack on his shoulders)*

ACTS *(trying unsuccessfully to move away from him)* No! Get away from me.

BLOOD *(trying to continue massage)* Be still.

ACTS Kinda rough there, aren't you, "Blood"?

BLOOD *(poking* ACTS*)* Is the pain here? Or there?

ACTS Let me go! Ouch! Ow!

Another look passes between them.

BLOOD Oh, I'm sorry, man.

ACTS Walter, don't you know when you're hurting someone?

BLOOD I'm not sure what you want, Dad.

ACTS I want you to stop, Son.

BLOOD *(gives* ACTS *a final, painful shoulder jab)* There! Doesn't that feel better?

ACTS Holy shit. What the hell is going on here?

BLOOD Every movement, every touch means something. *(suddenly releasing* ACTS *and running toward the car)*

ACTS Get back. Don't touch it. Keep away.

BLOOD It's a beautiful car. Just beautiful. *(he begins to disarrange various parts of the car)*

ACTS That's not it! That's not it at all! Get away from the damn thing. Stand back. *(pushing* BLOOD *away from the car)* Just look at it and don't touch a damn thing.

BLOOD *stands for several beats, looking at the car. He holds his hands together as if in prayer. Then he suddenly begins to pick up the peelings and fruit from the floor and carries them to* AWILDA's *candles on the mantelpiece, where he spreads them while mumbling in a strange language.* ACTS *watches him, fascinated.*

BLOOD It's a ritual.

ACTS Ritual?

BLOOD Yes. For your forgiveness.

ACTS Mine?

BLOOD Yes.

ACTS Why?

BLOOD *(searching)* Because . . . because . . . you broke the windows! WHY DID YOU BREAK THEM?

ACTS That was because your mother started on me about her "Pastor." I went off. The ground parted. Quick flashes of lightning stabbed at my head. My blood boiled.

BLOOD I know the feeling.

ACTS Be careful. It's in our blood.

BLOOD What's it called?

ACTS It ain't a disease. It's a condition. A condition I tell you. All of us are thinking about one thing. A boy brought up in the city and killed by wild dogs. *(returning to his car)* But when I am working on this car I don't feel a thing. I feel clean. I feel strong. I feel free.

BLOOD I feel like shit!

ACTS Get away from your mother's candles.

BLOOD My mother! What do you care about her?

ACTS I do. A lot. But she's with her "Pastor" now.

BLOOD *(exploding, violently blowing out candles)* Shit on her Pastor! *(blows out more candles)* I hate Sunday con men! *(blows out the last candles)* And their wicked trickerations!

ACTS Don't do that! What gives you the right?

BLOOD Pops, let's leave here. Let's not stay here. We should just take that money and run. You and me and Mom should get outta this place. Make a new start.

ACTS Oh yeah? Where, for instance?

BLOOD Let's go to Mexico.

ACTS Mexico? What they got down there for me besides refried beans and the worthless peso?

BLOOD You could get land cheap down there. In less than ten years it's worth three times what you paid. You could build cars down there. I know a special spot down there. A city in the mountains.

ACTS That's your world. My world is right here. A world where all the cars that my mind can conjure up is brought to life.

BLOOD Forget it man.

ACTS So . . . you liked it down in Mexico?

BLOOD I didn't get in trouble with the police if that's what you mean.

ACTS Then why did you come back this time?

BLOOD We're family. We're chained together.

ACTS Then why are you leaving?

BLOOD I can't stay here. Do you know what it means to be the surviving brother? You never talk about the morning that Linus was killed. You were with him when he got killed but you don't tell what really happened.

ACTS You know Walter, you'll be okay once you get yourself together. Take care of your own self. You need to get a mojo and don't worry about me none. The right mojo will give you the sayso. Put you in the driver's seat. The right mojo will take you over those moments of terror, doubt or even surprise. Nothing surprises me no more. I'm ready to take it all on.

At this moment we hear the singing, talking and laughing voices of AWILDA *and* PASTOR DELROY *offstage. Blackout.*

Scene 2

The stage slowly lights up as AWILDA *and* PASTOR DELROY *enter the room, still singing.* AWILDA, *radiant and nervous as a young girl on a date, is carrying a bouquet of multicolored gladioli. The* PASTOR *wears a clerical collar, robe and white gloves.*

AWILDA Mr. Benjamin! Walter! You two, we have special company. Oh Pastor, what a voice you have. Deep and rich and full like a . . . a . . . man! You could have been a singer with millions of fans instead of a man of God. In church I can hear your voice over all the others. *(to* WALTER *and* ACTS*)* What a lovely service. You two should have been there. Going to church is like going to a garden where beautiful music grows. And the beautiful carnations and gladiolas on the altar. I brought some home because church flowers are special.

PASTOR Brothers Benjamin, senior and junior. Peace and love. Our lovely sister Awilda asked me to stop by.

ACTS Oh yeah?

PASTOR I see you are still working on your car? Imagine that. Looks like you'll even be finished soon. *(makes a gesture to touch the car)*

ACTS *(ferociously)* Don't touch him.

PASTOR *(backing away, frightened)* Brother Acts. I've always felt that you fear me. There is no need to. Don't you know that "He that feareth is not made perfect in love"?

ACTS Don't you know that he that fucketh around with my car will be made perfect in death?

PASTOR Brother Benjamin, you can't mean that I'm not welcome here?

ACTS You never had any trouble feeling comfortable before. The wife seems to fry chicken just the way you like it.

PASTOR You don't expect me to refuse the gracious invitations of the lovely saints of my congregation, do you?

ACTS I have a line in my mind that divides the killer beast from the gentle man. Be careful. You are stepping awfully near the edge.

AWILDA There's something wrong in here. I felt it as soon as I walked in. New windows? All written over in red paint, AND WHAT IS THIS SHIT AROUND MY CANDLES? Who blew them out? What the Devil is going on around here now?

BLOOD *(going toward her, trying to calm her)* Easy Ma, let me explain.

AWILDA *(shrinking back from him)* That's all right. I should have known. Every time you're around I never know what is going to happen.

BLOOD I'll . . . I'll scrub the paint off . . . before I split.

AWILDA No! Don't leave. Today is Linus's anniversary.

BLOOD LINUS IS DEAD!

AWILDA *is lighting all the candles as if to revive him.*

PASTOR Sister, do not despair. Linus is near us, though unseen. His spirit depends on us to remember him in special ways.

ACTS Back off, Delroy! You are stepping on my line.

PASTOR I feel Linus nearer and nearer. Sometimes I can see him. I can see him standing large as life in front of me. He never looks at me. He's just there.

BLOOD *(to* AWILDA*)* Can't you see it's just an act?

PASTOR I tell you sister, there is no death. "The stars go down to rise upon some fairer shore. And bright in heaven's jeweled crown they shine, forevermore!"

ACTS *(grabbing him)* You have just crossed the equator. Get the hell out!

AWILDA Pastor should be here.

BLOOD I'm sorry about the windows. I was only trying to communicate with my father.

AWILDA I wanted Pastor here when I told you about the money.

PASTOR Amen.

ACTS What . . . about . . . the . . . money?

AWILDA Linus is getting a memorial.

PASTOR Praise Him!

BLOOD It's a damn shame.

AWILDA What are you saying?

BLOOD It's a damn shame that I'm alive and Linus isn't.

PASTOR I tell you all that Linus is alive and we must remember him.

ACTS We need to be alone right now, Delroy.

AWILDA No.

PASTOR *(seductively)* Awilda.

ACTS Awilda,. Awilda, now you listen. I been thinking. This car is gonna be finished soon. Then we gonna leave. All of us. We gonna slip out easy like a soft wind. When folks catch on that ain't nobody in this house anymore you know what they gonna do? They gonna break in and I leave everything to all of them. My rubber galoshes, my old brown leather longshoremen's jacket with the lamb's-wool lining, my checkerboard, my dream-books, my fishing poles—I'll get new ones—my Gene Ammons' seventy-eights and my tools. Let them take my acetylene torch, cutters, dollies and hammers, my balancers and hydraulic pressers, my reamers, hones and wrenchers, my gauges and gappers, and place them in the middle of Springfield Boulevard and burn them! Any second, this car will be finished and we'll all get in. I want you to put on the blue dress you was wearing at the Silver Fly that day I first seen you. And Walter's gonna wear his Mexican shirt. The car radio's gonna be on. The dial will be set. Chuck Berry, Ivory Joe Hunter and Nat King Cole will be bluesing around. Little Esther is wanting a "Sunday Kind of Love." Jimmy Garrison is on bass. Max is on drums. Monk is on piano. The Orioles. The Moonglows. Little Willie John and Aretha. All the sounds of all the ages coming together in my car.

AWILDA I remember how I used to love driving with you, listening to music, feeling the wind against my cheeks.

PASTOR Seek ye not the vain pleasures of this world, sister. Remember Linus.

AWILDA Ever since the money came I been thinking. We need something money can't buy. That's why I . . . I . . .

PASTOR You want me to hold your hand while you tell them?

AWILDA No.

PASTOR You want me to tell them for you?

AWILDA No.

PASTOR All right, then tell them!

AWILDA I'm giving the money to Pastor's church in Linus's name.

PASTOR Amen.

ACTS *begins a slow, dangerous laugh.*

There is no greater memorial.

ACTS *lunges at* PASTOR *and narrowly misses him.*

(remaining calm as he sidesteps ACTS *and speaks in a soft, sanctimonious voice, full of righteous piety)* "He delivereth me from my enemies. Yea, from those that rise up against me. Verily I say unto you, 'He delivereth me from the violent man.'" My poor, sinful brethren. You are consumed with hypocrisy and greed. "And the greedy man shall retch up his desire for it is an unclean thing." And the hypocrites shall burn! burn! in the lower depths. Rise! Cleanse yourselves and admit that you want that money. You don't want God to have it. You lust after each dollar and have silent plans how to spend every cent.

Remember, beloved, "Lying lips are an abomination and the liars shall all be stripped of their foul pretense." Why do you denounce my church? Why do you rail against my religion? Why do you attack all that is upright and righteous in this ungodly world full of evil fornicators? Why do you attack me?

My only concern is Linus and his immortality. Do not let the world forget him. He who was crushed by the forces of wickedness! He who was the fairest among boys. He who was snatched from us before the soft down of manhood kissed his cheeks. His loins yet girded with innocence. A bright-eyed, graceful manchild. O! Countless are the splendors of this world but none more splendiferous than was that fine, tender young boy!

BLOOD *(taking out his knife)* You weren't counting on murder, were you?

PASTOR Perhaps you're right. I'll just come back some other time.

PASTOR *tries to leave;* BLOOD *stops him with the knife.*

AWILDA Walter, stop it. I've been so afraid that you would hurt someone.

ACTS *(moving toward* AWILDA*)* Walter, put the knife away. I keep telling you, it's not a mojo.

BLOOD I have got to find a way to make you all listen to me. *(everyone is frozen)* I've got to find a way to make you all LISTEN TO ME!

Down in Mexico, in spots where I've been, some natives have a ritual for this kind of man. They believe in releasing the lies from his flesh. They just skin the poor devil alive. I've seen it done and it's just like skinning a fruit. Now listen up, your righteousness. I'm a-going to take my knife and slowly cut you from your larynx to your rectum. Then I'm going to flop you on your belly and peel away your lying skin in one piece just like a new suit of clothes. Just like an orange peel. *(everyone is terrified as he keeps talking. He menaces Pastor with the knife)* First, I'll work the skin over your skull and cut it with care so that it all comes off in one piece. Don't worry. I'll be careful when I cut around your eyes.

PASTOR *emits a terrified howl.*

I'll make an incision in your throat to a point midway in the calf of your leg.

ACTS Walter.

BLOOD I'll grab your scrotum. Or is it scrotii?

PASTOR Oh Jesus!

BLOOD And make an incision in each.

PASTOR *(doubling over in imagined pain, protecting his groin)* Ohhhhhhhhhhhhhhh.

BLOOD *(to* PASTOR*)* STRIP!

PASTOR *blinks frantically, not believing his ears.*

AWILDA Walter!

BLOOD Look at him. I want you to look. You won't look at me and you can't see through him. *(to* PASTOR*)* I . . . said . . . off . . . with . . . the . . . clothes, holiness.

PASTOR *slowly begins to remove his clerical collar, his white gloves and his robe. Around his neck is gleaming gold jewelry; he is dressed in a silk suit and other items of luxury. He has revealed himself as a "dandy man." When he takes off his white gloves he reveals the talons of a bird of prey with gleaming rings around them.* ACTS, BLOOD *and* AWILDA *are amazed at first and then* ACTS *and* BLOOD *double over, convulsed with laughter.*

AWILDA Pastor? Pastor?

BLOOD *(ridiculing him in a singsong chant)* "He took Ms. Johnson's money, poor old Miss Baker's Social Security, and made her throw in those diamonds he's wearing for an extra blessing."

ACTS Wife? Is this who you trust over me?

AWILDA *(in a daze)* No.

BLOOD Off with your clothes, reverent reverend.

PASTOR *continues to undress. He is wearing a jeweled G-string. S&M boots and other suggestive clothing.*

BLOOD "Jeanie Taylor, Diane Williams and little Dickie Hill were disgraced by his sexual conduct. But his congregation forgave him."

AWILDA *(gets nearer to* PASTOR *and inspects every inch of him)* Take it all off. Down to the bone. I want to see it all.

PASTOR *hesitates;* BLOOD *menaces him.*

BLOOD All off. You heard the lady, holy father.

As PASTOR *strips, he begins to take on the movements and rhythms of a vulture. He reveals a feathered body, a hook nose and webbed, claw feet. He makes vulture noises as he begins to execute broad, swooping circles around* AWILDA, *as if stalking his prey.*

AWILDA *(beating back the* PASTOR*/vulture as if exorcising something within her)* Scavenger! Bird of Prey! Vulture!

They both turn around in circles, he stalking her, she beating him off.

He has sharp eyes and a keen sense of smell. He can see dead animals from a great distance.

She tosses him her church flowers and white gloves, which he gobbles up, eating and retching at the same time.

He eats carrion, dead animals, dead things. He often vomits when feeding.

PASTOR*/vulture begins to stalk her once more.*

Drive back the unclean scavenger with living flesh. He only thrives on decay. Drive him out with living thoughts and a living heart. He only feeds on the dead. Only the living live in here. Out! Out! Out!

PASTOR*/vulture is driven out through the window. Exhausted,* AWILDA *collapses in the arms of* ACTS *and* BLOOD.

ACTS Awilda.

AWILDA Tell me what happened that night. Please.

BLOOD Go ahead, Pops. Tell her.

ACTS You are right, Son, I ran. I ran away.

BLOOD What!?

ACTS We both ran. The boy and I both ran.

ACTS *holds the check, inspecting the look, feel of it as he talks to it. Lights dim, candle flames grow higher as* ACTS *continues.* AWILDA *and* BLOOD *listen intently, for this is the first time they have ever heard the story.*

ACTS It's funny how it always comes back to money. It's funny how money is supposed to explain everything and make anything all right. It was a Saturday, right before dawn, and as you know, the boy and I were on our way to the yard. Fooling around with cars is in my bones so I figure since Linus takes after me in so many ways he could learn it real good and earn a little change too. So when he turned ten, he started coming with me on Saturday mornings 'cause the rest of the week he's in school like he's supposed to be. He was a nice boy. Very respectful. Very intelligent. He would have been a good mechanic some day.

I remember it was early spring but the dew made it cold. The sky was that light purplish gray you get right before dawn. We was both walking, not saying too much. I guess it was just too early to be doing a lot of talking. We walked down New York Boulevard through the vacant lot littered with broken glass, past the trees that rise right out of the trash and grow fifty feet tall. Suddenly two guys with plain clothes pull up in a plain car and yell at us, "Stop." Their car screams to a halt. I didn't even recognize them as humans so how should I know they was cops, creeping toward us, hissing, "Stop, you sons of bitches," laughing and drinking as they cursed us. Said in the papers they was looking for two grown burglars. My little son and I wasn't no burglars.

My wallet was bulging on my hip. I had just gotten paid. I had it all figured out. These drunken jokers are ordinary crooks trying to rob me. I figure the way they are drinking I can outrun both of them and you remember how Linus could outrun a chicken. "Run," I command, and we take off. Linus shoots out in front of me and I was right behind.

They didn't even chase us. A flat loud sound ripped the air and Linus fell and instantly became a red pool, his eyes a bright, white blank. They shot Linus in the back. They killed him! They shot my boy!

Always, always, in my head, "Should I have stood my ground and fought them? Was I trying to protect my money more than Linus?" Ain't no way I could run away and leave Linus alone, is there? LINUS RAN AHEAD OF ME AND LEFT ME! I know that's the way it happened. But sometimes a man can get confused and the way something awful happens isn't always the way you remember it. I play it back all the time in my head and my only thought that night was to protect Linus. At least that's the way I remember it.

He slowly tears the check to shreds. Suddenly the car headlights are blinking, the motor is running, the horn is honking and the radio is playing.

AWILDA *(coyly)* Mr. Benjamin, my blue dress is ready.

ACTS Blue dress?

AWILDA You know, the one I was wearing that day we first met.

She removes her church clothes and reveals her blue dress)

BLOOD *(dancing around and singing in a Spanish accent while revealing his Mexican shirt)* No more pain, no more blood, no more pain, no more blood.

ACTS *(taking off his mechanic's clothes, reveals his striped blue suit, rolled-collar shirt, diamond stickpin, leather wing tips, etc.)* I did it just like I said I would. It's crashproof, with an automatic fire extinguisher, electric shift and front-wheel drive, and rear seats that rise through the sunroof. A pretty machine nine hundred times as powerful as human man. It ain't even a machine. It's a force of nature, that's what it is. The Mojo 9. Built by a man who walked through iron times and is still kicking. See, look. My eyes are clear. My skin is tight and my body well-tuned for any situation. You all should trust me. Come with me. Mojo can take us anyplace. Mojo will get you through. I'll show you how to build an engine, boy, and you won't have to worry your head about nothing. Come on. What are you two standing there for? Get in. What are you waiting for?

ACTS, AWILDA *and* BLOOD *all climb in the car and the* MOJO *is driven straight through the door.*

(An Abridgment from)
FIRES IN THE MIRROR: CROWN HEIGHTS, BROOKLYN, AND OTHER IDENTITIES
1992

Anna Deavere Smith (1950–)

"The biggest, and the most surprising thing to me is that people are as interested in race as they are. I'm shocked. I'm shocked that this one-woman show about Blacks and Jews is interesting."[1]

—Anna Deavere Smith

In August 1991, a riot erupted in Crown Heights, Brooklyn, after the car in a Jewish Lubavitcher Rebbe's motorcade hit and killed a Black child named Gavin Cato. A Jewish scholar from Australia, Yankel Rosenbaum, was stabbed and killed by a Black man. (The man accused of his murder was later found innocent). The driver of the car escaped to Israel. These events ignited the racial fires that had been smoldering in the community for several years.

Smith took her tape recorder to Crown Heights and spoke with Blacks and whites, Jews and non-Jews, women and men, old and young to collect all points of view about the causes of the riot and what should be done to heal the community. "What I learned was that in an hour, which was the normal interview time, everybody does what I call 'talking in poetry'—which is saying something only they could possibly say, in a way that only they could say it."[2] Selecting those sections which captured the person's point of view,[3] Smith reproduced on stage his or her words verbatim.[4]

The full script of *Fires in the Mirror* (only

1. Barbara Lewis, "The Circle of Confusion: An Interview with Anna Deavere Smith." *Kenyon Review*, Fall 1993, p. 61.

2. Thulani Davis, "Anna Deavere Smith," an interview, *Bomb*, Fall 1992, p. 40.

3. "We don't see the whole interview in the show. I'm using just one minute; I'm taking a corner of the page and magnifying it for theater." Davis p. 40.

4. Richard Schechner, observed that Smith did not "act" the characters, she "incorporated" them. "Her way of working is less like that of a conventional Euro-American actor and more like that of African, Native American, and Asian ritualists. Smith works by means of deep mimesis." "Anna Deavere Smith, Acting as Incorporation," *The Drama Review* 37, Winter 1993, p. 63.

a representative portion is printed here) requires twenty-nine impersonations. Smith enacts each of them, working with small props, caps, jackets, and scarves. "Quick-change-artistry," once popular at the turn of the century, has a long standing African American tradition—exemplifed by Mercedes Gilbert, Pauline Myers, and Vinie Burrows, to name only a few. Additionally, Smith uses a television news style on stage, which audiences are already accustomed to accepting as trustworthy. However, Smith's "talking heads" only speak through her. She is not an objective camera; she allows the absent spirits to testify, to tell the living their conflicting stories, all truthful to their own points of view, but only through her good offices.[5]

According to the author, the fire images in the title of the show represent the many small, dormant fires of social unrest, which can flare up as a result of high-speed friction. The mirror is the stage, reflecting the fires back to us.[6]

After many years of work, Anna Deavere Smith has honed a miraculous talent. She began in 1979, with a performance series entitled *On the Road: A Search for American Identity.* Its segments include *Voices of Bay Area Women* (1988), *Gender Bending* (1989), *On Black Identity and Black Theatre* (1990), *Identities, Mirrors and Distortions I* (1991). In 1992, she added *Fires in the Mirror* and the next year, *Twilight: Los Angeles, 1992* (1993), based on the Los Angeles rebellion that pitted Koreans against Hispanics and Blacks.

Fires in the Mirror won an Obie, the Drama Desk and Lucille Lortel awards, and was runner-up for the Pulitzer Prize in Drama. In April 1993, George C. Wolfe directed Smith in the American Playhouse version for PBS television. The play may be so unique to time, and its creator, that few productions will be mounted without its author, although Smith has said she'd like to see another actor in her roles "on alternate nights." She also notes that an American audience might not accept a white actor playing the Black roles as readily as they accept Smith in white roles.

Smith has created her own genre of theatre—one "that is theatre, but it's also a community work in some ways. It's a kind of low anthropology, low journalism, it's a bit documentary. So it's not completely with the tradition."[7]

5 Carol Martin, "Anna Deavere Smith, The World Becomes You," an interview. *The Drama Review* 37, Winter 1993, p. 45.

6. Lewis, "Circle of Confusion," p. 57.

7. Lewis, "Circle of Confusion," p. 56.

from Fires in the Mirror

FROM IDENTITY

Ntozake Shange

The Desert

This interview was done on the phone at about four P.M. Philadelphia time. The only cue Ntozake gave about her physical appearance was that she took one earring off to talk on the phone. On stage we placed her upstage center in an armchair, smoking. Then we placed her standing, downstage.

Hummmm.
Identity—
it, is, uh . . . in a way it's, um . . . it's sort of, it's uh . . .
it's a psychic sense of place
it's a way of knowing I'm not a rock or that tree?
I'm this other living creature over here?
And it's a way of knowing that no matter where I put myself
that I am not necessarily
what's around me.
I am part of my surroundings
and I become separate from them
and it's being able to make those differentiations clearly
that lets us have an identity
and what's inside our identity
is everything that's ever happened to us.
Everything that's ever happened
to us as well as our responses to it
'cause we might be alone in a trance state,
someplace like the desert
and we begin to feel as though
we are part of the desert—
which we are right at that minute—
but we are not the desert,
uh . . .
we are part of the desert,
and when we go home
we take with us part of the desert that the desert gave us,
but we're still not the desert.
It's an important differentiation to make because you don't know
what you're giving if you don't know what you have and you don't
know what you're taking if you don't know what's yours and what's
somebody else's.

George C. Wolfe

101 Dalmatians

The Mondrian Hotel in Los Angeles. Morning. Sunny. A very nice room. George is wearing denim jeans, a light blue denim shirt and white leather tennis shoes. His hair is in a ponytail. He wears tortoise/wire spectacles. He is drinking tea with milk. The tea is served on a tray, the cups and teapot are delicate porcelain. George is sitting on a sofa, with his feet up on the coffee table.

I mean I grew up on a Black-
a one-block street—
that was Black.
My grandmother lived on that street
my cousins lived around the corner
I went to this
Black—Black—
private Black grade school
where
I was extraordinary.
Everybody there was extraordinary.
You were told you were extraordinary.
It was very clear
that I could not go to see *101 Dalmatians* at the Capital Theatre
because it was segregated.
And at the same time
I was treated like I was the most extraordinary creature that had
been born.
So I'm on my street in my house,
at my school—
and I was very spoiled too—
so I was treated like I was this special creature.
And then I would go beyond a certain point
I was treated like I was insignificant.
Nobody was
hosing me down or calling me nigger.
It was just that I was insignificant,

(slight pause)

You know what I mean?
So it was very clear

(Strikes teacup on saucer twice on "very clear")

where my extraordinariness lived.
You know what I mean.
That I was extraordinary as long as I was Black.
But I am—not—going—to place myself

(Pause)

in relationship to your whiteness.
I will talk about your whiteness if we want to talk about that.
But I,
but what,
that which,
what I—
what am I saying?
My Blackness does not resis— ex— re—
exist in relationship to your whiteness.

(Pause)

You know *(Not really a question, more like a "hmm")*

(Slight pause)

it does not exist in relationship *to*—
it *exists*
it exists.
I come—
you know what I mean—
like I said, I, I, I,
I come from—
it's a very *complex*,
con*fused*,
neu-rotic,
at times destructive
reality, but it is completely
and totally a reality
contained and, and,
and full unto itself.
It's complex.
It's demonic.
It's ridiculous. It's absurd.
It's evolved.
It's all the stuff.
That's the way I grew up.

(Slight pause)

So that *therefore*—
and then you're white—

(Quick beat)

and then there's a point when,
and then these two things come into contact.

MIRRORS

Aaron M. Bernstein

Mirrors and Distortions

Evening. Cambridge, Massachusetts. Fall. He is a man in his fifties, wearing a sweater and a shirt with a pen guard. He is seated at a round wooden table with a low-hanging lamp.

Okay, so a mirror is something that reflects light.
It's the simplest instrument to understand,
okay?
So a simple mirror is just a flat
reflecting
substance, like,
for example,
it's a piece of glass which is silvered on the back,
okay?
Now the notion of distortion also goes back into literature, okay?
I'm trying to remember from art—
You probably know better than I.
You know you have a pretty young woman and she looks in a mirror
and she's a witch

(He laughs)

because she's evil on the inside
Thats not a real mirror,
as everyone knows—
where
you see the inner thing.
Now that really goes back in literature.
So everyone understood that mirrors don't distort,
so that was a play
not on words
but on a concept.
But physicists do
talk about distortion.
It's a big
subject, distortions.
I'll give you an example—
if you wanna see the
stars
you make a big

reflecting mirror—
that's one of the ways—
you make a big telescope
so you can gather in a lot of light
and then it focuses at a point
and then there's always something called the circle of confusion.
So if ya don't make the thing perfectly spherical or perfectly
parabolic
then,
then, uh, if there are errors in the construction
which you can see, it's easy, if it's huge,
then you're gonna have a circle of confusion,
you see?
So that's the reason for making the
telescope as large as you can,
because you want that circle
to seem smaller,
and you want to easily see errors in the construction.
So, you see, in physics it's very practical—
if you wanna look up in the heavens
and see the stars as well as you can
without distortion.
If you're counting stars, for example,
and two look like one,
you've blown it.

RHYTHM

Monique "Big Mo" Matthews
Rhythm and Poetry

In reality this interview was done on an afternoon in the spring of 1989, while I was in residence at the University of California, Los Angeles, as a fellow at the Center for Afro-American Studies. Mo was a student of mine. We were sitting in my office, which was a narrow office, with sunlight. I performed Mo in many shows, and in the course of performing her, I changed the setting to a performance setting, with microphones. I was inspired by a performance that I saw of Queen Latifah in San Francisco and by Mo's behavior in my class, which was performance behavior, to change the setting to one that was more theatrical, since Mo's everyday speech was as theatrical as Latifah's performance speech.

Speaking directly to the audience, pacing the stage.

And she say, "This is for the fellas,"
and she took off all her clothes and she had on a leotard
that had all cuts and stuff in it,
and she started doin' it on the floor.
They were like
"Go, girl!"
People like, "That look really stink,"
But that's what a lot of female rappers do—
like to try to get off,
they sell they body or pimp they body
to, um, get play.
And you people like Latifah who doesn't, you know,
she talks intelligent.
You have Lyte who's just hard and people are scared by her
hardness,
her strength of her words.
She encompasses that whole, New York-street sound.
It's like, you know, she'll like . . .
what's a line?
What's a line
like "Paper Thin"
"IN ONE EAR AND RIGHT OUT THE OTHUH."
It's like,
"I don't care what you have to say,
I'm gittin' done what's gotta be done.
Man can't come across me.
A female she can't stand against me.
I'm just the toughest, I'm just the hardest/You just can't come up
against me/if you do you get waxed!"
It's like a lot of my songs,
I don't know if I'm gonna get blacklisted for it.
The image that I want is a strong strong African strong Black woman
and I'm not down with what's going on, like Big Daddy Kane had a song
out called "Pimpin' Ain't Easy," and he sat there and he talk for the
whole song, and I sit there I wanna slap him, I wanna slap him so
hard, and he talks about, it's one point he goes, yeah
um,
"Puerto Rican girls Puerto Rican girls call me Papi and
White girls say
even White girls say I'm a hunk!"
I'm like,

"What you mean 'even'"?
Oh! Black girls ain't good enough for you huh?"
And one of my songs has a line that's like
"PIMPIN' AIN'T EASY BUT WHORIN' AIN'T PROPER. RESPECT AND
CHERISH THE ORIGINAL MOTHER."
And a couple of my friends were like,
"Aww, Mo, you good but I can't listen to you 'cause you be Men
bashin'."
I say,
"It ain't men bashin', it's female assertin'."
Shit.
I'm tired of it.
I'm tired of my friends just acceptin'
that they just considered to be a ho.
You got a song.
"Everybody's a Hotty."
A "hotty" means you a freak, you a ho,
and it's like Too Short
gets up there and he goes,
"B I AYYYYYYYYYYYYE."
Like he stretches "bitch" out for as long as possible,
like you just a ho and you can't be saved,
and 2 Live Crew . . . "we want some pussy," and the girls! "La le la le la le la,"
it's like my friends say,
"Mo, if you so bad how come you don't never say nothin' about 2
Live Crew?"
When I talk about rap,
and I talk about people demeaning rap,
I don't even mention them
because they don't understand the fundamentals of rap.
Rap, rap
is basically
broken down
Rhythm
and Poetry.
And poetry is expression.
It's just like poetry; you release so much through poetry.
Poetry is like
intelligence.
You just release it all and if you don't have a complex rhyme
it's like,
"I'm goin' to the store."
What rhymes with store?
More, store, for, more, bore,
"I'm goin' to the store I hope I don't get bored,"
it's like,
"WHAT YOU SAYIN', MAN? WHO CARES?"
You have to have something that flows.
You have to be def,
D-E-F.
I guess I have to think of something for you that ain't slang.
Def is dope, def is live
when you say somethin's dope
it means it is the epitome of the experience
and you have to be def by your very presence
because you have to make people happy.
And we are living in a society where people are not happy with their everyday lives.

FROM SEVEN YEARS

Letty Cottin Pogrebin

Near Enough to Reach

Evening. The day before Thanksgiving, 1991. On the phone. Direct, passionate confident, lots of volume. She is in a study with a roll-top desk and a lot of books.

I think it's about rank frustration and the old story
that you pick a scapegoat
that's much more, I mean Jews and Blacks,
that's manageable,
because we're near,
we're still near enough to each other to reach!
I mean, what can you do about the people who voted for David Duke?
Are Blacks going to go there and deal with that?
No, it's much easier to deal with Jews who are also panicky.
We're the only ones that pay any attention

(Her voice makes an upward inflection)

Well, Jeffries did speak about the Mafia being, um,
Mafia,
and the Jews in Hollywood.
I didn't see
this tremendous outpouring of Italian
reaction.
Only *Jews* listen,
only *Jews* take Blacks seriously,

only *Jews* view Blacks as full human beings that you should *address*
in their rage
and, um,
people don't seem to notice that.
But Blacks, it's like a little child kicking up against Arnold
Schwarzenegger
when they, when they have anything to say about the dominant culture
nobody listens! Nobody reacts!
To get a headline,
to get on the evening news,
you have to attack a Jew.
Otherwise you're ignored.
And it's a shame.
We all play into it.

FROM CROWN HEIGHTS, BROOKLYN

Michael S. Miller

"Heil Hitler"

A large airy office in Manhattan on Lexington in the 50s. Mr. Miller sits behind a big desk in a high-backed swivel chair drinking coffee. He's wearing a yarmulke. Plays with the swizzle stick throughout. There is an intercom in the office, so that when the receptionist calls him, you can hear it, and when she calls others in other offices, you can hear it like a page in a public place, faintly.

I was at Gavin Cato's funeral,
at nearly every public event
that was conducted by the Lubavitcher community and the Jewish
community as a whole
words of comfort
were offered to the family of Gavin Cato.
I can show you a letter that we sent
to the Cato family expressing, uh,
our sorrow over the loss,
unnecessary loss, of their son.
I am not aware of a word
that was spoken at that funeral.
I am not aware of a—
and I was taking notes—
of a word that was uttered
of comfort to the family of Yankele Rosenbaum.
Frankly this was a political rally rather than a funeral.
The individuals you mentioned—
and again,
I am not going to participate in verbal acrimony,
not only
were there cries of "Kill the Jews"
or,
"Kill the Jew,"
there were cries of, "Heil Hitler."
There were cries of, "Hitler didn't finish the job."
There were cries of,
"Throw them back into the ovens again."
To hear in *Crown Heights*—
and Hitler was no lover of Blacks—
"Heil Hitler"?
"Hitler didn't finish the job"?
"We should heat up the ovens"?
From *Blacks?*
Is more inexplicable
or unexplainable
or any other word that I cannot fathom.
The hatred is so
deep-seated
and the hatred
knows no boundaries.
There is no boundary
to anti-Judaism.
The anti-*Judaism*—
if people don't want me
to use,
hear me use the word anti-Semitism.
And I'll be damned it,
if preferential treatment is gonna
be the excuse
for every bottle,
rock,
or pellet that's, uh, directed
toward a Jew
or the window of a Jewish home
or a Jewish store.
And, frankly,
I think the response of the Lubavitcher community was relatively
passive.

Norman Rosenbaum

My Brother's Blood

A Sunday afternoon. Spring. Crisp, clear and windy. Across from City Hall in New York City. Crowds of people, predominantly Lubavitcher, with placards. A rally that was organized by Lubavitcher women. All of the speakers are men, but the women stand close to the stage. Mr. Rosenbaum, an Australian, with a beard, hat and wearing a pinstripe suit, speaks passionately and loudly from the microphone on a stage with a podium. Behind him is a man in an Australian bush hat with a very large Australian flag which blows dramatically in the wind. It is so windy that Mr. Rosenbaum has to hold his hat to keep it on his head.

Al do lay achee so achee aylay alo dalmo
My brother's blood cries out from the ground.
Let me make it clear
why I'm here, and why you're here.
In August of 1991,
as you all have heard before today,
my brother was killed in the streets of Crown Heights
for no other reason
than that he was a Jew!
The only miracle was
that my brother was the only victim
who paid for being a Jew with his life.
When my brother was surrounded,
each and every American was surrounded.
When my brother was stabbed four times,
each and every American was stabbed four times
and as my brother bled to death in this city,
while the medicos stood by
and let him bleed
to death, it was the gravest of indictments against this country.
One person out of twenty gutless individuals
who attacked my brother has been arrested.
I for one am not convinced that it is beyond the ability of the New York Police
to arrest others.
Let me tell you, Mayor Dinkins,
let me tell you, Commissioner Brown:
I'm here,
I'm not going home,
until there is justice.

Richard Green

Rage

Two P.M. in a big red van. Green is in the front. He has a driver. I am in the back. Green wears a large knit hat with reggae colors over long dreadlocks. Driving from Crown Heights to Brooklyn College. He turns sideways to face me in the back and bends down, talking with his elbows on his knee.

Sharpton, Carson, and Reverend Herbert Daughtry
didn't have any power out there really.
The media gave them that power.
But they weren't turning those youfs on and off.
Nobody knew who controlled the switch out there.
Those young people had rage like an oil-well fire
that has to burn out.
All they were doin' was sort of orchestratin' it.
Uh, they were not really the ones that were saying, "Well
stop, go, don't go, stop, turn around, go up."
It wasn't like that.
Those young people had rage out there,
that didn't matter who was in control of that—
that rage had to get out
and that rage
has been building up.
When all those guys have come and gone,
that rage is still out here.
I can show you that rage every day
right up and down this avenue.
We see, sometimes in one month, we see three bodies
in one month. That's rage,
and that's something that nobody has control of.
And I don't know who told you that it was preferential treatment for
Blacks that the Mayor kept the cops back . . .
If the Mayor had turned those cops on?
We would still be in a middle of a battle.
And
I pray on both sides of the fence,
and I tell the people in the Jewish community the same thing,
"This is not something that force will hold."
Those youfs were running on cops without nothing in their hands,
seven- and eight- and nine- and ten-year-old boys were running at
those cops
with nothing,
just running at 'em.
That's rage.
Those young people out there are angry
and that anger has to be vented,
it has to be negotiated.
And they're not angry at the Lubavitcher community
they're just as angry at you and me,
if it comes to that.
They have no
role models,
no guidance
so they're just out there growin' up on their own,
their peers are their role models,

their peers is who teach them how to move
what to do, what to say
so when they see the Lubavitchers
they don't know the difference between "Heil Hitler"
and, uh, and uh, whatever else.
They don't know the difference.
When you ask 'em to say who Hitler was they wouldn't even be able
to tell you.
Half of them don't even know.

(Mobile phone rings; he picks it up)

"Richard Green, can I help?
Aw, man I tol' you I want some color
up on that wall. Give me some colors.
Look, I'm in the middle of somethin'."

(He returns to the conversation)

Just as much as they don't know who Frederick Douglass was.
They know Malcolm
Because Malcolm has been played up to such an extent now
that they know Malcolm.
But ask who Nat Turner was or Mary McCleod Bethune or Booker T.
Because the system has given 'em
Malcolm is convenient and
Spike is goin' to give 'em Malcolm even more.
It's convenient.

Carmel Cato

Lingering

Seven P.M. The corner where the accident occurred in Crown Heights. An altar to Gavin is against the wall where the car crashed. Many pieces of cloth are draped. Some writing in color is on the wall. Candle wax is everywhere. There is a rope around the area. Cato is wearing a trench coat, pulled around him. He stands very close to me. Dark outside. Reggae music is in the background. Lights come from stores on each corner. Busy intersection. Sounds from outside. Traffic. Stores open. People in and out of shops. Sounds from inside apartments, televisions, voices, cooking, etc. He speaks in a pronounced West Indian accent.

In the meanwhile
It was two.
Angela was on the ground
but she was trying to move. Gavin was still.
They was able to pound him.
I was the father.
I was 'it, chucked, and pushed,
and a lot of
sarcastic words were passed towards me
from the police
while I was trying to explain: It was my kid!
These are my children.
The child was hit you know.
I saw everything, everything,
the guy radiator burst
all the hoses,
the steam,
all the garbage buckets goin' along the building.
And it was very loud,
everything burst.
It's like an atomic bomb.
That's why all these people
comin' round
wanna know what's happening.
Oh it was very outrageous.
Numerous numbers.
All the time the police sayin'
you can't get in,
you can't pass,
and the children laying on the ground.
He was hit at exactly eight-thirty.
Why?
I was standing over there.
There was a little child—
a friend of mine
came up with a little child—
and I lift the child up
and she look at her watch at the same time
and she say it was eight-thirty.
I gave the child back to her.
And then it happen.
Umh, Umh, *(Sharp utterances)*
My child, these are the things I never dream about.
I take care of my children.
You know it's a funny thing,
if a child get sick and he dies
it won't hurt me so bad,
or if a child run out into the street and get hit down,
it wouldn't hurt me.
That's what's hurtin' me.
The whole week
before Gavin died
my body was changing,
I was having different feelings.
I stop eating,

I didn't et
nothin',
only drink water,
for two weeks;
and I was very touchy—
any least thing that drop
or any song I hear
it would affect me.
Every time I try to do something
I would have to stop.
I was
lingering, lingering, lingering, lingering,
all the time.
But I can do things,
I can see things,
I know that for a fact.
I was telling myself,
"Something is wrong somewhere,"
but I didn't want to see,
I didn't want to accept,
and it was inside of me,
and even when I go home I tell my friends,
"Something coming I could feel it
but I didn't want to see,"
and all the time I just deny deny deny,
and I never thought it was Gavin,
but I didn't have a clue.
I thought it was one of the other children—
the bigger boys
or the girl,
because she worry me,
she won't et—
but Gavin 'ee was 'ealtee,
and he don't cause no trouble.
That's what's devastating me even until now.
Sometimes it make me feel like it's no justice,
like, uh,
the Jewish people,
they are very high up,
it's a very big thing,
they runnin' the whole show
from the judge right down.
And something I don't understand:
The Jewish people, they told me
there are certain people I cannot be seen with
and certain things I cannot say
and certain people I cannot talk to.
They made that very clear to me—the Jewish people—
they can throw the case out
unless
I go to them with pity.
I don't know what they talkin' about.
So I don't know what kind of crap is that.
And make me say things I don't wanna say
and make me do things I don't wanna do.
I am a special person.
I was born different.
I'm a man born by my foot.
I born by my foot.
Anytime a baby comin' by the foot
they either cut the mother
or the baby dies.
But I was born with my foot.
I'm one of the special.
There's no way they can empower me.
No there's nothing to hide,
you can repeat every word I say.

BIBLIOGRAPHIES

Selected Bibliography of Books on Black Drama and Its Theatre Artists

Carter, Steven R. *Hansberry's Drama: Commitment amid Complexity*. Urbana: University of Illinois Press, 1991.

Coleman, Gregory D. *We're Heaven Bound: Portrait of a Black Sacred Drama*. Athens: University of Georgia Press, 1994.

Cooper, Ralph. *Amateur Night at the Apollo*. New York: HarperCollins, 1990.

Dictionary of Literary Biography. Vols. 5, 33, 38, 50, 51, 76. Detroit: Gale Research, 1980s.

Fabre, Geneviève, Michel Fabre, William French, and Amritjit Singh. *Afro-American Poetry and Drama, 1760–1975. A Reference Guide*. Detroit: Gale Research, 1979.

Fletcher, Tom. *100 Years of the Negro in Show Business!* New York: Burdge & Co., 1954. Reprint, New York: Da Capo Press, 1984.

Fraden, Rena. *Blueprints for a Black Federal Theatre 1935–1939*. New York: Cambridge University Press, 1994.

Gray, John, ed. *Black Theatre and Performance: A Pan-African Bibliography*. Westport, CT: Greenwood Press, 1990.

Grupenhoff, Richard. *The Black Valentino: The Stage and Screen Career of Lorenzo Tucker*. Metuchen, NJ: Scarecrow Press, 1988.

Haskins, James. *Black Theater in America*. New York: Thomas Y. Crowell, 1982.

Hatch, James V. *Sorrow Is the Only Faithful One: The Life of Owen Dodson*, Urbana: University of Illinois Press, 1993.

Hay, Samuel A. *African American Theatre: An Historical and Critical Analysis*. New York: Cambridge University Press, 1994.

Heath, Gordon. *Deep Are the Roots: Memoirs of a Black Expatriate*. Amherst, MA: University of Massachusetts Press, 1992.

Hill, Errol. *Shakespeare in Sable: A History of Black Shakespearean Actors*. Amherst, MA: University of Massachusetts Press, 1984.

———. *The Theatre of Black Americans*. New York: Applause Theatre Book Publishers, 1987.

Hughes, Langston, and Milton Meltzer. *Black Magic*. Englewood Cliffs, NJ: Prentice-Hall, 1968.

Kellner, Bruce, ed. *The Harlem Renaissance: A Historical Dictionary for the Era*. Westport, CT: Greenwood Press, 1984.

Klotman, Phyllis Rauch. *Frame by Frame: A Black Filmography*. Bloomington: Indiana University Press, 1979.

Lester, Neal A. *Ntozake Shange: A Critical Study of the Plays*. New York: Garland Publishing, 1995.

Mapp, Edward. *Directory of Blacks in the Performing Acts*, 2d ed. Metuchen, NJ: Scarecrow Press, 1978.

Molette, Carlton W., and Barbara J. *Black Theatre: Premise and Presentation*, 2d ed. Bristol, IN: Wyndham Hall Press, 1992.

Neal, Larry. *Visions of a Liberated Future: Black Arts Movement Writings*. New York: Thunder's Mouth Press, 1989.

Newman, Richard. *Black Access: A Bibliography of Afro-American Bibliographies*. Westport, CT: Greenwood Press, 1984.

Ortolani, Benito, ed. *International Bibliography of Theatre:* New York: Theatre Research Data Center, 1982. Also volumes published in 1983, 1984, 1985, 1986, 1987, 1988–89, 1990–91, 92–93.

Peterson, Jr., Bernard L., *Contemporary Black American Playwrights and Their Plays*. Westport, CT: Greenwood Press, 1988.

———. *Early Black American Playwrights and Dramatic Writers.* Westport, CT: Greenwood Press, 1990.

———. *A Century of Musicals in Black and White: An Encyclopedia of Musical Stage Works By, About, or Involving African Americans.* Westport, CT: Greenwood Press, 1993.

Riis, Thomas L. *Just before Jazz: Black Musical Theater in New York 1890–1915.* Washington, DC: Smithsonian Institute Press, 1989.

Rush, Theressa G., Carol F. Myers, and Esther S. Arata. *Black American Writers, Past and Present: A Biographical and Bibliographical Dictionary,* 2 vols. Metuchen, NJ: Scarecrow Press, 1975.

Sampson, Henry T. *Blacks in Blackface: A Source Book on Early Black Musical Shows.* Metuchen, NJ: Scarecrow Press, 1980.

———. *The Ghost Walks: A Chronological History of Blacks in Show Business, 1865–1910.* Metuchen, NJ: Scarecrow Press, 1988.

Schiffman, Jack. *Uptown: The Story of Harlem's Apollo Theatre.* New York: Cowles Book Company, 1971.

Southern, Eileen. *Biographical Dictionary of Afro-American and African Musicians.* Westport, CT: Greenwood Press, 1983.

———, ed. *African American Theater: Out of Bondage* (1876) and *Peculiar Sam; or, The Underground Railroad* (1879). New York: Garland Publishing, 1994.

Southern, Eileen, and Josephine Wright. Compiled by *African-American Traditions in Song, Sermon, Tale, and Dance, 1600s–1920: An Annotated Bibliography of Literature, Collections, and Artworks.* Westport, CT: Greenwood Press, 1990.

Szwed, John, and Roger D. Abrahams. *Afro-American Folk Culture: An Annotated Bibliography of Materials from North, Central, and South America and the West Indies,* 2 vols. Philadelphia: Institute for the Study of Human Issues, 1978.

Tanner, Jo A. *Dusky Maidens: The Odyssey of the Early Black Dramatic Actress.* Westwood, CT: Greenwood Press, 1992.

Toll, Robert C. *Blacking Up: The Minstrel Show in Nineteenth-Century America.* New York: Oxford University Press, 1974.

Watkins, Mel. *On the Real Side: Laughing, Lying, and Signifying: The Underground Tradition of African American Humor that Transformed American Culture, from Slavery to Richard Pryor.* New York: Simon & Schuster, 1994.

Williams, Mance. *Black Theatre in the 1960s and 1970s: A Historical-Critical Analysis of the Movement.* Westport, CT: Greenwood Press, 1985.

Woll, Allen. *Dictionary of the Black Theatre.* Westport, CT: Greenwood Press, 1983.

———. *Black Musical Theatre From Coontown to Dreamgirls.* Baton Rouge: Louisiana State University Press, 1989.

Selected Bibliography of Anthologies Containing Scripts by Black Playwrights

Baraka, Amiri. *Four Black Revolutionary Plays.* Indianapolis, IN: Bobbs-Merrill, 1969.

———. *The Motion of History and Other Plays.* New York: Morrow, 1977.

Branch, William, ed. *Black Thunder.* New York: Mentor, 1992.

Brasmer, William, and Dominick Consolo, eds. *Black Drama: An Anthology.* Columbus, OH: Merrill, 1970.

Brown-Guillory, Elizabeth, ed. *Wines in the Wilderness.* Westport, CT: Greenwood Press, 1990.

Bullins, Ed. *Five Plays by Ed Bullins.* Indianapolis, IN: Bobbs-Merrill, 1968.

———. *Four Dynamite Plays.* New York: William Morrow, 1971.

———. *The Theme Is Blackness.* New York: William Morrow, 1973.

Carter, Steve. *Plays by Steve Carter.* New York: Broadway Play Publishing, 1986.

Dean, Phillip Hayes. *The Sty of the Blind Pig and Other Plays.* Indianapolis, IN: Bobbs-Merrill, 1973.

Edmonds, Randolph. *The Land of Cotton and Other Plays.* Washington, DC: Associated Publishers, 1942.

Flynn, Joyce, and Joyce Occomy Stricklin, eds. *Frye Street & Environs: The Collected Works of Marita Bonner.* Boston: Beacon Press, 1987.

Hamalian, Leo, and James V. Hatch, eds. *Roots of African American Drama.* Detroit: Wayne State University Press, 1991.

Hansberry, Lorraine. *A Raisin in the Sun/The Sign in Sidney Brustein's Window.* New York: New American Library, 1966.

Hatch, James V., and Leo Hamalian, eds. *Lost Plays of the Harlem Renaissance.* Detroit: Wayne State University Press, in press.

Hill, Errol, ed. *Black Heroes, 7 Plays.* New York: Applause Theatre Book Publishers, 1989.

Kennedy, Adrienne. *Adrienne Kennedy in ONE ACT.* Minneapolis: University of Minnesota Press, 1988.

———. *The Alexander Plays.* Minneapolis: University of Minnesota Press, 1992.

King, Woodie, and Ron Milner, eds. *Black Drama Anthology.* New York: Columbia University Press, 1972.

Mahone, Sydne, ed. *Moonmarked & Touched by the Sun.* New York: Theatre Communications Group, 1994.

Nemiroff, Robert, ed. *Les Blancs: The Collected Last Plays of Lorriane Hansberry.* New York: Random House, 1972.

Oliver, Clinton, and Stephanie Sills, eds. *Contemporary Black Drama.* New York: Scribner, 1971.

Ostrow, Eileen, ed. *Center Stage: An Anthology of 21 Contemporary Plays.* Oakland, CA: Sea Urchin Press, 1981.

Oyamo [Charles Gordon]. *Hillbilly Liberation.* New York: Ujamaa, 1976.

Patterson, Lindsay, ed. *Black Theater.* New York: Dodd, Mead, 1971.

Perkins, Kathy, ed. *Female Black Playwrights.* Bloomington: Indiana University Press, 1989.

Richardson, Willis, ed. *Plays and Pageants from the Life of the Negro,* 2d ed. Jackson MI.: University Press of Mississippi, 1994.

Shange, Ntozake. *Three Pieces.* New York: St. Martin's Press, 1981.

Smalley, Webster, ed. *Five Plays by Langston Hughes.* Bloomington: Indiana University Press, 1963.

Turner, Darwin T., ed. *Black Drama in America,* 2d ed. Washington, DC: Howard University Press, 1994.

Walcott, Derek. *Dream on Monkey Mountain and Other Plays.* New York: Farrar, Straus & Giroux, 1970.

———. *Three Plays.* New York: Farrar, Straus & Giroux, 1986.

White, Edgar. *The Crucificado: Two Plays.* New York: William Morrow, 1973.

———. *Lament for Rastafari and Other Plays.* London: Marion Boyars, 1983.

Wilson, August. *Three Plays.* Pittsburgh: University of Pittsburgh Press, 1991.

Wilkerson, Margaret B., ed. *9 Plays by Black Women.* New York: New American Library, 1986.

Selected Bibliography of Authors in *The Recent Period*

Baldwin, James. *Blues for Mister Charlie.* New York: Samuel French, 1965. Black and white reaction to the murder of a young Black man by a white bigot in a small southern town.

Baraka, Amiri (LeRoi Jones). *The Baptism* and *The Toilet.* New York: Grove Press, 1967. *The Baptism* presents a confrontation between a Black preacher and a homosexual devil over the soul of a young Black Christ figure. In *The Toilet,* a gang of Black youth attack a white homosexual who has written a love letter to one of their members.

———. *The Slave.* In *Black Theater USA.* Edited by James V. Hatch. New York: The Free Press, 1974. A Black militant murders his white ex-wife's husband during a riot, then leaves her and their children to die as their home is destroyed.

———. *General Hag's Skeezag.* In *Black Thunder.* Edited by William Branch. New York: Mentor, 1992.

Bullins, Ed. *In New England Winter.* In *New Plays from the Black Theatre.* Edited by Ed Bullins. New York: Bantam, 1969. A study of Black lifestyle and survival.

———. *The Electronic Nigger and Other Plays by Ed Bullins.* London: Faber & Faber, 1970. *The Electronic Nigger* is a satire about a pretentious Black man's attempt to be white.

———. *The Taking of Miss Janie.* In *Black Thunder.* Edited by William Branch. New York: Mentor, 1992. A Black "poet" meets a white female classmate after many years and rapes her.

Childress, Alice. *Mojo.* New York: Dramatists Play Service, 1971. A middle-aged divorced couple are brought together by a cancer operation.

———. *Trouble in Mind.* In *Black Theater.* Edited by Lindsay Patterson. New York: Dodd, Mead, 1971. A Black actress refuses to play a stereotyped role.

———. *Wedding Band.* In *Black Thunder.* Edited by William Branch. New York: Mentor, 1992. A Black woman and white male find love and trouble in South Carolina during World War I.

Dodson, Owen. *The Garden of Time.* Unpublished typewritten script in the James Weldon Johnson Memorial Collection at Yale University (1939). A retelling of the Medea story set in the American South.

———. *Divine Comedy.* In *Black Theater USA.* Edited by James V. Hatch. New York: The Free Press, 1974. A poetic drama about the appeal of a charismatic Apostle of Light for the hungry and tired sufferers during the Great Depression.

——— and Countee Cullen. "The Third Fourth of July," *Theatre Arts Magazine,* August 1946.

———. *Amistad.* Unpublished manuscript in Yale University Library, 1939. The story of Cinque's rebellion aboard ship.

———. *Bayou Legend.* In *Black Drama in America: An Anthology.* Edited by Darwin T. Turner. Revised. Washington, D.C.: Howard University Press, 1994. About a Black vagabond hero of the Peer Gynt legend set in Louisiana.

Elder, Lonne, III. *Charade on East Fourth Street.* In *Black Drama Anthology.* Edited by Woody King, Jr., and Ron Milner. New York: New American Library, 1971. Black youth urged to use legal means to combat police corruption.

Hansberry, Lorraine. *The Sign in Sidney Brustein's Window.* In *Lorraine Hansberry's A Raisin in the Sun and The Sign in Sidney Brustein's Window.* New York: Signet, 1966. Does not focus on Black characters and themes; concerns the need for individuals to take a stand against moral corruption, comformity, and alienation.

———. *To Be Young, Gifted and Black.* New York: Samuel French, 1971. A self-portrait of the author's life from childhood through her maturity as a writer.

———. *The Drinking Gourd* in *Black Theater USA.* Edited by James V. Hatch. New York: The Free Press, 1974. A slave mother chooses her son's life over loyalty to a "beloved" master.

———. *Les Blancs.* In *Lorraine Hansberry: The Collected Last Plays.* Edited by Robert Nemiroff. New York: New American Library, 1983. Truths unfold about Black/white and Black/Black relationships during and impending revolution in Africa.

Hill, Abram. *Liberty Deferred.* In *Black Theatre USA,* vol. 1 (revised and expanded ed.). New York: The Free Press, 1996. An epic history of African Americans.

———. *Walk Hard.* In *Black Theater USA.* Edited by James V. Hatch. New York: The Free Press, 1974. The story of a boxer who has to submit to the mob or get out of the ring.

Hughes, Langston. *Simply Heavenly.* In *Five Plays by Langston Hughes.* Edited by Webster Smalley. Bloomington: Indiana University Press, 1968. A musical based on the adventures of Jesse B. Semple.

———. *Soul Gone Home.* In *Five Plays by Langston Hughes.* Edited by Webster Smalley. Bloomington: Indiana University Press, 1968. A one-act funeral monologue of a son for his prostitute mother.

———. *Emperor of Haiti.* In *Black Drama in America,* 2d ed. Edited by Darwin T. Turner. Washington, DC: Howard University Press, 1994. A drama about Jean Jacques Dessalines, a Black rebel who rose to power as a general and an emperor during the Haitian rebellion against Napoléon Bonaparte.

———. *Em-Fuehrer Jones.* In *Lost Plays of the Harlem Rensaissance.* Detroit: Wayne State University Press, in press. A parody of Hitler and Eugene O'Neill's play *The Emperor Jones.*

Kennedy, Adrienne. *The Owl Answers.* In *Adrienne Kennedy in One Act.* Minneapolis: University of Minnesota Press, 1988. A surreal drama of a woman of mixed race cannot find her identity.

———. *The Rat's Mass.* In *Adrienne Kennedy in One Act.* Minneapolis: University of Minnesota Press, 1988. A surreal struggle of two Black children to rid themselves of white Christianity.

———. *Sun.* In *Adrienne Kennedy in One Act.* Minneapolis: University of Minnesota Press, 1988. An experimental monologue poem about the scattering of a man's atoms into the cosmos.

Pawley, Thomas. *Jedgement Day.* In *The Negro Caravan.* Edited by Sterling Brown *et al.* New York: Citadel Press, 1941. A sinning husband, warned to repent, dreams that he is in hell.

———. *Crispus Attucks.* In *Experimental Productions of a Group of Original Plays.* Ph.D. diss., University of Iowa, 1949. Explores the reasons Attucks fought against the British.

Rahman, Aishah. *Lady Day* ("A Musical Tragedy"). A play about the life and career of Billie Holiday. Unpublished manuscript in the Hatch-Billops Collection, 1972.

———. *Unfinished Women Cry in No Man's Land While a Bird Dies in a Gilded Cage.* In *9 Plays by Black Women.* Edited by Margaret B. Wilkerson. New York: New American Library, 1986. Concerns unwed teenage mothers who must decide whether to keep their babies or give them up for adoption.

———. *The Mama.* A trilogy of one-act plays: *The Mama, a Folk's Tale,* 1974, *Portrait of a Blues Lady,* 1974, and *Mother to Son,* 1976. Unpublished manuscript in the Frank Silvera Writers' Workshop Archives, Schomburg Collection.

———. *Plays by Aishah Rahman,* New York: Broadway Play Publishing, 1996.

Salaam, Kalamu ya. "Destruction of the American Stage," *Black World,* April 1972. A set of nonbelievers shows how the American stage has been used to corrupt Black consciousness.

———. "Homecoming," *Nkombo,* August 1972. About the changes in attitude of a returning Black veteran after his experiences in the service.

———. *The Quest.* In *New Plays for the Black Theatre.* Chicago: Third World Press, 1989. A drama showing how racism causes a family to self-destruct.

———. "Malcolm My Son," *African American Review* (27) 1, Spring 1993. A gay son returns from college to confront his militant mother.

Shine, Ted. *Morning, Noon, and Night.* In *The Black Teacher and the Dramatic Arts.* Edited by William R. Reardon and Thomas D. Pawley. Westport, CT: Negro Universities Press, 1970. A peg-legged religious fanatic's attempt to make her young grandson a prophet.

———. *Herbert III.* In *Black Theatre USA.* Edited by James V. Hatch. New York: The Free Press, 1974. A husband and wife argue over the whereabouts of their missing son.

———. *The Old Woman Who Was Tampered with in Youth.* In *Center Stage.* Edited by Eileen Joyce Ostrow. Oakland, CA: Sea Urchin Press, 1981. An elderly woman confronts the man who molested her when she was a young girl.

Smith, Anna Deavere. *Twilight: Los Angeles, 1992.* New York: Anchor Books, 1994. A series of monologues taken from interviews with people of various races concerning the Los Angeles riot of 1992.

Ward, Douglas Turner. *The Reckoning.* New York: Dramatists Play Service, 1970. A southern governor is being blackmailed by his Black mistress and her pimp.

———. *Happy Ending.* In *Contemporary Black Drama.* New York: Scribner's, 1971. Two African American women who work as domestics and who have lived comfortably off of their unsuspecting employer now face a cut-off of funds.

Wolfe, George C. *Spunk.* New York: Theatre Communications Group, 1991. Three short stories by Zora Neale Hurston, as adapted by George C. Wolfe.

———. *Jelly's Last Jam.* New York: Theatre Communications Group, 1993. The story of how Jelly Roll Morton sold his soul for music.

ABOUT THE EDITORS

JAMES V. HATCH is a professor in the Graduate Theatre Program of the City University of New York. He is the author of several books on African American theatre, including the prize-winning biography *Sorrow Is the Only Faithful One: The Life of Owen Dodson.*

TED SHINE received his Ph.D. in theatre from the University of California, Santa Barbara. He currently teaches and directs in the Department of Music and Drama at A & M University, Prairie View, Texas. He is the author of more than thirty plays, including *Contribution* and *Morning, Noon, and Night.*